San Jose, CA, USA

May 7 - 12

CHI 2016 #chi4good

Association for Computing Machinery

SIGCHI

Proceedings

The 34th Annual CHI Conference on Human Factors in Computing Systems

San Jose Convention Center

https://chi2016.acm.org

Association for
Computing Machinery

Advancing Computing as a Science & Profession

The Association for Computing Machinery
2 Penn Plaza, Suite 701
New York, New York 10121-0701

ISBN: 978-1-4503-3362-7 (Digital)

ISBN: 978-1-4503-4632-0 (Print)

Additional copies may be ordered prepaid from:

ACM Order Department
PO Box 30777
New York, NY 10087-0777, USA

Phone: 1-800-342-6626 (USA and Canada)
+1-212-626-0500 (Global)
Fax: +1-212-944-1318
E-mail: acmhelp@acm.org
Hours of Operation: 8:30 am – 4:30 pm ET

Printed in the USA

CHI 2016 is the premier world-wide conference for Human-Computer Interaction (HCI) and this year took place in the heart of Silicon Valley, San Jose, California. The Proceedings and Extended Abstracts represent today's most innovative, novel and creative work in HCI. These Proceedings and Abstracts have added over one-thousand documents in the ACM Digital Library. Across all tracks, CHI received nearly 5000 submissions and accepted over 1000 that can be seen today. These include almost 600 rigorously reviewed papers and notes selected from over 2200 submissions. These Proceedings and Abstracts also document two days of workshops, symposia and meetings involving over 800 participants, a record number for CHI conferences.

The CHI 2016 conference includes two days of focused workshops and four days of technical content, including CHI's prestigious technical program, with 16 parallel sessions of rigorously reviewed research Papers, engaging Panels, Case Studies and Special Interest Groups (SIGs), Conference highlights also include student research, design, and game competitions, and last-minute SIGs for discussing current topics. The popular alt.chi forum enters its eleventh year of provocation within the HCI community. The conference also showcases Interactivity and Interactivity Research Demos, which are hands-on demonstrations of the best in technology and innovation. And we're particularly proud this year to include documents from our new Art Exhibition, held at the *Works/San Jose Gallery* in conjunction with the CHI conference.

We began our conference planning process with three core ideas: **"CHI in Silicon Valley"**: emphasizing local engagement in this vibrant community, **"#chiforgood"**: HCI in the community, both during the workshop time and at appropriate points during the conference, and a **"More Humane Conference and Planning Process"**: lots of transparency, early planning, no surprises, data-driven decisions and taking into account the importance of families, work/life balance, and the like.

From this, the overall theme of the conference emerged, **#chi4good**: addressing issues of social good through the innovation and creativity of the CHI community. To this end we held a Day of Service on the Saturday before the conference with hundreds of CHI attendees working on projects for non-profit and area arts organizations, and we have continued that theme throughout the conference by hosting the Diversity and Inclusion Lunch, brought childcare back to the conference for the first time in many years, and introduced the lunch@chi program to facilitate small group lunches on the first day of the conference. We've introduced CHI's first Diversity & Inclusion Statement, and our keynote speakers, represent the vibrancy, diversity and excitement of the wide field of HCI with particular emphasis on #chi4good. This year's speakers were chosen from among crowd-sourced suggestions from the CHI community and they are: Dayo Olopade, (Journalist and author of *The Bright Continent*); Kimberly Bryant (Founder, Black Girls Code), in conversation with Sarah Guthals, (Co-Founder of ThoughtSTEM); Marissa Meyer (President & CEO of Yahoo), in conversation with Terry Winograd (Professor Emeritus, Stanford University); Vishal Sikka (CEO of Infosys), in conversation with computing pioneer Alan Kay (Viewpoints Research Institute); and Salman Khan (founder, Khan Academy).

With careful consultation from the community, we have enhanced the CHI conference experience from submission and review processes, to more participation possibilities at the conference. Peer-reviewed papers have more space for references and will receive a wider range of better-matched reviews. There are more curated venues and more input into the selection of keynote speakers.

We are deeply indebted to an enormous number of volunteers, without whom CHI 2016 would not be possible, including over 4000 reviewers, 222 senior members of the program committee, nearly 100 members of the CHI 2016 conference organization committee and, of course, the more than 180 student volunteers.

The CHI conference is supported by the efforts of SIGCHI, (the Special Interest Group on Computer-Human Interaction) of the Association for Computing Machinery (ACM) and the ACM, and we are indebted for their ongoing support, organization, and leadership into the future.

Jofish Kaye, Yahoo, CHI 2016 General Conference Co-Chair

Allison Druin, University of Maryland / National Park Service, CHI 2016 General Conference Co-Chair

Cliff Lampe, University of Michigan, CHI 2016 Technical Program Chair

Dan Morris, Microsoft, CHI 2016 Papers Co-Chair

Juan Pablo Hourcade, University of Iowa, CHI 2016 Papers Co-Chair

Loren Terveen, University of Minnesota, President, ACM SIGCHI Executive Committee

Scooter Morris, University of San Francisco, ACM SIGCHI Vice President for Conferences

Table of Contents

VOLUME 1

Session: Social Media and Location Data

1 **I Know Where You Live: Inferring Details of People's Lives by Visualizing Publicly Shared Location Data**
Ilaria Liccardi, *University of Oxford & Massachusetts Institute of Technology,* Alfie Abdul-Rahman, Min Chen, *University of Oxford*

13 **Not at Home on the Range: Peer Production and the Urban/Rural Divide**
Isaac L. Johnson, Yilun Lin, *University of Minnesota*
Toby Jia-Jun Li, *University of Minnesota & Carnegie Mellon University,* Andrew Hall, *University of Minnesota,* Aaron Halfaker, *Wikimedia Foundation,* Johannes Schöning, *Hasselt University,* Brent Hecht, *University of Minnesota*

26 **App Movement: A Platform for Community Commissioning of Mobile Applications**
Andrew Garbett, Rob Comber, Edward Jenkins, Patrick Olivier, *Newcastle University*

38 **Generating Personalized Spatial Analogies for Distances and Areas**
Yea-Seul Kim, Jessica Hullman, *University of Washington,* Maneesh Agrawala, *Stanford University*

Session: How Fast Can You Type on Your Phone?

49 **IJQwerty: What Difference Does One Key Change Make? Gesture Typing Keyboard Optimization Bounded by One Key Position Change from Qwerty**
Xiaojun Bi, Shumin Zhai, *Google, Inc.*

59 **DualKey: Miniature Screen Text Entry via Finger Identification**
Aakar Gupta, Ravin Balakrishnan, *University of Toronto*

71 **One-Dimensional Handwriting: Inputting Letters and Words on Smart Glasses**
Chun Yu, Ke Sun, Mingyuan Zhong, Xincheng Li, Peijun Zhao, *Tsinghua University* Yuanchun Shi, *Tsinghua University & Qinghai University*

83 **A Cost–Benefit Study of Text Entry Suggestion Interaction**
Philip Quinn, *Google Inc. & University of Canterbury,* Shumin Zhai, *Google, Inc.*

Session: Front Stage on Social Media

89 **The Social Media Ecology: User Perceptions, Strategies and Challenges**
Xuan Zhao, Cliff Lampe, Nicole B. Ellison, *University of Michigan*

101 **Sharing Personal Content Online: Exploring Channel Choice and Multi-Channel Behaviors**
Manya Sleeper, William Melicher, Hana Habib, Lujo Bauer, Lorrie Faith Cranor, *Carnegie Mellon University,* Michelle L. Mazurek, *University of Maryland*

113 **Snap Decisions? How Users, Content, and Aesthetics Interact to Shape Photo Sharing Behaviors**
Sanjay Kairam, *Stanford University,* Joseph 'Jofish' Kaye, John Alexis Guerra-Gomez, David A. Shamma, *Yahoo Labs*

125 **Does Saying This Make Me Look Good? How Posters and Outsiders Evaluate Facebook Updates**
Yi-Chia Wang, *Carnegie Mellon University,* Hayley Hinsberger, *University of Oklahoma,* Robert E. Kraut, *Carnegie Mellon University*

Session: Families and Assistive Technology

130 **Designing Smart Objects with Autistic Children - Four Design Exposès**
Christopher Frauenberger, *Vienna University of Technology & University of Sussex,* Julia Makhaeva, Katharina Spiel, *Vienna University of Technology*

140 **Investigating the Influence of Avatar Facial Characteristics on the Social Behaviors of Children with Autism**
Elizabeth J. Carter, Jennifer Hyde, *Carnegie Mellon University,* Diane L. Williams, *Duquesne University,* Jessica K. Hodgins, *Carnegie Mellon University*

152 **Changing Family Practices with Assistive Technology: MOBERO Improves Morning and Bedtime Routines for Children with ADHD**
Tobias Sonne, Jörg Müller, *Aarhus University,* Paul Marshall, *University College London,* Carsten Obel, Kaj Grønbæk, *Aarhus University*

165 **Incloodle: Evaluating an Interactive Application for Young Children with Mixed Abilities**
Kiley Sobel, Kyle Rector, Susan Evans, Julie A. Kientz, *University of Washington*

Session: 3D Virtual Space

177 **Dynamic Stereoscopic 3D Parameter Adjustment for Enhanced Depth Discrimination**
Arun Kulshreshth, Joseph J. LaViola Jr., *University of Central Florida*

188 **Modeling the Impact of Depth on Pointing Performance**
Izabelle Janzen, *University of British Columbia,* Vasanth K. Rajendran, *Facebook* Kellogg S. Booth, *University of British Columbia,*

Table of Contents

200 Compensating for Distance Compression in Audiovisual Virtual Environments Using Incongruence
Daniel J. Finnegan, Eamonn O'Neill, Michael J. Proulx, *University of Bath*

213 miniStudio: Designers' Tool for Prototyping Ubicomp Space with Interactive Miniature
Han-Jong Kim, Ju-Whan Kim, Tek-Jin Nam, *Korea Advanced Institute of Science and Technology*

Session: Mining Human Behaviors

225 Unsupervised Clickstream Clustering for User Behavior Analysis
Gang Wang, Xinyi Zhang, Shiliang Tang, Haitao Zheng, *University of California, Santa Barbara,* Ben Y. Zhao, *University of California, Santa Barbara*

237 Augur: Mining Human Behaviors from Fiction to Power Interactive Systems
Ethan Fast, William McGrath, Pranav Rajpurkar, Michael S. Bernstein, *Stanford University*

248 Modeling and Understanding Human Routine Behavior
Nikola Banovic, Tofi Buzali, *Carnegie Mellon University,* Fanny Chevalier, *Inria,* Jennifer Mankoff, Anind K. Dey, *Carnegie Mellon University*

261 Setwise Comparison: Consistent, Scalable, Continuum Labels for Computer Vision
Advait Sarkar, *Microsoft Research Cambridge & University of Cambridge,* Cecily Morrison, *Microsoft Research,* Jonas F. Dorn, *Novartis Pharma AG,* Rishi Bedi, *Novartis Pharma AG & Stanford University,* Saskia Steinheimer, *Inselspital, Bern University Hospital,* Jacques Boisvert, *Novartis Pharma AG,* Jessica Burggraaff, *VU University Medical Center,* Marcus D'Souza, *University Hospital Basel,* Peter Kontschieder, Samuel Rota Bulò, *Microsoft Research,* Lorcan Walsh, *Norvatis Pharma AG,* Christian P. Kamm, *University Hospital Bern,* Yordan Zaykov, Abigail Sellen, Siân Lindley, *Microsoft Research*

Session: Behavioral Change

272 TimeAware: Leveraging Framing Effects to Enhance Personal Productivity
Young-Ho Kim, Jae Ho Jeon, *Seoul National University,* Eun Kyoung Choe, *The Pennsylvania State University,* Bongshin Lee, *Microsoft Research,* KwonHyun Kim, Jinwook Seo, *Seoul National University*

284 Personal Tracking of Screen Time on Digital Devices
John Rooksby, Parvin Asadzadeh, Mattias Rost, Alistair Morrison, Matthew Chalmers, *University of Glasgow*

297 Crowd-Designed Motivation: Motivational Messages for Exercise Adherence Based on Behavior Change Theory
Roelof A. J. de Vries, Khiet P. Truong, Sigrid Kwint, Constance H. C. Drossaert, Vanessa Evers, *University of Twente*

309 Understanding the Mechanics of Persuasive System Design: A Mixed-Method Theory-driven Analysis of Freeletics
Hanna Schneider, *University of Munich (LMU),* Kilian Moser, *Technical University Munich,* Andreas Butz, Florian Alt, *University of Munich (LMU)*

Session: Vulnerable Populations and Technological Support

321 Designing for Transient Use: A Human-in-the-loop Translation Platform for Refugees
Deana Brown, Rebecca E. Grinter, *Georgia Institute of Technology*

331 Syrian Refugees and Digital Health in Lebanon: Opportunities for Improving Antenatal Health
Reem Talhouk, *Newcastle University,* Sandra Mesmar, *American University of Beirut,* Anja Thieme, *Microsoft Research,* Madeline Balaam, Patrick Olivier, *Newcastle University,* Chaza Akik, Hala Ghattas, *American University of Beirut*

343 A Real-Time IVR Platform for Community Radio
Konstantinos Kazakos, *Newcastle University,* Siddhartha Asthana, *Indraprastha Institute of Information Technology,* Madeline Balaam, *Newcastle University,* Mona Duggal, *PGIMER,* Amey Holden, *Newcastle University,* Limalemla Jamir, *PGIMER,* Nanda Kishore Kannuri, *Indian Institute of Public Health,* Saurabh Kumar, *PGIMER,* Amarendar Reddy Manindla, Subhashini Arcot Manikam, GVS Murthy, *Indian Institute of Public Health,* Papreen Nahar, Peter Phillimore, *Newcastle University,* Shreyaswi Sathyanath, *A J Institute of Medical Sciences,* Pushpendra Singh, *Indraprastha Institute of Information Technology,* Meenu Singh, *PGIMER,* Pete Wright, *Newcastle University,* Deepika Yadav, *Indraprastha Institute of Information Technology,* Patrick Olivier, *Newcastle University*

355 Contextualizing Intermediated Use in the Developing World: Findings from India & Ghana
Ishita Ghosh, *University of California, Berkeley*

Session: Online Behaviors

360 Could This Be True? I Think So! Expressed Uncertainty in Online Rumoring
Kate Starbird, Emma Spiro, Isabelle Edwards, Kaitlyn Zhou, Jim Maddock, Sindhuja Narasimhan, *University of Washington*

Table of Contents

372 **Order in the Warez Scene – Explaining an Underground Virtual Community with the CPR Framework**
Priyank Chandra, *University of Michigan*

Session: Collaborative Fabrication: Making Much of Machines

384 **Understanding Newcomers to 3D Printing: Motivations, Workflows, and Barriers of Casual Makers**
Nathaniel Hudson, Celena Alcock, Parmit K. Chilana, *University of Waterloo*

397 **How Novices Sketch and Prototype Hand-Fabricated Objects**
Adrien Bousseau, *Inria,* Theophanis Tsandilas, *Inria & Univ Paris-Sud, CNRS (LRI) & Université Paris-Saclay,* Lora Oehlberg, *University of Calgary & Inria & Univ Paris-Sud, CNRS (LRI),* Wendy E. Mackay, *INRIA & Univ Paris-Sud, CNRS (LRI) & Université Paris-Saclay*

409 **RetroFab: A Design Tool for Retrofitting Physical Interfaces using Actuators, Sensors and 3D Printing**
Raf Ramakers, *Autodesk Research & Hasselt University - tUL IMinds,* Fraser Anderson, Tovi Grossman, George Fitzmaurice, *Autodesk Research*

420 **HotFlex: Post-print Customization of 3D Prints Using Embedded State Change**
Daniel Groeger, Elena Chong Loo, Jürgen Steimle, *Max Planck Institute for Informatics*

Session: Learning Feedback

433 **Effects of Pedagogical Agent's Personality and Emotional Feedback Strategy on Chinese Students' Learning Experiences and Performance: A Study Based on Virtual Tai Chi Training Studio**
Yulong Bian, *Shandong University & Shandong Normal University,* Chenglei Yang, Dongdong Guan, Sa Xiao, *Shandong University,* Fengqiang Gao, *Shandong Normal University,* Chia Shen, *Harvard University,* Xiangxu Meng, *Shandong University*

445 **MapSense: Multi-Sensory Interactive Maps for Children Living with Visual Impairments**
Emeline Brule, *CNRS, Telecom ParisTech, & Paris-Saclay University,* Gilles Bailly, *LTCI, CNRS, Télécom ParisTech, Université Paris-Saclay,* Anke Brock, *Inria,* Frederic Valentin, *CNRS, Telecom ParisTech, & Paris-Saclay University,* Grégoire Denis, *IJA,* Christophe Jouffrais, *CNRS & University of Toulouse*

458 **Framing Feedback: Choosing Review Environment Features that Support High Quality Peer Assessment**
Catherine M. Hicks, Vineet Pandey, C. Ailie Fraser, Scott Klemmer, *University of California, San Diego*

470 **Revising Learner Misconceptions Without Feedback: Prompting for Reflection on Anomalies**
Joseph Jay Williams, *Harvard University,* Tania Lombrozo, *University of California, Berkeley,* Anne Hsu, *Queen Mary, University of London,* Bernd Huber, *Harvard University,* Juho Kim, *Stanford University*

Session: Visual Design Principles for Unconventional Displays

475 **Designing Visual Complexity for Dual-screen Media**
Timothy Neate, *Swansea University,* Michael Evans, *British Broadcasting Corporation,* Matt Jones, *Swansea University*

487 **Hidden in Plain Sight: an Exploration of a Visual Language for Near-Eye Out-of-Focus Displays in the Peripheral View**
Kris Luyten, Donald Degraen, Gustavo Alberto Rovelo Ruiz, Sven Coppers, Davy Vanacken, *Hasselt University - tUL iMinds*

498 **Investigating Text Legibility on Non-Rectangular Displays**
Marcos Serrano, *University of Toulouse – IRIT,* Anne Roudaut, *University of Bristol,* Pourang Irani, *University of Manitoba*

509 **The Effect of Focus Cues on Separation of Information Layers**
Patrick Bader, *University of Stuttgart & Stuttgart Media University,* Niels Henze, *University of Stuttgart,* Nora Broy, *BMW Group,* Katrin Wolf, *BTK - University for Art & Design*

Session: Privacy - Social and Geolocated

515 **The Geography and Importance of Localness in Geotagged Social Media**
Isaac L. Johnson, Subhasree Sengupta, *University of Minnesota,* Johannes Schöning, *Hasselt University,* Brent Hecht, *University of Minnesota*

527 **Usability and Security of Text Passwords on Mobile Devices**
William Melicher, Darya Kurilova, Sean M. Segreti, Pranshu Kalvani, Richard Shay, Blase Ur, Lujo Bauer, Nicolas Christin, Lorrie Faith Cranor, *Carnegie Mellon University,* Michelle L. Mazurek, *University of Maryland*

Table of Contents

540 **Evaluation of Personalized Security Indicators as an Anti-Phishing Mechanism for Smartphone Applications**
Claudio Marforio, Ramya Jayaram Masti, *ETH Zurich,* Claudio Soriente, *Telefónica Research,* Kari Kostiainen, Srdjan Čapkun, *ETH Zurich*

552 **Computationally Mediated Pro-Social Deception**
Max Van Kleek, *University of Oxford,* Dave Murray-Rust, Amy Guy, *University of Edinburgh,* Kieron O'Hara, *University of Southampton,* Nigel R. Shadbolt, *University of Oxford*

Session: Social Media Engagement

564 **Changes in Engagement Before and After Posting to Facebook**
Nir Grinberg, *Cornell Tech,* P. Alex Dow, Lada A. Adamic, *Facebook Inc,* Mor Naaman, *Cornell Tech*

575 **Fast, Cheap, and Good: Why Animated GIFs Engage Us**
Saeideh Bakhshi, David A. Shamma, Lyndon Kennedy, Yale Song, Paloma de Juan, Joseph 'Jofish' Kaye, *Yahoo labs*

587 **Engineering Information Disclosure: Norm Shaping Designs**
Daphne Chang, Erin L. Krupka, Eytan Adar, *University of Michigan,* Alessandro Acquisti, *Carnegie Mellon University*

598 **A Market in Your Social Network: The Effects of Extrinsic Rewards on Friendsourcing and Relationships**
Haiyi Zhu, *University of Minnesota, Twin Cities,* Sauvik Das, Yiqun Cao, Shuang Yu, Aniket Kittur, Robert Kraut, *Carnegie Mellon University*

Session: Computer Supported Parenting

610 **LGBT Parents and Social Media: Advocacy, Privacy, and Disclosure during Shifting Social Movements**
Lindsay Blackwell, Jean Hardy, Tawfiq Ammari, Tiffany Veinot, Cliff Lampe, Sarita Schoenebeck, *University of Michigan*

623 **Information Seeking Practices of Parents: Exploring Skills, Face Threats and Social Networks**
Betsy DiSalvo, Parisa Khanipour Roshan, Briana Morrison, Georgia Institute of Technology

635 **"Best of Both Worlds": Opportunities for Technology in Cross-Cultural Parenting**
Svetlana Yarosh, *University of Minnesota, Twin Cities,* Sarita Schoenebeck, *University of Michigan,* Shreya Kothaneth, *SPARK Experience,* Elizabeth Bales, *University of California, San Diego*

648 **Screen Time Tantrums: How Families Manage Screen Media Experiences for Toddlers and Preschoolers**
Alexis Hiniker, Hyewon Suh, Sabina Cao, Julie A. Kientz, *University of Washington*

Session: Personal Informatic: Dear Data

661 **GenomiX: A Novel Interaction Tool for Self-Exploration of Personal Genomic Data**
Orit Shaer, *Wellesley College,* Oded Nov, *New York University,* Johanna Okerlund, *Wellesley College,* Martina Balestra, *New York University,* Elizabeth Stowell, Lauren Westendorf, Christina Pollalis, Jasmine Davis, Liliana Weston, *Wellesley College,* Madeleine Ball, *PersonalGenomes.org*

673 **Taking 5: Work-Breaks, Productivity, and Opportunities for Personal Informatics for Knowledge Workers**
Daniel A. Epstein, *FXPAL & University of Washington,* Daniel Avrahami, Jacob T. Biehl, *FX Palo Alto Laboratory, Inc.*

685 **Metadating: Exploring the Romance and Future of Personal Data**
Chris Elsden, Bettina Nissen, Andrew Garbett, David Chatting, David Kirk, John Vines, *Newcastle University*

699 **Design Opportunities in Three Stages of Relationship Development between Users and Self-Tracking Devices**
Da-jung Kim, Yeoreum Lee, Saeyoung Rho, Youn-kyung Lim, *Korea Advanced Institute of Science and Technology*

VOLUME 2

Session: Older Adult Support

721 **Designing for the Other 'Hereafter': When Older Adults Remember about Forgetting**
Laura Ramos, *University of Technology Sydney & Australian Research Council Centre of Excellence in Cognition and its Disorders,* Elise van den Hoven, *University of Technology Sydney & Eindhoven University of Technology & Australian Research Council Centre & Univ of Dundee,* Laurie Miller, *Royal Prince Alfred Hospital & Australian Research Council Centre & University of Sydney*

733 **Typing Tutor: Individualized Tutoring in Text Entry for Older Adults Based on Input Stumble Detection**
Toshiyuki Hagiya, Toshiharu Horiuchi, Tomonori Yazaki, *KDDI R&D Laboratories, Inc.*

Table of Contents

745 Not For Me: Older Adults Choosing Not to Participate in a Social Isolation Intervention
Jenny Waycott, Frank Vetere, *The University of Melbourne,* Sonja Pedell, *Swinburne University of Technology,* Amee Morgans, *RDNS Institute,* Elizabeth Ozanne, Lars Kulik, *The University of Melbourne*

Session: Real Reality Interfaces

758 The Augmented Climbing Wall: High-Exertion Proximity Interaction on a Wall-Sized Interactive Surface
Raine Kajastila, Leo Holsti, Perttu Hämäläinen, *Aalto University*

770 BitDrones: Towards Using 3D Nanocopter Displays as Interactive Self-Levitating Programmable Matter
Antonio Gomes, Calvin Rubens, Sean Braley, Roel Vertegaal, *Queen's University*

781 Pmomo: Projection Mapping on Movable 3D Object
Yi Zhou, Shuangjiu Xiao, Ning Tang, Zhiyong Wei, Xu Chen, *Shanghai Jiaotong University*

791 Combining Shape-Changing Interfaces and Spatial Augmented Reality Enables Extended Object Appearance
David Lindlbauer, *TU Berlin,* Jens Emil Grønbæk, Morten Birk, Kim Halskov, *Aarhus University,* Marc Alexa, *TU Berlin,* Jörg Müller, *Aarhus University*

Session: Sociotechnical Assemblage: Participation, Interaction & Materiality

803 The Ethics of Unaware Participation in Public Interventions
Annika Waern, *Uppsala University*

815 The Poetics of Socio-Technical Space: Evaluating the Internet of Things Through Craft
Jessica Lingel, *University of Pennsylvania*

827 Object-Oriented Publics
Tom Jenkins, Christopher A. Le Dantec, Carl DiSalvo, Thomas Lodato, Mariam Asad, *Georgia Institute of Technology*

840 Repurposing Bits and Pieces of the Digital
Vygandas 'Vegas Simbelis, *Mobile Life @ Royal Institute of Technology,* Pedro Ferreira, *Mobile Life @ KTH,* Elsa Vaara, *SICS,* Jarmo Laaksolahti, *Mobile Life @ SICS,* Kristina Höök, *KTH - Royal Institute of Technology*

Session: Thinking Critically

852 Five Provocations for Ethical HCI Research
Barry Brown, *University of Stockholm,* Alexandra Weilenmann, *University of Gothenburg,* Donald McMillan, Airi Lampinen, *University of Stockholm*

864 Acting with Technology: Rehearsing for Mixed-Media Live Performances
Louise Barkhuus, Chiara Rossitto, *Stockholm University*

Session: Prototyping for Fabrication: 3D Designing, Modelling & Printing

876 What you Sculpt is What you Get: Modeling Physical Interactive Devices with Clay and 3D Printed Widgets
Michael D. Jones, Kevin Seppi, Dan R. Olsen, *Brigham Young University*

887 On-The-Fly Print: Incremental Printing While Modelling
Huaishu Peng, Rundong Wu, Steve Marschner, François Guimbretière, *Cornell University*

897 CardBoardiZer: Creatively Customize, Articulate and Fold 3D Mesh Models
Yunbo Zhang, Wei Gao, Luis Paredes, Karthik Ramani, *Purdue University*

908 ChronoFab: Fabricating Motion
Rubaiat Habib Kazi, Tovi Grossman, Cory Mogk, Ryan Schmidt, George Fitzmaurice, *Autodesk Research*

Session: Learning @ School

919 Lessons Learned from In-School Use of rTAG: A Robo-Tangible Learning Environment
Victor Girotto, Cecil Lozano, *Arizona State University,* Kasia Muldner, *Carleton University,* Winslow Burleson, *New York University,* Erin Walker, *Arizona State University*

931 Human Proxies for Remote University Classroom Attendance
Clarissa Ishak, Carman Neustaedter, Dan Hawkins, Jason Procyk, *Simon Fraser University,* Michael Massimi, *Facebook*

944 Ingenium: Engaging Novice Students with Latin Grammar
Sharon Zhou, Ivy J. Livingston, Mark Schiefsky, Stuart M. Shieber, Krzysztof Z. Gajos, *Harvard University*

Session: Learning Facilitation

957 Social Situational Language Learning through an Online 3D Game
Gabriel Culbertson, Shiyu Wang, Malte Jung, Erik Andersen, *Cornell University*

969 Using Gamification to Motivate Students with Dyslexia
Daniel Gooch, *The Open University & Institute of Education,* Asimina Vasalou, Laura Benton, *Institute of Education,* Rilla Khaled, *Concordia University*

981 Local Standards for Sample Size at CHI
Kelly Caine, *Clemson University*

Table of Contents

993 **A Comparative Evaluation on Online Learning Approaches using Parallel Coordinate Visualization**
Bum Chul Kwon, *University of Konstanz,* Bongshin Lee, *Microsoft Research*

Session: Paying Attention to Smartphones

998 **Lock n' LoL: Group-based Limiting Assistance App to Mitigate Smartphone Distractions in Group Activities**
Minsam Ko, *Korea,* Seungwoo Choi, *Korea Advanced Institute of Science and Technology,* Koji Yatani, *University of Tokyo,* Uichin Lee, *Korea Advanced Institute of Science and Technology*

1011 **"Silence Your Phones": Smartphone Notifications Increase Inattention and Hyperactivity Symptoms**
Kostadin Kushlev, *University of Virginia,* Jason Proulx, Elizabeth W. Dunn, *University of British Columbia*

1021 **My Phone and Me: Understanding People's Receptivity to Mobile Notifications**
Abhinav Mehrotra, *University of Birmingham & University College London,* Veljko Pejovic, *University of Ljubljana,* Jo Vermeulen, *University of Calgary & University of Birmingham,* Robert Hendley, Mirco Musolesi, *University College London*

Session: Interaction Design for Audio Interfaces

1033 **Voices from the War: Design as a Means of Understanding the Experience of Visiting Heritage**
Daniela Petrelli, Nick Dulake, Mark T. Marshall, *Sheffield Hallam University,* Anna Pisetti, *Museo Storico Italiano Della Guerra,* Elena Not, *Fondazione Bruno Kessler*

1045 **Simplified Audio Production in Asynchronous Voice-Based Discussions**
Venkatesh Sivaraman, *Bexley High School,* Dongwook Yoon, *Cornell University,* Piotr Mitros, *edX*

1055 **Tap the ShapeTones: Exploring the Effects of Crossmodal Congruence in an Audio-Visual Interface**
Oussama Metatla, *Queen Mary University of London,* Nuno N. Correia, *Goldsmiths, University of London,* Fiore Martin, Nick Bryan-Kinns, Tony Stockman, *Queen Mary University of London*

1067 **Maps and Location: Acceptance of Modern Interaction Techniques for Audio Guides**
Philipp Wacker, Kerstin Kreutz, Florian Heller, Jan Borchers, *RWTH Aachen University*

Session: Living Healthy

1072 **Staying the Course: System-Driven Lapse Management for Supporting Behavior Change**
Elena Agapie, Daniel Avrahami, *FXPAL & University of Washington,* Jennifer Marlow, *FX Palo Alto Laboratory, Inc.*

1084 **Designing for Future Behaviors: Understanding the Effect of Temporal Distance on Planned Behaviors**
Minhyang (Mia) Suh, Gary Hsieh, *University of Washington*

1097 **ClimbAware – Investigating Perception and Acceptance of Wearables in Rock Climbing**
Felix Kosmalla, Frederik Wiehr, Florian Daiber, Antonio Krüger, *German Research Center for Artificial Intelligence (DFKI) & Saarland University,* Markus Löchtefeld, *Aalborg University*

1109 **Beyond Abandonment to Next Steps: Understanding and Designing for Life after Personal Informatics Tool Use**
Daniel A. Epstein, Monica Caraway, Chuck Johnston, An Ping, James Fogarty, Sean A. Munson, *University of Washington*

Session: Designing Quality in Social Media

1114 **Supporting Comment Moderators in Identifying High Quality Online News Comments**

1126 **"Popcorn Tastes Good": Participatory Policymaking and Reddit's**
Alissa Centivany, *University of Michigan & University of Toronto,* Bobby Glushko, *University of Toronto*

1138 **Going Dark: Social Factors in Collective Action Against Platform Operators in the Reddit Blackout**
J. Nathan Matias, *Microsoft Research*

1152 **Surviving an "Eternal September": How an Online Community Managed a Surge of Newcomers**
Charles Kiene, *University of Washington,* Andrés Monroy-Hernández, *Microsoft Research,* Benjamin Mako Hill, *University of Washington*

1157 **"This Post Will Just Get Taken Down": Characterizing Removed Pro-Eating Disorder Social Media Content**
Stevie Chancellor, Zhiyuan (Jerry) Lin, Munmun De Choudhury, *Georgia Institute of Technology*

Table of Contents

Session: Physical and Digital Collections

1163 Accountable Artefacts: The Case of the Carolan Guitar
Steve Benford, Adrian Hazzard, Alan Chamberlain, Kevin Glover, Chris Greenhalgh, Liming Xu, Michaela Hoare, Dimitrios Darzentas, *The University of Nottingham*

1176 Things We Own Together: Sharing Possessions at Home
Jane Gruning, *University of Texas at Austin,* Siân Lindley, *Microsoft Research*

1187 Mailing Archived Emails as Postcards: Probing the Value of Virtual Collections
David B. Gerritsen, Dan Tasse, Jennifer K. Olsen, Tatiana A. Vlahovic, Rebecca Gulotta, *Carnegie Mellon University,* William Odom, *Simon Fraser University,* Jason Wiese, *FX Palo Alto Laboratory, Inc.,* John Zimmerman, *Carnegie Mellon University*

1200 Finding Email in a Multi-Account, Multi-Device World
Marta E. Cecchinato, *University College London,* Abigail Sellen, Milad Shokouhi, Gavin Smyth, *Microsoft Research*

Session: Augmented AR and VR Experiences

1211 Novel Optical Configurations for Virtual Reality: Evaluating User Preference and Performance with Focus-tunable and Monovision Near-eye Displays
Robert Konrad, *Stanford University,* Emily A. Cooper, *Dartmouth College,* Gordon Wetzstein, *Stanford University*

1221 Augmenting the Field-of-View of Head-Mounted Displays with Sparse Peripheral Displays
Robert Xiao, *Microsoft Research & Carnegie Mellon University,* Hrvoje Benko, *Microsoft Research*

1233 SnapToReality: Aligning Augmented Reality to the Real World
Benjamin Nuernberger, *Microsoft Research & University of California, Santa Barbara,* Eyal Ofek, Hrvoje Benko, Andrew D. Wilson, *Microsoft Research*

1245 Virtual Objects as Spatial Cues in Collaborative Mixed Reality Environments: How They Shape Communication Behavior and User Task Load
Jens Müller, *University of Konstanz,* Roman Rädle, *University of Konstanz & Microsoft Research,* Harald Reiterer, *University of Konstanz*

1250 VR-STEP: Walking-in-Place using Inertial Sensing for Hands Free Navigation in Mobile VR Environments
Sam Tregillus, Eelke Folmer, *University of Nevada, Reno*

Session: Technological Care for Autism

1256 "Will I always be not social?": Re-Conceptualizing Sociality in the Context of a Minecraft Community for Autism
Kathryn E. Ringland, Christine T. Wolf, Heather Faucett, *University of California, Irvine,* Lynn Dombrowski, *Indiana University - Purdue University Indianapolis,* Gillian R. Hayes, *University of California, Irvine*

1270 Anxiety and Autism: Towards Personalized Digital Health
Will Simm, Maria Angela Ferrario, Adrian Gradinar, Marcia Tavares Smith, Stephen Forshaw, Ian Smith, Jon Whittle, *Lancaster University*

1282 EnhancedTouch: A Smart Bracelet for Enhancing Human-Human Physical Touch
Kenji Suzuki, Taku Hachisu, Kazuki Iida, *University of Tsukuba*

1294 "This is how I want to learn": High Functioning Autistic Teens Co-Designing a Serious Game
Benoît Bossavit, *Public University of Navarre,* Sarah Parsons, *University of Southampton*

Session: Sustainability, Design and Environmental Sensibilities

1300 Challenging the Car Norm: Opportunities for ICT to Support Sustainable Transportation Practices
Hanna Hasselqvist, Mia Hesselgren, Cristian Bogdan, *KTH-Royal Institute of Techonology*

1312 Learning from Green Designers: Green Design as Discursive Practice
Earl Friedberg, Edward Lank, *University of Waterloo*

1324 Understanding and Mitigating the Effects of Device and Cloud Service Design Decisions on the Environmental Footprint of Digital Infrastructure
Chris Preist, Daniel Schien, *University of Bristol,* Eli Blevis, *Indiana University Bloomington*

1338 MyPart: Personal, Portable, Accurate, Airborne Particle Counting
Rundong Tian, Christine Dierk, Christopher Myers, Eric Paulos, *University of California, Berkeley*

Session: Authentication and Privacy

1349 Evaluating the Influence of Targets and Hand Postures on Touch-based Behavioural Biometrics
Daniel Buschek, Alexander De Luca, Florian Alt, *University of Munich (LMU)*

Table of Contents

1362 Enhancing Mobile Content Privacy with Proxemics Aware Notifications and Protection
Huiyuan Zhou, Khalid Tearo, Aniruddha Waje, Elham Alghamdi, *Dalhousie University,* Thamara Alves, Vinicius Ferreira, *Federal University of Sao Carlos,* Kirstie Hawkey, Derek Reilly, *Dalhousie University*

1374 CalendarCast: Setup-Free, Privacy-Preserving, Localized Sharing of Appointment Data
Florian Echtler, *Bauhaus-Universität Weimar*

1379 SkullConduct: Biometric User Identification on Eyewear Computers Using Bone Conduction Through the Skull
Stefan Schneegass, *University of Stuttgart,* Youssef Oualil, *Saarland University,* Andreas Bulling, *Max Planck Institute for Informatics*

1385 Use Your Words: Designing One-time Pairing Codes to Improve User Experience
Sarah Wiseman, *Goldsmiths, University of London,* Gustavo Soto Mino, Anna L. Cox, Sandy J. J. Gould, *University College London,* Joanne Moore, Chris Needham, *BBC*

Session: (Re)understanding Making: A Critical Broadening of Maker Cultures

1390 Reconstituting the Utopian Vision of Making: HCI After Technosolutionism
Silvia Lindtner, *University of Michigan,* Shaowen Bardzell, Jeffrey Bardzell, *Indiana University Bloomington*

1403 Values in Repair
Lara Houston, Steven J. Jackson, *Cornell University,* Daniela K. Rosner, *University of Washington,* Syed Ishtiaque Ahmed, *Cornell University,* Meg Young, *University of Washington,* Laewoo Kang, *Cornell University*

1415 Making Community: The Wider Role of Makerspaces in Public Life
Nick Taylor, *University of Dundee,* Ursula Hurley, *University of Salford,* Philip Connolly, *Disability Rights UK*

1426 Continuing the Dialogue: Bringing Research Accounts Back into the Field
Sarah Fox, Daniela K. Rosner, *University of Washington*

VOLUME 3

Session: Learning Programming

1449 Programming, Problem Solving, and Self-Awareness: Effects of Explicit Guidance
Dastyni Loksa, Andrew J. Ko, *University of Washington,* Will Jernigan, Alannah Oleson, Christopher J. Mendez, Margaret M. Burnett, *Oregon State University*

1462 Understanding Conversational Programmers: A Perspective from the Software Industry
Parmit K. Chilana, *University of Waterloo,* Rishabh Singh, *Microsoft Research,* Philip J. Guo, *University of Rochester*

1473 Blind Spots in Youth DIY Programming: Examining Diversity in Creators, Content, and Comments within the Scratch Online Community
Gabriela T. Richard, *The Pennsylvania State University,* Yasmin B. Kafai, *University of Pennsylvania*

1486 Skill Progression in Scratch Revisited
J. Nathan Matias, Sayamindu Dasgupta, *Massachusetts Institute of Technology,* Benjamin Mako Hill, *University of Washington*

Session: Tracking Fingers

1491 SkinTrack: Using the Body as an Electrical Waveguide for Continuous Finger Tracking on the Skin
Yang Zhang, Junhan Zhou, Gierad Laput, Chris Harrison, *Carnegie Mellon University*

1504 Finexus: Tracking Precise Motions of Multiple Fingertips Using Magnetic Sensing
Ke-Yu Chen, Shwetak N. Patel, *University of Washington,* Sean Keller, *Oculus Research*

1515 FingerIO: Using Active Sonar for Fine-Grained Finger Tracking
Rajalakshmi Nandakumar, Vikram Iyer, *University of Washington,* Desney Tan, *Microsoft Research,* Shyamnath Gollakota, *University of Washington*

1526 DigitSpace: Designing Thumb-to-Fingers Touch Interfaces for One-Handed and Eyes-Free Interactions
Da-Yuan Huang, *National Taiwan University,* Liwei Chan, *Keio University & National Taiwan University,* Shuo Yang, Fan Wang, Rong-Hao Liang, *National Taiwan University,* De-Nian Yang, *Academia Sinica,* Yi-Ping Hung, Bing-Yu Chen, *National Taiwan University*

Session: VR for Collaboration

1538 Head Mounted Projection Display & Visual Attention: Visual Attentional Processing of Head Referenced Static and Dynamic Displays while in Motion and Standing
Çağlar Genç, Shoaib Soomro, Yalçın Duyan, Selim Ölçer, Fuat Balcı, Hakan Ürey, Oğuzhan Özcan, *Koç University*

Table of Contents

1548 Stabilized Annotations for Mobile Remote Assistance
Omid Fakourfar, Kevin Ta, Richard Tang, *University of Calgary,* Scott Bateman, *University of New Brunswick,* Anthony Tang, *University of Calgary*

1561 Parallel Eyes: Exploring Human Capability and Behaviors with Paralleled First Person View Sharing
Shunichi Kasahara, *University of Tokyo & SonyCSL,* Mitsuhito Ando, Kiyoshi Suganuma, *YCAM interlab,* Jun Rekimoto, *University of Tokyo & Sony CSL*

1573 Gaze Augmentation in Egocentric Video Improves Awareness of Intention
Deepak Akkil, Poika Isokoski, *University of Tampere*

Session: I Want to Know my Data: Democratizing, Opening and Comprehending Data

1585 Open Data in Scientific Settings: From Policy to Practice
Irene V. Pasquetto, Ashley E. Sands, *University of California Los Angeles,* Peter T. Darch, *University of Illinois at Urbana-Champaign,* Christine L. Borgman, *University of California Los Angeles*

1597 The Datacatcher: Batch Deployment and Documentation of 130 Location-Aware, Mobile Devices That Put Sociopolitically-Relevant Big Data in People's Hands: Polyphonic Interpretation at Scale
William Gaver, Andy Boucher, Nadine Jarvis, David Cameron, Mark Hauenstein, Sarah Pennington, John Bowers, James Pike, Robin Beitra, Liliana Ovalle, *Goldsmiths, University of London*

1608 Physikit: Data Engagement Through Physical Ambient Visualizations in the Home
Steven Houben, Connie Golsteijn, Sarah Gallacher, Rose Johnson, *University College London,* Saskia Bakker, *Eindhoven University of Technology,* Nicolai Marquardt, Licia Capra, Yvonne Rogers, *University College London*

1620 Accountable: Exploring the Inadequacies of Transparent Financial Practice in the Non-Profit Sector
Matthew Marshall, David S. Kirk, John Vines, *Newcastle University*

Session: The Economics of Being Online

1632 Designing for Labour: Uber and the On-Demand Mobile Workforce
Mareike Glöss, *Uppsala University,* Moira McGregor, Barry Brown, *Mobile Life @ Stockholm University*

1644 'MASTerful' Matchmaking in Service Transactions: Inferred Abilities, Needs and Interests versus Activity Histories
Hyunggu Jung, *University of Washington & Palo Alto Research Center,* Victoria Bellotti, *Palo Alto Research Center & University of California, Santa Cruz,* Afsaneh Doryab, *Carnegie Mellon University,* Dean Leitersdorf, *Technion Israel Institute of Technology,* Jiawei Chen, Benjamin V. Hanrahan, Sooyeon Lee, *The Pennsylvania State University,* Dan Turner, *Palo Alto Research Center,* Anind K. Dey, *Carnegie Mellon University,* John M. Carroll, *The Pennsylvania State University*

1656 Of Two Minds, Multiple Addresses, and One Ledger: Characterizing Opinions, Knowledge, and Perceptions of Bitcoin Across Users and Non-Users
Xianyi Gao, Gradeigh D. Clark, Janne Lindqvist, *Rutgers University*

1669 Hosting via Airbnb: Motivations and Financial Assurances in Monetized Network Hospitality
Airi Lampinen, *Stockholm University,* Coye Cheshire, *University of California, Berkeley*

Session: Designing Physical Games

1681 Digitally Augmenting Sports: An Opportunity for Exploring and Understanding Novel Balancing Techniques
David Altimira, *RMIT University & University of Canterbury,* Florian "Floyd" Mueller, *RMIT University,* Jenny Clarke, Gun Lee, *University of Canterbury,* Mark Billinghurst, *University of South Australia,* Christoph Bartneck, *University of Canterbury*

1692 SwimTrain: Exploring Exergame Design for Group Fitness Swimming
Woohyeok Choi, Jeongmin Oh, *Korea Advanced Institute of Science and Technology,* Darren Edge, *Microsoft Research Asia,* Joohyun Kim, Uichin Lee, *Korea Advanced Institute of Science and Technology*

Session: Work, Multitasking, and Distraction

1705 Influence of Display Transparency on Background Awareness and Task Performance
David Lindlbauer, Klemen Lilija, *TU Berlin,* Robert Walter, *Telekom Innovation Laboratories, TU Berlin,* Jörg Müller, *Aarhus University*

1717 Email Duration, Batching and Self-interruption: Patterns of Email Use on Productivity and Stress
Gloria Mark, *University of California, Irvine,* Shamsi T. Iqbal, Mary Czerwinski, Paul Johns, *Microsoft Research,* Akane Sano, *Massachusetts Institute of Technology,* Yuliya Lutchyn, *Microsoft Research*

Table of Contents

1729 'Don't Waste My Time': Use of Time Information Improves Focus
Steve Whittaker, *University of California, Santa Cruz,* Vaiva Kalnikaite, *Interactables,* Victoria Hollis, Andrew Guydish, *University of California, Santa Cruz*

1739 Neurotics Can't Focus: An *in situ* Study of Online Multitasking in the Workplace
Gloria Mark, *University of California, Irvine,* Shamsi T. Iqbal, Mary Czerwinski, Paul Johns, *Microsoft Research,* Akane Sano, *Massachusetts Institute of Technology*

Session: Physical Disability and Assistive Technologies

1745 An Intimate Laboratory? Prostheses as a Tool for Experimenting with Identity and Normalcy
Cynthia L. Bennett, Keting Cen, Katherine M. Steele, Daniela K. Rosner, *University of Washington*

1757 The Design of Assistive Location-based Technologies for People with Ambulatory Disabilities: A Formative Study
Kotaro Hara, Christine Chan, Jon E. Froehlich, *University of Maryland, College Park*

1769 Helping Hands: Requirements for a Prototyping Methodology for Upper-limb Prosthetics Users
Megan Hofmann, *Colorado State University & Carnegie Mellon University,* Jeffrey Harris, Scott E. Hudson, Jennifer Mankoff, *Carnegie Mellon University*

1781 Motivating Stroke Rehabilitation Through Music: A Feasibility Study Using Digital Musical Instruments in the Home
Pedro Kirk, Mick Grierson, *Goldsmiths University of London,* Rebeka Bodak, *Goldsmiths, University of London, Aarhus University & The Royal Academy of Music,* Nick Ward, Fran Brander, Kate Kelly, *The National Hospital for Neurology and Neurosurgery,* Nicholas Newman, *Hounslow and Richmond Community Health Care NHS Trus,* Lauren Stewart, *Goldsmiths, University of London, Aarhus University & The Royal Academy of Music*

Session: Citizenry and the Sciences: Design as Inquiry and Participation

1786 Everyday Food Science as a Design Space for Community Literacy and Habitual Sustainable Practice
Stacey Kuznetsov, Christina J. Santana, Elenore Long, *Arizona State University*

1798 You Put What, Where? Hobbyist Use of Insertable Devices
Kayla J. Heffernan, Frank Vetere, Shanton Chang, *The University of Melbourne*

1810 On Looking at the Vagina through Labella
Teresa Almeida, Rob Comber, Gavin Wood, Dean Saraf, Madeline Balaam, *Newcastle University*

1822 Citizens for Science and Science for Citizens: The View from Participatory Design
Danial Qaurooni, Ali Ghazinejad, Inna Kouper, Hamid Ekbia, *Indiana University*

1827 To Sign Up, or not to Sign Up? Maximizing Citizen Science Contribution Rates through Optional Registration
Caroline Jay, Robert Dunne, David Gelsthorpe, Markel Vigo, *University of Manchester*

Session: Evaluating Technological Application in Education

1833 Facilitator, Functionary, Friend or Foe? Studying the Role of iPads within Learning Activities Across a School Year
Anne-Marie Mann, Uta Hinrichs, *University of St Andrews,* Janet C. Read, *University of Central Lancashire,* Aaron Quigley, *University of St Andrews*

Session: Quantifying Efficiency of Input Methods

1846 Modeling the Steering Time Difference between Narrowing and Widening Tunnels
Shota Yamanaka, *Meiji University & Japan Society for the Promotion of Science,* Homei Miyashita, *Meiji University*

1857 Modelling Error Rates in Temporal Pointing
Byungjoo Lee, Antti Oulasvirta, *Aalto University*

Session: Mobile Behaviors

1869 Monetary Assessment of Battery Life on Smartphones
Simo Hosio, Denzil Ferreira, Jorge Goncalves, Niels van Berkel, Chu Luo, Muzamil Ahmed, Huber Flores, Vassilis Kostakos, *University of Oulu*

1881 Technology at the Table: Attitudes about Mobile Phone Use at Mealtimes
Carol Moser, Sarita Y. Schoenebeck, Katharina Reinecke, *University of Washington*

1893 "I thought she would like to read it": Exploring Sharing Behaviors in the Context of Declining Mobile Web Use
Frank R. Bentley, S. Tejaswi Peesapati, Karen Church, *Yahoo*

1904 Forget-me-not: History-less Mobile Messaging
Mattias Rost, Christos Kitsos, Alexander Morgan, Martin Podlubny, Pietro Romeo, Edoardo Russo, Matthew Chalmers, *University of Glasgow*

Table of Contents

Session: Touchscreen Interactions

1909 Detecting Swipe Errors on Touchscreens using Grip Modulation
Mohammad Faizuddin Mohd Noor, *University of Glasgow & Universiti Kuala Lumpur,* Simon Rogers, John Williamson, *University of Glasgow*

1921 Characterizing How Interface Complexity Affects Children's Touchscreen Interactions
Julia Woodward, Alex Shaw, Annie Luc, *University of Florida,* Brittany Craig, *St. Catherine University,* Juthika Das, Phillip Hall Jr., *University of Florida,* Akshay Holla, *User Testing, Inc., Baltimore County,* Danielle Sikich, *Western Oregon University,* Quincy Brown, *Bowie State University,* Lisa Anthony, *University of Florida,* Germaine Irwin, *University of Maryland*

1934 Smart Touch: Improving Touch Accuracy for People with Motor Impairments with Template Matching
Martez E. Mott, *University of Washington,* Radu-Daniel Vatavu, *University Stefan cel Mare of Suceava,* Shaun K. Kane, *University of Colorado Boulder,* Jacob O. Wobbrock, *University of Washington*

1947 Indirect 2D Touch Panning: How Does It Affect Spatial Memory and Navigation Performance?
Henri Palleis, Heinrich Hussmann, *University of Munich (LMU)*

1952 EyeSwipe: Dwell-free Text Entry Using Gaze Paths
Andrew Kurauchi, *University of São Paulo,* Wenxin Feng, Ajjen Joshi, *Boston University,* Carlos Morimoto, *University of São Paulo,* Margrit Betke, *Boston University*

Session: VR & Feedback

1957 Annexing Reality: Enabling Opportunistic Use of Everyday Objects as Tangible Proxies in Augmented Reality
Anuruddha Hettiarachchi, Daniel Wigdor, *University of Toronto*

1968 Haptic Retargeting: Dynamic Repurposing of Passive Haptics for Enhanced Virtual Reality Experiences
Mahdi Azmandian, *Microsoft Research & University of Southern California,* Mark Hancock, *Microsoft Research & University of Waterloo,* Hrvoje Benko, Eyal Ofek, Andrew D. Wilson, *Microsoft Research*

1980 HaptoClone (Haptic-Optical Clone) for Mutual Tele-Environment by Real-time 3D Image Transfer with Midair Force Feedback
Yasutoshi Makino, Yoshikazu Furuyama, Seki Inoue, Hiroyuki Shinoda, *The University of Tokyo*

1991 Dexmo: An Inexpensive and Lightweight Mechanical Exoskeleton for Motion Capture and Force Feedback in VR
Xiaochi Gu, *University of Cambridge & Dexta Robotics,* Yifei Zhang, Weize Sun, Yuanzhe Bian, Dao Zhou, *Dexta Robotics,* Per Ola Kristensson, *University of Cambridge*

1996 SwiVRChair: A Motorized Swivel Chair to Nudge Users' Orientation for 360 Degree Storytelling in Virtual Reality
Jan Gugenheimer, Dennis Wolf, Gabriel Haas, Sebastian Krebs, Enrico Rukzio, *Ulm University*

Session: Gamification

2001 Personality-targeted Gamification: A Survey Study on Personality Traits and Motivational Affordances
Yuan Jia, *Indiana University at Indianapolis,* Bin Xu, *Cornell University,* Yamini Karanam, *Indiana University (IUPUI),* Stephen Voida, *University of Colorado & Indiana University,*

2014 Gamer Style: Performance Factors in Gamified Simulation
Surabhi Gupta, *University of Western Australia,* Tim Coles, *Wild Runners,* Cedric Dumas, *Mines Telecom Institute,* Simon J. McBride, DanaKai Bradford, *CSIRO*

2026 Don't Whip Me With Your Games" – Investigating "Bottom-Up" Gamification"
Pascal Lessel, *DFKI GmbH,* Maximilian Altmeyer, Marc Müller, Christian Wolff, Antonio Krüger, *DFKI GmbH & Saarland University*

2038 'Choose a Game': Creation and Evaluation of a Prototype Tool to Support Therapists in Brain Injury Rehabilitation
Cynthia Putnam, Jinghui Cheng, *DePaul University,* Feng Lin, Sai Yalla, Stephanie Wu, *Rosalind Franklin University of Medicine and Science*

Session: Displays and Shared Interactions

2050 Negotiating for Space? Collaborative Work Using a Wall Display with Mouse and Touch Input
Mikkel R. Jakobsen, Kasper Hornbæk, *University of Copenhagen*

2062 An Actionable Approach to Understand Group Experience in Complex, Multi-surface Spaces
Roberto Martinez-Maldonado, *University of Technology Sydney & The University of Sydney,* Peter Goodyear, Judy Kay, *The University of Sydney,* Kate Thompson, *University of Technology Sydney & Griffith University,* Lucila Carvalho, *University of Technology Sydney*

Table of Contents

2075 Shared Interaction on a Wall-Sized Display in a Data Manipulation Task
Can Liu, *Univ Paris-Sud, CNRS & Inria and Telecom ParisTech,* Olivier Chapuis, Michel Beaudouin-Lafon, *University Paris-Sud & CNRS and INRIA,* Eric Lecolinet, *Telecom ParisTech – CNRS LTCI UMR 5141*

2087 Creating Your Bubble: Personal Space On and Around Large Public Displays
James R. Wallace, Nancy Iskander, Edward Lank, *University of Waterloo*

2093 Gaze-based Notetaking for Learning from Lecture Videos
Cuong Nguyen, Feng Liu, *Portland State University*

Session: Mental Health in Technology Design and Social Media

2098 Discovering Shifts to Suicidal Ideation from Mental Health Content in Social Media
Munmun De Choudhury, *Georgia Institute of Technology,* Emre Kiciman, *Microsoft Research,* Mark Dredze, *Johns Hopkins University,* Glen Coppersmith, *Qntfy.io,* Mrinal Kumar, *Georgia Institute of Technology*

2111 Recovery Amid Pro-Anorexia: Analysis of Recovery in Social Media
Stevie Chancellor, Tanushree Mitra, Munmun De Choudhury, *Georgia Institute of Technology*

2124 Health Technologies 'In the Wild': Experiences of Engagement with Computerised CBT
Stefan Rennick-Egglestone, *The University of Nottingham,* Sarah Knowles, *The University of Manchester,* Gill Toms, *University of Bangor,* Penny Bee, Karina Lovell, Peter Bower, *The University of Manchester*

2136 Challenges for Designing new Technology for Health and Wellbeing in a Complex Mental Healthcare Context
Anja Thieme, *Microsoft Research,* John McCarthy, *University College Cork,* Paula Johnson, Stephanie Phillips, *Calderstones Partnership NHS Foundation Trust,* Jayne Wallace, *Northumbria University,* Siân Lindley, *Microsoft Research,* Karim Ladha, Daniel Jackson, Diana Nowacka, Ashur Rafiev, Cassim Ladha, Thomas Nappey, Mathew Kipling, Peter Wright, *Newcastle University,* Thomas D. Meyer, *University of Texas,* Patrick Olivier, *Newcastle University*

Session: Visual Impairment and Technology

2150 Haptic Wave: A Cross-Modal Interface for Visually Impaired Audio Producers
Atau Tanaka, Adam Parkinson, *Goldsmiths, University of London*

2162 "I Always Wanted to See the Night Sky": Blind User Preferences for Sensory Substitution Devices
Giles Hamilton-Fletcher, Marianna Obrist, Phil Watten, *University of Sussex,* Michele Mengucci, *Laboratory for Interaction and Orality,* Jamie Ward, *University of Sussex*

2175 Linespace: A Sensemaking Platform for the Blind
Saiganesh Swaminathan, *Potsdam,* Thijs Roumen, Robert Kovacs, David Stangl, Stefanie Mueller, Patrick Baudisch, *Hasso Plattner Institute*

2186 Tangible Reels: Construction and Exploration of Tangible Maps by Visually Impaired Users
Julie Ducasse, *University of Toulouse & CNRS,* Marc J-M Macé, *CNRS – IRIT,* Marcos Serrano, *University of Toulouse & CNRS; IRIT,* Christophe Jouffrais, *CNRS - IRIT*

Session: What Lies Beyond? Design and Infrastructure through a Critical Lens

2198 Breaking Down While Building Up: Design and Decline in Emerging Infrastructures
Stephanie B. Steinhardt, *Cornell University*

2209 Logistics as Care and Control: An Investigation into the UNICEF Supply Division
Margaret Jack, Steven J. Jackson, *Cornell University*

2220 The Ins and Outs of HCI for Development
Nicola Dell, *Cornell Tech,* Neha Kumar, *Georgia Institute of Technology*

2233 Design(ing) 'Here' and 'There': Tech Entrepreneurs, Global Markets, and Reflexivity in Design Processes
Seyram Avle, Silvia Lindtner, *University of Michigan*

Session: Design, Labour and the Invisible Perils of Crowdsourcing

2246 "Why would anybody do this?" Understanding Older Adults' Motivations and Challenges in Crowd Work
Robin Brewer, *Northwestern University,* Meredith Ringel Morris, *Microsoft Research,* Anne Marie Piper, *Northwestern University*

2258 The Knowledge Accelerator: Big Picture Thinking in Small Pieces
Nathan Hahn, Joseph Chang, *Human-Computer Interaction Institute,* Ji Eun Kim, *Bosch Corporate Research,* Aniket Kittur, *Carnegie Mellon University*

Table of Contents

2271 **Taking a HIT: Designing around Rejection, Mistrust, Risk, and Workers' Experiences in Amazon Mechanical Turk**
Brian McInnis, Dan Cosley, Chaebong Nam, Gilly Leshed, *Cornell University*

Session: HCI and Physiological Interactions

2283 **Framework for Electroencephalography-based Evaluation of User Experience**
Jérémy Frey, *University Bordeaux,* Maxime Daniel, Julien Castet, *Immersion SAS,* Martin Hachet, Fabien Lotte, *Inria*

2295 **Intelligent Agents and Networked Buttons Improve Free-Improvised Ensemble Music-Making on Touch-Screens**
Charles Martin, Henry Gardner, Ben Swift, Michael Martin, *The Australian National University*

Session: In-Air Gesture

2307 **M.Gesture: An Acceleration-Based Gesture Authoring System on Multiple Handheld and Wearable Devices**
Ju-Whan Kim, Han-Jong Kim, Tek-Jin Nam, *Korea Advanced Institute of Science and Technology*

2319 **Do That, There: An Interaction Technique for Addressing In-Air Gesture Systems**
Euan Freeman, Stephen Brewster, *University of Glasgow,* Vuokko Lantz, *Nokia Technologies*

2332 **EMPress: Practical Hand Gesture Classification with Wrist-Mounted EMG and Pressure Sensing**
Jess McIntosh, Charlie McNeill, Mike Fraser, *University of Bristol,* Frederic Kerber, Markus Löchtefeld, Antonio Krüger, *German Research Center for Artificial Intelligence (DFKI) & Saarland University*

2343 **Skeletons and Silhouettes: Comparing User Representations at a Gesture-based Large Display**
Christopher Ackad, Martin Tomitsch, Judy Kay, *The University of Sydney*

2348 **Proactive Sensing for Improving Hand Pose Estimation**
Dun-Yu Hsiao, *University of Washington,* Min Sun, *National Tsing Hua University,* Christy Ballweber, *University of Washington,* Seth Cooper, *Northeastern University,* Zoran Popović, *University of Washington*

VOLUME 4

Session: Curation and Algorithms

2371 **First I like" it then I hide it: Folk Theories of Social Feeds**
Motahhare Eslami, Karrie Karahalios, *University of Illinois at Urbana-Champaign,* Christian Sandvig, *University of Michigan,* Kristen Vaccaro, *University of Illinois at Urbana-Champaign,* Aimee Rickman, *California State University, Fresno,* Kevin Hamilton, *University of Illinois,* Alex Kirlik, *University of Illinois at Urbana-Champaign,*

2383 **Accounting for Taste: Ranking Curators and Content in Social Networks**
Haizi Yu, Biplab Deka, *University of Illinois at Urbana-Champaign,* Jerry O. Talton, *Apropose, Inc.,* Ranjitha Kumar, *University of Illinois at Urbana-Champaign*

2390 **How Much Information? Effects of Transparency on Trust in an Algorithmic Interface**
René F. Kizilcec, *Stanford University*

2396 **Communities Found by Users – not Algorithms: Comparing Human and Algorithmically Generated Communities**
Alexandra Lee, Daniel Archambault, *Swansea University*

2401 **Hashtag Drift: Tracing the Evolving Uses of Political Hashtags Over Time**
Kyle Booten, *University of California, Berkeley*

Session: Contextual Awareness

2406 **The Impact of the Encoding View in Location-Based Reminders: Improving Prospective Remembering**
Yao Wang, *Virginia Tech,* Mark Schlager, *Samsung Research America,* Manuel Pérez-Quinones, *University of North Carolina, Charlotte*

2417 **Technology and the Politics of Mobility: Evidence Generation in Accessible Transport Activism**
Sunil Rodger, John Vines, Janice McLaughlin, *Newcastle University*

2430 **Supporting Opportunities for Context-Aware Social Matching: An Experience Sampling Study**
Julia M. Mayer, Starr Roxanne Hiltz, *New Jersey Institute of Technology,* Louise Barkhuus, *New Jersey Institute of Technology & Cornell Tech,* Kaisa Väänänen, *Tampere University of Technology,* Quentin Jones, *New Jersey Institute of Technology*

Table of Contents

2442 Helping Computers Understand Geographically-Bound Activity Restrictions
Marcus Soll, Philipp Naumann, *University of Hamburg,* Johannes Schöning, Pavel Samsonov, *Hasselt University - tUL – iMinds,* Brent Hecht, *University of Minnesota*

Session: Distance Still Matters

2447 RAMPARTS: Supporting Sensemaking with Spatially-Aware Mobile Interactions
Paweł Woźniak, *Chalmers University of Technology,* Nitesh Goyal, *Cornell University,* Przemysław Kucharski, *Lodz University of Technology,* Lars Lischke, Sven Mayer, *University of Stuttgart,* Morten Fjeld, *Chalmers University of Technology*

2461 Far but Near or Near but Far? The Effects of Perceived Distance on the Relationship between Geographic Dispersion and Perceived Diversity
Lionel P. Robert, *University of Michigan*

2474 Ritual Machines I & II: Making Technology at Home
David S. Kirk, David Chatting, *Newcastle University,* Paulina Yurman, Jo-Anne Bichard, *Royal College of Art*

2487 Office Social: Presentation Interactivity for Nearby Devices
Debaleena Chattopadhyay, *Microsoft Research & Indiana University,* Kenton O'Hara, Sean Rintel, Roman Rädle, *Microsoft Research*

2492 Gazed and Confused: Understanding and Designing Shared Gaze for Remote Collaboration
Sarah D'Angelo, Darren Gergle, *Northwestern University*

Session: Enabling End-Users and Designers

2497 Using and Exploring Hierarchical Data in Spreadsheets
Kerry Shih-Ping Chang, Brad A. Myers, *Carnegie Mellon University*

2508 Airways: Optimization-Based Planning of Quadrotor Trajectories according to High-Level User Goals
Christoph Gebhardt, *ETH* Benjamin Hepp, Tobias Nägeli, *ETH Zurich,* Stefan Stevšić, *ETH,* Otmar Hilliges, *ETH Zurich*

2520 SelPh: Progressive Learning and Support of Manual Photo Color Enhancement
Yuki Koyama, Daisuke Sakamoto, Takeo Igarashi, *University of Tokyo*

2533 A Live, Multiple-Representation Probabilistic Programming Environment for Novices
Maria I. Gorinova, Advait Sarkar, *University of Cambridge,* Alan F. Blackwell, *Computer Laboratory, University of Cambridge,* Don Syme, *Microsoft Research Cambridge*

Session: Interventions to Design Theory

2538 Dynamics, Multiplicity and Conceptual Blends in HCI
Susanne Bødker, Clemens Nylandsted Klokmose, *Aarhus University*

,2549 From Research Prototype to Research Product
William Odom, *Simon Fraser University,* Ron Wakkary, *Simon Fraser University & Eindhoven University of Technology,* Youn-kyung Lim, *Korea Advanced Institute of Science and Technology,* Audrey Desjardins, *Simon Fraser University,* Bart Hengeveld, *Eindhoven University of Technology,* Richard Banks, *Microsoft Research*

2562 Designing Media Architecture: Tools and Approaches for Addressing the Main Design Challenges
Peter Dalsgaard, Kim Halskov, *Aarhus University,* Alexander Wiethoff, *University of Munich (LMU)*

Session: HCI and Gender

2574 An Archive of Their Own: A Case Study of Feminist HCI and Values in Design
Casey Fiesler, *University of Colorado – Boulder,* Shannon Morrison, *College of Charleston,* Amy S. Bruckman, *Georgia Institute of Technology*

2586 Finding Gender-Inclusiveness Software Issues with GenderMag: A Field Investigation
Margaret Burnett, Anicia Peters, Charles Hill, *Oregon State University,* Noha Elarief, *Hewlett Packard*

2599 HCI and Intimate Care as an Agenda for Change in Women's Health
Teresa Almeida, Rob Comber, Madeline Balaam, *Newcastle University*

2612 A Feminist HCI Approach to Designing Postpartum Technologies: "When I first saw a breast pump I was wondering if it was a joke."
Catherine D'Ignazio, *Emerson College & Massachusetts Institute of Technology,* Alexis Hope, *Massachusetts Institute of Technology,* Becky Michelson, *Emerson College,* Robyn Churchill, *Clinton Health Access Initiative,* Ethan Zuckerman, *Massachusetts Institute of Technology*

Session: Complex Tasks and Learning in Crowdsourcing

2623 Toward a Learning Science for Complex Crowdsourcing Tasks
Shayan Doroudi, *Carnegie Mellon University,* Ece Kamar, *Microsoft Research,* Emma Brunskill, *Carnegie Mellon University,* Eric Horvitz, *Microsoft Research*

Table of Contents

2635 **Learning from the Crowd: Observational Learning in Crowdsourcing Communities**
Lena Mamykina, *Columbia University,* Thomas N. Smyth, *Sassafras Tech Collective,* Jill P. Dimond, *Sassafras Tech Collective,* Krzysztof Z. Gajos, *Harvard University*

2645 **Atelier: Repurposing Expert Crowdsourcing Tasks as Micro-internships**
Ryo Suzuki, *University of Colorado Boulder,* Niloufar Salehi, Michelle S. Lam, Juan C. Marroquin, Michael S. Bernstein, *Stanford University*

2657 **Supporting Collaborative Writing with Microtasks**
Jaime Teevan, Shamsi T. Iqbal, Curtis von Veh, *Microsoft Research*

Session: Game and Design

2669 **Designing Brutal Multiplayer Video Games**
Joe Marshall, *University of Nottingham,* Conor Linehan, *University College Cork,* Adrian Hazzard, *University of Nottingham*

2681 **Thighrim and Calf-Life: A Study of the Conversion of Off-the-Shelf Video Games into Exergames**
Mallory Ketcheson, Luke Walker, T.C. Nicholas Graham, *Queen's University*

Session: Crowdsourcing and Creation: Large-scale Ideas and Content Production

2693 **Enabling Designers to Foresee Which Colors Users Cannot See**
Katharina Reinecke, *University of Washington,* David R. Flatla, *University of Dundee,* Christopher Brooks, *University of Michigan*

2705 **Scaffolding Community Documentary Film Making using Commissioning Templates**
Tom Bartindale, *Newcastle University,* Guy Schofield, *University of York,* Peter Wright, *Newcastle University*

2717 **Comparing Different Sensemaking Approaches for Large-Scale Ideation**
Joel Chan, Steven Dang, *Carnegie Mellon University,* Steven P. Dow, *University of California, San Diego*

2729 **Improving Comprehension of Numbers in the News**
Pablo J. Barrio, *Columbia University,* Daniel G. Goldstein, Jake M. Hofman, *Microsoft Research*

Session: Embodied Interaction

2740 **Sketching Shape-changing Interfaces: Exploring Vocabulary, Metaphors Use, and Affordances**
Majken K. Rasmussen, *University of Aarhus,* Giovanni M. Troiano, *University of Copenhagen,* Marianne G. Petersen, *Aarhus University,* Jakob G. Simonsen, Kasper Hornbæk, *University of Copenhagen*

2752 **Understanding Affordance, System State, and Feedback in Shape-Changing Buttons**
John Tiab, Kasper Hornbæk, *University of Copenhagen*

2764 **Materiable: Rendering Dynamic Material Properties in Response to Direct Physical Touch with Shape Changing Interfaces**
Ken Nakagaki, Luke Vink, Jared Counts, Daniel Windham, Daniel Leithinger, Sean Follmer, Hiroshi Ishii, *Massachusetts Institute of Technology*

2773 **High-Low Split: Divergent Cognitive Construal Levels Triggered by Digital and Non-digital Platforms**
Geoff Kaufman, *Carnegie Mellon University,* Mary Flanagan, *Dartmouth College*

2778 **ShapeCanvas: An Exploration of Shape-Changing Content Generation by Members of the Public**
Aluna Everitt, Faisal Taher, Jason Alexander, *Lancaster University*

Session: Big Data and Local Society

2783 **Finding the Way to OSM Mapping Practices: Bounding Large Crisis Datasets for Qualitative Investigation**
Marina Kogan, Jennings Anderson, Leysia Palen, Kenneth M. Anderson, Robert Soden, *University of Colorado Boulder*

2796 **Infrastructure in the Wild: What Mapping in Post-Earthquake Nepal Reveals about Infrastructural Emergence**
Robert Soden, Leysia Palen, *University of Colorado, Boulder*

2808 **Why and How Traffic Safety Cultures Matter when Designing Advisory Traffic Information Systems**
MinJuan Wang, Sus Lundgren Lyckvi, Fang Chen, *Chalmers University of Technology*

2819 **It's Just My History Isn't It? Understanding Smart Journaling Practices**
Chris Elsden, Abigail C. Durrant, David S. Kirk, *Newcastle University*

Table of Contents

Session: Touch Interaction

2832 Expressy: Using a Wrist-worn Inertial Measurement Unit to Add Expressiveness to Touch-based Interactions
Gerard Wilkinson, Ahmed Kharrufa, *Newcastle University,* Jonathan Hook, *University of York,* Bradley Pursglove, Gavin Wood, Hendrik Haeuser, Nils Y. Hammerla, *Newcastle University* Steve Hodges, *Microsoft Research,* Patrick Olivier, *Newcastle University*

2845 Partially-indirect Bimanual Input with Gaze, Pen, and Touch for Pan, Zoom, and Ink Interaction
Ken Pfeuffer, Jason Alexander, Hans Gellersen, *Lancaster University*

2857 Hammer Time! A Low-Cost, High Precision, High Accuracy Tool to Measure the Latency of Touchscreen Devices
Jonathan Deber, *Tactual Labs,* Bruno Araujo, Ricardo Jota, Clifton Forlines, *University of Toronto & Tactual Labs,* Darren Leigh, Steven Sanders, *Tactual Labs,* Daniel Wigdor, *University of Toronto*

2869 Pre-Touch Sensing for Mobile Interaction
Ken Hinckley, *Microsoft Research,* Seongkook Heo, *Microsoft Research & Korea Advanced Institute of Science and Technology,* Michel Pahud, Christian Holz, Hrvoje Benko, Abigail Sellen, Richard Banks, Kenton O'Hara, Gavin Smyth, William Buxton, *Microsoft Research*

Session: Managing Design for Life Disruptions

2882 Transition Resilience with ICTs: 'Identity Awareness' in Veteran Re-Integration
Bryan C. Semaan, Lauren M. Britton, Bryan Dosono, *Syracuse University*

2895 Digital Footprints and Changing Networks During Online Identity Transitions
Oliver L. Haimson, *University of California, Irvine,* Jed R. Brubaker, *University of Colorado Boulder,* Lynn Dombrowski, *Indiana University - Purdue University Indianapolis,* Gillian R. Hayes, *University of California, Irvine*

2908 Legacy Contact: Designing and Implementing Post-mortem Stewardship at Facebook
Jed R. Brubaker, *University of Colorado Boulder & Facebook,* Vanessa Callison-Burch, *Facebook*

2920 "PS. I Love You": Understanding the Impact of Posthumous Digital Messages
Sue Jamison-Powell, *Sheffield Hallam University,* Pam Briggs, Shaun Lawson, *Northumbria University,* Conor Linehan, *University College Cork,* Karen Windle, Harriet Gross, *University of Lincoln*

Session: Civic Tech, Participation and Society

2933 Data and the City
Donald McMillan, Arvid Engström, Airi Lampinen, Barry Brown, *Stockholm University*

2945 Reflections on Deploying Distributed Consultation Technologies with Community Organisations
Ian G. Johnson, John Vines, *Newcastle University,* Nick Taylor, *University of Dundee,* Edward Jenkins, *Newcastle University,* Justin Marshall, *Falmouth University*

2958 Re-Making Places: HCI, 'Community Building' and Change
Clara Crivellaro, *Newcastle University,* Alex Taylor, *Microsoft Research Cambridge,* Vasillis Vlachokyriakos, Rob Comber, Bettina Nissen, Peter Wright, *Newcastle University*

2970 Data, Design and Civics: An Exploratory Study of Civic Tech
Kirsten Boehner, Carl DiSalvo, *Georgia Institute of Technology*

Session: Players' Motivations in Games

2982 Fostering Intrinsic Motivation through Avatar Identification in Digital Games
Max V. Birk, Cheralyn Atkins, Jason T. Bowey, Regan L. Mandryk, *University of Saskatchewan*

2996 Negative Emotion, Positive Experience? Emotionally Moving Moments in Digital Games
Julia Ayumi Bopp, Elisa D. Mekler, Klaus Opwis *University of Basel*

3007 The Effects of Social Exclusion on Play Experience and Hostile Cognitions in Digital Games
Max V. Birk, *University of Saskatchewan,* Benjamin Buttlar, *University of Trier,* Jason T. Bowey, *University of Saskatchewan,* Susanne Poeller, *University of Trier,* Shelby C. Thomson, *University of Saskatchewan,* Nicola Baumann, *University of Trier,* Regan L. Mandryk, *University of Saskatchewan*

3020 Designing Closeness to Increase Gamers' Performance
Lucas Colusso, Gary Hsieh, Sean A. Munson, *University of Washington*

Session: Workplace Social Performance

3025 What is Your Organization 'Like'? A Study of Liking Activity in the Enterprise
Ido Guy, *Yahoo Labs,* Inbal Ronen, Naama Zwerdling, *IBM Research – Haifa,* Irena Zuyev-Grabovitch, *Yahoo Labs,* Michal Jacovi, *IBM Research - Haifa*

Table of Contents

3038 **Find an Expert: Designing Expert Selection Interfaces for Formal Help-Giving**
Sharoda A. Paul, *GE Global Research*

3049 **The Role of ICT in Office Work Breaks**
Anya Skatova, Ben Bedwell, *University of Nottingham,* Victoria Shipp, *The Insight Lab & University of Nottingham,* Yitong Huang, Alexandra Young, Tom Rodden, *University of Nottingham,* Emma Bertenshaw, *Unilever R&D*

3061 **Let's Stitch Me and You Together! Designing a Photo Co-creation Activity to Stimulate Playfulness in the Workplace**
Di Lu, *University of Pittsburgh,* Casey Dugan, *IBM T.J. Watson Research Center,* Rosta Farzan, *University of Pittsburgh,* Werner Geyer, *IBM T.J. Watson Research Center*

Session: Patients' Participation in Online and Offline Settings

3066 **The Quantified Patient in the Doctor's Office: Challenges & Opportunities**
Peter West, Richard Giordano, *University of Southampton,* Max Van Kleek, Nigel Shadbolt, *University of Oxford*

3079 **Breaking the Sound Barrier: Designing for Patient Participation in Audiological Consultations**
Yngve Dahl, Geir Kjetil Hanssen, *SINTEF ICT*

3091 **Who's the Doctor? Physicians' Perception of Internet Informed Patients in India**
Rajesh Chandwani, Vaibhavi Kulkarni, *Indian Institute of Management*

3103 **"Not Just a Receiver": Understanding Patient Behavior in the Hospital Environment**
Sonali R. Mishra, Shefali Haldar, *University of Washington,* Ari H. Pollack, *University of Washington & Seattle Children's Hospital,* Logan Kendall, Andrew D. Miller, Maher Khelifi, Wanda Pratt, *University of Washington*

Session: User Experience and Performance

3115 **The Impact of Causal Attributions on System Evaluation in Usability Tests**
Adelka Niels, *University of Applied Sciences,* Sascha R. Guczka, *University of Hamburg,* Monique Janneck, *Luebeck University of Applied Sciences*

3126 **Personality of Interaction: Expressing Brand Personalities Through Interaction Aesthetics**
Peter Tolstrup Aagesen, Clint Heyer, *Malmö University*

3131 **Somaesthetic Appreciation Design**
Kristina Höök, Martin P. Jonsson, *KTH,* Anna Ståhl, Johanna Mercurio, *SICS*

Session: Microtasks and Crowdsourcing

3143 **Chain Reactions: The Impact of Order on Microtask Chains**
Carrie J. Cai, *Massachusetts Institute of Technology,* Shamsi T. Iqbal, Jaime Teevan, *Microsoft Research*

3155 **How One Microtask Affects Another**
Edward Newell, Derek Ruths, *McGill University*

3167 **Embracing Error to Enable Rapid Crowdsourcing**
Ranjay A. Krishna, Kenji Hata, Stephanie Chen, Joshua Kravitz, *Stanford University,* David A. Shamma, *Yahoo Research,* Li Fei-Fei, Michael S. Bernstein, *Stanford University*

3180 **Alloy: Clustering with Crowds and Computation**
Joseph Chee Chang, Aniket Kittur, Nathan Hahn, *Carnegie Mellon University*

Session: Software and Programming Tools

3192 **Towards Providing On-Demand Expert Support for Software Developers**
Yan Chen, Steve Oney, Walter S. Lasecki, *University of Michigan*

3204 **The Social Side of Software Platform Ecosystems**
Cleidson R. B. de Souza, *Vale Institute of Technology & Federal University of Pará,* Fernando Figueira Filho, *Federal University of Rio Grande do Norte,* Mu?:ler Miranda, Renato Pina Ferreira, *Federal University of Pará,* Christoph Treude, *University of São Paulo,* Leif Singer, *University of Victoria*

3215 **Tales of Software Updates: The process of updating software**
Kami Vaniea, *The University of Edinburgh,* Yasmeen Rashidi, *Indiana University Bloomington*

3227 **Trigger-Action Programming in the Wild: An Analysis of 200,000 IFTTT Recipes**
Blase Ur, *Carnegie Mellon University,* Melwyn Pak Yong Ho, Stephen Brawner, Jiyun Lee, *Brown University,* Sarah Mennicken, *University of Zurich,* Noah Picard, Diane Schulze, Michael L. Littman, *Brown University*

Table of Contents

3232 **Using Runtime Traces to Improve Documentation and Unit Test Authoring for Dynamic Languages**
Jan-Peter Krämer, *RWTH Aachen University & Adobe Research,* Joel Brandt, *Adobe Research,* Jan Borchers, *RWTH Aachen University*

Session: Did You Feel the Vibration? Haptic Feedback Everywhere

3238 **Cross-Field Aerial Haptics: Rendering Haptic Feedback in Air with Light and Acoustic Fields**
Yoichi Ochiai, *University of Tsukuba,* Kota Kumagai, *Utsunomiya University,* Takayuki Hoshi, *Nagoya Institute of Technology,* Satoshi Hasegawa, Yoshio Hayasaki, *Utsunomiya University*

3248 **HapTurk: Crowdsourcing Affective Ratings of Vibrotactile Icons**
Oliver S. Schneider, Hasti Seifi, Salma Kashani, Matthew Chun, Karon E. MacLean, *University of British Columbia*

3261 **AmbiVibe: Design and Evaluation of Vibrations for Progress Monitoring**
Jessica R. Cauchard, Janette L. Cheng, *Stanford University,* Thomas Pietrzak, *University Lille,* James A. Landay, *Stanford University*

3272 **Motion Guidance Sleeve: Guiding the Forearm Rotation through External Artificial Muscles**
Chia-Yu Chen, Yen-Yu Chen, Yi-Ju Chung, Neng-Hao Yu, *National ChengChi University,*

3277 **GauntLev: A Wearable to Manipulate Free-floating Objects**
Asier Marzo, *Sussex University & Bristol University*

Volume 5

Session: Designing for Attention and Multitasking

3299 **Spatio-Temporal Modeling and Prediction of Visual Attention in Graphical User Interfaces**
Pingmei Xu, *Princeton University,* Yusuke Sugano, Andreas Bulling, *Max Planck Institute for Informatics*

3311 **Now Check Your Input: Brief Task Lockouts Encourage Checking, Longer Lockouts Encourage Task Switching**
Sandy J. J. Gould, Anna L. Cox, Duncan P. Brumby, Alice Wickersham, *University College London*

3324 **Getting Users' Attention in Web Apps in Likable, Minimally Annoying Ways**
Dan Tasse, *Carnegie Mellon University,* Anupriya Ankolekar, *Hewlett Packard Labs,* Joshua Hailpern, *HP Labs & HP ArcSight*

3335 **Window Shopping: A Study of Desktop Window Switching**
Andrew Warr, Ed H. Chi, Helen Harris, Alexander Kuscher, Jenn Chen, Robert Flack, Nicholas Jitkoff, *Google, Inc.*

Session: Politics on Social Media

3339 **Constructing the Visual Online Political Self: An Analysis of Instagram Use by the Scottish Electorate**
Jamie Mahoney, *University of Lincoln,* Tom Feltwell, *Northumbria University,* Obinna Ajuruchi, *University of Lincoln,* Shaun Lawson, *Northumbria University*

3352 **#Snowden: Understanding Biases Introduced by Behavioral Differences of Opinion Groups on Social Media**
Q. Vera Liao, Wai-Tat Fu, *University of Illinois at Urbana-Champaign,* Markus Strohmaier, *GESIS-Leibniz Institute for the Social Sciences*

3364 **ICT Use by Prominent Activists in Republika Srpska**
Borislav Tadic, Markus Rohde, Volker Wulf, David Randall, *University of Siegen*

3378 **Gender and Ideology in the Spread of Anti-Abortion Policy**
Amy X. Zhang, *Massachusetts Institute of Technology,* Scott Counts, *Microsoft Research*

Session: Gesture Elicitation and Interaction

3390 **Between-Subjects Elicitation Studies: Formalization and Tool Support**
Radu-Daniel Vatavu, *University Stefan cel Mare of Suceava,* Jacob O. Wobbrock, *University of Washington*

3403 **User Elicitation on Single-hand Microgestures**
Edwin Chan, Teddy Seyed, *University of Calgary,* Wolfgang Stuerzlinger, *Simon Fraser University,* Xing-Dong Yang, *Dartmouth College,* Frank Maurer, *University of Calgary*

3415 **PathSync: Multi-User Gestural Interaction with Touchless Rhythmic Path Mimicry**
Marcus Carter, *The University of Melbourne,* Eduardo Velloso, *Lancaster University,* John Downs, *The University of Melbourne,* Abigail Sellen, Kenton O'Hara, *Microsoft Research,* Frank Vetere, *The University of Melbourne*

3428 **Machine Learning of Personal Gesture Variation in Music Conducting**
Alvaro Sarasua, *Universitat Pompeu Fabra & Escola Superior de Música de Catalunya* Baptiste Caramiaux, Atau Tanaka, *Goldsmiths, University of London,*

Table of Contents

3433 Fingers of a Hand Oscillate Together: Phase Syncronisation of Tremor in Hover Touch Sensing
John Williamson, *University of Glasgow*

Session: Supporting Player Performance

3438 The Mimesis Effect: The Effect of Roles on Player Choice in Interactive Narrative Role-Playing Games
Ignacio X. Domínguez, Rogelio E. Cardona-Rivera, *North Carolina State University,* James K. Vance, *University of Wisconsin-Stout,* David L. Roberts, *North Carolina State University*

3450 Scaffolding Player Location Awareness through Audio Cues in First-Person Shooters
Colby Johanson, Regan L. Mandryk, *University of Saskatchewan*

3462 How Disclosing Skill Assistance Affects Play Experience in a Multiplayer First-Person Shooter Game
Ansgar E. Depping, Regan L. Mandryk, Chengzhao Li, Carl Gutwin, Rodrigo Vicencio-Moreira, *University of Saskatchewan*

3473 Using an International Gaming Tournament to Study Individual Differences in MOBA Expertise and Cognitive Skills
Justin W. Bonny, Lisa M. Castaneda, Tom Swanson, *foundry10*

Session: End-User Programming

3485 Crossed Wires: Investigating the Problems of End-User Developers in a Physical Computing Task
Tracey Booth, Simone Stumpf, Jon Bird, Sara Jones, *City University London*

3498 LondonTube: Overcoming Hidden Dependencies in Cloud-Mobile-Web Programming
Christopher Scaffidi, *Oregon State University,* Andrew Dove, *National Instruments,* Tahmid Nabi, *Oregon State University*

3509 Foraging Among an Overabundance of Similar Variants
Sruti Srinivasa Ragavan, *Oregon State University,* Sandeep Kaur Kuttal, *Oregon State University & University of Tulsa,* Charles Hill, Anita Sarma, David Piorkowski, Margaret Burnett, *Oregon State University*

3522 Chronicler: Interactive Exploration of Source Code History
Moritz Wittenhagen, Christian Cherek, Jan Borchers, *RWTH Aachen University*

Session: Health Support

3533 AugKey: Increasing Foveal Throughput in Eye Typing with Augmented Keys
Antonio Diaz-Tula, Carlos H. Morimoto, *University of São Paulo*

3545 "Counting on the Group" Reconciling Online and Offline Social Support among Older Informal Caregivers
Matthieu Tixier, Myriam Lewkowicz, *Troyes University of Technology*

3559 A Sociotechnical Mechanism for Online Support Provision
Joshua Introne, *Michigan State University,* Bryan Semaan, *Syracuse University,* Sean Goggins, *University of Missouri*

3572 HaptiColor: Interpolating Color Information as Haptic Feedback to Assist the Colorblind
Marta G. Carcedo, *National University of Singapore & Chalmers University of Technology,* Soon Hau Chua, *National University of Singapore,* Simon Perrault, *Yale-NUS College & National University of Singapore,* Paweł Woźniak, *Chalmers University of Technology,* Raj Joshi, *National University of Singapore,* Mohammad Obaid, *Chalmers University of Technology & Koç University,* Morten Fjeld, *Chalmers University of Technology,* Shengdong Zhao, *National University of Singapore*

Session: Participating in Well-Being and Family

3584 Shared Language and the Design of Home Healthcare Technology
Alison Burrows, Rachael Gooberman-Hill, *University of Bristol,* David Coyle, *University College Dublin*

3595 Children's Perspectives on Ethical Issues Surrounding Their Past Involvement on a Participatory Design Team
Brenna McNally, Mona Leigh Guha, Matthew Louis Mauriello, *University of Maryland,* Allison Druin, *HCIL*

3607 The Evolution of Engagements and Social Bonds During Child-Parent Co-design
Jason C. Yip, *University of Washington,* Tamara Clegg, June Ahn, *University of Maryland,* Judith Odili Uchidiuno, *Carnegie Mellon University,* Elizabeth Bonsignore, Austin Beck, Daniel Pauw, Kelly Mills, *University of Maryland*

3620 Youth Advocacy in SNAs: Challenges for Addressing Health Disparities
Farnaz Irannejad Bisafar, Herman Saksono, Priscilla Baquerizo, *Northeastern University,* Dana Moore, *Winthrop University,* Andrea G. Parker, *Northeastern University*

Table of Contents

3625 **ThoughtCloud: Exploring the Role of Feedback Technologies in Care Organisations**
Andy Dow, John Vines, Rob Comber, Rob Wilson, *Newcastle University*

Session: Input Technology

3637 **Make It Big! The Effect of Font Size and Line Spacing on Online Readability**
Luz Rello, *Carnegie Mellon University,* Martin Pielot, *Telefonica Research,* Mari-Carmen Marcos, *Universitat Pompeu Fabra*

3649 **Fitts' Law and the Effects of Input Mapping and Stiffness on Flexible Display Interactions**
Jesse Burstyn, Juan Pablo Carrascal, Roel Vertegaal, *Queen's University*

Session: Comprehension through Visualization

3659 **Towards Understanding Human Similarity Perception in the Analysis of Large Sets of Scatter Plots**
Anshul Vikram Pandey, Josua Krause, Cristian Felix, Jeremy Boy, Enrico Bertini, *New York University*

3670 **Telling Stories about Dynamic Networks with Graph Comics**
Benjamin Bach, *Microsoft Research-Inria Joint Centre,* Natalie Kerracher, *Edinburgh Napier University,* Kyle Wm. Hall, Sheelagh Carpendale, *University of Calgary,* Jessie Kennedy, *Edinburgh Napier University,* Nathalie Henry Riche, *Microsoft Research*

Session: Haptic Sensation Meets Screens

3683 **Direct Manipulation in Tactile Displays**
Aakar Gupta, *University of Toronto,* Thomas Pietrzak, *University Lille,* Nicolas Roussel, *Inria,* Ravin Balakrishnan, *University of Toronto*

3694 **HapThimble: A Wearable Haptic Device towards Usable Virtual Touch Screen**
Hwan Kim, Minhwan Kim, Woohun Lee, *Korea Advanced Institute of Science and Technology*

3706 **Haptic Edge Display for Mobile Tactile Interaction**
Sungjune Jang, Lawrence H. Kim, Kesler Tanner, *Stanford University,* Hiroshi Ishii, *Massachusetts Institute of Technology Media Laboratory,* Sean Follmer, *Stanford University*

3717 **Tactile Presentation to the Back of a Smartphone with Simultaneous Screen Operation**
Sugarragchaa Khurelbaatar, Yuriko Nakai, Ryuta Okazaki, Vibol Yem, Hiroyuki Kajimoto, *University of Electro-Communications*

Session: Smartphone Authentication

3722 **Free-Form Gesture Authentication in the Wild**
Yulong Yang, Gradeigh D. Clark, Janne Lindqvist, *Rutgers University,* Antti Oulasvirta, *Aalto University*

3736 **SnapApp: Reducing Authentication Overhead with a Time-Constrained Fast Unlock Option**
Daniel Buschek, Fabian Hartmann, Emanuel von Zezschwitz, Alexander De Luca, Florian Alt, *University of Munich (LMU)*

3748 **Do Users' Perceptions of Password Security Match Reality?**
Blase Ur, *Carnegie Mellon University,* Jonathan Bees, *The Pennsylvania State University,* Sean M. Segreti, Lujo Bauer, Nicolas Christin, Lorrie Faith Cranor, *Carnegie Mellon University*

3761 **On-Demand Biometrics: Fast Cross-Device Authentication**
Christian Holz, *Microsoft Research,* Frank R. Bentley, *Yahoo*

Session: Shape Changing Displays

3767 **TableHop: An Actuated Fabric Display Using Transparent Electrodes**
Deepak Ranjan Sahoo, *University of Sussex,* Kasper Hornbæk, *University of Copenhagen,* Sriram Subramanian, *University of Sussex*

3781 **An Evaluation of Shape Changes for Conveying Emotions**
pn2495-file3.m4v
Paul Strohmeier, *Queen's University & University of Copenhagen,* Juan Pablo Carrascal, Bernard Cheng, Margaret Meban, Roel Vertegaal, *Queen's University*

3793 **Emergeables: Deformable Displays for Continuous Eyes-Free Mobile Interaction**
Simon Robinson, *Swansea University,* Céline Coutrix, *Université Grenoble Alpes,* Jennifer Pearson, *Swansea University,* Juan Rosso, *Université Grenoble Alpes,* Matheus Fernandes Torquato, *Swansea University,* Laurence Nigay, *Université Grenoble Alpes,* Matt Jones, *Swansea University*

3806 **DefSense: Computational Design of Customized Deformable Input Devices**
Moritz Bächer, *Disney Research Zurich,* Benjamin Hepp, *ETH Zurich,* Fabrizio Pece, *ETHZ,* Paul G. Kry, *McGill University,* Bernd Bickel, *IST Austria,* Bernhard Thomaszewski, *Disney Research Zurich,* Otmar Hilliges, *ETH Zurich*

Session: Fat Fingers, Small Watches

3817 **WatchWriter: Tap and Gesture Typing on a Smartwatch Miniature Keyboard with Statistical Decoding**
Mitchell Gordon, *University of Rochester,* Tom Ouyang, Shumin Zhai, *Google, Inc.*

Table of Contents

3822 Exploring Non-touchscreen Gestures for Smartwatches
Shaikh Shawon Arefin Shimon, Courtney Lutton, Zichun Xu, Sarah Morrison-Smith, Christina Boucher, Jaime Ruiz, *Colorado State University*

3834 WearWrite: Crowd-Assisted Writing from Smartwatches
Michael Nebeling, Alexandra To, Anhong Guo, Adrian A. de Freitas, *Carnegie Mellon University,* Jaime Teevan, *Microsoft Research,* Steven P. Dow, Jeffrey P. Bigham, *Carnegie Mellon University*

3847 Serendipity: Finger Gesture Recognition using an Off-the-Shelf Smartwatch
Hongyi Wen, *Tsinghua University,* Julian Ramos Rojas, *Carnegie Mellon University,* Anind K. Dey, *Carnegie Mellon University*

3852 B2B-Swipe: Swipe Gesture for Rectangular Smartwatches from a Bezel to a Bezel
Yuki Kubo, Buntarou Shizuki, Jiro Tanaka, *University of Tsukuba*

Session: Online Communities - Identities and Behaviors

3857 Anonymity, Intimacy and Self-Disclosure in Social Media
Xiao Ma, *Cornell Tech,* Jeff Hancock, *Stanford University,* Mor Naaman, *Cornell Tech*

3870 Look Before You Leap: Improving the Users' Ability to Detect Fraud in Electronic Marketplaces
Johannes Sänger, *University of Regensburg,* Norman Hänsch, *University of Erlangen-Nuremberg,* Brian Glass, *University College London,* Zinaida Benenson, Robert Landwirth, *University of Erlangen-Nuremberg,* M. Angela Sasse, *University College London*

Session: Affording Collective Action in Social Media

3883 Mediating the Undercurrents: Using Social Media to Sustain a Social Movement
Yong Ming Kow, *City University of Hong Kong,* Yubo Kou, *University of California, Irvine,* Bryan Semaan, *Syracuse University,* Waikuen Cheng, *City University of Hong Kong*

3895 Designing Cyberbullying Mitigation and Prevention Solutions through Participatory Design With Teenagers
Zahra Ashktorab, Jessica Vitak, *University of Maryland*

3906 Understanding Social Media Disclosures of Sexual Abuse Through the Lenses of Support Seeking and Anonymity
Nazanin Andalibi, *Drexel University,* Oliver L. Haimson, *University of California, Irvine,* Munmun De Choudhury, *Georgia Institute of Technology,* Andrea Forte, *Drexel University*

3919 Dear Diary: Teens Reflect on Their Weekly Online Risk Experiences
Pamela Wisniewski, *University of Central Florida,* Heng Xu, Mary Beth Rosson, Daniel F. Perkins, John M. Carroll, *The Pennsylvania State University*

Session: Designing New Player Experiences

3931 Contextual Autonomy Support in Video Game Play: A Grounded Theory
Sebastian Deterding, *University of York*

3944 Sensation: Measuring the Effects of a Human-to-Human Social Touch Based Controller on the Player Experience
Mert Canat, Mustafa Ozan Tezcan, Celalettin Yurdakul, Eran Tiza, Buğra Can Sefercik, İdil Bostan, Oğuz Turan Buruk, Tilbe Göksun, Oğuzhan Özcan, *Koç University*

3956 "I Love All the Bits": The Materiality of Boardgames
Melissa J. Rogerson, Martin Gibbs, Wally Smith, *The University of Melbourne*

3970 Destructive Games: Creating Value by Destroying Valuable Physical Objects
David Eickhoff, Stefanie Mueller, Patrick Baudisch, *Hasso Plattner Institute*

Session: Usability and User Burden

3975 Understanding the Relationship between Frustration and the Severity of Usability Problems: What can Psychophysiological Data (Not) Tell Us?
Anders Bruun, *Aalborg University,* Effie Lai-Chong Law, Matthias Heintz, *Leicester University,* Lana H.A. Alkly, *University of Leicester*

3988 Developing and Validating the User Burden Scale: A Tool for Assessing User Burden in Computing Systems
Hyewon Suh, Nina Shahriaree, *University of Washington,* Eric B. Hekler, *Arizona State University,* Julie A. Kientz, *University of Washington*

4000 COGCAM: Contact-free Measurement of Cognitive Stress During Computer Tasks with a Digital Camera
Daniel J. McDuff, Javier Hernandez, Sarah Gontarek, Rosalind W. Picard, *Massachusetts Institute of Technology*

Table of Contents

4005 When Bad Feels Good: Assistance Failures and Interface Preferences
Philip Quinn, Andy Cockburn, *University of Canterbury*

4011 Using fNIRS in Usability Testing: Understanding the Effect of Web Form Layout on Mental Workload
Kristiyan Lukanov, *Fadata AD & The University of Nottingham,* Horia A. Maior, Max L. Wilson, *University of Nottingham*

Session: Reflection on UX Design

4017 Stereotypes and Politics: Reflections on Personas
Nicola Marsden, Maren Haag, *Heilbronn University*

4032 Pushing the Limits of Design Fiction: The Case for Fictional Research Papers
Joseph Lindley, Paul Coulton, *Lancaster University*

4044 "It's More of a Mindset Than a Method": UX Practitioners' Conception of Design Methods
Colin M. Gray, *Purdue University*

4056 Why Design Method Development is Not Always Carried Out as User-Centered Design
Gary Dickson, Erik Stolterman, *Indiana University*

Session: Display and Visualizations

4061 'A bit like British Weather, I suppose' Design and Evaluation of the Temperature Calendar
Enrico Costanza, *University of Southampton,* Ben Bedwell, *University of Nottingham,* Michael O. Jewell, *University of Southampton,* James Colley, Tom Rodden, *The University of Nottingham*

4073 iVoLVER: Interactive Visual Language for Visualization Extraction and Reconstruction
Gonzalo Gabriel Méndez, Miguel A. Nacenta, Sebastien Vandenheste, *University of St Andrews*

Session: Reward Me! Motivating and Incentivising Crowdsourcing

4086 Novices Who Focused or Experts Who Didn't?: How Effort and Expertise Cues Affect Judgments of Crowd Work
Y. Wayne Wu, Brian P. Bailey, *University of Illinois at Urbana-Champaign*

4098 Curiosity Killed the Cat, but Makes Crowdwork Better
Edith Law, *University of Waterloo,* Ming Yin, *Harvard University,* Joslin Goh, Kevin Chen, Michael A. Terry, *University of Waterloo,* Krzysztof Z. Gajos, *Harvard University*

4111 Pay It Backward: Per-Task Payments on Crowdsourcing Platforms Reduce Productivity
Kazushi Ikeda, *KDDI R&D Laboratories, Inc.,* Michael S. Bernstein, *Stanford University*

4122 Investigating the Impact of 'Emphasis Frames' and Social Loafing on Player Motivation and Performance in a Crowdsourcing Game
Geoff Kaufman, *Carnegie Mellon University*, Mary Flanagan, Sukdith Punjasthitkul, *Dartmouth College*

Session: Making Interfaces Work for Each Individual

4129 We Need Numbers! - Heuristic Evaluation during Demonstrations (HED) for Measuring Usability in IT System Procurement
Mari Tyllinen, Johanna Kaipio, *Aalto University & City of Helsinki,* Tinja Lääveri, *Helsinki University Hospital and University of Helsinki & Oy Apotti Ab,* Marko H.T. Nieminen, *Aalto University*

4142 Interface Design Optimization as a Multi-Armed Bandit Problem
J. Derek Lomas, *University of California, San Diego,* Jodi Forlizzi, Nikhil Poonwala, Nirmal Patel, Sharan Shodhan, Kishan Patel, Ken Koedinger, Emma Brunskill, *Carnegie Mellon University*

4154 Anchored Customization: Anchoring Settings to the Application Interface to Afford Customization
Antoine Ponsard, Joanna McGrenere, *University of British Columbia*

4166 Heterogeneity in Customization of Recommender Systems by Users with Homogenous Preferences
Jacob Solomon, *University of Michigan*

Volume 6

Session: Everyday Objects as Interaction Surfaces

4189 TouchTokens: Guiding Touch Patterns with Passive Tokens
Rafael Morales González Caroline, Appert, *Inria and Univ Paris-Sud & CNRS,* Gilles Bailly, *LTCI, CNRS, Télécom ParisTech, Université Paris-Saclay,* Emmanuel Pietriga, *INRIA & INRIA Chile and Univ Paris-Sud & CNRS*

4203 Designing a Willing-to-Use-in-Public Hand Gestural Interaction Technique for Smart Glasses
Yi-Ta Hsieh, Antti Jylhä, *University of Helsinki,* Valeria Orso, Luciano Gamberini, *University of Padova,* Giulio Jacucci, *University of Helsinki & Aalto University*

Table of Contents

4216 Project Jacquard: Interactive Digital Textiles at Scale
Ivan Poupyrev, Nan-Wei Gong, Shiho Fukuhara, Mustafa Emre Karagozler, Carsten Schwesig, Karen E. Robinson, *Google, Inc.*

4228 GaussMarbles: Spherical Magnetic Tangibles for Interacting with Portable Physical Constraints
Han-Chih Kuo, Rong-Hao Liang, Long-Fei Lin, Bing-Yu Chen, *National Taiwan University*

4233 GaussRFID: Reinventing Physical Toys Using Magnetic RFID Development Kits
Rong-Hao Liang, Han-Chih Kuo, Bing-Yu Chen, *National Taiwan University*

Session: Fingers and Technology

4238 The Flat Finger: Exploring Area Touches on Smartwatches
Ian Oakley, *Ulsan National Institute of Science and Technology,* Carina Lindahl, *Technical University of Denmark,* Khanh Le, *Jacobs University,* DoYoung Lee, MD Rasel Islam, *Ulsan National Institute of Science and Technology*

4250 The Performance and Preference of Different Fingers and Chords for Pointing, Dragging, and Object Transformation
Alix Goguey, *Inria Lille,* Mathieu Nancel, *University of Waterloo,* Géry Casiez, *Université de Lille,* Daniel Vogel, *University of Waterloo*

4262 How We Type: Movement Strategies and Performance in Everyday Typing
Anna Maria Feit, Daryl Weir, Antti Oulasvirta, *Aalto University*

4274 Finger-Aware Shortcuts
Jingjie Zheng, Daniel Vogel, *University of Waterloo*

Session: Privacy over Time and Relationships

4286 Autonomous and Interdependent: Collaborative Privacy Management on Social Networking Sites
Haiyan Jia, Heng Xu, *The Pennsylvania State University*

4298 "We're on the Same Page": A Usability Study of Secure Email Using Pairs of Novice Users
Scott Ruoti, *Brigham Young University & Sandia National Laboratories,* Jeff Andersen, *Brigham Young University,* Scott Heidbrink, Mark O'Neill, *Brigham Young University & Sandia National Laboratories,* Elham Vaziripour, Justin Wu, Daniel Zappala, Kent Seamons, *Brigham Young University*

4309 Enhancing Lifelogging Privacy by Detecting Screens
Mohammed Korayem, *CareerBuilder,* Robert Templeman, *Naval Surface Warfare Center,* Dennis Chen, *Olin College,* David Crandall, Apu Kapadia, *Indiana University*

4315 Sharing Steps in the Workplace: Changing Privacy Concerns Over Time
Nanna Gorm, Irina Shklovski, *IT University of Copenhagen*

4320 You Can't Watch This! Privacy-Respectful Photo Browsing on Smartphones
Emanuel von Zezschwitz, Sigrid Ebbinghaus, Heinrich Hussmann, Alexander De Luca, *University of Munich (LMU)*

Session: Supporting Player Social Experiences

4325 Revisiting Computer-Mediated Intimacy: In-Game Marriage and Dyadic Gameplay in *Audition*
Jeffrey Bardzell, *Indiana University Bloomington*
Shaowen Bardzell, *Indiana University Bloomington*

4337 Ping to Win? Non-Verbal Communication and Team Performance in Competitive Online Multiplayer Games
Alex Leavitt, *University of Southern California*
Brian C. Keegan, *Harvard University*
Joshua Clark, *University of Southern California*

4351 The Proficiency-Congruency Dilemma: Virtual Team Design and Performance in Multiplayer Online Games
Jooyeon Kim, *Korea Advanced Institute of Science and Technology,* Brian C. Keegan, *Harvard University,* Sungjoon Park, Alice Oh, *Korea Advanced Institute of Science and Technology*

4366 Design and Evaluation of a Multi-Player Mobile Game for Icebreaking Activity
Pradthana Jarusriboonchai, Aris Malapaschas, Thomas Olsson, *Tampere University of Technology*

Session: How Does It Look? Evaluating Visual Design

4378 An EEG-based Approach for Evaluating Graphic Icons from the Perspective of Semantic Distance
Fu-Yin Cherng, Wen-Chieh Lin, Jung-Tai King, Yi-Chen Lee, *National Chiao Tung University*

Table of Contents

4390 Aesthetic Appeal and Visual Usability in Four Icon Design Eras
Johanna M. Silvennoinen, Jussi P. P. Jokinen, *University of Jyvaskyla*

4401 The Effect of Thermal Stimuli on the Emotional Perception of Images
Moses Akazue, *Glasgow Caledonian University,* Martin Halvey, *University of Strathclyde,* Lynne Baillie, *Heriot-Watt University,* Stephen Brewster, *University of Glasgow*

4413 Using Crowd Sourcing to Measure the Effects of System Response Delays on User Engagement
Brandon Taylor, Anind K. Dey, Daniel Siewiorek, Asim Smailagic, *Carnegie Mellon University*

Session: Participatory Design (PD) and Applications

4423 Multi-lifespan Design Thinking: Two Methods and a Case Study with the Rwandan Diaspora
Daisy Yoo, Katie Derthick, Shaghayegh Ghassemian, *University of Washington,* Jean Hakizimana, *Global Solidarity Corporation,* Brian Gill, *Seattle Pacific University,* Batya Friedman, *University of Washington*

4435 Participation Gestalt: Analysing Participatory Qualities of Interaction in Public Space
Peter Dalsgaard, Kim Halskov, Ole Sejer Iversen, *Aarhus University*

4447 Designing Movement-based Play With Young People Using Powered Wheelchairs
Kathrin Gerling, Kieran Hicks, Michael Kalyn, *University of Lincoln,* Adam Evans, *University of Copenhagen,* Conor Linehan, *University College Cork*

4459 Participatory Design through a Learning Science Lens
Betsy DiSalvo, *Georgia Institute of Technology*

Session: Health Support & Management

4464 Speeching: Mobile Crowdsourced Speech Assessment to Support Self-Monitoring and Management for People with Parkinson's
Róisín McNaney, Mohammad Othman, Dan Richardson, Paul Dunphy, Telmo Amaral, Nick Miller, Helen Stringer, Patrick Olivier, John Vines, *Newcastle University*

4477 Investigating the Heart Pump Implant Decision Process: Opportunities for Decision Support Tools to Help
Qian Yang, John Zimmerman, Aaron Steinfeld, *Carnegie Mellon University,* Lisa Carey, James F. Antaki, *Department of Biomedical Engineering*

4489 Finding Significant Stress Episodes in a Discontinuous Time Series of Rapidly Varying Mobile Sensor Data
Hillol Sarker, *University of Memphis,* Matthew Tyburski, *National Health Institute,* Md Mahbubur Rahman, *University of Memphis,* Karen Hovsepian, *Troy University,* Moushumi Sharmin, *Western Washington University,* David H. Epstein, Kenzie L. Preston, *National Health Institute,* C. Debra Furr-Holden, *Johns Hopkins Bloomberg School of Public Health,* Adam Milam, *Johns Hopkins University,* Inbal Nahum-Shani, *University of Michigan,* Mustafa al'Absi, *University of Minnesota,* Santosh Kumar, *University of Memphis*

4502 Designing Guidelines for Mobile Health Technology: Managing Notification Interruptions in the ICU
Preethi Srinivas, Anthony Faiola, *IUPUI,* Gloria Mark, *University of California, Irvine*

Session: UX and Usability Methods

4509 Momentary Pleasure or Lasting Meaning? Distinguishing Eudaimonic and Hedonic User Experiences
Elisa D. Mekler, *University of Basel,* Kasper Hornbæk, *University of Copenhagen*

4521 Researcher-Centered Design of Statistics: Why Bayesian Statistics Better Fit the Culture and Incentives of HCI
Matthew Kay, Gregory L. Nelson, *University of Washington,* Eric B. Hekler, *Arizona State University*

4533 Utilizing Employees as Usability Participants: Exploring When and When Not to Leverage Your Coworkers
Joanne Locascio, *PubMatic,* Rushil Khurana, *Carnegie Mellon University,* Yan He, Jofish Kaye, *Yahoo*

Session: Backstage of Crowdsourcing: Legitimacy, Performance and Crowd Support

4538 The Power of Collective Endorsements: Credibility Factors in Medical Crowdfunding Campaigns
Jennifer G. Kim, Ha Kyung Kong, Karrie Karahalios, Wai-Tat Fu, Hwajung Hong, *Ulsan National Institute of Science and Technology*

4550 Legitimacy Work: Invisible Work in Philanthropic Crowdfunding
Katie G. Tanaka, *Indiana University,* Amy Voida, *University of Colorado Boulder*

Table of Contents

4562 Extracting Heart Rate from Videos of Online Participants
Thomas Muender, Matthew K. Miller, Max V. Birk, Regan L. Mandryk, *University of Saskatchewan*

4568 Highly Successful Projects Inhibit Coordination on Crowdfunding Sites
Jacob Solomon, *University of Michigan,* Wenjuan Ma, Rick Wash, *Michigan State University*

4573 Stories We Tell About Labor: Turkopticon and the Trouble with "Design"
Lilly C. Irani, *University of California, San Diego,* M. Six Silberman, *IG Metall*

Session: Expressive HCI

4587 Storeoboard: Sketching Stereoscopic Storyboards
Rorik Henrikson, Bruno De Araujo, *University of Toronto,* Fanny Chevalier, *Inria & University of Toronto,* Karan Singh, Ravin Balakrishnan, *University of Toronto*

4599 Skuid: Sketching Dynamic Illustrations Using the Principles of 2D Animation
Rubaiat Habib Kazi, Tovi Grossman, Nobuyuki Umetani, George Fitzmaurice, *Autodesk Research*

4610 Object-Oriented Drawing
Haijun Xia, Bruno Araujo, *University of Toronto,* Tovi Grossman, *Autodesk Research,* Daniel Wigdor, *University of Toronto*

Session: Search and Discovery

4622 Pick me! Getting Noticed on Google Play
Aliaksei Miniukovich, Antonella De Angeli, *University of Trento*

4634 Diving in at the Deep End: The Value of Alternative In-Situ Approaches for Systematic Library Search
Uta Hinrichs, *University of St Andrews,* Simon Butscher, Jens Müller, Harald Reiterer, *University of Konstanz*

4647 Empath: Understanding Topic Signals in Large-Scale Text
Ethan Fast, Binbin Chen, Michael S. Bernstein, *Stanford University*

4658 Peek-a-View: Smartphone Cover Interaction for Multi-Tasking
Koeun Choi, *Seoul National University & Samsung Electronics,* Hyunjoo Song, Kyle Koh, Jinwook Bok, Jinwook Seo, *Seoul National University*

Session: Interaction with Small Displays

4663 Faster Command Selection on Touchscreen Watches
Benjamin Lafreniere, *Autodesk Research,* Carl Gutwin, *University of Saskatchewan,* Andy Cockburn, *University of Canterbury,* Tovi Grossman, *Autodesk Research*

4675 Doppio: A Reconfigurable Dual-Face Smartwatch for Tangible Interaction
Teddy Seyed, *University of Calgary,* Xing-Dong Yang, *Dartmouth College,* Daniel Vogel, *University of Waterloo*

4687 Supporting Transitions to Expertise in Hidden Toolbars
Katherine Schramm, Carl Gutwin, *University of Saskatchewan,* Andy Cockburn, *University of Canterbury*

4699 Investigating Effects of Post-Selection Feedback for Acquiring Ultra-Small Targets on Touchscreen
Chun Yu, Hongyi Wen, Wei Xiong, *Tsinghua University,* Xiaojun Bi, *Google, Inc.,* Yuanchun Shi, *Tsinghua University*

Session: How can Smartphones Fit Our Lives?

4711 A Systematic Assessment of Smartphone Usage Gaps
Niels van Berkel, Chu Luo, Theodoros Anagnostopoulos, Denzil Ferreira, Jorge Goncalves, Simo Hosio, Vassilis Kostakos, *University of Oulu*

4722 Journeys & Notes: Designing Social Computing for Non-Places
Justin Cranshaw, Andrés Monroy-Hernández, S. A. Needham, *Microsoft Research*

4734 PowerShake: Power Transfer Interactions for Mobile Devices
Paul Worgan, *University of Bristol,* Jarrod Knibbe, *University of Bristol & University of Copenhagen,* Mike Fraser, *University of Bristol,* Diego Martinez Plasencia, *University of Bristol & Sussex University*

4746 MyTime: Designing and Evaluating an Intervention for Smartphone Non-Use
Alexis Hiniker, Sungsoo (Ray) Hong, Tadayoshi Kohno, Julie A. Kientz, *University of Washington*

Session: Video Sharing

4758 Motives and Concerns of Dashcam Video Sharing
Sangkeun Park, Joohyun Kim, *Korea Advanced Institute of Science and Technology,* Rabeb Mizouni, *Khalifa University,* Uichin Lee, *Korea Advanced Institute of Science and Technology*

Table of Contents

4770 Meerkat and Periscope: I Stream, You Stream, Apps Stream for Live Streams
John C. Tang, Gina Venolia, Kori M. Inkpen, *Microsoft Research*

4781 The Tyranny of the Everyday in Mobile Video Messaging
Sean Rintel, *Microsoft Research,* Richard Harper, *Social Shaping Research,* Kenton O'Hara, *Microsoft Research*

4793 Impact of Video Summary Viewing on Episodic Memory Recall – Design Guidelines for Video Summarizations
Huy Viet Le, *University of Stuttgart,* Sarah Clinch, Corina Sas, *Lancaster University,* Tilman Dingler, Niels Henze, *University of Stuttgart,* Nigel Davies, *Lancaster University*

Session: Privacy and Security Interfaces

4806 The Anatomy of Smartphone Unlocking: A Field Study of Android Lock Screens
Marian Harbach, *International Computer Science Institute,* Alexander De Luca, *Google,* Serge Egelman, *University of California, Berkeley*

4818 On Multiple Password Interference of Touch Screen Patterns and Text Passwords
Weizhi Meng, *Institute for Infocomm Research,* Wenjuan Li, Lijun Jiang, Liying Meng, *City University of Hong Kong*

4823 Keep on Lockin' in the Free World: A Multi-National Comparison of Smartphone Locking
Marian Harbach, *International Computer Science Institute,* Alexander De Luca, *Google,* Nathan Malkin, Serge Egelman, *University of California, Berkeley*

Session: Detecting User Emotion

4828 AniSAM & AniAvatar – Animated Visualizations of Affective States
Andreas Sonderegger, *EPFL Lausanne,* Klaus Heyden, Alain Chavaillaz, Juergen Sauer, *University of Fribourg*

4838 Hot Under the Collar: Mapping Thermal Feedback to Dimensional Models of Emotion
Graham Wilson, Dobromir Dobrev, Stephen A. Brewster, *University of Glasgow*

4850 UX Heatmaps: Mapping User Experience on Visual Interfaces
Vanessa Georges, François Courtemanche, Sylvain Senecal, *HEC Montréal,* Thierry Baccino, *University Paris 8,* Marc Fredette, Pierre-Majorique Leger, *HEC Montréal*

Session: Diverse Disabilities and Technological Support

4861 Universal Design Ballot Interfaces on Voting Performance and Satisfaction of Voters with and without Vision Loss
Seunghyun "Tina" Lee, Yilin Elaine Liu, Ljilja Ruzic, Jon Sanford, *Georgia Institute of Technology*

4872 SayWAT: Augmenting Face-to-Face Conversations for Adults with Autism
LouAnne E. Boyd, *University of California, Irvine,* Alejandro Rangel, *CICESE,* Helen Tomimbang, Andrea Conejo-Toledo, Kanika Patel, *University of California, Irvine,* Monica Tentori, *CICESE,* Gillian R. Hayes, *University of California, Irvine*

4884 The AT Effect: How Disability Affects the Perceived Social Acceptability of Head-Mounted Display Use
Halley Profita, *University of Colorado,* Reem Albaghli, *University of Colorado Boulder,* Leah Findlater, Paul Jaeger, *University of Maryland,* Shaun K. Kane, *University of Colorado Boulder*

4896 Tickers and Talker: An Accessible Labeling Toolkit for 3D Printed Models
Lei Shi, *Cornell Tech,* Idan Zelzer, *Cornell Tech & Shenkar College of Engineering and Design,* Catherine Feng, *Cornell Tech & University of Washington,* Shiri Azenkot, *Cornell Tech*

Session: Robot Personalities

4908 The Effect of Displaying System Confidence Information on the Usage of Autonomous Systems for Non-specialist Applications: A Lab Study
Jhim Kiel M. Verame, Enrico Costanza, Sarvapali D. Ramchurn, *University of Southampton*

4921 Why That Nao? How Humans Adapt to a Conversational Humanoid Robot in Taking Turns-at-Talk
Hannah R. M. Pelikan, *University of Osnabrück,* Mathias Broth, *Linköping University*

4933 ID-Match: A Hybrid Computer Vision and RFID System for Recognizing Individuals in Groups
Hanchuan Li, *Disney Research & University of Washington,* Peijin Zhang, *Disney Research & Carnegie Mellon University,* Samer Al Moubayed, *Disney Research,* Shwetak N. Patel, *University of Washington,* Alanson P. Sample, *Disney Research*

4945 Help Me Please: Robot Politeness Strategies for Soliciting Help from Humans
Vasant Srinivasan, *Texas A&M University,* Leila Takayama, *Willow Garage & Google*

Table of Contents

Session: Problem-solving or Not? The Boundaries of HCI Research

4956 HCI Research as Problem-Solving
Antti Oulasvirta, *Aalto University,* Kasper Hornbæk, *University of Copenhagen*

4968 Anti-Solutionist Strategies: Seriously Silly Design Fiction
Mark Blythe, *Northumbria University,* Kristina Andersen, *STEIM,* Rachel Clarke, Peter Wright, *Newcastle University*

4979 Designing Speculative Civics
Carl DiSalvo, Tom Jenkins, Thomas Lodato, *Georgia Institute of Technology*

4991 Experimental Systems in Research through Design
Peter Dalsgaard, *Aarhus University*

4997 Social Inequality and HCI: The View from Political Economy
Hamid Ekbia, *Indiana University,* Bonnie Nardi, *University of California, Irvine*

Session: Visualization Methods and Evaluation

5003 Egocentric Analysis of Dynamic Networks with EgoLines
Jian Zhao, Michael Glueck, *Autodesk Research & University of Toronto,* Fanny Chevalier, *Inria & University of Toronto,* Yanhong Wu, *Hong Kong University of Science and Technology,* Azam Khan, *Autodesk Research*

5015 ResViz: Politics and Design Issues in Visualizing Academic Metrics
Chris Elsden, Sebastian Mellor, Patrick Olivier, Pete Wheldon, David Kirk, Rob Comber, *Newcastle University*

5028 Evaluating Information Visualization via the Interplay of Heuristic Evaluation and Question-Based Scoring
Marti A. Hearst, Paul Laskowski, *University of California, Berkeley,* Luis Silva, *University of California Merced*

5034 A Comparison of Cooperative and Competitive Visualizations for Co-located Collaboration
Sarah Tausch, Stephanie Ta, Heinrich Hussmann, *University of Munich (LMU)*

5040 The Effect of Richer Visualizations on Code Comprehension
Dimitar Asenov, Otmar Hilliges, Peter Müller, *ETH Zurich*

Volume 7

Session: Transportation and HCI

5063 Peer-to-Peer in the Workplace: A View from the Road
Syed Ishtiaque Ahmed, *Cornell University,* Nicola J. Bidwell, *University of Namibia,* Himanshu Zade, *Microsoft Research India,* Srihari H. Muralidhar, *Indian Institute of Technology Madras,* Anupama Dhareshwar, *P.E.S. Institute of Technology,* Baneen Karachiwala, *Indendent Consultant,* Cedrick N. Tandong, *Three Wheels United,* Jacki O'Neill, *Microsoft*

5076 A Design Space to Support the Development of Windshield Applications for the Car
Renate Haeuslschmid, Bastian Pfleging, Florian Alt, *University of Munich (LMU)*

5092 When (ish) is My Bus? User-centered Visualizations of Uncertainty in Everyday, Mobile Predictive Systems
Matthew Kay, *University of Washington,* Tara Kola, *Tufts University,* Jessica R. Hullman, Sean A. Munson, *University of Washington*

5104 Error Recovery in Multitasking While Driving
Ja Young Lee, Madeleine C., John D. Lee, *University of Wisconsin, Madison*

Session: Interaction Techniques for Mobile Interfaces

5114 Personalized Compass: A Compact Visualization for Direction and Location
Daniel Miau, Steven Feiner, *Columbia University*

5126 SymmetriSense: Enabling Near-Surface Interactivity on Glossy Surfaces using a Single Commodity Smartphone
Chungkuk Yoo, *Korea Advanced Institute of Science and Technology,* Inseok Hwang, *IBM Research,* Eric Rozner, *IBM Research,* Yu Gu, *IBM Watson Health,* Robert F. Dickerson, *IBM Mobile Innovation Lab*

5138 FlexCase: Enhancing Mobile Interaction with a Flexible Sensing and Display Cover
Christian Rendl, *University of Applied Sciences Upper Austria,* David Kim, *Microsoft Research,* Patrick Parzer, *University of Applied Sciences Upper Austria,* Sean Fanello, *Microsoft Research,* Martin Zirkl, Gregor Scheipl, *Joanneum Research,* Michael Haller, *University of Applied Sciences Upper Austria,* Shahram Izadi, *Microsoft Research*

Table of Contents

5151 **Evaluation of a Smart-Restorable Backspace Technique to Facilitate Text Entry Error Correction**
Ahmed Sabbir Arif, *Ryerson University,* Sunjun Kim, *Korea Advanced Institute of Science and Technology,* Wolfgang Stuerzlinger, *Simon Fraser University,* Geehyuk Lee, *Korea Advanced Institute of Science and Technology,* Ali Mazalek, *Ryerson University*

5163 **TapBoard 2: Simple and Effective Touchpad-like Interaction on a Multi-Touch Surface Keyboard**
Sunjun Kim, *Korea Advanced Institute of Science and Technology*
Geehyuk Lee, *Korea Advanced Institute of Science and Technology*

Session: Eye Gaze

5169 **Building a Personalized, Auto-Calibrating Eye Tracker from User Interactions**
Michael Xuelin Huang, Tiffany C. K. Kwok, Grace Ngai, Stephen C. F. Chan, Hong Va Leong, *Hong Kong Polytechnic University*

5180 **Can Eye Help You? Effects of Visualizing Eye Fixations on Remote Collaboration Scenarios for Physical Tasks**
Keita Higuch, Ryo Yonetani, Yoichi Sato, *The University of Tokyo*

5191 **Gaze-Contingent Manipulation of Color Perception**
Michael Mauderer, *University of St Andrews,* David R. Flatla, *University of Dundee,* Miguel A. Nacenta, *University of St Andrews*

5203 **Spotlights: Attention-Optimized Highlights for Skim Reading**
Byungjoo Lee, Olli Savisaari, Antti Oulasvirta, *Aalto University*

Session: Mental Models of Privacy

5215 **If You Put All The Pieces Together..." – Attitudes Towards Data Combination and Sharing Across Services and Companies"**
Igor Bilogrevic, Martin Ortlieb, *Google*

5228 **Privacy Personas: Clustering Users via Attitudes and Behaviors toward Security Practices**
Janna Lynn Dupree, Richard Devries, Daniel M. Berry, Edward Lank, *University of Waterloo*

5240 **It's Creepy, But It Doesn't Bother Me**
Chanda Phelan, Cliff Lampe, Paul Resnick, *University of Michigan*

5252 **Make it Simple, or Force Users to Read? Paraphrased Design Improves Comprehension of End User License Agreements**
T. Franklin Waddell, *The Pennsylvania State University,* Joshua R. Auriemma, *DramaFever,* S. Shyam Sundar, *The Pennsylvania State University*

5257 **Behavior Ever Follows Intention? A Validation of the Security Behavior Intentions Scale (SeBIS)**
Serge Egelman, Marian Harbach, *International Computer Science Institute,* Eyal Peer, *Bar-Ilan University*

Session: Living in Smart Environments

5262 **It is too Hot: An In-Situ Study of Three Designs for Heating**
Alper T. Alan, *University of Southampton,* Mike Shann, *University of Zurich,* Enrico Costanza, Sarvapali D. Ramchurn, *University of Southampton,* Sven Seuken, *University of Zurich*

5274 **Living in a Prototype: A Reconfigured Space**
Audrey Desjardins, *Simon Fraser University,* Ron Wakkary, *Eindhoven University of Technology*

5286 **"Like Having a Really Bad PA": The Gulf between User Expectation and Experience of Conversational Agents**
Ewa Luger, Abigail Sellen, *Microsoft Research*

5298 **LivingDesktop: Augmenting Desktop Workstation with Actuated Devices**
Gilles Bailly, Sidharth Sahdev, *Université Paris-Saclay,* Sylvain Malacria, *Inria,* Thomas Pietrzak, *University Lille*

Session: Design for Health Care

5311 **Technological Caregiving: Supporting Online Activity for Adults with Cognitive Impairments**
Anne Marie Piper, Raymundo Cornejo, Lisa Hurwitz, Caitlin Unumb, *Northwestern University*

5324 **Closing the Gap: Supporting Patients' Transition to Self-Management after Hospitalization**
Ari H. Pollack, *University of Washington & Seattle Children's Hospital,* Uba Backonja, Andrew D. Miller, Sonali R. Mishra, Maher Khelifi, Logan Kendall, Wanda Pratt, *University of Washington*

5337 **Care Partnerships: Toward Technology to Support Teens' Participation in Their Health Care**
Matthew K. Hong, Lauren Wilcox, Daniel Machado, *Georgia Institute of Technology,* Thomas A. Olson, Stephen F. Simoneaux, *Children's Healthcare of Atlanta*

Table of Contents

Session: Representing User Experience

5350 **Data-driven Personas: Constructing Archetypal Users with Clickstreams and User Telemetry**
Xiang Zhang, *North Carolina State University,* Hans-Frederick Brown, Anil Shankar, *Platfora Inc.*

5360 **Evaluating the Paper-to-Screen Translation of Participant-Aided Sociograms with High-Risk Participants**
Bernie Hogan, Joshua R. Melville, *University of Oxford,* Gregory Lee Phillips II, Patrick Janulis, Noshir Contractor, Brian S. Mustanski, Michelle Birkett, *Northwestern University*

Session: Making Music on the Brain

5372 **Learn Piano with BACh: An Adaptive Learning Interface that Adjusts Task Difficulty Based on Brain State**
Beste F. Yuksel, Kurt B. Oleson, *Tufts University,* Lane Harrison, *Worcester Polytechnic Institute & Tufts University,* Evan M. Peck, *Bucknell University,* Daniel Afergan, *Tufts University & Google Inc.,* Remco Chang, Robert JK Jacob, *Tufts University*

5385 **#Scanners: Exploring the Control of Adaptive Films using Brain-Computer Interaction**
Matthew Pike, Richard Ramchurn, Steve Benford, Max L. Wilson, *University of Nottingham*

5397 **Inspect, Embody, Invent: A Design Framework for Music Learning and Beyond**
Xiao Xiao, Hiroshi Ishii, *Massachusetts Institute of Technology*

Session: Natural User Interfaces for InfoVis

5409 **TimeFork: Interactive Prediction of Time Series**
Sriram Karthik Badam, *University of Maryland,* Jieqiong Zhao, *Purdue University,* Shivalik Sen, *Birla Institute of Technology and Science,* Niklas Elmqvist, *University of Maryland,* David Ebert, *Purdue University*

5421 **The Effect of Visual Appearance on the Performance of Continuous Sliders and Visual Analogue Scales**
Justin Matejka, Michael Glueck, Tovi Grossman, George Fitzmaurice, *Autodesk Research*

5433 **Making Sense of Temporal Queries with Interactive Visualization**
Leilani Battle, *Massachusetts Institute of Technology,* Danyel Fisher, Robert DeLine, Mike Barnett, Badrish Chandramouli, Jonathan Goldstein, *Microsoft Research*

5444 **Investigating Time Series Visualisations to Improve the User Experience**
Muhammad Adnan, *University of Leeds,* Mike Just, Lynne Baillie, *Heriot-Watt University*

Session: Multi-Device Interaction

5456 **Smartwatch <i>in vivo</i>**
Stefania Pizza, *Sapienza University of Rome,* Barry Brown, Donald McMillan, Airi Lampinen, *University of Stockholm*

5470 **When Tablets meet Tabletops: The Effect of Tabletop Size on Around-the-Table Collaboration with Personal Tablets**
Johannes Zagermann, Ulrike Pfeil, Roman Rädle, *University of Konstanz* Hans-Christian Jetter, *Campus Hagenberg,* Clemens Klokmose, *Aarhus University,* Harald Reiterer, *University of Konstanz*

5482 **Enhancing Cross-Device Interaction Scripting with Interactive Illustrations**
Pei-Yu (Peggy) Chi, *Google Inc. & University of California, Berkeley,* Yang Li, *Google Inc.,* Björn Hartmann, *Google Inc. & University of California, Berkeley*

5494 **XDBrowser: User-Defined Cross-Device Web Page Designs**
Michael Nebeling, Anind K. Dey, *Carnegie Mellon University*

Session: Social Media and Health

5506 **"With most of it being pictures now, I rarely use it": Understanding Twitter's Evolving Accessibility to Blind Users**
Meredith Ringel Morris, *Microsoft Research,* Annuska Zolyomi, *University of Washington,* Catherine Yao, *Microsoft Research & Massachusetts Institute of Technology,* Sina Bahram, *North Carolina State University,* Jeffrey P. Bigham, *Carnegie Mellon University,* Shaun K. Kane, *University of Colorado Boulder*

5517 **Sleep Debt in Student Life: Online Attention Focus, Facebook, and Mood**
Gloria Mark, Yiran Wang, Melissa Niiya, Stephanie Reich, *University of California, Irvine*

5529 **"Tell It Like It Really Is": A Case of Online Content Creation and Sharing Among Older Adult Bloggers**
Robin Brewer, Anne Marie Piper, *Northwestern University*

5543 **Social Media Image Analysis for Public Health**
Venkata Rama Kiran Garimella, *Aalto University,* Abdulrahman Alfayad, *Carnegie Mellon University,* Ingmar Weber, *Qatar Computing Research Institute*

Table of Contents

5548 **It Matters If My Friends Stop Smoking: Social Support for Behavior Change in Social Media**
Corbin Reno, Erika S. Poole, *The Pennsylvania State University*

Volume 8

Session: Engaging Players in Games

5571 **Designing Engaging Games Using Bayesian Optimization**
Mohammad M. Khajah, Brett D. Roads, Robert V. Lindsey, *University of Colorado,* Yun-En Liu, *University of Washington,* Michael C. Mozer, *University of Colorado*

5583 **Operationalising and Evaluating Sub-Optimal and Optimal Play Experiences through Challenge-Skill Manipulation**
Madison Klarkowski, Daniel Johnson, Peta Wyeth, Mitchell McEwan, Cody Phillips, Simon Smith, *Queensland University of Technology*

5595 **How to Present Game Difficulty Choices? Exploring the Impact on Player Experience**
Jan D. Smeddinck, *University of Bremen,* Regan L. Mandryk, Max V. Birk, *University of Saskatchewan,* Kathrin M. Gerling, *University of Lincoln,* Dietrich Barsilowski, Rainer Malaka, *University of Bremen*

5608 **Peak-End Effects on Player Experience in Casual Games**
Carl Gutwin, Christianne Rooke, *University of Saskatchewan,* Andy Cockburn, *University of Canterbury,* Regan L. Mandryk, *University of Saskatchewan,* Benjamin Lafreniere, *Autodesk Research*

Session: Food as Method and Inquiry

5620 **"My Doctor is Keeping an Eye on Me!": Exploring the Clinical Applicability of a Mobile Food Logger**
Yoojung Kim, Sookyoung Ji, Hyunjeong Lee, *Seoul National University,* Jeong-Whun Kim, Sooyoung Yoo, *Seoul National University Bundang Hospital,* Joongseek Lee, *Seoul National University*

5632 **Crumbs: Lightweight Daily Food Challenges to Promote Engagement and Mindfulness**
Daniel A. Epstein, Felicia Cordeiro, James Fogarty, Gary Hsieh, Sean A. Munson, *University of Washington*

5645 **Evaluation of a Food Portion Size Estimation Interface for a Varying Literacy Population**
Beenish M. Chaudhry, *University of Notre Dame,* Christopher Schaefbauer, *University of Colorado,* Ben Jelen, Katie A. Siek, Kay Connelly, *Indiana University Bloomington*

5658 **Examining Unlock Journaling with Diaries and Reminders for In Situ Self-Report in Health and Wellness**
Xiaoyi Zhang, Laura R. Pina, James Fogarty, *University of Washington*

Session: Medical Device Sensing

5665 **Delineating the Operational Envelope of Mobile and Conventional EDA Sensing on Key Body Locations**
Panagiotis Tsiamyrtzis, *Athens University of Economics and Business,* Malcolm Dcosta, Dvijesh Shastri, Eswar Prasad, Ioannis Pavlidis, *University of Houston*

5675 **SpiroCall: Measuring Lung Function over a Phone Call**
Mayank Goel, Elliot Saba, *University of Washington,* Maia Stiber, *Inglemoor High School,* Eric Whitmire, Josh Fromm, *University of Washington,* Eric C. Larson, *Southern Methodist University,* Gaetano Borriello, Shwetak N. Patel, *University of Washington*

5686 **Interacting with Predictions: Visual Inspection of Black-box Machine Learning Models**
Josua Krause, *New York University,* Adam Perer, Kenney Ng, *IBM T.J. Watson Research Center*

5698 **Musically Informed Sonification for Chronic Pain Rehabilitation: Facilitating Progress & Avoiding Over-doing**
Joseph W. Newbold, Nadia Bianchi-Berthouze, Nicolas E. Gold, *University College London,* Ana Tajadura-Jiménez, *University College London & Universidad Loyola Andalucía,* Amanda CdC Williams, *University College London*

5704 **KeDiary: Using Mobile Phones to Assist Patients in Recovering from Drug Addiction**
Chuang-Wen You, Ya-Fang Lin, Cheng-Yuan Li, Yu-Lun Tsai, *National Taiwan University,* Ming-Chyi Huang, *Taipei City Hospital Songde Branch* Chao-Hui Lee, *Taipei City Hospital Songde Branch,* Hao-Chuan Wang, *National Tsing Hua University,* Hao-Hua Chu, *National Taiwan University*

Session: Supporting Information Seeking

5710 **The 32 Days of Christmas: Understanding Temporal Intent in Image Search Queries**
Frank R. Bentley, Joseph Jofish' Kaye, David A. Shamma, John Alexis Guerra-Gomez, *Yahoo*

Table of Contents

5715 Influence of Content Layout and Motivation on Users' Herd Behavior in Social Discovery
Yanzhen Yue, *Agency for Science, Technology and Research,* Xiaojuan Ma, *Hong Kong University of Science and Technology,* Zhenhui Jiang, *National University of Singapore*

5720 Age-related Differences in the Content of Search Queries when Reformulating
Saraschandra Karanam, Herre van Oostendorp, *Utrecht University*

Session: Designing New Materials and Manufacturing Techniques

5731 Steel-Sense: Integrating Machine Elements with Sensors by Additive Manufacturing
Tatyana Vasilevitsky, *The Hebrew University of Jerusalem,* Amit Zoran, *Hebrew University*

5743 xPrint: A Modularized Liquid Printer for Smart Materials Deposition
Guanyun Wang, *Zhejiang University,* Lining Yao, Wen Wang, Jifei Ou, Chin-Yi Cheng, Hiroshi Ishii, *Massachusetts Institute of Technology*

5753 Cilllia - 3D Printed Micro-Pillar Structures for Surface Texture, Actuation and Sensing
Jifei Ou, Gershon Dublon, Chin-Yi Cheng, Felix Heibeck, *Massachusetts Institute of Technology,* Karl Willis, *Addimation, Inc.,* Hiroshi Ishii, *Massachusetts Institute of Technology*

5765 Foldem: Heterogeneous Object Fabrication via Selective Ablation of Multi-Material Sheets
Varun Perumal C, Daniel Wigdor, *University of Toronto*

Session: Eye Tracking Applications

5776 A Model Relating Pupil Diameter to Mental Workload and Lighting Conditions
Bastian Pfleging, *University of Munich (LMU) & University of Stuttgart,* Drea K. Fekety, *Clemson University,* Albrecht Schmidt, *University of Stuttgart,* Andrew L. Kun, *University of New Hampshire*

5789 Pointing while Looking Elsewhere: Designing for Varying Degrees of Visual Guidance during Manual Input
Baris Serim, *Helsinki Institute for Information Technology HIIT & Aalto University,* Giulio Jacucci, *University of Helsinki & Aalto University*

5801 EyeGrip: Detecting Targets in a Series of Uni-directional Moving Objects Using Optokinetic Nystagmus Eye Movements
Shahram Jalaliniya, Diako Mardanbegi, *IT University of Copenhagen*

5812 Eye-Trace: Segmentation of Volumetric Microscopy Images with Eyegaze
Thomas Templier, Kenan Bektas, Richard H. R. Hahnloser, *University of Zurich & ETH Zurich*

Session: Large Display Interaction

5824 The Bicycle Barometer: Design and Evaluation of Cyclist-Specific Interaction for a Public Display
Sandy Claes, Karin Slegers, Andrew Vande Moere, *KU Leuven*

5836 HandMark Menus: Rapid Command Selection and Large Command Sets on Multi-Touch Displays
Md. Sami Uddin, Carl Gutwin, *University of Saskatchewan,* Benjamin Lafreniere, *Autodesk Research*

5849 Glowworms and Fireflies: Ambient Light on Large Interactive Surfaces
Florian Perteneder, Eva-Maria Beatrix Grossauer, Joanne Leong, *University of Applied Sciences Upper Austria,* Wolfgang Stuerzlinger, *Simon Fraser University,* Michael Haller, *University of Applied Sciences Upper Austria*

5862 Off-Limits: Interacting Beyond the Boundaries of Large Displays
Anders Markussen, Sebastian Boring, Mikkel R. Jakobsen, Kasper Hornbæk, *University of Copenhagen*

Session: IoT and HCI ASAP!

5874 Pressing Not Tapping: Comparing a Physical Button with a Smartphone App for Tagging Music in Radio Programmes
Lianne Kerlin, Jasmine Cox, Stephen Jolly, Michael Evans, *British Broadcasting Corporation,* George Green, David Regan, *Amberlight Partners Limited*

5885 PaperID: A Technique for Drawing Functional Battery-Free Wireless Interfaces on Paper
Hanchuan Li, *Disney Research, Pittsburgh & University of Washington,* Eric Brockmeyer, Elizabeth J. Carter, *Disney Research,* Josh Fromm, *University of Washington,* Scott E. Hudson, *Disney Research & Carnegie Mellon University,* Shwetak N. Patel, *University of Washington,* Alanson Sample, *Disney Research*

5897 RapID: A Framework for Fabricating Low-Latency Interactive Objects with RFID Tags
Andrew Spielberg, *Disney Research & Massachusetts Institute of Technology,* Alanson Sample, *Disney Research,* Scott E. Hudson, Jennifer Mankoff, *Disney Research & Carnegie Mellon University,* James McCann, *Disney Research*

Table of Contents

5909 Snap-to-It: A User-Inspired Platform for Opportunistic Device Interactions
Adrian A. de Freitas, Michael Nebeling, Xiang 'Anthony' Chen, *Carnegie Mellon University,* Junrui Yang, *Peking University,* Akshaye Shreenithi Kirupa Karthikeyan Ranithangam, *Coimbatore Institute of Technology,* Anind K. Dey, *Carnegie Mellon University*

Session: Smart Homes, Devices and Data

5921 "She'll just grab any device that's closer": A Study of Everyday Device & Account Sharing in Households
Tara Matthews, Kerwell Liao, Anna Turner, Marianne Berkovich, Robert Reeder, Sunny Consolvo, *Google*

5933 "Just whack it on until it gets hot": Working with IoT Data in the Home
Joel E. Fischer, Andy Crabtree, Tom Rodden, James A. Colley, *University of Nottingham,* Enrico Costanza, Michael O. Jewell, Sarvapali D. Ramchurn, *University of Southampton*

5945 Designing for Domestic Memorialization and Remembrance: A Field Study of Fenestra in Japan
Daisuke Uriu, *Keio University,* William Odom, *Simon Fraser University*

5958 Integrating the Smart Home into the Digital Calendar
Sarah Mennicken, *University of Zurich,* David Kim, *Microsoft Research,* Elaine May Huang, *University of Zurich*

Session: Seams of Craft, Design and Fabrication

5970 Expanding on Wabi-Sabi as a Design Resource in HCI
Vasiliki Tsaknaki, Ylva Fernaeus, *KTH - Royal Institute of Technology*

5984 The Hybrid Bricolage - Bridging Parametric Design with Craft through Algorithmic Modularity
Tamara Anna Efrat, *Bezalel Academy of Arts and Design,* Moran Mizrahi, *The Hebrew University of Jerusalem,* Amit Zoran, *Bezalel Academy of Arts and Design & The Hebrew University of Jerusalem*

5996 ExoSkin: On-Body Fabrication
Madeline Gannon, *Autodesk Research & Carnegie Mellon University,* Tovi Grossman, George Fitzmaurice, *Autodesk Research*

6008 Mimetic Machines: Collaborative Interventions in Digital Fabrication with Arc
Hidekazu Saegusa, Thomas Tran, Daniela K. Rosner, *University of Washington*

Session: Body and Fashion

6014 Embodied Sketching
Elena Márquez Segura, Laia Turmo Vidal, *Uppsala University,* Asreen Rostami, *Stockholm University,* Annika Waern, *Uppsala University*

6028 "I don't want to wear a screen": Probing Perceptions of and Possibilities for Dynamic Displays on Clothing
Laura Devendorf, Joanne Lo, Noura Howell, Jung Lin Lee, *University of California, Berkeley,* Nan-Wei Gong, M. Emre Karagozler, Shiho Fukuhara, Ivan Poupyrev, *Google ATAP,* Eric Paulos, Kimiko Ryokai, *University of California, Berkeley*

6040 BeUpright: Posture Correction Using Relational Norm Intervention
Jaemyung Shin, Bumsoo Kang, *Korea Advanced Institute of Science and Technology,* Taiwoo Park, *Michigan State University,* Jina Huh, *University of California, San Diego,* Jinhan Kim, Junehwa Song, *Korea Advanced Institute of Science and Technology*

6053 Body Integrated Programmable Joints Interface
Sang-won Leigh, Pattie Maes, *Massachusetts Institute of Technology*

6058 Mirror Mirror: An On-Body T-shirt Design System
Daniel Saakes, Hui-Shyong Yeo, Seung-Tak Noh, Gyeol Han, Woontack Woo, *Korea Advanced Institute of Science and Technology*

6064 Author Index

Peer-to-peer in the Workplace: A View from the Road

Syed Ishtiaque Ahmed
Cornell University
Ithaca, USA
sa738@cornell.edu

Nicola J. Bidwell
U. of Namibia U. of Pretoria
Windhoek, Namibia South Africa
nic.bidwell@gmail.com

Himanshu Zade
Microsoft
Bangalore, India
t-hizad@microsoft.com

Srihari H. Muralidhar
IIT Madras
Tamil Nadu, India
hmsrihari@gmail.com

Anupama Dhareshwar
P.E.S.I.T
Bangalore, India
anupamadhareshwar@gmail.com

Baneen Karachiwala
Independent Consultant,
Bangalore, India
baneenk@gmail.com

Tandong N. Cedrick
Three Wheels United
Bangalore, India
Cedrick@twu-india.com

Jacki O'Neill
Microsoft
Bangalore, India
Jacki.oneill@microsoft.com

ABSTRACT
This paper contributes to the growing literature on peer-to-peer (P2P) applications through an ethnographic study of auto-rickshaw drivers in Bengaluru, India. We describe how the adoption of a P2P application, Ola, which connects passengers to rickshaws, changes drivers work practices. Ola is part of the 'peer services' phenomenon which enable new types of ad-hoc trade in labour, skills and goods. Auto-rickshaw drivers present an interesting case because prior to Ola few had used Smartphones or the Internet. Furthermore, as financially vulnerable workers in the informal sector, concerns about driver welfare become prominent. Whilst technologies may promise to improve livelihoods, they do not necessarily deliver [57]. We describe how Ola does little to change the uncertainty which characterizes an auto drivers' day. This leads us to consider how a more equitable and inclusive system might be designed.

Author Keywords
Workplace studies; ethnography; P2P technology; auto-rickshaws; peer services; peer economy; ridesharing, ICTD

ACM Classification Keywords
H.5.m. Information interfaces and presentation (e.g., HCI), H.5.3 Group and Organization Interfaces, Collaborative Computing, K.4.3 Organizational Impacts

INTRODUCTION
The recent proliferation of 'peer services' has enabled new types of ad-hoc trade in labour, skills, knowledge and material goods [e.g. 26,53,31,2] using web and mobile technologies with peer-to-peer (P2P) architectures. Services range from hospitality [26] to lending a helping hand [53] to transportation [34,32] and are often, collectively, called the 'gig', 'alternative', 'collaborative', 'peer' or 'sharing' economy [2,38,58]. Whilst all use P2P architectures, these groups include diverse sets of practices involving exchanging varied resources, for monetary or non-monetary gain, and for employment or not. We are interested in the use of peer services in the workplace and in this paper examine Ola Auto, an implementation to connect customers and auto-rickshaw (auto) drivers. Olacabs, an Indian start-up, added Ola Auto (or Ola) to its taxi-booking services in November 2014. Like Uber its closest competitor, Olacabs does not own taxis or autos but links customers to owner-drivers for specific trips with P2P technology, similar to apps that enable ride-sharing.

We conducted an ethnographic study of auto drivers in Bengaluru, India. By focusing on their adoption of Ola, we aim to understand where and how the app impacts auto-driving for the purposes of design. HCI has long been interested in the impact of new technologies on work-practices [7,8,25,54]. Introducing technology changes existing practices and typically brings both benefits and disruptions [e.g. 7,10,25]. By examining in detail how the work is achieved in, and through, people's actions and interactions with technology and one another, workplace studies draw attention to the knowledge and skills of workers [49,50,55]. Such studies open up spaces for (re)designing technology to better support that work [9,5,15,45].

We focus on how drivers use P2P technology as part of their work. What makes this setting unique is that auto-rickshaw drivers in India have had little exposure to computing technologies, such as the smartphones on which Ola runs. For most drivers using Ola was their first use of smartphones and the first and only way they accessed the Internet. Furthermore drivers are classified as urban poor [40], working in the informal sector [13], which means their welfare is an important concern when introducing new technologies. Autos provide 13% of the city's total trips [59], and auto-driving is the source of livelihood for approximately 125,000 drivers and their families in Bengaluru alone. Many people who travel by auto also do not use smartphones, that is the technology is not yet pervasive among drivers or their passengers. In this study we observed both drivers who had and had not adopted Ola to understand how Ola was changing existing practice. As far

CHI'16, May 07 - 12, 2016, San Jose, CA, USA
Copyright is held by the owner/author(s). Publication rights licensed to ACM.
ACM 978-1-4503-3362-7/16/05 $15.00
DOI: http://dx.doi.org/10.1145/2858036.2858393

as we are aware this is the first study of this type of peer service for work outside of the Global North.

Olacabs, like Uber, acts as a 'Digital Middleman' [28] to connect customers and drivers through the algorithms, networks and data they control. They set fares, receive ride requests, offer and assign rides to drivers, and use real-time and historical data to manage assignment and, possibly, payment rates. The distribution of computing at the driver and customer ends of the P2P architecture is limited to requesting, accepting, paying for and rating rides. Whilst the introduction of new technology into such a setting might offer hope in improving livelihoods, it also brings concerns. New technology can create new poorly paid and unregulated markets [20,27,6,11] and various ICTD studies show that technology deployments in developing countries often fail to produce sustained positive changes in the life of vulnerable populations (see [57] for an extensive list). Our study enables examining the impact of a P2P transportation platform on the auto drivers' work. We found that drivers use Ola alongside their usual methods to find passengers and, despite incentives, do not prioritize Ola over traditional passengers. Ola introduces new elements of competition and evaluation, but does little to change the uncertainty characterizing an auto drivers' day. These insights prompted us to consider redesign of the system, to better support drivers' expertise, literacies and skills, and how P2P architectures might be used in optimal mediation to benefit all actors - drivers, customers and digital middlemen. We are motivated by a view, held by the original P2P movement, that superior solutions involving diverse peers can be achieved provided there is a sense of fairness in distributing resources [41]. Here, we orient our in-depth understanding of work practices, with and without Ola, towards new design ideas for a more equitable and inclusive system.

RELATED WORK

Workplace technologies in the transportation sector

Peer services that link passengers to drivers join a range of computer technologies in the transport industry, and add to debates about their effects on skills and freedoms in workplaces. Automated dispatch systems, that remotely monitor pickup and drop-off and use optimisation algorithms, became prevalent in taxis in many countries in the 1990s and GPS a decade later [47]. Debate about the effects of such systems becomes more complex for a peer economy involving financially vulnerable workers in developing regions.

Analysis of US vehicle ownership in taxi firms suggests that computerised dispatch systems promote central organisation and unskilled labour because key routines are more efficient and firms can lease more cars to drivers who are unfamiliar with the spatial and temporal patterns of the business [47]. However, several extensive ethnographic studies suggest transformations are more nuanced and GPS-enabled systems do not change jobs from skilled to unskilled [24,22]. Contrary to studies on London's taxi drivers [19] and the opinions of some experienced local drivers [24], technologies can induce various innovative practices amongst drivers. Drivers in Barcelona, for instance, acquired a "Satnav literacy" in mastering skills to interpret, assess and tackle the varying accuracy of GPS information [22]. GPS modified only part of drivers' practices and, while transforming practices in learning, lost usefulness when drivers were familiar with areas [22]. Indeed, in New York drivers tuned their use of Uber and Lyft's ridesharing apps to accommodate their local knowledge [32]. Meanwhile, in Singapore, a GPS-enabled taxi-dispatch system obliged drivers to move beyond their former geographic haunts and gain new temporal and spatial knowledge [24]. This enabled some to reach places unknown to other drivers, and some to gain insights about precise 'hot-spots' to 'capture', not wait for, customers.

Just as GPS-enabled systems change, rather than eliminate, wayfinding skills, they can change social skills [22,33]. Not needing to ask for route information can limit drivers' conversations with passengers, colleagues and locals [22]. On the other hand, drivers used GPS-enabled systems as guides to places where there are interesting customers to talk with [24] and to propose alternate routes for customers to choose from to avoid complaints [22]. Meanwhile, Lyft and Uber's ridesharing apps provoked social interactions, online and in streets, to reduce the effects of algorithmic 'errors' [32].

Technologies for the workers

Designing workplace technologies to be inclusive is not simple. Consider how Uber or Lyft drivers with more technical expertise and social capital often benefited most from collaboratively tackling issues arising due to the ridesharing app's algorithms [32]. Consider also how drivers with most knowledge about a dispatch systems' functionality earned highest incomes and had lower costs and those with less knowledge worked longer hours or maintained only a basic income [24]. Indeed, the competitive pressure that the system induced constrained some drivers, who were older, could not read the system's texts easily, were disturbed by it, and only used the system in a perfunctory way.

Inclusion in workplaces that are mediated by technology requires both access to those technologies and literacies in the representations and communication forms they use. Many efforts in India have tackled exclusion amongst low-income communities by designing text-free interfaces [42,43]. For example, Medhi et al. [37] designed a mobile phone interface for a job portal for service workers who typically have limited print and technological literacy.

Whilst accessible devices and interfaces are important for the auto drivers, they are not sufficient in fairly distributing resources across peers. Toyama [57] proposes that technologies in development contexts can, in fact, magnify existing differences in society. Even in developed countries, the peer economy often disadvantages, or provides few benefits to, people on no/low-incomes or in economically poorer communities [e.g. [16,56,28, 29]. They are most susceptible to exploitation, subjected to low wages, underpayment or adverse working conditions and incur relatively more expensive liabilities and insurances [39,28]. Concerns about workers' rights are common for many digital micro-task crowdsourcing platforms, such as TaskRabbit and Amazon Mechanical Turk (AMT) [27, 35]. Technology platforms often create new working relationships, where digital middlemen [28], like AMT and Uber, operate in something of a grey area of poorly regulated labour markets [20,11] in which they do not identify as employers [46].

Accounting for the diverse experience, knowledge and skills workers have, or develop with technology, is also vital for inclusion; and an opportunity to achieve superior services. Recognising experience, knowledge and skills requires shifting focus towards workers' practices and away from technological platforms, which inherently privilege certain literacies [e.g. 3]. A body of research on micro-task work has begun to rectify prior emphasis on technology in examining crowdsourcing [27,35,23,30]. Thus, as is customary in workplace studies, we use ethnographic methods to understand the technology in use [9, 25, 45] and take the workers' perspective [50,55].

Two key issues that arise when taking the workers' perspective are choice and control. Providing workers with sufficient information about how a system works enables informed choice while opacity leads to distrust. Consider, for instance, the suspicions that some drivers in New York expressed because Uber's and Lyft's ride assignment algorithms were unclear [32]. Distrust and resistance often arise in the transport sector when in-vehicle computers are introduced, partly in response to the surveillance that many afford [44]. Trust is easily compromised in employment relationships [see 24] and, so too, in peer systems. For instance, drivers were dissatisfied with Uber and Lyft's customer ratings, which many found unfair [32] or arbitrary [48]. Choice and control are also integral to the original P2P movement's ethos and to considering the effects of workplace technologies on economically vulnerable people in developing regions. Sen defined development as a freedom both in constitutive and instrumental ways [52]. Taxi drivers note that they appreciate the freedom to schedule their itineraries and select destinations and types of passengers permitted by some dispatch systems [24]. This sense of freedom associates with fully understanding the system [24], which is not always true for Uber or Lyft's apps and some drivers prefer their regular taxi dispatch systems because they enable seeing and choosing freely between incoming requests [32].

In this paper we describe Ola's effects on the practices of auto drivers, both as a P2P service in dispatching rides and as the drivers' first experience of workplace technology. After explaining our methods and the context, we show how Ola fits into, and changes, drivers' practices. We conclude by considering the implications of these insights to designing a P2P service that might offer more effective, and also more inclusive and equitable, dispatch.

METHOD AND FIELD SITE

We conducted an ethnographic study of auto drivers in Bengaluru, April-July 2015. We used observation and in-situ and semi-structured interviewing to get a rich picture of drivers' practices, concerns and perceptions of technology. We observed 23 drivers (12 using Ola), during 14 days in the field, and conducted 48 semi-structured interviews (21 using Ola). Our population consists of 66 individual drivers, as we both observed and interviewed a few drivers. All field encounters were conducted in the official language of Karnataka state, Kannada, by a researcher fluent in it.

Drivers were recruited to our study by Three Wheel United (TWU), a social enterprise that helps auto drivers to buy their own autos; and Peace Auto, a network of auto drivers which campaigns for their rights. Recruitment was based on availability and willingness to take part and use or non-use of Ola. Drivers gave verbal consent to participate, with separate agreements to audio recording and photographs.

We observed the auto drivers as they went about their normal business, looking for and carrying passengers, taking breaks and so on. To avoid interfering with the process of picking up passengers, we followed behind an auto in a second auto. We identified pairs of drivers and hired the following auto to carry us at a fixed rate, set by TWU. For the first part of the day we sat in one auto and then changed to the other. The observed driver went about his normal business, whilst we followed, hopping out for short in situ interviews when the occasion arose (traffic lights, tea breaks, etc.). If the driver was using Ola, he signaled to us when he got an Ola ride and we got into his auto to drive to the passenger's destination. In the separate semi-structured interviews, we asked drivers about their biographical data, technology use, financial situation and work. For those using Ola we focused on the impact of Ola in their life, how they understood it and started using it, etc.

Data was collected through field-notes, audio recordings and photographs. The interviews were translated and transcribed. Our analysis took a broadly ethno-methodologial (EM) perspective [21]. EM ethnographies explicate the knowledgeable, artful ways in which participants orient to their work and reveal the ways in which technologies and other arfefacts are used as part of the accomplishment of work (see e.g. [10,49]). These rich insights have proved useful in informing the (re-) design of technologies to support or transform work [15,12,45].

DRIVER DEMOGRAPHICS AND DRIVING CONTEXT

The auto industry is male dominated and all 66 drivers in our study are male. Their average age was 39 years and 76% were 30-50 years old, which is representative of auto drivers in general [14]. As well as Kannada, most drivers speak at least one other language (typically Hindi, Tamil or Telugu) and 36 had some understanding of three or more languages, often including English. Most did not own a personal smart phone, and almost none had accessed the Internet, although two got their children to look up things for them. Ten participants had never been to school, 20 dropped out after primary school, 28 completed high school, and 8 studied beyond high school.

Participants had an average of 14 years driving experience and the most experienced had 38 years of auto driving experience. Surveys typically classify Indian auto drivers as urban poor (based on housing and income) [40]. The average daily income of the majority of participants, after fuel and maintenance costs, was 600-800 INR (approx. USD8-11). An exceptional few earned more than 1000INR. Most were the sole earners in their families. Typically, drivers had enough income to cover their daily expenses but few were able to save though most wished to. With no buffer if events incurred additional costs, like [40] we classify the majority of drivers in our study as financially vulnerable.

Each city in India has its own norms about rickshaw drivers' use of meters, and use is hotly contested. Drivers in Bengaluru should use their meters but, while a considerable proportion do, use varies for different parts of the city, times of day and types of ride. Customers may have to approach multiple autos to find one prepared to use the meter. Drivers in our study almost always used their meter, as all were associated with TWU, who like Ola, require meter use. Ola passengers pay a 'convenience charge' on top of the meter fare, which varies at peak and off-peak times. Ola also pays an incentive to drivers if they carry a set number of Ola passengers in a day. This scheme changes regularly and drivers complained that incentives have declined. Being an auto driver (without Ola)

Driving an auto in Bengaluru is a hot, noisy, polluted business, in frequent heavy traffic, with typically long hours. 12-hour days, excluding breaks, are common. Drivers reported two busy periods, from 7am to midday and from 4pm to 8pm and many take a break during the hottest part of the day. The primary orientation of drivers is to find passengers, as they often struggle to get enough rides to make an adequate daily wage. Passengers and drivers locate each other by sight: drivers cruise slowly near the pavement at promising locations, i.e. where there are people on the street. They may be flagged down, by a hand wave, shout, and/or eye contact, or just slow down for people who are standing by the roadside or carrying baggage. They favor particular locations such as bus stops, schools, hospitals, etc., often planning a route , in whichever vicinity they happen to be in, to pass these places.

Autonomy, control and uncertainty

Auto drivers appreciate their independence. Each driver works for himself. Thus drivers can choose their hours and structure their day according to their priorities and preferences, e.g. taking their children to school. However, an important caveat to this flexibility is that they are not earning when they are not working. Furthermore, drivers have no control over passengers' availability and they often drive empty for some unpredictable period of the day. Their tight financial circumstances, limits the choices they actually make when out on the road. Despite preferring long or short rides or particular locations, drivers typically go wherever passengers want to go, except for the end of the day when tiredness or the need to get home may intervene.

As Mr. A says "*Just because I prefer not take some rides doesn't mean I don't. If I haven't gotten many rides, then I will have to take it, whether I like it or not. In the afternoon, I do not refuse anybody*"

Only 3 of 23 participants declined passengers during our observations. This arose when driver and passenger did not know the destination; passengers outnumbered seats, and would not pay enough extra; or, the ride was 'too short' (although other drivers prefer short rides). Being an auto driver is thus characterized by control over some aspects of working life but also by uncertainty and inconsistency.

Dealing with Uncertainty

Since drivers do not know for sure where they will find their next passenger, they employ various tactics to manage the uncertainty 1) Driving around ('rounding') is the most common tactic and many drivers said they did not like to stop in one place for long.

"*I only do rounding to find passengers. I don't wait at any stands because it's a waste of time and then we feel lazy to drive passengers' around*" (Mr. B)

Drivers' decisions about what to do next account for a set of factors. These include the need to find passengers; the need for rest/to escape the sun; the payoff between using petrol in 'rounding' vs missing passengers and a losing momentum while stationary. 2) Drivers use their local knowledge of where and when they might find passengers in deciding what to do next. Mr. C picked up a passenger driving on a quite narrow internal lane. When we asked how he knew to come into this area, he said "*I know the area really well since I live around here and where I might find passengers*". Drivers have certain places they like to head to at particular times, such as hospitals, schools, cinemas, bus stops, offices, shopping malls. Yet none are guaranteed and drivers are not surprised if unsuccessful. 3) Drivers organize themselves to cover both peak hour periods, and some like to drive when others do not, such as on religious holidays or at midday when many take a break.

STARTING OLA

When auto drivers' sign-up, Olacabs gives them a locked smart phone, running the Ola app, in English, Kannada or Hindi. This is the first smartphone most drivers have used. Ola runs a 2-hour training program on "*how to use the device, how you should accept if you get a ride, how to keep your auto, how to behave with the passengers*" (Mr. D). Most drivers in our study mastered the device and the app, often after putting some effort into learning to use them.

MR. E: "*I found it difficult to use for a couple of days but now it's easy. It's in Kannada. I find it easy to understand*"

Some drivers reported getting help from fellow drivers and we saw drivers discussing troubles with the device. However, drivers have different levels of education and access to support when they have a problem. Even simple problems can be a barrier and not all drivers will ask for help. One driver had been unable to logon to his device for 2 weeks until a fieldworker spotted and fixed a simple number entry error, whereupon he logged in and got a ride. Drivers can call Olacabs, but they are not always very helpful or can forfeit up to a whole day's work by going to and waiting at the often busy office. Thus, drivers may delay going, preferring to drive without Ola than to lose a day's wages.

Most drivers in our study who tried to use Ola were able to learn, including at least one auto driver who had not been to school. However, education did seem to play a role in how easy Ola was to master, and concern about being unable to use it was a barrier to adoption for some non-users. A few drivers told us they would not join Ola as they might not be able to use the app because they had not been to school.

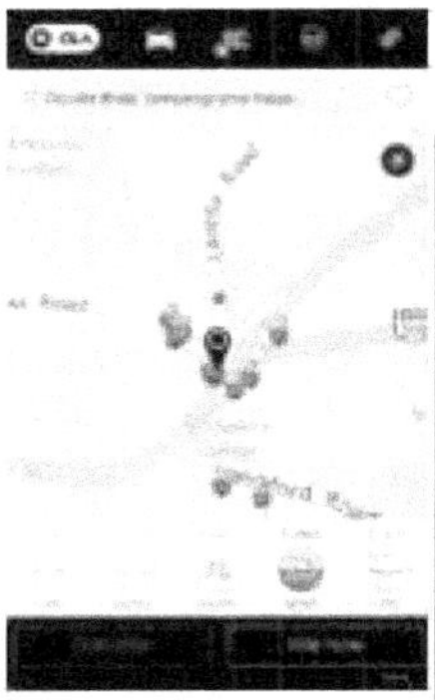

Figure 1: Passenger interface

Figure 2: Ola device mounted in auto-rickshaw

FINDING PASSENGERS WITH OLA

The most obvious changes when using Ola are the ways drivers and customers find one another and negotiate (Fig 1). Without Ola, drivers locate passengers by sight, negotiate whether to take them then set off towards their destination. Typically, this interaction takes just a few seconds. Ola changes the dynamics as drivers must first accept the passenger's request then physically locate them, and do not negotiate with the customer.

Once a customer confirms they want an auto, a request is broadcast to available drivers within a radius determined by the Ola algorithm, which appears to start at 2km. The driver is notified of the request by a loud beep and a pop-up box on the screen showing the pick-up and drop locations, labeled as area names. The driver has 30 seconds to respond to the request if no one else accepts the ride but, as drivers are usually competing, they often have just a few seconds to respond. Since only one driver can accept a request a split second can make all the difference. To enable them to see and respond rapidly to requests, drivers mount the device on a holder attached to their windscreen (Fig 2).

Being available for Ola requests

To be able to accept an Ola passenger, drivers must make themselves available for Ola requests. To do so they must be both in the radius to receive the request and free to accept it. Firstly, with regards to being within the request radius, Ola customers are not distributed evenly across the city. As customers must have a smart phone and Internet access to use the app, they concentrate in certain areas, which we call Ola Hotspots. Hotspots include software companies, certain business areas and areas "*where auto drivers refuse to take passengers or demand a lot over the meter*" (Mr. F). Drivers determine where Hotspots are because they hear many Ola beeps when they drive through them. Thus, although the technology mediates the search for passengers the auto drivers still actively 'seek out' Ola passengers. Some drivers changed their habits to spend more time in Hotspots. However, just as there may be many passengers in these Hotspots there were also many drivers. Other drivers just carried on as normal – if they are in those areas they will get Ola rides, if they are not they will find passengers the traditional way. There is no guarantee of getting a ride in these areas either. For instance, Mr. D stops at an Ola Hotspot every day outside a business school; yet, during our observations he waited 50 minutes before getting a non-Ola passenger. On another day whilst cruising around a different area Mr. R expressed surprise at not receiving any Ola requests at that hour. It was peak hour and he usually hears tens of requests there.

Secondly, all the drivers in our study used Ola alongside their traditional methods of picking up passengers. They do not accept new requests that come in when they have non-Ola passengers in their autos. However, Ola cannot detect a non-Ola passenger and depicts any driver that is logged in and not already engaged in an Ola ride as available. This means customers often see a representation of autos in their vicinity that is imprecise and may see autos on the map when being notified that there are no available autos.

Accepting Ola requests

Most drivers tried to accept the rides that came when they were available. However, they accounted for various factors in accepting a request. This includes the customer's pick-up and drop-off and their own location, traffic conditions and time of day. Travelling to the customer takes fuel and time and most drivers are unwilling to travel more than 2km to pick-up. Ola passengers pay the driver a 'convenience charge' of 10 INR over the meter, which compensates for the extra costs in fuel and phone calls, as discussed below.

"*If the passenger is a short distance away say, 1-1.5Kms, I can travel there and pick him up because I will at least get the extra 10 rupees from the customer. If the customer is over 2.5Kms, then it's a loss for me*" (Mr. G)

Drivers do not always have enough information to make a good decision. Mr. H explains, "*Now, the catch is the device doesn't show how far away the driver is from the pickup address. Sometimes we end up accepting it and then realize the distance of the pickup location from ours. The initial message [...] only shows the area*". Areas vary widely in scale, from just 1Km to 5km across. Drivers most common tactic is to accept and then, if it is too far, cancel or ask the passenger to cancel. Cancellations can, however, impact drivers' ratings, as we discuss later. Another tactic is to ignore rides when traffic conditions are poor. One driver reported how he and other drivers did not accept Ola rides in peak hours "*Because Ola will send a message to the passenger assuring that the driver will arrive in 5 minutes but it is not possible to reach a pickup location which is 1.5-2 Km away in such a short span of time".*

Drivers said that they only refused Ola rides on the basis of drop location at the end of the day, unless the destination was unknown. This reflects their practices with traditional passengers, although without Ola they can check if the passenger knows the destination.

Picking up the passenger

Having won an Ola ride, auto drivers must locate their passenger. As Ola does not give the exact pick-up location it often took 3-4 phone calls between drivers and customers to achieve a pick-up. Typically, drivers start heading towards the pick-up, following the map, to give customers time to call. If the customer does not contact them most drivers will call but some just cancel. Keeping an adequate credit balance on their phones is necessary for drivers to use Ola effectively but a financial burden. Drivers' preference for customers to call them fits expectations that people with more money call those with less [17,4]. However, the nature of the service transaction confounds this, particularly since drivers of taxis almost always call passengers.

Ola introduces a new uncertainty into the transaction: will the customer actually be at pick-up location? Since passengers can jump into any passing auto, waiting for an Ola auto is more burdensome, particularly since Ola's estimation of arrival time is often inaccurate. Thus, customers cancel their ride or, in the worst-case, leave before the driver arrives. As Mr. I reports "*I have never gone to the passengers and get complaints from them about me being late. They don't even wait that long, they just book another ride and I don't find the passenger there when I go there." "This has happened to me 4-5 times. [...] This upsets me a lot.*"

Negotiation

The Ola app replaces the need to negotiate fares, which is a clear benefit for the customer. One customer said, *"no negotiations need to be done which is what I like. If I take a regular auto [...] 95% of them charge me one and a half time during the day"*. Drivers in our study typically charge by the meter and take any passenger, thus almost no negotiation with the passenger occurred even without Ola and little has changed by moving this 'negotiation' onto the app. However, as we mentioned, when the driver does not know the destination the app precludes any compromise, as the driver has little choice but to turn down the ride.

INTERWEAVING OLA WITH TRADITIONAL RIDES

Despite changing how customers and drivers find each other in some ways, much of the work of auto driving remains the same. Drivers incorporated Ola into existing routines and use it alongside their existing methods for getting passengers. On first glance, this is because drivers do not get enough Ola rides for it to be their sole means of business. Most drivers reported getting 2-5 Ola rides a day, and the next largest category was 6-8 rides. Yet, there is more to it than this. Drivers typically accept only a few of the many requests they hear day in Ola Hotspots. As Mr. J explains *"In a day, I get around 10-20 rides but I can't attend to all the 20 rides because I will have passengers in my auto.* [...] *Some days I get 2 rides* [...] *The most I have got is 5 rides*". Ola passengers compete with traditional passengers for rides, and most Ola requests come during the peak hours, when auto drivers are already busiest. Few come in when drivers most need to find passengers, as Mr. A describes *"Very rarely do we get 1 or 2 Ola rides in the afternoon*".

To encourage drivers to take Ola requests, Olacabs pays drivers an incentive of 10 INR off-peak and 40 INR on-peak per ride, if they get three or more rides a day. Nonetheless drivers do not choose to wait for an Ola request if they can get a traditional passenger instead. This is partly because getting Ola passengers is just as unpredictable as getting traditional passengers, as Mr. K says "*It depends on our luck*". Mr. L explains "*if you wait for Ola rides to come in when you are waiting at a particular location [...] you end up waiting all day without getting either normal or Ola passengers*". Added to this are the extra costs and the risk the passenger might not wait. Mr. I confirms, "*In the evening too, if I'm near a company, I get rides on the street from them, who will go 1-2 kms to pick up somebody else from Ola? At these times, it doesn't really come of use.*" Most drivers therefore continue to do rounds, only waiting during the quiet part of the day, just as they would for non-Ola passengers. To adapt an old idiom, a passenger in the hand is worth two in the bush.

Some drivers don't even make enough rides to get the incentives. Some long-term users reported that increasing competition had reduced rides per day. "*I can't guarantee that I might get incentives"* Mr. G said "*because they have 3 rides as a minimum for incentives and I don't get 3 rides every day"*. Even the promise of incentives will not make drivers wait for an Ola passenger. Obtaining the incentives involves elements of chance: being in the right place at the right time, without a passenger. This unpredictability combines with the unpredictability of getting traditional passengers and the constraints drivers operate under - the need to get enough rides to cover their living costs.

To conclude, whilst some drivers were very positive, saying Ola has increased their earnings or reduced their hours, others reported little impact on earnings or hours. Most were rather muted in their appreciation. They were glad of the extra rides, especially in quiet periods or places but, since most Ola rides come at busy times and in busy areas, Ola did not produce a big change in their working lives.

COMPETITION

Drivers compete for non-Ola passengers at the side of the road. They rush towards potential passengers and negotiations start on a roughly first-come-first-served basis. Interrupting an ongoing negotiation can result in fights and rarely happens. A driver's success largely depends on his ability to locate a potential passenger, quickly reach them, and the outcome of the previous negotiation. With Ola drivers compete through the app, rushing to be the first to hit accept. The Ola competition introduces new elements.

First, whereas previously they only competed with the autos in sight of a passenger, now drivers compete with all Ola drivers in the request radius. Second, Ola's algorithm intervenes in this competition by influencing a drivers' chance of getting a ride. The drivers do not know how the request is distributed. In fact it is unclear whether the request is broadcast simultaneously to all drivers in the radius or from nearest to farthest over time, or to drivers with higher passenger- or Ola- ratings. Indeed, the algorithm is likely to change over time. What is important here is that it is Ola who controls the algorithm and its workings are not transparent to the drivers, as [32] also reported.

Finally, this new competition is only available by using Ola and, thus, disproportionately impacts on drivers who cannot, or do not believe they can, use the system. Consider Mr. B, a driver of 35 years who never went to school and cannot read and write. He is skilled at locating passengers and prides himself on knowing every nook and cranny of the city and alternative routes. Mr. B thinks Ola lets inexperienced drivers win rides that would otherwise be his:

"Look at all these young and new auto drivers! They do not even know the roads and places. Yet, they are now getting the passengers using this new mobile phone. They take the rides, and then ask people on the road about the routes. [...] If they did not have that phone, they would never get these passengers, when they did not know the destinations."

Although none of the drivers in our study took rides when they did not know the destination, it is true that the app does not distinguish between drivers' expertise. Of course, even knowledgeable, experienced and highly skilled auto drivers cannot get Ola rides if they do not use the app. Further, whilst the app is relatively easy to use by people with schooling, drivers with little formal education are less able to use it and also may lack confidence in trying. Some, particularly older drivers, were unwilling to attempt to use it.

The introduction of Ola and Uber also puts auto drivers in more direct competition with cabs. Only autos can pick-up passengers directly from the side of the road, making them the 'go to' transport for immediate journeys. However, peer services have changed the dynamics of taxi booking, showing which cabs are nearby and enabling booking on a click. This, plus reduced cab fares for Ola taxis, make taxis a more attractive choice than previously. Whilst autos have a lower minimum fare, above that threshold cabs are cheaper per Km. A number of drivers mentioned their concern. "*The rate of the car has become less and is very competitive to the auto prices. The only reason a passenger might prefer an auto over a car because we can zip through traffic if need be. [...] They are also increasing the number of cabs on the road which results in less business for us*" (Mr. M). Although not all drivers were concerned e.g. Mr. J "*People who prefer Ola cabs book Ola cabs and people who book Ola autos book Ola autos*".

From one perspective the Ola Auto app puts autos and cabs on a little more equal footing. However, some auto drivers were suspicious that Olacabs might be biased towards cabs while assigning rides. A couple complained that Ola intentionally shows less autos and more cabs, to encourage passengers to take cabs. Although there is no concrete evidence to support it, the drivers' claim shows mistrust in Ola and concern that it is not working to their benefit.

EVALUATION

Drivers are evaluated by their passengers and by Olacabs. When a passenger logs onto the app after completing a ride, they are prompted to select 1-5 stars and give a rationale from a pre-defined list. The driver sees a cumulative rating (number of stars) on the front page of his app. All the drivers had noticed the stars, but they were not always sure about how they worked. Some drivers did not even know they were from the passengers, but even if they did, they found it hard to understand why their ratings changed.

Mr. N said, "*The Ola people have said that the stars are related to the customer rating the driver. Sometimes in the afternoon, I have lesser stars and it increases in the evening. Some days when I have accepted lots of rides, I get lesser stars and some days when I barely have any passengers, I get rated high. I am not entirely sure why this happens.*"

Features of the implementation make understanding the stars difficult as drivers cannot associate a change in rating with a ride. They do not see individual passengers' ratings and because updates in ratings depend on when customers next open the app, there are erratic time intervals between rides and ratings. Further, drivers are unclear about how Olacabs rates them, as illustrated by Mr. O, "*I have seen the rating but do not know much about it. They just told us that our ratings go up when we take more rides and will go down if we cancel or reject a ride.*" Olacabs rates the drivers on certain aspects of their performance, such as number of accepted rides per day, number of cancellations, etc. However, it is unclear which, if any, of these aspects feed into the stars and whether the ratings feed into ride request algorithms or will do in the future. In the absence of concrete information, some drivers based their hypotheses on the partial information that they received from Ola and their own observations, similar to [32]. Some described customer ratings, some described Olacabs ratings, some described a bit of both, e.g. Mr. A "*It increases if we take on more rides and/or if any customer gives me a 5 rating*".

Living with ratings

Drivers expressed varied opinions on the rating system, however the majority thought that it had some impact on them, even if they were not always sure what. Some saw it as a reflection of their performance, e.g. Mr. P said, "*If we get 4 stars it means we are the best driver*", and some could be quite affected by a poor rating. Mr. Q explained, "*When I reject the ride, my stars go down. I then get very upset and switch off the phone and put it away.*". Others, who understood the system well, even reminded passengers to rate them, e.g. Mr. A said, "*I tell them at the end of each ride to give a rating. But sometimes they forget*". One driver, Mr. J, believed the rating was connected to the number of rides he got, "*If my stars increase, I get more rides.*". Interestingly Mr. J also said he was indifferent to the stars "*If these stars points change it doesn't really affect me much. Yesterday it was 3.9, today it's 3 but that doesn't make any difference to me*". A few drivers said this, however even if Mr. J is indifferent he still keeps track of what his rating actually is. Finally, similar to [32], a few drivers were critical that the rating system did not capture the reasons for accepting or rejecting a ride. That is, the measurements were too gross to capture drivers' real performance.

DISCUSSION

Auto drivers are a financially vulnerable population that works long hours in a physically demanding job. Drivers' primary orientation is to find enough passengers each day to cover their basic living costs. Potentially, peer services, like Ola, may offer ways to increase drivers' livelihoods or improve their quality of life. Insights into how drivers incorporated Ola into their work practices and the advantages and problems they experienced in using Ola can inform ideas for a more equitable and inclusive system that, ultimately, will offer a superior solution for passengers, drivers and the digital middlemen.

Despite its potential Ola does not seem to appreciably transform the situation for drivers. While passengers get an auto service to their doorstep with a few key presses and phone calls, drivers carry the burden of locating a passenger in a timely manner once they have won a request. Only a few reported that using Ola had increased their earnings or reduced the number of hours they worked, and some reported that initial improvements in earnings declined over time.

Perhaps most importantly, Ola has not reduced the uncertainty of an auto driver's day. This is largely because they do not get enough Ola rides per day and crucially most Ola rides are requested when they are already busy. Interestingly, even the peak hour incentive of 40INR per passenger, after 3 rides, is not enough to persuade drivers to prefer Ola over traditional passengers. Although they get many Ola requests during peak hours when in Hotspots, drivers continue to take traditional passengers as normal and only accept Ola requests if they happen to come when they are empty. This is because getting an Ola passenger is no more predictable than getting a traditional passenger. Indeed Ola introduces new elements of uncertainty around getting enough rides to make the incentives, when a request will come in, winning requests, how far away the request is, whether and for how long the passenger will wait at the pick-up point and whether a drop-off will be far-off or in an Ola Hotspot.

Changing skills?

Before Ola, finding passengers on the road was mostly dependent on the driver's expertise. Like taxi drivers [47], a skilled auto driver is one who possesses knowledge about the spatial and temporal variation in demand and knowledge about routes around Bengaluru, including shortcuts through, and locations within, warrens of small internal streets that crisscross many areas. Ola introduces digital and print literacy alongside driver's existing passenger-finding and wayfinding literacies. Despite ease of use, Ola is not equally accessible in the auto driver community and excludes some drivers based on their (perceived) capability to adopt the technology, not their auto-driving skills. Further, it is possible that Ola may enable unskilled drivers to win rides they would not have got previously, which could result in a poorer service for customers. There is no evidence in our study of this, other than Mr. B's experience, as no participant was a newly qualified drivers. The drivers using Ola employed their geographical expertise just as they would without it. In fact, Ola tested drivers' geographical skills and knowledge more because they have less information to go on. Firstly, they must decide to accept or reject an Ola request without knowing the exact destination; and secondly, Ola removes collaborations that ensure at least one person in the auto knows the destination.

P2P in the workplace

Control

Choice and control is integral to the P2P movement's ethos and is vital in considering the effects of workplace technologies on economically vulnerable people in developing regions. While auto drivers value the independence and flexibility offered by their jobs, in reality the financial constraints on their operation limit the choices they actually make, both with and without Ola. At the moment, the drivers in our study maintained their independence largely because, like CabLink drivers [24], they could use the system as one in a set of ways to get passengers. However, using Ola could erode drivers' independence if Ola passengers dominate the marketplace to advance the role of the middleman and the influence of Ola's algorithm in mediating the passenger-driver relationship. Drivers' experience and knowledge, about when and where to find passengers, routes and locations, does not influence Ola's algorithm or the role it plays, and drivers have little understanding of how the system works. Such a shift in the marketplace is likely to be some way off in Bengaluru, given the socio-economic situation of many who use autos. Nonetheless to some extent Ola erodes drivers' freedom and control, with little benefit so far. Yet, this does not have to be the case. Both [24] and [32] described taxi dispatch systems that enabled greater freedom and choice, and appropriations that support local knowledge.

Transparency

There are three places in which a lack of transparency in the Ola app impacts on drivers. Firstly, the working of the Ola algorithm is not transparent. For example, drivers do not have enough information about the distance between their current and the pick-up location to consistently make good decisions on whether or not to accept a ride. They assume that requests tend to be broadcast in a 2km radius, and should be fine to accept. Yet sometimes requests are broadcast much further and even 2km can be too far in peak hours. This can lead drivers or passengers to cancel rides, with penalties to a driver's ratings if he cancels.

Secondly, most drivers still prefer rounding to find passengers. This is partly because they rely on a mixture of Ola and traditional passengers and also because Ola Hotspots can be quite large and may increase competition. Currently, drivers understand the Ola landscape from personal experience. It is only by driving around that they come across where requests often/never come in, and where and when they have good/poor chances of winning a request. The mass of information that the Ola system produces from the collectivity of drivers and customers is currently not used, at least not for the benefit of the drivers. In theory this information could be made available to, and improved upon, by drivers who already organize themselves to cover quiet times, holidays and so on.

Thirdly, drivers poorly understand the rating system. Both passengers and Ola rate the drivers on various factors but, like the drivers, we do not know whether and how such ratings feed into ride assignments. This leads us to ask who is the rating system for? In its current form is not actionable by drivers, who have little idea why their ratings change in seemingly random ways. Thus, even if drivers want to act to improve their performance they cannot do so. If it is not for the drivers then, presumably, it is for Ola to determine who are good or bad drivers and identify dissatisfied customers. However, the ambiguous and subjective nature of the ratings makes it impossible for drivers to determine what is required to be a good driver.

There is also a deeper issue involved here that relates to introducing an evaluation system into drivers' daily work. While all are aware of the rating schema, drivers respond in different ways. Some try to adapt to this new culture, e.g. by reminding customers to rate them, whereas others profess indifference. This raises a second question around whether Ola is correctly measuring driver performance. Since Ola does not provide enough information for drivers to make a well informed choice on ride acceptance, they are often 'late', miss passengers, or cancel rides. All of these effects can impact drivers' ratings. Lee et al's [32] study on the Uber and Lyft drivers in USA shows that drivers in the shared economy are concerned about their rating, and critical about the perceived errors produced by algorithms for rating. The online social network of those drivers provides a platform for them to get united, blacklist misbehaving passengers, and thus develop a communal effort to balance the power equation. However, with limited Internet access, infra-structural support and digital literacy, such online unity is unlikely be common amongst Indian auto drivers. It is also reminiscent of crowd-workers who receive little useful feedback on their work and, thus, find it hard to improve or to challenge misconceptions built into a platform [23,35].

Another interesting aspect of Ola's evaluation system involves the power dynamics in the relationship between the drivers and passengers. Some studies in developing contexts suggest that technology amplifies difference [57]. If ratings feed into ride assignments, they could affect a driver's earnings. Since our study Olacabs has introduced driver ratings of passengers, which may balance the situation a little. However, passengers are unlikely to suffer the same impact from bad ratings. While the rating may affect the chance of a passenger to get a ride or make her pay more for it, for a driver it is a question of livelihood.

DESIGN REFLECTIONS

Recently we have seen the emergence of new types of technologically-mediated marketplaces creating new forms of organization. Studies of crowdwork show that for all their apparent novelty, markets such as AMT recreate existing hierarchies. For example, favoring employers over employees [27] or enabling different experiences in different populations [36]. The strident media debate about sectors of the peer economy such as Uber raise parallel concerns [6,28,38,39]. In both these markets workers are portrayed as independent contractors. Our study shows how Ola actually reduces the independence of drivers, by mediating between them and customers, but does little too reduce the uncertainty of auto-driving. Like a growing group of researchers studying crowdsourcing [36,51], we believe it does not have to be this way. More equitable re-design that takes seriously the rights and requirements of the workers could produce more sustainable marketplaces and benefit all the parties in the equation (e.g. drivers, customers and Ola). In speaking to notions of choice and control and the problems that arise from the lack of transparency, our findings echo those of studies of another technologically-mediated marketplace, AMT. Thus, to spark design ideas we compare what is hidden and revealed in AMT and Ola along three axis.

1. Making the work visible

Unlike AMT, Ola does not make all **work** visible to all involved. Drivers see specific jobs one-at-a-time, as Ola alerts them, and only drivers with print literacy can read the jobs. One set of design reflections, therefore, concern making work more visible by improving accessibility, providing better information about individual rides and comprehensively representing rides, autos and spatiotemporal patterns of rides. Access could be widened by designing for low print literacy [see e.g. 37]; for example, notifying with spoken place names instead of Ola's beep. To support drivers' decision-making about individual rides, ride requests could contain more information e.g. show the pick-up as a sector on the map or providing estimates of time to pick-up.

Greater potential benefits could result from sharing information about patterns in Ola and non-Ola ride requests, available autos and traffic conditions. Information about Ola ride request patterns (e.g. volume, frequency, location) currently resides only with Ola, while information about real-time non-Ola passengers and traffic conditions is fragmented across drivers on the road. Empowering drivers to share real-time, information that adds to the data Ola already collects, stands to improve services to both Ola and non-Ola passengers. For instance, drivers could contribute to shared, dynamic images of the distribution of potential passengers and areas of congestion by sending alerts about surges in by-the-road passengers and/or traffic conditions in particular areas. Drivers seeking customers could access a view of surge areas or otherwise browse the 'ride map' of their locality. Meanwhile, Ola could improve time estimates to customers by accounting for the likely availability of autos based on recent busyness in an area. The reliability of updates about surge areas might be represented according to the number of drivers reporting a surge (e.g. darker shaded area for more reports).

2. Maximizing relationships

Whereas AMT hides **relationships between actors** (employer/workers) causing problems and workarounds [e.g.23], in Ola there is greater visibility, since drivers directly interact with individual customers, albeit transiently. Nonetheless, more could be done to enhance and benefit from customer-driver relationships. For example, individual drivers and customers have particular preferences and needs for particular rides. Drivers may know some areas better, be more flexible about waiting or driving short/long distances and most speak multiple languages. Similarly, customers may be in a hurry, require a certain language or a driver who knows the route; or have time to spare or be willing to navigate themselves. Incorporating preferences into the system could enable more sensitive ride assignment.

In current implementations, evaluation is a key part of the relationship but has little use since the rating system is not actionable and thus does not improve service. Drivers should be able to see the ratings of their last 2-3 customers, for instance, as well as their cumulative score. They should be encouraged to rate their customers, and customers who neither wait nor cancel a pick-up should face consequences. Olacabs should also make more visible the parameters of its own rating system and the effect they have on drivers. Finally, to support drivers in addressing barriers of technological literacy, a 'help me' request could enable drivers to identify others nearby able and prepared to assist in trouble-shooting or learning to use the system. This idea bears some similarities to a system that enabled rickshaw pullers in Dhaka, Bangladesh to get help in operating their mobile phones from their garage owner [1].

3. Making the role of the P2P provider visible

Current P2P and crowdsourcing services tend to position workers as independent agents or micro-entrepreneurs. This associates with a view is that P2P technologies allow greater freedom to workers as they ostensibly more directly connect customers with drivers. However, this view does not account for the influence of the service provider. Like Uber, Ola plays a powerful role in the market's operation, which directly impacts worker freedom. In Ola's case this substantially threatens to erode the freedom of drivers who previously operated independently. We do not argue that working independently is always optimal, but that the particular manifestation of power and control in these P2P systems is problematic. As Raval and Dourish note [46] crowdsourcing and P2P platform providers tend to hide their role in the marketplace in terms of both how much and how they operate. Digital middlemen, like Ola and Uber, can become pseudo-employers that manipulate the market to some extent without assuming any contractual responsibilities [23,27,35]. A fairer system to enable greater worker agency, by increasing the visibility of the P2P provider's role, is not, however, a simple proposition and is likely to be the topic of much future research.

Designing for multiple stakeholders

Whilst our design reflections largely focus on drivers' concerns, we are not oblivious to the concerns of the other stakeholders, notably the customers and Ola themselves. We believe that our suggestions should improve the customer experience. Our study revealed that customers are most concerned about price (specifically paying a fair price for the ride) and have low tolerance for waiting (e.g. they cancel rides or leave before the driver arrives). Our designs would enable customers to make more informed choices, based on better estimates of pick-up time and a view of the spatiotemporal landscape, and improve service due to less cancellation by drivers or passengers. Further, accounting for customer and driver preferences should improve the customer experience and worker satisfaction. More content workers are likely to produce a more robust and sustainable service. Certainly, Ola's rather fragile reputation with the driver community stands to benefit from improving the auto drivers' lot.

In summary

Design ideas that improve services might create few extra rides for auto drivers. However, enabling drivers to gain more insight about the ride landscape and better control in responding to this insight might help to ameliorate some of the uncertainty of their day and improve the quality of life, by reducing stress, such as found for some taxi-dispatch systems [22]. Perhaps, more generally, these design ideas illustrate the broader potential for P2P services to support the reasoned agency of all those interacting with them [49].

REFERENCES

1. Syed Ishtiaque Ahmed, Maruf Zaber, Mehrab Bin Morshed, Md. Habibullah Bin Ismail, Dan Cosley, and Steven J. Jackson. 2015. Suhrid: A Collaborative Mobile Phone Interface for Low Literate People. In Proceedings of ACM Symposium on Computing for Development (DEV'15), ACM, New York, NY, USA, 1085-1094.
2. Victoria Bellotti, Alexander Ambard, Daniel Turner, Christina Gossmann, Kamila Demkova, and John M. Carroll. 2015. A Muddle of Models of Motivation for Using Peer-to-Peer Economy Systems. In *Proceedings of the 33rd Annual ACM Conference on Human Factors in Computing Systems* (CHI '15). ACM, New York, NY, USA, 1085-1094.
3. Nicola J. Bidwell. "Moving the centre to design social media in rural Africa." *AI & SOCIETY* (2014): 1-27.
4. Nicola J Bidwell, Mounia Lalmas, Gary Marsden, Bongiwe Dlutu, Senzo Ntlangano, Azola Manjingolo, William D. Tucker, Matt Jones, Simon Robinson, and Elina Vartiainen. "Please call ME. NU 4EVER: designing for 'callback'in rural Africa." (2011).
5. Pernille Bjørn, and Nina Boulus-Rødje. "The multiple intersecting sites of design in CSCW research." *Computer Supported Cooperative Work (CSCW)* 24, no. 4 (2015): 319-351.
6. Josh Borstein. 2015. *The great Uber fairness fallacy: as a driver, how do you bargain with an app?* Article. Retreived on 24/9/15 from http://www.theguardian.com/technology/2015/aug/24/uber-fairness-independent-contractors-employees-rights
7. John Bowers, Graham Button, and Wes Sharrock. "Workflow from within and without: technology and cooperative work on the print industry shopfloor." In *Proceedings of the Fourth European Conference on Computer-Supported Cooperative Work ECSCW'95*, pp. 51-66. Springer Netherlands, 1995.
8. Graham Button. (1993). *Technology in working order: Studies of work, interaction, and technology*. Routledge
9. Graham Button. (2000). The ethnographic tradition and design. *Design studies*. 21. 319-333
10. Graham Button and Wes Sharrock (1997). The production of order and the order of production: possibilities for distributed organisations, work and technology in the print industry. In *Proceedings of the Fifth European Conference on Computer Supported Cooperative Work* (pp. 1-16). Springer Netherlands
11. Bryant Cannon and Hanna Chung, *A Framework for Designing Co-Regulation Models Well-Adapted to Technology-Facilitated Sharing Economies*, 31 Santa Clara High Tech. L.J. 23 (2015). Retrieved on 23/9/15 from http://digitalcommons.law.scu.edu/cgi/viewcontent.cgi?article=1589&context=chtlj
12. Stefania Castellani, Antonietta Grasso, Jacki O'Neill and Frederic Roulland. (2009). Designing technology as an embedded resource for troubleshooting. *JCSCW*, 18(2-3), 199-227.
13. Radha Chanchani and Fagun Rajkotia (CiSTUP). *A study of the Auto-Rickshaw sector in Bangalore City - Suggestions for Improved Governance*. 20012. Retrieved on 22/09/15 from http://cistup.iisc.ernet.in/pdf/newsandevents/Autorickshaws-Blore_FinalReport_Dec12_Cistup.pdf
14. Civitas Consultancies Pvt Ltd for City Connect Foundation Chennai (CCCF). *Study on the Auto-rickshaw sector in Chennai*. December 2010. Retrieved on 24/09/15 from http://chennaicityconnect.com/wp-content/uploads/2011/03/Auto-Study-Chennai.pdf
15. Andy Crabtree. 2003. Designing Collaborative Systems: A Practical Guide to Ethnography, Springer
16. Tawanna R. Dillahunt and Amelia R. Malone. 2015. The Promise of the Sharing Economy among Disadvantaged Communities. *Proceedings of CHI '15*. ACM, New York, NY, USA, 2285-2294.
17. Jonathan Donner. "The rules of beeping: exchanging messages via intentional "missed calls" on mobile phones." *Journal of Computer-Mediated Communication* 13.1 (2007): 1-22.
18. Paul Dourish and Genevieve Bell. 2011. *Divining a Digital Future: Mess and Mythology in Ubiquitous Computing*. MIT Press. Cambridge, Mass, London, England
19. Silvia Elaluf-Calderwood and Carsten Sørensen. *420 years of mobility: ICT enabled mobile interdependencies in London hackney cab work*. Routledge, 2008.
20. Alek Felstiner. 2011. Working the crowd: employment and labor law in the crowdsourcing industry. *Berkeley Journal of Employment and Labor Law,* Vol. 32, No. 1, 2011.
21. Harold Garfinkel (1967) *Studies in ethnomethodology*. Englewood Cliffs, NJ: Prentice-Hall
22. Fabien Girardin and Josep Blat. "The co-evolution of taxi drivers and their in-car navigation systems." *Pervasive and Mobile Computing* 6.4 (2010): 424-434.
23. Neha Gupta, David Martin, Benjamin V. Hanrahan, and Jacki O'Neill. "Turk-Life in India." In *Proceedings of the 18th International Conference on Supporting Group Work*, pp. 1-11. ACM, 2014.
24. Ruey-Lin Hsiao, Se-Hwa Wu, and Sheng-Tsung Hou. "Sensitive cabbies: Ongoing sense-making within technology structuring." *Information and Organization* 18.4 (2008): 251-279.
25. John Hughes, Val King, Tom Rodden, and Hans Andersen. "Moving out from the control room: ethnography in system design." In *Proceedings of the*

1994 ACM conference on Computer supported cooperative work, pp. 429-439. ACM, 1994.

26. Tapio Ikkala and Airi Lampinen. "Monetizing Network Hospitality: Hospitality and Sociability in the Context of Airbnb." In *Proceedings of the 18th ACM Conference on Computer Supported Cooperative Work & Social Computing*, pp. 1033-1044. ACM, 2015.
27. Lilly C. Irani and M. Six Silberman. 2013. Turkopticon: interrupting worker invisibility in amazon mechanical turk. In *Proceedings of CHI '13*. ACM, New York, NY, USA, 611-620.
28. Emily Isaac (2014) Disruptive Innovation: Risk-Shifting and Precarity in the Age of Uber. Berkeley Roundtable on the International Economy BRIE Working Paper 2014-7. December 7, 2014. brie.berkeley.edu
29. Benjamin Jen, Jashanjit Kaur, Jonathan De Heus, and Tawanna R. Dillahunt. 2014. Analyzing employment technologies for economically distressed individuals. In *CHI '14 Extended Abstracts on Human Factors in Computing Systems (CHI EA '14)*. ACM, New York, NY, USA, 1945-1950.
30. Aniket Kittur, Jeffrey V. Nickerson, Michael Bernstein, Elizabeth Gerber, Aaron Shaw, John Zimmerman, Matt Lease, and John Horton. "The future of crowd work." In *Proceedings of the 2013 conference on Computer supported cooperative work*, pp. 1301-1318. ACM, 2013.
31. Airi MI.Lampinen, Account sharing in the context of networked hospitality exchange. *Proceedings of the 17th ACM conference on Computer supported cooperative work & social computing*. ACM, 2014.
32. Min Kyung Lee, Daniel Kusbit, Evan Metsky, and Laura Dabbish. 2015. Working with Machines: The Impact of Algorithmic and Data-Driven Management on Human Workers. In *Proceedings of CHI '15*. ACM, New York, NY, USA, 1603-1612.
33. Gilly Leshed, Theresa Velden, Oya Rieger, Blazej Kot, and Phoebe Sengers. "In-car gps navigation: engagement with and disengagement from the environment." In *Proceedings of the SIGCHI Conference on Human Factors in Computing Systems*, pp. 1675-1684. ACM, 2008.
34. Moira McGregor, Barry Brown and Mereike Gloss. 2015 Disrupting the cab: Uber, Ridesharing and the Taxi Industry. *Journal of Peer Production*. Issue 6. Retrieved on 23/09/15 from http://peerproduction.net/issues/issue-6-disruption-and-the-law/essays/disrupting-the-cab-uber-ridesharing-and-the-taxi-industry/
35. David Martin, Benjamin V. Hanrahan, Jacki O'Neill, and Neha Gupta. "Being a turker." In *Proceedings of the 17th ACM conference on Computer supported cooperative work & social computing*, pp. 224-235. ACM, 2014.
36. David Martin, Jacki O'Neill, Neha Gupta, Benjamin V. Hanrahan (In press). Turking in a Global Labour Market. To appear in *JCSCW 2016*. 25 (1). Springer.
37. Indrani Medhi, Aman Sagar, and Kentaro Toyama. "Text-free user interfaces for illiterate and semi-literate users." *Information and Communication Technologies and Development, 2006. ICTD'06. International Conference on*. IEEE, 2006
38. Toon Meelan and Koen Frenken. 2015. *Stop Saying Uber Is Part Of The Sharing Economy*. Blog. Retrieved 22/09/15 from http://www.fastcoexist.com/3040863/stop-saying-uber-is-part-of-the-sharing-economy
39. Evgeny Morozov *The 'sharing economy' undermines workers' rights*. Blog retrieved on 23/9/15 from http://www.ft.com/intl/cms/s/0/92c3021c-34c2-11e3-8148-00144feab7de.html
40. Subhashree Natarajan and T.K.T Sheik Abdullah. Social Organizations: Decongesting the Muddled Economies of Auto-Rickshaw Drivers in India. In *World Applied Sciences Journal* 30 (7): 831-837, 2014.
41. P2P Foundation. *Peer*. Retrieved on 23/09/15 from http://p2pfoundation.net/peer
42. Tapan Parikh, Kaushik Ghosh, and Apala Chavan. 2003. Design studies for a financial management system for micro-credit groups in rural India. In *Proceedings of the ACM Conference on Universal Usability* (CUU'03), 15-22.
43. Neil Patel, Deepti Chittamuru, Anupam Jain, Paresh Dave, and Tapan Parikh. 2010, Avaaj otalo: A field study of an interactive voice forum for small farmers in rural India. In *Proceedings of the SIGCHI Conference on Human Factors in Computing Systems* (CHI'10), 733-742.
44. Gary Pritchard, John Vines, Pam Briggs, Lisa Thomas, and Patrick Olivier. "Digitally driven: how location based services impact the work practices of London bus drivers." In *Proceedings of the SIGCHI Conference on Human Factors in Computing Systems*, pp. 3617-3626. ACM, 2014.
45. David Randall, Richard Harper, and Mark Rouncefield. *Fieldwork for design: theory and practice*. Springer Science & Business Media, 2007.
46. Noopur Raval and Paul Dourish. Standing Out from the Crowd: Emotional Labor, Body Labor, and Temporal Labor in Ridesharing. To appear in P. Bjorn and D. Konstan (Eds): *Proceedings of Computer-Supported Cooperative Work 2016, February 27 – March 2 2016*. New York: ACM press.Robinson, W. I. (2009) Saskia Sassen and the Sociology of Globalization: A Critical Appraisal. Sociological Analysis. Spring 2009

47. Evan Rawley and Timothy S. Simcoe (2012) Information Technology, Productivity, and Asset Ownership: Evidence from Taxicab Fleets. Organization Science Articles in Advance, pp. 1–15
48. Lisa Rayle, Susan Shaheen, Nelson Chan, Danielle Dai, and Robert Cervero. 2014. App-Based, On-Demand Ride Services: Comparing Taxi and Ridesourcing Trips and User Characteristics in San Francisco, University of California: Berkeley
49. Mark Rouncefield, John A. Hughes, Tom Rodden, and Stephen Viller. "Working with "constant interruption": CSCW and the small office." In *Proceedings of the 1994 ACM conference on Computer supported cooperative work*, pp. 275-286. ACM, 1994.
50. Patricia Sachs (1995). Transforming Work: Collaboration, Learning and Design. *Communica-tions of the ACM*, Vol. 38, No 9. 36-44
51. Niloufar Salehi, Lilly Irani, Michael Bernstein, Ali Alkhatib, Eva Ogbe, and Kristy Milland (2015). We Are Dynamo: Overcoming Stalling and Friction in Collective Action for Crowd Workers. In B. Begole and J. Kim (Eds): *Proceedings of CHI 2015, Seoul, South Korea, April 18-23, 2015*. New York: ACM press, pp. 1621-1630
52. Amartya Sen. 2001. *Development As Freedom*. Oxford University Press
53. Patrick C.Shih, Victoria Bellotti, Kyungsik Han, and John M. Carroll. "Unequal Time for Unequal Value: Implications of Differing Motivations for Participation in Timebanking." In *Proceedings of the 33rd Annual ACM Conference on Human Factors in Computing Systems*, pp. 1075-1084. ACM, 2015.
54. Lucy A. Suchman. 1987. *Plans and Situated Actions: The Problem of Human-Machine Communication*. Cambridge University Press
55. Lucy Suchman "Making work visible." *Communications of the ACM* 38.9 (1995): 56-ff.
56. Jacob Thebault-Spieker, Loren G. Terveen, and Brent Hecht. 2015. Avoiding the South Side and the Suburbs: The Geography of Mobile Crowdsourcing Markets. In *Proceedings CSCW '15*. ACM, New York, NY, USA, 265-275.
57. Kentaro Toyama. 2015. Geek Heresy: Rescuing Social Change from the Cult of Technology. PublicAffairs.
58. Stacco Troncoso. 2014 *Is Sharewashing the new Greenwashing?* Blog retrieved on 22/9/2014 from http://blog.p2pfoundation.net/is-sharewashing-the-new-greenwashing/2014/05/23
59. Urban Mass Transit Company Limited. *Bangalore Mobility Indicators* 2010-11. Submitted to Directorate of Urban Land Transport (DULT). Dec 2011. Retrieved 22/09/2015 from http://www.urbantransport.kar.gov.in/Bangalore%20Mobility%20Indicators_(22-12-2011).pdf

A Design Space to Support the Development of Windshield Applications for the Car

Renate Haeuslschmid
University of Munich (LMU)
Munich, Germany
renate.haeuslschmid@ifi.lmu.de

Bastian Pfleging
University of Munich (LMU)
Munich, Germany
bastian.pfleging@ifi.lmu.de

Florian Alt
University of Munich (LMU)
Munich, Germany
florian.alt@ifi.lmu.de

ABSTRACT
In this paper we present a design space for interactive windshield displays in vehicles and discuss how this design space can support designers in creating windshield applications for drivers, passengers, and pedestrians. Our work is motivated by numerous examples in other HCI-related areas where seminal design space papers served as a valuable basis to evolve the respective field – most notably mobile devices, automotive user interfaces, and interactive public displays. The presented design space is based on a comprehensive literature review. Furthermore we present a classification of 211 windshield applications, derived from a survey of research projects and commercial products as well as from focus groups. We showcase the utility of our work for designers of windshield applications through two scenarios. Overall, our design space can help building applications for diverse use cases. This includes apps inside and outside the car as well as applications for specific domains such as fire fighters, police, ambulance.

Author Keywords
Windshield display; head-up display; in-vehicle interfaces; automotive interfaces; design space

ACM Classification Keywords
H.5.2 Information Interfaces and Presentation: User Interfaces

INTRODUCTION
Today, drivers perform many activities while driving. This goes far beyond just maneuvering the vehicle, which is still the primary driving task. Besides, drivers want to adjust comfort features such as tuning the air conditioning, accessing entertainment features (e.g., radio, music player), communicating (phone calls, text messages), and retrieving information (e.g., navigation, vehicle information) [11, 76].

For many of these activities, the driver needs to receive visual feedback or information. A multitude of displays has been established in the car to provide visual output. Traditionally, such information is displayed in the instrument cluster or

CHI'16, May 07 - 12, 2016, San Jose, CA, USA

ACM 978-1-4503-3362-7/16/05...$15.00
DOI: http://dx.doi.org/10.1145/2858036.2858336

Figure 1. Windshield displays enable novel applications – not only for drivers but also for people outside the vehicle. One example is a navigation system that can be used by pedestrians passing by. We chart the design space for such applications and show how designers could benefit when creating novel WSD applications.

on the center stack (central information display, CID). More recently, head-up displays (HUDs) find their ways into cars. Their advantage is that they are close to the drivers' focus point as they observe the road. Hence, information can be quickly accessed while still being able to keep track of the road.

Windshield displays (WSDs) extend the display real estate[1]. This is not only helpful for meeting the ever-increasing demand for new functions for drivers – provided by the car itself or through external apps – but such displays create novel opportunities also for applications that can be seen and interacted with from the outside of the car, both while parking and while driving. In the near future these needs may become even more pronounced with highly-automated and autonomous driving, allowing the user to engage in new driving and non-driving-related tasks [75]. WSDs may come in handy, particularly in situations where drivers need to take over control, since their view is already directed towards the windshield.

While research is starting to take up on such displays, the focus of in-car functions now changes from safety and navigation (as will be shown later) to discover more entertainment functions – in particular social interaction. To bridge that gap, we suggest a categorization for windshield display apps as well as a design space meant to support the creation and design of future apps.

[1]In the remainder of this work we refer to windshield displays (WSDs) as any type of display using (parts of) the vehicle's windshield – independent of where it is visible from (inside/outside) and by whom (driver, passenger, or passerby) – as opposed to head-up displays (HUD) that are only visible from the driver inside the car and show information close to the usual viewpoint.

We combine findings from reviews of research projects, papers, patents, and commercial products with a series of focus groups to present a categorization of windshield display applications. Furthermore, we explore core dimensions of a design space for WSDs – including display technology, interaction, visualization, context, and user. This is meant to support the designer's creativity for the development of novel ideas as well as design decisions towards the implementation of certain systems. Based on sample applications taken from these categories, we demonstrate the usability of the design space by discussing two thought experiments on exemplary applications.

CONTRIBUTION STATEMENT

We present a categorization of specific WSD applications that were derived from a literature review and focus groups. Furthermore, we contribute a design space for WSD applications for use inside and outside of vehicles. Our research is complemented by showcasing how designers are supported by the design space, when it comes to creating WSD applications.

BACKGROUND AND RELATED WORK

During the design and development of in-car applications and in-vehicle information systems (IVIS) the involved parties are urged to consider a comprehensive set of guidelines, rules, laws, and standards [4]. Many of them intend to facilitate the interaction with the IVIS, limit the driver's distraction from the primary driving task [21], and thus ensure safe driving. They contain recommendations and enforcements regarding interaction design and support the design process, e.g., by providing hints regarding location and installation of displays and controls, font sizes, or feedback about the system status.

While guidelines and standards provide beneficial hints to avoid creating distracting interfaces, they often do not support the designer when exploring different design options for a specific context. The importance of exploring design spaces has been emphasized in the human-computer interaction (HCI) community: Describing and analyzing design spaces helps to understand differences between designs but also to find and propose new opportunities [24]. Early work concentrated on basic HCI aspects, such as a classification and taxonomy of input devices [22, 25]. Similarly, design spaces have also been proposed for InfoVis [24, 29] and for various subfields of HCI. In particular, the latter ones are a valuable basis for the development of the corresponding field. For example, Ballagas et al. [12] explore the design space for mobile phone input. Mueller et al. explore public displays [67], and Nigay et al. did so for multimodal interaction [72]. Also, automotive user interfaces are subject to design space explorations. Kern and Schmidt [55] present a general design space for driver-based automotive UIs. Their goal is to provide a tool that comprehensively describes, analyzes, compares, and discusses different UI arrangements (car-related input / output devices). Also, it can be used to identify new interaction opportunities and placements for controls.

For automotive augmented reality, Ng-Thow-Hing et al. [70] present a user-centered process and principles for creating and evaluating designs for AR displays. Most closely related to our research is the work of Tönnis et al. who provide an early design space for augmented reality (AR) apps for HUDs [98]. In contrast, our work considers a comprehensive set of design-relevant dimensions for WSDs in general, such as technology, interaction, content, and user. In this way we cover the entire process of developing windshield display applications rather than focussing exclusively on information presentation.

WINDSHIELD DISPLAY APPLICATIONS

At the outset of our research we collected a set of possible applications and use cases for windshield displays through a comprehensive literature review and focus groups. This resulting set helped us to understand the variety of applications and served as a basis for the design space presented later.

Methodology

Literature and Patents Review

We performed an extensive literature and patents review (> 125 papers and patents) on applications based on the terms *windshield display*, *head-up display/HUD*, and also *car side and rear windows* (to find related issues), based on the information retrieval process proposed by Galvan [41]. We used those general terms in order not to exclude early approaches or proposals by simply searching for too specific terms. We searched through search engines, such as Google Scholar, ResearchGate, ACM Digital Library, IEEE Xplore. Furthermore, we iteratively went through all citing and cited references of both papers and patents. We then selected the ones related to use cases for the aforementioned displays and windows.

From the literature we then identified use cases, ideas, prototypes, and applications and collected them in an Excel file. We documented name and description of the idea, graphics (if available), used window/display, and development status (idea, simulation, prototype, market launch) as well as reference type (literature or patent), author(s), and year. We documented each use case. If we found a use cases several times we documented it with a cross-reference, only counting it once.

Focus Groups

We complemented our collection by conducting three focus groups. The focus groups concentrated on the desires of current but also future users, particularly in the entertainment and communication area. We recruited students with valid driver's licenses for all focus groups. One focus group was conducted with participants familiar with the topic of WSDs and existing literature; the remaining participants were unfamiliar with WSDs and came from different fields. Altogether, 14 students took part (six female) with 4 to 6 participants per focus group. The participants were aged 21 to 26 with a mean age of 24.

To conduct the focus groups, we derived rules and best practices for focus groups and collected them in the form of guidelines for the semi-structured sessions [61, 99]. Furthermore, we prepared a discussion outline and nine questions to encourage and guide the exploration phase. Those questions varied slightly to cover different aspects and reduce the number of redundant use cases. The overall procedure was the same for all groups. After the introduction, three initiation questions were asked to encourage discussion: *What do you do while driving? What would you like to do? What situations are strongly annoying for you?*

Subcategory	Description	Examples
	Category	
Safety		
Vision Extension	extension of the driver's view by displaying occluded objects	wall-see through [103], transparent pillars (FG)
Vision Enhancement	enhancement of the driver's vision in bad viewing or lighting conditions	night and pedestrian vision [85], automatic sun shade (FG)
View Point	display of the views of virtual or real cameras; often replacing mirrors	virtual rear mirror [66], virtual side mirror (FG)
Spatial Awareness	improvement of the driver's understanding of the space around the car	safety grid showing the distance to vehicles [90], marshaller (FG)
Monitoring Surroundings	safety-relevant information about the environment	crash warning [58], approaching police (FG)
Driver Monitoring	driver performance and physical state observation	driver drowsiness alert [94] (FG)
Lane Change & Intersection	support in turning or changing lanes safely	overtaking assistant [38], driving on the right lane requirement (FG)
Breakdown	they help the driver in breakdown situations	warning triangle [86] (FG)
Specific Support Systems	systems directed at a specific party, support several tasks, or provide various information	racing car assistance [65], elderly visualization with integrated visual acuity (FG)
Vehicle Monitoring		
Vehicle Status	information about vehicle parts and the momentary status of the engine	monitoring of specialized vehicles [17], dashboard (FG)
Supervision	support in supervising the vision of the vehicle's sensors; most of they aim to increase trust	autonomous driving and ACC detection display [16]
Fuel & Battery	information about the current fuel or battery status	battery reach [31], charging status (FG)
Navigation & geo IS		
Path Finding	support in finding the way to the target	3D arrows [96], navigation with map and registered hints (FG)
Car-Following	support when following a car	projected virtual car [69], car mark up (FG)
Traffic & Street Signs	display of traffic signs currently applying; street signs and names	speed compliance warning [28], green traffic light continue (FG)
Points of Interest	additional on-route information to find people, shops or services	roadside objects [40], mountaintop peak display (FG)
Public Transport	support for commuters who switch to public transportation	BusMobile with schedules and park&rail and waiting passenger information (FG)
Entertainment & Communication		
Commercials	commercials for products or services, e.g. restaurants or promotions of stores	Taximedia, an advertising system for cab fares [8], drive-through menu ordering (FG)
Economy & Costs	economical driving and costs display	economical recommender system [53] (FG)
Work & Tasks	information about general tasks or activities or (office) work tasks	location-based reminders [64], activity suggestion generator (FG)
Driver Mood & Status	observation of the driver's status to promote a specific mood or physical state	Breakaway, a break recommender system [51], cheering-up display for construction zones (FG)
Education	the driver can gain knowledge or learn a specific behavior	CarCoach; feedback on driving performance [89], language learner application (FG)
Gaming	game play alone or together with others	car racing [100] or name or city guessing (FG)
Multimedia & Web	general information; music or video player; access to the Internet or news; specific for passenger entertainment and waiting times	passenger entertainment and information system [63], karaoke (FG)
Arts & Photography	picture or arts presentation, applications which enable drawing and taking photos	a road scene illustrator [95], photo app with slide shows and an outside targeting camera (FG)
Atmosphere	creation of a different atmosphere in the car by displaying different surroundings or ambient lights	candlelight [17], sleepover atmosphere (FG)
Public Display	public information to the outside	an outside projection of the parking ticket [17], passers-by navigation (FG)
Observation	observation of a person, normally relatives, or an object and its state	CareNet to observe elderly relatives [30], self-mirror (FG)
Social Interaction	social interaction with other parties than drivers	video conferencing on Skype (FG)
Driver 2 Driver Communication	communication with other drivers	Last Gentlement (rewards) [59], single driver marking (FG)
Internet of Things	access to or control of things	smart home (FG)

Table 1. This tables explains our classification of windshield display applications into five main categories and several subcategories. Also, it provides two examplary applications for each subcategory, one from literature and one identified in the focus groups (marked with "FG")

After the initiation phase, the moderator led over to the exploration phase: *If there were no technological or safety constraints, what information would you personally like to be conveyed to you during driving?* When the count of created ideas bottomed out, the moderator further encouraged the discussion by asking how a WSD could support them in one of the three scenarios: *While commuting, on a long highway journey, and during a vacation in an unfamiliar city*. Next, more specific trends and topics were introduced to the discussion: *information about other vehicles, the surroundings, the own (electric) car, support for elderly people, or being on-line*. In addition, one of the following applications was explained: (1) *social status sticker* (driver share short status texts which are visible as stickers on the WSDs of other drivers [83]), (2) *entertainment channel* (information such as emails are accessible during waiting times at traffic lights on the WSD [6]), or (3) *roadside objects* (information about the environment can be accessed by means of the WSD [40]). Lastly, the moderator asked for ideas or statements not mentioned so far.

Each focus group lasted for roughly one hour. The sessions were audio recorded to ensure the moderator can focus on leading the group and to document ideas comprehensively and correctly. All participants gave permission in the beginning.

Finally, we collected all mentioned use cases including name, description, and utilized window/display in a spreadsheet. Use cases that came up several times were documented only once.

Results

We collected 96 different ideas; 71 ideas were found in literature and 25 ideas from patents. 31 % of the ideas are *safety*-related, 43 % belong to *entertainment and communication*, 4 % of the ideas support the driver in *monitoring* the *vehicle*,

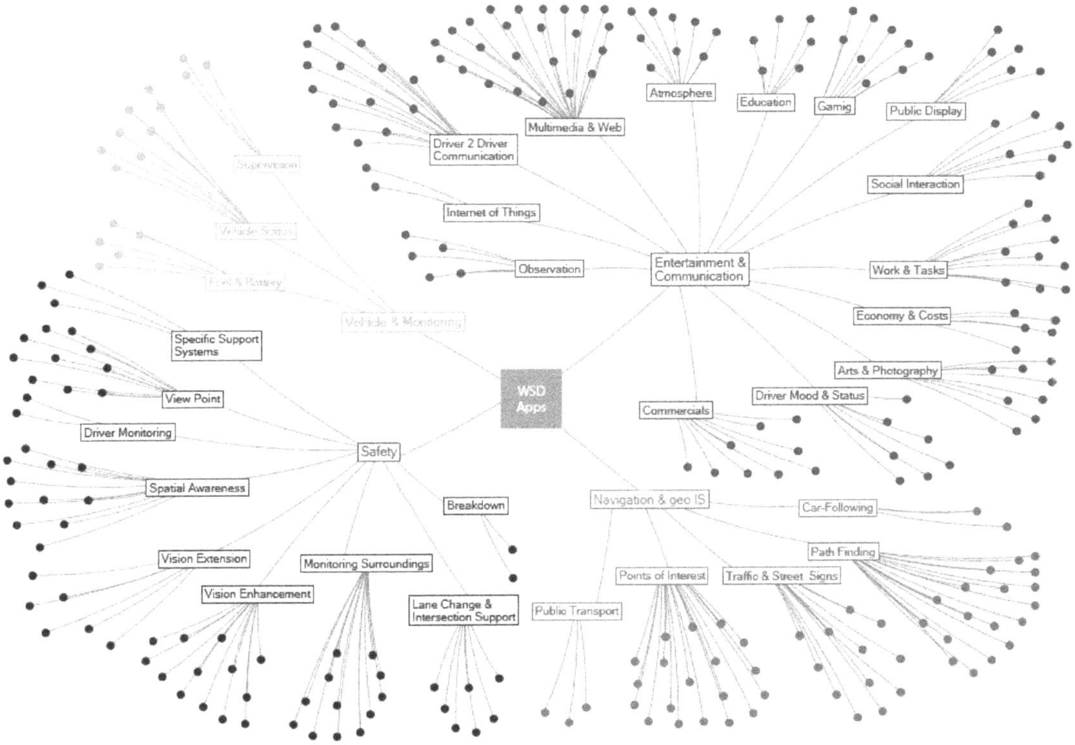

Figure 2. Overview of collected use cases: Safety (blue), Vehicle & Monitoring (yellow), Entertainment & Communication (magenta), Navigation (green).

and 22 % in *navigational tasks*. From the focus groups we collected 115 new ideas. Use cases are distributed as follows: 14 % *safety*, 3 % *vehicle monitoring*, 11 % *navigation & geo IS*, 47 % *entertainment & communication*. We also derived 28 use cases for special vehicles (police/ambulance) (24 %).

As a next step, we ordered all ideas by allocating them to predefined first-level categories. We based these first-level categories on the ones proposed by Brandt [19] with slight modifications, so as to reflect the application areas of WSDs:

Entertainment & communication. Information systems which enable communication and are entertaining.

Vehicle monitoring. Information about the vehicle itself.

Navigation & geo information systems (IS). information about the trip or path.

Safety. Information about the surroundings with the purpose to increase driving safety.

We subdivided the first-level categories (Table 1), adapting and extending the classification presented by Schroeter at al. [84]. The table presents all subcategories and provides a short description for each subcategory. It also lists one application derived from literature and one suggested in a focus group, respectively. Figure 3 provides an overview of the different categories and the distribution of all ideas among the categories.

DESIGN SPACE

Based on the list of applications we derived a design space for windshield display applications. For the design space, we did not only consider literature on use cases for windshield displays but also on WSD presentation, interaction with WSDs, and technological approaches to realize such displays. Furthermore, we reviewed existing design spaces, guidelines, surveys, and classifications related to HUDs, general in-vehicle displays, in-car interaction, and (AR) information presentation. We merged proposed classification and categorization approaches suitable for windshield displays. Moreover, we added categories and dimensions to our collection based on well-known (or novel) approaches or proposals in application and technology papers. Doing so, we focused also on characteristics of WSD currently popular in research: large size and 3D-registered images. Furthermore, the potential observers and persons possibly interacting received particular attention: A large-sized display could superimpose its image also to other parties than the driver, inside and outside of the car. Finally, we ordered and grouped all aforementioned aspects into dimensions and categories to complete the design space.

We defined five dimensions for our design space: (1) *User*, (2) *Context*, (3) *Visualization*, (4) *Interaction*, and (5) *Technology*. Each dimension consists of two to five categories. All categories, dimensions and characters are listed with a short description and an example reference in the following.

User

Currently, WSDs are usually targeted at a single person – the driver – with regard to interaction and observation. However, with increasing projection space, future systems may also allow the presentation of content to other passengers in the car, or – with outside projections – by other road users. Thus, we distinguish three different aspects in this dimension.

User	User Mode*	Single User	Multi User			
	Observer	Driver	Co-Driver / Passengers	Road Users / Passers-by		
	Actor(*)	Driver	Co-Driver / Passengers	Road Users & Passers-by	Nobody	
Context	Application Purpose	Safety	Navigation & geo IS	Vehicle Monitoring	Entertainment	
	Information Context	Environment	Vehicle	Person	Time	
	Driving Mode*	Driving	Waiting	Parking		
	Level of Automation	Manual	Semi-automated	Autonomous		
	Privacy*	Public	Personal	Private		
Visualization	Level of Augmentation	Reality & loose Information	Augmeted Reality	Virtual Reality		
	Registration*	Unregistered	2D registered	3D registered	Gaze-dependent	
	Field of View Position	Foveal	Central	Peripheral / Ambient		
	Presentation	Symbolic	Naturalistic			
	Graphic Design Factors	Color	Transparency	Size	Motion	
Inter-action	Input Modality	Touch & Controls	Gestures	Gaze	Speech	Behaviour
	Multimodal Feedback	Visual	Haptic/Tactile	Audtiory	Olfactory	
Technology	Image Generation	Image reflected on windshield	Image on windshield			
	Size*	HUD (rather small)	WSD (rather large)			
	Depth*	Single-layer (2D)	Multi-layer	Continuous (3D)		
	Display Factors	Color depth	Transparency	Brightness	Resolution	

Figure 3. The design space we propose consists of four core dimensions – content, visualization, interaction, and technology (*exclusive selection).

User Mode
While many common WSDs (such as a head-up display) can be used exclusively by the driver (*single user*), larger WSDs could enable *multi-user* interaction (e.g., for other passengers, people in other cars, or on the sidewalk). Application areas are game play or car-to car-communication.

Observer
This category describes the WSD observers. Depending on the selected technology, the image may be visible to the *driver* only, to the *co-driver or passengers*, or to *other road users including passers-by* on the side walk. The classic HUD is only visible to the driver when his eyes are within the eye-box – a predefined 3D space depending on the HUD position. Using other approaches to generate the image on the windshield could also make it visible to other occupants and to other road users or passersby, for example for ads [5, 86].

Actor
If the display is visible to a particular person, this does not necessarily mean that this person can also control the display. Hence, we distinguish between *observer* and *actor*. As actors we consider the *driver* as a main user, the *co-driver & passengers* as alternative actors inside the car, and other *road users & passersby* as potential actors outside of the car. Furthermore, there may be apps exclusively controlled by the system itself (for example, crash warnings), making the system the actor.

Context
Depending on the current context, WSD applications might provide different features and options or behave differently. This relates, for instance, to the purpose of the application, context information of the environment, whether the car is moving or not and the current level of automated driving.

Application Purpose
This category is directly based on our application classification. We distinguish between *safety*, *geo IS & navigation*, *vehicle monitoring*, and *entertainment & communication* applications.

Information Context
The information context may be relevant for placement and visualization (for example, dynamics). Based on two context collections from related work [82, 92], we came up with the following information contexts: *environment* (e.g. weather, GPS position) [82, 92], *vehicle* (e.g. tire pressure, temperature) [82], *person* (e.g. blood pressure, SMS) [82, 92], and *time* (e.g. current time, countdown) [92].

Driving Mode
The driving mode represents the current status of the vehicle. Selker, Burleson and Arroyo [88] differentiate between driving and non-driving condition and propose separate applications for each condition. This is important to differentiate in order to consider the driver's tasks, and therefore mental and physical workload when the application is used. In our design space, we differentiate three modes: In the *driving* mode, the vehicle is moving. The *waiting* mode is limited to the waiting time when the car is stopped (e.g., at traffic lights). It is in a way comparable to semi-automated driving since the driver is free to perform additional tasks but still has to monitor the surroundings. A car is *parking* when standing in a parking lot with engine off and no person inside.

Level of Automation
Automated driving can be divided into five support levels [3, 50]: no-automation (level 0), function-specific automation (1), combined function automation (2), limited self-driving automation (3), full self-driving automation (4).

Windshield displays and autonomous driving are technologies that fit well together: autonomous driving and new driver assistance systems give the user spare time while sitting in the car: they perform more non-driving related tasks [34]. In automation levels 1 to 3, the driver needs to monitor the vehicle or take over control. Hence, the car interior cannot completely be modified for autonomous driving. On the other hand, current cockpits need new concepts to enable new interaction possibilities when less attention to the road is required. The windshield display suits both, the driver-controlled and autonomously controlled vehicles, and can be the perfect match for the transformation: It can support the driver in controlling the vehicle and in performing completely unrelated non-driving-related tasks, but most importantly, it allows for easy task switches.

For the design of WSD applications it is very important to know which driving-related tasks the user has to perform. The level of automation gives insights in how much the driver has to be involved in driving, mentally and physically. Furthermore, it is important to also consider the driver's supervision task and the moment of the take-over-request when the control is handed back to the driver. These tasks are very demanding and safety-critical [44, 78] and are important for the design.

In our windshield display design space, we differentiate the following levels of driving automation: *manual*, corresponding to level 0 automation, *semi-automated* (level 1 to level 3), and *autonomous*, corresponding to level 4 automation. When designing an application for semi-automated driving, the level of automation has to be considered in more detail, but also the automated control units, as mentioned earlier. As there are more variables than only the level of control, we summed up the levels 1 to 3 to *semi-automated driving*.

Privacy

Information accessible by everyone is visible to the *public* (e.g., news). *Personal* information is restricted to the observer and a particular group of people (e.g. Facebook status posts). *Private* information is exclusively accessible by the current observer (e.g. private messages).

Visualization

When it comes to the visual output itself, designers have a large set of options. Tönnis et al. [98] defined six classes categorizing AR systems, which we adapted for our work.

Augmentation

Tönnis et al. also proposed the 'frame of reference', characterized by egocentric and exocentric presentation, as AR HUD presentation dimension. While the egocentric view corresponds to the driver's view, the exocentric view can be any other viewing position, e.g., the bird's eye perspective. The two frames of reference are included in the dimension *Augmentation* of our design space: *Reality & loose Information* includes the exocentric view, but also additional information that has no specific frame of reference, such as time. The egocentric view is part of *Augmented Reality (AR)* and *Virtual Reality (VR)*. *AR* corresponds to digital information merged into a person's view on the real world (spatially registered). *VR* is the immersive experience in a simulated world, the digital version of the real world or a completely virtual world.

Placement Strategy

This category describes the relative and absolute spatial placement of information. In their classification of AR HUD information presentation principles, Tönnis et al. [98] propose the class registration. They subdivide it into unregistered, registered and contact-analog. *Unregistered* information is placed without spatial relation to an environmental or in-vehicle object. Registered information is aligned with the real world but presented rather symbolic than naturalistic, according to Tönnis et al. On the other hand, contact-analog information is smoothly integrated into the real world and naturalistic; in a way that it looks and behaves like a real object.

'Contact-analog' is a term used exclusively in the car domain and often misused and confused with registered information placement. To address this, we propose the terms *2D registered* and *3D registered* and to distinguish naturalistic and symbolic information *presentation*. As *2D registered* we define information placed spatially close to a related object but not meeting its depth. As *3D registered* we define information placed at the same depth of and spatially close to a related object.

Tönnis et al. also propose glance behavior related information presentation [97, 98], which we consider here as a relative positioning strategy as well. *Gaze-dependent* information is placed relative to the observer's momentary visual focus point.

Field of View Position

We included this category in our design space as the windshield display wil – due to its size – not only address *foveal* and *central* vision but also *peripheral* vision. This is particularly important since humans' visual perception varies strongly within the field of view (FoV) [49, 60, 98]. In the area of *foveal* vision (up to 2 ° from line of sight) the human has the fastest and sharpest visual perception. Within the *central* field of view (up to 10 °) colors, contours, and contrasts are still perceptible. In the *periphery* (beyond 10 °) the human perception is mainly limited to movements, light alteration, and recognition of very simple objects and their orientation. When the driver looks straight at the road, the windshield ends approximately at 50 °; this is where stereo-vision ends [1, 45].

One may argue that standard in-vehicle displays (instrument panels / CIDs) are also placed in the periphery when the driver looks straight on the road. However, the WSD may be too large to be fully perceived. Independent of where the user is looking, parts of the display are in the periphery. Furthermore, information on those standard displays is small-sized and thereby only perceptible by directly looking. In contrast, the WSD offers a lot of space to either display simple information large enough to make them perceptible, even with the limited peripheral perceptional abilities [49] (e.g. ambient information), or is actually meant to attain the driver's attention and lead it towards a hazard [47]. Of course, peripheral perception can be highly distracting and therefore needs to be used and designed carefully (see Haeuslschmid [46, 47] for a discussion).

Presentation

As already mentioned in category Placement Strategy, the information can be presented in a symbolic and a naturalistic way. *Symbolic information* 'embeds abstract symbols' [98].

This includes standard graphical elements such as text, (shapeless) forms, icons, abstract graphics, pictures, videos. *Naturalistic information* should not be identifiable as augmented to reality at first glance. It smoothly merges with the real world and looks and behaves like a real world object.

Graphic Design Factors

At first, this dimension only addresses graphics design, not the display technology. The standard design factors are dimensions by itself but grouped here to one since they are continuous or have few manifestations. Yet, designer need to be aware of them, when creating information for the windshield displays: *color*, *transparency*, *size*, and *motion*.

Color needs to be chosen carefully in the context of use (e.g., daytime), FoV position, and environment [14, 23, 39]. A common environment is a white to blue sky with a grey asphalt on the ground, possibly with greenish or brownish fields or also white or colored buildings to its sides. It is clear that colors which are well distinguishable from the background should be chosen to ensure recognizability. Furthermore, the cultural meaning of colors need to be considered [48].

Transparency is important since presented content can occlude the driving scene [74, 98]. It may be the case that driving-relevant objects in the surroundings should be highlighted (e.g. by light), but those objects should never be completely invisible to the driver. Here, transparency comes into play.

As mentioned earlier, objects placed in the periphery may have to be of larger *size* to be well perceivable and recognizable, independent of if they aim to gain attention or not. Research has to be performed in order to identify optimal sizes for information throughout the windshield display area.

Motion is directly related to relative information display. If information is displayed relative to an environmental object or also the driver's gaze, it is most likely that this information will have to move. Also animations, videos, and on-growing or blinking information belongs into this category. Motion is very distracting and has to be used carefully [14, 39].

Interaction

To enable interactive WSD applications, the potential WSD users also need to have the chance to interact with the system. The design space therefore also comprises dimensions that consider how to provide input to the system as well as additional (multimodal) output/feedback channels.

Input Modality

Kern and Schmidt [55] describe input and output modalities. They based their automotive design space on an analysis of the interior of modern (in 2007) and old cars and current trends. New interaction techniques, such as gesture and speech, are mentioned in the paper but not yet integrated into the design space due to the state of development at that time. Therefore, we now update this design space as follows:

The category *touch & controls* represents hand-based, haptic input techniques such as button, slider, knob, stalk control, thumbwheel, pedal, multifunctional controller, and touchscreens as mentioned by Kern et al. [55]. Charissis et al. investigated the control of a single-layer windshield displays using buttons [27]. Whether these controls are suitable to interact with multi-layer or continuous windshield displays has to be investigated. In particular, when the image is partially (3D) registered and unregistered and thereby dynamic and unstructured, far away from the common hierarchical layouts, it will be challenging to map controls with so limited dimensions. One possible approach is to mirror the driver's view through the windshield onto a touch sensitive display, as already proposed for other domains [87]. Touch on the windshield itself is not recommended due to the driver's limited range of motion and the size and orientation of the windshield. However, one could combine it for instance with (remote) touch interaction such as touch gestures on the steering wheel [35, 77].

Gestures, such as midair or micro gestures, are investigated intensively for in-car use. According to Fujimura et al. [40] and Rümelin et al. [79], pointing gestures are a good approach to interact with registered information such as points of interest. Though, it is unclear if gestures are suitable for more than one-handed interaction such as selection. Until (partially) autonomous driving is available, all users but the driver are free to perform two-handed gestures. Furthermore, entering text with gestures is problematic. More research has to performed to see if gesture-based input techniques (cf. Ni et al. [71]) are practicable and usable also in cars.

Speech is an input methodology of growing importance [9, 10]. It is a useful input method in cars but can most probably not be a stand-alone input method either, but, for example, be complementary to gestural interaction [77]. Since natural language understanding and analysis are not yet perfect and comprehensive in vocabulary, it will be difficult to select (the right) object by announcing it. Object manipulation and text input may be less problematic, though.

Gaze interaction is nowadays robust enough to be integrated in cars [73]. The driver's eyes are already tracked for apps such as drowsiness warning [104, 105]; this can be accounted as indirect input. Similarly, by implicitly storing and highlighting the screen location last looked at, attention switches away from and back to the screen can be accelerated [54]. Performing gaze interaction while performing another visual, safety-critical task requiring constant supervision is challenging. *Behaviour* can only serve as an indirect method of control for adaptive applications.

For interaction with the WSD from outside, future apps can draw from public display research. Most notably, touch, midair gestures, and phone-based interaction have beed explored in previous work [7, 33, 68]. More recently, also gaze was used as an interaction modality in public [56, 106].

Multimodal Feedback

According to Ablassmeier et al. [2], WSDs have a great potential for multimodal interaction concepts. We bases this dimension again on the design space by Kern et al. [55]. As the windshield display itself is a platform for *visual* output, here we only describe output modalities as extension to this. Visual feedback to a user action can of course be also displayed on other displays, e.g. a status LED, a head down display or also the windshield display of other road users. *Haptic and tactile* feedback can be given to the driver by means of vibration (e.g. seat belt or steering wheel) and also by airflow. *Auditory* feedback is given by means of loudspeaker and can range from a simple status change sound to a played music. *Olfactory* output has not been matter of research by now. Kern et al. propose to use it for ambient information [55].

Technology

In order to design the physical part of WSD apps, designers can choose from different technological options. These relate to how the image is generated, at which depth it is displayed, the WSD size as well as additional display factors.

Image Generation

By now, there are two major ways of generating a WSD image [46]: The first and simplest approach is to generate the *image directly on the windshield* itself: Either a (laser) projector is directed onto the windshield [36, 57, 102] or a transparent display such as OLEDs are integrated into the windshield [17]. This approach is advantageous compared to standard head down displays as the driver can keep the head up and the road situation in view while reading the display.

The second approach is based on the *reflection of a display or a projection surface on a transparent mirror*, called combiner, or the windshield. The image of a reflected light source seems to float above the road. The advantage is that the image distance is increased, which allows for faster eye accommodation and, hence, faster reaction time. Head-up displays are based on the principle of reflection: Betancur [15] describes several variations for constructing HUDs and WSDs. Also, the HUDs of major car manufacturers and contractors rely on this principle: Continental constructs HUDs for BMW, Audi, and Mercedes and describes the basic construction online [43]. Sato et al. [81] also used reflection but positioned a projector on the vehicle's roof, thereby enabling real world studies with a WSD of intermediate size. Takaki et al. [101] proposed a 3D HUD based on a reflected autostereoscopic multi-view display and reached a continuous image depth. The Pioneer HUD is a mobile realization which reflects the image to float 2.5 m behind the combiner, based on a DLP projector and a LED light source [37]. Lastly, there is research regarding future technology, e.g., 3D holographic image generation, which may soon find their way into cars.

Depth

Head-up displays normally present the image on a *single-layer* in front of the windshield [42] – perpendicular or angular to the road. This enables a 2D but no 3D registered information display. For a full AR feeling, digital information has to meet the depth of analog environmental objects. Hence, HUD research focuses on *continuous* depth presentation. Continuous displays are able to place images at various levels, which are not distinguishable for the observer, or at continuous depth. Therefore, the distances between the layers have to be within the boundaries of just noticeable depth difference (JNDD) [52]; Cutting et al. [32] provides measurements of JNDD based on monoscopic and stereoscopic depth cues. Furthermore, we propose to use the term *continuous* only in relation with a wide depth range, meaning that information can be presented 3D-registered to other road users.

Takaki et al. [101] built a WSD prototype enabling image presentation at distances up to 100 m. Broy et al. [20] and Charissis et al. [26], performed user studies on 3D HUDs with stereoscopic and hence (limited) continuous displays. Bark et al. [13] evaluated a vehicular navigation aid that uses a see-thru 3D volumetric HUD. However, these displays were only prototypes and cannot be integrated into production cars due to spatial requirements or limitations.

Between *single-layer* and *continuous*, we suggest the category of *multi-layer* technology. The layers of a display within that category are distinguishable for the observer and do not mandatorily have to be generated by the same technology. For example, a HUD can be combined with an OLED display. An example of information on two depth layers was presented by Blume et al. [16] and Continental [43].

Size

As mentioned before, WSDs can cover the entire windshield whereas HUDs are limited in and vary in size.

BMW HUDs have a size of $7.5 \times 17.5\, cm$ (in 2012) [18], Mercedes reports a reflected image size of $21 \times 7\, cm$ (in 2014) [62], and Pioneer documents a 29" projection image at a distance of 2.5 m [37]. In 2014, Continental announced HUDs at a size of 3.1" as new advancement as well as an AR HUD with an image size of $130 \times 60\, cm$ at a distance of 7.5 m [43]. In science, the size of the used display is rarely documented. Also, the constructional approach, such as the used light source, lenses, and image path, strongly influence the image size visible to the driver. Here, measuring the visible image in degrees (field of view) would be more self-explaining and independent of image distance.

We propose to categorize displays with a coverage of minimum 40 % horizontally and minimum 40 % vertically of the driver's windshield FoV as windshield displays. For displays of a smaller size we suggest to refer to them as head-up displays. We decided for a separation at 40 %, as smaller displays are most probably not able to cover the central road scene.

Display Factors

Standard display factors are dimensions by themselves but grouped since they are continuous or have few manifestations and so as to keep the design space concise. The light source (a display or projector) needs to fulfill requirements specific for in-car use. First, the light source has to be very bright to be visible in direct sunlight. HUDs have a luminance higher than $10{,}000\, cd/m^2$ [43, 62]. Furthermore, the *brightness* has to be adjustable to not glare at night, if the application is not daytime-dependent (e.g. night-vision). Another display factor to be considered is the display *transparency*. Currently, the windshield itself has to transmit at least 70 % of the outside luminance [80]. Technologies based on reflection or projection do not influence the light transparency of the windshield unless foils or covers are used. However, this does not mean that the visibility of outside objects is always ensured. With autonomous driving, this requirement may become less important. When the driver does not have to drive or supervise the car (level 4 automation), immersive virtual reality could be provided in cars. Together with more complex illustrations and larger display sizes, also the *resolution* and the *color space* of the display may need to increase. Current HUDs provide resolutions between 800×480 pixels [43] and 480×240 pixels (60 pixel per degree) [62]. As a final factor in this section, we also consider *color depth*. Display-based solutions normally feature full-color [37, 43, 62]. However, also uni- and bicolor laser-projector-based solutions exist [93].

USING THE DESIGN SPACE

We envision that the presented design space facilitates the design of interactive (windshield display) applications in and around the car. We seek to support the designers' creativity when designing novel systems for a specific use case. Using the design space, they can easily explore the multiple dimensions for windshield displays in order to define the technical implementation. By comparing and discussing the available options in each dimension, differences between designs can be understood. Also, by considering the multitude of options new ideas, use cases, and approaches may be identified.

In the following we present two exemplary thought experiments to showcase how the design space may support the design process for interactive vehicular applications. For both examples, we first present a motivation and explanation of the use case. We then present the discussion of the use case from a designer's point of view.

Example 1: Pedestrian Navigation

Navigation is a frequent task when driving a car. Today, various solutions for navigation exist, including convenient WSD applications and visualizations. Navigation is also of interest to pedestrians and cyclists who often use their smartphone for this purpose. Considering the option to display information to people outside the car, WSDs may also be beneficial for the latter user group: Constantly pulling out and unlocking the phone is annoying. Furthermore, it can be cumbersome to view a larger map or plan a longer trip on the small phone display. Using the outside WSD of a car, one could create a new navigation system for pedestrians which integrates the outside projection windshield display as an extension to the personal phone (see also Figure 1).

Paul is a designer, using our design space to develop the presented WSD application. He imagines the following scenario: A group of people walks around an unfamiliar city to explore its sights. They want to locate themselves and find the shortest way to the central square. Using a printed map is old-fashioned and so is it to use the smartphone for navigation. Instead, the group steps towards a parked car and one of the group's phones connects to the car. The outside WSD displays the city map. Once someone enters the next destination, the map presents the most interesting or shortest route to get there. The group then starts out to the central square.

How could this application look like? When the scenario is defined, Paul explores how the application idea could be further expanded and designed. 'In my scenario a *group of people* walks through the city', Paul thinks. 'Of course, it could also be a *single* person. Would it make a difference in designing the application? Probably not, as long as everybody is *inside or outside* the car – and the *display technology* enables it, of course. And also, only because there are several *observers*, it does not mean that everybody wants to interact with the system. Actually, does anyone need to interact with the system once the destination is entered? This depends on which other functions the system provides. Are there other ways to *visualize* the path? Once the group starts, cars on the way could *dynamically* light the way to the central square – serving as *ambient* displays. Does this also work on driving cars, or only with *parked* ones? Well, it could work with both. Those displays could also react to the pedestrian's *gaze* – maybe by presenting an arrow that points to the right direction. But eye tracking might be difficult to implement: Light conditions could impede the detection. And: sensors need to be clean. At least I don't have to be concerned about *privacy* issues when the application only presents general information which is not even obviously connected to a particular person. What if several groups are walking around the city using the same app? That's definitely something I have to consider carefully–later. Let's discuss another dimension. Which other content or features can be nice and practical for visitors? The application should be more *entertaining*! That helps to make the journey more fun and adventurous. When exploring the city, it could be nice to get historical information – or to see how this particular place looked like a century ago. Even better, the group could be on a treasure hunt. I always enjoy treasure hunting. The app could only tell where to turn next when a question was answered correctly. It could actually *tell* the directions by giving *auditory feedback*. Maybe the users talk with an avatar. Which other *input modality* could they use? To move the map or to select something, touch would be perfect. But wait, the hood is in the way. Actually, I wouldn't like to have greasy finger prints on my freshly washed car. What happens if the owner of the car is still inside? Maybe (s)he is also interacting with the display – looking up when it will stop raining. Well, better no touch interaction on the windshield. But maybe touch interaction on the personal phone? But I wouldn't want to take it out of my pocket. So, maybe *speech* and *gestures* could do. Okay, that's good for now. '

Example 2: Driver Training

Most car accidents (appr. 90 %) are caused by human error [91]. That is why a lot of effort is spent on training – particularly young drivers but there are also specific driver training for all drivers to train for emergency situations. However, the reason for an accident is often the driving behavior, for instance hubris or underestimation of danger.

'When I was young, I already felt being a good driver – a bit arrogant maybe – and I even drove intoxicated sometimes. My girlfriend instead was shy and overcautious – anything but a good driver. Now that I think about it, I would have actually needed a resolute girlfriend rather than more training. I am pretty sure that there are many people who are like I was back then. How could I design an application for a *single user* suitable for both, arrogant and overcautious drivers?'

'First, new drivers need to familiarize with the car regarding size, steering, and reversing. Virtual lines and arrows could help the student. This *visualization* already exists – but actually it is boring. I think the application also has the *purpose* to *entertain*. When drivers are emotionally involved, they benefit more from this training session. So let's look for something unconventional – something they enjoy. Let's replace the virtual lines – maybe by coins just like in Super Mario. When drivers perfectly keep the lane, they get feedback by this nice sound of rattling coins. Let's see some other feedback *modalities*: We could use haptic feedback in addition to that. For instance, the steering wheel vibrates if the driver performs badly.

I think that is a nice start when learning to drive but after a certain *time* it is not challenging anymore. What is really difficult is to learn is how to react in emergency situations. It's hard to fake them. But when they happen in real life, you better know what to do. Since *AR* is already available, there might be the opportunity to artificially create such situations, for example, in a playful application during automated driving – wild animals or pedestrians that cross the road could appear. But where should they appear? The design space says, visual perception is limited in the *periphery* – so why not there? And the student has to detect them and to react properly. But to display one after the other is not surprising. This should depend on something. Let's look at the *input modalities* for this: bad *behaviour* and *gaze* – looking away from the road – can trigger the emergency. But the *presentation* has to be very naturalistic, otherwise it is too easy to spot that it is artificial.

Are there advantages or new opportunities when using *VR* instead of AR? Yes – we could completely influence their vision by that! When already creating emergency situations, we could use VR to demonstrate how dangerous intoxicated driving is. The windshield could be *blurred and dimmed* around the driver's *gaze* point. That could be tested at *night* when they are tired. In this condition, they have to repeat the previous test and see how their spatial and hazard detection performance is impeded.'

Summarizing the two presented thought experiments, 'Paul' explored the dimensions and characters of the design space which encouraged him to look at the ideas from different angles. With the proposed design space at hand, he created a lot of new ideas for already existing concepts.

DISCUSSION AND LIMITATIONS

Based on our extensive literature research and patents review, we defined our design space to be as inclusive and comprehensive as possible. However, we are aware that neither the list of applications nor the categorization provided may be complete.

Due to the composition of our focus groups, the findings reflect the view of a rather young age group with a strong focus on communication and entertainment. However, we believe young, tech-savvy drivers to be a major user group of WSD apps. At the same time, conducting additional focus groups with other age groups may identify further use cases. While middle aged users may be interested in applications related to or supporting their work, older users may benefit from applications that focus on increasing road and driving safety.

Windshield displays is still a young research field. Only as the technology required to build interactive, large-sized windshields matures it will become possible to investigate the impact of technical properties (e.g., depth continuity). Furthermore, with advances in technology, new opportunities and ideas will arise and lead to an extension of our initial categorization of the design space. Examples include, but are not limited to new interaction devices or novel output technology (for instance holography) or changes with regard to mobility concepts (car sharing, electric vehicles). Also, we are aware that not all provided options may be in compliance with legal requirements at the time of publication of this work. For instance, there may be limitations with regard to the degree of transparency of the WSD, its (dynamic) content and its brightness towards the outside of the vehicle.

To show how the design space could support designers in creating novel applications for WSDs, we provided two example use cases. As these showcases are only thought experiments, it is still unclear how the design space will actually be used and how designers benefit from it.

CONCLUSION

Based on two examples, we showcased how the design space for windshield display applications presented in this paper can aid the design process for future vehicle systems, in particular by enabling design alternatives to be compared and discussed as well as by encouraging and supporting the designer in exploring novel aspects. Furthermore, we presented the different application categories which supports the ideation process as practitioners and researchers explore novel application areas.

The design space allows to explore the different dimensions, both for inside and outside WSD. As the idea of using windshield displays from the outside further evolves, we see a tight connection to the research area of public displays. Researchers need to think of how to attract the attention of passersby and how to communicate that interaction is possible with the windshield display – which currently nobody would expect. Further, such displays would need to offer easy-to-use and easy-to-understand interaction techniques – presumably beyond touch, as has been stressed before – and such displays would need to motivate people to approach and use them. Ultimately, novel business models emerge where vehicle owners could be reimbursed for sharing the interaction space – both by the providers of applications as well as by the users of these applications.

ACKNOWLEDGMENTS

We thank Sven Osterwald for his support in conducting the focus groups and collecting the use cases.

REFERENCES

1. DIN 15996:2008. 2008. Bild- und Tonbearbeitung in Film-, Video- und Rundfunkbetrieben - Grundsätze und Festlegungen für den Arbeitsplatz. (2008).

2. Markus Ablassmeier, Gregor Mcglaun, and Gerhard Rigoll. 2005. Evaluating the Potential of Head-Up Displays for a Multimodal Interaction Concept in the Automotive Environment. In *Proceedings of the 9th World Multi-Conference on Systemics, Cybernetics and Informatics (WMSCI 2005)*, Vol. X. IIIS.

3. National Highway Traffic Safety Administration. 2013. Preliminary Statement of Policy Concerning Automated Vehicles. National Highway Traffic Safety Administration (NHTSA), Washington, DC.

4. Motoyuki Akamatsu, Paul Green, and Klaus Bengler. 2013. Automotive Technology and Human Factors Research: Past, Present, and Future. *International Journal of Vehicular Technology* 2013, Article 526180 (2013), 27 pages. DOI:http://dx.doi.org/10.1155/2013/526180

5. Florian Alt, Christoph Evers, and Albrecht Schmidt. 2009. Users' View on Context-Sensitive Car Advertisements. In *Proceedings of 7th International Conference on Pervasive Computing (Lecture Notes in Computer Science)*, Hideyuki Tokuda, Michael Beigl, Adrian Friday, A.J.Bernheim Brush, and Yoshito Tobe (Eds.), Vol. 5538. Springer Berlin Heidelberg, 9–16. DOI: http://dx.doi.org/10.1007/978-3-642-01516-8_2

6. Florian Alt, Dagmar Kern, Fabian Schulte, Bastian Pfleging, Alireza Sahami Shirazi, and Albrecht Schmidt. 2010. Enabling Micro-entertainment in Vehicles Based on Context Information. In *Proceedings of the 2nd International Conference on Automotive User Interfaces and Interactive Vehicular Applications (AutomotiveUI '10)*. ACM, New York, NY, USA, 117–124. DOI: http://dx.doi.org/10.1145/1969773.1969794

7. Florian Alt, Alireza Sahami Shirazi, Thomas Kubitza, and Albrecht Schmidt. 2013. Interaction Techniques for Creating and Exchanging Content with Public Displays. In *Proceedings of the SIGCHI Conference on Human Factors in Computing Systems (CHI '13)*. ACM, New York, NY, USA, 1709–1718. DOI: http://dx.doi.org/10.1145/2470654.2466226

8. Florian Alt, Alireza Sahami Shirazi, Max Pfeiffer, Paul Holleis, and Albrecht Schmidt. 2009. TaxiMedia: An Interactive Context-Aware Entertainment and Advertising System. In *GI Jahrestagung*. 3933–3940.

9. Ignacio Alvarez, Aqueasha Martin, Jerone Dunbar, Joachim Taiber, Dale-Marie Wilson, and Juan E. Gilbert. 2010. Voice Interfaced Vehicle User Help. In *Proceedings of the 2nd International Conference on Automotive User Interfaces and Interactive Vehicular Applications (AutomotiveUI '10)*. ACM, New York, NY, USA, 42–49. DOI:http://dx.doi.org/10.1145/1969773.1969782

10. Ignacio Alvarez, Aqueasha Martin, Jerone Dunbar, Joachim Taiber, Dale-Marie Wilson, and Juan E Gilbert. 2011. Designing driver-centric natural voice user interfaces. In *Adjunct Proceedings Proceedings of the 3rd International Conference on Automotive User Interfaces and Interactive Vehicular Applications (AutomotiveUI '11)*. 42–49.

11. Media-und Sozialforschungsgesellschaft mbH ARIS Umfrageforschung Markt. 2011. Studie Automobil. online (slides). (2011). http://www.bitkom.org/files/documents/BITKOM_Studie_Automobil_-_ITK_im_Auto_und_Elektromobilitaet.pdf

12. Rafael Ballagas, Michael Rohs, Jennifer G. Sheridan, and Jan Borchers. 2008. *The Design Space of Ubiquitous Mobile Input*. IGI Global, Hershey, PA, USA, 386–407. DOI: http://dx.doi.org/10.4018/978-1-59904-871-0.ch024

13. Karlin Bark, Cuong Tran, Kikuo Fujimura, and Victor Ng-Thow-Hing. 2014. Personal Navi: Benefits of an Augmented Reality Navigational Aid Using a See-Thru 3D Volumetric HUD. In *Proceedings of the 6th International Conference on Automotive User Interfaces and Interactive Vehicular Applications (AutomotiveUI '14)*. ACM, New York, NY, USA, Article 1, 8 pages. DOI: http://dx.doi.org/10.1145/2667317.2667329

14. Lyn Bartram, Colin Ware, and Tom Calvert. 2003. Moticons:: detection, distraction and task. *International Journal of Human-Computer Studies* 58, 5 (2003), 515 – 545. DOI: http://dx.doi.org/10.1016/S1071-5819(03)00021-1

15. J. Alejandro Betancur. 2011. *Augmented Reality - Some Emerging Application Areas*. InTech, Chapter Physical Variable Analysis Involved in Head-Up Display Systems Applied to Automobiles. DOI: http://dx.doi.org/10.5772/25849

16. Jochen Blume, Thorsten Alexander Kern, and Pablo Richter. 2014. Head-up-Display–Die nächste Generation mit Augmented-Reality-Technik. In *Vernetztes Automobil*, Wolfgang Siebenpfeiffer (Ed.). Springer, 137–143. DOI: http://dx.doi.org/10.1007/978-3-658-04019-2_20

17. Lorenz Bohrer, Stefan Henze, Matthias Hoping, Hans-Hermann Johannes, Wolfgang Kowalsky, Henning Krautwald, Michael Kröger, Jens Meyer, Thomas Riedl, and Heino Wengelnik. 2008. Transparente Anzeigevorrichung für ein Kraftfahrzeug. DE Patent DE200,710,012,571. (17 January 2008). https://register.dpma.de/DPMAregister/pat/PatSchrifteneinsicht?docId=DE102007012571A1 Filed March 13, 2007.

18. John Brandon. 2012. Top 5 huds in mordern cars today. Website. (2012). Retrieved September 19, 2015 from http://www.techradar.com/news/car-tech/top-5-huds-in-modern-cars-today-1092312.

19. Tobias Brandt. 2013. Information Systems in Automobiles - Past, Present, and Future Uses. In *19th Americas Conference on Information Systems, AMCIS 2013, Chicago, Illinois, USA, August 15-17, 2013.* http://aisel.aisnet.org/amcis2013/GreenIS/GeneralPresentations/1

20. Nora Broy, Simone Höckh, Annette Frederiksen, Michael Gilowski, Julian Eichhorn, Felix Naser, Horst Jung, Julia Niemann, Martin Schell, Albrecht Schmid, and Florian Alt. 2014. Exploring Design Parameters for a 3D Head-Up Display. In *Proceedings of the International Symposium on Pervasive Displays (PerDis '14)*. ACM, New York, NY, USA, Article 38, 6 pages. DOI: http://dx.doi.org/10.1145/2611009.2611011

21. Heiner Bubb. 2003. Fahrerassistenz - primaer ein Beitrag zum Komfort oder fuer die Sicherheit?. In *Der Fahrer im 21. Jahrhundert : Anforderungen, Anwendungen, Aspekte für Mensch-Maschine-Systeme; Tagung Braunschweig, 2. und 3. Juni 2003 (VDI-Berichte ; 1768)*. VDI-Verlag, Düsseldorf, Germany, 25–44. http://bvbr.bib-bvb.de:8991/F?func=service&doc_library=BVB01&doc_number=010423777&line_number=0001&func_code=DB_RECORDS&service_type=MEDIA

22. William Buxton. 1983. Lexical and Pragmatic Considerations of Input Structures. *SIGGRAPH Comput. Graph.* 17, 1 (Jan. 1983), 31–37. DOI: http://dx.doi.org/10.1145/988584.988586

23. Nilgün Camgöz, Cengiz Yener, and Dilek Güvenç. 2004. Effects of hue, saturation, and brightness: Part 2: Attention. *Color Research and Application* 29, 1 (2004), 20–28. DOI:http://dx.doi.org/10.1002/col.10214

24. Stuart K. Card and Jock D. Mackinlay. 1997. The Structure of the Information Visualization Design Space. In *Proceedings of the 1997 IEEE Symposium on Information Visualization (InfoVis '97)*. IEEE Computer Society, Washington, DC, USA, 92–999. DOI: http://dx.doi.org/10.1109/INFVIS.1997.636792

25. Stuart K. Card, Jock D. Mackinlay, and George G. Robertson. 1991. A Morphological Analysis of the Design Space of Input Devices. *ACM Trans. Inf. Syst.* 9, 2 (April 1991), 99–122. DOI: http://dx.doi.org/10.1145/123078.128726

26. Vassilis Charissis and Martin Naef. 2007. Evaluation of Prototype Automotive Head-Up Display Interface: Testing Driver's Focusing Ability through a VR Simulation. In *IEEE Intelligent Vehicles Symposium*. IEEE Computer Society, 560–565. DOI: http://dx.doi.org/10.1109/IVS.2007.4290174

27. Vassilis Charissis, Martin Naef, Stylianos Papanastasiou, and Marianne Patera. 2007. Designing a Direct Manipulation HUD Interface for In-vehicle Infotainment. In *Proceedings of the 12th International Conference on Human-computer Interaction: Interaction Platforms and Techniques (HCI'07)*. Springer-Verlag, Berlin, Heidelberg, 551–559. http://dl.acm.org/citation.cfm?id=1757268.1757333

28. Shinko Y. Cheng, Anup Doshi, and Mohan M. Trivedi. 2007. Active Heads-up Display based Speed Compliance Aid for Driver Assistance: A Novel Interface and Comparative Experimental Studies. In *2007 IEEE Intelligent Vehicles Symposium*. IEEE Computer Society, 594–599. DOI: http://dx.doi.org/10.1109/IVS.2007.4290180

29. Ed H. Chi. 2000. A taxonomy of visualization techniques using the data state reference model. In *IEEE Symposium on Information Visualization (InfoVis 2000)*. IEEE Computer Society, 69–75. DOI: http://dx.doi.org/10.1109/INFVIS.2000.885092

30. Sunny Consolvo, Peter Roessler, and Brett E. Shelton. 2004. The CareNet display: lessons learned from an in home evaluation of an ambient display. In *UbiComp 2004: Ubiquitous Computing*, Nigel Davies, ElizabethD. Mynatt, and Itiro Siio (Eds.). Lecture Notes in Computer Science, Vol. 3205. Springer, Berlin Heidelberg, Germany, 1–17. DOI: http://dx.doi.org/10.1007/978-3-540-30119-6_1

31. David Curbow. 2001. User Benefits of Connecting Automobiles to the Internet. In *CHI '01 Extended Abstracts on Human Factors in Computing Systems (CHI EA '01)*. ACM, New York, NY, USA, 1–2. DOI: http://dx.doi.org/10.1145/634067.634069

32. James E. Cutting and Peter M. Vishton. 1995. Perceiving layout and knowing distances: The integration, relative potency, and contextual use of different information about depth.. In *Perception of space and motion. Handbook of perception and cognition (2nd. ed.)*., William Epstein and Sheena J. Robers (Eds.). Academic Press, San Diego, CA, USA, 69–117. DOI:http://dx.doi.org/doi/10.1016/B978-012240530-3/50005-5

33. Nigel Davies, Sarah Clinch, and Florian Alt. 2014. Pervasive displays: understanding the future of digital signage. *Synthesis Lectures on Mobile and Pervasive Computing* 8, 1 (2014), 1–128. DOI: http://dx.doi.org/10.2200/S00558ED1V01Y201312MPC011

34. Joost C. F. de Winter, Riender Happee, Marieke H. Martens, and Neville A. Stanton. 2014. Effects of adaptive cruise control and highly automated driving on workload and situation awareness: A review of the empirical evidence. *Transportation Research Part F: Traffic Psychology and Behaviour* (Aug. 2014). DOI: http://dx.doi.org/10.1016/j.trf.2014.06.016

35. Tanja Döring, Dagmar Kern, Paul Marshall, Max Pfeiffer, Johannes Schöning, Volker Gruhn, and Albrecht Schmidt. 2011. Gestural Interaction on the Steering Wheel: Reducing the Visual Demand. In *Proceedings of the SIGCHI Conference on Human Factors in Computing Systems (CHI '11)*. ACM, New York, NY, USA, 483–492. DOI:http://dx.doi.org/10.1145/1978942.1979010

36. A. Doshi, Shinko Yuanhsien Cheng, and M.M. Trivedi. 2009. A Novel Active Heads-Up Display for Driver Assistance. *IEEE Transactions on Systems, Man, and Cybernetics, Part B: Cybernetics* 39, 1 (Feb 2009), 85–93. DOI:http://dx.doi.org/10.1109/TSMCB.2008.923527

37. Pioneer Europe. year unknown. NavGate Head-Up Display - SPX-HUD01. Website. (year unknown). Retrieved September 19, 2015 from http://www.pioneer.eu/eur/products/archive/SPX-HUD01/page.html.

38. Michel Ferreira, Pedro Gomes, Michelle Kruger Silveria, and Fausto Vieira. 2013. Augmented Reality Driving Supported by Vehicular Ad Hoc Networking. In *2013 IEEE International Symposium on Mixed and Augmented Reality (ISMAR'13)*. IEEE Computer Society, 253–254. DOI:http://dx.doi.org/10.1109/ISMAR.2013.6671791

39. Steven L. Franconeri and Daniel J. Simons. 2003. Moving and looming stimuli capture attention. *Perception and Psychophysics* 65, 7 (2003), 999–1010. DOI: http://dx.doi.org/10.3758/BF03194829

40. Kikuo Fujimura, Lijie Xu, Cuong Tran, Rishabh Bhandari, and Victor Ng-Thow-Hing. 2013. Driver Queries Using Wheel-constrained Finger Pointing and 3-D Head-up Display Visual Feedback. In *Proceedings of the 5th International Conference on Automotive User Interfaces and Interactive Vehicular Applications (AutomotiveUI '13)*. ACM, New York, NY, USA, 56–62. DOI: http://dx.doi.org/10.1145/2516540.2516551

41. Jose L. Galvan. 2006. *A Guide for Students of the Social and Behavioral Sciences*. Pyrczak Publishing.

42. K. W. Gish and L. Staplin. 1995. Human Factors Aspects of Using Head Up Displays in Automobiles: A Review of the Literature. National Highway Traffic Safety Administration (NHTSA) (report no: DOT HS 808 320), Washington, DC.

43. Continental Automotive GmbH. 2014. Head-up Displays. Website. (2014). Retrieved September 19, 2015 from http://continental-head-up-display.com/.

44. Christian Gold, Daniel Damböck, Lutz Lorenz, and Klaus Bengler. 2013. "Take over!" How long does it take to get the driver back into the loop?. In *Proceedings of the Human Factors and Ergonomics Society Annual Meeting*, Vol. 57. 1938–1942. DOI: http://dx.doi.org/10.1177/1541931213571433

45. Herbert Hagendorf, Joseph Krummenacher, Hermann-Josef Müller, and Torsten Schubert. 2011. *Wahrnehmung und Aufmerksamkeit: Allgemeine Psychologie für Bachelor*. Springer, Berlin Heidelberg, Germany. DOI: http://dx.doi.org/10.1007/978-3-642-12710-6

46. Renate Häuslschmid, Sven Osterwald, Marcus Lang, and Andreas Butz. 2015a. Augmenting the Driver's View with Peripheral Information on a Windshield Display. In *Proceedings of the 20th International Conference on Intelligent User Interfaces (IUI '15)*. ACM, New York, NY, USA, 311–321. DOI: http://dx.doi.org/10.1145/2678025.2701393

47. Renate Häuslschmid, Laura Schnurr, Julie Wagner, and Andreas Butz. 2015b. Contact-analog Warnings on Windshield Displays Promote Monitoring the Road Scene. In *Proceedings of the 7th International Conference on Automotive User Interfaces and Interactive Vehicular Applications (AutomotiveUI '15)*. ACM, New York, NY, USA, 64–71. DOI: http://dx.doi.org/10.1145/2799250.2799274

48. Eva Heller. 2009. *Psychologie de la couleur - Effets et symboliques*. Editions Pyramyd. 39–63 pages.

49. M. J. M. Houtmans and A. F Sanders. 1984. Perception of signals presented in the periphery of the visual field. *Acta Psychologica* 55, 2 (1984), 143–155. DOI: http://dx.doi.org/10.1016/0001-6918(84)90064-7

50. SAE International. 2014. Taxonomy and Definitions for Terms Related to On-Road Motor Vehicle Automated Driving Systems (Standard J3016 201401). SAE International (SAE).

51. Nassim Jafarinaimi, Jodi Forlizzi, Amy Hurst, and John Zimmerman. 2005. Breakaway: An Ambient Display Designed to Change Human Behavior. In *CHI '05 Extended Abstracts on Human Factors in Computing Systems (CHI EA '05)*. ACM, New York, NY, USA, 1945–1948. DOI: http://dx.doi.org/10.1145/1056808.1057063

52. Seung-Won Jung and Sung-Jea Ko. 2012. Depth sensation enhancement using the just noticeable depth difference. *IEEE Transactions on Image Processing* 21, 8 (2012), 3624–3637. DOI: http://dx.doi.org/10.1109/TIP.2012.2191569

53. Hannu Karvonen, Tuomo Kujala, and Pertti Saariluoma. 2006. In-Car Ubiquitous Computing: Driver Tutoring Messages Presented on a Head-Up Display. In *IEEE Intelligent Transportation Systems Conference 2006 (ITCS '06)*. IEEE, IEEE Computer Society, 560–565. DOI: http://dx.doi.org/10.1109/ITSC.2006.1706800

54. Dagmar Kern, Paul Marshall, and Albrecht Schmidt. 2010. Gazemarks: Gaze-based Visual Placeholders to Ease Attention Switching. In *Proceedings of the SIGCHI Conference on Human Factors in Computing Systems (CHI '10)*. ACM, New York, NY, USA, 2093–2102. DOI: http://dx.doi.org/10.1145/1753326.1753646

55. Dagmar Kern and Albrecht Schmidt. 2009. Design Space for Driver-based Automotive User Interfaces. In *Proceedings of the 1st International Conference on Automotive User Interfaces and Interactive Vehicular Applications (AutomotiveUI '09)*. ACM, New York, NY, USA, 3–10. DOI: http://dx.doi.org/10.1145/1620509.1620511

56. Mohamed Khamis, Andreas Bulling, and Florian Alt. 2015. Tackling Challenges of Interactive Public Displays Using Gaze. In *Adjunct Proceedings of the 2015 ACM International Joint Conference on Pervasive and Ubiquitous Computing and Proceedings of the 2015 ACM International Symposium on Wearable Computers (UbiComp/ISWC'15 Adjunct)*. ACM, New York, NY, USA, 763–766. DOI: http://dx.doi.org/10.1145/2800835.2807951

57. Javid Khan, Chi Can, Alan Greenaway, and Ian Underwood. 2013. A real-space interactive holographic display based on a large-aperture HOE, In Practical Holography XXVII: Materials and Applications. *Proc. SPIE* 8644 (2013). DOI: http://dx.doi.org/10.1117/12.2021633

58. Hyungil Kim, Xuefang Wu, Joseph L. Gabbard, and Nicholas F. Polys. 2013. Exploring Head-up Augmented Reality Interfaces for Crash Warning Systems. In *Proceedings of the 5th International Conference on Automotive User Interfaces and Interactive Vehicular

Applications (AutomotiveUI '13). ACM, New York, NY, USA, 224–227. DOI: http://dx.doi.org/10.1145/2516540.2516566

59. Martin Knobel, Marc Hassenzahl, Simon Männlein, Melanie Lamara, Josef Schumann, Kai Eckoldt, Matthias Laschke, and Andreas Butz. 2013. Become a Member of the Last Gentlemen: Designing for Prosocial Driving. In *Proceedings of the 6th International Conference on Designing Pleasurable Products and Interfaces (DPPI '13)*. ACM, New York, NY, USA, 60–66. DOI: http://dx.doi.org/10.1145/2513506.2513513
60. H. H. Kornhuber. 1978. Blickmotorik. In *Physiologie des Menschen. Band 13: Sehen (Sinnesphysiologie III)*, Kramer (Ed.). Schwarzenbeck, München, Wien, Baltimore, 357–426.
61. Richard A Krueger and Mary Anne Casey. 2002. Designing and conducting focus group interviews. *Social Analysis, Selected Tools and Techniques, Krueger, RA, MA Casey, J. Donner, S. Kirsch and JN Maack* (2002), 4–23.
62. Jochen Kruse. 2014. Head up: information in the driver's field of view. Website. (2014). Retrieved September 19, 2015 from http://next.mercedes-benz.com/en/hud-en/.
63. Jiannan Li, Ehud Sharlin, Saul Greenberg, and Michael Rounding. 2013. Designing the Car iWindow: Exploring Interaction Through Vehicle Side Windows. In *CHI '13 Extended Abstracts on Human Factors in Computing Systems (CHI EA '13)*. ACM, New York, NY, USA, 1665–1670. DOI: http://dx.doi.org/10.1145/2468356.2468654
64. Pamela J. Ludford, Dan Frankowski, Ken Reily, Kurt Wilms, and Loren Terveen. 2006. Because I Carry My Cell Phone Anyway: Functional Location-based Reminder Applications. In *Proceedings of the SIGCHI Conference on Human Factors in Computing Systems (CHI '06)*. ACM, New York, NY, USA, 889–898. DOI: http://dx.doi.org/10.1145/1124772.1124903
65. Roy J. Mathieu, Thomas A. Seder, Joesph F. Szczerba, and Dehua Cui. 2013. Driving maneuver assist on full windshield head-up display. US Patent 8,514,101. (20 August 2013). https://www.google.com/patents/US8514101 Filed December 2, 2011.
66. Toru Miyamoto, Itaru Kitahara, Yoshinari Kameda, and Yuichi Ohta. 2006. Floating Virtual Mirrors: Visualization of the Scene Behind a Vehicle. In *Advances in Artificial Reality and Tele-Existence*, Zhigeng Pan, Adrian Cheok, Michael Haller, RynsonW.H. Lau, Hideo Saito, and Ronghua Liang (Eds.). Lecture Notes in Computer Science, Vol. 4282. Springer, 302–313. DOI: http://dx.doi.org/10.1007/11941354_31
67. Jörg Müller, Florian Alt, Daniel Michelis, and Albrecht Schmidt. 2010. Requirements and Design Space for Interactive Public Displays. In *Proceedings of the International Conference on Multimedia (MM '10)*. ACM, New York, NY, USA, 1285–1294. DOI: http://dx.doi.org/10.1145/1873951.1874203
68. Jörg Müller, Robert Walter, Gilles Bailly, Michael Nischt, and Florian Alt. 2012. Looking Glass: A Field Study on Noticing Interactivity of a Shop Window. In *Proceedings of the SIGCHI Conference on Human Factors in Computing Systems (CHI '12)*. ACM, New York, NY, USA, 297–306. DOI: http://dx.doi.org/10.1145/2207676.2207718
69. Wolfgang Narzt, Gustav Pomberger, Alois Ferscha, Dieter Kolb, Reiner Müller, Jan Wieghardt, Horst Hörtner, and Christopher Lindinger. 2006. Augmented reality navigation systems. *Universal Access in the Information Society* 4, 3 (2006), 177–187 DOI: http://dx.doi.org/10.1007/s10209-005-0017-5
70. Victor Ng-Thow-Hing, Karlin Bark, Lee Beckwith, Cuong Tran, Rishabh Bhandari, and Srinath Sridhar. 2013. User-centered perspectives for Automotive Augmented Reality. In *2013 IEEE International Symposium on Mixed and Augmented Reality - Arts, Media, and Humanities (ISMAR-AMH '13)*. IEEE Computer Society, 13–22. DOI: http://dx.doi.org/10.1109/ISMAR-AMH.2013.6671262
71. Tao Ni, Doug Bowman, and Chris North. 2011. AirStroke: Bringing Unistroke Text Entry to Freehand Gesture Interfaces. In *Proceedings of the SIGCHI Conference on Human Factors in Computing Systems (CHI '11)*. ACM, New York, NY, USA, 2473–2476. DOI: http://dx.doi.org/10.1145/1978942.1979303
72. Laurence Nigay and Joëlle Coutaz. 1993. A Design Space for Multimodal Systems: Concurrent Processing and Data Fusion. In *Proceedings of the INTERACT '93 and CHI'93 Conference on Human Factors in Computing Systems (CHI '93)*. ACM, New York, NY, USA, 172–178. DOI:http://dx.doi.org/10.1145/169059.169143
73. Takehiko Ohno, Naoki Mukawa, and Atsushi Yoshikawa. 2002. FreeGaze: A Gaze Tracking System for Everyday Gaze Interaction. In *Proceedings of the 2002 Symposium on Eye Tracking Research and Applications (ETRA '02)*. ACM, New York, NY, USA, 125–132. DOI: http://dx.doi.org/10.1145/507072.507098
74. Jason Orlosky, Kiyoshi Kiyokawa, and Haruo Takemura. 2013. Dynamic Text Management for See-through Wearable and Heads-up Display Systems. In *Proceedings of the 2013 International Conference on Intelligent User Interfaces (IUI '13)*. ACM, New York, NY, USA, 363–370. DOI: http://dx.doi.org/10.1145/2449396.2449443
75. Bastian Pfleging and Albrecht Schmidt. 2015. (Non-) Driving-Related Activities in the Car: Defining Driver Activities for Manual and Automated Driving. In *Workshop on Experiencing Autonomous Vehicles: Crossing the Boundaries between a Drive and a Ride at CHI'15* (2015-04-01). http://www.hcilab.org/wp-content/uploads/pfleging-2015-drivingrelatedactivities1.pdf

76. Bastian Pfleging, Stefan Schneegass, Dagmar Kern, and Albrecht Schmidt. 2015. Vom Transportmittel zum rollenden Computer - Interaktion im Auto. *Informatik Spektrum* 37, 5 (October 2015), 1–5. DOI: http://dx.doi.org/10.1007/s00287-014-0804-6

77. Bastian Pfleging, Stefan Schneegass, and Albrecht Schmidt. 2012. Multimodal Interaction in the Car: Combining Speech and Gestures on the Steering Wheel. In *Proceedings of the 4th International Conference on Automotive User Interfaces and Interactive Vehicular Applications (AutomotiveUI '12)*. ACM, New York, NY, USA, 155–162. DOI: http://dx.doi.org/10.1145/2390256.2390282

78. Ioannis Politis, Stephen Brewster, and Frank Pollick. 2015. Language-based Multimodal Displays for the Handover of Control in Autonomous Cars. In *Proceedings of the 7th International Conference on Automotive User Interfaces and Interactive Vehicular Applications (AutomotiveUI '15)*. ACM, New York, NY, USA, 3–10. DOI: http://dx.doi.org/10.1145/2799250.2799262

79. Sonja Rümelin, Chadly Marouane, and Andreas Butz. 2013. Free-hand Pointing for Identification and Interaction with Distant Objects. In *Proceedings of the 5th International Conference on Automotive User Interfaces and Interactive Vehicular Applications (AutomotiveUI '13)*. ACM, New York, NY, USA, 40–47. DOI:http://dx.doi.org/10.1145/2516540.2516556

80. SAE International (SAE). 1997. Safety Glazing Materials for Glazing Motor Vehicles and Motor Vehicle Equipment Operating on Land Highways - Safety Standard (ANSI Z26.1 1997th Edition). SAE International (SAE), 46.

81. Akihiko Sato, Itaru Kitahara, Yoshinari Kameda, and Yuichi Ohta. 2006. Visual navigation system on windshield head-up display. In *In Proceedings of 13th World Congress on Intelligent Transport Systems*.

82. Bill Schilit, Norman Adams, and Roy Want. 1994. Context-Aware Computing Applications. In *First Workshop on Mobile Computing Systems and Applications, 1994 (WMCSA 1994)*. IEEE Computer Society, 85–90. DOI: http://dx.doi.org/10.1109/WMCSA.1994.16

83. Ronald Schroeter and Andry Rakotonirainy. 2012. The future shape of digital cars. In *Proceedings of the 2012 Australasian Road Safety Research, Policing and Education Conference*. Australian College of Road Safety (ACRS), 1–11.

84. Ronald Schroeter, Andry Rakotonirainy, and Marcus Foth. 2012. The Social Car: New Interactive Vehicular Applications Derived from Social Media and Urban Informatics. In *Proceedings of the 4th International Conference on Automotive User Interfaces and Interactive Vehicular Applications (AutomotiveUI '12)*. ACM, New York, NY, USA, 107–110. DOI: http://dx.doi.org/10.1145/2390256.2390273

85. Thomas A. Seder, Joseph F. Szczerba, and Dehua Cui. 2012. Night vision on full windshield head-up display. US Patent 8,164,543. (24 April 2012). https://www.google.com/patents/US8164543 Filed May 18, 2009.

86. Thomas A. Seder, Joseph F. Szczerba, and Dehua Cui. 2013. External presentation of information on full glass display. US Patent 8,606,430. (10 December 2013). https://www.google.com/patents/US8606430 Filed October 8, 2010.

87. Jack A. Segal, William Allen Yates, Steven B. Branton, and Jeff Mossontte. 2004. Remote control having touch pad to screen mapping. US Patent 6,765,557. (20 July 2004). https://www.google.com/patents/US6765557 Filed April 10, 2000.

88. Ted Selker, Winslow Burleson, and Ernesto Arroyo. 2002. E-windshield: a study of using. In *Extended abstracts of the 2002 Conference on Human Factors in Computing Systems, CHI 2002, Minneapolis, Minnesota, USA, April 20-25, 2002*. 508–509. DOI: http://dx.doi.org/10.1145/506443.506453

89. Taly Sharon, Ted Selker, Lars Wagner, and Ariel J. Frank. 2005. CarCoach: a generalized layered architecture for educational car systems. In *Proceedings of IEEE International Conference on Software-Science, Technology and Engineering (SWSTE '05)*. IEEE Computer Society, 13–22. DOI: http://dx.doi.org/10.1109/SWSTE.2005.9

90. Srinath Sridhar and Victor Ng-Thow-Hing. 2012. Generation of virtual display surfaces for in-vehicle contextual augmented reality. In *IEEE International Symposium on Mixed and Augmented Reality (ISMAR'12)*. IEEE Computer Society, 317–318. DOI: http://dx.doi.org/10.1109/ISMAR.2012.6402592

91. Maria Staubach. 2009. Factors correlated with traffic accidents as a basis for evaluating Advanced Driver Assistance Systems. *Accident Analysis & Prevention* 41, 5 (9 2009), 1025–1033. DOI: http://dx.doi.org/10.1016/j.aap.2009.06.014

92. Jie Sun, Zhao-hui Wu, and Gang Pan. 2009. Context-aware smart car: from model to prototype. *Journal of Zhejiang University SCIENCE A* 10, 7 (2009), 1049–1059. DOI: http://dx.doi.org/10.1631/jzus.A0820154

93. Sun Innovations. 2015. FW-HUD. Website. (2015). Retrieved September 19, 2015 from http://www.sun-innovations.com/index.php/products/fw-hud/laser-scanning-fw-hud.

94. Joseph F. Szczerba, Dehua Cui, and Thomas A. Seder. 2013. Driver drowsy alert on full-windshield head-up display. US Patent 8,344,894. (1 January 2013). https://www.google.com/patents/US8344894 Filed September 21, 2009.

95. Joesph F. Szczerba, Thomas A. Seder, and Dehua Cui. 2014. Augmented road scene illustrator system on full windshield head-up display. US Patent 8,633,979. (21 January 2014). https://www.google.com/patents/US8633979 Filed December 29, 2010.

96. Marcus Tönnis, Leslie Klein, and Gudrun Klinker. 2008. Perception thresholds for augmented reality navigation schemes in large distances. In *7th IEEE/ACM International Symposium on Mixed and Augmented Reality (ISMAR '08)*. IEEE Computer Society, 189–190. DOI:http://dx.doi.org/10.1109/ISMAR.2008.4637360

97. Marcus Tönnis and Gudrun Klinker. 2014. Boundary Conditions for Information Visualization with Respect to the User's Gaze. In *Proceedings of the 5th Augmented Human International Conference (AH '14)*. ACM, New York, NY, USA, Article 44, 8 pages. DOI: http://dx.doi.org/10.1145/2582051.2582095

98. Marcus Tönnis, Marina Plavšić, and Gudrun Klinker. 2009. Survey and Classification of Head-Up Display Presentation Principles. In *Proceedings the 17th World Congress on Ergonomics*. International Ergonomics Association. CD-ROM Proceedings.

99. Armin Töpfer and Steffen Silbermann. 2008. Einsatz von Kunden-Fokusgruppen. In *Handbuch Kundenmanagement*, Armin Töpfer (Ed.). Springer Berlin Heidelberg, 267–279. DOI: http://dx.doi.org/10.1007/978-3-540-49924-4_10

100. Stephen Uphill, Christopher Francis, Dominic Jackson, James Whittamore, and Ashleigh J. Pook. 2011. Heads-up display for a gaming environment. US Patent App. 12/868,512. (11 August 2011). https://www.google.com/patents/US20110193773 Filed August 25, 2010.

101. Yohei Urano, Shinji Kashiwada, Hiroshi Ando, Koji Nakamura, and Yasuhiro Takaki. 2011. Super-multiview windshield display for driving assistance. *Journal of Information Display* 12, 1 (2011), 43–46. DOI: http://dx.doi.org/10.1080/15980316.2011.563060

102. Wen Wu, Fabian Blaicher, Jie Yang, Thomas Seder, and Dehua Cui. 2009. A Prototype of Landmark-based Car Navigation Using a Full-windshield Head-up Display System. In *Proceedings of the 2009 Workshop on Ambient Media Computing (AMC '09)*. ACM, New York, NY, USA, 21–28. DOI: http://dx.doi.org/10.1145/1631005.1631012

103. Hiroshi Yasuda and Yoshihiro Ohama. 2012. Toward a practical wall see-through system for drivers: How simple can it be?. In *2012 IEEE International Symposium on Mixed and Augmented Reality (ISMAR '12)*. IEEE Computer Society, 333–334. DOI: http://dx.doi.org/10.1109/ISMAR.2012.6402600

104. Jung-hack Yeo. 2000. Driver's eye detection method of drowsy driving warning system. US Patent 6,130,617. (10 October 2000). http://www.google.com/patents/US6130617 Filed June 9, 1999.

105. Jung-hack Yeo. 2001. Driver's drowsiness detection method of drowsy driving warning system. US Patent 6,243,015. (5 June 2001). http://www.google.com/patents/US6243015 Filed June 17, 1999.

106. Yanxia Zhang, Jörg Müller, Ming Ki Chong, Andreas Bulling, and Hans Gellersen. 2014. GazeHorizon: Enabling Passers-by to Interact with Public Displays by Gaze. In *Proceedings of the 2014 ACM International Joint Conference on Pervasive and Ubiquitous Computing (UbiComp '14)*. ACM, New York, NY, USA, 559–563. DOI:http://dx.doi.org/10.1145/2632048.2636071

When (ish) is My Bus? User-centered Visualizations of Uncertainty in Everyday, Mobile Predictive Systems

Matthew Kay
CSE | dub
University of Washington
mjskay@uw.edu

Tara Kola
Computer Science
Tufts University
tara.kola@tufts.edu

Jessica R. Hullman
iSchool | dub
University of Washington
jhullman@uw.edu

Sean A. Munson
HCDE | dub
University of Washington
smunson@uw.edu

ABSTRACT
Users often rely on realtime predictions in everyday contexts like riding the bus, but may not grasp that such predictions are subject to uncertainty. Existing uncertainty visualizations may not align with user needs or how they naturally reason about probability. We present a novel mobile interface design and visualization of uncertainty for transit predictions on mobile phones based on discrete outcomes. To develop it, we identified domain specific design requirements for visualizing uncertainty in transit prediction through: 1) a literature review, 2) a large survey of users of a popular realtime transit application, and 3) an iterative design process. We present several candidate visualizations of uncertainty for realtime transit predictions in a mobile context, and we propose a novel discrete representation of continuous outcomes designed for small screens, quantile dotplots. In a controlled experiment we find that quantile dotplots reduce the variance of probabilistic estimates by ~1.15 times compared to density plots and facilitate more confident estimation by end-users in the context of realtime transit prediction scenarios.

Author Keywords
End-user visualization; transit predictions; mobile interfaces; dotplots; uncertainty visualization.

INTRODUCTION
Quantitative predictions are increasingly ubiquitous in everyday life. Many such data come in the form of point estimates designed to aid decision-making, such as when the next bus is going to arrive, how long a road trip will take, whether and when it will rain, or what the high temperature will be. Often, people access these predictions on their mobile phones to make in-the-moment decisions that are time-constrained (providing little opportunity for training, interpretation, or complex interaction) using interfaces that are space-constrained (due to screen size).

CHI'16, May 07 - 12, 2016, San Jose, CA, USA

ACM 978-1-4503-3362-7/16/05 $15.00
DOI: http://dx.doi.org/10.1145/2858036.2858558

For example, Susan might refer to a bus's predicted arrival time on a smartphone application to check if she has time to get coffee before her bus to work arrives. She sees that the bus is running a few minutes late and is predicted to arrive in five minutes There is no line at the coffee shop, so she steps in to order. However, the bus makes up lost time and arrives only two minutes later: Susan, still waiting for coffee, misses her bus and is late for a meeting.

Susan based her decision on a point estimate of arrival time, as presented in many predictive systems for bus arrival, flight time, or car travel. Her decision is reasonable given the point prediction she saw, but real-world predictions are subject to uncertainty (e.g., her bus is most likely to come in 5 minutes but may come in as little as 1 minute or as much as 9 minutes). Designers and analysts are responsible for reporting uncertainty with predictions to help people make decisions that align with their goals [5,33], yet most visualizations of predictions present the data as if it were true (Finger & Bizantz [10] as cited in Cook & Thomas [5]). Had Susan's application presented her with a more complete representation of the predicted arrival time—perhaps noting that arrival times earlier than 5 minutes are also quite probable—she may not have risked getting coffee.

Many attempts to communicate uncertainty rely on complex visual representations of probability distributions. For example, error bars and probability densities require prior experience with statistical models to correctly interpret [2,6]. People can better understand probabilistic information when it is framed in terms of discrete events. For instance, Hoffrage & Gigerenzer [16] found that more medical experts could accurately estimate the positive predictive value (precision) of a test when presented with discrete counts or outcomes. Discrete-event representations have been used to improve patient understanding of risk, e.g., by showing the uncertainty in a medical diagnosis as discrete possible outcomes (number of true positive, false positives, false negatives, and true negatives) [11]. However, visualizing discrete approaches to presenting probability distributions typically requires a large amount of space or time to communicate the set of possible outcomes [17]. It is not clear how to effectively communicate discrete outcomes on small screens such as mobile devices.

We study user needs for communicating predictions and then design and evaluate novel, goal-directed visualizations of hypothetical outcomes in a time- and space-constrained mobile application, realtime transit prediction. As a setting where users have direct, day-to-day experience with uncertainty, transit prediction provides a representative context in which to evaluate how well people can use different uncertainty visualizations. The specific goals of our work are to see if and for what reasons people want uncertainty information in a bus setting; to identify effective uncertainty visualizations for realtime decision-making on a smartphone; and to test for differences in how precisely and confidently people extract probabilities from different visualizations of uncertainty.

Our three contributions based on these goals are to:

1. Develop **general and domain-specific design requirements and a rich description of user needs** for visualizing uncertainty in transit arrival times based on (i.) an analysis of the literature and (ii.) an initial survey of 172 people who use a popular realtime transit application.
2. Propose **design layouts and discrete-event visualizations of uncertainty** for conveying bus arrival time predictions on small screens based on an iterative design process. We introduce **quantile dotplots**, a novel modified dotplot that is a discrete analog to the common probability density plot.
3. Identify through a large user study of transit application users how accuracy and precision in estimating probability compares across several visualizations. Unlike previous work in communicating uncertainty in continuous outcomes [6,14], our study is the first to compare static discrete-outcome visualizations of probability distributions to continuous representations. We find that a **quantile dotplot depicting a small number of outcomes has ~ 1.15 times lower variance than a density plot**, making probability estimates 1-3 percentage points more precise.

Our results further understanding of how to communicate prediction uncertainty to non-experts in everyday, mobile decision-making contexts. Specifically, we recommend using low-density dotplots (due to lower variance and higher user confidence) or density plots (which have only slightly higher variance, but were more visually appealing) for visualizing uncertainty in space-constrained environments.

BACKGROUND & MOTIVATION

In this section, we use prior work to establish baseline requirements for the effective communication of uncertainty.

Improving trust by communicating uncertainty

Research indicates that displaying uncertainty can improve trust and decision-making in everyday contexts. Kay *et al.* [23] studied trust in body weight measurements, arguing that single point estimates without uncertainty decrease trust and tend to be interpreted as being more precise than they actually are. Kay *et al.* suggest **avoiding false precision in single point estimates** by displaying the uncertainty associated with weight data to improve trust. Similarly, Jung *et al.* [21] found that displaying the estimated remaining range of an electric vehicle as a gradient plot (i.e., with uncertainty) reduced range anxiety in a driving task compared to a single point estimate.

Joslyn & LeClerc [19] found that displaying uncertainty in weather predictions can lead to more optimal decision-making and trust in a forecast. When asked to make decisions about whether to salt roads (given a virtual budget, cost for salting, and cost for failing to salt when they should have), people made more optimal decisions when given point estimates with probabilistic information. Subjects with access to probabilistic information even made more optimal decisions than subjects who were explicitly told the optimal decision based on a cot-benefit analysis. While the decision suggested by a cost-benefit analysis will give the best choice on average, always applying the decision will sometimes lead people to take precautions that seem unnecessary (e.g., salting the roads when the weather ultimately does not require it). After experiencing a such few errors, people may begin to distrust the strategy and ignore the suggested course of action. Probabilistic information, on the other hand, provides a more transparent form of information for decision making, leading to greater trust. We believe this insight also applies to realtime transit prediction: even if we could develop a system to make recommendations like "leave now to make your bus on time", **a more transparent communication of uncertainty** will maintain trust over the long term and leave people the agency to make mistakes.

Visualizing uncertainty

As extrinsic annotation

A common approach to visualizing uncertainty is as an *extrinsic* annotation to a plot of the distribution's location (mean, median, or mode). For example, error bars representing confidence intervals or prediction intervals[1] can be superimposed on bar charts [2]. These intervals are extrinsic to other properties like the mean or mode since they are not integrated into the same encoding. By contrast, the probability density and mode are intrinsic to each other in a density plot, since the mode is visually encoded as the maximum of the density. Other distributional properties may be represented in summary plots using a series of marks (e.g., specific quantiles in a boxplot or modified box plot as in [6,18,28]).

Extrinsic representation can result in interpretation errors because the statistical construct (such as one standard error or a 95% confidence interval) is poorly understood [2,18],

[1] In contrast to a *confidence interval*, which describes the precision of an inferred model parameter (e.g. population mean), a *prediction interval* is an interval that a given percentage of specific instances are predicted to fall into. While much of the literature focuses on confidence intervals (of interest to scientists using models for inference), we are more concerned with prediction intervals (of interest to an individual who wishes to know how likely their bus is to arrive in a specific instance).

because individuals apply heuristics that are not correct (such as assuming that overlapping confidence intervals always indicate a non-significant difference [7]), or because the representation is ambiguous (such as an error bar being used to encode standard deviation, standard error, or 95% confidence interval). Finally, individuals tend to underweight probabilistic information (such as sample size or variance) when making judgments in favor of heuristic attributes like representativeness [35]. By separating the marks encoding underlying data from those encoding uncertainty, extrinsic representations are at risk of being viewed as peripheral, and consequently discounted when making judgments. Thus, to avoid ambiguity, simplify interpretation, and encourage users not to underweight probability information, we believe that **uncertainty should be intrinsic to the representation.**

Further, while a given prediction interval corresponds to a specific risk tolerance, a user may have differing risk thresholds in different contexts. For example, Susan may be willing to be late to her meeting 1/20 times, translating to a one-sided 95% prediction interval for estimated arrival time, yet she may tolerate more risk in different contexts like social gatherings or less important meetings. Different individuals are also likely to have different risk tolerances. Therefore, we believe that effective visualizations of uncertainty in this context should **allow users to apply situation-dependent risk tolerance**.

As abstract, continuous outcomes

Many other abstract, static representations encode a predictive distribution's probability density function (PDF) intrinsically as *retinal variables* (e.g., color, shape, texture) [3]. For example, density plots encode the PDF as distance from the *x*-axis, violin plots encode it as width [1,22,31], and gradient plots encode it as opacity. Several studies that include variants of density and gradient plots find little evidence of a performance difference between the two [6,18]. Opacity is a less effective encoding than height, width, or area [26]. As a result, we do not test the gradient plot.

Not all encodings of continuous outcomes using retinal variables make distributional properties intrinsic. Ibrekk & Morgan [18] compare density plots to plots of cumulative density functions (CDFs), amongst several other encodings. CDFs encode cumulative density as distance from the *x*-axis, allowing the probability of intervals to be estimated from height. They found that CDFs were unfamiliar to participants and required training. Not surprisingly, people had particular difficulty in using CDFs to estimate means, most likely because there is no simple visual variable that corresponds to mean (nor mode) on a CDF.

As hypothetical, discrete outcomes

We use *discrete outcomes* to refer to techniques that employ draws from a probability distribution rather than abstract probabilities of events. Discrete approaches were initially found to improve reasoning in textual communication. Gigerenzer and Hoffrage [12] found that statistical word problems described in terms of *natural frequencies* (e.g., 10/100) rather than probabilities (10%) were more likely to elicit inferences according to Bayes' rule in laypeople. Past work on visualizing uncertainty through hypothetical, discrete outcomes uses spatial or temporal bandwidth to communicate. For example, Garcia-Retamero and Cokely [11] reviewed studies of several types of visual aids for communicating health risks, including discrete outcome charts that illustrate treatment risk: they found that displaying *icon arrays* (a grid of pictograms, each representing a patient who lived or died) improved the accuracy of people's risk assessment. Hullman *et al.* use animation to display discrete outcomes more compactly in space [17], finding that animated discrete outcomes (called *hypothetical outcome plots*, or HOPs) support more accurate probability estimates than static alternatives (violin plots and error bars) for some tasks. However, by presenting outcomes over time, animated techniques bring a time-precision trade-off: to make more precise inferences, a user must view more outcomes, taking more time [ibid].

From the evidence in both visual communication and statistical reasoning, we believe that **discrete outcomes can improve decision making under uncertainty**. However, because transit decisions are often made quickly in real time we focused on developing non-animated presentations of discrete outcomes that are **glanceable** yet compact enough for a mobile phone display, in which it is typical to visualize the upcoming arrival of ~10 buses on one screen [9].

Visualization in space-constrained environments

To display many buses simultaneously on a mobile phone screen, we require our visualizations to be **compact**. Techniques like horizon graphs [15] and sparklines [34] have been proposed for visualizing time-series data in space-constrained environments. Visualizing uncertainty in transit arrival predictions encounters similar issues as these approaches; for example, a probability density function of predicted arrival time will become quite tall as its variance decreases (particularly, close to the predicted arrival time the prediction will become very precise). Our work demonstrates possible solutions for the specific context of visualizing PDFs on mobile phone displays.

SURVEY OF EXISTING USERS

Our reading of the literature provides an initial grounding for our design work, but to apply these results to a user-centered uncertainty visualization we also need to understand user goals. To establish design criteria for representations of uncertainty based on user needs, we surveyed users of one popular realtime transit application, OneBusAway [9].

Method

We conducted a survey to identify 1) how users currently use realtime bus arrival predictions and 2) their unaddressed needs for goal-oriented uncertainty information. We surveyed 172 users of OneBusAway, recruited via social media and department mailing lists.

Users' existing goals

To identify important user scenarios to address and what types of information are most important to those scenarios, we asked people about the *primary goals* they have when using OneBusAway. We developed a set of possible questions (e.g., "When should I start walking to the bus stop to catch my bus?"[2]) that people may ask using the interface using observations from previous studies of OneBusAway [20], our own reflections on using the system, from informal interviews with a small group (~15) of other users at our university, and through piloting the survey. We presented participants with a list of 9 such questions, and asked how often (on a 7-point scale from "never" to "always") they try to answer each question using OneBusAway. We also asked them if there are other ways they use OneBusAway in an open-ended question.

Problems with OneBusAway and unaddressed needs

We similarly presented participants with a list of types of information not currently provided by OneBusAway and asked them to rate the *potential helpfulness* of these (on a 5 point scale from "not helpful at all" to "very helpful"). We also provided an open-ended question asking about needs for uncertainty information not in this list. Finally, we asked people to describe the *worst experience* they have had using OneBusAway's predictions.

Results and Discussion

Users' existing goals

The top 5 highest-rated questions users currently ask are:

- **When to leave**: When should I start walking to my bus?
- **Wait time**: If I leave now, how long will I have to wait at the bus stop?
- **Time to next bus**: I missed my bus, how long will I have to wait for the next one to come?
- **Schedule risk:** Will I get to a meeting/event on time despite bus delays? This relates to a commonly-described worst experience of buses coming later than expected. For example:

  A more recent bad experience was when I was waiting for the 511 or 512 for over an hour. At least five buses should have passed, but they either did not show up or they were full and didn't let anyone on

- **Schedule opportunity:** Will I have enough time to do ____ before the bus arrives? This relates to a commonly-described *worst experience* of the bus coming earlier than expected after someone has used the prediction to decide to do something else before going to the bus; e.g.:

  It showed delays on a bus due to which I didn't leave home as I didn't want to wait at the bus stop for long (the bus stop is 4 mins from my home), but it suddenly came on time and I missed it. Sometimes, it even comes early when it shows delay.

[2] The full survey is available in our supplementary material.

Problems with OneBusAway and unaddressed needs

The top three questions users would like to be able to ask, but which are not well-supported by the current OneBusAway interface, are:

- **Status probability:** What is the chance OBA is showing the correct arrival status? This problem was also reflected in a commonly-described *worst experience*, wherein the bus never shows up and people have to make alternative plans. For example:

  My bus is perpetually 9 minutes away...while I watch alternative buses pass me thinking that oh, mine is going to be here soon only to eventually see "no information" for my bus. I could have been on my backup bus a half hour ago!!!

  It was common for people to report their worst experiences were related to status probability: for example, OneBusAway said "departed", but the bus had not arrived; it said "arriving" but had already departed. Any noisy estimate reduced to a categorical status will exhibit these types of errors which could be mitigated by conveying status probabilistically.

- **Prediction variance:** What is the chance the predicted arrival time will change unexpectedly?
- **Schedule frequency:** How frequently do buses arrive at various times in the day?

DESIGN REQUIREMENTS

Based on our literature review and user survey, we identified the following necessary design elements:

Point estimate of time to arrival: To support *glanceability*, we think that the point estimate of arrival time is necessary: people often use OneBusAway to make fast decisions about when to arrive at the bus stop. In addition, previous work has found that even when providing probabilistic estimates, people still want a point estimate. The existing point estimate of OneBusAway supports estimation tasks from our survey like *when to leave*, *wait time*, and *time to next bus*, though without communicating risk.

Probabilistic estimate of time to arrival: While people often want a point estimate of arrival time, a point estimate without uncertainty will often convey a *false precision.* A probabilistic estimate will help users understand that there is a chance the bus will come earlier or later than the point estimate. This helps people assess *schedule risk* and *schedule opportunities*. A probabilistic estimate also allows people to make conservative estimates while planning for meetings, or less conservative estimates for low risk situations – that is probabilistic estimates *allow situation-dependent risk tolerance*. This will help people better answer questions about *when to leave*, *wait time*, and *time to next bus* (the highest rated goals) and prepare people for commonly-reported *worst experiences* like a bus coming unexpectedly early or late.

Probabilistic estimate of arrival status: For example, what is the chance the bus has already arrived? Among questions not currently supported by OneBusAway, survey respondents most wanted support for this question (*status probability*), and commonly reported *worst experiences* related to it.

Data freshness: Because OneBusAway does not currently give probabilistic estimates, one of the only available signals for expert users to assess risk is the *freshness* of the data: OneBusAway indicates the time of the last update for realtime predictions and whether the current prediction is based on realtime data (it reflects the scheduled arrival time when realtime data is not available). This freshness information should either be provided to users in a redesigned interface, or should be incorporated into any models driving probabilistic estimates.

We believe these design elements will address each goal identified in the user survey with the exception of the goal of knowing *schedule frequency*. We felt that this goal is better addressed through a separate interface, such as a trip planner or schedule explorer in a mapping application. Schedule frequency is less relevant to in-the-moment decision-making than it is to long-term planning (can I rely on a bus arriving within some amount of time?). When schedule frequency is relevant to in-the-moment decisions, it typically reduces to other goals, like *time to next bus*.

DESIGN

We conducted an iterative design process focused on the design requirements set out above. This process began with a wide exploration of ideas through sketching, followed by paper prototyping in increasing fidelity, and culminated in digital mockups. These phases were informed by ongoing user feedback gained through informal down-the-hall testing with a total of 24 users. During informal testing, we presented users with hypothetical scenarios of use and asked them to think aloud as they interpreted the display.

Many of the design issues we encountered are somewhat orthogonal to specific of encodings of probability: given a particular timeline layout, for example, we could encode probability in many ways (e.g., as area, discrete events, a gradient). We first present our proposed set of designs and their rationale, then discuss possible techniques for encoding probability on small screens.

Proposed designs and rationale

Our proposed designs, instantiated with one particular visualization of uncertainty (density plot) out of several possible, are shown in Figure 1. Here we describe decisions we made to resolve design tensions and to match user goals.

Different layouts better serve different use cases

We developed two alternative layouts, *bus-timeline* and *route-timeline*. The *bus-timeline* layout gives a timeline for a single bus on each row, similar to how the existing OneBusAway app displays a single row per bus, sorted by predicted time to arrival. This simplifies understanding and

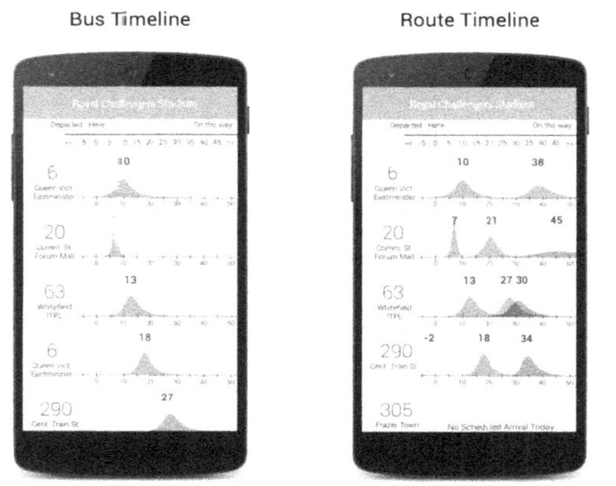

Figure 1. Alternative layouts we developed. (a) Bus Timeline: Each row (timeline) shows one predicted bus. (b) Route Timeline: Each row shows all predicted buses from a given route.

navigation, but is less compact in addressing problems like assessing *schedule frequency,* and, once the probabilistic visualizations are added, less compact than the current application. *Route-timeline*, by contrast, creates a more complex display and navigation (requiring navigation in two dimensions), but more easily aids understanding of *schedule frequency* (how often is the bus) and *schedule opportunity* (since if one is considering the risk associated with missing the next bus, it is easier to see how soon the bus after that is coming and factor that into one's decision).

Point estimates and probabilistic estimates should coincide spatially

We explored several tradeoffs between prominent point estimates versus probabilistic estimates, what we call the **glanceability/false precision tradeoff**. A too-prominent display of the point estimate causes users to ignore the probabilistic one, thus still giving a false sense of precision; a less-glanceable point estimate will be difficult to skim and frustrating to use. We want a display that is *glanceable* but which also does not convey false precision. To resolve this, we concluded that these two elements should coincide spatially: that is, *looking at the point estimate should encourage the user to also be looking at the probabilistic estimate.* We had considered designs in which the point estimate was along the right-hand edge of the display (Figure 3), as in the original OneBusAway. We concluded that this facilitated glanceability, but also allowed users to pay too little attention to the probabilistic estimates. Moving the point estimate onto the probability distribution resolved this tension.

Annotated timelines give probabilistic estimates of status "for free"

While we considered designs that more explicitly communicate the probability that the bus has arrived, we realized that an annotated timeline combined with probabilistic predictions communicates this implicitly. By denoting areas that correspond to "departed", "now", and "on the way" on the timeline, users can directly read these probabilities from the distributions depicted; see the timeline annotations across the top of Figure 1.

When to leave is implicit in time to arrival
We considered designs that communicated when someone should leave to catch their bus; i.e. designs that directly addressed the *when to leave* goal. However, there are several difficulties with this approach: first, when to leave is not the only goal for which people use OneBusAway; thus it would need to be integrated into displays communicating information like time to arrival (or alternate designs developed for both goals). This exacerbates space issues. Estimating when to leave also requires substantial knowledge about the users' plans, and introduces further uncertainty (e.g., how long does it take to walk to the stop?).

Data freshness may be subsumed by an improved model
OneBusAway often does not have truly realtime information, but instead updates when buses check in. As noted previously, expert users often refer to the last check-in time as a way to evaluate how much they trust the application's prediction. To facilitate this use, we considered several designs that included indicators of data freshness or last update times. Ultimately we decided not to include this information, as the model used to generate the probabilistic arrival information should **take data freshness into account to provide better estimates to all users**, rather than continuing to support a workaround used by expert users.

Synchronized timelines allow comparison between buses
In our designs, the axis of the timeline in each row is synchronized to the other rows, facilitating comparison between buses. We considered designs with each row having its own time range depending on the prediction (e.g., one row with low variance might show a density plot covering 5-10 minutes from now; another with high variance might have an axis covering 5-15 minutes from now). However, such relative timelines are very difficult to compare between buses on different rows—buses with different variance might look similar because the relative timeline would also cause the density to be scaled.

Encoding probability in space-constrained environments
Given our chosen design, we need an effective way to encode probability at small sizes. We considered several approaches (Figure 4). Most of these are drawn from the literature, including density plots, violin plots, and gradient plots. We also propose variants of two existing discrete plots for visualizing predictive distributions as discrete outcomes, stripeplots and dotplots.

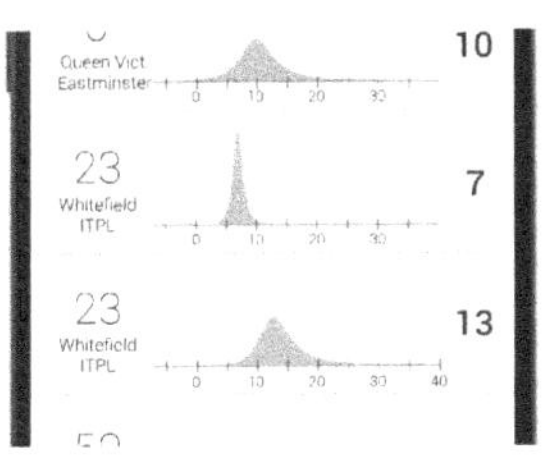

Figure 3. An example of a design we rejected for placing point predictions (along the right side) outside the context of uncertainty, making it more likely to give users a false sense of precision.

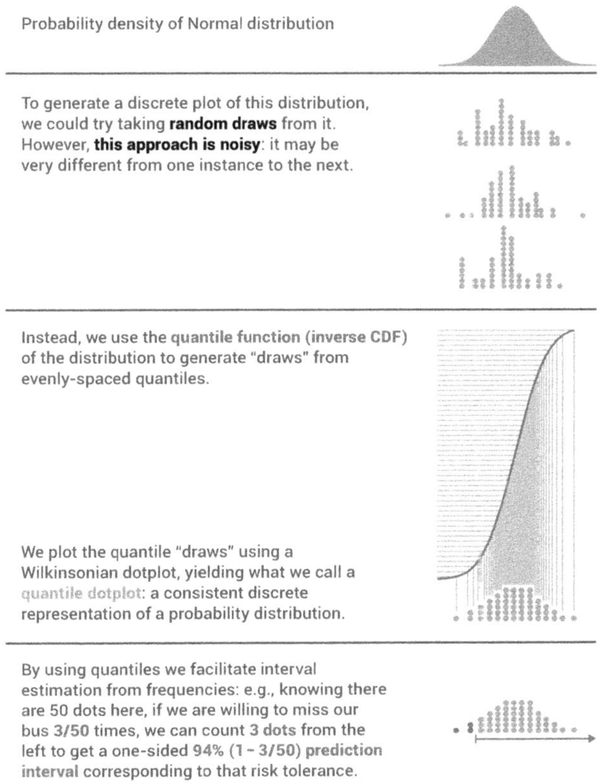

Figure 2. Explanation of quantile dotplots.

Discrete outcome visualizations of continuous variables
We explored several ways to convey a continuous predictive probability distribution as discrete outcomes. The first is based on Wilkinson's dotplots [37], which are typically used to communicate the distribution of experimental samples (e.g., [27]). We instead adopt these plots to display theoretical quantiles from a predictive distribution. As Wilkinson notes, correctly-produced dotplots have the desirable property of also conveying the density of the distribution. Our **quantile dotplots** have this property, as well as the additional property of allowing direct estimation of arbitrary (to a certain precision) predictive intervals through counting (see Figure 2). We believe that this form of natural reasoning about predictive intervals—as frequencies—should allow people to obtain precise estimates of predictive intervals in a way that is easily understood.

We also use **stripeplots** [8] of theoretical quantiles to communicate a continuous probabilistic prediction as hypothetical outcomes. In these, the density of stripes in a region encodes probability density, and as in quantile dotplots (though less easily), predictive intervals can be estimated directly through counting. Where dotplots are a discrete analog to a density plot, stripeplots can be thought of as the discrete analog to a gradient plot.

Tight densities require special attention on small screens
Displaying many rows of predictions on a small screen necessitates relatively small row height. Unfortunately, distributions with low variance will become very tall, exceeding

the row height. Traditional solutions include horizon charts [15] (which we suspect are unfamiliar to lay users), or normalizing all density plots to the same height (which makes comparison difficult). This problem is most pronounced on buses with tight variance, i.e., the most precise predictions. Consequently, for density plots we adopted the compromise approach of scaling down the max height only when it exceeds the row height. This adjustment affects only the predictions of which the model is most certain, so fine-grained resolution of probability becomes less important to most goals. This adjustment is required only for *density*, *dotplot-50*, and *dotplot-100* (in the dense dotplots, instead of scaling we reduce the dot-spacing). Dotplot-20 and stripeplot have the advantage of a *consistent representation of probability in tight densities*: they need not be modified.

Countability may vary from tails to body

Care must be taken in deciding how many hypothetical *draws* (quantiles) to include in discrete plots. Figure 4 compares some of the tradeoffs here: With few draws, as in *dotplot-20*, it is easy to count the dots in the tails and body of the distribution, but the density is less well-resolved. With many dots, as in dotplot-100, counting in the tails is often still easy, but in the body overwhelming; however, density is very well-resolved.

Selected encodings

To select the encodings to evaluate for our final design, we constructed the matrix shown in Figure 4 comparing various properties of the encodings. We selected *density*, *stripeplot*-50, *dotplot-20*, and *dotplot-100* as representing a wide range of possible trade-offs suggested by this matrix.

EXPERIMENT

We conducted an online survey to evaluate the effectiveness of our designs in conveying uncertainty. The goal of this survey was to assess how well people can interpret probabilistic predictions from the visualizations and to elicit their preferences for how the data should be displayed.

Method

To assess how well people can judge probability from our visualizations, we adopted an approach similar to that of Ibrekk and Morgan [18], who presented various representations of uncertainty for weather forecasts and asked subjects to report probabilities (e.g., snowfall >2 inches, or between 2 and 12 inches).

We created four scenarios based on the goals identified in our user survey, each with two questions about the probability of bus arrival. For example, in one scenario the respondent is waiting for a bus, and must decide if they have enough time to get coffee before the bus arrives. They are asked what the chance is that the bus will arrive 10 minutes or earlier, and respond using a visual analog scale, a 100-point slider from 0/100 to 100/100. We call their response the *estimated p* (in contrast to the *true p*, which we calculate from the underlying probability distribution). A bubble on the response slider shows this chance expressed in all three denominators used by the various visualization types (e.g.

	Density	Stripeplot	Density+ Stripeplot	Dotplot(20)	Dotplot(50)	Dotplot(100)
shows discrete, countable events		●	●	●	●	●
fast counting in tails		●		●	●	●
fast counting in body				●		
directly estimate density	●	●	●		●	●
directly estimate quantiles		●	●	●	●	●
tight densities drawn consistently		●		●		
project to axis		●				
easily assess range (min/max)	●	●			●	●
easily assess mode	●		●	●	●	●

Figure 4. Comparison of various encodings of probability we considered for use in our designs.

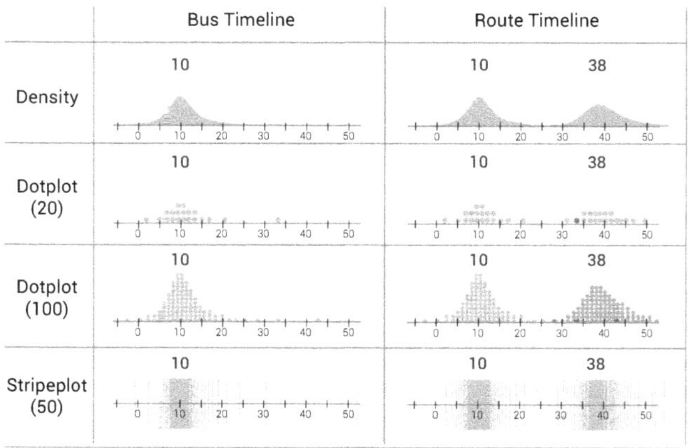

Figure 5. The four types of visualizations selected for evaluation.

"20/100, 10/50, 4/20"), so that participants do not have to do mental arithmetic in the dotplot and stripeplot conditions. The predictions in each scenario were generated from models based on Box-Cox *t* distributions [29] fit to ~2 weeks worth of arrival time data for actual buses in Seattle, but the buses were given fake route names. Participants are also asked how *confident* they are in each probability they estimate. At the end of the survey they rate the *ease of use* and *visual appeal* of each visualization. All subjective ratings are made on 100-point visual analog scales.

Scenario order was randomized between participants. Each participant saw each *visualization type* (*density, stripeplot, dotplot-20, or dotplot-100*) once. Before each scenario, they were also given a brief tutorial explaining the encoding they were about to use. Pairings between scenario and visualization type were also randomized. Participants were also randomly assigned to see all visualizations in the *bus-timeline* or *route-timeline layout*. A full version of the survey can be found in the supplementary material.

Participants

We recruited participants from a variety of locations, including department mailing lists, a local transit blog, and a local forum on reddit.com. Participants were entered into a raffle for 1 $100 Amazon.com gift card and an additional

$25 gift card per 100 participants. Since our primary research questions were about the effect of visualization types, not layout, we ran the first 100 participants only on the *bus-timeline* condition. This threshold was chosen based on a power analysis of data from Hullman *et al.* [17], which suggested a power of at least .8 with our design for detecting similar effect sizes to that study after 100 participants. After reaching 100 participants in the *bus-timeline* layout, the remainder of participants were randomly assigned to either the *bus-timeline* or *route-timeline layout*. After removing 9 participants for incomplete data, we had 320 participants in the *bus-timeline* and 221 participants in the *route-timeline* layouts. Our participants skewed male (71% male). 90% were existing OneBusAway users.

Results

To understand how well each visualization performs, we can examine the *error* in people's probability estimates. We break error into *bias* (do people over- or under- estimate probabilities on average?) and *variance* (how *self-consistent* are people's estimates, whether biased or not?). **So long as the bias is low, we believe that variance is the more important component of error in this task**: over time people can adjust their risk tolerance to a small but consistent bias, but they cannot do so if their estimates are not consistent. We consider overall error, bias, and variance in turn.

Overall error in participants' probability estimates

We start by looking at the overall shape of participants' *estimation error*: logit(*estimated p*) – logit(*true p*) for each question.[4] Figure 6A shows the density of those differences, broken down by visualization type. The *bias* in responses is consistently low and positive across conditions: note that the error distributions all peak in approximately the same place, slightly to the right of 0 (the dashed line). *Variance* appears to be lower in *dotplot-20* compared to the other visualizations: the distribution of error is narrower. However, this does not necessarily equate to more *self-consistent* responses. We therefore use a model to assess bias and variance more systematically and to account for within participant effects.

Regression model for bias and variance

We fit a beta regression to participants' estimated probabilities, which assumes responses are distributed according to a beta distribution. This distribution is defined on (0, 1) and naturally accounts for the fact that responses on a bounded interval have non-constant variance.[5] In other words, the variance of *estimated p* changes with the probability being estimated. For example, at *probability* = 0.5 one can guess 0.5 + 0.4 = 0.9; at *probability* = 0.9 one cannot guess 0.9 + 0.4 = 1.3 (it is greater than 1.0), so responses "bunch up" [30] under 1.0 and variance is lower. Beta regression has been shown to be better-suited to this type of data than linear regression [30].

Our regression uses a submodel for the mean (in logit-space) and the dispersion (proportional to variance, in log-space) [30]. This allows us to model the bias of people's *estimated p* as effects on the mean of their responses, and the variance as effects on the dispersion of their responses. Specifically, we include *visualization*, logit(*true p*), and their interaction as fixed effects on mean response. We include *visualization, layout,* and *gender* as fixed effects on the dispersion (in other words, some visualizations or layouts may be harder to use, resulting in more variable responses; and men may be better or worse at this task). We also include *participant* and *participant* × *visualization* as random effects (some people may be worse at this task, or worse at this task on specific visualizations), and *question* as a random effect (some questions may be harder).

We use a Bayesian model, which allows us to build on previous results by specifying prior information for effects, and report results primarily as posterior distributions with 95% credibility intervals (the Bayesian analog to a confidence interval) [24,25]. We derive priors from fitting a similar model to the data from Hullman *et al.*[17], which had a similar task (estimating cumulative probabilities on three visualizations: a violin plot, animated hypothetical outcomes, and error bars). We set Gaussian priors for fixed effects in our model that capture the sizes of effects seen in the Hullman *et al.* data within 1-2 standard deviations, with skeptical means (0 for intercept and 1 for slope in logit-logit space, corresponding to an unbiased observ`er). We use the posterior estimate of the variance of the random effect of participant in that model as the prior for the variance of random effects in our analysis. Full priors and posterior estimates are available with our data. [6]

Bias in respondent probability estimates

Consistent with Figure 6A, our regression found that estimates were slightly biased on average, and these biases were similar across conditions (more details in supplementary material). Our beta regression model accounts for this bias when estimating the variance of participant responses. The slight overestimation here may be because all of our distributions are right-tailed (positively skewed). This is generally true of transit arrival time data; thus, if the skew is the source of this bias we should expect to see this effect in real-world situations in our domain but perhaps not others. Skewness of distributions is known to affect risk aver-

[4] The logit function is an s-shaped function that transforms probabilities into log-odds, often used when to simplify the analysis of probabilities by transforming them onto the unbounded real line.

[5] Because 0 and 1 are not defined in the beta distribution, we treat answers of 0 and 1 from our visual analog scales as 0.001 and 0.999.

[6] Note that similar results were obtained using more default priors, showing our results are not highly sensitive to choice of priors here. The model was fit using Stan [32], with 16 chains having 20,000 iterations each (half warmup), thinned at 8, for a final sample size of 20,000. Parameters of interest all had effective sample sizes > 10,000 and potential scale reduction factor < 1.001. See https://github.com/mjskay/when-ish-is-my-bus for survey data and code (DOI: 10.6084/m9.figshare.2061876)

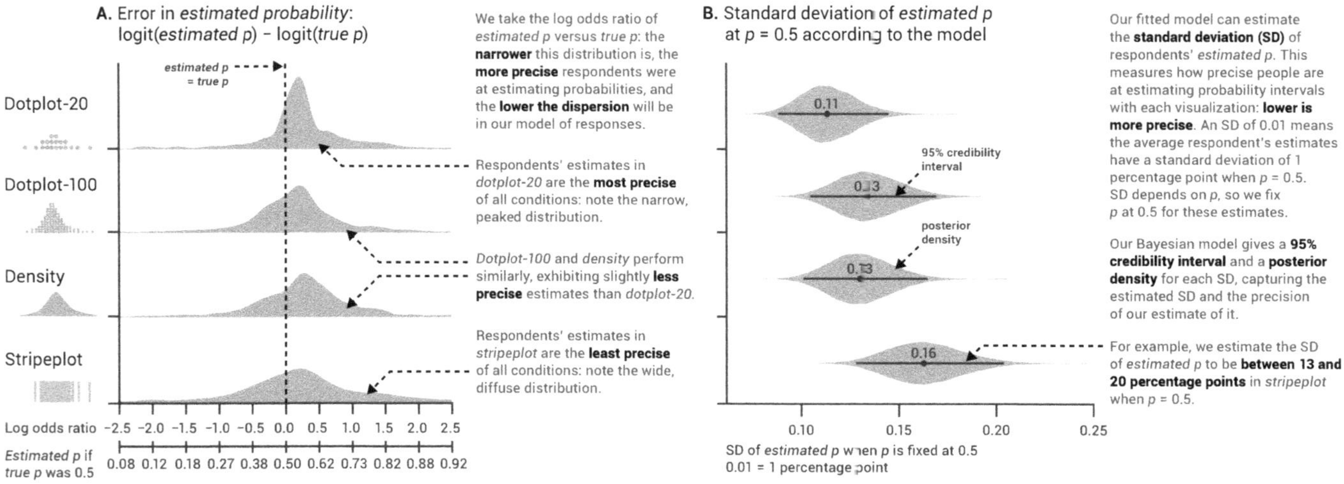

Figure 6. Variance of respondent estimates of probability intervals, (A) as raw data and (B) as estimated by our model.

sion in financial decisions made from density plots [36]; these biases may be related.

Variance in participant probability estimates

As noted above, we believe that variance is more important than bias in this task, as low variance would allow people to adjust their behavior to a consistent bias over long-term usage. We estimate the variance associated with each visualization as a standard deviation in *estimated p* if *p* is fixed at 0.5 (Figure 6B). Figure 7 shows pairwise comparisons of SD for all visualizations (pair specified in left column). *Dotplot-20* has the lowest estimated variance (SD of ~11 percentage points), being about 1.15 times more precise than *density* plots. By contrast, *dotplot-100* has similar variance to *density*, consistent with people estimating area instead of counting dots, perhaps because there are more dots than they may be willing to count.

Confidence

Ideally, greater confidence in a given answer would be associated with less error, indicating that people are able to self-assess their accuracy. We used a similar beta regression to model *confidence* in estimates depending on *visualization*. Participants expressed higher confidence in their estimates on average in the *dotplot-20* condition (mean = 81/100, 95% CI: [77, 83]) than the next-most-confident condition, *dotplot-100* (mean = 73, 95% CI: [71, 76]). At the same time, confidence in the *dotplot-20* condition correlated negatively with *absolute estimation error* (Spearman's $\rho = -0.18$, 95% CI: [−0.13, −0.25]), an association we did not see in other conditions. At least with *dotplot-20*, people have some ability to assess how good their own estimates are. We suspect that this may be due to the fact that with *dotplot-20* one can choose either to be precise (by counting dots) or to give a less precise, less confident answer (by approximating density or area instead of counting).

Ease of use and visual appeal

We also analyzed ease of use and visual appeal using beta regression. *Density* had the highest visual appeal (mean = 66, 95% CI: [64, 67]); *dotplot-20* was less visually appeal-

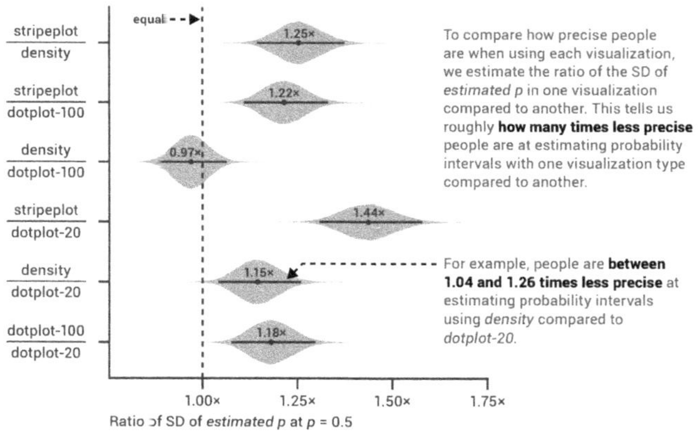

Figure 7. Differences in variance for each visualization type.

ing (mean = 43, 95% CI: [42, 45]). However, despite these differences, ease of use for all visualizations except *stripeplot* was ~60 (*stripeplot* mean = 35, 95% CI: [33, 36]), suggesting only *stripeplot* was found consistently difficult to use. This may reflect *stripeplot's* much higher estimation variance than the other visualizations (higher standard deviation by about 4-5 percentage points when *probability* = 0.5—Figure 6B—or about 1.44 times the SD of *dotplot-20*—Figure 7).

DISCUSSION

Discrete outcomes work best in small numbers

Our results suggest that discrete-outcome visualizations of uncertainty can improve probability estimation in space-constrained visualizations of continuous outcomes if care is taken in their instantiation. While *dotplot-20* improved estimation variance over *density*, *dotplot-100* performed very similarly to *density*. In addition, *Stripeplot* performed very poorly. We believe this may reflect the principle that *discrete plots with too many outcomes converge to continuous encodings*: since counting dots is arduous in *dotplot-100* and *stripeplot-50*, people are more likely to read them like density plots and gradient plots (respectively), nullifying the value of the discrete outcomes. In *dotplot-20*, people can count quickly by using *subitizing*, the ability to quickly recognize rather than count groups of items in number < ~5 [4,13]. Since the vertical groups of dots in dotplot-20 are rarely are over 5 dots high, interval judgements (particularly close to the tails) are often reduced to quick, accurate judgments through subitizing. Thus, **we recommend discrete outcome plots with few enough outcomes to take advantage of subitizing**.

Implications for design and future work

The value of communicating uncertainty

In the first survey, users described goals and unfortunate experiences in OneBusAway that information about uncertainty could help mitigate. In the second survey, most respondents said they appreciated the idea of representing uncertainty. They said this information could help them make better decisions, alleviate their anxiety when the app's information does not match their knowledge, or help them with a problem they commonly experience with OneBusAway.

A minority of respondents said they did not care about the uncertainty information: that point estimates are sufficient. In contrast to respondents who said the information could help, these respondents tended to say the point prediction presented in OneBusAway was consistently accurate. An additional minority actively did not want to receive any information about uncertainty. Several of these people compared evaluating probability information in visualizations to statistics courses. Five feared that, if given uncertainty information, they would become responsible for making decisions, and would have to take responsibility for the wrong decision: "*you're more likely to be unhappy than if you missed the bus and can just blame the app.*" While this represents a small number of participants, we believe that future work is necessary to see how widespread such reactions may be in real-world deployments.

Navigating the precision versus glanceability tradeoff

Designers should attend to the balance of precision and glanceability in representing uncertainty. Participants were divided over whether our visualizations were appropriately glanceable for a transit mobile app. While some said the new designs were easy and clear, more described feeling overwhelmed at least in the context of our experiment and the majority of commenters expressed doubts about being able to use these visualizations while walking to a bus stop. Despite respondent concerns about whether they or others could understand the visualizations, our survey results overwhelmingly show that people understood them.

The designs presented here should be evaluated in longitudinal field studies to assess actual acceptability and use. For example, survey respondents were concerned that the dot plots would compel them to count, but in practice they may find that they count when they want precise estimates but are able to get a good overview from a quick glance. As transit prediction is an everyday practice for many, more sophisticated use of the visualizations may develop over time, making learning an important component to understand in this space.

The designs we evaluated also did not fully exploit interactivity, which might enhance the glanceability of the current static visualizations while preserving uncertainty information. For example, we prototyped a "risk slider" that lets people move the point estimate to match a specific risk threshold; this would allow them to fit the point estimate to their overall preferences or change it to match a specific situation. This feature can be incorporated into any of our proposed designs and should be evaluated as a technique to help resolve the glanceability/false precision tradeoff.

Our research demonstrates that our visualizations can help people accurately, precisely, and confidently evaluate uncertainty, laying the groundwork for future studies evaluating the effects of differences in precision on behavioral measures.

Visual appeal vs. estimation tradeoff

Related to the precision/glanceability tradeoff, people were also divided about preferring the dot plots or the density plots. The dotplots, while ~1.15 times more precise than the density plots and yielding higher confidence, were also rated less visually appealing. We do not know if this is a consequence of unfamiliarity, or if it is because the dotplots are visually busier. It is worth investigating whether the improvement from dotplots is worth decreased visual appeal, or if participants might get used to the dotplots over time.

CONCLUSION

In this paper, we identify general design requirements for visualizing uncertainty on mobile applications as well as domain-specific design requirements for visualizing uncertainty in transit arrival times. From these, we propose a mobile interface for communicating uncertainty in realtime transit predictions in a way that supports users' goals. We developed and evaluated candidate visualizations, including a novel discrete representation of continuous outcomes designed for small screens, quantile dotplots. In a controlled experiment, quantile dotplots improved probabilistic estimates over traditional density plots and facilitated more confident estimation by end-users. Researchers and designers can apply and evaluate these interfaces in the field, with particular attention to opportunities to employ interactivity and other techniques to balance precision and glanceability.

ACKNOWLEDGMENTS

This work was supported by a Google Faculty Award, the Intel Science and Technology Center for Pervasive Computing, the Computing Research Association's Distributed Research Experiences for Undergraduates program, and the Robert Wood Johnson Foundation Health Data Exploration program. We especially thank Martin Wattenberg for valuable feedback.

REFERENCES

1. Nicholas J Barrowman and Ransom A Myers. 2003. Raindrop Plots: A New Way to Display Collections of Likelihoods and Distributions. *The American Statistician* 57, 4: 268–274. http://doi.org/10.1198/0003130032369
2. Sarah Belia, Fiona Fidler, Jennifer Williams, and Geoff Cumming. 2005. Researchers misunderstand confidence intervals and standard error bars. *Psychological methods* 10, 4: 389–96. http://doi.org/10.1037/1082-989X.10.4.389
3. Jacques Bertin. 1983. *Semiology of Graphics: Diagrams, Networks, Maps*.
4. H Choo and S L Franconeri. 2014. Enumeration of small collections violates Weber's law. *Psychonomic bulletin & review* 21, 1: 93–9. http://doi.org/10.3758/s13423-013-0474-4
5. Kristin A Cook and James J Thomas. 2005. *Illuminating the path: The research and development agenda for visual analytics*. Pacific Northwest National Laboratory (PNNL), Richland, WA. Retrieved from http://vis.pnnl.gov/pdf/RD_Agenda_VisualAnalytics.pdf
6. Michael Correll and Michael Gleicher. 2014. Error bars considered harmful: Exploring alternate encodings for mean and error. *IEEE transactions on visualization and computer graphics* 20, 12: 2142–2151. http://doi.org/10.1109/TVCG.2014.2346298
7. Geoff Cumming. 2009. Inference by eye: reading the overlap of independent confidence intervals. *Statistics in medicine* 28, 2: 205–220.
8. Eric D. Feigelson and G. Jogesh Babu (eds.). 1992. *Statistical Challenges in Modern Astronomy*. Springer New York, New York, NY. Retrieved September 25, 2015 from http://www.springerlink.com/index/10.1007/978-1-4613-9290-3
9. Brian Ferris, Kari Watkins, and Alan Borning. 2010. OneBusAway: results from providing real-time arrival information for public transit. *Proceedings of the 28th international conference on Human factors in computing systems - CHI '10*, ACM Press, 1807. Retrieved July 13, 2015 from http://dl.acm.org/citation.cfm?id=1753326.1753597
10. Richard Finger and Ann M. Bisantz. 2002. Utilizing graphical formats to convey uncertainty in a decision-making task. *Theoretical Issues in Ergonomics Science* 3, 1: 1–25. http://doi.org/10.1080/14639220110110324
11. R. Garcia-Retamero and E. T. Cokely. 2013. Communicating Health Risks With Visual Aids. *Current Directions in Psychological Science* 22, 5: 392–399. http://doi.org/10.1177/0963721413491570
12. Gerd Gigerenzer and Ulrich Hoffrage. 1995. How to improve Bayesian reasoning without instruction: Frequency formats. *Psychological Review* 102, 4: 684–704. http://doi.org/10.1037//0033-295X.102.4.684
13. Ernst von Glasersfeld. 1982. Subitizing: The role of figural patterns in the development of numerical concepts. *Archives de Psychologie* 50, 194: 191–218.
14. Theresia Gschwandtnei, Markus Bogl, Paolo Federico, and Silvia Miksch. 2016. Visual Encodings of Temporal Uncertainty: A Comparative User Study. *IEEE Transactions on Visualization and Computer Graphics* 22, 1: 539–548. Retrieved January 8, 2016 from http://www.ncbi.nlm.nih.gov/pubmed/26529717
15. Jeffrey Heer, Nicholas Kong, and Maneesh Agrawala. 2009. Sizing the horizon: the effects of chart size and layering on the graphical perception of time series visualizations. *Proceedings of the 27th international conference on Human factors in computing systems - CHI 09*, ACM Press, 1303. http://doi.org/10.1145/1518701.1518897
16. U Hoffrage and G Gigerenzer. 1998. Using natural frequencies to improve diagnostic inferences. *Academic medicine : journal of the Association of American Medical Colleges* 73, 5: 538–540. http://doi.org/10.1097/00001888-199805000-00024
17. Jessica Hullman, Paul Resnick, and Eytan Adar. 2015. Hypothetical Outcome Plots Outperform Error Bars and Violin Plots for Inferences about Reliability of Variable Ordering. *PloS one* 10, 11. http://doi.org/10.1371/journal.pone.0142444
18. Harald Ibrekk and M.Granger Morgan. 1987. Graphical Communication of Uncertain Quantities to Nontechnical People. *Risk Analysis* 7, 4: 519–529. http://doi.org/10.1111/j.1539-6924.1987.tb00488.x
19. S. Joslyn and J. LeClerc. 2013. Decisions With Uncertainty: The Glass Half Full. *Current Directions in Psychological Science* 22, 4: 308–315. http://doi.org/10.1177/0963721413481473
20. Harshath JR 2015. Redesigning the OneBusAway Mobile Experience.
21. Malte F Jung, David Sirkin, and Martin Steinert. 2015. Displayed Uncertainty Improves Driving Experience and Behavior : The Case of Range Anxiety in an Electric Car. *Proceedings of the 33rd Annual ACM Conference on Human Factors in Computing Systems (CHI '15)*: 2201–2210. http://doi.org/10.1145/2702123.2702479
22. Peter Kampstra. 2008. Beanplot: A Boxplot Alternative for Visual\nComparison of Distributions. *Journal of Statistical Software* 28, code snippet 1: 1–9. Retrieved from http://www.jstatsoft.org/v28/c01/paper

23. Matthew Kay, Dan Morris, Mc Schraefel, and Julie A Kientz. 2013. There's No Such Thing as Gaining a Pound: Reconsidering the Bathroom Scale User Interface. *Ubicomp '13*: 401–410.
24. John K. Kruschke. 2010. Bayesian data analysis. *Wiley Interdisciplinary Reviews: Cognitive Science* 1, 5: 658–676. http://doi.org/10.1002/wcs.72
25. John K. Kruschke. 2011. *Doing Bayesian Data Analysis*. Elsevier Inc.
26. Jock Mackinlay. 1986. Automating the design of graphical presentations of relational information. *ACM Transactions on Graphics* 5, 2: 110–141. Retrieved May 26, 2015 from http://dl.acm.org/citation.cfm?id=22949.22950
27. S. S. Pak, J. B. Hutchinson, and N. B. Turk-Browne. 2014. Intuitive statistics from graphical representations of data. *Journal of Vision* 14, 10: 1361–1361. Retrieved January 8, 2016 from http://jov.arvojournals.org/article.aspx?articleid=2145239
28. K. Potter, J. Kniss, R. Riesenfeld, and C. R. Johnson. 2010. Visualizing summary statistics and uncertainty. *Computer Graphics Forum* 29, 3: 823–832. http://doi.org/10.1111/j.1467-8659.2009.01677.x
29. Robert A Rigby and D Mikis Stasinopoulos. 2006. Using the Box–Cox <I>t</I> distribution in GAMLSS to model skewness and kurtosis. *Statistical Modelling* 6, 3: 209–229. Retrieved September 25, 2015 from http://smj.sagepub.com/content/6/3/209.abstract
30. Michael Smithson and Jay Verkuilen. 2006. A better lemon squeezer? Maximum-likelihood regression with beta-distributed dependent variables. *Psychological methods* 11, 1: 54–71. Retrieved August 27, 2015 from http://www.ncbi.nlm.nih.gov/pubmed/1659476
31. David J Spiegelhalter. 1999. Surgical Audit: Statistical Lessons from Nightingale and Codman. *Journal of the Royal Statistical Society. Series A (Statistics in Society)* 162: 45–58. http://doi.org/10.1111/1467-985X.00120
32. Stan Development Team. 2015. *Stan Modeling Language: User's Guide and Reference Manual*.
33. Barry N. Taylor and Chris E. Kuyatt. 1994. *Guidelines for Evaluating and Expressing the Uncertainty of NIST Measurement Results*.
34. Edward R Tufte. 2006. *Beautiful Evidence*.
35. Amos Tversky and Daniel Kahneman. 1975. Judgment under uncertainty: Heuristics and biases. *Science* 185, 4157: 1124–1131. Retrieved June 20, 2013 from http://link.springer.com/chapter/10.1007/978-94-010-1834-0_8
36. Dennis Vrecko, Alexander Klos, and Thomas Langer. 2009. Impact of Presentation Format and Self-Reported Risk Aversion on Revealed Skewness Preferences. *Decision Analysis* 6, 2: 57–74. Retrieved September 25, 2015 from http://dl.acm.org/citation.cfm?id=1555872.1555874
37. Leland Wilkinson. 2012. Dot Plots. *The American Statistician*. Retrieved September 25, 2015 from http://amstat.tandfonline.com/doi/abs/10.1080/00031305.1999.10474474

Error Recovery in Multitasking While Driving

Ja Young Lee
University of Wisconsin-Madison
Madison, WI, USA
jayoung.lee@wisc.edu

Madeleine C. Gibson
University of Wisconsin-Madison
Madison, WI, USA
mcgibson2@wisc.edu

John D. Lee
University of Wisconsin-Madison
Madison, WI, USA
john.d.lee@wisc.edu

ABSTRACT
Human-technology interactions involving errors undermine acceptance and performance. The effect of errors and the ability to recover from them represent a particularly important consideration for design in safety-critical multitasking situations. However, few studies have considered the recovery process of errors in multitasking situations, such as their contribution to driver distraction. This paper investigates errors that drivers make interacting with an infotainment system. In this study, participants (N = 46) drove a stimulated vehicle and performed word entry tasks on a touch screen. Errors undermined driving and task performance. We also identified four different error recovery strategies and found that the accumulated information related to the driving situation and the characteristics of an infotainment system affected the choice of strategy. Implications for in-vehicle interface design, driver models, and general multitasking design are discussed.

Author Keywords
Task switching; distraction; driving; error; multitasking; interruption.

ACM Classification Keywords
H.5.2. [Information interfaces and presentation (e.g., HCI)]: User Interfaces - *Evaluation/methodology*.

INTRODUCTION
Interaction between humans and computer systems are rarely perfect and precise. Users fail to enter intended information, and systems produce unexpected outcomes in response to the users' input. Regardless of the source, errors can disrupt task completion. Errors often extend task durations, prevent people from achieving a desired goal, impair the overall system performance, and increase annoyance or frustration [19]. In the driving domain, errors in interacting with the in-vehicle interface can jeopardize vehicle control and even lead to fatal crashes. Thus, it is wise to take errors into account when designing the structure and elements of interaction. A large body of literature on human error focused on either the nature of human errors and contributing factors [21,24], or methods to reduce error rates [13]. Other studies produced models of human errors resulting from imperfect memory retrieval or lack of working memory capacity [8,16]. From these studies, we can glean insights for good interface design, such as providing good feedback about the current mode, having consistent menu structure throughout the system, distinguishing actions between unrelated functions, or minimizing memory load.

CHI'16, May 07-12, 2016, San Jose, CA, USA
© 2016 ACM. ISBN 978-1-4503-3362-7/16/05$15.00
DOI: http://dx.doi.org/10.1145/2858036.2858238

When it comes to the interaction with in-vehicle displays, human errors have been largely ignored. For instance, the National Highway Traffic Safety Administration (NHTSA) provides guidelines on visual manual interaction and recommends removing tasks that cause errors during more than 50 percent of test trials [1]. Many empirical studies exclude trials with errors from analyses, and driver models implicitly assume that drivers perform the secondary task accurately (e.g., [10,23]). To the best of the authors' knowledge, no study has considered the consequences of drivers' errors in performing a secondary task, except for a computational model that considered errors in a multitasking scenario [12]. Nevertheless, errors can affect how well drivers interleave secondary tasks with driving tasks, jeopardizing driving performance [7]. To understand how secondary task errors affect driving, we need to study the reaction of drivers to the errors.

Compared to error prevention, how people react to or recover from errors has received relatively little attention. Zapf and Reason [28] questioned the error prevention approach and described the error handling process by dividing the process into error occurrence, detection, explanation, solution development, and recovery. Among these subprocesses, Mo and Crouzet [20] reviewed error recovery and its modes, such as undoing the current error, finding an intermediate stable state, buying time to find a better solution, or using other resources to bring the system to the desired state. Skantze [26] suggested that the consequence of errors depends on the response. From the design perspective, Kontogiannis [15] proposed five factors that can help people recover from errors, including memory cues, perceptual cues, and previous experience in errors. These studies considered only errors that occurred during single-task situations, and cannot explain how errors might affect people in multitasking situations where they must interleave multiple tasks. To bridge the gap, this study describes how errors and recovery from errors affect multitasking performance.

To account for error recovery in multitasking, we can borrow concepts from studies of interruptions, because errors interrupt users' intended sequence of actions by requiring them to correct the error before proceeding to the next action. Thus, the 'error correction task' acts as an interrupting task. According to interruption studies, an interruption can be characterized by four critical events: alert to an oncoming interrupting task, beginning of interrupting task, end of interrupting task, and resumption of interrupted task [27]. The time between the alert and the beginning of an interrupting task (i.e., interruption lag) depends on a user's reaction to the interruption, while the time between the end of the interrupting task and the resumption of the original task (i.e., resumption lag) is influenced by preparation for the interruption, duration of the interruption, complexity of the interrupting task, and the timing of interruption [5].

These concepts from interruption literature can be applied to people's reaction to errors. The time between the end of error correction and the return to the original task (analogous to resumption lag) may depend on the complexity of the error, urgency and priority of the task, the timing of error, and so forth. The difference between interruptions and errors is that errors are involuntary interruptions initiated by external events, while the interruptions can arise from both external and internal sources. Additionally, the goal of the correcting error (interrupting task) is aligned with the goal of the task that the error occurred (interrupted task), while the goal of interrupting task does not always match the goal of interrupted task in general. Thus, when an error occurs in a multitasking situation, we can assume that an additional interruption task is added to the original task sequence.

Driving includes many elements that are representative of many multitasking situations. Drivers often strategically interleave the primary driving task and the secondary task to balance their two goals: to maintain vehicle stability and to complete the secondary task [11]. They tend to interleave two tasks at natural break points of the secondary task, defined by the contents of the task or the interaction structure of the task [3,10,17]. Those break points tend to be subtasks boundaries, or the end of a small discrete task decomposed from the entire task that is characterized by small memory carryover, edge of a decomposed task at higher level, or change in difficulty [9]. Computational driver models delineate these subtask boundaries where the drivers interleave two tasks and predict drivers' performance on driving and secondary task, based on the time the drivers spend on each of two tasks.

When an error interrupts a task, however, recovering actions may interfere with typical task switching behavior. There are two possible effects of errors on drivers' behavior while resolving and recovering from errors: the driver can defer a response to the secondary task error and switch attention back to driving earlier than usual, or engage in completing the secondary task and spend more time on it than usual. The former assumes that the error acts as a subtask boundary that encourages people to switch attention [4,10], and the latter assumes that the error further activates the task goal and motivates task completion [2].

In this paper, we study how people switch between the primary driving task and a secondary word entry task when an error interrupts the secondary task. By investigating the word entry errors that naturally occur during trials, we address (1) how errors interrupt multitasking performance, operationalized as vehicle control and glance patterns, (2) how error recovery strategies influence overall performance, and (3) what influences error recovery strategy adoption. We measured drivers' vehicle control with the variability in lateral and longitudinal control of a vehicle. To measure the task performance, we calculated the total time to complete a task. The durations of single glance off road and the total eyes off road time (TEORT) while completing a task were used as measures of attention drawn away from the safety-critical driving tasks. In other word, it measures driver distraction, which is defined as "a diversion of attention away from activities critical for safe driving toward a competing activity" (p.34) [22]. Finally, we summarize implications of this study for reducing the distraction potential of in-vehicle systems.

METHODS

Participants

48 participants from four different age groups (18-24, 25-39, 40-54, and 55+ years old, 12 from each age group) with an equal number of males and females (6 from each gender) completed the study. Two participants were removed from the data analyses due to recording errors.

Driving Task and Apparatus

The simulator used for the study was the NADS MiniSim, and the driving scenario used was defined by the NHTSA visual-manual guidelines. The NADS MiniSim consists of one 65" screen placed at a distance of about 54" from the driver and includes a standard steering and pedal setup. Following the NHTSA visual-manual guidelines, participants were instructed to drive in the right lane at a speed of 50 mph until the lead vehicle appeared. Participants were instructed to maintain a fixed following distance of 220 feet for the entire experiment. The simulated environment was an undivided, four-lane highway with a shoulder on each side. A GoPro camera was mounted to record drivers' head and eye movements.

Secondary Task and Apparatus

Participants completed a word entry task on a 7" touchscreen attached at a typical center-stack position (Figure 1). This display had a text block on the top that shows letters entered and a keyboard on the bottom (Figure

2). The participants could use backspace key (←) to delete a letter. All participants performed the task in two system conditions: one with a delay and the other without a delay. The system with delay showed the result of each entry only after a delay of 500-1200ms, which was drawn from a uniform. However, participants were able to type multiple letters ahead. The order of system condition (delayed or non-delayed) was counterbalanced, and the trials within a system condition were randomized. Participants completed 12 trials for each system: 6 with short words (4 letters) and 6 with long word (12 letters). Words for the tasks were selected from the text reading and text input assessment study conducted by Boyle et al.[6].

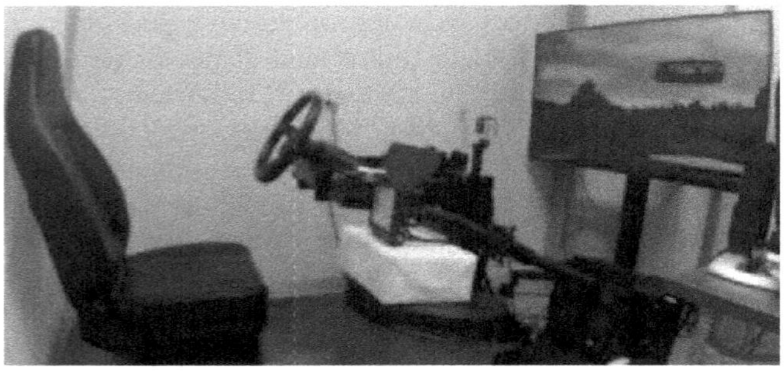

Figure 1 Driving simulator with a touchscreen at center-stack position.

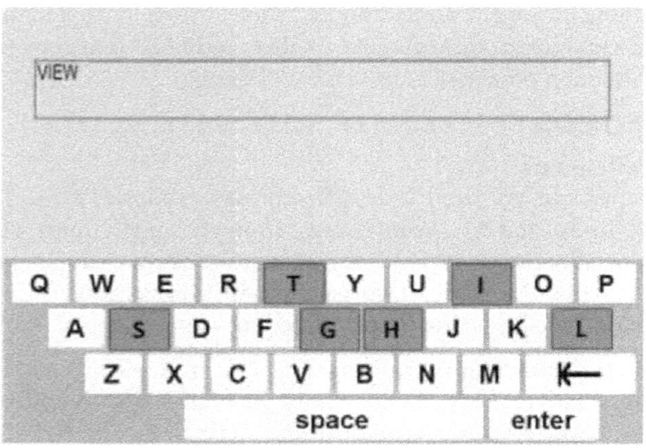

Figure 2 Touchscreen text entry task on the center stack of the driving simulator.

Procedure

Upon arrival, participants read and signed the informed consent form and completed a demographics and driving history survey. The experimenter orally reviewed the instructions for the tasks and participants were shown examples of each task. Each participant completed a three-minute practice drive and received feedback on their performance maintaining a 220-foot following distance from the lead vehicle. Participants repeated the practice drive until they felt comfortable with the task. When the practice ended, participants completed a wellness questionnaire to assess prevalence of simulator sickness symptoms. Then participants performed the data collection trials blocked by condition. Each condition began with four practice trials, followed by twelve data collection trials. Each trial lasted one minute, thus each condition took approximately 16 minutes to complete. When the data collection ended, participants were compensated for their time.

Data Preparation

Driving measures were directly collected by the NADS MiniSim. We measured vehicle control performance by the standard deviation of lane position and the standard deviation of headway distance, which were calculated according to SAE J2944 [29]. The lane position is defined as the offset of vehicle center from the center of the lane (in feet), indicating lateral instability of a vehicle. The headway distance is calculated as the distance between the front bumper of the following vehicle and the front bumper of the lead vehicle (in feet). Because the lead vehicle was driving at a constant speed, variability in headway distance indicates imperfect speed control. We sampled both the lane position and the headway distance at 60Hz.

Eye glance data was manually coded following the NHTSA visual-manual guidelines using a video logging tool Morae®. A glance is defined as the time from the moment at which the direction of gaze moves toward the touchscreen to the moment it moves away from it [30].

We used durations of individual glance and the sum of multiple glance durations within each trial (i.e., total eyes off road time, TEORT). These measures are defined in the visual-manual NHTSA driver distraction guidelines for in-vehicle electronic devices and used to evaluate the level of distraction associated with secondary tasks [1]. The glance duration affects many aspects of safe driving such as lane keeping, headway maintenance, or detection and response to events on the road. The TEORT is a measure of the total visual demand of the task and has been related to crash risk [14,18]. If a driver adopts shorter, but more glances, the single glance duration is reduced, but the TEORT may be increased.

RESULTS

In this study, errors were defined as 'when a participant became aware of an input (letter) that did not match his/her intended goal (word) and pressed backspace key (←) to erase the input'. The errors that were not caught by participants—those where the participant did not use the backspace key were excluded from this analysis. Thus, the interrupted task was a word entry task, and the interrupting task was the correction of an error in that task. The error correction task goal was achieved by pressing a backspace key, and resumption of the original task was achieved by pressing the first correct key after removing the incorrectly entered letter.

For all of the statistical analysis, we used alpha level 0.05 and fit linear mixed effects model with the lme4 package of R. The degrees of freedom were adjusted to reflect differences in sample variances (i.e., Satterthwaite approximation), resulting in fractional degrees of freedom. The degrees of freedom in ANOVA test were also adjusted based on the random effect of participants and tested words. When the random effect influenced the value of dependent variable, the random effect was included in the model and the degrees of freedom were reduced. If the random effect was negligible, the random effect was removed from the model and degrees of freedom were increased.

Errors Occur Frequently

298 letter entry errors naturally occurred in the 24 trials of each of the 46 participants. Out of 24 trials, 12 involved a system delay and 12 did not. For each delay condition, half of the trials involved entering a long word with 12 letters, and the other half of the trials involved entering a short word with 4 letters. 156 errors occurred in the delay condition and the other 142 errors occurred in no delay condition. 108 errors occurred in the short words and 190 errors occurred in the long words. All 46 participants made at least one error during the experiment, and participants made an average of 6.48 errors throughout the experiment (SD = 2.89). The mean number of errors was 1.21 (SD = 0.47) per trial. An error occurred at least once in 22.6% of the all trials. For each letter, the probability of being typed wrong was 2.9%.

Errors Disrupt Multitasking

Black solid lines in Figure 3 show that errors increased total task time ($F(3, 1046.1) = 132.8$, $p < 0.01$), with different magnitude in the two systems ($F(3, 1044.0) = 4.91$, $p < 0.01$). The task time was also influenced by the length of words ($F(1, 98.9) = 31.0$, $p < 0.01$). Each error increased the task time by 4.6 seconds. This includes time to detect an error, to determine how to correct the error, to correct the error by pressing backspace key, and to press the correct letter key. If the driver decided to defer error correction, the time the driver looked forward and focused on the driving task before returning to correct the error is also included in this value. The increased task time indicates that errors substantially increase the demands of secondary task engagement. Extending the secondary task duration may lead the task to overlap high demand road segments (e.g., highway to exit ramp) leading the driver to engage in secondary tasks in situations in a way that the driver did not originally intend.

The blue dashed lines in Figure 3 show that the total-eyes-off-road-time (TEORT) also increased with the number of errors ($F(3, 1040.0) = 152.6$, $p < 0.01$), and the increment magnitude was different for the two systems ($F(3, 1039.0) = 7.20$, $p < 0.01$). The length of words also influenced the TEORT ($F(1, 330.1) = 67.0$, $p < 0.01$). Compared to the effect of errors on task time, the increased TEORT suggests a more direct increase in task total demand of the secondary task and higher crash risk.

Overall driving performance measures, such as standard deviation of lane position (Figure 4, top) and standard deviation of headway distance (Figure 4, bottom) worsened with the occurrence of errors. Both the occurrence of error and the length of word significantly influenced standard deviation of lane position ($F(1, 1071.8) = 56.8$, $p < 0.01$; $F(1, 1057.4) = 110.0$, $p < 0.01$) and standard deviation of headway distance ($F(1, 18.6) = 25.5$, $p < 0.01$; $F(1, 1065.6) = 36.5$, $p < 0.01$). These results indicate that errors undermine vehicle control.

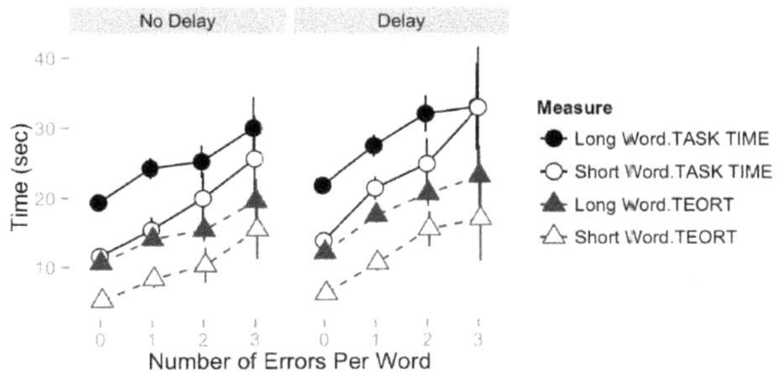

Figure 3 The total task time (solid lines and circles) and the total eyes off road time (dashed lines and triangles) as a function of the number of errors that occurred in each trial and length of the word with and without delays. Vertical lines indicate 95% confidence intervals.

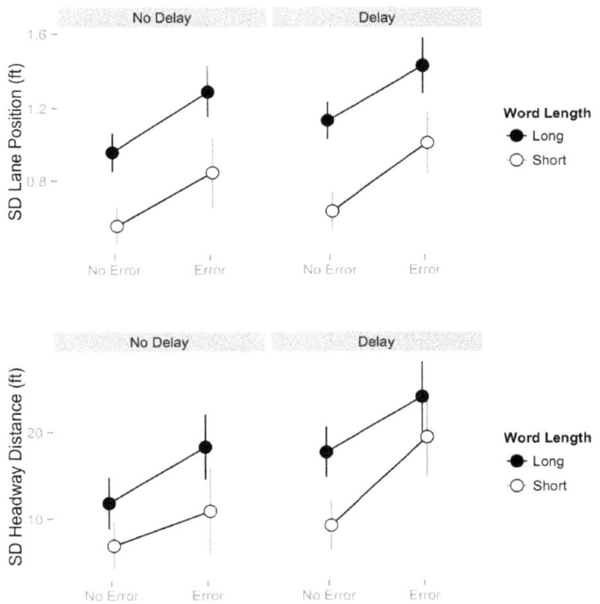

Figure 4 The standard deviation of lane position (top) and headway distance (bottom) as a function of error occurrence and the length of the word with and without delay. Vertical lines indicate 95% confidence intervals.

When participants perceived that they made an error, many decided to switch attention from the word entry display to the road. This means that the drivers chose to switch attention before error correction. The odds ratio of switching attention at the error was 1.85 (confidence interval = [1.41, 2.46]). However, this attention switch did not lead to shorter off-road eye glances. The top row of

Figure 5 shows that the average single glance duration increased with the occurrence of error ($F(1, 6388.4) = 41.6$, $p < 0.01$). There was an interaction of delay and word length ($F(1,6386.1) = 4.2$, $p = 0.04$). Increased duration of a single glance might have contributed to the increased total task time, along with the greater number of glances.

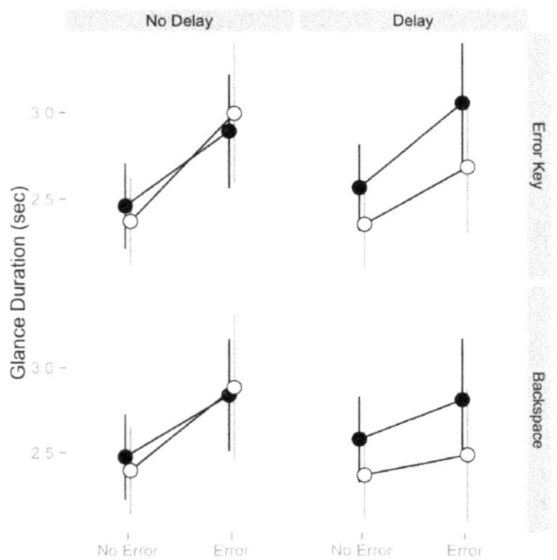

Figure 5 The glance duration to the secondary task associated with error occurrence (top) and error correction (bottom) as a function of error occurrence and the length of the word with and without delay. Vertical lines indicate 95% confidence intervals.

A similar tendency was observed after the participants corrected the error. After pressing the backspace key, they tended to switch attention back to the road with odds ratio 1.80 (confidence interval = [1.36, 2.37]), and glance duration was again longer as shown in the bottom row of Figure 5 ($F(1, 5602.2) = 15.8$, $p < 0.01$). This might have also contributed to the increased total task time. The bottom row of Figure 5 shows the average glance duration associated with error correction by pressing a backsapce key. Both results indicate the error increases the probability of switching attention back to the roadway, but these switches do coincide with shorter glances away from the road, compared to normal glance switching pattern.

Drivers Adopt Four Different Error Recovery Strategies

We classified drivers' task switching behaviors into four strategies based on the task switching decisions that drivers make at two pivotal moments: the first is after perceiving and before correcting the error, and the second is after correcting the error and before resuming the secondary task. This is as if an error interrupts the secondary task and adds 'error correction' task to the task sequence with a constraint that the secondary task cannot be resumed until the error correction task is complete.

There were four strategies that a driver can adopt after making an error (Figure 6). First, the driver can continue performing the secondary task without switching attention back to the road. This requires longer glances away from the road, but saves time to relocate attention by reducing the number of glances. Second, the driver can switch attention to the road and perform the driving task after perceiving the error and before correcting the error, and continue to resume the task after correcting the error. Third, the driver can switch attention after correcting the error and before the resuming the task. Finally, the driver can switch attention whenever possible, both before and after correcting the error. This strategy directs attention back to the road and sample visual information more frequently, but at the same time, it requires time to relocate attention repeatedly.

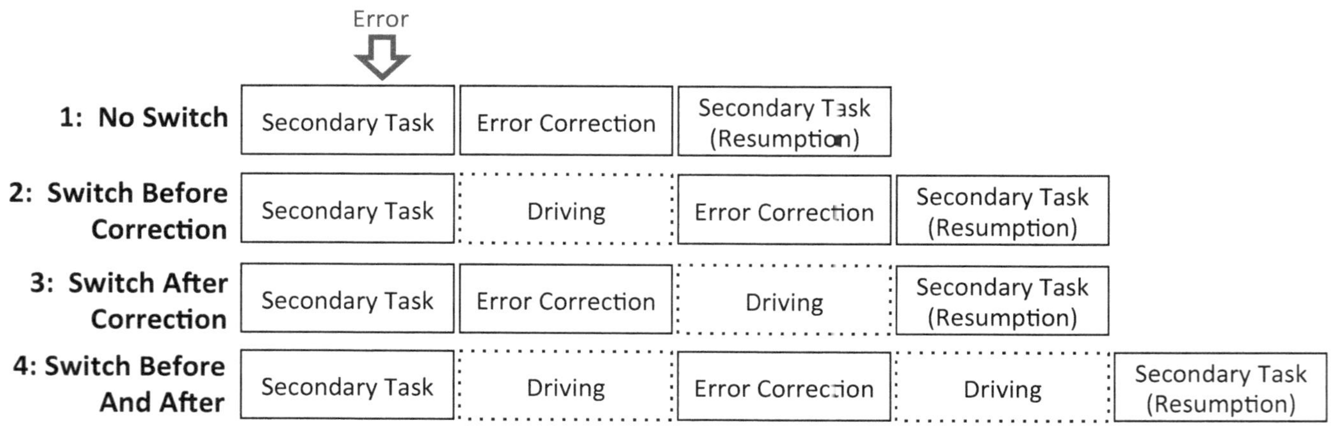

Figure 6 Four error recovery strategies defined according to the task switching decisions before and after correcting the error. Here we have the primary driving task, the secondary task, and an error correction task.

For clearer analyses, we selected cases with the following button press sequence: letter – backspace – letter. If the trial terminated after pressing the backspace (without further entering any letter), the trial was excluded from the analyses. As a result, the proportion of each of the four error recovery strategies was 12.6% (No Switch), 18.6% (Switch Before Correction), 25.1% (Switch After Correction), and 43.7% (Switch Before and After

Correction). Drivers most frequently adopted the fourth strategy, switch attention before and after correcting an error.

System characteristics influenced strategy selection. In the delay condition, drivers switched more often and used more of the 'switch before and after' strategy and less of the 'no switch' strategy (Figure 7). The fact that the driver was not immediately able to see inputs and errors might have influenced strategy selection.

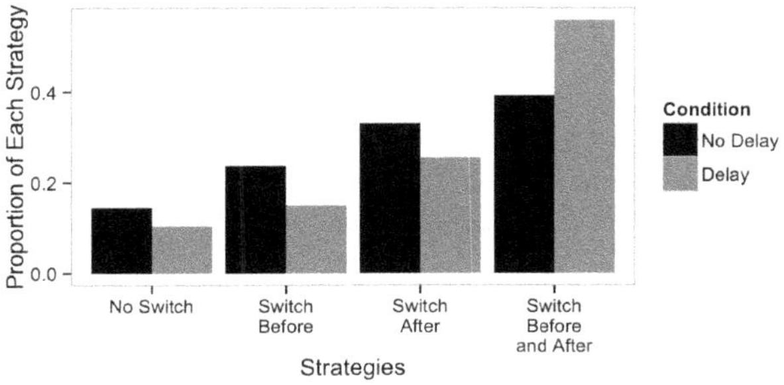

Figure 7 The proportion of each error recovery strategy in No-Delay condition and Delay condition.

Figure 8 shows the total task time and TEORT for each error recovery strategy. Each point denotes a single eye glance observed during the experiment, and box range is from the 25th to 75th percentile of the data, with the median marked with a horizontal line. For this analysis only, we used trials with only one error to avoid multi-strategy trials. The task time and TEORT differed by strategy ($F(1, 167.4) = 9.4, p < 0.01$; $F(1,161.6) = 11.4, p < 0.01$). As indicated in the graph, more frequent switch of visual attention (e.g., switch before and after) lead to longer task time and TEORT. It shows that the strategy of not switching attention led to shorter task time and shorter TEORT.

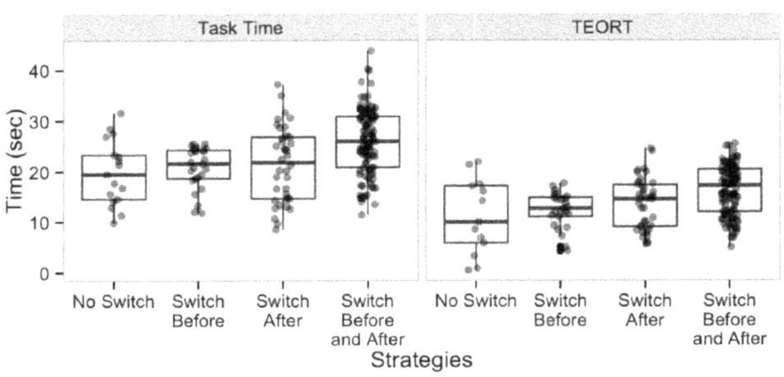

Figure 8 The total task time and the total eyes off road time by error recovery strategy.

Figure 9 shows individual off road glance glance duration with the occurrence of error. The duration of glance was shorter in the no switching condition, ($F(3, 439.7) = 13.7, p < 0.01$). While 'no switch' had one long glance to the display, 'two switches' had at least three short glances to the display. Yet, the glance durations were mostly longer than the mean glance duration away from the road ($M = 1.79$, $SD = 0.99$). This implies that errors can provoke long glances when drivers try to correct without letting the error interrupt the secondary task with a glance back to the road.

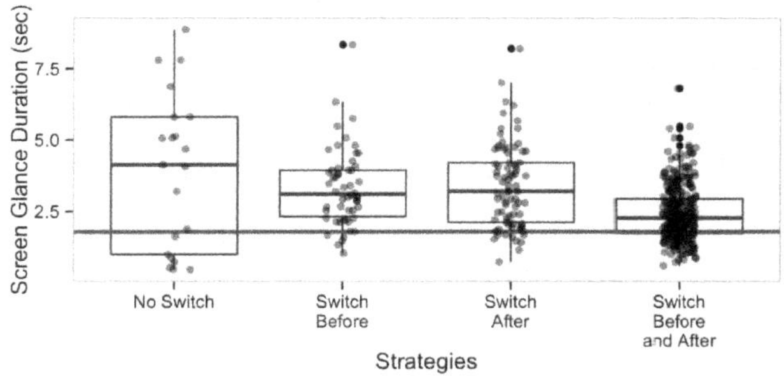

Figure 9 Duration of individual glances to the secondary task display. Red horizontal line indicates the mean duration of all glances away from the road from the current experiment.

Although the single glance duration differed in four strategies, vehicle control remained similar. The vehicle stability measures (standard deviation of lane deviation and headway distance) did not significantly differ among four cases ($F(3, 230.1) = 0.44, p = 0.73$; $F(3, 234.0) = 0.57, p = 0.64$) during the time between making an error and resuming the secondary task.

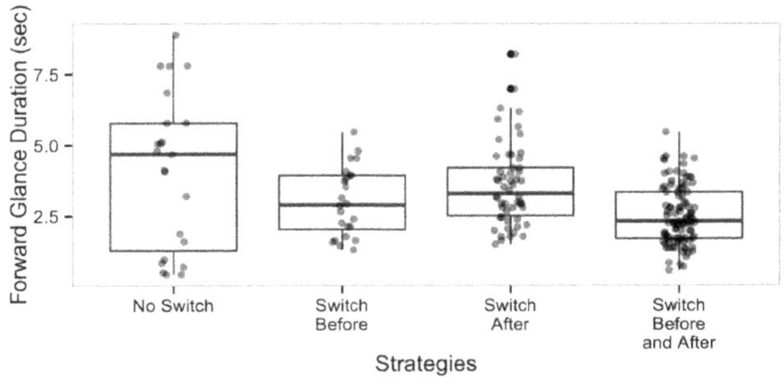

Figure 10 Forward glance before the first decision (after making error and before correcting error).

While it is important to identify the different strategies, it is perhaps more crucial to understand what leads drivers to adopt these strategies. We examined the time drivers spent on the driving task prior to each switch decision. Interestingly, forward glance duration before each error was associated with strategy selection. When the forward glance was long, before the error, participants tended to continue the secondary task and fix the error by pressing the backspace. Figure 10 shows the forward glance duration before the occurrence of secondary task error, for each strategy. When the forward glance was longer, people continued to correct the error without switching attention (as in 'no switch' and 'switch after correction').

This effect continued after correcting the error. Figure 11 shows the effect of the most recent forward glance duration carried over to the second decision of task switching, after correcting the error and before resuming the secondary task. We compared 'no switch' versus 'switch after correction' and 'switch before correction' versus 'switch before and after correction' separately, because the forward glances in the former took place even before they made an error, while the forward glances in the latter took place in between the error and the correction. When comparing 'no switch' and 'switch after correction' (left), the forward glance of 'switch after correction' was shorter ($F(1, 69.3) = 4.1$, $p < 0.05$). As the label implies, drivers switched attention after correction when the forward glance was shorter. When comparing the forward glance between 'switch before correction' and 'switch before and after correction' (right), the forward glance duration of 'switch before and after correction' was shorter ($F(1, 118.9) = 41.4$, $p < 0.01$), and thus drivers switched visual attention after correction.

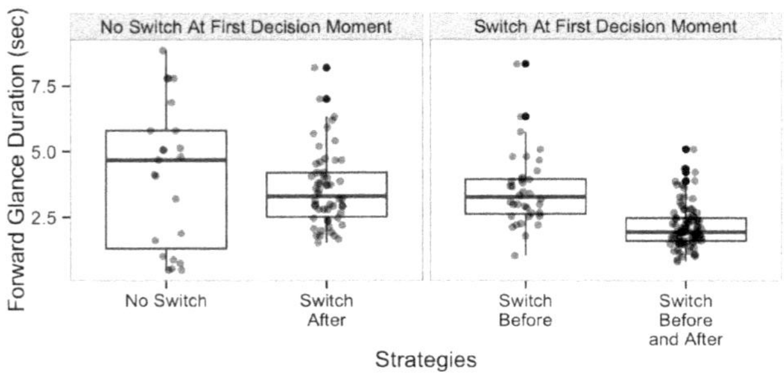

Figure 11 Forward glance before the second decision (after correcting error and before resuming the secondary task).

On the contrary, the time drivers spent on the display did not affect their decision to switch attention (i.e., longer glances away from the road did not always lead to an attention switch). This implies that the task switching decision depends more on the amount of time they spent looking at the forward roadway than the time they looked away. Therefore, these data suggest that people accumulate roadway information as a function of "glance duration$^{1.5}$" and that the information decays over time. Also, these data suggest that the attention switch depends on how this information relates to their internal threshold, resembling Senders and others' study [25]. At a pivotal moment, such as after making one key press, if the amount of roadway information the driver has is lower than the threshold, then the driver will switch attention back to the roadway to obtain information about the roadway situation. However, if the amount of roadway information remaining is higher than the threshold, the driver will continue looking at the secondary screen. Figure 12 depicts such information accumulation and dissipation and its effect on task switching.

Figure 13 shows that the amount of roadway information drivers has influences task switching. The amount of information is operationalized as 1.5^{th} power of forward glance duration minus off-road glance duration. Left facet of the graph show the relationship between the amount of information and the switching decision at the moment of first decision (i.e., before error correction). Drivers tended not to switch attention when the amount of information exceeded a hypothetical threshold ('no switch' and 'switch after correction') but did switch attention when there was not enough information left ('switch before correction' and 'switch before and after correction'). The right facet of the graph shows the amount of information at the moment of second decision (i.e. after error correction), and drivers followed a similar pattern. They continued the task with more information ('no switch' and 'switch before correction') but switched tasks with less information ('switch after correction' and 'switch before and after correction').

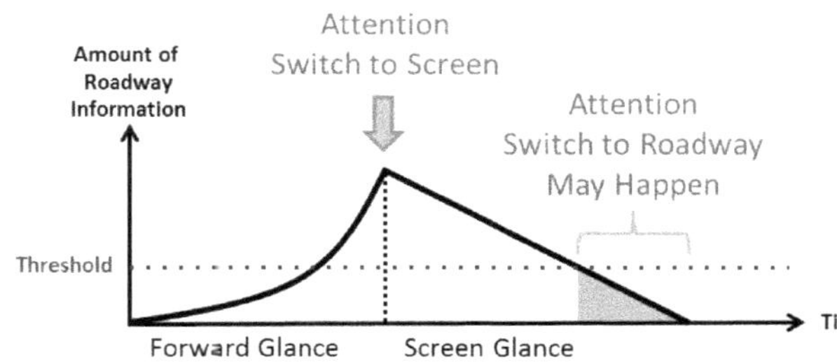

Figure 12 Information accumulates during forward glance exponentially and exhausts linearly during glance away from the road. If the amount of information at a pivotal decision moment is under threshold, the driver may switch attention back to the roadway.

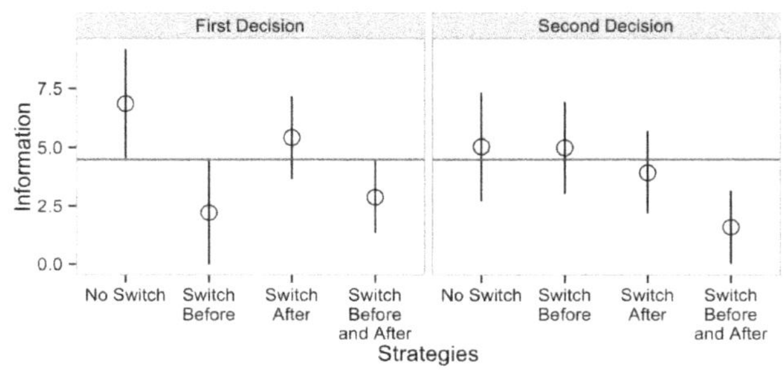

Figure 13 The amount of information (= forward glance duration$^{1.5}$ – time occuluded$^{1.0}$) at the moment of the first decision (left) and the second decision (right). Red horizontal line indicates potential threshold of decision.

Lastly, we calculated the resumption lag, which was the duration from the backspace key press to the correct key press, assuming that the drivers resumed the secondary task by pressing the correct key. We only took the duration that drivers looked at the in-vehicle display. The glance time spent on the secondary screen was longer in 'no switch' and 'switch before correction', where drivers continued to the secondary task after correcting the error (Figure 14). The difference in time between the first two groups (i.e., no switch of attention after correcting an error) and the last two groups (i.e., switch of attention after correcting an error) suggests that the process of resuming the secondary task happened not only when the drivers' visual attention was on the display, but also while they were gazing at the forward roadway.

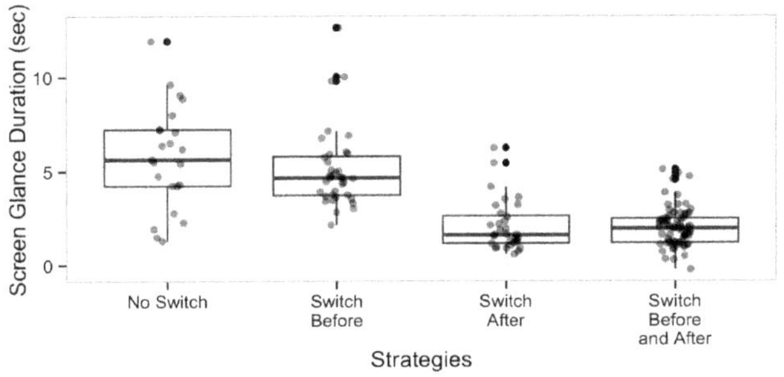

Figure 14 Total glance duration towards the secondary task screen while resuming the task (between backspace and the next key press for task resumption).

DISCUSSION

In the current experiment, error in a word typing task was fairly common, and the effect of the errors was troublesome. Occurrence of an error increased the total task time, the total duration of attention away from the roadway, and the overall vehicle instability. Increase in task time indicates that the drivers are not fully engaged in the driving task for a longer period, and longer individual glances away from the road implies a higher probability of missing unexpected events on the roadway. Poor lane and speed keeping performance is directly related to the risk of accident. It is notable that the duration of each glance away from the road was longer with errors, even though the odds ratio of switching attention back to the road was higher. This indicates that the error encourages drivers to switch attention as if it were a subtask boundary rather than encouraging a continuation, but it does not shorten the glance duration to promote safe driving. Thus, we can conclude that errors, regardless of recovery strategy, impair safe driving.

We borrowed and applied the concept of task interruption to predict potential ways of interleaving driving and secondary task. The 'error correction' task is added to the original sequence of tasks with a constraint that the 'error correction' task needs to be done before resuming the secondary task. With such restriction, we identified four error recovery behaviors based on task switching decisions at two moments, before and after the error correction, to better understand the process of error recovery. In almost half of the cases, drivers switched visual attention after each action, even though such a decision increased the total task time and total eyes off road time compared to less switching strategies. With this switching decision, however, drivers could reduce the duration of each glance away from the road, compared to continuing decision. It was beneficial in that the drivers could collect information more frequently from the roadway, and they are less likely to miss unexpected events on the forward roadway. As suggested in the other studies [7], because the single glance time is more important than the total time distracted from driving, in-vehicle interface should facilitate the strategy that allows more frequent breaks in the task for safer driving.

We also observed that people adapted behavior to system design and switched more often when there was a delay in the letter entry system interface. Delays in the system did not provide immediate feedback on the result of each letter entry and removal. Hence, holding visual attention on the secondary task display was a waste of attentional resource for the drivers. This suggests that moments that do not require visual resource nudge drivers to look back on the road. In other words, immediate feedback makes drivers visually focus longer on the task.

Findings from the task resumption process led to similar conclusions. Even though there was a perceptual cue on the screen (i.e., last letters entered), the time drivers spent looking at the screen was shorter when attention switched back to the road between error correction and task resumption. It means that drivers' internal reconstruction of the task also occurred while attention was on the road. The perceptual cue used in the task was simple and latent and required little attention. If the visual cue required more attention, drivers would have spent more time on the screen. Hence, to prevent extensive engagement in the secondary task, sufficient but not greater than necessary visual information should be provided to let the drivers focus on driving for the rest of the time.

From this line of analysis, we also gained insight into the underlying forces of task switching decisions -- preceding forward glance durations largely influenced decisions to switch attention. If drivers have a clear mental model of the road due to long forward glances to the roadway, they stay longer on the secondary task. This clear mental model means the drivers' roadway information does not need to be urgently updated, hence drivers are distracted for a longer period.. We could explain the decision by partially adapting Senders and others' uncertainty model [25], which assumes that drivers switch attention when the information accumulated during the forward glance is exhausted (i.e. from looking away). With a higher demand for updated information on roadway, drivers switched attention. Our results show that more weight was placed on information accumulation during the driving task than the word entry task. To generalize, task switching decisions may depend on the demand of higher priority tasks.

Additionally, this experiment showed the disruptiveness of errors on driving and task performance. Theoretically, the recovery process of error was understood from interruption. This approach is applicable to more complicated situations, such as multitasking between more than two tasks or errors that have more than one recovery method (e.g., deleting and retyping a letter to correct an error or auto correction). Practically, the experiment showed that the strategies adaption was influenced by system characteristics (i.e., delay) and task demands (i.e., information needed). The performance of each error recovery process suggested that in-vehicle technologies should support more frequent task switching by providing visual-free moments for safer driving. In addition, future design research should not mindlessly include or exclude error trials, as they have distinct pattern associated with driving and task characteristics.

Errors may affect distraction more than other design features. The scenario we used on the experiment was fairly simple and less complex than reality. If the demand of the roadway increases, drivers may choose to adapt behavior accordingly and switch attention more often. However, even though a driver switches attention often, the driver would still take time fixing errors and reconstructing the task. During this process, an interface design may promote safer interaction strategies when an error occurs and provide easier means to recover. Another design may hold the users' attention on the screen by promoting longer paths to error recovery. If interactions will occur during driving, the interface should be designed to easily recover from errors, beyond trying to prevent errors. These findings translate to mobile devices, as drivers today use devices such as smartphones or tablets as their primary in-vehicle interactive display. Any device that draws driver visual attention and distracts them from the roadway should not only prevent errors but also provide means for quick recovery from errors, without requiring a great amount of effort. Thus, evaluation of interfaces should also consider their robustness to error.

To date, computational driver models have not taken human error into consideration. However, the ability to predict the possibility of error and the subsequent reaction to errors will help models better replicate reality and enable models to evaluate the potential for distraction of an interface in the context of human errors. Not including errors in driver models could severely underestimate the potential for distraction of future designs. This study may help extend such cognitive model to account for the recovery from errors. As the results suggests, system characteristics and the demand of tasks may act as guiding parameters in the model in predicting driver behavior and evaluating the interface designs. Incorporating the results of the current study will enhance the usefulness of driver models.

The results of this study can be extended to any multitasking situations where people have different options to recover from errors, and the interruption approach can reframe the approach to human errors. This experiment demonstrated that the primary task information and secondary task structure influences the user behavior when they realize an error. For example, imagine designing an email alarm system with a sorting function on a smartphone; users might make an error such as accidentally sorting an email to a wrong folder. Such error could influence the performance of the email alert system and primary task. In this case, what steps do they need to go through to correct the error? Interruption approach to error recovery can help make a list of strategies that the users can choose from. Would such steps direct users' attention to email sorting system immediately or let them finish a primary task and return to re-sort the email? The key findings of this experiment suggest that a less urgent primary task and an immediate feedback of the email alert system would engage users into correcting an error. Overall, this study shifts the approaches of previous studies about predicting or preventing errors to recovering from errors and suggests the importance of evaluating users' performance in the face of errors.

ACKNOWLEGMENTS

Data used in this paper is derived from research supported by the U.S. Dept. of Transportation – National Highway Traffic Safety Administration under Contract No. DTNH22-11-D-00237. Any opinions, findings, and conclusions or recommendations expressed in this publication are those of the authors and do not necessarily reflect the views of the NHTSA or the U.S. DOT.

REFERENCES

1. National Highway Traffic Safety Administration. 2013. *Visual-Manual NHTSA Driver Distraction Guidelines for In-Vehicle Electronic Devices (Docket No. NHTSA-2010-0053).*
2. Erik M. Altmann and J. Gregory Trafton. 2002. Memory for goals: An activation-based model. *Cognitive science* 26, 1: 39–83.
3. John R. Anderson and Dan Bothell. 1998. An Integrated Theory of List Memory. *Journal of Memory and Language* 38, 4: 341–380.
4. Jelmer P. Borst, Niels A. Taatgen, and Hedderik van Rijn. 2010. The problem state: a cognitive bottleneck in multitasking. *Journal of experimental psychology. Learning memory, and cognition* 36, 2: 363–82.
5. Jelmer P. Borst, Niels A. Taatgen, and Hedderik van Rijn. 2015. What Makes Interruptions Disruptive? *Proceedings of the 33rd Annual ACM Conference on Human Factors in Computing Systems - CHI '15*, ACM Press, 2971–2980.
6. L N Boyle, J D Lee, Y Peng, et al. Text Reading and Text Input Assessment in Support of the NHTSA Visual-Manual Driver Distraction Guidelines.
7. Duncan P. Brumby, Dario D. Salvucci, and Andrew Howes. 2007. An empirical investigation into dual-task trade-offs while driving and dialing. *Proceedings of the 21st British HCI Group Annual Conference on People and Computers: HCI...but not as we know it - Volume 2*, British Computer Society, 11–14.
8. Michael D. Byrne and Susan Bovair. 1997. A Working Memory Model of a Common Procedural Error. *Cognitive Science* 21, 1: 31–61.
9. Shamsi T. Iqbal and Brian P. Bailey. 2006. Leveraging characteristics of task structure to predict the cost of interruption. *Proceedings of the SIGCHI conference on*

Human Factors in computing systems - CHI '06, ACM Press, 741.

10. Christian P. Janssen, Duncan P. Brumby, and Rae Garnett. 2012. Natural Break Points: The Influence of Priorities and Cognitive and Motor Cues on Dual-Task Interleaving. *Journal of Cognitive Engineering and Decision Making* 6, 1: 5–29.
11. Christian P. Janssen and Duncan P. Brumby. 2010. Strategic adaptation to performance objectives in a dual‐task setting. *Cognitive science* 34, 8: 1548–1560.
12. Christian P. Janssen and Duncan P. Brumby. 2015. Strategic adaptation to task characteristics, incentives, and individual differences in dual-tasking. *PLoS One*.
13. George R. Kim, Allen R. Chen, Robert J. Arceci, et al. 2006. Error reduction in pediatric chemotherapy: computerized order entry and failure modes and effects analysis. *Archives of pediatrics & adolescent medicine* 160, 5: 495–8.
14. Sheila G. Klauer, Feng Guo, Bruce G. Simons-Morton, Marie Claude Ouimet, Suzanne E. Lee, and Thomas A. Dingus. 2014. Distracted driving and risk of road crashes among novice and experienced drivers. *New England Journal of Medicine* 370, 1: 54–59.
15. Tom Kontogiannis. 1999. User strategies in recovering from errors in man–machine systems. *Safety Science* 32, 1: 49–68.
16. Christian Lebière, John R. Anderson, and Lynne M. Reder. 1994. Error Modeling in the ACT-R Production System. *Proceedings of the Sixteenth Annual Conference of the Cognitive Science Society*, 555–559.
17. Ja Young Lee, Madeleine Gibson, and John D. Lee. 2015. Secondary task boundaries influence drivers' glance durations. *Proceedings of the 7th International Conference on Automotive User Interfaces and Interactive Vehicular Applications - AutomotiveUI '15*, ACM Press, 273–280.
18. Y. Liang, John D. Lee, and L. Yekhshatyan. 2012. How Dangerous Is Looking Away From the Road? Algorithms Predict Crash Risk From Glance Patterns in Naturalistic Driving. *Human Factors: The Journal of the Human Factors and Ergonomics Society* 54, 6: 1104–1116.
19. Helena Mentis and Geri Gay. 2003. User recalled occurrences of usability errors. *CHI '03 extended abstracts on Human factors in computing systems - CHI '03*, ACM Press, 736–737.
20. Jin Mo and Yves Crouzet. 1996. Human error tolerant design for air traffic control systems. In *Probabilistic Safety Assessment and Management'96*. 400–405.
21. Donald A. Norman. 1983. Design rules based on analyses of human error. *Communications of the ACM* 26, 4: 254–258.
22. Michael A. Regan, John D. Lee, and Kristie L. Young. 2008. *Driver Distraction: Theory, Effects, and Mitigation*. CRC Press.
23. Dario D. Salvucci, M Zuber, Ekaterina Beregovaia, and Daniel Markley. 2005. Distract-R: Rapid prototyping and evaluation of in-vehicle interfaces. *Proceedings of the SIGCHI Conference on Human Factors in Computing Systems*, 581–589.
24. Nadine B. Sarter and David D. Woods. 1995. How in the World Did We Ever Get into That Mode? Mode Error and Awareness in Supervisory Control. *Human Factors: The Journal of the Human Factors and Ergonomics Society* 37, 1: 5–19.
25. J W Senders, A B Kristofferson, W H Levison, C W Dietrich, and J W McDonald. 1967. *The attentional demand of automobile driving*.
26. Gabriel Skantze. 2005. Exploring human error recovery strategies: Implications for spoken dialogue systems. *Speech Communication* 45, 3: 325–341.
27. J. Gregory Trafton, Erik M. Altmann, Derek P. Brock, and Farilee E. Mintz. 2003. Preparing to resume an interrupted task: effects of prospective goal encoding and retrospective rehearsal. *International Journal of Human-Computer Studies* 58, 5: 583–603.
28. Dieter Zapf and James T. Reason. 1994. Introduction: Human Errors and Error Handling. *Applied Psychology* 43, 4: 427–432.
29. SAE J2944 Operational Definitions of Driving Performance Measures and Statistics.
30. SAE J2396 Definitions and Experimental Measures Related to the Specifications of Driver Visual Behavior Using Video Based Techniques.

Personalized Compass: A Compact Visualization for Direction and Location

Daniel Miau **Steven Feiner**
Columbia University
New York, NY, USA
{dmiau, feiner}@cs.columbia.edu

ABSTRACT

Maps on mobile/wearable devices often make it difficult to determine the location of a point of interest (POI). For example, a POI may exist outside the map or on a background with no meaningful cues. To address this issue, we present Personalized Compass, a self-contained compact graphical location indicator. Personalized Compass uses personal *a priori* POIs to establish a reference frame, within which a POI in question can then be localized. Graphically, a personalized compass combines a multi-needle compass with an abstract overview map. We analyze the characteristics of Personalized Compass and the existing Wedge technique, and report on a user study comparing them. Personalized Compass performs better for four inference tasks, while Wedge is better for a locating task. Based on our analysis and study results, we suggest the two techniques are complementary and offer design recommendations.

Author Keywords

Visualization; small screens; spatial cognition, maps.

ACM Classification Keywords

H.5.2. [Information Interfaces and Presentation]: User Interfaces—Graphical user interfaces (GUI)

INTRODUCTION

As the display area of an information space becomes smaller, information is often left out. When important information required by a spatial cognition task is not displayed, an otherwise reasonable task could become difficult (e.g., route planning to an off-screen destination [18]). A small display also increases the probability of Desert Fog [24]—a condition in which the display information is devoid of meaningful cues to assist users in making decisions. These two issues are often discussed separately in the literature. In this paper, we refer to them together as the "Where is x?" problem, occurring whenever some POI x is off display, or on display but with Desert Fog present.

The "Where is x?" problem is frequently encountered on a map, a common information space that is the focus of this paper. Driven by the growth of mobile and wearable devices, as well as the demand of accessing geospatial data on these devices, the ever decreasing size of maps makes the "Where is x?" problem an increasingly frustrating issue.

CHI'16, May 07–12, 2016, San Jose, CA, USA
© 2016 ACM. ISBN 978-1-4503-3362-7/16/05$15.00.
DOI: http://dx.doi.org/10.1145/2858036.2858068

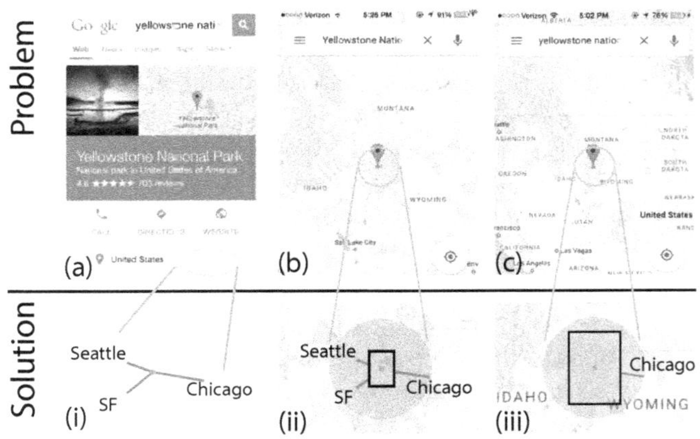

Figure 1: Where is Yellowstone National Park? Answering this question from a mobile search result often involves (a–b) unnecessary application switching and (b–c) repetitive zooming. (i–iii) A P-Compass uses important POIs to provide a first-order approximation to the answer, and can function independently or with a map. (a–c) Screenshots from a smartphone. (i–iii) Proposed P-Compass visualizations to be superimposed on the screenshots at the designated locations.

Take location search as an example. Figure 1(a) shows a search result for the keywords "Yellowstone National Park" on a smartphone. The embedded stamp-size map is rich in information. Ironically, due to Desert Fog, it fails to communicate *where* Yellowstone National Park is. To find out the answer, users may tap the stamp-size map to switch to a map app and then continue fighting Desert Fog by repeatedly zooming out (Figure 1b–c). When a satisfying overview is eventually reached (Figure 1c), details such as Yellowstone Lake are no longer visible, and the original application context (the web search engine) has been dismissed. Similar "Where is x?" problems are often encountered in social media, Internet articles, and local business reviews—whenever a stamp-size map is presented. For obvious reasons, the issue occurs even when the area of a map reduces to zero, as when users try to determine the location indicated by a geo-tag, a zip code, an address, or GPS coordinates. The "Where is x?" issue is ubiquitous, with or without a map.

Now suppose we ask a knowledgeable person the same question, "Where is Yellowstone National Park?" They may first gauge the geographic knowledge of the questioner, either via a mental assessment or verbal questions. Based on the initial evaluation, they may then describe the location of Yellowstone National Park in relation to other geographical entities (e.g., Yellowstone National Park is located *k* miles northwest of *abc*; Yellowstone National Park is located between *abc* and *def*).

We make two observations based on this scenario. First, the person constructs an answer from assumed *a priori* knowledge of the questioner. Second, in terms of information complexity (measured in bits), the information provided in the answer is very compact, to the degree that it can be effectively transmitted via language. Put a different way, an approximated answer to the "Where is *x*?" question, provided in a frame of reference known by the questioner, requires surprisingly little information.

Inspired in part by these observations, we present Personalized Compass (P-Compass), a compact graphical representation that communicates the location of *x* with the support of personal *a priori* POIs. Figure 1(i) shows P-Compass as a standalone location indicator. It uses three major U.S. cities to establish a reference frame, which in turn indicates the location of Yellowstone National Park. Note that a P-Compass can occupy a relatively small footprint.

P-Compass can also be integrated into the zooming interface, as seen in Figure 1(ii–iii). The black rectangle in the center of the compass indicates the boundary of the visible map. As a user zooms in the map, the size of the black rectangle updates accordingly, providing immediate feedback on the relative scale of the visible map to the distances to the three major cities.

We integrated P-Compass and Wedge [18], a well-known technique to visualize off-display POIs[1], into a customized iOS/OS-X map app and used the app regularly in daily life for over a year. Based on our field experience, we analyzed the characteristics of Wedge and P-Compass, and designed and ran a formal user study to compare the two. To ensure a fair comparison, our study used a common set of fictional POIs, instead of personalizing the POIs for each participant.

Our analysis and study reveal that P-Compass and Wedge complement each other. Wedge's strength, which is P-Compass's weakness, is to place an off-screen POI at its absolute location. However, the need to locate an off-screen POI makes it difficult to perform certain inference tasks, which are better carried out with P-Compass. In addition, as the distance to an off-screen POI increases, and/or the size of a display decreases, we show that the benefits of P-Compass eventually outweigh those of Wedge.

This paper thus makes the following contributions: 1) P-Compass, a compact graphical location indicator designed to address the "Where is *x*?" problem; 2) An analysis of P-Compass and Wedge; 3) A formal user study comparing these two approaches with tasks derived from our field experience, showing the advantages of P-Compass for inference tasks; and 4) Recommendations to designers, based on our analysis and study results.

[1]Wedge is also a frequent baseline technique in previous studies (e.g., [5, 7, 21]), which is why we chose it for comparison.

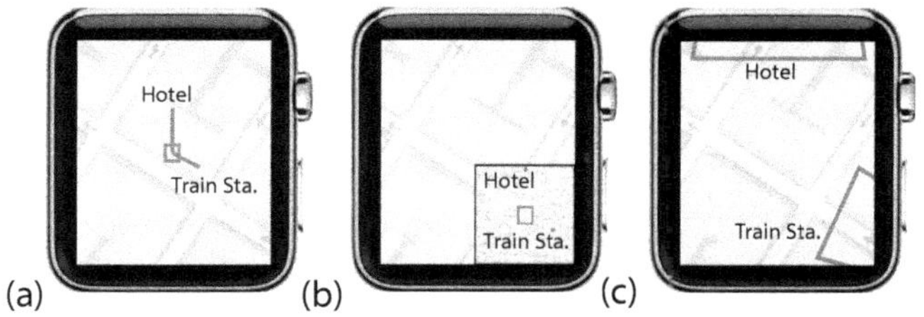

Figure 2: Where am I? Localization on a smartwatch form factor using (a) P-Compass, (b) Overview+Detail, and (c) Wedge. The two off-screen POIs are 6 cm ("Hotel") and 4 cm ("Train Sta.") from the centroid of the display. (In true scale.)

RELATED WORK

A large body of work has been dedicated to approaches for presenting overview and detail on a limited display area. Cockburn et al. [10] categorize these into four basic schemes:

Overview+Detail. This scheme, also referred to as *spatial separation* [10], presents an information space at different scales side-by-side (Figure 2b). Variants include stacking representations of an information space at different scales on top of each other [26], providing the user a magnified view [37, 25] with which to interactively explore an information space, and allowing the user to interactively build hierarchies of different regions of interest at different scales [23].

Zooming. Zooming [3, 20] separates information at different scales temporally, so it is also referred to as *temporal separation*. While zooming is well suited to interactively exploring an information space, it requires an unnecessary round trip between detail and overview for a user to gain context while focusing on detail. In Figure 1(c), for example, a reverse zoom is required if the users wants to confirm that they saw a lake in the park. Zooming can also be challenging when a user is mobile or their hands are busy.

Focus+Context. This scheme aims to blend the seams between overview and detail. Distortion [31, 4] and folding [12, 21] are typically applied to emphasize or deemphasize certain portions of an information space. Two representative frameworks [8, 14] have been proposed to include a wide range of approaches. However, it is often difficult to perform metric measurements from the modified information space.

Cue-Based. The cue-based scheme uses proxies to selectively visualize POIs that may not be visible in the displayed information space [1, 18, 21, 28, 19, 6]. A representative technique in this category is Wedge [18] (Figure 2c). A Wedge is a partially clipped isosceles triangle, whose invisible apex is located at an off-screen POI. Users estimate the location of that POI by visually completing the shape (Figure 3).

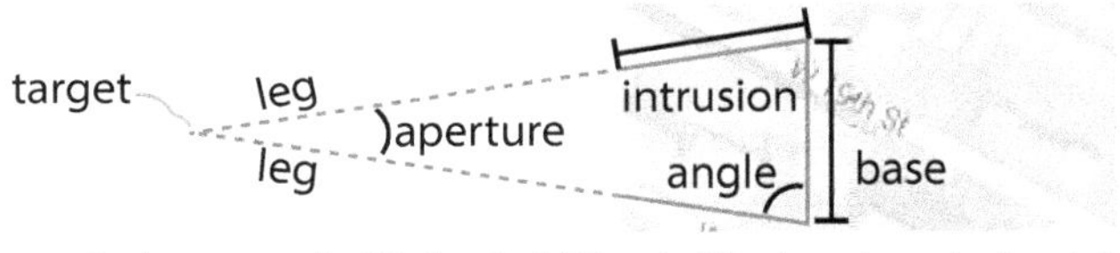

Figure 3: Anatomy of a Wedge (solid lines). The target can be located using visual shape completion (dashed lines).

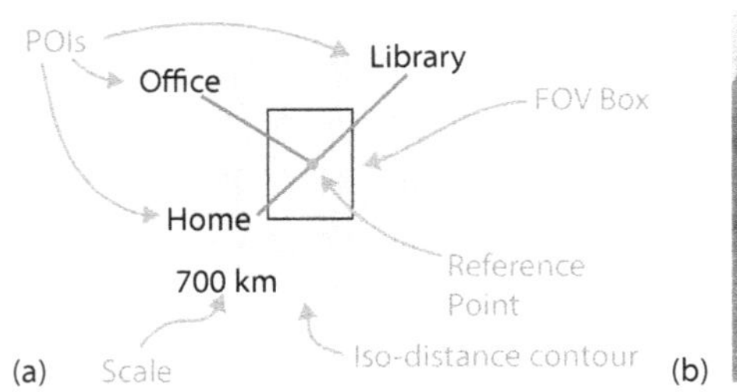

Figure 4: (a) Anatomy of a P-Compass. (b) P-Compass prototype.

P-Compass is a hybrid technique that integrates spatial separation and cue-based techniques, and can be incorporated into a zooming interface. Figure 2 compares P-Compass, Wedge and overview map. While P-Compass and overview map both add an overview to the underlying detail view (Figure 2a,b), the use of POI cues allows P-Compass to reduce the amount of occlusion. Furthermore, while P-Compass and Wedge both use proxies to indicate off-screen POIs (Figure 2a,c), the overview provided by P-Compass allows it to communicate the relationship between multiple off-screen POIs.

Several researchers have proposed variants of compasses that point to POIs instead of magnetic north [13, 11, 35, 9]. However, P-Compass is more than a specialized compass; P-Compass visualizes the direction and *location* of a POI in relation to personal a priori POIs (e.g., landmarks). Personal a priori POIs have been exploited in generating personalized routes [30], tourist maps [16], and textual descriptions of a POI [2]. In contrast, we propose a compact graphical location indicator that can be used with or without a map.

Much research aims to visualize a potentially large number of off-screen POIs [1, 18, 5, 7]. Instead, our focus is on using as few off-screen POIs as possible to answer the question "Where is *x*?" Furthermore, we are interested in a solution that can scale to distant off-screen POIs.

PERSONALIZED COMPASS

The anatomy of a P-Compass can be seen in Figure 4(a). A P-Compass consists of a reference point, and one or more needles to communicate the direction and distance to POIs. When a P-Compass is shown on a map, a field of view (FOV) box—a 2D scale, can be added as an additional cue to indicate the location of an off-display POI with respect to the boundary of the display. The needles can extend into the FOV box, to signify the reference point, or stop at the edge of the FOV box, as shown in Figure 1. As the user zooms into the map, the FOV box decreases in size, eventually becoming a dot. An optional iso-distance contour assists the user in comparing distances to POIs (and separates P-Compass from the background), while an optional numerical scale denotes the distance to the iso-distance contour.

A central idea of P-Compass is the use of personal, a priori POIs to establish a frame of reference. Personal POIs have been known to play an important role in cognitive maps [36] (mental representations of environments). As a POI—be it a landmark, an intersection, a store, or a city—becomes known to a person, the POI becomes a reference with which they reason and continue to develop their cognitive maps. The use

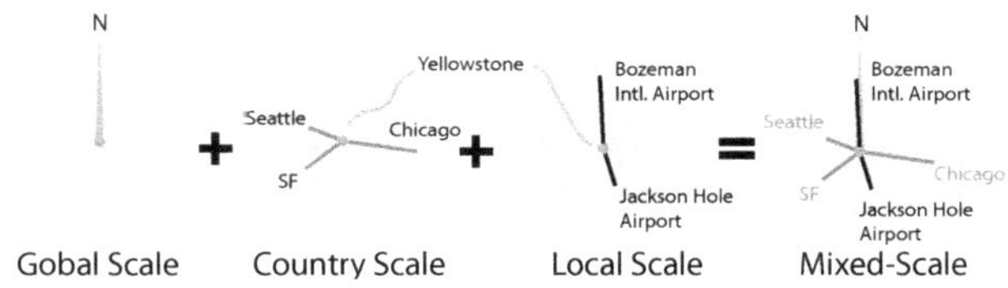

(a) Location of Yellowstone National Park and its nearest airports.

(b) Location of Yosemite National Park.

Figure 5: Stackability. Information at multiple scales is combined into a single P-Compass. (a) Information at each scale is read independently. (b) Information at all scales is related.

of personal POIs can effectively provide a frame of reference for the user [15, 34], while significantly reducing the amount of information needed to be shown on a graphical representation. As a result, a P-Compass occupies a compact footprint, and can work alone or in conjunction with a map.

Proof-of-Concept Prototype

We implemented a custom iOS/OS-X map application incorporating a P-Compass (Figure 4b). The application, using Apple MapKit, supports zoom, pan, rotate, and location search. The P-Compass, implemented in OpenGL, updates dynamically as the user interacts with the map, and can be resized and translated with simple gestures.

We manually entered a master list of personal POIs for our field prototype. Other methods to collect a-priori POIs could include drawing them from personal GPS [38] and cellular network [22] location history, or from social network traces (e.g., Facebook check-ins and Google Maps Saved Places), and inferring them from public sources (e.g., Flickr) by data mining [32, 33]. These methods could be combined and continuously refined using machine learning.

We apply a simple greedy algorithm (detailed in the supplementary material [29]) to select *n* POIs that are roughly equally distributed in orientation to automatically form a P-Compass. Alternatively, the POIs can be selected manually by the user. We also implemented Wedge [18] in the same application. The user can toggle between P-Compass and Wedge, or show both simultaneously.

For over a year, the first author used this application in daily life on an iPhone, as well as an iPad, laptop, and desktop, to explore the characteristics and design space of P-Compass. Below, we describe the design and analysis of P-Compass, with references to real-world scenarios as well as comparisons with Wedge.

Stackability

P-Compass allows multiple scales of information to be stacked on top of each other (Figure 5). Thus, a compass can be converted into a P-Compass *in place* simply by stacking relevant information on top. Users can access information at different scales simultaneously. Figure 5(a) shows three scales combined in a single P-Compass. POIs at each scale serve a different purpose—global-scale information indicates the orientation of the diagram; country-scale information indicates the location of Yellowstone National Park; local-scale information visualizes which local airport is closer.

Representing *related* information in multiple scales can enhance readability. The P-Compass at the left of Figure 5(b) displays all POIs at the same scale. Since Yosemite National Park is much closer to San Francisco and Les Vegas than to New York City, two of the compass needles are nearly invisible. The P-Compass at the right presents a multi-scale view of the same information. The scale indicator is essential in this case, and indicates the ratio of the two scales is 1:9. Presenting information at mixed-scale can increase the complexity of a visualization. Design techniques (e.g., color coding) can be applied to distinguish information at different scales.

Optimized for Personal Use

In the context of a mobile map application, there is often one particular POI, a reference point, that a user cares about (e.g, the location of the user in a "you-are-here" map). P-Compass, a centralized representation, is optimized for tasks involving *n* (off-screen) POIs-to-1 reference point.

Let *VD* be a virtual display formed by Figures 6–7. *VD* contains four Wedges and four P-Compasses, together visualizing four off-screen POIs (see Figure 7 for definitions of terms). It is trivial to use PC_{r_a} (Figure 6) to draw inferences from $r1$ and $r2$ with respect to reference point O_a (e.g., between $r1$ and $r2$, determining which one is closer and by how much). PC_{r_a} also makes it easy to estimate the direction of $r1$ or $r2$—a common pedestrian and vehicle navigation task. In contrast, it could be difficult to perform these tasks using W_{r1} (Figure 6) and W_{r2} (Figure 7), since a user cannot draw inferences from a POI without first estimating its absolute location.

Wedge is optimized for placing a POI near the boundary of a display. W_{r1} provides direct visual guidance near the edge of *VD* so a user can place $r1$ at its absolute location. Knowing the absolute locations of off-screen POIs can help perform tasks involving *m* (off-screen) POIs-to-*n* reference points. For example, determining which of the *n* on-screen hospitals is farthest away from the *m* off-screen traffic jams [18].

In comparison, it could be difficult to use a P-Compass to place a POI at its absolute location. Using PC_{r_a}, a user will need to first estimate the relative location of $r1$ with respect to the FOV box, and then transfer the estimate to the actual scale. In addition, two P-Compasses, each optimized for a different reference point, could differ significantly, as can be seen from comparing PC_{r_a} and PC_{r_d}. It could be challenging to use a P-Compass to perform tasks with respect to a non-optimized point.

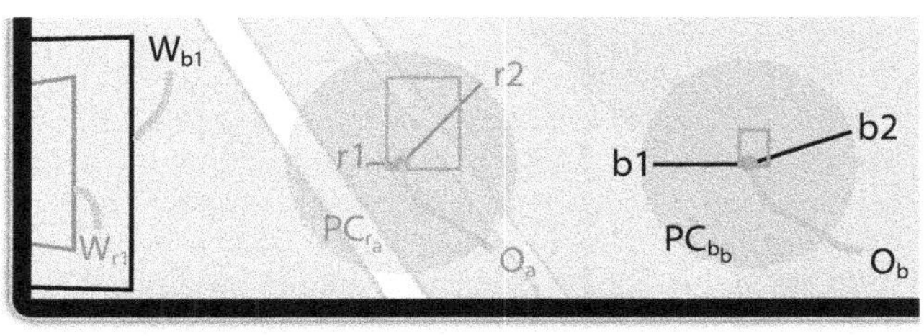

Figure 6: This figure and Figure 7 together form two corners of a virtual display nearly the size of this page. See Figure 7 caption for details.

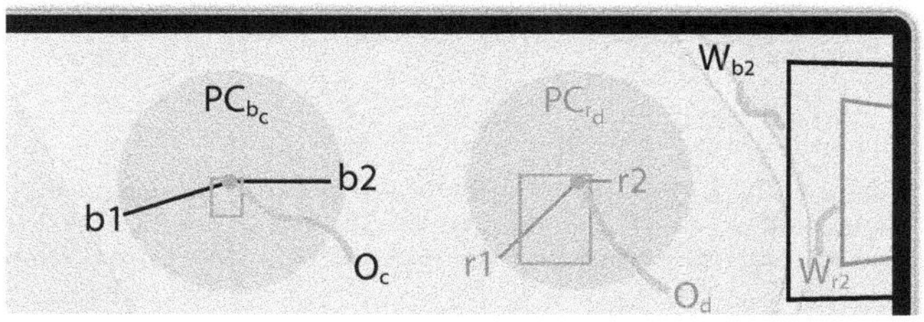

Figure 7: P-Compass vs. Wedge. Figure 6 and Figure 7 are the lower-left and upper-right corners of a virtual display (drawn in true scale). Wedges (prefixed with "W") and P-Compasses (prefixed with "PC") indicate locations of four off-display POIs, $r1$, $r2$, $b1$ and $b2$ (r* and b* are 4 cm and 50 cm off-display, respectively). P-Compasses are better for drawing inferences from POIs, while Wedges are better for locating POIs.

This reference-point dependency diminishes as the distance of an off-screen POI increases. Comparing the two pairs of P-Compasses PC_{r_a} and PC_{r_d}, PC_{b_b} and PC_{b_c}, shows that distant off-screen POIs make the latter pair more similar to the former pair. In other words, for distant off-screen POIs, a single P-Compass is approximately valid for all reference points on a display[2]. On the other hand, distant off-screen POIs significantly reduce the usability of Wedge. It becomes impossible to use W_{b1} and W_{b2} to estimate the locations of $b1$ and $b2$.

In short, P-Compass is better for drawing inferences from off-screen POI(s) with respect to a single reference point, while Wedge is better for locating a nearby off-screen POI. As the distance to an off-screen POI increases, the benefits of P-Compass eventually outweigh those of Wedge.

Issues of Scalability

Scalability refers to how the performance of a visualization technique is affected by the distance to an off-screen POI [17]. While scalability is rarely discussed, it is important for two reasons: Not all off-screen POIs are near the display, as often assumed in the literature; further, with sufficient zoom any nearby off-screen POI becomes distant.

Wedge and P-Compass both have issues with scalability. Wedge is limited mostly to nearby off-screen POIs. As the distance to an off-screen POI increases, the angles between the base and the two legs increase nonlinearly and the rate of change quickly becomes indistinguishable. Beyond a certain distance, the two legs of a Wedge essentially appear parallel [17]. The FOV box of a P-Compass, which becomes visually indistinguishable from a point for sufficiently distant POIs, does not scale either. In a sense, these two approaches both aim to *extend* the effective area of a display. Therefore, we refer to them as *display extension* methods.

The extended display area achieved this way is finite. Simply put, the probability that an off-screen POI falls into the small extended display area could be small. Most important, while

[2] A good example is the conventional magnetic compass: it is correct for all reference points on a local map regardless of its placement.

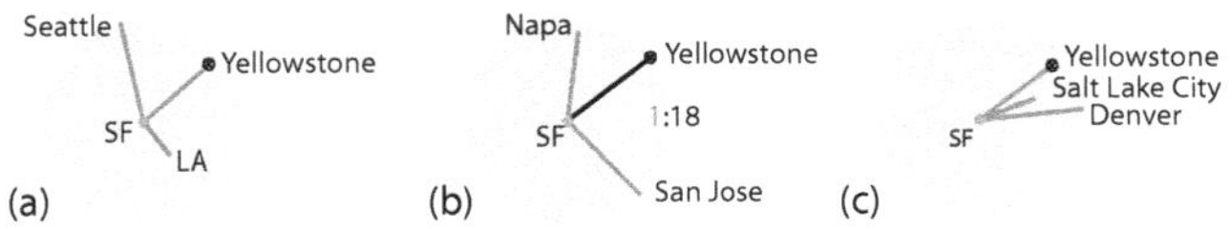

Figure 8: (a) Using supporting POIs to *extrapolate* an unknown POI (Yellowstone). (b–c) Two alternatives: (b) Emphasizes nearby POIs (mixed-scale representation); (c) Emphasizes POIs close to Yellowstone.

it may not seem obvious, display extension methods require a relatively large display. The smaller the display area, the smaller the extended display area that can be achieved. (The Wedge max base length and P-Compass FOV box size are both bounded by the size of the display.) Clearly, a different approach is needed to visualize off-screen POIs.

Using POIs to Overcome Scalability

P-Compass achieves scalability by using *a priori* POIs as references to communicate the location of an unknown POI x. We refer to this method as the POI-reference method. In the "Where is Yellowstone National Park?" example (Figure 1), multiple POIs are enlisted to *interpolate* an on-screen x (Yellowstone National Park). A similar strategy could be applied to *extrapolate* an off-screen x. Figure 8(a) shows a P-Compass in which the reference point is at San Francisco, and the off-screen x (Yellowstone National Park) is at the periphery. Unlike display extension methods, this strategy is invariant to the distance of POIs, the scale of the information space, and the size of a display.

The use of POIs creates an interesting design space for P-Compass. Different P-Compasses can answer the same "Where is x?" question. A system can tailor the message of a P-Compass through its choice of POIs. Figure 8(b–c) shows two alternatives to Figure 8(a). Note that different distributions (distance, orientation) and numbers of POIs can affect the estimation accuracy of x. While our initial prototype uses a simple algorithm to select POIs, we leave exploration of this space to future work.

USER STUDY

Apparatus

We performed a study that uses the prototype application described earlier; however, all test cases shown to participants are static, with all map interactions disabled. Two types of displays were used in the study: (1) A Dell 24-inch monitor (U2412M) displayed instructions and (for one task) an emulated smartphone to match a previously proposed setup; (2) An Apple iPhone 5 supported additional smartphone tasks (application area: W 50 mm × H 75 mm) and also emulated a circular smartwatch (36 mm diameter) for smartwatch tasks.

Design and Tasks

We are interested in how P-Compass and Wedge could assist users in resolving the "Where is x?" problem in daily life. Based on the first author's year of field experience, we developed a "day in the city" scenario comprising five navigation tasks. A preliminary pilot study of nine participants, who were researchers not associated with our lab, was first conducted to evaluate the tasks and gather feedback. Below we describe the five tasks and their motivations.

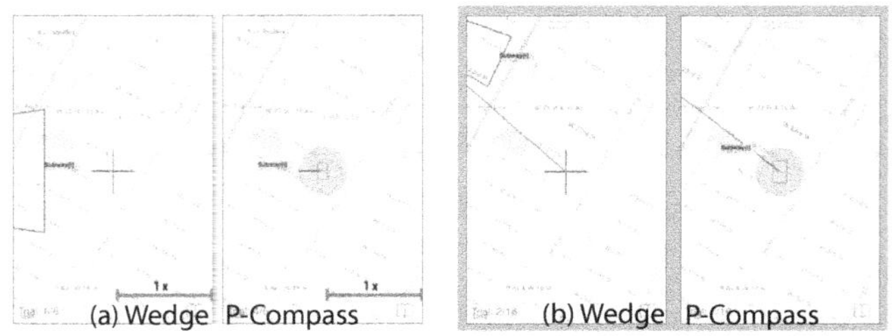

Figure 9: (a) LOCATE and DISTANCE. (LOCATE was performed on a desktop monitor with no map background.) (b) ORIENTATION.

LOCATE: Where is the subway station?

LOCATE asks a user to estimate the location of an off-screen subway station. This task is similar to one proposed by Gustafson et al. [18], and, like it, is performed with an emulated smartphone on a desktop monitor. On a blank canvas, a user sees a wireframe rectangle representing the boundary of the smartphone display (W×H: 67 mm×105 mm, 1.3× the size of the custom map app on iPhone), along with a visualization to indicate the location of a subway station (Figure 9a). The user must move a mouse cursor to the estimated location of the subway station.

The two within-subject factors in this task are visualization type (P-Compass and Wedge) and off-screen POI distance (six distances: 5–30 cm). We constrained all off-screen POIs to be on the short axis (the axis passing through the centroid of the display and parallel to the shorter display edge). The goal is to investigate *scalability*—how the error may change as a function of off-screen distance. From our field experience, we noticed that an off-screen POI was often not located near the display edge, yet studies of Wedge [18, 5, 7] focus mostly on nearby off-screen POIs.

DISTANCE: How far is the subway station?

DISTANCE asks a user to estimate the distance to an off-screen subway station in terms of an integral multiple of the half-screen width—a simplified scale. The user sees the visualization on an iPhone 5 (Figure 9a), and enters the answer on a nearby desktop computer. The goal is to investigate whether a visualization can support the use of a scale. In our field experience, we used other objects as the basis for measurement (e.g., a city block or a baseball field). For simplicity, we use a half-screen width for this task.

The two within-subject factors in this task are visualization type (P-Compass and Wedge) and off-screen POI distance (six off-screen distances: 7.5–32.5 cm). All off-screen POIs are on the short axis. Since the task may rapidly increase in difficulty with the distance to a POI, we asked participants to provide their best estimate.

ORIENTATION: Which direction is the subway station?

ORIENTATION asks a user to estimate the direction of an off-screen subway station with respect to the display center. The user sees the visualization on an iPhone 5 and uses their finger to rotate a blue line on the screen (Figure 9b) to indicate the answer. In our field experience, inquiring the direction of a POI was one of the most frequent questions in pedestrian and vehicle navigation. While map applications are typically able

Figure 10: Setup for LOCALIZE and LOCATE+.

to show that "you are here," they do not show the *direction* to a POI from that location.

The three within-subject factors in this task are visualization type (P-Compass and Wedge), the distance to a POI (near and far) and the location of a POI (edge and corner). Near POIs are roughly 5 cm from the display edge, and far POIs are roughly 20 cm from the display edge.

LOCALIZE: Where am I? LOCATE+: Where is the Cafe?

In these two tasks, the user needs to estimate an unknown location x from the locations of two known POIs, P_1 and P_2. The user wears a smartwatch (emulated on a wrist-worn iPhone 5), which displays the relationship between x, P_1 and P_2. The user marks the estimated location of x on a desktop monitor, on which only P_1 and P_2 are displayed on a blank background (Figure 10).

In LOCALIZE, x is visible and located at the center of the smartwatch (P_1 and P_2 are both off-smartwatch; see Figure 11a). The user's task is to *interpolate* x on the desktop monitor. In LOCATE+, P_1 is visible and located at the smartwatch center (x and P_2 are both off-smartwatch; see Figure 11b). The user must *extrapolate* x on the desktop monitor.

LOCALIZE is motivated by the scenario in which a user must determine where she is with respect to two off-screen landmarks. The mobile location search scenario (Figure 1) provides additional motivation. LOCATE+ is motivated by the same scenario as LOCATE. Rather than asking the user to estimate the *physical* location of x, LOCATE+ asks the user to estimate x with respect to a reference frame consisting of POIs.

To study how the distribution of P_1 and P_2 may affect estimating x, the two tasks include 12 different P_1 and P_2 locations as exploratory conditions (detailed in the Results section). However, visualization type (P-Compass and Wedge) is the only within-subject factor used in data analysis.

Fair Comparison

How can one control the sizes of Wedge and P-Compass to allow them to be compared fairly? In addition, for a rectangular display, the location of an off-screen POI, x, could affect the fairness of a comparison—the best case scenario for P-Compass is when x lies along the long axis (the axis passing through the centroid of the display and parallel to the longer display edge), since the long edge of the FOV box would then be used as the standard for estimation. In contrast, the best case scenario for Wedge is when the object lies along the short axis, since a Wedge would then have the maximal length to use for its base. We are interested in the general use of P-Compass and Wedge, not their optimal cases. So we fix compass radius at $\frac{1}{8}$ screen width, Wedge intrusion at $\frac{1}{7}$ screen width, and maximal Wedge base at $0.9 \times min(W, H)$. For LOCATE and DISTANCE, we constrain all POIs on the short axis.

In our experiment, Wedge covers a greater area than P-Compass. (The biggest Wedge occupies roughly 2.7× the area of the P-Compass.) We considered reducing maximal base length so that both cover the same area. However, the two Wedge legs could then become almost parallel, making it impossible to estimate the location of an off-screen POI.

For LOCALIZE and LOCATE+, we use a circular watch face (36 mm diameter), rather than a rectangular display. These two tasks require users to estimate the distance ratio and directional difference of two off-screen POIs. Our pilot study indicated it could be challenging to use Wedge on a rectangular display to estimate the direction of off-screen POIs. With a circular display, we constrain the bases of all Wedges perpendicular to lines radiating from the display centroid. This Wedge implementation is optimized for direction estimation, but may result in overlap for POIs with small angular differences. We chose POIs with big enough angular differences to eliminate Wedge overlap. All Wedges are guaranteed to have a fixed intrusion of 4.5 mm ($\frac{1}{4}$ of the radius). The maximal base is fixed at 22 mm, which is 90% of the chord when the chord is $\frac{1}{4}$ radius away from the centroid. The maximal needle length of the P-Compass is fixed at 6.25 mm. A single Wedge could occupy up to 13.2% of the display area (two Wedges are shown in each trial), while a P-Compass occupies 12% of the display area.

While it is possible to scale Wedge **I**ntrusion, or **B**ase length (IB for short; see Figure 3 for definitions) to directly reflect the true off-screen distance ratio between POIs, this method requires some of the Wedges to reduce their IBs. Doing so could negatively impact the accuracy of Wedge, and goes against the suggestions made by Gustafson et al. [18]. Additionally, this (off-screen distance) encoding scheme does not help users infer the relationship between POIs, especially with respect to an on-screen reference point. For example, to know the distance ratio of a set of off-screen POIs with

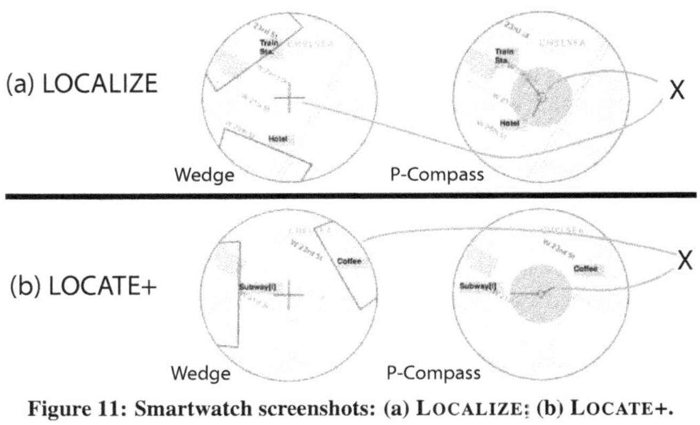

Figure 11: Smartwatch screenshots: (a) LOCALIZE; (b) LOCATE+.

respect to an on-screen reference point, users will still need to mentally combine the on-screen distance to the off-screen distance for each off-screen POI.

One may argue that it is also possible to scale IB to directly reflect the *true* distance ratio between each POIs with respect to a point. This (true distance) encoding scheme could negatively impact the accuracy of Wedge, as mentioned earlier. Furthermore, this encoding scheme could cause confusion for a non-circular display. For example, on a smartphone display with unequal width and height, two off-screen POIs of the same distance from an on-screen reference point, one on the short axis and other on the long axis, could have different off-screen distance. Yet the two Wedges, representing these two off-screen POIs, will have the same IBs according to the (true distance) encoding scheme. Therefore, we implement Wedge by following the algorithm suggested by Gustafson et al. [18], so each Wedge uses its maximal IB.

Hypotheses

We formulated five hypotheses:

H.1. *For* LOCATE, *Wedge will yield higher accuracy for close POIs, while P-Compass will yield higher accuracy for distant POIs.* Shape completion (Wedge) is effective for close POIs, in which case only a small portion of the triangle is hidden. For distant POIs, the mostly hidden triangle, the nearly parallel Wedge legs, and the nonlinear angle-to-distance mapping[3] could put Wedge at a disadvantage, in comparison with P-Compass, which offers a linear distance cue[4].

H.2. *For* DISTANCE, *P-Compass will yield more accurate estimates.* Users can use P-Compass as an abstract overview map to perform distance estimation. With Wedge, however, users need to first estimate the off-screen POI's location, memorize the location, and then use the scale to measure the distance. This process induces heavier cognitive load and is more error prone.

H.3, H.4. *For* LOCALIZE (H.3) *and* LOCATE+ (H.4), *P-Compass will yield more accurate results.* P-Compass is a centralized reference-point representation that allows users to see the relationship among multiple POIs at once, bypassing the need to first estimate physical locations of off-screen POIs, as in the case of Wedge.

H.5. *For all tasks except* LOCATE, *users will prefer P-Compass.* The difference between LOCATE and the other tasks is that LOCATE requires a user to estimate the physical location of an off-screen POI, which is Wedge's strength. For the other tasks, knowing the physical location of an off-screen POI is not a prerequisite, and may even complicate the tasks. The map-like property of a P-Compass makes the other tasks easier.

Since direction indication is exactly what a compass is designed for, we did not formulate an hypothesis for ORIENTATION, but did include it as an investigational task and report its results for completeness. In addition, it is possible to modify the Wedge layout algorithm to optimize direction estimation with respect to a reference point. (In fact, we did so for LOCALIZE and LOCATE+, as mentioned earlier.) Potential issues for this alternative layout algorithm are overlaps and increased Wedge footprint (for rectangular displays), which the original Wedge layout algorithm [18] tries to avoid.

[3]Wedge angles scale nonlinearly as the distance to a POI changes.
[4]The ratio (size of FOV box)/(compass needle length) scales linearly as the distance to a POI changes.

	P-Compass	Wedge
LOCATE	64.89 mm (53.70)	63.30 (48.96)
DISTANCE	2.02 x (2.28)	2.96 (2.49)
ORIENTATION	0.44 deg (0.42)	6.30 (6.01)
LOCALIZE	17.82 mm (11.65)	29.29 (16.87)
LOCATE+	14.84 mm (8.82)	34.67 (20.74)

Table 1: Summary of error results (s.d.).

	P-Compass	Wedge
LOCATE	11.98 sec (8.00)	6.82 (5.43)
DISTANCE	15.30 sec (11.89)	12.06 (5.34)
ORIENTATION	4.12 sec (3.10)	8.16 (6.58)
LOCALIZE	11.31 sec (7.56)	11.67 (7.35)
LOCATE+	9.03 sec (5.97)	9.94 (5.01)

Table 2: Summary of completion times (s.d.).

Procedure

26 participants (13 female), ages 20–39 ($\bar{x}$ = 25.5, s = 4.9), were recruited from the general population pool of our institution for a single-session (one hour) experiment in return for a small cash compensation. All participants were familiar with mobile map applications (e.g., Google Maps). All except one owned a smartphone and used it multiple times a day. Only one had a smartwatch and used it daily.

Each participant was seated at a desk for all tasks, and instructed to imagine performing the tasks as if in an outdoor urban environment—taking a quick glance at a visualization and then providing rough estimations. Participants were also told all POIs and the background image were fictional. For smartphone/smartwatch tasks, participants were asked to hold/wear the device; they were not allowed to place the device on the desk or use both hands to assist in measurements, as this would not be possible in many outdoor situations.

The study was blocked by visualization type; half the participants started with tasks using Wedge, and the other half started with tasks using P-Compass. At the start of each block, the study coordinator introduced the idea of the corresponding visualization. The participant then followed on-screen instructions for a practice block for all tasks using the corresponding visualization (3 LOCATE + 4 ORIENTATION + 3 DISTANCE + 3 LOCALIZE + 3 LOCATE+ = 16 practice trials per visualization). At the end of each practice trial, the participant could view the ground truth, but not during the actual trials. The participant next followed on-screen instructions to complete one block for each of the five tasks.

Task blocks were fully counterbalanced, with the constraint that LOCATE, ORIENTATION and DISTANCE were grouped together, and LOCALIZE and LOCATE+ were grouped together (to minimize the number of device switches). The conditions of the non-visualization factor were randomized. Each participant was given a total of 2 (visualization) × (6 LOCATE + 15 ORIENTATION + 6 DISTANCE + 12 LOCALIZE + 12 LOCATE+) = 104 timed trials.

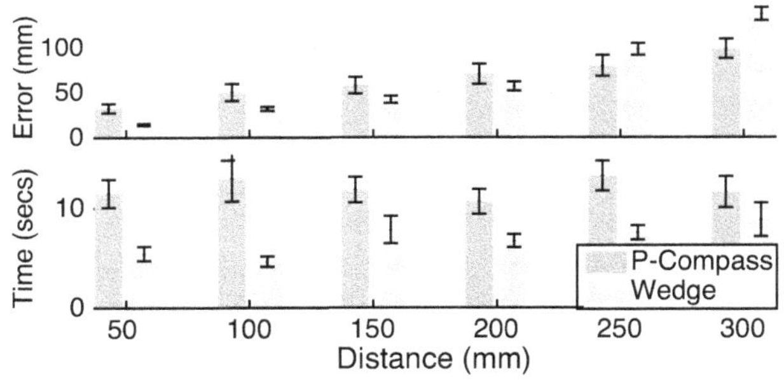

Figure 12: LOCATE Results. Errors (top), completion time (bottom).

RESULTS

Errors and task completion times were collected during the study (Tables 1–2). Since error definition differs by task, it is described along with the results of each task. Completion time is computed from trial start to participant answer. All analyses were conducted with $\alpha = 0.05$. Since each task was carried out independently, we discuss them separately.

LOCATE

Error for LOCATE (Figure 12 top) was defined as Euclidean distance between the estimated answer and ground truth. A 2×6 (Visualization $\times$ Distance Level) ANOVA on error indicates no significant main effect on visualization ($F_{1,25} = 0.06, p = 0.81$). However, there is significant interaction between visualization and distance levels ($F_{5,125} = 7.67, p < 0.001$). With post-hoc *t*-tests using Bonferroni correction, we found significant differences at 5 cm and 30 cm (both $p < 0.003$), supporting **H.1**. A similar 2×6 (Visualization $\times$ Distance Level) ANOVA was performed on completion time (Figure 12 bottom), showing a significant main effect on visualization ($F_{1,25} = 37.22, p < 0.001$), but no interaction between visualization and distance levels ($F_{5,125} = 1.29, p = 0.27$).

DISTANCE

At the farthest two distance levels, we found three participants consistently made large estimation errors using P-Compass (greater than three times the quartile), so we excluded their data from analysis. Interviewing one of the three, we learned that this participant had used the gap between the reference point and the FOV box as the basis for estimation, instead of the FOV box as expected. The FOV box almost overlapped the reference point at the farthest two levels. There was no gap as the base of estimation. The participant acknowledged that their answers were random guesses.

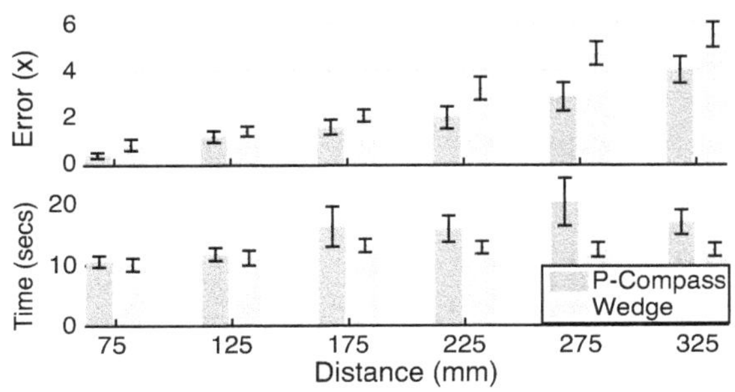

Figure 13: DISTANCE Results. Errors (top), completion time (bottom).

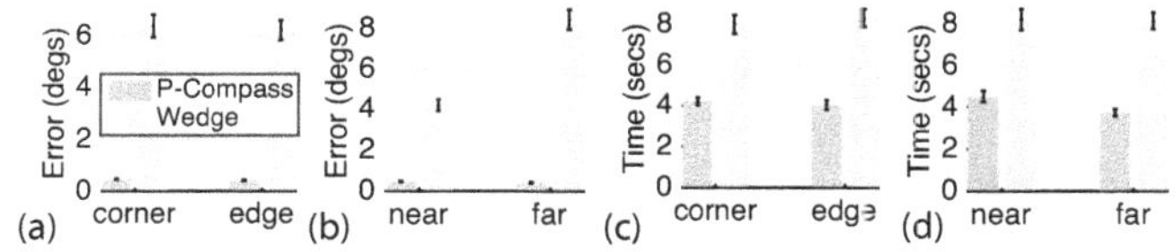

Figure 14: ORIENTATION Results.

Figure 13 (top) shows the errors of DISTANCE. The error is defined as the absolute difference between the estimated distance (in integer multiples of half-screen width) and the ground truth. A 2×6 (Visualization $\times$ Distance Level) ANOVA on error shows a significant main effect on visualization ($F_{1,22} = 7.25, p = 0.013$). This result supports **H.2**. No interaction between visualization and distance level was found ($F_{5,110} = 1.89, p = 0.10$). A similar 2×6 (Visualization $\times$ Distance Level) ANOVA was performed on completion time. There is a significant main effect on visualization ($F_{1,25} = 11.44, p = 0.003$), but no interaction between visualization and distance levels ($F_{5,110} = 1.34, p = 0.25$).

ORIENTATION

Errors for ORIENTATION (Figure 14a–b) were defined as angular distance between the estimated answer and the ground truth. A $2 \times 2 \times 2$ (Visualization $\times$ Distance $\times$ Position) ANOVA on error indicates a significant main effect on visualization ($F_{1,25} = 89.06, p < 0.001$), no significant interaction between visualization and position ($F_{1,725} = 0.16, p = 0.68$), but significant interaction between visualization and distance ($F_{1,725} = 78.85, p < 0.001$). An ANOVA was performed on completion time (Figure 14c–d), showing a significant main effect on visualization ($F_{1,25} = 69.18, p < 0.001$), no significant interaction between visualization and position ($F_{1,725} = 0.07, p = 0.79$), and no significant interaction between visualization and distance ($F_{1,725} = 1.21, p = 0.27$).

LOCALIZE

Figure 15 (top) shows errors for LOCALIZE. The *x*-axis of the figure indicates the parameters of the exploratory conditions. The top row indicates the distance ratio of two off-screen POIs (base length 7.79 cm), and the bottom row indicates the angular difference in degrees between the two off-screen POIs, all with respect to the display centroid. Error is defined as Euclidean distance between the estimated answer and the ground truth. A one-way (Visualization) ANOVA on errors indicates a significant main effect on visualization ($F_{1,25} = 69.97, p < 0.001$), supporting **H.3**. A similar one-way (Visualization) ANOVA was performed on completion

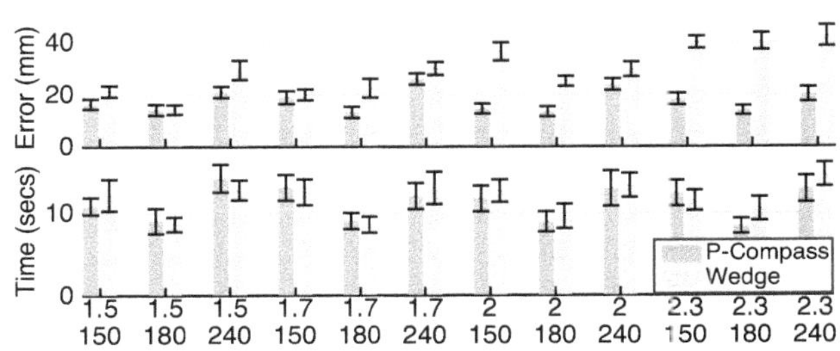

Figure 15: LOCALIZE Results. Errors (top), completion time (bottom). The *x*-axis indicates the parameters of the exploratory conditions (see text for details).

time, and found no significant main effect on visualization ($F_{1,25} = 0.097, p = 0.75$).

LOCATE+

Figure 16 (top) shows errors for LOCATE+. The x-axis of the figure indicates the parameters of the exploratory conditions (the same as in the LOCALIZE task). Error is also defined as in LOCALIZE. We performed a one-way (Visualization) ANOVA on errors and found a significant main effect on visualization ($F_{1,25} = 49.53, p < 0.001$), supporting **H.4**. A similar one-way (Visualization) ANOVA was performed on completion time, and found no significant main effect on visualization ($F_{1,25} = 1.87, p = 0.18$).

Subjective Preferences and User Comments

At the end of the session, the participant was asked to choose their preferred technique for each task and provide comments. Table 3 summarizes participants' preferences. Chi-Square tests reveal P-Compass was preferred for ORIENTATION, LOCALIZE, and LOCATE+ (all $p < 0.005$). No significant preferences are found for LOCATE ($p = 0.67$) and DISTANCE ($p = 0.06$). These results partially support **H.5**.

It is interesting to note the preference difference between LOCATE and DISTANCE, because the two share a similar setup but ask different questions (Figure 9). The preference reversal suggests that characteristics of a technique could make certain types of tasks more or less difficult, as also pointed out by participant 23 (P23) in a comment on Wedge, "I felt like I had trouble estimating distances well, but the tasks involving locations felt easier."

Regardless of the technique, all participants expressed frustration with LOCATE and DISTANCE, especially for distant off-screen POIs. P27 commented on Wedge, "It's hard to tell small differences in the angle at the base of the triangle, especially when it is very close to perpendicular." P14 said about P-Compass, "I found it very hard to determine the distance when the mini screen [FOV box] is very small."

For ORIENTATION, the majority of the participants preferred P-Compass and commented on the difficulty of using Wedge. P18 remarked, "it needed physical measurement help from my fingers to get the location of the tip of triangle."

Most participants preferred P-Compass for LOCALIZE and LOCATE+. However, we were puzzled by a small number

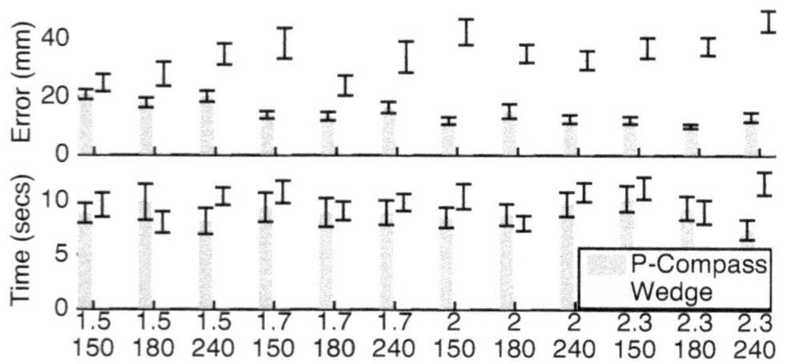

Figure 16: LOCATE+ Results. Errors (top), completion time (bottom). The x-axis indicates the parameters of the exploratory conditions (see text for details).

	P-Compass	Wedge	No Preference
LOCATE	10	12	4
DISTANCE	16	7	3
ORIENTATION	25	0	1
LOCALIZE	23	3	0
LOCATE+	19	5	2

Table 3: Participants' preferences on each task.

who preferred Wedge, even though quantitative data suggests P-Compass allowed them to achieve higher accuracy in comparable time. We later learned from the comments that those participants were more comfortable when all off-screen POIs were presented at the same scale as the displayed content, and they felt Wedge performed better. Indeed, in this study we limited all POIs to a distance range where Wedge can be functional. It is possible within this setup that individual preferences overshadow the strengths of P-Compass.

DISCUSSION

The study results offer strong evidence to support **H.1–H.4**. **H.5** was partially supported by significant preferences for three out of the four predicted tasks.

In terms of scalability, the errors of LOCATE and DISTANCE support our analysis that the display extension method does not scale. This is also reflected in participants' frustration, as revealed in the comments. Putting the results in real-life context, one can see that it is only meaningful to perform LOCATE and DISTANCE when a POI is at the display boundary. In LOCATE and DISTANCE, the farthest off-screen POI is 30 cm, which corresponds to half the height of New York's Central Park at the scale of 1 cm per city block—a reasonable distance for a tourist or a city resident, yet the average error at this distance amounted to 10 cm (10 city blocks). This underscores the importance of having the POI-reference method.

In terms of task type, the results support our analysis that the characteristics of each visualization technique make them suitable for different tasks. While users could use Wedge to achieve better accuracy for LOCATE (especially when off-screen distance was less than 20 cm), the same performance advantage was not observed for DISTANCE. Similarly, Wedge's advantage for locating an off-screen POI becomes a disadvantage for ORIENTATION, LOCALIZE, and LOCATE+. As reported in previous research [21] and participants' comments, participants in the Wedge condition often used fingers to denote an imaginary POI, or shift the smartphone/smartwatch away to have a better overview. The need to use fingers could make Wedge difficult for hands-busy, mobile, or dynamic scenarios.

For ORIENTATION, the results show it is more challenging for a user to estimate the direction of a distant POI than a nearby one using Wedge, but surprisingly the position condition (edge/corner, Figure 14a) does not yield a significant result. The reason could be due to our implementation of Wedge. We provide ample intrusion at edges and corners; the minimal intrusion at corners is the same as the maximal intrusion at edges. For LOCALIZE and LOCATE+, the exploratory conditions offer interesting patterns, suggesting that future work could investigate how the distribution of POIs may affect estimation accuracy.

Regarding completion time, on average we found using P-Compass took roughly twice as much time as Wedge for LOCATE. This could be due to the more complicated mental process required by P-Compass, as described earlier. It also took longer on average to complete DISTANCE using P-Compass. It is possible that Wedge users gave up when a POI was beyond some distance (which could explain the relatively flat completion time, Figure 13 bottom), while P-Compass users held on longer. Note that we asked users to provide a rough estimate if they were unable to provide a good answer. For ORIENTATION, LOCALIZE, and LOCATE+, P-Compass completion time was either shorter or similar to that of Wedge.

Design Recommendations

Based on the analysis and study results, we make the following design recommendations:

Replace a compass with a P-Compass. The results show P-Compass helps users infer the directions and locations of off-screen POIs, and resolves Desert Fog. The added benefits require little modification to a conventional compass.

Use P-Compass for distant off-screen POIs. P-Compass yields more accurate results for distant POIs, and was preferred by most study participants. Distant POIs let a single P-Compass accommodate all reference points on a display.

Use Wedge for nearby off-screen POIs. Wedge essentially extends the effective area of a display, and has the benefit of presenting POIs at the same scale as the displayed content. While our formal study focused on more distant POIs, in our field experience and pilot study we observed that Wedge appeared to offer similar or better performance, especially for POIs close to the display edge. Previous studies [17, 5] have also reported the effectiveness of Wedge for nearby POIs.

Take display size into account. Wedge's effective zone gets smaller as display area decreases. Designers should take display size into account to determine the distance at which to switch between Wedge and P-Compass.

Give users control. In practice, a gray area, rather than a clear line, may exist between effective zones for Wedge and P-Compass. In addition, depending on the task, a specific user may prefer one technique over another. Application designers should provide the option to switch between visualizations.

Transition between P-Compass and Wedge

Our analysis suggests that Wedge and P-Compass are complementary. In fact, a P-Compass can be smoothly transformed into a set of Wedges, and vice versa. As a set of Wedges are pulled in from the periphery of a display to a single reference point, and each triangle is reduced to a needle during the process, a P-Compass is formed. An inverse transformation can convert a P-Compass to a set of Wedges.

Limitations

P-Compass requires personal a priori knowledge of a space. The more detailed knowledge a user has, the better estimation a P-Compass can provide. Overlapping POIs can reduce the readability of a P-Compass. However, the primary aim of a P-Compass is to use *minimal* information to answer the "Where is *x*?" question. For a small number of overlapping POIs, varying the color or thickness of compass needles could be a potential solution.

CONCLUSIONS AND FUTURE WORK

We introduced P-Compass, a compact graphical location indicator to address the "Where is *x*?" problem, which generalizes the problems of off-screen POIs and Desert Fog. P-Compass uses personal *a priori* POIs to establish a reference frame in which the POI *x* can then be localized. A P-Compass can be integrated into a map or accompany visual content. As an extreme example, the standalone P-Compass in Figure 1(i) can even be directly embedded into text, much like an inline equation: [Seattle; SF; Yellowstone; Chicago].

We examined the characteristics of P-Compass and Wedge, and conducted a formal user study to compare the two. The results showed P-Compass performs better for the four inference tasks, while Wedge is better for the locating task. Based on the analysis and study results, we suggested the two techniques are complementary and offered design recommendations. As a rule of thumb, as the display size becomes smaller, and/or the distance of a POI increases, the benefits of P-Compass eventually outweigh those of Wedge.

There are several directions for future work. We would like to explore how the distribution of POIs on a P-Compass may affect readability and estimation accuracy, and develop a POI-selection algorithm. We would also like to distribute our P-Compass app and test it in the wild. P-Compass need not be restricted to the described setups and tasks. How well would P-Compass do for large displays, dynamic scenarios, or on-screen POIs? How could P-Compass be extended to 3D environments, for example, to support VR or AR applications?

We are also interested in evaluating the multi-scale feature. For independent information in mixed scales (Figure 5a), we could ask participants to use information at a single scale to perform any of the five tasks. For related information in mixed scales (Figure 5b), we could ask participants to localize a POI (LOCALIZE and LOCATE+), using information from two or more scales. Factors could be number of scales, ratio of scales, and distributions of POIs. The control condition could present all information at a single scale, and completion time, errors and preferences could be collected.

We believe P-Compass is an important step toward realizing a visualization technique we term *spacepiece*, which could answer "Where is *x*?" with a single glance, much how a *timepiece* answers "What time is it?" In addition to POIs, we are interested in incorporating entities such as paths, districts, and boundaries, which are important to wayfinding [27].

ACKNOWLEDGEMENTS

This research was funded in part by NSF Grants DGE-1144854, IIS-0905569, and IIS-1514429. We thank Mengu Sukan and Barbara Tversky for discussions.

REFERENCES

1. Patrick Baudisch and Ruth Rosenholtz. 2003. Halo: a technique for visualizing off-screen objects. In *Proc. CHI*. 481–488.
2. Patrick M Baudisch and John C Krumm. 2013. Location-to-landmark. (Dec. 31 2013). US Patent 8,620,570.
3. Benjamin B Bederson, James D Hollan, Ken Perlin, Jonathan Meyer, David Bacon, and George Furnas. 1996. Pad++: A zoomable graphical sketchpad for exploring alternate interface physics. *Journal of Visual Languages & Computing* 7, 1 (1996), 3–32.
4. John Brosz, Miguel A Nacenta, Richard Pusch, Sheelagh Carpendale, and Christophe Hurter. 2013. Transmogrification: causal manipulation of visualizations. In *Proc. UIST*. 97–106.
5. Stefano Burigat and Luca Chittaro. 2011. Visualizing references to off-screen content on mobile devices: A comparison of Arrows, Wedge, and Overview+ Detail. *Interacting with Computers* 23, 2 (2011), 156–166.
6. Stefano Burigat, Luca Chittaro, and Silvia Gabrielli. 2006. Visualizing locations of off-screen objects on mobile devices: a comparative evaluation of three approaches. In *Proc. MobileHCI*. 239–246.
7. Stefano Burigat, Luca Chittaro, and Andrea Vianello. 2012. Dynamic visualization of large numbers of off-screen objects on mobile devices: an experimental comparison of wedge and overview+ detail. In *Proc. MobileHCI*. 93–102.
8. M Sheelagh T Carpendale and Catherine Montagnese. 2001. A framework for unifying presentation space. In *Proc. UIST*. 61–70.
9. Luca Chittaro and Stefano Burigat. 2004. 3D location-pointing as a navigation aid in Virtual Environments. In *Proc. Working Conference on Advanced Visual Interfaces*. ACM, 267–274.
10. Andy Cockburn, Amy Karlson, and Benjamin B Bederson. 2008. A review of overview+ detail, zooming, and focus+ context interfaces. *ACM Computing Surveys (CSUR)* 41, 1 (2008), 2.
11. Mark Egenhofer. 1999. Spatial information appliances: A next generation of geographic information systems. In *1st Brazilian workshop on geoinformatics, Campinas, Brazil*.
12. Niklas Elmqvist, Nathalie Henry, Yann Riche, and Jean-Daniel Fekete. 2008. Melange: space folding for multi-focus interaction. In *Proc. CHI*. 1333–1342.
13. Steven Feiner, Blair MacIntyre, Tobias Höllerer, and Anthony Webster. 1997. A touring machine: Prototyping 3D mobile augmented reality systems for exploring the urban environment. *Personal Technologies* 1, 4 (1997), 208–217.
14. George W Furnas. 2006. A fisheye follow-up: further reflections on focus+ context. In *Proc. CHI*. 999–1008.
15. Reginald G Golledge. 1999. Human wayfinding and cognitive maps. *Wayfinding Behavior: Cognitive Mapping and Other Spatial Processes* (1999), 5–45.
16. Floraine Grabler, Maneesh Agrawala, Robert W. Sumner, and Mark Pauly. 2008. Automatic Generation of Tourist Maps. *ACM Trans. Graph.* 27, 3, Article 100 (Aug. 2008), 11 pages.
17. Sean Gustafson. 2008. *Visualizing off-screen locations on small mobile displays*. Master's thesis. Department of Computer Science, University of Manitoba.
18. Sean Gustafson, Patrick Baudisch, Carl Gutwin, and Pourang Irani. 2008. Wedge: clutter-free visualization of off-screen locations. In *Proc. CHI*. 787–796.
19. Sean Gustafson and Pourang P Irani. 2007. Comparing visualizations for tracking off-screen moving targets. In *CHI Extended Abstracts*. 2399–2404.
20. Takeo Igarashi and Ken Hinckley. 2000. Speed-dependent automatic zooming for browsing large documents. In *Proc. UIST*. 139–148.
21. Alexandra Ion, Y-L Betty Chang, Michael Haller, Mark Hancock, and Stacey D Scott. 2013. Canyon: providing location awareness of multiple moving objects in a detail view on large displays. In *Proc. CHI*. 3149–3158.
22. Sibren Isaacman, Richard Becker, Ramón Cáceres, Stephen Kobourov, Margaret Martonosi, James Rowland, and Alexander Varshavsky. 2011. Identifying important places in peoples lives from cellular network data. In *Pervasive Computing*. Springer, 133–151.
23. Waqas Javed, Sohaib Ghani, and Niklas Elmqvist. 2012. Polyzoom: multiscale and multifocus exploration in 2D visual spaces. In *Proc. CHI*. 287–296.
24. Susanne Jul and George W Furnas. 1998. Critical zones in desert fog: aids to multiscale navigation. In *Proc. UIST*. 97–106.
25. Dominik P Käser, Maneesh Agrawala, and Mark Pauly. 2011. FingerGlass: efficient multiscale interaction on multitouch screens. In *Proc. CHI*. 1601–1610.
26. Henry Lieberman. 1994. Powers of ten thousand: navigating in large information spaces. In *Proc. UIST*. 15–16.
27. Kevin Lynch. 1960. *The image of the city*. MIT Press.
28. J Mackinlay, Lance Good, P Zellweger, Mark Stefik, and Patrick Baudisch. 2003. City Lights: Contextual views in minimal space. In *Proc. CHI*. 838–839.
29. Daniel Miau and Steven Feiner. 2016. Personalized Compass Supplementary Material. (2016). `http://dx.doi.org/10.1145/2858036.2858068`.
30. Kayur Patel, Mike Y Chen, Ian Smith, and James A Landay. 2006. Personalizing routes. In *Proc. UIST*. 187–190.

31. Manojit Sarkar and Marc H Brown. 1992. Graphical fisheye views of graphs. In *Proc. CHI*. 83–91.

32. Noah Snavely, Rahul Garg, Steven M Seitz, and Richard Szeliski. 2008. Finding paths through the world's photos. In *ACM Trans. Graph.*, Vol. 27.

33. Noah Snavely, Steven M Seitz, and Richard Szeliski. 2006. Photo tourism: exploring photo collections in 3D. In *ACM Trans. Graph.*, Vol. 25. 835–846.

34. Molly E Sorrows and Stephen C Hirtle. 1999. The nature of landmarks for real and electronic spaces. In *Spatial Information Theory. Cognitive and Computational Foundations of Geographic Information Science*. Springer, 37–50.

35. Riku Suomela and Juha Lehikoinen. 2000. Context compass. In *The Fourth International Symposium on Wearable Computers*. IEEE, 147–154.

36. Edward C Tolman. 1948. Cognitive maps in rats and men. *Psychological Review* 55, 4 (1948), 189.

37. Colin Ware and Marlon Lewis. 1995. The DragMag image magnifier. In *Conference Companion on Human Factors in Computing Systems*. ACM, 407–408.

38. Changqing Zhou, Nupur Bhatnagar, Shashi Shekhar, and Loren Terveen. 2007. Mining personally important places from GPS tracks. In *IEEE 23rd International Conference on Data Engineering Workshop*. 517–526.

SymmetriSense: Enabling Near-Surface Interactivity on Glossy Surfaces using a Single Commodity Smartphone

Chungkuk Yoo* School of Computing, KAIST Daejeon, Republic of Korea ckyoo@nclab.kaist.ac.kr

Inseok Hwang† IBM Research Austin, TX, USA ihwang@us.ibm.com

Eric Rozner IBM Research Austin, TX, USA erozner@us.ibm.com

Yu Gu IBM Watson Health Austin, TX, USA yugu@us.ibm.com

Robert F. Dickerson IBM Mobile Innovation Lab Austin, TX, USA rfdickerson@us.ibm.com

ABSTRACT
Driven to create intuitive computing interfaces throughout our everyday space, various state-of-the-art technologies have been proposed for near-surface localization of a user's finger input such as hover or touch. However, these works require specialized hardware not commonly available, limiting the adoption of such technologies. We present SymmetriSense, a technology enabling near-surface 3-dimensional fingertip localization above arbitrary glossy surfaces using a single commodity camera device such as a smartphone. SymmetriSense addresses the localization challenges in using a single regular camera by a novel technique utilizing the principle of reflection symmetry and the fingertip's natural reflection casted upon surfaces like mirrors, granite countertops, or televisions. SymmetriSense achieves typical accuracies at sub-centimeter levels in our localization tests with dozens of volunteers and remains accurate under various environmental conditions. We hope SymmetriSense provides a technical foundation on which various everyday near-surface interactivity can be designed.

Author Keywords
Near-surface input; computing interfaces; fingertip localization; smartphone; single commodity camera.

ACM Classification Keywords
H.5.2. User Interfaces: Input devices and strategies (e.g., mouse, touchscreen)

*This work was done when the first author was on an internship at IBM Research - Austin.
†The corresponding author.

CHI'16, May 07 - 12, 2016, San Jose, CA, USA

ACM 978-1-4503-3362-7/16/05$15.00
DOI: http://dx.doi.org/10.1145/2858036.2858286

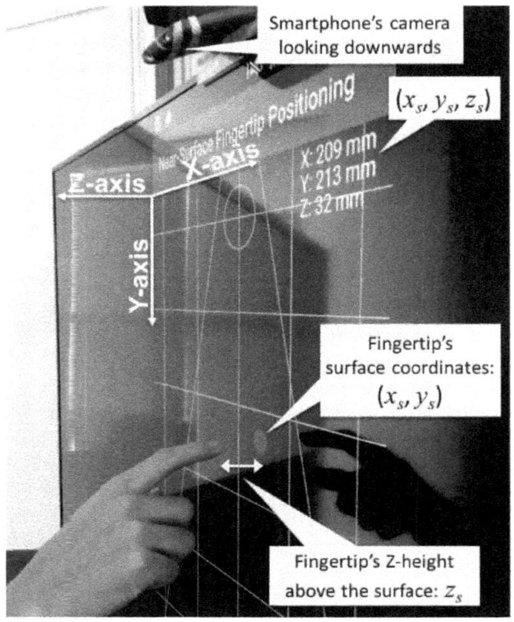

Figure 1: SymmetriSense pinpoints the fingertip's (x, y, z) position near a glossy surface with a single camera.

INTRODUCTION
A major vision of ubiquitous computing is to create seamless computing interfaces throughout the space of our everyday life. In this light, various technologies instrumenting everyday objects with on-surface or near-surface inputs have been proposed [5, 12, 14, 24, 28, 29, 34, 39, 40]. These technologies enable finger or hand movements to provide input either through contact or floating above the surfaces of instrumented target objects. Despite the advantages of these technologies, they require using dedicated hardware which can limit adoption of touch or near-touch interfaces for the user's surrounding objects.

We present *SymmetriSense*, a single camera-based technology that enables near-surface 3-D fingertip localization closely above arbitrary glossy surfaces. SymmetriSense is uniquely advantageous in that it requires only a single commodity camera such as one from a smartphone to instrument a glossy surface, meaning that the technology is immediately available to almost everyone today. Examples of glossy surfaces include various home or office items such as wall mirrors, television screens with protective glass, or even kitchen countertops with a high gloss finish. By mounting the smartphone at the edge of the target surface as shown in Figure 1, SymmetriSense captures the real-time 3-D position of the user's fingertip within the near-surface space (i.e., the fingertip's X- and Y-coordinates on the surface and its Z-height up to several centimeters from the surface). SymmetriSense achieves a sub-centimeter accuracy on small form-factor surfaces (e.g., 5-inch diagonal) and still retains a centimeter accuracy on much larger surfaces (e.g., 60-inch diagonal).

A key challenge for enabling near-surface fingertip localization with a single regular camera is that an image taken from the camera's field of view lacks the precise distance to the finger. Without the distance, the fingertip's position cannot be uniquely determined with respect to the surface area. Although using cameras with depth-sensing features such as infrared or stereoscopy may resolve this issue [12, 14, 18, 19, 24, 30, 39], such specialized devices are still not as ubiquitous as a regular camera built in every smartphone. Their limited availability could significantly hinder many users from adopting such near-surface input technology throughout their everyday space. SymmetriSense presents a novel approach from the state-of-the-art by utilizing the principle of reflection symmetry and the fingertip's natural reflection cast upon a glossy surface. The glossy surface naturally creates a flipped image of the fingertip at a mirrored position in the camera's field of view. The principle of reflection symmetry provides a geometric condition of the pair-wise positions of the original and reflected fingertips, allowing us to obtain a unique solution for the fingertip's (x, y, z) position near the surface.

We expect SymmetriSense can serve as a platform on which hover, touch, or other kinds of finger gestures can be applied to various everyday items without the addition of new dedicated hardware devices. For example, a user may opt to use her own smartphone to instantly and temporarily enable this interface, or for a more permanent installation, she may use a recycled old smartphone and mount it to a granite countertop or a dressing table mirror. SymmetriSense can then create interfaces like virtual touch, proximity sensing, or drawing a pattern on particular regions of the dressing table mirror. Many applications could be designed to respond to such inputs in cooperation with IoT or connected home technologies, for example illuminating the room or narrating today's weather. SymmetriSense can also turn conventional displays like televisions or desktop monitors into interactive displays which respond to the user's finger inputs. SymmetriSense's sufficiently high localization accuracy allows for an interface design that accommodates multiple interactive buttons or regions, which may be sized and spaced similarly to those in interactive tablets or tabletops.

We present our design and implementation of a working SymmetriSense prototype using an off-the-shelf smartphone as well as a prototype that uses a 60-inch flat panel television. While our implementation and evaluation are focused on the smartphone, it should be noted that SymmetriSense can be implemented on any other platform supporting a regular camera and reasonable computing power. We evaluate SymmetriSense by reporting the basic localization accuracies with a group of users, as well as the impacts on accuracy over diverse environmental factors. To be specific, its finger-localization accuracy has been evaluated with volunteers of different ages, genders, and ethnic groups. Our evaluation also includes a robustness test under different lighting conditions and different surface colors and brightness. It is noteworthy that our particular implementation of SymmetriSense does not rely on parameters specific to human skin colors or textures; it can work with any long-shaped pointer in a finger-like dimension, such as a pen or a finger in a glove. We believe the evaluations outline the capabilities and limitations of SymmetriSense, delivering design considerations for developers to build interfaces on top of SymmetriSense.

The key advantages of SymmetriSense are threefold: (1) it offers a negligible barrier-to-entry because SymmetriSense can be built on single-camera commodity platforms such as a smartphone; (2) it features versatile applicability on various glossy surfaces providing a modest reflection; (3) its fingertip localization typically achieves a centimeter accuracy even on a large form-factor surfaces, enabling a fine-grained, sophisticated surface interface design.

In the next section, we outline related work in ubiquitous touch interactivity and near-surface interaction. We then describe our localization technique, which is inspired by the principle of reflection symmetry. Next we present our implementation process along with various engineering choices, and we then report the evaluation results in terms of localization accuracy and robustness. We conclude after discussing the limitations and remaining issues of SymmetriSense.

RELATED WORK

There exists a large body of pre-existing work to enable surface interactivity. In spite of this, SymmetriSense offers a unique advantage by allowing any user with a single commodity camera, such as a smartphone, to enable near-surface 3-D fingertip localization on various surfaces. Below we present a summary of major related works and differentiate SymmetriSense from them.

Surface Instrumentation for Ubiquitous Touch Interfaces

Bringing computing interfaces out of a few dedicated boxes to everyday space has been a major interest of ubiquitous computing and human-computer interaction. Along with the recent proliferation of touch-screen devices, instrumenting various everyday surfaces to respond to users' touch-like inputs has received much attention. A number of works addressed ubiquitous surface instrumentation by localizing the pointer on various surfaces. PlayAnywhere [39] uses infrared light sources and cameras with infrared pass filters to locate touches and hovers of fingertips on arbitrary surfaces. OmniTouch [14] and PointPose [19] use a depth camera oriented towards a surface to detect a larger set of finger input types like hover, touch, tilt, and rotation. Inverted FTIR [12] uses a sheet of special acrylic glass with a laterally mounted infrared light source and takes advantage of frustrated total internal reflection to sense multi-touch locations on a display. WorldKit [40] makes a large ordinary surface instantly touch-interactive by deploying a paired projector and depth camera above the target. SMART Board [5] implements a touch-sensitive whiteboard which localizes the pointer by four cameras at each corner and determines a touch event by analyzing the pointer's on-surface reflection. Several other works instrumented surfaces for different types of surface interactivity not relying on fine-grained pointer locations: Touché [29] determined single- or multi-touch on conductive objects, Scratch Input [15] and Toffee [41] sensed on-surface scratch inputs, SurfaceLink [13] sensed on-surface directional motion of a pointer, and uTouch [7] sensed touch and hover over an LCD display by tapping on the powerline.

Different from the ubiquitous surface instrumentation works above, SymmetriSense presents a novel technology requiring only a single commodity camera to localize the user's near-surface fingertip with respect to an arbitrary reflective surface. Importantly, SymmetriSense is deployable as a smartphone app, making it highly practical for many end users.

Above-surface Input Technologies

Input technologies above a surface extend the input space beyond the discrete boundary of a conventional 2-D touch area. Diverse technologies have been proposed, including those designed for near-surface interactions in close proximity to the surface to others that support relatively distant interactions from the surface. For the space up to a few centimeters above a surface, SmartSkin [28] determines the depth information from a user's hand to the surface by a surface equipped with capacitive sensor grids, while Z-depth [34] senses the depth by multi-layered laser planes over the surface. Very recently a few smartphone models come with built-in hover-sensing screens like Samsung Air View [37] or Sony Floating Touch [36]. By using different types of touchscreen panels and/or different capacitance calibrations, they enable the phones to detect a hovering fingertip close to the screen. FlexAura [20] supports proximity sensing from an arbitrary object by wrapping the target object with a flexible-PCB sensor circuit. For relatively higher altitudes like several tens of centimeters above a surface, RetroDepth [18] uses a pair of stereoscopic infrared cameras to enable precise inputs on and above a retro-reflective material. Similarly, LeapMotion [24] uses an infrared transceiver device to detect multi-finger gestures in the space above the device. Sharp et al. [30] present a Kinect-based system tracking the detailed mid-air motion of a user's hand. Medusa [1] installs 138 proximity sensors around the perimeter of a tabletop to enrich the tabletop interaction with the user's body and arm location contexts.

SymmetriSense targets the near-surface space, i.e., a few centimeters above the surface. Within this space, SymmetriSense pinpoints the fingertip in terms of its spatial coordinates with respect to the surface area, at an accuracy comparable to those provided by the commercial devices with special hover-sensing screens such as Samsung Air View. SymmetriSense also provides the fingertip's height information above the surface which is not supported by those commercial devices. Later in the paper, we show the accuracy of SymmetriSense in comparison with Samsung Air View.

Designing Near-surface Interaction

With the emergence of near-surface input technologies, new interfaces and interaction guidelines incorporating on- and near-surface space have been studied. Hilliges et al. [16] explored interactions seamlessly switching between on a tabletop surface and above it. Spindler et al. [33] and Wacharamanotham et al. [38] studied the vertical thickness guidelines to design mid-air gestures within the near-surface space. Marquardt et al. [21] addressed the notion of continuous interaction space, treating the space on and above the surface as a continuum, and categorized various interactions making use of the space. Detailed interface examples include selective information exposure upon a hovering event [3], preselection guides to improve touch accuracy on small targets [25], hover-responsive dynamic user interfaces [8], and so on.

We clarify that crafting or assessing user interfaces designed on top of SymmetriSense is beyond the scope of this paper. We introduce the technical foundations of SymmetriSense and analyze its performance metrics to benefit future interface designs and usability assessments.

CHALLENGES AND KEY APPROACH

In this section, we first address the key challenge of localizing the fingertip with respect to the surface using only a single regular non-depth camera. Then we present our novel technique utilizing the natural reflection of the fingertip appearing on a glossy surface. The principle of reflection symmetry ensures the original image and its reflected image appear symmetric with respect to the plane of reflection, which is the interacting surface in our case. We will describe how we leverage this property to derive the 3-D spatial coordinates of the fingertip from a single 2-D image from the camera's field of view (FoV hereinafter).

Single Vision Challenge in Fingertip Localization

Figure 1 shows a possible placement of the camera (i.e., the smartphone) with respect to the target surface. The phone is simply placed at an edge of the television's bezel with a simple acrylic mount. This placement allows the phone's camera to see the perspective horizontal view of the surface, the fingertip, and the near-surface space in between. Also, placing the phone right at an edge of the target surface makes SymmetriSense easier and more intuitive to use, rather than placing the phone at a distant location such as on the ceiling. For the rest of the paper, we use the definitions of X-, Y-, and Z-axes as shown on Figure 1.

Figure 2 shows that fingertips at two different positions near a matte surface appear as the same points in the camera's FoV. Figure 3 depicts its sagittal cross-section diagram without the notion of reflection, explaining the uncertainty of the true position of the fingertip along the line of sight passing from the camera to the fingertip. One might wonder if the use of the fingertip's shadow casted on the surface would help. It may

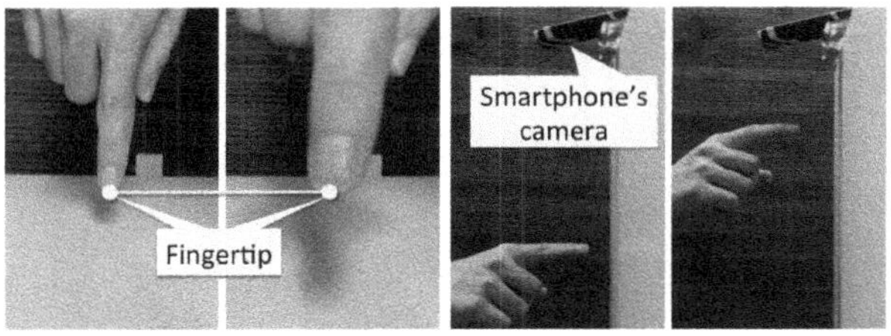

(a) Viewed from the camera. (b) Viewed from the side.

Figure 2: Fingertips at two different locations appear at the same points in the camera's FoV.

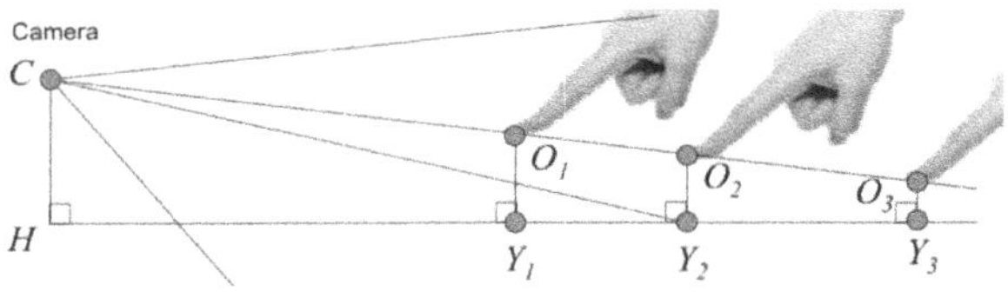

Figure 3: Uncertainty in localizing fingertips.

narrow the area in which the fingertip possibly exists, but it still does not pinpoint the fingertip's position as the shadow can be arbitrarily displaced depending on the fingertip's Z-axis height and the directions of external lighting sources.

Pinpointing Fingertip by Leveraging Reflection Symmetry

Figure 4 demonstrates how the reflected fingertip makes it possible to pinpoint the fingertip's location. The figures are taken from our high-gloss 60-inch LCD TV screen under the illuminance of 150 lux, a typical office lighting condition [23]. Basically, the fingertips at two different locations along the camera's line of sight still appear at the same points in the camera's FoV. However, their reflected counterparts appear at different points from each other. This property can be described by a set of geometric equations, from which we can pinpoint the true location of the fingertip. Note that glossy surfaces with reasonable reflection are very common in our everyday space. Figure 5 demonstrates reflected fingertips on four different surfaces, i.e., a restroom mirror, an office window, a granite kitchen countertop, and a white board.

Our goal is to compute the near-surface coordinates of the fingertip (x_s, y_s, z_s) (denoted in Figure 1) with respect to the surface using the on-camera coordinates (x_{co}, y_{co}) and (x_{cr}, y_{cr}), the coordinates of the original and the reflected fingertip seen from the camera's FoV, respectively (denoted in Figure 7). Note that we presume a few constants of known values, such as the vertical and horizontal angles of the camera's FoV (denoted by Θ_v and Θ_h, respectively), its mounting angle (denoted by Θ_{HM}), the camera's offset distances from the surface edges (denoted by D_x and D_y, respectively), the Z-axis height of the camera above the surface, and so on. We discuss how to derive those constants in Discussion section.

Determining the Y-axis coordinate

For easier understanding, we begin with a simpler case where x_{co} and x_{cr} are zero, i.e., the fingertip is on a straight line from the camera in parallel with Y-axis. Figure 6 depicts the

(a) Viewed from the camera. (b) Viewed from the side.

Figure 4: Fingertips at two different locations still appear at the same points in the camera's FoV but their reflected counterparts do not appear at the same locations.

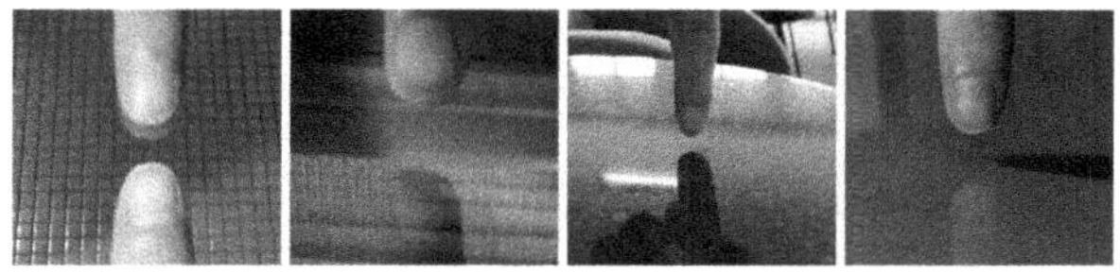

Figure 5: Fingertips reflected on (from left to right): a restroom mirror, an office window, a granite kitchen countertop, and a white board.

sagittal cross-section diagram of such a case, along the line from the camera to the fingertip. Now the problem is to find y_s, which can be expressed from Figure 6:

$$y_s = \overline{HC}\tan(\Theta_{HM} + \theta_{MY}) - D_y \quad (1)$$

where $\overline{HC}$ is the height between the camera and the surface.

To obtain the unknown angle θ_{MY}, we first use the property given by reflection symmetry: $\overline{OY} = \overline{RY}$ in Figure 6. This means that $\frac{1}{2}\left(\overline{RY_C} - \overline{OY_C}\right) = \overline{RY_C} - \overline{YY_C}$, which can be expressed by:

$$\frac{1}{2}(\tan\theta_{RY_C} - \tan\theta_{OY_C}) = \tan\theta_{RY_C} - \tan\theta_{YY_C} \quad (2)$$

$$\text{where } \theta_{YY_C} = \frac{\pi}{2} - (\Theta_{HM} + \theta_{MY}),\ \theta_{RY_C} = \frac{\pi}{2} - (\Theta_{HM} + \theta_{MR}),$$

$$\theta_{OY_C} = \frac{\pi}{2} - (\Theta_{HM} + \theta_{MO}) \quad (3)$$

Equation (2) is equivalent to:

$$\tan\theta_{YY_C} = \frac{1}{2}(\tan\theta_{RY_C} + \tan\theta_{OY_C}) \quad (4)$$

By using the definition of θ_{YY_C} in (3) on (4),

$$\theta_{MY} = \frac{\pi}{2} - \Theta_{HM} - \arctan(\tan\theta_{RY_C} + \tan\theta_{OY_C}) \quad (5)$$

Therefore, we can evaluate y_s in Equation (1) by using (5) and (3). Note that θ_{MR} and θ_{MO} can be obtained from y_{cr} and y_{co}, respectively. If we assume an ideal pinhole camera without a nonlinear distortion [11], it gives the following relation for θ_{MR}:

$$\frac{y_{cr}}{Y_{FOV}/2} = \frac{\tan\theta_{MR}}{\tan(\Theta_v/2)}$$

$$\text{Or equivalently, } \theta_{MR} = \arctan\left(\frac{y_{cr}}{Y_{FOV}/2}\tan\frac{\Theta_v}{2}\right) \quad (6)$$

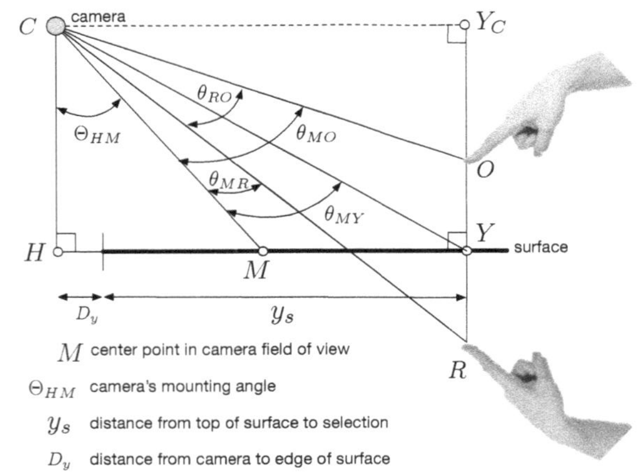

Figure 6: Sagittal cross-section diagram of a near-surface finger and its reflection.

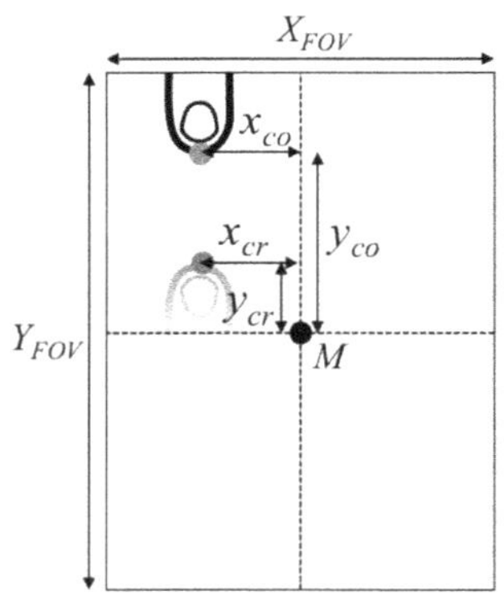

Figure 7: Notations to denote the on-camera coordinates of the original fingertip (x_{co}, y_{co}) and the reflected fingertip (x_{cr}, y_{cr}) as seen by the camera, with respect to the center (M) of the camera's FoV.

where Y_{FOV} is the vertical length of the camera's full FoV, as denoted in Figure 7.

The expression of θ_{MO} is analogous to (6). We applied a polynomial radial distortion correction in our actual implementation.

Determining the X- and Z-axis coordinates

The general case with nonzero x_{co} and x_{cr} is depicted in Figure 8. Once we obtain y_s, it is rather straightforward to compute the remaining near-surface coordinates, i.e., x_s and z_s. Note that z_s is equal to $\overline{OY} = \overline{YY_C} - \overline{OY_C}$. In turn, this difference is represented by the difference between two tangent values:

$$z_s = (y_s + D_y)\,(\tan\theta_{YY_C} - \tan\theta_{OY_C})$$

which can be evaluated with (3), (5), and θ_{MO}'s version of (6). Finally, x_s is given by the Pythagorean theorem:

$$x_s = \sqrt{\overline{HC}^2 + (y_s + D_y)^2}\,\tan\theta_{YX} + D_x$$

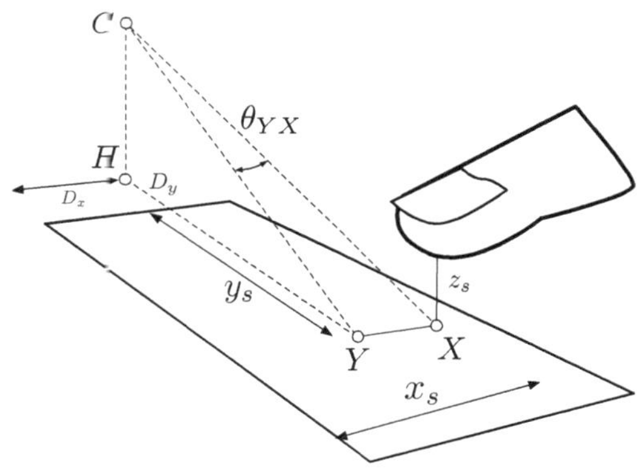

Figure 8: General case of localizing the fingertip in 3-D space.

(a) (b) (c) (d) (e)

Figure 9: Finger extraction. (a), (b): Raw images seen by the camera at two successive frames; (c): Finger extraction by applying skin color ranges; (d): Finger extraction by inter-frame differentials; (e): Computing convex hulls.

where the expression of θ_{YX} is analogous to (6), in terms of x_{cr}, X_{FOV}, and Θ_h.

IMPLEMENTATION

We present the issues and considerations in implementing a working prototype of SymmetriSense. While our prototype is built on Samsung Galaxy S5 with Android 5.0, it could be built on other phones or various off-the-shelf mobile platforms having a single regular camera combined with a embedded computer such as Arduino [2] or Rasberry Pi [27].

Extracting Finger Parts

The approach presented in the previous section assumes that we can extract the original and reflected finger parts out of the image seen from the camera's FoV. Our first attempt was to extract finger parts whose color values belong to the representative color range of the human skin [32]. We further specified the YCbCr color range between (0, 77, 133) and (255, 127, 173) [26]. However, we observed this technique is highly susceptible to background objects similar to skin colors; Figure 9c demonstrates this issue for the given raw image of Figure 9a. It is also unable to support non-finger pointers such as a hand in glove or pen.

To overcome the limitations of the color-based technique, we adopted alternative techniques based on frame differences [22]. When the user moves her finger near the surface, we extract the differentials between successive frames. Figure 9d demonstrates the differentials evaluated from two successive

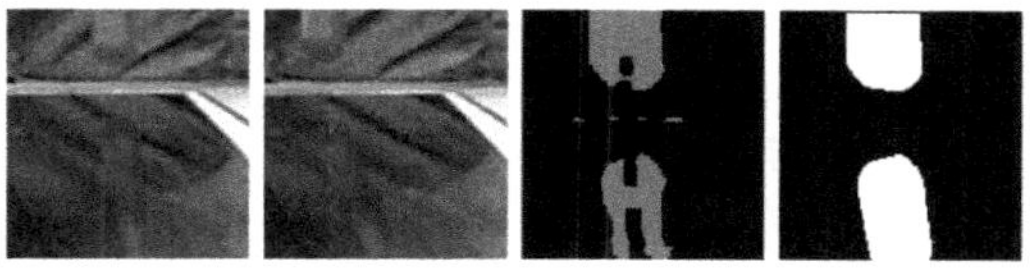

(a) (b) (c) (d)

Figure 10: Pen extraction. (a), (b): Raw images at two successive frames; (c) Inter-frame differentials; (d) Computing convex hulls around the pair of pen images.

frames shown in Figure 9a and 9b. We set empirically-determined threshold values to classify a motion at a certain position on the FoV. To suppress false-positives from non-finger motions in the background, we find a contour of the differential area between the frames and compute a convex hull enclosing the contour as shown in Figure 9e. We classify the differential area as a finger only for a convex hull larger than a threshold size. We used the Android OpenCV library to find contours and compute convex hulls. Another advantage in this technique is the ability to extract not only a fingertip but also many different long-shaped pointers, as shown in Figure 10.

Note that finger extraction is not a part of the novelty we claim; we integrated well-known, relatively simple image processing techniques to build a working prototype of SymmetriSense. Rather than simply using frame differences, there may be more advanced object-tracking techniques proposed in the field of image processing [42, 9, 31]. In particular, Cucchiara et al. [9] proposed a method to precisely extract a moving object without its shadow included, which may be applied to SymmetriSense to further improve the finger extraction performance. However, such advanced techniques are beyond the scope of this paper.

Detecting Fingertips from Finger Parts

In our camera-mounting configuration, the original finger appears in the top part of the view, while the reflected finger appears in the bottom part. We first find the original fingertip by searching for the bottom-most tangential point in the original finger part (indicated by the red arrow in Figure 9e). Starting from this point, we define a narrow rectangular space stretching downwards to search for the reflected fingertip.

To reduce computation, we leverage the locality of the moving fingertip. We define a region of interest (ROI) centered at the previously detected location on the FoV, only in which we perform fingertip detection. We empirically found an appropriate camera resolution to ensure real-time responsiveness and practical localization accuracy. We used 320×240 pixels for the camera resolution and its quarter size for the ROI. We apply these detected locations into the equations in the previous section to localize the fingertip's (X, Y, Z) coordinates. Detection is done at 30 frames per second.

Suppressing Image Noises and Localization Errors

Under low brightness conditions, we observed random noises on images regardless of a moving object due to the camera's ISO settings. We applied a blur filter for higher noise-robustness. To ensure sufficiently large differentials, we compute the difference between the current frame and a past one four frames behind. We also performed morphology operations (dilate and erode) to acquire well-connected finger shapes.

Due to the relatively low camera resolution of 320×240, a single pixel error often results in momentary hopping of a fingertip's locations. To alleviate such behaviors, we applied a 10-frame weighted moving average to smooth the fingertip's trajectory. Given the 10 points from those frames, we further rule out the largest outlier to improve accuracy. All combined, our localization pipeline takes 8.7 ms to compute each frame (not including the moving average filter lag). Due to the inherent causality of the moving average filter, real-time localization introduces a slight noticeable lag. Note that quadrupling the resolution would halve the impact of single pixel error, allowing a shorter moving average to do the equivalent smoothing effect, and thereby shorten the response lag. However, all these improvements are at the cost of extra computation. We will discuss these details in the Discussion section.

We observed subtle localization errors which tend to grow at outer regions of the camera's FoV. This is known as radial distortion [11] due to the non-ideal curvature of the camera's lens. We implemented additional correction based on the polynomial approximation model [11, 6]. As the correction parameters are variables in terms of the focal length, we disabled Android's auto-focus feature. In fact having a constant focal length is necessary in localizing the fingertip as it effectively fixes the camera's FoV.

EVALUATION

The goal of our experiments is to report the basic fingertip localization accuracies of SymmetriSense under a wide range of participants as well as environmental conditions. We believe this provides numerical implications or guidelines for future interface designs on top of SymmetriSense. First, we describe our evaluation settings and then present the results.

Evaluation Settings

We perform three classes of experiments: a fingertip localization accuracy experiment on a smartphone, a fingertip localization accuracy experiment on a 60-inch television, and finally a set of microbenchmarks to analyze the accuracy under a variety of environmental conditions.

While SymmetriSense supports a wide array of arbitrary glossy surfaces, we include a smartphone experiment to compare against an alternative near-surface localization technology in the market, i.e., Samsung Air View. The Samsung Galaxy S5's Air View is a built-in hover sensing feature enabled by extended capacitive sensing supported in its specific display hardware. The experiment is a set of finger-hovering tasks on targets shown on different positions of the display. Upon a participant's fingertip above a target, we have SymmetriSense and Air View independently compute the fingertip's location. We consider the locations from Air View as the ground truth, and evaluate the fingertip localization accuracies of SymmetriSense by measuring the offset distance between SymmetriSense-computed locations and

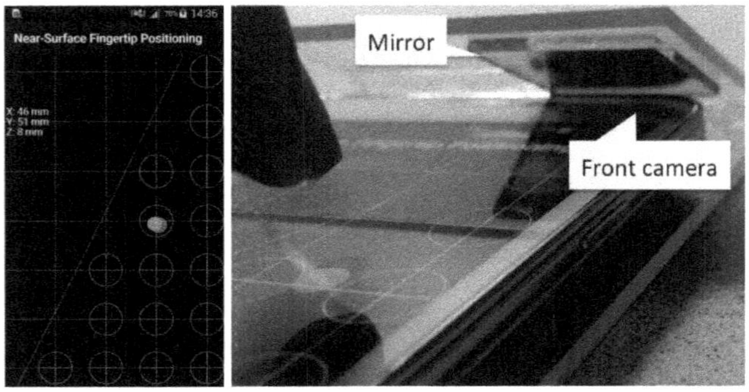

(a) Test app screenshot on phone. (b) A phone case with mirror.

Figure 11: Phone experiment settings.

the ground truth locations from Air View. One might wonder why we do not simply measure the offset distance between SymmetriSense-computed locations and the corresponding target locations shown on the display. The reason is to rule out possible human errors; the participants may not have perfectly positioned their fingertips on the targets. By measuring SymmetriSense-vs-Air View differences, we evaluate the accuracies of SymmetriSense comparative to those of Air View and irrespective of human errors.

In the TV experiment, we report only the localization results from SymmetriSense with respect to on-screen targets due to the absence of an alternative built-in localization technology. Therefore, the localization errors in TV experiments may include not only the errors from SymmetriSense technology itself but also human errors. Given that the phone experiment has shown the localization accuracies free from human errors, the TV experiment mainly demonstrates the efficacy of SymmetriSense on much larger surfaces.

To incorporate diverse finger shapes, skin colors, and pointing poses in the smartphone and TV experiments, we recruited 18 participants for each experiment. To be specific, the participants of the phone experiments include 4 females out of 18 and were 38.3 years old on average (std: 10.5 years). Those of the TV experiments include 4 females out of 18 and were 40.2 years old on average (std: 9.6 years). Our participants pool consists of left- and right-handed users, and mixed ethnicity of Asians, African Americans, Hispanics, and Whites.

Lastly, the microbenchmarks demonstrate if SymmetriSense is susceptible to various environmental conditions. To be specific, a series of small case studies were performed over varying conditions of surface colors, ambient lighting, and screen brightness. These experiments were conducted on the phone to use Air View as the ground truth.

Detailed setup for smartphone experiment. A Samsung Galaxy S5 phone was placed on a desk in a large corporate office. To retrieve the localization results from both technologies at minimal time differences, we slightly engineered the phone's exterior to make SymmetriSense localize a fingertip near the phone's own surface, where Air View is running as well. Figure 11b shows our phone on a custom acrylic mount with a mirror above its front camera. This setup produces geometrically similar effects as having the camera mounted at an edge of the target surface (as depicted in Figure 8).

18 volunteers were asked to perform a sequence of positioning tasks on our test application (shown in Figure 11a). The test application shows 16 circular targets which are placed within the camera's FoV. The circles were 5 mm in radius and the centers of adjacent circles were separated by 15 mm on both the X- and Y-axes. For each circle, the participants were instructed to point at the center of the circle with a hovering fingertip for 5 seconds. During the experiment, two small dots were shown: a red dot, which corresponds to the location of the hovering finger as determined by the built-in Air View feature, and a blue dot, which corresponds to the location of the finger based on SymmetriSense. Participants were told to center the red dot in the circle. The process continued to show 16 circles, all of which are located within the camera's FoV. One might think the presence of the dots may influence a participant's targeting behaviors, e.g., trying to center the blue dot instead. Our metric is invariant in spite of such a participant; we consider the Air View's locations as the ground truth, and report the offset distances between SymmetriSense-computed locations and the ground truth. If a participant does not follow the instruction and purposely moves a finger elsewhere, AirView will displace the red dot to track the finger. It is impossible for the participant to manipulate the distance in between.

Detailed setup for TV experiment. A phone was affixed atop a 60-inch LCD TV in an office, and connected via an HDMI output. Figure 1 shows the setup, where the phone's rear camera is angled toward the TV surface. The mounting angle Θ_{HM} was 63.8 degrees, but SymmetriSense allows different mounting angles. Users were asked to stand in front of the TV and repeat an experiment similar to the phone experiment. Due to differences in surface areas, camera mounting positions, and camera vantage points, the TV experiment had a different number and placement of circles. A total of 22 circles were shown, each of which had a 25 mm radius and was separated by 75 mm on the X and Y axes. As there is no other technology available for ground truth, we report the offset distances between each circle center and the corresponding SymmetriSense-computed fingertip locations. No dots were displayed to avoid potential influences on the participants' targeting behaviors.

We additionally performed a single participant study to measure the Z-height accuracy. We mounted a ruler below the pointing finger and instructed the participant to hold the fingertip at several predetermined discrete heights. We visually inspected the ground truth heights from the recorded pictures and compared them with the Z-height measured by SymmetriSense. Note that Air View does not provide Z-heights.

Evaluation Results

Localization accuracies on a smartphone. The raw data of fingertip localization over all users and all circles is shown in Figure 12. Figures 12a and 12b show the locations of the

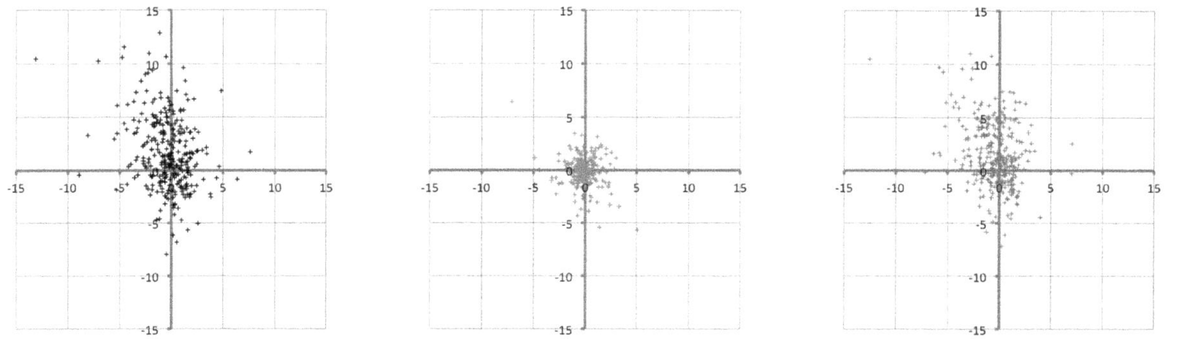

(a) SymmetriSense offset to Air View. (b) Air View offset to circle centers. (c) SymmetriSense offset to circle centers.

Figure 13: Offset, in millimeters, for Air View and SymmetriSense on the phone.

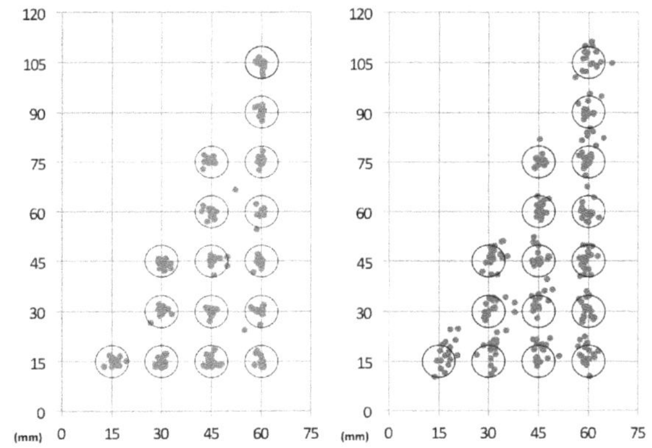

(a) Samsung Air View. (b) SymmetriSense.

Figure 12: Location estimates on the phone for all users.

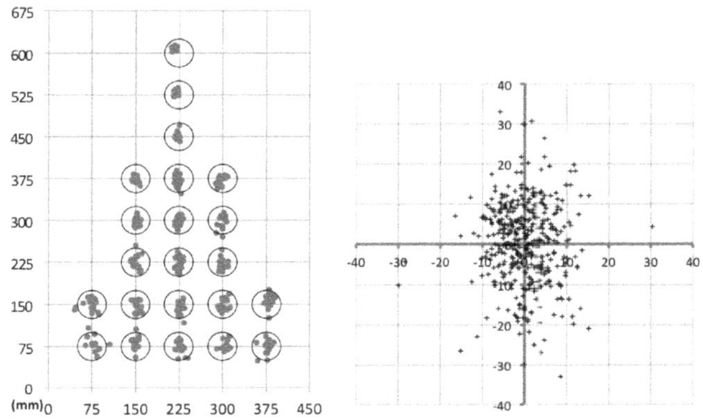

(a) Location estimates. (b) Offset, in mm, to circle centers.

Figure 14: Location estimates on the TV surface and offsets.

fingertip hovering above each target, retrieved from Air View and SymmetriSense, respectively. The gridlines and circles corresponding to the actual screen content are also shown for reference. Our main evaluation metric, i.e., the offset distance between SymmetriSense-computed locations and Air View's ground truth locations, is shown in Figure 13a. For information purposes, Figure 13b and 13c present scatter plots of the locations from Air View and SymmetriSense respectively relative to each circle's center. As we discussed earlier, the results in Figures 13b and 13c may contain human error.

The amount of error is relatively small; the average offset distance between SymmetriSense-computed locations and the corresponding Air View's ground truth locations is 3.61 mm (std=2.55). As shown in Figure 13a, the errors on the X-axis are generally lower than the errors on the Y-axis (1.53 mm vs 2.63 mm average). Furthermore, the largest errors in SymmetriSense come from the furthest points from the camera: the furthest row has an average distance of 4.38 mm from their Air View counterparts, while the closer points have an average error of 2.55 mm. These limitations are addressed in the Discussion section.

Finally, we examine how SymmetriSense performs if we apply a *snap-to-grid* feature, i.e., snapping the estimated fingertip position to the closest circle center. We post-process the data to see if any estimate snaps to a wrong circle. The Air View estimates are 100% correct. SymmetriSense misclassifies only 2.78% (8 out of 288 samples). All of these errors occur on the two rows furthest from the camera.

Localization accuracies on a 60-inch TV. Figure 14 shows the X, Y accuracy results from the TV experiment. Figure 14a shows SymmetriSense's estimated locations and Figure 14b shows the offset of the estimated locations from the circle centers. As discussed earlier, part of the error from the circle centers is introduced by the users themselves. Regardless, the relative error is small: the average distance from the circle centers to our estimate is only 10.04 mm (std=6.20). Even though these errors are larger than the phone experiment, the error relative to the screen size is much smaller in this experiment. None of the snap-to-grid points are misclassified. We see similar trends as the phone experiment, with the average error on the Y-axis (7.89 mm) being higher than the average error on the X-axis (4.70 mm).

Figure 15 shows the the Z-height test results. The user hovered his finger 10, 30 and 50 mm above the screen and the Z-height estimate was captured. For each distance, 22 data

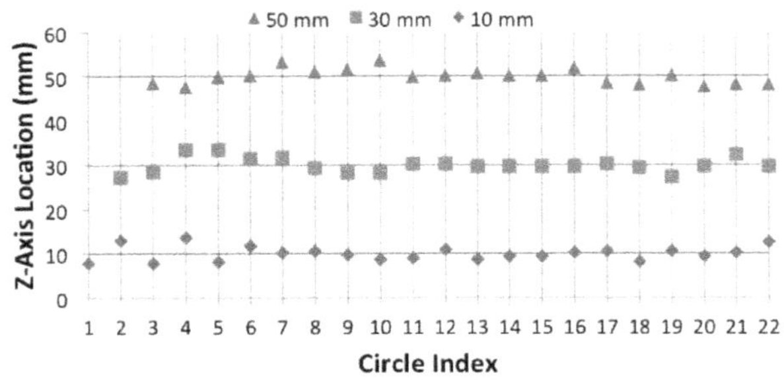

Figure 15: Z-axis estimate for 10, 30, and 50 mm.

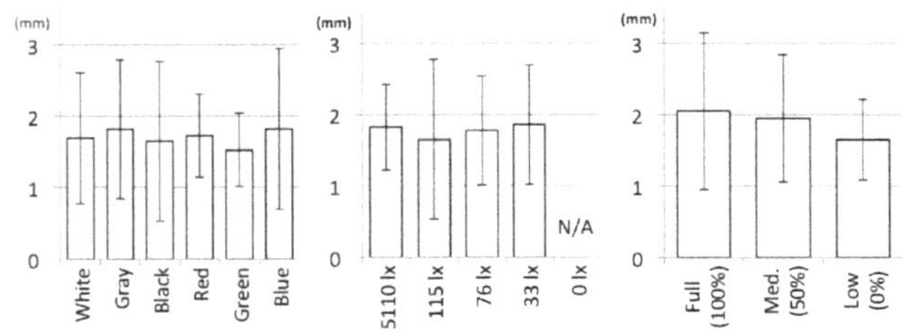

(a) Errors over background colors. (b) Errors over lighting conditions. (c) Errors over screen brightness.

Figure 16: Environmental benchmark results.

points were captured, one for each circle center. We index the circles from 1-22, from left to right, and then top to bottom. For example, the top circle in Figure 14a is Circle 1, the 2nd-to-top is Circle 2, the bottom-left is Circle 18, and the bottom-right is Circle 22. Note that we are only able to capture the Z-heights that lie within the camera's vertical FoV. This means that for 30 mm height, we cannot capture Circle 1 (which is closest to the camera), and for 50 mm height, we cannot capture Circles 1 and 2. Overall, however, SymmetriSense does an effective job tracking the Z-height of a user's finger. The average error at the 10 mm height is 1.26 mm (std=0.99), at the 30 mm height is 1.24 mm (std=1.15) and at the 50 mm height is 1.35 mm (std=1.06). These results indicate that SymmetriSense can effectively estimate a user's 3-D fingertip location, which is a powerful primitive with only a single commodity camera.

Environmental benchmarks. The first microbenchmark is changing the color of the screen. The surface color in our earlier tests was black. To study the effectiveness of SymmetriSense on a variety of surface colors, a single user repeated the previous phone test on the surface colors of white, gray, black, red, green, and blue. Figure 16a shows the X, Y accuracies for each color in terms of the distance between AirView's and SymmetriSense's locations with one standard deviation error bars. SymmetriSense stays reasonably consistent across surface colors ($F_{5,90} = 0.240$, $p > 0.943$), indicating that the technology is fairly robust to surface colors.

Figure 16b shows the average error over varying ambient lighting conditions. Our earlier experiments on the phone and the TV were done under 115 lux and 150 lux, respectively, which are typical office illuminance levels [23]. To diversify the illuminance conditions, a single participant conducted tests on five conditions, i.e., in an office lighting (115 lux), in full sun in mid-afternoon (5100 lux), in a small conference room with a full set of lights on (76 lux), the same room with only the dimmer lights on (33 lux), and in complete darkness. Figure 16b shows similar errors across the conditions ($F_{3,60} = 0.180$, $p > 0.909$), usually ranging from 1-3 mm, indicating SymmetriSense can effectively deal with a range of ambient lighting conditions. Our scheme does not work in complete darkness.

Last, Figure 16c shows the average error for SymmetriSense over varying screen brightness settings. The same user repeated the experiments at 0%, 50% and 100% screen brightness. The screen background color was set to white. We see that screen brightness makes little difference ($F_{2,45} = 0.909$, $p > 0.410$), with low brightness giving slightly larger errors. Regardless, the results indicate that SymmetriSense can deal with varying screen brightness.

DISCUSSION

Limitations

Significant CPU utilization. In the camera resolution of 320 × 240, SymmetriSense shows a steady CPU utilization around 25%. It is the full CPU utilization for a single-threaded application on a quad-core CPU, which is the case of our Galaxy S5. This can be alleviated by increasing smartphones' computing power, exploiting parallelism, or computational offload to GPGPU or external devices [10]. As discussed in the Implementation section, the camera resolution affects several real-time performance metrics, including: (1) localization errors along the Y-axis and (2) the real-time localization lag resulted from the moving average filter length. We analyze the effects on (1) in detail below.

Larger localization errors along the Y-axis. In the evaluations we observed larger localization errors along the Y-axis than the X-axis, and growing Y-axis errors near the surface's distal edge from the camera. It is not surprising; the tangent function in Equation (1) takes the camera's mounting angle Θ_{HM}, in addition to the variable θ_{MY}. Because the tangent function diverges near $\pi/2$, the existence of Θ_{HM} makes the tangent function very sensitive to a small change of θ_{MY}. This sensitivity increases around the surface's distal edge where θ_{MY} is greater. Still, Θ_{HM} should be large enough to ensure a sufficient view of the surface from the camera.

To alleviate this sensitivity, processing the input images at a higher pixel-density would help. For example, in our setting with a 60-inch LCD television and camera resolution of 320 × 240 pixels, a single pixel width is converted into 25 mm of Y-axis distance at the farthest edge (60 cm away from the camera in our settings). In a future implementation with additional CPU power available, we can quadruple the pixel density (640 × 480) so that the converted distance per pixel is improved to 12 mm, giving smaller localization errors.

Limited FoV. SymmetriSense introduces near-surface interactivity only for part of the surface within the camera's FoV;

on a Galaxy S5 phone, the FoVs are 79.69° for the front camera and 62° for the back camera at maximum. Accordingly, designing an interface on top of SymmetriSense should follow a guideline such as placing interactive regions within this area. We may further extend the interactive area with a fish-eye lens and image deformation techniques [17].

Largely dynamic on-surface content. Our implementation leverages moving object tracking techniques to extract the fingertip from the scene. We have observed SymmetriSense performs well when applied on a static surface or a display with modest content changes. Some dynamic content is tolerated because screen content viewed from the edge-mounted camera often appears severely blurred and much dimmer. Still, applying SymmetriSense on a display with large dynamic contents might interfere with the finger extraction. A potential resolution is to evaluate the symmetry of a moving object and discard non-symmetric parts because content changes only appear on the screen side. We may also apply advanced image processing techniques such as optical feature-based image tracking on digital surfaces [4], or separating an object's reflection from a single image [35].

Battery consumption. The smartphone's battery consumption has not been a major consideration in our initial development. We acknowledge the smartphone running heavy vision tasks requires nontrivial energy. In our implementation, the battery drop is roughly 20% per hour if the phone is unplugged. Given this energy requirement, desirable application scenarios would be an instant, short-term interaction with a user's primary phone, or a permanent instrumentation with a plugged, possibly recycled, phone.

Design guidelines and considerations. While our results show SymmetriSense can accurately localize a fingertip, a few limitations were also brought to light. The goal of our accuracy studies is to provide developers with a series of best practices when using our system. For example, certain touch- or hover-sensitive regions should be separated by a safe distance. Alternatively, coarse-grained interactions, such as scrolling or swiping, can be implemented over areas with lower pin-point accuracy. For larger surfaces like TVs or mirrors, this may not be a big burden. This work aims to provide a first-order evaluation of SymmetriSense with the hope that future algorithms, uses and techniques can be refined.

Open Issues and Future Works

Deriving form-factor constants. SymmetriSense relies on a few constants like the camera's FoV, mounted height from the surface, and mounted angle. The camera's FoV angles are obtainable at runtime, e.g., via `Camera.Parameters` APIs of Android. The other constants can be obtained through a one-time calibration sequence after mounting the camera device, such as instructing the user to point to a few predetermined positions. In some cases, SymmetriSense may not need to convert the fingertip's position into real-world distance metrics, making a calibration sequence unnecessary. For example, an application letting the user define her own interactive regions on her dressing table mirror that respond to her finger's proximity to a region to execute various tasks. The design of a runtime calibration sequence is future work.

Incorporating a touch feature. SymmetriSense's touch support depends on how strictly we define a touch. We observed that SymmetriSense often does not clearly distinguish a finger physically contacting the surface from one floating very close, e.g., 1-2 mm above the surface. The reasons are (1) low camera resolution makes such a tiny gap unclear, and (2) a fat fingertip often obstructs the line of sight from the gap to the camera, making the camera see the fingertip's original image and reflected image slightly connected. If we accept a touch only if the fingertip physically contacts the surface (i.e., only when Z-height is 0.0 mm), SymmetriSense may generate non-trivial false positives. If we accept a relaxed definition of touch (e.g., if the gap is under 2 mm), we can say SymmetriSense supports touch. This may not be a radical assumption given that even capacitive touch screens sometimes misclassify a touch upon a very closely floating fingertip. Due to the delicate issue of touch definitions, we chose not to justify our redefinition of a touch in this study, and focused on pinpointing a user's fingertip within a near-surface space. Still, incorporating physical touches and near-surface interaction by a single uniform technology makes SymmetriSense more attractive, and a rigorous extension towards touch support and/or an equivalent touch definition is our future work.

Alternate input mechanisms. While most of our evaluation focused on locating a fingertip, we believe SymmetriSense will work with other input objects. We informally tested pens, styluses and gloves with our approach and the performance was promising. Our localization scheme relies on motion and convex hull detection, which allows for a wide variety of input objects. We leave detailed analysis to future work.

CONCLUSION

In this paper, we presented SymmetriSense, a technology that enables near-surface 3-D fingertip localization above arbitrary glossy surfaces, using a single commodity camera such as one from a smartphone. Unlike the state-of-the-art, SymmetriSense achieves localization by using only a commodity device which is ubiquitously available. To address the challenge using a single camera, we presented a novel technique utilizing the fingertip's natural reflection and the principle of reflection symmetry. We reported the implementation details and built a working prototype. Our performance evaluation shows sub-centimeter 3-D localization accuracy in most cases, even as environmental conditions change. We believe that SymmetriSense can serve as a platform that can instrument various everyday glossy surfaces with near-surface interactivity to enable new ubiquitous computing applications.

REFERENCES

1. Michelle Annett, Tovi Grossman, Daniel Wigdor, and George Fitzmaurice. Medusa: a proximity-aware multi-touch tabletop. In *Proc. UIST 2011*. ACM, 337–346.

2. Arduino. Retrieved September 24, 2015 from `https://www.arduino.cc`.

3. Aras Balali Moghaddam, Jeremy Svendsen, Melanie Tory, and Alexandra Branzan Albu. Integrating touch and near touch interactions for information visualizations. In *Proc. CHI 2011 Extended Abstracts*. ACM, 2347–2352.
4. Dominikus Baur, Sebastian Boring, and Steven Feiner. Virtual projection: exploring optical projection as a metaphor for multi-device interaction. In *Proc. CHI 2012*. ACM, 1693–1702.
5. SMART Board. Retrieved December 28, 2015 from http://education.smarttech.com/.
6. Camera calibration with OpenCV. Retrieved December 26, 2015 from http://docs.opencv.org/2.4/doc/tutorials/calib3d/camera_calibration/camera_calibration.html.
7. Ke-Yu Chen, Gabe A Cohn, Sidhant Gupta, and Shwetak N Patel. uTouch: sensing touch gestures on unmodified LCDs. In *Proc. CHI 2013*. ACM, 2581–2584.
8. Victor Cheung, Jens Heydekorn, Stacey Scott, and Raimund Dachselt. Revisiting hovering: Interaction guides for interactive surfaces. In *Proc. ITS 2012*. ACM, 355–358.
9. Rita Cucchiara, Costantino Grana, Massimo Piccardi, and Andrea Prati. Detecting moving objects, ghosts, and shadows in video streams. *Pattern Analysis and Machine Intelligence, IEEE Transactions on* 25, 10 (2003), 1337–1342.
10. Eduardo Cuervo, Aruna Balasubramanian, Dae-ki Cho, Alec Wolman, Stefan Saroiu, Ranveer Chandra, and Paramvir Bahl. MAUI: making smartphones last longer with code offload. In *Proc. MobiSys 2010 (MobiSys '10)*. ACM, New York, NY, USA, 49–62. DOI: http://dx.doi.org/10.1145/1814433.1814441
11. Frederic Devernay and Olivier Faugeras. Straight lines have to be straight. *Machine vision and applications* 13, 1 (2001), 14–24.
12. Florian Echtler, Andreas Dippon, Marcus Tönnis, and Gudrun Klinker. Inverted FTIR: easy multitouch sensing for flatscreens. In *Proc. ITS 2009*. ACM, 29–32.
13. Mayank Goel, Brendan Lee, Md Tanvir Islam Aumi, Shwetak Patel, Gaetano Borriello, Stacie Hibino, and Bo Begole. SurfaceLink: using inertial and acoustic sensing to enable multi-device interaction on a surface. In *Proc. CHI 2014*. ACM, 1387–1396.
14. Chris Harrison, Hrvoje Benko, and Andrew D Wilson. OmniTouch: wearable multitouch interaction everywhere. In *Proc. UIST 2011*. ACM, 441–450.
15. Chris Harrison and Scott E Hudson. Scratch input: creating large, inexpensive, unpowered and mobile finger input surfaces. In *Proc. UIST 2008*. ACM, 205–208.
16. Otmar Hilliges, Shahram Izadi, Andrew D Wilson, Steve Hodges, Armando Garcia-Mendoza, and Andreas Butz. Interactions in the air: adding further depth to interactive tabletops. In *Proc. UIST 2009*. ACM, 139–148.
17. Pan Hu, Guobin Shen, Liqun Li, and Donghuan Lu. ViRi: view it right. In *Proc. MobiSys 2013*. ACM, 277–290.
18. David Kim, Shahram Izadi, Jakub Dostal, Christoph Rhemann, Cem Keskin, Christopher Zach, Jamie Shotton, Timothy Large, Steven Bathiche, Matthias Nießner, and others. RetroDepth: 3D silhouette sensing for high-precision input on and above physical surfaces. In *Proc. CHI 2014*. ACM, 1377–1386.
19. Sven Kratz, Patrick Chiu, and Maribeth Back. Pointpose: finger pose estimation for touch input on mobile devices using a depth sensor. In *Proc. ITS 2013*. ACM, 223–230.
20. Shenwei Liu and François Guimbretière. FlexAura: a flexible near-surface range sensor. In *Proc. UIST 2012*. ACM, 327–330.
21. Nicolai Marquardt, Ricardo Jota, Saul Greenberg, and Joaquim A Jorge. The continuous interaction space: interaction techniques unifying touch and gesture on and above a digital surface. In *Proc. INTERACT 2011*. Springer, 461–476.
22. Davide A Migliore, Matteo Matteucci, and Matteo Naccari. A revaluation of frame difference in fast and robust motion detection. In *Proc. 4th ACM international workshop on Video surveillance and sensor networks, 2006*. ACM, 215–218.
23. Evan Mills and Nils Borg. Trends in recommended illuminance levels: an international comparison. *Journal of the Illuminating Engineering Society* 28, 1 (1999), 155–163.
24. Leap Motion. Retrieved September 24, 2015 from https://www.leapmotion.com.
25. Anna Ostberg and Nada Matic. Hover cursor: Improving touchscreen acquisition of small targets with hover-enabled pre-selection. In *Proc. CHI 2015 Extended Abstracts*. ACM, 1723–1728.
26. Son Lam Phung, Abdesselam Bouzerdoum, and Douglas Chai. A novel skin color model in ycbcr color space and its application to human face detection. In *Proc. International Conference on Image Processing, 2002*, Vol. 1. IEEE, I–289.
27. Rasberry Pi. Retrieved September 24, 2015 from https://www.raspberrypi.org.
28. Jun Rekimoto. SmartSkin: an infrastructure for freehand manipulation on interactive surfaces. In *Proc. CHI 2002*. ACM, 113–120.
29. Munehiko Sato, Ivan Poupyrev, and Chris Harrison. Touché: enhancing touch interaction on humans, screens, liquids, and everyday objects. In *Proc. CHI 2012*. ACM, 483–492.

30. Toby Sharp, Cem Keskin, Duncan Robertson, Jonathan Taylor, Jamie Shotton, David Kim Christoph Rhemann Ido Leichter, Alon Vinnikov Yichen Wei, Daniel Freedman Pushmeet Kohli Eyal Krupka, Andrew Fitzgibbon, and Shahram Izadi. Accurate, robust, and flexible real-time hand tracking. In *Proc. CHI 2015*. ACM, 3633–3642.

31. Jeongho Shin, Sangjin Kim, Sangkyu Kang, Seong-Won Lee, Joonki Paik, Besma Abidi, and Mongi Abidi. Optical flow-based real-time object tracking using non-prior training active feature model. *Real-Time Imaging* 11, 3 (2005), 204–218.

32. Jie Song, Gábor Sörös, Fabrizio Pece, Sean Ryan Fanello, Shahram Izadi, Cem Keskin, and Otmar Hilliges. In-air gestures around unmodified mobile devices. In *Proc. UIST 2014*. ACM, 319–329.

33. Martin Spindler, Marcel Martsch, and Raimund Dachselt. Going beyond the surface: studying multi-layer interaction above the tabletop. In *Proc. CHI 2012*. ACM, 1277–1286.

34. Yoshiki Takeoka, Takashi Miyaki, and Jun Rekimoto. Z-touch: an infrastructure for 3d gesture interaction in the proximity of tabletop surfaces. In *Proc. ITS 2010*. ACM, 91–94.

35. Robby T Tan and Katsushi Ikeuchi. Separating reflection components of textured surfaces using a single image. *Pattern Analysis and Machine Intelligence, IEEE Transactions on* 27, 2 (2005), 178–193.

36. Sony Floating Touch. Retrieved September 24, 2015 from `http://developer.sonymobile.com/knowledge-base/technologies/floating-touch`.

37. Samsung Air View. Retrieved September 24, 2015 from `http://www.samsung.com/us/support/answer/ANS00044011/997407174/`.

38. Chat Wacharamanotham, Kashyap Todi, Marty Pye, and Jan Borchers. Understanding finger input above desktop devices. In *Proc. CHI 2014*. ACM, 1083–1092.

39. Andrew D Wilson. PlayAnywhere: a compact interactive tabletop projection-vision system. In *Proc. UIST 2005*. ACM, 83–92.

40. Robert Xiao, Chris Harrison, and Scott E Hudson. WorldKit: rapid and easy creation of ad-hoc interactive applications on everyday surfaces. In *Proc. CHI 2013*. ACM, 879–888.

41. Robert Xiao, Greg Lew, James Marsanico, Divya Hariharan, Scott Hudson, and Chris Harrison. Toffee: enabling ad hoc, around-device interaction with acoustic time-of-arrival correlation. In *Proc. MobileHCI 2014*. ACM, 67–76.

42. Alper Yilmaz, Omar Javed, and Mubarak Shah. Object tracking: A survey. *ACM Computing Surveys (CSUR)* 38, 4 (2006), 13.

FlexCase: Enhancing Mobile Interaction with a Flexible Sensing and Display Cover

Christian Rendl[1], David Kim[2], Patrick Parzer[1], Sean Fanello[2], Martin Zirkl[3], Gregor Scheipl[3], Michael Haller[1], Shahram Izadi[2]

[1]Media Interaction Lab, University of Applied Sciences Upper Austria
[2]Microsoft Research, Redmond, WA, USA
[3]Institute of Surface Technologies and Photonics, Joanneum Research

Figure 1. FlexCase is a novel flip cover for smartphones, which combines a flexible sensor and e-paper display to enhance interaction with existing mobile phones. The cover can be used in a variety of configurations and it augments phone's existing input and output capabilities with a variety of new interaction techniques, such as bimanual and back-of-device interaction or the incorporation of different grips for mode-switching.

ABSTRACT
FlexCase is a novel flip cover for smartphones, which brings flexible input and output capabilities to existing mobile phones. It combines an e-paper display with a pressure- and bend-sensitive input sensor to augment the capabilities of a phone. Due to the form factor, FlexCase can be easily transformed into several different configurations, each with different interaction possibilities. We can use FlexCase to perform a variety of touch, pressure, grip and bend gestures in a natural manner, much like interacting with a sheet of paper. The secondary e-paper display can act as a mechanism for providing user feedback and persisting content from the main display. In this paper, we explore the rich design space of FlexCase and present a number of different interaction techniques. Beyond, we highlight how touch and flex sensing can be combined to support a novel type of gestures, which we call *Grip & Bend*. We also describe the underlying technology and gesture sensing algorithms. Numerous applications apply the interaction techniques in real-world examples, including enhanced e-paper reading and interaction, a new copy-and-paste metaphor, high degree of freedom 3D and 2D manipulation, and the ability to transfer content and support input between displays in a natural and flexible manner.

Author Keywords
Flexible, input, output, sensor, deformation, grip detection

http://dx.doi.org/10.1145/2858036.2858314

ACM Classification Keywords
H.5.2. [Information interfaces and presentation]: User Interfaces: Input Devices and Strategies, Interaction Styles.

INTRODUCTION
The smartphone has revolutionized computing, making interacting with digital information as simple as reaching into your pocket. Although the hardware continually improves, many of the interactions are still reduced to touching and sliding our fingers on a rigid piece of glass.

To remove these bounds on 2D input on the front of the display and to avoid occluding (often valuable) pixels on screen, researchers have explored interaction on the back [6, 53], above [29], or around the device [9]. Further, researchers have looked at using flexible sensors [41] or even the combination of flexible display and input [15, 19, 22, 27, 28, 47, 48] to bring more paper-like physical interactions to mobile devices.

Another trend extends the output space of smartphones by using electronic paper (e-paper) displays in conjunction with the phone's regular screen [5, 35, 38, 55]. These e-paper displays are very power-efficient as they only need to be powered while the screen content is being updated, and exhibit a paper-like reading experience, which can remove aspects of eye strain. However, none of the aforementioned systems support rich flexible and gestural interactions between the two screens or make use of the combined extended screen space.

In this paper, we present FlexCase, a flexible interactive flip cover that augments the input and output capabilities of smartphones with novel paper-like and gestural interactions. As shown in Figure 1, a cover housing both our novel sensor and e-paper display is attached to the phone without compromising the form factor. We utilize a custom-made flexible touch, pressure and bend sensor, combined with a flexible e-paper display that turns the phone cover into a versatile input and output device. The cover provides interactive mechanisms to move content between displays. It allows the secondary display to be used as a peripheral surface for input and output. It also enables rich physical paper-like interactions with the cover using touch, pressure and various flex gestures. The ability to simultaneously detect touch and complex deformation of the surface allows for gestures, which we call *Grip & Bend*, that provide a variety of novel paper-like interactions. We explore the design space for FlexCase in detail, demonstrating a variety of new applications.

While we consider the novel form factor and the resulting interaction techniques as the main contributions of this paper, we also present technical novelty with a sensor that combines multiple modes of input. The flexible input sensor is built on a touch and pressure-sensitive printed piezoelectric film [40, 56], which recently demonstrated its ability to sense complex deformations [41]. In contrast to this prior work that utilizes a sparse arrangement of sensors around the periphery, we use a matrix-like sensor layout to sense touch, pressure, and complex deformations with only a single sensor. Summarizing, the main contributions of this paper are:

- A concept of a novel flip cover form factor that augments existing mobile interaction with flexible output and input, including touch and bend input.
- Exploration of the design space for our system with its reconfigurable multi-display and multi-input form factor.
- Novel interaction techniques, which arise from the combination of touch, pressure, grip, and bend sensing.
- A custom input sensor, which enables bi-directional bending and touch on both sides; and a new-machine learning algorithm for leveraging grip sensing for richer bend input.
- A set of application scenarios demonstrating novel interaction possibilities with our proposed design.

We will firstly discuss the design rationales for the FlexCase form factor and its resulting design space. We will then introduce the hardware architecture, the sensing principles and the algorithms of our system. Further, we will present a compelling set of novel application scenarios arising from our proposed design and its input modalities. Finally, we will conclude with a discussion, limitations and future work.

RELATED WORK

Our work relates to many areas of HCI research, including work on flexible displays and mobile interaction. In this section, we will introduce the most important work for each field, starting with a review of devices combining traditional touchscreens and e-paper displays. Then we discuss work dealing with flexible display interaction and interactions with multiple displays. Finally, we discuss possibilities of extending input around and behind the device.

Combination of Touchscreen & E-Paper Display

Nook [5] was one of the first commercial E-Readers, which combined an electronic paper display with an additional smaller LCD touchscreen. The secondary display was mainly used for more dynamic interactions such as animated menus. More recent products, like Yotaphone [55], InkCase [35], or PopSlate [38], use e-paper displays as a secondary, more power-efficient ambient display. Although these products show compelling scenarios, the secondary display is not used as an additional input device nor as direct extension of the main display, thus both screens are mostly used in isolation. In contrast, Dementyev et al. [14] showed wirelessly powered display tags, which can serve as mobile phone companion displays. However, they were not attached to a smartphone.

Flexible Display Interaction

Bendable interfaces, such as ShapeTape [13], Gummi [42], PaperPhone [28], or MorePhone [18] demonstrate many novel interaction scenarios based on making a mobile device with flexible sensing or input and output capabilities.

ShapeTape is a thin long tape subdivided into a series of fiber-optic bend sensors, each detecting bend and twist. Balakrishnan et al. [3] demonstrated modeling 3D curves with this technology. PaperPhone [28] was one of the first prototypes that coupled flexible input and output into one self-contained device. PaperTab [49] is a self-contained electronic reader with a flexible touchscreen and two bi-directional bend sensors for input. In contrast, the Kinetic Phone [27] demonstrates a full-color bendable phone, providing both gentle twist and bend gestures. In a follow-up study Ahmaniemi et al. [1] demonstrated the utility of bidirectional continuous bend gestures. More recently, FlexView [8] augmented predominant touch input on flexible devices with a set of bending interaction techniques for navigation in 3D (along the Z-axis).

Researchers have also used external devices, generally in form of cameras and projectors to prototype flexible interactions. Examples include high-fidelity input [47], foldable [25, 30], and rollable displays [26]. These however are limited to a non-self-contained form-factor, requiring heavyweight input and output capabilities to be placed in the environment.

Multi-Display Interaction

Both Hinkley et al. [20] and Chen et al. [10] have shown multi-display interaction in the context of handheld tablet devices. However, none of them utilized bending as additional input metaphor. Recently, Duet [11] explored new interaction possibilities on mobile phones by coupling a mobile phone with a smartwatch. The watch acts as an active element in the interaction, where its orientation and acceleration are used to control the interaction on the mobile phone.

Several researchers explored paper-like interaction with flexible interactive displays. Holman et al. [22] presented a desktop-windowing environment, which projects desktop windows on flexible sheets of paper. By tracking their motions, simple paper sheets become fully interactive. DisplayStacks [16] allows the physical stacking of e-paper displays. These displays are tracked relative to each other, enabling cross-device interaction for moving content or displaying contextual information. More recently, Paperfold [19] presents a configurable multi-device concept based on e-paper displays. The detachable displays can be arranged to a wide variety of different device configurations. Although, Paperfold shows multi-display interaction for e-paper based mobile devices, our work explores the use of novel flexible input and output combined with a regular phone.

Input Around and Behind the Device

One common problem is that interactions on handheld devices are limited due to the small form factor. Researchers have systematically explored the space around and behind the device for further input possibilities.

SideSight [9], for example, uses optical sensors embedded into the side of a device to track multi-touch around the device. Besides interactions around the periphery of the device, our flip cover form factor also enables input behind the device. LucidTouch [53] introduced the idea of a tablet-sized see-through display, where some interactions are performed at the back of the device. A user study showed that many prefer this technique over touching on the front due to reduced occlusion and higher precision. Baudisch and Chu took this concept further and explored the possibility of back-of-device interaction on very small displays [6]. More recently, Löchtefeld et al. [32] explored the combination of front- and back-of-device interaction with one hand. An evaluation showed, that although it is slower compared to traditional front-of-device input, it allows for accurate input. Finally, [46] explore the 3D space behind the smartphone leveraging the existing camera. Unlike prior work, FlexCase allows for continuous flexible input behind the display, in combination with touch. This adds tangible and physical qualities to these types of back-of-device interactions.

Utilizing Grips and Bimanual Input on Mobile Devices

Another interesting approach for extending input is to utilize grips, e.g. for implicit mode switching. This idea was shown for mobile phones [12, 17, 54], multi-touch pens [45] and mice [51]. Recently, Ansara and Girouard [2] proposed the idea of overloading bend gestures with different modes by pressing pressure-sensitive keys with the non-dominant hand. In contrast, FlexCase extracts grip information from how a user is touching the device before bending and utilizes this information to assign different meanings to bend gestures.

Prior work has also shown that desktop-based bimanual interaction techniques increase both performance and accuracy [4, 24]. More recently, this idea was also applied to handheld devices [34, 52] and flexible devices [8]. Wagner et al. [52] used touches of the thumb or fingers of the grasping hand for implicit mode-switching while Burstyn et al. [8] used the thumb of the grasping hand for scrolling on flexible devices. FlexCase tries to take the idea of bimanual interaction further, and combines touch interaction with the one hand with continuous bend input with the other hand.

DESIGN RATIONALE

As highlighted, our work overlaps with many areas of interaction research, and this is because of the richness, flexibility, and diverse capabilities that our flip cover configuration affords. In this section, we give insights on the design process leading to this kind of form factor.

There is clearly compelling work in the area of flexible sensors and displays, with a large focus on mobile interaction. The

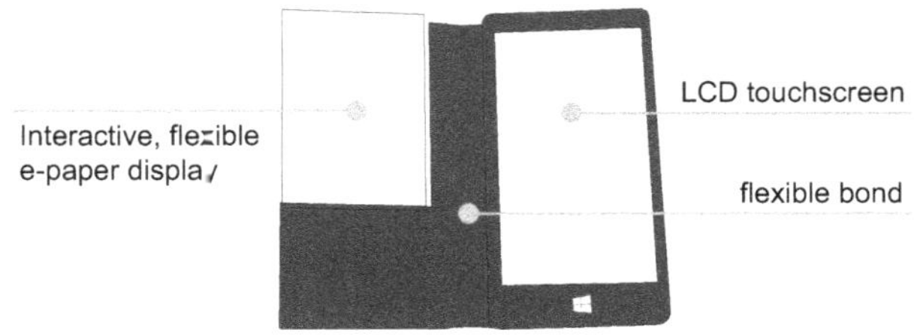

Figure 2. The FlexCase form factor. The usage of a flip cover-like form factor allows for different configurations with only one additional device.

majority of this work has, however, looked at replacing the smartphone with a flexible display or leveraging an e-paper display as a peripheral display with limited interaction. Our work preserves the interactive qualities of existing smartphones and augments their capabilities with additional input and output, in the form of a highly interactive, bendable flip cover.

The following high level design goals underpinned the development of FlexCase:

- **Compactness:** Preserving the compact form factor of current mobile devices - while enhancing interaction.
- **Versatility:** Allow the device to adapt to various usage scenarios - through simple adjustment of the form factor.
- **Expressiveness:** Enable richer input - through touch and other direct physical manipulations.
- **Mobility and Portability:** The flip cover should be an unobtrusive companion of the smartphone, which should not significantly decrease battery life or increase weight.

In order to fulfill the specified design goals, we evaluated a number of different form factors. We experimented with fixed displays at the backside of the smartphone (as other e-paper products do) as well as displays, which were attachable to the side of the smartphone. Detachability is an interesting concept since it increases the ability to reuse the flexible display for different smartphones and it allows even more different form factors. However, early user tests revealed that this also raises a number of issues, particularly mounting and subsequent stability issues. We therefore chose to focus on integrating the flexible display into an existing phone accessory rather than requiring two separate devices. By integrating an additional, flexible device into a flip cover (see Figure 2), various physical configurations are possible while being folded and enable the smart cover to be used as a versatile input and output device for existing mobile phones (*cf. Compactness & Versatility*). By further embedding a thin-film sensor into the device, we can enable flexible and continuous input for existing phones.

In choosing our configuration, we developed a new iteration of a printed piezoelectric sensor film that combines shape deformation [41] with touch and pressure [40, 56]. A major advantage of this technology based on PyzoFlex sensors [23] is, that we are able to achieve both touch [40] and complex bend sensing [41] with one single sensor (*cf. Expressiveness*). In contrast to multiple sensor layers, the advantage of a single layer is that it greatly reduces the rigidity of the layer stack and therefore improves flexibility for bend interaction.

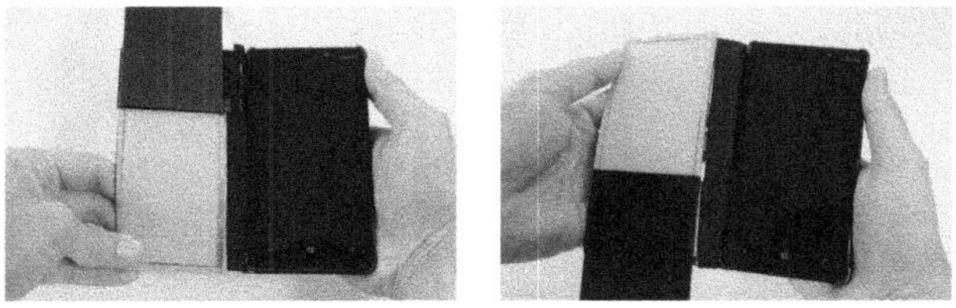

Figure 3. The final layout was evaluated with early mockups. For ergonomic reasons, given the hand position and hand mobility, we decided for arranging the display at the top left side of the flip cover (Right).

For output, we decided to focus on slower framerate, but ubiquitous e-paper displays rather than emerging OLED displays. Whilst work on flexible OLEDs is incredibly promising, it is still not broadly available due to ongoing research on improving durability and robustness [31, 36]. Furthermore, e-paper displays have already begun to appear on mainstream phone products, have demonstrated long lifetime and power efficiency, and also provide an interesting challenge of combining higher framerate input with slower output. For instance, the main phone display has the advantage of being able to render high-fidelity colors with a high framerate, but the secondary e-paper display offers good readability while preserving power and reducing eye strain (cf. *Mobility and Portability*). Instead of merely using the e-paper display for displaying 'offline' and ambient content, the flip cover form factor gives us the possibility to actively use the second screen in conjunction with the main display of the phone for interactive scenarios to combine the best of the two worlds. For example, the phone screen can be used to give instant visual feedback for continuous flex interactions, while the flexible e-paper output can actively guide and control the users' interactions.

Flexible displays suffer from inflexible parts, such as the lamination with the e-paper display's rigid driving electronics, which usually requires one edge to be rigid. In our case, it is the short display edge, as this affected the flexibility least. Furthermore, we decided to detach the long edge from the flip cover's bond to additionally increase flexibility and to allow rich deformations (otherwise only one corner would be available for flex interactions). The final form factor including some design considerations can be found in Figure 3.

DESIGN SPACE

In this section, we explore the different physical configurations and interactive modalities the flip cover form factor affords.

Configurations

FlexCase enables the following configurations (cf. Figure 4):

Book. This configuration provides extended screen space, allowing specific content to be offloaded to the second screen. Since the e-paper display has a lower resolution and a lower refresh-rate, it makes sense to offload static content to the secondary display, providing instant access to otherwise hidden menu items and reducing clutter on the main screen. The secondary display can be used for displaying persistent information without battery drain but can also act as a high-fidelity input device for continuous interaction.

Laptop. By rotating the display into a landscape configuration, the interactive display can be seen as a keyboard-like input

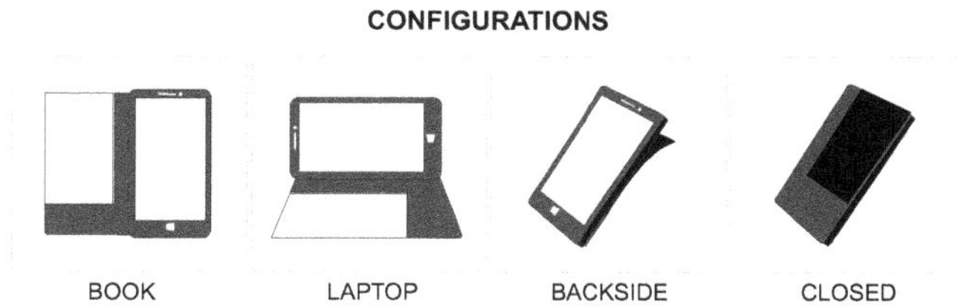

Figure 4. The design space derives from the combination of various different physical configurations and interactive modalities. The e-paper display can be used next to (*Book*), below (*Laptop*), behind (*Backside*), and above the smartphone (*Closed*).

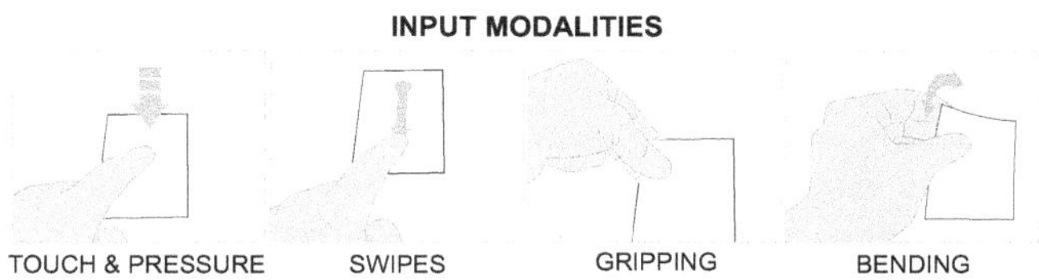

Figure 5. From an interaction point of view, the device allows for touch and pressure interaction, swipe gestures, recognition of grips, and high fidelity bending.

device. For specific input, we can also turn the secondary display into a versatile direct input device with dynamically changeable visual feedback.

Backside. By flipping the cover behind the main screen, we support a configuration that allows for tap and slide gestures behind the mobile phone's screen. Beyond this, the interactive display enables continuous bend input for the main display. The affordance of having a flexible, interactive display behind the device helps to reduce existing problems of today's mobile phones (e.g. fat-finger problem [44]) but also gives the possibility to interact with, for example, zoomable or browsable user interfaces in a more natural way.

Closed. When closed, the backside of the flip cover still provides interaction possibilities. From an interaction point of view, this configuration can be used for very explicit interactions, e.g. copying content between two screens or putting the phone into silent mode.

Input Modalities

The sensor foil within the FlexSense flip cover can detect *pressure* and *touch* location, allowing simple *tapping*, *sliding* or *rubbing* gestures, as well as detecting how the device is being *gripped*. This is combined with the ability to reconstruct continuous *bending* of the surface (cf. Figure 5).

Touch & Pressure. Users can perform taps on the interactive display. Furthermore, the piezoelectric input sensor gives the possibility to detect the strength of a certain tap, both continuously or for distinguishing different pressure levels. Beyond this, the input sensor can detect whether the user is tapping on the display or on the back of the display. Users can also perform basic *swipe* gestures in four directions.

Gripping. Given the matrix-like layout of the input sensor, the sensor can detect where, how and how strong a user is gripping the device. This becomes an important modality for input and is described later.

Bending. Users are able to perform complex deformations in both directions. The strength of bending gestures can be used for continuous operations (e.g. zooming) but also for triggering specific actions (e.g. corner bend for page turning).

Output Modality

The interactive e-paper display provides also a possibility to enhance interactions with appropriate feedback. This can be used to either show persistent information without battery drain, or can accompany input with changeable output to guide the users' interactions (e.g. changeable soft keyboard layout).

Compatibility of configurations and modalities

Although the form factor offers a wide variety of different configurations and modalities, not every modality is compatible and useful in each configuration. Table 1 shows a detailed correlation of configurations and modalities.

	Front Touch	Back Touch	Pressure	Swipes	Gripping	Bending	Output
Closed	-	+	+	+	o	o	-
Backside	+	-	o	+	+	+	+
Laptop	+	-	+	+	-	o	+
Book	+	o	o	o	+	+	+

Table 1. Designers should bare in mind that not every combination of configurations and modalities is compatible and useful.

For instance, it is inconvenient to use different grip gestures when the interactive e-paper display rests on a table in laptop mode, as it lacks the affordance of grasping in this configuration. In contrast, given the flexible cover, it is also important to consider that interaction in mid-air would make some interactions, such as accurate pressure input, impractical. When creating and designing new interactions, it is important to keep this compatibility of configurations and modalities in mind.

INTERACTION TECHNIQUES

In the previous section, we described various device configurations that FlexCase can be used in and we also described a number of different interaction modalities, such as swiping, gripping, bending and touch. As it can be seen in Table 1, each device configuration affords a certain set of interaction modalities better than other device configurations. There is no one form factor that could serve all usage scenarios equally well. However, a unique feature of FlexCase is that it allows the user to quickly combine and switch between a number of different configurations and modalities. In this section, we will describe the interactive modalities in more detail. Later in the paper, these will be showcased in the context of fully working application scenarios.

Force-sensitive & Dual-sided Touch

The sensor capabilities can be utilized to enrich traditional touch interaction. The addition of pressure information alongside touch can be used for quick actions, e.g. for switching between upper- and lowercase typing [33]. The touch sensitivity on the backside can be further utilized for indirect manipulations, e.g. *Rubbing* by sliding over the backside of the cover for pinning content.

Continuous Bend Input

Given the flexibility of the input sensor, the flip cover can act as a novel input device for existing smartphones. Existing smartphones can be enhanced with continuous bend input, which could be used for all sorts of linear navigational tasks in existing phone applications, e.g. zooming a map [1]. The smartphone display provides instant feedback, which is necessary to ensure smooth user interactions.

These types of bend gestures can naturally map to 3D navigation tasks [8], bringing these capabilities to existing (rigid) smartphones. Beyond this, FlexCase can map paper-like actions to the digital world, e.g. making a *Dog Ear* by bending the top right corner to memorize a page.

Back-of-device & Background Interaction

When the interactive and flexible display is folded back to the rear of the smartphone, it allows for back-of-device [6, 53] interactions, all without requiring any other modifications to the phone or additional sensors. This can be used for one-dimensional navigation tasks, such as list scrolling, with the benefit of not occluding the screen while browsing. Another possibility is to use discrete gestures at the backside to perform background tasks without needing to change the foreground app (e.g. performing swipes to switch music). The combination of bend gestures with back-of-device interaction can enable the user to change or manipulate UI layers or enable zoomable user interfaces [37], just by bending the cover.

Bi-manual Interaction

The possibility to have two screens next to each other also enables bi-manual interaction using the dominant and non-dominant hand simultaneously. Researchers have shown the usefulness of such an interaction both for speed and accuracy [4, 24]. For instance, users can use the thumb of the grasping hand to pan on the smartphone while performing continuous bend gestures with the other hand. Bending affords an easy way for changing a linear parameter [8] and greatly reduces the clutching issue [43] and screen occlusions due to pinching.

Interaction Across Screens

The output capability of FlexCase creates the possibility of sharing interactions, UI, and content between displays. This can be, for example, utilized to transfer static or temporary content from the main screen to the e-paper display and vice versa. One example is a clipboard, where the secondary display can reduce the clutter on the main screen while keeping the user informed about what is stored on the clipboard.

Grip & Bend

The touch and bending fidelity of our input sensor allows for a novel gesture where the user first *grips* the flexible display in different ways prior to bending in order to perform different actions. The e-paper display can act as a mechanism to preview the gesture or provide feedback to the user prior to when bending begins. This type of gesture is only feasible given the touch and bending fidelity of our sensor, where different grips can be detected robustly and combined with different types of bending deformations. This allows for a single edge of the display to be used for different gestures simply by adjusting

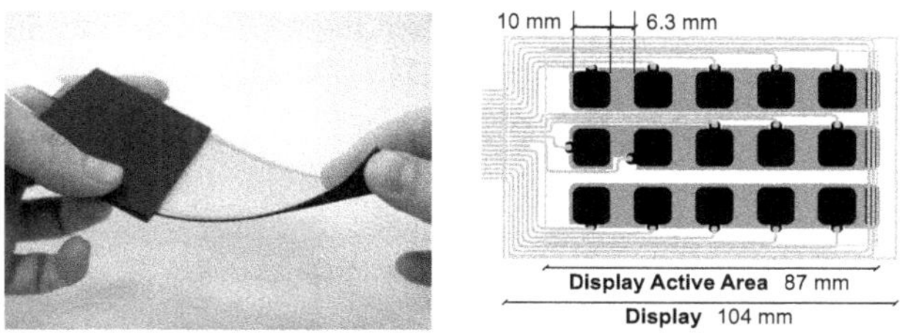

Figure 6. The layer stack of FlexCase consists of (I) an electrophoretic display on top, (II) a piezoelectric input sensor and (III) a self-adhesive protection layer behind (left). The input sensor layout consists of a 3 × 5 matrix of piezoelectric sensors, which is capable of sensing high-fidelity bending, pressure-sensitive touch and grip detection (right).

the user's grasp. Researchers have shown the usefulness of incorporating grasping for input on styluses and tablets [17, 21, 45], which is also enabled in FlexCase by combining grip detection with *bend* gestures to support rich mobile interactive possibilities.

The initial grip (comprising touch and pressure information) can be used to overload bend gestures with different meanings, such as mode switching, depending on which initial grip gesture was used. This concept is particularly interesting for flexible devices with a smaller form factor, where the variety of possible bend gestures is limited due to physical constraints.

IMPLEMENTATION DETAILS

The hardware implementation of the FlexCase prototype consists of a flexible, electrophoretic display and a piezoelectric input sensor on its backside (cf. Figure 6).

Display

We use an electrophoretic ink display (EPD) in our FlexCase prototype. These displays suffer from slow screen update rates, however, their power consumption is low since only refreshing the displayed content consumes energy. For FlexCase, we chose a flexible, monochrome 4 inch electrophoretic display manufactured by FlexEnable. The active area of the display is 87 × 54 mm and it provides a resolution of 400 × 240 pixel, which corresponds to a pixel density of 85 ppi. The display features 16 gray levels and performs a complete full-screen refresh in < 900 ms.

Sensor

For input, we used a low-resolution 3 × 5 matrix of printed piezoelectric sensors (cf. Figure 6). When deformed, a piezoelectric sensor creates a surface charge, which correlates with the applied mechanical deformation. This sensing principle has been used for touch and pressure input [40] as well as complex bi-directional bend [41]. FlexCase brings these capabilities together, in one single sensor. In contrast to multiple sensor layers or technologies, this is particularly beneficial for reducing the rigidity of the layer stack.

During our experiments with deformation of piezoelectric sensors, we found pressure induced by touch creates small, local deformations triggering one or a few adjacent sensors (cf. Figurin 7, left). In contrast, bending the sensor usually results in global deformations, triggering a greater number of sensors across a larger surface area (cf. Figure 7, right). Given this fact

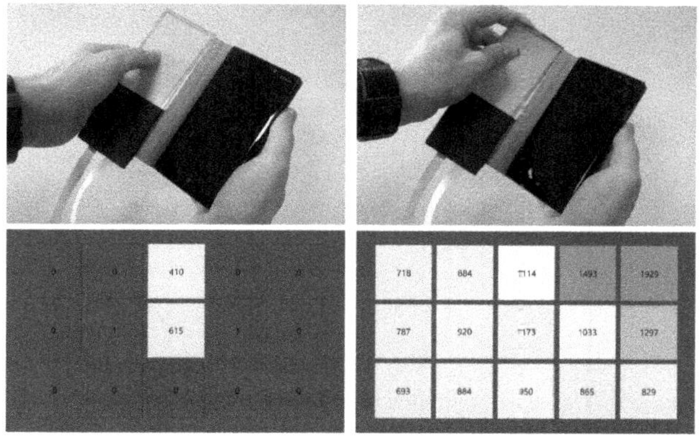

Figure 7. FlexCase utilizes one single sensor for both touch (left) & bend (right) sensing. The distinction is based upon a simple function incorporating the number of active sensors and the standard deviation across all readings.

and in contrast to prior work [41], we were able to use a sensor matrix for both touch & bend sensing without any additional optimization of the layout. A distinction between touch and bend can be easily identified based on a simple function that incorporates the number of active sensors and the standard deviation across all readings:

$$\theta = N \cdot \sqrt{\frac{\sum_{k=1}^{n}(s_k - \mu)^2}{n}} \tag{1}$$

where N is the number of activated sensors, s the set of all integrated sensor signals, n the total number of sensors, and μ the population mean. The smaller the value of θ, the less variance and active sensors, indicating a touch. A high value indicates a large variance with a high number of activated sensors, which corresponds to a bend gesture. The threshold for robust distinction between touch and bend can be then empirically defined.

Grip Detection

In the interaction techniques section we introduced a new concept called *Grip & Bend*. In the following, we will explain the learning-based algorithm we used for detecting different grips in detail, to aid reproducibility.

Figure 8 shows the temporal signature for grip and bend. Note a strong peak when performing bending across all sensors. At a high-level our algorithm detects that a bending gesture has started by identifying these peaks, and then backtracks to recognize the grip, by analyzing a sliding window across previous sensor readings. Given the range of different gestures we wished to support, and to better deal with changes in the temporal sequence due to different execution speed of users, we decided to use a learning-based algorithm to achieve high recognition accuracy (as opposed to heuristic-based approaches). Note that our algorithm incorporates both location of the grip as well as polarity (touched side).

We can assume that we have to infer the grip label y from a small sequence $\mathbf{X} \in \mathbb{R}^{15 \times T}$, where $T = 50$, which is the number of observations (in ms) used for the grip classification.

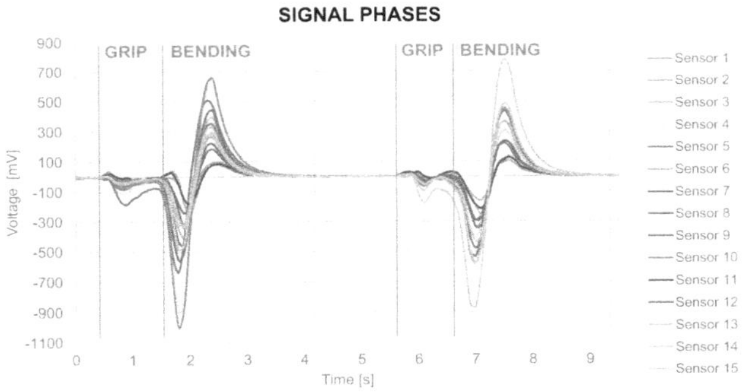

Figure 8. The chart highlights the two signal phases of Grip & Bend. If a bend gesture is recognized the grip gets evaluated based on the last set of observed sensor signals. Colors denote each of the sensors.

Single frames $\mathbf{x}_t \in \mathbb{R}^{15}$ were too noisy to be used directly as a feature descriptor: instead, we use an average pooling operator to aggregate frames of P descriptors. Consequently, our feature vector $\mathbf{f}_t \in \mathbb{R}^{15}$ for the frame t becomes:

$$\mathbf{f}_t = \frac{1}{P} \sum_{p=t-P}^{t} \mathbf{x}_p. \tag{2}$$

Given the set of tuples $\{(\mathbf{f}_t, \mathbf{y}_t)\}_{t=1}^{N}$ we want to learn the class model $\mathbf{W} \in \mathbb{R}^{15 \times n}$ minimizing the following objective function:

$$E = \frac{1}{N} \sum_{t=1}^{N} \mathcal{L}(\mathbf{W}, \mathbf{f}_t, y_t) + \mathcal{R}(\mathbf{W}), \tag{3}$$

which represents the sum of a loss function $\mathcal{L}(\circ)$ and a regularization term $\mathcal{R}(\circ)$ that gives a tradeoff between the accuracy and the complexity of the model. Since we want to detect grip gestures with a certain probability, our loss function and regularizer are defined using a standard softmax model [7] and the optimization is carried out using Stochastic Gradient Descent (SGD), which could be also employed for online learning of new grip gestures.

The learned model $\mathbf{W}$ is only able to describe linear dependencies in the data, however grip gestures can share non-linear relations and a better classifier must be used. Non-linear classifiers are usually expensive from the computational viewpoint, thus we use *Random Features* to approximate a non-linear kernel [50, 39]. The idea of random features consists of using a non-linear mapping $\Phi(\mathbf{\Omega}, \mathbf{f})$ to transform a non-linear separable problem into a linear separable one. After this mapping is computed, simple linear classifiers can solve the problem efficiently. Following [39] we define:

$$\Phi(\mathbf{\Omega}, \mathbf{f}) = \frac{1}{\sqrt{F}} [\exp(-i\omega_1 \mathbf{f}), \ldots, \exp(-i\omega_F \mathbf{f})], \tag{4}$$

where the parameters $\mathbf{\Omega} \in \mathbb{R}^{F \times 15}$ ($F = 128$ total number of random features) are sampled from a random distribution. Finally, the objective function $E = \frac{1}{N} \sum_{t=1}^{N} \mathcal{L}(\mathbf{W}, \Phi(\mathbf{\Omega}, \mathbf{f}_t), y_t) + \lambda ||\mathbf{W}||^2$ is optimized using SGD.

Given the current observations $\mathbf{X} \in \mathbb{R}^{15 \times T}$, to recognize the grip y we first compute the descriptors $\mathbf{f}_t$ with $t = P, \ldots, T$. These $T - P$ descriptors are then mapped into a non-linear space using the random features $\mathbf{\Omega}$ as described before. Finally, we compute the label $\hat{y}$ using the probability scores as follow:

$$\hat{y} = \arg\max_i \frac{\sum_t \exp(\Phi(\mathbf{f}_t, \Omega)\mathbf{w}_i)}{C_t}, \tag{5}$$

where $C_t = \sum_i \exp(\Phi(\mathbf{f}_t, \Omega)\mathbf{w}_i)$ is a normalization constant.

Technical Evaluation

To be able to evaluate the precision of our grip detection, we performed an elicitation study with the primary goal to extract common grip gestures that are both ergonomically feasible and comfortable to users. The goal of the study was not to find the most natural grips without any constraints, but a distinctive set of common grips, which can be used to train and test our learning-based algorithm.

We asked eight unpaid participants aged between 25-36 years ($M = 27.5$) from a local academic research lab (two female; all right-handed) to grip several regions of the device as naturally as possible. The task was performed in two different configurations, namely *Book* and *Backside* configurations, for four obvious regions of interest (*top left corner*, *top right corner*, *side edge* and *whole display*), resulting from the physical limitations of the flip cover. The grips were video-taped from two perspectives and later transcribed for analysis.

Results revealed that although the available area for gripping is limited, participants found a large variety of different gestures (on average 10.1 different grips per condition, $SD = 3.79$). To extract a distinctive set of grips from this large number of candidates, we decided to nominate the two grips with the highest number of occurrences and diversity for each condition (see Figure 9).

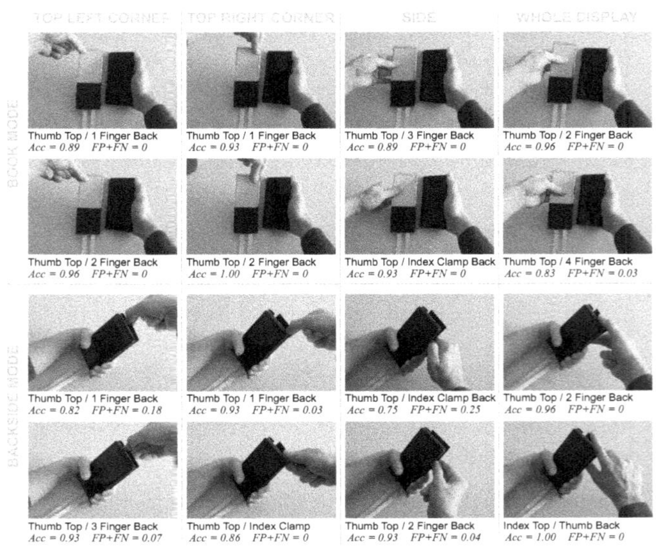

Figure 9. The resulting subset of grip gestures of the elicitation study was used to evaluate our learning-based grip detection algorithm. The *Acc* values indicate accuracy and *FN + FP* the miss classifications and false positives per class with non-linear feature mapping.

The extracted set of grips was then used for evaluating our learning-based algorithm. The $n = 8$ grip gestures for each configuration were performed by different participants, resulting in an overall of 50 examples per condition. We evaluated the algorithm on 10 new sequences of 25 gestures. For the *Book* set of grips, the linear method achieved 70% accuracy on the test set, while the non-linear feature mapping approach reached 92.5% accuracy on the same test set. For the *Backside* grips we reached 69% with the linear classifier, whereas the random feature method achieved 89% of accuracy. Figure 9 shows the accuracy and false positives/negatives for each condition in detail. These results clearly confirm the benefit of using non-linear classifiers and in particular a random features approach as used in our approach.

Interoperability

Both the input sensor as well as the display are connected to external driver electronics, which both offer a custom-made communication API via TCP/IP for smartphone applications. On the input side, an application receives raw input sensor data as well as pre-processed gesture information such as tap, grip, and bend gestures. For displaying content onto the secondary display, an application can use the display API to either render parts of the phone UI or upload images to the e-paper display.

Power consumption

In the current configuration, our sensor electronics consumes 81.3 mW with a refresh rate of 100 Hz. The typical update energy for refreshing the EPD display is 206 mJ (power consumption for microprocessor excluded).

APPLICATIONS

In this section and supplementary video, we present a number of novel application scenarios that show the benefits of our interactive flip cover for enhancing interaction with traditional mobile phones. The demonstrated applications try to combine the high-level interaction techniques, which were presented in this paper, in convincing real-world scenarios. Beyond scenarios where each of the two screens is used in isolation (e.g. the e-paper display for displaying persistent data such as a boarding pass), we were more interested in applications where the two screens actively support and enrich each other. Further, the system is shown in different physical configurations.

Document Reading

While e-paper displays are optimized for reading with low eye-strain and outdoor conditions, LCDs are well-suited for displaying dynamic media. For document readers, the benefits of the two worlds can be combined by using the secondary display for text and the smartphone screen for media content such as videos or animations (cf. Figure 10).

Grip & Bend. In order to switch to the next or previous page, the user can bend the top left corner forward or backward. To quickly browse through a greater number of pages, the user can - like with a book - bend the entire left edge of the cover. The LCD shows a live preview to overcome the slow update rate of e-paper displays and thus ensure a fluid interaction.

Bi-Manual Interaction. While flipping through the virtual pages, the user can tap onto the desired page on the LCD to select and to display it on the e-paper display.

Interaction Across Screens. If rich media is linked to the displayed page on the e-paper display, the resolution and color fidelity of the LCD display can be utilized to display it directly on the smartphone screen instead. For videos, another *Grip & Bend* gesture can be used to continuously navigate within a video figure, avoiding the use of small touch-based widgets on the main screen.

Figure 10. Document Reader. Left: The user can flip through the pages of a document on the LCD by bending the flexible display. Middle: A page gets selected by touch on the LCD and gets pushed over to the secondary e-paper display. Right: The fidelity of the LCD screen can be utilized to show rich media linked in text pages on the e-paper display.

Content Transfer

We also see a lot of potential in simplifying tasks on the main screen by using the two screens in unison, for instance for copy & paste tasks.

Interactions Across Screens. The secondary screen can be used as a *visual* clipboard where snapshots and texts can be easily copied and pasted (cf. Figure 11).

Bi-Manual Interaction. The clipboard is rendered on the e-paper display and contains several slots where information can be stored. By simultaneously tapping an information asset on the main screen and a clipboard slot a user can copy the information to the clipboard. To paste data, a user first double taps a clipboard item and then taps on the target location on the main screen. This not only provides visual feedback, it also allows for multiple clipboard entries to be stored unlike standard copy and paste mechanisms.

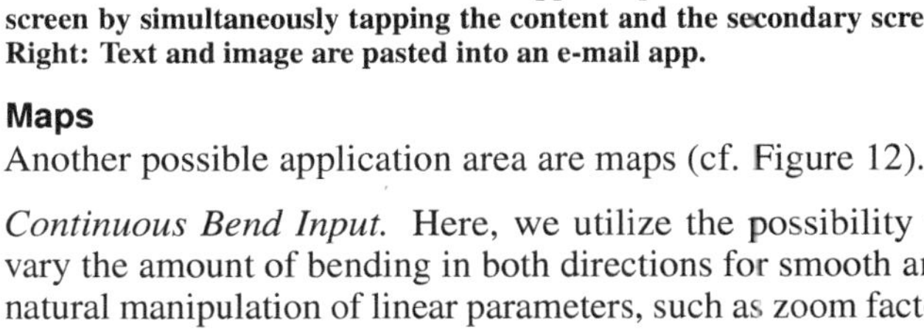

Figure 11. Clipboard. Left: A recommender app is temporarily opened. Middle: Content in the recommender app is copied onto the secondary screen by simultaneously tapping the content and the secondary screen. Right: Text and image are pasted into an e-mail app.

Maps

Another possible application area are maps (cf. Figure 12).

Continuous Bend Input. Here, we utilize the possibility to vary the amount of bending in both directions for smooth and natural manipulation of linear parameters, such as zoom factor, rotation angle and tilt angles. This type of high degree-of-freedom 3D navigation is often challenging to perform on a touchscreen without numerous overloaded gestures. With our proposed method, these interactions can be performed using different *Grip & Bend* gestures.

Grip & Bend. The user can zoom the map in and out by gripping and bending the whole display backward or forward, or can change the rotation angle by bending the left corner, or changing the tilt of the map by bending the right corner.

Interaction Across Screens. Additionally, the map allows for easy transfer of information to the secondary display, which is used as an extended visual clipboard. In our example, the user is able to store routes from the map onto the secondary display for quick previews of the stored routes.

Dual-Sided Touch. To store a route, the user can close the flip cover to put the two displays above each other and can, like with traditional blueprint paper, perform a rubbing gesture on the backside of the secondary display to transfer the content between the displays.

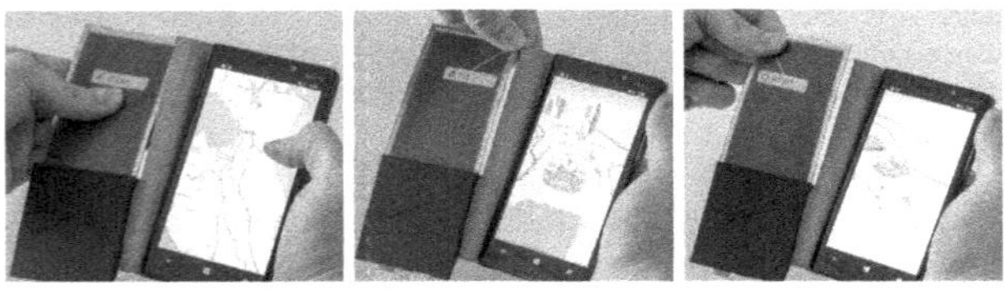

Figure 12. Maps. Different Grip & Bend gestures can be used to continuously control zoom (Left), tilt (Middle) and rotation (Right) in a map.

Photos

Another mode of operation is to use the secondary screen mainly for visualizing icons and widgets, which provides extended space on the primary display. This allows users to have faster access to the phone functions by not having to navigate through clutter. This can be applied for instance to media players or camera applications, where the user often wants to see the full image of the phone display (cf. Figure 13).

Continuous Bend Input. Various camera parameters can be selected, and the bending angle is used to input linear settings (e.g. zoom, aperture, exposure).

Figure 13. Camera. Capture settings are visualized on the secondary screen, leaving the primary display free of clutter. Functions, such as flash settings (Left), can be activated via touch or linear parameters, such as aperture (Middle) or exposure (Right), can be selected and controlled with different grips.

Grip & Bend. Grip & Bend gestures can be used, for example, to control different functions. By bending the corner of the display with a single finger, the user can control the zoom level, while different grips for the corners can accordingly adjust aperture or brightness settings. Speed can be controlled by varying the amount of bending.

Pressure Input & Gaming

In Laptop mode, the secondary display can also be used as a customizable, pressure-sensitive keyboard or gamepad.

Force-sensitive Touch. In our example, we use this configuration for PIN number input, where the user uses a combination of touch and pressure to enter a PIN (cf. Figure 14, left). This could also be extended to support pressure sensitive keyboard input for text entry [33].

Continuous Bend Input. This configuration is also useful in gaming scenarios, where the secondary display can be used as a novel input controller. Besides the possibility to show gamepad-like touch controls on the display, bending could be used as an additional input modality to enable more degrees of freedom (cf. Figure 14, right). In Jump&Run games, bending could be mapped to the jump of the character, while the magnitude of bending defines the height of a jump, allowing other buttons to be used for shooting or other actions.

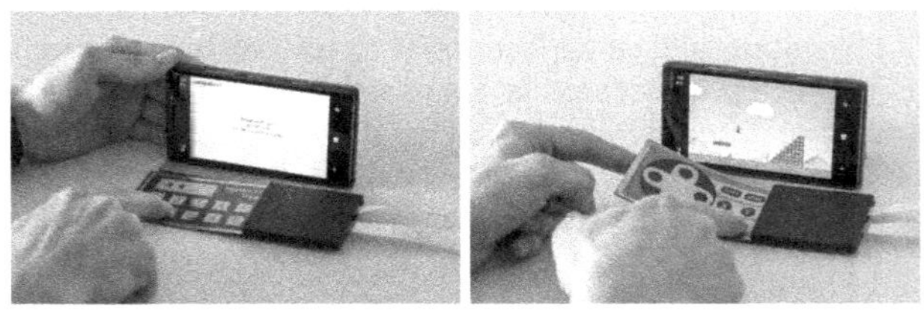

Figure 14. Left: Input of a combination of digits and pressure information for increasing security in public areas. Right: Showing a flexible gamepad layout with touch-enabled buttons and bend sensing.

Background Interaction

Backside mode is particularly interesting for performing background tasks, which are not related to the foreground application (e.g. controlling a music player). For example, a user can use swipe gestures on the back of the device for changing to the previous or next song, while bending the corners either decrease or increase the music player's volume. This allows these settings to be set without even switching the application or interacting with the phone screen (cf. Figure 15).

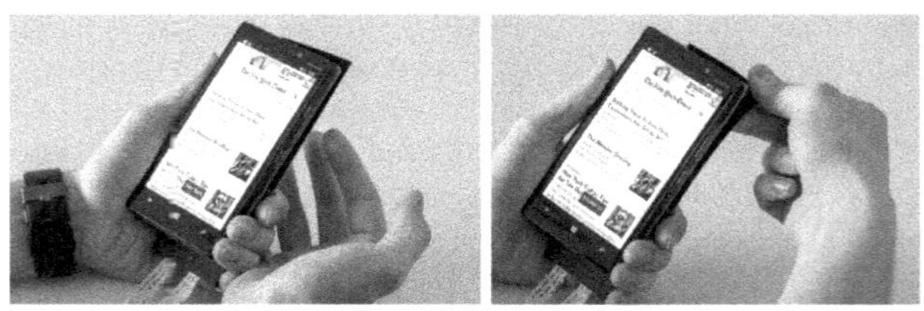

Figure 15. Left: A swipe gesture on the back of the device plays the next song in a music player running in the background. Right: The volume is adjusted with a corner Grip & Bend gesture.

Navigation

Another possibility of the Backside mode is adding a richer, more physical way for navigating through content on rigid displays or zoomable user interfaces [37].

Back-of-device Interaction & Continuous Bend Input. The backside configuration allows the user to literally push back the user interface to gain an overview of running applications (cf. Figure 16, left). A similar approach uses bending for enhancing digital interaction with metaphors known from the real world, such as digital flip-book animations. Although the main display is completely rigid and provides only touch input, FlexCase adds a physical interaction layer which is very similar to an analog flip-book (cf. Figure 16, right).

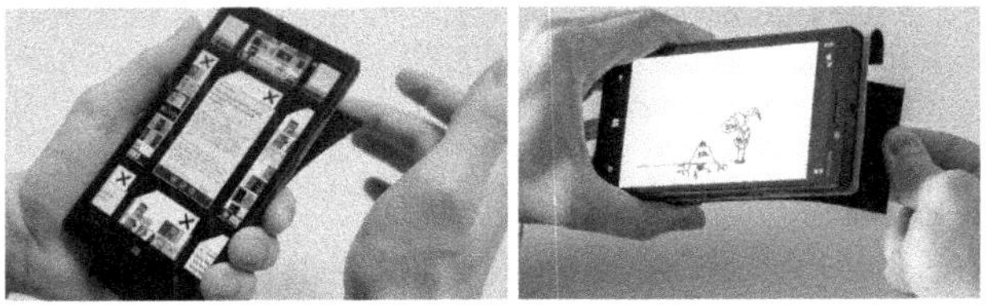

Figure 16. Left: Zooming out of the user interface by bending the cover. Left: Flipbook animation on the LCD with back-of-device bend input.

DISCUSSION & LIMITATIONS

In this paper, we have focused on a new mobile interaction concept called FlexCase. Although we gained promising feedback from informal evaluation sessions with FlexCase, a quantitative comparison is clearly needed in the future, but was simply out of scope for this paper, where we focus on the interactive capabilities of our system. However, this is an important area to address in future work.

From an interaction point of view, we see novelty in incorporating grips for overloading continuous bend gestures and see this concept as a good avenue to further extend the interaction space when bend gestures are physically limited due to the compact mobile form factor. However, one issue of the *Grip & Bend* technique is that the mapping of different grips to their related digital task can be unintuitive. Ideally, the grips would show a strong physical correlation to their related digital task, but would also allow more abstract mappings to be memorized by the users, especially if different regions are incorporated (e.g. zoom, tilt, rotate in the map scenario). Moreover, the e-paper output gives the possibility to guide those interactions, e.g. by displaying mappings. However, we acknowledge that this requires the user to learn mappings. One possible improvement of the technique could be to let the user assign grips to different actions to improve memorability.

If the cover is interactive at all times, one problem could be false activations. An additional protective cover for the flexible display could decrease unwanted interactions, but may also decrease the flexibility of the display. Another solution could involve optimizing and activating touch & bend sensing for specific use cases. For example, if an application supports slide gestures on the backside, the cover should refuse all other input such as taps, grips, or bends. While false activations were not a big issue in our preliminary user studies, it is worth to explore this topic more systematically in future work.

The current prototype was wired to an external driver box for rapid prototyping and evaluation of the different interaction concepts. While this was sufficient for this paper, mobility is till a crucial part of this interaction concept. Further, the mechanical mounting of the e-paper driver electronics limits the use of one side of the flip cover. This could be addressed in the future by embedding the electronics directly between the FlexCase cover and phone (much like a spine of a book). One shortcoming of the FlexCase form factor is the flexible bond, which requires some fixation with the hand to hold the device in a certain configuration. This could be solved by using a shape-retaining material in the bond, which is easily bendable but keeps the device in the intended form.

Our e-paper display clearly suffers from a low refresh rate. However, as demonstrated in our application scenarios, we see how the combination of LCD and e-paper display can be used to exploit the best of both worlds. Therefore, while flexible OLED displays, of course, will provide additional value and different possibilities for FlexCase, we already see a great deal of potential in the inclusion of the e-paper display, which makes this not just an interim solution until fast full-color flexible displays are bistable, robust and lower-power.

In the previous section and accompanying video, we have hopefully demonstrated numerous compelling applications and interaction techniques for FlexCase. The richness of the design space is illustrated by the large body of application and interactive scenarios, and we feel this is just the beginning, and our hope is that practitioners and researchers will develop these scenarios further.

CONCLUSIONS AND FUTURE WORK

In this paper, we presented a novel flip cover concept for smartphones, which combines a purpose-built touch, pressure and flex sensor with an e-paper display. It is designed specifically to enable a range of reconfigurable uses and modalities, where our novel input and output surface augments the standard touch and display capabilities on the phone. Users can use our system to perform a variety of touch, pressure, grip and bend gestures in a natural manner, much like interacting with a sheet of paper, without occluding the main screen.

The secondary e-paper display can act as a mechanism for providing user feedback and persisting content from the main display. We provided insights about the design process for the form factor as well as the interaction techniques and systematically explored the design space, resulting from the different configurations and modalities. We have demonstrated many interactive and application capabilities, and highlighted how touch and flex sensing can be combined in a novel way, e.g. the Grip & Bend technique. We feel this ability to combine touch and bend interaction in one single interaction is compelling and novel. The range of applications already shown suggests a rich design space for researchers and practitioners to explore in the future.

For future work, we currently work on a fully mobile version and plan to experiment with different materials in order to further improve the form factor, e.g. a shape-retaining bond. On interaction side, we plan to conduct quantitative and qualitative evaluations to highlight the performance and benefit of our system compared to more traditional forms of interaction.

ACKNOWLEDGEMENTS

We acknowledge Florian Perteneder, Andreas Tschepp and Barbara Stadlober for their invaluable input. The research leading to these results has received funding from the European Union, Seventh Framework Programme FP7/2007-2013 under grant agreement N° 611104.

REFERENCES

1. Teemu T. Ahmaniemi, Johan Kildal, and Merja Haveri. 2014. What is a Device Bend Gesture Really Good for?. In *Proceedings of the 32Nd Annual ACM Conference on Human Factors in Computing Systems (CHI '14)*. ACM, New York, NY, USA, 3503–3512. http://doi.acm.org/10.1145/2556288.2557306
2. Rufino Ansara and Audrey Girouard. 2014. Augmenting Bend Gestures with Pressure Zones on Flexible Displays. In *Proceedings of the 16th International Conference on Human-computer Interaction with Mobile Devices & Services (MobileHCI '14)*. ACM, New York, NY, USA, 531–536. http://doi.acm.org/10.1145/2628363.2634228
3. Ravin Balakrishnan, George Fitzmaurice, Gordon Kurtenbach, and Karan Singh. 1999. Exploring Interactive Curve and Surface Manipulation Using a Bend and Twist Sensitive Input Strip. In *Proceedings of the 1999 Symposium on Interactive 3D Graphics (I3D '99)*. ACM, New York, NY, USA, 111–118. http://doi.acm.org/10.1145/300523.300536
4. Ravin Balakrishnan and Ken Hinckley. 1999. The Role of Kinesthetic Reference Frames in Two-handed Input Performance. In *Proceedings of the 12th Annual ACM Symposium on User Interface Software and Technology (UIST '99)*. ACM, New York, NY, USA, 171–178. http://doi.acm.org/10.1145/320719.322599
5. Barnes and Noble International LLC. 2015. http://www.nook.com. (2015).
6. Patrick Baudisch and Gerry Chu. 2009. Back-of-device Interaction Allows Creating Very Small Touch Devices. In *Proceedings of the SIGCHI Conference on Human Factors in Computing Systems (CHI '09)*. ACM, New York, NY, USA, 1923–1932. http://doi.acm.org/10.1145/1518701.1518995
7. Christopher M. Bishop. 2006. *Pattern Recognition and Machine Learning (Information Science and Statistics)*. Springer-Verlag New York, Inc.
8. Jesse Burstyn, Amartya Banerjee, and Roel Vertegaal. 2013. FlexView: An Evaluation of Depth Navigation on Deformable Mobile Devices. In *Proceedings of the 7th International Conference on Tangible, Embedded and Embodied Interaction (TEI '13)*. ACM, New York, NY, USA, 193–200. http://doi.acm.org/10.1145/2460625.2460655
9. Alex Butler, Shahram Izadi, and Steve Hodges. 2008. SideSight: Multi-"Touch" Interaction Around Small Devices. In *Proceedings of the 21st Annual ACM Symposium on User Interface Software and Technology (UIST '08)*. ACM, New York, NY, USA, 201–204. http://doi.acm.org/10.1145/1449715.1449746
10. Nicholas Chen, Francois Guimbretiere, and Abigail Sellen. 2012. Designing a Multi-slate Reading Environment to Support Active Reading Activities. *ACM Trans. Comput.-Hum. Interact.* 19, 3, Article 18 (Oct. 2012), 35 pages. http://doi.acm.org/10.1145/2362364.2362366
11. Xiang 'Anthony' Chen, Tovi Grossman, Daniel J. Wigdor, and George Fitzmaurice. 2014. Duet: Exploring Joint Interactions on a Smart Phone and a Smart Watch. In *Proceedings of the SIGCHI Conference on Human Factors in Computing Systems (CHI '14)*. ACM, New York, NY, USA, 159–168. http://doi.acm.org/10.1145/2556288.2556955
12. Lung-Pan Cheng, Meng Han Lee, Che-Yang Wu, Fang-I Hsiao, et al. 2013. IrotateGrasp: Automatic Screen Rotation Based on Grasp of Mobile Devices. In *Proceedings of the SIGCHI Conference on Human Factors in Computing Systems (CHI '13)*. ACM, New York, NY, USA, 3051–3054. http://doi.acm.org/10.1145/2470654.2481424
13. Lee A Danisch, Kevin Englehart, and Andrew Trivett. 1999. Spatially continuous six-degrees-of-freedom position and orientation sensor. In *Photonics East (ISAM, VVDC, IEMB)*. International Society for Optics and Photonics, 48–56.
14. Artem Dementyev, Jeremy Gummeson, Derek Thrasher, Aaron Parks, Deepak Ganesan, Joshua R. Smith, and Alanson P. Sample. 2013. Wirelessly Powered Bistable Display Tags. In *Proceedings of the 2013 ACM International Joint Conference on Pervasive and Ubiquitous Computing*. ACM, New York, NY, USA, 383–386. http://doi.acm.org/10.1145/2493432.2493516
15. David T. Gallant, Andrew G. Seniuk, and Roel Vertegaal. 2008. Towards More Paper-like Input: Flexible Input Devices for Foldable Interaction Styles. In *Proceedings of the 21st Annual ACM Symposium on User Interface Software and Technology (UIST '08)*. ACM, New York, NY, USA, 283–286. http://doi.acm.org/10.1145/1449715.1449762
16. Audrey Girouard, Aneesh Tarun, and Roel Vertegaal. 2012. DisplayStacks: Interaction Techniques for Stacks of Flexible Thin-film Displays. In *Proceedings of the SIGCHI Conference on Human Factors in Computing Systems (CHI '12)*. ACM, New York, NY, USA, 2431–2440. http://doi.acm.org/10.1145/2207676.2208406
17. Mayank Goel, Jacob Wobbrock, and Shwetak Patel. 2012. GripSense: Using Built-in Sensors to Detect Hand Posture and Pressure on Commodity Mobile Phones. In *Proceedings of the 25th Annual ACM Symposium on User Interface Software and Technology (UIST '12)*. ACM, New York, NY, USA, 545–554. http://doi.acm.org/10.1145/2380116.2380184
18. Antonio Gomes, Andrea Nesbitt, and Roel Vertegaal. 2013. MorePhone: A Study of Actuated Shape Deformations for Flexible Thin-film Smartphone Notifications. In *Proceedings of the SIGCHI Conference on Human Factors in Computing Systems (CHI '13)*.

ACM, New York, NY, USA, 583–592. http://doi.acm.org/10.1145/2470654.2470737

19. Antonio Gomes and Roel Vertegaal. 2015. PaperFold: Evaluating Shape Changes for Viewport Transformations in Foldable Thin-Film Display Devices. In *Proceedings of the Ninth International Conference on Tangible, Embedded, and Embodied Interaction (TEI '15)*. ACM, New York, NY, USA, 153–160. http://doi.acm.org/10.1145/2677199.2680572

20. Ken Hinckley, Morgan Dixon, Raman Sarin, Francois Guimbretiere, and Ravin Balakrishnan. 2009. Codex: A Dual Screen Tablet Computer. In *Proceedings of the SIGCHI Conference on Human Factors in Computing Systems (CHI '09)*. ACM, New York, NY, USA, 1933–1942. http://doi.acm.org/10.1145/1518701.1518996

21. Ken Hinckley, Michel Pahud, Hrvoje Benko, Pourang Irani, et al. 2014. Sensing Techniques for Tablet+Stylus Interaction. In *Proceedings of the 27th Annual ACM Symposium on User Interface Software and Technology (UIST '14)*. ACM, New York, NY, USA, 605–614. http://doi.acm.org/10.1145/2642918.2647379

22. David Holman, Roel Vertegaal, Mark Altosaar, Nikolaus Troje, and Derek Johns. 2005. Paper Windows: Interaction Techniques for Digital Paper. In *Proceedings of the SIGCHI Conference on Human Factors in Computing Systems (CHI '05)*. ACM, New York, NY, USA, 591–599. http://doi.acm.org/10.1145/1054972.1055054

23. Joanneum Research Forschungsgesellschaft mbH. 2016. http://www.joanneum.at/en/materials/research-areas/pyzoflexr.html. (2016).

24. Paul Kabbash, William Buxton, and Abigail Sellen. 1994. Two-handed Input in a Compound Task. In *Conference Companion on Human Factors in Computing Systems (CHI '94)*. ACM, New York, NY, USA, 230–. http://doi.acm.org/10.1145/259963.260425

25. Mohammadreza Khalilbeigi, Roman Lissermann, Wolfgang Kleine, and Jürgen Steimle. 2012. FoldMe: Interacting with Double-sided Foldable Displays. In *Proceedings of the Sixth International Conference on Tangible, Embedded and Embodied Interaction (TEI '12)*. ACM, New York, NY, USA, 33–40. http://doi.acm.org/10.1145/2148131.2148142

26. Mohammadreza Khalilbeigi, Roman Lissermann, Max Mühlhäuser, and Jürgen Steimle. 2011. Xpaaand: Interaction Techniques for Rollable Displays. In *Proceedings of the SIGCHI Conference on Human Factors in Computing Systems (CHI '11)*. ACM, New York, NY, USA, 2729–2732. http://doi.acm.org/10.1145/1978942.1979344

27. Johan Kildal, Susanna Paasovaara, and Viljakaisa Aaltonen. 2012. Kinetic Device: Designing Interactions with a Deformable Mobile Interface. In *CHI '12 Extended Abstracts on Human Factors in Computing Systems (CHI EA '12)*. ACM, New York, NY, USA, 1871–1876. http://doi.acm.org/10.1145/2212776.2223721

28. Byron Lahey, Audrey Girouard, Winslow Burleson, and Roel Vertegaal. 2011. PaperPhone: Understanding the Use of Bend Gestures in Mobile Devices with Flexible Electronic Paper Displays. In *Proceedings of the SIGCHI Conference on Human Factors in Computing Systems (CHI '11)*. ACM, New York, NY, USA, 1303–1312. http://doi.acm.org/10.1145/1978942.1979136

29. Mathieu Le Goc, Stuart Taylor, Shahram Izadi, and Cem Keskin. 2014. A Low-cost Transparent Electric Field Sensor for 3D Interaction on Mobile Devices. In *Proceedings of the 32Nd Annual ACM Conference on Human Factors in Computing Systems (CHI '14)*. ACM, New York, NY, USA, 3167–3170. http://doi.acm.org/10.1145/2556288.2557331

30. Johnny C. Lee, Scott E. Hudson, and Edward Tse. 2008. Foldable Interactive Displays. In *Proceedings of the 21st Annual ACM Symposium on User Interface Software and Technology (UIST '08)*. ACM, New York, NY, USA, 287–290. http://doi.acm.org/10.1145/1449715.1449763

31. Flora M. Li, Sandeep Unnikrishnan, Peter van de Weijer, Ferdie van Assche, et al. 2013. Flexible Barrier Technology for Enabling Rollable AMOLED Displays and Upscaling Flexible OLED Lighting. *SID Symposium Digest of Technical Papers* 44, 1 (2013), 199–202. http://stacks.iop.org/0268-1242/26/i=3/a=034001

32. Markus Löchtefeld, Christoph Hirtz, and Sven Gehring. 2013. Evaluation of Hybrid Front- and Back-of-device Interaction on Mobile Devices. In *Proceedings of the 12th International Conference on Mobile and Ubiquitous Multimedia (MUM '13)*. ACM, New York, NY, USA, Article 17, 4 pages. http://doi.acm.org/10.1145/2541831.2541865

33. David C. McCallum, Edward Mak, Pourang Irani, and Sriram Subramanian. 2009. PressureText: Pressure Input for Mobile Phone Text Entry. In *CHI '09 Extended Abstracts on Human Factors in Computing Systems (CHI EA '09)*. ACM, New York, NY, USA, 4519–4524. http://doi.acm.org/10.1145/1520340.1520693

34. Ross McLachlan and Stephen Brewster. 2013. Can You Handle It?: Bimanual Techniques for Browsing Media Collections on Touchscreen Tablets. In *CHI '13 Extended Abstracts on Human Factors in Computing Systems (CHI EA '13)*. ACM, New York, NY, USA, 3095–3098. http://doi.acm.org/10.1145/2468356.2479619

35. Oaxis Inc. 2015. http://www.inkcase.com. (2015).

36. Jin-Seong Park, Heeyeop Chae, Ho Kyoon Chung, and Sang In Lee. 2011. Thin film encapsulation for flexible AM-OLED: a review. *Semiconductor Science and Technology* 26, 3 (2011), 034001. http://dx.doi.org/10.1002/j.2168-0159.2013.tb06178.x

37. Ken Perlin and David Fox. 1993. Pad: An Alternative Approach to the Computer Interface. In *Proceedings of the 20th Annual Conference on Computer Graphics and Interactive Techniques (SIGGRAPH '93)*. ACM, New York, NY, USA, 57–64. http://doi.acm.org/10.1145/166117.166125

38. popSLATE Media, Inc. 2015. http://www.popslate.com. (2015).

39. Ali Rahimi and Benjamin Recht. 2007. Random features for large-scale kernel machines. In *Advances in neural information processing systems*. 1177–1184.

40. Christian Rendl, Patrick Greindl, Michael Haller, Martin Zirkl, et al. 2012. PyzoFlex: Printed Piezoelectric Pressure Sensing Foil. In *Proceedings of the 25th Annual ACM Symposium on User Interface Software and Technology (UIST '12)*. ACM, New York, NY, USA, 509–518. http://doi.acm.org/10.1145/2380116.2380180

41. Christian Rendl, David Kim, Sean Fanello, Patrick Parzer, et al. 2014. FlexSense: A Transparent Self-sensing Deformable Surface. In *Proceedings of the 27th Annual ACM Symposium on User Interface Software and Technology (UIST '14)*. ACM, New York, NY, USA, 129–138. http://doi.acm.org/10.1145/2642918.2647405

42. Carsten Schwesig, Ivan Poupyrev, and Eijiro Mori. 2004. Gummi: A Bendable Computer. In *Proceedings of the SIGCHI Conference on Human Factors in Computing Systems (CHI '04)*. ACM, New York, NY, USA, 263–270. http://doi.acm.org/10.1145/985692.985726

43. Andrew Sears and Ben Shneiderman. 1991. High Precision Touchscreens: Design Strategies and Comparisons with a Mouse. *Int. J. Man-Mach. Stud.* 34, 4 (April 1991), 593–613. http://dx.doi.org/10.1016/0020-7373(91)90037-8

44. Katie A. Siek, Yvonne Rogers, and Kay H. Connelly. 2005. Fat Finger Worries: How Older and Younger Users Physically Interact with PDAs. In *Human-Computer Interaction - INTERACT 2005*, MariaFrancesca Costabile and Fabio Patern (Eds.). Lecture Notes in Computer Science, Vol. 3585. Springer Berlin Heidelberg, 267–280. http://dx.doi.org/10.1007/11555261_24

45. Hyunyoung Song, Hrvoje Benko, Francois Guimbretiere, Shahram Izadi, et al. 2011. Grips and Gestures on a Multi-touch Pen. In *Proceedings of the SIGCHI Conference on Human Factors in Computing Systems (CHI '11)*. ACM, New York, NY, USA, 1323–1332. http://doi.acm.org/10.1145/1978942.1979138

46. Jie Song, Gábor Sörös, Fabrizio Pece, Sean Ryan Fanello, et al. 2014. In-air Gestures Around Unmodified Mobile Devices. In *Proceedings of the 27th Annual ACM Symposium on User Interface Software and Technology (UIST '14)*. ACM, New York, NY, USA, 319–329. http://doi.acm.org/10.1145/2642918.2647373

47. Jürgen Steimle, Andreas Jordt, and Pattie Maes. 2013. Flexpad: A Highly Flexible Handheld Display. In *CHI '13 Extended Abstracts on Human Factors in Computing Systems (CHI EA '13)*. ACM, New York, NY, USA, 2873–2874. http://doi.acm.org/10.1145/2468356.2479555

48. Taichi Tajika, Tomoko Yonezawa, and Noriaki Mitsunaga. 2008. Intuitive Page-turning Interface of e-Books on Flexible e-Paper Based on User Studies. In *Proceedings of the 16th ACM International Conference on Multimedia (MM '08)*. ACM, New York, NY, USA, 793–796. http://doi.acm.org/10.1145/1459359.1459489

49. Aneesh P. Tarun, Peng Wang, Audrey Girouard, Paul Strohmeier, et al. 2013. PaperTab: An Electronic Paper Computer with Multiple Large Flexible Electrophoretic Displays. In *CHI '13 Extended Abstracts on Human Factors in Computing Systems (CHI EA '13)*. ACM, New York, NY, USA, 3131–3134. http://doi.acm.org/10.1145/2468356.2479628

50. Andrea Vedaldi and Andrew Zisserman. 2012. Efficient Additive Kernels via Explicit Feature Maps. *IEEE Transactions on Pattern Analysis and Machine Intelligence* 34, 3 (March 2012), 480–492.

51. Nicolas Villar, Shahram Izadi, Dan Rosenfeld, Hrvoje Benko, et al. 2009. Mouse 2.0: Multi-touch Meets the Mouse. In *Proceedings of the 22Nd Annual ACM Symposium on User Interface Software and Technology (UIST '09)*. ACM, New York, NY, USA, 33–42. http://doi.acm.org/10.1145/1622176.1622184

52. Julie Wagner, Stéphane Huot, and Wendy Mackay. 2012. BiTouch and BiPad: Designing Bimanual Interaction for Hand-held Tablets. In *Proceedings of the SIGCHI Conference on Human Factors in Computing Systems (CHI '12)*. ACM, New York, NY, USA, 2317–2326. http://doi.acm.org/10.1145/2207676.2208391

53. Daniel Wigdor, Clifton Forlines, Patrick Baudisch, John Barnwell, and Chia Shen. 2007. Lucid Touch: A See-through Mobile Device. In *Proceedings of the 20th Annual ACM Symposium on User Interface Software and Technology (UIST '07)*. ACM, New York, NY, USA, 269–278. http://doi.acm.org/10.1145/1294211.1294259

54. Raphael Wimmer and Sebastian Boring. 2009. HandSense: Discriminating Different Ways of Grasping and Holding a Tangible User Interface. In *Proceedings of the 3rd International Conference on Tangible and Embedded Interaction (TEI '09)*. ACM, New York, NY, USA, 359–362. http://doi.acm.org/10.1145/1517664.1517736

55. Yota Devices. 2015. http://yotaphone.com. (2015).

56. Martin Zirkl, Anurak Sawatdee, Uta Helbig, Markus Krause, et al. 2011. An All-Printed Ferroelectric Active Matrix Sensor Network Based on Only Five Functional Materials Forming a Touchless Control Interface. *Advanced Materials* 23, 18 (2011), 2069–2074. http://dx.doi.org/10.1002/adma.201100054

Evaluation of a Smart-Restorable Backspace Technique to Facilitate Text Entry Error Correction

Ahmed Sabbir Arif[1], Sunjun Kim[3], Wolfgang Stuerzlinger[2], Geehyuk Lee[3], Ali Mazalek[1]

[1]Ryerson University
Toronto, Ontario, Canada
{asarif, mazalek}@ryerson.ca

[2]Simon Fraser University
Surrey, British Columbia, Canada
http://ws.iat.sfu.ca

[3]KAIST
Daejeon, South Korea
{kuaa.net, geehyuk}@gmail.com

ABSTRACT

We present a new smart-restorable backspace technique to facilitate correction of "overlooked" errors on touchscreen-based tablets. We conducted an empirical study to compare the new backspace technique with the conventional one. Results of the study revealed that the new technique improves the overall text entry performance, both in terms of speed and operations per character, by significantly reducing error correction efforts. In addition, results showed that most users preferred the new technique to the one they use on their tablets, and found it easy to learn and use. Most of them also felt that it improved their overall text entry performance, thus wanted to keep using it.

Author Keywords

Text entry; virtual keyboard; predictive text; touchscreen; errors; error correction; backspace.

ACM Classification Keywords

H.5.m. Information interfaces and presentation (e.g., HCI): Miscellaneous; H.5.2 User Interfaces (D.2.2, H.1.2, I.3.6): Input devices and strategies (e.g., mouse, touchscreen).

INTRODUCTION

Recent market research suggests that tablet computers will gradually overtake desktop and laptop computers in the near future [11]. Tablets have become lighter and smaller over the years, with substantial advances in power, functionality, and performance. Nowadays, one can be productive with tablets for tasks that previously required the "power" of a desktop or a laptop. Text entry with tablets, however, is still relatively difficult due of their smaller screen sizes and the absence of a physical keyboard. Although many have addressed these issues by developing new and improved text entry techniques, almost no work has focused on the error correction process. Most current techniques allow users to correct errors in three different ways. First, navigating to the position where a mistake was made by using direct touch cursor control, correcting the mistake by replacement, insertion, or deletion, and then repositioning the cursor to the end of the text. Second, using the virtual cursor control keys, which requires navigating to the error position by repetitively tapping on virtual cursor control keys (if they are available), correcting the mistake, and then repositioning the cursor to the end of the text. Finally, through the backspace key, which involves deleting all characters following the error position, correcting the mistake, and then re-inputting the deleted text.

While these methods work reasonably well for immediate error corrections, *i.e.*, when an error is noticed and corrected immediately after committing it or within the entry of three characters following the error, they all suffer from usability issues when users attempt to correct a missed or overlooked error in the text. In such a scenario, with direct cursor control, users are required to tap outside of the virtual keyboard, *i.e.*, on the text area, to precisely place the cursor to the intended position, correct the mistake, and then reposition the cursor to the end of the text. This increases the cognitive load and the index of difficulty (ID, a function of the target size and distance in Fitts' law [14]) for the task. Such an action has been shown to require on average 4.5 seconds [16]. Besides, positioning the cursor among small characters is error prone and increases the possibility of further errors [7].

Both backspace and cursor control keys are more precise and accurate than direct cursor control, but require potentially many repetitive keystrokes. For instance, to position the cursor five characters behind the current position, users have to tap the cursor-right key five times. Then after fixing the error, have to navigate back to the original position with five additional keystrokes. Thus ten plus the corrective keystrokes are required to fix a single error. Similarly, with the backspace key, users have to delete all text following the error, and after correcting it, have to re-input the deleted text, requiring the same number of keystrokes as the cursor control key method.

To facilitate such error correction episodes, we present here a new smart-restorable backspace technique for touchscreen-based tablets. The reminder of the paper is organized as follows. It starts with a brief discussion of related work in the area. Then, it introduces a basic version of the new approach, justifies the design decisions, and evaluates it in a pilot study that provides further insights into the human error correction process and indications on how to improve the technique. The paper then presents an improved approach, compares it with the conventional backspace method in the main user

CHI'16, May 07-12, 2016, San Jose, CA, USA
© 2016 ACM. ISBN 978-1-4503-3362-7/16/05$15.00
DOI: http://dx.doi.org/10.1145/2858036.2858407

study, and discusses the results. Finally, it ends with a conclusion and speculations on future work.

RELATED WORK

Previous research has focused on touchscreen text editing [16], where users modify on an already completed text, and error prevention [3, 10, 12, 18], where the system attempts to prevent an error from occurring. Yet, not much work has focused on error correction itself, where users correct their mistakes as they type. In fact, the only major development in the area is a feature that is now default in almost all virtual predictive keyboards, which enables users to restore the originally inputted text by pressing the backspace key immediately after an autocorrection [11].

A recent mobile keyboard, KeuKey [24], permits users to correct typos by entering the correct word at the end of the text, and performing a down gesture on the keyboard to replace the incorrect word with the correct one. It simply compares the last inputted word with the rest of the text, and replaces the word with the best match score. If multiple words match, it replaces the most recent word, but permits the user to navigate to the correct word with additional down gestures. With this technique, users are often forced to enter a complete word even when they only made a single mistake. Fleksy [15] allows users to delete text word by word by performing left gestures on the keyboard. While this permits users to quickly reach an error position, it still requires them to delete the correct portion of the text and to re-input it later.

The new Apple iOS 9 provides support for indirect cursor control using two-finger gestures [1] and 3D touch [2] on the virtual keyboard. While this enables users to move the cursor in any direction by words or lines, prior investigations have found such approach less accurate than direct touch [27].

THE SMART-RESTORABLE BACKSPACE

The smart-restorable backspace utilizes the existing predictive system of a virtual keyboard to accommodate the correction of overlooked spelling mistakes in a text entry episode. It does not account for in-vocabulary (IV) errors, such as an incorrect autocorrection. While spelling mistakes and typos are less frequent in most current predictive techniques due to forceful autocorrection, they are mostly independent of the predictive method. Yet they still impact the user experience. The goal of our work is to enable users to correct such mistakes with fewer keystrokes than the default backspace. In this section, we discuss the design and implementation of our technique.

Determining Correction Positions

When the predictive system finds a likely misspelled word, the smart-restorable backspace compares it with the most probable correct word to find the position(s) where a single-character operation, *i.e.*, insertion, deletion, or substitution, is necessary to change the incorrect word to the correct one; referred to as correction positions (*CP*). The system uses the Levenshtein distance [25] and a string comparison algorithm [20] to determine these *CPs*. Then, it records the earliest correction position for future smart deletion. For example, if the user enters "*exapla*" instead of "*example*", the system will detect two potential correction positions, an insertion after the third character (*CP* 3), and the replacement of the last character (*CP* 5), but will record only the earliest one (*CP* 3).

Basic Smart Deletion

The basic smart-restorable backspace method behaves like the conventional backspace for the first three repetitive taps to accommodate immediate error corrections. For instance, when users notice a mistake almost immediately after committing it, *i.e.*, within the entry of three characters following the mistake, they can quickly make the necessary correction and continue with text entry. The system automatically triggers smart deletion only on the fourth backspace tap, provided that the text contains at least one misspelled word. In such a case, the technique deletes all input following the latest correction position. For example, if the user inputs the phrase, "*exaple has more folloes than reason*" instead of "*example has more followers than reason*", the first three backspaces will delete the last three characters ("*son*") but the fourth one will delete all input after the correction position for the latest misspelled word, *i.e.*, "*folloes*" instead of "*follows*", *CP* 21, and the user will then see "*exaple has more follo*".

In order to correct multiple misspelled words in the text, the user has to keep tapping on the backspace key. Then on each fourth tap the system will delete all input following the previous correction position. In the above example, the user can continue tapping on the backspace key to delete the text after the first correction position, *i.e.*, "*exapla*" instead of "*example*", corresponding to *CP* 3, "*exa*". This enables the user to delete 32 characters with only 8 backspace taps.

The system also accounts for direct cursor positioning. If the user moves the cursor to before the last misspelled word, the system disregards all correction positions following the cursor. *E.g.*, if the user moves the cursor before the last misspelled word, *i.e.*, "*folloes*" in the above example, the technique will disregard "*folloes*" and only account for the mistakes that precede the cursors, *i.e.*, "*exapla*".

The system also permits users to delete multiple characters by long-pressing the backspace key. When the user holds the backspace key for more than 750 milliseconds, the system starts deleting one character every 150 milliseconds, until the user lifts his/her finger. These thresholds are commonly used in mobile and Web interfaces.

Smart Restoration

One issue with smart deletion is that after deleting a chunk of text, users then have to re-input the correct portions. Our restoration feature builds on Kim and Lee's idea [23], and addresses this by keeping a separate record of the deleted text and later suggesting the correct remainder of it in the prediction panel when the user attempts to re-input it, *i.e.*, when the user inputs at least two characters which match previously entered text following the correction. If the deleted text contains errors, the system trims the text based on each correction position to avoid the entry of incorrect text. For instance, in the above example, let us assume that after deleting all text until the first correction position, "*exa*", the user corrects the spelling of "*example*", and then enters a space and two characters of the next word, "*example ha*". In this case, the system will find a match for "*ha*" in the deletion record "*has more folloes than reason*", but will trim it to avoid the entry of a likely misspelled word "*folloes*" to display only the correct portion "*s more follo*" in the prediction panel. The user then can restore this text by tapping on it in the prediction panel. The system removes a *CP* and a deleted chunk from the record as soon as the user corrects a spelling and/or restores a chunk of text, to avoid recurrences.

The system uses the characters entered after the correction of a misspelled word, *i.e.*, two characters or more, to find a match in the deleted text to suggest a smart restoration. For instance, in the above example, when the user enters "*ha*" after correcting the misspelled word "*example*", the system searches the record for "*ha*". As there is only one occurrence of the key in the deleted text, the system simply suggests the restoration of the reminder of the text. However, in case of multiple occurrences of the search term, the system uses the Levenshtein distance [25] to find the best match. For instance, if "*she had coffee*" was also in the record, the system would have found two matches for "*ha*", one in "*le has more folloes than reason*" and another in "*she had coffee*". Nevertheless, as the recently entered text "*mple ha*" would yield a lower Levenshtein distance for "*le ha*" (distance: 2) than "*she ha*" (distance: 3), the former text would have been suggested for restoration. Figure 1 illustrates an example error correction episode with the smart-restorable backspace.

Word Prediction and Autocorrection

We developed a simple word prediction and autocorrection system using the most frequent 10,000 words in the English language [30]. Similar to the default Android predictive system, it displays a panel above the virtual keyboard to suggest three candidates: the original text in the left, the most probable prediction in the center (highlighted with underline), and the second most probable one in the right. Illustrated in Figure 1. The system permits users to enter a candidate by pressing the space key, which inputs the highlighted candidate, or by tapping on the candidate word in the panel.

For a likely misspelled word, the system autocorrects it with the most probable correct word, *i.e.*, the underlined candidate in the prediction panel. However, to replicate the default Android keyboard with its "aggressive" autocorrection, both of the following must hold to trigger an autocorrection.

- The length difference between the entered and the candidate word is less than two characters. That is, the inputted word is of the same length or one character longer or shorter than the candidate word.
- The Levenshtein distance [25] between the inputted and the candidate word is less than two operations.

If the above parameters are not met, the system highlights the likely misspelled word with a red underline. See Figure 1 (a). Users can still override an autocorrection by tapping on the original text in the panel, *i.e.*, the left candidate. Then, the system does not consider the word as misspelled and does not underline it. Users can also replace an autocorrected word with the original text by tapping on the backspace key directly after the autocorrection. Then the system does not autocorrect that word on the second input or correction attempt.

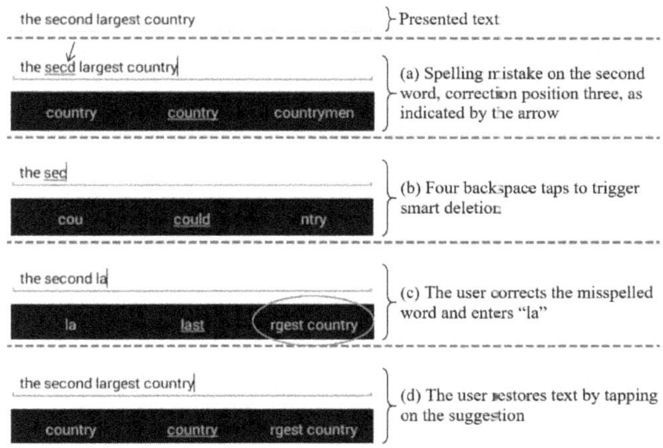

Figure 1. Four steps of an example error correction episode with smart backspace and restoration: (a) the user makes a spelling mistake on the second word, (b) taps backspace four times to delete the text after the latest correction position, (c) corrects the misspelled word and then enters two characters "la", which displays a restoration suggestion on the right of the prediction panel, then (d) restores previously deleted text by tapping on the suggestion.

We informally tested the custom predictive system with some experienced Android OS users. None of them noticed potential differences between the custom and the default Android prediction.

STUDY SETUP

To increase the external validity of the user studies evaluating the new smart-restorable backspace technique, we conducted an informal survey to identify the most used text entry positions and predictive features on touchscreen-based tablets. The survey involved 24 experienced users who owned and frequently used tablets for text entry. Ages were from 18 to 38 years, average 23.5 (SD = 5.7). 62.5% of them were female. Results revealed that about 92% of them use word prediction and 79% use autocorrection.

Almost all users input text by placing the device on flat surfaces, such as a table, and input text using their index fingers (54%), thumbs (29%), or all fingers but thumbs (8%). The remaining 9% hold the device with their hands and input text using their thumbs. Based on this, we placed the device on a table during the studies but allowed users to input text using their preferred posture. Similarly, as the survey showed that almost all users use word prediction and autocorrection, we enabled these features.

In another pilot, we evaluated an earlier version of the backspace technique *without* prediction. Three novices (one female), average age 26 years (SD=3.54), entered 70 short English phrases [26] with each technique, in counterbalanced order, on a first generation Apple iPad. Results revealed that the smart-restorable backspace increased text entry speed by 32.5% and reduced total error rate by 57.4%. This suggests the new technique substantially improves entry performance for novices when word prediction and autocorrection features are *disabled*. Yet, this is not ecologically valid and we re-enabled these features after this pilot.

A PILOT STUDY

We evaluated the basic smart-restorable backspace technique in a pilot study. The purpose was to fine-tune the technique's performance, to get user feedback, and also to guide the final study design [8].

Apparatus

We used a custom application developed with the Android SDK on an ASUS MeMO Pad HD 7 at 800×1280, 196.8× 120.6×10.8 mm. The device used the default Google keyboard and logged all interactions. See Figure 1 (a). The device was attached to a desk with a custom dock to tilt it to a comfortable typing position at ~15°. See Figure 1 (b).

Participants

Twelve participants, aged from 19 to 38 years, average 23, participated in the pilot. Seven of them were female and one was left-handed. They all owned a tablet for at least a year and frequently used it for text entry.

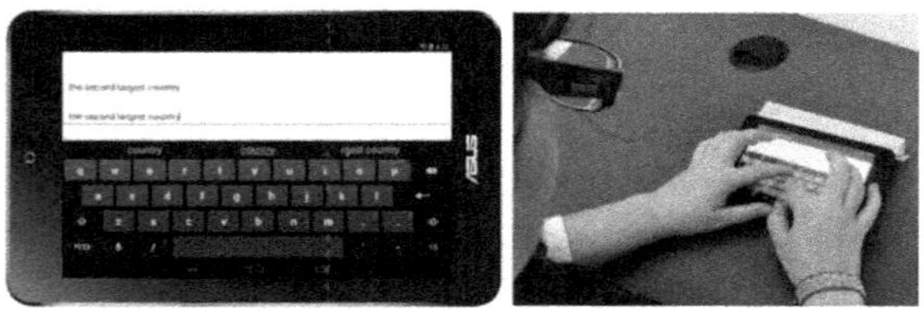

(a) (b)

Figure 2. (a) The device and the custom application used during the pilot study and (b) a participant inputting text using the custom application during the pilot study.

Procedure and Design

We used a within-subjects design. The two factors were the conventional and the smart-restorable backspace. During the study, participants were asked to enter short English phrases from the MacKenzie and Soukoreff set [26] with both techniques. These phrases were shown in random order on the display, all in lowercase. We instructed each participant to read and understand the phrases in advance, then to enter them as quickly and accurately as possible. When finished, they had to press the enter key to see the next phrase. Error correction was *forced*. That is, participants had to correct all mistakes before submitting a phrase, otherwise the system made a "ding" noise to notify them of any existing error and did not accept the submission. The reasons behind this is that we observed that some users simply ignore some or all of the errors. The cause of this may be that current correction efforts are too high (a core motivation for our work). While sending erroneous text may be acceptable in some situations, this is not desirable in all contexts. To address the potential confound, we decided to force users to correct all errors.

Participants could use any comfortable posture in landscape position to input text. During the study, most of them (92%) used both hands. We provided them with two practice phrases before each condition to make sure that they were moderately familiar with the techniques and protocol. They could extend this practice period on request. They were informed that they could rest between conditions, blocks, or trials. Timing started from the entry of the first character and ended with the last. In summary, the design was:

12 participants ×
2 conditions (*conventional* and *new*, *counterbalanced*) ×
36 short phrases (excluding practice phrases)
= 864 submissions, in total.

Metrics

We calculated the following metrics during the study.

- **Words per minute (wpm):** the total number of words entered in a minute. This metric measures text entry speed.
- **Operations per character:** denotes the average number of operations it requires to input one character. This metric is similar to keystrokes per character (KSPC), but considers all operations, including taps and gestures.
- **Backspace rate (%):** signifies the average percentage of backspace action necessary to produce error free text. This was calculated as the ratio of the total number of backspace keys used to the length of the transcribed text.

Results

We used repeated-measures ANOVA for all analysis.

An ANOVA failed to find a significant effect of technique on entry speed ($F_{1,11} = 0.58$, ns). The average entry speed with the conventional and new backspace were 23.5 (SE = 1.55) and 22.68 wpm (SE = 1.5), respectively. We filtered the data for cases where users committed at least one spelling mistake (64% of all transcribed phrases), but failed again to identify an effect ($F_{1,11} = 0.04$, ns).

An ANOVA failed to find a significant effect of technique on operations per character ($F_{1,11} = 1.57$, ns). On average the conventional and smart-restorable backspace required 1.2 (SE = 0.05) and 1.2 (SE = 0.04) operations per character, respectively. There was no significant effect for cases where users committed at least one mistake ($F_{1,11} = 1.26$, ns).

There was no significant effect of technique on backspace rate ($F_{1,11} = 3.51$, ns). The average backspace rate for the conventional and smart-restorable backspace were 13.58 (SE = 2.22) and 10.72% (SE = 1.41), respectively. There was no significant effect for cases where users committed at least one mistake ($F_{1,1} = 4.67$, $p = .05$).

Discussion

Due to the inclusion of predictive features, we did not expect to observe a significant effect of technique on entry speed, accuracy, and backspace rate. Results revealed that although the backspace rate was about 21% less with the new smart-restorable backspace, both techniques needed about the same number of operations per character. This suggests that despite using fewer backspaces than the conventional technique, users needed additional operations. More surprisingly, results showed that the entry rate with smart-restorable was 3.5% less. Through more analysis, we found several reasons for this.

First, participants had (too) few occasions to use the smart-restorable features when transcribing short English phrases. In an entire text entry episode, there were only about 29% cases where they *could* use the smart-restorable backspace. This corresponds to a previous finding [6], which showed that about 79% of all errors are noticed and then corrected within the entry of three characters following the mistake. This was also apparent in the post-study interviews, where many users commented that they did not notice any difference between the conventional and the smart-restorable backspace.

Second, the smart deletion feature disrupted the natural flow of text entry. It deleted chunks of text automatically, and often unexpectedly, not allowing users to mentally prepare for the change. As a result, the entry of a character following a smart deletion required more time. According to our logs users took on average 2.1 seconds to continue with text entry after smart deletion was triggered.

Third, the restore feature was rarely used by participants; most probably due to inadequate visual feedback. The system displayed all restorable chunks in the prediction panel, which required users to shift their focus from the text area to the panel. Besides, the restore feature did not record texts deleted with regular or tap-hold backspacing, *i.e.*, *only* with smart backspace, which caused confusion.

IMPROVED SMART-RESTORABLE BACKSPACE

Based on the findings of the above pilots and Kim and Lee's early exploration [23], we made several improvements to the smart-restorable backspace behavior.

First, we provide the users with more control over the smart deletion feature by disabling automatic deletions. Instead, we permit users to activate smart deletion on demand. For that, we used a tap and gesture hybrid approach, where users tap on the backspace key for regular backspace behaviors and perform a right to left gesture on the key to activate the smart-restorable backspace (Figure 3). If the inputted text contains multiple errors, the improved smart-restorable backspace targets the last committed one. To reach an error before that, the user has to smart-delete again, and so forth. This is to address the case that an error was intentionally left uncorrected, *e.g.*, an out-of-vocabulary word. In case of multiple errors within the same word, it deletes all letters following the earliest error, as this likely affects everything else in the word, too. In contrast, if the inputted text does not contain a spelling mistake, the smart-restorable backspace acts like the regular backspace, that is, deletes one character per gesture. This not only reduces the possibility of accidental and unexpected deletions but also the number of operations required to activate smart deletion. Now, only a single "left" stroke is necessary, while four backspaces were needed for smart deletion previously.

We also considered using long-press and double-tap on the key to activate smart deletion but decided against these, as they again interfere with the regular backspace behavior. In regular backspacing, long-press usually enables continuous character deletion, a feature also supported by the smart-restorable backspace. With double-tap, on the other hand, it is difficult to differentiate whether the intention was to activate smart deletion or to quickly delete two characters. Gestures do not suffer from this ambiguity. Besides, the fact that users are able to quickly learn and adapt to keyboards augmented with gestures [11], also motivated us to use this option.

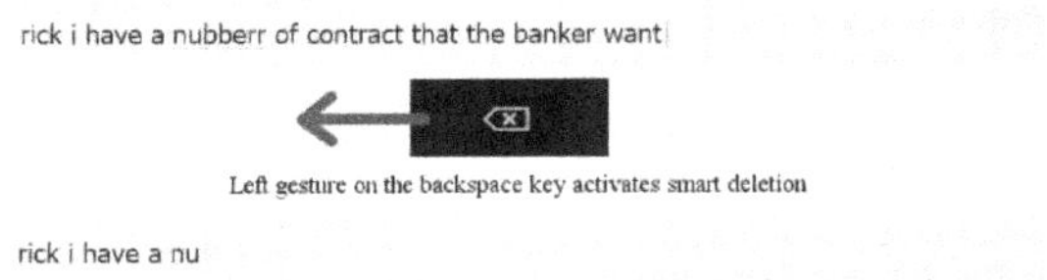

Figure 3. Activating smart deletion through a left gesture on the backspace key.

The new system also permits users to include a non-dictionary word into the dictionary by tapping on it in the text area. Once added to the dictionary, the system does not consider it as a misspelled word, eliminating the possibility of future accidental smart deletion. Similarly, users can delete the word from the dictionary by re-tapping on it.

Moreover, we improved the smart restoration feature by enabling it even for regular backspace operations. In the previous version of this feature, chunks of text that were deleted with repetitive keystrokes or long-press were not available for restoration. The improved version, in contrast, records all deleted text, increasing the restoration possibilities for the user. We also reduced the minimum key length from two to one character to display a restore suggestion earlier and with the minimum number of keystrokes possible. To facilitate access to smart restoration, we map activation to a right swipe on the backspace key. See Figure 4. We limit the smart deletion and smart restoration gestures, left and right swipes respectively, to the backspace key to account for the fact that some virtual keyboards map other functionalities to gestures [11], which makes our new method compatible with other keyboard systems.

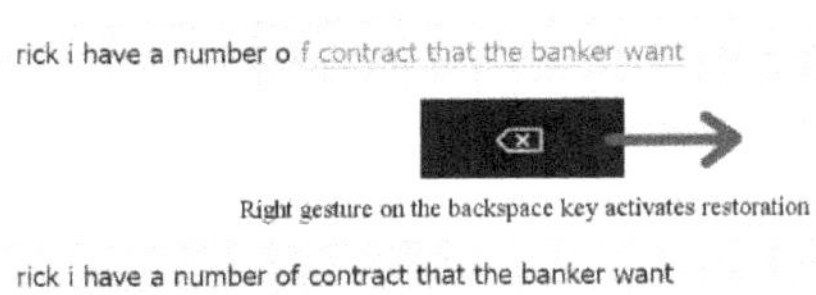

Figure 4. Visual feedback on a restorable text and smart restoration using a right gesture on the backspace key.

Finally, the improved smart restoration feature provides additional visual feedback for potentially restorable chunks.

To address the issue that users did not notice the prediction in the panel, the new version provides visual feedback for a restorable chunk directly in the text area in a grayed-out font (Figure 4). Then, the user can accept the suggestion by either performing a right gesture on the backspace key or tapping on the prediction in the prediction panel.

A USER STUDY

We conducted a user study to test the following hypotheses, which apply when users did not notice an error immediately after committing it:

H_1: *The smart-restorable backspace performs better than the conventional backspace in terms of speed and efforts.*

H_2: *The smart-restorable backspace is easy to learn and use, and users prefer it to the conventional backspace.*

Apparatus

We used multiple Microsoft Surface Pro 3 tablets, Intel Core i5 processor, 29.21×20.14×0.91 cm, and 798 grams, for the study, with Windows 8.1 at 2160×1440 resolution.

The Custom Application

We developed a custom Web application using HTML5 and JavaScript. We used the jQuery Mobile library to provide support for touch and gestures [22]. All text entry operations were processed on the client side to avoid delays. However, all user interactions were recorded in a MySQL/PHP database when the user pressed the enter key to submit a phrase. Figure 5 shows the device(s) and the application used in the study.

Figure 5. The device and the custom application used during the final user study.

Phrase Set

During the study, participants were asked to enter English phrases from the Enron set [28]. We used transcription tasks to increase the internal validity [29]. We decided to use the Enron corpus for two reasons. First, it is a collection of phrases written by actual mobile users on mobile devices, which increases the external validity of the study. Second, unlike most other sets, it contains phrases of various lengths, allowing us to test the new technique with relatively longer phrases. During the study we used a 775 phrase subset of the corpus, with 14-102 characters (5-15 words), and an average length of 41.45 (SD = 15.96). All phrases were presented in lowercase, without punctuation and special characters.

Design

We used a *between*-subjects design for the study. There were two groups (conditions): *conventional* backspace and the (improved) *smart-restorable* one. Participants were assigned to one of the two groups. Both groups had the same number of participants. We used a between-subjects design to collect as much data for each technique as possible, and to avoid any potential interference. There were two sessions, with roughly 24 hour gap in between. During the first session participants transcribed 80 random phrases. In the second session they transcribed 40 random phrases in two steps: first without and then with injected errors. Thus, there were 80 input attempts, as in the first session. In summary, the design was:

2 groups (*conventional* and *smart-restorable*) ×
10 participant per group ×
2 sessions, with about 24 hour gap in between ×
Session 1: 80 phrases (excluding practice phrases) +
Session 2: 40 phrases × (without + with injected error)
= 6,400 submissions, in total.

Error Injection

The purpose of the smart-restorable backspace is to facilitate the correction of "overlooked" errors, where the user did not notice or correct one or more mistake/s immediately after committing it. A prior investigation [6] found that such occurrences are infrequent, only 20-30% of a text entry episode, as also confirmed through post-hoc analysis of our pilot data. This makes it difficult to evaluate the new technique in a user study. Therefore, we artificially replicated error correction scenarios by injecting synthetic errors on the transcription. When users submit an error-free text by tapping on the enter button, the system injects an insertion, omission, substitution, or transposition error on the longest word. This is based on an observation that longer words are more prone to spelling errors. Besides, error injection on shorter words often results in other dictionary words, *e.g.*, "mam" to "man", making injected errors unnoticeable. If the maximum length occurs in multiple words in a phrase, the system randomly injected an error on one of the words. No errors were injected on text that already contained a spelling error.

We use these types of errors, as a prior study [21] showed that such errors represent about 90% of all those committed by experienced users. That study also resembled our use case the best, as we use comparatively large virtual keys (2.4×1.5 cm) and permit bimanual input. As in previous work [21], we simulate how such errors occur in the real-life, *i.e.*, 80% substitution errors replace a letter with a surrounding one from the same row. We also match the rates at which they occur, *i.e.*, 50% insertion, 26% substitution, 16% omission, and 8% transposition errors.

Participants

We recruited 20 paid participants from the university community. They were all experienced mobile touchscreen users. That is, they own and have been using a touchscreen-based mobile device on a daily basis, for at least three years. They were also experienced in mobile text entry, as all of them enter text on their mobile devices, *i.e.*, smartphone or tablet, almost every day. We randomly assigned them to each group, but made an effort to maintain roughly the same age range and gender ratio in the two groups.

Conventional: Ten participants were assigned to this group. Three were female. Their age ranged from 19 to 23, average 20.5 years (SD = 1.35). Seven were right-handed, one left-handed, and one ambidextrous.

Smart-Restorable: Ten participants were assigned to this group. Two were female and age ranged from 19 to 28, average 22 years (SD = 3.35). All were right-handed.

Procedure

At the start of the first session, we demonstrated the technique corresponding to their group to them. We made sure they understood and knew how to use all features. Then, we asked them to practice with the system, where they had to enter at least three phrases using "their" technique. However, they were allowed to extend this practice period on request. The intention was to make sure they felt confident using the technique. The main study started after that, where we asked the participants to transcribe eighty English phrases from our phrase set, which were shown in random order on the display. We instructed participants to read and understand the phrases in advance, then to enter them as quickly and accurately as possible. When finished, they had to press the enter key to see the next phrase. Error correction was *forced* during the study and participants had to correct all mistakes before submitting it, otherwise the system made a "ding" noise to notify them of any existing error. While, the system supported direct cursor control, we disabled this in the study to eliminate a potential confound. Hence, participants were asked to exclusively use backspace for error correction. We permitted them to position the tablet on the table in any comfortable landscape position (Figure 6). We also allowed participants to use any posture they felt conformable with for text entry. All of them ended up using both hands.

Figure 6. A participant inputting text using the custom application during the final user study.

The second session started the next day and followed the same procedure as the first one. In addition, error injection was added to each submission attempt. That is, the system injected an insertion, substitution, omission, or transposition error on the longest word of the phrase upon submission. However, users were only informed that errors would occur on a random word. Participants had to correct that mistake and resubmit to see the next phrase. We decided to inject errors on each submitted phrase to reduce the effort for reading and understanding a new phrase. Participants were informed of this behavior ahead of time to avoid any surprise effects. We explained that this was designed to simulate a situation where they overlooked a mistake. Participants were able to test this in a practice period, where they were asked to enter at least three phrases. They could extend this practice period upon request.

Upon completion of the study, participants were asked to fill out a short questionnaire where they could rate the technique they used on a seven-point Likert scale and also to comment on the techniques and study procedure.

Metrics

In addition to calculating words per minute (wpm), operations per character, and backspace rate as in the pilot study, here we also calculated the following metrics.

- **Visual scan time (milliseconds):** denotes the average time it takes to verify an inputted phrase. This was calculated by measuring the interval between the last character entry and the enter key press [5].
- **Backspace time (milliseconds):** denotes the average time it takes the user to perform a backspace. This metric was calculated by measuring the interval between the last character entry and a backspace. Apart from the decision, preparation, and action time for the backspace, this also includes the visual scan for the last character. We did not separate these human processes as cognitive modeling is outside the scope of our work. This metric excludes long-press backspace incidents.
- **Post-backspace time (milliseconds):** signifies the average time it takes to input a character after performing a backspace. This was calculated by measuring the interval between a backspace and the next character. This metric is the compound of the verification time for the backspace and the decision, preparation, and action time for the next character.

RESULTS

We analyzed the data with mixed ANOVA for the effect of technique (between subjects) and session (within). In the figures, error bars represent ±1 standard error.

Entry Speed

An ANOVA revealed that there was no significant effect of technique on text entry speed ($F_{1,18}$ = 0.1, ns) across all sessions. Average entry speeds for conventional and smart-restorable were 27.75 (SE = 0.28) and 28.36 wpm (SE = 0.27), respectively. There was a significant effect of session ($F_{1,18} = 27.21, p < .0001, \eta^2 = .03$), but no technique × session interaction ($F_{1,18}$ = 0.2, ns). Figure 7 shows average entry speed for both techniques during the two sessions.

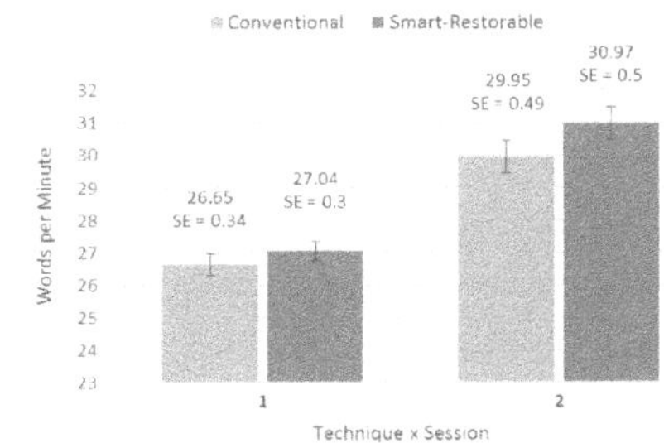

Figure 7. Average entry speed for both techniques by session.

An ANOVA identified a significant effect of technique on entry speed for phrases with injected errors ($F_{1,18} = 4.49$, $p < .05$, $\eta^2 = .03$). Average entry speeds for conventional and smart-restorable were 18.75 (SE = 0.46) and 21.83 wpm (SE = 0.4), respectively. See Figure 8.

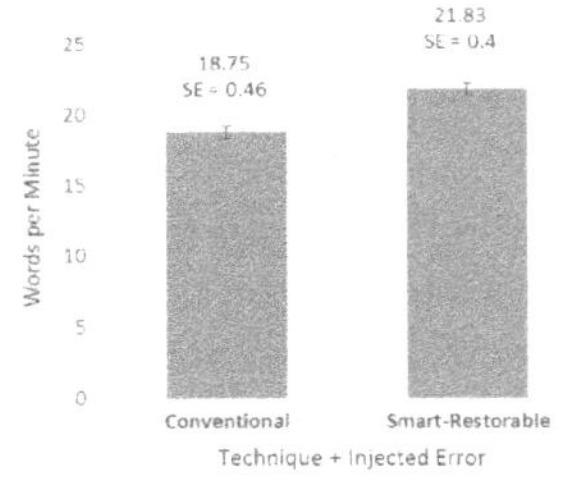

Figure 8. Average entry speed for both techniques in the injected error block.

Operations per Character

There was no significant effect of technique on operations per character ($F_{1,18} = 0.11$, ns). On average conventional and smart-restorable required 1.2 (SE = 0.01) and 1.2 (SE = 0.01) operations per character, respectively. There was also no significant effect of session ($F_{1,18} = 1.92$, $p > .05$) and the interaction was not significant, either. Figure 9 displays average operations per character for both techniques during the two sessions.

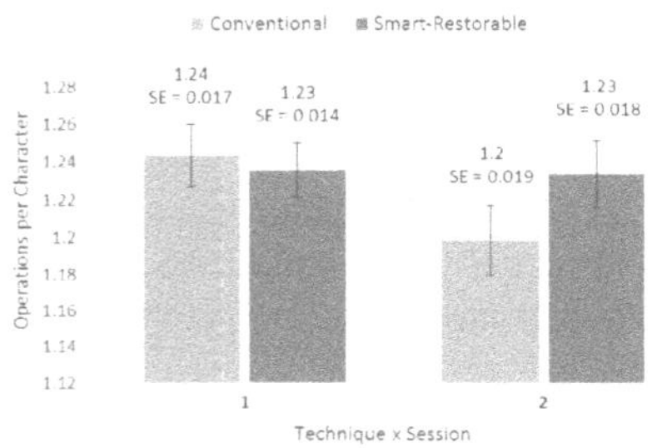

Figure 9. Average operations per character for both techniques by session.

An ANOVA identified a significant effect of technique on operations per character for phrases with injected errors ($F_{1,18} = 72.14$, $p < .00001$, $\eta^2 = .16$). Average operations per character with injected error for conventional and smart-restorable were 2.1 (SE = 0.04) and 1.52 (SE = 0.02), respectively. See Figure 10.

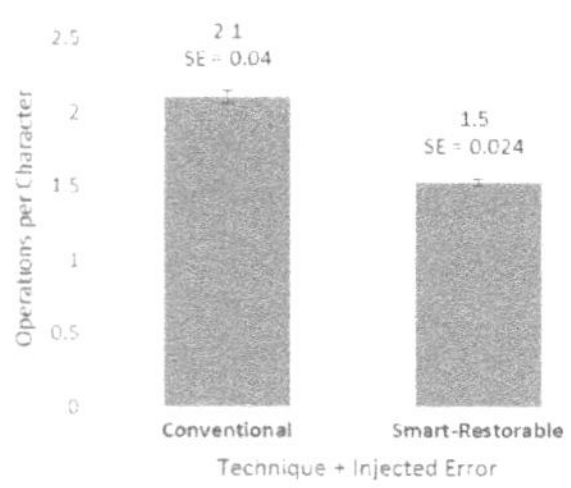

Figure 10. Average operations per character for both techniques in the injected error block.

Backspace Rate

An ANOVA did not find a significant effect of technique on backspace rate ($F_{1,18} = 1.79$, $p > .05$). On average 7.71 (SE = 0.24) and 8.96% (SE = 0.28) of all keystrokes were backspaces for conventional and smart-restorable, respectively. There was also no significant effect of session ($F_{1,18} = 2.68$, $p > .05$) or technique × session ($F_{1,18} = 0.19$, ns). Figure 11 shows the average backspace rate for both methods in the two sessions.

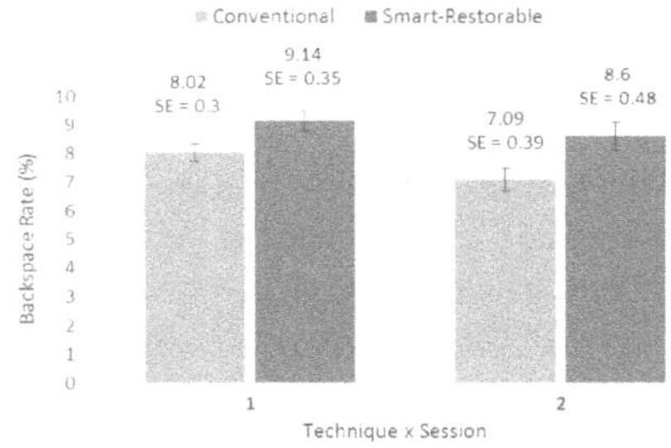

Figure 11. Average backspace rate for both techniques by session.

There was a significant effect of technique on backspace rate for phrases with injected errors ($F_{1,18} = 142.99$, $p < .00001$, $\eta^2 = .22$). Average backspace use was 23.6 (SE = 0.56) and 12.3% (SE = 0.5) for conventional and smart-restorable, respectively. Figure 12 illustrates this.

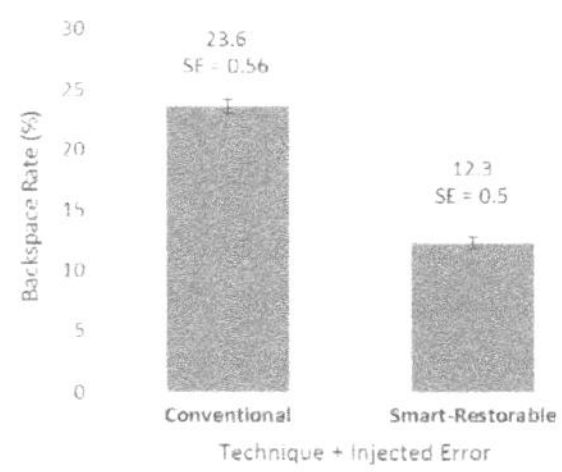

Figure 12. Average backspace rate for both techniques in the injected error block.

A deeper investigation revealed that in the conventional condition about 6.82% and 1% of all inputted characters were deleted using the regular and tap-hold methods, respectively. Interestingly, smart-restorable had similar results, where about 7.6%, 1.3%, and 0.1% of all entered characters were deleted using regular, tap-hold, and the smart gesture, respectively. Also, about 1.32% of all characters were restored using the smart restore feature. As expected, these rates increased with injected errors.

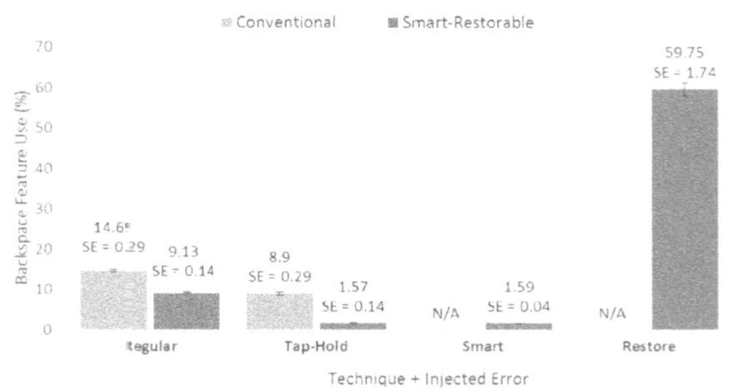

Figure 13. Average backspace feature distribution for both techniques in the injected error block.

A Mann-Whitney U test revealed that the rates in which regular and tap-hold methods were used, were significantly different for different techniques for phrases with injected errors. Both regular ($U = 36413.0$ $Z = -13.339$, $p < .0001$) and tap-hold ($U = 53170.0$ $Z = -10.982$, $p < .0001$) rates reduced significantly for smart-restorable. Yet, about 1.59% of all inputted characters were deleted using the smart gesture and 60% were restored using the smart restore feature (Figure 13).

Visual Scan Time

An ANOVA did not find a significant effect of technique on visual scan time ($F_{1,18} = 0.83$, ns). The average visual scan time for conventional and smart-restorable were 840.22 (SE = 17.3) and 743.22 (SE = 16.027) ms, respectively. However, there was also a significant effect of session ($F_{1,18} = 9.41$, $p < 0.01$, $\eta^2 = .01$) but not on technique × session ($F_{1,18} = 1.80$, $p > .05$). Figure 11 shows the average backspace rate for both techniques during the two sessions.

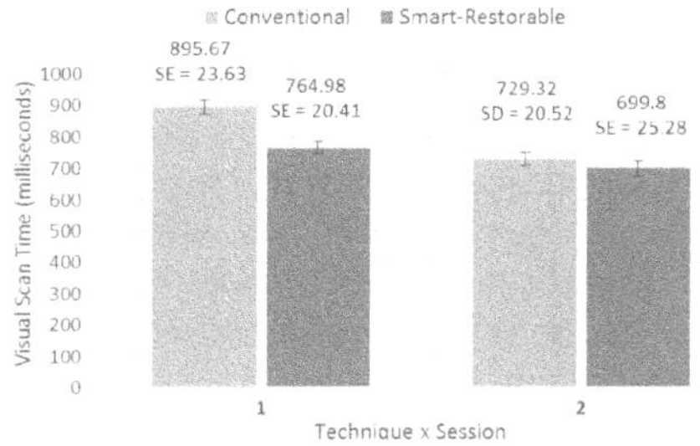

Figure 14. Average visual scan time for both techniques by session.

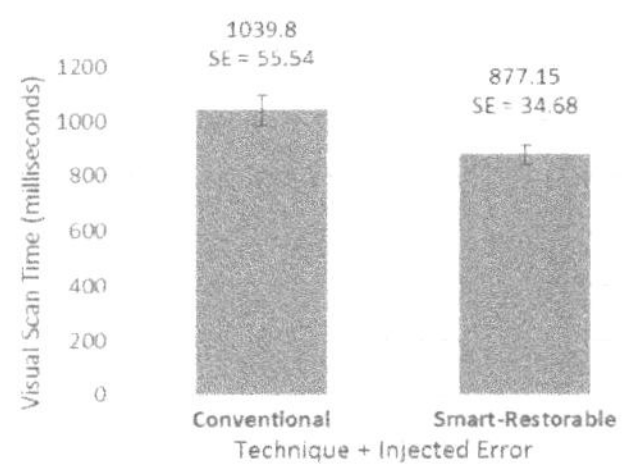

Figure 15. Average visual scan time for both techniques in the injected error block.

There was no significant effect of technique on visual scan time with injected errors ($F_{1,18} = 2.51$, $p > .05$). Average visual scan times with injected error were 1039.8 (SE = 55.5) and 877.15 (SE = 34.7) ms for conventional and smart-restorable, respectively. Figure 15 illustrates this.

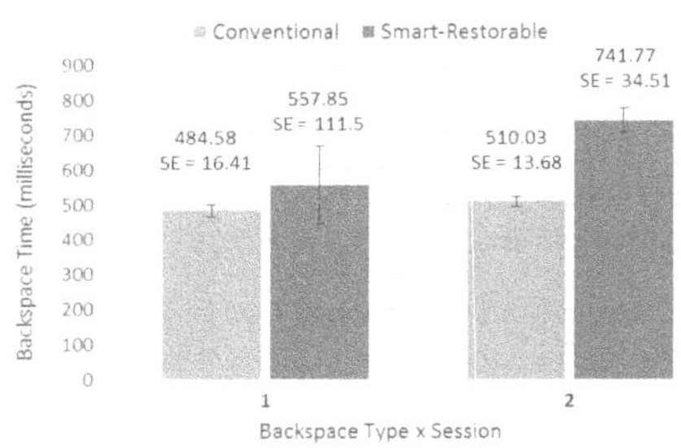

Figure 16. Average backspace time for both backspace types by session.

Backspace Time

An ANOVA failed to find a significant difference between backspace type in terms of operation time ($F_{1,18} = 1.45$, $p > .05$). On average performing the conventional and the smart-restorable backspace took 495.6 (SE = 11.04) and 717.08 (SE = 33.5) ms, respectively. An ANOVA also failed to find a significant effect of session ($F_{1,18} = 1.19$, $p > .05$) or backspace type × session ($F_{1,18} = 0.68$, ns). Figure 16 illustrates average backspace times for both techniques during the two sessions.

Post-Backspace Time

An ANOVA identified a significant effect of backspace type on post-backspace time ($F_{1,18} = 9.10$, $p < .01$, $\eta^2 = .002$). On average operations following the conventional and the smart-restorable required 580.3 (SE = 8.96) and 1171.5 (SE = 55.4) ms, respectively. However, there was no significant effect of session ($F_{1,18} = 3.83$, $p = .06$) or technique × session ($F_{1,18} = 1.9$, $p > .05$). Figure 17 shows the average post-backspace time for the two backspace methods during the two sessions.

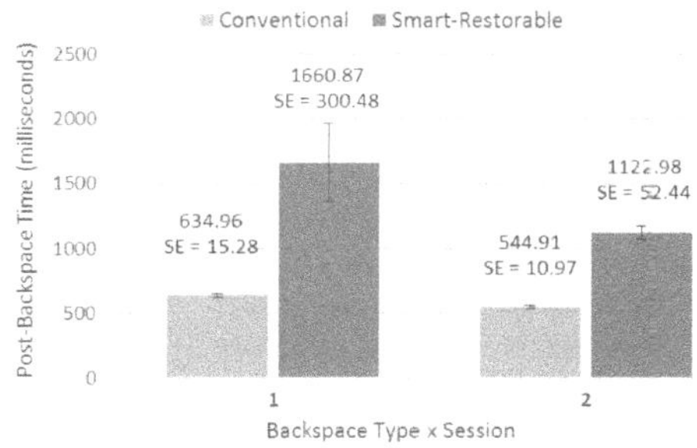

Figure 17. Average post-backspace operation time for both backspace types by session.

Prediction Behaviors

An ANOVA did not find a significant effect of technique on accepted prediction ($F_{1,18} = 0.83$, ns) or autocorrection ($F_{1,18} = 0.90$, ns) rates. On average 8.97 and 8.04% of all predicted words were accepted in conventional and smart-restorable, respectively. Similarly, about 5.5 and 6.9% of all supposedly misspelled words were autocorrected in conventional and smart-restorable, respectively (Figure 18). However, in both techniques, about 1.7% (SE = 0.10) words were incorrectly autocorrected. These rates were similar with injected errors.

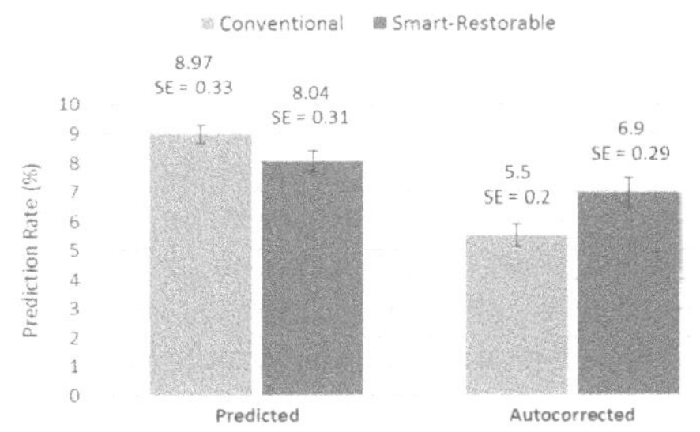

Figure 18. Average predictive feature distribution for both techniques.

User Feedback

We converted all seven-point scales to three-point scales using linear transformation to calculate ratios (%), which is common practice in statistics [13].

Conventional Backspace: Most participants, 90%, agreed that error correction is difficult with the conventional backspace, while the remaining 10% disagreed. Besides, 50% believed that conventional backspace compromises their entry speed, while 30% did not think that it has any impact on their performance. The remaining 20% participants were neutral regarding this. Yet, none of them were fully satisfied with the current backspace technique, and 90% wanted a better correction method, while 10% were impartial.

Smart and Restorable Backspace: Participants were mostly positive about the smart-restorable backspace. Almost all of them (90%) found it easy to learn and use, while the remaining 10% were neutral. Nonetheless, all of them (100%) thought that it made error correction faster and easier than the methods they use on their mobile devices. 90% thought that it increased their overall entry speed, while the remaining 10% were impartial. Overall, 90% participants liked smart-restorable more than the techniques they use, and wanted to keep using it. The remaining 10% were neutral.

DISCUSSION

The results reveal that the two examined techniques were not significantly different in terms of speed and operations per character. We expected this, as error correction, which the new technique addresses, occurs relatively infrequently in text entry. There was a significant effect of session on speed, suggesting that with practice entry speed improves substantially for both techniques. Also, the smart-restorable backspace yielded on average 2.2% better entry speed than the conventional technique, with a comparable number of operations per character. This is an obvious improvement over our pilot, where the new technique had lower entry speed. This indicates that the redesign improved the technique's performance. Also, as predicted, both speed and operations per character improved significantly with injected errors. That is, in situations where users attempted to correct an "overlooked" error, the new technique improves entry speed by 16.5% and reduces operation per character by 27.6%.

Backspace rates were not significantly different for the investigated techniques. However, with injected errors, the new technique yielded a significantly (48%) lower backspace rate than the conventional one. A deeper analysis revealed that about 60% of all backspace gestures were used to restore text. This suggests that with the smart-restorable backspace, users used the backspace gestures more to restore text than to delete it. This is most probably due to the fact that the smart restore feature splits deleted text based on the *CP*s to avoid restoration of incorrect texts, which provides the user with restoration options for each error correction. This suggests that users benefited the most from this feature. Thus we recommend its inclusion in all predictive keyboards. Interestingly, there was no significant effect of technique on visual scan time, even with injected errors, which means users did not take additional time to verify an input using the new technique, even when the input contained errors.

Apart from these metrics, we also analyzed the performance of different backspace actions. While there was no significant difference, performing a smart-backspace required on average *only* about 222 milliseconds more than the regular backspace. This is surprising, as prior studies found gesture-based input to be significantly slower than tap-based input [4]. We speculate that the reason is that we instructed our participants to perform the gestures "on the backspace key", instead of "on the keyboard", which reduced the average length of a gesture, resulting in faster operation time. The fact that we only recruited experienced touchscreen users may have contributed to this as well, as studies showed that users tend to use shorter gestures with experience [9]. However, there was a significant effect of backspace type on post-backspace operation time. On average users took 591 milliseconds more time to perform an operation following a smart-backspace. The most probable reason is that users needed extra time to prepare for the next step, after deleting a chunk of text. Yet, this time reduced by 32% in the second session, suggesting that post-backspace time for the smart-restorable backspace may reduce further with practice. In the second session and for the backspace and post-backspace time combined, the smart-restorable backspace required about 810 milliseconds more time than the conventional one, which is an obvious improvement from the pilot's 2.1 second overhead. Thus, the new technique improves the overall text entry performance, by significantly reducing correction efforts for "overlooked" mistakes, which supports acceptance of H_1.

Almost all participants (90%) in the conventional group were unhappy with the technique and felt the necessity for a better approach. 50% of them also felt that it reduces their text entry performance. Participants in the smart-restorable group were mostly positive about the examined technique. All of them (100%) rated it higher than the method they use on their tablets and most of them (90%) wanted to keep using it. Most of them (90%) also found it easy to learn and use, and improved their overall text entry performance. These results support the acceptance of H_2.

CONCLUSION AND FUTURE WORK

We presented a new smart-restorable backspace technique to facilitate the correction of "overlooked" errors. We compared the technique with the conventional backspace in a user study. Results showed that the new technique improves the overall text entry performance, in terms of speed and operation per character, by significantly reducing error correction efforts for "overlooked" mistakes. Results also revealed that most users liked the new approach better than the one they use on their devices, and found it easy to learn and to use. Most of them also felt that it improves their overall text entry performance and wanted to keep using it.

In the future we intend to explore the possibility of a word-based deletion feature to address cases where the system fails to identify an error, such as an incorrectly autocorrected word.

ACKNOWLEDGMENTS

We thank the attendees of the CHI '15 Workshop on Text Entry on the Edge [19] for their feedback on the study design. This work has been supported in part by the Canada Research Chairs program, NSERC, and NCE.

REFERENCES

1. Apple Insider. First Look: iOS 9's New Cursor-Controlling Gesture Keyboard on iPad. 2015. Retrieved August 22, 2015 from http://appleinsider.com/articles/15/06/11/first-look-ios-9s-new-cursor-controlling-gesture-keyboard-on-ipad
2. Apple Insider. How to use iOS 9's keyboard as a trackpad with 3D Touch on iPhone 6s. 2015. Retrieved December 30, 2015 from http://appleinsider.com/articles/15/10/11/how-to-use-ios-9s-keyboard-as-a-trackpad-with-3d-touch-on-iphone-6s-
3. Ahmed Sabbir Arif, Mauricio H. Lopez, Wolfgang Stuerzlinger. 2010. Two new mobile touchscreen text entry techniques. *Poster at the 36th Graphics Interface Conference* (GI '10). CEUR-WS.org/Vol-588.
4. Ahmed Sabbir Arif, Michel Pahud, Ken Hinckley, and Bill Buxton. 2014. Experimental study of stroke shortcuts for a touchscreen keyboard with gesture-redundant keys removed. In *Proceedings of Graphics Interface 2014* (GI '14). Canadian Information Processing Society, Toronto, Ont., Canada, Canada, 43-50.
5. Ahmed Sabbir Arif and Wolfgang Stuerzlinger. 2009. Analysis of text entry performance metrics. In *Proceedings of IEEE Toronto International Conference on Science and Technology for Humanity* (TIC-STH '09). IEEE, Washington, DC, USA, 100-105.
6. Ahmed Sabbir Arif and Wolfgang Stuerzlinger. 2010. Predicting the cost of error correction in character-based text entry technologies. In *Proceedings of the SIGCHI Conference on Human Factors in Computing Systems* (CHI '10). ACM, New York, NY, USA, 5-14.
7. Ahmed Sabbir Arif and Wolfgang Stuerzlinger. 2013. Pseudo-pressure detection and its use in predictive text entry on touchscreens. In *Proceedings of the 25th Australian Computer-Human Interaction Conference: Augmentation, Application, Innovation, Collaboration* (OzCHI '13), Haifeng Shen, Ross Smith, Jeni Paay, Paul Calder, and Theodor Wyeld (Eds.). ACM, New York, NY, USA, 383-392.
8. Ahmed Sabbir Arif, Wolfgang Stuerzlinger, Ali Mazalek, Sunjun Kim, and Geehyuk Lee. 2015. A smart-restorable backspace to facilitate text entry error correction. In *CHI 2015 Workshop on Text Entry on the Edge* (April 18, 2015). Seoul, South Korea.
9. Ahmed Sabbir Arif, Wolfgang Stuerzlinger, Euclides Jose de Mendonca Filho, and Alec Gordynski. 2014. Error behaviours in an unreliable in-air gesture recognizer. In *Proceedings of the Extended Abstracts of the 32nd Annual ACM Conference on Human Factors in Computing Systems* (CHI EA '14). ACM, New York, NY, USA, 1603-1608.
10. Geoffroy Aulagner, Romain François, Benoît Martin, Dominique Michel, and Mathieu Raynal. 2010. Floodkey: increasing software keyboard keys by reducing needless ones without occultation. In *Proceedings of the 10th WSEAS International Conference on Applied Computer Science* (ACS' 10), Hamido Fujita and Jun Sasaki (Eds.). World Scientific and Engineering Academy and Society (WSEAS), Stevens Point, Wisconsin, USA, 412-417.
11. Matt Bolton. 2014. How to Improve iOS Autocorrect. Mac Life. Retrieved July 21, 2015 from http://www.maclife.com/article/howtos/how-improve-autocorrect
12. James Clawson, Kent Lyons, Alex Rudnick, Robert A. Iannucci, Jr., and Thad Starner. 2008. Automatic whiteout++: correcting mini-QWERTY typing errors using keypress timing. In *Proceedings of the SIGCHI Conference on Human Factors in Computing Systems* (CHI '08). ACM, New York, NY, USA, 573-582.
13. John G. Dawes. 2008. Do data characteristics change according to the number of scale points used? An experiment using 5 point, 7 point and 10 point scales. *International Journal of Market Research 51*, 1.
14. Paul M. Fitts. 1954. The information capacity of the human motor system in controlling the amplitude of movement. *Journal of Experimental Psychology* 47, 6: 262-269.
15. Fleksy Keyboard. 2015. Retrieved August 12, 2015 from https://fleksy.com
16. Vittorio Fuccella, Poika Isokoski, and Benoit Martin. 2013. Gestures and widgets: performance in text editing on multi-touch capable mobile devices. In *Proceedings of the SIGCHI Conference on Human Factors in Computing Systems* (CHI '13). ACM, New York, NY, USA, 2785-2794.
17. Gartner, Inc. Forecast: PCs, Ultramobiles, and Mobile Phones, Worldwide, 2011-2018, 2Q14 Update. 2015. Retrieved July 21, 2015 from https://www.gartner.com/doc/3077322/forecast-pcs-ultramobiles-mobile-phones
18. Joshua Goodman, Gina Venolia, Keith Steury, and Chauncey Parker. 2002. Language modeling for soft keyboards. In *Proceedings of the 7th International Conference on Intelligent User Interfaces* (IUI '02). ACM, New York, NY, USA, 194-195.
19. James Clawson, Ahmed Sabbir Arif, Stephen Brewster, Mark Dunlop, Per Ola Kristensson, and Antti Oulasvirta. 2015. Text Entry on the Edge. In *Proceedings of the 33rd Annual ACM Conference Extended Abstracts on Human Factors in Computing Systems* (CHI EA '15). ACM, New York, NY, USA, 2381-2384.

20. Google Code. The Diff Match and Patch Libraries. 2012. Retrieved August 10, 2015 from https://code.google.com/p/google-diff-match-patch
21. Jonathan T. Grudin. 1983. Error patterns in novice and skilled transcription typing. In *Cognitive Aspects of Skilled Typewriting*, W. E. Cooper (Ed.). Springer-Verlag, 121-143.
22. jQuery Mobile. A Touch-Optimized Web Framework. 2015. Retrieved March 12, 2015 from https://jquerymobile.com
23. Sunjun Kim and Geehyuk Lee. 2012. Restorable backspace. In *Adjunct proceedings of the 25th annual ACM symposium on User interface software and technology* (UIST Adjunct Proceedings '12). ACM, New York, NY, USA, 73-74.
24. KeuKey Keyboard. 2014. Retrieved July 21, 2015 from http://www.keukey.com
25. Vladimir I. Levenshtein. 1966. Binary codes capable of correcting deletions, insertions, and reversals. In *Soviet Physics Doklady 10*, 8: 707-710.
26. I. Scott MacKenzie and R. William Soukoreff. 2003. Phrase sets for evaluating text entry techniques. In *CHI '03 Extended Abstracts on Human Factors in Computing Systems* (CHI EA '03). ACM, New York, NY, USA, 754-755.
27. Dominik Schmidt, Florian Block, and Hans Gellersen. 2009. A Comparison of Direct and Indirect Multi-touch Input for Large Surfaces. In *Proceedings of the 12th IFIP TC 13 International Conference on Human-Computer Interaction: Part I* (INTERACT '09), Tom Gross, Jan Gulliksen, Paula Kotzé, Lars Oestreicher, Philippe Palanque, Raquel Oliveira Prates, and Marco Winckler (Eds.). Springer-Verlag, Berlin, Heidelberg, 582.
28. Keith Vertanen and Per Ola Kristensson. 2011. A versatile dataset for text entry evaluations based on genuine mobile emails. In *Proceedings of the 13th International Conference on Human Computer Interaction with Mobile Devices and Services* (MobileHCI '11). ACM, New York, NY, USA, 295-298.
29. Keith Vertanen and Per Ola Kristensson. 2014. Complementing text entry evaluations with a composition task. *ACM Transactions on Computer-Human Interaction* 21, 2, Article 8 (February 2014), 33 pages.
30. Wiktionary. The Most Common Words in Project Gutenberg: Frequency lists/PG/2006/04/1-10000. 2006. Retrieved July 21, 2015 from https://en.wiktionary.org/wiki/Wiktionary:Frequency_lists/PG/2006/04/1-10000

TapBoard 2: Simple and Effective Touchpad-like Interaction on a Multi-Touch Surface Keyboard

Sunjun Kim and Geehyuk Lee
School of Computing, KAIST
Daejeon 305-701, Republic of Korea
{kuaa.net, geehyuk}@gmail.com

ABSTRACT
We introduce TapBoard 2, a touchpad-based keyboard that solves the problem of typing and pointing disambiguation. The pointing interaction design of TapBoard 2 is nearly identical to natural touchpad interaction, and its shared workspace naturally invites bimanual pointing interaction. To implement TapBoard 2, we developed a novel gesture representation scheme for a systematic design and gesture recognizer. A user evaluation showed that TapBoard 2 successfully supports collocated pointing and typing interaction. It was able to disambiguate typing and pointing actions with an accuracy of greater than 95%. In addition, the typing and pointing performance of TapBoard 2 were comparable to that of a separate keyboard and mouse. In particular, the bimanual pointing operations of TapBoard 2 are highly efficient and strongly favored by participants.

Author Keywords
TapBoard; pointing; typing; multi-touch; gesture; touch screen; touch pad; text entry system.

ACM Classification Keywords
H.5.2. Information interfaces and presentation (e.g., HCI): User Interface

INTRODUCTION
The keyboard and mouse have been the de facto standard input devices for text entry and pointing. One common concern is the burden of frequently switching between devices and the extensive space that they require [4]. To address these concerns, many studies have tried to unify the keyboard and mouse control spaces [3,4,7,18,19]. One simple approach is to integrate an isometric joystick into a keyboard [13]. However, an isometric joystick is not as efficient as isotonic pointing devices [17].

Another approach to unifying keyboard and mouse control spaces is to add a finger-tracking function to a keyboard. FingerMouse [11], AirMouse [12], and FlowMouse [20] all utilize a down-looking camera and set pointing space above the typing space. For "on-the-keyboard" interaction, DGTS [7], Touch & Type [4], Moky [3], and FlickBoard [18] embed touch sensors on the keyboard and enable touchpad-like interactions. In these cases, typing and pointing share the same input space (the keyboard surface), and a method of disambiguating strokes for typing and pointing is employed. The disambiguating methods vary: a separate mode button [3,4,20], special hand shape [11,12], or software classifier [7,18] have been studied. However, the current sensor on a physical keyboard is not sufficiently fast and accurate for fluent cursor manipulation. In addition, common concerns exist regarding irregular touch surfaces [7] and limited touch sensor sensitivity because of thick keyboard buttons [4].

Yet another approach to unifying keyboard and mouse spaces is to use a large touch surface. A representative work in this field is that of Westerman [19], which is based on a FingerWorks TouchStream product. This touchpad-based approach provides a precise and smooth pointing operation compared to pointing on a physical keyboard. It uses a two-finger drag and tap gesture for mouse operations. However, a two-finger tap occasionally conflicts with consecutive overlapping taps during fast typing [19]. Multi-touch gestures on a flat keyboard are also used for different purposes besides pointing. These include menu invocation [5,8], alternative character insertion [1,5], and caret manipulation [6,9]. Moving distance [1,6,8], dwell time [9], and multi-touch [5,6,9] are often used to discriminate keystrokes and gestures.

In this study, we introduce TapBoard 2, which solves the problem of typing and pointing disambiguation by the TapBoard concept of Kim et al. [9]. They showed that people usually type on a touchscreen keyboard by tapping and that a tapping-only soft keyboard is as fast and accurate as an ordinary soft keyboard. These results may also be valid with respect to a touchpad-based keyboard and motivated us to implement a tapping-only soft keyboard on a touchpad. One result is that we can use dragging gestures longer than a tap threshold (450 ms and 5 mm) for pointing, thereby solving the typing and pointing disambiguation problem without requiring a mode key or special gestures.

The purpose of the current study is to verify the feasibility and benefits of TapBoard 2. First, we show that the concept of TapBoard effectively solves the typing and pointing disambiguation problem. Second, we show that typing and

CHI'16, May 07-12, 2016, San Jose, CA, USA
© 2016 ACM. ISBN 978-1-4503-3362-7/16/05...$15.00
DOI: http://dx.doi.org/10.1145/2858036.2858452

pointing performance is preserved after the two inputs share the same control space. Third, we display the benefit of a large keyboard-sized touch surface that invites natural bimanual touch operations. As an example, we show the advantage of dividing pointing and clicking operations between the two hands.

TAPBOARD 2

We implemented a TapBoard 2 prototype using a touchscreen tablet computer that embeds a fast (100 fps) and high-resolution (sub-millimeter) multi touch surface. The tablet always displays a keyboard pattern and functions as an external keyboard and mouse device for a host computer.

TapBoard Gesture Recognizer

As shown in Figure 1, a touch point exists in any one of the following three phases: *Touched*, *Dwelling*, and *Moving*. A touch point starts at the *Touched* phase upon finger touchdown. After a time threshold τ (450 ms [9]), it automatically transitions to the *Dwelling* phase. Whether in the *Touched* or *Dwelling* phase, when a touch point travels more than a distance threshold δ (5 mm [1,9]), it enters the *Moving* phase. At the *Moving* phase, touch point does not change its phase until finger lift-off. The gesture recognizer enumerates the number of touch points in each phase. We define a system state as having three consecutive numbers such as `213`, which denotes two *Touched* points, one *Dwelling* point, and three *Moving* points.

A state sequence then defines a TapBoard gesture. For example, `{000,100,000}` defines a tap gesture, `{000,100,001}` defines a drag gesture, and `{000,100,200,101,002}` defines a two-finger dragging gesture. The system declares that a gesture has been detected when the latest state history matches the state sequence of the gesture. For ease of illustration, consider a simple gesture keyboard that moves a text caret with a one-finger dragging gesture and scrolls the document with a two-finger dragging gesture. Gesture definitions of such a keyboard are shown in Table 1.

This historical record of gestures may prevent conflicts between gestures more effectively than can state-based gesture recognition. Suppose that a naïve gesture recognizer maps `001` (one-finger moving) as a caret-move gesture and `002` (two-finger moving) as a scroll gesture. After performing a scroll gesture, a user may then release two fingers separately within a fraction of a second. In this case, the recognizer may detect a caret-move gesture, which results in an unintended small caret movement. In our system, the state sequence of the caret-move gesture `{000,100,001}` does not match the state history of releasing two fingers `{002,001,000}` and, thus, this type of erratic caret movement cannot occur. This problem may be addressed using a timer or context variable. However, our approach enables a more systematic and compact gesture recognizer implementation.

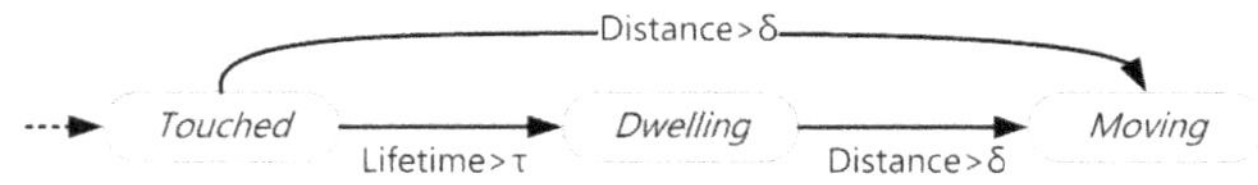

Figure 1. Three phases of a touch point. We set τ = 450 ms and δ = 5 mm for our implementation.

Gesture	Description
{000,100,000}	Keystroke
{000,100,001}	Caret move
{000,100,200,101,002}	Document scroll

Table 1. Simple gesture keyboard showing TapBoard gesture representation

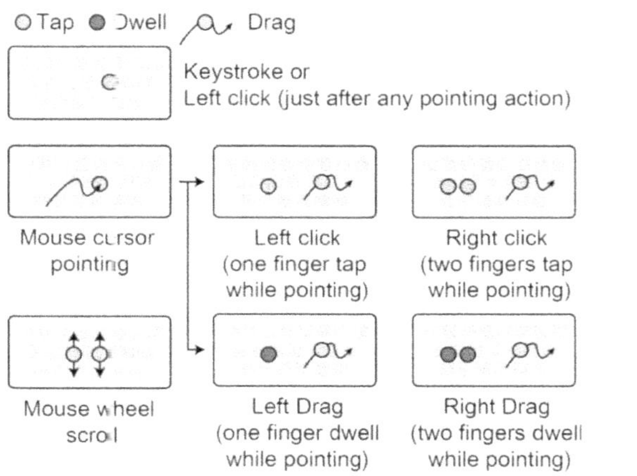

Figure 2. Designed touchpad-like pointing interaction.

Gesture	Description
{100,000},{200,100},{300,200}	Keystroke
{100,001},{100,010}	Mouse cursor move
{000,100,000}, {010,110,010},{001,101,001}	Mouse left-button click
{000,100,200,100,000}, {001,101,201,101,001}, {010,110,210,110,010}	Mouse right-button click
{101,011},{110,011}, {011,002},{110,020,011}	Mouse left-button press and drag
{201,111,021},{120,021}, {021,012},{021,012,003}	Mouse right-button press and drag
{011,001},{010,000},{001,000}	Mouse left and right release (if pressed)
{200,101,002}	Mouse-wheel scroll

Table 2. Interaction represented by TapBoard gesture definitions. Underlined items represent conflicting gestures (see text).

Touchpad-like Pointing Interaction on a Keyboard

Using the TapBoard gesture recognizer, we designed a touchpad-like pointing interaction (Figure 2) that can coexist with a tapping-only keyboard. Tapping functions as a keystroke except when it follows a pointing gesture. For our system, mapping a release-and-tap gesture to a left-click event was required because this is a general touchpad skill. However, this matches both keystroke `{100,000}` and left-button `{000,100,000}` gestures and, thus, represents a conflict. We treated this as an exception and have the system execute a left-button gesture instead of keystroke only for a tap within one second and 15 mm from the previously touched pointing gesture. The other mouse operations are defined without conflicts. One-finger dragging is used to control a mouse cursor. Two-finger dragging is used for mouse-wheel scrolling. During one-finger dragging, additional finger touches function as mouse-button clicks, a one-finger tap functions as a left click, and a two-finger tap functions as a right click. Dragging with a button pressed is supported similarly by including *Dwelling* touches. The other hand should preferably perform these mouse-button gestures. In addition, we include dwell+taps as mouse-button gestures to enable a click without a cursor move.

EVALUATION

To evaluate the proposed design, we conducted a within-subject user study to answer the following questions.

1) Does pointing interfere with typing or vice versa?
2) Does the combined pointing-typing design impair typing and pointing performance?
3) Does bimanual interaction offer any advantages regarding pointing performance?

Tasks and Metrics

We designed a task that requires frequent switching between pointing and typing (Figure 3). First, a start point appears at the screen center, and clicking it starts a 2D Fitts' law pointing task [16]. We used three distance (D = 100, 200, and 800 px) and three target diameter (W = 40, 60, and 80 px) levels. Index of difficulty (ID) was calculated using the Shannon formulation $ID = \log_2(D/W+1)$. We designed IDs to be distributed evenly from 1.0 to 4.5. Clicking a target point ends the pointing task. An effective index of difficulty (IDe) was calculated based on [16]. Following the pointing task, a textbox appears that begins a typing task. A word preview appears during the pointing task to minimize the effect of cognitive load on task time. Words of 5-7 characters are randomly chosen from the Enron corpus [10]. Pressing the Enter key ends the typing task.

In our study, as the two tasks were repeated, we measured the following metrics. For transition cost metrics, we measured the interval between the start of the new task – in other word, end of the typing task – and the first mouse move event (i.e., *Typing to Pointing transition time* or *T2P*), and the interval between successful target selection and the first keystroke (i.e., *Pointing to Typing transition time or P2T*). For pointing performance metrics, we calculated *Throughput* = *MT* (movement time) / *IDe*, and the number of failed target selections (*Targeting Error*). For typing performance metrics, we measured *Typing Speed* in word per minute (WPM) and *Total Error Rate* [15]. For interference metrics, we measured *Keyboard Error*, which counts the number of keystrokes during the Fitts' law test, and *Mouse error*, which counts the number of mouse move or click events during typing. Finally, we measured the total task completion time (*Total Time*).

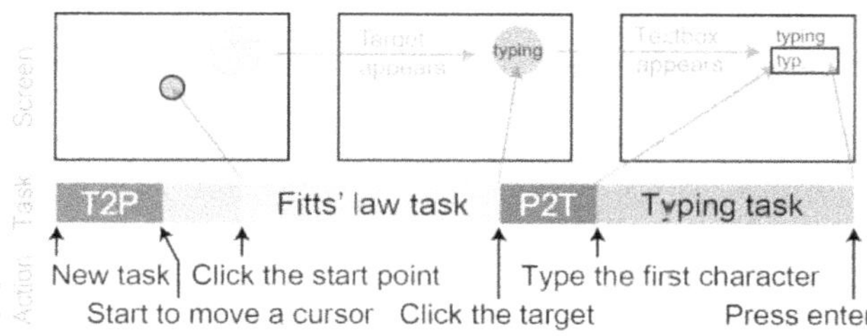

Figure 3. Task sequence consists of pointing and typing

Conditions and Apparatus

We established three *Conditions*: **Separated-Tap (ST)**, **Combined-Tap (CT)**, and **Combined-AddFinger (CA)**.

ST is the base condition that simulates a separate touchpad and keyboard configuration. It uses two tablet devices adjacently placed. One device simulates a soft keyboard and the other simulates a touchpad. The keyboard device interprets all touches as keystrokes, and the touchpad device interprets a drag gesture as a mouse move and a tap as a click gesture.

CT and **CA** are test conditions that use the proposed combined pointing-typing method. A single tablet device functions as both keyboard and touchpad. Both conditions share the same implementation. The sole difference concerns click-gesture choice. In our study, we instructed users to employ release-and-tap with **CT** and an additional finger tap with **CA** for the left-click gesture.

We implemented **ST**, **CT**, and **CA** on Microsoft Surface Pro 3 touchscreen tablets. To mimic touchpad-like appearance, we configure the tablets to show only a QWERTY layout with 18.2 x 18.6 mm keys, except the touchpad device for **ST** that displays only a black screen. The tablets generated keyboard and mouse events, and an Arduino Leonardo board interpreted these events to legacy USB keyboard and mouse packets. A separate laptop conducted the experiment tasks driven by the USB packets. The measured latency between the tablets and laptop were 50 ms on average. In our system, a keystroke highlights the corresponding soft key and generates a short beep sound (800 Hz tone, 10 ms). In **CT**, a small circle indicating the "clickable" area for the release-and-tap gesture is shown on the keyboard. Mouse acceleration, keyboard size, and device orientation were identical across conditions and participants.

Procedure

We recruited 18 paid participants (nine males and nine females, average age of 21.5) who were familiar with QWERTY keyboards. All participants were right-handed and operated a mouse with that dominant hand. A "block" in our study consists of all three conditions and 27 trial runs of pointing and typing tasks for each condition. Each participant completed three blocks. Thus, 243 trials (3 x 3 x 27) in total were conducted. We counterbalanced the order of conditions across the participants. The first block was a practice block, and we analyzed the data from the last two blocks.

Results

Metrics	ST	CT	CA
T2P Time (ms)	497	473	469
Targeting Error (%)	2.6	1.9	2.2
Throughput (bits/s)	3.1	2.9	**3.9**
Keyboard Error (%)	**0.7**	**1.2**	3.9
P2T Time (ms)	579	**490**	640
Typing Speed (WPM)	39.6	37.6	37.4
Total Error Rate (%)	5.6	6.9	7
Mouse Error (%)	**0.6**	3.4	2.9
* Mouse Click Error (%)	0.4	0.3	0.2
Total Task Time (ms)	4944	4868	4761

Table 3. The average results of blocks 2 and 3 (Boldface values indicate the best performance groups.)

Table 3 shows the average results of the second and third blocks ordered by the task flow illustrated in Figure 3. The study was a 2 (*Block*) × 3 (*Condition*) within-subject design. We performed a repeated measures ANOVA. *Condition* exhibited significant main effects on *Throughput*, *Keyboard Error*, *P2T*, *Typing Speed* and *Mouse Error*. *Block* exhibited significant main effects on *T2P* and *Throughput*. There were significant *Condition* * *Block* interaction on *T2P* and *P2T*. For the detailed results, refer to Appendix 1.

As a post hoc test, we performed pairwise Tukey's HSD tests between *Conditions* with $\alpha = 0.05$. Boldfaced values in Table 3 indicate the best performance groups. We summarize the major findings below.

- For *T2P*, the pairwise comparison failed to find a difference between conditions. For *P2T*, the fastest condition was **CT**, followed by **ST** and **CA**.
- For pointing performance, **CA** exhibited the highest *Throughput*. No difference was found in *Targeting Error*.
- For typing performance, the pairwise comparison failed to find a difference between conditions, although *Condition* exhibited a main effect on *Typing Speed*. No difference was found in *Total Error Rate*.
- For interference metrics, **CA** produced more *Keyboard Errors* than did **ST** and **CT**. **CT** and **CA** generated more *Mouse Errors* than did **ST**.

Subjective Ratings

We asked participants to rank the exposed conditions. We then collected comments about conditions. The average ranks were 1.22 (**CA**), 2.22 (**CT**), and 2.56 (**ST**). **CA** was the most favored (15 of 18 participants ranked it as first).

Afterwards, we provided instructions on mouse operations (Figure 2). Participants rated the ease of use on a seven-point Likert scale. Left click received a score of 6.78, left drag 6.00, right click 5.89, and right drag 5.16.

Discussion

ST is better in disambiguation and typing performance. However, frequent device switching caused participant fatigue. **CT** improves transition time and is comparable to **ST** regarding pointing and typing performance. Participants appreciated short hand movements, but timeout-based click interaction produced strain. Bimanual interaction generated the best *Throughput* but the slowest *P2T* times for **CA**. Forcing a left finger to release to complete a mouse clicks may reduce *P2T* time in **CA**, whereas other conditions enabled participants to prepare left-hand keys. **CA** also exhibits the worst *Keyboard Error*. Raw log analysis showed that participants often release two fingers simultaneously for left-button click gestures, which records as `{001,101,100,000}` and fails to match predefined gestures. Participants then typed a word, which generated keystrokes before successful target selection. Nevertheless, participants mostly favored **CA** for its combined workspace and continuous bimanual target selection method.

Both **CT** and **CA** exhibited more *Mouse Errors* than did **ST**, but 88% of errors were move events. Participants sometimes move their fingers away from a key in order to cancel a keystroke and then swipe on the backspace key to remove an entire word. **ST** ignores such dragging movements, whereas **CT** and **CA** interpreted them as mouse-move events. Filtering out these mouse-move errors eliminated *Mouse Error* differences (Table 3 *).

The cursor-moving gesture requires some slack (5 mm) or dwelling (450 ms). Most participants initiated a cursor move by means of a shaking gesture [2], in which case the spatial slack becomes less pronounced. However, some participants complained that the system was unresponsive during subtle cursor manipulation. Here, the moved distance falls within the slack threshold and dwelling activates the cursor. We may address this limitation in the future by incorporating a probabilistic approach [14].

CONCLUSION

We developed TapBoard 2, a pointing-typing keyboard based on a systematic gesture recognizer. In our study, the system distinguished typing and pointing with over 95% accuracy. Moreover, typing and pointing performance with the combined interface was comparable to that of the base condition **ST**. Finally, because of bimanual interaction, **CA** outperformed other conditions in pointing *Throughput*, and participants strongly favored this.

A future study will extend the application of our design. TapBoard 2 functionality can be easily embedded in many touch-sensing platforms such as touchscreen tablets, tabletops, laser projection keyboards, flat keyboards such as Microsoft Surface Touch Cover, and glass keyboards. This design can also be applied to physical keyboards as soon as they are equipped with a fast and reliable touch-sensing technology.

ACKNOWLEDGMENTS

This work was supported by Hancom Inc. Its intellectual property rights reserved by KAIST and Hancom.

REFERENCES

1. Ahmed Sabbir Arif, Michel Pahud, Ken Hinckley, and Bill Buxton. 2014. Experimental study of stroke shortcuts for a touchscreen keyboard with gesture-redundant keys removed. In *Proceedings of GI '14*. Canadian Information Processing Society, Toronto, Ont., Canada, Canada, 43-50.
2. Robert Ball and Chris North, Analysis of user behavior on high-resolution tiled displays. 2005. *Human-Computer Interaction-INTERACT* 2005.Vol 3585 of the series Lecture Notes in Computer Science: 350-363. http://doi.org/10.1007/11555261_30
3. Enyoung Cho, Moky: invisible touchpad keyboard. 2015. Retrieved Sep. 7, 2015 from https://www.indiegogo.com/projects/moky-invisible-touchpad-keyboard
4. W. Fallot-Burghardt, M. Fjeld, C. Speirs, S. Ziegenspeck, H. Krueger, and T. Läubli. 2006. Touch&Type: a novel pointing device for notebook computers. In *Proceedings of NordiCHI '06*. 465-468. http://doi.acm.org/10.1145/1182475.1182538
5. Leah Findlater, Ben Lee, and Jacob Wobbrock. 2012. Beyond QWERTY: augmenting touch screen keyboards with multi-touch gestures for non-alphanumeric input. In *Proceedings of CHI '12*. ACM, 2679-2682. http://dx.doi.org/10.1145/2207676.2208660
6. Vittorio Fuccella, Poika Isokoski, and Benoit Martin. 2013. Gestures and widgets: performance in text editing on multi-touch capable mobile devices. In *Proceedings of CHI '13*. ACM, 2785-2794. http://dx.doi.org/10.1145/2470654.2481385
7. Iman Habib, Niklas Berggren, Erik Rehn, Gustav Josefsson, Andreas Kunz, and Morten Fjeld. 2009. Dgts: Combined typing and pointing. *Human-Computer Interaction-INTERACT* 2009, Vol. 5727 of the series Lecture Notes in Computer Science: 232-235. http://doi.org/10.1007/978-3-642-03658-3_30
8. Poika Isokoski. 2004. Performance of menu-augmented soft keyboards. *In Proceedings of CHI '04*. ACM, 423-430. http://dx.doi.org/10.1145/985692.985746
9. Sunjun Kim, Jeongmin Son, Geehyuk Lee, Hwan Kim, and Woohun Lee. 2013. TapBoard: making a touch screen keyboard more touchable. In *Proceedings of CHI '13*. ACM, 553-562. http://doi.acm.org/10.1145/2470654.2470733
10. Bryan Klimt and Yiming Yang. 2004. The enron corpus: A new dataset for email classification research. *Machine learning:* ECML. Springer Berlin Heidelberg, 217-226. http://doi.org/10.1007/978-3-540-30115-8_22
11. Thomas A. Mysliwiec, 1994. Fingermouse: A freehand computer pointing interface. In *Proceeding of International Conference on Automatic Face and Gesture Recognition*, 372-277. http://citeseerx.ist.psu.edu/viewdoc/summary?doi=10.1.1.54.4906
12. Michael Ortega and Laurence Nigay. 2009. AirMouse: Finger gesture for 2D and 3D interaction. *Human-Computer Interaction–INTERACT* 2009. Springer Berlin Heidelberg, 214-227. http://doi.org/10.1007/978-3-642-03658-3_28
13. Joseph D. Rutledge and Ted Selker. 1990. Force-to-motion functions for pointing. In *Proceedings of INTERACT '90*. 701-706.
14. Julia Schwarz, Scott Hudson, Jennifer Mankoff, and Andrew D. Wilson. 2010. A framework for robust and flexible handling of inputs with uncertainty. In *Proceedings of UIST '10*. ACM, New York, NY, USA, 47-56. http://dx.doi.org/10.1145/1866029.1866039
15. R. William Soukoreff and I. Scott MacKenzie. 2003. Metrics for text entry research: an evaluation of MSD and KSPC, and a new unified error metric. In *Proceedings of CHI '03*, ACM, 113-120. http://doi.acm.org/10.1145/642611.642632
16. William Soukoreff and I. Scott MacKenzie. 2004. Towards a standard for pointing device evaluation, perspectives on 27 years of Fitts' law research in HCI. *International journal of human-computer studies*, 61, 6 (December 2004): 751-789. http://dx.doi.org/10.1016/j.ijhcs.2004.09.001
17. Christian Sutter and Martina Ziefle, 2005. Interacting with notebook input devices: An analysis of motor performances and user's expertise. *Human Factors*, 47: 169-187. http://doi.org/10.1518/0018720053653893
18. Ying-Chao Tung, Ta Yang Cheng, Neng-Hao Yu, Chiuan Wang, and Mike Y. Chen. 2015. FlickBoard: Enabling Trackpad Interaction with Automatic Mode Switching on a Capacitive-sensing Keyboard. In *Proceedings of CHI '15*. ACM, 1847-1850. http://doi.acm.org/10.1145/2702123.2702582
19. Wayne Westerman. 1999. *Hand tracking, finger identification, and chordic manipulation on a multi-touch surface*. Doctoral dissertation, University of Delaware.
20. Andrew D. Wilson, and Edward Cutrell. 2005. FlowMouse: a computer vision-based pointing and gesture input device, *Human-Computer Interaction-INTERACT*. Springer Berlin Heidelberg, 565-578. http://doi.org/10.1007/11555261_46

APPENDIX

We present the per block results, the repeated measures (RM) ANOVA results, and the post hoc test results, which we omitted in Table 3, in the following tables.

	Block 2			Block 3		
Metrics	ST	CT	CA	ST	CT	CA
T2P Time (ms)	510	493	472	483	**454**	**465**
Targeting Error (%)	2.7	1.6	1.4	2.5	2.1	2.9
Throughput (bits/s)	3.08	2.88	**3.79**	3.12	2.98	**4.00**
Keyboard Error (%)	**1.0**	**1.0**	4.1	**0.4**	**1.4**	3.7
P2T Time (ms)	591	**489**	645	567	**492**	634
Typing Speed (WPM)	39.7	37.7	36.5	39.5	37.5	38.2
Total Error Rate (%)	5.3	6.7	6.7	5.8	7.1	7.2
Mouse Error (%)	**0.4**	3.7	3.3	**0.8**	3.1	2.5
* Mouse Click Error (%)	0.4	0.4	0.2	0.4	0.2	0.2
Total Task Time (ms)	4961	4846	4807	4926	4889	4715

Table 4. Complete results from blocks 2 and 3

	Condition F(2,16), α =.05		Block F(1,17), α =.05		Interaction F(2,16), α =.05	
Metrics	*F*-val	*p*-val	*F*-val	*p*-val	*F*-val	*p*-val
T2P Time (ms)	0.72	.500	15.2	**< .001**	3.72	**.047**
Targeting Error (%)	.516	.607	.938	.346	.991	.393
Throughput (bits/s)	74.3	**< .001**	12.3	**.002**	1.53	.247
Keyboard Error (%)	8.54	**.003**	.321	.578	.634	.543
P2T Time (ms)	25.0	**< .001**	.783	.388	25.0	**< .001**
Typing Speed (WPM)	8.75	**.003**	.511	.484	1.73	.208
Total Error Rate (%)	2.52	.112	.994	.333	0.01	.989
Mouse Error (%)	5.63	**.014**	.747	.395	.974	.399
* Mouse Click Error (%)	1.60	.233	.191	.668	.056	.946
Total Task Time (ms)	1.70	.214	.232	.636	.579	.572

Table 5. RM-ANOVA results

<table>
<tr><th>Metrics</th><th>Block 2</th><th>Block 3</th></tr>
<tr><td>T2P Time (ms)</td><td>ST = CT = CA</td><td>ST = CT = CA</td></tr>
<tr><td>Throughput (bits/s)</td><td colspan="2">CA > ST = CT</td></tr>
<tr><td>Keyboard Error (%)</td><td colspan="2">CA > ST = CT</td></tr>
<tr><td>P2T Time (ms)</td><td>ST = CA > CT</td><td>CA=ST, ST=CT
CA > CT</td></tr>
<tr><td>Typing Speed (WPM)</td><td colspan="2">ST = CT = CA</td></tr>
<tr><td>Mouse Error (%)</td><td colspan="2">CT = CA > ST</td></tr>
</table>

Table 6. Conditions sorted by Tukey's HSD test results. The insignificant metrics according to RM-ANOVA results are excluded. We performed block-wise analyses for T2P and P2T, which exhibited *Condition*Block* interactions according to RM-ANOVA results.

Building a Personalized, Auto-Calibrating Eye Tracker from User Interactions

Michael Xuelin Huang, Tiffany C.K. Kwok, Grace Ngai, Stephen C.F. Chan, Hong Va Leong
Department of Computing, Hong Kong Polytechnic University
Hong Kong, China
{csxhuang,csckkwok,csgngai,csschan,cshleong}@comp.polyu.edu.hk

ABSTRACT

We present PACE, a Personalized, Auto-Calibrating Eye-tracking system that identifies and collects data unobtrusively from user interaction events on standard computing systems without the need for specialized equipment. PACE relies on eye/facial analysis of webcam data based on a set of robust geometric gaze features and a two-layer data validation mechanism to identify good training samples from daily interaction data. The design of the system is founded on an in-depth investigation of the relationship between gaze patterns and interaction cues, and takes into consideration user preferences and habits. The result is an adaptive, data-driven approach that continuously recalibrates, adapts and improves with additional use.

Quantitative evaluation on 31 subjects across different interaction behaviors shows that training instances identified by the PACE data collection have higher gaze point-interaction cue consistency than those identified by conventional approaches. An *in-situ* study using real-life tasks on a diverse set of interactive applications demonstrates that the PACE gaze estimation achieves an average error of 2.56°, which is comparable to state-of-the-art, but without the need for explicit training or calibration. This demonstrates the effectiveness of both the gaze estimation method and the corresponding data collection mechanism.

Author Keywords

Gaze estimation; implicit modeling; data validation; gaze-interaction correspondence

ACM Classification Keywords

H.1.2 [Models and Principles]: User/Machine Systems-Human factors; I.5.m [Pattern Recognition]: Miscellaneous

INTRODUCTION

Gaze information, as a reflection of human attention and cognition, has great potential applications in a large number of domains, including diagnostics, crowdsourcing, market research and education. The potential of gaze-aware systems for daily human-computer interaction and social interaction has increased with the growing pervasiveness of camera systems. Therefore, there has been, and continues to be, much research in gaze estimation [8].

With few exceptions, most gaze estimation methods require calibration and non-periodical re-calibration to accommodate lighting and head pose variances [26], which is obviously cumbersome and inconvenient in real use [22]. Since there is likely a strong correlation between eye gaze and interaction cues, such as cursor and caret locations, it seems to make sense that the mapping between gaze features and the gaze point can be collected implicitly from normal computer interactions and used to recalibrate or retrain gaze estimation models. However, while a number of studies have demonstrated a correlation between gaze and cursor [10][15], there have been few efforts in using noisy daily interaction data for webcam gaze learning. One notable exception is that of Sugano et al. [22], which collects mouse clicks for incremental gaze learning.

Given the massive amounts of time spent interacting with the computer, we believe it makes sense to explore the use of regular human computer interactions with mouse and keyboard for gaze learning. This can potentially make available a much larger amount of data, which accelerates the learning process and improves performance. Specifically, we are interested in data that can be obtained unobtrusively using conventional off-the-shelf equipment.

Most previous work [6][13][22] makes the assumption that users are looking at where they click, or, to put it more broadly, that users are looking at the interaction cue at the moment that the interaction is triggered. However, this assumption may be not valid in real-use situations, due to factors such as eye blink, mind-absence, response delay, individuality and task difference. We therefore propose to apply behavior-informed and data-driven approaches to identify reliable training instances from daily-use interaction data and webcam video.

To the best of our knowledge, there is no prior work that seeks to automatically identify and validate noisy interaction and webcam video data for gaze model learning. The exception is Huang et al [12], which addresses gaze-

CHI'16, May 07-12, 2016, San Jose, CA, USA
© 2016 ACM. ISBN 978-1-4503-3362-7/16/05$15.00
DOI: http://dx.doi.org/10.1145/2858036.2858404

related feature extraction and tentative data validation, but with more restrictive and rigid constraints.

This paper presents PACE, a Personalized, Auto-Calibrating Eye-tracking system, which is designed to enable high-performing gaze estimation in standard computing systems with no additional equipment. We (1) conduct an in-depth experimental study to investigate and quantify the gaze-interaction consistency across different behaviors; (2) propose an unobtrusive, adaptive, interaction-informed method that identifies the gaze-interaction alignment in daily computer use; and (3) demonstrate the effectiveness of PACE in multi-person evaluations across diverse interactive tasks.

RELATED WORK

The best-performing gaze estimation systems are model-based approaches [28], which use specialized equipment such as multiple cameras, light sources, or infrared, but the costs and equipment requirements make them infeasible for wide-range application on a large scale. In contrast, appearance-based approaches [1][16][18][21][23][24] that estimate gaze from single images are more versatile and easily deployed. However, they are sensitive to noise from lighting conditions, head pose, and individuality. Hansen and Ji [8] present an extensive review of such approaches.

Generalizing From Limited Data

Making good use of limited data is key to improving performance while reducing the calibration effort. Williams et al. [23] developed a semi-supervised method to use unlabeled calibration data. Their method requires users to follow an animated spot on the screen. Lu et al. [16] introduced compensations to correct the head pose biases for gaze estimation. Their calibration requires the user to rotate his/her head while fixating on each calibration point. To reduce the amount of calibration needed, Lu et al. [17] synthesized training samples for unseen head poses from multiple reference images where the user's head position changes while the eye rotation is held constant.

Although these methods reduce the amount of total calibration data, they all require a tedious, explicit initialization procedure. In addition, human error during calibration, such as eye blinks [18] or distracted saccades, may cause unexpected performance drop. It is not difficult to see that a method that implicitly collects good training data can also be used in conjunction with the above approaches to further improve gaze modeling.

Implicit Collection of Incremental Data

Some approaches bypass the cumbersome and lengthy calibration phase by implicitly collecting data from daily computer usages. One popular solution uses a saliency model that assumes that the user is more likely to look at the salient region of an image or video frame. Sugano et al. [21] applied the saliency map of video frames to estimate gaze based on images captured by a monocular camera. The problem with this approach is that the consistency between image saliency and real gaze location is often influenced by the attributes of visual stimuli, such as complexity and semantics. Apart from these uncertainties, the computation saliency models often do not match the actual human gaze movement [14]. Alnajar et al. [1] therefore made a different assumption that infers the calibration of a new user based on previously-collected gaze data from a group of individuals. This method makes use of inter-personal similarity for visual attention. However, the correlation between visual attention and image conspicuity is also affected by differences between individuals.

There has been some work into adopting interaction information to facilitate gaze learning. Hornof et al. [9] suggested a strategy that looks for interactions with known fixation points for run-time recalibration of the eye tracking model. Zhang et al. [27] further identified probable fixation locations to account for instances that cannot be clearly mapped to a known fixation point. Their work, however, relies on an infrared eye tracker to detect eye fixations, and knowledge of the visual context, including target locations and layout irregularity.

Sugano et al [22] proposed an alternative model which collected mouse click points as ground truth data to incrementally update the gaze model. Jacob [13] used click data to correct gaze tracking results. Similarly, Fares et al. [6] proposed to use mouse-click data as dynamic local calibration data. These approaches all assume that the location of the click point is the location of the user's gaze. However, in unconstrained real-use situations, this assumption may not always hold.

Investigating Gaze-Cursor Correlation

Gaze-cursor consistency is a perennially popular topic of study, especially for web browsing behaviors. Chen el al. [4] suggested that there is a strong correlation between gaze and saccade-like mouse movement. Rodden et al. [19] reported strong alignments between gaze and cursor during active mouse usages, including using the cursor as a reading aid (in both horizontal and vertical directions) and to mark particular results. Guo et al. [7] proposed a set of mouse features to identify the moments with strong gaze and cursor alignment during browsing. They achieved an average accuracy of 77%, 3% higher than the baseline. Liebling et al. [15] showed that gaze and mouse coordination contain complex and nuanced characteristics in real-life scenarios. Huang et al. [11] found that there is a certain correlation between gaze and cursor, but with substantial variation whereby the distance between the eye gaze and the mouse click location is smallest one second before the click occurs for one third of the subjects, in a "cursor lags behind gaze" phenomenon [10]. These findings suggest that the conventional hypothesis that "gaze is well approximated by cursor" may be naïve. It also shows that temporal alignments varied significantly across individuals, which argues for a personalized approach.

Interaction event	Human intention	*Potential* gaze pattern
Mouse click	Link or button selection	Fixation on the mouse cursor
Mouse double-click	Word selection in document editing	Fixation on the mouse cursor
Mouse button up after drag	Paragraph selection in document editing	Fixation on the mouse cursor
Keyboard letter key down	Word typing	Fixation/smooth pursuit on the typing caret

Table 1. Examples of gaze patterns from common interaction behaviors.

INVESTIGATING CONSISTENCY BETWEEN GAZE AND INTERACTION

In order for PACE to be feasibly integrated into real-world computing systems, the gaze model must be robust to natural head movement, not require explicit calibration, and not require the use of specialized equipment. Our approach is therefore to unobtrusively identify and collect training instances from daily interaction data. We start by evaluating the assumed correspondence between gaze and interaction from previous work [6][13][22]. Our findings will guide the identification of reliable data for gaze learning.

We hypothesize that the moment of strongest gaze-interaction correlation depends on the nature of the interaction, the context, user habits and preferences. Some activities require a more explicit demonstration of human intention, which results in a higher gaze-cursor consistency. For example, the positions of the eye gaze and the mouse cursor are better aligned during a mouse click event, compared to when the mouse cursor is being used as a reading aid [10]. The context also affects the correlation. It is easy to see that clicking to select a single character in a paragraph of text would require a more purposeful and precise gaze than clicking on photo thumbnails to scroll through photo albums. Some tasks may actually require or encourage the user to look at a part of the screen away from the cursor, e.g. pausing the playback of a video at a precise moment during video editing.

Experiment Setup

Our investigation focuses on four commonly encountered interaction activities, as shown in Table 1. We use the Tobii EyeX tracker to provide us with the "ground truth" of the user's gaze point. The Tobii tracker uses infra-red technology with 60 Hz tracking frequency and an accuracy within 1° visual angle (corresponding to 30-50 pixels on our 22" monitor at 1680×1050 resolution and a reading distance ≈500~800mm), and can be considered to be state-of-the-art.

We recruited 31 subjects (16 female, ages 20-30 yrs, mean 25.1, standard deviation 2.5) for this study. The subjects were university students and staff. 24 of them are capable of touch-typing, at least for the letter keys.

Subjects were asked to work naturally, which meant free movement of head and body. They were allowed to change the chair position and height, but to keep their head-to-monitor distance within the valid range (≈500~800mm) of the monitor. Three experiments were designed to generate the necessary interaction behaviors:

Correlation between visual attention and click targets: The first experiment requires the subject to click on targets of different shapes and sizes. Observations of common mouse usage patterns show that mouse clicks usually involve (1) long slim targets, (2) small targets and (3) large targets.

To obtain data on (1) and (2), a list of academic papers with long titles (≥ 3/4 of the screen width) was prepared in advance. The subjects were asked to search for each paper on Google Scholar, and to click on the hyperlinks for the title and authors for each paper. Since Google abbreviates authors' first names, author hyperlinks are usually short and button-like (small targets), and the hyperlinks with the paper titles give long slim targets. The large targets were obtained by asking the subjects to search for and click on photos in Flickr that they found interesting. The width of the photos occupied around one third of the screen.

Correlation between visual attention and mouse drag actions: The second experiment considers a different kind of mouse activity – dragging. Subjects were asked to select sentences from a given PDF document by dragging the mouse. To ensure that they would actually pay attention to what they were doing, they were required to select complete sentences or phrases (ending with a period or comma.)

Correlation between visual attention and keyboard usage: For the third experiment, subjects were asked to type a short paragraph into a text file. They could type anything they wanted, as long as it was a syntactically correct paragraph that made sense semantically. We collected only letter keys ("a"-"z", "A"-"Z", spaces), because most people, even those who can touch-type, are actually only able to touch type the letter keys, not the number or function keys.

Each of the experiment subjects was required to generate at least 50 instances of each interaction activity. The occurrence of a clicking event was defined as the press of the left mouse button, dragging events as the release of the left mouse button, and keypresses as the depression of a letter key. Each interaction event triggered a screenshot that was saved for data validation and event classification. In total, we collected 1915 clicking events on long slim targets, 2344 on small targets, 1955 on large targets, 2029 dragging events and 4863 typing events.

Evaluation of the Correspondence Assumption

To investigate the correlation between visual attention and interaction event, we study the 3 seconds of data from the Tobii tracker *preceding* each interaction event. The focus on pre-interaction behavior is informed by previous work

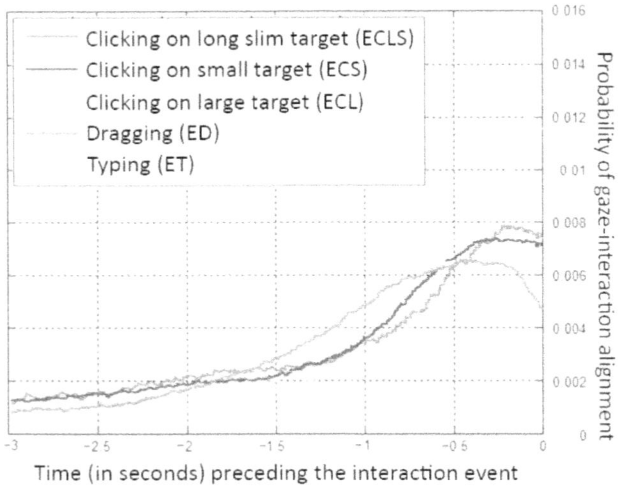

Figure 1. Probability of gaze-interaction alignment – i.e. the likelihood that visual attention is spatially located at the interaction event, as a function of time *preceding* the event.

[10], which reports that in general, the position of the cursor lags behind the gaze point, not the other way around.

For simplicity, we will use the following abbreviations when referring to events of: clicking on small targets (ECS), long slim targets (ECLS), large targets (ECL), dragging (ED) and typing (ET).

The eye tracker returns the position of the user's gaze on the screen as a temporal sequence of (*x*, *y*) screen coordinates. To allow for inherent error from the eye tracker, we choose a small distance threshold γ (=60 pixels), which matches the equipment error. The position of the user's gaze and the location of the interaction event are considered to be *aligned* when their *displacement*, or the distance between them, is less than this threshold, *i.e.* $D(\boldsymbol{g}_t(t_p), \boldsymbol{c}) < \gamma$, where $D(\boldsymbol{g}_t(t_p), \boldsymbol{c})$ indicates the Euclidean distance between the tracker-measured gaze point $\boldsymbol{g}_t$ and the interaction point $\boldsymbol{c}$, and t_p represents the time preceding an interaction event.

Figure 1 shows the probability of *gaze-interaction* (i.e. gaze-cursor or gaze-caret) *alignment* as we approach the moment of interaction, *i.e.* $Pr(D(\boldsymbol{g}_t(t_p), \boldsymbol{c}) < \gamma)$. The *x*-axis shows the time in seconds *before* the interaction event. As expected, the probability of the gaze-interaction consistency generally increases as we get closer to the interaction event. However, the moment of highest probability for gaze-interaction alignment does not necessarily occur at the moment of the interaction. For example, the likelihood distribution of gaze-interaction alignment peaks at t_p=-0.01s for ET, -0.07s for ECL, -0.20s for ECLS, -0.25s for ECS, and -0.43s for ED. In particular, for mouse drag events (ED), the probability of gaze-interaction alignment *falls off significantly* in the moments just before the interaction event happens. It would seem that typing events (ET) are the only ones in which the assumption that "the user is looking where he/she is interacting" is consistently upheld.

Figure 2 presents the *gaze-interaction displacement* *i.e.* $D(\boldsymbol{g}_t(t_p), \boldsymbol{c})$ or the distance between the location of the user's gaze and the eventual location of the interaction event. It can be seen that the displacement (mainly: the grey and blue regions) generally decreases as we get closer to the time of the interaction event, but the distributions are quite dissimilar. Unsurprisingly, the displacement is largest for ECL (clicking on large targets). However, the interaction activity with the second largest displacement is ET (typing), which also has a large range of displacement values (wide blue and grey regions). This implies that even though

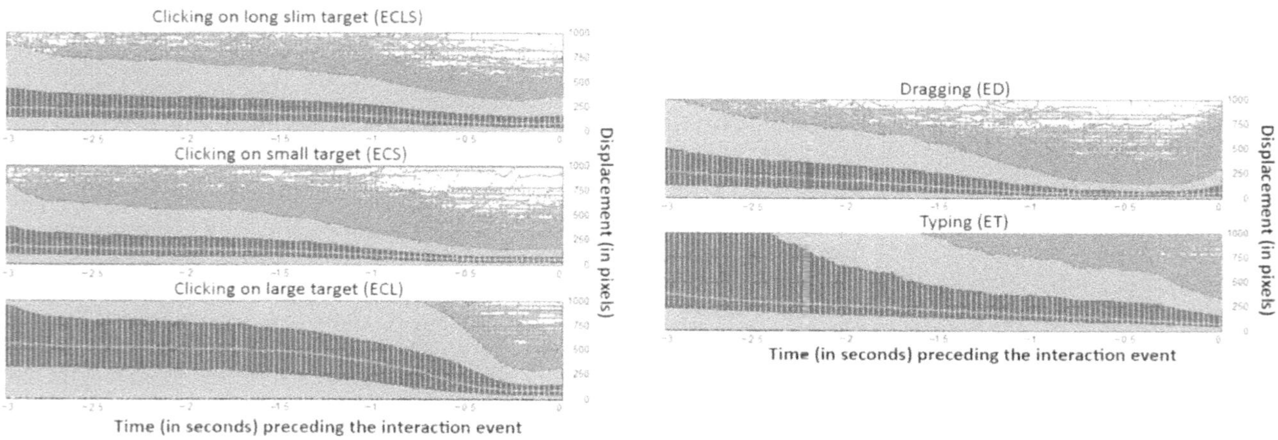

Figure 2. Displacement between gaze and interaction cues (cursor/caret) as a function of pre-interaction event time for different interaction activities. The *x*-axis indicates the time before the event, the *y*-axis shows Euclidean distance between location of event (i.e. where the mouse is actually clicked or where the character appears on the screen) and gaze coordinates collected by eye tracker. The green line shows the median distance. The blue region shows values that fall within $[p_{25}, p_{75}]$, *i.e.* the 25th and 75th percentiles. The grey area indicates the range of the data points that are not considered as outliers. The red points are the individual outliers, defined as values located beyond $[2.5p_{25} - 1.5p_{75},\ 2.5p_{75} - 1.5p_{25}]$.

Figure 1 suggests that people are *generally* looking at the caret when they type, there is still much variation across different events, and hence, using the raw typing-informed data for gaze model training would introduce much noise and error into the system.

The distribution of the outliers (the red regions) is also of interest. Figure 2 shows that there is much variation in the user's gaze. Furthermore, the *range* of these locations is very great, ranging to 1000 pixels away from the interaction position. This further corroborates our hypothesis that the correspondence assumption is not valid in real-use situations. This means that a naïve use of raw interactional-informed data for gaze model learning is not likely to produce optimal results.

Inspecting the non-outlier data reveals some interesting findings. For ED (dragging), a U-shape distribution starts to form around one second before the interaction event. This indicates that in most cases, subjects start looking elsewhere before the drag event is complete. A similar phenomenon happens during ECLS. This suggests that if we could identify the point of least displacement, this would potentially be a better indicator of eye gaze than simply collecting the data at the moment of the event.

Another interesting finding comes from the *densities* of the displacement distributions across the different behaviors. Although the *range* of the displacements, *i.e.* the upper boundaries of the grey region, is fairly large, 75% of the data stays within half of the range, as evidenced by the fact that the upper boundary of the blue regions lies close to the middle of the grey regions. Similarly, the green median line lies below the middle of the blue region for almost all behaviors, which indicates that the data is very compactly distributed. This is especially true for typing events (ET). This implies that the majority of the data exhibits strong gaze/interaction consistency, even in real-use situations.

In addition to the data analysis, observations of the subjects' behavior during the experiment and the post-experiment interviews also reveal some interesting insights and provide possible explanations for the data distribution.

Clicking: We observed two distinct ways in which people usually click on long slim links. Some people start moving the cursor towards a link only after reading its context and deciding to click on it. In this case, the user's gaze tends to stay close to the last word they read and that is usually also where they click. However, sometimes the user perceives that there is a high probability that a certain link would be relevant, even before reading it. In these cases, they often move the cursor to hover over the link before actually reading the words. Once they finish reading, they click the mouse without moving it again. In these cases, the displacement between gaze and click could be quite unpredictable, depending on where the cursor hovers and where the link ends.

Dragging: Dragging generally results in high consistency between gaze and interaction-informed data. Since the nature of the action requires precision, people are more likely to spend more time and care to ensure that the context selection is correct. However, by the time a drag has been completed, users may already be looking for the next target, such as the "highlight" button. This may be the main reason that the probability of gaze-cursor alignment drops as we get closer to the moment of the event as shown in Figure 1 and that the corresponding large displacement causes the U-shape distribution as shown in Figure 2. The context is also important. When the selected sentence ends a paragraph, the PDF viewing application automatically snaps the end of the drag to the end of the paragraph. Therefore, subjects are often more careless when selecting such sentences, thus creating a large distance displacement.

Typing: For users who can touch type, their gaze normally follows the caret, *i.e.* the location of the character being typed. However, we observed that when they are thinking hard, many (11 out of 24 in our case) touch-typers look elsewhere on the screen while continuing to type. For users with limited touch-typing skills, the gaze switches between the monitor and keyboard. Both of these behaviors create large displacement, and explain the presence of the large number of outliers for this interaction activity.

IDENTIFYING GOOD INTERACTION DATA FOR EYE TRACKING

Our behavior study suggests that interaction data corresponds with the gaze to a certain degree, which implies that it is feasible to use everyday user interactions as data to build a gaze tracking system. However, the findings also show that the moment of best alignment varies across different interaction activities, the context of each interaction, and the individuality of the users. This argues for a more refined approach to using interaction-informed data for training. It also suggests that a *personalized* approach would be the most effective; since it would automatically adapt to user preferences and constraints.

We hypothesize that it is possible to use *knowledge of common gaze patterns* and *analysis of visual signals* to identify the point at which user gaze and interaction event are most likely to be aligned. In other words, we postulate that there are periods when user gaze-interaction event alignment is likely, and it is possible to detect these periods in an automated fashion.

Overall System Flow and Methodology

Figure 3 gives an overview of our PACE approach. A standard webcam captures video of the user's head and shoulders while mouse movements and keystrokes are tracked by the system. Two tracking models extract the gaze feature vector $\boldsymbol{v}$ from face and eye landmarks identified in the frames of the video stream.

Upon the trigger of an interaction event $\boldsymbol{c}$, gaze feature vectors from the 3-second window preceding the interaction

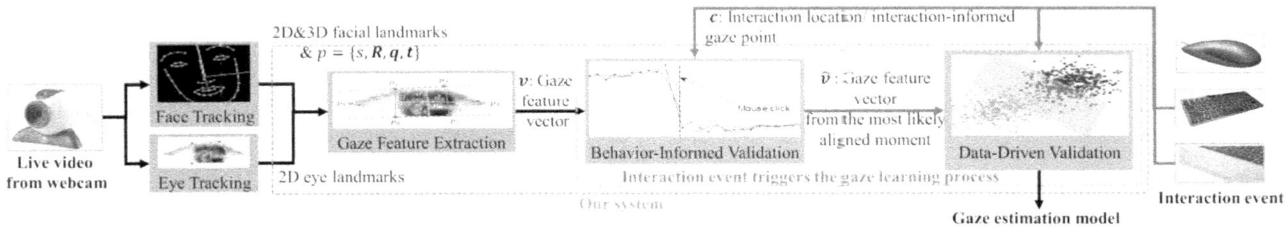

Figure 3. Overview of the PACE methodology: combining interaction data and webcam video for eye gaze modeling.

are sent to a *behavior-informed validation* engine and a *data-driven validation* engine. The behavior-informed validation engine selects one vector $\tilde{\boldsymbol{v}}$ that corresponds to the moment when the user's gaze is most likely to be aligned with the interaction event. The data-driven validation engine then further checks the validity of $\tilde{\boldsymbol{v}}$, based on the previous training samples. If $\tilde{\boldsymbol{v}}$ passes both of these validation steps, $[\tilde{\boldsymbol{v}}, \boldsymbol{c}]$ will be used as training data to update the gaze estimation model. Otherwise the data is retained for re-evaluation after the next update.

Extracting Gaze Features from Video

To obtain accurate locations of the facial landmarks and head pose information, we use Constrained Local Models (CLM) [20] to obtain 3D vertices of 66 facial landmarks. Procrustes alignment [5] is used to normalize the rigid transformation and Principal Component Analysis (PCA) to approximate the non-rigid deformation of the given face images. Supervised Descent Method (SDM) is then used to optimize 48 facial landmarks [25] to improve the localization accuracy and facilitate head pose estimation.

To model the user's eyes, we follow Huang et al. [12] and use facial landmarks on the iris contour and eyelid corners to calculate the location of the pupil center inside the eye image. This gives 3 eye features representing the eye yaw and pitch rotation, and the degree of openness of the eye.

The facial and eye features are combined into a 12-feature gaze vector $\boldsymbol{v} = [s, \boldsymbol{R}, \boldsymbol{t}, \boldsymbol{e}_r, \boldsymbol{e}_l]^T$, where $s, \boldsymbol{R}, \boldsymbol{t}$ are the head pose features and $\boldsymbol{e}_r, \boldsymbol{e}_l$ the features from right and left eyes, respectively.

Using Human Behavior to Inform Data Validation

Human gaze patterns can be categorized into four behaviors: *fixation*, *smooth pursuit*, *saccade* and *blink* [8]. Fixation indicates a stationary gaze. Smooth pursuit denotes relatively slow gaze movements, while saccades are eye movements that rapidly direct towards a stationary target.

Figure 4 shows the change in an example feature signal (eye yaw) around a mouse click. The gaze pattern contains 2 short fixations, 2 saccades and 1 smooth pursuit. The black dashed line indicates the moment of the mouse click. The figure shows that the user's gaze was originally focused on one point (1st fixation), then rapidly moved towards a short link (1st saccade), which took approximately 1 second to read (smooth pursuit). She then clicked on the link and her attention shifted (2nd saccade) elsewhere (2nd fixation). This behavior is consistent across multiple instances, with the mouse click usually occurring at the end of the smooth pursuit, the beginning of the 2nd saccade or even the beginning of the 2nd fixation. This clearly illustrates how the user's fixation is not always located at the point of the interaction event.

The behavior-informed validation in PACE identifies moments at which the user's gaze aligns with the cursor/caret when interaction activity is triggered. Based on knowledge of human gaze patterns and our observations, this is most likely during periods of fixation or smooth pursuit. For simplicity, we refer to these periods as $\boldsymbol{S}_S$ and the state of the gaze feature during these periods as being "stationary with small trend", or "stationary". The problem then is to determine $\boldsymbol{S}_S$ automatically from the webcam data.

Signal Smoothing and Filtering

Based on our previous findings, we focus on the user signals collected in the 3 seconds prior to the interaction event. Linear interpolation is used to resample the signal to 100Hz, giving us 300 samples per feature per interaction event. Since the raw webcam signals contain much high-frequency visual noise, a standard low-pass filter is used to remove some of the noise prior to analysis [2].

Figure 4 demonstrates the effects of filtering in the frequency and temporal domains. While both filtering methods remove much of the high-frequency noise, filtering in the temporal domain results in the loss of some critical information, such as the dynamic overshoot glissade that occurs before the 1st rapid saccade. We therefore filter in the frequency domain to remove the high frequency temporal jitter while maintaining the shape of the main

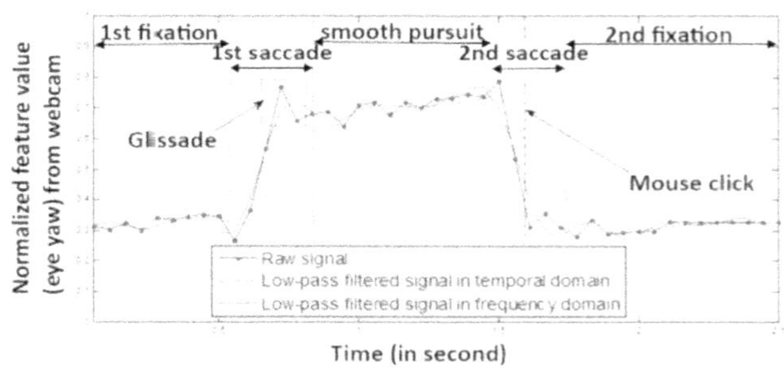

Figure 4. Raw and filtered webcam signals from a sample mouse click event (user is reading from left to right).

Input: Matrix $\boldsymbol{F}$ of gaze feature vectors from the 3-second window before the interaction event.	
Output: The stationary period $\boldsymbol{S}_s$ and the feature vector $\widetilde{\boldsymbol{v}}$ at the most likely moment of gaze-interaction alignment.	
1	Calculate the low-pass frequency-domain filtered signal $\hat{\boldsymbol{f}}_j$ for each gaze feature signal $\boldsymbol{f}_j$
2	Iteratively search for the stationary period using an incremental threshold $\boldsymbol{\varepsilon} \in [\boldsymbol{r}/1000, \boldsymbol{r}/100]$, where $\boldsymbol{r} \in \Re^{n\times 1}$ is the range of each feature over the window.
3a	Initialize the overall stationary period with the frame index $\boldsymbol{S} = [1, \ldots, m]$.
3b	Calculate the overall stationary period $\boldsymbol{S}$ according to Equation (1); set S_i to 0 if the condition is not satisfied.
3c	Backward search $\boldsymbol{S}$ for the first series of consecutive frame indices $\boldsymbol{S}_s$ whose corresponding duration is longer than the minimum fixation duration (80ms) [8].
3d	If t_s, the last moment of $\boldsymbol{S}_s$, occurs within 0.5 seconds before the event, then break.
	Else increment $\boldsymbol{\varepsilon}$ by $\boldsymbol{r}/1000$.
	End
4	Perform line fitting for each feature signal $\hat{\boldsymbol{f}}_j$ in $\boldsymbol{S}_s$ to approximate the final gaze feature vector $\widetilde{\boldsymbol{v}}$.

Table 2. Adaptively Extracting a Stationary Feature Vector.

component with minimal distortion.

Extracting a stationary feature vector

To identify the stationary period $\boldsymbol{S}_s$ and the corresponding estimated feature vector $\widetilde{\boldsymbol{v}}$, our approach adaptively searches for candidate periods occurring close to the point of the event that do not exhibit high signal variance.

To identify these candidate periods, PACE uses a novel adaptive method that searches for a *relatively stationary* period close to the event. The algorithm is similar to that of Huang et al [12], which uses a threshold to determine if the signal change is small enough to be considered "stationary", but their approach requires a truly fixed gaze and will fail if the user's gaze is not truly still, which would be problematic for real-world contexts where the eye is rarely truly stationary.

Table 2 presents our algorithm. Basically, we analyze the changes between consecutive frames in the 3-second window prior to the interaction event. An adaptive threshold $\boldsymbol{\varepsilon}$, which is based on the range of each feature, is used to identify candidate frames whose feature vectors satisfy the following condition:

$$\prod_{j=1}^{n} H(\varepsilon_j^2 - \dot{\hat{f}}_{ij}^2) = 1 \quad (1)$$

where $H(x) = (1 + \mathrm{sgn}(x))/2$ is the Heaviside step function and $\dot{\hat{f}}_{ij}$ is the ith frame value of the derivative of $\hat{\boldsymbol{f}}_j$ with respect to the sample time. These frames are considered to be potentially within the stationary period.

After all frames in the window have been tested, a backward search is performed to locate $\boldsymbol{S}_s$. Linear regression is used to approximate the gaze feature vector $\widetilde{\boldsymbol{v}}$ corresponding to the last moment of $\boldsymbol{S}_s$, which under our assumptions is also the moment when the user's gaze is most likely to be aligned with the interaction event. If no fixation or smooth pursuit is detected at all during the 3-second time window, that interaction event is considered to be not suitable for training and is discarded.

Data-driven validation

The behavior-informed validation looks for the stationary period corresponding to the received interaction event. However, there is a possibility that even though the user's gaze is fixated on something, the gaze point may not be anywhere near the location of the interaction event – for example, when the user is watching a movie with the mouse pointer poised over the "pause" button, or typing a chat message while reading the previous incoming responses. To accommodate these types of interactions, PACE uses data-driven validation as an additional layer of validation to determine the goodness of the feature vector $\widetilde{\boldsymbol{v}}$ and the corresponding assumed interaction-informed gaze point $\boldsymbol{c}$ based on previously validated data.

We use random forest [3] to build the gaze regression models for both x- and y-coordinates. The gaze feature vectors $\widetilde{\boldsymbol{v}}$ are used as features and the corresponding interaction points $\boldsymbol{c}$ as the "truth". Each model generates 100 trees and each tree considers 4 random gaze features. The initial model is trained on the first 100 interaction instances in which the moment of the interaction occurs within a fixation period.

When the most-recently collected feature vector $\widetilde{\boldsymbol{v}}$ is passed through the gaze model, it outputs a webcam estimated gaze point $\boldsymbol{g}_W$. If $D(\boldsymbol{g}_W, \boldsymbol{c}) \le \lambda$, ($\lambda$ = 1/12 of the screen diagonal length in our work), the instance $[\widetilde{\boldsymbol{v}}, \boldsymbol{c}]$ is considered validated and can be used as training data. For efficiency, the gaze model is updated in a batch mode; upon the collection of 150 valid instances of new training data, the random forest regression model is retrained on all the validated data. To make full use of all potential data, instances that fail the current validation are also retained and re-evaluated after each update of the gaze model.

In summary, PACE uses a dual-level validation First, by looking for the stationary gaze features corresponding to an interaction event, the behavior-informed validation uses knowledge of gaze movement patterns and user interaction to identify the moment when user gaze and interaction point are most closely aligned. The data-driven validation further applies prior knowledge of the particular user to account for user individualities and contextual differences.

Correctness of Assumptions on User Gaze Patterns

The PACE approach makes some assumptions about the characteristics of user gaze patterns to identify good data points that can be used to train a gaze model. We are interested in whether these data points really correspond to moments when user gaze aligns with interaction event.

We use the eye gaze coordinates collected by the Tobii EyeX tracker as the gold standard for this evaluation. For each interaction event, we compare its location $\boldsymbol{c}$ with the Tobii-measured gaze coordinates $\boldsymbol{g}_t$ at the moment identified by the behavior-informed validation mechanism as the point of closest alignment. The error of our PACE method, $error_{PACE}$, is calculated as the displacement (Euclidean distance) between $\boldsymbol{g}_t$ and $\boldsymbol{c}$. We also calculate $error_{naive}$, which is the error that would result if we take the naïve assumption and simply choose the moment of the interaction event as the moment of best alignment, as in previous work [22]. As another point of reference, we compute $error_{min}$, which is the minimum possible error that we could achieve if we somehow knew the exact moment of best gaze-interaction alignment in the 3-second window; and $error_{minf}$, which is the minimum error achieved after discarding the obvious errors, defined as points where the displacement is larger than 1/12 of the screen diagonal length (≈240 pixels). These usually correspond to instances in which the user is clearly not looking at the interaction point – for example, when he/she is looking for a key on the keyboard.

Figure 5 compares the performance achieved by the three different approaches on the data described in the previous experiment. The color bars indicate the displacement values, and the circles denote the percentage of data that is retained after outliers are removed.

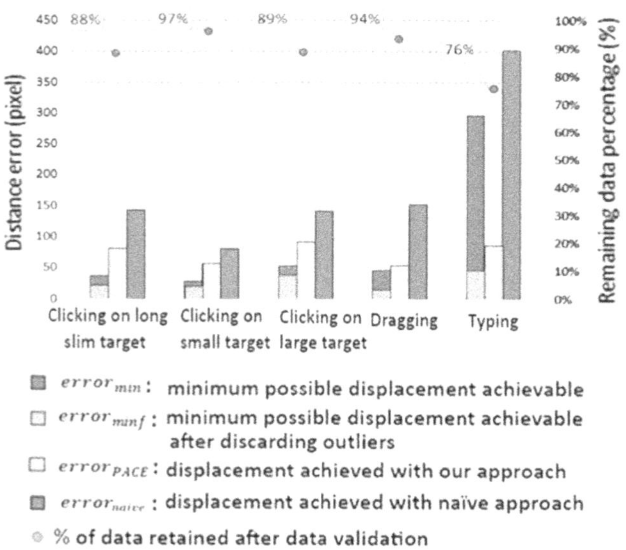

Figure 5. Displacement between gaze points identified with different approaches and location of corresponding interaction events.

The results are encouraging. As expected, $error_{min}$ (blue) can be very small, with an average of 41.1 pixels over all mouse interactions. For keyboard events, $error_{min}$ is much larger at 401.8 pixels. This is caused by the instances in which the user was not looking at what was being typed at all – i.e. the gaze was either wandering about the screen, or he/she was looking at the keyboard. When outliers are discarded, the keyboard event error decreases to 86.7 pixels. Discarding outliers for all events brings the error down to 27.8 pixels. However, this is the best achievable result, which is extremely difficult to achieve in practice.

In comparison, $error_{naive}$ (red) from the naïve approach is larger than $error_{PACE}$ (green) from our approach, across all interaction behaviors. The reason is obvious when one considers the U-shape pattern seen in most of the interaction behaviors (Figure 2), as the displacement falls to a minimum before the event, and then actually rises again just before the event. For example, with mouse drags, using the point at the event moment gives $error_{naive}$ of 153.3 pixels, while $error_{PACE}$, at 53 pixels, approaches the lowest possible $error_{min}$ (46 pixels). On average, $error_{naive}$ is 184.2 pixels while $error_{PACE}$ is 73.6 pixels.

It is also interesting to consider the amount of data that is retained after the two-layer validation process. We find that on average, 88.8% of the data is retained. The exception is typing, which has a low retention rate (76%), which is due to the large number of outliers. Incidentally, both the unfiltered $error_{min}$ and $error_{naive}$ are very large for typing interactions. However, our method is able to successfully identify these problematic data points, hence achieving a small $error_{PACE}$, which is close to that of mouse events. This is promising as keypress events are usually more numerous than mouse events, and hence it makes sense to find a means to include them as interaction-informed data.

Our results suggest that the proposed validation mechanism can effectively and precisely identify the reliable interaction-informed data, significantly outperforming the method based on the conventional assumption.

EVALUATION IN REAL-USE CONTEXTS

To evaluate the accuracy and effectiveness of the PACE system, we recruited 10 subjects (university students, 6 female, aged 20-33) for a focus study. Subjects were asked to choose at least 3 of the following tasks for the data collection: browsing websites, coding in Visual Studio, writing in Notepad, creating a figure using Microsoft Paint, and playing a shooting game (the House of the Dead). These tasks were chosen to cover a diverse range of common user interaction activities and applications, and to contain diverse interaction types. For example, some of the tasks will involve relatively dense keypresses while others contain mainly mouse events, like clicking and dragging.

The experiments were run on an i7-2600MHz PC with 4GB RAM, a 22" monitor and a standard off-the-shelf webcam

Methods	Error	Calibration	Data Required / Method Used
PACE	**2.56°**	**Implicit, Automatic**	**mouse/keyboard interactions**
Sugano et al.[22]	4°-5°	Implicit	click
Lu et al.[16]	2°-3°	Explicit	video
Lu et al.[17]	2°-3°	Explicit	image synthesis

Table 3. Performance of our approach, compared with state-of-the-art appearance models that allow free head motion.

capable of recording at 30fps. Running PACE on this setup achieves a frame rate of 22fps and performing a model update with 1500 data points takes less than 500ms. The gold standard eye gaze position is measured by the Tobii EyeX tracker. Approximated by our face tracker, the head-to-monitor distance ranges from 372~892mm (mean: 663mm; SD: 35.2mm); and head-to-camera pitch from -9.6°~56.6° (mean: 14.2°; SD: 8.9°).

At least 1500 events were collected from each subject. Each mouse click and press of a letter key logs the gaze feature data from the preceding 3 seconds. Subjects were allowed to pause and continue the experiment as needed, even over multiple days if necessary. They were also free to adjust head pose, body posture and chair position/height. The experiment lasted from 2 to 18 hours, depending on how long it took for the needed interaction events to be generated. On average, the subjects took around 4 hours to generate the required number of interaction points.

Table 3 shows the performance achieved by our method, as compared against similar state-of-the-art appearance-based methods that rely on webcam signals. The performance is measured as the average error over all collected instances and subjects. It is encouraging to see that our method achieves an average error of 30.9mm (*i.e* 2.56° visual error, calculated using the approach in Sugano et al [22]), which is comparable to state-of-the-art approaches that require explicit calibration. This is a promising result, given that PACE (1) does not require explicit calibration and will

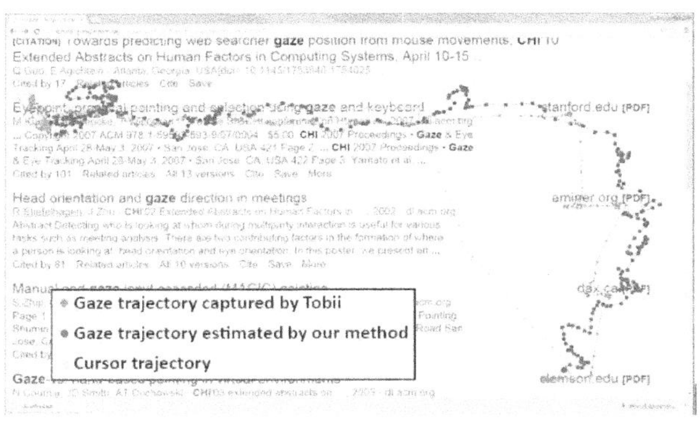

Figure 6. Trajectories of user gaze as estimated by PACE (blue) and as captured by the Tobii EyeX eye tracker (red). The cursor trajectory (green) is included for reference.

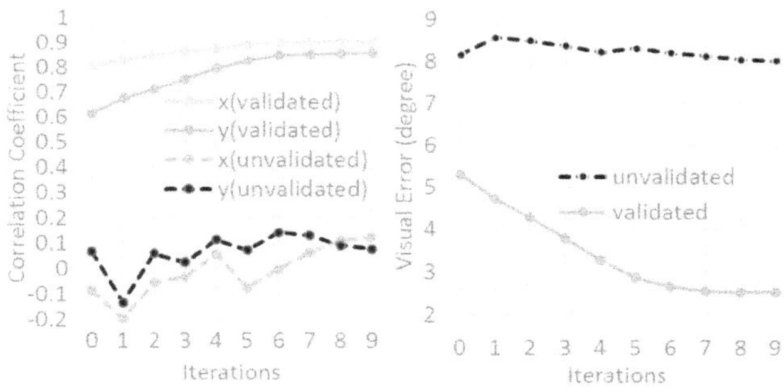

Figure 7. Comparison of PACE and naïve models. Change in performance (Correlation and Visual Error) as data increases. Each iteration consists of 150 interaction events.

automatically update itself to account for changes in light and posture variance, even across multiple sessions spanning over multiple days, (2) uses conventional off-the-shelf equipment that is commonplace in work environments, and (3) is tested using real applications and activities.

Figure 6 shows a graphical example of the performance of our system during a browsing activity. The blue line shows the eye movement estimated by PACE, while the red line denotes the true trajectory, measured by the Tobii tracker. It is seen that the PACE eye positions closely approximate that from the Tobii for the majority of the time, without using any additional equipment.

It is informative to consider the improvement in performance as the amount of data increases. We train two models using the same random forest algorithm. One is trained on data collected under the naïve assumption. The other is the PACE model, trained on data identified through the 2-step validation process. The models are updated and retrained every 150 interaction events (mouse clicks or keypresses). This means that the naïve model gets 150 new data instances per iteration, but the PACE model will get fewer instances, as the data-driven validation will invariably filter out some unreliable data points.

Figure 7 compares the performance (correlation and visual error) of the two models. Along the x-axis, each point represents one iteration of 150 interaction events. The performance of the naïve model fluctuates considerably – the visual error hovers around 8°, and the correlation never increases beyond 0.2. The performance of PACE, on the other hand, improves monotonically as additional training data is provided. The correlation reaches an impressive 0.90 and 0.85 for the x- and y-coordinates respectively, and the visual error drops steadily to 2.56°. This is further evidence that shows that our validation mechanism is effective as well as necessary for collecting interaction-informed training data in real-use situations.

CONCLUSION

This paper describes PACE, a Personalized, Auto-Calibrating Eye-tracking system that can be integrated into standard interactive computing systems. The assumptions behind PACE are informed by an in-depth study on the relationship between eye gaze and interaction location for several common types of interactive behaviors. Based on the results of the study, we then develop a novel approach that automatically identifies the moment of best gaze-interaction alignment, and a further data validation mechanism that accounts for user differences and context.

Experimental evaluations demonstrate that PACE can effectively extract good training data from daily interaction activities to build a reliable eye tracker with automatic updating and re-calibration. The performance thus achieved is comparable to those from similar state-of-the-art methods. However, PACE has the advantage that it automatically updates and re-calibrates itself and is therefore able to adjust to variances in conditions over multiple days and sessions.

In future work, we plan to probe further into different types of interaction behaviors, and also to take the semantics of the interaction (e.g. the functionality of the button that was clicked, or the type of the key that was pressed) and/or the history of the interaction into account. We also plan to investigate the impact of focus and attention on human eye gaze patterns and the performance of the eventual gaze tracking system. In addition, since it is also not difficult to see how the underlying data validation method could be combined with other gaze estimation techniques, we also plan to investigate the effectiveness of collecting training data in a similar way for appearance-based techniques using webcam video, or even for model-based techniques that work on infrared devices.

ACKNOWLEDGMENTS

We would like to thank all the experiment subjects for their help. We also thank the anonymous reviewers for their constructive comments and suggestions. This work was partially supported by grants PolyU 5235/11E and PolyU 5222/13E from the Hong Kong Research Grants Council.

REFERENCES

1. Alnajar, F., Gevers, T., Valenti, R. and Ghebreab, S. 2013. Calibration-Free Gaze Estimation Using Human Gaze Patterns. 2013 IEEE International Conference on Computer Vision (Dec. 2013), 137–144.
2. B. A. Shenoi 2005. Introduction to Digital Signal Processing and Filter Design. Wiley.
3. Breiman, L. 2001. Random forests. Machine Learning. 45, (2001), 5–32.
4. Chen, M.C., Anderson, J.R. and Sohn, M.H. 2001. What can a mouse cursor tell us more? CHI '01 extended abstracts on Human factors in computing systems - CHI '01 (New York, New York, USA, 2001), 281.
5. Cootes, T.F., Edwards, G.J. and Taylor, C.J. 2001. Active appearance models. IEEE Transactions on Pattern Analysis and Machine Intelligence. 23, 6 (Jun. 2001), 681–685.
6. Fares, R., Fang, S. and Komogortsev, O. 2013. Can we beat the mouse with MAGIC? Proceedings of the SIGCHI Conference on Human Factors in Computing Systems - CHI '13 (New York, New York, USA, 2013), 1387.
7. Guo, Q. and Agichtein, E. 2010. Towards predicting web searcher gaze position from mouse movements. Proceedings of the 28th of the international conference extended abstracts on Human factors in computing systems - CHI EA '10 (New York, New York, USA, 2010), 3601.
8. Hansen, D.W. and Ji, Q. 2010. In the eye of the beholder: a survey of models for eyes and gaze. IEEE transactions on pattern analysis and machine intelligence. 32, 3 (Mar. 2010), 478–500.
9. Hornof, A J. and Halverson, T. 2002. Cleaning up systematic error in eye-tracking data by using required fixation locations. Behavior research methods, instruments, & computers : a journal of the Psychonomic Society, Inc. 34, (2002), 592–604.
10. Huang, J., White, R. and Buscher, G. 2012. User see, user point: gaze and cursor alignment in web search. Proceedings of the 2012 ACM annual conference on Human Factors in Computing Systems - CHI '12 (New York, New York, USA, 2012), 1341.
11. Huang, J., White, R.W. and Dumais, S. 2011. No clicks, no problem: using cursor movements to understand and improve search. Proceedings of the 2011 annual conference on Human factors in computing systems - CHI '11 (New York, New York, USA, 2011), 1225.
12. Huang, M.X., Kwok, T.C.K., Ngai, G., Leong, H.V. and Chan, C.F.S. 2014. Building a Self-Learning Eye Gaze Model from User Interaction Data. ACM Multimedia (2014).
13. Jacob, R.J K. 1990. What you look at is what you get: eye movement-based interaction techniques. Proceedings of the SIGCHI conference on Human factors in computing systems Empowering people - CHI '90 (New York, New York, USA, 1990), 11–18.
14. Judd, T., Ehinger, K., Durand, F. and Torralba, A. 2009. Learning to predict where humans look. 2009 IEEE 12th International Conference on Computer Vision (Sep. 2009), 2106–2113.
15. Liebling, D.J. and Dumais, S.T. 2014. Gaze and mouse coordination in everyday work. Proceedings of the 2014 ACM International Joint Conference on Pervasive and Ubiquitous Computing Adjunct Publication - UbiComp '14 Adjunct (2014), 1141–1150.

16. Lu, F., Okabe, T., Sugano, Y. and Sato, Y. 2014. Learning gaze biases with head motion for head pose-free gaze estimation. Image and Vision Computing. 32, 3 (Mar. 2014), 169–179.

17. Lu, F., Sugano, Y., Okabe, T. and Sato, Y. 2012. Head pose-free appearance-based gaze sensing via eye image synthesis. International Conference on Pattern Recognition (ICPR), (2012), 1008 – 1011.

18. Lu, F., Sugano, Y., Okabe, T. and Sato, Y. 2014. Inferring Human Gaze from Appearance via Adaptive Linear Regression. IEEE Transactions on Pattern Analysis and Machine Intelligence. (2014), 1–1.

19. Rodden, K., Fu, X., Aula, A. and Spiro, I. 2008. Eye-mouse coordination patterns on web search results pages. Proceeding of the twenty-sixth annual CHI conference extended abstracts on Human factors in computing systems - CHI '08 (New York, New York, USA, 2008), 2997.

20. Saragih, J.M., Lucey, S. and Cohn, J.F. 2009. Face alignment through subspace constrained mean-shifts. 2009 IEEE 12th International Conference on Computer Vision (Sep. 2009), 1034–1041.

21. Sugano, Y., Matsushita, Y. and Sato, Y. 2013. Appearance-based gaze estimation using visual saliency. IEEE transactions on pattern analysis and machine intelligence. 35, 2 (Feb. 2013), 329–41.

22. Sugano, Y., Matsushita, Y., Sato, Y. and Koike, H. 2008. An Incremental Learning Method for Unconstrained Gaze Estimation. 10th European Conference on Computer Vision, ECCV' 2008 (2008), 656–667.

23. Williams, O., Blake, A. and Cipolla, R. Sparse and Semi-supervised Visual Mapping with the S^3GP. 2006 IEEE Computer Society Conference on Computer Vision and Pattern Recognition - Volume 1 (CVPR'06) 230–237.

24. Wood, E. and Bulling, A. 2014. EyeTab. Proceedings of the Symposium on Eye Tracking Research and Applications - ETRA '14 (New York, New York, USA, 2014), 207–210.

25. Xiong, X. and De la Torre, F. 2013. Supervised Descent Method and Its Applications to Face Alignment. 2013 IEEE Conference on Computer Vision and Pattern Recognition (Jun. 2013), 532–539.

26. Zhang, Y. and Hornof, A.J. 2014. Easy post-hoc spatial recalibration of eye tracking data. Proceedings of the Symposium on Eye Tracking Research and Applications - ETRA '14 (2014), 95–98.

27. Zhang, Y. and Hornof, A.J. 2011. Mode-of-disparities error correction of eye-tracking data. Behavior research methods. 43, (2011), 834–842.

28. Zhu, Z., Ji, Q. and Bennett, K.P. 2006. Nonlinear Eye Gaze Mapping Function Estimation via Support Vector Regression. 18th International Conference on Pattern Recognition (ICPR'06) (2006), 1132–1135.

Can Eye Help You?: Effects of Visualizing Eye Fixations on Remote Collaboration Scenarios for Physical Tasks

Keita Higuch[1], **Ryo Yonetani**[1], and **Yoichi Sato**[1]

[1]The University of Tokyo

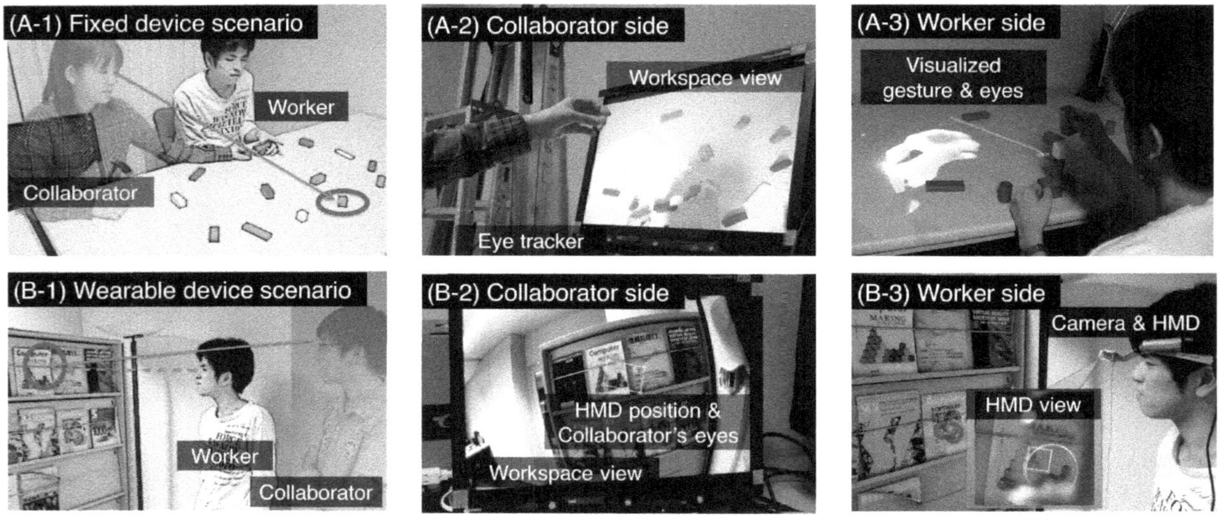

Figure 1: Conceptual figures and implementations of our remote collaboration framework under two different scenarios: (A-1) **fixed device** scenario offers remote collaboration experience for physical tasks on a small workspace. (A-2) a remote collaborator monitors a workspace through a fixed point-of-view camera and provides instructions to a worker using his/her eye fixations and hand gestures. (A-3) the system then visualizes a history of collaborator's point of gaze (green line) as well as hands directly in front of the worker. (B-1) **wearable device** scenario addresses remote collaboration in larger workspaces. (B-2) the system provides the view of a wearable camera worn by the worker. (B-3) the worker was allowed to see the relative direction and position of collaborator's eye fixations through an optical see-through head-mounted display.

ABSTRACT

In this work, we investigate how remote collaboration between a local worker and a remote collaborator will change if eye fixations of the collaborator are presented to the worker. We track the collaborator's points of gaze on a monitor screen displaying a physical workspace and visualize them onto the space by a projector or through an optical see-through head-mounted display. Through a series of user studies, we have found the followings: 1) Eye fixations can serve as a fast and precise pointer to objects of the collaborator's interest. 2) Eyes and other modalities, such as hand gestures and speech, are used differently for object identification and manipulation. 3) Eyes are used for explicit instructions only when they are combined with speech. 4) The worker can predict some intentions of the collaborator such as his/her current interest and next instruction.

CHI'16, May 07-12, 2016, San Jose, CA, USA

http://dx.doi.org/10.1145/2858036.2858438

Author Keywords

Remote Collaboration; Gaze

ACM Classification Keywords

H.5.3. Group and Organization Interfaces: Computer-supported cooperative work

INTRODUCTION

Remote collaboration is a form of interaction among two or more people at remote locations, who interact with each other to achieve a goal. Supporting remote collaboration by systems (*i.e.*, computer-supported cooperative work; CSCW) is a long-standing topic in HCI and is beneficial in various fields. For example, novice workers at a factory production line can gain the abilities of experienced people at another factory, making craftsmanship potentially ubiquitous. Remote collaboration at home enables people to take online classes while sharing their work in progress with a remote teacher. People may even casually consult on remote partners in their daily life as elders ask their children about the use of smartphones.

In particular, we are interested in a specific scenario where a worker involved in a physical task is supported by another remote collaborator who sees the worker's work in progress via video. One important technique in this scenario is the transmission of the collaborator's intentions and instructions to the worker such as what objects the collaborator is currently focusing on and how he/she wants the worker to manipulate these objects. Prior work does this by using different modalities including speech, annotations [10, 12, 17, 20, 36], and hand gestures [16, 30, 34] displayed to a physical work space to show the explicit instructions given by the collaborator.

In this study, we investigate how remote collaboration by a worker and a remote collaborator will change if the collaborator's eye fixations on a physical workspace are presented to the worker. We track the collaborator's points of gaze on a screen monitoring a workspace (Figure 1 (A-2), (B-2)) and project them on the space by a projector (A-3) or through an optical see-through head-mounted display (HMD) (B-3). Prior work has revealed the effectiveness of using eyes in both physical tasks [24, 32] and virtual tasks [41, 49]. We expect that people will also effectively use their eyes to accomplish a task in the context of remote collaboration. We will also see how the role of existing modalities, such as speech and hand gestures, will change when they are used in combination with eye fixations.

The proposed systems facilitate remote collaboration as follows: A physical workspace is first captured by a camera and transferred to a display screen monitored by a remote collaborator. The collaborator's points of gaze on the screen are then captured by an eye tracker and visualized directly onto the workspace. We design several ways of visualization to address two major scenarios of remote collaboration, which introduce 1) a pair of fixed point-of-view (POV) camera and a projector for monitoring relatively small workspaces, and 2) a wearable head-mounted camera and an optical see-through HMD to cope with larger workspaces.

The contribution of this work can be summarized by the following four main findings obtained from three user studies:

- Eye fixations visualized on a physical workspace serve as a fast and precise pointer, allowing collaborators to reduce the number of incorrect directions or to decrease the task completion time. This feature further leads to joint pointing to multiple objects in a static scene captured by a fixed POV camera or stable pointing in a dynamic scene with large motion caused by a moving wearable camera.

- We observe the different roles of eyes and other modalities. Instructions given by eye fixations are mainly used for identifying objects of the collaborator's interest. On the other hand, the collaborator uses hand gestures for describing object manipulation such as rotation and attachment.

- Eye fixations are used for providing explicit instructions only when these fixations are combined with speech. The worker can therefore distinguish such instructions easily even if the eye fixations are visualized throughout a task in a non-salient manner.

- Eye fixations indicate the collaborator's implicit intentions. In particular, the worker can predict what the collaborator is interested in and what his/her next instruction will be.

RELATED WORK

Remote Collaboration

Prior work on remote collaboration, as typified by [34], has sought a method to enhance the abilities of the worker with respect to physical tasks, *e.g.*, construction, navigation, and decision making, with support from the collaborator. Systems to support the remote collaboration are characterized by a camera device used for monitoring a physical workspace such as fixed POV camera systems [1, 2, 20, 30, 43, 50] and mobile camera systems [10, 12, 17, 26, 33, 36, 47]. In particular, Fussell *et al.* studied the effect of camera settings on a remote collaboration scenario [14, 15]; they observed that fixed POV cameras providing a static view of workspaces offered valuable visual information to a collaborator. Fussell also suggested that wearable cameras could be used to capture wider workspaces than the fixed cameras. These findings have inspired our use of the collaborator's eye fixations for providing instructions as eyes can be used for quickly scanning the workspaces.

Gaze-based Interfaces

After the pioneering work by Jacob on eye movement-based interaction techniques [22], eye movements have been adopted in a wide range of applications such as GUI manipulation [38, 25], daily life [8, 21], emergency guidance [40], and robot operation [35], as high-accuracy eye tracking has become available at a low cost. A considerable amount of recent work has focused on the enhancement of touch/gesture interaction with gaze information [42, 48, 51], demonstrating that users can use their eyes to quickly point at target objects and enhance the precision and speed of touch/gesture interactions. We expect that this ability of the eyes can also effectively work in object identification tasks in the context of remote collaboration.

Eye-tracking for collaborative tasks

Eye-tracking technologies have already been used in the field of CSCW, but in a different configuration. Dual eye-tracking (DUET) studies use an eye tracker for two workers to visualize their points of gaze on a shared screen [9, 11, 23, 39, 41, 44, 49]. Another method of using eye tracking is to present the eye movements of a worker involved in a physical task to a collaborator [31]; this has revealed a close relationship between the worker's gaze and the collaborator's verbal instructions. We will use the eye fixations of a remote collaborator for remote collaboration on physical tasks, standing for a complementary work to [31]. Our work also attempts to combine eye fixations and hand gestures used along with speech [34, 10, 16, 30].

PROPOSED REMOTE COLLABORATION FRAMEWORK

Assume that two persons at remote locations are trying to collaborate with each other to perform a physical task, including fine operations on physical objects such as cooperatively assembling implements at a factory production line or building a showcase of items at a store, *etc.*In this setting, we consider the following two roles to establish remote collaboration: 1) a *worker* who faces a workspace in physical spaces (*e.g.*, a workbench or an entire factory) to perform a task, and 2) a *collaborator* who monitors the workspace through a camera and instructs the worker.

The key question of this work is how the interactions between a collaborator and a worker working together will change if the collaborator's eye fixations on a monitor screen are physically presented onto the workspace. As the collaborator and the worker are physically separated, it is important through interaction to share objects of interest to manipulate them toward the goal of the task. Therefore, many user studies with a remote-collaboration setting have consisted of object identification (*e.g.*, [26, 31]) and manipulation (*e.g.*, [14, 34]).

In particular, we are interested in how systems can facilitate remote collaboration when remote collaborators wish to manifest their intentions or instructions, such as what objects they are currently focusing on and how they want a worker to manipulate these objects. In previous studies, remote collaborators did this explicitly using hand gestures [10, 26, 30, 34], annotations [12, 17, 20, 36], and so on. While these modalities are capable of describing detailed instructions, such as object manipulation or the overall context of a task, they have also been used only for identifying the objects of focus.

Our proposal to this end is to allow collaborators to use their eyes together with their hands and speech for describing their intentions and instructions. We hypothesize that if the eye fixations and the hand gestures of the collaborators are visualized in front of a worker, the collaborators will mainly use their eyes to identify the objects of interest, and use their hands and speech for describing other detailed instructions such as object manipulation. In fact, we see objects implicitly before manipulating them by hand [24], and such implicit gaze behavior alone is often critical for identifying which objects should be of the collaborator's interest [3, 7, 19]. To help workers infer the collaborator's intentions from such implicit behavior, we visualize eye fixations on the workspaces throughout the tasks, while keeping them less salient so as to not distract the workers.

Another advantage of using eye fixations is to enable fast pointing to objects, as we have already reviewed in the related work section. Even if the eye fixations are visualized in a less-salient way, they can be used for supporting the other modalities (*i.e.*, speech and hands) in the form of specifying the objects being referred to.

In the remainder, we will further discuss how eye fixations potentially work on more specific scenarios such as when using fixed POV cameras and wide field-of-view projectors, or when using wearable head-mounted cameras and relatively narrow field-of-view optical see-through displays. We will also present how to visualize eye fixations tailored to each of the scenarios.

Visualizing Eye Fixations with Fixed POV Devices

We first consider a specific scenario where a fixed POV camera and a projector are installed to deal with relatively small workspaces. In this scenario, a sequence of the remote collaborator's eye fixations can be visualized on the workspaces, enabling the collaborator to instruct a worker on more than a single object of current interest.

Some psychological studies have revealed that eye movements were indicative of their background factors such as critical points in the manipulation tasks [24], task-relevant locations in a scene [18, 52], next set of manipulations [6], types of tasks [5, 45, 52], and conversational cues [4, 28]. We can therefore expect that workers will be able to infer some of the intentions from the collaborator's eye movements. For example, eye fixations that traverse an entire workspace region implicitly indicate that the collaborator is not sure of which objects to process at that moment. In contrast, sequential fixations on several objects could allow workers to predict the next set of objects to focus on.

Another possible behavior enabled by a sequence of eye fixations is a joint reference of two or more objects. This behavior can help collaborators to describe the relationships between objects (*e.g.*, screws to attach and boards to be attached).

Visualizing Eye Fixations with Wearable Devices

When workspaces are larger than what a worker can see at once, we choose to use a pair of wearable head-mounted camera and an optical see-through HMD for the worker to interact with his/her collaborator. Unlike other camera devices, such as shoulder-mounted cameras [33] and portable computers [17], the head-mounted cameras allow the worker to use his/her hands for physical operations. The optical see-through HMD also has an advantage in physical tasks over display tools, such as immersive video see-through displays, particularly when the worker is involved in fine operations on physical objects.

As the field-of-view of HMDs is often considerably narrower than that of wearable head-mounted cameras, a collaborator's instructions on the object outside the display view cannot be directly transmitted to a worker. This constraint makes it difficult or the collaborator to use his/her hands for manifesting the instructions; when pointing out the objects of interest, the collaborator must change his/her hand poses frequently to describe the relative direction of the objects as the head-mounted cameras move according to head motions of the worker.

Therefore, we design an indicator for the direction and distance of an eye fixation from the current view of the worker as if the worker and the collaborator were focusing on the same objects, as depicted in Figure 1 (B-1). The collaborator can then specify the objects of interest just by seeing them, making it easier to give instructions by other modalities such as speech and hand gestures.

From the worker's perspective, the eye fixations of the collaborator are not always salient as the worker sometimes averts his/her eyes from the HMD. Fixations will explicitly work only when they are used for instructions in combination with the other modalities.

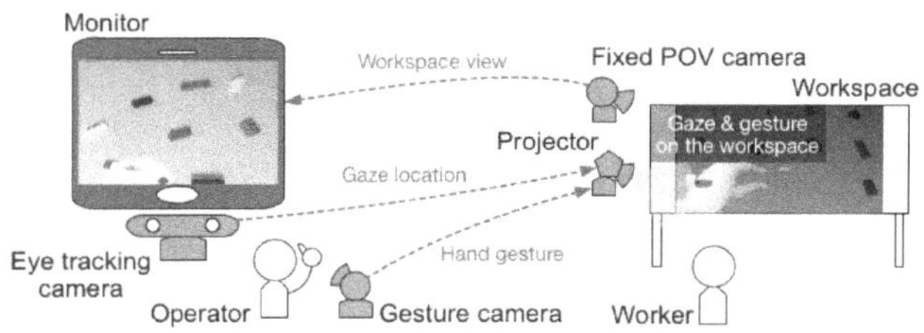

Figure 2: Overview of the system with fixed POV devices

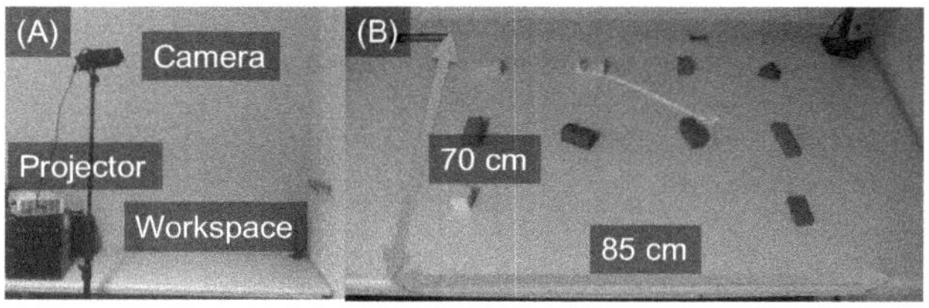

Figure 3: (A) Workspace captured by a fixed POV camera (B) Dimensions of the fixed device setting

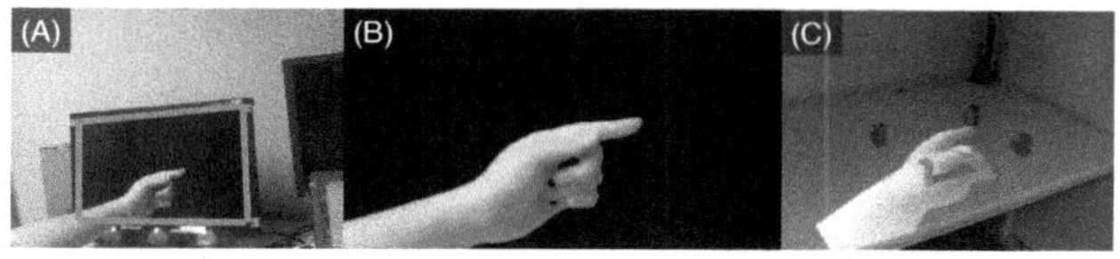

Figure 4: Visualizing Hand Gestures: (A) Video from web camera with a polarized filter (B) Cropped hand (C) Projected hand on the workspace

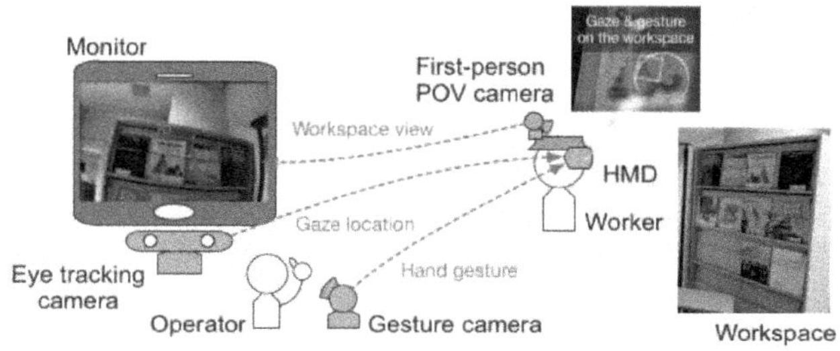

Figure 5: Overview of the system with wearable devices

IMPLEMENTATIONS

Implementation with Fixed POV Devices

We first introduce the implementation of our framework aimed for relatively small workspaces with a pair of a fixed POV camera and a projector (see Figure 2 for its overview).

Figure 3 shows the physical setup of the worker side; here, the system is based on a homographic projection mapping method. The dimensions of the setup are 85 (width) × 70 (depth) centimeter, but these dimensions can be extended by changing the projector and camera positions.

Projector-camera calibration

To map the collaborator's eye fixations on a display monitor onto the physical workspace of a worker, we computed the perspective projection between a projector and a camera by manually pointing where markers placed on the workspace appear in the view of the camera and the projector.

Visualizing eye fixations

The collaborator's eye and hand movements are captured using an off-the-shelf eye tracker (Tobii EyeX) and a webcam (Microsoft LifeCam), respectively. The eye tracker measures the collaborator's 2D eye position on the display at 30 fps. The current point of gaze is displayed as a green circle together with five preceding points of gaze shown with a polyline, which corresponds to approximately a 0.2-s history of eye movements (Figure 3 (B)).

Visualizing hand gestures

To visualize hand-based instructions, such as hand gestures, we referred to previous researches [13, 37]. Polarized light from an LCD monitor is blocked by a polarized filter attached to the camera, while an unpolarized light reflection from a hand is still visible. This makes it easy to find the hand regions irrespective of what is being displayed on the monitor (Figure 4). Then, the system visualizes the hand gestures onto the workspace.

Implementation with Wearable Devices

As shown in Figure 5, we adopt the same implementation for the collaborator's side for wearable-device scenarios tailored to larger workspaces. The main difference is that the worker wears a head-mounted camera (Panasonic A1H) and a light-weighted optical see-through HMD (Brother AirScouter WD-200S). The HMD is placed in front of the wearer's line-of-sight to achieve better task performance [53].

HMD-Camera Calibration

The system uses optical see-through HMD-based mobile augmented reality (AR) technologies that require a calibration process to map collaborator's eye fixations onto the HMD view from a worker. To do this, we followed [27] and asked an HMD wearer (worker) to align an AR marker at several locations specified in the HMD view by moving his/her head. We could then achieve the HMD-camera calibration by seeing the marker through the head-mounted camera.

Visualization in optical see-through displays

As the HMD has a considerably narrower field of view than the camera, the collaborator's eye position on the display showing the view from the wearable camera may be outside of the HMD's view. In such cases, the direction of and the distance to the collaborator's eye position is visualized on the HMD as shown in Figures 6 (A) and (B). The direction of eye positions from the center of the HMD's view is indicated by a circular edge, where the number of red edges increases as the eye positions get closer. When the collaborator sees inside the HMD's view, the eye positions are indicated by a green square (Figure 6 (C)). The worker is expected to see whether he/she and the collaborator can share the view or not.

The collaborator's hands are also shown on the HMD. The system crops hand images by using the same technology as the fixed device system (see Visualizing hand gestures). The system also directly visualizes the cropped hand images on the HMD (Figure 6 (D)).

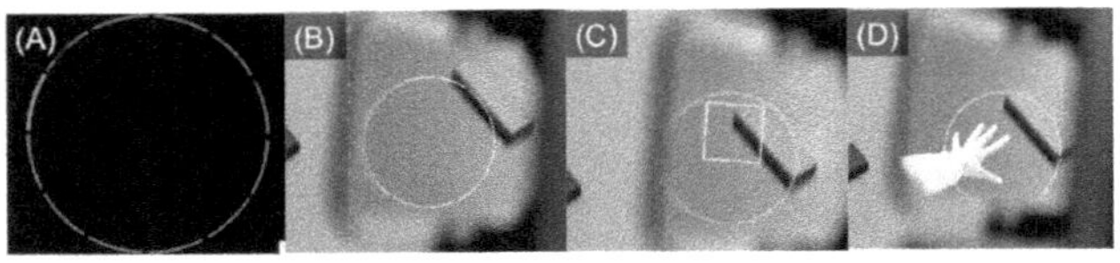

Figure 6: Visualizations through an optical see-through HMD: (A) and (B) circular-edge indicators to show the direction of the collaborator's points of gaze, (C) point of gaze inside the HMD view indicated by a green square, and (D) hand gestures

USER STUDY 1: ASSEMBLING TARGET OBJECTS UNDER FIXED DEVICE SCENARIO

In this section, we first report how eye fixations work on a fixed POV device scenario. Similar to [43, 46], participants were asked to perform remote collaboration to assemble a certain object (*e.g.*, a building) with the blocks scattered on a desk. We found the statistical evidence on fast pointing by eye fixations. We also obtained some feedback that implied the capability of eye fixations, enabling multiple pointing and conveying the collaborator's intentions.

Task and Procedure

In this user study, we compared the following two conditions to see how eye fixations were used for collaboration and how the use of the other modalities changed: a **Gesture** condition where a collaborator was allowed to use hand gestures and speech and a **Gesture + Eye** condition where eye fixations are also available for the collaborator. We recruited eight participants who were students or postdoctoral researchers at a graduate school of computer science; they belonged to the age group of 20 to 30 years and had limited experience on computer-supported remote collaboration.

Four pairs of participants were asked to complete an assembly task by using the following steps. First, one of the participants in each pair assigned the role of a remote collaborator saw the as-built drawings of a target object. Then, the collaborator instructed the other participant (*i.e.*, a worker) on how to assemble the target object by using blocks. Each participant took turns playing the collaborator and the worker for each condition, and the order of conditions was randomized to maintain the counterbalance (*i.e.*, each pair conducted four sessions in total). For each session, the participants were given an additional 5 min in advance for practice with an instruction to use our remote collaboration system by an experimenter. In the

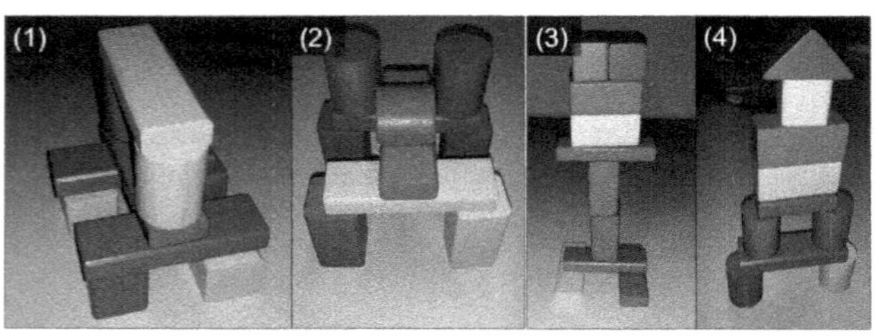

Figure 7: Four target objects used in User Study 1

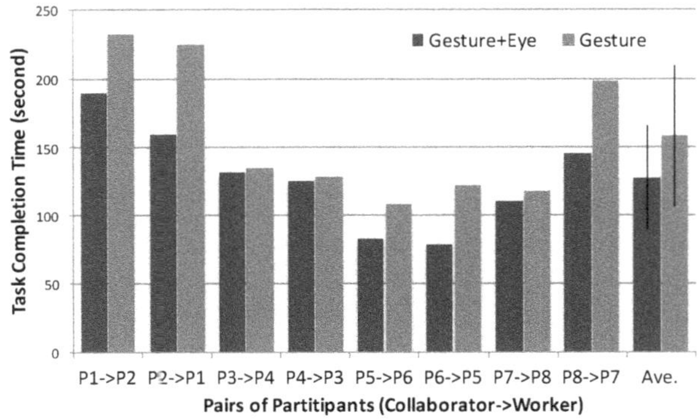

Figure 8: Task completion times in User Study 1. Bars show standard deviation.

case of the **Gesture + Eye** condition, we calibrated the eye tracker before each session.

The target objects were randomly chosen from the four depicted in Figure 7. They all consisted of 10 blocks from 25 candidate blocks with a variety of shapes and colors. The as-built drawings of the target objects were the photographs of these same objects taken from three different points of view so that the collaborators could easily figure out the component blocks.

Evaluations

The time taken to complete a task was measured for each session to observe the statistical difference between the conditions. We hypothesized that the task completion time would decrease in the **Gesture + Eye** condition than in the **Gesture** condition owing to the fast pointing by eye fixations. We validated this hypothesis by using a paired t-test as standardized test statistic.

After each session, the participants answered the list of questions presented in Figure 9 with a seven-point scale (disagree = 1, agree = 7). We also investigated using the Wilcoxon matched-pair signed-rank test as a non-parametric statistical hypothesis test whether there were significant differences in the participants' experience. Finally, we interviewed the participants regarding their experience with our remote collaboration system at the end of the experiment.

Results

Figure 8 shows the task completion time for each session. We confirmed the statistical significance in the task completion time ($p = 0.01$), indicating that the eye fixations were certainly used as a fast pointer. This finding was also supported by the statistical significance obtained in the case of the questionnaire shown in Figure 9 ($p \leq 0.05$). We also confirmed that the participants successfully shared the instructions and intentions, on the basis of the responses to questions.

Observation and Feedback

Under the **Gesture + Eye** condition, most participants serving as a collaborator used eye fixations together with speech to instruct a worker regarding a block position. They quickly

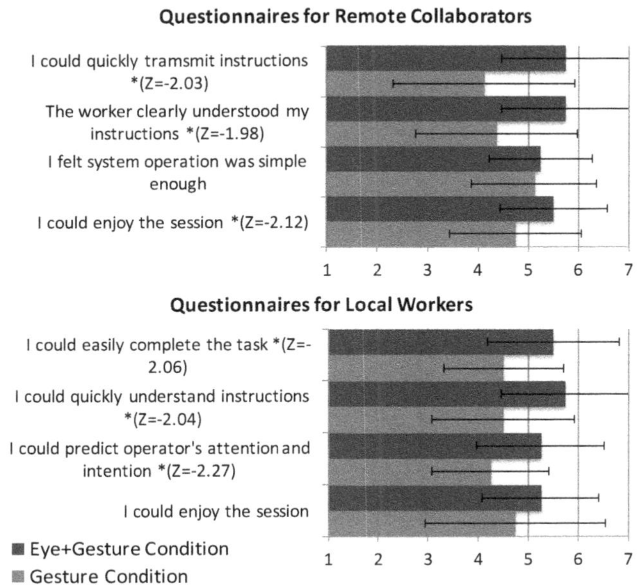

Figure 9: Questionnaires in User Study 1: Pairwise Wilcoxon signed-rank tests. "*" indicates the significance. Bars show standard deviation.

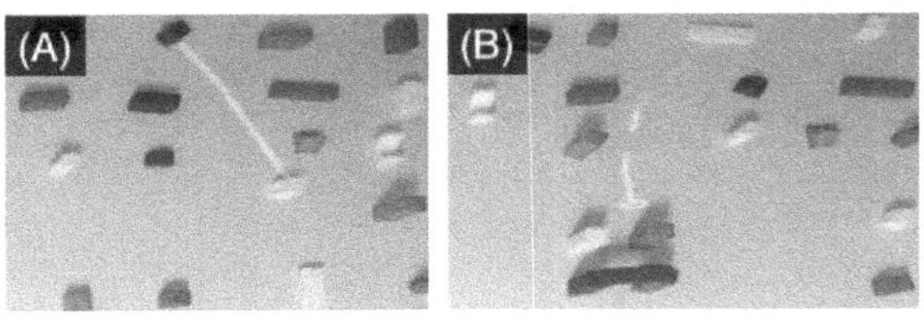

Figure 10: Multiple pointing in User Study 1 (A) Two blocks (B) Block and its destination

looked at a target block and gave simple instructions: *"I felt the worker knew my gaze position, so I just said* ***take this*** *to identify an object* [1]*."*

We also observed a particular role of hand gestures. The collaborators mainly used hand gestures to provide detailed instructions of a manipulation of blocks such as rotations and attachments: *"pointing by eye fixation is very easy and fast, but it can only describe locational information. So, I used gestures for describing the posture of blocks."*

Further, we sometimes observed multiple pointing by using eye fixations; the collaborators looked at several positions at a time. *"I could easily point out two blocks with my eyes"* and *"I pointed the block and destination positions together."* Multiple pointing is a characteristic capability of visualizing eye fixations in a fixed device setting that might support fast instructions for shorter task completion times (Figure 10).

The workers almost correctly understood the collaborator's instructions in the **Gesture + Eye** condition: *"I understood the blocks looked at by the collaborator. I just took these blocks in time with the collaborator's speech."*

The workers could also distinguish the collaborator's instructions from other eye movements: *"I followed the collaborator when he/she spoke some instructions,"* and *"I was able to predict the next instruction from a history of collaborator's eye positions."*

We received negative feedback mostly on projection problems because of the incorrect projection size and the 2D projection: *"The size of the collaborator's hands was unnatural to me; it was too large."* In addition, blocks rarely occluded instructions provided by visualized eyes from the workers: *"Sometimes, I lost the collaborator's eyes by occlusion"* and *"When the worker lost my eyes, I needed to keep looking at the target block to describe its position."*

USER STUDY 2: OBJECT IDENTIFICATION UNDER WEARABLE DEVICE SCENARIO

Next, we evaluated our remote collaboration system in a wearable device setting. We aimed to see how fast and precisely the collaborators could use gaze to specify the target objects captured with a head-mounted camera of a worker. We designed a simple task since it was unclear whether people could point objects reliably when the view of a camera changed dynamically with a worker's movement.

Task and Procedure

Two conditions were compared in this experiment, where a collaborator could use eye fixations (**Eye** condition) or hand gestures (**Gesture** condition). The eight participants had the same background as those in User Study 1. This time, the participants all played the role of the collaborator, while one experimenter served as a worker.

We performed the following simplified task where only a collaborator pointed to objects. As shown in Figure 11 (A), the worker was asked to stand in front of the 18 blocks placed on a desk. When a session began, the image shown in Figure 11 (B), which indicated one of the 18 blocks, was first presented to a collaborator. The collaborator then navigated the worker to the indicated block, by seeing it or describing its location by hand. The worker moved his/her head to place an object inside the view of an HMD and confirmed whether it was the correct target. This pair of navigation and confirmation was repeated until the collaborator reached the correct target. The collaborators were allowed to say "yes" or "no" to tell whether the worker correctly found the target. The number of mistakes were measured by counting the number of "no" responses in nine sessions. Please note that multiple mistakes could occur in a single session.

For each participant, we conducted the aforementioned procedure nine times for each condition preceded by three additional trials for practice. We calibrated an eye tracker once before the **Eye** condition. The order of conditions was randomized to maintain the counterbalance. We also performed experimental sessions to use wearable devices for the experimenter in advance in order to reduce the learning effects.

[1]In this paper, italic fonts in double quotations denote translated speech from Japanese.

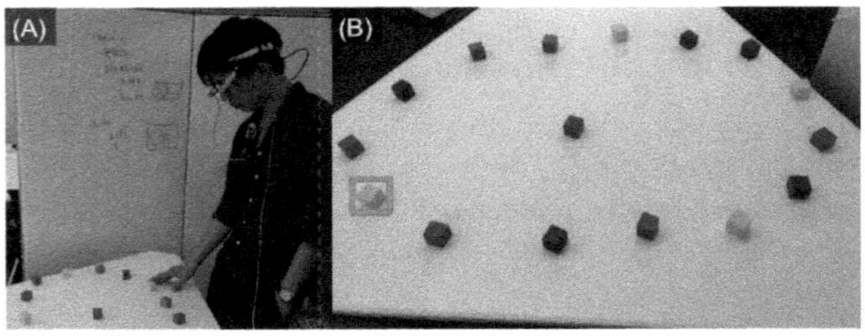

Figure 11: (A) Experimental setting for User Study 2 (B) example of a target block picture presented to participants

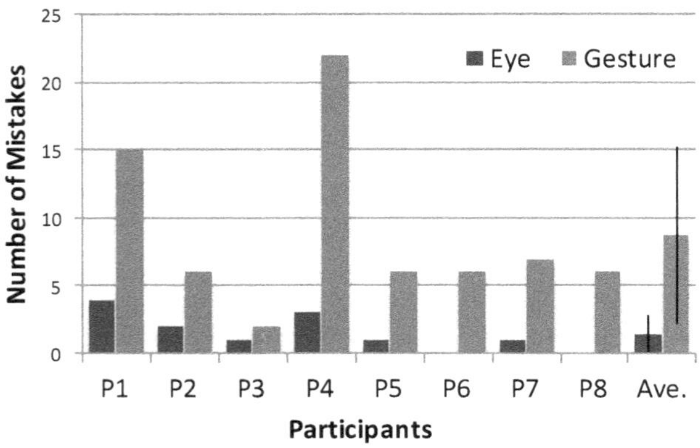

Figure 12: The number of mistakes in User Study 2. Bars show standard deviation.

Evaluations and Results

As an evaluation measure, we counted the number of times where the worker failed to specify the object navigated by a collaborator, accumulated over nine trials. We also measured the total task completion time in the nine sessions. We expected the number of mistakes and the total time to decrease in the **Eye** condition and tested them by the paired t-test.

Figure 12 shows the total number of mistakes for each participant. Overall, all the participants precisely specified the target objects with eye fixations, which was supported by the paired t-test at $p = 0.01$.

Figure 13 also shows the total task completion times for each participant. Some participants quickly specified the target objects with eye fixations, which was supported by the paired t-test at $p = 0.05$.

USER STUDY 3: ARRANGING SHOWCASES OF BROCHURES UNDER WEARABLE DEVICE SCENARIO

We further evaluated our system with wearable devices qualitatively to see how eye fixations affected the remote collaboration experience in a practical task. We again recruited eight participants who had the same background as those in User Studies 1 and 2. Four pairs of participants were asked to arrange a showcase of brochures for travel fairs, as shown in Figure 15, and to answer the interview questions on their experience of the task.

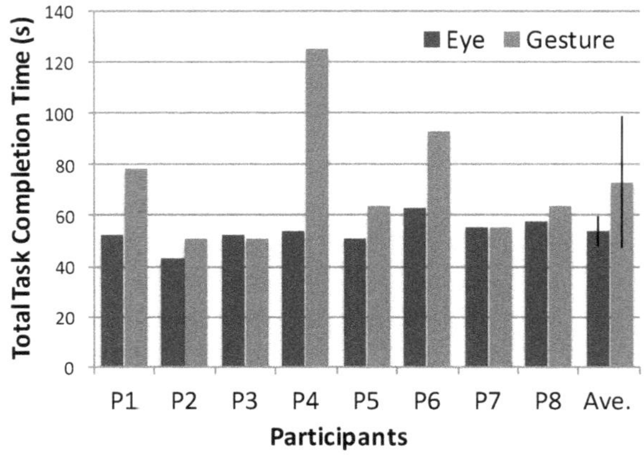

Figure 13: The task completion times in User Study 2. Bars show standard deviation.

Task and Procedure

This experiment was conducted with a larger workspace than that in the previous two user studies. As illustrated in Figure 14, the workspace consisted of a working desk, a shelf, and a whiteboard that could not all be captured at once by a wearable camera without moving the worker's head. A set of brochures was placed on the working desk. Various decorations and tools were stored on the shelf. The worker was able to attach them on the whiteboard to arrange a showcase.

The task proceeded as follows: First, we explained the use of our system and the goal of the task to a pair of participants. They then decided their role (the worker or the collaborator). We performed HMD-camera calibration for the worker and eye tracker calibration for the collaborator. During a session, the participants first checked all the travel brochures and discussed the concept of the showcase (*e.g.*, trip to Europe). Once the concept was fixed, they started to decorate the whiteboard by using brochures and tools on the showcase space. The task continued until participants were satisfied.

Interviews

At the end of the task, we interviewed the participants for 10 min. Our interviews were semi-structured to focus on the experience as a worker and a collaborator. First, we asked to the collaborator, "*Did you use your eyes for providing instructions, and if so, when?*" Next, we asked to the worker, "*Did you understand the collaborator's eye positions?*"and "*How did you find the visualization on the HMD?*" We then reviewed their showcase together and asked the participants to comment on their experience freely.

Observation and Feedback

All the pairs of participants were able to successfully realize their concept of travel fairs and satisfactorily arrange their showcases, as shown in Figure 15. The task completion times were between 22 min and 51 min. They enjoyed the remote collaboration experience: "*I really enjoyed this collaboration. I was able to realize our concept with my partner*" and "*We were satisfied with this showcase.*"

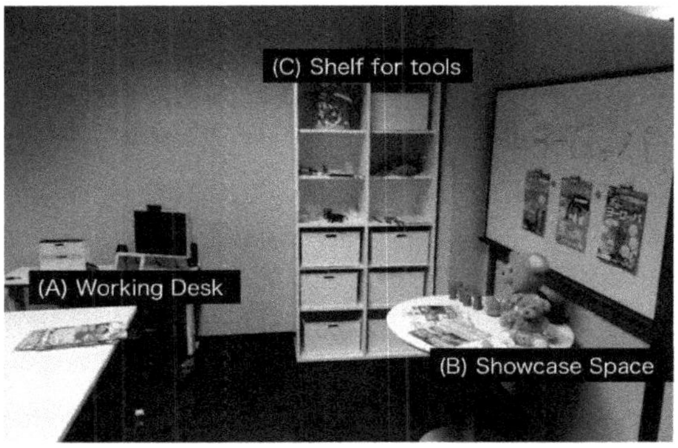

Figure 14: Experimental setting of User Study 3

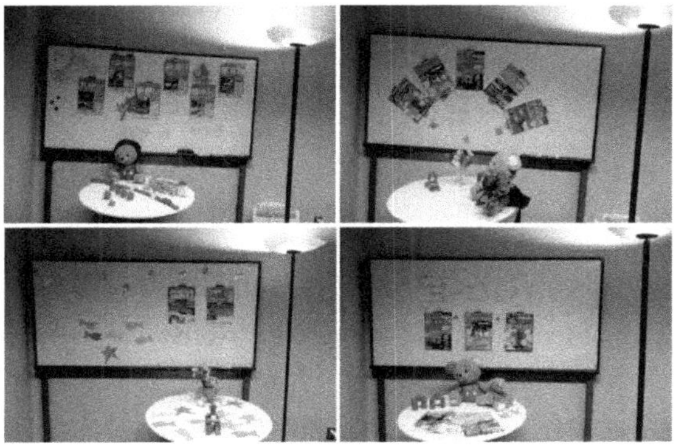

Figure 15: Results of User Study 3: each picture shows a result of the showcase arranged by each pair.

The collaborator used eye fixations for pointing objects and some locations in the workspaces to facilitate joint attention with the worker (Figure 16). The worker could specify the objects mentioned by the collaborator before manipulating the objects: *"I felt the instructions provided by my eyes simple"* and *"I could look at the objects looked at by the collaborator."* In all the pairs, instructions with eye fixations were provided frequently when a worker moved around and the workspace visible to a collaborator completely changed. The collaborators were able to track the target objects/locations by their eyes under dynamic scenes.

Similar to the fixed device scenario evaluated in User Study 1, we found that the workers were able to distinguish explicit instructions from eye fixations continuously presented through an optical see-through HMD as such instructions were always accompanied with speech: *"I checked the HMD to receive instructions when my partner used speech."*

The visualization of eye fixations sometimes indicated the collaborator's interests: *"Sometimes, I saw the HMD to check the collaborator's interests"* and *"I could figure out where my partner was interested in."*

Hand gestures were used for describing various object manipulations such as attaching brochures on a whiteboard, moving a toy, and cutting paper decorations. The workers felt that the hand gestures were more noticeable than eye fixations: *"I like seeing hand gestures. They are more attractive"* and *"I felt the eye movements non-salient compared to gestures."*

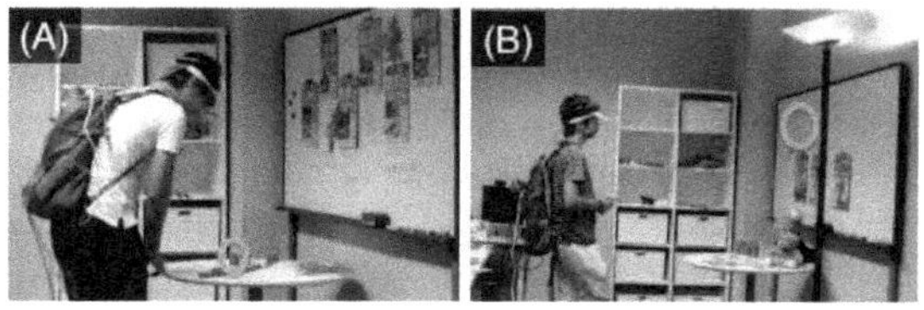

Figure 16: Pointing instructions with eye fixations in User Study 3: (A) Object (B) Location. Blue circles show collaborator's eye positions.

The participants who played the role of workers mostly liked our system setup and visualization: *"This setup is simple. I didn't feel a fatigue in this experiment."* We also received negative feedback from a few participants about the HMD-camera calibration process. The process needed trial and error for precise calibration that took up to 10 min: *"The calibration process was difficult for me; I wish it were easier."* On the other hand, the other participants were able to perform this calibration process quickly.

DISCUSSION

In this section, we discuss how remote collaborator's eye fixations visualized on a workspace can work for remote collaboration. Overall, we confirmed the effectiveness of visualizing eye fixations both in the user studies with fixed POV and wearable devices. In particular, we found the following features of the fixations in remote collaboration.

Finding 1: fast and precise pointing by fixations

Eye fixations visualized by both a projector (User Study 1) and a HMD (User Studies 2 and 3) show a fast and precise pointing capability over hand gestures. This feature of fast pointing further enables joint pointing to multiple objects at a time when the history of fixations is visualized in the fixed device scenario. Precise pointing effectively works in the wearable device scenario where workspaces monitored through a wearable camera often change dynamically.

Finding 2: different roles in fixations and hand gestures

Collaborators used their eyes and hands in different ways to instruct workers. Eye fixations were used mainly for identifying the objects of interest, while hand gestures were used for providing instructions regarding the manipulation of the identified objects. In User Studies 1 and 3, remote collaborators described the object locations by gaze, often followed by their hand gestures, to describe how they wanted the worker to manipulate the object of focus.

Finding 3: explicit instructions enabled by the combination of fixations and speeches

In User Studies 1 and 3, eye fixations were used for providing explicit instructions (*e.g.*, object identification) only when they were combined with speech. This feature allowed workers to easily distinguish instructions from the other unmeaningful eye movements even if the points of gaze were visualized throughout a task, in a non-salient manner. This feature was related to the finding in [31] that the collaborator's verbal instructions affected the worker's attention.

Finding 4: indicating collaborator's implicit intentions

Continuous visualization of the collaborator's points of gaze was also indicative of the implicit intentions of the collaborator such as his/her interest and future instructions. Indeed, some participants in User Study 1 reported that the history of points of gaze could be used for predicting the current state of the collaborator such as comparing multiple objects in the workspace and trying to provide the next instruction. In addition, the worker was able to see whether his/her interest aligned with that of a collaborator in User Study 3.

LIMITATION

In User Study 1, we observed the problems of projection mapping related to the size of the projected hands and the occlusions by blocks, because the fixed device system used a 2D projection mapping method (*i.e.*, homographic projection mapping). We believe that 3D projection mapping technologies will be able to address these problems.

The result of User Study 2 revealed fast and precise pointing of visualizing eye fixations in a wearable device setting. However, User Study 2 did not clarify the effectiveness of the collaborator's eye fixations from a worker's perspective, because the participants played only the role of the collaborator. Even so, the participants of User Study 3 used eye fixations for object and position identification in a practical task. We believe that this observation can support Finding 1. Additional studies will help to generalize the effectiveness of the proposed framework under different conditions (e.g., different person and target sizes).

CONCLUSIONS AND FUTURE WORK

In this study, we investigated how remote collaboration between a local worker and a remote collaborator changed if the eye fixations of the collaborator were presented to the worker. Through a series of user studies, we found some typical ways of using eyes for remote collaboration and how they effectively worked to accomplish physical tasks. Our findings can be enabled just by adding an off-the-shelf eye tracker on the collaborator's side. It covers not only the remote collaboration in small workspaces enabled by a pair of a fixed POV camera and a projector but also that for larger workspaces that require wearable devices.

Extending the visualization of eye fixations to the collaborator's side like [31] leads to a novel dual eye-tracking study. One promising direction is to install a pair of wearable head-mounted eye tracker and an HMD on both the people in the remote collaboration for two individual physical tasks. While this setting has the potential of enhancing their non-verbal interaction, it also raises a new question: How will people distribute their attention to their own workspace and that of their partner's visualized through the HMD.

Another direction is to apply our framework to considerably larger workspaces, such as an entire building or a city, where more than two workers will move around to perform a physical task. This application involves several important topics in CSCW, such as efficient monitoring and provision of instructions to multiple workers, long-term assistance with remote collaboration, and heterogeneous monitoring of workspaces by using smartphones [17, 29] as well as fixed POV and wearable cameras.

ACKNOWLEDGMENTS

This research was supported by CREST, JST. We thank Kei Nitta and Kana Misawa for their support.

REFERENCES

1. Matt Adcock, Stuart Anderson, and Bruce Thomas. RemoteFusion: Real Time Depth Camera Fusion for Remote Collaboration on Physical Tasks *(VRCAI '13)*.
2. Matt Adcock, Dulitha Ranatunga, Ross Smith, and Bruce H. Thomas. Object-based Touch Manipulation for Remote Guidance of Physical Tasks *(SUI '14)*.
3. Antti Ajanki, DavidR. Hardoon, Samuel Kaski, Kai Puolamk, and John Shawe-Taylor. 2009. Can eyes reveal interest? Implicit queries from gaze patterns. *User Modeling and User-Adapted Interaction* (2009).
4. Michael Argyle, Roger Ingham, Florisse Alkema, and Margaret McCallin. 1973. The Different Functions of Gaze. *Semiotica* 7 (1973).
5. Roman Bednarik, Shahram Eivazi, and Hana Vrzakova. 2013. A Computational Approach for Prediction of Problem-Solving Behavior Using Support Vector Machines and Eye-Tracking Data. In *Eye Gaze in Intelligent User Interfaces*. 111–134.
6. Roman Bednarik, Hana Vrzakova, and Michal Hradis. 2012. What Do You Want to Do Next: A Novel Approach for Intent Prediction in Gaze-based Interaction *(ETRA '12)*.
7. Boris Brandherm, Helmut Prendinger, and Mitsuru Ishizuka. 2007. Interest Estimation Based on Dynamic Bayesian Networks for Visual Attentive Presentation Agents *(ICMI '07)*.
8. Andreas Bulling, Daniel Roggen, and Gerhard Tröster. It's in Your Eyes: Towards Context-awareness and Mobile HCI Using Wearable EOG Goggles *(UbiComp '08)*.
9. Jean Carletta, Robin L Hill, Craig Nicol, Tim Taylor, Jan Peter De Ruiter, and Ellen Gurman Bard. 2010. Eyetracking for Two-Person Tasks with Manipulation of a Virtual World. *Behavior Research Methods* 42, 1 (2010).
10. Sicheng Chen, Miao Chen, Andreas Kunz, Asim Evren Yantaç, Mathias Bergmark, Anders Sundin, and Morten Fjeld. SEMarbeta: Mobile Sketch-gesture-video Remote Support for Car Drivers *(AH '13)*.

11. Mauro Cherubini, Marc-Antoine Nüssli, and Pierre Dillenbourg. Deixis and Gaze in Collaborative Work at a Distance (over a Shared Map): A Computational Model to Detect Misunderstandings *(ETRA '08).*

12. Andrew J. Davison, Walterio W. Mayol, and David W. Murray. 2003. Real-Time Localisation and Mapping with Wearable Active Vision. In *Proceedings of the 2Nd IEEE/ACM International Symposium on Mixed and Augmented Reality (ISMAR '03).* 18–.

13. Kentaro Fukuchi, Toshiki Sato, Haruko Mamiya, and Hideki Koike. 2010. Pac-pac: Pinching Gesture Recognition for Tabletop Entertainment System *(AVI '08).* ACM, 267–273.

14. Susan R. Fussell, Leslie D. Setlock, and Robert E. Kraut. Effects of Head-mounted and Scene-oriented Video Systems on Remote Collaboration on Physical Tasks *(CHI '03).*

15. Susan R. Fussell, Leslie D. Setlock, and Elizabeth M. Parker. Where Do Helpers Look?: Gaze Targets During Collaborative Physical Tasks *(CHI EA '03).*

16. Susan R. Fussell, Leslie D. Setlock, Jie Yang, Jiazhi Ou, Elizabeth Mauer, and Adam D. I. Kramer. 2004. Gestures over Video Streams to Support Remote Collaboration on Physical Tasks. *Human–Computer Interaction* (2004).

17. Steffen Gauglitz, Benjamin Nuernberger, Matthew Turk, and Tobias Höllerer. World-stabilized Annotations and Virtual Scene Navigation for Remote Collaboration *(UIST '14).*

18. Mary Hayhoe and Dana Ballard. 2005. Eye Movements in Natural Behavior. *Trends Cogn. Sci. (Regul. Ed.)* 9, 4 (2005), 188–194.

19. Takatsugu Hirayama, Dodane Jean-Baptiste, Hiroaki Kawashima, and Takashi Matsuyama. 2010. Estimates of User Interest Using Timing Structures between Proactive Content-Display Updates and Eye Movements. *IEICE Trans. Inf. & Syst.* 93, 6 (2010).

20. Shinsaku Hiura, Kenji Tojo, and Seiji Inokuchi. 3DD Tele-direction Interface Using Video Projector.

21. Yoshio Ishiguro, Adiyan Mujibiya, Takashi Miyaki, and Jun Rekimoto. Aided Eyes: Eye Activity Sensing for Daily Life *(AH '10).*

22. Robert J. K. Jacob. 1990. What You Look at is What You Get: Eye Movement-based Interaction Techniques *(CHI '90).*

23. Patrick Jermann, Darren Gergle, Roman Bednarik, and Susan Brennan. Duet 2012: Dual Eye Tracking in CSCW. In *Proceedings of the ACM 2012 conference on Computer Supported Cooperative Work Companion.* 23–24.

24. Roland S. Johansson, Gran Westling, Anders Bckstrm, and J. Randall Flanagan. 2001. Eye-Hand Coordination in Object Manipulation. *JOURNAL OF NEUROSCIENCE* 21, 17 (2001), 6917–6932.

25. Yvonne Kammerer, Katharina Scheiter, and Wolfgang Beinhauer. Looking My Way Through the Menu: The Impact of Menu Design and Multimodal Input on Gaze-based Menu Selection *(ETRA '08)*

26. Shunichi Kasahara and Jun Rekimoto. JackIn: Integrating First-person View with Out-of-body Vision Generation for Human-human Augmentation *(AH '14).*

27. Hirokazu Kato and Mark Billinghurst. Marker Tracking and Hmd Calibration for a Video-based Augmented Reality Conferencing System *(IWAR '99).*

28. Adam Kendon. 1967. Some Functions of Gaze-Direction in Social Interaction. *Acta Psychologica* 26 (1967).

29. Seungwon Kim, Gun Lee, Nobuyasu Sakata, and Mark Billinghurst. Improving Co-presence with Augmented Visual Communication Cues for Sharing Experience through Video Conference *(ISMAR'14).*

30. David Kirk and Danae Stanton Fraser. Comparing Remote Gesture Technologies for Supporting Collaborative Physical Tasks *(CHI '06).*

31. Nikolina Koleva, Sabrina Hoppe, Mohammed Mehdi Moniri, Maria Staudte, and Andreas Bulling. On the Interplay between Spontaneous Spoken Instructions and Human Visual Behaviour in an Indoor Guidance Task *(COGSCI '15).*

32. Robert E. Kraut, Susan R. Fussell, and Jane Siegel. 2003. Visual Information As a Conversational Resource in Collaborative Physical Tasks. *Human–Computter Interaction* 18, 1 (2003).

33. Takeshi Kurata, Nobuchika Sakata, Masakatsu Kourogi, Hideaki Kuzuoka, and Mark Billinghurst. Remote Collaboration using a Shoulder-worn Active Camera/Laser *(ISWC '04).*

34. Hideaki Kuzuoka. Spatial Workspace Collaboration: A SharedView Video Support System for Remote Collaboration Capability *(CHI '92).*

35. Hemin Omer Latif, Nasser Sherkat, and Ahmad Lotfi. Teleoperation Through Eye Gaze (TeleGaze): A Multimodal Approach *(ROBIO'09).*

36. Taehee Lee and Tobias Hollerer. Viewpoint Stabilization for Live Collaborative Video Augmentations *(ISMAR '06).*

37. Kana Misawa and Jun Rekimoto. Wearing Another's Personality: A Human-surrogate System with a Telepresence Face *(ISWC '15).*

38. A. Monden, K. Matsumoto, and M. Yamato. 2005. Evaluation of Gaze-Added Target Selection Methods Suitable for General GUIs. *Int. J. Comput. Appl. Technol.* 24, 1 (2005).

39. Romy Müller, Jens R Helmert, Sebastian Pannasch, and Boris M Velichkovsky. 2013. Gaze Transfer in Remote Cooperation: Is it always Helpful to See What Your Partner Is Attending to? *The Quarterly Journal of Experimental Psychology* 66, 7 (2013), 1302–1316.

40. Hideyuki Nakanishi, Satoshi Koizumi, Toru Ishida, and Hideaki Ito. Transcendent Communication: Location-based Guidance for Large-scale Public Spaces *(CHI '04)*.
41. Jiazhi Ou, Lui Min Oh, Jie Yang, and Susan R. Fussell. Effects of Task Properties, Partner Actions, and Message Content on Eye Gaze Patterns in a Collaborative Task *(CHI '05)*.
42. Ken Pfeuffer, Jason Alexander, Ming Ki Chong, and Hans Gellersen. Gaze-touch: Combining Gaze with Multi-touch for Interaction on the Same Surface *(UIST '14)*.
43. Abhishek Ranjan, Jeremy P. Birnholtz, and Ravin Balakrishnan. Dynamic Shared Visual Spaces: Experimenting with Automatic Camera Control in a Remote Repair Task *(CHI '07)*.
44. Kshitij Sharma, Patrick Jermann, Marc-Antoine Nüssli, and Pierre Dillenbourg. Gaze evidence for different activities in program understanding.
45. Jaana Simola, Jarkko Saloj"arvi, and Ilpo Kojo. 2008. Using Hidden Markov Model to Uncover Processing States from Eye Movements in Information Search Tasks. *Cognitive Systems Research* 9, 4 (2008), 237–251.
46. Rajinder S. Sodhi, Brett R. Jones, David Forsyth, Brian P. Bailey, and Giuliano Maciocci. BeThere: 3D Mobile Collaboration with Spatial Input *(CHI '13)*.
47. Aaron Stafford, Wayne Piekarski, and Bruce Thomas. Implementation of God-like Interaction Techniques for Supporting Collaboration Between Outdoor AR and Indoor Tabletop Users *(ISMAR '06)*.
48. Sophie Stellmach and Raimund Dachselt. Look & Touch: Gaze-supported Target Acquisition *(CHI '12)*.
49. Cara A. Stitzlein, Jane Li, and Alex Krumm-Heller. Gaze Analysis in a Remote Collaborative Setting *(OZCHI '06)*.
50. Chiew Seng Sean Tan, Johannes Schöning, Kris Luyten, and Karin Coninx. Investigating the Effects of Using Biofeedback As Visual Stress Indicator During Video-mediated Collaboration *(CHI '14)*.
51. Jayson Turner, Jason Alexander, Andreas Bulling, and Hans Gellersen. Gaze+RST: Integrating Gaze and Multitouch for Remote Rotate-Scale-Translate Tasks *(CHI '15)*.
52. Alfred Yarbus. 1967. Eye Movements and Vision. *Plenum* (1967).
53. Xianjun Sam Zheng, Cedric Foucault, Patrik Matos da Silva, Siddharth Dasari, Tao Yang, and Stuart Goose. Eye-Wearable Technology for Machine Maintenance: Effects of Display Position and Hands-free Operation *(CHI '15)*.

Gaze-Contingent Manipulation of Color Perception

Michael Mauderer
University of St Andrews, UK
mm285@st-andrews.ac.uk

David R. Flatla
University of Dundee, UK
d.flatla@dundee.ac.uk

Miguel A. Nacenta
University of St Andrews, UK
mans@st-andrews.ac.uk

ABSTRACT
Using real time eye tracking, gaze-contingent displays can modify their content to represent depth (e.g., through additional depth cues) or to increase rendering performance (e.g., by omitting peripheral detail). However, there has been no research to date exploring how gaze-contingent displays can be leveraged for manipulating perceived color. To address this, we conducted two experiments (color matching and sorting) that manipulated peripheral background and object colors to influence the user's color perception. Findings from our color matching experiment suggest that we can use gaze-contingent simultaneous contrast to affect color appearance and that existing color appearance models might not fully predict perceived colors with gaze-contingent presentation. Through our color sorting experiment we demonstrate how gaze-contingent adjustments can be used to enhance color discrimination. Gaze-contingent color holds the promise of expanding the perceived color gamut of existing display technology and enabling people to discriminate color with greater precision.

Author Keywords
Eye tracking; gaze-contingent displays; color perception; simultaneous contrast; local contrast enhancement

ACM Classification Keywords
H.1.2 Models and Principles: User/machine Systems; I.3.3 Computer Graphics: Picture/Image Generation

INTRODUCTION
Inexpensive and easy-to-use eye tracking (e.g., Eye Tribe[1], Gazepoint[2]) is entering the mass market for gaming hardware through dedicated products, such as the Sentry Eye Tracker [37], and has long been used in marketing and user experience research [40]. Building on stand-alone eye tracking, gaze-contingent rendering and gaze-contingent multi-resolution displays are appearing in the wild [8] and in applications that aim to enhance immersion and realism [9].

Other facets of gaze-contingent displays (GCDs) have received less attention; in particular, gaze-contingent color manipulation has yet to be adequately explored. GCD-based luminance manipulation has been developed for displaying High Dynamic Range (HDR) images [32]; however, there is no quantitative evidence of its benefits yet and GCDs have yet to be extended to properties of color beyond luminance. We propose that gaze-contingent color manipulation can be used beyond gaze-based luminance adjustments to virtually enhance the entire gamut of a display in both luminance and chromaticity.

Gaze-contingent (GC) color manipulation could allow us to virtually expand the perceivable color gamut of a display (e.g., allowing more vivid colors in photographs) and increase user color discrimination abilities (e.g., improved color differentiability in information visualization tasks that involve color).

To explore GC color manipulation, we conducted two experiments to provide insights into how GCDs can influence color appearance. Both experiments used gaze-contingency to manipulate simultaneous contrast (SC), which is the phenomenon in which the color of an object's surroundings influences our perception of the object's color (see Figure 1).

In our first experiment, participants manipulated the color of a target patch to match a reference patch in both static and gaze-contingent conditions. We found that gaze-contingent color presentation preserved the SC effect in general but also found minor differences in the magnitude of the SC effect between the static and gaze-contingent conditions.

In our second experiment, participants sorted colored patches into a gradient using both static and gaze-contingent presentation techniques. We found that gaze-contingent techniques allowed participants to sort colors with fewer errors than in the naive static condition, although not directly through SC background manipulation.

This paper makes three contributions. First, we provide the first quantitative analysis of the effects of gaze-contingent color manipulation. Second, we provide data that supports the feasibility of techniques that (a) use simultaneous contrast to extend the apparent display gamut and (b) manipulate peripheral patches to improve color differentiation. Finally, we provide general insights into how color changes in the visual periphery can influence the perception of color on a GCD, which has implications for the use of GCDs in general and color manipulations specifically.

BACKGROUND
This section provides basic information on color perception, simultaneous contrast, and the CIE L*a*b* color space.

Color Perception
Color perception is a process in which the visual system interprets light-wave stimulation in the eye to differentiate

[1] `https://theeyetribe.com/`, retrieved September 25, 2015
[2] `http://www.gazept.com/`, retrieved September 25, 2015

CHI '16, May 07–12, 2016, San Jose, CA, USA
ACM 978-1-4503-3362-7/16/05...$15.00
DOI: http://dx.doi.org/10.1145/2858036.2858320

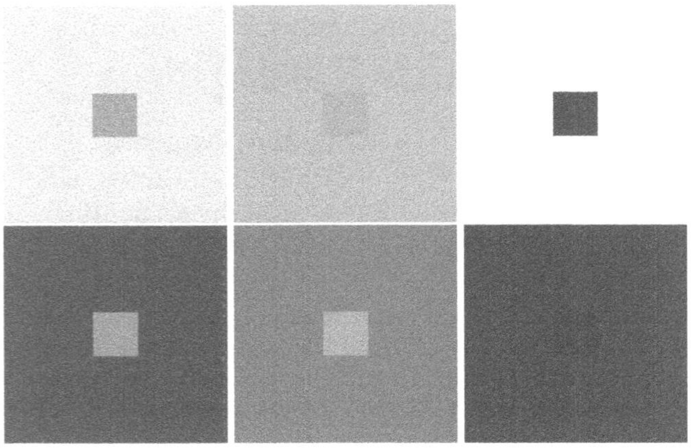

Figure 1. Simultaneous contrast: Central patches in the top row contain the same color as the patches of the bottom row but are perceived differently (in chromaticity and lightness) due to their surround.

between objects with varying reflective properties [13]. Although the spectrum of light that an object reflects into our eyes can vary substantially depending on the sources of light and the environment, we are able to reliably identify objects and their color [10]. This stability, often referred to as *color constancy* [13], is achieved through a combination of perceptual processes which we are generally unaware of until certain anomalous situations or stimuli make them obvious or puzzling, such as the recent "Dressgate" viral phenomenon [41].

At the core of our work is one of these perceptual anomalies: simultaneous contrast (SC). SC refers to how the appearance of a color patch is often influenced by the color that surrounds it (see Figure 1) and has been previously explored using color matching experiments in which participants compare patches of colors surrounded by different colors (e.g., [2, 18]).

SC and other color perception phenomena are described in Color Appearance Models (CAMs) that predict the appearance of a color given extrinsic viewing conditions [10]. A range of CAMs exist, including the application-oriented CIECAM02 [26], the comprehensive Hunt's model [16, 17], and other recent computational approaches [28]. These CAMs assume static viewing conditions, so they might not generalize to the temporally-dynamic conditions of gaze-contingent color manipulations, motivating our first experiment.

Color spaces

Color perception research requires precise ways to represent colors, typically by using *color spaces* which are multidimensional coordinate spaces in which each unique color maps to a unique location. In this paper, we use the 1976 CIE L*a*b* color space (CIELAB) [33, 34] because it is approximately perceptually uniform (Euclidean distance corresponds to perceptual difference), is well-known, and is based on opponent color channels [10, 13] which are closely related to simultaneous contrast effects [10]. CIELAB describes colors using lightness (L*: dark to bright), an a* axis (green to red), and a b* axis (blue to yellow), as shown in Figure 2.

RELATED WORK

Color perception has been applied to the development of graphics [1], interfaces [20], visualizations [12, 36], and image com-

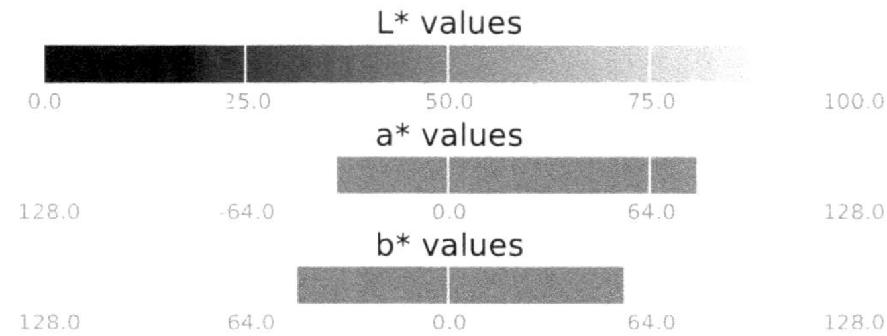

Figure 2. Sample gradients along the CIELAB axes (relative to D65). The L* gradient assumes a* = b* = 0, the a* and b* gradients assume L* = 50 and a* = 0 or b* = 0 respectively. Colors are truncated to sRGB.

pression [35, 39]. Of particular importance to our work are *tone mapping* and *gaze-contingent displays*.

Tone Mapping

When moving images between devices, tone mapping is used to adjust the colors of the image so that they are displayable or printable on the target device (e.g., displaying an image from a camera with a wide color gamut and HDR sensors on an LDR display with a smaller color gamut [32]). The two main approaches to tone mapping are global and local. Global operators are applied to each value in an image equally, e.g., by logarithmic transformation. Local tone mapping operators take into account the surround for each point in the image. To preserve the overall impression of a scene and create a realistic rendition of the HDR data, many advanced tone mapping techniques use knowledge of visual perception to influence how colors are perceived, e.g., by using simultaneous contrast to make colors appear brighter through an adapted surround [4, 19]. Most tone mapping approaches produce a static image; examples of gaze-contingent tone mapping are reviewed next.

Gaze-contingent Displays (GCDs)

GCDs leverage real-time eye tracking to manipulate display content in reaction to the user's eye gaze. GCDs have been used to reduce the computational cost of rendering [6, 14, 22, 27, 31]), to compensate for visual problems such as scotoma [6], or to add additional depth cues [25, 38].

There have also been attempts to use GCDs to influence brightness and luminance perception. Jacobs et al. [7] simulated loss of acuity, aftereffects and other visual phenomena with a GCD and found that brightness perception can be altered. Cheng and Badano [3] describe a gaze-based luminance and contrast algorithm for medical imaging, but do not provide an evaluation. Yamauchi, Mikami and Ouda [42] investigated global tone mapping operators driven by parameters derived from the focal area and compared them in a subjective task, but their comparison had no baseline nor showed statistically-reliable effects. Similar gaze-contingent tone mapping approaches have been proposed (e.g., [24, 30]), but without empirical evaluation. As a result, there is no evidence that gaze-contingent tone mapping provides any benefit over static tone mapping.

Our work furthers the state-of-the-art in gaze-contingent perceptual manipulation in two main ways: 1) we provide reliable empirical evidence about the perceptual effects and feasibility of gaze-contingent manipulation of color, and; 2) we extend the idea beyond luminance to also include chromaticity.

OVERARCHING GOALS AND RESEARCH QUESTIONS

We aim to lay the foundation for the use of gaze-contingent displays to achieve a *perceived* gamut that is wider than what the same display could produce without gaze contingency. For example, consider the range of sRGB colors in the a* axis (center row, Figure 2). Existing knowledge of the simultaneous contrast effect [2] tells us that the green sRGB color displayed at the left end of the a* axis can be perceived equivalently (i.e., *matched* in color-matching experiments) to a green further left on the axis (not displayed in the figure) *if a suitable surrounding color is provided* for the original green. We call this a *color shift*. For example, the left-end green can be made to appear more green by surrounding it with a contrasting color (e.g., red) even if the green being perceived or, more precisely, the green that we would have to generate to match our original green's perception is actually out of the gamut that the display can produce. In simplified terms, the more contrasting the surrounding color is (the redder or further right in the a* axis in our example), the further the SC models predict the color will shift outside the existing gamut.

We can achieve this effect on static displays for a single color by manipulating the colors in the surround to have higher chromatic contrast (e.g., make them more red in our green example above); however, to actually enlarge the perceived gamut of a display, we have to be able to manipulate the colors in the surround for any color at the edge of the gamut. A gaze-contingent display could help us shift the surrounding colors according to the position of gaze, but this assumes that the simultaneous contrast effect is robust to gaze-contingent changes in the display. This leads to our first research question (addressed in Experiment 1): Does gaze-contingent presentation of color preserve the simultaneous contrast effect, and if so, to what extent? Assuming that gaze contingency manifests SC, our second research question (addressed in Experiment 2) is: Do GC-based techniques increase a user's ability to discriminate colors?

COMMON TERMINOLOGY AND GC-MANIPULATIONS

Accurate reproduction of color in this document requires calibrated media (i.e., a color-calibrated display). Descriptions of colors in this paper are in CIELAB coordinates. Ideally our experiments would test the different manipulations at samples covering the whole CIELAB space at regular intervals, but this is unfeasible at this stage for our multi-technique comparison and is not necessary at the proof-of-concept stage. Instead, we sample the space at two points of each of the CIELAB axes by testing our hypotheses with colors on the L* axis at low and high values (dark and light greys), the a* axis at the green (low) and red (high) ends, and the b* axis at the blue (low) and yellow (high) ends (Figure 2 provides a reference). When testing each axis, the other axes stay at default values which are L*=50 and a*=b*=0. This means that if we refer to a color by one of its values (e.g., a*=43) its full coordinates are L*=50, a*=43, b*=0, or $(50, 43, 0)$.

Our experiments use uniform color patches as stimuli as is customary in color science and color appearance model research. Patches will be denoted by P with a subscript modifier that denotes their role in the experiment (e.g., P_{match} for a patch that the participant controls to match another patch). Patches have a color which can vary depending on the experiment circumstances and the gaze of the participant. Patches appear within a background B that also has a precisely-identified color. Both patches and background colors can be *static* or *gaze-contingent (GC)*. If they are gaze-contingent, they will change color depending on whether the participant is looking at the patch (*attended* patch – the coordinates of the gaze location are within the boundaries of the presented patch) or not (*unattended* patch).

In general we investigate two types of gaze-contingent color manipulations: background manipulation and peripheral patch manipulation. Background manipulation changes the color of the background area(s) depending on which area is looked at, i.e., a global change in the scene. This will be used to explore inducing different degrees of simultaneous contrast in different areas of the screen. Unattended patch manipulations change the color of patches that are not currently being looked at, i.e., a local peripheral change of specific objects. This will be used to explore increasing contrast between objects, e.g., to make peripheral objects easier to differentiate from the attended one.

REPLICABILITY

The analyses presented in this paper were performed in Python/R on a Vagrant virtual machine. We provide configuration files to recreate the virtual machine, as well as the data and code of the analyses (ACM DL). We hope that making our data and analyses available in this way will promote openness and reliability, and encourage other researchers to use our data to further analyze our experiments and to facilitate replication.

STATISTICAL APPROACH

The main statistical outcomes take two forms: effect sizes of factors from omnibus tests of repeated measures linear models and pairwise comparisons between conditions.

The factor effects from the repeated measures linear models are reported as η_p^2 (proportion of explained variance when excluding other factors). For the pairwise comparisons, we report effect sizes as mean paired differences M_D in CIELAB units and as standardized mean changes d_{diff} (M_D divided by the standard deviation). M_D is useful as it gives an impression of change between two variables in color units, while the standardized values are useful to make the effect sizes comparable regardless of the measure and experiment. Together with the 95% confidence intervals (CI) generated through the Bias-Corrected Accelerated Non-Parametric bootstrapping algorithm[3] they allow us to interpret the results and their reliability without depending on p-values and significance testing, which are strongly argued against in the current statistical and psychological literature (see [5, 21] for more details).

Although we do not discuss them in detail, we do report ANOVA omnibus significance test results (with repeated measures linear models over the experimental factors) for completeness and reference for those accustomed to these procedures. When the data was found to be not spherical (i.e., failed Mauchly's test), we applied a Greenhouse-Geisser correction that can be identified by the non-integer values in the resulting tests' degrees of freedom.

[3] `https://github.com/cgevans/scikits-bootstrap`

Figure 3. Example stimuli from Exp. 1. Left shows a static trial; each patch has its own background. Center and right show a GC trial with the left (matching) patch and the right (reference) patch being attended.

EXPERIMENT 1 — COLOR MATCHING

The goal of Exp. 1 is to test whether SC persists with gaze-contingent presentation of color when an object's color or its background change while the object itself is unattended. To test this we use a standard color matching experimental paradigm and compare several GC presentation conditions to a static one. We hypothesize that:

H1.1: Gaze-contingent simultaneous-contrast presentations of color patches will result in color shifts of the matched colors.
H1.2: Color shifts of the matched colors will be similar in GC conditions and the static condition.

Rejecting H1.1 implies that GC-SC is an unpromising avenue for our goal. H1.2 tells us whether we can use existing CAMs (e.g., [16, 17]) to predict color appearance.

Stimuli & Task

In each trial we presented a display that contained two circular color patches: the reference patch on the right P_{ref} and the adjustable matching patch on the left P_{match}. Each patch had a local background color (B_l and B_r) (see Figure 3). The rest of the screen was white (the display white point). Each color patch had a diameter of 2° visual angle and the patches were separated by 15° visual angle. Each half of the background had a width of 15° horizontally and 30° vertically.

We used a color matching task common in color appearance research (e.g., [15, 10]). The participants used a physical slider to control the color of P_{match} until it matched the appearance of P_{ref}. The available color range controlled by the slider depended on the trial (e.g., a range from green to red for a* trials). We instructed participants to compare the appearance of the patches by directly looking at them and collected eye tracking data to verify that this instruction was followed.

Experimental Design & Manipulations

We chose five experimental factors in a $3 \times 2 \times 2 \times 2 \times 3$ design with a single repetition per participant, resulting in a total of 1728 trials (72 per participant). These factors controlled the appearance and behaviour of the stimuli as follows:

Color Space Axis (C_{dim}) – To provide a degree of generality we explored the three axes of CIELAB. We look at each axis independently; that is, each trial shows colors from only one axis. Colors in one trial were thus either reddish/greenish (a*), yellowish/blueish (b*) or greys (L*).

Reference Patch Color (C_C) – For each axis, participants matched colors at one of the two ends of each axis. We refer to these reference patch colors as "low" and "high". The two values were equidistant to the center value in CIELAB space $(50, 0, 0)$, but were not at the very edge of the display gamut for methodological reasons; if the perceived reference color was shifted outside the display's physical gamut, we would not be able to provide a range that contained a match. The color values used were 42.18 (■) and 57.81 (■) for L*, and -20 (■ / ■) and $+20$ (■ / ■) for a* and b*.

Reference Patch Background Color (C_B) – To manipulate the reference patch color's appearance through SC, we manipulated the background color. The background could be one of two colors that we chose from within the range defined by the two reference extremes in each axis (previous paragraph). One of these background colors was near to the reference color and one was far, enabling the experiment to differentiate between different levels of simultaneous contrast intensity (e.g., background colors that are more distant should shift the perceived reference color more strongly away from the background color, towards the outside of the gamut). The background colors were 46.09 (■) and 53.91 (■) for L*, and -10 (■ / ■) and $+10$ (■ / ■) for a* and b*, respectively.

Background Manipulation (B_M) – This factor compared two presentation modes for the background: *static* and *gaze-contingent (GC)*. In the static condition, the display was divided in the middle as shown in Figure 3. The background to the left (around the matching patch) was neutral $(50, 0, 0)$ and the background to the right had the reference patch background color. In the GC background condition, B_l and B_r had the same color resulting in a uniform background, but the color varied with the participant's gaze location. When looking at (or to the right of) the reference patch, the background had the *reference patch background color* and when looking at (or to the left of) the matching patch, the background was neutral grey. The background was linearly interpolated between the reference patch background color and the neutral grey when looking between the patches.

Reference Patch Manipulation (C_δ) – So far we have assumed that viewers switch gaze between the reference patch and the matching patch to compare colors, and that they use their impression of the color of a patch while it is centered on the fovea to accomplish the matching task; however, it is also possible that viewers use information from their peripheral vision to perform matching. To control for this possibility, we introduced a manipulation that affects only the GC condition; the color of the reference patch was changed by an offset C_δ when unattended (by adding the offset to the CIELAB coordinate). The color of the patch was linearly interpolated between its base value and the modified value as in the Background Manipulation above. We chose two different values for the offset, one negative and one positive (both along the trial's axis), resulting in three possible levels of C_δ: one negative, one zero (static) and one positive. The values used for L*, a* and b* respectively are: $-3.91/+3.91$, $-10/+10$, $-10/+10$.

Apparatus

We used a monocular EyeLink 1000 eye tracker that provided gaze data at 1000 Hz with a nominal 1.4 ms delay. The tracker was installed in a tower mount configuration with a chin rest that kept the participant's face at a stable distance from the screen (40 cm).

The display was an Iiyama HM204DT 22 inch CRT display with a resolution of 1280 px × 1024 px running at 100 Hz. We calibrated the color output of the screen by using a PR-650 SpectraScan spectroradiometer to measure the screen through the eye tracker's hot mirror. We took measurements for the white point, R/G/B primaries and 25 luminance values along each R/G/B channel. These values were used to create a monitor calibration profile for PsychoPy[4], ensuring linear luminance values along each R/G/B channel, as well as a monitor-specific RGB color space specification for color computations.

Participants controlled the matching patch color through a custom-built physical input slider and a capacitive plate that served as a button to confirm input. The slider controlled the color along the same axis being tested (e.g., the slider made the matching patch go between green and red when testing a*, blue and yellow when testing b*, and between dark and light when testing L*).

The experiment took place in a darkened room with the area surrounding the display covered with a matte black surface to avoid visual distraction from the monitor's face plate.

The experimental software was built using PsychoPy [29] and colors were calculated using Colour [23]. We provide the code for this experiment in the supplemental material.

Participants

24 participants (15 female, aged 18 to 65, M=25.54, SD=10.66) took part in the experiment. All had normal or corrected-to-normal vision, 14 were right-eye dominant, 19 were right-handed. Eye dominance was determined using the Miles test, acuity with a Snellen chart, and absence of color vision deficiency with the Ishihara test using hidden digit plates. An additional six participants were tested but excluded from the analysis due to severe problems with the eye-tracking. Another participant was excluded because they did not follow the experimental instructions.

Procedure

After a brief introduction and obtaining written ethical consent (in compliance with the local committee) participants answered a demographic questionnaire and performed the vision tests. Then participants learned the five-point gaze-calibration procedure through a tutorial which also explained the basic task. The time spent on the tutorial and calibration (about 5 to 10 minutes) allowed for adaptation to the screen and room.

Each trial began with a fixation cross in the center of the screen and started when the participant looked at it. The participant controlled the matching patch's color with the slider according to our instructions (exact phrasing is available through the supplemental materials). Once a trial was complete, the participant had to reset the slider position to the bottom of the input device before proceeding to next trial.

Trial order was randomized for each participant. After half the trials, there was a break. After the break we checked the eye tracker calibration for changes in accuracy and re-calibrated if the average error was more than 1 degree. No change in room lighting happened during the break. The experiment took about 60 minutes. After the trials were complete, the participant was debriefed and compensated.

[4]http://www.psychopy.org/general/monitors.html

Measures and Statistical Analysis

The main raw measure for each trial was the CIELAB coordinate of the matching patch color along the given axis, which was recorded along with the specific condition (i.e., the reference patch color and its manipulations). We also recorded gaze-patterns to validate participant behavior.

To detect SC, we derived a measure called *simultaneous contrast effect* (δC) calculated as the difference (in CIELAB units) between the colors matched for a given reference color when using the two different backgrounds of the *reference patch background color factor* (C_B). This value will be non-zero if SC exists as different background colors will have changed the appearance of the reference patch color.

For completeness, we also computed a measure we call *absolute color appearance* ($\overline{C}$) which was the average across both background colors (C_B) of the matched color (all other conditions being equal), giving us an SC-independent measure. This allows us to make simple comparisons in CIELAB units between conditions (for H1.2). For example, by looking at absolute color appearance we can learn how much more green the green reference patch appears in the GC condition than in the static condition.

We noticed some severe outliers that appeared to be caused by resetting the slider before confirming the input. To address this, we trimmed the data to 3σ in each cell, affecting 17 trials ($\sim$1% of all trials).

Results

We report results by measure: simultaneous contrast effect (δC) and then absolute color appearance ($\overline{C}$).

Simultaneous Contrast Effects

We analyze δC per axis. Large δC values indicate a large shift in matched color due to SC. Results of the omnibus RM analysis are summarized in Table 1. The intercept of the model has a special meaning as it tells us whether SC appeared at all.

The large effect size of the intercept for the L* axis (M=−3.56 CI[−3.81, −3.30]) indicates that SC was present overall. All other factors and interactions had small effects. This means that the static and gaze-contingent manipulations were not very different in terms of SC effects. We did not observe large effect sizes in factors or interactions related to gaze-contingent manipulations. This is evidence that gaze-contingent manipulations did not negate simultaneous contrast.

We observe a small effect for the interaction $B_M \times C_C$, which could indicate a systematic (if small) difference between GC and static background manipulation for specific colors. The GC condition showed a larger SC effect than the static condition for the dark end of the L* axis (Figure 4). The effect sizes for the GC-vs-static difference are M_D=−1.1, d_{diff}=−0.43 for low and M_D=−0.12, d_{diff}=−0.050 for high.

Results on the a* axis are similar to those on the L* axis. The intercept (measure of SC effect) is weaker than in L* (although clearly present M=−3.43 CI[−4.22, −2.69]).

Factors	df	$\widetilde{df}$	F	p	η_p^2
*Results for L**					
$(Intercept)$	1.00	22.00	219.52	<0.01	0.75
B_M	1.00	22.00	4.93	0.04	0.03
C_C	1.00	22.00	0.40	0.53	<0.01
C_δ	2.00	44.00	0.68	0.51	<0.01
$B_M \times C_C$	1.00	22.00	5.17	0.03	0.02
$B_M \times C_\delta$	2.00	44.00	2.63	0.08	0.01
$C_C \times C_\delta$	2.00	44.00	0.12	0.89	<0.01
$B_M \times C_C \times C_\delta$	2.00	44.00	3.26	0.05	0.01
*Results for a**					
$(Intercept)$	1.00	22.00	44.04	<0.01	0.24
B_M	1.00	22.00	1.33	0.26	<0.01
C_C	1.00	22.00	12.98	<0.01	0.11
C_δ	1.51	33.25	1.99	0.16	<0.01
$B_M \times C_C$	1.00	22.00	0.29	0.59	<0.01
$B_M \times C_\delta$	2.00	44.00	0.06	0.95	<0.01
$C_C \times C_\delta$	2.00	44.00	0.56	0.57	<0.01
$B_M \times C_C \times C_\delta$	2.00	44.00	0.91	0.41	<0.01
*Results for b**					
$(Intercept)$	1.00	22.00	198.78	<0.01	0.56
B_M	1.00	22.00	4.47	0.05	0.02
C_C	1.00	22.00	45.58	<0.01	0.22
C_δ	2.00	44.00	1.33	0.27	<0.01
$B_M \times C_C$	1.00	22.00	12.92	<0.01	0.05
$B_M \times C_\delta$	2.00	44.00	0.23	0.79	<0.01
$C_C \times C_\delta$	2.00	44.00	2.37	0.10	0.02
$B_M \times C_C \times C_\delta$	2.00	44.00	0.59	0.56	<0.01

Table 1. Results of the repeated measure ANOVA of simultaneous contrast effect in Experiment 1, split by CIELAB axis.

As in L*, GC-related factors did not show effects. The effect on C_C simply shows that SC is not homogeneous along the axis, a result in agreement with exiting CAMs.

The SC effect is also evident in the b* axis through the intercept with M=−7.28, CI[−8.17, −6.37]. As in a*, the C_C effect shows that SC varies along the axis.

In b* there are two interactions with small effect sizes. $B_M \times C_C$ and $C_C \times C_\delta$ are plotted in Figure 5. The former shows that the SC effect is slightly reduced in the GC condition for the high color case M_D=4.7, d_{diff}=0.47. The latter, which suggests that different values of peripheral offset (C_δ) affect the low and high ends of the axis differently, is probably of little practical importance judging from the CIs and the small differences.

Absolute Color Appearance

This section looks at the $\overline{C}$ measure, which ignores the SC contrast effect to focus on absolute color appearance shifts. Results of the omnibus RM analysis are summarized in Table 2. The large effect of C_C is trivial since if we show a different color, people will match it to a different color.

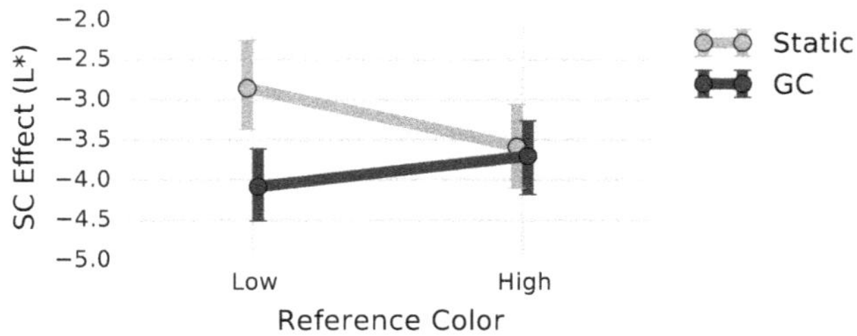

Figure 4. Plot of the $B_M \times C_C$ interaction on the L* axis for SC effect.

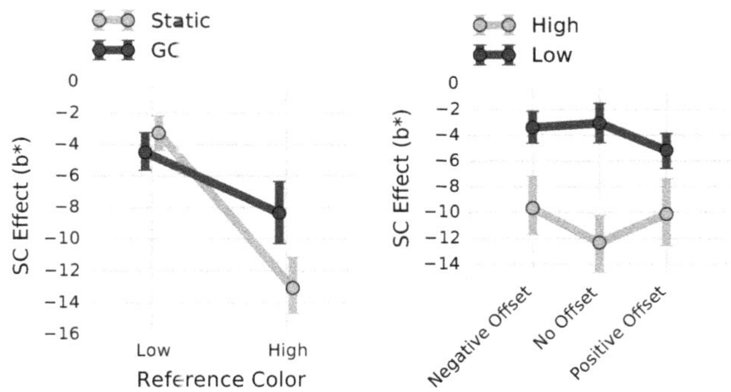

Figure 5. Plots of the interactions observed for the simultaneous contrast effect in the b* axis. $B_M \times C_C$ (Left), $C_C \times C_\delta$ (right).

Across all axes we also see a small but consistent main effect of the peripheral gaze-contingent manipulation (C_δ). Participants matched their stimulus with a small influence of peripheral color change (see Figure 6).

There are two small interactions in the b* axis that involve C_δ: the first one with C_C and the second one with B_M (Figure 6). We see that the difference between C_δ positive and negative persisted, but the no-offset condition seemed to deviate for C_C high and B_M GC. These findings show that there are exceptions to the effect of C_δ in very specific conditions.

Discussion

The strong effect sizes of the intercept for all axes indicate that Exp. 1 was able to replicate the simultaneous contrast effect and, more importantly, that gaze-contingent presentations of the stimuli cause simultaneous contrast as well (H1.1 is supported). Looking at it in terms of $\Delta_{CIE2000}$, the absolute measures indicate that SC can induce changes in color appearance in the range of 3 or 4 $\Delta_{CIE2000}$ units depending on the axis. The results also showed some small differences between gaze-contingent and static presentation, but only in the b* axis. H1.2 is consequently only partially supported; there are systematic effects that might prevent us from applying current SC models directly to GC-SC.

The results also show that SC does not take place uniformly across the CIELAB space. One might be tempted to think that since CIELAB is designed to be perceptually uniform, SC would happen uniformly across the space as well; however, our data suggest that this is not the case.

We have also learned that changing the reference color patch while in the periphery (reference patch manipulation) can also produce shifts in the matched color. Although these shifts are

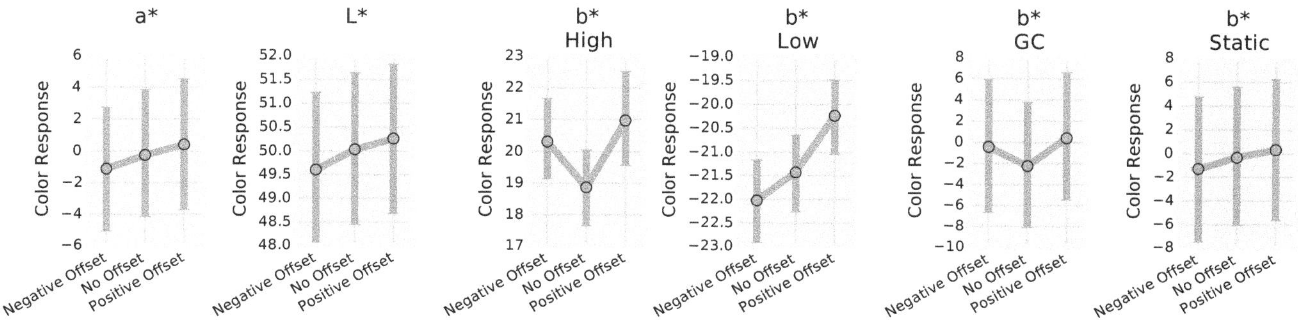

Figure 6. Plots of baseline color response modulated by C_δ. From left to right the results are for the a* axis, the L* axis, followed by the b* axis split by C_C (high and low) and then the b* column split by B_M (GC and static).

Factors	df	$\widetilde{df}$	F	p	η_p^2
*Results for L**					
(*Intercept*)	1.00	22.00	506881.52	<0.01	1.00
B_M	1.00	22.00	0.95	0.34	<0.01
C_C	1.00	22.00	5158.22	<0.01	0.98
C_δ	2.00	44.00	8.20	<0.01	0.06
$B_M \times C_C$	1.00	22.00	1.21	0.28	<0.01
$B_M \times C_\delta$	1.48	32.48	0.78	0.43	<0.01
$C_C \times C_\delta$	2.00	44.00	0.28	0.75	<0.01
$B_M \times C_C \times C_\delta$	2.00	44.00	1.05	0.36	<0.01
*Results for a**					
(*Intercept*)	1.00	22.00	1.76	0.20	0.01
B_M	1.00	22.00	0.02	0.88	<0.01
C_C	1.00	22.00	3532.09	<0.01	0.98
C_δ	2.00	44.00	6.34	<0.01	0.04
$B_M \times C_C$	1.00	22.00	1.62	0.22	<0.01
$B_M \times C_\delta$	2.00	44.00	1.43	0.25	<0.01
$C_C \times C_\delta$	1.60	35.21	0.73	0.46	<0.01
$B_M \times C_C \times C_\delta$	2.00	44.00	0.02	0.98	<0.01
*Results for b**					
(*Intercept*)	1.00	22.00	4.01	0.06	0.02
B_M	1.00	22.00	0.79	0.38	<0.01
C_C	1.00	22.00	2441.87	<0.01	0.97
C_δ	2.00	44.00	6.00	<0.01	0.03
$B_M \times C_C$	1.00	22.00	1.53	0.23	<0.01
$B_M \times C_\delta$	2.00	44.00	5.22	<0.01	0.02
$C_C \times C_\delta$	2.00	44.00	2.50	0.09	0.01
$B_M \times C_C \times C_\delta$	2.00	44.00	0.27	0.77	<0.01

Table 2. Results of the repeated measure ANOVA of absolute color appearance in Experiment 1, split by CIELAB axis.

small compared to the SC effect and are modulated by the patch's color, they deserve further exploration and open an interesting possibility of gaze-contingent manipulation which we explore further in Experiment 2.

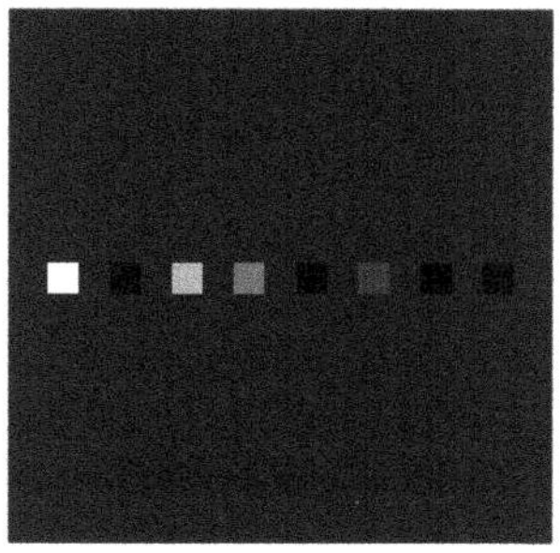

Figure 7. Example of stimulus setup. Relatively high-contrasting L* axis colors are shown for illustrative purposes; differences between patches were much subtler in real trials.

EXPERIMENT 2 — COLOR SORTING

Exp. 2 investigates if GC techniques (simultaneous contrast and the peripheral color adjustment discussed in Exp.1) can enhance color discrimination. Although Exp. 1 showed that GC manipulations can be used to shift how a color is perceived, we now consider whether this can be leveraged to increase the differentiability of color steps perceived by viewers.

To test this we use a gradient sorting task similar to a Farnsworth-Munsell 100 hue test [11] where participants are asked to arrange a shuffled sequence of color patches in order according to their color. We hypothesize that:

H2.1: Gaze-contingent simultaneous contrast presentation of color will result in fewer errors in the ordering of the sequences.
H2.2: Peripheral manipulation of colors will result in fewer errors in the ordering of the sequences.

Stimuli & Task

The stimuli in this task consisted of eight square color patches, each covering $2° \times 2°$ visual angle. The patches were placed horizontally with a gap separation of 2° (see Figure 7) within a square background of $35° \times 35°$. Outside of this area the display was white. The patch colors were from a gradient of similar colors (see Table 3). The leftmost and rightmost patches were fixed in position and showed the color extremes. The other patches could be re-arranged via mouse input using drag-and-drop. While dragging, a patch only showed as a black outline to prevent a participant from moving squares for comparison. After moving a patch, a small white line below the patch flashed to indicate change. This reassured participants that changes had occurred when they were working with very small color differences.

	Color Patch Gradients						Background Gradients		
	L*		a*		b*		L*	a*	b*
	low	high	low	high	low	high			
Lower	39.10	54.19	-23.84	16.16	-23.84	16.16	45.50	-5.76	-5.76
Upper	45.10	60.19	-16.16	23.84	-16.16	23.84	54.50	5.76	5.76
$\Delta_{CIE2000}$	5.44	5.50	4.59	4.59	4.04	4.04	9.00	10.62	15.97

Table 3. Color Gradients used in Experiment 2 and $\Delta_{CIE2000}$ differences between them. Values denote upper and lower ends of the gradients along the relevant color axis in CIELAB space. Intermediate values where interpolated linearly. Color swatches provided for illustration might not correspond to the exact color displayed in the experiment, and can vary depending on viewing medium.

The task was to arrange the patches from left to right according to their color so that they formed a gradient between the fixed patches at the extremes. Accuracy was measured through an error score taken from the original Farnsworth task [11]. Each patch was assigned a number according to its actual position along the gradient. For each patch in the participant-determined order, we added the absolute difference of the patch's number with respect to the numbers of the patches on its left and right, subtract two, and then summed the sub-scores for all patches. A perfect order gives a score of zero.

At the start of the trial the patches appeared in a randomized arrangement with an error score of 21. This kept the baseline error score sufficiently high and consistent between participants, and avoided varying difficulty between trials.

Color Gradients and Backgrounds

As in the previous experiment, we sampled along each CIELAB axis. The exact gradients are described in Table 3. The gradients contained very similar colors that were hard to distinguish. If the task had been too easy the different manipulations would not show differences due to ceiling effects. $\Delta_{CIE2000}$ (a measure of perceptual differences) of the extremes of the gradient was about 5, where a value of 1 corresponds approximately to a *just noticeable difference*.

Each gradient had a corresponding background gradient (also in Table 3) for the GC-SC manipulation. To choose these, we balanced the goal of maximizing simultaneous contrast effects (according to the data that we obtained from Exp. 1) while keeping the experiment simple (by using a single background gradient for both ends of the axis). These background gradients were thus chosen to be broad but centred around the middle point of each axis.

Techniques

We tested five different color presentation techniques. These corresponded to all combinations of absent or present manipulations of the background (i.e., the simultaneous contrast manipulation) and the peripheral object color manipulation, plus an additional static technique that served as control.

Static (S_u) – This was the baseline, with no manipulations. It displayed the color gradient on a background of static uniform middle grey (L*=50, a*=0, b*=0).

GC patches (GC_{patch}) – Peripheral patches changed their color to increase contrast in relation to the currently-attended patch. We used this function to compute the colors to display:

$$r(c_i) = \begin{cases} c_i & \text{for } i = i_a \\ \text{interp}(c_0, \max(c_0, c_a - \Delta c), \frac{i}{i_a}), & \text{for } i < i_a \\ \text{interp}(\min(c_7, c_a + \Delta c), c_7, \frac{i-i_a}{7-i_a}), & \text{for } i > i_a \end{cases}$$

where $r(c_i)$ is the resulting L*/a*/b* value for the current trial, c_i is the color along the gradient at index i (c_0 is the lower end of the gradient and c_7 the upper end), i_a is the color index of the currently attended patch, interp(a,b,x) is a linear interpolation function at x (in $[0,1]$) between $(0,a)$ and $(1,b)$, and Δc is a constant value that depended on the CIELAB axis (3 for L* and 3.84 for a* and b*).

Since the visual space between patches is very small, we chose not to use continuous interpolation for gaze position between patches, but instead used a hysteresis-based approach; a patch would only be considered attended once the gaze position was measured inside of its visible area on the screen.

GC background (GC_{bg}) – This technique changed the background based on the attended patch, i.e., it applied simultaneous contrast. The currently attended patch was determined as in GC_{patch}.

GC background and patches ($GC_{bg+patch}$) – This technique combined both GC_{patch} and GC_{bg} simultaneously.

Static with Frames (S_f) – This technique was similar to S_u, but each patch was enclosed by a 0.25° wide frame. The colors of the frames were picked from the background gradient to enhance the difference between patches through SC. This technique provided SC-enhanced color in a static form, but is somewhat artificial because it is feasible only for specific spatial arrangements, adds visual noise, and is consequently of limited utility in realistic scenarios.

Consistent with our hypotheses, we expected the three gaze-contingent techniques to reduce errors compared to the baseline. We also suspected that the static with frames technique (S_f) would perform well due to the additional visual information included in the frame, which could be used in addition to the patch color to inform ordering.

Experimental Design

The design was a $3 \times 2 \times 5$ (color axis $\times$ color $\times$ technique) within-subjects design with two repetitions per cell, resulting in 60 trials per participant. The presentation of trials was

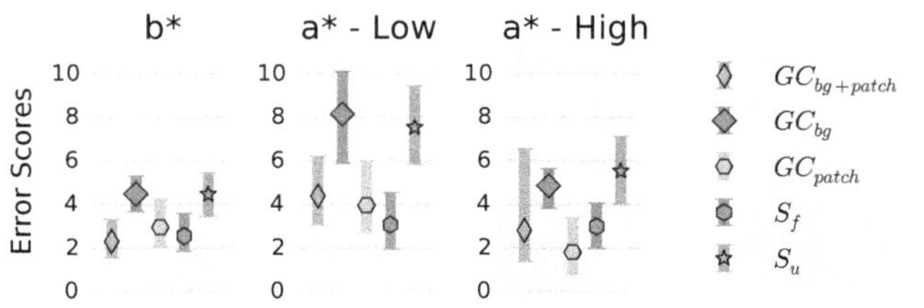

Figure 8. Error scores on the a* and b* axis for each technique.

blocked by technique, block order was balanced between participants using Latin squares.

Apparatus

The apparatus is identical to Exp. 1 except that, due to lab requirements for another experiment, the screen was replaced with an Iiyama MM904UT 19 CRT running at 1280 px × 1024 px and 85 Hz. This setup was re-calibrated using the same procedure as the previous one. The participants provided responses through a keyboard and mouse.

Participants

We tested 20 participants (14 female, aged 18 to 39, M = 23.85, SD = 6.32, all had normal or corrected-to-normal vision, 15 were right-eye dominant, 16 were right-handed). Screening of the participants proceeded as in Exp. 1. Two participants where excluded from the analysis due to severe problems with their eye tracking.

Procedure

Participants gave written consent in compliance with the local ethics regulations. We collected demographic information through a preliminary questionnaire and then performed the vision screening tests.

The participants then sat at the eye tracker, learned the task through a tutorial (four trials with easy black to white gradients), and performed a five point calibration procedure. Each trial began when the participant looking at a cross. After each block there was a short break. After each break, we checked the calibration for changes in accuracy and re-calibrated if the average error was more than 1 degree. The main part of the experiment lasted about 45 minutes.

Measures and Statistical Analysis

The main measure was the error score derived from the final configuration of the patches. The error responses were not expected to be normally distributed (skewed towards perfect performance). Although we use a parametric model for the omnibus test, the comparison analysis and the confidence intervals are non-parametric and therefore robust.

Results

Table 4 shows the results of the RM-ANOVA. We focus on the *technique* factor, which is directly related to our hypotheses. The effect sizes of Technique on the number of errors are smaller than in Exp. 1, but still sizable in all axes (η_p^2 of 0.21, 0.61 and 0.56 for L*, a* and b* respectively). This indicates that the different techniques affected accuracy and justifies further comparisons between techniques.

Unfortunately, when looking at error scores according to axis we found that performance with the L* axis was close to perfect for most participants, despite of its gradients having equivalent $\Delta_{CIE2000}$ ranges to the other axes. This ceiling effect masks the differences between techniques, making pairwise comparisons uninformative; therefore, we omit the L* axis in the following analysis. These data and analysis are still available through the supplemental material.

Factors	df	$\widetilde{df}$	F	p	η_p^2
*Results for L**					
(Intercept)	1.00	19.00	25.77	<0.01	0.21
Color	1.00	19.00	<0.01	0.97	<0.01
Technique	2.86	54.38	5.13	<0.01	0.10
Color × Technique	2.27	43.06	0.35	0.73	<0.01
*Results for a**					
(Intercept)	1.00	19.00	68.26	<0.01	0.61
Color	1.00	19.00	10.97	<0.01	0.06
Technique	4.00	76.00	15.11	<0.01	0.17
Color × Technique	4.00	76.00	1.97	0.11	0.02
*Results for b**					
(Intercept)	1.00	19.00	55.84	<0.01	0.56
Color	1.00	19.00	0.09	0.77	<0.01
Technique	4.00	76.00	7.62	<0.01	0.09
Color × Technique	4.00	76.00	0.56	0.69	<0.01

Table 4. Results of the RM-ANOVAs of error scores in Exp. 2.

	S_f		GC_{patch}		$GC_{bg+patch}$		GC_{bg}	
	M_D	d_{diff}	M_D	d_{diff}	M_D	d_{diff}	M_D	d_{diff}
a*	-3.50	-1.04	-3.64	-1.05	-2.93	-0.61	-0.03	-0.01
b*	-1.92	-0.49	-1.50	-0.42	-2.15	-0.74	0.01	0.00

Table 5. Differences in error scores of each technique compared to the baseline technique S_u.

The performance of the individual techniques in the a* and b* axes (Figure 8) reveals a clear pattern: in both axes the S_u and GC_{bg} condition had the highest error scores, while the three other techniques had low error scores. This pattern is evident for both color axes. The differences in error scores compared to the baseline S_u appear in Table 5, where we observe lower error rates for all techniques except GC_{bg}.

Effect sizes of other interactions are not large enough to be of practical relevance except for the interaction of color and technique in the a* axis, which is small but we decided to investigate nonetheless. A closer look revealed some outliers in the a*-high condition. Otherwise both a*-high as well as a*-low show the same pattern (see Figure 8). The effect of color in the a* axis indicates that one of the gradients was more difficult than the other M_D=1.8, d_{diff}=0.44.

Discussion

Exp. 2 results show that gaze-contingent techniques that manipulate peripheral patches (GC_{patch} and $GC_{bg+patch}$) improve performance in a color ordering task with respect to the uniform background S_u, which is the baseline technique (H2.2

is supported). Surprisingly, gaze-contingent manipulation of only the background (i.e., only with SC) does not seem to help with color differentiation as the GC_{bg} technique did not show a comparable advantage (H2.1 is *not* supported).

Therefore, it is likely that the advantages in the ordering task of Exp. 2 are due to peripheral color manipulation. Although this is not strictly an SC effect, it is still a valid way to take advantage of gaze-contingency.

The static technique with the SC frames is interesting and deserves further investigation. As we mentioned above, it is not feasible for full-range displays, but it might result in better color differentiability for reduced ranges if properly harnessed. This technique showed error scores comparable to the best GC-based techniques.

Overall, this experiment found that we can improve color discrimination using gaze-contingent techniques, only not through the use of simultaneous contrast induced through the change of the overall background. Perhaps a more targeted background adjustment (similar to the static individual background) that partially preserves relative background might lead to improvements, however, this kind of technique will have to be investigated in future work.

GENERAL DISCUSSION

The results from our two experiments provide insights into properties and benefits of color perception on gaze-contingent displays in general and simultaneous contrast (SC) specifically. We provide the first empirical data on gaze-contingent SC showing that SC can be induced through background manipulations of attended objects, and that SC persists even if the background changes when an object is unattended. We also provide the first empirical evaluation of a technique that uses gaze-contingent peripheral contrast enhancement to successfully increase color discrimination in a color sorting task.

Gaze-contingent SC could be used to create a new kind of High Dynamic Range (HDR) rendering technique. Since the appearance of a color can be moved along the CIELAB axes, colors at the edge of the display gamut can be pushed outside of the physical gamut of the screen, essentially increasing its perceivable gamut size. This could be used to display images with higher perceived luminance ranges (as suggested by [3, 24]), but also higher perceived chromaticity, allowing the display to render more vivid photographs or display medical images (e.g., MRI, X-ray) with more observable detail.

While we focused on SC as the main driver of changes in color appearance, in Exp. 2 we found that techniques based on changing the appearance of peripheral objects (enhancing local contrast) improved color discrimination, whereas the purely SC-based technique did not. We expected to see the gamut extended through GC-SC of Exp. 1 to have a similarly beneficial effect in the color ordering task of Exp. 2, but found otherwise. This indicates that our color matching task and color ordering tasks are affected by gaze-contingency in different ways.

The results of Exp. 2 are nevertheless useful since they suggest that GC peripheral changes can help color discrimination. This type of technique could be used to increase the number of categorical colors for encoding information in information visualisations or make the reading of color scales more precise.

Open Questions and Future Work

Our findings provide a base to further explore the application of gaze-contingent techniques for perceived gamut expansion and improved color differentiability; however, our ability to take advantage of these techniques in realistic scenarios requires further empirical and practical work. It is necessary to generalize the manipulations described in this paper to work in more complex displays that go beyond the carefully-controlled stimuli of our investigations. Application areas include GC-based gamut-enhanced photos and movies.

Two related outstanding issues are screen flicker and the noticeability of the gaze-contingent changes. We did not design our studies to detect or measure these, but these are obviously important matters for the feasibility of GC color manipulation techniques. Our own experience with our system suggests that flicker was not an issue in our experiments, but flicker and noticeability certainly need to be considered in future extensions and applications of our GC-SC based techniques.

Finally, our measurements of the effects of gaze-contingent manipulation are not exhaustive as they only cover a limited number of points on the CIELAB axes. The precise control of perceived color with gaze-contingent techniques might require a higher-density sampling of the color space, perhaps leading to a model that accounts for differences due to the gaze-contingency of the display. Our findings of differences between SC effects in GC and non-GC presentation, as well as asymmetries across different axes and values, highlight the need for more comprehensive knowledge in this area.

CONCLUSION

In this paper, we presented an empirical evaluation of gaze-contingent manipulation of colors through simultaneous contrast and peripheral object color manipulation. We conducted two experiments that provide insight into general perceptual properties and benefits of gaze-contingent color presentation.

We contribute evidence that gaze-contingent simultaneous contrast can be used to change the appearance of colors, which could be used to extend the perceived gamut of a display. We also show that changing the appearance of peripheral objects can be used to improve color differentiability. Our results can be used to inform future work on gaze-contingent color manipulations to extend the capabilities of displays or on manipulation of perceived colors to enhance the user's color discrimination ability.

ACKNOWLEDGEMENTS

We want to thank the reviewers and members of SACHI for their helpful comments on this work. This research is supported by the EU's Marie Curie Program: CIG - 303780.

REFERENCES

1. Dirk Bartz, Douglas Cunningham, Jan Fischer, and Christian Wallraven. 2008. The Role of Perception for Computer Graphics. *Eurographics state-of-the-art-reports* (2008), 65–86. DOI: http://dx.doi.org/10.2312/egst.20081045

2. K. Tiplitz Blackwell and G. Buchsbaum. 1988. The effect of spatial and chromatic parameters on chromatic induction. *Color Research & Application* 13, 3 (1988), 166–173. DOI:http://dx.doi.org/10.1002/col.5080130309

3. Wei-Chung Cheng and Aldo Badano. 2010. A gaze-contingent high-dynamic range display for medical imaging applications. *SPIE Medical Imaging* 7627 (March 2010), 76270A–76270A–6. DOI: http://dx.doi.org/10.1117/12.845782

4. Ken Chiu, Michael Herf, Peter Shirley, S. Swamy, Changyaw Wang, and Kurt Zimmerman. 1993. Spatially nonuniform scaling functions for high contrast images. In *In Proceedings of Graphics Interface*. 245–253.

5. Geoff Cumming. 2013. *Understanding the new statistics: Effect sizes, confidence intervals, and meta-analysis*. Routledge.

6. Andrew T. Duchowski and Tiras D. Eaddy. 2009. A gaze-contingent display compensating for scotomata. *Eurographics* (2009).

7. David E. Jacobs, Orazio Gallo, Emily A. Cooper, Kari Pulli, and Marc Levoy. 2015. Simulating the Visual Experience of Very Bright and Very Dark Scenes. *ACM Transactions on Graphics* 34, 3 (May 2015), 25:1–25:15. DOI:http://dx.doi.org/10.1145/2714573

8. Eyexblog.tobii.com. 2015a. Avalanche Studios has you literally looking to bag your next trophy | Tobii EyeX Blog. (2015). http://eyexblog.tobii.com/avalanche-studios-has-you-literally-looking-for-your-next-kill/

9. Eyexblog.tobii.com. 2015b. Foveated Rendering in VR = easy peasy with Tobii & Starbreeze new collaboration. | Tobii EyeX Blog. (2015). http://eyexblog.tobii.com/starvr/

10. Mark D. Fairchild. 2013. *Color Appearance Models* (3 ed.). Wiley. 408 pages.

11. Dean Farnsworth. 1943. The Farnsworth-Munsell 100-Hue and Dichotomous Tests for Color Vision. *Journal of the Optical Society of America* 33, 10 (Oct. 1943), 568. DOI:http://dx.doi.org/10.1364/JOSA.33.000568

12. David R. Flatla and Carl Gutwin. 2010. Individual Models of Color Differentiation to Improve Interpretability of Information Visualization. In *Proceedings of the SIGCHI Conference on Human Factors in Computing Systems (CHI '10)*. ACM, New York, NY, USA, 2563–2572. DOI: http://dx.doi.org/10.1145/1753326.1753715

13. E. Bruce Goldstein. 2013. *Sensation and perception*. Wadsworth, Cengage Learning.

14. Brian Guenter, Mark Finch, Steven Drucker, Desney Tan, and John Snyder. 2012. Foveated 3D graphics. *ACM Transactions on Graphics* 31, 6 (2012), 1. DOI: http://dx.doi.org/10.1145/2366145.2366183

15. Robert W. G. Hunt. 1952. Light and dark adaptation and the perception of color. *JOSA* 42, 3 (1952), 190–199.

16. Robert W. G. Hunt. 1987. A model of colour vision for predicting colour appearance in various viewing conditions. *Color Research & Application* 12, 6 (1987), 297–314. DOI:http://dx.doi.org/10.1002/col.5080120605

17. Robert W. G. Hunt. 1994. An improved predictor of colourfulness in a model of colour vision. *Color Research and Application* 19, 1 (1994), 23–26. DOI: http://dx.doi.org/10.1111/j.1520-6378.1994.tb00056.x

18. Dorothea Jameson and Leo M. Hurvich. 1961. Opponent chromatic induction: experimental evaluation and theoretical account. *Journal of the Optical Society of America* 51, 1 (1961), 46–53. DOI: http://dx.doi.org/10.1364/JOSA.51.000046

19. Daniel J. Jobson, Zia-ur Rahman, and Glenn A. Woodell. 1996. Retinex image processing: Improved fidelity to direct visual observation. In *Color and Imaging Conference*, Vol. 1996. Society for Imaging Science and Technology, 124–125.

20. Gordon Kindlmann, Erik Reinhard, Sarah Creem, and Sarah Kindlmann, Gordon and Reinhard, Erik and Creem. 2002. Face-based luminance matching for perceptual colormap generation. In *Proceedings of the conference on Visualization (VIS '02)*. IEEE, IEEE Computer Society, Washington, DC, USA, 299–306. DOI: http://dx.doi.org/10.1109/VISUAL.2002.1183788

21. Rex B. Kline. 2004. Beyond significance testing: Reforming data analysis methods in behavioral research. (2004).

22. Sheng Liu and Hong Hua. 2008. Spatialchromatic Foveation for Gaze Contingent Displays. In *Proceedings of the 2008 Symposium on Eye Tracking Research & Applications (ETRA '08)*. ACM, New York, NY, USA, 139–142. DOI:http://dx.doi.org/10.1145/1344471.1344507

23. Thomas Mansencal, Michael Mauderer, and Michael Parsons. 2015. Colour 0.3.6. (Aug. 2015). DOI: http://dx.doi.org/10.5281/zenodo.27234

24. Radoslaw Mantiuk and Mateusz Markowski. 2013. Gaze-Dependent Tone Mapping. In *Image Analysis and Recognition*. 426–433. DOI: http://dx.doi.org/10.1007/978-3-642-39094-4_48

25. Michael Mauderer, Simone Conte, Miguel A. Nacenta, and Dhanraj Vishwanath. 2014. Depth perception with gaze-contingent depth of field. In *Proceedings of the SIGCHI Conference on Human Factors in Computing Systems*. ACM, 217–226. DOI: http://dx.doi.org/10.1145/2556288.2557089

26. Nathan Moroney, Mark D. Fairchild, Robert W. G. Hunt, Changjun Li, M. Ronnier Luo, and Todd Newman. 2002. The CIECAM02 color appearance model. In *Color and Imaging Conference*, Vol. 2002. Society for Imaging Science and Technology, 23–27. http://dx.doi.org/10.1002/col.20227

27. Hunter Murphy and Andrew T. Duchowski. 2001. Gaze-contingent level of detail rendering. *Eurographics* (2001).

28. Xavier Otazu, Olivier Penacchio, and Laura Dempere-Marco. 2012. Brightness induction by contextual influences in V1: a neurodynamical account. *Journal of Vision* 12, 9 (Aug. 2012), 1208–1208. DOI: http://dx.doi.org/10.1167/12.9.1208

29. Jonathan W Peirce. 2009. Generating stimuli for neuroscience using PsychoPy. *Frontiers in Neuroinformatics* 2, 10 (2009). DOI: http://dx.doi.org/10.3389/neuro.11.010.2008

30. Susanto Rahardja, Farzam Farbiz, and Corey Manders. 2009. Eye HDR: Gaze-adaptive system for displaying high-dynamic-range images. *SIGGRAPH ASIA Art Gallery & Emerging Technologies* (2009), 68–68. DOI: http://dx.doi.org/10.1145/1665137.1665187

31. Eyal M Reingold, Lester C Loschky, George W McConkie, and David M Stampe. 2003. Gaze-contingent multiresolutional displays: an integrative review. *Human factors* 45, 2 (June 2003), 307–328. DOI: http://dx.doi.org/10.1518/hfes.45.2.307.27235

32. Erik Reinhard, Wolfgang Heidrich, Paul Debevec, Sumanta Pattanaik, Greg Ward, and Karol Myszkowski. 2010. *High dynamic range imaging: acquisition, display, and image-based lighting* (1 ed.). Morgan Kaufmann. 520 pages.

33. Alan R. Robertson. 1977. The CIE 1976 Color-Difference Formulae. *Color Research & Application* 2, 1 (1977), 7–11. DOI: http://dx.doi.org/10.1002/j.1520-6378.1977.tb00104.x

34. Alan R. Robertson. 1990. Historical development of CIE recommended color difference equations. *Color Research & Application* 15, 3 (1990), 167–170. DOI: http://dx.doi.org/10.1002/col.5080150308

35. Athanassios Skodras, Charilaos Christopoulos, and Touradj Ebrahimi. 2001. The JPEG 2000 still image compression standard. *Signal Processing Magazine* 18, 5 (2001), 36–58. DOI: http://dx.doi.org/10.1109/79.952804

36. Ian Spence, Natasha Kutlesa, and David L. Rose. 1999. Using Color to Code Quantity in Spatial Displays. *Journal of Experimental Psychology: Applied* 5, 4 (1999), 393–412. DOI: http://dx.doi.org/10.1037/1076-898X.5.4.393

37. Steelseries.com. 2015. sentry gaming eye tracker | SteelSeries. (2015). https://steelseries.com/gaming-controllers/sentry-gaming-eye-tracker

38. Margarita Vinnikov and Robert S. Allison. 2014. Gaze-contingent Depth of Field in Realistic Scenes: The User Experience. In *Proceedings of the Symposium on Eye Tracking Research and Applications (ETRA '14)*. ACM, New York, NY, USA, 119–126. DOI: http://dx.doi.org/10.1145/2578153.2578170

39. Gregory K. Wallace. 1991. The JPEG still picture compression standard. *Commun. ACM* 34, 4 (1991), 30–44.

40. Michel Wedel and Rik Pieters. 2008. A review of eye-tracking research in marketing. *Review of marketing research* 4, 2008 (2008), 123–147. DOI: http://dx.doi.org/10.1108/S1548-6435(2008)0000004009

41. Wikipedia. 2015. The dress (viral phenomenon). (2015). https://en.wikipedia.org/wiki/The_dress_(viral_phenomenon)

42. Takuya Yamauchi, Toshiaki Mikami, and Osama Ouda. 2011. Improvement and evaluation of real-time tone mapping for high dynamic range images using gaze information. *Computer Vision - ACCV 2010 Workshops* (2011), 440–449. DOI: http://dx.doi.org/10.1007/978-3-642-22822-3_44

Spotlights: Attention-Optimised Highlights for Skim Reading

Byungjoo Lee
Aalto University, Finland
bjlee1985@gmail.com

Olli Savisaari
Aalto University, Finland
olli.savisaari@aalto.fi

Antti Oulasvirta
Aalto University, Finland
antti.oulasvirta@aalto.fi

ABSTRACT
The paper contributes a novel technique that can improve user performance in skim reading. Users typically use a continuous-rate-based scrolling technique to skim works such as longer Web pages, e-books, and PDF files. However, visual attention is compromised at higher scrolling rates because of motion blur and extraneous objects with overly brief exposure times. In response, we present Spotlights. It complements the regular continuous technique at high speeds (2–20 pages/s). We present a novel design rule informed by theories of the human visual system for dynamically selecting objects and placing them on transparent overlays on top of the viewer. This improves the quality of visual processing at high scrolling rates by 1) limiting the number of objects, 2) ensuring minimal processing time per object, and 3) keeping objects static to avoid motion blur and facilitate gaze deployment. Comprehension levels for long documents were comparable with those in continuous-rate-based scrolling, but Spotlights showed significantly better scrolling speed, gaze deployment, recall, lookup performance, and user-rated comprehension.

ACM Classification Keywords
H.5.2. Information Interfaces and Presentation (e.g. HCI): User Interfaces – Interaction styles

Author Keywords
Skim reading; comprehension; scrolling techniques; attention brokering; visual attention; attentional blink

INTRODUCTION
This paper presents *Spotlights*, a novel technique to facilitate *skim reading* of long documents. The explosion of digital content on the Internet has made rapid comprehension of complex information important for users [24, 9]. Our goal is to improve the most commonly used interaction technique for documents, *continuous-rate-based scrolling*, which has become the *de facto* standard in browser and viewer applications. Scrolling rate is typically controlled by a scroll wheel, scrollbar, touchpad, or touchscreen.

The design of Spotlights addresses three factors that degrade information gain in continuous scrolling at high scrolling speeds: 1) too many objects competing for visual selection, 2) overly brief per-object exposure times, and 3) motion blur [17, 30]. These drawbacks compromise users' ability to find information (lookup), explore contents, and comprehend documents when scrolling quickly. In particular, visual processing suffers if attention must be shifted too soon. This effect is called *attentional blink*. Current understanding is that about 500 ms of processing time is required to avoid it [29]. Although the phenomenon is more complex than this [26], the 'minimum 500 ms rule' provides a starting point for our approach. Spotlights is designed to complement continuous scrolling by giving a greater chance of spotting interesting objects at high scrolling speed. In our design, continuous scrolling takes place as normal below the rate of 2 pages/second (pps), Above this rate, Spotlights is triggered. It selects a few objects for static, semi-transparent layers (spotlights) rendered in the viewer window (see Figure 1). Their transparency allows the user to maintain a global view

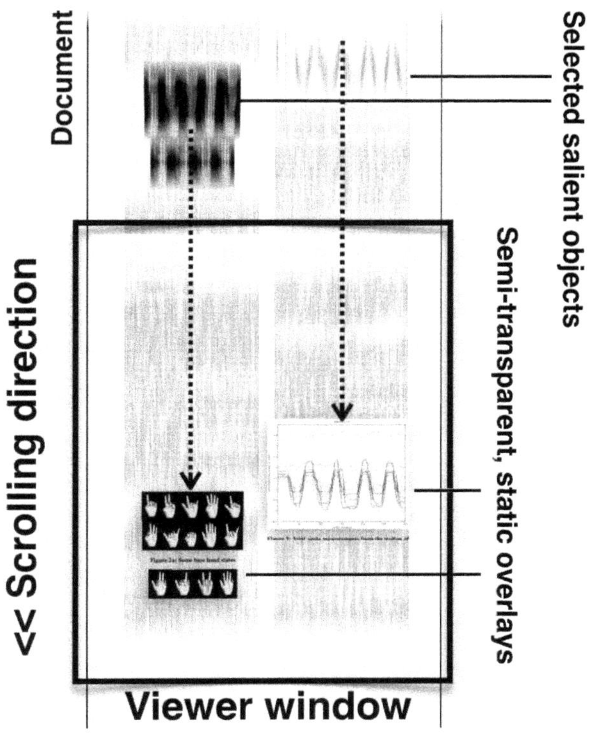

Figure 1. Spotlights supports skim reading with continuous scrolling in document viewers. In scrolling down at a high scrolling rate, Spotlights selects important objects into semi-transparent overlays (spotlights) that stay static for a prolonged time before fading away. Thereby, the user can maintain visual attention on objects from previous pages.

CHI'16, May 07–12, 2016, San Jose, CA, USA
Copyright © 2016 ACM. ISBN 978-1-4503-3362-7/16/05 ...$15.00
DOI: http://dx.doi.org/10.1145/2858036.2858299

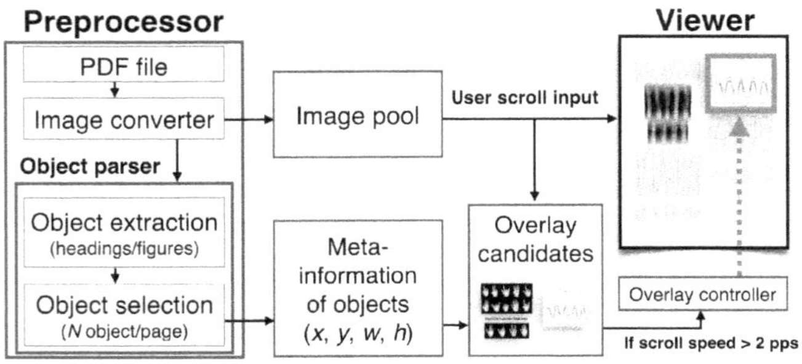

Figure 2. System overview: Spotlights extracts objects from a document in a series of preprocessing steps and renders them as an overlay in the renderer (viewer). The preprocessor saves only the meta-information of headings and figures to select overlay candidates from the image pool. The candidate objects can be highlighted as static overlays while the background image is scrolling.

of the scrolling document and spot potentially interesting objects underneath the layers. The spotlights remain on long enough to allow visual processing before fading away. Attention then is guided to another one appearing in the viewer. The detail-level behaviour of the technique is highly dynamic and responds to factors such as scrolling speed, clicking, and object type. Our approach requires no special hardware or expensive real-time computation. It can be integrated into a viewer that uses continuous scrolling. The only requirement is (lightweight) preprocessing of documents (see Figure 2).

Our technical contribution builds on and extends existing interaction techniques that select objects for attention at higher scrolling rates. We present a novel *design rule* to find the optimal spatial–temporal trade-off for human visual attention. More precisely, it determines 1) whether to show objects in spotlights / how many to show and 2) for how long. We claim that this supports visual attention in four ways: 1) divided attention is supported by limiting the number of objects for attention, 2) selective attention is supported by presenting the overlays in a predictable location, 3) motion blur is minimised by keeping overlays static (the gaze need not pursue them), and 4) attentional blink is avoided via an enforced minimum exposure time of 500 ms. The benefit to the user is that attention can be deployed to more objects and maintained longer at high scrolling rates.

To evaluate Spotlights, we followed a replicate-and-extend strategy wherein we repeated a set core task but implemented slight changes to conditions and dependent variables. To increase realism, we did not force users to use Spotlights but allowed them to control the scrolling rate in all studies. The three evaluation studies allow us to compare Spotlights to regular continuous-rate-based scrolling in terms of four central aspects of skim reading:

- Recall of contents (Study 1)
- Dynamics of scrolling (studies 1 and 2)
- Comprehension, self-reported (Study 1) and indicated by a questionnaire (Study 2)
- Lookup performance (Study 3)

The results are favourable. Spotlights not only supports keeping user attention on objects but improves interactions *during* scrolling. As users spot interesting items more reliably, they tend to do more backward scrolling. They are also faster in finding items they are looking for, and their recall of content improves. In other respects, scores were equal between Spotlights and the continuous-scrolling technique. We conclude the paper by discussing opportunities to exploit the properties of human visual attention in skim reading.

In the following discussion, we describe the design and implementation of Spotlights. We discuss how to handle issues such as masking and how to support page backtracking.

PREVIOUS WORK

We give a brief overview of skim reading, then position Spotlights in relation to existing scrolling techniques.

Definitions of skim reading describe it as being about *absorbing information* [11], wherein the defining feature is the aim of comprehending a new document in minimal time [24]. In addition to this main goal, skim reading involves sub-goals closer to the interaction. Firstly, it is an activity often involving *visual search tasks* wherein the goal is to find an object known in advance [24, 33, 7]. This emphasises *visual recognition* of objects during scrolling. Skim reading also involves *target acquisition*: after an interesting object is identified, it should be selected with the mouse or attended visually ([15]). Interestingly, empirical studies of unassisted skim reading suggest that most users are not efficient in it [3]. It has been noted that users exhibit a satisficing strategy wherein they jump ahead in the text when information gain falls below some threshold [9]. This is manifested in erratic scrolling rates.

Spotlights contributes to a body of techniques designed to support interaction with visual spaces that exceed the size of the viewport. These techniques typically target 1D visual spaces and documents. Five individual approaches can be distinguished. One is to make scrolling performance more robust for particular situations, such as dealing with varying lengths of documents ([6]) or single-handed mobile interaction ([25]). Secondly, the transition between pages can be enhanced. It has been found that users benefit from an animated transition more than page-flipping [22]. Rapid serial visual presentation (*RSVP*) is an alternative to page-based presentation that can minimise the motion blur in scrolling. It shows only static fragments of a document (e.g., words, phrases, or figures) at a time but at a very rapid pace. Thirdly, one can improve rate control, as with *hopping* [18] or *advance visual cues* [20]. A *wear-based scrollbar* [1] supports revisiting by visualising cues about previous visits to a page. Kim et al. [21] implemented a pseudo-haptic technique that creates an illusionary sensation of friction around important objects to alert users. Fourthly, one can relax the assumption that the document must be navigated linearly. Most 1D techniques here can be characterised via a scale–space diagram [10], including *Flipper*, which switches from continuous scrolling to flipping at 2 pps, and *Speed-Dependent Automatic Zooming* (*SDAZ*) [17] adaptively zooms out as scrolling rate increases. However, both suffer from decreasing resolution at higher rates, making it hard to read headings and decipher figures. *Semantic rendering and zooming* have been proposed; these retain or enhance selected objects when the rate increases [19, 4, 27]. The fifth approach, which is orthogonal, is to train users to skim read more efficiently. Yi [31] presented *Qn-DReview*, a reading technique that facilitated rapid comprehension of scientific (CHI) papers.

Spotlights is a mono-scale technique that is best understood not in terms of scale but on the temporal dimension. As RSVP does, it selects objects for attention. Spotlights builds on RSVP by keeping these objects static, in overlays, but it mixes them with a rate-controlled background. As SDAZ's does, its behaviour changes with scrolling rate, but its selection and adaptation follow a novel design rule that prevents exceeding the limits of visual attention. This allows continuous scrolling at average rates of up to 10 pps, which pose a problem for existing techniques. Flipper, for example, prevents rates over 2 pps. Although our focus here is on the dynamic management of overlays, Spotlights is compatible with many of the above-mentioned techniques, including semantic zooming, advance cues, and hopping. One advantage of Spotlights is that no additional widgets or interactions are needed: it works in the familiar framework of a document viewer simply upon scrolling. Of the existing techniques, *Froggy GX* [32] comes closest. Aimed at enhancing Web page skimming for non-native learners of English, it uses content overlays, along with masking and filtering. However, it too lacks a solution to avoid overloading the visual attention.

OVERLAYS: DESIGN AND IMPLEMENTATION

The overlays in Spotlights are transparent, rendered in or near the position of the corresponding object on the original page, and fade out as a function of time. They are filled sequentially in first-come, first-served fashion, starting at the top of the display when multiple objects are shown simultaneously. We implemented the technique for documents composed of textual and graphical elements. However, the principles can be adapted for other types.

Extraction of Objects on a Page for Overlays

We automatically parse candidate objects for overlay that are likely to be interesting and descriptive. Previous work on skim reading suggests that users devote more gaze time to

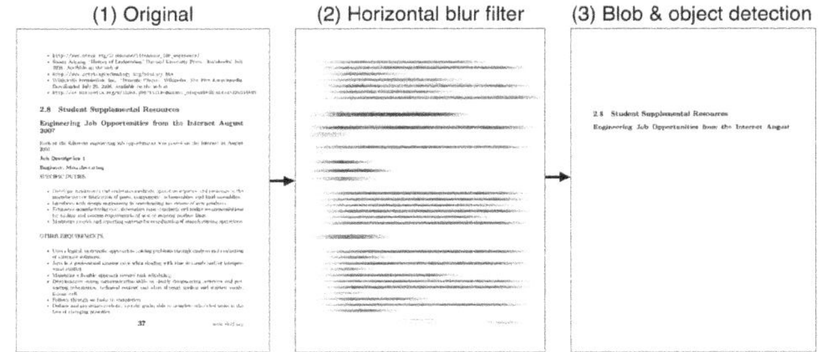

Figure 3. Spotlights extracts objects for overlays by using horizontal Gaussian blur and blob detection. This identifies objects that are larger than their context.

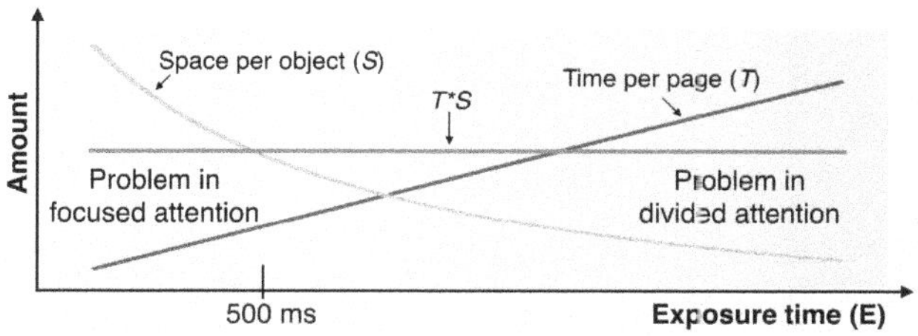

Figure 4. Spotlights maximises performance by obtaining optimal exposure time E. Prolonged exposure allows more processing time for visual attention but causes overloading in the viewer window. Each object is guaranteed a minimum of 500 ms exposure, to avoid attentional blink.

titles, headings, pictures, and figures than plain text [24, 16, 9]. We used this fact as a guide in creating an object parser.

Our parser extracts headings and figures from a PDF page, using a two-step process. Firstly, the PDF file is converted to a set of images. Then, *horizontal* Gaussian blur is applied to each image. The result is a set of 'smudged' horizontal lines, as depicted in Figure 3. In the second step, we group these lines via a blob-detection process. We assume that there is a standard line spacing defined for a document, and those blobs of greater height than this line spacing are selected as possible important objects. Titles, headings, and figures are larger vertically than plain text and are likely to be selected in this process. Lastly, we sort the objects on a page in order of decreasing height, which allows us to select only the largest 1–2 objects per page for the overlays.

This parser is implemented in Java and works well for relatively homogenous content types (for other content, we may need a smarter extraction algorithm [5]). It reaches a processing speed of 100 pages per 40 seconds on a regular laptop. The technique is demonstrated in the supplementary video.

The Design Rule for Optimal Exposure Time E

After choosing objects, we render them in the location they originally had on the page. Here, we describe a design rule to decide how many objects to select and how long they should be displayed in overlays. The insight is that there is a trade-off between attention's *spatial* resources – that is, space per object – and its *temporal* resources – that is, the time allowed per page. On one hand, it is beneficial if an object is shown for a long time. On the other, if exposure time is increased, more objects end up crowding the view. Therefore, exposure time should be increased only if there are few upcoming objects. Our design rule searches for the optimal exposure time for overlays, which maximises attentional performance while minimising other possible problems. We shall now describe the rule more formally.

Let us assume that a user is scrolling with N_{obj} important objects per page and a scrolling speed of v_p pps. From the visual attention perspective, this context affords $1/v_p$ seconds per page (T, the temporal resource) and $1/N_{obj}$ of space (or area) per object (S, the spatial resource). Spotlights affects T and S by choosing how long the objects remain there even after the page that contained them is no longer visible. Let us call this E, for exposure time of overlays. With longer E, more pages in the past leave objects in the current viewer space, hence increasing the total number of objects per page. The changes in T and S due to exposure time E can be formulated in detail thus:

$$T = 1/v_p + E \text{ and } S = 1/(N_{obj}v_pE + N_{obj}) \quad (1)$$

However, if we multiply T and S, we always get the same value, no matter the changes in E, indicating temporal–spatial trade-off in the design space of Spotlights (see Figure 4):

$$T \times S = 1/(N_{obj}v_p) \quad (2)$$

Next, we explain the user perspective on the design rule. Let us say that the user is achieving a certain amount of attentional performance A with the given resources (T, S) and a given scrolling context (v_p, N_{obj}). Using Equation 1, we can express the function as shown below:

$$\text{Attentional performance} = A(T, S, v_p, N_{obj}) = A(E, v_p, N_{obj}) \quad (3)$$

If attentional performance is already at maximum and no bottleneck is occurring due to excess temporal and spatial resources, changes in E or other context parameters do not affect attentional performance, $A(E)$. In other words, the only bottleneck is in the user's attentional gate. However, here we suggest a design rule that first assumes a *temporal* bottleneck in the conventional scrolling context. It gradually increases E until we find that no more relief of the temporal bottleneck is available (see Algorithm 1). This 'staircasing' procedure is similar to just-noticeable difference (JND) methodology in psychophysics and was used in a previous study of layered user interfaces [12].

Algorithm 1 Design Rule to Find Optimal E

```
Define N_obj, v_p, ΔE, E_0 and Threshold_E
procedure SEARCH
top:
    E_i ← E_{i-1} + ΔE
    Observe A_i = A(E_i)
    if (A_i − A_{i-1}) < Threshold_E then
        return E_i
    else
        i ← i + 1
        goto top.
```

In practice, the design rule can be parameterised in a user experiment. Firstly, N_{obj}, v_p, E_0, and ΔE should be predefined on the basis of the scrolling context that we are striving to optimise. N_{obj} and v_p should not be extreme but represent the target range and type of documents. For E_0, we would like to start at 500 ms to avoid attentional blink [28, 29]. Finally, the user's attentional performance should be appropriately observed. One of our studies used an eye tracker to measure attentional performance.

Dynamic Overlay Control

We adapt exposure time E for an overlay dynamically, in real time, in line with scrolling speed and user behaviour (see Figure 6). If the scrolling rate exceeds 2 pps, the overlay function is triggered. After triggering of the overlay, its transparency is linearly decreased until the set time expires. When transparency is high, it acts as a trigger for visual attention to move

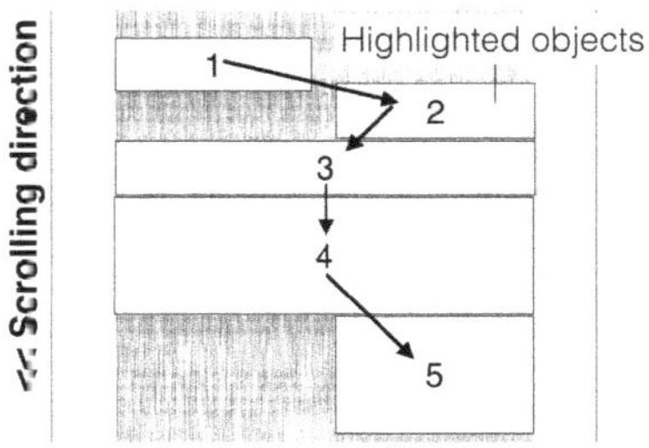

Figure 5. When two or more overlays from the same location compete, they are 'stacked' in first-come, first-served fashion. An object's horizontal position is maintained.

on to the next object; also, it allows the attention to select the 'freshest' objects easily to focus on. The user can eliminate the overlays at any time by stopping the scrolling.

Our overlay control is content-specific. Taking into account the fact that textual information takes longer to comprehend [23], we obtain parameter E separately for graphical vs. textual objects, as described in the calibration section.

The overlay functions were implemented by means of an OpenGL framebuffer object. A frame rate of 60 Hz was achieved for 1050-pixel height with A4 or US-letter-sized documents.

Minimising Masking with Transparency

During scrolling, the movement of the document in the background layer is not meaningless; it gives the user a sense of scrolling speed and global position [22]. Hence, an overlay should not mask too much of the scrolling background. To minimise masking yet achieve high legibility of the overlay, we utilised an empirical result from a past study [12]. That finding was that a foreground opacity of 20% is required for obtaining good performance with both focused and divided attention. In our case, the overlay should get more focus than the background layer.

Stacking Objects

We also address competition for the same space among highlighted objects. This can occur when two overlays, from two or more previous pages, overlap in position. Titles and figures, for example, tend to be in the top half of a page. In this case, Spotlights tries to retain original positions, except that it treats the vertical and the horizontal dimension differently. Vertical positions for overlays are filled sequentially in first-come, first-served fashion, starting at the top of the display. In contrast, the horizontal position is kept as it was,

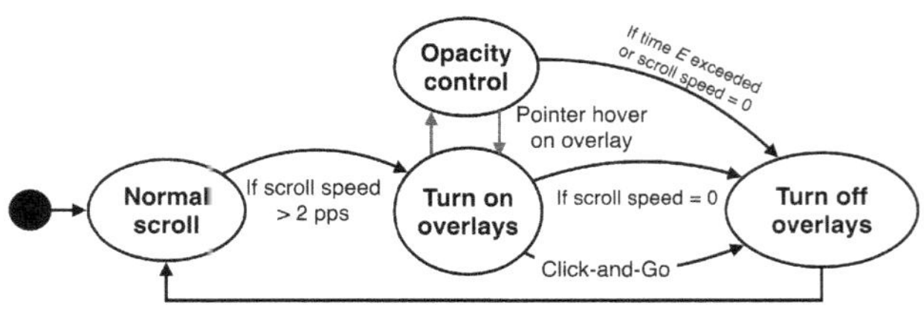

Figure 6. State diagram of the dynamic overlay control function in the Spotlightssystem.

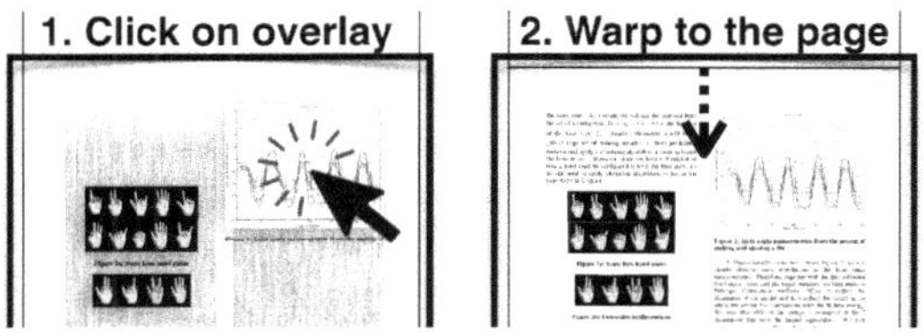

Figure 7. Click-and-Go: The page containing the highlight can be warped to by clicking on it. This reduces the time for backtracking to spotted objects.

to retain some memory for object locations. When the document is crowded, the overlays are 'stacked'. Figure 5 shows an example. The fact that the overlays are static and close to each other may aid in selective attention: a more predictable location may make it easier to find the next targets.

Click-and-Go: Page Warping with Selections

The overlays are selectable with the cursor. Before selection, the opacity control is turned off from the mouse-hover event (see Figure 6). Selection takes the viewer to the page containing the object in the overlay, in order to reduce the time for backtracking. Just after the warp, old highlights are removed from the viewer. Figure 7 illustrates this.

THE CALIBRATION STUDY

Here, we describe empirically obtaining exposure time E for textual and graphical objects. We applied our design rule (see Algorithm 1) for the following target scrolling scenario:

- N_{obj} = 1–2 objects per page
- v_p = 10 pps (averaged over 2–20 pps)
- $Threshold_E$ will be statistically tested with Helmert contrast
- E_0 = 500 ms, to avoid attentional blink
- ΔE = 250 ms

Optimal exposure time E differs among various types of objects in a document. What matters is how quickly the user can recognise the object, absorb its 'gist', and attribute some value or importance to it. Our case is focused on two object types – headings (text) and graphical objects – but the procedure can be replicated for other types of object.

The experimental task was to follow rapidly scrolling symbols (shapes) or words. Users were asked to report which object variant (e.g., a green triangle) was the most frequent.

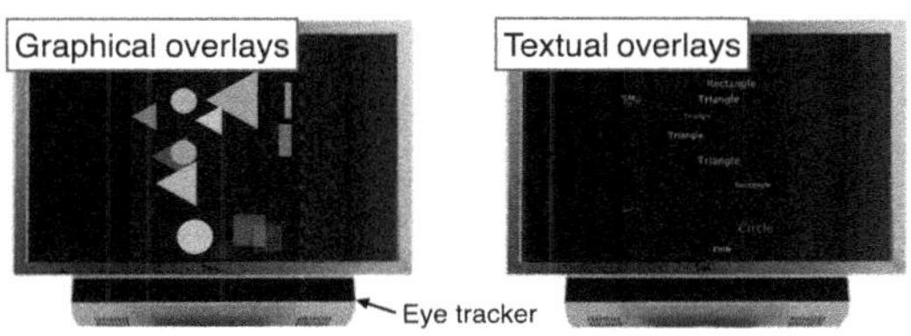

Figure 8. We obtained the optimal exposure time E for symbols (on the left) and textual objects (at right). Users were asked to attend a rapidly scrolling display to assess which of the three elements (e.g., rectangles, circles, and triangles) was the most common.

However, we did not examine this; we looked at only how long they needed to process an item before moving on to the next one. Figure 8 shows the task. As stimuli, we use simple symbols such as triangles and basic words. The reason is to obtain a *lower, optimistic boundary* for E, the minimal time for obtaining the gist of an object in rapid viewing.

Method

Participants: Four people (1 male, 3 female) were recruited from the local campus to participate. Their average age was 28.75 years (SD = 2.98), and three had corrected vision. All were familiar with scrolling.

Experimental design: The experiment followed a 2×2×6 within-subjects design. The object-type conditions (2) and number-of-objects-per-page conditions (2) were balanced across participants. The duration of E was increased in six ascending levels, to avoid abrupt or surprising changes (this presumed that users get accustomed to the technique). We varied the type of object with two levels (word and symbol). The number of objects per page too was varied on two levels (1 and 2). The six levels for exposure time were 500, 750, 1000, 1250, 1500, and 1750 ms. The dependent measure of user performance was the time spent gazing at objects as a percentage of the trial's duration (50 s).

Task and materials: We implemented a prototype of Spotlights using symbols (shapes) and words. We used a page size of 743×1050 pixels (a typical ratio for documents). Scrolling speed was fixed at 10 pps. Three variations of shape existed for the symbol condition: triangle, square, and circle. For the text mode, the name of the shape was displayed as a string (e.g., 'triangle' or 'rectangle'; see Figure 8). The location and the colour of each object were randomly assigned when the page was generated. The object size was 50–150 pixels for a symbol. Font sizes between 25 and 50 pixels were used for text. Each trial presented 500 pages of objects generated randomly by the algorithm.

Procedure: Participants were asked to find a comfortable posture. The display was then set perpendicular to the field of view at a distance of 50 cm. After eye-tracker calibration, the experimenter explained the procedure. The participants were asked to attend to as many targets as possible during scrolling and at the end report which had been the most frequent shape during their scrolling. This task was devised to ensure that participants really attended to the stimuli. In reality, all shapes had the same probability. After the instruction, the experimenter started a trial consisting of scrolling through 500 pages. Because scroll speed was set to 10 pps, it took about 50 seconds to complete one trial. In total, it took about 30 minutes to complete the full 24 trials.

Apparatus: An SMI eye tracker (RED, 250 Hz) was installed just below an LCD monitor (Dell 21-inch with 60 Hz refresh rate; see Figure 8). A Java application on a laptop (MacBook Pro, late 2012, 15-inch, 2.2 GHz Intel Core i7, with Intel Iris Pro 1536 MB graphic card) generated and controlled the stimulus. Gaze location and the colour of the pixel at that location were saved in real time. We used colour information to extract the user's attention to the highlighted objects.

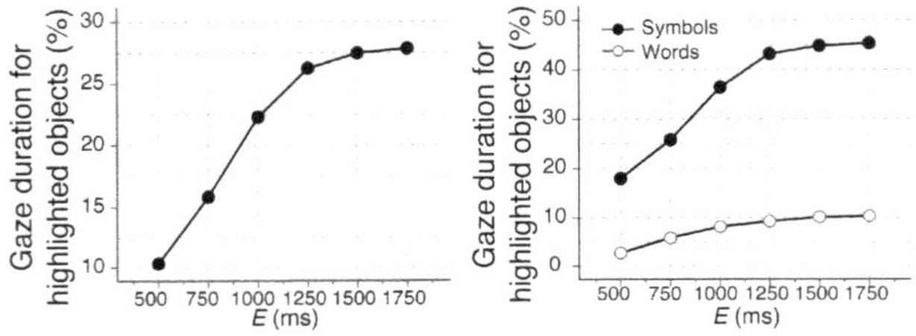

Figure 9. At right, the optimal exposure time *E* for words vs. graphical objects. The estimates were obtained from eye-tracking data showing how long users were able to attend to highlighted layers as the number of objects and the exposure times changed. On the left, the average over the two object types.

Results

We used repeated-measures ANOVA with an alpha level of 0.05. Exposure duration showed a significant effect on the duration of attention to highlighted objects: $F(5,15) = 22.43$, $p = 0.001$. In particular, it increased with exposure time. However, the Helmert contrast shows no effect beyond Level 4 (1250 ms) of E ($p = 0.42$). Figure 9 presents this effect. The interaction effect between highlight duration and object type was also significant: $F(5,15) = 8.84$, $p < 0.001$. Pairwise comparisons prove no longer significant after Level 3 (1000 ms, $p = 0.11$) for symbols and Level 4 (1250 ms, $p = 0.08$) for words. This difference may stem from the differences in required withdrawal times between object types [23]. We conclude that words required 250 ms more exposure time.

The interaction effect between exposure duration and the number of objects on the page was not significant ($p = 0.16$). We conclude that at such a rapid rate, attention is already at its maximum with just a single object in an overlay.

STUDY 1: RECALL

Study 1 was informed by empirical research on skim reading, which emphasises the influence of 1) time pressure, 2) complex documents, and 3) focus on comprehension (as opposed to search). Our study imposed a time limit and used long documents (300+ pages). To assess comprehension, we asked users to recall keywords and figures, numerically rating their comprehension also. For directly testing whether Spotlights improves ability to attend to objects during scrolling, we also collected data on gaze and scrolling behaviour.

Method

Participants: Twelve individuals were recruited from the local university. Average participant age was 26.9 years (*SD* = 6.44). All had experience with scrolling. All reported being comfortable with the specific touchpad used for the study. Four users had corrected vision. The users were compensated with cinema tickets for participation. None reported having background knowledge of the materials.

Experimental design: The experiment followed a 2×2 mixed design with Scrolling Method and Book Set as factors. To mitigate order effects, we created two distinct sets of documents, and these were balanced between the two techniques. Each set consisted of three unrelated documents, and the order of inner documents was counter-balanced. Scrolling Method was set as a within-subject factor while Book Set was set as a between-subject factor. Dependent measures included the number of figures and keywords recalled by the participants, participant-reported confidence in comprehension, the number of minutes the users would need to complete the skim reading, mean and maximum speed of scrolling, the amount of downward and backward scrolling, and depth of scrolling.

Task and materials: The participants were instructed to skim the whole document to get an overview. They could control scrolling speed as they wished. Participants were allowed to select their strategy for skim reading but asked to maximise global understanding of the document. Each trial was ended automatically after 90 seconds.

To increase realism, the materials used were books from various fields. The documents were chosen to have many pages ($M = 333$ pages, $SD = 195$). The books are listed below. Book Set 1 consisted of the first three books listed, and Book Set 2 was made up of the last three.

- *Architecture and Mathematics from Antiquity to the Future*, 723 pages (0.41 headings/page, 0.32 figures/page)
- *Higher Education in Sport in Europe: From Labour Market Demand to Training Supply*, 194 pages (0.98 headings/page, 0.29 figures/page)
- *Functional Programming in JavaScript*, 261 pages (0.55 headings/page, 0.019 figures/page)
- *Architectures: Modernism and After*, 270 pages (0.29 headings/page, 0.085 figures/page)
- *New Media, Old News: Journalism & Democracy in the Digital Age*, 233 pages (0.83 headings/page, 0.15 figures/page)
- *R Packages: Organize, Test, Document and Share Your Code*, 318 pages (0.52 headings/page, 0.054 figures/page)

These densities were computed by means of the object extractor of Spotlights. The average number of objects per page was 0.78 (*SD* = 0.33).

Spotlights was automatically triggered in the range of 2 to 20 pps. We used the parameters obtained in the calibration study. Because the average object density of the books used (0.75 objects/page) were below 1, we could use the empirically obtained E from the calibration study. Objects with a width-to-height ratio above 20 were regarded as textual objects and given 1500 ms of exposure time. Others were treated as figures and provided with 1250 ms. During the exposure period, the opacity of the background layer was decreased linearly from 1.0 to 0.2 on the basis of the instantaneous scrolling speed. For each page, the object with the greatest height was chosen as the candidate for Spotlights.

Procedure: The procedure was the same as in the calibration study, with the following exceptions. Participants controlled the scrolling with a touchpad on a laptop at a desk. The two-finger scrolling method (of Mac OS X) was used. The directional mapping was changed to suit the preferences of the user. After eye-tracker calibration, the experimenter demonstrated both scrolling methods in detail. Then, user was pro-

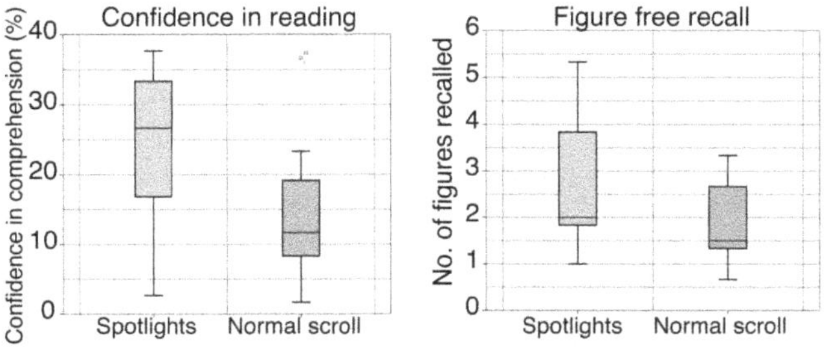

Figure 10. Study 1: Spotlights users reported higher confidence in their memory for objects ($p = 0.028$, left). Spotlights increased recall accuracy for graphical objects (right).

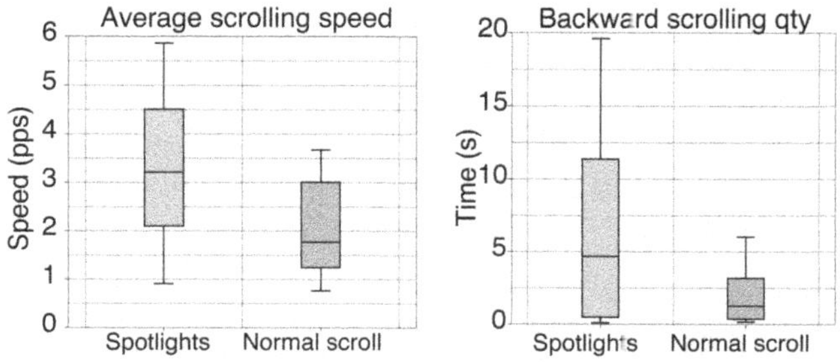

Figure 11. Study 1: Participants scrolled faster with Spotlights (left). Thanks to spotting more interesting objects, participants used more time scrolling backwards with Spotlights to revisit a passed object.

vided with five minutes for training with each method. A dummy document was used. After training, the experimenter explained the purpose of the study and the user's goal in it. Each trial lasted 90 seconds, and the Click-and-Go feature was turned off for this study.

Apparatus: We used the same set-up as in the calibration study.

Post-trial data collection: After each trial, four questions about understanding were asked. Two involved free recall and addressed memory for keywords and figures. The other two were about perceived comprehension. Participants were asked to rate their confidence in the level of comprehension they achieved on a 100-point scale. The quality of recall was not assessed, only the number of items.

Results

We used repeated-measures ANOVA with an alpha level of 0.05. Benjamini–Hochberg correction [2] was applied to correct for multiple testing, and all pairwise statistics used Bonferroni correction.

Free Recall

Memory of content improved with Spotlights. Scrolling method had a borderline effect on the number of figures recalled by the participants: $F(1,10) = 3.66$, $p = 0.11$. In particular, the mean for Spotlights was 2.69 (SD = 1.38) and for continuous scrolling 1.81 (SD = 0.85). However, no significant effect was found on the number of keywords recalled: $F(1,10) = 0.642$, $p = 0.50$. Overall, 7.73 keywords were reported (SD = 2.81). Scrolling Method × Book Set had a significant effect on the number of figures recalled: $F(1,10) = 6.914$, $p = 0.025$. Pairwise comparison showed that more figures were recalled ($p = 0.009$) when book set 1 was read with Spotlights ($M = 3.22$, $SD = 1.66$) than with normal scrolling ($M = 1.11$, $SD = 0.34$). For book set 2, there was no difference between scrolling methods.

Confidence

Users had more confidence in their comprehension with Spotlights: $F(1,10) = 6.61$, $p = 0.04$. In particular, Spotlights gained a 23.86% confidence score (SD = 11.9), while continuous scrolling received 15.33% (SD = 11.2).

No significant effect was found for the number of minutes users estimated they would need to complete the skim reading: $F(1,10) = 0.303$, $p = 0.59$. Participants reported, on average, that 10.79 minutes (SD = 9.8) would be required per document.

Pattern of Scrolling

Scrolling was faster with Spotlights. Mean scrolling speed differed significantly between the scrolling methods: $F(1,10) = 20.62$, $p = 0.009$. With Spotlights it was 3.26 pps (SD = 1.53), whereas continuous scrolling yielded 2.03 pps (SD = 14.74). Maximum scrolling speed too was significantly different: ($F(1,10) = 7.47$, $p = 0.047$). Spotlights showed maximum speeds of 35.19 pps, with continuous scrolling reaching only 25.64 pps.

Also, when using Spotlights, users scrolled significantly more in the downward direction: $F(1,10) = 9.97$, $p = 0.049$ – specifically, for 34.65 seconds (SD = 12.74) with Spotlights and 24.67 seconds (SD = 16.96) with continuous scrolling. However, the backward-scrolling time too was higher for Spotlights. Spotlights showed more backward scrolling ($M = 6.33$ s, $SD = 6.56$) than continuous scrolling did ($M = 2.04$ s, $SD = 2.08$) at rates exceeding 2 pps: $F(1,10) = 7.43$, $p = 0.038$. The effect of scrolling method on scrolling depth was also significant: ($F(1,10) = 9.83$, $p = 0.033$). Spotlights users scrolled through 209 pages (SD = 68.3), continuous-system users 157 pages (SD = 79).

Pattern of Gaze

We show eye-tracking data in Figure 12. The plot presents the movement speed of gaze vs. scroll speed. This figure shows

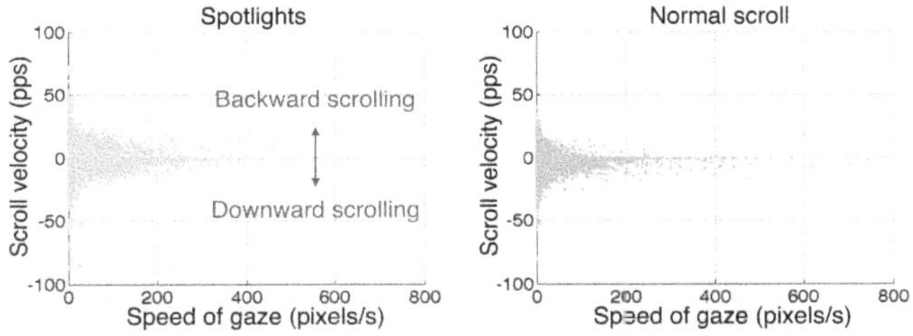

Figure 12. Study 1: Eye-tracking data show a more active gaze pattern for Spotlights. The amount of backward and forward scrolling in particular was more balanced with Spotlights (left), showing more vertical symmetry of shape than the normal scrolling condition did (right). In this plot, downward scrolling is expressed as negative scrolling speed.

that Spotlights allowed richer use of visual attention to objects, especially in fast scrolling. In other words, users could maintain visual attention longer on a larger number of objects in the document. Furthermore, the amount of backward and forward scrolling was more balanced with Spotlights, showing a vertically more symmetrical form than normal scrolling.

STUDY 2: COMPREHENSION

Our second study compared Spotlights to normal scrolling in a questionnaire-based comprehension test accompanied by standard workload metrics.

We learned from the recall study that participants employed more backward tracking. We wanted to assist in this behaviour by turning on the Click-and-Go feature (see Figure 7). When an object is highlighted, the user can select that item by clicking it with the cursor. This warps the user to that object in the document and removes any other highlighted objects from view. The user is able to return to potentially important and interesting objects within the document.

Method

Participants: Sixteen peoples were recruited from local universities. Most participants were women (3 male, 13 female), and ages ranged from 20 to 34, with an average of 25.6 (SD = 4.3). Six participants had corrected vision. Twelve of them assessed their English skills as high enough for comprehending documents. The other four reported their skills in English as at medium level. None had background knowledge of the testing materials. All participants were volunteers, and each was rewarded with one cinema ticket for this 60-minute study.

Experimental design: We followed a $2 \times 2 \times 2$ mixed design. Scroll Mode was varied on two levels (Spotlights and normal scrolling), as was Reading Time (2 minutes and 10 minutes). Also, two separate books were chosen, to create two distinct reading conditions:

- Condition 1: Reading an engineering book with Spotlights and an HCI book with normal scrolling
- Condition 2: Reading an engineering book with normal scrolling and an HCI book with Spotlights

Scroll Mode and Reading Time were set as within-subject factors, while Reading Condition was set as a between-subject factor. Order of conditions was fully balanced among participants.

Task and materials: The task was to skim read through two books, using the continuous-scrolling method while trying to comprehend as much information as possible. The task was carried out for two books: *Engineering: An Introduction for High School* and *Human-Computer Interaction (3rd Edition)*. Properties of the books are shown below:

- *Engineering: An Introduction for High School*, 220 pages (0.84 headings/page, 0.58 figures/page)
- *Human–Computer Interaction (3rd Edition)*, 255 pages (Chapter 1 to 7, 0.53 headings/page, 0.51 figures/page)

Participants were told to prepare for a post-reading questionnaire. Before proceeding to the actual experiment, participants used a demo application to gain familiarity with Spotlights.

Multiple-choice questionnaire for comprehension: The questionnaires were generated to assess skim reading comprehension, emphasising literal and reorganisational comprehension[8]. To simplify scoring, all questions were multiple-choice items with three alternatives, of which one was correct. This made the expected score one third the number of questions if a participant was guessing. The purpose was to measure comprehension of important aspects and content of the two books. The questions were devised to pertain to larger themes, body text, headers, figures, and graphs. No type of content was especially favoured or ignored. The goal in creation of the questions was to cover all important material and produce a test-like setup for measuring comprehension.

After all questions were ready, they were split into two distinct question sets per book (of 22 and 21 questions for the engineering book and of 18 questions each for the HCI book). This was done by separating them into beginning-, middle-, and end-of-book questions, then picking the same number of questions randomly from all three categories. Thus the entire book was represented in each of the question sets. Although the questions were picked randomly, their order was preserved such that it reflected the order in which topics were presented in the books.

The questionnaire was administered via an online form, which automatically recorded the responses. Some of the questions involved a picture to which a link was embedded in the questionnaire.

Procedure: The experiment was conducted in a noise-free room, with participants seated at a desk where they were asked to find a comfortable posture. A background questionnaire was presented to examine age, field of studies, level of English skills etc. Participants were first told the general structure of the experiment and then instructed on how to use Spotlights. The experiment was carried out with a laptop. Each participant practised using the software for five minutes or as long as needed for feeling comfortable with it. Continuous scrolling was facilitated by the touchpad, with two-finger use.

After the practice, participants proceeded to the skim reading task. During the reading, a scrollbar indicating the current location of the viewing window was shown at the right edge of the document. The time left for reading was visualised also, at the left edge of the document, via a vertical progress bar. Participants were instructed to rest if there was any test time left after answering all questions. The experiment lasted one hour.

Apparatus: We used the same laptop as in Study 1, with the same Java application. The only difference was in the Click-and-Go function, which was turned on. The effective frame rate of the application was 60 Hz.

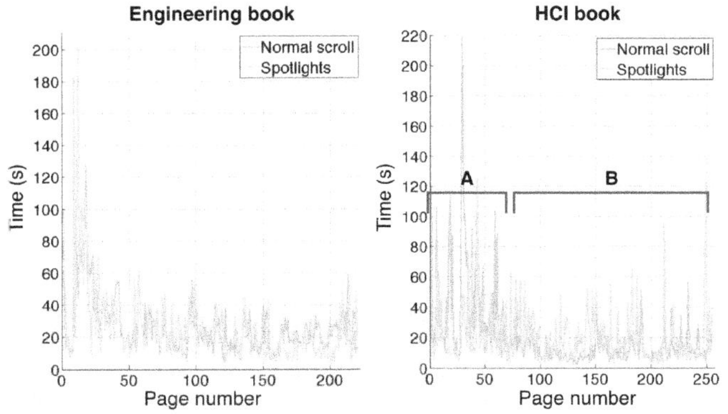

Figure 13. Time spent on reading, plotted against page number. Participants showed deeper exploration of documents when using Spotlights for the HCI book (right).

Post-trial data collection: After each reading task, the questionnaire was administered, related to the book. Question-set order was balanced among participants. Answering time was limited to eight minutes, which was sufficient for all participants. Absolute scores were divided by the total number of questions in the set to gauge comprehension. When the participant was done with one mode, the corresponding workload was measured with a NASA-TLX form [14] in addition to the questionnaire, and answering time was increased to 10 minutes. We used Raw TLX values [13] to simplify the experimental procedure.

Results

Repeated-measures ANOVA with an alpha level of 0.05 was used for statistical testing. All pairwise statistics used Bonferroni correction. One participant gave no answer to five questions on the engineering book and three on the HCI book. An 'Incorrect' response was recorded for these.

Comprehension Scores

Reading time had no significant effect on reading scores ($F(1,14) = 0.072$, $p = 0.79$). The score was 58% for two-minute reading ($SD = 9.4$), 61% ($SD = 10$) for the 10-minute condition. Scroll Mode had no significant effect on reading scores ($F(1,14) = 0.30$, $p = 0.60$). Spotlights showed an average score of 60% ($SD = 11$), and normal scrolling scored 61% ($SD = 7$). Reading Condition had no significant effect on reading scores ($F(1, 14) = 3.80$, $p = 0.071$). The average score with the engineering book was 61% ($SD = 9$); that for the HCI book was 59% ($SD = 11$).

Figure 13 visualises the reading time spent on each page of the books for all participants. We found that for books that were predictable to them (e.g., *Engineering for High School*), users tended to rely more on normal scrolling. For less familiar books (e.g., *Human–Computer Interaction*), users tended to move around the entire document freely, using Spotlights, until finding something interesting to investigate further.

To understand possible effects of the differences in reading pattern shown in Figure 13, we further divided all questions into two groups: difficult (under 50% correct answers) and easy (above 50%). Of the 43 questions for the engineering book, 16 were regarded as difficult, and 11 out of 36 were regarded as difficult for the HCI one. For difficult questions, Scroll Mode × Reading Condition significantly affected comprehension score: $F(1,14) = 8.57$, $p = 0.01$. Most notably, Spotlights showed a 3.3% higher score ($p = 0.024$) than normal scrolling for reading condition 1. For reading condition 2, the difference was not significant. Scroll Mode × Reading Condition effect on score was not significant for easy questions: $F(1,14) = 0.38$, $p = 0.55$. We conclude that Spotlights helps users orient better to unfamiliar content, particularly by helping them understand the high-level structure of a book quickly.

Workload

None of the components in the TLX scale were significant: mental demand ($F(1,15) = 0.396$, $p = 0.54$), physical demand ($F(1,15) = 0.089$, $p = 0.77$), temporal demand ($F(1,15) = 0.016$, $p = 0.90$), performance ($F(1,15) = 0.791$, $p = 0.39$), effort ($F(1,15) = 0.127$, $p = 0.727$), and frustration ($F(1,15) = 0.281$, $p = 0.60$). Mean mental demand was 64.38 for Spotlights ($SD = 21.44$) and 66.56 ($SD = 20.63$) for normal scrolling. Physical demand with Spotlights was 27.19 ($SD = 25.03$), while that in normal scrolling was 25.63 ($SD = 23.16$); The result for temporal demand for Spotlights was 74.38 ($SD = 17.97$), 75 ($SD = 15.06$) for normal scrolling. For performance, Spotlights rated 65.31 ($SD = 20.37$), normal scrolling 61 ($SD = 21.49$). Effort was 68.44 for Spotlights ($SD = 17.49$) and 67.5 ($SD = 15.92$) for normal scrolling. Lastly, the corresponding figures for frustration were 52.81 ($SD = 23.59$) and 51.25 ($SD = 24.80$), respectively.

Usage Statistics for the Click-and-Go Feature

For the engineering book, participants used the Click-and-Go feature 7.06 ($SD = 7.19$) times with Spotlights. For the HCI book, they used this feature of Spotlights 11.56 ($SD = 9.63$) times.

STUDY 3: LOOKUP PERFORMANCE

The final study considered skim reading done for lookup and filtering purposes. A target was given and the user had to locate it in the document. Consider, for example, skimming the CHI proceedings to spot interesting articles for later reading. For such cases, scroll speed could be expected to be higher than in Study 2 (on comprehension), on account of the sparse distribution of interesting objects in the document. We again compare performance to continuous scrolling.

Participants: The same users who took part in Study 2 completed this study. Different materials and tasks were used, to avoid carry-over effects. Because of data loss caused by a technical error, two participants' results had to be discarded, making the number of eligible participants 14. All were compensated with one cinema ticket for the 30-minute-long study.

Experimental design: Scroll Mode was the only factor in this within-subjects experiment. The conditions (Spotlights and normal scrolling) were balanced across participants.

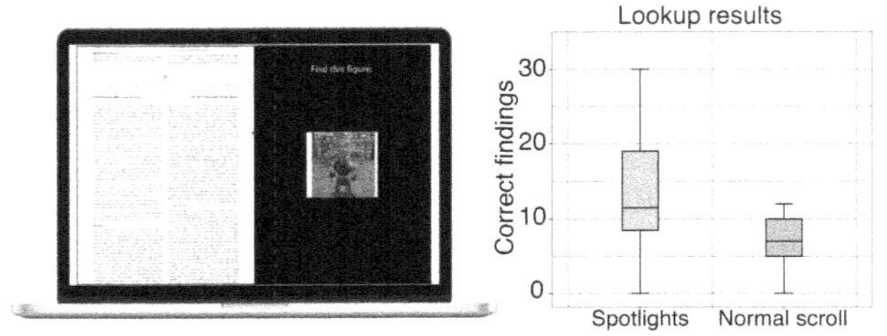

Figure 14. Study 3: Lookup task screen for finding figures in 20 CHI full papers. A target figure was shown in the right portion of the screen, and the user's task was to find it by scrolling the document on the left. Spotlights users were twice as successful in localising targets as those using normal scrolling.

Task and materials: The document used in the task was a compilation of 40 CHI full papers from 2014 and 2015. They were randomly divided into two groups of papers thus:

- Group 1: 20 CHI full papers (200 pages, 0.38 figures/page)
- Group 2: 20 CHI full papers (198 pages, 0.65 figures/page)

The task was to find a given target figure by using the continuous-scrolling method. We limited the target type to figures because searches of the textual information could be done conventionally with the Find feature (Ctrl+F) of the PDF viewer. Thanks to their fixed similar formatting, CHI papers are good for our purposes.

A figure was randomly chosen from the entire range of documents and displayed at the right side of the viewer to specify the current target (see Figure 14). If a document was full of figures, as with an object density above 2 figures/page, Spotlights had to skip some figures to avoid overlap between overlays. However, such extreme cases were rare.

Procedure: The apparatus and the experimental setting were the same as for Study 2. The task here was to find as many figures as possible from the set of scientific articles. Each scrolling method was used for 10 minutes, with a short break between them, for a total task duration of just over 20 minutes. To indicate finding the figure, the Tab key was pressed on a keyboard. For a successful hit to be registered, the entire picture had to be inside the viewing window. If the key was pressed at any other time, a result of 'Incorrect' was recorded. At the beginning of the task for each method, the viewer showed the first page of the document. After each key press, a new picture was shown. The simplicity of the task meant that no practice session was needed.

The order of the pictures was randomised, and both mode order and document group were balanced between participants.

Results

We used repeated-measures ANOVA with an alpha level of 0.05 for the analysis. The scrolling method had a significant effect on the number of correctly found targets ($F(1,13) = 15.87$, $p = 0.002$). With Spotlights, users ($M = 15.5$, $SD = 7.76$) were twice as successful in localising targets as they were in normal scrolling ($M = 7.57$, $SD = 3.08$). The number of false positives did not differ significantly between scrolling modes ($F(1,13) = 1.41, p = 0.26$). The mean of 'Incorrect' finds was 2.21 ($SD = 3.55$) for Spotlights and 1.00 ($SD = 1.03$) for normal scrolling.

SUMMARY AND FUTURE WORK

In this paper, we have presented a novel technique to support skim reading. It 'brokers' visual attention to objects in very fast scrolling of a document. As the user scrolls, it finds a balance between how many objects to show and how long to expose them. The benefits to users are threefold: 1) Even at high scrolling rates, some visual attention can be maintained and objects recognised. 2) The technique can be integrated into any application that uses continuous scrolling, on the assumption that (lightweight) preprocessing of documents is permissible. 3) It is intuitive and easy to learn. Our users learned it in five minutes during the study.

At a higher level, this paper has shown that we can approach the design of interaction techniques for skim reading in a systematic manner by considering the known limitations of visual attention. The results from our empirical study are positive and confirm that this approach deserves more attention. Specifically, we hypothesise that the attentional cost of shifting between overlays and background did not degrade performance through attentional blink, which prevents obtaining content-level information from underlying document at scrolling speeds over 2 pps. In summary, the results for Spotlights show that 1) users scroll 60% faster (3.26 pps vs. 2.03 pps) and scroll more; 2) they find more objects and track back more often to look at them; 3) they recall more figures, with a mild trend, and 4) are more confident in their level of comprehension; and 5) they succeed 100% better in lookup tasks when searching for given figures.

We see many opportunities to develop the technique further. Firstly, our exposure parameters were adjusted for a single scrolling speed. It is reasonable to assume that better performance would result if parameters were obtained for other rates too. Secondly, we observed that some users exhibit strategies that counteract our technique. Some users shifted attention to the middle of the screen instead of actively trying to find the best upcoming spotlight. It is useful to consider various techniques to guiide attention almost automatically to the next object. The challenge is to do this in such a way that the document scrolling in the background is still legible. Thirdly, we did not consider how the complexity (or unpredictability) of an object affects visual processing requirements. Objects could be preprocessed for complexity and the exposure time modulated accordingly. Fourthly, we can imagine that models of individual-specific preferences or relevance could improve object selection. Fifthly, techniques such as advance cues or semantic zooming could be considered, to improve performance further.

ACKNOWLEDGEMENTS

The project has received funding from the Academy of Finland project COMPUTED and the European Research Council (ERC) under the European Union's Horizon 2020 research and innovation programme (grant agreement 637991).

REFERENCES

1. Jason Alexander, Andy Cockburn, Stephen Fitchett, Carl Gutwin, and Saul Greenberg. 2009. Revisiting read wear: analysis, design, and evaluation of a footprints scrollbar. In *Proc. CHI09*. ACM, 1665–1674.
2. Yoav Benjamini and Yosef Hochberg. 1995. Controlling the false discovery rate: a practical and powerful approach to multiple testing. *Journal of the Royal Statistical Society. Series B (Methodological)* (1995), 289–300.
3. George Buchanan and Fernando Loizides. 2007. *Investigating document triage on paper and electronic media*. Springer.
4. George Buchanan and Tom Owen. 2008. Improving skim reading for document triage. In *Proc. IIiX08*. ACM, 83–88.
5. Christopher Clark and Santosh Divvala. 2015. Looking Beyond Text: Extracting Figures, Tables and Captions from Computer Science Papers. In *Workshops at the Twenty-Ninth AAAI Conference on Artificial Intelligence*.
6. Andy Cockburn, Philip Quinn, Carl Gutwin, and Stephen Fitchett. 2012. Improving Scrolling Devices with Document Length Dependent Gain. In *Proc. CHI12 (CHI '12)*. ACM, 267–276.
7. Andy Cockburn and Joshua Savage. 2004. Comparing speed-dependent automatic zooming with traditional scroll, pan and zoom methods. In *People and Computers XVIIDesigning for Society*. Springer, 87–102.
8. Richard R Day and Jeong-suk Park. 2005. Developing Reading Comprehension Questions. *Reading in a foreign language* 17, 1 (2005), 60–73.
9. Geoffrey B Duggan and Stephen J Payne. 2011. Skim reading by satisficing: evidence from eye tracking. In *Proc. CHI11*. ACM, 1141–1150.
10. George W Furnas and Benjamin B Bederson. 1995. Space-scale diagrams: Understanding multiscale interfaces. In *Proc. CHI15*. ACM Press/Addison-Wesley Publishing Co., 234–241.
11. Yves Guiard, Yangzhou Du, and Olivier Chapuis. 2007. Quantifying degree of goal directedness in document navigation: Application to the evaluation of the perspective-drag technique. In *Proc. CHI07*. ACM, 327–336.
12. Beverly L Harrison, Hiroshi Ishii, Kim J Vicente, and William AS Buxton. 1995. Transparent layered user interfaces: An evaluation of a display design to enhance focused and divided attention. In *Proceedings of the SIGCHI conference on Human factors in computing systems*. ACM Press/Addison-Wesley Publishing Co., 317–324.
13. Sandra G Hart. 2006. NASA-task load index (NASA-TLX); 20 years later. In *Proceedings of the human factors and ergonomics society annual meeting*, Vol. 50. Sage Publications, 904–908.
14. Sandra G Hart and Lowell E Staveland. 1988. Development of NASA-TLX (Task Load Index): Results of empirical and theoretical research. *Advances in psychology* 52 (1988), 139–183.
15. Ken Hinckley, Edward Cutrell, Steve Bathiche, and Tim Muss. 2002. Quantitative analysis of scrolling techniques. In *Proc. CHI02*. ACM, 65–72.
16. Jukka Hyönä, Robert F Lorch Jr, and Johanna K Kaakinen. 2002. Individual differences in reading to summarize expository text: Evidence from eye fixation patterns. *Journal of Educational Psychology* 94, 1 (2002), 44.
17. Takeo Igarashi and Ken Hinckley. 2000. Speed-dependent automatic zooming for browsing large documents. In *Proc. UIST00*. ACM, 139–148.
18. Pourang Irani, Carl Gutwin, and Xing Dong Yang. 2006. Improving selection of off-screen targets with hopping. In *Proc. CHI06*. ACM, 299–308.
19. Edward W. Ishak and Steven K. Feiner. 2006. Content-aware scrolling. In *Proc. UIST06*. ACM, New York, NY, USA, 155–158.
20. Victor Kaptelinin, Timo Mäntylä, and Jan ström. 2002. Transient visual cues for scrolling: an empirical study. In *Ext. Abst. CHI'02*. ACM, 620–621.
21. Juho Kim, Amy X Zhang, Jihee Kim, Robert C Miller, and Krzysztof Z Gajos. 2014. Content-aware kinetic scrolling for supporting web page navigation. In *Proceedings of the 27th annual ACM symposium on User interface software and technology*. ACM, 123–127.
22. Christian Klein and Benjamin B Bederson. 2005. Benefits of animated scrolling. In *CHI'05 Extended Abstracts on Human Factors in Computing Systems*. ACM, 1965–1968.
23. Theresa J Babbitt Kline, Laura M Ghali, Donald W Kline, and Steven Brown. 1990. Visibility distance of highway signs among young, middle-aged, and older observers: Icons are better than text. *Human Factors: The Journal of the Human Factors and Ergonomics Society* 32, 5 (1990), 609–619.
24. Fernando Loizides and George Buchanan. 2009. An Empirical Study of User Navigation during Document Triage. *Interfaces* (2009).
25. Takashi Miyaki and Jun Rekimoto. 2009. GraspZoom: zooming and scrolling control model for single-handed mobile interaction. In *Proc. MobileHCI09*. ACM, 11.
26. Mark R Nieuwenstein, Mary C Potter, and Jan Theeuwes. 2009. Unmasking the attentional blink. *Journal of Experimental Psychology: Human Perception and Performance* 35, 1 (2009), 159.
27. Tom Owen, George Buchanan, Parisa Eslambochilar, and Fernando Loizides. 2010. *Supporting early document navigation with semantic zooming*. Springer.

28. Jane E Raymond, Kimron L Shapiro, and Karen M Arnell. 1992. Temporary suppression of visual processing in an RSVP task: An attentional blink? *Journal of Experimental Psychology: Human Perception and Performance* 18, 3 (1992), 849.

29. Kimron L Shapiro, JE Raymond, and KM Arnell. 1997. The attentional blink. *Trends in cognitive sciences* 1, 8 (1997), 291–296.

30. Matteo Valsecchi, Karl R Gegenfurtner, and Alexander C Schütz. 2013. Saccadic and smooth-pursuit eye movements during reading of drifting texts. *Journal of vision* 13, 10 (2013), 8.

31. Ji Soo Yi. 2014. QnDReview: Read 100 CHI papers in 7 hours. In *Ext. Abst. CHI'14*. ACM, 805–814.

32. Chen-Hsiang Yu and Robert C. Miller. Enhancing web page skimmability. In *Ext. Abst. CHI'12*. ACM, 2655–2660.

33. Jian Zhao, R William Soukoreff, Xiangshi Ren, and Ravin Balakrishnan. 2014. A model of scrolling on touch-sensitive displays. *International Journal of Human-Computer Studies* 72, 12 (2014), 805–821.

"If You Put All The Pieces Together..." – Attitudes Towards Data Combination and Sharing Across Services and Companies

Igor Bilogrevic
Google
Zurich, Switzerland
ibilogrevic@google.com

Martin Ortlieb
Google
Zurich, Switzerland
mortlieb@google.com

ABSTRACT
Online services often rely on processing users' data, which can be either provided directly by the users or combined from other services. Although users are aware of the latter, it is unclear whether they are comfortable with such data combination, whether they view it as beneficial for them, or the extent to which they believe that their privacy is exposed. Through an online survey (N=918) and follow-up interviews (N=14), we show that (1) comfort is highly dependent on the type of data, type of service and on the existence of a direct relationship with a company, (2) users have a highly different opinion about the presence of benefits for them, irrespectively of the context, and (3) users perceive the combination of online data as more identifying than data related to offline and physical behavior (such as location). Finally, we discuss several strategies for companies to improve upon these issues.

Author Keywords
Privacy; Attitudes; User Study; Data Combination; Data Sharing.

ACM Classification Keywords
H.5.m. Information Interfaces and Presentation (e.g. HCI): Miscellaneous

INTRODUCTION
The online experience of users is more personalized and contextual than ever. From accurate movies recommendations to virtual, voice-operated assistants, online services are able to tailor the content provided to users by extracting relevant information derived from their interactions with the services.

Usually, the extent and limits to the collection and use of users' data are described in the provider's data or privacy policies, which are part of the general "Terms of Use" of the service. By agreeing to such terms, users give consent to the collection and processing of their data in accordance with the data policy. Over time, online services can undergo a series of changes, either in terms of their functionality or as a consequence of mergers, acquisitions or new laws, which can result in updates to their data policy [17, 20, 31]. In spite of the fact that such policies are nominally written for the users, they are often unread or perceived as being unclear [3, 53], mainly due to overly complex language that is beyond the grasp of most of the Internet users [25, 36].

The collection of personal data often raises privacy concerns, as users of all ages find it difficult to understand the benefits they get from such a collection [3, 30, 41, 58]. Furthermore, the use of multiple accounts from different providers to manage personal and professional identities makes it even more challenging to have a correct representation of where different types of data are stored and who can access them [13]. As a result, users often struggle to understand what could be the consequences of online information sharing [22].

Several studies investigated the concerns raised by online users regarding their sensitivity when sharing different types of personal data with third-parties [3, 11, 18, 62]. For instance, [33] showed that data related to health, communications, location and online browsing are considered as highly sensitive. As nowadays more and more data is combined from different services under a more unified privacy policy (e.g., through mergers and acquisitions), different data types can be combined in a single service to provide an enhanced experience for the users. Yet, little is known about their privacy attitudes when different types of data are combined and shared across different services and companies, or about how risky different combinations of data could be in terms of user re-identification.

In this paper, we answer these two questions by means of a brand-blind, online survey with 918 participants, followed by in-depth interviews with 14 participants. Specifically, we investigate users' privacy attitudes when multiple types of personal data are shared and combined across different online services and companies. By quantifying their comfort with sharing data, as well as the perceived benefits and re-identification risks of several combinations of individual data types, we provide a comprehensive assessment of privacy attitudes that is representative for the three most popular online domains (search engines, social networks and shopping services) [39]. Finally, based on our data, we propose mitigation strategies for companies that could increase users' comfort when sharing data and perceived benefits. To the best of our

CHI'16, May 07-12, 2016, San Jose, CA, USA
ACM 978-1-4503-3362-7/16/05.
http://dx.doi.org/10.1145/2858036.2858432.

knowledge, this is the first study to investigate users' privacy attitudes towards data combination and sharing across different services and companies.

Our results show that, in general, comfort with sharing data with third-parties depends on the type of data, the type of service and the existence of a direct relationship with the service provider. One additional aspect that emerges as a positive driver for user comfort is expected liability for first-party data holders in case of a possible information leak by third-party companies who may have received parts of users' data. In terms of perceived benefits, users unsurprisingly believe that there is an imbalance between the benefits that they experience, as compared to the benefits that the company gets when accessing and sharing their data. Furthermore, across the three different online scenarios, a combination of not-so-identifying pieces of information is perceived as being more personally identifying than the single most identifying type of data, suggesting that the availability of different complementary information is a significant aspect of the data collection context that determines sensitivity, and that it should be an important factor in defining communication strategies about user data practices.

Our work focuses on dimensions related to users' perceptions and attitudes towards privacy when combining information. Technical solutions to provide privacy for data aggregation and inference, although important, are only of marginal interest for the presentation of this paper. Hence, we refer the reader to [16, 19, 27, 65] for a comprehensive treatment of some of the technical solutions.

The remainder of the paper is structured as follows. First, we introduce the related work, by treating three different subgroups of studies focusing on personalization, data sensitivity and re-identification. Next, we define the research questions and describe the study methodology. Afterwards, we present the results and discuss their implications, before concluding the paper and outlining the future work.

RELATED WORK

Prior studies that investigated the challenges related to people's privacy attitudes towards data combination can be grouped, from a high-level perspective, into three different categories. First, we start by providing some background about (i) online users' attitudes towards personalization and privacy [5, 6, 14, 56, 58, 60], which is directly related to users' opinions about (ii) data sensitivity and aggregation [4, 9, 28, 33, 34, 62]. Finally, we tackle the topic of (iii) user re-identification [7, 23, 24, 32, 42, 48, 54, 55, 57] , as it follows the previous two (personalization and aggregation) by exploring users' concerns about one potential negative consequence of personalization and data aggregation.

Personalization and Privacy Attitudes

Awad et al. [6] are among the first to discover the existence of an apparent paradox between online privacy and personalization: Users who value transparency (a dimension of privacy) are also less willing to be profiled (thus resisting personalization). The authors posit that, instead of developing features for the users who value privacy, firms should focus on those who value personalization. In addition to transparency, Chellappa et al. [14] identified trust as a dimension of privacy that positively influences users' willingness to use personalization services. In particular, the authors recommend that companies shall build user trust and allow different levels of personalization, in order to acquire and use users' information. By taking a broader perspective towards technology, Toch et al. [60] point to three emerging areas of privacy risks for personalization services, which are social-based personalization, behavioral profiling (through the aggregation of online data from different sources) and location-based personalization. To mitigate such risks, the authors propose strategies based on data anonymization, client-side processing and algorithmic privacy-preserving solutions. Moreover, Acquisti [1] shows how the latter can be used to enhance the aggregate welfare when used for personalization. Regarding client-side personalization, Sutanto et al. [56] studied how users' comfort with using personalized services changes depending on where the personalization takes place, i.e., locally on the mobile device or in a marketer's datacenter. By building on the uses and gratifications theory (UGT, [37, 49]), they show that users can both benefit from personalization and mitigate their privacy concerns if their data is stored and processed locally on their mobile device, instead of being processed by a third-party marketer. Our work explores personalization aspects related to comfort with sharing data, perceived benefits and re-identification risks for the users.

Data Sensitivity and Aggregation

Numerous studies have shown that different types of data (such as age, financial information, health records and location) have different levels of sensitivity for the users [11, 33, 34, 62], and that sensitivity depends on the situation in which the data is collected and used [4, 28, 34]. According to a recent study conducted in the US [33], the most sensitive pieces of data for online users are (in decreasing order): social security number, health record, content of communications and location. In order to capture the nuances in sensitivity across different contexts, in this study we focus on the three most popular online contexts [39]: search engines, social networks and online shopping services. Within each of these contexts, we study users' comfort with sharing different types of data with third parties.

User Re-identification

Re-identification of users from publicly available information is a topic that has received significant attention from the research community. From the initial work by Sweeney [57], based on US Census data from 1990, to more recent de-anonymization attacks on search queries [7], movie ratings [42], music listening history [32] and genomic data [23, 24, 29], researchers have shown that it is possible to identify an individual or some of her traits with high precision, by accessing data that is easily (and most of the time publicly) available on the Internet. For instance, a combination of [5-digit US ZIP code, gender, date of birth] is sufficient to uniquely identify 87% of the US citizens [57], individuals could be identified from a set of 650,000 anonymized search queries [7], and genomic data released by one member of a family can be used to infer health predispositions of the other members via side-channel information (such as kin relationships, available on online social networks [23]). As a complement to prior studies, our work provides a user-centric assessment of their perceptions about the re-identification risks, by analyzing both individual data types (such as age, financial information and location), as well as their combinations.

STUDY GOAL AND METHODOLOGY

The goal of our study was to identify and quantify users' privacy concerns when their data is used and shared across different online services and companies. As users' perceptions about privacy vary according to the context, we focused on a comprehensive but limited set of data types and online contexts, as described in the following subsection.

Privacy as Data Sensitivity, Benefits and Risks

As privacy is a multi-faceted concept for which there is no single definition [40, 63], we needed to frame it in clear and understandable terms for the purpose of this study. To this end, we chose to focus on a subset of data types in a limited set of popular online contexts [39]. In particular, we solicited our participants' opinions about the following 5 categories of personal data, which include most of the sensitive data types listed in [33]: Information about you (such as age, gender and interests), contact details (such as home address and phone number), online browsing history (the list of websites you visited), online search history (the terms you searched for) and payment details. For each of the aforementioned data categories, we elicited responses with respect to (i) data sensitivity (by quantifying users' comfort with sharing their data with different types of online services), (ii) incentives (by quantifying the perceived benefits for the users and for the company when sharing users' data) and (iii) users' perceived risk of re-identification (by quantifying and ranking different data categories and combinations thereof in terms of their potential to identify a single user).

Experimental Scenarios: Search Engine, Online Social Network and Online Shopping Service

In order to reduce inter-subject variability when answering our questions, and to retain as much contextual integrity as possible [8, 43] we assigned each participant to one of the following three popular online scenarios: (1) Search engine, (2) social network, (3) shopping service. In each scenario, the participant was told that a fictitious company runs three different services: The main service (i.e., the company SearchCo/SocialCo/RetailCo that runs the search engine/social network/shopping service, respectively), and two other secondary services (e.g., SearchCo runs its main service, the search engine, as well as a social network and a shopping service). Moreover, in each scenario, participants were told to assume that they have an account on the main service, but not on the secondary services of the same company. For instance, Figure 1 shows the diagram for the search engine scenario. We chose to assign a participant to only one of the three scenarios to reduce respondents' fatigue and cognitive load, as well as to increase focus during the study.

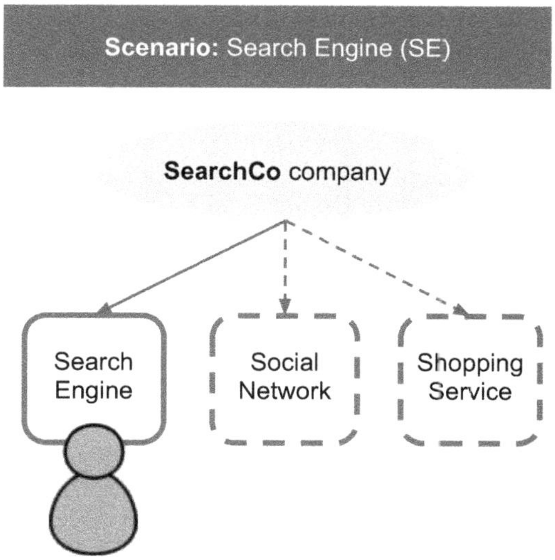

Figure 1. Search Engine scenario diagram, where the participant is assumed to have an account on the main service, (Search Engine) of SearchCo, but not on the other two secondary services (Social Network and Shopping service).

User Study

We structured the study in two phases. In Phase I, we explored the breadth of the research question by eliciting responses in an online survey; in Phase II, we performed an in-depth analysis of the salient findings and trends that we observed in the previous phase, by means of semi-structured interviews, which aimed to provide greater details and interpretation cues as to the previous findings.

Phase I: Online Survey

We created an online survey to elicit a broad range of responses about users' comfort with sharing personal data, the perceived benefits for them and for companies when sharing users' data, and the risks of user re-identification from individual data types and for some of their combinations. We administered our survey through a third-party online vendor, where we removed any logo or text that would link our survey with our company, in order to preserve brand-blindness and avoid any response bias due to factors such as brand reputation and past experience. All subjects were recruited on the Amazon Mechanical Turk (MTurk) platform, a widely-used service in the research community to recruit subjects for human-intelligence tasks [26, 35]. In order not to have any association with our company account or prior reputation, we created and used a new MTurk account for this study.

Survey structure: The survey had a total of 26 questions, including a screener, data access expectations, scenario-specific questions related to comfort and benefits, followed by questions about risks of re-identification when sharing data, demographics and Internet usage (the full questionnaire can be found as a Supplementary Information (SI) document). The format of the possible answers included free-text, multiple-choice selections and 5-point ordinal scales. [1] The struc-

[1] More details about each specific scale will be provided where appropriate.

ture of the survey was the following. First, a participant was randomly assigned to one of the three scenarios (i.e., either search engine, social network or shopping service), where she answered a question related to how she normally uses the main service. For example, in the search engine scenario, a participant answered the multiple-choice question "How do you normally use Online Search Engines (e.g., Google, Bing, Yahoo, Baidu, AOL)?" with either "I do not use Online Search Engines", or "I use at least one of them but I do not have an account on it", or "I use at least one of them but I do not sign in with my account", or "I use at least one of them and I sign in with my account". Participants that selected either one of the two last possible choices were allowed to continue with our survey, whereas those who selected either one of the first two choices were screened out. This approach would ensure that all participants are familiar with providing some personal information (such as email, name, address, interests) to the online service, as usually required during the account set-up process.

Participants who passed the screener question were first presented with 3 questions in which we asked them to rate, on a 6-point scale (where 1 means "multiple times per day" and 6 means "never") how often they expected their data to be accessed by the main service and shared with other companies. Next, they provided answers on a 5-point ordered scale (from "Not at all comfortable" to "Extremely comfortable") to a set of scenario-specific questions about their comfort when different types of data are accessed and shared by different services of the same company. Following that, participants were presented with questions related to the perceived benefits that there for them and for the company, when it accesses and shares different types of data with other companies. The answers to these questions were coded on a 5-point Likert scale as to the agreement with, for example, the statement "There is a benefit for me/SearchCo if it has access to my contact details (e.g., name, home address, email, photo)".

After the scenario-specific questions about comfort and benefits, the participants answered a set of common questions about the risks of re-identification for 10 individual types of personal information and for 4 combinations of these 10 individual types of information. In other words, they were asked to rank, from the most to the least personally identifying, 10 types of personal information, such as email address, ZIP code of their home, age, gender, interests, trace of GPS position over the last week and browsing history. Finally, they finished the survey with a set of demographics and Internet usage questions.

Survey validation: We assessed and refined the questionnaire by means of 3 cognitive walk-throughs, 2 expert checks and a pilot with 30 survey participants on MTurk. To detect possible misbehavior, we relied on the time to complete of the survey (as compared to the average) and we provided a survey completion code after participants submitted their last answer. We did not include any verification (or "dummy") questions, as prior work has shown this has does not significantly increase the quality of the responses [11, 12]. To qualify for our survey, MTurk participants were required to have at least 1 previous HIT approved and not to have previously participated in our pilot survey. Finally, several researchers with privacy and ethics training reviewed the survey questions before the experiment.

Participants recruitment: We recruited our participants on the MTurk platform, as privacy-related concerns from MTurk participants are found to be in between those from participants recruited through other providers [50]. The target population was comprised of US adults who reported having an account on at least one of the three online services (search engine, social network or shopping service). Each participant was remunerated with $2 for completing the survey (avg. completion time of 17 minutes, which corresponds to $7.1/hour).

Phase II: Semi-structured interviews

We structured the interviews that we conducted in Phase II with the goal of focusing on specific patterns and concepts that emerged from the analysis of the survey results from Phase I (more details are provided in the next section). We followed a similar structure as we did in Phase I, i.e., the same three online scenarios, but we allowed participants to articulate their opinions to a greater extent, and we invested more time for in-depth discussions of specific statements.

Interview structure: We created an interview script for each of the three online scenarios (search engines, social networks and shopping services). According to the answer to a pre-interview screening question (which is the same as the online interview screening question), we assigned each interviewee to one of the three online scenarios. We then followed the script and took short notes about the participants' answers in a separate document.

Logistics and participants recruitment: We informed the participants that we would be recording the audio and video of the session, and that they were free to stop the interview at any time, or to skip any question they wanted. Each interview lasted approximately 60 minutes, and participants were given an appreciation token of $75 in the form of a coupon. We recruited participants through an internal panel of human subjects volunteering to be part of user studies conducted by our company. Each participant was informed about the logistics of the study, signed a Non-Disclosure Agreement (NDA) and gave written consent to participate to this study.

Dataset Description

During Phase I of our study (September 15th – 23rd, 2014), 954 participants completed the survey, out of the 987 participants that started it. The average survey completion time was 17 minutes, with a standard deviation of 15 minutes. Out of the 954 who completed the survey, we registered 31 screen-outs (3%) and 4 exclusions due to potential cheating (2 with a wrong completion code, and 2 with a completion time smaller than 3 minutes, i.e., one standard deviation from the average) and 1 invalid entry in our database. In the end, we collected 918 valid survey response sets (96% of the total). In terms of demographics, 53% of the respondents were male, 68% were between 24 – 40 years of age, 13% reported working in science, IT or engineering, 9% were students and 98% stated that they use the Internet more than 1 hour per day. Following the random scenario assignment, we obtained 32% of all the valid responses for the Search Engine scenario, 24% for the Online Social Network scenario, and 44% for the Online Shopping scenario.

In Phase II (November 18th – 21st, 2014) we conducted 14 semi-structured remote interview sessions with US adults, lasting 60 minutes each, via a proprietary video-conferencing application. The participants were selected from a large internal pool and had similar demographics as the ones of Phase I. To keep a balanced split across the three scenarios, we assigned 4 participants to the Search Engine scenario, and 5 to both the Online Social Networks and the Online Shopping scenario. The first author conducted and coded all the interviews, and the video recordings were used to complete the related notes. After the interviews, the authors presented the summary of the notes to our research group, and together we open-coded the notes (16 codes in total). Next, the authors clustered the codes into concepts, and we iteratively analysed the concepts to identify and refine the topics that we report hereafter.

RESULTS

In the following, we present our results by themes rather than by the study phases, as it enables us to present the findings from both phases within their context.

Comfort with Sharing Data

Overall, participants reported feeling the least comfortable with sharing information about their payment details (such as bank account and credit card numbers); on average, 78% of the respondents answered "Not at all comfortable" (on the 5-point scale [Not at all / Slightly / Moderately / Very / Extremely comfortable]) to a question related to their comfort when different services and companies access such information (question #8 of the questionnaire). Next, we find online search history (61%), browsing history (60%), contact details (59%) and information about you (45%). Interestingly, the level of comfort for the online search and browsing histories, two aspects related to the online identity and persona, was lower as compared to two aspects related to the physical world (contact details and generic demographic and behavioral information). We discuss this aspect further in the subsection "Risks of re-identification".

A within-scenario analysis shows that the differences in the comfort level across information types are significant, in all three scenarios (Figure 2). [2] In general, we notice a sharp difference between the first row (i.e., other company) and the last 3 rows (secondary and main service of the first-party company) across all scenarios, indicating that respondents' opinions are markedly influenced by the presence of a direct interaction with the company. The follow-up interviews revealed that for 50% (7 out of 14) of the interviewees, the absence of a first-party interaction with a third-party company makes them significantly less comfortable in knowing that it could access some of their data. For instance, participant #10 (P10) stated:

P10: *"Well... if I'm not even interacting with that company online, I don't really... I don't want them to have my info."*

In addition to a first-hand relationship with a company, interviewees mentioned four factors that influence their comfort level: (i) The control over the access to information (57% - in particular P3-P5,P7,P10-P13), (ii) whether their data is anonymized before being shared by a third-party company (43% - P1,P5,P7,P12-P14), (iii) the transparency about what information is accessed and for what purpose (29% - P3,P7,P9,P13), and (iv) the level of trust in the third-party company (29% - P2,P7,P12,P13). Moreover, participants often mentioned a combination of the aforementioned factors when explaining their lack of comfort.

Regarding control and transparency, interviewees noted that

P7: *"... if it [access to information] is, like, without my consent or something, or if it's automated or something, I probably would be 2 or 1 [on the 5-point scale where 1 means "Not at all comfortable" and 5 means "Extremely comfortable"]. But if it's like an option... that might be ok, only if it's like something that is brought to my attention."*

P4: *"It's about what you've allowed... I think it's when you... when you don't know that you're allowing all these people to access it [information about you], is the problem."*

Control and transparency are usually implemented through forms of notice and consent [2, 64], by which users are informed about the modalities of data access and have a choice on whether to agree to it. Often, however, such a choice is limited, as companies are under legal obligation to store data about user interactions for a fixed amount of time, hence reducing the level of perceived control for users over their online data.

With respect to anonymization, P13 stated that:

P13: *"That [level of comfort] depends on whether or not it [the information] is linked to me. If it's... if the person is anonymous... uhm... if... they could figure out who I am, it's something that I'm uneasy about."*

Similarly, P7 and P12 raised concerns about the possibility of linking their online information with their identity, in which case the comfort level would drop from 5 to 1 and from 5 to 2, respectively.

Finally, four interviewees mentioned trust as a driving factor for their comfort level. In particular, P12 argued that:

P12: *"... I actually care for what company is running it [the main service], and when I sign up for that, I actually place a bit of trust in the company, and when a third-party is using it, I am not exactly sure who these third-parties are or maybe I just don't trust them as much as I would...*

According to Unsworth [61], the challenges in managing trust in cloud environments are mainly due to the uncertainty about

[2]Cochran's Q test results across information types are as follows: Search Engine (89.6 < Chi-sq < 258.32, df = 4, adjusted $p < .001$ with Bonferroni correction), Online Social Network (54 < Chi-sq < 182.3, df = 4, adjusted $p < .001$), Online Shopping (123.6 < Chi-sq < 290.2, df = 4, adjusted $p < .001$).

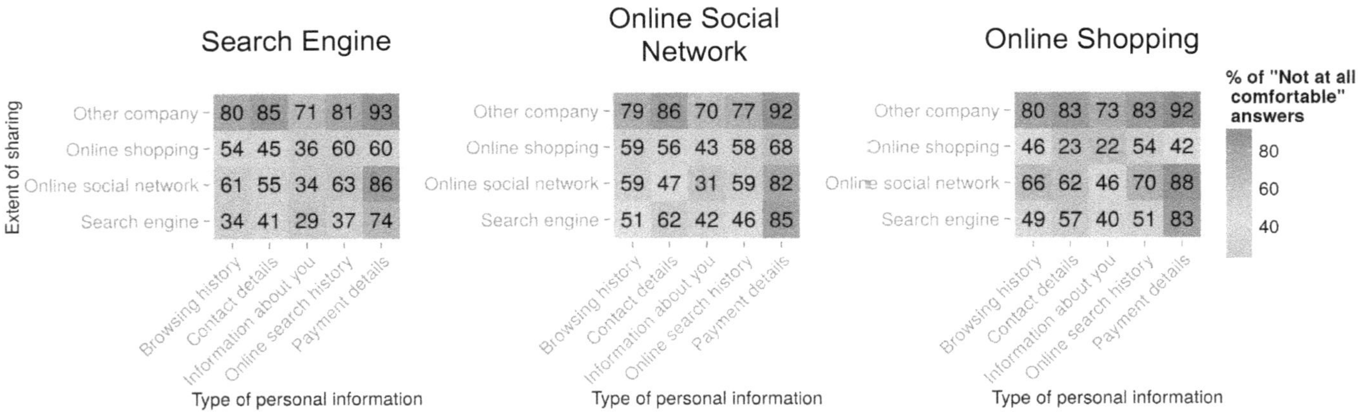

Figure 2. Discomfort with sharing different types of information, for each scenario (left - Search Engine, middle - Online Social Network, right - Online Shopping). The values are rounded for enhanced readability.

and lack of knowledge of third-party data policies, two dimensions of transparency. As users often have limited control over cloud resources and about the data that can be accessed by a third-party, they need to rely on contracts stipulating what use can be performed over users' data, and on the possibility of compensations for the affected users in the event of inappropriate and unauthorized data leakage [47].

In the following, we present findings related to comfort with sharing different types of data within each of the three considered scenarios.

Search Engine Scenario

In the search engine scenario, the participants are overall the least comfortable when their information is accessed by a third-party company: 82% chose the "Not at all comfortable" answers (on average across all 5 information types), followed by the secondary service "Online social network" belonging to the first-party company (60%), the shopping service (51%) and finally by the search engine (43%, the main service). Figure 2 (left) shows the breakdown per information type for this scenario. [3] With respect to the different information types, 78% of the respondents were (on average) not at all comfortable with sharing payment details, 60% with sharing their online search history, 57% with their online browsing history, 56% with their contact details and 43% with information about them (such as age, gender, interests), which is also the type of information that exhibits the least amount of variability across all secondary services (max − min = 7.8%). A post-hoc analysis [4] indicates that the difference between the comfort level of the information type "payment details" and each other type is significant, across all sharing extents (adjusted $p < .001$), except from "Browsing history" and "Online search history" when accessed by the shopping service.

Unsurprisingly for this scenario, we see that the survey respondents are quite comfortable if the search engine accessed their search history, as it is required to provide them with relevant results. However, they seem to be quite comfortable also for other types of information, except for payment details. In the follow-up interviews, the participants in this scenario stated that they could see the value in receiving personalized ads and services based on their browsing history. However, they were quite sensitive when it came to having such information publicly accessible and associated with them, especially by close social circles such as family and friends, as stated by P9:

P9: *"So... if I'm gonna like... look at some porn, I wouldn't want it to... like... immediately coming up on my shopping site for things that I wanna buy... I'll be like... oh no, I'm shopping with my mom and that's really awkward... but... if it's being used in a more subtle way that that I don't mind."*

Online Social Networks Scenario

As shown in Figure 2 (middle), respondents to the survey in the online social network scenario are in general less comfortable with sharing any kind of personal information with the main service (social network), as compared to the previous scenario (search engine). In fact, the difference in the number of responses with the lowest comfort score between these two scenarios is 12.6% (on average, for the same type of information), with the largest single difference occurring for the online search history, where there are 59% more users that are not at all comfortable with the primary service accessing such information in the Online Social Network scenario as compared to the Search Engine scenario, even if they have an account on it. One concern that emerged from the interviews is related to the scope of the search history that could potentially reach the social circles of the users, if used for advertising and personalization. For instance, P2 stated that:

P2: *"...I'd be a little less comfortable with the social network... providing information to... ah... large groups of people... you know... or my grandma."*

[3]Note that the number in each cell represents the percentage of users who replied "Not at all comfortable" for a given information type (column) being accessed by a given entity (row). Hence, each of the cells corresponds to a question/answer item in the questionnaire.

[4]A post-hoc series of McNemar's tests conducted using the Bonferroni correction for all pairwise comparisons can be found in in the Supplementary Information document, together with the full questionnaire.

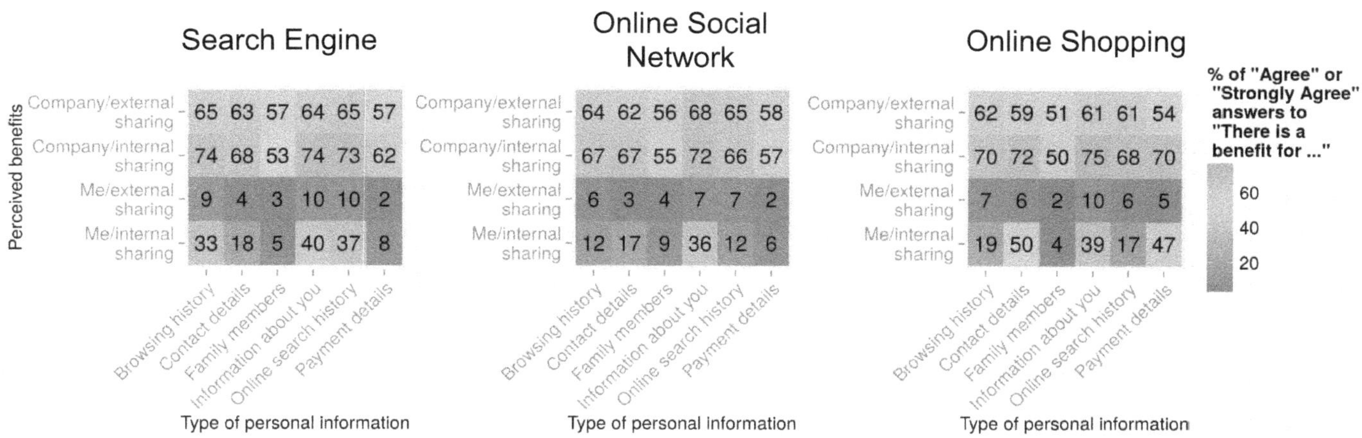

Figure 3. Perceived benefits for either users (i.e., Me/) or the first-party company (i.e., Company/) when personal information is used only internally (i.e., /no sharing) or shared with a third-party company (i.e., /sharing), for each scenario (left - search engine, middle - online social network, right - online shopping). The values are rounded for enhanced readability

For the other types of information, participants reported having the same ranking in terms of comfort as they have in the search engine scenario.

Online Shopping Scenario

In this scenario, Figure 2 (right) shows that, overall, only a minority (42%) of the users are not at all comfortable if the main service (online shopping) accesses their payment details, and such a ratio drops even further (22%) for the contact details, as most of the time these are required for processing and shipping online purchases. For the remaining information type, the respondents follow the same trend as in the other two scenarios.

It is interesting to notice that even though payment details are usually processed by the shopping service in order to provide the service or good to the user, there is still a non-negligible fraction of the respondents (42%) who are not at all comfortable with that. During our interviews, participants pointed to the risks of identity and financial theft (P4, P14), as experienced by one of our interviewees. In particular, P14 stated:

P14: *"I do not pay unless I can use [popular online payment system A or B]. I had... personal situations where my account information was used... without me knowing. I just don't want that to happen again... it's just too easy."*

In other scenarios, participants raised the issue of explicit consent for payment details being accessed and shared even internally within a company. As payment details can be linked to financial transactions, a notoriously sensitive topic for online users, it is unsurprising to see that users would prefer to exert more control over the flow of such information, in order to increase their comfort.

Benefits from Sharing Data

After asking participants about their comfort level with knowing that different services and companies would access and share their personal data, we now focus on the second dimension of users' attitudes towards online data combination and sharing, i.e., the benefits that there could be for users if their data gets shared. To capture their opinions, we ask them about the extent to which they agree that there are benefits for them if (i) different types of data (the same ones as before) are shared by the first-party company with its secondary services, and if (ii) different types of data are shared with a third-party company (questions #12 – #17 of the questionnaire).

Figure 3 shows the ratio of responses "Agree" or "Strongly agree", on a 5-point Likert scale from "Strongly disagree" to "Strongly agree", to 4 statements about the 4 possible combinations of beneficiaries and sharing; for example, one such statement in the search engine scenario is "There is a benefit for me if the Search Engine has access to... [6 different types of information]". We included "family members", in addition to the previous 5 information types, as online services may rely on social features to provide value for the users.

In general, the figure shows that users clearly distinguish between the presence of benefits for them as opposed to the first-party company (i.e., top vs. bottom two rows of the figure). The majority of respondents agree that there is a benefit for the company when it either uses or shares users' data with its own secondary services or with another company; yet, only a minority of users feels the same about the benefits for themselves, if the first-party company uses and shares their data with another company. A Cochran's Q test shows that, within each scenario, the difference across beneficiaries is statistically significant. [5] During our interviews, however, participants struggled to find a real-world example in which a company would clearly benefit from such an activity and a user would not. For instance, P12 stated:

P12: *"I know that a lot of company already do this, so it must be beneficial... otherwise they wouldn't be doing so."*

On average, 66% of the survey respondents agree that there is a benefit for the first-party company if it accesses users' personal information, and 61% agree that there is a benefit for

[5]Cochran's Q test results across information types are as follows: Search Engine (55.5 < Chi-sq < 252.4, df = 5, adjusted $p < .001$ with Bonferroni correction), Online Social Network (20.9 < Chi-sq < 129.5, df = 5, adjusted $p < .01$), Online Shopping (42 < Chi-sq < 416.1, df = 5, adjusted $p < .001$).

the same company if it shares users' data with a third-party company However, only 23% of the respondents agree that there is a benefit for them if the company uses their information, and only 6% agree to the same if the company shares their information with another company. For example, in the interviews candidates suggested unprompted that a better purchasing experience, such as 1-click purchases, and the convenience of not having to manually enter the contact details are two notable benefits that there are for them, if the first-party company made use of their personal information. If sharing such information with a third-party company, however, participants could perceive some benefits for them in terms of a larger and complementary choice of services/products that the first-party company does not offer. The convenience factor seems to arise from the survey responses of the online shopping scenario (Figure 3 - right), where we notice a highly diverse percentage of respondents who agree that there is a benefit for them if such data does not get shared with a third-party company, for different types of personal information. For example, about half of the respondents agree or strongly agree with that statement for their contact and payment details. Our results provide further evidence of the existence of a relationship between perceived benefits and comfort with allowing access to data, which has been observed in a recent study [58]. Although important, the quantification of such a relationship is outside of the scope of this paper, and further research is needed to evaluate its strength.

Risks of Re-identification

The goal of the last part of our survey is to understand how users perceive the risk of re-identification from 10 different types of data. [6] First, we asked users to rank the different types of data in terms of the re-identification risk that they pose (question #18 of the questionnaire), from the most to the least personally identifying type of data. Second, we asked users to indicate, on a scale from 1 to 5 where 1 means "Not at all identifying" and 5 means "Extremely identifying", the extent to which they feel that 4 different combinations of the 10 individual data types can be used to uniquely identify them (question #19).

Individual Data Types

As shown in Figure 4, the "GPS trace over the last week" is perceived as being the most personally identifying type of data (ranked 1st or 2nd in 74% of the responses), followed by their email address (60%) and ZIP code (21%). At the end of the ranking, we find "marital status", "gender" and "interests", aspects related to demographics and personality. Dimensions pertaining to the online behavior ("browsing history" and "online purchases") are present in the middle. A Friedman rank sum test indicates that the differences in the rankings across the different data types are statistically significant. [7]

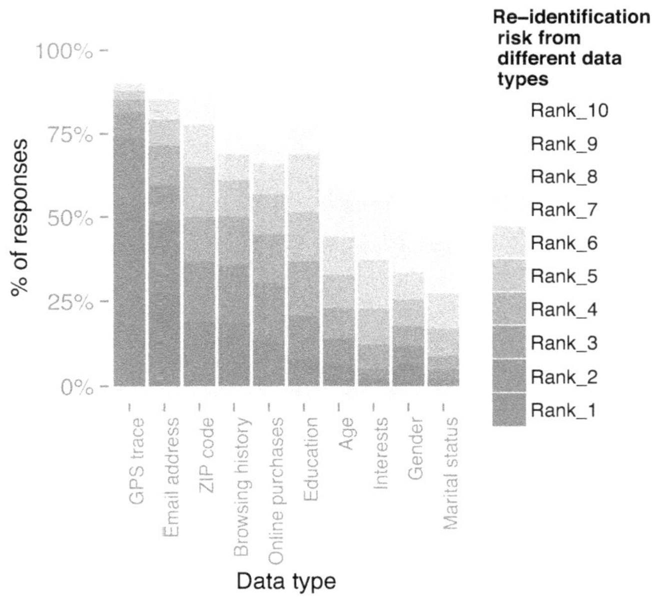

Figure 4. Re-identification risk from different data types, ranked from Rank_1 (most personally identifying) to Rank_10 (least personally identifying). The types are ordered from left to right according to their average ranking, from the highest to the lowest, respectively.

In the interviews, participants expressed concerns about their physical safety when explaining the risk of re-identification from location information. In particular, P2 stated:

P2: *"GPS position over the last week, that clearly shows my patterns... where I live, where I work, where my kids go to school... it's not that you know where I am, but if you start drawing that pattern... that draws a very good picture of physically where I am. If real-time, if I get close to a store with the GPS, send my location... but tracking me, storing that information is where... you know... I start having problems with that.'*

In addition to physical safety and tracking concerns, P3 mentioned concerns about inferring the personality and larger social group of people to whom she belongs to:

P3: *"I live in an area where region strongly defines identity... [with GPS] you can identify the individual but also identify what kind of person they are likely to be, based on the region that they're in."*

Moreover, P8 pointed out that a GPS trace can be used to infer some of the other types of information without having to access them directly:

P8: *"I feel like... for GPS position, that could easily define a lot about what our interests are... who we go to see... it could easily... give you a range... you could easily figure out ZIP code from house you get to visit every night, possibly the gender based on where shopping occurs, interests from where different things happen, where education occurs... "*

Location data, which is often used by online services and mobile applications in order to provide context-related services, has received a significant attention by both media [46, 59]

[6]The data types we considered are: Trace of the GPS position over the last week, email address, ZIP code, browsing history, list of all items purchased online, education (schools you went to), age, interests, gender, and marital status.

[7]Friedman Chi-sq = 2451, df = 9, $p < .001$.

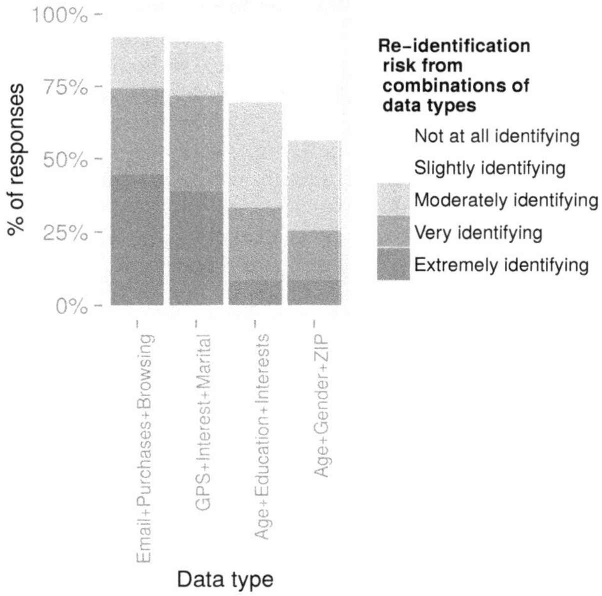

Figure 5. Re-identification risk from different combinations of data types. The combinations are ordered from left to right according to their average ranking, from the highest to the lowest, respectively.

and the research community [10, 27, 45, 51], due to its early adoption and popularity among smartphone users. Research scholars have shown how location data, even if discretized and anonymized, can be used to de-anonymize users successfully 95% of the time [15].

Two aspects related to users' online behavior, i.e., browsing history and list of online purchases, are ranked at the 4th and 5th place, respectively. Interviewees noted that such data can be collected and used passively to infer what the users like, without them knowing about it. For instance, P7, who ranked browsing history as being the most personally identifying type of data, stated that:

P7: *"That [browsing history] is the most ... like ... quantitative and qualitative data, it's a lot of detail as well as breadth... just knowing one day's worth of browsing history is a lot."*

In the literature, Olejnik et al. [44] have analysed the uniqueness of users' browsing histories, showing that 69% of the users in their experiment had a unique browsing history, and that only 4 websites are enough to uniquely identify 97% of the users. In addition to browsing history, Soroush et al. [55] have shown how throughput data related to music streaming on a mobile device can leak one's location trajectory, and similarly Michalevsky et al. [38] have relied on the power consumption of a mobile device to track users' whereabouts.

Combinations of Different Data Types

In addition to the evaluating the perceived risk of re-identification from individual data types, we asked our respondents a similar question related to four different *combinations* of individual data types. Specifically, we wanted to study how such a risk is related to the other types of data it is combined with. We asked respondents to rate on a scale from 1 to 5, where 1 means "Not at all identifying" and 5 means "Extremely identifying", different combinations of data types.

Figure 5 shows the opinions of the respondents for this question. Differences across the combinations are statistically significant. [8] An interesting finding is that, as opposed to the individual case, the combination containing GPS information is not perceived as being the most personally-identifying one. [9] When combined, data related to online activities is perceived by the users as being (on average) the most personally identifying, followed by offline data containing GPS, users' interests, marital status, age, gender and ZIP code. When reasoning about these two combinations during the interviews, the tension was evident:

P5: *"My email address is exactly the same as my legal given name... purchasing and browsing history would tell you quite a bit more. Interest and GPS and marital status are...slightly more anonymous, although because you're throwing in GPS...you probably know where the person lives..."*

43% of the interviewees alluded to the concept of k-anonymity while explaining their thought process for rating the 4 combinations of data types. Although research has shown that such a concept might provide only limited location privacy [52, 66], especially when combined with other publicly-available information (such as the census data), participants often resorted to this concept in order to rationalize their choice.

DISCUSSION

Our study investigated online users' opinions and concerns about data combination that happens across different Internet services and companies. In particular, we (1) analysed users' comfort with knowing that a service or company might access and share some of their data with other services or third-party companies, (2) evaluated the perceived benefits for users and companies from the users' perspective, and (3) studied users' the perceived risk of re-identification for different data types.

The results indicate that the level of comfort with sharing data depends on the data type, the domain in which the first-party company operates and whether users have a direct relationship with the third-party that could be accessing their data. Users are the least comfortable when their financial information is accessed or shared, followed by their online behavior (browsing and search history) and finally by contact details demographic information (age, gender, interests). Although such ranking holds across the three scenarios we considered (search engine, online social network and online shopping service), there are notable differences in relative values within each one of them. In order to increase users' comfort, according to the opinions that emerged during our interviews, first-party companies should adopt more comprehensive commu-

[8] Friedman Chi-sq = 898.2, df = 3, $p < .001$.

[9] Post-hoc Wilcoxon signed rank tests with Bonferroni correction show that the differences across all pairs are statistically significant, with adjusted $p \in [10^{-82}, .049]$.

nication strategies based on a greater transparency (i.e., what and how data is used or shared), provide more control over the data access to users (e.g., through intuitive settings and an opt-in approach) and clarify the extent of data anonymization before it is being shared. According to our participants, the interaction of these three factors would positively affect their comfort when data is accessed and shared. Moreover, the users' trust in the third-party company is especially relevant when such a company accesses users' data, which can be managed through clear and understandable data policies indicating the purpose and scope of the data access, as well as the security mechanisms in place to safeguard data and the liability clauses in case of unintended data leakage.

In terms of perceived benefits, users clearly differentiate between benefits for them versus benefits for the company, where the former are significantly lower (23%) with respect to the latter (66%). Moreover, users feel that there is no significant difference for them in terms of perceived benefits, irrespectively of whether the first-party company shares their data with a third-party company (61%) or not (66%). However, our interview participants often struggle to describe clear examples of benefits the first-party company may get from accessing and sharing users' data. In order to mitigate this perceived imbalance, one possible approach for the companies could be to put forward a better communication strategy, by exemplifying the benefits of accessing and sharing data with both first- and third-party services. As mentioned by our participants, this could include a better user experience through 1-click purchases, more complementary services or goods not offered by the first-party company, and higher relevance of search results by accessing the browsing history.

Unintended consequences due to data leakage can be detrimental for both users and companies. The perceived risk of re-identification of different types of data can be analysed from two perspectives. First and foremost, users often mention concerns related to the physical safety when explaining what they perceive as being the most personally-identifying piece of information: The user's GPS trace over the last week. However, concerns are not limited to physical safety. Personality traits, such as interests, preferences and habits, are almost as important, indicating that behavior (including online behavior) is perceived as having a moderate potential to re-identify a person (as highlighted in [21]). Furthermore, our results show that combinations of moderate-risk data types related to online behavior (such as browsing history, email address and list of online purchases) are perceived as bearing more risk than the combination of offline (or physical and demographics) data, such as the GPS trace, interests, age and gender. According to several of our interviewees, one plausible explanation for this significant difference is that online data can potentially reveal personality traits of an individual which provide a greater amount of detail about one's intents their evolution over time. As compared to the physical location, for instance, online behavior could be used to reveal a user's current state and future plans, which could be inferred to a greater extent from her/his browsing history as compared to the regular location and travel patterns.

Some of the limitations of this study are as follows. First, the participants were recruited either directly on MTurk or through an internal participants panel. In both cases, participants needed to opt-in to participate to human-subject studies, which could introduce selection bias in the sample that was recruited. Second, in order to limit participants' fatigue when responding to the questionnaire, we omitted low-sensitivity questions that could have been useful to calibrate the responses to the high-sensitivity questions that were presented. Finally, our participants were asked questions about a hypothetical scenario, which demanded a non-negligible effort to remember; future work should address these issues in a more realistic setting, for instance by focusing more about users' actual experiences rather than imagined situations.

CONCLUSION

The use of online services often requires users to create accounts and to provide some information about them to the service providers. Even though users are aware that such information is stored and processed by the service they register with, they might not be fully aware of the possibility that their data could flow and be aggregated across different services of that company or even with a third-party company. In order to better understand users' perceptions and feelings about data sharing across online services and companies, we conducted an online survey and follow-up interviews to quantify users' comfort level with sharing different types of data with different types of services, the perceived benefits and the risks of re-identification for different combinations of their data.

Based on 918 survey respondents and 14 interviews, our results indicate that users' comfort level is influenced by three contextual factors, which are the type of service, the type of data, and the existence (or not) of a direct relationship with a third-party company. More polarised, users feel that there is a significant imbalance in the perceived benefits from data access for them, irrespectively of the context, as compared to the company. In terms of re-identification potential of different types of data, our results show that location information is the single piece of information that is perceived as being the most personally identifiable; however, that is not true when data is combined. Inadvertently leaking information pertaining to online behavior (such as browsing history and online purchases) has a similar if not higher risk for the users as leaking other types of data that include location.

Our findings suggest that, in order to address these challenges, companies should actively improve their communication to users (by providing them with more transparency about their data practices), provide a more concrete value proposition for the users, and greater controls over third-party access to data about them.

ACKNOWLEDGEMENTS

We would like to express our sincere gratitude to Sunny Consolvo, Allison Woodruff, Sebastian Schnorf, Miguel Malheiros, Pauline Anthonysamy, as well as to the anonymous reviewers for the precious feedback that greatly improved the quality of this work.

REFERENCES

1. Alessandro Acquisti. 2006. Price Discrimination, Privacy Technologies, and User Acceptance. *CHI Workshop on Personalization and Privacy* (2006).
2. A. Acquisti, I. Adjerid, and L. Brandimarte. 2013. Gone in 15 Seconds: The Limits of Privacy Transparency and Control. *IEEE Security Privacy* 11, 4 (July 2013), 72–74.
3. Alessandro Acquisti, Laura Brandimarte, and George Loewenstein. 2015. Privacy and human behavior in the age of information. *Science* 347, 6221 (2015), 509–514.
4. Anne Adams and Martina Angela Sasse. 2001. Privacy in multimedia communications: Protecting users, not just data. In *People and Computers XVInteraction without Frontiers*. Springer, 49–64.
5. Lalit Agarwal, Nisheeth Shrivastava, Sharad Jaiswal, and Saurabh Panjwani. 2013. Do not embarrass: re-examining user concerns for online tracking and advertising. In *Proceedings of the Ninth Symposium on Usable Privacy and Security*. ACM, 8.
6. Naveen Farag Awad and M. S. Krishnan. 2006. The personalization privacy paradox: an empirical evaluation of information transparency and the willingness to be profiled online for personalization. *MIS quarterly* (2006), 13–28.
7. Michael Barbaro, Tom Zeller, and Saul Hansell. 2006. A face is exposed for AOL searcher no. 4417749. *New York Times* 9, 2008 (2006).
8. Louise Barkhuus. 2012. The mismeasurement of privacy: using contextual integrity to reconsider privacy in HCI. In *Proceedings of the SIGCHI Conference on Human Factors in Computing Systems*. ACM, 367–376.
9. Alastair R Beresford, Dorothea Kübler, and Sören Preibusch. 2012. Unwillingness to pay for privacy: A field experiment. *Economics Letters* 117, 1 (2012), 25–27.
10. Alastair R Beresford and Frank Stajano. 2003. Location privacy in pervasive computing. *IEEE Pervasive computing* 1 (2003), 46–55.
11. Igor Bilogrevic, Kévin Huguenin, Berker Agir, Murtuza Jadliwala, Maria Gazaki, and Jean-Pierre Hubaux. 2015a. A machine-learning based approach to privacy-aware information-sharing in mobile social networks. *Pervasive and Mobile Computing* (2015).
12. Igor Bilogrevic, Kévin Huguenin, Stefan Mihaila, Reza Shokri, and Jean-Pierre Hubaux. 2015b. Predicting Users' Motivations behind Location Check-Ins and Utility Implications of Privacy Protection Mechanisms. In *22nd Network and Distributed System Security Symposium (NDSS" 15)*.
13. Joseph Bonneau and Sren Preibusch. 2010. The privacy jungle: On the market for data protection in social networks. In *Economics of information security and privacy*. Springer, 121–167.
14. Ramnath K. Chellappa and Raymond G. Sin. 2005. Personalization versus privacy: An empirical examination of the online consumers dilemma. *Information Technology and Management* 6, 2-3 (2005), 181–202.
15. Yves-Alexandre de Montjoye, César A Hidalgo, Michel Verleysen, and Vincent D Blondel. 2013. Unique in the Crowd: The privacy bounds of human mobility. *Scientific reports* 3 (2013).
16. Cynthia Dwork. 2011. Differential privacy. In *Encyclopedia of Cryptography and Security*. Springer, 338–340.
17. Facebook. 2015. Updating Our Terms and Policies: Helping You Understand How Facebook Works and How to Control Your Information. (2015).
18. Adrienne Porter Felt, Serge Egelman, and David Wagner. 2012. I've got 99 problems, but vibration ain't one: a survey of smartphone users' concerns. In *Proceedings of the second ACM workshop on Security and privacy in smartphones and mobile devices*. ACM, 33–44.
19. Oded Goldreich. 1998. Secure multi-party computation. *Manuscript. Preliminary version* (1998).
20. Google. 2012. Updating our privacy policies and terms of service. (2012).
21. Serge Gutwirth, Ronald Leenes, Paul de Hert, and Yves Poullet. 2012. *European data protection: coming of age*. Springer Science & Business Media.
22. Mark Halper. 2015. Isabelle Falque-Pierrotin: Privacy Needs to Be the Default, Not an Option. (June 2015).
23. Mathias Humbert, Erman Ayday, Jean-Pierre Hubaux, and Amalio Telenti. 2013. Addressing the concerns of the lacks family: quantification of kin genomic privacy. In *Proceedings of the 2013 ACM SIGSAC conference on Computer & communications security (CCS '13)*. ACM, New York, NY, USA, 1141–1152.
24. Mathias Humbert, Erman Ayday, Jean-Pierre Hubaux, and Amalio Telenti. 2014. Reconciling Utility with Privacy in Genomics. In *Proceedings of the 13th Workshop on Privacy in the Electronic Society (WPES '14)*. ACM, New York, NY, USA, 11–20.
25. Carlos Jensen and Colin Potts. 2004. Privacy Policies As Decision-making Tools: An Evaluation of Online Privacy Notices. In *Proceedings of the SIGCHI Conference on Human Factors in Computing Systems (CHI '04)*. ACM, New York, NY, USA, 471–478.
26. Aniket Kittur, Jeffrey V. Nickerson, Michael Bernstein, Elizabeth Gerber, Aaron Shaw, John Zimmerman, Matt Lease, and John Horton. 2013. The future of crowd work. In *Proceedings of the 2013 conference on Computer supported cooperative work*. ACM, 1301–1318.

27. John Krumm. 2009. A survey of computational location privacy. *Personal and Ubiquitous Computing* 13, 6 (2009), 391–399.

28. Ponnurangam Kumaraguru and Lorrie Cranor. 2006. Privacy in India: Attitudes and awareness. In *Privacy Enhancing Technologies*. Springer, 243–258.

29. David Lazer, Alex (Sandy) Pentland, Lada Adamic, Sinan Aral, Albert Laszlo Barabasi, Devon Brewer, Nicholas Christakis, Noshir Contractor, James Fowler, Myron Gutmann, Tony Jebara, Gary King, Michael Macy, Deb Roy, and Marshall Van Alstyne. 2009. Life in the network: the coming age of computational social science. *Science* 323, 5915 (Feb. 2009), 721–723.

30. Pedro Giovanni Leon, Blase Ur, Yang Wang, Manya Sleeper, Rebecca Balebako, Richard Shay, Lujo Bauer, Mihai Christodorescu, and Lorrie Faith Cranor. 2013. What matters to users?: factors that affect users' willingness to share information with online advertisers. In *Proceedings of the Ninth Symposium on Usable Privacy and Security*. ACM, 7.

31. Linkedin. 2015. Updating LinkedIns Privacy Policy. (2015).

32. Jen-Yu Liu and Yi-Hsuan Yang. 2012. Inferring Personal Traits from Music Listening History. In *Proceedings of the Second International ACM Workshop on Music Information Retrieval with User-centered and Multimodal Strategies (MIRUM '12)*. ACM, New York, NY, USA, 31–36.

33. Mary Madden. 2014. Americans Consider Certain Kinds of Data to be More Sensitive than Others. (2014).

34. Miguel Malheiros, Sren Preibusch, and M. Angela Sasse. 2013. "Fairly truthful": The impact of perceived effort, fairness, relevance, and sensitivity on personal data disclosure. In *Trust and Trustworthy Computing*. Springer, 250–266.

35. Winter Mason and Siddharth Suri. 2012. Conducting behavioral research on Amazons Mechanical Turk. *Behavior research methods* 44, 1 (2012), 1–23.

36. Aleecia M Mcdonald, Robert W Reeder, Patrick Gage Kelley, and Lorrie Faith Cranor. 2009. A comparative study of online privacy policies and formats. In *Privacy enhancing technologies*. Springer, 37–55.

37. William J. McGuire. 1974. Psychological motives and communication gratification. *The uses of mass communications: Current perspectives on gratifications research* 3 (1974), 167–196.

38. Yan Michalevsky, Gabi Nakibly, Aaron Schulman, and Dan Boneh. 2015. PowerSpy: Location Tracking using Mobile Device Power Analysis. *USENIX Security* (2015).

39. Kate Moody. 2012. Internet usage amongst British consumers. (2012).

40. James Moor. 1989. How to invade and protect privacy with computers. *The information web: Ethical and social implications of computer networking* (1989), 57–70.

41. Anthony Morton. 2015. *Age shall not wither them: But It Will Change Their Priorities About Protecting Their Information Privacy*. Working Paper. Academy of Science and Engineering,USA.

42. Arvind Narayanan and Vitaly Shmatikov. 2009. De-anonymizing social networks. In *Security and Privacy, 2009 30th IEEE Symposium on*. IEEE, 173–187.

43. Helen Nissenbaum. 2004. Privacy as contextual integrity. *Washington law review* 79, 1 (2004).

44. Lukasz Olejnik, Claude Castelluccia, and Artur Janc. 2012. Why johnny can't browse in peace: On the uniqueness of web browsing history patterns. In *5th Workshop on Hot Topics in Privacy Enhancing Technologies (HotPETs 2012)*.

45. Alexandra-Mihaela Olteanu, Kévin Huguenin, Reza Shokri, and Jean-Pierre Hubaux. 2014. Quantifying the effect of co-location information on location privacy. In *Privacy Enhancing Technologies*. Springer, 184–203.

46. Matthew Panzarino. 2011. Its not just the iPhone, Android stores your location data too. (Aug. 2011).

47. S. Pearson and A. Benameur. 2010. Privacy, Security and Trust Issues Arising from Cloud Computing. In *2010 IEEE Second International Conference on Cloud Computing Technology and Science (CloudCom)*. 693–702.

48. Vasile Claudiu Perta, Marco Valerio Barbera, and Alessandro Mei. 2014. Exploiting Delay Patterns for User IPs Identification in Cellular Networks. In *Privacy Enhancing Technologies*. Springer, 224–243.

49. Alan M. Rubin. 1985. Uses and gratifications: Quasi-functional analysis. *Broadcasting research methods* (1985), 202–220.

50. Sebastian Schnorf, Aaron Sedley, M Ortlieb, and A Woodruff. 2014. A comparison of six sample providers regarding online privacy benchmarks. In *SOUPS Workshop on Privacy Personas and Segmentation*.

51. Reza Shokri, George Theodorakopoulos, Jean-Yves Le Boudec, and Jean-Pierre Hubaux. 2011. Quantifying location privacy. In *Security and Privacy (SP), 2011 IEEE Symposium on*. IEEE, 247–262.

52. Reza Shokri, Carmela Troncoso, Claudia Diaz, Julien Freudiger, and Jean-Pierre Hubaux. 2010. Unraveling an old cloak: k-anonymity for location privacy. In *Proceedings of the 9th annual ACM workshop on Privacy in the electronic society*. ACM, 115–118.

53. Internet Society. 2012. Global Internet User Survey. (2012).

54. Chaoming Song, Zehui Qu, Nicholas Blumm, and Albert-Laszlo Barabasi. 2010. Limits of predictability in human mobility. *Science* 327, 5968 (2010), 1018–1021.

55. Hamed Soroush, Keen Sung, Erik Learned-Miller, Brian Neil Levine, and Marc Liberatore. 2013. Turning Off GPS is Not Enough: Cellular location leaks over the Internet. In *Privacy Enhancing Technologies*. Springer, 103–122.

56. Juliana Sutanto, Elia Palme, Chuan-Hoo Tan, and Chee Wei Phang. 2013. Addressing the personalization-privacy paradox: an empirical assessment from a field experiment on smartphone users. *Mis Quarterly* 37, 4 (2013), 1141–1164.

57. Latanya Sweeney. 2000. Simple demographics often identify people uniquely. *Health (San Francisco)* 671 (2000), 1–34.

58. Teradata. 2015. Balancing the Personalisation and Privacy Equation The Consumer View. (2015).

59. New York Times. 2014. How your iPhone is tracking your every move. (Aug. 2014).

60. Eran Toch, Yang Wang, and Lorrie Faith Cranor. 2012. Personalization and privacy: a survey of privacy risks and remedies in personalization-based systems. *User Modeling and User-Adapted Interaction* 22, 1-2 (2012), 203–220.

61. Kristene Unsworth. 2014. Questioning trust in the era of big (and small) data. *Bul. Am. Soc. Info. Sci. Tech.* 41, 1 (Oct. 2014), 12–14.

62. Yang Wang, Gregory Norice, and Lorrie Faith Cranor. 2011. Who is concerned about what? A study of American, Chinese and Indian users privacy concerns on social network sites. In *Trust and trustworthy computing*. Springer, 146–153.

63. Samuel D Warren and Louis D Brandeis 1890. The right to privacy. *Harvard law review* (1890), 193–220.

64. Edgar A. Whitley. 2009. Informational privacy, consent and the control of personal data. *Information security technical report* 14, 3 (2009), 154–159.

65. Sergey Yekhanin. 2010. Private Information Retrieval. *Commun. ACM* 53, 4 (April 2010), 68–73.

66. Hui Zang and Jean Bolot. 2011. Anonymization of location data does not work: A large-scale measurement study. In *Proceedings of the 17th annual international conference on Mobile computing and networking*. ACM, 145–156.

Privacy Personas: Clustering Users via Attitudes and Behaviors toward Security Practices

Janna Lynn Dupree, Richard DeVries, Daniel M. Berry, and Edward Lank
Cheriton School of Computer Science, University of Waterloo
Waterloo, ON, Canada
jannaweber@gmail.com, red3141@gmail.com, dberry@uwaterloo.ca, lank@uwaterloo.ca

ABSTRACT
A primary goal of research in usable security and privacy is to understand the differences and similarities between users. While past researchers have clustered users into different groups, past categories of users have proven to be poor predictors of end-user behaviors. In this paper, we perform an alternative clustering of users based on their behaviors. Through the analysis of data from surveys and interviews of participants, we identify five user clusters that emerge from end-user behaviors—Fundamentalists, Lazy Experts, Technicians, Amateurs and the Marginally Concerned. We examine the stability of our clusters through a survey-based study of an alternative sample, showing that clustering remains consistent. We conduct a small-scale design study to demonstrate the utility of our clusters in design. Finally, we argue that our clusters complement past work in understanding privacy choices, and that our categorization technique can aid in the design of new computer security technologies.

Author Keywords
Persona, Security; Privacy; Interviews; User differences.

INTRODUCTION
Many security and privacy researchers have noted that end-users differ in the effort they are willing to make to protect themselves, in their knowledge of tools and risks, in the context of use of their computer systems, and in the way they tradeoff convenience for privacy [3, 5, 12, 16, 25]. To understand differences between users, past research has frequently divided users into three categories based on an analysis of their privacy concerns: the Marginally Concerned, the Fundamentalists, and the Pragmatic Majority [1, 5, 9, 10, 26, 33, 41]. These clusters were originally defined by Dr. Allen Westin using survey responses to three Likert questions. The three questions explored consumer control of data, trust in business's use of data, and trust in existing laws [26]. To cluster participants, specific levels of concern were assigned for Fundamentalists and specific levels of unconcern were assigned for Marginally Concerned with mixed responses resulting in an assignment as the Pragmatic Majority. Recent work continues to leverage these clusters as one primary mechanism for identifying different types of security and privacy end-users [9, 41]. However, much research has also found these categories to be poor predictors of user behavior [10, 21, 41].

The goal of this paper is to explore more deeply the issue of categorizing or segmenting end-users into groups based upon security or privacy attitudes and behaviors. Our approach to address this issue is to examine user-categorization as a bottom-up rather than a top-down process, i.e. rather than starting with Westin's categories as others do [9, 21], we collect data on attitude and behavior from a participant sample and explore what categories arise naturally from a clustering process. Is there coherence to bottom-up clusters? How do these clusters differ from Westin's categorizations?

To address these questions, this paper first presents the result of surveys and interviews that capture the behaviors of 32 university-educated, twenty-two to thirty-five year old participants. We identify five categories among our participants: The Fundamentalist; The Lazy Expert; The Technician; The Amateur; and The Marginally Concerned. To develop these categories, we first clustered participants around similarities in low-level behaviors, yielding five clusters. We then examined attributes of the clusters, and grouped attributes using the themes of knowledge and motivation. Finally, using a rating of knowledge and motivation for participants in the clusters, we labeled the clusters descriptively.

To verify the coherence of our clusters, we conducted a follow-on study of 200 participants, using a set of online survey questions inspired by our participant clustering. The goal of this survey was to determine whether the coherence of classes observed during our initial clustering was preserved, i.e. if the set of attributes of individual clusters continued to be linked together. We found that clustering

CHI'16, May 07 - 12, 2016, San Jose, CA, USA

ACM 978-1-4503-3362-7/16/05…$15.00
DOI: http://dx.doi.org/10.1145/2858036.2858214

our survey data yielded five similar clusters, i.e. that clustering persisted.

Finally, to explore design implications of our clusters, we explored differences in behavior of design teams using user categories generated from our user clusters versus Westin's cluster. We found, first, that designers were more comfortable describing themselves using our categories, whereas they had to qualify their membership in any specific user cluster for Westin's earlier three-level categorization. Second, during analysis and redesign, designers leveraged our participant clusters, whereas they simply noted that they were designing for the pragmatic majority and subsequently ignored participant categories when using Westin's categories of users.

The remainder of this paper is organized as follows. We first review research in security and privacy behaviors and categories. We then describe our three study methodologies and results. Finally, we discuss the implications of our work to the field of security and privacy.

RELATED WORK

A significant body of HCI research has explored privacy and security practices (see [11] for a good overview). In this section, we focus specifically on research that seeks to understand why users act in different ways. We first examine research focused on understanding motivations for different user actions. We then examine research that seeks to specifically categorize users into different groups.

Differences in Privacy and Security Behaviors

Several researchers have analyzed factors affecting the different security and privacy behaviors of users, but results are often contradictory. For example, Friedman et al. [18] and Sheehan [33] explored factors that might influence security practices. Friedman et al. [18] looked at 72 individuals from three different geographical and technological communities in hopes of seeing some differences in security practices based on location or technological demographics. However, they observed that "the high-technology participants did not always have more accurate or sophisticated conceptions of Web security than did their [less-technical] counterparts." They concluded that differences are not a result of demographic factors. In contrast Sheehan [33] conducted an email survey and found that there were demographic factors that affected survey responses. For example, Sheehan noted that older users were typically either unconcerned or extremely concerned about privacy and security, and younger users (under 45) were more likely to be pragmatists. More recently, Kang et al. [20] examined the interaction of technical knowledge and behavior. They compared 17 lay participants with 11 technical participants and found "little difference in the actions that people with more technical Internet knowledge took versus the actions of lay participants used except that technical participants were slightly more likely to secure their (internet) connections."

Conti and Sobiesk [11], Berendt et al. [5] Olson et al. [31], and Acquisti and Grossman [2] used survey data to assess participants' comfort with information disclosure. Conti and Sobiesk [11] surveyed 352 university students and 25 older adults to determine privacy expectations, and found that most were not concerned about a loss of privacy because they believed they had nothing to hide. In contrast, Berendt et al. [5] found that participants they surveyed were highly concerned about loss of privacy, but that participants' actions did not match their privacy concerns: Participants quickly forgot privacy concerns and released a large amount of personal information on an instrumented e-commerce site. Olson et al. [31] explore the effect that recipients play on information sharing, noting the existence of classes of recipients, analogous to social circles [28].

Lee et al. [27] found that a desire to protect oneself was not sufficient to promote secure or privacy-preserving behaviors; participants in their study needed to believe themselves capable of performing protective actions (self-efficacy) and needed to believe that those protective measures would be sufficient (response efficacy) before protedting themselves. More recently, Wash and Rader [38] explored the link between beliefs and behaviors using a large survey of US households. They found a similar link between behavior and belief. For example, if an individual believed that viruses would cause visible problems and that anti-virus software would protect their computer, that individual was more likely to install anti-virus software.

One reason for the contradictory results observed in past studies is that users, even demographically homogeneous users, have different tolerances for information disclosure. Acquisti and Grossman [2] explore this dichotomy in depth. They note that "the vast majority of expressed privacy concerns and still traded-off privacy for other (small) advantages." They also explored the distinction between protecting one's privacy and exchanging one's privacy for a reward, noting that this distinction seems immaterial because privacy conscious individuals claimed to be willing to pay to protect their privacy, but then do not follow through, instead trading their privacy for minor gain (e.g. a slightly lower price). Finally, Joinson et al. [19] explored the link between privacy concern and level of trust in requestor, noting that these two dimensions appear to interact when assessing an individual's willingness to disclose information.

Beyond variable tolerances, users also act based on context. Each time a user discloses information, they make a choice to disclose that information. To describe how users make these choices, Dourish and Anderson [16] identified three models describing user privacy decisions: Privacy as Economic Rationality; Privacy as Practical Action; and Privacy as Discursive Practice. They hypothesize that user decision making is driven either by a risk versus reward analysis, an ad-hoc decision made in the moment, or some notion of acceptable action. These models are essentially models of social decision making, where a user answers the question: "Should I release this information to this entity?" These models have been explored in the literature. For example, Angulo et al. [4], delving into issues of economic rationality, showed that participants were willing to give up significant control of their personal data in exchange for saving a modest amount of time registering for a cloud-based service. Exploring privacy as discursive practice, Knijnenburg et al. [23] noted that users reveal information using a *privacy calculus*, where subjective distance between different levels of location sharing biases whether they reveal more or less information.

Finally, issues of control and transparency have been explored with respect to privacy behaviors. Acquisti and Grossman [2] examined students' privacy awareness levels with respect to Facebook use to determine if intentions matched actions. They found that many participants were more concerned about controlling who could see information rather than limiting the information available. However, in later work these researchers [8] note the existence of both a control paradox, where more control of privacy settings may actually lead to more release of sensitive information, and transparency limits, where even minor misdirection (e.g. an irrelevant distractor question) can negate the benefits of transparency. In other words, while users want control over the release of information, such control may be counter-productive to preserving privacy; good defaults may be a better option [8].

Categorizing Users

Security and privacy research has attempted to identify the different types of users that exist. The most commonly cited set of user categories for privacy was developed by Westin from a set of over 30 different consumer surveys he conducted (see Kumaraguru and Cranor [26] for an overview of Westin's surveys). Of particular note in Westin's surveys is a classification of users into three groups based on their privacy concerns: the Marginally Concerned or minimalists, the Pragmatists or moderates, and the Fundamentalists or highly concerned.

Several researchers have made use of Westin's surveys to analyze user types. Based upon concerns that Westin's 3-Likert-Question categorization of users might be insufficient, Ackerman et al. [1] developed a survey to evaluate participants using Westin's scale and found that 27% of respondents were Marginally Concerned, 56% were Pragmatists, and 17% were Fundamentalists. Ackerman et al.'s survey included a mix of closed and open-ended questions. Participants were asked to rate their concerns regarding particular practices, how they would respond to scenarios, and their general attitudes and demographics. To simplify classification of individuals into Weston's categories, Sheehan [33] conducted an email based survey that asked respondents to rate on a Likert scale their concerns about a set of specified situations (e.g. an awareness of monitoring, how others will use information you provide, etc.) and their frequency of engaging in a set of seven behaviors (reading spam, registering with a website, etc.). Urban and Hoofnagel [36] critique Westin's scales and note the importance of knowledge or information in assessing users' practices. Other researchers have performed small manipulations to Westin's categorizations [5, 26] or have found varying percentages. However, most classifications of users into distinct groups use Westin's categories as the basis for their categorization.

Various researchers have explored how Westin's categories intersect with behaviors. Consolvo et al. [10] analyzed users' propensity to release information to others and found little correlation between Westin's categories and a willingness to release information (with fundamentalist sometimes more willing to share information than the unconcerned). King [21] examined demographics, privacy knowledge, privacy behaviors, and privacy attitudes to determine whether any factors significantly varied with respect to Westin's categories. King, sampling 907 participants, notes that "it is surprising that [Westin's] categories were not reliably associated with any of my three privacy measures." Woodruff et al. [41] explore several scenarios with respect to Westin's categories, and, again, shows a lack of correlation. In constrast, Chancary and Chiasson [9] did find statistical correlation between Westin's categories and a stated willingness to share demographic, financial, and location information. However, Chancary and Chiasson also demonstrate how freely participants share: 85% of Fundamentalists were willing to share demographic information (vs 90% of others); 50% were willing to share financial information (vs 70%); and 65% were willing to share location information (vs 85%).

The idea of user segmentation and privacy has seen increased focus recently through a workshop series dedicated specifically to this topic, the Privacy Personas and Segmentation Workshop (PPS), held, in 2014 and 2015, with the Symposium on Usable Privacy and Security (SOUPS). One benefit of this increased focus on personas and user segmentation has been a re-examination of user segmentation or personas in designing privacy and security tools [24, 30, 40]. A second benefit of this workshop is that it provides guidance on the factors that may influence security and privacy behaviors. Authors have examined mental models [12], risk perception [14], knowledge [25], advertising perception [32] and impression management strategies [37], to name only a few of the factors potentially at play. Coventry et al. [14] and Kraus et al. [25] note the link between knowledge or risk awareness and concern with respect to behavior; specifically, concerned *and* risk-aware or knowledgeable participants were more likely to take care than unconcerned participants or concerned but less knowledgeable participants.

In summary, there is ample criticism of Westin's categorization of users, both from a methodological perspective (how users are segmented) and an application/analysis perspective (what purpose his categories can serve). Segmentation of end-users remains an important and current problem.

METHODOLOGY

To explore alternative clusters of participants, we conducted a qualitative study using surveys and interviews to assess differences between a set of participants in regard to their privacy and security practices. In this section, we describe our study methodology.

Participants

To better develop our understanding of users' privacy and security concerns, we collected data from 32 participants (17 male, mean age 26.3, standard deviation 5.9) over a four-month period.

We sourced participants for our initial study from a relatively narrow demographic of university-educated digital natives, i.e. participants who had been exposed to computers since childhood. Our rational for using this group is that they represent a set of digital natives, i.e. users who grew up with technology in their everyday lives. They are thus familiar with technology, but also have very diverse and rich practices with that technology. As well, demographic uniformity among our participants still yields a high-value data point: If, despite their demographic homogeneity, we see categories that differ from Westin's, that allows us to contrast categories and thus diagnose the pitfalls of Westin's three-category view of participants.

Nineteen of our participants were recruited from the non-Computer Science graduate student population at our institution. These participants represent a convenience sample: They are easily accessible and vary widely in their knowledge of security and privacy. As a check on our grad-student participants, we also conducted an additional set of thirteen Skype interviews with participants recruited from across North America. In reporting our data, we note that P1 – P13 are our on-line, non-student participants, and P14 – P32 are our local, student participants. During our analysis, we found no significant differences between local and remote participants. As a result, data from both local and remote participants were combined and treated uniformly during analysis. To anonymize gender we use arbitrary pronouns when reporting results.

Data Collection

Data were sourced from our participants in two ways. Participants completed a survey on-line. Participants were also interviewed in person (for local participants) or via Skype (for remote participants).

Our survey asked participants to describe security concepts (cookies, certificates, WPA/WEP, etc.), to rate their concern for certain situations (monitoring, how others use information they provide, etc.), and to describe their use of security tools (virus scanners, firewalls, anonymous browsing, WPA/WEP, etc.). The goal of this survey was to replicate survey-based classification of participants and to provide complementary data on each of our participants.

Interviews with participants typically occurred after the survey. Interviews lasted approximately one hour for in-person participants, and approximately 45 minutes for remote participants. The interview format was semi-structured, exploring:

- Participants' knowledge of security/privacy concepts.
- Participants' specific security practices, e.g. their password schemes, software used, network security.
- Participants' privacy protection practices, i.e. analysis of their use of social networking sites, their attitude toward electronic monitoring and eavesdropping, etc.
- Participants concerns about security and privacy, i.e. what they were concerned about, how they protected themselves, and why.
- Participants' assessment of their own vulnerability or invulnerability vis a vis the security of their computers and data and/or their privacy.

A typical progression for any issue in the interview was to first explore participants' understanding of a concept. For example, we would ask participants to describe the concept of employer monitoring or the concept of a cookie. If participants understood the concept, we would then engage in a discussion to elicit their opinion of the issue, the actions they might take, or their use of different pieces of software, depending on the issue being explored. If they did not understand the concept, we would briefly explain it, and then explore their impressions of the concept given the limited information we provided.

Similar to Ackerman et al.'s [1] surveys, we also asked three scenario-based questions, depending on topics already covered in the interview, to gauge participants' responses to violations of their privacy and/or security. For example, we asked our participants how their behavior would change if there was a 50-50 chance that someone was monitoring what they did on their computer.

Data Analysis

To analyze our data, interviews were transcribed manually, an initial open coding was performed, and salient quotes were extracted from the raw interview data [34]. Survey responses were added to the coded interview data. The coded data were then clustered using an affinity diagram. Data clusters were labeled, and labels were analyzed for higher-level themes. We use the term *traits* to refer to low-level grouped behaviors in our affinity, and we cluster these traits into a set of *concepts* [34].

Clustering Participants

Using traits from our affinity diagram, we clustered participants by creating a weighted graph across all participants. The goal of creating a weighted graph was to allow us to visualize the connections between participants. Edge-weights between participants were set equal to the number of traits shared by the two participants.

More formally, for each participant, p_i, we create a vector over all traits, T, such that an entry in the vector, t_i, is 1 if the participant shares or exhibits that trait and 0 if the participant does not. The similarity measure between two participants, which is equivalent to the edge-weight in the weighted graph, is the dot-product of the two participants' trait vectors. While some traits were shared by only a small subset of participants, other traits were shared by many participants. During clustering, if a trait was shared by too many emergent clusters, we eliminated the trait from the weighted graph and reclustered. Our participant clustering procedure was inspired by *Latent Semantic Analysis* (LSA), a textual analysis technique that calculates a similarity measure between documents [29].

DATA VALIDITY

Assessing the validity and completeness of qualitative data is challenging. There are three questions which must be addressed to determine data validity: accuracy of data, accuracy of coding, and completeness of data (i.e. *saturation* [7, 15, 34]).

Accuracy

In terms of accuracy, the basic question posed is whether the information participants share with a researcher represents actual behaviors, or, instead, represents an idealized representation of how participants believe they should describe their behaviors to a security researcher.

Fields as diverse as software design [6, 13] and social science [39] have explored the question of data validity for interviews (see, for example, [39] pp. 147 – 150). In our interviews, we grounded our data collection in actual behaviors. Participants described their password schemes or practices for websites as they accessed those websites. We watched either shoulder surfacing or screen sharing as they performed tasks or demonstrated configurations on their own computers, and we asked detailed questions about settings and configurations. We used walkthroughs of tasks early in the interview to develop trust between participant and researcher so that our more open-ended inquiries would be answered based upon a shared rapport that evolved over the course of the interview [39]. We validated our interpretations with participants to correct and refine our data. Our role was to understand behaviors and rationales for those behaviors [3]; as such, we did not provide any feedback on behaviors or suggestions for new practices to protect privacy or security.

Qualitative Data Coding

Open coding was performed separately by the first two authors, and any conflicts were addressed collaboratively. Given, the relatively straightforward nature of much of the information collected (knowledge of security concepts, password schemes, software used, privacy practices on on-line sites, attitudes toward monitoring and eavesdropping, etc.) agreement was virtually universal for our initial open coding. The process of linking traits into concepts was performed collaboratively by the research team. As we noted earlier, we used an affinity diagram to cluster traits. The affinity diagram revealed 24 concepts (Table 1). 85 traits (or low-level clusters) resided within these concepts.

Completeness of Data: Saturation

The goal of sampling in qualitative research is to selectively add participants until *saturation* occurs, i.e. no new data is added by additional participants [7, 15, 34]. Bowen [7] argues that, while many qualitative research papers claim that saturation occurred, researchers rarely discuss the meaning of saturation from the perspective of their study.

Personal Assessments	Determining Trust On-line	Fallback Authentication
Knowledge Indicators	Data Concerns	Helping Others
Home Network (Trust)	Types of Attacks (hackers, ID theft, etc)	Learning Source
Changing Behaviors	Monitoring	Proactive/Not
Rationales	Number of Passwords	Password Layers
Censoring Information	Security vs Convenience	Social Networking Use
Social vs Privacy	System Protection	Website Settings
View of Others	Writing Passwords	Source of Threats (local or remote)

Table 1: Concepts in our affinity diagram.

As we noted earlier, the goal of this research was to understand potential problems with top-down clustering of participants, and, in particular, to understand the challenges in applying Westin's three-category characterization of participants. When we looked for saturation in our data set, we considered two different factors. The first involved full coverage of the space of concepts in our data, i.e. the traditional definition of saturation. For each concept we identified from low-level traits, we analyzed the concept to ensure that the range of possible traits within each concept was represented in our data set.

Concern	Attribute	Categorization
Low/No Concern	No Worries I'm not very secure	Marginally Concerned (P7, P9, P12, P16, P28)
Moderate Concern	I try but don't know how Companies are a target I don t matter You can't find me I know it when I see it I used to be very insecure I take extra care with my bank I treat it like its public	Pragmatist (all other participants)
High Concern	I monitor very closely	Fundamentalist (P14, P31)

Table 2: Expanding on Personal Assessment

The second factor we examined was how well our participant population coincided with data from past studies using Westin's categories. While we did not use the three Likert questions of Westin in our survey, in our affinity diagram the concept of Personal Assessments mimicked the data collected by Ackerman et al. [1] and Sheehan [33] when they clustered into Westin's categories. As a result, we leveraged this data to classify participants on a continuum from least to most concerned. Our data also incorporated rationales (similar to Ackerman et al.'s open-ended questions) for levels of concern. Table 2 lists the traits under Personal Assessment for Low/No to High Concern. Our division of participants into the marginally concerned, pragmatists, and fundamentalists is also shown.

	Our study	Sheehan	Consolvo	Ackerman
Marginally Concerned	16%	16%	19%	27%
Pragmatists	78%	81%	69%	56%
Fundamentalists	6%	3%	12%	17%

Table 3: Comparison of our participants to past studies.

Based upon our segmentation into Westin's user clusters, we found that 16% of our participants were marginally concerned, 78% were pragmatists, and 6% were fundamentalists. Table 3 compares this split to past studies, finding reasonable agreement. We continued sampling until each concept in our affinity was saturated, and at least two participants were identified in each of Westin's categories.

CLUSTERING PARTICIPANTS

Defining New Participant Clusters

To develop our new clustering of participants, we first made use of the traits in our affinity diagram. Five clusters of participants resulted from our analysis. Clusters are shown as a condensed graph in Figure 1. Figure 1 shows the connectivity of each group, i.e. the number of edge-weights shared by a plurality of members of the group, as weights on the self-referencing arcs. The number of shared traits is represented as the between-cluster edge weights.

We generated clusters using an iterative, agglomerative clustering approach, beginning with participants with high connectivity and iteratively adding participants to clusters and merging highly connected clusters until clusters stabilized and singleton participants were eliminated.

Examining Figure 1 closely, we see that the sum of the within cluster and between cluster edges is 64 in the condensed graph. 52 of our traits were unique to a participant cluster. 12 were shared between two participant clusters. The remaining 21 were shared by more than two participant clusters and were not eliminated during clustering. Figure 2 depicts the traits that define each cluster and the traits shared between clusters.

Linking Clusters to User Categories

While traits allowed clustering, it is also useful to explore whether there are higher-level attributes of a cluster's participants [34] that unify each cluster's participants. Westin, for example, uses motivation both to segment participants into categories and as a common attribute of each category's participants [26]. Two attributes that we identified during qualitative coding that provide insight into participants' behaviors are their knowledge of privacy and security versus the effort they expend to protect their privacy or security, i.e. their motivation. We examined other themes including: pragmatism, trust, risk awareness, desire for automation, understanding relationships, precision of practices, software protection steps, risk mitigation steps, and responses to triggers. Knowledge and motivation attributes are common in past privacy and security research [12, 14, 18, 25, 26] and were most encompassing of our data.

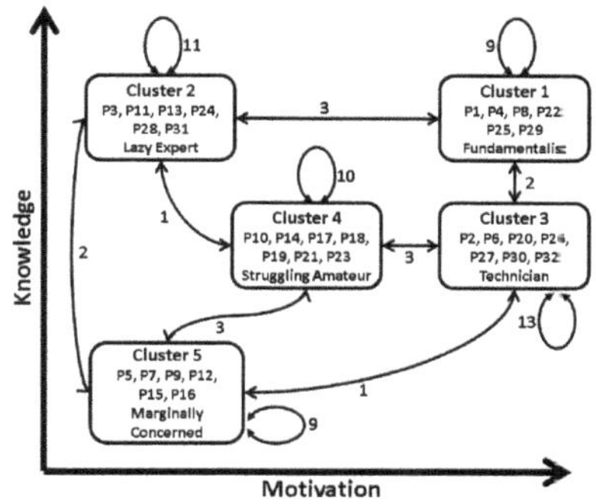

Figure 1: Participant clusters.

We evaluated each participant's knowledge of concepts and their motivation to take actions using our interview data. We subjectively rated each participant as having low, medium, or high knowledge, and low, medium or high motivation. We then determined an overall rating for each cluster. For example, consider Cluster 2 (P3, P11, P13, P24, P28, and P31). In our analysis, P11, P13, and P31 had high knowledge and low motivation scores, P3 and P28 had high knowledge and medium motivation, and P24 had medium knowledge and low motivation. We assigned the cluster an overall score of high knowledge and low motivation because these were the most common ratings for cluster 2's participants. The axes in Figure 1 show a knowledge-versus-motivation "user-space" for our clusters.

Using the knowledge and motivation ratings, we label our participant clusters as: Fundamentalists, Lazy Experts, Self-Educated Technicians, Amateurs, and the Marginally Concerned. Two of these categories (Fundamentalists and Marginally Concerned) are borrowed directly from Westin [26]. The other three labels segment Westin's *Pragmatic Majority*, and were selected to replicate the tone and descriptive nature of Westin's category labels. A brief synopsis of each category follows.

Fundamentalists (High Knowledge, High Motivation)

Fundamentalists are reluctant helpers. They view others as uneducated and unsecure. These participants have little or no trust of security technology and watch carefully for security indicators on websites they visit. Fundamentalists have multi-layer password schemes, and important passwords are unique. They may also extend protection beyond the computer, for example by encrypting external storage devices. They are highly concerned about privacy: They may refuse to sign up for accounts and do not like corporate monitoring. Finally, they have wide ranging security concerns. Fundamentalists have advanced security knowledge and advanced software manipulation skills. They need fine-grained access to security settings.

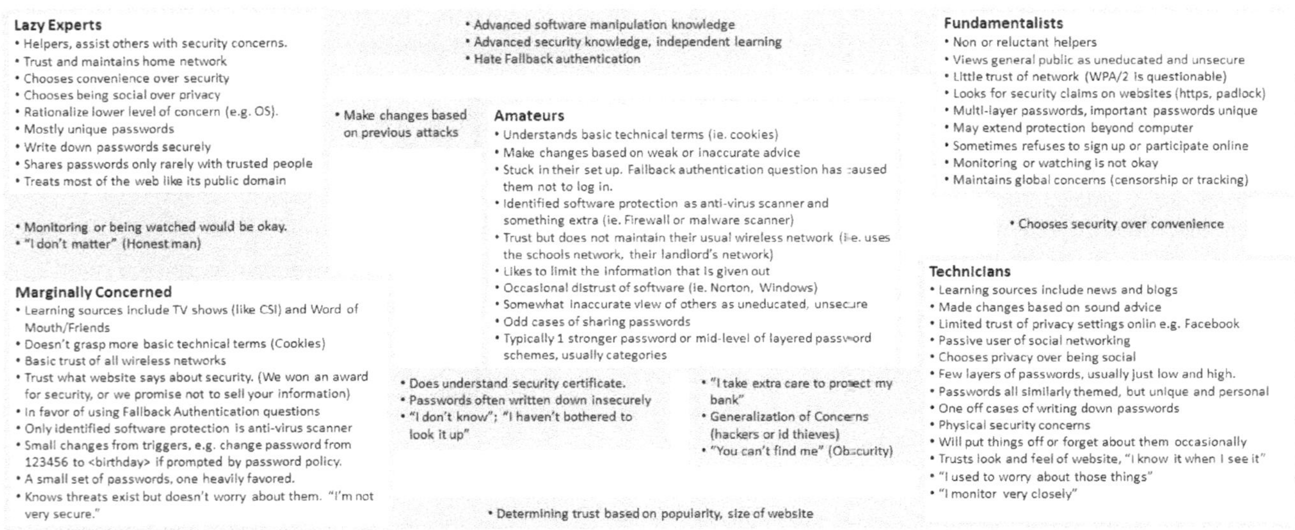

Figure 2: Attributes (traits) in our participant clusters. Attributes shared between clusters are pictured in shaded boxes linking two participant clusters together.

Lazy Experts (High Knowledge, Low Motivation)
Lazy Experts are knowledgeable. They are often helpers because they have a positive view of others' efforts (rather than, as Fundamentalists, viewing others as uneducated). They choose convenience over security, being social over privacy. They rationalize inaction through a belief that they are not a target. They do, however, take certain actions to protect themselves: Their password schemes are strong; they write down passwords securely or not at all; they only share passwords with those they trust; and they treat all information they put online as public domain. While they have advanced software manipulation skills, they use this ability to limit their need to interact with security.

Technicians (Medium Knowledge, High Motivation)
Technicians are highly motivated but have less knowledge than Lazy Experts and Fundamentalists. They read online news and blogs to inform themselves about security, and they try to understand information before they act on it. They have limited trust of privacy settings on sites like Facebook, are passive users of social networking, and choose privacy over being social online. Passwords are weaker than Lazy Experts or Fundamentalists: participants in this group commonly had just low and high security passwords, and, though unique and personal, passwords were based off of one thing. While technicians have physical security concerns (e.g. intrusion, viruses), they may also put things off or forget about them, despite being concerned. They tend to trust their impressions, stating they will *"know that stuff when I see it."* If given enough information, they are willing to change their behaviors.

Amateurs (Medium Knowledge, Medium Motivation)
Amateurs have begun learning about security concepts. The challenge is that these participants are not sufficiently motivated and/or knowledgeable to distinguish good advice from bad, and so still make changes to their practices based on weak or inaccurate advice. Although they have limited motivation, they use some software tools to protect their security, usually an anti-virus and something else—e.g. a built-in firewall or an ad blocker. They trust but often do not maintain wireless networks they use. They place some limits on the information they give out. They view others (somewhat inaccurately) as uneducated and unsecure compared to them. They typically have one stronger or some mid-level set of layered passwords. Finally, again despite limited motivation, given enough information, they will act to protect themselves.

The Marginally Concerned (Low Knowledge, Motivation)
Marginally concerned participants have limited knowledge of security concepts and what they do know they learned from word of mouth or some other informal source. They trust wireless networks and websites that claim to be secure. These participants like Fallback Authentication. Their only identified software protection is anti-virus. They make changes based on triggers: A common example was switching their password because of a password policy. They have a small set of passwords, with one heavily favoured. These participants know threats exist, but don't worry about them; they feel it is unlikely something will happen to them, and so are not motivated to do or learn more about security.

STABILITY ANALYSIS OF PARTICIPANT CLUSTERS

To assess how susceptible our participant clusters were to participant sample, we conducted a follow-on study using a popular on-line survey website. We targeted participants living in the United States aged between 18 and 65 years of age. Participants were remunerated via the web site's remuneration policy.

Figure 3 depicts the topics explored in our survey. We first asked participants to rate themselves on Westin's privacy scale as per King [21] (three Likert questions). Next we asked participants to self-assess their knowledge and motivation. Then, leveraging the attributes identified in our earlier interviews, we asked a series of multiple choice questions that mapped onto similar topics as in Figure 2.

As shown in Figure 3, there were 16 topic areas for survey questions, and each of the 16 topic areas had multiple sub-questions. As well, multi-stage questions frequently made use of branching logic provided by the survey site. For example, to assess participants' use of security tools (third oval), we first asked participants to list tools they used to protect their system (free text). Then, on a new page without backtracking, we asked them a series of specific questions on security tools (firewall, anti-virus, ad-blocker, anti-malware). Finally, for each tool used, we asked questions on configuration changes and knowledge questions to assess understanding of the role of each tool. Similarly, for online behaviors and beliefs, we first asked them what tasks they performed on home networks (text list then selected tasks), then configuration/security/setup questions associated with home networking, then questions on public Wi-Fi use (free form list for their last session), then provided a list of tasks with recency, and finally a ranking question ordering tasks from safest to least safe with a short free-text justification of ranking.

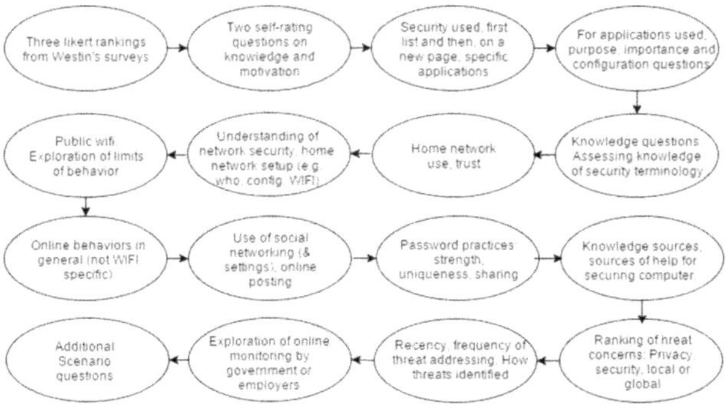

Figure 3: Topics explored in our survey.

Results

Over a 48-hour period, 212 participants (117 female) completed our survey. Using demographic data from the survey site, the median age of our participants was between 50 and 55 years of age. 98.5% had completed highschool, 40% a college or university degree, and 20.6% a graduate degree. Based upon 2014 census data, our participant population has higher education than expected based upon a random sample of United States citizens (88.3% high school, 41.9% Bachelor's degree, 8% graduate degree), possible due to the under-65 restriction. Based upon Westin's privacy categories (first three questions on our survey), our participant population consisted of 26% fundamentalist, 58% pragmatists, and 16% marginally concerned.

Given the survey data from participants, we clustered participants into categories. To cluster, we used manual coding of free-form text answers, and then used a script to parse data in spreadsheet form, calculate similarity scores between participants, and perform agglomerative clustering on our data. Figure 4 summarizes our placement of participants into clusters based upon the data we collected.

First, in similarities, we again identify five clusters of participants. Second, in clustering, we find that knowledge level questions provide a clear distinction between Lazy Experts and Technicians versus amateurs and the marginally concerned, while motivation and scenario questions discriminate between lazy experts and marginally concerned versus the other three categories.

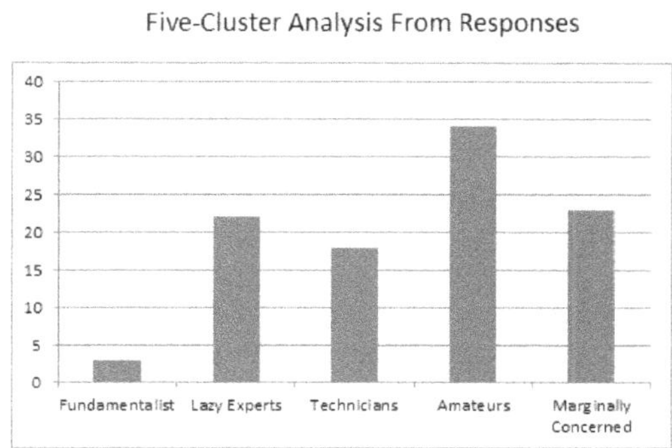

Figure 4: Clustering of our survey data based upon extracted survey data.

The repeated finding of five clusters may surprise the reader. However, recent research performed concurrently with ours in the area of privacy clustering also identified five clusters of participants. Morton and Sasse [30] use Q-Methodology to assess privacy concerns. In Q-Methodology, participants rank a series of statements in order of importance, and these rankings then segment participants into groups. Applying Q-Methodology to 58 participants ranking 40 statements, Morton and Sasse [30] identify five principal clusters that encompass 40 of their 58 participants: Benefits Seekers, Information Controllers, Crowd Followers, Security Concerned, and Organizational Assurance Seekers. These categories echo, respectively, our Lazy Experts, Fundamentalists, Marginally Concerned, Technicians, and Amateurs.

Returning to our survey data, there were differences between our survey clusters and our prior clusters. Most significant was the absence of fundamentalists in our survey participants: Five participants were in a cluster that exhibited high knowledge and high software manipulation skills, avoided public wifi and social networking, and practiced pro-active, well-informed security behaviors. We hypothesize that this may be a characteristic of participants who participate in on-line survey sites, i.e. participants in online surveys are willing to share information. One implication of this result is that online surveys may under-represent highly security- and privacy-conscious web users.

Alongside the distribution of our participant population, differences arose in the specific data that segmented clusters. In particular, differences existed in software used (Marginally Concerned used more software, making this point less useful for segmentation), areas of concern (many participants had broad areas of concern, requiring a ranking of concerns to aid clustering), and password practices (some low security participants had good password practices; some lazy experts had a single password).

DESIGN IMPLICATIONS: A FORMATIVE STUDY

The purpose of categorizing users is to aid in the design of security and privacy tools. Much research in clustering assumes, a priori, that clusters will enhance the design of security and privacy tools [24, 30, 40], but we know of no research that validates this assumption. To explore the potential impact of user categories on design discourse, we conducted a final experiment, a design review of a popular social networking platform's privacy settings.

Participants

Twelve participants (one female) recruited from within the local technology community took part in our study. All had at least one year of software development experience, and all had participated in software design discussions as part of their work experience. None of the participants had knowledge of Westin's privacy categories.

Procedure

Participants worked in pairs: Three pairs were provided with Westin's categorization, obtained from Kumaraguru and Cramer [26], and three were provided with our clusters using text from the previous section. Design pairs D1, D2, and D3 received Westin's categorizations, and pairs D4, D5, and D6 received our clusters. Note, e.g., D1 consisted of two participants, D1.1 and D1.2. The design task was to explore how privacy settings on the target social networking platform could be modified to better accommodate university students studying in a co-operative education program. We indicated to participants that we had performed research to segment our user population into the following groups of users, and then provided participants with categories of users (ours or Westin's depending on designation). Participants were given 30 minutes to perform their analysis.

Post design exercise, participants completed a short survey. Participants were first asked to assess the participant categories they used during the design exercise. Participants were then provided with the second classifications of users (the one they did not use) and asked to contrast the second classification with the one used during the design exercise.

The design discussion was audio-recorded and observed by one member of the research team. Audio recordings were transcribed for analysis and matched with field notes. As our goal was to assess the design discourse (not designs), final designs were not collected, though field notes on attributes of the designs were captured.

Results

Based on an analysis of field notes and discussion, the design discussion proceeded as follows (for all design pairs). First, the design teams read and discussed the user categorizations and discussed how they, themselves, would fit into each of the categories. This process took an average of five minutes. Because of the number of participant categories, it took qualitatively longer for design pairs to read and discuss the 5-category view of participants.

During this initial discussion of participant categories and self-characterization, we noted that participants given Westin's cluster had difficulty self-identifying. None of our participants self-identified as Fundamentalists or the Marginally Concerned. Instead, participants would note that they were Pragmatists, but would shade their answers:

[D1.1] I feel like I'm closer to the Fundamentalist side of the Pragmatic Majority.

Participants given the 5-category view had an easier time self-identifying:

[D5.1] I would say I'm a lazy expert.

However, even with the five-category view, one participant, D5B, indicated some ambiguity with self-categorization:

[D5.2] I kinda see myself as a mix between an Amateur and a Lazy Expert.

When we subsequently probed this participant (post-study), we found that the challenge with self-identification typically occurred when participants self-assessed as having a significant attribute that differed from their primary categorization. For example, D5.2 perceived his or her knowledge as lower than he or she believed was required of an 'expert'. However, this lower knowledge level typically arose because of a self-assessment relative to security experts, rather than against non-technical users. When we noted that the user community did not consist of computer scientists, but instead consisted of a more general population, their self-assessment changed.

When participants performed their analysis of privacy settings, we noted that, in all cases, Fundamentalists and the Marginally Concerned were immediately eliminated as design targets; the consensus among all design teams was that Fundamentalists would not use social networking, and the Marginally Concerned would not bother adjusting settings. One design pair did discuss defaults for the Marginally Concerned.

For teams that started with Westin's categories, given the single class of participant remaining, the pragmatic majority, the three design teams discussed a variable tolerance for this group. The idea of sliding bar for privacy settings was raised by two of the design groups to allow for finer control within this group.

In contrast, discussions with the five-category view focused on the groups individually. D4 typified this behavior:

[D4.1] [Lazy Experts] might want the [...] very quick decisions and things that don't have a lot of consequences at the top level....

[D4.2] [For Technicians] We could almost have, like, a special kind of, like, how-to section <drawing>....

[D4.1] [For Amateurs] The first time they log in, if there's some change to [the security settings...] notify them, [...] enough that they know that it's there so they can actually go seek it out.

In the post-study questionnaire, D1, D2, and D3 all noted problems with Westin's categorization, specifically the vagueness of the pragmatic majority. D6 noted that Westin's 3-category view was *simpler [D6.2]*, but *vague [D6.1]*, and that it might be possible to combine the Amateur and Technician into a single group as both might need similar privacy features in social networking.

DISCUSSION

We address two issues in our discussion: Privacy vs. security and the contrast with past clusters.

Privacy vs Security Categories?

Our participant clusters are mapped onto a knowledge-motivation space, so the semantics of the clusters we generate are privacy-focused, as are Westin's categories. Our categories also incorporate rationales in how we structure and assign meaning to data. Rationales naturally bias data toward social context rather than remaining in the purely technical, i.e. privacy, not security, clusters [16].

Despite the privacy-base of our categories, we treat security and privacy issues cohesively in analysis. There is debate among researchers about whether privacy and security should be studied separately: Dourish and Anderson [16] note the dangers of segmenting security from privacy and dealing with each issue 'in-the-small'. To ensure privacy, users wish to limit access by others to personal data (e.g. the messages in their email account, their credit card number, their address). They limit this access using security tools (the *how*, e.g. passwords, SSL connections).

One reason for our combined treatment of security and privacy is inherent in our data. In interviews, our participants did not separate the concept of security from privacy. The actions they take and tools they use are motivated by a desire to protect themselves and their systems and data. As a result, whether they described technologies to protect the integrity of their system and data (security) or expressed concerns about limiting the exposure of personal information (privacy) was immaterial; despite the end result of privacy categories, both security and privacy issues were incorporated into our analysis.

Contrasts with Westin's Categories

Past research has frequently identified a shortcoming of the common categorization of users that appears in security and privacy research [1, 5, 6, 17, 21, 33], and our original goal was to determine whether an alternative classification technique would yield different categories. It did, but why?

The challenge with Westin's categories may be inherent in the concept of *pragmatism.* For example, if you feel that you have lost control of your personal information, that it will be used badly by businesses, and that laws do little to protect you, the typical response might not be increased proactivity. Lee et al.'s [27] observation of self-efficacy and response efficacy argues for this point: Only if you both feel that you have the ability and that exercising that ability will yield positive results will you act to protect yourself. King also observed a lack of correlation between any privacy measures and Westin's categories [21].

The final point we address is the stability of the five-cluster view of participants. Our initial goal in this research was never to propose a definitive clustering of participants. Our belief is that any clustering performed should be done in the context of a tangible goal, i.e. a specific user community for which you are building software or a specific threat you wish to understand and address. However, both we and Morton and Sasse [30] observe a five-way segmentation of participants. Overall, we posit that the domain of user-segmentation would continue to benefit from additional inquiry to verify whether this five-way segmentation is an artifact of the contemporary privacy context (e.g. social networking, mobile computing, pervasive connectivity, terrorism and security, etc.) or if it is, indeed, a more accurate segmentation than Westin's prior categories.

CONCLUSION

We report a novel clustering of a set of 32 participants based on their security and privacy behaviors. While past user categories have identified Fundamentalists, the Pramatic Majority, and the Marginally Concerned, in our analysis of qualitative interview data, participants fragment into five distinct groups. Organizing these clusters into broader themes of knowledge and motivation allowed us to identify a set of security categories: Fundamentalists, Lazy Experts, Technicians, Amateurs, and the Marginally Concerned. While the Fundamentalists and Marginally Concerned echo past categorization, we note that the Pragmatic Majority fragments into three distinct groups around different sets of behaviors and levels of knowledge and motivation.

We also conducted two follow-on studies to assess stability and utility of our clusters. The first, a survey focusing specifically on whether behavior, attitude, and knowledge attributes remained consistent, found high agreement with our clusters. The second exploring implications for the design of security and privacy tools, found that designers were more comfortable leveraging our five participant categories, both for self-assessment and during design.

ACKNOWLEDGEMENTS

The research described in this grant was funded by the Natural Science and Engineering Research Council of Canada through the Discovery Grant Program. We thank all participants in our studies. The research methodologies used were approved by a University of Waterloo Research Ethics Review Committee.

REFERENCES

1. Mark S. Ackerman, Lorrie Faith Cranor, and Joseph Reagle. 1999. Privacy in e-Commerce: Examining User Scenarios and Privacy Preferences. *Proceedings*

of the 1st ACM Conference on Electronic Commerce, ACM, 1–8. http://doi.org/10.1145/336992.336995

2. Alessandro Acquisti and Ralph Gross. 2006. Imagined Communities: Awareness, Information Sharing, and Privacy on the Facebook. In *Privacy Enhancing Technologies*, George Danezis and Philippe Golle (eds.). Springer Berlin Heidelberg, 36–58.
3. Anne Adams and Martina Angela Sasse. 1999. Users Are Not the Enemy. *Commun. ACM* 42, 12: 40–46. http://doi.org/10.1145/322796.322806
4. Julio Angulo, Erik Wästlund, and Johan Högberg. 2014. What Would It Take for You to Tell Your Secrets to a Cloud? In *Secure IT Systems*. Springer, 129–145.
5. Bettina Berendt, Oliver Günther, and Sarah Spiekermann. 2005. Privacy in e-Commerce: Stated Preferences vs. Actual Behavior. *Commun. ACM* 48, 4: 101–106. http://doi.org/10.1145/1053291.1053295
6. Hugh Beyer and Karen Holtzblatt. 1997. *Contextual design: defining customer-centered systems*. Elsevier.
7. Glenn A. Bowen. 2008. Naturalistic inquiry and the saturation concept: a research note. *Qualitative Research* 8, 1: 137–152. http://doi.org/10.1177/1468794107085301
8. Laura Brandimarte, Alessandro Acquisti, and George Loewenstein. 2013. Misplaced Confidences Privacy and the Control Paradox. *Social Psychological and Personality Science* 4, 3: 340–347. http://doi.org/10.1177/1948550612455931
9. Farah Chanchary and Sonia Chiasson. 2015. User Perceptions of Sharing, Advertising, and Tracking. *Eleventh Symposium On Usable Privacy and Security (SOUPS 2015)*, 53–67.
10. Sunny Consolvo, Ian E. Smith, Tara Matthews, Anthony LaMarca, Jason Tabert, and Pauline Powledge. 2005. Location Disclosure to Social Relations: Why, when, & What People Want to Share. *Proceedings of the SIGCHI Conference on Human Factors in Computing Systems*, ACM, 81–90. http://doi.org/10.1145/1054972.1054985
11. Gregory Conti and Edward Sobiesk. 2007. An Honest Man Has Nothing to Fear: User Perceptions on Web-based Information Disclosure. *Proceedings of the 3rd Symposium on Usable Privacy and Security*, ACM, 112–121. http://doi.org/10.1145/1280680.1280695
12. Alan Cooper. 1999. *The Inmates are Running the Asylum*. Macmillan.
13. Kovila Coopamootoo and Thomas Gross. 2014. Mental Models: An Approach to Model Privacy Concern and Behavior. *Workshop on Privacy Personas and Segmentation, PPS 2014*, held with *SOUPS 2014*. See: http://cups.cs.cmu.edu/soups/2014/workshops/privacy/s2p2.pdf
14. Lynne Coventry, Debora Jeske and Pam Briggs. 2014. Combining privacy and risk perceptions to better understand user behavior. *Workshop on Privacy Personas and Segmentation, PPS 2014*, held with *SOUPS 2014*. See: http://cups.cs.cmu.edu/soups/2014/workshops/privacy/s2p3.pdf
15. John W. Creswell. 2013. *Research Design: Qualitative, Quantitative, and Mixed Methods Approaches,* 2nd Edition, Sage.
16. Paul Dourish and Ken Anderson. 2006. Collective Information Practice: Emploring Privacy and Security As Social and Cultural Phenomena. *Hum.-Comput. Interact.* 21, 3: 319–342. http://doi.org/10.1207/s15327051hci2103_2
17. Dinei Florencio and Cormac Herley. 2007. A Large-scale Study of Web Password Habits. *Proceedings of the 16th International Conference on World Wide Web*, ACM, 657–666. http://doi.org/10.1145/1242572.1242661
18. Batya Friedman, David Hurley, Daniel C. Howe, Edward Felten, and Helen Nissenbaum. 2002. Users' Conceptions of Web Security: A Comparative Study. *CHI '02 Extended Abstracts on Human Factors in Computing Systems*, ACM, 746–747. http://doi.org/10.1145/506443.506577
19. Adam N. Joinson, Ulf-Dietrich Reips, Tom Buchanan, and Carina B. Paine Schofield. 2010. Privacy, Trust, and Self-Disclosure Online. *Human–Computer Interaction* 25, 1: 1–24. http://doi.org/10.1080/07370020903586662
20. Ruogu Kang, Laura Dabbish, Nathaniel Fruchter, and Sara Kiesler. 2015. "My Data Just Goes Everywhere:" User Mental Models of the Internet and Implications for Privacy and Security. In *Eleventh Symposium On Usable Privacy and Security (SOUPS 2015)* (pp. 39-52).
21. Jennifer King. 2014. Taken Out of Context: An Empirical Analysis of Westin's Privacy Scale. *Workshop on Privacy Personas and Segmentation, PPS 2014*, held with *SOUPS 2014*. See: http://cups.cs.cmu.edu/soups/2014/workshops/privacy/s1p1.pdf.
22. Predrag Klasnja, Sunny Consolvo, Jaeyeon Jung, et al. 2009. "When I Am on Wi-Fi, I Am Fearless": Privacy Concerns & Practices in Eeryday Wi-Fi Use. *Proceedings of the SIGCHI Conference on Human Factors in Computing Systems*, ACM, 1993–2002. http://doi.org/10.1145/1518701.1519004
23. Bart P. Knijnenburg, Alfred Kobsa, and Hongxia Jin. 2013. Preference-based Location Sharing: Are More Privacy Options Really Better? *Proceedings of the SIGCHI Conference on Human Factors in Computing Systems*, ACM, 2667–2676. http://doi.org/10.1145/2470654.2481369
24. Bart P. Knijnenburg, Alfred Kobsa, and Hongxia Jin. 2013. Dimensionality of information disclosure behavior. *International Journal of Human-Computer Studies* 71, 12: 1144–1162. http://doi.org/10.1016/j.ijhcs.2013.06.003

25. Lydia Kraus, Ina Wechsung and Sebastian Möller. 2014. A Comparison of Privacy and Security Knowledge and Privacy Concern as Influencing Factors for Mobile Protection Behavior. *Workshop on Privacy Personas and Segmentation, PPS 2014*, held with *SOUPS 2014.* See: http://cups.cs.cmu.edu/soups/2014/workshops/privacy/s2p4.pdf
26. Ponnurangam Kumaraguru and Lorrie Faith Cranor. 2005. Privacy Indexes: A Survey of Westin's Studies. *Technical Report CMU-ISRI-5-138,* December 2005, Carnegie Mellon University.
27. Doohwang Lee, Robert Larose, and Nora Rifon. 2008. Keeping our network safe: a model of online protection behaviour. *Behaviour & Information Technology* 27, 5: 445–454. http://doi.org/10.1080/01449290600879344
28. Ryan Lytle. 2013. The Beginner's Guide to Google+. http://mashable.com/2013/10/27/google-plus-beginners-guide/.
29. Tomasz Miaskiewicz, Tamara Sumner, and Kenneth A. Kozar. 2008. A Latent Semantic Analysis Methodology for the Identification and Creation of Personas. *Proceedings of the SIGCHI Conference on Human Factors in Computing Systems*, ACM, 1501–1510. http://doi.org/10.1145/1357054.1357290
30. A. Morton and M.A. Sasse. 2014. Desperately seeking assurances: Segmenting users by their information-seeking preferences. *2014 Twelfth Annual International Conference on Privacy, Security and Trust (PST)*, 102–111. http://doi.org/10.1109/PST.2014.6890929
31. Judith S. Olson, Jonathan Grudin, and Eric Horvitz. 2005. A Study of Preferences for Sharing and Privacy. *CHI '05 Extended Abstracts on Human Factors in Computing Systems*, ACM, 1985–1988. http://doi.org/10.1145/1056808.1057073
32. Sai Teja Peddinti, Allen Collins, Aaron Sedley, Nina Taft, Anna Turner and Allison Woodruff. 2015. Perceived Frequency of Advertising Practices. *Workshop on Privacy Personas and Segmentation, PPS 2015*, held with *SOUPS 2015.* See: https://cups.cs.cmu.edu/soups/2015/papers/ppsPeddinit i.pdf
33. Kim Bartel Sheehan. 2002. Toward a Typology of Internet Users and Online Privacy Concerns. *The Information Society* 18, 1: 21–32. http://doi.org/10.1080/01972240252818207
34. Anselm Leonard Strauss and Juliet M. Corbin. 1990.*Basics of Qualitative Research: Grounded Theory Procedures and Techniques*. Sage
35. Colleen Swanson, Ruth Urner, and Edward Lank. 2010. Naïve Security in a Wi-Fi World. In *Trust Management IV*, Masakatsu Nishigaki, Audun Jøsang, Yuko Murayama and Stephen Marsh (eds.). Springer Berlin Heidelberg, 32–47.
36. Jennifer Urban and Chris Hoofnagle. 2014. The Privacy Pragmatic as Privacy Vulnerable, *Workshop on Privacy Personas and Segmentation, PPS 2014*, held with *SOUPS 2014.* See: http://cups.cs.cmu.edu/soups/2014/workshops/privacy/s1p2.pdf
37. Jessica Vitak. 2015. Balancing Privacy Concerns and Impression Management Strategies on Facebook. *Workshop on Privacy Personas and Segmentation, PPS 2015*, held with *SOUPS 2015.* See: https://cups.cs.cmu.edu/soups/2015/papers/ppsVitak.pd f
38. Rick Wash and Emilee Rader. 2015. Too Much Knowledge? Security Beliefs and Protective Behaviors Among United States Internet Users. In *Eleventh Symposium On Usable Privacy and Security (SOUPS 2015)* (pp. 309-325).
39. Robert S. Weiss. 1995. *Learning from strangers: The art and method of qualitative interview studies*. Simon and Schuster.
40. Pamela Wisniewski, Bart Knijnenburg and Heather Richter Lipford. 2014. Profiling facebook users' privacy behaviors. *Workshop on Privacy Personas and Segmentation, PPS 2014*, held with *SOUPS 2014.* See: http://cups.cs.cmu.edu/soups/2014/workshops/privacy/s2p1.pdf
41. Allison Woodruff, Vasyl Pihur, Sunny Consolvo, Lauren Schmidt, Laura Brandimarte, and Alessandro Acquisti. 2014. Would a privacy fundamentalist sell their dna for $1000... if nothing bad happened as a result? the westin categories, behavioral intentions, and consequences. In *Symposium on Usable Privacy and Security (SOUPS)*.

It's Creepy, But It Doesn't Bother Me

Chanda Phelan **Cliff Lampe** **Paul Resnick**
University of Michigan School of Information
Ann Arbor, Michigan
{cdphelan,cacl,presnick}@umich.edu

ABSTRACT
Undergraduates interviewed about privacy concerns related to online data collection made apparently contradictory statements. The same issue could evoke concern or not in the span of an interview, sometimes even a single sentence. Drawing on dual-process theories from psychology, we argue that some of the apparent contradictions can be resolved if privacy concern is divided into two components we call *intuitive concern*, a "gut feeling," and *considered concern*, produced by a weighing of risks and benefits. Consistent with previous explanations of the so-called privacy paradox, we argue that people may express high considered concern when prompted, but in practice act on low intuitive concern without a considered assessment. We also suggest a new explanation: a considered assessment can override an intuitive assessment of high concern without eliminating it. Here, people may choose rationally to accept a privacy risk but still express intuitive concern when prompted.

Author Keywords
Privacy; social media; privacy paradox; trust; social awareness

ACM Classification Keywords
H.5.3 Group and Organization Interfaces – Web-based Interaction

INTRODUCTION
Sharing personal information is an everyday occurrence online, and weighing the tradeoffs between convenience and privacy is an inescapable reality of using the internet. For designers of online systems, much of the difficulty in establishing the acceptability of data collection practices lies in the uncertainty surrounding consumers' preferences: people's views of online privacy are full of contradictions. One such contradiction is the commonly observed mismatch between people's stated privacy concern and behavior, a phenomenon often referred to as the *privacy paradox* [29], but contradictions exist even in the way people speak about their concern.

To explore the source of contradictions in privacy concern, we conducted semi-structured interviews with undergraduates at a large university to study how individuals make sense of privacy concern in specific disclosure decisions. We find that people often seem to contradict themselves when talking about their concern, e.g. describing an intrusion as creepy but denying that it bothers them. The apparent incoherence vanishes when we decompose privacy concern into two parts: an initial "gut feeling," which we call *intuitive concern*, and a subsequent deliberate weighing of costs and benefits, resulting in what we call *considered concern*.

We argue that the two ways that people talk about concern correspond well to the two systems proposed by the dual process model of cognition popularized by Daniel Kahneman [17], making the two-system view a useful analysis framework for privacy concern. System 1 is the fast, automatic process that generates impressions and feelings; System 2 is the deliberate, reasoning process that one identifies as the conscious self. System 1 is efficient but vulnerable to influences that should be irrelevant to a rational decision, and strongly influences System 2 despite System 2's outward appearance of rationality. We find that the qualities of intuitive concern correspond to a System 1 process, and those of considered concern to a System 2 process.

Additionally, we identify three factors that commonly affected participants' privacy concern: trust, social presence of agents collecting data, and using the belief that nothing is private online as a reference frame to assess marginal risk. The three factors have different impacts on the two types of concern. While trust in the organization collecting data affects both, the collector's social presence affects only intuitive concern and marginal risk affects only considered concern. We additionally conclude that a dual process model of privacy concern sheds light on the privacy paradox. There are two ways in which a privacy paradox can occur in this model. In one, individuals act on their intuitive concern without assessing considered concern; they are usually unaware of the paradox because it arises from an incomplete understanding of the relevant risks. In the other, individuals ignore their high intuitive concern because they are able to establish low considered concern; in this case, they usually recognize the paradox but find it

CHI'16, May 07-12, 2016, San Jose, CA, USA
© 2016 ACM. ISBN 978-1-4503-3362-7/16/05…$15.00
DOI: http://dx.doi.org/10.1145/2858036.2858381

unproblematic because they view it as irrelevant to their decision, even though it can lead to lingering discomfort.

BACKGROUND

Privacy is a broad subject studied in a number of fields, many of which understand privacy differently. There is no universally agreed-upon direct measure of privacy. A common proxy measure in empirical research is *privacy concern* [37], specifically as related to the collection, unauthorized secondary use, errors in, and improper access of personal data [38]. Using privacy concern as a proxy measure for disclosure intentions or behavior has proven problematic. First, privacy concern has been often measured as an individual's tendency to worry about privacy *in general*, which ignores the effect of context cues like a website's trustworthiness. Second, privacy concern is not predictive of disclosure behavior or even disclosure intention [29]; though often conflated in the past, they are three separate constructs.

Treating privacy concern, disclosure intention, and disclosure behavior as interchangeable assumes that privacy decision-making is an assessment of risks and benefits connected to disclosure, called the *privacy calculus* [12, 13]. This model assumes that people are rational, meaning they "have stable individual preferences for privacy and disclosure, and…will consistently react to changes in the objective risks and benefits" [6]. Under this model, the difference between intentions and actual behavior is negligible, making privacy concern a perfectly acceptable substitute for actual behavior.

More recent research has found that people's behavior is only partly a result of a privacy calculus, introducing a central puzzle of privacy research: people tend to say they have higher levels of privacy concern than is indicated by their behavior. This contradiction is referred to as the *privacy paradox* [29]. Ackerman et al. [1] found that though 39% of survey respondents claimed to be "very concerned" about online privacy, only half of those respondents reported behavior that classified them as such. Other studies have found that people who claim high privacy concern are willing to sell their personal information for small incentives, such as coupons [5].

Several possible sources of the privacy paradox have been proposed. Some have argued that the paradox is simply a methodological quirk, a result of measuring general privacy concern and ignoring how costs and benefits can change in specific disclosure decisions [3]. This explanation is unsatisfactory, as individuals' behavior can diverge from their stated concern even when asked about their concern in specific scenarios [4]. Other explanations of the privacy paradox argue that privacy decisions are affected by bounded rationality, meaning that a person's ability to perform the privacy calculus is bounded by incomplete information and cognitive limitations [3, 21]. This makes it unrealistic to expect that people will behave rationally when making privacy-related decisions [2].

Bounded rationality presents two other possible sources of the privacy paradox. First, privacy decisions are nearly always clouded by uncertainty about risk, making it all but impossible for individuals to understand their own privacy preferences, let alone report them with any accuracy [3]. Second is the use of heuristics, or mental shortcuts, as a means of avoiding effortful cognitive processing [3]. For example, consumers use the presence of a privacy seal on a website as a safety heuristic and fail to assess the objective risks of disclosure [23]. Heuristics are efficient and often lead to satisfactory outcomes, but they are also susceptible to factors that would be discarded as irrelevant in the risk/benefit calculation of the privacy calculus model, such as website design [16], affect [21], or others' observed behavior [27]. For example, people tend to disclose less when they are assured of confidentiality because it draws their attention to and thus heightens privacy concern [16].

System 1 and System 2: a model of cognition

A two-system view of thought developed by Daniel Kahneman and Amos Tversky distinguishes intuition and reasoning as separate mental processes. It is often applied as an explanation of apparent contradictions in decisions made under conditions of uncertainty [17]. Given the high levels of uncertainty in privacy decisions, applying this model to information privacy yields useful insights.

The systems, named System 1 and System 2 by Stanovich and West [39], refer to two parallel thought processes. System 1—the intuitive process—is automatic, fast, and often emotionally charged [17]. It generates *impressions* based on associations and heuristics with no sense of voluntary control. System 1 activities include recognizing anger in a voice or knowing the answer to 2+2=? [18]. System 2—the reasoning process—is slower, effortful, and may be governed by logic. It generates *judgments* based on consciously controlled mental activity [17]. System 2 activities include monitoring one's behavior in a social setting and evaluating a logical argument [18].

As System 2 is conscious, it is more capable of rationality, and so part of its function is to act as quality control for the impressions generated by System 1. System 2 is costly, though; it takes effort to allocate and sustain attention. Therefore, System 2 monitors System 1 only lightly [19]. During normal operation, System 1's impressions are usually adopted without modification by System 2. Kahneman calls these *intuitive judgments* [43]. If System 1 runs into difficulty—for example, when surprised by a sudden sound—it can call on System 2 to take over. Even when System 2 is fully engaged, it is heavily influenced by System 1's impressions. Further, System 1's impressions are inaccessible to introspection, so System 2 is unaware of its influence. Instead, System 2 fills in the gaps itself: people are able to provide rational explanations for their choices even when their behavior indicates they are following a System 1 heuristic [45].

Previous privacy literature has introduced a particular two-system model called the elaboration likelihood model (ELM). It describes how various persuasive cues are more or less effective depending on whether System 1 (the peripheral route in the ELM) or System 2 (the central route) is engaged. ELM has been used to explain the inconsistent effects of factors such as message framing [7, 23, 47, 48], brand reputation, information quality [47,48] and individual trait anxiety [49] on privacy behavior and/or intentions. In contrast, our focus is on how a two-system model can help us understand different types of privacy concerns, and thus resolve apparent incoherence among statements about concerns as well as inconsistency between stated concerns and behaviors.

Factors contributing to privacy concern

Privacy concern can be influenced by many factors. For example, studies have found that giving users more control over their data can reduce privacy concern [46], while another study found that targeted advertising is considered "creepy" and raises privacy concern [44]. The factors' effects often interact with each other. One study found that people are concerned about sharing location information from their mobile devices, a concern amplified by the perceived lack of control over access to their location [40]. Further complications arise from the fact that the factors are not always rational; the lighting in the room can affect privacy concern, for instance [11]. Factors may cause an emotional reaction, which can also interfere with rationality: a study of user responses to mobile apps' data collection found that the users said they were "creeped out" by them; the authors argue creepiness is "an emotional response to a sense of wrongness that is difficult to articulate" and is not necessarily related to objective risks [36], which suggests a System 1 response.

Participants in our study were affected by a complex array of factors found in previous literature. Of these, we chose three of the most common factors to analyze in detail. We examine the background for each here.

Trust

Trust's effect on privacy concern has been widely studied as a crucial factor in e-commerce and other information disclosure behavior [31]. Research on trust in online environments usually focuses on institutional trust, which refers to a consumer's belief that a data collector will not misuse personal data [15, 21]. This trust tends to be formed based on the reputation of the company as a whole rather than its privacy policies specifically: Earp and Baumer [14] found that consumers are more likely to intend to disclose information if the site is well-known.

Trust has an extremely powerful influence on both privacy concern and behavior. In a survey, the majority of respondents said that whether a site was run by a trusted company was a very important factor in their general privacy concern [1]. Another study found that building trust was more effective in encouraging information disclosure than attempting to reduce privacy concern directly [26]. In concrete privacy decisions, trust can overrule an individual's general privacy concern and increase disclosure behavior [29]. While the importance of trust in online privacy is well-established, its precise role remains unclear: trust has been alternately modeled as an antecedent to privacy concern, an outcome of privacy concern, a mediating variable between privacy concern and disclosure behavior, or a moderator of the influence of privacy concern on disclosure [37].

The importance of trust to online consumers is a rational response, to an extent; trust is most important when there is uncertainty [25], a common characteristic of online privacy decisions. Consumer response to trust can extend beyond what is strictly rational, though. Previous research has found that people can use trust as a heuristic to guide their behavior [35]. This strategy saves time and is less cognitively taxing, but can lead to errors. For example, interventions meant to protect privacy can be too effective in establishing trust: a 2009 survey found that 62% of its respondents incorrectly believed that the simple existence of a privacy policy meant that a site could not share personal information with third parties [42].

Social presence

Social presence describes the feeling of being with another in mediated communication [10]. Whether the other is human or artificial intelligence is immaterial [9]. According to the Computers as Social Actors (CASA) model, humans are predisposed to treat most everything like social entities, including virtual computer agents [27, 28]. The effect is particularly strong if the computer agent possesses characteristics of language and interactivity, but they are not a requirement [22]: targeted advertisements can create social presence [28]. Social presence can also be created by surveillance [41], though it fades if the intrusion does not change over time [24, 30].

Treating computers as social is an automatic response, so people are largely unaware of their behavior. They do not believe that computer agents are literally human [22, 27]. There is some variation in the propensity to feel social presence—gender [34] can have an effect, as can mood [22]—but even so, social presence is pervasive [28].

In research on online learning [41] or remote collaboration [8], social presence is often studied as a desirable occurrence, but the expectations of CASA suggest that social presence may increase privacy concern. Treating computers as social entities entails more than simply feeling presence. It also means holding the agent to the expectations of a social being [22]. People are polite to computers, and expect computer agents to be polite to them [32]. A machine that violates social norms is perceived to be socially—not technologically—deficient. Unsolicited social presence online is likely to be met with the same negative response as another person looking over their shoulder as they browse.

Experimental evidence of the effect of social presence on privacy behavior has produced conflicting results. One study, which used interactivity and vivid visual cues in banner advertisements to induce social presence, found human-seeming agents caused over-disclosure of personal information [3]. In contrast, evidence from another study showed that agents meant to create social presence caused decreased disclosure of personal information if they were perceived to be violating social norms [14].

Marginal risk

Individuals tend to assess outcomes as losses or gains relative to a reference frame, rather than the absolute level of the outcome [20]. In the case of online privacy, this would mean that individuals judge the risk of a new privacy intrusion by comparing it to their understanding of how exposed they already are. Studies examining the effect of marginal risk on privacy concern and behavior are recent and still relatively sparse, but there is evidence of marginal risk assessments affecting online privacy behavior. For example, Acquisti et al. [5] found that people will pay much less to protect information that would otherwise be public than the amount they will accept to disclose information that would otherwise be private.

A closely related but distinct concept is relative risk, judgment of the risk of a privacy intrusion relative to a specific similar intrusion that is close to mind. For example, a recent study found that subjects assessing the intrusiveness of two surveys had lower privacy concern when the level of protection increased from the first to the second survey, rather than when it decreased [6]. The same study also found that relative risk had an effect on both disclosure intention and actual privacy behavior, but was more pronounced in actual behavior.

METHOD

Recruitment

Participants were recruited from an introductory undergraduate course on information studies at Large University. Anyone enrolled in the class was eligible to participate, and received credit in the course for doing so. Students were invited by email to sign up for an interview. Students had access to alternative exercises for points. The study was approved by the university institutional review board.

Procedure

Three weeks before the invitations to participate in the current study were sent out, students were invited to sign up for a separate research study about social media use, called the Media Monitor (MM) for the purposes of this narrative, in exchange for class credit. To participate, students visited MM's recruiting website and downloaded a Chrome browser extension that could be perceived as privacy invasive: the extension logged visits to social media and other popular websites, collecting the URL, time, and duration of their visit. The data was collected pseudonymously: participants created accounts with their email addresses, which were stored separately. All gave their informed consent to install MM. Of the 230 students in the class, 181 (79%) signed up.

Later, students received another email inviting them to participate in this privacy study, again in exchange for class credit. Students who had not signed up for MM were particularly encouraged to participate.

Semi-structured interviews with 37 undergraduates were conducted in person over a period of three weeks, each lasting 23-56 minutes (median 35 minutes). During the first stage of the interview, the study was disguised as a user experience interview for MM; the true focus of the study, to elicit views on privacy, was concealed. In this first stage, participants were not asked about privacy directly, and were instead asked to talk about their experience signing up for and using MM, as well as social media habits more generally. When participants brought up privacy in one of their responses, the interviewer asked exploratory questions but allowed the participant to direct the conversation. The concealment accomplished two things: it discouraged priming participants to over-report privacy concern [29], and it anchored the discussion to a real, specific privacy choice, which is important in capturing privacy concern accurately [37].

In the second stage of the interview, participants were informed of the concealment and given the opportunity to retract their consent (none did). With privacy revealed as a topic, participants were asked to talk about their general privacy concern, a common measure of privacy that has been demonstrated to be inaccurate [3]. Its inaccuracy was what made general privacy concern important to the study design: when contrasted with the more reliable method of questioning in the first stage, it encouraged contradictory responses and created an opportunity to observe if and how the participants resolved those contradictions for themselves.

The interviewer never defined online privacy in either stage. This was essential for us, because we wanted to see what factors would emerge as important to them, rather than forcing a focus on factors that we had pre-selected. A disadvantage of this strategy was that it was difficult to gauge how privacy concern may have been affected by an individual's understanding of privacy issues.

Audio of the interview was recorded and later transcribed. Interview transcripts were analyzed using inductive coding to iteratively identify themes. We first coded for anything that affected a participant's perception of a privacy intrusion, subsequently identifying a number of factors that commonly affected participants. These factors included the type of data being collected, trust in the entity collecting data, and their perceived level of control over their data. During this stage we noticed that participants differentiated between factors that affected how *comfortable* they were, and how *acceptable* they considered the intrusion to be. We coded for these two themes. We then refined the codes for each factor contributing to privacy concern over several iterations.

Once we had refined the contributing factors, we delved more deeply into the characteristics of the themes *acceptable* and *comfortable* and found they corresponded to the characteristics of System 1 and System 2. Three of the most common factors were chosen to be analyzed in detail and were catalogued according to the type of privacy concern they affected. In a final round of analysis, transcripts were examined for counter evidence for our interpretation of each of these factors.

Participants

Interviews were conducted with 37 undergraduates (18 female). The majority, 62%, were studying a technology-related field, though all were enrolled in an introduction to information studies course. Nearly all reported having an account on multiple social media platforms, though most said they were primarily active on Facebook. One participant had recently deactivated his social media accounts to reduce distractions. All of the participants had signed up for MM. One reported uninstalling it before the interview, and three more said they planned to uninstall it.

RESULTS

Most participants were fairly content with their level of privacy on Facebook and other social media. They were largely aware that nothing on social media was truly private but found this unproblematic because *"I keep everything to myself that I don't want people [on Facebook] to know in the first place"* (S28). Most were similarly unworried by government surveillance, accepting it as an inevitability they believed was unlikely to ever affect them personally. In contrast, there was a lot of variation in participants' level of concern regarding the collection of browsing data by entities like MM or private companies such as Google. There was no common standard of what constituted a comfortable level of data collection or which risks were most salient.

Intuitive and considered privacy concern

The way participants spoke about their privacy concern sometimes appeared contradictory, simultaneously acknowledging and distancing themselves from their concern when reflecting on it. For example, S35's statement, *"The more I think about [data collection], the more disturbing it is, I guess. Personally, I'm not that worried right now,"* or S08's reaction to Facebook's data collection practices, "*I don't think it is that big of a deal. [...] I just think it's the fact that they're able to do that [...] is what scares me a little bit.*"

These statements were not simply evidence of confusion. Rather, they were examples of participants' tendency to divide their overall privacy concern into two separate components: whether a given data collection practice was "*creepy,*" and whether they were "*bothered*" by it. This is evident in S17 speaking of targeted advertisements: *"It's kind of strange for me, [but] it doesn't necessarily bother me. [...] it's just kind of like, 'This is weird.'"* A number of other participants phrased their concern in a similar way, such as S34: *"It doesn't really bother me. [...] It gets you thinking, 'Wow, that's annoying that's weird, but whatever, I guess. That's fine.'"*

Though participants used particular words differently, when examined in context it appeared that participants were referring to two distinct components to their concern. The first component was the result of an emotional response to an intrusion—most frequently described using such words as "*annoying,*" "*weird,*" "*creepy,*" or "*disturbing*"—while the second was the result of a more deliberate assessment of how problematic the intrusion was—most frequently described as the participant being "*bothered*" or "*worried.*" The distinction can be observed in S23's response to targeted ads:

> *"I don't like the outcome 'cause that's annoying. But once you see the outcome, you realize what they're doing, and then that starts to bother you. If you [...] don't know that they're manipulating you, you're just annoyed with them [...] But once I started learning about the manipulation, that started to bother me."*

As tended to be the case with participants generally, whether the intrusion was bothersome was the most important in explaining behavior when reflecting on past choices; the intrusion's creepiness was largely dismissed.

Another difference between the two components was time. When presented with new, specific privacy intrusions during the interviews, participants tended to respond immediately with an emotional reaction, with more deliberate consideration following after. This exchange between the interviewer and S05 illustrates:

> *Interviewer: [...] Would [reading your Facebook messages] change how you felt about [MM]?*
>
> *S05: Oh, definitely. That's pretty invasive and, or at the very least someone who agrees that would probably be not, would probably censor themselves a bit and act kind of differently.*
>
> *Interviewer: [...] What do you think is different?*
>
> *S05: [pause] Good question. I don't... [know] how to explain it. It's just... I guess it's a matter of knowing who is going to see it. [...] I just feel like I would need to censor myself. It would be kind of, just like... I don't know, it just kinda makes me less comfortable.*

S05 knew his feelings immediately but had trouble articulating the reasons for his concern, an indication that he moved to the second stage of consideration only after being prompted. The sequence was generally the same for all participants when establishing overall privacy concern.

Upon encountering a new privacy intrusion, a "gut feeling" formed immediately, based on a first impression often established before learning many details about objective privacy risks. As a result, it could be affected by factors that should have been irrelevant, and the participant did not always appear to understand which factors affected her gut feeling. When discussing past choices as well, participants named factors that should have been irrelevant, even though they were sometimes unsure as to why those factors mattered; this suggests the gut feeling was also formed in real privacy choices. We identified this gut feeling using the participants' emotional responses to an intrusion, i.e. how the intrusion made them feel. We call this *intuitive concern.*

After establishing intuitive concern, a participant sometimes engaged in a second stage of deliberate assessment, resulting in what we call *considered concern.* In this stage, participants identified possible privacy risks and considered whether they were worth taking, given the intrusion's benefits (e.g. class credit for installing MM).

Participants only assessed considered concern under certain conditions, namely when intuitive concern was high but there were benefits to accepting the intrusion anyway. In other cases, participants skipped assessing considered concern entirely. For privacy choices presented during the interview, participants usually had to be prompted to engage in a considered evaluation of concern. When intuitive concern was high and no benefits were apparent (e.g. a version of MM run by Facebook with no class credit) participants followed their intuition and rejected the intrusion; if intuitive concern was sufficiently low, participants accepted, again without further consideration. Participants who made a choice based only on intuitive concern usually had clear feelings but were unable to articulate the reasons with confidence.

Many factors contributed to participants' concern about their privacy; some affected assessments of both intuitive and considered concern, while others primarily affected just one. Therefore, intuitive concern and considered concern were related but ultimately independent components of overall concern, which explained the apparent contradictions in some responses. Participants could achieve low considered concern even if intuitive concern was high, but if they were unable to address the factors contributing to their intuitive concern, their intuitive concern remained high. This resulted in responses such as S08 earlier referring to data collection on Facebook as both "*scary*" and "*[not] that big of a deal*" in the same thought.

Factors contributing to privacy concern

The way a factor tended to affect participants provided clues as to whether it had an impact on intuitive concern, considered concern, or both. In the following sections, we identify three of the most common factors and how they contribute to each concern component.

Trust

Trust appeared to affect both intuitive and considered concern; it also appeared to have the strongest effect on participants of all the identified factors. Trust's proposed effect on concern is modeled in Figure 1; see Figure 4 for the full model with all factors included. Both institutional trust and interpersonal trust were discussed in the interviews, primarily in the context of the MM sign-up decision. Institutional trust in Large University was mentioned more frequently than interpersonal trust in their professor, but it is not possible to untangle the two entirely. Consequently, we refer to trust generally here.

Effect of trust on intuitive concern: Trust had a powerful effect on keeping participants' intuitive concern about MM low. Nearly all participants felt comfortable sharing their data with MM even if they disliked the idea in other contexts, like S36:

> *"I already think [academic department] is really cool. So anything that they're putting out [...] it's really easy to just be like, 'Oh, well, you're cool. [...] Whereas I feel like I'd maybe just put more thought into it if it was coming from someone I don't know."*

A number of participants failed to recognize MM as a potential privacy intrusion, an indication that trust had kept their intuitive assessment of concern so low that they had bypassed assessing considered concern before signing up. About half of the participants said they had no hesitation about signing up for MM (even when they were otherwise concerned about their privacy) and they usually did not have a complete understanding of MM's data collection practices. S08 said he did not realize that MM collected data at all, initially:

> *"I was just flipping through, yay, whatever, install, and then when I went and looked back [...] I was like, 'Wow. They must be collecting something in my computer.' [...] I feel like that's not their motive, to collect personal information from me. [...] Especially when it's coming from professors from the university, they're trustworthy people" (S08).*

In S08's case, he eventually investigated what data was being collected. Many others did not, and even though they had gone through MM's informed consent process,

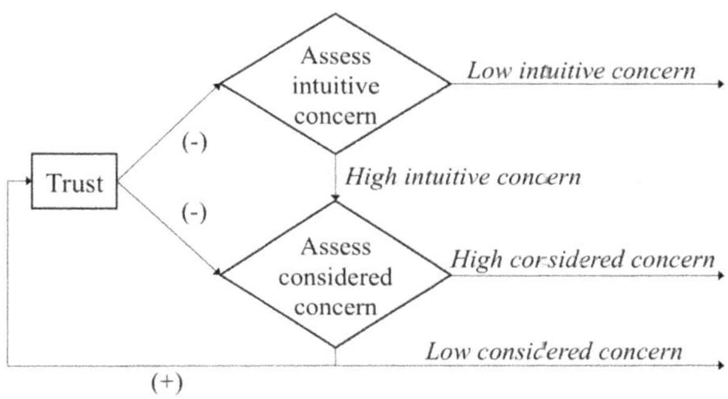

Figure 1: Effect of trust on privacy concern.

they were surprised to learn about MM's data collection. These participants never evaluated the objective privacy risks of MM, suggesting they did not engage in the second stage of assessing considered concern.

Effect of trust on considered concern: Trust also appeared to have a major impact on participants' considered assessment of concern. It was the most commonly-cited reason for why participants were comfortable sharing their data with MM. The ease with which most participants were able to explain their lack of intuitive concern was more evidence trust affected both components of concern.

Trust was important in dampening considered concern primarily because participants felt they could trust that the creators' intentions were good and the application truthfully described exactly what it did. Together, these significantly reduced the perceived risks of signing up. Participants felt they could reasonably infer what they were agreeing to from the university context without investing the time to investigate MM itself in much detail. Consequently, most participants who reported initial reservations about the app did not express any regret about their choice to install MM.

Social presence of data collectors

Social presence was the most difficult factor to identify; it affected primarily intuitive concern, so participants were unlikely to cite it directly as a factor. Instead, its existence was inferred through participants' descriptions of their emotional response to data collectors. Though not all participants felt social presence, it seemed to have a powerful effect on those who did, and led to lingering privacy concern even if their considered concern overruled their intuitive concern and they chose to accept an intrusion. The proposed effect of social presence is modeled in Figure 2.

Identifying social presence: Data collectors were generally unpopular among participants, but some participants had an appreciably higher level of concern than others about data collectors and tended to have a strong negative emotional reaction to them. Even these participants commonly had trouble identifying their issue with data collectors. For example, S27 had trouble thinking of what data she wanted to be kept private:

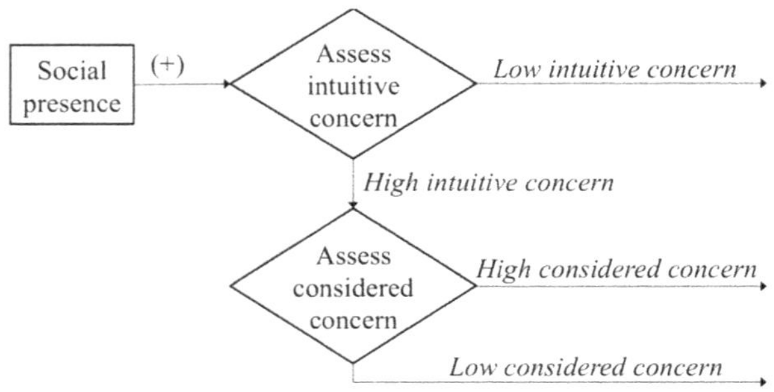

Figure 2: Effect of social presence on privacy concern.

"That's a good question. I want to say location but... Like I'm always on campus, so where would I go? I don't know. That's a good question. It's hard to pinpoint."

As a result, in most cases it was not possible to directly identify what made these participants more concerned about data collectors than others. Instead, social presence was inferred by participants describing data collectors as making them *feel watched.* Participants who felt watched brought up a specific browsing experience in which they became aware of a data collector's presence in real time (usually through targeted advertising) *and* used language of surveillance to describe the experience:

> *"I do still use Google and stuff, but it's definitely opened my eyes to see, okay, they are pretty much watching, they're watching."* (S35)
>
> *"[I don't like] the fact that people know where I've been to [...] the fact that there's somebody behind me, trailing me, it's just a little scary."* (S27)

No one described feeling watched constantly. Most reported feeling negatively about the data collectors only intermittently while browsing; for example, after being reminded by targeted advertisements. Many participants, including those who showed no signs of feeling social presence generally, reported an initial feeling of being under surveillance after installing MM that faded quickly. For those who tended to feel social presence, the feeling returned more frequently and intensely. In addition, when otherwise comfortable participants were asked to describe their "nightmare" privacy scenario, it usually involved not feeling alone while browsing. For similar reasons, many participants said they would be more concerned about more invasive versions of MM, like one that tracked all browsing: "*It just creates a level of transparency where we feel like we're being watched... where people are so scared of the level of surveillance they're under that they are afraid to do certain things"* (S30).

Effect of social presence on intuitive concern: There were a number of indications that social presence primarily influenced the intuitive assessment of concern. Take S04 describing his response to social presence:

> *"[The collection of browsing data is] a weird subject for me. I don't know. Sometimes, when I'm researching things that [...] would seem sketchy then I have concerns about privacy, but I would say that that's a very small way I use the internet. [...] But it's just like a weird thing to think about that someone's sort of watching you, whatever you're doing."*

This implies intuitive concern because his concern was rooted in an emotional reaction (the discomfort he felt about a data collector watching him). This would explain why he did not state social presence as a factor outright: as the concern stemmed from the sensation itself, rather than any concrete risks, he was unable or unwilling to use social presence as a factor during his assessment of considered concern and struggled to find an alternative explanation ("*[It's] a weird subject for me. I don't know*"). He attempted to minimize his concern ("*that's a very small way I use the internet*") but remained unsettled, unable to resolve his intuitive concern.

Social presence had a pronounced effect on overall concern and was one of the few factors that convinced participants to take protective action. S35 reported switching to the no-tracking search engine DuckDuckGo when she felt uncomfortable, one of the few instances where participants described accepting inconvenience for more privacy. Similarly, the one participant who reported uninstalling MM did so because *"I didn't want to have something checking up on me"* (S24) and said he *"definitely"* felt less watched after uninstalling it. Several other participants said they planned to uninstall MM, all because the app made them feel watched.

Effect of social presence on considered concern: Social presence was not frequently discussed as a factor contributing to considered concern. Instead, some participants discussed their strategies for ignoring or avoiding intuitive concern caused by social presence. A number of participants said that their lack of concern about data collectors was contingent on not being reminded of them. S15 was one: *"I knew that they could [target ads], but the fact that I keep seeing it keeps reminding me of it. As long as it's out of sight, out of mind."* S06 was another: *"The Facebook advertising thing creeps me out [...] I don't like to think about it. That's just having it right there and [I think to myself], 'Oh, don't look at it!'"* These participants tended to have lower overall privacy concern than participants who were affected by social presence; it may be they simply had better strategies for ignoring feelings of social presence.

Marginal risk

Some participants gauged their concern by evaluating the additional risk of a new intrusion compared to their current perceived level of exposure, namely the belief that nothing on the Internet is private. S30 used this to justify his lack of concern about MM: *"All you guys were asking for was monitoring my sites and my hits, and basically a lot of other sites already do that without my permission."* Figure 3 models the proposed effect of marginal risk.

Effect of marginal risk on intuitive concern: There was little evidence that marginal risk reduced intuitive concern. Indeed, some subjects explicitly described feeling intuitive concern despite believing that marginal risk was minimal. For example, S06 said:

> *"I just hate the idea of...I don't know, just having [browsing activity] recorded, although, I'm sure it's recording somewhere else right now, but just I guess visualizing it and giving it to someone else is just weird to me. It just freaks me out."*

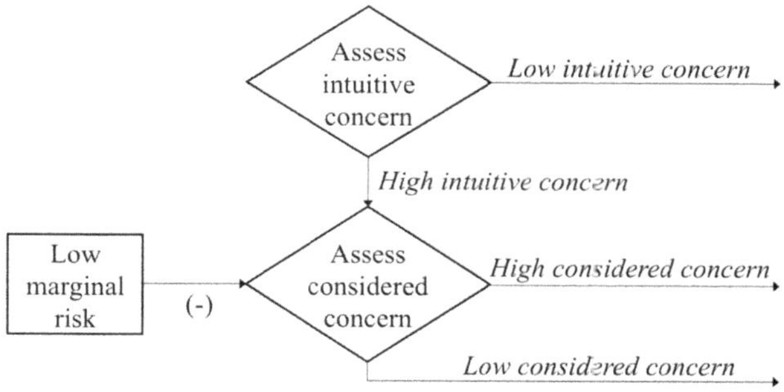

Figure 3: Effect of marginal risk on privacy concern.

S33 was similarly unsatisfied with low marginal risk as a reason to be less concerned when appraising a hypothetical version of MM run by Google: *"I might have been a little bit more skeptical [...] It's like, 'I already give Google so much of my information, so why am I really concerned?' I don't know. It's a good question."* Not being able to explain the residual concern suggests that the residual concern was intuitive, not considered.

Effect of marginal risk on considered concern: Some participants used marginal risk arguments to justify discarding intuitive concern upon further deliberation, signaling considered concern. For example, S11:

> *"I'm just numb to the fact that people can get information about me. I guess, it did occur to me like, 'Oh, what if they can see my Facebook and see my interactions with other people?' [...] [but in the end] I just signed up for it."*

S23 expressed a similar sentiment:

> *"I probably wouldn't prefer to have a big corporation have all that information stored about me, [...] but it's not like I would be in an uproar about it. I'm pretty content that they already have a lot of information, so it wouldn't be that much more."*

Further evidence that marginal risk affected considered assessments of concern was that it was often employed in an explicit cost-benefit analysis. S25 was one participant who did this: *"I think just with the way that times have changed, it's impossible to really [keep personal information offline] and stay in touch with everything. So I think you just have to accept that reality."*

Interestingly, S33, who denied minimal marginal risk was a satisfactory reason to discard intuitive concern in a specific choice, *did* use low marginal risk to justify lower considered concern: *"People get so angry [about privacy][...] it's like, whatever, I'm already giving the Internet all this information about me. I can't even think of what they can do to that really, really make me angry."*

Unlike trust, low considered concern based on assessment of minimal marginal risk did not have a mechanism for reducing intuitive concern. Intuitive concern remained even after a considered assessment of low concern.

DISCUSSION

Based on the results of the interviews, we developed a model of privacy concern with two semi-independent pieces, which we call intuitive concern and considered concern. The model explains apparent contradictions in our student respondents' expressed privacy concerns.

As we analyzed the characteristics of intuitive and considered concern, we found that they correspond to the results of assessments by the two systems of a dual process model of cognition. Intuitive concern results from a process of the intuitive System 1: emotional, formed immediately, and affected by factors that are irrelevant to objective privacy risk. Considered concern results from a process of the reasoning System 2: conscious, slower, and more likely to engage in an explicit cost-benefit analysis using factors that are relevant to objective risk.

A two-system view can explain why individuals only assess considered concern under certain conditions. System 2 processes take up more cognitive resources, so they do not engage unless System 1 raises a warning; otherwise, System 2 adopts the intuitive judgment without modification. As this would predict, in situations where there is conflict in an intuitive assessment of concern—namely, if intuitive concern is high but there is some apparent benefit to be gained by accepting the intrusion anyway—individuals assess considered concern. Otherwise, when intuitive concern is very low or no obvious benefit exists that is worth the extra cognitive effort, an evaluation of considered concern is bypassed for the sake of efficiency. The impression generated by the intuitive assessment of concern is then adopted without modification. Switching between the two types of assessment occurs invisibly, usually without the person being aware they are moving between the two systems.

The two-system view also predicts that intuitive concern, as a product of a System 1 process, would be more influential in determining overall concern than considered concern, the product of a System 2 process. As Kahneman put it, though System 2 "believes itself to be where the action is," it is System 1 that is really in charge [18]. This is consistent with the findings of the interviews: it would explain why factors affecting considered concern are most effective when they also address intuitive concern, as was the case with the trustworthiness of MM. Participants who were intuitively concerned about MM's data collection were able to alleviate their intuitive concern through considered concern because once they decided that MM's creators were trustworthy, subsequent intuitive assessments produced lower intuitive concern. The two-system view also explains why factors *unable* to address intuitive concern were likely to lead to residual intuitive concern even if considered concern was low, as was the case with marginal risk.

Further, because the impressions generated by System 1 processes usually cannot be articulated, individuals evaluating considered concern may not understand the influence of intuitive concern. Therefore, if the benefits of disclosure are sufficiently large or they can achieve low considered concern, they may disregard their lingering intuitive concern. However, as a System 2 process, an assessment of low considered concern can override System 1's conclusion of high intuitive concern, but cannot disregard its influence; they therefore remain concerned. This can have long-term consequences on an individual's privacy attitudes and behavior: every participant who discussed uninstalling MM did so because trust in Large U was insufficient to allay the intuitive concern caused by social presence. The complete model is summarized in Figure 4.

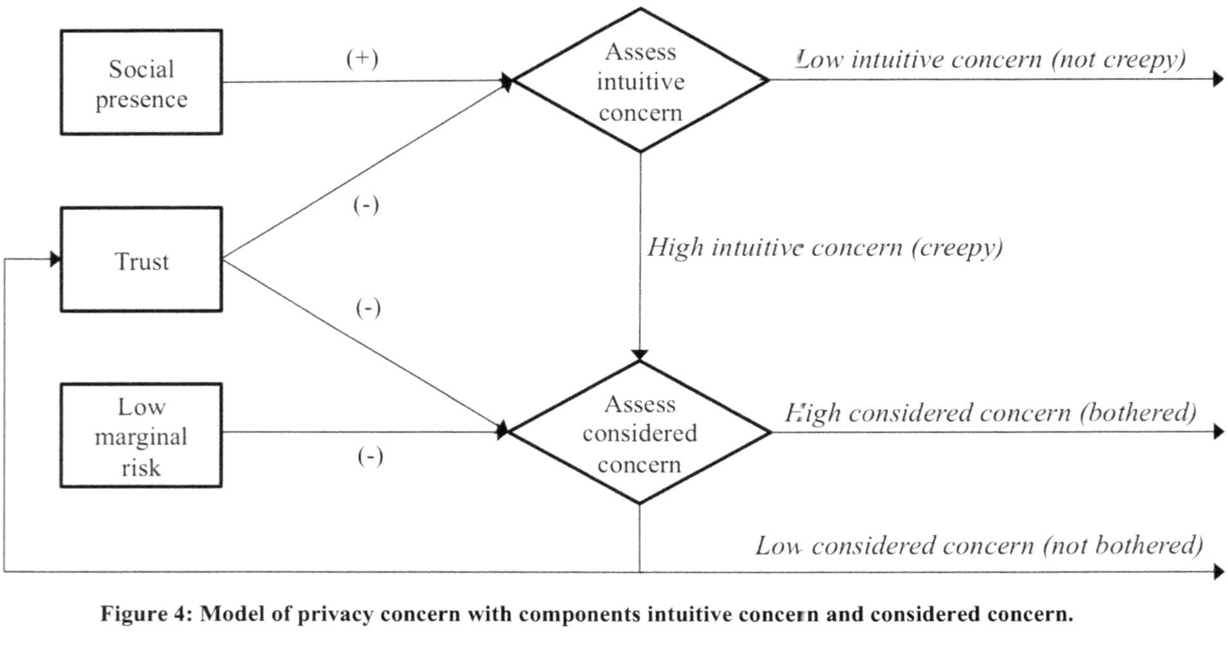

Figure 4: Model of privacy concern with components intuitive concern and considered concern.

The privacy paradox in the dual process model

This dual process model of privacy concern additionally contributes to our understanding of the privacy paradox. The model shows there are two ways in which a mismatch in preferences and behavior can be created:

1) An individual bypasses considered assessment of concern entirely and acts only on System 1's intuitive assessment. The intuitive concern assessment may be at odds with a considered assessment of concern when that is undertaken.
2) An individual accepts an intrusion because of low considered concern, overriding (but not reducing) System 1's assessment of high intuitive concern.

The first type provides insight into privacy paradox findings of existing research. For example, John et al. [16] found that people were more likely to disclose sensitive information when privacy concern was suppressed, even when the website was judged as high in disclosure danger by others. That is, people with low intuitive concern skipped assessing considered concern and were thus susceptible to errors caused by heuristic thinking. The same study also found that people are less vulnerable to the effect of interface design on disclosure if their privacy concern is activated, an indication that considered assessment of concern will override the mistaken impressions of intuitive concern more often under those conditions.

The second source of the paradox described above appears to be a new finding. It is of special interest because the intuitive concern, though overruled, is not erased. It may have lingering effects on behavior and should therefore be a special concern for designers.

Design implications

System designers naturally rely on people to *tell* them what privacy practices users want; as a result, they design for considered concern. The dual process model demonstrates that this is problematic: people may be rationally okay with an intrusion, according to their considered concern, but still be intuitively uncomfortable. Ensuring low marginal risk is one example of a factor that looks like an attractive target to lower privacy concern, since people say it is important. However, it is unable to make people *feel* good about a privacy intrusion, weakening its effect on overall concern.

People are less likely to think of or state their intuitive concerns when asked to think about their concerns. This makes it harder for designers to identify factors that affect assessments of intuitive concern. Nonetheless, it is this type of concern that designers should target to help people make privacy choices they can be happy with when they are no longer rationally considering them. This poses a difficulty, as strategies that target considered concern directly—such as emphasizing confidentiality before a disclosure decision—are often ineffective or even counterproductive in addressing intuitive concern [16]. An alternate approach would be to offset factors that raise intuitive concern with factors that lower it. MM achieved this by offsetting the social presence it caused with high levels of institutional and interpersonal trust, for example; the same effect might be achieved by improving users' mood whenever they are making disclosure decisions [21] or using website design that is perceived as trustworthy [16].

Limitations and future work

This study has several limitations. The participants were drawn from a population that was non-representative even of undergraduate students; it is likely that they were more knowledgeable than average about privacy issues. Further, the only specific, real privacy choice discussed was the MM sign-up decision. It may therefore be the case that participants' reflections on other privacy choices were inaccurate, which would limit the strength and generalizability of our findings. In addition, all participants had installed MM, even though we encouraged participation by students who had not consented to MM. Those students may have had higher privacy concern, been less trusting, or otherwise differed significantly from the students who participated in the interviews. However, qualitative work like this does not claim generalizability as a contribution, and we see the themes uncovered as important.

As our evidence is preliminary, further work is necessary to test the validity of our proposed model. Future research can investigate how well a dual process model of privacy concern predicts the impact of other factors. It would be particularly useful to test if one type of concern is more closely connected to behavior than the other, and if one type of concern is particularly effective in producing preference-consistent behavior.

CONCLUSION

We propose a dual process model of privacy concern, where privacy concern can be decomposed into intuitive concern, one's "gut feeling," and considered concern, a deliberate calculation of risks and benefits. In this model, high intuitive concern can be overruled by low considered concern, but residual concern can remain. Consequently, there are two ways that a privacy paradox can occur: if an individual fails to engage in considered concern, or if an individual engages in considered concern and is unable to adequately address the factors contributing to intuitive concern. The challenge for future designers is to differentiate between the two causes of a privacy paradox in particular situations and respond with appropriate strategies that help people make better privacy choices.

ACKNOWLEDGMENT

We gratefully acknowledge financial support from Google's Social Interactions Focused Program.

REFERENCES

1. Mark S Ackerman, Lorrie Faith Cranor and Joseph Reagle. (1999) Privacy in e-commerce: examining user scenarios and privacy preferences. in *Proceedings of the 1st ACM conference on Electronic commerce*, ACM, 1-8.
2. Alessandro Acquisti. (2004) Privacy in electronic commerce and the economics of immediate gratification. in *Proceedings of the 5th ACM Conference on Electronic Commerce*, ACM, 21-29.
3. Alessandro Acquisti, Laura Brandimarte and George Loewenstein. (2015) Privacy and human behavior in the age of information. *Science*, 347 (6221). 509-514.
4. Alessandro Acquisti and Ralph Gross. (2006) Imagined communities: Awareness, information sharing, and privacy on the Facebook. in *Privacy Enhancing Technologies*, Springer, 36-58.
5. Alessandro Acquisti, Leslie K John and George Loewenstein. (2013) What is privacy worth? *The Journal of Legal Studies*, 42 (2). 249-274.
6. Idris Adjerid, Eyal Peer and Alessandro Acquisti. Beyond the privacy paradox: Objective versus relative risk in privacy decision making. *Available at http://www.krannert.purdue.edu/academics/MIS/workshop/Idris%20Adjerid_RDJournalPaper-Purdue_Final.pdf.*
7. Corey M Angst and Ritu Agarwal. (2009) Adoption of electronic health records in the presence of privacy concerns: the elaboration likelihood model and individual persuasion. *MIS Quarterly*, 33 (2). 339-370.
8. Mark Billinghurst and Hirokazu Kato. (2002) Collaborative augmented reality. *Communications of the ACM*, 45 (7). 64-70.
9. Frank Biocca. (1997) The cyborg's dilemma: progressive embodiment in virtual environments. *Journal of Computer-Mediated Communication*, 3 (2). 0-0.
10. Frank Biocca, Chad Harms and Judee K Burgoon. (2003) Toward a more robust theory and measure of social presence: Review and suggested criteria. *Presence*, 12 (5). 456-480.
11. Alan L Chaikin, Valerian J Derlega and Sarah J Miller. (1976) Effects of room environment on self-disclosure in a counseling analogue. *Journal of Counseling Psychology*, 23 (5). 479-481.
12. Mary J Culnan and Pamela K Armstrong. (1999) Information privacy concerns, procedural fairness, and impersonal trust: An empirical investigation. *Organization science*, 10 (1). 104-115.
13. Tamara Dinev and Paul Hart. (2006) An extended privacy calculus model for e-commerce transactions. *Information Systems Research*, 17 (1). 61-80.
14. Julia B Earp and David Baumer. (2003) Innovative web use to learn about consumer behavior and online privacy. *Communications of the ACM*, 46 (4). 81-83.
15. Ellen Garbarino and Olivia F Lee. (2003) Dynamic pricing in internet retail: effects on consumer trust. *Psychology & Marketing*, 20 (6). 495-513.
16. Leslie K John, Alessandro Acquisti and George Loewenstein. (2011) Strangers on a plane: Context-dependent willingness to divulge sensitive information. *Journal of Consumer Research*, 37 (5). 858-873.
17. Daniel Kahneman. (2003) A perspective on judgment and choice: mapping bounded rationality. *American Psychologist*, 58 (9). 697-720.
18. Daniel Kahneman. (2011) *Thinking, fast and slow*. Macmillan.
19. Daniel Kahneman and Shane Frederick. (2002) Representativeness revisited: Attribute substitution in intuitive judgment. *Heuristics and biases: The psychology of intuitive judgment*, 49-81.
20. Daniel Kahneman and Amos Tversky. (1979) Prospect theory: An analysis of decision under risk. *Econometrica: Journal of the Econometric Society*. 263-291.
21. Flavius Kehr, Tobias Kowatsch, Daniel Wentzel and Elgar Fleisch. (2015) Blissfully ignorant: the effects of general privacy concerns, general institutional trust, and affect in the privacy calculus. *Information Systems Journal*. 25 (6). 607-635.
22. Kwan Min Lee and Clifford Nass. (2003) Designing social presence of social actors in human computer interaction. in *Proceedings of the SIGCHI Conference on Human Factors in Computing Systems*, ACM, 289-296.
23. Paul Benjamin Lowry, Greg Moody, Anthony Vance, Matthew Jensen, Jeff Jenkins and Taylor Wells. (2012) Using an elaboration likelihood approach to better understand the persuasiveness of website privacy assurance cues for online consumers. *Journal of the American Society for Information Science and Technology*, 63 (4). 755-776.
24. David Lyon. (2002) Everyday surveillance: Personal data and social classifications. *Information, Communication & Society*, 5 (2). 242-257.
25. Roger C Mayer, James H Davis and F David Schoorman. (1995) An integrative model of organizational trust. *Academy of Management Review*, 20 (3). 709-734.
26. George R Milne and Maria-Eugenia Boza. (1999) Trust and concern in consumers' perceptions of marketing information management practices. *Journal of Interactive Marketing*, 13 (1). 5-24.
27. Youngme Moon. (2000) Intimate exchanges: Using computers to elicit self-disclosure from consumers. *Journal of Consumer Research*, 26 (4). 323-339.
28. Clifford Nass, Jonathan Steuer and Ellen R Tauber. (1994) Computers are social actors. in *Proceedings of the SIGCHI conference on Human Factors in Computing Systems*, ACM, 72-78.

29. Patricia A Norberg, Daniel R Horne and David A Horne. (2007) The privacy paradox: Personal information disclosure intentions versus behaviors. *Journal of Consumer Affairs*, 41 (1). 100-126.
30. Antti Oulasvirta, Aurora Pihlajamaa, Jukka Perkiö, Debarshi Ray, Taneli Vähäkangas, Tero Hasu, Niklas Vainio and Petri Myllymäki. (2012) Long-term effects of ubiquitous surveillance in the home. in *Proceedings of the 2012 ACM Conference on Ubiquitous Computing*, ACM, 41-50.
31. Paul A Pavlou. (2003) Consumer acceptance of electronic commerce: Integrating trust and risk with the technology acceptance model. *International Journal of Electronic Commerce*, 7 (3). 101-134.
32. Byron Reeves and Clifford Nass. (1996) *The media equation*. Cambridge University Press.
33. Nora J Rifon, Robert LaRose and Sejung Choi. (2005) Your privacy is sealed: Effects of web privacy seals on trust and personal disclosures. *Journal of Consumer Affairs*, 39 (2). 339-362.
34. Paul Schermerhorn, Matthias Scheutz and Charles R Crowell. (2008) Robot social presence and gender: Do females view robots differently than males? in *Proceedings of the 3rd ACM/IEEE International Conference on Human Robot Interaction*, ACM, 263-270.
35. John T Scholz and Mark Lubell. (1998) Trust and taxpaying: Testing the heuristic approach to collective action. *American Journal of Political Science*. 398-417.
36. Irina Shklovski, Scott D Mainwaring, Halla Hrund Skúladóttir and Höskuldur Borgthorsson. (2014) Leakiness and creepiness in app space: Perceptions of privacy and mobile app use. in *Proceedings of the 32nd annual ACM conference on Human factors in computing systems*, ACM, 2347-2356.
37. H Jeff Smith, Tamara Dinev and Heng Xu. (2011) Information privacy research: an interdisciplinary review. *MIS Quarterly*, 35 (4). 989-1016.
38. H Jeff Smith, Sandra J Milberg and Sandra J Burke. (1996) Information privacy: measuring individuals' concerns about organizational practices. *MIS Quarterly*. 20 (2). 167-196.
39. Keith E Stanovich and Richard F West. (2000) Individual differences in reasoning: Implications for the rationality debate. *Behavioral and Brain Sciences*, 23 (5). 645-665.
40. Janice Y Tsai, Patrick Gage Kelley, Lorrie Faith Cranor and Norman Sadeh. (2010) Location-sharing technologies: Privacy risks and controls. *ISJLP*, 6. 119.
41. Chih-Hsiung Tu. (2002) The measurement of social presence in an online learning environment. *International Journal on E-learning*, 1 (2). 34-45.
42. Joseph Turow, Jennifer King, Chris Jay Hoofnagle, Amy Bleakley and Michael Hennessy. (2009) Americans reject tailored advertising and three activities that enable it. *Available at SSRN 1478214*.
43. Amos Tversky and Daniel Kahneman. (1974) Judgment under uncertainty: Heuristics and biases. *Science*, 185 (4157). 1124-1131.
44. Blase Ur, Pedro Giovanni Leon, Lorrie Faith Cranor, Richard Shay and Yang Wang. (2012) Smart, useful, scary, creepy: perceptions of online behavioral advertising. in *Proceedings of the Eighth Symposium on Usable Privacy and Security*, ACM, 4.
45. PC Wason and J St BT Evans. (1975) Dual processes in reasoning? *Cognition*, 3 (2). 141-154.
46. Heng Xu, Hock-Hai Teo, Bernard CY Tan and Ritu Agarwal. (2009) The role of push-pull technology in privacy calculus: the case of location-based services. *Journal of Management Information Systems*, 26 (3). 135-174.
47. Shu-Chen Yang, Wan-Chiao Hung, Kai Sung and Cheng-Kiang Farn. (2006) Investigating initial trust toward e-tailers from the elaboration likelihood model perspective. *Psychology and Marketing*, 23 (5). 429-445.
48. Tao Zhou. (2012) Understanding users' initial trust in mobile banking: An elaboration likelihood perspective. *Computers in Human Behavior*, 28 (4). 1518-1525.

Make it Simple, or Force Users to Read? Paraphrased Design Improves Comprehension of End User License Agreements

T. Franklin Waddell
College of Communications
Penn State University
tfw119@psu.edu

Joshua R. Auriemma
Drama Fever
Philadelphia, PA
allocate@gmail.com

S. Shyam Sundar
College of Communications
Penn State University
sss122psu.edu

ABSTRACT
Users often react negatively towards applications that track their personal information, even though they have consented to such tracking by hitting the "I Agree" button on the application's end user license agreement (EULA). This is because most users do not read the EULA carefully. The language and presentation of EULAs are often dull, dense and inaccessible. Researchers have proposed design options for heightening comprehension of EULA content, but the effectiveness of these suggestions is unclear. To address this gap, we conducted an experiment that examined how users' attitudes towards EULAs are affected by paraphrased and forced EULA formats. Paraphrased EULA presentations increased the time spent on reading the EULA. Moreover, they elicited more positive attitudes toward the EULA, which in turn predicted better comprehension. These findings hold implications for design of EULAs by showing that complex content displayed in simple terms across multiple windows can increase reader comprehension.

Author Keywords
End user license agreement (EULA); interface design

ACM Classification Keywords
H.5; K.5

INTRODUCTION
It is generally assumed that users accept the terms and services of computer and mobile programs without comprehending the actual content of the legal agreement in question [1]. Given that users are increasingly concerned about the terms and services associated with program use, there is a corresponding interest in the ways that EULAs can be made more accessible and user-friendly for the general population. Past work has found that reducing verbosity and replacing legal jargon with simpler words and phrases enhances individuals' understanding of legal contracts [7]. Along similar lines, Nielsen [8] suggests that web-based legal contracts should be parsimonious and distribute information across multiple pages to promote user comprehension. In line with these suggestions, Bernstein [2] designed a EULA prototype that displays EULA content in a paraphrased manner using accessible, jargon-free language across multiple presentation windows. However, while this EULA prototype conforms to the design recommendations advocated in prior research on legal contract comprehensibility [7], there is no direct empirical test of its psychological effects on users.

CHI'16, May 07-12, 2016, San Jose, CA, USA
© 2016 ACM. ISBN 978-1-4503-3362-7/16/05...$15.00
DOI: http://dx.doi.org/10.1145/2858036.2858149

Related research on EULA comprehension has found that variations of EULA presentation type can affect users' subsequent responses to EULA content. For example, Kay and Terry [6] found that licensing agreements that used symbols and vignettes to complement EULA content elicited longer exposure times and higher EULA comprehension than plain-text EULA presentations. Other presentation factors, such as providing a brief summary of EULA content [6] or adjusting the style of EULA request to be polite rather than direct [3], also has been related to less frequent EULA consent. Thus, prior research suggests that EULA presentation factors can affect users' comprehension and attention to EULA content, although little research to date has directly tested the proposed "best practices" for EULA design identified in prior research [2,8]. One possible design strategy is to force users to view the entire EULA by scrolling down the page before they are allowed to consent. Alternatively, other scholars [2,8] have suggested a 'paraphrased" presentation style that displays legal content across multiple windows using simple, non-legal language. To test the relative efficacy of these two solutions, the current study examined the effect of a paraphrased EULA and forced-exposure EULA, as compared with traditional EULA, on users' attitudes, attention, and comprehension.

METHOD

Fifty-two participants were recruited from undergraduate courses in interactive media at a large US university to participate in a three-condition experiment (traditional EULA, paraphrased, forced-exposure), approved by the Institutional Review Board of the University. The average age of participants was 19.37 (SD = 1.34). The sample was primarily male (83%). All participants provided implied consent on an online questionnaire before participating in the study.

Stimuli

Participants were asked to install a program ("Reflexology") on their computer under the cover story that the program would be used to measure their reflexes. Before the program began installation, one of three possible EULAs was presented, asking participants if they agreed to the terms and services of the program.

In the traditional EULA condition, participants viewed the EULA agreement in a single window that displayed the text of the agreement and a set of options at the bottom of the window that allowed the user to either "Accept" or "Decline" the EULA. By comparison, the "paraphrased EULA" condition was designed based on the prototype proposed by Bernstein [5] following the best practices for legal contracts identified in past research [4]. Specifically, the paraphrased EULA condition displayed the terms with bullet-point statements using everyday, non-legal language, while the traditional EULA condition presented the full agreement in paragraph form using legal terminology. The paraphrased EULA condition and traditional EULA conditions also varied according to display style, such that the "paraphrased EULA" condition summarized the EULA's terms of service across four separate windows (participants started on window 1, then navigated to subsequent windows using the "next" button) while the "traditional EULA" condition displayed the legal content via one single page (see Figure 1). This manipulation is distinct from Good et al. [4], who tested the effect of one (rather than multiple) paraphrased windows.

In the "forced exposure" condition, participants were required to view the entire EULA by scrolling down the page before the terms of service could be accepted. If the effect of EULA presentation is simply due to novelty, then we would expected both the paraphrased and forced exposure EULA conditions to elicit higher comprehension levels because they both deviate from the traditional EULA style. However, if adapted layout is key, then we would expect that only the paraphrased EULA will elicit greater levels of comprehension. Thus, comparing the effects of the paraphrased and forced exposure EULAs allows us to determine the specific traits of EULA presentation that may affect EULA attitudes and comprehension.

Figure 1. Traditional vs. Paraphrased EULA

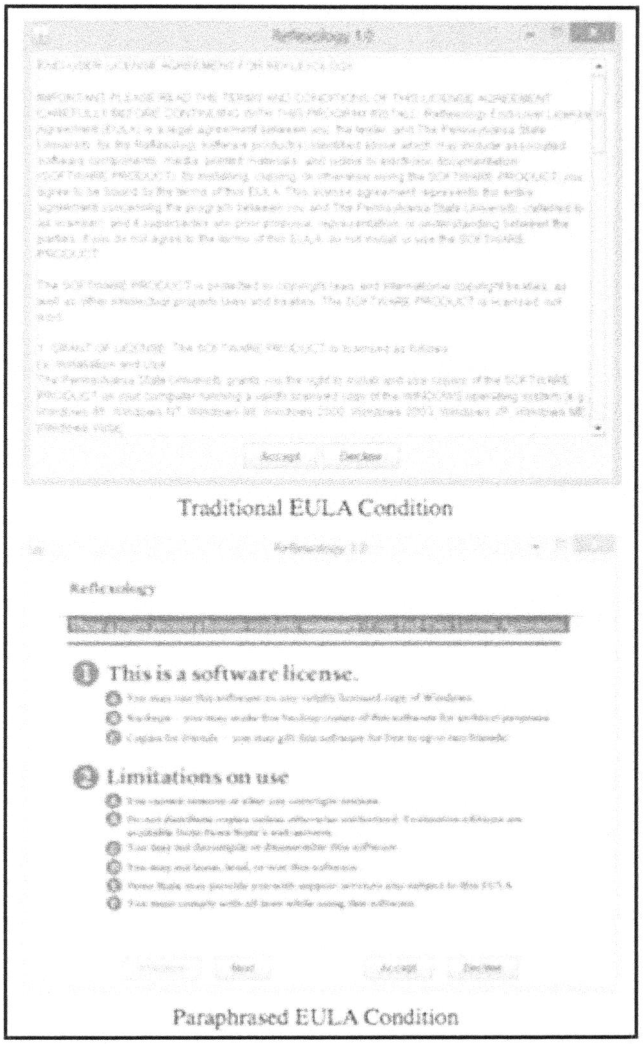

Measures

EULA attitudes. Two Likert-type items examined users' attitudes towards the EULA: "The EULA was visually appealing" and "The EULA was easy to understand." These two measures of EULA attitudes were significantly correlated ($r = .52$, $p < .001$), so an index was formed by combining them ($M = 1.90$, $SD = .84$) rather than considering them as distinct attributes.

EULA Exposure. The total time that participants viewed the EULA agreement was unobtrusively measured by the application while participants viewed the EULA. Specifically, the total number of seconds that expired between the appearance of the EULA and the acceptance of the agreement was recorded by the program ($M = 3.80$, $SD = .39$).

EULA Comprehension. Six closed-ended questions assessed participants' comprehension of EULA content, including "How many copies of the program can you distribute as a gift?" (4.1% of respondents) "What are the terms for the programs' warranty?" (20.4%)"How many backup copies of the program are you allowed to create?" (4.1%) "Who are you entering into an agreement with?" (18.4%) "Who owns the application?" (16.3%) and "What is the scope of the user agreement?" (40.8%). The total number of correct answers out of six was averaged to create a total comprehension score (M = 1.04, SD = 1.24).

Procedure

Participants took part in the study individually in a laboratory. Upon arrival at the lab, participants were greeted and told that they would take part in an experiment that measured their reflexes. After providing informed consent, participants were told that they would be asked to install a program ("Reflexology") from an external hard drive provided by the researcher. In order to increase the perceived importance of the installation activity and improve the ecological validity of the study procedure, participants were asked to install the program on their own personal laptop computer and were also informed that the university was not responsible for any potential harm to their computer that resulted from the installation.

Once the application was installed and opened by the participant, one of three possible EULAs were displayed, as determined by random assignment. Participants were free to navigate the EULA at their own pace without supervision by the researcher. The application unobtrusively began recording the total time that participants viewed the EULA between the time of first exposure and when participants selected either "Accept" or "Decline" (No participants declined the EULA). Following their response to the EULA, participants were advanced to the so-called "Reflexology" program that required participants to track a red dot using their mouse for several minutes. After participants completed the "reflex" activity, they were directed to a post-exposure questionnaire that measured their attitudes towards the EULA, comprehension of the EULA, and basic demographic information. Participants were escorted to a different room, debriefed about the purpose of the study and thanked for their participation, following the completion of the post-exposure questionnaire.

RESULTS

EULA Attitudes

A one-way ANOVA with EULA presentation style as the independent variable and EULA attitudes as the dependent variable was significant, F (2, 46) = 5.63, p = .006, η_p^2 = .20. Participants in the paraphrased EULA condition (M = 2.44) evaluated the EULA more positively than participants in the traditional EULA condition (M = 1.66) or the forced exposure EULA condition (M = 1.65).

EULA Exposure

A one-way ANOVA with EULA presentation as the independent variable and EULA exposure as the dependent variable was significant, F (2, 46) = 3.17, p = .05, η_p^2 = .12. Participants in the paraphrased EULA condition (M = 3.92) spent more time viewing the EULA than participants in the standard EULA condition (M = 3.60). Along similar lines, participants in the forced exposure EULA condition (M = 3.82) spent more time viewing the EULA than participants in the traditional EULA condition.

EULA Comprehension

In order to examine the effect of EULA presentation on EULA comprehension via EULA attitudes and time of EULA exposure, two parallel mediation models were estimated using ordinary least squares path analysis with 5,000 bootstrapped samples and 95% bias adjusted confidence intervals [5].

The first model examined the effect of the paraphrased EULA presentation (0 = traditional EULA, 1 = paraphrased EULA) on EULA comprehension, while controlling for participants in the forced exposure EULA condition. As shown in Figure 2, participants in the paraphrased EULA condition reported more positive EULA attitudes (a_1 = .39) than participants in the traditional group, and more positive EULA attitudes were correlated with a higher level of reading comprehension (b_1 = .53). The indirect effect of the paraphrased EULA presentation on reading comprehension (a_1b_1 = .21) was significant because the bootstrap confidence interval for the indirect effect did not include zero (.02, .53). There was no evidence that the paraphrased EULA presentation had an effect on reading comprehension indirectly via time of EULA exposure (a_2b_2 = .10; CI: -.03, .39) or independent of the effect through EULA attitudes (c' = -.37 p = .11)

Figure 2. Indirect Effect of Paraphrased EULA on Comprehension

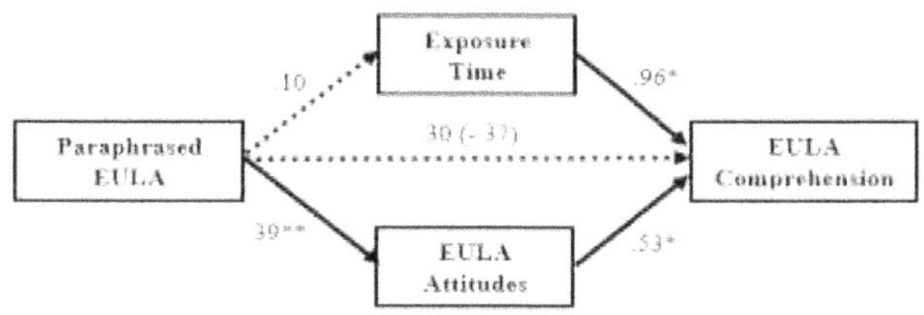

* p < .05 ** p < .01 *** p < .0001

Note: .30 is total effect of all paths. -.37 is remaining effect controlling for exposure time and EULA attitudes. 0 = Standard EULA, 1 = Paraphrased EULA condition

The second model examined the effect of the forced exposure EULA presentation on EULA comprehension (0 = standard EULA, 1 = paraphrased EULA) while controlling for participants in the paraphrased EULA condition. The indirect effect of the forced exposure EULA presentation on EULA comprehension via EULA attitudes (a_1b_1 = -.00; -.018, .13) or time of EULA exposure (a_2b_2 = .08; -.05, .36) was not significant. In addition, there was no evidence of an indirect effect of the forced exposure EULA on EULA comprehension while controlling for EULA attitudes and time of EULA exposure (c' = -.35, p = .14). In other words, there was no evidence that the forced exposure EULA presentation had a significant direct or indirect effect on EULA comprehension compared to the standard EULA presentation.

Summary

In sum, the paraphrased EULA elicited more positive attitudes and longer exposure times than the traditional EULA. Furthermore, our results show that attitudes and EULA comprehension were positively related. By comparison, the forced exposure condition did not affect EULA attitudes or comprehension relative to control.

DISCUSSION

There is a growing interest in improving users' attention and comprehension of end user license agreements (EULAs). Following the design recommendations identified in prior research, the current study examined the effect of EULA presentation type on users' EULA attitudes, time of EULA exposure, and EULA comprehension. Our results suggest that EULA presentation style can affect a range of users' attitudinal and behavioral responses to EULAs, as summarized below:

- The paraphrased EULA, which displayed legal information in an abbreviated manner across multiple windows, elicited more positive EULA attitudes and a longer time of exposure than the traditional EULA presentation.
- A series of parallel mediation models found that the paraphrased EULA presentation affected EULA comprehension indirectly by promoting more positive EULA attitudes. By comparison, there was no evidence of an indirect effect of the paraphrased EULA through total exposure. In other words, it appears that eliciting positive attitudes through EULA presentation is more likely to increase EULA comprehension than increased time of EULA exposure.

These findings hold several implications for effective design of EULA presentations. First, it appears that summarizing EULA content across multiple windows elicits more favorable EULA attitudes and longer EULA exposure than EULA presentations that require forced exposure. It should be noted that this effect does not appear to be explained by novelty of the paraphrased EULA, as the forced exposure EULA condition did not elicit more favorable user responses than the traditional EULA condition despite its novelty. Instead, it appears that other differences between the two EULA conditions, such as the presentation format of the EULA content, elicited more positive EULA attitudes and longer times of EULA exposure. Therefore, rather than implementing options that require users to scroll through all presented EULA content (as tested in the forced exposure EULA condition), our findings suggest that paraphrased EULAs which display content using simple terms across multiple windows are more likely to elicit positive EULA attitudes and behaviors among prospective users.

Second, the current study also examined the relative impact of 1) EULA attitudes and 2) time of exposure on users' comprehension of EULA content. Based on our findings, it appears that eliciting favorable attitudes towards EULAs is more likely to be positively related with increased EULA comprehension than simple time of exposure. Thus, designers should be aware that EULA features that affect users' attitudes (e.g., visually pleasing layout, paraphrased content that is easy to understand) are more likely to increase EULA comprehension than design features aimed at increasing total time of EULA exposure (e.g., forced exposure, timed agreements). Given that participants generally spent no more than eight seconds viewing EULA content, designers should consider adopting EULA design styles similar to the paraphrased EULA condition that summarize legal terms in such a way that comprehension is possible even when EULA exposure is brief.

Our findings should be contextualized according to several limitations. First, it is possible that the threat of information leakage or hardware malfunction associated with program installation may have been relatively low because participants assumed their information and hardware were secure, given the artificial nature of the experimental setting. Although our study attempted to maintain a high level of ecological validity (e.g., participants installed the program on their own computer; the researcher waived responsibility for potential hardware damage), future research should attempt to replicate our results using a setting with a higher perceived threat for information leakage or hardware failure. Another limitation is that our study was conducted with young adults who are generally more technologically savvy than the general population. Therefore, our results should be replicated with other user populations that may have higher levels of security vulnerability, such as youth or older adults. Finally, while we attempted to control for novelty by including the forced exposure condition, future research should directly measure perceptions of novelty as a statistical control, given that forced-exposure EULAs are more widely used (and thus less novel) than before. These avenues for future research will complement our results, which suggest that subtle manipulations of EULA presentation can have a significant effect on users' subsequent EULA attitudes and comprehension.

REFERENCES

1. Ben-Shahar, O. The myth of the "opportunity to read" in contract law. *European Review of Contract Law, 5*, 1(2009), 1-28.
2. Bernstein, G. R. The fine print: Redesigning legal contracts for the digital environment. Retrieved from http://typographichub.org/images/uploads/downloads/the_fine_print.pdf

3. Böhme, & Köspell, S. Trained to accept? A field experiment on consent dialogues. *Proceedings of the SIGCHI Conference on Human Factors in Computing Systems,* 2010, 2403-2406.
4. Good, N. S., Grossklags, J., Mulligan, D. K., & Konstan, J. A. Noticing notice: A large-scale experiment on the timing of software licensing agreements. *Proceedings of the SIGCHI Conference on Human Factors in Computing Systems*, 2007, 607-616.
5. Hayes, A., & Preacher. Statistical mediation analysis with a multicategorical independent variable. *British Journal of Mathematical and Statistical Psychology*, in press.
6. Kay, M., & Terry, M. Textured agreements: Re-envisioning electronic consent. *Proceedings of the Sixth Symposium on Usable Privacy and Security, 2010.*
7. Masson, M E. J., & Waldron, M. A. Comprehension of legal contracts by non-experts. *Applied Cognitive Psychology, 8*, 1(1994), 67-85.
8. Nielsen, J. *Designing Web Usability*. Berkeley: New Riders 2000.

Behavior Ever Follows Intention?

A Validation of the Security Behavior Intentions Scale (SeBIS)

Serge Egelman[1], Marian Harbach[1], Eyal Peer[2]
[1]International Computer Science Institute, Berkeley, CA
[2]Bar-Ilan University, Ramat Gan, Israel
{egelman,mharbach}@icsi.berkeley.edu, eyal.peer@biu.ac.il

ABSTRACT
The Security Behavior Intentions Scale (SeBIS) measures the computer security attitudes of end-users. Because intentions are a prerequisite for planned behavior, the scale could therefore be useful for predicting users' computer security behaviors. We performed three experiments to identify correlations between each of SeBIS's four sub-scales and relevant computer security behaviors. We found that testing high on the *awareness* sub-scale correlated with correctly identifying a phishing website; testing high on the *passwords* sub-scale correlated with creating passwords that could not be quickly cracked; testing high on the *updating* sub-scale correlated with applying software updates; and testing high on the *securement* sub-scale correlated with smartphone lock screen usage (e.g., PINs). Our results indicate that SeBIS predicts certain computer security behaviors and that it is a reliable and valid tool that should be used in future research.

Author Keywords
Security behavior; measurement; user studies

ACM Classification Keywords
J.4. Social and Behavioral Sciences: Psychology; K.6.5. Management of Computing and Information Systems: Security and Protection

INTRODUCTION AND RELATED WORK
Understanding users' computer security attitudes is important for researchers because it helps to contextualize users' observed behaviors, as well as to potentially predict their future behaviors. For example, an understanding of a given user's attitudes may shed light on the likelihood that she will comply with a given security mitigation; a user with poor security attitudes is unlikely to take steps to comply. Similarly, if a user has strongly stated security intentions, yet exhibits poor security behaviors, this may indicate usability problems (i.e., Norman's "Gulf of Execution" [9]). Thus, when studying users' computer security behaviors, it is incumbent on researchers to evaluate the gap between attitudes and behaviors.

CHI'16, May 07 - 12, 2016, San Jose, CA, USA

ACM 978-1-4503-3362-7/16/05...$15.00
DOI: http://dx.doi.org/10.1145/2858036.2858265

Within the privacy literature, researchers have long studied users' privacy attitudes: various privacy concerns scales have been developed to measure users' privacy preferences (e.g., [11, 6, 3, 7]). Measuring users' attitudes has allowed for the study of the "privacy paradox," which is the gap between self-reported attitudes and observed privacy-preserving behaviors [1]. For instance, Egelman *et al.* showed that more usable user interfaces can help close this gap [5].

One challenge to applying these methods to computer security behaviors is that up until very recently, there has not existed a reliable metric to gauge users' computer security attitudes. This changed in 2015, when Egelman and Peer introduced the Security Behavior Intentions Scale (SeBIS) [4], which is a 16-item instrument scored on a 5-point Likert scale that measures a computer user's self-reported intent to comply with "good" security practices spanning four dimensions:

- **Awareness**: Do users pay attention to contextual cues, such as the web browser URL bar or various security iconography?
- **Passwords**: Do users create unique passwords that exceed minimum requirements and are therefore difficult to crack?
- **Updating**: Do users apply software security updates in a timely manner?
- **Securement**: Do users secure their devices with secret codes, such as using smartphone secure lock screens (i.e., requiring a PIN) or password-protected screen savers on desktops and laptops?

Understanding computer security intentions is important, because intentions are a prerequisite of planned behavior [2]. In their original paper, Egelman and Peer showed how computer security intentions—as measured by SeBIS—are correlated with various well-studied psychological constructs, and that SeBIS exhibits high internal reliability [4]. However, one shortcoming of their work was that they did not demonstrate criterion validity; that is, does SeBIS actually predict computer security behavior? And if so, to what extent?

We are unaware of any prior published research that has attempted to correlate the four SeBIS sub-scales (or any other measure of computer security intentions) with observed computer security behaviors. Thus, we contribute the following:

- We show that testing high on the *awareness* sub-scale is significantly correlated with the ability to correctly identify a phishing website.

- We show that testing high on the *passwords* sub-scale is significantly correlated with the ability to create passwords that cannot be cracked in a reasonable amount of time.
- We show that testing high on the *updating* sub-scale is significantly correlated with applying important software updates in a timely manner.
- We show that testing high on the *securement* sub-scale is significantly correlated with the use of smartphone locking mechanisms (e.g., PINs or drawing a pattern).

In performing this study, we conducted three experiments. Our first experiment used a single cohort of online participants and was designed to examine the *awareness* and *passwords* sub-scales. Our second experiment used a new cohort of online participants to examine the *updating* sub-scale, and our third experiment was a field study of smartphone users in order to examine the *securement* sub-scale. Examining each of SeBIS's sub-scales involved measuring very different types of behaviors, and therefore one single experiment is unlikely to examine all four dimensions with any sort of ecological validity. As a result, the remainder of this paper is divided into three sections based on these experiments, concluding with discussion.

AWARENESS AND PASSWORDS

Our first experiment was performed entirely online using Amazon's Mechanical Turk and was designed to examine the *awareness* and *passwords* SeBIS sub-scales.

The SeBIS *awareness* dimension is designed to measure the extent to which users claim to be aware of various contextual cues. This includes indicators such as a web browser's URL bar, which may yield information about the website being visited, such as whether it uses encryption or whether the domain name matches the user's expectations. The latter can be used to detect phishing websites. As such, we designed an experiment to test the following hypothesis:

> $H_{awareness}$: *Users who correctly use the URL bar to identify a phishing website will test significantly higher on the awareness sub-scale than users who do not correctly identify a phishing website.*

The SeBIS *passwords* dimension is designed to measure the extent to which users claim to create strong and unique passwords. We examined the following hypothesis:

> $H_{passwords}$: *Users who create passwords that cannot easily be cracked will test significantly higher on the passwords scale than users whose passwords can be cracked.*

Methodology

We recruited participants from Amazon's Mechanical Turk to complete an online task in two parts, with a two-week gap in between. In this section, we describe how we used this experiment to examine behaviors that we hypothesized would correlate with the SeBIS's *awareness* and *passwords* sub-scales. We also describe the followup task, which included administering SeBIS and collecting demographics.

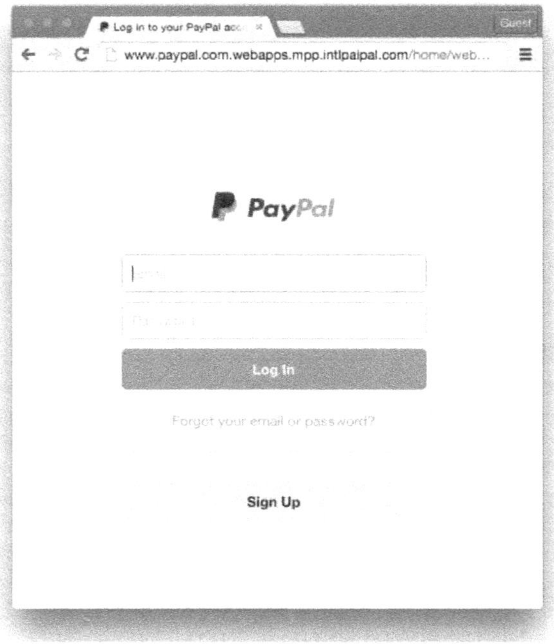

Figure 1. We showed participants a screenshot of this website and asked them to describe it in an open-ended response. Those who used the included URL bar to realize that it was a phishing website scored significantly higher on the SeBIS *awareness* sub-scale.

Awareness

As part of a different study, participants completed a series of psychometric scales in exchange for $1.00. To prevent fatigue and detect attempts at cheating, between each scale, we displayed a screenshot of a website and asked them to describe the website pictured using the text box provided. They performed this task three times; the first two screenshots were of the legitimate Amazon and Twitter websites, whereas the third screenshot was of a phishing website spoofing PayPal (Figure 1). The only way of identifying the phishing website was by examining the URL bar in the screenshot.

Passwords

At the end of this set of tasks, we asked each participant to create a password, which we told them they would need to enter when returning two weeks later to complete the second half of the study. Because we wanted to examine the extent to which participants' passwords would go beyond any minimum requirements, we set the requirements to be relatively weak: 6 characters with at least 1 digit or symbol. (We also wanted to see whether participants would reuse existing passwords, and therefore chose minimum requirements that were likely to be weaker than those found on other websites.)

The reason for the two-week gap was that we were concerned that if we immediately presented participants with SeBIS right after the website identification and password creation tasks, the scale might be biased by participants' recollections of their behaviors. Similarly, we were also concerned that participants may discuss the security nature of the study in various online forums, thereby tainting future participants.

As a result, two weeks after participants had completed the initial task, we used Amazon's internal messaging system to invite them to complete SeBIS for a $2.00 bonus payment.

To analyze the passwords participants created in the first part, we uploaded them to CMU's Password Guessability Service (PGS)[1] [12], which hashed the passwords and then attempted to crack them using four different approaches. We used the minimum number of guesses it took to crack each password across all four approaches as our strength metric. Ur *et al.* used this approach and concluded that it represents "a conservative estimate for the performance of an experienced professional attacker who uses all techniques, wordlists, tools, and dynamic updates at his/her disposal" [12]. Additionally, in our exit survey (administered at the same time as SeBIS), we asked participants whether they had used this password on other websites.

Exit Survey and Demographics

Two weeks after completing the first part of the study, 718 participants returned (we discarded the data of 260 participants who did not attempt to return). We gave them three attempts to enter their passwords, after which the survey simply let them in. We decided on this policy so that we could balance the conflicting requirements of testing password memorability with minimizing attrition from the study as a whole due to forgotten passwords. That is, 206 participants (28.7% of 718) could not remember their passwords two weeks later within three attempts, and therefore we removed their data from the *password* sub-scale evaluation—but still used it as part of the *awareness* evaluation—because we could not know the reasons for their authentication failures (e.g., they may not have created passwords that they intended to remember, and therefore these passwords would not be representative of passwords used in real life), whereas failure to remember the password was unlikely to impact their non-password behaviors. Thus, our password analysis included 512 subjects who successfully recalled their passwords.

We first examined the internal validity of participants' SeBIS responses and found that they were consistent with the original paper [4]: Cronbach's $\alpha_{total} = 0.81$, $\alpha_{securement} = 0.77$, $\alpha_{passwords} = 0.74$, $\alpha_{awareness} = 0.65$, $\alpha_{updating} = 0.70$. Regarding demographics, our 718 participants were split roughly evenly between 370 males (51.5%) and 348 females (48.5%), with a mean age of 35 (range of 19-69). All participants were from the U.S. and had completed at least 500 previous tasks on Mechanical Turk with an approval rating of 95% or higher [10]. The demographics of our subset of 512 participants who successfully remembered their passwords did not significantly differ from the superset.

Results

Awareness

To examine *awareness* behaviors, two independent coders examined the open-ended responses to the phishing website description question for correctness (Cohen's $\kappa = .83$) and identified 22 participants (3.1% of 718) who correctly identified the phishing website. While this number was small, these 22 participants had mean *awareness* sub-scale scores that were larger than those who were unable to identify the phishing website: 4.31 vs. 3.68. A t-test (data was normally distributed) indicated that this difference was statistically significant ($t = 5.22$, $p < 0.0005$) with a large effect size (Cohen's $d = 0.92$). Upon correcting for multiple testing, none of the other sub-scales yielded statistically significant differences. Thus, $H_{awareness}$ is supported.

Passwords

Of the 512 passwords that we uploaded to PGS for cracking, 75 could not be cracked (14.7%). Participants whose passwords could be cracked had average *passwords* sub-scale scores of 3.21, whereas participants whose passwords could not be cracked had average sub-scale scores of 3.56. This difference was statistically significant ($t = 3.47$, $p < 0.001$) with a medium effect size (Cohen's $d = 0.41$). This effect was not present with any of the other SeBIS sub-scales.

In the exit survey, 196 participants (38.3% of 512) reported that they reused an existing password that they use on other websites. Not surprisingly, these participants scored significantly lower on the *passwords* sub-scale than participants who claimed to have created a new password: 2.94 vs. 3.46 ($t = 6.94$, $p < 0.0005$), respectively. This effect was relatively large (Cohen's $d = 0.63$). However, we were surprised to find that participants who claimed to create new passwords scored significantly higher on each of the three other sub-scales, with medium effect sizes, even after correcting for multiple testing:

- Securement: $t = 3.66$, $p < 0.0005$, $d = 0.32$
- Awareness: $t = 4.79$, $p < 0.0005$, $d = 0.43$
- Updating: $t = 3.87$, $p < 0.0005$, $d = 0.35$

These results suggest that not only is $H_{passwords}$ supported, but that users who claim to create unique passwords intend to engage in better security practices across the other areas measured by SeBIS.

UPDATING

The SeBIS *updating* dimension is designed to measure the extent to which users claim to apply security updates in a timely manner. We examined the following hypothesis:

> $H_{updating}$: *Users who promptly apply software updates will test significantly higher on the updating scale than users who delay applying software updates.*

During our previous experiment, we wanted to examine the *updating* sub-scale after we serendipitously discovered that critical operating system updates—those requiring a reboot—were released between the first and second parts of our experiment. However, only 50 subjects were eligible for these updates, which did not yield enough statistical power. As a result, we decided to perform an additional experiment to specifically examine updating behaviors.

Methodology

On October 20, 2015, three weeks after Mac OS X 10.11 came out (requiring manual installation), we deployed a new survey on Mechanical Turk, which was only available to Mac

[1]https://pgs.ece.cmu.edu/

users who had previously not completed SeBIS. We asked participants to complete SeBIS as well as to provide demographics and the model and owner of the Mac they were using. We screened for Mac OS based on the `user-agent` string. We paid participants $0.50, and they took about 3 minutes on average. We excluded participants who were not completing the survey on their own Mac (self-report) and who were ineligible for the update, based on the model information (as copied from the "About This Mac" dialogue). Finally, we determined whether or not the update was installed based on the version of Mac OS X reported by their web browser's `user-agent` string.

Result

Of the 359 participants who successfully completed our survey, 281 (56.2% female, median age = 28) were eligible for the update. We found a statistically significant difference between participants who had installed the update within three weeks (24.2% of 281) vs. those who had not ($M = 3.52$ vs. 3.02, $t = 4.11$, $p < 0.0001$), with a medium effect size (Cohen's $d = 0.59$). Thus, $H_{updating}$ is supported.

SECUREMENT

The SeBIS *securement* dimension measures the extent to which users claim to secure their electronic devices when not in use. This amounts to enabling password-protected screensavers on desktops and laptops, manually locking screens when stepping away, enabling secure lock screens on mobile devices (e.g., requiring a PIN, pattern, or biometric), and so forth. We examined the following hypothesis:

> $H_{securement}$: *Users who employ secure lock screens on smartphones will test significantly higher on the securement scale than users not employing secure lock screens.*

Methodology

We performed a third experiment using an entirely different sample recruited from PhoneLab [8].[2] PhoneLab is an experimental platform maintained by researchers at the University of Buffalo, consisting of a panel of about 200 Android smartphone users who have agreed to have their smartphones instrumented for research purposes. We deployed instrumentation to the PhoneLab panelists that collected data about whether or not they employed a secure lock screen on their Android device. We recorded whether each participant unlocked his or her phone via either entering a PIN or drawing a pattern, or using the insecure "slide-to-unlock" method, which does not require entering a secret (i.e., typing a PIN or drawing a pattern). This instrumentation occurred transparently to participants and therefore was unlikely to prime them to think about security.

After collecting our data on participants' unlock methods, we emailed them a link to an online exit survey. The exit survey consisted of SeBIS and various demographic questions. As an incentive to complete the survey, we created a drawing for a $100 Amazon gift card. Of the 71 participants who completed the exit survey, 50.1% were female and the median age was 35, with a range of 19-70 years.

[2]https://www.phone-lab.org/

Result

Our 71 participants were split between PIN users (25.4% of 71), pattern users (25.4% of 71), and those using the insecure slide-to-unlock method (49.3% of 71). While we observed no difference in SeBIS *securement* scores between those using either PINs or patterns, we did observe that the mean SeBIS scores of slide-to-unlock users was a full point below users of either of the two secure unlock methods: 2.75 vs. 4.25. A Wilcoxon rank sum test (SeBIS scores were not normally distributed, which we attribute to the relatively small sample size) indicated that this difference was statistically significant ($W = 169$, $p < 0.0005$) with a large effect size ($r = 0.63$). Thus, $H_{securement}$ is supported.

DISCUSSION

In this study, we examined the criterion validity of the Security Behavior Intentions Scale (SeBIS) to see whether participants' self-reported security intentions, as measured by the scale, predicted their security behaviors. We observed that participants' SeBIS sub-scale scores for all four sub-scales were predictive of very specific security behaviors.

Our results show that SeBIS does in fact predict particular security behaviors, and in many cases, the effect sizes were large. At the same time, our study had several limitations. The behaviors that we examined were relatively narrow in scope and were also chosen to align with concepts specifically mentioned in SeBIS (e.g., SeBIS directly asks about the locking behavior that we observed). Further research is therefore needed to examine a wider spectrum of security-related behaviors. For instance, are individuals who test high on *securement* more likely to log out of websites? Do scores on the *passwords* scale predict usage of password managers? Are individuals testing low on *awareness* more likely to delegate computer maintenance to others? Are individuals testing high on *updating* more discriminating with regard to provenance when choosing software to install?

Furthermore, we only examined password creation behaviors for relatively low-risk accounts; it is therefore not clear how these behaviors might generalize to high-risk accounts. Participants' password reuse was also self-reported; future studies may be needed to further examine these behaviors.

Despite the shortcomings outlined above, we contribute to the literature by demonstrating that SeBIS is predictive of certain computer security behaviors. While further studies are needed, we conclude that SeBIS is a useful tool for researchers who need to assess users' computer security attitudes and related behaviors.

ACKNOWLEDGEMENTS

We would like to thank the PhoneLab team at the University of Buffalo and the Password Guessability Service at Carnegie Mellon University for their support in gathering the data. This work was supported by the FITweltweit program of the German Academic Exchange Service (DAAD); U.S. National Science Foundation awards CNS-1343433, CNS-1343451, and CNS-1528070; U.S. National Security Agency Lablet contract H98230-14-C-0140; and U.S.-Israel Binational Science Foundation award 2014626.

REFERENCES

1. A. Acquisti and R. Gross. 2006. Imagined Communities: Awareness, Information Sharing, and Privacy on the Facebook. In *Privacy Enhancing Technologies Workshop (PET '06) (Lecture Notes in Computer Science)*, Vol. 4258. Springer-Verlag, Berlin / Heidelberg, Germany, 36–58.

2. Icek Ajzen. 1991. The theory of planned behavior. *Organizational behavior and human decision processes* 50, 2 (1991), 179–211.

3. Tom Buchanan, Carina Paine, Adam N Joinson, and Ulf-Dietrich Reips. 2007. Development of measures of online privacy concern and protection for use on the Internet. *Journal of the American Society for Information Science and Technology* 58, 2 (2007), 157–165.

4. Serge Egelman and Eyal Peer. 2015. Scaling the Security Wall: Developing a Security Behavior Intentions Scale (SeBIS). In *Proceedings of the 33rd Annual ACM Conference on Human Factors in Computing Systems (CHI '15)*. ACM, New York, NY, USA, 2873–2882. DOI: http://dx.doi.org/10.1145/2702123.2702249

5. Serge Egelman, Janice Tsai, Lorrie Faith Cranor, and Alessandro Acquisti. 2009. Timing is Everything?: The Effects of Timing and Placement of Online Privacy Indicators. In *Proceedings of the SIGCHI Conference on Human Factors in Computing Systems (CHI '09)*. ACM, New York, NY, USA, 319–328. DOI: http://dx.doi.org/10.1145/1518701.1518752

6. Ponnurangam Kumaraguru and Lorrie Faith Cranor. December, 2005. *Privacy Indexes: A Survey of Westin's Studies*. Technical Report CMU-ISRI-5-138. Carnegie Mellon University. http://reports-archive.adm.cs.cmu.edu/anon/isri2005/abstracts/05-138.html.

7. Naresh K. Malhotra, Sung S. Kim, and James Agarwal. 2004. Internet Users' Information Privacy Concerns (IUIPC): The Construct, The Scale, and A Causal Model. *Information Systems Research* 15, 4 (December 2004), 336–355.

8. Anandatirtha Nandugudi, Anudipa Maiti, Taeyeon Ki, Fatih Bulut, Murat Demirbas, Tevfik Kosar, Chunming Qiao, Steven Y. Ko, and Geoffrey Challen. 2013. PhoneLab: A Large Programmable Smartphone Testbed. In *Proceedings of First International Workshop on Sensing and Big Data Mining (SENSEMINE'13)*. ACM, New York, NY, USA, Article 4, 6 pages. DOI: http://dx.doi.org/10.1145/2536714.2536718

9. Donald A. Norman. 1986. Cognitive Engineering. In *User Centered System Design: New Perspectives on Human-Computer Interaction*, Donald A. Norman and Stephen W. Draper (Eds.). Lawrence Erlbaum Associates, London, Chapter 3, 31–62.

10. Eyal Peer, Joachim Vosgerau, and Alessandro Acquisti. 2014. Reputation as a sufficient condition for data quality on Amazon Mechanical Turk. *Behavior Research Methods* 46, 4 (December 2014), 1023–1031.

11. Sören Preibusch. 2013. Guide to Measuring Privacy Concern: Review of Survey and Observational Instruments. *International Journal of Human-Computer Studies* 71, 12 (Dec. 2013), 1133–1143. DOI: http://dx.doi.org/10.1016/j.ijhcs.2013.09.002

12. Blase Ur, Sean M. Segreti, Lujo Bauer, Nicolas Christin, Lorrie Faith Cranor, Saranga Komanduri, Darya Kurilova, Michelle L. Mazurek, William Melicher, and Richard Shay. 2015. Measuring Real-World Accuracies and Biases in Modeling Password Guessability. In *24th USENIX Security Symposium (USENIX Security 15)*. USENIX Association, Washington, D.C., 463–481. https://www.usenix.org/conference/usenixsecurity15/technical-sessions/presentation/ur

It is too Hot: An In-Situ Study of Three Designs for Heating

Alper T. Alan[1], Mike Shann[2], Enrico Costanza[1], Sarvapali D. Ramchurn[1], Sven Seuken[2]
[1]University of Southampton
Southampton, United Kingdom
{ata1g11, ec, sdr1}@ecs.soton.ac.uk
[2]University of Zurich
Zurich, Switzerland
{shannm, seuken}@ifi.uzh.ch

ABSTRACT
Smart energy systems that leverage machine learning techniques are increasingly integrated in all aspects of our lives. To better understand how to design user interaction with such systems, we implemented three different smart thermostats that automate heating based on users' heating preferences and real-time price variations. We evaluated our designs through a field study, where 30 UK households used our thermostats to heat their homes over a month. Our findings through thematic analysis show that the participants formed different understandings and expectations of our smart thermostat, and used it in various ways to effectively respond to real-time prices while maintaining their thermal comfort. Based on the findings, we present a number of design and research implications, specifically for designing future smart thermostats that will assist us in controlling home heating with real-time pricing, and for future intelligent autonomous systems.

Author Keywords
Heating; field study; design; smart grid; real-time pricing; autonomous systems; internet of things.

ACM Classification Keywords
H.5.m. Information Interfaces and Presentation (e.g. HCI): Miscellaneous

INTRODUCTION
We live in a world where smart energy systems form an important part of our lives, not only within workplaces, but also at home [9]. These systems sense information about their users, learn from this information, and exploit what they have learned to make decisions on their users' behalf. Examples include smart thermostats that learn households' occupancy behaviour for automating heating of their house (e.g., Nest). Consistent with the improvements in these technologies, our ways of consuming energy change day by day.

Meanwhile, the energy market is undergoing significant changes with penetration of renewables, including wind turbines and solar farms [23]. Energy production from these renewables fluctuates depending on the weather. Such variable energy generation puts more strain on the energy market to

CHI'16, May 07-12, 2016, San Jose, CA, USA.
© 2016 ACM ISBN 978-1-4503-3362-7/16/05...$15.00.
http://dx.doi.org/10.1145/2858036.2858222

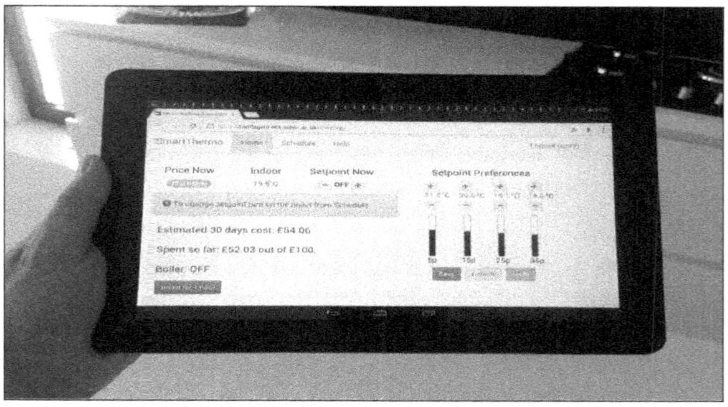

Figure 1. One of our smart thermostat designs running on a tablet.

balance supply with demand. One way to overcome this issue is to use real-time pricing schemes, where energy prices vary over short time intervals, typically hourly [3]. These real-time prices significantly change the role of consumers and offer lower energy bills. However, consumers are required to continuously monitor the changing prices to take the advantage of them. While this task might be daunting for people, it is well-suited for a smart system that can learn user preferences, monitor the prices, and respond to them autonomously. Prior HCI studies about renewable resources [4] and real-time pricing [8] have shown that autonomous computing systems can help people shift their loads by providing them with recommendations. However, in these studies the tasks were not fully automated by the systems, therefore user reactions towards agency was limited to the only suggestions received.

Against this background, in this study we aim to explore how households adopt to and interact with a home smart thermostat designed to help them manage heating given real-time energy prices. To do so we developed and deployed three different smart thermostats: a *manual* one through which participants explicitly specify how the heating should respond to price changes, and two *learning-based* ones that employ an artificial intelligence (AI) algorithm to automate the temperature settings based on learned households' preferences. We conducted a field study with 30 UK households over a month. As the smart thermostat responded to the varying prices on the households' behalf, it caused a real impact on the comfort of its users. More specifically, in this study, we aim to observe people's feelings and expectations towards a smart thermostat that controls their home heating given real-time prices, and how they interact with such a thermostat in their everyday lives.

BACKGROUND

Interdisciplinary knowledge and research is vital to facilitate a better understanding of how user interactions can be designed for smart energy systems. The work we present in this paper lies at the boundary of AI and HCI. Hence, in this section, we briefly review prior literature on models and algorithms for smart heating, field studies of autonomous systems, and interaction with machine learning.

Models and Algorithms for Smart Heating

The combination of mathematical models and computer algorithms form the backbone of making systems smart. The literature includes numerous models and algorithms developed with different approaches for energy efficient heating. Some approaches focused on the models of the environment (e.g., the weather) to create an efficient heating schedule [30, 14]. Other approaches used motion sensing to detect people's presence, and control the heating based on the occupancy models of buildings [21, 11, 15].[1]

Shann and Seuken [22] presented a learning algorithm that elicits users' preferred temperatures for different energy prices and creates a comfort-cost trade-off model for each user. Lam et al. [10] introduced a thermal comfort model that updates based on the user's comfort feedbacks. However, all these studies have simulation based results. They do not have a real smart thermostat that is physically deployed to enable its users to interact with it to control their actual heating.[2]

Field Studies with Autonomous Systems

Conducting field studies has been considered a significant way of evaluating computing systems to better understand the social context and user experience [19]. Increasingly, researchers are taking AI technologies from labs to field deployments, where algorithms are used to bring autonomous systems to life in different forms, such as social robots, virtual agents and software agents. In this respect, Sauppé and Mutlu [20] conducted an ethnographic field study with robots in manufacturing sites, and showed that human workers approached the robot co-workers as social entities.

Yang and Newman [28] examined the real-world uptake of a smart thermostat with 23 participants. They highlighted how sub-optimal decisions taken by a smart thermostat are likely to cause frustration for users and may lead them to abandon the technology. Their follow-up study [29] has investigated users' long term interactions with the smart thermostat. Their findings suggest that users' interactions faded over time and resulted in unrealised energy saving opportunities. They also propose that an alternative design (i.e., a mixed-initiative system) might improve the sustainability of user engagement and the system's usefulness.

Bourgeois et al. [4] deployed energy-aware washing machines that provide users with suggestions on when to do their laundry based on the availability of green energy. They studied various intervention techniques with 18 households for 8 months, and showed that proactive suggestions sent by a software agent via text messages are more effective than the agent's email interventions. Similarly, Costanza et al. [8] proposed 'Agent B', a software agent that also helps users book their washing machine in a scenario where electricity prices change every 15 minutes. In a field experiment, 10 participants used Agent B for one month. The results suggest that Agent B helped users defer their laundry in response to real-time prices.

Alan et al. [1] proposed 'Tariff Agent', an agent that helps users select electricity tariffs on a daily basis. It provides three levels of autonomy (fully autonomous, semi-autonomous, and manual), and users can change the level at any time. In a field experiment with 10 users, Tariff Agent was used over a period of 12 days. The results indicate that people are willing to delegate some decisions to an agent but at the same time there is also a desire to stay in control. In a 6-week follow-up study with 12 users, they showed that the users took responsibility for undesired outcomes if the system's autonomy level could be adjusted flexibly [2].

Our study builds on this literature, but extends it in two key ways. First, while prior studies only made the autonomous operation of the systems tangible to participants only through financial rewards, in our study the system also directly influences the participants' thermal *comfort* by controlling the heating setpoint given real-time prices. Second, we evaluate three different UI designs for smart thermostats in the wild.

Interaction with Machine Learning

HCI researchers have long been using machine learning techniques in their studies [13]. The main area of these studies has focused on classification methods, and visualisation of machine learning algorithms. The underlying aim is to improve accuracy of classifiers through enabling users to explore data and interact with machine learning algorithms [26]. However, even though machine learning is becoming an important part of our everyday lives, and significantly changing the way we live (e.g., smart thermostats), there have been few studies that examine how users could interact with machine learning systems, beyond accuracy judgements [25].

In fact, to date no studies have examined how different designs of learning systems may impact people's perceptions. There is a significant gap in our understanding of how we should design interactions with machine learning systems, especially for the ones that might possibly intrude upon our daily activities. In this paper, we present a field study that aims to close this gap by focusing on households' perceptions of and interactions with two designs of a smart thermostat exploiting machine learning, and draw implications for the design of future smart energy systems.

SMARTTHERMO IN THE WILD

We aim to explore how to best design user interactions with a smart thermostat that is designed to automate home heating control when energy price varies in real-time. To do so we prototyped a smart thermostat based on envisioning [17], and evaluated it with a field study. To make the experience of the smart thermostat relevant to the participants of our

[1] Indeed, there are commercial thermostats that utilise occupancy detection (e.g., tado.com).)

[2] We note that Lam et al. deployed a mobile system but it was only for getting users' comfort feedbacks.

Table 1. Participants' profiles.

	Thermostat	Age	Occupation	Others
P1	Indirect L.	40	PhD Student	1 Child
P2	Manual	63	Maintenance Eng.	1 Adult
P3	Direct L.	37	Antiques Dealer	1 Ad., 2 Ch.
P4	Direct L.	43	PhD Student	1 Ad., 2 Ch.
P5	Manual	50	Estate Mng.	1 Ad., 1 Ch.
P6	Manual	36	Nanny	1 Ad., 1 Ch.
P7	Indirect L.	76	Retired	1 Adult
P8	Indirect L.	32	Radiographer	2 Ad., 1 Ch.
P9	Direct L.	44	Teacher	1 Ad., 2 Ch.
P10	Direct L.	62	Retired	2 Adults
P11	Manual	44	Teacher	1 Ad., 2 Ch.
P12	Indirect L.	50	Office Mng.	1 Adult
P13	Manual	40	Education	2 Ad., 1 Ch.
P14	Indirect L.	60	Lecturer	1 Adult
P15	Manual	53	Photographer	2 Ad., 1 Ch.
P16	Direct L.	60	Self Employed	1 Adult
P17	Indirect L.	58	Charity Mng.	1 Adult
P18	Manual	40	Accountant	1 Ad., 4 Ch.
P19	Direct L.	71	Retired	1 Ad.
P20	Indirect L.	56	Database Admin.	2 Adults
P21	Indirect L.	26	Contract Mng.	1 Ad., 1 Ch.
P22	Direct L.	22	Student	1 Adult
P23	Indirect L.	28	Sport Mng.	2 Adults
P24	Direct L.	69	Retired	1 Adult
P25	Direct L.	49	Gas Engineer	1 Adult
P26	Manual	64	Engineer	1 Adult
P27	Manual	91	Retired	1 Adult
P28	Direct L.	73	Retired	1 Adult
P29	Manual	75	Retired	Na
P30	Indirect L.	28	PhD Student	1 Ad. , 1 Ch.

study, we defined a real-time pricing scenario, based on actual historical spot prices in the UK electricity market in January 2014.[3] Following a study design proposed in prior work [8], this scenario was made tangible to participants through financial rewards, as detailed further below. For convenience, we removed extreme outliers from the historical pricing data making the prices range from 5 pence to 35 pence. During our field study the energy price was changed every 30 minutes, similarly to the UK market. In the following sections, we present the details of our study, including our study procedure and participants, descriptions of the thermostat designs, and the data collection and analysis methods we used.

Study Design

In order to gain an understanding of how to best design a smart thermostat for real-time prices, we decided to explore three thermostat designs:

1. Manual: This design aims to provide manual operation and involves no machine learning algorithm. Hence, in this design, users are required to manually specify how the temperature is going to be set at different prices through adjusting a number of setpoint sliders.

2. Direct Learning: This design uses the machine learning algorithm introduced in a prior work [22],[4] and aims to automate users' temperature decisions for different prices.

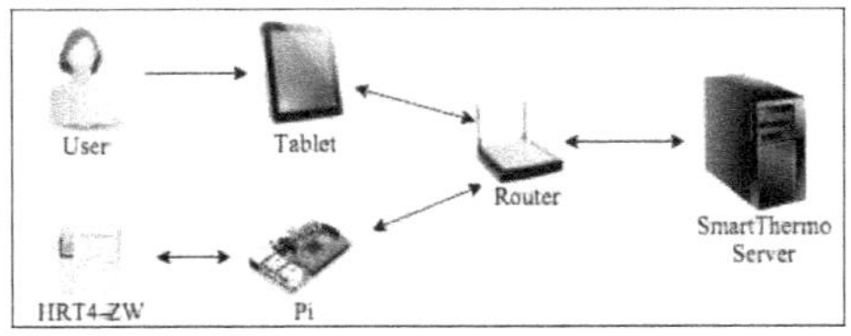

Figure 2. Overall system diagram.

When users make changes in the temperature, the learning algorithm correlates these changes with the prices and generates a user model. Thus, rather than requiring the user to manually specify the setpoint sliders, the learning algorithm automatically arranges them. Each time the user submits a temperature, the algorithm updates the user's model and the thermostat directly heats to the optimal temperature of the user model based on the current price. The aim of this design is to help users understand that the setpoints that they save are being learned by the smart thermostat for future use to determine the setpoint based on varying prices.

3. Indirect Learning: Similar to the direct learning thermostat, the same learning algorithm is used in this design. However, the rationale behind this design is to enable users to temporarily override the learning, and in this way hide from the users the complexity of the algorithm. Thus, in this design, each time the user submits a temperature, the algorithm updates the user model but the thermostat first heats to the inputted temperature - rather than heating to the optimal temperature of the model. Though, after one hour it goes back to auto-mode and sets the setpoint to the optimal temperature of the user model based on the then current price.

We conducted a study with 30 UK households (see Table 1) over a period of four weeks during February-March 2015. To recruit participants we distributed approximately 3000 study invitation letters around the city. We recruited households who had a broadband Internet connection and a central heating control, based on a first-come first-served basis. Participants were assigned to three groups, each corresponding to one thermostat design, one by one in the order 1, 2, 3. An online budget of £100 was then allocated to each household and participants started to use our system for heating their house. Their heating cost is calculated based on the number of hours their boiler was on, and subtracted from their online budget on each day. After four weeks, when the study ended, they received the amount left in their budget as experimental reward. By so doing, we aimed to encourage participants to respond to the prices, and make savings have a tangible impact. The idea of using monetary incentives to simulate real-time pricing is inspired by an early study where participants received payments of the value of electricity saved [24].

Technology

We equipped each household with a Horstmann HRT4-ZW thermostat, a Raspberry Pi (RPi) and an Android 4.4 tablet. Figure 2 shows the connections among different entities. The Horstmann thermostat is a standard room thermostat but can

[3]For practicality we recorded the prices about a year earlier than our study took place, that is in February-March 2015.

[4]There might be more advanced algorithms giving better results. We chose this algorithm due to its simplicity and robustness.

Figure 3. Manual - home page.

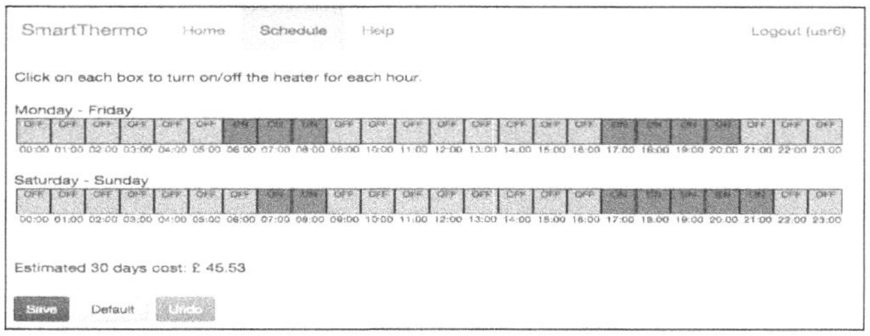

Figure 4. Manual - schedule page.

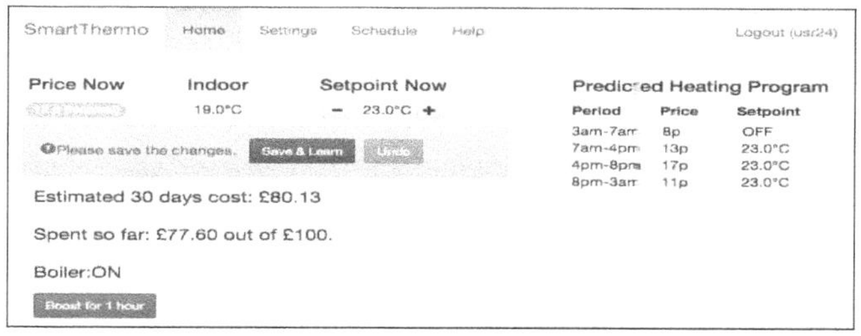

Figure 5. Direct learning - home page.

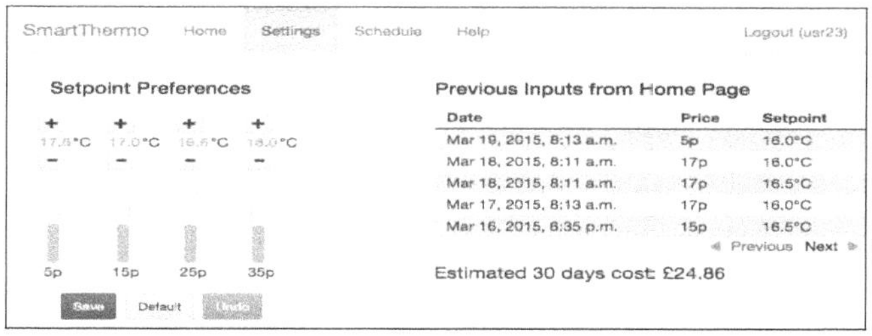

Figure 6. Direct learning - setting page.

be wirelessly controlled over the Z-Wave communication protocol from the RPi (through a RaZberry daughter card[5]). The RPi also connects through the home wireless broadband router to our web server, where the smart thermostat algorithm and UIs run. The RPi regularly pulls the indoor temperature from the thermostat (every 5 minutes), sends the temperature data to our server, and receives the latest individual heating plan. Based on the plan the RPi then controls the setpoint of the thermostat. The tablet allows participants to access our web application through the broadband connection, and to manipulate their own heating plan. Each tablet was installed with a software called Kiosk Browser Lockdown and our web application was set as the default one. We also added the application as a bookmark on the home screen of participants own devices (tablet or smart phone), if they wished.

Design Variations

Manual Thermostat

On the home page (Figure 3), users can see the current energy price and indoor temperature, and adjust the setpoint by pressing the *+/- buttons* next to it. Each press increases/decreases the setpoint by half a degree. To provide context for the current value, a label indicates whether the price is *normal* (bottom of the range), *high* (mid-range) or *very high* (top of the range). The price value and the label are color coded green, yellow or red for emphasis. At the bottom left of the home page users can find the *boost button*, which allows them to turn the heating on continuously for 1 hour, temporarily overriding the setpoint.

On the right side of the page, four *setpoint sliders* enable users to specify how the setpoint should be changed at different prices. In other words, these sliders allow users to directly specify how to trade off comfort and cost. These are positioned on the home page to make them easily visible and accesible, even at the risk of increasing the complexity of the page.

The schedule page (Figure 4) is another page that the manual thermostat users could access. This page allows the users to program the heating schedule that defines the boiler's on and off times. Due to the screen size of our tablets we decided to divide the schedule of a day into hourly-based time slots and group the days as weekdays and weekend. To change the boiler's status for a period of time the user only needs to touch on the time slots corresponding to the period. We provided this schedule page since we anticipated that users would expect such a functionality from a smart thermostat.

Both the home and the schedule pages display the 'Estimated 30 days cost' that reflects how the current settings on the setpoint sliders and the schedule impact the monthly cost of heating. When users make a change in the sliders or in the schedule, the estimated cost updates accordingly. Also it is important to note that users need to save any changes that they make in order to register that change into the system.

Direct Learning Thermostat

In this thermostat design (Figure 5), users directly interact with the machine learning algorithm. When the user presses the +/− buttons, the learning algorithm updates the user's model and displays the optimal setpoint based on the model. The algorithm uses Bayesian inference to update the model, which means it considers the user's individual temperature inputs as noisy data. Thus, the user might need to press the +/− buttons several times to change the setpoint a half degree, depending on the model's prior knowledge. However, to visualise the impact of each press, a pop-up message appears with two buttons, by which users can save or undo the setpoint change. Additionally, each press synchronously affects the 'Estimated 30 days cost' as well as a table called 'Predicted Heating Program'. This table shows the average temperatures that will be set by the thermostat, based on the

[5] `http://razberry.z-wave.me/`

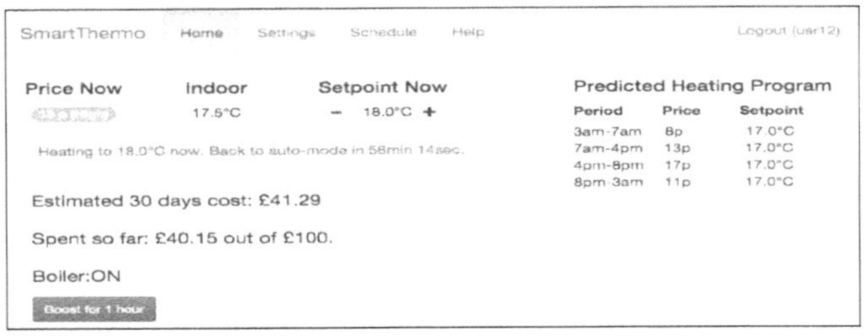

Figure 7. Indirect learning - home page.

predicted average prices at four time periods. The setpoint displayed for each time period changes dynamically according to the updates in the user model. Similar to the manual thermostat, the home page also contains the boost button, which turns the heating on continuously for 1 hour. The boost button does not influence the learning: it was designed as a way to define exceptions to the preferences.

With this thermostat design, users also have one additional page called settings. The settings page (Figure 6) aims to provide users an additional level of control and transparency on the learning algorithm. Similar to the home page of the manual design, there are four sliders representing the user's learnt temperature preferences for each price band. We moved the sliders into the settings page because the focus of the learning thermostat is simplicity of use. The user can see how these sliders are arranged by the thermostat by looking at a history table. The table lists the user's previous temperature inputs together with correlated prices. The user can adjust the sliders to specify his own preferences. By so doing, the user resets the learning algorithm and clears the table of previous inputs. Therefore, a confirmation pop-up is shown before the user saves any changes made in the sliders. The schedule page provided in the manual thermostat is also accessible by the users of the direct learning thermostat.

Indirect Learning Thermostat

In this design, the temperature input that users provide temporarily overrides the setpoint that the algorithm would set based on the user's model and the current price. Thus, the +/− buttons work exactly in the same way as in the manual thermostat (each press increases/decreases the setpoint by half a degree). Once the user saves the new setpoint, the algorithm updates the user model based on the new input. Then, it waits for an hour to take the control back and change the setpoint to the learned one according to the then current price. Meanwhile, the thermostat heats to the inputted temperature. This process was explained with a pop-up message including a countdown timer, starting from 60 minutes, in the UI (Figure 7). Users can still change the setpoint and save it before the countdown finishes, which will restart the count down with the new setpoint. As in the direct learning thermostat, the home page also contains a boost button, which does not influence the learning. The settings and schedule pages are also provided for the indirect learning thermostats.

Method

During the course of the study, we recorded all users' interactions with the thermostat application. For instance, we recorded when participants changed the setpoint or the heating schedule, or when they used the boost button. Additionally, we collected detailed quantitative data about the heating habits of each household, including the temperatures the users set in response to real-time prices and how indoor temperatures varied over the course of the study. However, it was difficult to derive conclusions about the impact of the different thermostat designs on these data, since there are other factors affecting people's heating preferences (e.g., weather and home insulation) [16]. Therefore, in this paper, we focused on the qualitative data collected during the interviews.

Interviews

We conducted semi-structured exit interviews with family members at their homes. We interviewed 26 households.[6] The interviews were mostly held with the participant that signed the consent form at the beginning of the study, however some interviews also involved the participant's partner. In the interviews we asked participants open questions about their use, adoption and understanding of the thermostat. All interviews were audio-recorded, and lasted on average of 34 minutes (SD: 8 minutes, min: 18 minutes, max: 52 minutes).

Analysis

The interviews were fully transcribed and analysed through thematic analysis [5]. Four researchers were involved in this, while the coding was performed by two researchers. The analysis started by categorising the material at the sentence level through open codes. Initially 93 open codes were used, later grouped in broader categories that we discuss in the following section.

FINDINGS

In this section we first present an overview of the quantitative analysis we performed on the overall system usage, based on the automatic interaction logs. Secondly, we report the major findings of our thematic analysis. The analysis revealed six key themes: (1) orientation towards the thermostat's agency, (2) reactions to different UI features, (3) managing the home heating with real-time prices, (4) mental models of the thermostat's learning feature, (5) balancing cost and thermal comfort, and (6) limitations of the thermostat's learning model. We present the categories that revealed these themes in the following subsections. In excerpts, we use "F" for female and "M" for male to denote the gender of the household member.

Overview of Quantitative Analysis

Users of each thermostat design heated their home using our system for a month. They mostly interacted with the system via the tablet we provided or the tablet they already had. Some of these participants additionally used their mobile phones to access the system. Table 2 includes the overall data of system usage. We performed one-way ANOVA tests on the quantitative data. However, we could not find any significant differences or long-term effects in user interactions across the three deployed designs. This was also the case for the analysis of other quantitative data collected (i.e., setpoints and indoor temperatures). The analysis did not reveal

[6] Other 4 participants were not available for the interview.

Table 2. Overall quantitative data analysis.

	Manual		Direct L.		Indirect L	
	M	SD	M	SD	M	SD
Setpoint Changes from Home Page	36.7	52.8	13.3	14.4	18.5	22.8
Setpoint Changes from Settings Page	-	-	6.4	7.4	2.5	3
Schedule Changes	18.2	14.8	47.8	51.3	21.8	19.4
Boost Activations	17.5	14.1	7.3	4.3	14.2	11.3
Spent from Budget	£55	£22	£55	£33	£30	£15
Demand Response	36%	19%	34%	17%	47%	24%

Note. M = Mean. SD = Standard Deviation.

any significant differences in users' demand-responses or savings, which might be understandable given the interpersonal, contextual, and environmental differences of the users.

Orientation towards the Thermostat's Agency

All participants commented that they were happy with the thermostat autonomously responding to real-time prices on their behalf. The following is a typical response that we received in the interviews, when we asked participants about their feelings towards the agency of the system.

> **P18 (M):** "I'm happy with that if the thermostat understands that at this price I would rather avoid heating the house, and at this price I would like to heat the house, then I'm happy for it to take over that control, as long as it's very straightforward for me to override."

We observed that they felt in control overall and were also mostly confident with the way the thermostat was working.

> **Analyst:** "To what degree did you feel like the system worked for you, or it required you to do the work?"

> **P13 (F):** "So basically I just order the system to do the things for me and the system does the whole thing. "

Reactions to Different UI Features

In the interviews we observed that most participants understood well how to use the UI elements (e.g., the +/− buttons) of each thermostat design. Nearly all participants commented that the thermostat was easy to understand and use. All participants appeared to understand the functionality of the setpoint sliders and mostly appreciated their use.

The users of the direct learning thermostat were mostly aware of the fact that sometimes they were required to press the +/− buttons multiple times to achieve the desired setpoint value. However, they did not explicitly state that this was due to the learning feature.

> **P3 (F):** "The estimated cost would change before the degree thing changed. So, you press it. Sort of, like, Wow it needs four presses per half degree or something, and I was like, because I could see this number here was changed. It was doing something. Then I thought it must be incremental, must be in tenths rather than in halves."

The indirect learning thermostat users mostly explained the way the 60 minutes countdown works as though it goes back to the previously saved setpoint rather than the learned setpoint based on the price at the time after 60 minutes.

> **P23 (F):** "So then there's a countdown for 60 minutes and after that the temperature will resume to what was set previously. Occasionally I would reset the temperature again within those 60 minutes."

Managing the Home Heating with Real-time Prices

Here we detail how and why participants used the thermostat in different ways to heat their house with real-time prices.

Setpoint Preferences

Most participants of all three thermostat designs reported preferring to change 'setpoint now' from home page to control the indoor temperature with real-time prices. They also fiddled with the setpoint sliders, but the number of times was relatively low compared to the changes made in the 'setpoint now'. Interviews revealed that most participants were happy with the arrangement of the sliders and therefore they did not feel the need to alter them often. Also a few participants found the sliders complex, which led them to play with the 'setpoint now' more.

We had constrained the setpoint sliders to present a straight line corresponding to users' heating preferences. Therefore, changes made to one of the sliders affected the values of others. Overall the participants who interacted with the sliders found them easy to adjust and appreciated their use. In the interviews, only one participant griped about this linear relationship among the sliders. However, we noticed that this user only played with the first slider throughout the study, therefore they could make only parallel shift on the slider values without being able to change the slope of the line.

> **P15 (F):** "If we could've adjusted them differently and made our own decisions on these rather than they just go up automatically when you change one of the others, we would've preferred that."

Most participants kept the configuration of the sliders in descending order, starting with higher temperature at lower price and lowering the setpoint as the price increases. Two users calibrated the four sliders to have the same setpoint. In other words, they opted for a specific temperature setpoint to heat their house over the course of the study regardless of the heating cost.

> **P29 (M):** "You should be prepared to pay more, a higher rate, if you wanted to be more comfortable. I could change it as when I wanted it, but if I wanted to go to a higher temperature, it could cost me more. But, because I had set it at a flat rate, I wasn't bothered."

Also, participants reported that they did not need to change the sliders once they found their limit for how much comfort they could sacrifice to save money. The process of finding such a limit was generally a matter of trial and error:

> **P11 (F):** "It was freezing cold and it must've broken. I checked and that's when I saw it was on 35p and that's when I changed the lowest set point."

Some participants were more conscious of and certain about their tolerance limit for temperature even in the early stages of the field study. Therefore, once these participants arranged the sliders early on in the study, they stopped interacting with the sliders, and used other interface features, such as the schedule, to adjust the heating.

> **P16 (M):** "When we first got it, we looked at the pricing bands and made some decisions at that stage. We did it once and I don't think we revisited it. What we did visit, then, pretty regularly, probably every day, and maybe more often than once a day, we did revisit the schedule."

Schedule

Most participants told us how it was easier to access and change the heating program through our system compared to their previous programmable heating controls. Being able to easily turn on and off the heating by touching on the displayed hourly time slots, and being able to have different programs for weekdays and weekends, seemed to meet participant's favour.

> **P21 (F):** "We changed it most days because it was so easy to access. If I was going out and I knew that we wouldn't be home until five, I'd set it to come on at four. Whereas previously, we wouldn't even touch it on a normal one."

Here she refers to the "normal one" as a wall-mounted programmable thermostat that she had before taking part in our study. Her comment suggests that people may engage more with their heating systems when the systems are easy to control and access. Specifically, among the users of all UI designs, most participants liked being able to control the heating remotely from anywhere in the house or anywhere outside via their Internet-connected devices - rather than walking to a wall-mounted thermostat each time.

> **P23 (F):** "It was just useful to be able to change the temperature from wherever I was really. I could do it from work and quite often did or if I went from work to the supermarket and then came home, you could do it from the supermarket. So yes, it was really *clever*."

In the interviews, we observed that occupancy was the major factor affecting the way participants modified the schedule. They mostly tended to turn off the heating when no one was around, and turn it on if someone was at home. Participants who had regular lifestyles reported that they didn't need to change the schedule often, whereas some participants altered the schedule quite often due to their irregular lifestyles.

> **P28 (M):** "I did change this one [schedule] at the very beginning, but other than that I haven't touched it at all because, I've been working with this time limits for the boiler on and off for 25 years. It's suited my lifestyle. I'm a creature of habit really."

> **P10 (F):** "I'm retired so could be at home all day but at the last minute suddenly go off somewhere and we're three adults. So it's three people leading separate lives in a way rather than if we were a family with children and you'd know you would be in the house until half past eight go to school picking up. So our lifestyle is quite *erratic*."

We also observed that some participants used the schedule as a medium to respond to changing energy prices. For example, in the following quote, P9 (F) indicates that she moved the time that the thermostat normally comes on in the mornings nearly one hour earlier to benefit from lower prices.

> **Analyst:** "How do you feel about the real-time prices for heating energy?"

> **P9 (F):** "I noticed that it [price] was cheaper before 7am. Previously, I'd been putting the heating on like maybe 6:45 because we get up about 7:00, then leaving it on while we're getting ready for work and school and then turning it off. I changed that and started putting it on earlier, putting it on at 6:00 and then having it go off at 7:00, and it still kept the house warm enough until we went out sort of an hour or so later."

There were other factors that influenced participants' heating program, such as their daily activities or weather conditions. Participants mostly turned the heating on at times that they usually took showers, or turned it off when they used the oven. While on cold days participants arranged the schedule to make the thermostat come on for more time slots, they had fewer time slots on for milder days.

Boost

After deciding how to balance comfort and cost, participants tended to use the "boost" button for exceptional situations to turn the heating on instead of changing the setpoints on the sliders.

> **P2 (M):** "I tended to be comfortable with the settings that I had on it and sort of left it. The only time if it was really cold in the mornings when we got up, I'd press the boost to boost it and it probably only went on for an hour or two."

Some participants also commented that they used the boost button just to heat their home a bit more when the prices were lower.

> **P21 (F):** "I liked when it said £0.05 and I was like; yes, put the heating on, boost it!"

Mental Models of the Thermostat's Learning Feature

Only the users of direct and indirect thermostats were exposed to the machine learning algorithm. These users were required to click the save and learn button that appears every time they make a change in the setpoint from home page in order to register their preferred temperature into the thermostat. Including the text 'learn' in the save button seemed to be successful at conveying the fact that the thermostat was learning. However, when we asked the users' opinion about what the thermostat was learning in the interviews, three users reported that they had not thought about it before and therefore that they had no comment.

Among the participants who formed opinions about the learning feature, most participants appeared to have an understanding that is well-matched with the actual underpinnings of the thermostat's learning feature. Most participants were aware of the fact that the thermostat was trying to correlate their preferred setpoints to varying prices. It seemed that the display of previous inputs in the settings page supported their comprehension. Though, conceivably, no one seemed to be interested in how the thermostat was actually calculating the setpoint based on their previous inputs

Analyst: "If you had to explain the learning feature to one of your friends, how would you explain it?"

P3 (F): "It [thermostat] learns your tolerance for an increase in price. It learns your habits and your behaviours in terms of the price versus the temperature, and then it applies those, reapplies them for future events when the unit price goes up."

P23 (M): "As you input your set point changes according to the prices and then the system starts to understand what your views are of that cost I suppose. That is what you think is expensive and that is what you think is cheap, and then make changes."

In these quotes, the participants are very clear about what the thermostat was trying to learn. They explain that the thermostat was learning their temperature preferences for different prices based on their previous inputs. Also, the participants express that the thermostat was learning in order to be able to autonomously respond to the changing prices on their behalf.

On the other hand, some participants had another interesting mental model description of the learning feature, which was neglecting the effect of the prices. These participants described the thermostat as though it was matching their preferred temperatures with the times and the days of the previous temperature inputs that they provided.

Analyst: "So can you tell me what happens when you click to the save and learn button after you change the setpoint?"

P21 (M): "Well, it [thermostat] updates and it changes the kind of the setpoint to what it is going to heat to, but it also learns what you have done. So, I am guessing that later on, if you are doing that at a certain point every day then it's going to learn that."

P30 (M): "If I play a particular temperature as the setpoint and then click on save and learn, from what I understand is the system will take this reading to consideration for whether to turn the boiler on or off but at the same time try to see that at this particular time of the day, whether it's weekday or weekend and then try to replicate that during other days."

This misinterpretation of the learning feature was more prevalent among the indirect learning thermostat users than among the users of the Direct Learning Thermostat. Further exploration also revealed that none of the participants having the misinterpretation was familiar with the Nest thermostat, or in fact any other smart thermostats that exist in the energy market. We can therefore assume that they were not biased.

Balancing Cost and Thermal Comfort

Even though seeing the current price of energy had mostly impacted on how our participants heated their home over the course of the study, there were other significant factors that played key roles in the decisions of the participants for maintaining their thermal comfort at home. One of these key factors was occupancy. Most of our participants commented that they tended to turn off the heating for the times that no one was at home. Another important factor was outside weather as opposed to the indoor temperature: the colder the weather was, the longer the heating was on. Lastly, daily activities at home seemed to substantially influence the participants' heating preferences. While sitting still or having a shower caused participants to turn on the heating, cooking or other physical activities led them to keep the heating off.

P2 (M): "I generally go out by nine o'clock I had the heating going off at eight o'clock in the morning. So it sort of warmed us up to have our showers and be comfortable in the morning, and weekends it depended whether we were in or out as to whether we left it on or knocked it off. So it revolved around our lifestyle and work patterns and things. And the temperature outside. If it was really cold outside then we would have it on longer."

P1 (M): "Most of the time I tried to connect the schedule with my daily activities. For instance, I take shower in the morning, and sometimes I work here at home between 9 and 11. So these are the times that I turn on the heating. Most of the time between 12 and 3, I cook and turn off the heating, because it really doesn't feel cold."

Another interesting finding that emerged from the interviews was the ways participants attempted to maintain their thermal comfort at home without using our heating system. The most prevalent attempt was putting on one more layer of clothing (generally a jumper), or using a blanket when the energy prices are high. Also some participants took the advantage of their other heating sources such as wood-burning stoves, which is typical in small town houses in the UK.

P8 (M): "I think we have probably spent less on our heating in general than we would have done normally. Normally we heat the house pretty much all the time in the winter. We did at times just put another jumper on."

Limitations of the Thermostat's Learning Model

As it is clear in the previous excerpts, the price was not the only factor affecting our participant's setpoint preferences. However, the learning algorithm used in both direct and indirect learning thermostats was only considering two inputs: the setpoint registered and the price at that current time. Therefore, the thermostat was automating the setpoint control only based on the price. This limited learning capability resulted in dissatisfaction among a few participants since the setpoint automatically set by the thermostat was not always the right temperature for its owner. The following quotes are the only ones from which we received such feedback from the participants.

P3 (F): "There were times when I came in and I was like. Hang on a sec. My house is really warm and it must have been because it had learned something that. To do with the temperature. So, it must have said all the prices are this, so they like it warm when it's like this. It's like. Hell no. It's too hot!"

P9 (F): "Well, if I understood the intention that it was trying to set my temperature according to the price, that didn't really work for me. I kind of wanted a combination. I kind of could see the point of that. But like I said, at night, I didn't want it so warm, though perhaps I quite sort of would like it to keep it a degree or two cooler when the temperature's high to save money or something like that. But I also wanted it to let me decide more and not decide for me all the time."

DISCUSSION

In this section, we revisit the major findings of our study, and discuss them in light of prior literature. We also present implications for interaction design of smart energy systems and for future research.

Designing a Thermostat for Real-Time Prices

Any thermostat designed for real-time prices will need to automate the heating at some level, as otherwise it would be a very difficult task for a human to monitor every price change and alter the heating accordingly. Prior research on autonomous systems suggests that these systems should allow their users to easily override the automated decisions at any point in time, without completely disabling the system's autonomy [1]. In this vein, in our study we observed that some participants used the boost button as a means to temporarily override their temperature preferences for exceptional situations, rather than resetting the learned preferences. These exceptional situations not only occurred when users felt cold and wanted to heat the house despite the high prices, but also happened when users wanted to heat the house a bit more than they would do normally in order to benefit from low prices (typically termed the rebound effect).

One of the most-liked features was the display of 'Estimated 30 days cost'. As P28-m said, "I've watched also my estimated cost each day, to see whether it varied at all. I had taken an interest in it, every day really, I've become almost fixated by it." We observed that the participants used it as a 'sandbox' area [12], by which they could view the consequences of different settings on the cost before approving them. Another well-liked feature was the ability to control the thermostat remotely. Participants commented that this feature affords them a high degree of convenience for heating their home. Most of them reported that they monitored their house (whether the heating was on or off) while they were away, or turned the heating on just before coming home. Furthermore, they found the use of it handy even within the house. For instance, one of our participants commented that she liked being able to take the tablet with her to bed so that she could turn the heating on in cold mornings without having to leave the bed.

Most participants found the thermostat's heating schedule easy to access and program. However, some participants perceived its hourly time slots as limiting their scheduling plan. This is understandable when one considers that today most heating controls provide finer resolutions (e.g., 10 to 30 minutes). Additionally, grouping the daily heating program by weekdays and weekend was not convenient for all participants to accommodate their occupancy patterns. As an example, one participant said her Saturdays and Sundays are totally different. We also had some participants who did not have any occupancy patterns at all and had to adjust the schedule quite a few times in a day. Therefore, further research is needed to address how to best design heating programs for people with unpredictable lifestyles.

Our field study showed that participants could use our thermostats to effectively manage their home heating and create temperature preferences based on real-time prices. As we expected these temperature preferences varied for different individuals. While most participants set lower temperatures at peak prices compared to lower price periods, two households kept the same temperature for all price bands. Furthermore, our participants adopted different strategies to respond to real-time prices. While most participants used the setpoint and the setpoint sliders for reacting to changing prices, some participants interestingly used the boost and the schedule features more than adjusting the setpoint for heating their home with real-time prices. This is in line with a previous study that examined people's use and mental model of their heating system [18], and revealed that setpoint adjustment was less prevalent among their participants compared to the adjustments of other devices, such as the programmer, override button and radiator valves.

Finally, we noted the several ways that our participants used to maintain their thermal comfort, especially when the prices were high, without using our heating systems, such as putting on one more layer of clothing or using a blanket. These observations show similarity to the findings of previous work [7, 6], which examine students' daily heating habits and report the similar activities without any financial benefits.

Expectations from Smart Home Heating Systems

While most participants perceived the thermostat as "smart" because of its learning capability of preferred temperatures and its ability to automate home heating based on changing prices, for some participants it was enough to describe the thermostat as smart just because of its remote control capability and its programmable schedule. This perception was due to the fact that these functionalities were mostly new to the participants. More importantly they experienced improvement in their quality of life as these functionalities assisted and facilitated their heating task. This finding is in line with prior research suggesting that computing technologies would be perceived to be "smart" if they offer an advantage for the users' daily tasks [12].

Regarding the learning feature of the thermostats, participants had different explanations and mental models. While some participants described the system as one that was trying to match their temperature preferences with changing prices, other participants thought that the system was learning the times of days that they set temperatures. Interestingly, participants who used the direct learning thermostat and had no technical background (e.g., P3, an antiques dealer) described more accurate mental models compared to the participants of the indirect learning thermostat with more technical background (e.g., P1-m and P30-m, both computer science PhD students). A previous study examining non-technical users' understandings of an intelligent system suggests that people's initial mental models and misconceptions stayed relatively constant over their study [27]. Therefore, we asked our participants, who had this misconception, if they were aware of any commercial smart thermostats, such as Nest that learns your schedule, in order to see if they had any initial knowledge that would have affected their mental models. However, they all reported that they had not heard of any smart thermostat before. This then may suggest that exposing users directly to the outcomes of learning algorithms may help users to create better mental models. Furthermore, while showing the correlation between previous temperature inputs and prices supported the users' understanding, a more useful method could be a notification system that periodically states what has been learned by the system. We believe these results highlight an important implication for future research in interaction with "smart" energy systems to try and discover the source of people's mental models and learning expectations.

Our system learns users' preferred temperatures at different prices to automate home heating. However, from the interviews, it was clear that the price was not only the factor that our users considered for heating their home. Other key factors were outside weather, occupancy and daily activities within the house. Some participants explicitly stated that the use of the thermostat could be more convenient if it could learn their occupancy patterns. Also, outside weather and the activities that they perform during a day within the house have a significant impact on how people feel the indoor temperature. For instance, most of our participants preferred to have the heating on when they shower and have the heating off when they use their oven or perform physical activities. Therefore, future design of learning thermostats should not only take into account occupancy patterns and outdoor temperatures [16], in addition to people's price preferences, but also people's daily routines (e.g., times that they shower and cook).

Studying Future Smart Energy Systems

In order to let participants experience a future scenario, we prototyped our system based on envisioning [17]. Our scenario depicts an energy market in which consumers can respond to real-time prices by using a smart thermostat that automatically controls heating on their behalf. Participants' statements about their perception and adoption of the smart thermostat indicate that combining experimental reward with a deployed prototype is an effective way to convey a future scenario to participants and allow them to obtain real life experience, echoing recent studies of future scenarios [1, 2, 8]. Extending these recent studies, our participants experienced the autonomous actions of the smart energy system not only through financial incentives, but also through the thermostat's automatic temperature changes. Such changes could directly influence our participants' comfort. Yet, similar to the results of previous studies, our participants mostly felt in control of their heating system and demonstrated a generally positive attitude towards the thermostat. Hence, we believe this finding reinforces those from those previous studies, revealing the potential of future autonomous smart energy systems.

One of the prerequisites for taking part in our study was to have a central heating system with a single boiler. However, we did not define any requirements on the type of thermostat previously installed, such as programmable or non-programmable, digital or analog. Our findings revealed that the type of thermostat familiar to our participants influenced their perception and use of our system. In particular, participants not used to a programmable thermostat focused mostly on the schedule feature of our system, since this was a new and significant feature for them. This circumstance turned out to steer attention away from our primary interest: the ability of our thermostats to automatically react to real-time prices. Hence, future research should take user fragmentation into account in the recruiting process of participants in order to improve the effectiveness of system designs and to obtain more focused results.

CONCLUSION

Smart energy systems that leverage machine learning techniques are increasingly integrated in all aspects of our lives, and they are changing the way that we perform our daily activities. The design of these systems plays a key role in how we adapt to and interact with them. To better understand how to design user interaction with such systems, we implemented three different smart thermostats that automate heating based on users' heating preferences and real-time prices. We evaluated our designs through a field study, where 30 UK households used our thermostats to heat their homes over a month.

Our findings through thematic analysis show that the participants formed different understandings and expectations of our smart thermostat, and used it in various ways to effectively respond to real-time prices while maintaining their thermal comfort. Based on the findings, we provided a number of design and research implications, specifically for designing future smart thermostats that will assist us in controlling home heating with real-time pricing, and for future intelligent autonomous systems. These recommendations will assist designers in improving user experience with smart energy systems, which in return will help us to more smoothly integrate them into our everyday lives and actually benefit from them.

ACKNOWLEDGMENTS

Thanks to our participants for the courage of taking part in our study. Work partially supported by the EPSRC ORCHID project (EP/I011587/1), through a PhD scholarship from the Turkish Government, and by the SNSF (Swiss National Science Foundation) project #147211. Data URL: `http://doi.org/bbpr`. Study approved by University of Southampton FPSE Ethics Committee (ref: 13417).

REFERENCES

1. Alper T. Alan, Enrico Costanza, Joel Fischer, Sarvapali D. Ramchurn, Tom Rodden, and Nicholas R. Jennings. 2014. A Field Study of Human-agent Interaction for Electricity Tariff Switching. In *Proceedings of the 2014 International Conference on Autonomous Agents and Multi-agent Systems (AAMAS '14)*. International Foundation for Autonomous Agents and Multiagent Systems, Richland, SC, 965–972. http://dl.acm.org/citation.cfm?id=2615731.2617400

2. Alper T. Alan, Sarvapali D. Ramchurn, Tom Rodden, Enrico Costanza, Joel Fischer, and Nicholas R. Jennings. 2015. Managing Energy Tariffs with Agents: A Field Study of a Future Smart Energy System at Home. In *Adjunct Proceedings of the 2015 ACM International Joint Conference on Pervasive and Ubiquitous Computing and Proceedings of the 2015 ACM International Symposium on Wearable Computers (UbiComp/ISWC'15 Adjunct)*. ACM, New York, NY, USA, 1551–1558. DOI: http://dx.doi.org/10.1145/2800835.2801626

3. Galen L. Barbose, Charles A. Goldman, and Bernie Neenan. 2004. A Survey of Utility Experience with Real Time Pricing. (12 2004), 127.

4. Jacky Bourgeois, Janet van der Linden, Gerd Kortuem, Blaine A. Price, and Christopher Rimmer. 2014. Conversations with My Washing Machine: An In-the-wild Study of Demand Shifting with Self-generated Energy. In *Proceedings of the 2014 ACM International Joint Conference on Pervasive and Ubiquitous Computing (UbiComp '14)*. ACM, New York, NY, USA, 459–470. DOI: http://dx.doi.org/10.1145/2632048.2632106

5. Virginia Braun and Victoria Clarke. 2006. Using thematic analysis in psychology. *Qualitative Research in Psychology* 3, 2 (2006), 77–101.

6. Adrian Clear, Adrian Friday, Mike Hazas, and Carolynne Lord. 2014. Catch My Drift?: Achieving Comfort More Sustainably in Conventionally Heated Buildings. In *Proceedings of the 2014 Conference on Designing Interactive Systems (DIS '14)*. ACM, New York, NY, USA, 1015–1024. DOI: http://dx.doi.org/10.1145/2598510.2598529

7. Adrian K. Clear, Janine Morley, Mike Hazas, Adrian Friday, and Oliver Bates. 2013. Understanding Adaptive Thermal Comfort: New Directions for UbiComp. In *Proceedings of the 2013 ACM International Joint Conference on Pervasive and Ubiquitous Computing (UbiComp '13)*. ACM, New York, NY, USA, 113–122. DOI: http://dx.doi.org/10.1145/2493432.2493451

8. Enrico Costanza, Joel E. Fischer, James A. Colley, Tom Rodden, Sarvapali D. Ramchurn, and Nicholas R. Jennings. 2014. Doing the Laundry with Agents: A Field Trial of a Future Smart Energy System in the Home. In *Proceedings of the SIGCHI Conference on Human Factors in Computing Systems (CHI '14)*. ACM, New York, NY, USA, 813–822. DOI: http://dx.doi.org/10.1145/2556288.2557167

9. Nicholas R. Jennings, Luc Moreau, David Nicholson, Sarvapali Ramchurn, Stephen Roberts, Tom Rodden, and Alex Rogers. 2014. Human-agent Collectives. *Commun. ACM* 57, 12 (Nov. 2014), 80–88. DOI: http://dx.doi.org/10.1145/2629559

10. Abraham Hang-yat Lam, Yi Yuan, and Dan Wang. 2014. An Occupant-participatory Approach for Thermal Comfort Enhancement and Energy Conservation in Buildings. In *Proceedings of the 5th International Conference on Future Energy Systems (e-Energy '14)*. ACM, New York, NY, USA, 133–143. DOI: http://dx.doi.org/10.1145/2602044.2602067

11. Jiakang Lu, Tamim Sookoor, Vijay Srinivasan, Ge Gao, Brian Holben, John Stankovic, Eric Field, and Kamin Whitehouse. 2010. The Smart Thermostat: Using Occupancy Sensors to Save Energy in Homes. In *Proceedings of the 8th ACM Conference on Embedded Networked Sensor Systems (SenSys '10)*. ACM, New York, NY, USA, 211–224. DOI: http://dx.doi.org/10.1145/1869983.1870005

12. Sarah Mennicken, Jo Vermeulen, and Elaine M. Huang. 2014. From Today's Augmented Houses to Tomorrow's Smart Homes: New Directions for Home Automation Research. In *Proceedings of the 2014 ACM International Joint Conference on Pervasive and Ubiquitous Computing (UbiComp '14)*. ACM, New York, NY, USA, 105–115. DOI: http://dx.doi.org/10.1145/2632048.2636076

13. Vassilis Moustakis. 1997. Do People in HCI Use Machine Learning?. In *Design of Computing Systems: Social and Ergonomic Considerations, Proceedings of the Seventh International Conference on Human-Computer Interaction, (HCI International '97), San Francisco, California, USA, August 24-29, 1997, Volume 2*. 95–98.

14. F. Oldewurtel, A. Parisio, C. N. Jones, M. Morari, D. Gyalistras, M. Gwerder, V. Stauch, B. Lehmann, and K. Wirth. 2010. Energy Efficient Building Climate Control using Stochastic Model Predictive Control and Weather Predictions. In *American Control Conference*. Baltimore, USA. http://control.ee.ethz.ch/index.cgi?page=publications;action=details;id=3551

15. Athanasios Aris Panagopoulos, Muddasser Alam, Alex Rogers, and Nicholas R. Jennings. 2015. AdaHeat: A General Adaptive Intelligent Agent for Domestic Heating Control. In *Proceedings of the 2015 International Conference on Autonomous Agents and Multiagent Systems (AAMAS '15)*. International Foundation for Autonomous Agents and Multiagent Systems, Richland, SC, 1295–1303. http://dl.acm.org/citation.cfm?id=2772879.2773317

16. Therese Peffer, Marco Pritoni, Alan Meier, Cecilia Aragon, and Daniel Perry. 2011. How people use thermostats in homes: A review. *Building and*

Environment 46, 12 (2011), 2529 – 2541. DOI: http://dx.doi.org/10.1016/j.buildenv.2011.06.002

17. Stuart Reeves. 2012. Envisioning Ubiquitous Computing. In *Proceedings of the SIGCHI Conference on Human Factors in Computing Systems (CHI '12)*. ACM, New York, NY, USA, 1573–1582. DOI: http://dx.doi.org/10.1145/2207676.2208278
18. Kirsten M.A. Revell and Neville A. Stanton. 2014. Case studies of mental models in home heat control: Searching for feedback, valve, timer and switch theories. *Applied Ergonomics* 45, 3 (2014), 363 – 378. DOI: http://dx.doi.org/10.1016/j.apergo.2013.05.001
19. Yvonne Rogers, Helen Sharp, and Jenny Preece. 2011. *Interaction design: beyond human-computer interaction*. Wiley.
20. Allison Sauppé and Bilge Mutlu. 2015. The Social Impact of a Robot Co-Worker in Industrial Settings. In *Proceedings of the 33rd Annual ACM Conference on Human Factors in Computing Systems (CHI '15)*. ACM, New York, NY, USA, 3613–3622. DOI: http://dx.doi.org/10.1145/2702123.2702181
21. James Scott, A.J. Bernheim Brush, John Krumm, Brian Meyers, Michael Hazas, Stephen Hodges, and Nicolas Villar. 2011. PreHeat: Controlling Home Heating Using Occupancy Prediction. In *Proceedings of the 13th International Conference on Ubiquitous Computing (UbiComp '11)*. ACM, New York, NY, USA, 281–290. DOI: http://dx.doi.org/10.1145/2030112.2030151
22. Mike Shann and Sven Seuken. 2013. An Active Learning Approach to Home Heating in the Smart Grid. In *Proceedings of the Twenty-Third International Joint Conference on Artificial Intelligence (IJCAI '13)*. AAAI Press, 2892–2899. http://dl.acm.org/citation.cfm?id=2540128.2540545
23. Will Simm, Maria Angela Ferrario, Adrian Friday, Peter Newman, Stephen Forshaw, Mike Hazas, and Alan Dix. 2015. Tiree Energy Pulse: Exploring Renewable Energy Forecasts on the Edge of the Grid. In *Proceedings of the 33rd Annual ACM Conference on Human Factors in Computing Systems (CHI '15)*. ACM, New York, NY, USA, 1965–1974. DOI: http://dx.doi.org/10.1145/2702123.2702285
24. Robert E. Slavin, John S. Wodarski, and Bernard L. Blackburn. 1981. A Group Contingency for Electricity Conservation in Master-Metered Apartments. *Journal of Applied Behavior Analysis* 14, 3 (1981), 357–97. DOI: http://dx.doi.org/10.1901/jaba.1981.14-357
25. Simone Stumpf, Vidya Rajaram, Lida Li, Weng-Keen Wong, Margaret Burnett, Thomas Dietterich, Erin Sullivan, and Jonathan Herlocker. 2009. Interacting meaningfully with machine learning systems: Three experiments. *International Journal of Human-Computer Studies* 67, 8 (2009), 639 – 662. DOI: http://dx.doi.org/10.1016/j.ijhcs.2009.03.004
26. Justin Talbot, Bongshin Lee, Ashish Kapoor, and Desney S. Tan. 2009. EnsembleMatrix: Interactive Visualization to Support Machine Learning with Multiple Classifiers. In *Proceedings of the SIGCHI Conference on Human Factors in Computing Systems (CHI '09)*. ACM, New York, NY, USA, 1283–1292. DOI: http://dx.doi.org/10.1145/1518701.1518895
27. Joe Tullio, Anind K. Dey, Jason Chalecki, and James Fogarty. 2007. How It Works: A Field Study of Non-technical Users Interacting with an Intelligent System. In *Proceedings of the SIGCHI Conference on Human Factors in Computing Systems (CHI '07)*. ACM, New York, NY, USA, 31–40. DOI: http://dx.doi.org/10.1145/1240624.1240630
28. Rayoung Yang and Mark W. Newman. 2013. Learning from a Learning Thermostat: Lessons for Intelligent Systems for the Home. In *Proceedings of the 2013 ACM International Joint Conference on Pervasive and Ubiquitous Computing (UbiComp '13)*. ACM, New York, NY, USA, 93–102. DOI: http://dx.doi.org/10.1145/2493432.2493489
29. Rayoung Yang, Mark W. Newman, and Jodi Forlizzi. 2014. Making Sustainability Sustainable: Challenges in the Design of Eco-interaction Technologies. In *Proceedings of the SIGCHI Conference on Human Factors in Computing Systems (CHI '14)*. ACM, New York, NY, USA, 823–832. DOI: http://dx.doi.org/10.1145/2556288.2557380
30. Zhe Yu, Liyan Jia, Mary C. Murphy-Hoye, Annabelle Pratt, and Lang Tong. 2013. Modeling and Stochastic Control for Home Energy Management. *IEEE Trans. Smart Grid* 4, 4 (2013), 2244–2255. DOI: http://dx.doi.org/10.1109/TSG.2013.2279171

Living In A Prototype: A Reconfigured Space

Audrey Desjardins[1] and Ron Wakkary[2]
[1] Simon Fraser University, Surrey, British Columbia, Canada
[2] Eindhoven University of Technology, Eindhoven, Netherlands
{adesjard, rwakkary} @sfu.ca

ABSTRACT
In this paper, we present a twenty-three months autobiographical design project of converting a Mercedes Sprinter van into a camper van. This project allows us to investigate the complexities and nuances of a case where people engage in a process of making, transforming and adapting a space they live in. This example opens a radically different and productive context for revisiting concepts that are currently at the center of human-computer interaction (HCI) research: ubiquitous computing, home automation, smart homes, and the Internet of Things. We offer six qualities characterizing the evolving relationship between the makers and the lived-in environment: the van. We conclude with a discussion on the two themes of living *in* a reconfigured home and prototype qualities in a reconfigured space, and a critical reflection around the theme of the invariably unfinished home.

Author Keywords
Autobiographical design; Maker; making; lived-with; DIY; everyday design; IoT; Smart home.

ACM Classification Keywords
H.5.m. Information interfaces and presentation (e.g., HCI): Miscellaneous.

INTRODUCTION

We present a long-term autobiographical design project of converting a Mercedes Sprinter van into a camper van. Over the past twenty-three months, we have reconfigured the space in a cargo van to allow activities like cooking, eating, sleeping and entertaining during their biking and skiing trips. In this paper, we present this project as a way to examine further and critically reflect on how people imagine, design, make, and repair an environment they live in. The core goal of this paper is to interpret insights from this project in the context of future research in HCI on the design of technologies for the home, particularly smart homes and the Internet of Things (IoT).

CHI'16, May 07 - 12, 2016, San Jose, CA, USA

ACM 978-1-4503-3362-7/16/05···$15.00
DOI: http://dx.doi.org/10.1145/2858036.2858261

This project relates to previous research investigating how people live with design artifacts (digital or not) in everyday settings and how they creatively appropriate, remake, or modify them through ongoing practices. Ethnography and ethnomethodology works by Tolmie et al. [29], Crabtree et al. [10], Swan et al. [25], and Taylor and Swan [27] show how families organize, communicate, and coordinate their everyday lives through and with the help of a variety of artifacts and media in the home as part of their routines. Specifically, work by Wakkary et al. [32,34] has looked at how those artifact and system transformations are part of ongoing design processes and build on incremental engagements with artifacts and the surroundings. With design-in-use, everyday designers are able to adapt their artifacts and systems to the daily pressures of use and family members' individual needs [34]. Use is a strong motor for changes to occur, and the accessibility to resources and materials in the surroundings makes it possible for those changes to happen dynamically. While, at times, those changes can be tacit and unselfconscious [32], at other times home dwellers are aware of the value of those changes and intentionally plan and test out design variations for a specific need [34]. Our van conversion project is an example where the maker is aware of the design process and this project is a particularly rich example for how making, using, and living over time are inevitably linked.

The van conversion project offers a radically novel and productive context to explore questions regarding ongoing developments along the trajectory of research leading from ubiquitous computing [1] towards smart home research [14] and the IoT in the home [5]. As an extension of visions of ubiquitous computing [6], the IoT promises to reconfigure our everyday environments by sensing the world around us and providing connectivity to and between things, buildings, the city and beyond, our social network, and our own body [5]. Building on and extending ideas that emerged from ubiquitous and pervasive computing, the IoT also imagines how computation will continue to shift away from the desktop to becoming part of and disappear into the physical environment we inhabit, from graspable things to using architectural surfaces as active surfaces for computation [1]. As we describe later, the van conversion project is a unique example for how people can reconfigure a whole environment, its furniture, and its artifacts; *and live in it*. This project allows us to understand how all aspects of a reconfiguration are connected, and provides a strong starting point for reflecting on the current trajectory of the integration of technologies in the home.

For those who are advocates of IoT, there are still challenges for a widespread adoption. For instance, De Roeck et al. state: "in order for the IoT to really take off, end-users need to participate in the creation process on a larger scale. They need to have the power and control over the creation and use of applications for smart environments." [20:170]. As computing becomes more entangled with the things we live with and the places we dwell in, it also has the challenge of becoming highly unique, personal, and multifaceted to fit each of our lives. Proposed solutions include end-user development [28] and a do-it-yourself (DIY) approach [20] to allow users to take control over how, when and why they will integrate IoT 'things' in their lives.

Both end-user development and DIY are approaches that see people as being creators and designers instead of consumers or users [35]. The van conversion project offers a deep look into a DIY approach where people have become creators and makers. With this single case of autobiographical design, we are able to dive into details of how a complete environment is designed and made, and how the makers have lived with this space for almost two years. Although the camper van is not primarily a technological environment, nor an IoT project, it has the benefit of being easily customizable and transformable, and existing accessible tools and materials can seamlessly be used in the van conversion. The design conception and the physical transformations in the van could not have attained the same level of richness, fluidity, and detail compared to an existing technological environment or IoT system. This is mostly due to the nascent state of such systems, which currently do not sufficiently support off the shelf customization, adaptation, and transformation. We turn to the van conversion project as an illustration of a space that already encourages maker/user[1] practices as a way to investigate the complex, personal and evolving relationship that exists between the maker/user and the designed artifact or environment. This project opens a critical and reflective space for examining domestic technologies. In particular it can bring into focus qualities that may be overlooked in a more technocentric view of technology in the home. Our goal in this paper is to expand and provide details for future IoT for the home from both autobiographical researcher and maker/user perspectives.

In this paper we investigate making in an everyday context, particularly how makers live with the things they make over time. In this manner, we not only look at how one object is created or transformed, but also how it relates to other objects in the environment. Specifically, we ask the questions: *What can we learn from the evolving relationship between the maker/user and the designed lived in environment?* and *What critical perspective does the van conversion project offer on the current trajectory of the integration of technology in the home?*

[1] Throughout the paper, we use the term maker/user to refer to the people who simultaneously design and build a new artifact, system, or environment by creatively and resourcefully using materials and tools; and live with the designed artifact, system, or environment over long periods of time.

Our contribution to the human-computer interaction (HCI) community is two-fold. Firstly, we offer a description of six qualities of the relationship between the user/maker and the lived-in environment. This has specific implications for future research and design in the area of the IoT and computing environments like smart homes. Our second contribution is presented in our discussion: a reflection on the current trajectories of technologies in the home under three themes: living *in* a reconfigured home, prototype qualities in a reconfigured space, and the invariably unfinished nature of the home.

BACKGROUND

Before we present the van conversion project, we provide an overview of previous HCI related research that has investigated how everyday people and makers reconfigure their own spaces and environments. The ways in which people have engaged in those transformations range from being mundane, tacit, and unremarkable to being at the center of DIY and maker practices.

Everyday reconfigurations of the home

HCI and interaction design research has been interested in understanding people's routines and organization strategies in their most intimate space: the home (e.g. [10,19,25,27,29]). In those studies, researchers often found unique and personal practices where people reconfigure the space around them, including the artifacts within it, to fit their family's needs and activities. An important insight from these studies is that the systems created by families are often only intelligible to themselves and are so well integrated into routines that they often become invisible or unremarkable [29]. The study of everyday design [34] investigates the incremental and ongoing processes of living with design artifacts in the home, and particularly how people may creatively and resourcefully adapt or transform them to better fit their everyday routines and needs. The work on everyday design highlights that systems in the home are often heterogeneous, unique, dynamic, and personalized. This echoes findings by Taylor and Swan [27] who also bring attention to the lived experiences in the home and the material properties of artifacts in households. Collectively, this work emphasizes how design and making are ongoing processes that are part of everyday routines, how the material aspect of those practices are central to their working, and how everyone can be a designer and maker.

The study of mundane and tacit design coincides with the description of unselfconscious cultures described by architect Christopher Alexander [3]. In unselfconscious cultures, design and architecture are not professions, but rather something that is performed by everyone, following the traditions of family and ancestors. In those cultures, design is an integral part of everyday life, where small fixes and changes are performed in an ongoing manner as a way to reach a better design (or a goodness of fit between what is designed and the context). In [32], Wakkary et al. revisit characteristics of unselfconscious cultures and present the conceptual construct of unselfconscious interaction, a form of interaction that enables ongoing and incremental engagements with an everyday setting, leading to goodness of fit. A supporting notion to the construct is the quality of *lived-with*: the idea that it takes time for those interactions to emerge and take place, and that it is through co-inhabiting with artifacts that home dwellers can eventually see them as resources for further design action.

The analysis we present in this paper builds on this previous research. While the major design acts in the van conversion project are not tacit, unselfconscious, or mundane (they are rather in the realm of DIY practices, as we describe in the next section), some qualities of ongoing design processes and the long-term relationship between the maker and the environment as described here are central to what we have observed in the van.

Do-it-yourself reconfigurations of the home

Do-it-yourself (DIY) enthusiasts and makers share the common practices of designing, appropriating, and transforming existing products to better fit their own needs, lifestyle, or aesthetic tastes. Makers have been of interest to HCI for the alternative and critique to mass production and consumerism of personal technologies they provide (e.g. [2]). In addition, the study of makers has provoked deep reflections on the ways they expand both the definition of the user [35] and the definition of the designer [33]. In this paper, we refer to maker/users: a term that invites the reader to consider a user to be simultaneously using and making (or remaking) an artifact or a space, hence combining the two actions into a unique identity.

More specifically, studies of maker and DIY cultures push the boundaries of our understanding of the relationship between people and design artifacts and technologies by foregrounding themes such as identity, empowerment, creativity, and resourcefulness. In the past years, the HCI community has been studying maker individuals and communities to gain insight about how to create interactive technologies that better support their design and making practices (e.g. [15,17,21,26,36]) as well as to gain inspiration for designing future personal technologies. While DIY and maker ideologies aspire to inclusion and technology democratization [26], we wish to highlight the distinction between the types of reconfigurations that 'everyone' can do in the everyday (as presented in the section above) and more involved reconfigurations performed by makers or DIY enthusiasts [4,30], as illustrated in our van conversion project.

True to its origins in home improvement [24], DIY has been investigated in the context of smart home and home automation, and more recently as an approach to IoT in the home. In those contexts, DIY is not only about the reconfiguration of artifacts, but also spaces and environments. Dautriche et al. [11] champion the idea of bringing end-user development to smart home systems. In this way, they argue that people will have more control and will be able to create and adjust the system to their own needs. Commercially available systems like Twine [38] and Ninjablocks [39] are DIY kits that allow people to install sensors and actuators around their house and to program rules to activate them. Woo and Lim [37] have studied how people use these DIY kits for home automation in a three-week deployment study. They describe the usage cycle as follows: "*initial installation*, *motivation*, *implementation*, *use-through-routine*, *routinization*, and *removal*" [37:783]. In addition to DIY kits, we see in Casa Jasmina [40], a project by Arduino, an example of a house designed to be open source, connected, and part of the IoT. With this project, the team hopes to see how people can live within a space that encourages the making of artifacts that will become part of the home. These recent examples show that there is interest in incorporating a DIY approach to smart homes and other environments.

Through this brief literature review of HCI research on everyday and DIY reconfigurations of home, we have highlighted how people actively, sometimes tacitly, engage in the adaptation and transformation of their own artifacts and dwellings over time. This research foregrounds the role people have in shaping their environment to better fit their identities and needs. However, as Verbeek [31], a philosopher of technology, has articulated: those artifacts and technologies also have an impact and a role in mediating between people and their actions in the world. In this paper, we are interested in understanding the qualities of this two-way, co-shaping relationship between what is being made and the maker/users.

OUR STUDY

Our goal with this paper is to investigate what it is like to live in a reconfigured space for the maker/user. More specifically, we want to understand what are the qualities of the relationship between the maker/user and the design artifact that is built and lived in.

We want to note here that while this paper is a collaborative effort with multiple authors, Desjardins and Wakkary, the latter author did not participate in the van conversion. Further, Bérubé Lebrun, Desjardins' partner, participated in the van conversion and autobiographical design but is not an author or researcher in this paper. Despite these multiple and different contributions, we decided to use the authorial voice "we" to refer to both authors and participants. We feel justified in this approach since the first author, whose contributions we rely on the most in this paper, is both author and autobiographical design participant. This allows us to adhere to our methodological commitment to autobiographical design research (see Methodology) in which we report in the first-person perspective (in our case in the plural form), and acknowledges the fluidity of insights that occur during the experience of the autobiographical design by participants and on further reflection by participants and researchers.

The Van conversion project

This study reports on the first twenty-three months of building and living in the converted van. This is a project the first author Desjardins and her partner Bérubé LeBrun started alongside their day time jobs: Desjardins is an interaction design researcher trained in industrial design and Bérubé Lebrun is a landscape architect with eight years of professional experience and woodworking skills. The maker/users in this case have had extensive design training, which distinguishes them from non-expert designers.

We bought a Sprinter van in October 2013 with the intention of converting it into a camper van for camping and ski trips. The van was new with nothing else in it other than the driver and passenger seats. The walls were not finished; they were the bare metal sheets. The back of the van represented a space of approximately 6 feet wide by 10 feet long by 6 feet tall. The complete van conversion was planned over five years with different stages such as adding a complete kitchen unit, electricity, water, solar panels, etc. Each stage includes breaks that allow us to live in the van and go skiing, mountain biking, or camping; however small changes, additions, and repairs are ongoing, even while traveling with the van. To date, the van has been through four major building stages: insulating the walls, creating a back platform for storage, finishing the walls with cedar tongue-and-groove panels, and building a unit that serves as benches and a table that converts to a bed (see figure 1).

The van conversion autobiographical design project potentially offers deep insights into how a maker/user builds and lives in a delimited environment. We chose this case because we were able to follow each step as it occurred, from buying the van to the most recent build and trip. In addition, the van offers a circumscribed area where all the transformations and living occur. This enclosed, contained environment accentuates characteristics of living in a prototype over time. Although the van conversion project may share similarities to home improvement or home renovation projects, we note that a home is rarely renovated as a whole while people live in it. Finally, the van also allowed us to observe not only aesthetic transformations, but also functional and technical adaptations, such as the storage platform, the installation of a new radio and speakers, and reflections on the electrical system of the van. We reiterate here that we believe the van is a useful case to study as a way to understand the deeply personal and rich practice of maker/users in environments.

Methodology

The conversion of this van was never intended to be research; it was meant to be the process before we were ready to hit the road and travel, camp, ski, and bike. However, this project offers a rare opportunity to take an in-depth look at how people live with (and in) the things they make. It allows us to extract many of the sensibilities and nuances of the intertwined processes of making and living, and to identify qualities of the relationship that exists between the maker and the thing that is made. As the project moved forward, it became clear that it was revealing and illustrating issues and matters of concern that were relevant to HCI research. Hence, we use an autobiographical design approach to present those insights in this paper.

Autobiographical design is defined as "design research drawing on extensive, genuine usage by those creating or building the system" [18:514]. Neustaedter and Sengers [18] argue that successful autobiographical design needs to fulfill a genuine need, the system needs to be lived with over a long period of time, and the designer needs to be the user of the system. All those criteria are fulfilled with the van conversion project. Neustaedter and Sengers' study shows that this type of design research can support fast

Figure 1. Building steps: From top left: the empty van; step 1 – wall insulation; step 2 – back storage platform; step 3 – wall finishing with cedar panels; step 4: benches-table-bed unit in a) table position, b) bed position.

tinkering, requires and tests real systems beyond concepts, can provide detailed and experiential understanding of the system, and reveals the big effects of a system. Interestingly, in our view, the autobiographical designer is by definition a maker/user as well, because he or she embodies both the making aspect as well as the living with aspect of the maker/user.

Autobiographical design offers a lot of potential for studying complex, long-term, personal situations, such as the practices of maker/users in lived environments [12]. In addition, it allows us to gain insights into the making and design aspect of the van conversion, as well as the iterative experience of living with it over time.

Data collection

As Neustaedter and Sengers state, record keeping and data collection are unusual in autobiographical design [18], since projects are often not seen as research projects while they are being made or used. The van project conversion is an exception. We had an extensive process for gathering data about the fabrication of the van, the different steps of making, and about living in the van as well. The data gathered was not aimed at generating a research account, but rather to create documentation about the design process to share with other DIY enthusiasts and the community invested in converting campervans. The data gathered included:

- Tutorials on the Instructables web platform for each important fabrication stage. Tutorials were created for the wall insulation, the construction of a storage platform, the finishing of the walls with cedar panels, the construction of benches and a table that convert into a bed, and the making of cushions for the benches and bed.[2] The tutorials have received between 33,000 and 178,000 views to date.
- The Instructables tutorials required photos of each step in the making, including tools and materials. Those photos also show the finished product at each step.
- Within the Instructables tutorials were also added timelapse videos[3] of each day of building. Photos were taken every 30 seconds and then assembled to make short videos. There are a total of 17 videos to date.
- The Instructables tutorials also hold a record of readers' comments and questions, and the authors' answers (total of 169 comments and replies to date). Questions often led to reflections on design decisions and current living practices in the van.
- Short diary logs that record the dates, places, and important events of the trips made in the van.
- Photos of the van's interior while on trips, focusing on different activities like cooking, eating, playing games, sleeping, and getting ready for outdoor activities.
- Blog post of some of the trips on the site www.go-van.com as travel reports.

Data analysis

The data was organized by creating a thematic analysis that grouped data points following how they characterized and qualified the relationship between the maker/user and the environment of the van. Themes such as intimacy, shaping the maker, dialogue, arguing, taking care of, getting to know you, knowing you too much, dreaming up a future, pride, and timing were developed. In a second analysis iteration, those themes were revisited and some were combined into six qualities of living in a prototype, as presented in the following section.

QUALITIES OF LIVING IN A PROTOTYPE

In this section, we describe qualities, or characteristics, of living in a prototype. These qualities emerged during the process of making/using but concretized in later reflections and analysis of the experience and data. Those qualities describe the intimate relationship that has taken shape between the maker/users and the prototype, or in this case, between Desjardins and Bérubé Lebrun and the van as it is being converted.

Reciprocal shaping

In a long-term personal project, we have observed that not only the project changes over time, but we change as well. We call this quality of the relationship between the maker/users and the environment: *reciprocal shaping*. This is not far from the idea of reflective conversation, first theorized by Schön [22], but goes beyond the observation that materials may have a say in how they are formed and shaped. In the case of the van project, we have noticed that by living in the van as it is constructed, we have changed our expectations for what a van is (or should be), and our predicted or expected needs.

Firstly, we observed how our bodies (dimensions and flexibility) dramatically influenced how things were designed in the van. For example, when shopping for the van and doing a road test, we stopped the van and lay on the floor in different positions to imagine how the bed could be positioned. Later in the process, we also followed our personal bodily dimensions to balance the height and depth of the benches and table on the back platform. Decisions were made based on physical comfort, and it is important to note that in this case comfort was defined accordingly to the only two users who would live in this van.

Simultaneously, as we made decisions about how to build the van, the van itself gave hints and suggestions for how to build the next steps. By slowly designing and adding

---

[2] http://www.instructables.com/id/How-to-insulate-a-camper-van/
http://www.instructables.com/id/Storage-platform-for-the-back-of-your-Sprinter-van/
http://www.instructables.com/id/Cedar-paneling-for-van-interior/
http://www.instructables.com/id/Bed-Table-and-Benches-for-camper-van-All-in-one/
http://www.instructables.com/id/How-to-sew-cushions-for-a-camper-van/

[3] https://vimeo.com/album/2607513

Figure 2. Evolution of the furniture.

different parts to the environment we were living in, the time allowed for reflections on our needs. We started this project with expectations and ideas of what a converted van was and how it resembled a small recreational vehicle (RV). For example, for both of us, it was clear that the van would eventually need electricity through a secondary electric system to support lighting and a fridge. However, as a convenient solution while waiting for the time and resources to install an electrical system, we developed alternative strategies to support our electric needs such as small portable solar panels, rechargeable batteries, and a camping cooler for the food. After almost two years of living with the 'alternative' system, we realized that electricity (in the form we had envisioned) might not be necessary anymore. The realization that having less than expected might work better for us occurred only because we lived in the van over a long period of time, in a manner we had not imagined. The luxury of having time to deeply know our needs influenced greatly how the rest of the van was built.

Intimate knowledge and intimate frustration

The quality of *intimate knowledge and intimate frustration* refers to the deep personal connection we have with the van. It is a strong relationship and a profound understanding for how things are in the van. For example, when driving, we can hear different sounds like creaking and rattling depending on how things are positioned in the van. However these sounds vary with the temperature and the weather (heat and humidity make wood and metal expand and shrink at different rates). After twenty-three months of building, living, and driving in the van, we have learned where these noises come from, and we now know how to make them stop by rearranging objects in some cases.

However, with intimacy can also come frustration. As much as we know where the sounds come from when driving the van, there are some noises we know cannot be changed, since they are related to how the van was built, particularly how different sections are connected together (such as the storage platform and where it touches the cedar panel walls). Since the project follows a trial and error process, we are able to adjust the next steps in building to reduce noises, however for some noises it is impossible to go back and make adjustments now. In a way, the earlier builds served as prototypes for future builds where we were able to adjust the technique based on previous mistakes, and to share it with others through our Instructables tutorial:

"Also, ***more importantly****, we left at least a 1/4 inch between the benches and the walls. From our previous experience with the platform and the cedar walls, if things are too close together but not attached together, there is so much creaking and rubbing noises when we drive that it can drive us crazy! For the same reason, we also added small felt auto-adhesive pads between the side benches and the back bench, to prevent them from being too close together."*[4]

The intimate frustration is accentuated when we share our concerns with others who do not have the same intimate knowledge of the van. For example, after the first winter, the side door started to make more creaking noises when driving. These noises were quite specific, but they were happening at the same time as other noises were produced from the platform touching the cedar panel walls. We brought the van back to the van dealership to have the door checked. After two test runs, the mechanics still concluded that the noise was only coming from the wood platform and walls that were added. It was impossible to show or communicate the noise that we had heard.

Intimacy is also about developing routines for camping in the van that are gained over time. For example, knowledge for how to pack the van or knowledge for how to be most efficient when cooking comes from multiple days of living in the van. These are hard things to share with others who have not lived in the van, even if explained in words or with demonstrations. For example, on a weekend trip, one of our friends from out of town shared the van with us. Although we managed to do everything we needed to accomplish, things needed to be verbalized and explained with patience. This revealed the deep intimacy that is shared only between us and the van, something that is often invisible to the eyes of others.

Renewed novelty

The quality of *renewed novelty* describes the sensation of novelty experienced whenever a change is made in the van. This is a similar feeling to getting accustomed to a new piece of furniture in a home or the freshly painted walls of a room in a different color.

[4] http://www.instructables.com/id/Bed-Table-and-Benches-for-camper-van-All-in-one/

Renewed novelty was felt the strongest after making important changes to the van, such as adding the storage platform, finishing the walls, and adding the benches and table (see figure 2). In such cases, we had worked for a very long time on the making of each step before trying the results out. This meant that for two or three weekends in a row, we had been focusing on the making rather than the living in the prototype. Once a step was concluded, a palpable excitement was felt as we planned a weekend trip to try it out. Each first time living in the van again was also a rediscovery of the van itself, or perhaps it was a different version or iteration of the van.

Moreover, we noted that this sensation of renewed novelty was not only experienced with large changes, but also with small subtle additions to the van. The intimate knowledge of the van, as described earlier, is deeply tacit and any small change has an important effect on how we felt about the van. For example, in January 2015, more than one year after starting the conversion, we installed two hooks on the ceiling on the van to allow for hanging a light and its wire. Even though lights had been used and positioned in various places in the van previously, this slight change created a new feeling, one that was more homey, and that expressed how much more settled we were in the van at this point. That small change also transformed how other activities were performed, such as cooking, eating and hanging out.

After each incremental improvement, in addition to the feeling of accomplishment, we also found ourselves dreaming about the next building stages almost as soon as we tried current versions of the van. This imaginative process was catalyzed and supported by the now existing newly added pieces to the van. Instead of envisioning multiple steps ahead, the current version of the van offered a strong anchor to explore possibilities of future design and builds. This finding echoes recent literature on prototypes that argue that the value of the prototypes lies in how it manifests a design idea [16].

Ownership and change

One of the main qualities of our relationship to the van is ownership. Ownership influences how we manage and deal with changes in the van over time. Contrary to most research artifacts deployed in field studies, the van is something that we own. Knowing that the van cannot be returned to the store after its transformation provides a sense of freedom, while also adding more responsibilities. For instance, ownership has an important influence on the choice of the materials, the quality of the materials, the attention to the craftsmanship and detail that is put into making the different changes in the van. As we were making decisions about what material to use to finish the walls, we knew that this was going to be a main feature and would be value-added to the van. Even though tongue-and-groove cedar panels were a good choice for durability, sustainability and style, they were not an easy choice in terms of installation or price. We needed to drill into the metal frame of the van to install wood studs before nailing the cedar panels into place. Regardless, we were thoughtful when planning how we would install the cedar panels, made a small set of test pieces, and then spent over 25 hours installing the panels.

As owners, we also made decisions about how permanently or temporarily certain elements should be installed in the van. A balance between how committed we are about a change, the ease to install and uninstall, and the time and monetary resources has to be found before a change is made in the van. For example, with the cedar paneling, even though the installation was complicated and time consuming, the final result is intended to stay for the life of the van. The motivation to have beautiful and well-made walls was strong enough to encourage us to put the effort and time into crafting them purposefully and to think through all of the fabrication details.

Yet, in some cases, temporary solutions needed to be installed in the van to support important activities. For instance, a simple kitchen unit was necessary since the first trips to be able to prepare meals in the van when it is too cold or rainy outside. Before putting the time and effort into building a kitchen unit fully furnished with stove, fridge and sink, we wanted a temporary solution that would give us time to live in the van before making any decisions. We bought a pre-made simple kitchen unit (with 3 shelves and a counter top) from a large retail store (see figure 3). We simply used c-clamps and attached the unit's posts to the wall and floor with screws. This simple solution works well as a temporary solution, but also as a 'sketch' for what we could build when they create the 'real' kitchen unit.

In terms of ownership and the various versions of elements in the van, the van is not a traditional prototype, one that stands as a representation of something to be made in the future. Some decisions lead to permanent installations, which, in turn, influence how future elements are designed. At the same time, it seems also evident to 'prototype' within the van, to try elements of the future design, as exemplified by the kitchen unit. We return to the question of sketching and prototyping in the discussion section.

Figure 3. Kitchen unit as a temporary solution. (Left) as it was firstly installed, and (right) after the walls were finished.

Care and trust

The qualities of *care and trust* in the relationship between the prototype and the maker/users are strong underlying ties that take time to grow. Care included maintenance of the van, such as changing summer tires to winter tires, changing burned lights, and retouching the paint of the hood for rock chips. In this sense, we see maintenance as part of how we care for the van, similarly to how Gaver attended rapidly to a repair he needed to do on the Video Window [13] (another example of autobiographical design). Care was also about how we treat the van on the road, for example by being very cautious on backcountry roads that can be rocky, steep and snowy. When taking a challenging route, we felt proud when the van was able to transport them without any problems. By constantly driving the van, a sense of trust developed, the trust that the van can 'take it' and that it is possible to explore with it further and faster.

Trust also developed in and about ourselves. We learned how to secure and attach things to the van, how to build things in the most efficient and safe ways. Since this project is the first one both of us have ever done of this type, we needed to build trust in ourselves and with each other that we had the proper skills to transform the van the way we wanted. The first time we drilled in the van walls to install studs to support the cedar panels, it was a stressful moment, but we eventually realized that our technique was working and we could move along with the process. This trust in our own skills also relates back to the quality of *ownership and change* since the care for the van goes hand in hand with the sense of responsibility present with ownership. Care was also demonstrated when we wanted to make important changes to the van but did not believe we had the proper skills, such as cutting metal to add windows to the doors or a fan to the ceiling. In such cases, we hired professional help specialized in camper conversions to do the job. This is an example where the care for the van was strong enough to push us to seek external help.

Trust in our own skills was also assessed when writing the tutorials online. We were aware that we are amateurs and wanted to make sure readers of the tutorials did not take us for professionals. This is illustrated in the disclaimer that we added at the beginning of each tutorial:

Figure 4. Laser cut paper deer head and watercolor of the cabin that inspired the van conversion project.

"*DISCLAIMER: This is the first van conversion we are doing, so this is certainly a process of trial and error! We tried to describe at every step the reasons why we made the material choices we made, so hopefully you can see that we used common sense to design this process. I am an industrial designer and design researcher and my boyfriend is a landscape architect with some knowledge in wood working. We see this project as an experiment and as a wonderful place to try out some ideas about design, materials and fabrication.*"[5]

Growing uniqueness

The quality of *growing uniqueness* highlights how, as the prototype becomes more and more unique to the maker/users, it also becomes less and less suitable for any other users. The ongoing process of living and making in the van, augmented by the quality of *reciprocal shaping*, has led to a nuanced and detailed understanding of how to build for usability and functionality in the van. Similar to what has been observed in everyday design [34], systems used in the van are often only intelligible and make sense fully to its inhabitants. For example, every object has its own place in the storage bins and areas. These positions have been developed over time, based on space, size, but also on how noisy things are when driving, and when and how or when each thing has to be used in the van.

In addition to finely adjusted functionality, we are also designing for our own aesthetic taste, influenced by places we have lived in before, places we have visited, and our own preferences. In the case of the van, we had rented a small blue A-Frame cabin for 2 winters before buying the van. This A-frame was our ideal of what a cabin in the woods should be: cozy, filled with wood and with the smell of cedar. Our experience in that cabin, along with the memories it carries, was the inspiration for many decisions in the van, including the warm materials like cedar panel walls, the plaid curtains and cushions, as well as the wooden table. For example, this is how we presented the cedar panel step in the Instructables tutorial:

"*We love skiing. We love mountain life. We love the feel of rustic cabins. We love the smell of cedar. We wanted a real cabin on wheels. This means there was only one material we wanted to use for the walls and ceiling of the van: CEDAR PANELS!*"[6]

In addition, decorative elements such as a paper laser cut deer head and a watercolor painting of the initial blue A-frame cabin were added to the walls (figure 4). Although these elements can be visually appreciated by others, their real significance is only felt by us.

Six qualities of living in a prototype

The six qualities described above are unique to this autobiographical design project and were rarely pointed at

[5] http://www.instructables.com/id/How-to-insulate-a-camper-van/

[6] http://www.instructables.com/id/Cedar-paneling-for-van-interior/

in previous literature on smart homes or the IoT for the home. For us, this gap indicates an opportunity for future research in HCI, where researchers can use these qualities as lenses to orient their designs. The six qualities as a group highlight themes such as designing for and supporting household uniqueness, enhancing a sense of self and at the same time a sense of responsibility towards the space, and finally acknowledging how small and subtle changes in the space can have important and big impacts on the ways of living in the space. In addition, those six qualities speak to the maker/user *in a space* rather than *with* artifacts in isolation. The findings of this paper make clear the kind of qualities such a relation can have and this contributes to a reframing of discussions in the trajectory of the design of technology in the home, from ubicomp, to smart environments, to IoT, as we will outline below.

DISCUSSION

In this section, we use the six qualities of the relationship between the maker/user and the lived in environment to reflect on how the van project can support and move forward the research fields of IoT and smart home. With this discussion, we answer our first research question: *What can we learn from the evolving relationship between the maker/user and the designed lived in environment?* We present our reflection under the two themes of living *in* a reconfigured space and championing the prototype qualities of a reconfigured space.

While we see the potential and promise of IoT, the simple, slow, and piecemeal design process of the van can also trigger more critical reflections on the current trajectory of the design of technologies for the home. With these reflections, we address our second research question: *What critical perspective does the van conversion project offer on the current trajectory of the integration of technology in the home?* Our critical reflective view is articulated under the theme of the invariably unfinished nature of the home.

Living *in* a reconfigured home

Our understanding of the complex relations and connections existing between things and the environment of the van offers a constructive anchor to reflect on the evolving visions along the trajectory from ubicomp, to smart home design and IoT. We bring specific attention to the physical immersion in the space and the long-term engagement within the space.

Physical immersion

Living in a prototype means to be surrounded by the project, to be physically immersed in the thing that is being designed and built. This particularity transforms the maker/user's perspective by providing constant cues, no matter where he or she is looking, for what could be improved, changed, redesigned, or crafted in a better fashion. This sensation that everything could be changed is supported by the ability to control, conceive and build all aspects of the lived in environment. For instance, in the van we aimed at creating an overarching aesthetic, across the ensemble of different elements added. Similarly, functional relations between things are also central to living and building the prototype, with a particular focus on how things work together and how to prevent interference between things (e.g. the creaking noises in the van).

The current IoT discourse aims to connect things to things but often neglects to account for the broader lived-in environment where those things are situated. The immersive physical experience of living in the van suggests that while interaction designers certainly design the relation between computational things, they should also pay particular attention to their relation to the environment and other systems and non-computational things already in place.

Temporality

In addition, we see implications in terms of temporality and the long-term making, using and living cycles in the van. This particularly long design process (the van conversion project was planned over a five-year designing and building process) diverges importantly from the fast pace user-centered design model that is commonly used and reported on in HCI research. The scale of time allows for a different relationship to the project and for a rich co-shaping between the van and the maker/users to emerge.

As we described in the *reciprocal shaping* quality, the capacity to have time to live with multiple versions of the van before making decisions about next building stages is a luxury that is rare in the practice of design. By living with the prototype, and by reevaluating our needs, we, as the maker/users, are able to know exactly what we want to build, find the proper materials and tools, and then build it in unique self-determined ways. The time spent in the prototype also enables us, the maker/users, to become accustomed to it and to grow and nurture intimacy as versions of the van accumulate and change through incremental adaptations and reflections. It is the temporal aspect of living in a prototype that creates the relationship for the sensibility on what changes to make in the van. It is precisely this constant back and forth between living and making over time that makes the maker/user such an expert in designing a space for him or herself.

The long term and slow incremental process of living and making in the van suggests that time can allow for a deeper relationship to form with the reconfigured space. This is an interesting reflection that proposes that future IoT development should also support a longer temporal scale and allow for maker/users to engage and re-engage over time with the artifacts and systems created.

Prototype qualities in a reconfigured space

Throughout this paper, we have referred to the van as a space, an environment, and as a prototype. Even though the van is not a 'prototype' in the common definition of the term (it is not a version of another van that might exist in the future [8]), we have observed many similarities to qualities of prototypes and prototyping activities that allow us to rethink future developments in IoT for the home.

Firstly, the van, at every stage of the construction, is a manifestation of a design idea [16]. We saw that through its presence and existence, the van dramatically influences how we made and used it, as illustrated by the quality of *ownership and change*. However, the van is not a single artifact, it is a combination of a space, furniture, and artifacts, and each designed thing in the van can attain different levels of refinement, between roughly sketched ideas to polished details. This combination is rich in contrast and can also serve as a point of friction to spark new ideas, new iterations, and future designs in the designed environment. The van conversion project is a productive example of how prototypes (or sections of prototypes) can serve as filters [16] to focus on specific design elements of a larger project that can be iterated on, manipulated, widely explored and even polished, while still ignoring other unfinished details in the space.

Secondly, even though the van might not be a prototype in the traditional sense of the term, it is interesting to consider how prototyping or sketching activities occurred in the van. Examples include the pre-manufactured kitchen unit as a simple, cheap, and straightforward way to prototype a future kitchen, the quick and dirty enactments for our sleep positions in the van and an improvised solution for curtains while on trips as the start of a series of improvements. Through these examples, we noted how the level of craftsmanship varied depending on how 'sketched' an element was or not. Hence, when we knew an element would be changed eventually, we spent less time, energy, and care in giving it a high level of finish.

Our reflection on prototype qualities in the van conversion project reiterate the identity of maker/users, an identity that embraces roles beyond use and customization, to create a substantial role for an evolving design process within the space. We see an opportunity for future IoT research to support better prototyping activities with connected artifacts and spaces.

The invariably unfinished home

Our critical reflection on the current trajectory of the integration of technology in the home centers on the idea of unfinishedness: the notion that a lived in space (or parts of that space) might never attain a high level of finish. Similar to the common understanding that home improvements are never finished, we saw in the van conversion project a clear illustration of how it is part of the nature of living in a reconfigured space to want to continuously change and incrementally adapt to everyday living practices. This echoes the findings in early studies of home life (e.g. [9,25,27,34]). The notion of unfinishedness allows us to start to paint a new picture for what IoT systems and artifacts might be in the future that challenges current visions. By accepting unfinishedness, this new picture welcomes and creates space for the maker/user who has agency in the creation of the unique space of his or her home.

As we presented in the last section, the van project allows us to think about the reconfiguration of the home to include various ongoing stages of prototyping. It also showed how the prototyped and unfinished sections of the van became part of the everyday and how we, as maker/users, became familiar to the various levels of finish in the van. At the same time, this ability to grow accustomed to the prototype could eclipse unfinished details, missing parts, and even inconvenient parts of the design. Through exposing unfinished elements and by embracing an unfinished aesthetic in the van, we as the maker/users set the scene to allow for a unique and deeper relationship with the space to emerge. Similarly to how unfinished design can invite more creativity on the part of end-users (as suggested in [23]), we can imagine how championing unfinished smart homes and IoT systems can support better maker/user practices. Overall, this suggests a more piecemeal, long-term, and incremental pace for introducing and implementing various elements of the IoT in home dwellers' spaces.

CONCLUSION

By building on the autobiographical design project of converting a van into a camper van, we presented six qualities of the maker/user's relationship with a lived in prototype. This work deepens our understanding of maker/user practices in general, but more importantly sheds light on how maker/users reconfigure their dwellings. We see this work to be in line with broader ongoing initiatives in the HCI community to move beyond designing for usability and efficiency and towards leveraging and enabling the creativity that people might have with regards to their own practices of 'making home'.

Our reflection grounded in the van conversion project led to the two points of living in a reconfigured home and the prototype qualities in a reconfigured space. With this discussion, we see in our work a contrasting vision to smart home design and IoT developments with regards to the ways in which people (or rather maker/users) reconfigure their homes. As a final thought, we meditate on Bell and Dourish's [7] proposition that past visions of ubicomp and smart homes might not have materialized the way the HCI field has collectively imagined, and that future technologies for the home might never look or feel like those visions. Instead, for new visions and inspiration, we might need to turn to today's unfinished, sketched, simple, and rich instances of how people reconfigure their everyday environments around the complexities and nuances of everyday life.

ACKNOWLEDGMENTS

First, we want to thank Léandre Bérubé Lebrun since without him this converted van would not exist. This project is supported by the Social Sciences and Humanities Research Council of Canada (SSHRC).

REFERENCES

1. Gregory D. Abowd. 2012. What Next, Ubicomp?: Celebrating an Intellectual Disappearing Act. *Proceedings of the 2012 ACM Conference on Ubiquitous Computing*, ACM, 31–40. http://doi.org/10.1145/2370216.2370222
2. Binaebi Akah and Shaowen Bardzell. 2010. Empowering Products: Personal Identity Through the Act of Appropriation. *CHI '10 Extended Abstracts on Human Factors in Computing Systems*, ACM, 4021–4026. http://doi.org/10.1145/1753846.1754096
3. Christopher Alexander. 1964. *Notes on the Synthesis of Form*. Harvard University Press.
4. Morgan G. Ames, Jeffrey Bardzell, Shaowen Bardzell, Silvia Lindtner, David A. Mellis, and Daniela K. Rosner. 2014. Making Cultures: Empowerment, Participation, and Democracy - or Not? *CHI '14 Extended Abstracts on Human Factors in Computing Systems*, ACM, 1087–1092. http://doi.org/10.1145/2559206.2579405
5. Luigi Atzori, Antonio Iera, and Giacomo Morabito. 2010. The Internet of Things: A survey. *Computer Networks* 54, 15: 2787–2805. http://doi.org/10.1016/j.comnet.2010.05.010
6. Matthew P. Aylett and Aaron J. Quigley. 2015. The Broken Dream of Pervasive Sentient Ambient Calm Invisible Ubiquitous Computing. *Proceedings of the 33rd Annual ACM Conference Extended Abstracts on Human Factors in Computing Systems*, ACM, 425–435. http://doi.org/10.1145/2702613.2732508
7. Genevieve Bell and Paul Dourish. 2007. Yesterday's Tomorrows: Notes on Ubiquitous Computing's Dominant Vision. *Personal Ubiquitous Comput.* 11, 2: 133–143. http://doi.org/10.1007/s00779-006-0071-x
8. Marion Buchenau and Jane Fulton Suri. 2000. Experience Prototyping. *Proceedings of the 3rd Conference on Designing Interactive Systems: Processes, Practices, Methods, and Techniques*, ACM, 424–433. http://doi.org/10.1145/347642.347802
9. Andy Crabtree and Tom Rodden. 2004. Domestic Routines and Design for the Home. *Computer Supported Cooperative Work (CSCW)* 13, 2: 191–220. http://doi.org/10.1023/B:COSU.0000045712.26840.a4
10. Andy Crabtree, Tom Rodden, Terry Hemmings, and Steve Benford. 2003. Finding a Place for UbiComp in the Home. In *UbiComp 2003: Ubiquitous Computing*, Anind K. Dey, Albrecht Schmidt and Joseph F. McCarthy (eds.). Springer Berlin Heidelberg, 208–226. Retrieved February 14, 2014 from http://link.springer.com.proxy.lib.sfu.ca/chapter/10.1007/978-3-540-39653-6_17
11. Rémy Dautriche, Camille Lenoir, Alexandre Demeure, Cédric Gérard, Joëlle Coutaz, and Patrick Reignier. 2013. End-User-Development for Smart Homes: Relevance and Challenges. 6. Retrieved September 4, 2015 from https://hal.inria.fr/hal-00953369/document
12. Audrey Desjardins, Ron Wakkary, and William Odom. 2015. Investigating Genres and Perspectives in HCI Research on the Home. *Proceedings of the 33rd Annual ACM Conference on Human Factors in Computing Systems*, ACM, 3073–3082. http://doi.org/10.1145/2702123.2702540
13. W. Gaver. 2006. The Video Window: My Life with a Ludic System. *Personal Ubiquitous Comput.* 10, 2-3: 60–65. http://doi.org/10.1007/s00779-005-0002-2
14. Richard Harper (ed.). 2003. *Inside the smart home*. Springer, London ; New York.
15. Stacey Kuznetsov and Eric Paulos. 2010. Rise of the expert amateur: DIY projects, communities, and cultures. *Proceedings of the 6th Nordic Conference on Human-Computer Interaction: Extending Boundaries*, ACM, 295–304. http://doi.org/10.1145/1868914.1868950
16. Youn-Kyung Lim, Erik Stolterman, and Josh Tenenberg. 2008. The anatomy of prototypes: Prototypes as filters, prototypes as manifestations of design ideas. *ACM Trans. Comput.-Hum. Interact.* 15, 2: 7:1–7:27. http://doi.org/10.1145/1375761.1375762
17. Silvia Lindtner, Garnet D. Hertz, and Paul Dourish. 2014. Emerging Sites of HCI Innovation: Hackerspaces, Hardware Startups & Incubators. *Proceedings of the SIGCHI Conference on Human Factors in Computing Systems*, ACM, 439–448. http://doi.org/10.1145/2556288.2557132
18. Carman Neustaedter and Phoebe Sengers. 2012. Autobiographical Design in HCI Research: Designing and Learning Through Use-it-yourself. *Proceedings of the Designing Interactive Systems Conference*, ACM, 514–523. http://doi.org/10.1145/2317956.2318034
19. Jon O'Brien and Tom Rodden. 1997. Interactive Systems in Domestic Environments. *Proceedings of the 2Nd Conference on Designing Interactive Systems: Processes, Practices, Methods, and Techniques*, ACM, 247–259. http://doi.org/10.1145/263552.263617
20. Dries De Roeck, Karin Slegers, Johan Criel, et al. 2012. I Would DiYSE for It!: A Manifesto for Do-it-yourself Internet-of-things Creation. *Proceedings of the 7th Nordic Conference on Human-Computer Interaction: Making Sense Through Design*, ACM, 170–179. http://doi.org/10.1145/2399016.2399044
21. Daniela Rosner and Jonathan Bean. 2009. Learning from IKEA hacking: i'm not one to decoupage a tabletop and call it a day. *Proceedings of the SIGCHI Conference on Human Factors in Computing Systems*, ACM, 419–422. http://doi.org/10.1145/1518701.1518768

22. Donald A Schön. 1983. *The reflective practitioner: how professionals think in action*. Basic Books, New York.

23. Jin-min Seok, Jong-bum Woo, and Youn-kyung Lim. 2014. Non-finito Products: A New Design Space of User Creativity for Personal User Experience. *Proceedings of the SIGCHI Conference on Human Factors in Computing Systems*, ACM, 693–702. http://doi.org/10.1145/2556288.2557222

24. Elizabeth Shove, Matthew Watson, Martin Hand, and Jack Ingram. 2007. *The design of everyday life*. Berg, Oxford; New York.

25. Laurel Swan, Alex S. Taylor, and Richard Harper. 2008. Making Place for Clutter and Other Ideas of Home. *ACM Trans. Comput.-Hum. Interact.* 15, 2: 9:1–9:24. http://doi.org/10.1145/1375761.1375764

26. Joshua G. Tanenbaum, Amanda M. Williams, Audrey Desjardins, and Karen Tanenbaum. 2013. Democratizing Technology: Pleasure, Utility and Expressiveness in DIY and Maker Practice. *Proceedings of the SIGCHI Conference on Human Factors in Computing Systems*, ACM, 2603–2612. http://doi.org/10.1145/2470654.2481360

27. Alex S. Taylor and Laurel Swan. 2005. Artful systems in the home. *Proceedings of the SIGCHI Conference on Human Factors in Computing Systems*, ACM, 641–650. http://doi.org/10.1145/1054972.1055060

28. Daniel Tetteroo, Panos Markopoulos, Stefano Valtolina, Fabio Paternò, Volkmar Pipek, and Margaret Burnett. 2015. End-User Development in the Internet of Things Era. *Proceedings of the 33rd Annual ACM Conference Extended Abstracts on Human Factors in Computing Systems*, ACM, 2405–2408. http://doi.org/10.1145/2702613.2702643

29. Peter Tolmie, James Pycock, Tim Diggins, Allan MacLean, and Alain Karsenty. 2002. Unremarkable computing. *Proceedings of the SIGCHI Conference on Human Factors in Computing Systems*, ACM, 399–406. http://doi.org/10.1145/503376.503448

30. Austin L. Toombs, Shaowen Bardzell, and Jeffrey Bardzell. 2015. The Proper Care and Feeding of Hackerspaces: Care Ethics and Cultures of Making. *Proceedings of the 33rd Annual ACM Conference on Human Factors in Computing Systems*, ACM, 629–638. http://doi.org/10.1145/2702123.2702522

31. Peter-Paul Verbeek. 2005. *What Things Do: Philosophical Reflections on Technology, Agency, and Design*. Penn State Press.

32. Ron Wakkary, Audrey Desjardins, and Sabrina Hauser. 2015. Unselfconscious Interaction: A Conceptual Construct. *Interacting with Computers*: iwv018. http://doi.org/10.1093/iwc/iwv018

33. Ron Wakkary, Audrey Desjardins, Sabrina Hauser, and Leah Maestri. 2013. A sustainable design fiction: Green practices. *ACM Trans. Comput.-Hum. Interact.* 20, 4: 23:1–23:34. http://doi.org/10.1145/2494265

34. Ron Wakkary and Leah Maestri. 2007. The resourcefulness of everyday design. *Proceedings of the 6th ACM SIGCHI conference on Creativity & Cognition*, ACM, 163–172. http://doi.org/10.1145/1254960.1254984

35. Ron Wakkary and Karen Tanenbaum. 2009. A sustainable identity: the creativity of an everyday designer. *Proceedings of the SIGCHI Conference on Human Factors in Computing Systems*, ACM, 365–374. http://doi.org/10.1145/1518701.1518761

36. Tricia Wang and Joseph"Jofish" Kaye. 2011. Inventive leisure practices: understanding hacking communities as sites of sharing and innovation. *CHI '11 Extended Abstracts on Human Factors in Computing Systems*, ACM, 263–272. http://doi.org/10.1145/1979742.1979615

37. Jong-bum Woo and Youn-kyung Lim. 2015. User Experience in Do-it-yourself-style Smart Homes. *Proceedings of the 2015 ACM International Joint Conference on Pervasive and Ubiquitous Computing*, ACM, 779–790. http://doi.org/10.1145/2750858.2806063

38. Twine. Retrieved from http://supermechanical.com/twine/

39. NinjaBlocks. Retrieved from https://ninjablocks.com/

40. http://casajasmina.arduino.cc/. Retrieved September 2, 2015 from http://casajasmina.arduino.cc/

"Like Having a Really bad PA": The Gulf between User Expectation and Experience of Conversational Agents

Ewa Luger
Microsoft Research, UK
ewluge@microsoft.com

Abigail Sellen
Microsoft Research, UK
asellen@microsoft.com

ABSTRACT
The past four years have seen the rise of conversational agents (CAs) in everyday life. Apple, Microsoft, Amazon, Google and Facebook have all embedded proprietary CAs within their software and, increasingly, conversation is becoming a key mode of human-computer interaction. Whilst we have long been familiar with the notion of computers that speak, the investigative concern within HCI has been upon multimodality rather than dialogue alone, and there is no sense of how such interfaces are used in everyday life. This paper reports the findings of interviews with 14 users of CAs in an effort to understand the current interactional factors affecting everyday use. We find user expectations dramatically out of step with the operation of the systems, particularly in terms of known machine intelligence, system capability and goals. Using Norman's 'gulfs of execution and evaluation' [30] we consider the implications of these findings for the design of future systems.

Author Keywords
Conversational Agents; mental models; evaluation

ACM Classification Keywords
H.5.m. Information interfaces and presentation (e.g., HCI): Miscellaneous

INTRODUCTION
Framed as "dialogue systems often endowed with 'humanlike' behaviour" [43 p.357], conversational agents (CA) are becoming ever more common human-computer interfaces. The launch of Siri (Apple, 2011), Google Now (2012), Cortana (Microsoft, 2015), and Alexa (Amazon, 2015) indicate a spike in mainstream market commitment to this form of experience and, in a departure from their traditional services, even Facebook have thrown down the gauntlet by launching 'M'; a hybrid dialogue system that employs both artificial intelligence and human responses to task requests. Equally, such products are no longer solely tied to the handset. Both Siri and Cortana are now core components of their respective operating systems and Alexa finds its home in the form of Amazon Echo, giving us every reason to believe that spoken dialogue interfaces will become the future gateways to many key services.

CHI'16, May 07 - 12, 2016, San Jose, CA, USA

ACM 978-1-4503-3362-7/16/05...$15.00
DOI: http://dx.doi.org/10.1145/2858036.2858288

Whilst the past 4 years have clearly seen a reinvigoration of such systems, this is very much a return to an old idea; that conversation is the next natural form of HCI. It has also long been argued that "when speech and language interfaces become more conversational, they will take their place along with direct manipulation in the interface" [6]. Moreover, they will have the potential to enhance both the system usability and user experience [43]. However, despite these expectations, the weight of research has veered away from such single modalities and tended towards multimodal developments, with a focus upon embodiment and anthropomorphism rather than voice alone. Indeed, our fascination with computers that converse can be traced back as far as 1964 when, seeking to create the illusion of human interaction, Joseph Weizenbaum of MIT created Eliza [10], a computer program that responded on the basis of data gleaned only from human respondents' typed input. Whilst script-based, it is considered the first convincing attempt to simulate natural human interactions between a user and a computer. This chatterbot, rudimentary by today's standards, was designed in the form of a Rogerian psychotherapist and, due to the high level of emotional involvement exhibited by users, was hailed as the beginnings of an automated form of psychotherapy [45]. Fast-forward 50 years and, whilst psychotherapy-bots for the time being remain the stuff of science fiction, HCI is again seeing moves towards serious adoption of naturalistic human-computer dialogue systems.

However, despite tech giants vying to develop the most compelling experience, the field of HCI has developed little empirical knowledge of how such agents are used in everyday settings. Whilst CA research exists, it tends towards either technical papers related to architecture [37], CAs studied in experimental settings, or systems created for specific contexts, such as guiding users around a space [24], delivering information [41], or for the support of language learning [40]. Whilst each study brings us closer to understanding effective design, without concurrent knowledge of the pragmatics of everyday use, we fail to truly understand dynamics such as how and why such systems are used and "which factors influence acceptance and success in such scenarios" [24 p.329]. In light of this deficit, our paper seeks to understand user experience of CA systems by answering two simple questions; (a) what factors currently motivate and limit the ongoing use of CAs in everyday life, and (b) what should we consider in future design iterations? To this end we present the findings of 14 semi-structured interviews conducted with existing users of CA systems and, on the basis of our analysis, present four key areas where current systems fail to support effective user interaction.

PRIOR WORK

When considering human-machine dialogue from an HCI perspective, some of the earliest work can be traced back to vision statements and position papers such as JCR Licklider (1960), 'Man-machine symbiosis' [25] and the early work of Richard Bolt [4]. Whilst this work was visionary in nature, more recent studies have focussed around the development of CA systems for specific contexts or settings [24] with a preference towards multimodality, or embodiment, in order to more effectively simulate the nuances of human communication.

What is a conversational agent?

The notion of a humanlike virtual character has been framed and realised in many different ways. When using the term Conversational Agent, for example, one might think of a chatbot, virtual companion, "interface agent, embodied conversational agent, virtual assistant, autonomous agent, [or] avatar...often synonymously" [44 p.1641] and use these labels interchangeably, or so as to articulate particular subtle distinctions. In order to distinguish such terms more clearly, Wilks (2010) suggests a series of differentiating characteristics. From this perspective, CAs are distinct by their function; to carry out tasks. In contrast, "chatbots" have no memory or knowledge but instead mimic conversation; for example, Richard Wallace's Alice technology [1] or Microsoft's Xiaoice [13]. Digital companions on the other hand are not designed for any central or overriding tasks, have *long term* discourses and personal knowledge of the user, and are able to lay the foundations of a 'relationship' [47]. Although the emerging class of CAs may indeed have aspirations to become a user's artificial companion, their current functionality places them some way from realising this. In this paper we use the term 'Conversational Agent' to label the emergent form of dialogue system that is becoming increasingly embedded in personal technologies and devices. At a minimum, such spoken dialogue systems require "an automatic speech recognizer to perform speech to text conversion, some form of dialogue manager (controller) to control the interaction with the user, and a mechanism for conveying information to the user (e.g. text and/or speech generation" [15; 1]. These systems, whilst often accompanied by some form of graphic such as the Cortana ring or the wavy line that appears when Siri is activated, are not strictly speaking embodied. Neither is anthropomorphism their principal goal, nor is it to represent a specific person and as such they cannot be considered avatars. More accurately, these types of systems draw directly from the notion of the 'virtual/digital assistant', or 'virtual/digital butler' [32] in that their purpose is both support for real time task completion and to develop sufficient knowledge about the user in order to exert agency on their behalf. In this way, whilst they are not a 'companion', they might seek to exhibit a level of the associated characteristics in order to (a) better perform their function, (b) present a more compelling experience, or (b) mimic human-human relationships and build user trust [22]; setting behavioural realism as a principal goal.

Embodiment, multimodality and humanlike behaviour

Reflective of this, the weight of work in this area has tended towards embodiment and multimodality. Von der Pütten *et al* (2010) argue that the social influence of an autonomous agent relates strongly to the levels of behavioural realism it exhibits. From this perspective, an embodied conversation agent (ECA) will elicit significantly more sympathetic social behaviour than those agents without physical form, and even less than those exhibiting a high level of anthropomorphism, thereby framing embodiment as *the* means to natural interaction. This desire, to create the illusion of human-human dialogue, is catalogued through a range of experimental studies. Most prominent is the work of linguist/psychologist Justine Cassell (2000) who created Rea, an embodied CA that incorporated non-verbal behaviour to show that such modalities were key to sustaining convincing experiences. Unlike the emerging class of CAs, embodied agents take their own physical form with the intent of eliciting more natural human-computer communication. Embodied conversational agents are "specifically conversational in their behaviors, and specifically humanlike in the way they use their bodies in conversation" [9 p.29], though the requirements of such agents are arguably partly transferable to the non-embodied CA. Such requirements include (a) recognising/responding to verbal/non-verbal input (b) generating verbal and non-verbal output, (c) dealing with functions of conversation such as turn-taking, giving feedback, and repair mechanisms, (d) giving "signals that indicate the state of the conversation, as well as contribut[ing] to new propositions to the discourse" [10 p.29]. One example within this vein is Max, a museum guide that presents as an avatar on screen to guide visitors and answer questions [24]. Like many embodied CAs, Max is multimodal in that it employs manual gestures, gaze, facial expressions, locomotion and capability for small talk. Similar developments have been seen within a range of spheres such as gaming [19], mixed reality environments [14], tourism [29], train timetabling [41] and agents to support learning [23; 14]. Whilst it is clear that the anthropomorphic value of embodiment has driven much recent work in this field, focus upon a single modality has faded and subsequently the majority of HCI work around dialogue systems is somewhat dated.

The value of dialogue as interaction

It has been argued that the true value of dialogue interface systems over direct manipulation (GUI) can be found where task complexity is greatest [6]. Specifically, when used (a) to filter/browse or issue commands over large amounts of information/sets of things (b) to follow navigational paths (c) to allow negation and quantification (d) to distinguish individuals from kinds (e) to filter and request information in ways not predetermined by design, (f) to build a complex query that takes more than a single turn, (g) for referring to things that you cannot see or point to, or doing anything that's not in the here and now, and (h) for delegating complex or redundant actions. However, the realities of spoken language processing are such that "success is blighted by recognition errors, unintelligible responses and hard to navigate dialogues" [28 p.123], leaving us somewhere in the void between experience and potential. According to Moore, this gulf will remain unbridged until dialogue systems better understand user drivers and motivations, and are able link these meaningfully to their communicative behaviour. In this regard, the notion of a conversational agent might be considered something of a misleading concept. In line with Moore's assertions, the act of conversing with another person implicates a raft of transactions beyond the mere vocalising of words, more akin to what Harper (2010) describes as 'structural patternings', which are dictated by judgments made in response to certain social cues. He gives the following example - the opening 'hello' is actually preceded by a glance that allows the speaker to ascertain context, judge the mood of the recipient, and assess the correct tone to take in order to know, for example, whether one is interrupting. Framed in this way, even a simple conversational act becomes highly complex, inferentially fertile, and can be said to perform multiple functions. So, one might ask, is the principle design goal to replicate human-to-human interactions?

Conversing with Computers

In 1996, Reeves & Nass claimed that individuals respond to computer-based agents in the same way that they do to other humans during social interactions. Shechtman & Horowitz (2003) however found that in fact this was not the case. The authors highlighted three kinds of conversation goals: 1) *task goals*, in which conversation is used to achieve a joint activity, or construct a plan together; 2) *communication goals*, in which the goal is to ensure the conversation itself runs smoothly, and 3) *relationship goals*, in which people are driven to achieve a certain tone of conversation and maintain certain kinds of relationships (whether friendly, hostile, professional, intimate, etc). In order to assess interaction, subjects were blinded as to whether they were interacting with a human or computer. It was found that subjects put more effort into their conversations when they thought their partner was human, used more statements relating to their relationship, were more engaged in the conversation, and reacted more assertively to assertive responses from their partner. Wilkes confirms this view by suggesting that, whilst people expect politeness in human interactions, they are actually 'repelled' by excessive politeness and repetitions when they know the interaction is with a machine [48].

Whilst research has shown that people talk differently to humans and computers, there are still common requirements. Both cases require a degree of context dependence in the conversation, and users expect connectedness across the whole sequence of conversational turns rather than a response only to a single turn [6]. In addition, CAs need to exhibit 'social smarts' that enable engagement of the human in "an interesting and relevant conversation" [9 p.30], which should be both automatic and context appropriate. Prior work has shown that designing for human-computer dialogue is a complex space. However, it is also clear that if we are seeking to make CAs successful applications, we first "need to make them capable of interacting with naïve, uninformed humans in everyday situations" [24 p.329]. Having given an overview of cognate work, the following section outlines the methodology and results of our study.

METHODOLOGY

Within this paper we seek to understand the high-level factors that motivate and limit ongoing use of CAs in everyday life. To this end we conducted a series of semi-structured interviews [7] with 14 individuals who considered themselves 'regular' users of a CA. Fourteen users were interviewed; 9 male and 5 female, aged between 25 and 60. Interview durations ranged from 19:32 to 48:50. All interviews were conducted at a distance (telephone/Skype) between November 2014 and February 2015. Participants were recruited through an open call via email and social media, and were selected on the basis of having 'regularly' used a CA for at least one month. They included; a health telecare advisor, two consultants, a magazine editor, a data analyst, a lecturer, three managers, two researchers, a strategic advisor (educational policy), a homemaker and one PhD student. Twelve participants identified as British, one as American and one as a Czech national (see Fig.1).

Name	CA type	Age	Gender	Role
Adam	Siri	40-49	M	Lecturer
Viv	Siri	20-29	F	Researcher
Dan	G Now	30-39	M	Consultant
Allan	Siri	30-39	M	PhD student
Sam	Siri	50+	M	Strategic advisor
Richard	Siri	50+	M	Project manager
Graham	Siri/G Now	40-49	M	Consultant
Sarah	Siri	30-39	F	Magazine editor
Mike	Siri/ G Now	20-29	M	Researcher
Andy	Siri	40-49	M	Telecare advisor
Rob	G Now	30-39	M	Data analyst
Emily	G Now	30-39	F	Regional manager
Laura	Cortana	30-39	F	Homemaker
Denise	Siri	40-49	F	Account manager

Figure 1: Participants by age/gender/CA type/occupation

Definitions of CA 'use' were not prescribed, in order to allow a range of perspectives, and individuals self-identified as 'regular' users. A CA was described as a 'task-driven system or application that you interact with through speech' and examples were given. Respondents were predominately male and principally Siri users.

Transcripts were coded using a Thematic Network Analysis (TNA) approach in order to align with the interpretive epistemology of the wider research. The thematic network is a 'web-like coding structure' [2; 385] that allows for a rich understanding of the conceptual interplay occurring within the narrative. TNA organizes coded text into three types of theme; (i) basic (lowest order, coded statements or beliefs that related to organizing themes), (ii) organizing (that cluster basic themes into organizing issues) and (iii) global themes (super-ordinate themes that organize all codes into meta-groups or metaphor) [2]. Interview questions sought to elicit participants' technical knowledge, the broad frequency and duration of CA use, type of use, most/least complex tasks, use location, manner of use and emotions elicited by the experience, personal preferences, and perceived benefits/limitations in respect of their specific CA product. Participants were also prompted to describe at least one example in detail; 'describe step by step the way in which you [user-defined example]'. Transcripts were coded on an ongoing basis and new participants were sought until theoretical saturation was reached [17]. Themes were derived of the data, and drew from both the frequency of their occurrence and their perceived substantive significance. Having described the approach to recruitment, data collection, and analysis, the following section frames the findings in terms of stages of CA use.

FINDINGS

Participants were all daily users of technology (predominately smartphones, laptops and tablets) with mobile devices cited as those most frequently used. All but one owned a smartphone through which they accessed their CA; Mike was the only exception to this as he accessed Siri solely via his iPad. Only two participants made use of more than one CA; Mike and Graham, who used both Google Now and Siri. Overall, Siri was the most frequently used CA (10) followed by Google Now (5). Only one user made use of Cortana as the study was conducted prior to the UK launch date and our Cortana user had set her phone to United States settings specifically in order to access it.

Motivations and Type of Use

Whilst a third of users employed their CA only a few times a week, the majority made use of it on a daily basis, with only one user reporting the CA (Siri) as their preferred task interface. When asked about the most frequent type of CA use, the tasks reported were relatively simple; checking upcoming weather followed by reminders. When asked to describe these interactions in more detail, users reported using natural/colloquial language in the first instance (e.g. 'should I take an umbrella/my coat today'), but then simplifying language until the desired result was achieved. When describing their rationale for use, participants spoke of broadly similar motivations. Principal amongst these was the desire for the CA to enable multitasking, particularly where their hands were otherwise engaged. For example: Adam regularly cycled to work and made most use of the CA in that context; Sarah worked from home whilst looking after two small children, and wanted to be able to carry out multiple tasks; and, Rob spent a considerable amount of time driving to work and liked to use his CA for productivity in what would otherwise be dead time. Indeed, time-saving was a key related motivation *"I'm also constantly asking Siri to set appointments, reminders, alerts and alarms because on the iPhone each of those takes, you know, 4 to 7 steps, not including typing. So Siri is good for those things that would otherwise cause me to go to the keyboard"* (Graham).

Learning to Use the CA

When learning to use their CA, all participants described making use of a particular economy of language. Dropping words other than 'keywords', removing colloquial or complex words, reducing the number of words used, using more specific terms, altering enunciation, speaking more slowly/clearly and changing accent were the most commonly described tactics: *"I try to enunciate as much as I can and keep my requests to relatively simple words.....you know possibly in a very exaggerated, trying to speak in a very clear fashion....rinse and repeat as necessary until it works out what I mean"* (Rob). For over half of participants this was seen as affecting ease of use *"I think it would be easier...if you didn't have to enunciate everything or feel like you have to"* (Denise). In this way they reported 'learning' to speak to their CA as a process necessary for successful interaction. *"To a certain extent you have to change the language you use because sometimes it doesn't pick up certain words or it doesn't understand the inflection in your voice obviously...you have to say things in a particular way"* (Laura).

Several users noted that they had attempted to speak to their CA as though it were a person, though the majority were unlikely to engage in conversational-style interactions when in public. One user noted that he was more likely to speak to Siri colloquially when in private – indeed, there was a desire by several participants to be able to carry out more natural conversational interactions: *"Often, if I'm in private, I talk to it a bit more like it's a person. So, I'll say 'Siri, can you tell me what the weather's like today', whereas if I was on the street I'd just say 'directions from St Pancras to Waterloo station'"* (Allan). Despite attempting the use of more colloquial phrases, there was no sense that users spoke to the CA in the same way as one might to a human. Each interaction was uniquely framed and in the majority of cases participants commented on the lack of ability of the CA to bring to bear contextual understanding between interactions, even when they were temporally close. This was seen as limiting the tasks one might ask: *"I don't ask for more information from it. It tends not to be very good at that. You ask it to do one thing and you know that that's the one thing it knows how to do. Asking it to do sub-tasks, to follow up or to give you more information about something you've just asked it, it tends to be really bad at."* (Allan)

Effective use requires ongoing 'work' and investment

For all except three participants, Conversational Agents (CA) were considered an entertaining/gimmicky addition to their device rather than a key application; Graham and Andy were the only participants who defined themselves as 'serious' users. Both such users described a strong desire for their CA to function efficiently and were each prepared to do additional 'work' to ensure the most successful operation. Such work included researching the capability if the CA, introducing use of the CA within social/professional settings, considering and testing best strategies of use, training it to recognize key contextual variables such as locations/people, systematically testing appropriate speech syntax in order to 'speak its language' and create a dynamic mental model of its capabilities, and making time to test these capabilities: *"I found out through poking online out of curiosity about what Siri can do...I played around with it just to see how it worked... So, I tried a very simple test. I told Siri who my father and mother were and then I said, both of those entries have addresses and so, you know, after I drive from my mother's to my father's my mother wants me to let her know I arrived alive, and sometimes I forget, you know, because I'm an adult man and I forget to call my mother when I get to someplace after a perfectly normal drive. So I told Siri 'remind me, call mom when I get to my father's house'...so there was a pre-set up just to get to a point where I could ask something very basic."* (Graham)

This form of preparatory work resulted in the user being able to more easily ask complex tasks than those participants who used the CA less frequently. Such ongoing work also served to build user 'trust' in the system; a word frequently used. Andy, in particular, was prepared to invest time in discovery and set up because he wanted to know both whether the technology would be useful for his clients, and the extent to which it would be helpful for his own day-to-day life; *"I suppose ever since I got it I would probe it as much as I could so I suppose I am more serious about using it but I was serious I suppose from the beginning"* (Andy). Whilst a relatively recent (1 month) and less frequent user, Richard also sought to discover more features of his CA, though his motivation was stimulated by seeking common ground with his son, who also used Siri. Whilst the most effort was brought to bear by those who had a clear use case, all users engaged in some level of 'work' to ensure successful interaction (see 'learning to talk to computers'). As one might expect, the level of work/investment of time appeared to have a direct relationship with user satisfaction.

Those who used their CA frequently (at least daily) also found themselves becoming more successful in their use. This was reportedly due to (a) their growing accustomed to the types of commands the CA would respond to, and (b) the greater likelihood that a successful CA interaction would motivate them to search for other things their CA could do. *"I think by playing with it and understanding what it could do well and what it could do badly....through that I found that I developed a series of things that I used it for that were a quite discrete number of its functions"* (Allan). In this way, users' satisfaction with, and trust in, the product had a strong relationship to the extent to which they were prepared to invest time in both understanding what their CA could do, and practicing those interactions. Equally, the more personally compelling the described use proposition (primarily professional need), the more likely users were to frame task failure as forgivable.

'Play' as a point of entry

All users except one began their engagement through playful interactions such as finding 'Easter eggs' in the system; the inbuilt humorous responses triggered by specific phrases. This, they described, as allowing them to both better understand what Siri could do and enabling their familiarity with the interface. *"I started out in a playful thing simply because...you just don't know what you can ask it... and it was like 'can you do this'?"* (Dan). The only participant who did not start with play (Andy) approached Siri as an instrument to be used with his clients - people with physical and mental health issues. In this case, he was professionally motivated to find practical uses for Siri, which subsequently transferred to his day-to-day life. This user was also far more forgiving of errors or points of failure as his desire for the promise of a fully functioning CA raised his threshold of acceptable failure. *"It wasn't just an added feature on the phone.... I got (iPhone) especially for it and when I got it I was so excited that I could find the use for my clients"* (Andy). In the case of families with small children (3 participants), Siri and Cortana were a particular source of entertainment. *"Cortana has this function where she can sing to you... she does...if you ask her to sing you a song or tell you a joke, she'll sing to you or tell you a joke and we use that quite regularly.... I have numerous children so they play with my phone quite a lot"* (Laura). However, once the amusement had passed, levels of engagement dipped and the framing of Siri as a fallible but amusing tool pervaded much of the narrative: *'We played games with the kids when we first got it...we did ask it 'what the fox said'... and it said frakakakakaka, which is one of the lyrics from the song. Which made us all laugh. So that's my happiest story of using Siri so far"* (Adam). In most cases, these playful interactions resulted in longer-term use. This was particularly true where users felt they had time to invest in the product, or where the CA was seen as 'easier' or 'faster': *"My feeling originally with Siri was that it was a toy....you'd ask it to do stupid stuff and then you start to do certain things with it and it starts to work, you know, like putting stuff in your calendar, and then it just becomes like an easier way of doing things"* (Mike).

However, beyond the initial framing of 'playful' experiences, users became less forgiving of failure. As early successes resulted in sustained use, so early failures affected the frequency and type of on-going use, particularly where users expected the system to respond similarly to the way in which it had during play: *"I don't think maybe I was speaking clearly enough to it so it wasn't really getting it...she nailed the jokes though so I guess it was, you know, surprising"*

(Denise). When Siri failed to perform a key task more than a few times (reportedly between 2 and 6 in the majority of cases), user expectations were set. *"I gave it the benefit of the doubt…and then I thought no, you're always going to be rubbish"* (Sarah). Having failed at more complex tasks, the CA was often relegated to performing very basic tasks such as setting reminders. When asked to describe the factors that had affected use, participants most frequently cited misunderstanding of words or commands; *"I'd heard it had had difficulty recognising accents and I guess mine was amongst [those]"* (Emily). This was particularly the experience of the female users as all except one woman found the CA unable to dependably recognise their voice. Male users found this less of a consistent problem, though it was still the most commonly reported reason that CAs were perceived to fail. However, where users were aware of software updates or improvements, they reported subsequent improvements in voice recognition, though they were often uncertain as to the extent this was imagined. The two associated global themes, of a lack of awareness regarding the operation of the system, and the limitations of its 'intelligence', were recurrent across all participants.

'Hands free' as the principle use case

As one might expect, the principle use-case for the CA was 'hands free', which was tied strongly to the theme of time-saving and convenience. *"So I was walking through London and it was just more convenient to ask Siri how to get between St Pancras and Waterloo then it would be to stand in the street and type it in…it's quicker"* (Allan). Reasons for hands-free use were cited as when (a) hands were necessarily otherwise engaged, (b) hands were dirty (c) the handset couldn't be easily reached, (d) speech was felt to be faster, or (b) when attention was distributed, particularly during another primary activity: *"So, my main use case is when my hands are otherwise occupied, which is when I'm cycling into work typically"* (Adam). Time saving was also a global theme. *"In terms of economy of key presses, it's just an awful lot quicker"* (Richard). Indeed, where a desire for hands-free was not the motivating rationale, *perceived* time savings drove the preferred mode of interaction. However in such cases, when users felt they had not saved time, they fell back upon using the touchscreen, a practice they described as 'traditional', 'normal' or 'old-school'. In instances where the CA responded to task requests by defaulting to on-screen web-search results, this was universally seen as a failure.

Locus of attention and task complexity

Within the global theme of 'hands-free', the locus of user attention was a key organizing theme and use of the CA was rarely described as a primary activity. Participants made the CA their principal focus only when engaging it in playful interactions, or during preparatory or exploratory work/activities such as experimenting/teaching it/testing the limits of its capability. For occasional users, the CA was perceived to be most useful during activities that demanded high attentional resources such as cycling, driving, or looking after children. This desire by users, to employ their CA to support distribution of their cognition, was also reflected in the second most frequently cited task type, that of memory augmentation: *"I constantly have a really shitty memory…if I don't write it down I'll remember it a week later and it's like, oh that important thing I had to remember just came back to me…I travel a lot, I'm out and about a lot…so I pull out Siri and I just say 'set appointment tomorrow for 10am, call mom"* (Graham).

In line with our working definition, users viewed their CA principally as a simple task-based system and, other than Graham, they did not attempt complex tasks (particularly without visual confirmation) or tasks where they perceived a high social cost to failure. Simple tasks included asking the CA to check the weather, setting reminders, setting alarms, getting directions, making lists, adding notes, adding items to their calendar, searching the Internet, searching their address book, activating music playlists, or activating FaceTime. In contrast, more complex or socially sensitive tasks, such as launching a call or sending a long email, were mostly considered tasks with which the CA could not be trusted. In each case where use of the CA distracted the user from their primary task, or required manual intervention, it was seen as a failure, and recurrence was rarely forgiven: *"I've tried to use it when driving, I've tried to use it when I've got my hands full with the kids, I've tried to use it when I've kind of been engaged in other stuff and all that happens is that I've had to abandon what I was doing and sort of do it in the old-school way of actually typing in what I need and so I have by and large kind of given up on using it.* (Sarah). However, where users came to the CA with a clearly defined proposition for use, such as Graham or Andy, they were more willing to return to the application, consider ways in which they might improve the outcome, and set more complex tasks.

System Feedback and User Evaluation of CAs

With the exception of the more exogenous limitations of infrastructure or social context, the majority of reported issues during use related to a lack of system feedback/transparency. Half of users explicitly stated that they did not know what their CA could do. This resulted in them either feeling overwhelmed by the unknown potential, or led them to assume that the tasks they could accomplished were highly limited. *I felt let down that I didn't get any feedback from it…It has a captive audience it could have just told me…just to let you know, this is what we've done. Just a few examples of what could be done. The things it can do are so broad that I just feel lost"* (Dan). User understanding of the operation of the system was a key organizing theme within participant interviews. Insufficient feedback or visibility of both the limits and capabilities of the CA was often cited as a factor limiting users' ability to make the system work: *"I'd have put the [CA] down and never picked it up again, I know that. So there was quite a big barrier I think… I don't consciously know what I've done to change it"* (Richard). Specific factors limiting interaction included a lack of understanding of (a) what the system *could* do, (b) what it *was* doing (c) *how* it was doing it, (d) whether or not its capabilities altered over time, and (e) the extent to which that alteration was a direct result of user interaction; i.e. whether or not the CA learned from user behaviour. Indeed, the extent to which a CA could be said to 'know' or 'learn' things was mentioned by all participants. Additionally, users who had previously defined themselves as not/less technically knowledgeable, tended to have higher initial expectations of CA capability and intelligence. Equally, when tasks failed, they were more likely to see the CA as static and *unable* to learn, resulting in them being less experimental in the tasks they asked it to perform. *"I don't use it as a functional tool as it were…it's more sort of oooh look at this, I can speak through my phone. Then when I use it…to look up recipes for sloe gin or something like that it simply directs me to a website. That's it. It seems to be a very blunt tool. It's literally just replacing my finger on a keyboard in a kind of clever smoke and mirrors kind of way"* (Sam).

In contrast, where users were more technically knowledgeable, their expectations were relatively modest and they tended to be more forgiving when the CA failed. *"I think I'm probably quite forgiving because I know how hard voice recognition is as a problem, and especially in the time frame that it's attempting to work on, just a few seconds, I know how difficult a problem that is. So it doesn't really annoy me if it doesn't work it out because I assume it's not going to because I know how difficult it is"* (Rob). Such users were also more likely to persevere, doing further research or using different types of commands or syntax, until the task was accomplished: *" I know it's got like certain words that work. You just say 'weather' and it will work, you don't have to ask it a question. You know that it's searching for keywords and it doesn't care what you say around it really"* (Viv). Equally, those with a reportedly higher level of technical knowledge were more likely to locate task failure with the technology, whereas those who identified as non-technical were more likely to see the failure as their own: *"I wasn't using the right words and it would confuse words with things that I was looking for"* (Richard). This assignation of blame often resulted in users reporting feelings of being 'stupid', 'slow', 'unaware' or lacking in 'technical savvy': *"And it's all my fault because I haven't put the numbers in under the right, you know, headings and it's all like well if you'd have done the right thing…if you'd have done the right you wouldn't have made that mistake and you know it's making me feel really stupid right now"* (Dan).

Assessing system intelligence

In terms of perceptions of CA intelligence, all except the most highly technical users (Graham, Rob, Adam and Allan) felt unsure as to whether their CA had a capacity to learn, and even for those who were highly technical, this was not always clear: *"I don't know whether it learns or not, that was the other thing, I'm not sure whether it learns or not"* (Richard). This resulted in the majority of users being unsure as to the interaction dynamic; is the computer learning to adapt to the user or visa versa. However, for those with lower levels of technical knowledge, a combination of (a) the system's failure to learn/adapt to either their accents or the ways in which their questions were posed, and (b) its tendency to resort to web search, led them to frame the CA as simply a voice-based search engine extension. Even for those with technical knowledge, the tendency for their CA to default to search was a frustration: *' I've asked it about the weather today, say, and then I want to ask it about tomorrow….and it will just come back and say 'do you want me to do a web search for what about tomorrow, not to give me tomorrow's weather"* (Allan).

Whilst all users described a process of learning to speak to their CA, for those with lower levels of technical knowledge, there continued to be mismatch between their initially high expectations, and the perceived intelligence of the system. However, even where users described the system as failing, they were at the same time able to ascribe to it a high level of contextual understanding, sarcasm, anger or situational humor. *"There was one time I was very [sarcastic)] to it, I was like 'oh thanks that's really helpful' and it just said, I swear, in an equally sarcastic tone 'that's fine it's my pleasure'"* (Sarah). Irrespective of whether they believed the system capable, a fluid understanding of context was something considered key to making interactions appear more naturalistic. Users expected the CA to be able to infer, from all previous interactions, the context of the current task. In particular, once an interaction/task was complete, the majority of users expected the CA to remember the context of the preceding interaction. Equally, more positive 'conversational' experiences were reported when the CA was perceived to have understood the context of use, for example knowing that reading a message would likely lead to the user wanting to reply; *"It's brilliant that it reads messages to you and gives you the option would you like to reply…automatically, without pressing the button again it goes into what would you like to reply and it's almost like you're having a conversation with your co-driver"* (Andy).

In the context of Siri, those who took a more instrumental view of the CA, or reported high levels of technical understanding, tended to describe less anthropomorphic behaviour and referred to Siri using gender-neutral pronouns. In contrast, those who reported less technical knowledge were found to use both gendered pronouns and greater anthropomorphism in their descriptions: *"He was like a bad boyfriend that was just never going to make the grade"* or *"like having a really bad PA"* (Sarah). In many such cases users reasoned about perceived limitations of the system in terms of the CA being 'just' a computer. Indeed, the term 'computer was often thematically tied to pejorative language and was regularly set against human intellect; the latter framed as the superior form. Irrespective of user experience, the CAs were universally seen as a blunt instrument - limited in their capacity to learn. In all cases, even where improved performance was perceived, or failure was expected and forgiven, CAs were found to fail to live up to initial user expectations: *"So my expectations were always high, I adjusted them and the product improved, but …it's still not quite met with my original expectations or my adjusted expectations"* (Emily).

Issues Affecting Engagement and Ongoing Use

Where the capability or operation of the CA was felt to be unknown, so the issue of trust emerged. Asides from the two most frequent users who tended to be more experimental and forgiving, all of those interviewed raised issues of trust as limiting the tasks they would ask their CA to perform. For example, after several attempts Allan had not succeeded in getting Siri to book cinema tickets and had subsequently abandoned asking for help with this task. As in the case of most users, if Siri failed after successive attempts he felt compelled to abandon that task and now uses it *"only where I know I'm going to get a reasonably reliable result…. "After it's got it wrong a couple of times, oh I might as well just set it normally"* (Alan). This was particularly true where failure might result in social embarrassment. Within this theme, the most frequently-cited activity users would *not* use their CA for was to make a call on their behalf. *"I would never risk calling anyone because I know that that would not work for me and it'd end up being awkward because I'd end up calling someone I didn't want to call"* (Viv).

"I tend to not use it for dialing and stuff like that because I'm worried that it's going to ring the wrong person….and because you're not paying attention it sort of rings that person on your contact list that you haven't spoken to for 7 or 8 years. It's like 'hello darling how are you'….what?" (Allan). However, one participant (UK-based but whose family live in the US) noted that this may well relate to cultural context, his feeling being that people in the UK had a lower threshold of social embrassement than other cultures: *"Oooh God no, absolutely not…where I'm trying to get to here is the idea that just like ringing the wrong number, if it was a US thing, it's the opportunity to have a quick chat and that's fine. I just reached out and touched a friend. But in the UK, God no."* Irrespective of the activity, however, all users described seeking visual confirmation of complex tasks.

Precision and visual confirmation

In all cases, the issue of required precision was a factor linked to trust and reliability. Where precision was necessary, for example when drafting an email, users tended not to trust their CA to complete the task. Even amongst the two 'serious' users, 'send' would not occur without visual confirmation and intervention, and 'call' only where the respondent was well known. *"I'm not going to trust Siri where the language needs to be precise…but when it can be imprecise then I'll trust Siri"* (Graham). All users described this need, for visual confirmation that complex tasks had been carried out accurately. However for simpler tasks, such as setting an alarm, repeated successful completion was sufficient for them to trust spoken confirmation from the CA alone; the exception being when the alarm was important. Indeed where tasks did not require precision, such as setting reminders, alarms, or asking about the weather, visual confirmation was not always required. In contrast sending messages was considered a potentially more sensitive task, particularly when the audience was not family or friends. Here, despite the potential effort/time-saving of using a CA, users felt the need to return to the screen and check/amend errors before sending. *"I can sometimes make it read an incoming text, you know, a notification comes in and I can't see what it is because the phone's in my pocket, and I quite like the audio output. At the moment I certainly can't trust it to reply. You know, I can't rattle a reply off by speech and trust that it's got it right, and that whole interaction….of not being able to see the screen of what it's translating"* (Adam).

Google versus Siri

Whilst the purpose of this study was not to compare products, it was clear that there was a considerable difference in the ways that users approached use of Google Now compared to Siri or Cortana. Google Now was used predominantly as voice-activated search. Conversely, Siri was seen as having more of a personality, which was well received. Even in the case of 'serious' users or those who self-reported as technically skilled, there was recognition that it had been designed to give that impression. *"You know I tell Siri 'tell me a joke' and it has a few, you know…and my hope that Siri…I mean Siri is very much at the vanguard. I haven't asked Google like, you know, tell me a joke. Siri seems very much trying to be a personal thing whereas Google seems to me very much task-oriented"* (Graham). None of the users of Google Now referred to the product with either gendered pronouns or in any way that suggested humanlike characteristics, rather they framed it as a tool: *So with Google Now, because it's very tightly integrated into Google maps, you can ask it a place and it will show you where it is. Siri isn't as developed that way"* Mike).

DISCUSSION

In light of our findings it is clear that user expectations of CA systems remain far from the practical realities of use. This is illustrated by the level of effort users described when seeking to elicit the expected task response from their CA. Unlike human-human interactions, the nature of CA human-computer dialogue was, as one might suppose, limited. Our findings show that this is due to the manifest dissonance between user expectations and the pragmatics of CA communication, particularly regarding their assessment of system intelligence. This speaks to what Norman describes as the 'gulfs of execution and evaluation', understood as the degree to which the system representations can be perceived and decoded by the user into accurate expectations and intentions of use. The smaller the gulf, the more satisfying the user experience, and a small gulf is achieved "when the device provides information about its state in a form that is easy to get, is easy to interpret and matches the way the person thinks of the system" [30, p.39]. According to Cassell, there are three components that affect perceptions of intelligence in the design of a CA user interface; (a) how the system is represented through its interface, (b) how the system represents information (and the world) to the user, and (c) how the system's 'internal representation' impacts upon users' interactions with that system. Whilst the focus of Cassell's work has been multimodal representations of intelligence (physical gestures in addition to voice), the central concept, of the users' need to 'locate intelligence', and thereby the need to represent intelligence to the user, is equally salient here.

Setting realistic expectations scaffold the learning process

For all our participants, expectations of how to interact with the CA, its capability and operation, were out of step with reality. In the majority of cases users were unable to make accurate judgments about system capability. This varied in accordance with the referential frame of the user; for example, where users had knowledge of computer science then the gulf of execution and to some extent evaluation were much smaller. Here, users had a more developed mental model of system capability and were less likely to abandon tasks. For those without technical knowledge, however, the model upon which they drew tended towards that of human-human dialogue, illustrated by (a) beginning their interactions with fuller and more natural sentences, which they then amended (b) a tendency towards anthropomorphism, and (c) ungrounded attribution of intelligence. During conversation-based human interactions, we use a variety of cues to communicate intelligence, what Cassell describes as 'social interactional intelligence' such as initiation, appropriately interrupting a conversation, feedback, error-handing and turn-taking. In contrast our users described each interaction with their CA as clearly bounded, which problematized their instinctive approach to task commands and led them to desire more colloquial dialogue, more akin to Harper's 'structured patternings' [21]. In the absence of expected cues, our users tended towards two overlapping approaches; (a) to endow the system with imagined anthropomorphic qualities, such as an advanced understanding of context, or (b) to employ an economy of interaction, such as avoiding complex tasks, limiting the types of language used, and gradual abandonment of the CA for activities other than those they 'trusted' it to perform. Each of these approaches were problematic in their own way and, where they overlapped, served to confuse the user experience.

(a) CA design should reveal system intelligence: Whilst such economic interaction resulted in a much more effective approach to human-agent conversation and task completion, it was ultimately mechanistic and shut down opportunities for developing meaningful CA use. In contrast, anthropomorphism set unrealistic expectations that framed user perceptions of what constituted system failure. Our results showed that technically skilled participants were better able to see beyond artificial humanlike qualities to devise their own mental models of interaction. However, those with lower levels of knowledge described little alteration in their expectations and greater levels of frustration, leading them to question the 'intelligence' of the system, indicating that user expectations of CAs should be scaffold through more considered revelation of system intelligence through design.

System feedback and representation of intelligence – recognising humour as an indicator of state

Despite users actively engaging in the process of 'learning' to speak more simply to their CA, this did not seem to affect their high expectations of system intelligence. Even where users perceived CA failure, they continued to attribute elevated levels of episodic social intelligence to the system such as sarcasm or humour. One reason for this might be the expectations set by the act of conversation and use of humour as a form of interaction. When considering the nature of human-human/face-to-face interaction, "unique informational conditions prevail" [16, p33]. Humans expect to hear intonation and "mutual evaluations will be conveyed by very minor things" [16, p.33]. In this way it is possible that the familiar 'Easter Eggs' and humorous trigger responses to particular phrases or words may have conveyed a level of 'social smarts' that belied the true system capabilities. Expecting to hear sarcasm and humour in conversation then is perhaps unsurprising, although a concern arises where this expectation frames wider perceptions of system capability, resulting in dissatisfaction. This poses something of a conundrum. Whilst users are drawn into serious uses of the system through Easter eggs and playful interactions, our finding show that these interactions also act as affordances, in that they suggest the possibility of action/interaction. This is not entirely unexpected. It has been suggested that framing systems as anthropomorphic "raises user expectations about the extent of their capabilities for intelligence, language, judgement, autonomy, and social norms" [39, p 193]. For our non-technical participants, these expectations were cemented through the playful interactions which characterised initial engagement with these systems.

(b) Reconsidering the interactional promise made by humour: Whilst being a key mechanism for drawing users into more exploratory practices, these playful/humorous interactions had the effect of reinforcing anthropomorphic qualities, thus compounding users' expectations of CA capability. For example, where users were not familiar with the 'intelligence' of the system, or had no technical frame of reference, anthropomorphic language pervaded much of their descriptions of use. It also, however, framed their descriptions of failure and frustration. Equally, users of Google Now had more accurate expectations of the system and were able to reason fairly about what they felt Google did best. Here, Google Now was clearly understood as a hands free interface to a search facility and there were no expectations of wider intelligence or anthropomorphic qualities. In light of these findings, we suggest that future iterations reconsider the interactional promises made by humorous engagement and explore how such engagements could instead support user assessment of system intelligence.

Supporting user evaluation - revealing system capabilities

One of the overarching themes throughout our findings was the inability of users to assess the intelligence of the CA. During a human-human conversation, we use a series of physical indicators and indexical verbal shorthand in order to communicate not only concepts and our identity, but also our intelligence/ capability. Our conversational partner will seek to elicit such information through their interactions with us; what do we know, think or feel. In these instances our behaviour is tightly synchronised to our conversational partner and, as such, feels natural and immersive. Here, the listener is able to bring to bear a ready model of human interaction developed from prior experiences which allows them to either "map the speaker's behaviours onto richer underlying representations, functions, and conventions – to attribute intelligence to the other", [8 p.71] or to "reach an understanding with another person about something in the world" [20, p.215]. Our findings indicate that whilst users applied this mental model of human communication, it was revised in light of their CA experiences and reflected in their interactions. Whilst the need for this type of effort or learning is reported in other types of 'natural' user interfaces, such as those relying on gesture [31], the absence of any 'natural' means to interrogate and assess system capabilities or state meant that the gulf of evaluation remains too great to result in positive user experience. Within human-human dialogue, the 'internal nature' of the speaker is conveyed via speech.

(c) Consider new ways of conveying CA capability though interaction: Currently, the reality of CAs is such that the system response presents only task-related information to the user. In some cases this has the consequence of conveying capability, for example reverting to visual web-search as an indicator that the system is struggling, or through polite trigger responses that might tell you about limited connectivity. Where users were not able to draw from a technical frame of reference, they tended to find blame in themselves, and often abandoned particular types of task requests, a behaviour seen where systems present a gulf of execution [30]. If we are to truly reflect the expectations set by 'conversation' as interface, some thought should be given to how to convey system limitations and capabilities in instances other than the moment when the system has visibly failed in its task.

Supporting ongoing user engagement by clearly defining the goal of the system

Ideally a conversational interaction should be immersive, resulting in a 'binding hypnotic effect' (p.113) through 'joint spontaneous involvement'. However, the experience of using a CA is currently very far from this. Indeed, our research showed that the principle use-case of the CA was 'hands-free', meaning that an alternative primary task, rather than the conversation, was the focus of attention. Where cognition is split across two tasks, fluidity of user experience is critical to supporting interaction. The majority of our participants used a CA where their primary task required a high level of attention (e.g. driving, cycling, child-minding), what Preece *et al* describe as 'fast thinking' meaning that we "perceive, act, and react to events around us intuitively and effortlessly" [33, p.66]. In each use case described by participants, the activity was not only hands free but required a level of visual attention. Where participants felt they had to resort to 'old school' techniques, or where the CA reverted to screen-based response, the resulting stress and extra effort was seen as failure from their perspective. In contrast, where the user goal was successful operation of the system, then the extra work involved was acceptable and satisfaction of the system was greater. In the majority of cases, however, the primary user goal was not solely to use the CA, making the system a means to an end rather than an end in itself.

(d) Rethink system feedback and design goals in light of the dominant use case: It is clear that the majority of users engage with the system only up to the point that it ceases to provide utility. However, the way in which the system interacts, handles tasks and delivers information does not reflect the dominant use case. This begs the question, what are the design goal of current CA system and how might these be rethought to deliver a more compelling user experience.

Limitations of the study: This study is based upon a UK-centric sample of mostly male participants. Whilst every effort was made to balance gender, the greater number of users responding to the call were male. Though we found no meaningful differences between genders, and theoretical saturation was reached, the imbalance is acknowledged. Beyond this, Siri was the most commonly used system, reflective of the market at the time. Equally, our analysis focused upon interactional themes rather than specific capabilities. Whilst system capability influenced user experience, our study represents the state of the art at the time.

CONCLUSIONS

Overall, in the majority of instances, the operation of the CA systems failed to bridge the gap between user expectation and system operation. Our study showed that users had poor mental models of how their CA worked and that these were reinforced through a lack of meaningful feedback regarding system capability and intelligence. Equally, where playful aspects and trigger responses were programmed into the systems, these served to act as engagement mechanisms, whilst concurrently setting unrealistic expectations that framed the ongoing user experience. A deep 'gulf of evaluation' was also found. This was demonstrated through the extent to which users were consistently unable to ascertain the level of system intelligence, their need to visually confirm all but the simplest tasks, and their reluctance to use the CA for complex or sensitive activities. Finally, whilst the key use case for CAs was found to be 'hands free', system error handling made this largely untenable but for the most economic interaction, calling into question the design goals of such systems. Whilst CAs offer the promise of an engaging and natural user interface, much design and interaction work is required before this potential is realised. Without the humanlike cues and affordances relied upon by multimodal systems, CAs have a particular challenge. We suggest considering (a) ways to reveal system intelligence (b) reconsidering the interactional promise made by humorous engagement, (c) considering how best to indicate capability though interaction, and (d) rethinking system feedback and design goals in light of the dominant use case, as areas for future investigation and development.

REFERENCES

1. ALICE http://www.alicebot.org/bios/richardwallace.html Artificial Intelligence Foundation
2. Jennifer Attride-Stirling. 2001. Thematic networks: an analytic tool for qualitative research. Qualitative Research, 1(3), 385–405
3. Margaret A Boden. 2007. Conversationalists and Confidants. In *Proceedings of Artificial Companions in Society: Perspectives on the Present and Future*. Oxford Internet Institute. Retrieved from http://www.academia.edu/2669520/Artificial_Companions_in_Society_Perspectives_on_the_Present_and_Future
4. Richard, A Bolt. 1980. "Put-That-There": Voice and Gesture at the Graphics Interface, *In the proceedings of SIGGRAGH '80* Proceedings, 14, 3 (July 1980), 262-270. doi: 10.1145/800250.807503
5. Timothy Bickmore and Rosalind W Picard. 2005. Establishing and maintaining long-term human-computer relationships. *ACM Transactions on Computer-Human Interaction*. 12, 2: 293-327. doi: 10.1145/1067860.1067867
6. Susan Brennan. 1990. Conversation as direct manipulation: An iconoclastic view. In *The Art of Human-Computer Interface Design*. B.K. Laurel (Ed.), Reading, MA: Addison-Wesley.
7. Alan Bryman. 2004. Social Research Methods (2nd Ed). New York: Oxford University Press
8. Justine Cassell. 2001. Embodied Conversational Agent: Representation and Intelligence in User Interfaces. *AI Magazine*. 22, 4: 67-83. doi: http://dx.doi.org/10.1609/aimag.v22i4.1593
9. Justine Cassell. Tim Bickmore, Lee Campbell, Hannes Vihjalmsson & Hao Yan. 2000. Human Conversation as a System Framework: Designing Embodied Conversational Agents. *In Embodied Conversational Agents*. Justine Cassell. (ed) MIT Press: 29-63
10. Martin Davis. 2000. *Engines of Logic: Mathematicians and the Origin of the Computer*. W W Norton & Company
11. Anind Dey and Jennifer Mankoff. 2005. Designing mediation for context-aware applications. *ACM Transactions on Computer-Human Interaction* 12, 1: 53-80. doi 10.1145/1057237.1057241
12. Abbe Don, Susan Brennen., Brenda Laurel and Ben Shneiderman. 1992 Anthropomorphism: from Eliza to Terminator 2. Panel In Proc. CHI '92, Bauersfeld, P., Bennett, J., and Lynch, G. (eds.). ACM, 67-70
13. Jilian D'Onfro. 2015. *Microsoft Created a Chatbot in China that has Millions of Loyal Followers who talk to it like in the Movie 'Her'*. Business Insider UK. http://uk.businessinsider.com/microsoft-chatbot-xiaoice-2015-8?r=US&IR=T
14. Mauro Dragone, Thomas Holz, Brian R. Duffy, Greogory M.P. O'Hare. 2005. Social Situated Agents in Virtual, Real and Mixed Reality Environments. In *Intelligent Virtual Agents*. Themis Panayiotopoulos, Jonathan Gratch, Ruth Aylett, Daniel Ballin, Patrick Olivier & Thomas Rist (Eds.) Proceedings of 5th International Working Conference, IVA 2005 Kos, Greece, September 12-14, 2005. Springer: 166-177. doi: 10.1007/11550617_15
15. James R. Glass, 1999. Challenges for Spoken Dialogue Systems. *In the proceedings of IEEE Workshop on Automatic Speech Recognition and Understanding*. (ASRU), Colorado, USA
16. Erving Goffman. 1967. *Interaction Ritual: Essays on Face-to-Face Behaviour*. Pathenon
17. Aurthur Graesser, Haiying Li & Carol Forsyth. 2014. Learning by Communicating in Natural Language with Conversational Agents. Current Directions in Psychological Science. 23, 5: 374-380 doi: 10.1177/0963721414540680
18. Greg Guest, Arwen Bunce & Laura Johnson. 2006. How many interviews are enough? An experiment with data saturation and variability. *Field Methods*, 18, 1: 59-82. doi: 10.1177/1525822X05279903
19. Joakim Gustafson, Johan Boye, Morgan Fredriksson, Lasse Johanneson, Jürgen Königsmann. 2005. Providing Computer Game Characters with Conversational Abilities. In *Intelligent Virtual Agents*. Themis Panayiotopoulos, Jonathan Gratch, Ruth Aylett, Daniel Ballin, Patrick Olivier & Thomas Rist (Eds.) Proceedings of 5th International Working Conference, IVA 2005 Kos, Greece, September 12-14, 2005. Springer: 37-51 doi: 10.1007/11550617_4
20. Jürgen Habermas. 1998. *On the Pragmatics of Communication*. Cambridge: Polity Press.
21. Richard H. R. Harper. 2010. *Texture: Human Expression in the Age of Communications Overload*. MIT Press
22. Kerstin Heuwinkel. 2012. Framing the Invisible – The Social Background of Trust. In *Your Virtual Butler: The Making-of*. Robert Trappl (ed). Springer, 16-26. doi: 10.1007/978-3-642-37346-6_3
23. Ido A. Iurgel & Manuel Ziegler. 2005. Ask & Answer: An Educational Game Where It Pays to Endear Your Capricious Virtual Companion. In *Intelligent Virtual Agents*. Themis Panayiotopoulos, Jonathan Gratch, Ruth Aylett, Daniel Ballin, Patrick Olivier & Thomas Rist (Eds.) Proceedings of 5th International Working Conference, IVA 2005 Kos, Greece, September 12-14, 2005. Springer: 15-24 doi: 10.1007/11550617_2
24. Stephan Kopp, Lars Gesellensetter, Nicole, C. Krämer & Ipke Wachsmuth. 2005. A Conversational Agent as Museum Guide: Design and Evaluation of a Real-World Application. *Intelligent Virtual Agents*. 3661: 329-343 doi: 10.1007/11550617_28
25. Joseph Carl Robnett Licklider. Man-Computer Symbiosis . IRE Transactions on Human Factors in Electronics, HFE-1,(March, 1960), 4-11

26. Paul P. Maglio and Christopher S. Campbell. 2003. Attentive agents. *Communications of the ACM* 46, 3: 47-51 doi: 10.1145/636772.636797

27. Cade Metz. 2015. Get a Peek at Using Facebook's New Assistant, 'M'. *Wired*. Retrieved from http://www.wired.com/2015/09/get-peek-someone-using-facebooks-new-assistant-m/ (accessed 07.09.15)

28. Roger Moore. 2012. Spoken Language Processing: Where do we go from Here? In *Your Virtual Butler: The Making-of.* Robert Trappl (ed). Springer, 119-133 doi: 10.1007/978-3-642-37346-6_10

29. Andreea I Niculescu, Kheng Hui Yeo, Luis F D'Haro, Seokhwan Kim, Ridong Jiang & Rafael E Banchs. 2014. Design and evaluation of a conversational agent for the touristic domain. *In Proceedings of APSIPA' 14*: 1–10. doi:10.1109/APSIPA.2014.7041744

30. Don Norman. 2013. *The Design of Everyday Things*. Basic Books.

31. Kenton O'Hara, Richard Harper, Helena Mentis. Abigail Sellen and Alex Taylor. 2013. On the naturalness of touchless: putting the "interaction" back into NUI. *ACM Transactions on Computer-Human Interaction*. 20, 1 doi: 10.1145/2442106.2442111

32. Sabine Payr. 2012. Virtual Butlers and Real People: Styles and Practices in Long Term Use of a Companion. In *Your Virtual Butler: The Making-of.* Robert Trappl (ed). Springer, 134-178 doi: 10.1007/978-3-642-37346-6_11

33. Jenny Preece, Yvonne Rogers & Helen Sharp. 2015. *Interaction Design: Beyond Huma- Computer Interaction.* Wiley& Sons Ltd

34. Stephen Pulman. Johan Boye, Marc Cavazza, Cameron Smith & Raúl Santos de la Cámara. 2010. How was your Day? *In Proceedings of the 2010 Workshop on Companionable Dialogue Systems. Assoc. for Computational Linguistics*, Stroudsburg, PA, USA: 37-42

35. Byron Reeves & Clifford Nass. 1996. *The Media Equation: How People Treat Computers, Television, and New Media Like Real People and Places*. New York: Cambridge University Press.

36. Deborah Richards. 2012. Agent-based museum and tour guides: applying the state of the art. In *Proceedings of The 8th Australasian Conference on Interactive Entertainment: Playing the System (IE '12).* ACM (2012) doi: 10.1145/2336727.2336742

37. Lina Maria Rojas-Barahona and Christophe Cerisara. 2014. Bayesian Inverse Reinforcement Learning for Modelling Conversational Agents in a Virtual Environment. *Computational Linguistics and Intelligent Text Processing*. 8403: 503-514 doi: 10.1007/978-3-642-54906-9_41

38. Nicole Shechtman, and Leonard M Horowitz. 2003 Media Inequality in Conversation: How People Behave Differently when Interacting with Computers and People. *In Proceedings of the. SIGCHI Conference on Human Factors in Computing Systems (CHI '03).* ACM, (2003), 281-288 doi: 10.1145/642659.642661

39. Nathan Shedroff & Christopher Noessel. 2012. *Make it so: Interaction Design Lessons from Science Fiction.* Brooklyn, New York: Rosenfeld

40. Stergios Tegos, Stavros Demetriadis, Thrasyvoulos Tsiatsos. 2012. Using a Conversational Agent for Promoting Collaborative Language Learning In *Proceedings of Fourth International Conference on Intelligent Networking and Collaborative Systems*: 162-165 doi: 10.1109/iNCoS.2012.105

41. Janienke Sturm, Else den Os, Lou Boves. 1999. Issues in Spoken Dialogue Systems: Experiences with the Dutch ARISE System. *In the proceedings of ESCA Workshop on Interactive Dialogue in Multi-Modal Systems (UDS-99)*, Kolster Irsee, Germany.

42. Robert Trappl. 2012. From Jeeves Jeannie to Siri, and Then? In *Your Virtual Butler: The Making-of.* Robert Trappl (ed). Springer, 1-8 doi: 10.1007/978-3-642-37346-6_1

43. Giorgio Vassallo, Giovanni Pilato, Agnese Augello & Salvatore Gaglio. 2010. Phrase Coherence in Conceptual Spaces for Conversational Agents. In *Semantic Computing.* Sheu, Yu, Ramamoorthy, Joshi & Zadeh.(eds). IEEE: 357-371 doi: 10.1002/9780470588222.ch18

44. Astrid M. Von der Pütten, Nicloe C. Krämer, Jonathan Gratch & Sin-Hwa Kang. 2010. "It doesn't matter what you are!" Explaining Social Effects of Agents and Avatars. In *Computers in Human Behaviour*, 26: 1641-1650 doi: 10.1016/j.chb.2010.06.012

45. Joseph Weizenbaum. 1976. *Computer Power and Human Reason: From Judgement to Calculation*. W. H. Freeman

46. Joseph Weizenbaum. 1965. Eliza: A Computer Program for the Study of Natural Language Communication between Man and Machine. In *Communications of the ACM.* 9,1:36-45 doi: 10.1145/365153.365168

47. Yorick Wilks. 2010. Is a companion a distinctive kind of relationship with a machine? *.In Proceedings of the 2010 Workshop on Companionable Dialogue Systems (CDS '10).* Association for Computational Linguistics, Stroudsburg, PA, USA, 13-18

48. Yorick Wilks (ed.). 2010. *Close Engagements with Artificial Companions. Key social, psychological, ethical and design issues*. Amsterdam: John Benjamins.

LivingDesktop: Augmenting Desktop Workstation with Actuated Devices

Gilles Bailly[1] **Sidharth Sahdev**[1] **Sylvain Malacria**[2] **Thomas Pietrzak**[3]
[1]LTCI, CNRS, Telecom ParisTech, University Paris-Saclay, France
[2]Inria, France [3]Univ. Lille, France
{firstname.lastname} [1]@telecom-paristech.fr [2]@inria.fr [3]@univ-lille1.fr

ABSTRACT
We investigate the potential benefits of actuated devices for the desktop workstation which remains the most used environment for daily office works. A formative study reveals that the desktop workstation is not a fixed environment because users *manually* change the position and the orientation of their devices. Based on these findings, we present the *LivingDesktop*, an augmented desktop workstation with devices (mouse, keyboard, monitor) capable of moving autonomously. We describe interaction techniques and applications illustrating how actuated desktop workstations can improve ergonomics, foster collaboration, leverage context and reinforce physicality. Finally, the findings of a scenario evaluation are (1) the perceived usefulness of ergonomics and collaboration applications; (2) how the LivingDesktop inspired our participants to elaborate novel accessibility and social applications; (3) the location and user practices should be considered when designed actuated desktop devices.

Author Keywords
Augmented Desktop; Destkop Workstation; Actuated Devices; Mouse; Keyboard; Monitor

ACM Classification Keywords
H.5.m. Information Interfaces and Presentation (e.g. HCI): Miscellaneous

INTRODUCTION
Desktop workstation remains the most used interface for office work tasks such as text editing, CAD, data analysis or programming. Indeed, pointing with a *mouse*, typing text on a *physical keyboard* and visualizing digital content on relatively *large monitors* are well suited for single users performing office tasks requiring a high level of productivity for extended periods. While several studies investigated how users interact with their devices (e.g. pressing keyboard keys, moving the cursor, etc.), it is not clear how they arrange their devices on the desk and whether we can leverage existing users' behaviors.

CHI'16, May 07-12, 2016, San Jose, CA, USA
©2016 ACM. ISBN 978-1-4503-3362 -7/16/05...$15.00
DOI: http://dx.doi.org/10.1145/2858036.2858208

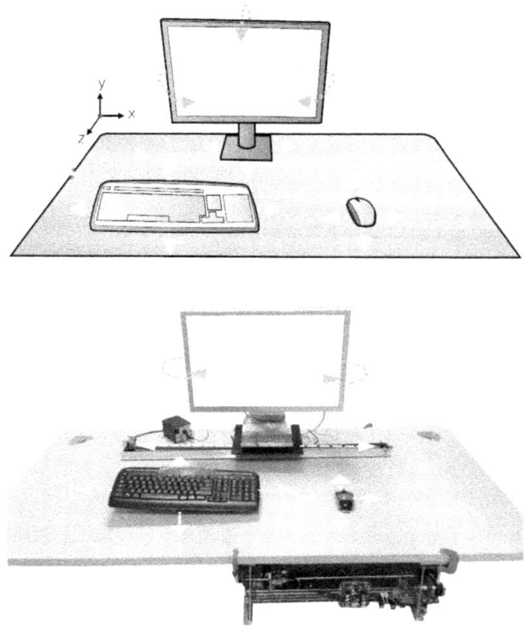

Figure 1. The LivingDesktop concept and proof-of-concept. The LivingDesktop is an augmented desktop with the mouse, keyboard and monitor capable of moving to improve ergonomics, foster collaboration, leverage context and reinforce physicality in the desktop workstation.

In this paper, we conduct a formative study investigating how users arrange and manipulate their desktop workstation devices (mouse, keyboard and monitor). While the desktop workstation is often considered as a *fixed* environment, our observations and interviews reveal that it is actually *semi-fixed* since users often change the position and the orientation of their devices. For instance, they can rotate the monitor to share contents, move the keyboard to adopt an ergonomic posture or move the keyboard and the mouse to make room for physical objects (e.g. food box, tablet).

Based on these findings, we investigate the potential benefits of actuated devices to create richer and more effective interaction on desktop workstations. Actuated interfaces are interfaces in which physical components move in a way that can be detected by the user [34]. They have shown promise in different applications such as tangible interaction [28], public displays [16] or virtual reality (VR) [41] but they have not been investigated in the traditional desktop workstation which has remained essentially the same for over thirty years.

We present the LivingDesktop (Figure 1), an augmented desktop with devices capable of moving autonomously. The LivingDesktop can control the position and orientation of the mouse, keyboard and monitors. It offers different degrees of control for both the system (autonomous, semi-autonomous) and the user (manual, semi-manual) as well as different perceptive qualities (visual, haptic) thanks to a large range of device motions.

The LivingDesktop has several advantages: (1) it improves *ergonomics* by continuously adjusting the position of its devices to help users adopting ergonomic postures and avoiding static postures for extended periods; (2) It facilitates *collaborative* works between local (e.g. located in the office) and remote co-workers. For instance, the teacher can control the mouse of a student during distant teaching; (3) it leverages context by reacting to the position of the user in the office, the presence of physical objects (e.g. tablets, food) or users' current activity to maintain a high level of comfort and (4) it reinforces physicality within the desktop workstation to increase immersion. For instance the monitor and the input devices shake when an explosion occurs in video games, providing both visual and haptic feedback.

We present a proof-of-concept of the LivingDesktop combining rail, robotic base and magnetism to control the position and orientation of the devices. We then conduct a scenario evaluation. Results show (1) the perceived usefulness of collaborative and ergonomics applications (2) how the LivingDesktop inspired our participants to elaborate novel applications including social communication or accessibility.

Our main contributions are 1) a proof-of-concept augmented desktop with devices capable of moving; 2) A set of interaction techniques and applications relying on the findings of a formative study; 3) Findings of a scenario evaluation.

RELATED WORK

The sustainability of the desktop workstation has encouraged researchers to explore ways to augment it. The most common approach is to augment the *software* aspect of the workstation such as new window managers (e.g. [7]). In comparison, little *physical* approaches have been investigated. When creating the LivingDesktop, we sought to build upon the related work in the area of augmented desktop and traditional devices (mouse, keyboard, monitor). We also discuss studies that have inspired the implementation of the LivingDesktop.

Augmented desktop workstation

The primary rationale of augmenting the desktop workstation is to better blend it in office activities. Several works aimed at enabling simultaneous work with *physical information* such as paper documents and digital information [1, 49]. The idea is to enhance paper documents that are cheap, familiar, easy to read, etc. with computation rather than replacing them with computers. For instance, the DigitalDesk [49] and InteractiveDesk [1] recognize and scan paper documents with a camera and augment them with videoprojection.

Other approaches make good use of *everyday human skills* to augment desktop workstation, typically designers who use Wacom tablets for drawing-like activities. In that respect, Hinckley *et al.* considers the ability of humans to use both hands in the real world and present a set of two-handed interaction techniques for desktop [14].

A final approach considers the *furnitures* surrounding the desktop workstation to extent peripheric interaction. For instance, office workers can use the desk as an input (touch or pen input for shortcuts) or output surface to extend the monitor display area with video-projection [3, 17, 45]. The chair can also be used as an input device to capture emotional data, gesture input and support office activities (e.g. [35, 36]).

Our approach also considers the desktop workstation as a whole that should be integrated in its environment, but our primary focus is on augmenting devices and their interaction.

Augmented devices

In parallel, several works augment independently input devices in order to provide novel input or output capabilities.

Some mouse prototypes introduce novel input modalities, for instance, to capture rotations [21, 24, 33] or multitouch input[1]. Others provide visual [50] or haptic [21, 22, 29] feedback. In particular, the Immersion FEELit mouse [37] is mounted on a pantograph to provide efficient haptic sensations but its displacements are limited to a few centimeters without the possibility to lift it. Park *et al.* embedded an electromagnet in a mouse operated over a metal plate to control the difficulty to move the mouse [29], but the mouse is not capable of moving.

Augmented keyboards have been proposed to sense gestures inputs [46, 52] or pressure inputs [9]. Other keyboards provide visual [4] or additional haptic feedback [2, 40].

Finally, actuated displays [6, 8, 20, 42, 44, 51] have been proposed in different contexts. For instance, TouchMover [44] is a touchscreen mounted onto a rail that exerts forces when users are pushing it in a VR context. In video-conferencing, tablet displays mounted on pan-tilt robotic platform have been proposed to increase immersion and telepresence [8, 20, 51]. RoCo [6] is a robotic display with 5 degrees of freedom to improve ergonomics.

Proxemic interaction and micro-mobility

The LivingDesktop is also related to Proxemic interaction and micro-mobility because it considers the distance between the desktop devices and: the user, the other devices, and possible objects on the desk. Proxemic interaction [11] describes the interaction between users and computing devices based on Hall's theory about people use of distance to mediate their interactions with other person [12]. Among others, Greenberg *et al.* describe the orientation and distance between persons or between a user and computing devices, as key measures mediating the interaction in the context of ubiquitous computing. Micro-mobility [23] is at a different scale and considers "*the way in which an artifact can be mobilized and manipulated for various purposes around a relatively circumscribed, or at hand, domain*".

[1] https://www.apple.com/magicmouse/

Objects capable of moving

In the literature on actuated devices [34, 38], the LivingDesktop is especially related to actuated tangibles on tabletops [5, 26, 28, 31, 32, 43, 48]. For instance, PsyBench [5] synchronizes the position of tangibles on a local and distant tabletop to enhance real time collaboration in distributed environment. Pico [31] moves tangibles and apply magnetic attraction and repulsion forces to users' movements to satisfy constraints between tangibles (e.g. relative distance) defined in software. TangibleBots [32] ensures physical/digital consistency when manipulating the digital model or allows efficient interaction with multiple tangibles. These works inspired some of the applications of the LivingDesktop (the category called Physicality) as well as the technologies to move objects: motorizing objects [32, 47] or augmenting the surface and using passive objects [28, 31, 48].

In summary, few physical interaction techniques have been proposed to augment the desktop workstation that has remained essentially the same for over thirty years. Some works enrich traditional devices with novel input or output modalities, but we still lack (1) insights on the potential of actuated mouse, keyboard and monitors and (2) how they can interact together in an unified desktop environment.

FORMATIVE STUDY: ARRANGING DESKTOP DEVICES

We conducted a formative study to understand how users currently arrange and manipulate their desktop devices.

Procedure

We collected data from two-month informal observations of desktop users in two laboratory institutions. We also conducted semi-structured interviews with 13 desktop users. The interview was divided into three parts. The first part included questions about personal information (age, profession, frequency of device use, etc.). The second part included questions related to their last working sessions and when, why and how did they arrange and manipulate their desktop devices. Finally, the interviewer presented the collected observations and discuss them with the interviewee.

The 13 participants (3 female), aged 19 to 43 ($\bar{x} = 30$) including knowledge workers, designers, researchers and students reported occasionally or frequently doing web surfing (100% of them), using office applications (100%), programming (75%), gaming (45%). 93% of the participants (respectively 86%) use the keyboard (respectively the mouse) more than 6 hours per day. Finally, 93% of the participants occasionally or frequently use a second monitor.

Findings

77% of respondents reported having moved either the mouse, keyboard or monitor during their last use of their desktop workstation, beyond the simple fact of controlling the cursor on the screen with the mouse, suggesting desktop devices are generally not adequately located on the desk. We collected respondents' different motivations and organized them into three categories:

1. Ergonomics. Half of respondents reported to frequently rotate their monitor when the luminosity conditions are changing. We observed that users frequently adjust the home position of the keyboard (and some extent the mouse) when correcting or changing their body postures (e.g. moving the chair). Three interviewees tend to rotate their display in order to plug devices. One participant said "*My monitor is quite heavy and far from me. So, I sometimes get up from my chair to access the back of it*".

2. Collaboration. Half of the interviewees often rotate their monitor in order to show its content to somebody else. For instance, one participant reported "*I can rotate my monitor several times per hour when discussing a project with my colleague*". This can also happen with remote users. "*I sometime rotate my monitor [with a embedded webcam] while skyping to show something to the people I chat with*". In the opposite, we observed one user systematically rotating the monitor to prevent other users from seeing it. Finally, we observed several participants passing on mouse and keyboard to grant input control to somebody else.

3. Situation. One respondent rotates his monitor when moving in his office from his desk to a companion table. One respondent also reported rotating the monitor at home when switching activities: "I *work on my desk, but when I watch a movie, I rotate the monitor so this is visible while leaning on my bed*". "*Sometimes, I rotate the monitor in portrait mode when active reading or editing a document. Otherwise I use the landscape mode*". Three users occasionally or frequently use a laptop with their desktop monitor and reported "*moving [their] desktop monitor to fit the virtual desktops configuration to the location of the physical screens*". Observations and interviews revealed that users move their keyboard and mouse back to a specific location every evening when leaving work. Rationale was either because (1) they are office workers working in an open-space environment, (2) their employer requested them to do so, (3) their devices were wireless and required to be charged on their stations. Finally, we observed some participants moving their mouse and keyboard to temporally make some room on the desk for other objects such as food, paper documents or tablets.

In conclusion, while the desktop workstation is often considered as a *fixed* environment, it is actually a semi-fixed one where users are arranging and manipulating the mouse, the keyboard and the monitor to accommodate an ongoing task or a specific activity. In this paper, we investigate whether actuated devices may be a promising approach to support users' behaviors and enrich the desktop interaction experience.

THE LIVINGDESKTOP

The LivingDesktop (Figure 1), is an augmented desktop with actuated devices having similar form factors (size, weight) than current devices (Figure 2). The LivingDesktop can control the position and orientation of the mouse, keyboard and monitors, offering different degrees of control for both the system and the user (from autonomous to manual control). It also offers different perceptive qualities (visual, haptic) thanks to a large range of device motions. Actuating a desktop workstation with the LivingDesktop implies the following design considerations.

Devices. A desktop workstation is composed of a combination of input (mouse, keyboard, tablet, etc.) and output devices (monitor, speakers) that could be actuated. Other devices, typically a phone, are also often on a desk, even though it is not entirely a device of the desktop workstation itself.

Degrees of freedom. This dimension expresses the type of motions users can expect from an actuated device. Ideally, each device should provide 6 *degrees of freedom* (DOFs) with 3 translations (T) and 3 rotations (R) to allow a wide class of applications. However, we will see in the next sections that simple actuations on the horizontal plan (T_x, T_z, R_y) already support a wide range of applications (see table 1).

Levels of perception. The design space of actuated device motions is huge and includes speed, directions and range of motion [30]. Here, we focus on how these motions can be perceived by people in the office. In particular, we distinguish four levels of perception: (1) motions that can be visually perceived by both the user and people around (e.g., rotating the monitor can draw co-workers attention to initiate a collaboration); (2) motions that can only be seen by the user (e.g., moving the keyboard on the desk); (3) motions that can be haptically perceived by the user (e.g., the mouse can provide haptic feedback by shaking or opposing resistance to users' motions); (4) motions that are not consciously perceived by the user (e.g., one application in ergonomics slowly shift devices over time to avoid static postures).

Degrees of control. This dimension is a continuum inspired by HoverPad [43] expressing the degree of control of the user (respectively the system) on the devices. On one end of the continuum, the devices can be *autonomous*. The monitor or a mouse can for instance shake when an explosion occurs in a video-game regardless of the actions of the user. On the other end of the continuum, the user has the full control of the devices actuation (*manual*). In between, we emphasize two degrees of control: semi-manual control occurs for instance when the user is manipulating the mouse and the resistance is partially defined by the system; semi-autonomous control occurs when the system moves the mouse to guide the user's hand. Note that supporting different degrees of control might require powerful actuators (e.g. motors).

Interaction. Users can *explicitly* request devices to move/rotate with different interaction techniques. They can directly manipulate the device itself. They can also perform indirect interaction. To rotate the screen, users can for instance move the mouse, perform a mid-air pointing gesture or simply press a dedicated key on the keyboard. Indirect interaction is especially useful in configurations where the devices is out of hand reach. The interaction can also be *implicit*. It occurs in situations where the user interacts without being aware of interacting. For instance, the monitor can automatically rotate when the user is moving to her companion table.

Sensing context. The LivingDesktop senses the desktop workstation and its surroundings to adapt to user activity. In particular, it is aware of the position and orientation of the devices and objects (e.g. books) on the desk, of user's position and of the applications running on the computer.

Figure 2. Living Desktop setup consisting of a mouse, keyboard and monitor as well as a depth camera to track their position on the desk.

Figure 3. Left. The monitor relies on a servo motor for rotation and a rail for translation. Right. The keyboard is augmented with a robotic base allowing translation (Txz) an rotation (Ry) of the device

PROOF-OF-CONCEPT

Our proof-of-concept comes out of several compromises. Despite the advances in robotics, we are not aware of technologies allowing rapid prototyping of such environments. Introducing actuated devices within the desktop workstation raises several long-term challenges such as (1) the miniaturization of the actuators to keep devices with the same form factor and weight; (2) the quality of the actuation (for instance, the device should quickly react to system instructions to maintain a high level of interactivity and provide enough strength to guide/resists to the users' motions); (3) It should also allow a large variety of motions, ideally 3 degrees of freedom (DoF) in translation and 3 DoF in rotation with a large range of motion; Finally, (4) for deployment, the autonomy and cost should accommodate widespread adoption.

The LivingDesktop setup (Figure 2) comprises three actuated devices (monitor, mouse and keyboard) and a depth sensor to track the locations of the devices and the user.

Monitor. A 65cm × 49cm monitor (2560×1440) rests on a horizontal base capable of rotating at 180 degrees per second speed using a servo motor (TowerPro digital servo Mg995). We brought its rotation speed down to 60 degrees per second to reduce centrifugal forces and prevent the screen from toggling when rotating. A robotic rail (100cm× 9cm) on the table allows the monitor to translate sideways along the desk

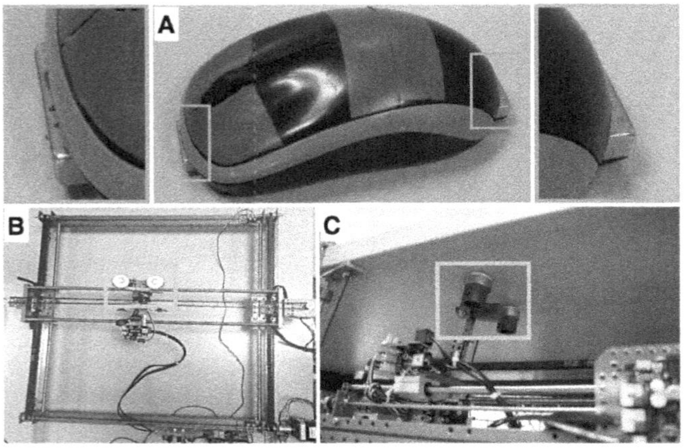

Figure 4. (A) Mouse augmented with two magnets. (B) A plotter under the desk control the position of the mouse. (C) A arm with two magnets to couple (or not) the mouse to the plotter

(Figure 3). The rail uses pulley and timing belt attached to a 12V dc motor with enough torque to translate the monitor screen sideways.

Keyboard. We augmented a wireless keyboard (Logitech MK320) with a robotic base that can translate and rotate (Figure 3). The base consists of a 12V DC motor driven differential drive system for locomotion and a 6V stepper motor for orientation control. The keyboard (6.8cm high) is slightly higher than traditional keyboard. The height may be reduced further depending on the choice of wheels and dc motors.

Mouse. A plotter (Makelblock XY-Plotter Robot Kit V2.0) is positioned under the desk to control the mouse position. Two strong magnets (2×1×0.5cm) are attached on the plotter arm and on the mouse (front and back) to magnetically couple these two elements on demand and maintain the orientation of the mouse. The strength of the magnetic field was chosen after several iterations to offer adequate resistance to the users movements without completely blocking their movements. Moreover, the actuator power should be stronger than the magnetic field to ensure that disengagement of the mouse is still possible. The working area is 310mm×390mm which is larger than common mouse pads.

Tracking devices, objects and hand gestures. We used a RGBD camera (Microsoft Kinect) fixed over the desk (Figure 2) and OpenCV to track the position and orientation of the devices. We consider all objects located less than 8cm over the desk on the depth image (Figure 5) as *objects* and then user colors tags to recognize the mouse and keyboard of other objects. Indeed, recognizing a device from its shape with the depth image may not be sufficient, especially because the hand can mask much of the device. We also ignore objects that are too small to be devices (typically, a pen). Feedback from the kinect sensor keeps track of the physical mouse and other devices on the table. From the depth image, the system can also recognize rectangular objects approaching the desk. Finally, it can recognize a pointing gesture performed by the user between 8 and 20 cm over the desk (see Figure 5).

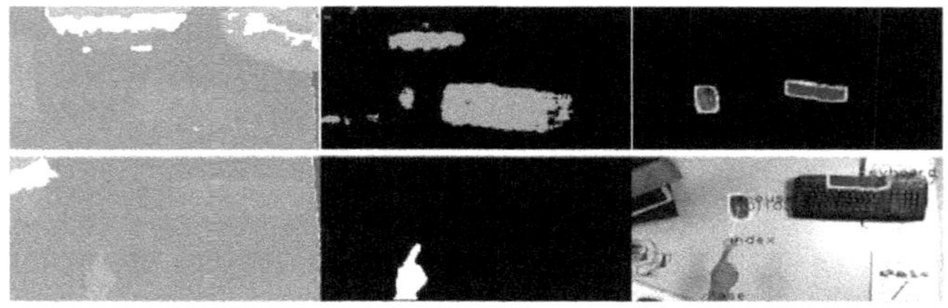

Figure 5. Top: The image is segmented by depth and color to track objects. Bottom: "pointing" gesture before and after depth segmentation.

Controller & Software. Devices communicate with our system using a Arduino micro-controller through an USB Serial port. Applications communicate with these devices thanks to a dedicated protocol. The system is then responsible for sending instructions to devices, analyzing the data from the depth camera, and relating that information with user activity. The prototype is based on Qt/C++/OpenCV and run under Linux. We developed a library that encapsulates the communication protocol, and provides a discovery protocol over serial ports to ease the detection and connection of devices.

APPLICATIONS

We foresee four main classes of applications that would benefit from the LivingDesktop. The first three directly result from the formative study. They describe *existing* users' behaviours and aim at improving ergonomics, fostering collaboration and leveraging context. The last class of applications is called "Physicality" and consists of bridging the gap between digital and physical desktop. The list of applications we are now presenting is not meant to be exhaustive but illustrates potential benefits of the LivingDesktop for each category. We will see in the section "Scenario Evaluation" that our participants also built on the LivingDesktop to elaborate novel usages. The applications are summarized in the table 1.

Ergonomics

Office work often requires people to remain in static positions for extended periods [13]. However, the restriction of movement leads to pain, fatigue and potential long-term injury such as the carpal tunnel syndrome[2], especially when people do not adopt the appropriate postures. The two following applications focus on these two problems: inappropriate postures (*Configuring*) and static postures (*Shifting*).

Configuring. When the user is sitting down in her working chair, the system detects her current posture either with sensors in the chair [35, 36] or computer vision system located above the desk (see implementation section). The system then moves the mouse, keyboard and monitors to ensure a safe working environment compatible with ergonomic postures: the monitor moves in front of the user, rises to have the top of the screen with the users' eyes and slightly tilt upward in order to avoid possible neck and shoulder pain [13]. The keyboard moves in front of the user just above the level of her lap. The mouse stays close to the keyboard to not have to reach far to grasp it. The keyboard can also slightly tilt away depending on the angle of the user's arm.

[2] Workers Health and Safety Centre (WHSC)

Application	Devices	DOFs	Perception	Control	Interaction	Sensing
ERGONOMICS						
Configuring *						
- **Initial configuration**		T_{xyz}, R_{xyz}	Visual	Autonomous	Implicit	User posture
- Adjust posture [6]		T_{xyz}, R_{xyz}	Visual	Autonomous	Implicit	User posture
- **Adjust brightness**		R_y	Visual	Autonomous	Implicit	Ambient light
Shifting		T_{xyz}, R_{xyz}	$\emptyset$	Autonomous	Implict	User posture
Pluging *		R_y	Visual	Manual	Explicit - Indirect	
COLLABORATION						
Co-Working *		R_y	Visual	Manual	Explicit-Indirect	
Video-conference [8, 20, 51]		R_y, R_z	Visual	Manual	Explicit-Indirect	Mid-air gesture
Distant control						
- Touchy Talkie [39]		T_{xz}	Haptic	Semi-autonomous	Explicit-direct	
- **Distant teaching**		T_{xz}	Haptic	Semi-autonomous	Explicit-direct	
SITUATION AND CONTEXT AWARNESS						
Following *		R_y	Visual	Autonomous	Implicit	User location
Tidying *						
- **Recharging devices**		T_{xz}	Visual	Autonomous	Implicit	Objects
- **Moving devices away**		T_{xz}	Visual	Autonomous	Implicit	Objects
Devices on demand						
- **Bringing devices**		T_{xz}, R_z	Visual	Autonomous	Implicit	Activity
- **Portrait/landscape mode**		T_{xz}, R_x	Visual	Autonomous	Implicit	Activity
PHYSICALITY						
Relief [27][44]		T_{xz}	Haptic	Semi-Manual	Explicit-Direct	
Shaking		T_{xz}, R_{yz}	Visual/haptic	Autonomous		
Virtual Space *						
- **Peephole display**		T_{xy}	Visual	Manual	Explicit-Indirect	
- **Displays arrangement**		T_{xy}	Visual	Manual	Explicit-Indirect	

Table 1. The seven features of the LivingDesktop for the proposed applications. (1) Applications inspired from the formative study are marked with *; Novel applications are in bold; (2) Device; (3) Degrees of freedom (DOFs); (4) modality related to levels of perception; (5) Degree of control; (6) Interaction; (7) Sensing context.

Inspired by Roco [6], the LivingDesktop can also dynamically adjust the user's posture. The devices can either move away until the user adopts an appropriate posture, or subtly move to a position so that the user has a tendency to mirror the movements of the devices and adopt a better posture.

Some systems adjust the monitor brightness according to ambient light. A LivingDesktop with luminosity sensors extends this feature by slightly changing the orientation of the monitor according to the direction of light to avoid uncomfortable light reflection.

Shifting. The devices *slightly* shift over time to force users to regularly adjust their positions and avoid static postures for extended periods and prevent repetitive stress injury.

Pluging. Tapping on a dedicated keyboard key makes the monitor rotate and come closer to ease plugging/unplugging a device. A second tap moves it back to its default configuration. This can be used with most of the monitors on the market which have various plugs (usb, firewire, ethernet, dvi, etc.) located at their back.

Collaboration

Co-working. The LivingDesktop allows users to easily rotate the monitor, either to share screen contents with co-workers located in the office (Figure 6-left) or to prevent shoulder surfing. Users press a dedicated key on the keyboard (e.g. Function key) to enter in the pseudo mode "Monitor control". They can then control the orientation of the screen by dragging the mouse. Users can also double tap on the key to rotate the monitor to a bookmarked angle such as both the user and the visitor (sitting on the visitor chair) can see the screen. Double tapping a second time, rotates the monitor back to its default orientation. Instead of using the keyboard, a button can be located on the monitor itself. While this functionality can be more easily discovered than a dedicated key, it is slower because it requires larger arm movements. Moreover, it does not work when the monitor is out of arm reach.

Video-conferencing. The LivingDesktop can enrich video-conferencing experience. When a local user wants to show an element in the office (e.g. an object on the desk, an equation on the whiteboard, etc.) during a video-conferencing, she presses the dedicated key and points towards this object

Figure 6. left. The user rotates the monitor to share screen content with his co-worker by using a dedicated key on the keyboard and moving the mouse. Right. The user presses a dedicated key and points towards an object to make sure that this object is inside the field of view of the webcam and visible from the remote user.

as shown on Figure 6-right. The livingDesktop then rotates the local monitor (equipped with a built-in camera) and makes sure that this object is inside the field of view of the embedded webcam. The user can also use the mouse instead her hand to rotate the monitor. In this scenario, the local monitor reacts *explicitly* to the actions of the *local* user. The local monitor could also *implicitly* react to the actions of the *distant* user. For instance, the motions of the monitor are coupled to the head movements of the distant user. This application, inspired by [8, 20] makes the telepresence more engaging because it gives natural feeling of head movement as in a face-to-face conversation. While this application relies on an actuated monitor, the next one uses an actuated mouse.

Distant Control. The idea of this application is to control the mouse of a distant user. The actuated mouse can be used as a "touchy Talkie" [39] to communicate a message through the haptic modality: the user moves her mouse to shape a "heart". When the distant user touches his mouse, the mouse reproduces the same path to communicate the "heart" [39].

The actuated mouse can also be used for remote teaching. When the remote teacher wants to attract the attention of a student on a specific element on the screen, he can take the control of her cursor but also the mouse to physically guide the hand of the user through haptic feedback. While traditional systems allow distributed users to share *digital* contents, the Living Desktop also allows them to share *physical* devices [5] and to assist them with haptic feedback.

Situation and Context awareness

Following. The monitor "follows" the user in her office (e.g. standing on his companion table) by changing its orientation. It displays notifications (e.g new emails, agenda alerts, missed calls, etc.) and adapts the size of what is displayed so it can be read regardless of the distance (Figure 7).

Tidying. To keep the desk tidy, the devices move away when the user shuts down the computer, when he leaves his office or after a period of inactivity (e.g. 10mn). Moreover, the devices can move to their charging stations. This is especially useful with state of the art wireless devices (e.g. keyboard with embedded screens [4] or actuators [2], shape-changing mouses [21]) using more energy than conventional devices.

The LivingDesktop can also make room for other objects (Figure 8). It detects (with computer vision) when the user

Figure 7. The monitor follows the user to be readable when working on her companion standing table.

Figure 8. The LivingDesktop anticipates when the user wants to put an object on the desk and make room for it.

carries an object in her hands (e.g lunch box, printed document, tablet, etc.) and anticipates whether she wants to put it on the desk by moving the devices on the sides. This scenario can be extended to virtual objects when the desk is used as a large output surface (with a tabletop or video-projection) [3]. For instance, the keyboard and the mouse masking important information (e.g. cities) of a virtual map move away to keep information visible.

Devices on demand. The LivingDesktop brings the desired pointing device at hand (or move it away) depending of the current activity. Indeed, some users have several pointing devices, depending of the task they perform, typically one graphic tablet for design tasks and one mouse for other activities (office work, games).

The orientation of the screen can also depends on the current activity: The monitor automatically rotates from the landscape mode to the portray mode when editing a digital portray on Adobe Photoshop or when activating the full screen mode of Adobe Reader with a portray format document in order to make reading more comfortable.

Physicality

A key feature of the Livingdesktop is to reflect digital changes into the physical world through the actuated desktop devices. Actuation has already been used in tangible interfaces to preserve consistency between digital information and physical object [28, 32]. For instance, the position of sliders in a sound mixer can be controlled by the system to be consistent with the current sound parameters. Similarly, the LivingDesktop aims at introducing more physicality in desktop interaction, either to decrease the inconsistency between desktop devices and the manipulated virtual data or to increase immersion by exploiting a larger range of perceptual qualities.

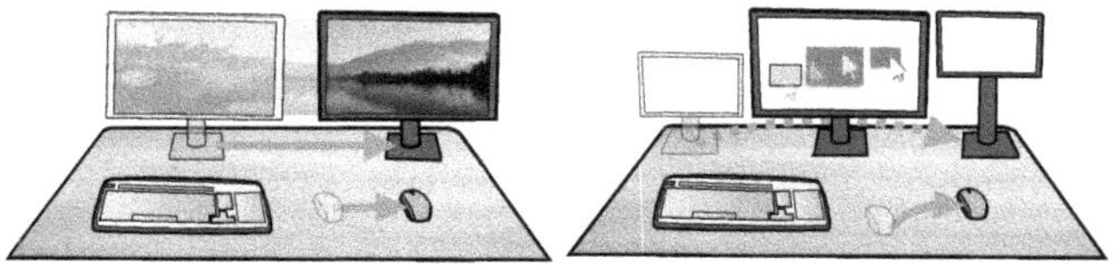

Figure 9. Left. The monitor acts as a *peephole display* over the virtual space. Right. The relative position of the secondary monitor fits the virtual spatial configuration.

The coupling between the physical mouse and the virtual cursor is usually one way: the mouse displacements control the position of the cursor. However, changes in the location of the cursor are not reflected by the mouse. The LivingDesktop allows bidirectional interaction to maintain consistency between digital information and the physical desktop devices (mouse, keyboard and monitor).

Relief. The LivingDesktop can make games or graphical information systems more tangible. For instance, the mouse behavior can simulate the depth on monitors. Depending on the position of the cursor, the system can change the coefficient of friction and constraint trajectories to act as physical gravity wells [27]: the "avatar" can shift along the slip of a ditch or provide resistance when rising a hill. This application illustrates how to reduce inconsistencies between the mouse and the cursor to increase immersion.

This application can be extended to touchscreens: The user touches and feels the relief of a map on the screen which moves on the z axis depending on the position of the finger on the map such as the TouchMover system[44].

Shaking. Applications can also rely on more autonomous behaviors. The mouse and the monitor could shake when explosion or a crash occurs in a game to simulate visual (monitor) and kineasthetic sensations (mouse, keyboard).

Virtual Spaces. LivingDesktop can also be used to navigate in very large documents such as images or maps that cannot be displayed entirely on the screen. When the cursor is approaching the border of screen, the navigation relies on rate-control. However, instead on moving the digital content within the frame of the monitor, the monitor is shifting as a window on the digital content. Thus, the monitor becomes a *peephole display* over the entire virtual space (Figure 9-left), which can theoretically increase spatial recall accuracy over the traditional *panning* approach [19]. We also considered *virtual desktops* which are supported by most recent operating systems. Typically, Mac OS X allows users to organize their applications and windows in virtual desktops arranged in an horizontal line. The LivingDesktop brings this concept into the physical world. It changes the physical position of the monitor depending on the current virtual desktop. For instance moving the monitor to the right when the user switches to the next virtual desktop.

In the same spirit, when users are editing the "Displays Arrangement" preferences, the physical relative position of the monitors is arranged automatically to match the configuration in the virtual space (Figure 9). If the user uses a laptop on his desk, the position of the second monitor can be updated according to the current position of the laptop on the desk.

Implementation

All the above described applications have been implemented for our LivingDesktop prototype. However, functionalities requiring to sense the environment remain limited. For instance, sensing user posture is limited to tracking user's head and hands. Moreover, user is only tracked in the vicinity of the desktop due to the limited field of view of the Microsoft Kinect. Advanced skeleton tracking and using wide-lenses (or raising the kinect when possible) could be used to better track user's activity and postures. Finally, the scenarios only use the available degrees of freedom of our prototype. For instance, the scenario changing the orientation of the monitor from landscape to portrait is incomplete but would be possible with a robotic arm.

SCENARIO EVALUATION

The goal of this study is to both collect feedback about the system and investigate whether the setup could trigger novel usage or applications. To achieve this, we deployed an online survey via mailing lists and social networks for evaluating a subset of 6 applications through videos. We chose a video-based evaluation to reduce the impact of the implementation on participants subjective feedbacks, because our prototype faces miniaturization and autonomy problems and may not be ready for extended use. We focused on applications where motions of devices was easy to perceive on videos, and took care to cover the four classes of applications. Each application was illustrated with a video showing the experimenter interacting with our Living Desktop proof-of-concept. The video was presented in an order that would make sense for an office worker. The scenario was the following:

(1) Bob enters in his office and the monitor rotates to indicate the time of his next meeting. (2) Bob then seats on his working chair. As his posture was not ergonomic, the keyboard and the mouse move away until he adopts a more ergonomic posture. (3) Bob decides to navigate within a large image. He drags the mouse to use his monitor as peephole display. After a break, (4) Bob seats back to his office and put his lunch box and the paper in front of him making the keyboard and the mouse move away to free the desk. When he has finished to read the paper, (5) Bob starts a video skype call with Linda to present his novel idea. When explaining the concept on the whiteboard, the monitor rotates so that the whiteboard is in the field of view of the embedded webcam. The skype call over, (6) Simon wants to help Bob to finalize his talk for this afternoon. Bob rotates the monitor with a dedicated key on the keyboard to share screen content with Simon. At the end of the day, Bob shuts down his computer and his devices move back in place to keep the desk tidy.

After each scenario, we asked (using a 7 item Likert scale) whether the presented scenario was liked, useful and amusing. They could also provide comments. Finally, at the end of the survey, one open question invites participants to suggest novel applications for the LivingDesktop system.

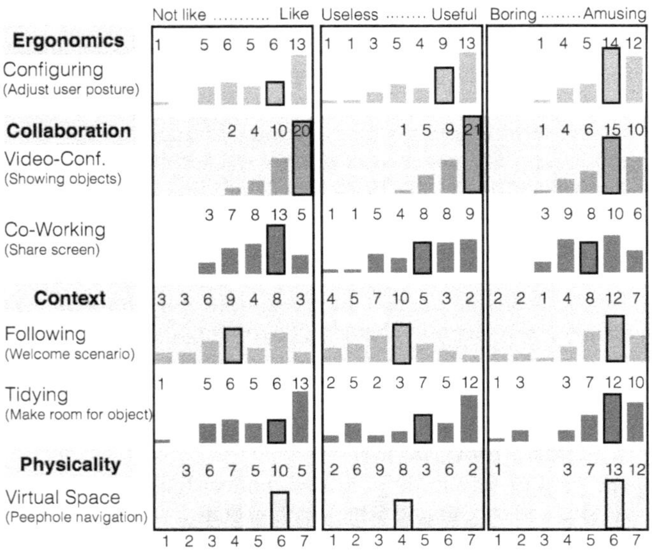

Figure 10. A summary of participants responses to the 7-point Likert scale questions with the median indicated.

Results

36 participants (11 female) aged 22 to 40 years (mean=28.8, SD=5.0) completed our online survey. Due to the growing concerns regarding null hypothesis significance testing [10], especially in the context of Likert-Scale measures [25, 18], we base our analysis on histogram distributions of ratings and medians (Figure 10). The distributions reveal that participants were particularly enthusiastic regarding three applications: Video-Conferencing (collaboration), Configuring (Ergonomics) and Tidying (context).

Video-conferencing. Video-conferencing received the highest subjective evaluations, especially for its perceived usefulness (median of 7). Participants reported they found it likely to be "*Very useful*", "*Useful in a closed office*"; they also found it was a "*Very good idea* because *rotating a monitor is every time very cumbersome while video-conferencing*".

Configuring. Participants also reported positive rates for this ergonomics application (median for 6 for all criteria). They mentioned "*I recognize myself and many people in this posture. This could encourage many people to adopt healthier habits*". "*It is a very nice way to improve the posture at work.*", "*This is a very good feature which I personally want to use, the problem is very practical and everyone in the office faces it.*". However, some respondents questioned the applicability of the approach: "*It could be useful, or not. Depending on what we're doing at the moment.*", highlighting the needs of being able to recognize user's posture and activity.

Tidying. Respondents liked the scenario where the devices make room for objects (median of 6) and found it amusing (median of 6). One stated "*I like it a lot. This is really good. I often move my keyboard to eat and I can completely relate to the use case.*". One also mentioned possible limitations when the desk is cluttered of documents: "*This might be difficult to achieve because of the clutter on the desktop*".

Co-Working. This application received strong divergences of opinions and was evaluated as moderately useful (median of 5) and amusing (median of 5) by participants. While some participants reported "*I think it is very useful. It is a very common problem in my job environment*" or "*This problem is finally solved*", others were less enthusiastic either because they "*do not think it would be useful*" or because they find it "*very easy to turn the screen*".

Virtual space. Participants were mixed regarding the usefulness of this application (median of 4), but still liked it (median of 6) because they found it amusing (median of 6). More precisely, they found it "Cool" and "Fun" and one participant said: "*I think this is really nice. If it can move forward and backward, it would be nice as well as that can be the zoom in/out.*". This result highlights the high potential of this application for playful applications and games.

Following. Participants did not like this application (median of 4) and were not enthusiastic about its usefulness (median of 4). They raised several potential privacy issues and were concerned whether it could "*be disturbing for other persons in the workspace*".

Untested techniques

Several participants suggested additional applications described in the paper but not tested in the user study. For instance, the monitor "*moves to not reflect the sun*" or moves back when the user is too close to "*ensure a minimum distance with the eyes and avoid eye fatigue*" (Ergonomic). One participant suggested to "*have one mouse for two seats*" or "*remote teaching scenarios*" (Collaboration). One considered the "Following" application "*useful at home. The screen lights up, rotates with me and provides information*" (Context). Two participants proposed to shake the mouse or the monitor in games (Physicality). Some participants also suggested applications we had not considered:

Accessibility. Two participants (one being a professional working with visually impaired people) reported that the LivingDesktop would be useful for people with disabilities. The *Configuring* application can be useful for people with motor impairments for moving the mouse in the vicinity of the user's hand. It can also be useful for visually impaired people to easily find the location of the input devices or to make the screen content readable by moving it closer.

Social Communication. Two participants suggested social communication applications for co-workers: "*Instead of sending an email to my co-worker, I will temporally show him my screen*" or "*I would attach post-its or other small objects on the mouse and 'order' it to visit my co-worker*". Another application was that when "*you want to speak to your colleague just behind the screen, it could go down a bit*".

Other. One respondent envisioned VR applications: "*When gaming with a VR headset, it can be difficult to grasp the keyboard. It could move towards my hands when I am trying to grab it*". One participant taking yoga video lessons would like the monitor to rotate to follow her postures when practicing. Finally, several participants wanted to actuate other objects such as a lamp or a phone.

DISCUSSION

The participants of our scenario evaluation were particularly enthusiastic with *ergonomics* and *collaborative* scenarios. The system also inspired them as they proposed various additional applications: some that we already considered but did not evaluate, and other novel applications in different domains including accessibility for people with visual or motor impairments or social communications with verbal or non verbal communications.

Our results also highlighted the critical importance of considering the context of interactions. Indeed, participants reported about the Following application that actuated monitor can be obtrusive and disturbing in a workspace. In the opposite, some participants see the LivingDesktop as an opportunity to have "*non-verbal communication between coworkers*". Others mentioned the efficiency of this system at home. Our evaluation was probably bias because the videos were performed in an open spaces with co-workers due to technical constraints. Results could have been different in a closed office or at home. It appears that the location should be seriously considered when deploying this technology.

We also observed strong divergences between participants regarding some applications, often because of different practices and habits between participants. For instance, while some participants found the Co-working application very useful, others found it useless because it can also be done manually. It seems, from the analysis of comments, that the perception of usefulness of this application is correlated to *user practices* and how frequently users perform this operation.

An other critical point highlighted by our scenario evaluation was the importance of not giving "too much" control to the LivingDesktop. This raises one key challenge of future actuated devices: How much should actuated devices be automated/ be controlled by the user? Table 1 shows that our applications cover several *degrees of control*: autonomous, semi-autonomous, semi-manual and manual. However, it appears that several participants were concerned that the system could be unpredictable due to its partial knowledge. We therefore recommend to carefully consider the *degree of control* with the LivingDesktop and to grant users full control of their desktop devices (contrary to adaptative interfaces). For instance, a dedicated key on the keyboard (or on the monitor) could be used to trigger the "Following" mode which can easily be cancelled if a second person enters in the office or if the user is leaving the office. This can for instance reduce the feeling of privacy issues or disturbance for others. However, Mixed initiative [15], which consists of sharing the control over the actuated interfaces between the user and the system, is a promising (but challenging) direction for future work.

A limitation of the LivingDesktop is of course when the desk is cluttered with objects, because the actuated devices are likely to be blocked by or to push objects away. Interestingly, two participants of our scenario evaluation reported that they already knocked objects when they *manually* rotated the monitor. In fact, we see the LivingDesktop as an opportunity to avoid knocking objects with desktop devices. One feature of the LivingDesktop is indeed to sense the presence of objects on the desk (our proof-of-concept using a Microsoft Kinect depth camera). A depth model of the desk and objects located on its surface can be used to prevent actuated monitors (e.g. robotic arms) to move, or make them take a different path in order to not knock objects.

Finally, we believe the results of our scenario evaluation have been strongly influenced by the current technologies used for implementing our proof-of-concept. Indeed, several participants commented that "*The monitor rail takes too much space on the desk*", that "*the keyboard is too high*" or that "*the mouse controller [plotter] could hurt my knees*". Some participants also hoped for smoother and faster motions of the actuated devices. While our prototype has been useful for exploring the potential of actuated desktop devices, we believe an evaluation conducted with better quality and miniaturized implementations would lead to better results. Different implementations could also lead to novel applications, thanks to additional degrees of freedom in our proof-of-concept. Typically, we envision applications where the monitor move front and back and is combined with zoom-based interfaces. Future work should also actuate other equipments and devices that are generally available on a desktop workstation such as a phone or a lamp as suggested by the participants. A promising one is the laptop which is more and more frequently used in workspaces, often combined with other desktop devices.

CONCLUSION

HCI designers just started to explore possible applications of actuated objects [30]. In this exploratory project, we investigated whether actuated devices may be a promising approach for one of most popular interactive environment: Desktop workstations.

We contributed a deeper understanding on how users are arranging their desktop devices. We also provide insights about actuated workstations by describing its main features as well as a set of applications including support for ergonomics, collaboration, context awareness and physicality. Finally, the scenario evaluation provides three main findings: (1) actuated desktop devices appear as a promising approach for applications such as ergonomics and collaboration; (2) Others contexts of application such as accessibility, or social communication could also benefit from actuated devices. Finally, (3) the environment and in particular the location and users practice should seriously be considered when designing actuated interfaces for desktop workstations.

ACKNOWLEDGEMENT

We thank Nicolai Marquadt, Juergen Steimle, Joerg Mueller, Anne Roudaut, Nicolas Roussel, Marcos Serrano, Aurelien Tabard, Kashyap Todi, Olivier Chapuis and IHM reviewers for their useful comments. We thank Patrick Bush, Gerard Mouret, Frederic Bouquet and Julien Bobroff for the technical help. This work was partly supported under the research programme EDiSon3D (ANR-13-CORD-0008-01) funded by ANR, the French State agency for research.

REFERENCES

1. Arai, T., Machii, K., Kuzunuki, S., and Shojima, H. Interactivedesk: A computer-augmented desk which responds to operations on real objects. In *Conference Companion on Human Factors in Computing Systems*, CHI '95, ACM (New York, NY, USA, 1995), 141–142.
2. Bailly, G., Pietrzak, T., Deber, J., and Wigdor, D. J. Métamorphe: Augmenting hotkey usage with actuated keys. In *Proceedings of the SIGCHI Conference on Human Factors in Computing Systems*, CHI '13, ACM (New York, NY, USA, 2013), 563–572.
3. Bi, X., Grossman, T., Matejka, J., and Fitzmaurice, G. Magic desk: Bringing multi-touch surfaces into desktop work. In *Proceedings of the SIGCHI Conference on Human Factors in Computing Systems*, CHI '11, ACM (New York, NY, USA, 2011), 2511–2520.
4. Block, F., Gellersen, H., and Villar, N. Touch-display keyboards: Transforming keyboards into interactive surfaces. In *Proceedings of the SIGCHI Conference on Human Factors in Computing Systems*, CHI '10, ACM (New York, NY, USA, 2010), 1145–1154.
5. Brave, S., Ishii, H., and Dahley, A. Tangible interfaces for remote collaboration and communication. In *Proceedings of the 1998 ACM Conference on Computer Supported Cooperative Work*, CSCW '98, ACM (New York, NY, USA, 1998), 169–178.
6. Breazeal, C., Wang, A., and Picard, R. Experiments with a robotic computer: body, affect and cognition interactions. In *Human-Robot Interaction (HRI), 2007 2nd ACM/IEEE International Conference on*, IEEE (2007), 153–160.
7. Chapuis, O., and Roussel, N. Metisse is not a 3d desktop! In *Proceedings of the 18th Annual ACM Symposium on User Interface Software and Technology*, UIST '05, ACM (New York, NY, USA, 2005), 13–22.
8. Chua, Y., Tee, K. P., Yan, R., Li, L., and Huang, Z. Towards more engaging telepresence by face tracking. In *Proceedings of the Workshop at SIGGRAPH Asia*, WASA '12, ACM (New York, NY, USA, 2012), 137–141.
9. Dietz, P. H., Eidelson, B., Westhues, J., and Bathiche, S. A practical pressure sensitive computer keyboard. In *Proceedings of the 22Nd Annual ACM Symposium on User Interface Software and Technology*, UIST '09, ACM (New York, NY, USA, 2009), 55–58.
10. Dragicevic, P., Chevalier, F., and Huot, S. Running an hci experiment in multiple parallel universes. In *CHI '14 Extended Abstracts on Human Factors in Computing Systems*, CHI EA '14, ACM (New York, NY, USA, 2014), 607–618.
11. Greenberg, S., Marquardt, N., Ballendat, T., Diaz-Marino, R., and Wang, M. Proxemic interactions: the new ubicomp? *interactions 18*, 1 (2011), 42–50.
12. Hall, E. T. The hidden dimension .
13. Healy, G., Lawler, S., Thorp, A., Neuhaus, M., Robson, E., Owen, N., and Dunstan, D. Reducing prolonged sitting in the workplace. *Human Factors and Ergonomics Society* (2012).
14. Hinckley, K., Czerwinski, M., and Sinclair, M. Interaction and modeling techniques for desktop two-handed input. In *Proceedings of the 11th Annual ACM Symposium on User Interface Software and Technology*, UIST '98, ACM (New York, NY, USA, 1998), 49–58.
15. Horvitz, E. Principles of mixed-initiative user interfaces. In *Proceedings of the SIGCHI Conference on Human Factors in Computing Systems*, CHI '99, ACM (New York, NY, USA, 1999), 159–166.
16. Ju, W., and Sirkin, D. Animate objects: How physical motion encourages public interaction. In *Proceedings of the 5th International Conference on Persuasive Technology*, PERSUASIVE'10, Springer-Verlag (Berlin, Heidelberg, 2010), 40–51.
17. Kane, S. K., Avrahami, D., Wobbrock, J. O., Harrison, B., Rea, A. D., Philipose, M., and LaMarca, A. Bonfire: A nomadic system for hybrid laptop-tabletop interaction. In *Proceedings of the 22Nd Annual ACM Symposium on User Interface Software and Technology*, UIST '09, ACM (New York, NY, USA, 2009), 129–138.
18. Kaptein, M. C., Nass, C., and Markopoulos, P. Powerful and consistent analysis of likert-type ratingscales. In *Proceedings of the SIGCHI Conference on Human Factors in Computing Systems*, ACM (2010), 2391–2394.
19. Kaufmann, B., and Ahlström, D. Studying spatial memory and map navigation performance on projector phones with peephole interaction. In *Proceedings of the SIGCHI Conference on Human Factors in Computing Systems*, CHI '13, ACM (New York, NY, USA, 2013), 3173–3176.
20. Kawaguchik, I., Kuzuoka, H., and Suzuki, Y. Study on gaze direction perception of face image displayed on rotatable flat display. In *Proceedings of the 33rd Annual ACM Conference on Human Factors in Computing Systems*, CHI '15, ACM (New York, NY, USA, 2015), 1729–1737.
21. Kim, S., Kim, H., Lee, B., Nam, T.-J., and Lee, W. Inflatable mouse: Volume-adjustable mouse with air-pressure-sensitive input and haptic feedback. In *Proceedings of the SIGCHI Conference on Human Factors in Computing Systems*, CHI '08, ACM (New York, NY, USA, 2008), 211–224.
22. Kudo, H., Suzumori, K., and Kanda, T. Force feedback mouse with differential mechanism for omni-traveling. In *Micro-NanoMechatronics and Human Science, 2007. MHS '07. International Symposium on* (Nov 2007), 430–435.

23. Luff, P., and Heath, C. Mobility in collaboration. In *Proceedings of the 1998 ACM Conference on Computer Supported Cooperative Work*, CSCW '98, ACM (New York, NY, USA, 1998), 305–314.

24. MacKenzie, I. S., Soukoreff, R. W., and Pal, C. A two-ball mouse affords three degrees of freedom. In *CHI '97 Extended Abstracts on Human Factors in Computing Systems*, CHI EA '97, ACM (New York, NY, USA, 1997), 303–304.

25. Marcus-Roberts, H. M., and Roberts, F. S. Meaningless statistics. *Journal of Educational and Behavioral Statistics 12*, 4 (1987), 383–394.

26. Nowacka, D., Ladha, K., Hammerla, N. Y., Jackson, D., Ladha, C., Rukzio, E., and Olivier, P. Touchbugs: Actuated tangibles on multi-touch tables. In *Proceedings of the SIGCHI Conference on Human Factors in Computing Systems*, CHI '13, ACM (New York, NY, USA, 2013), 759–762.

27. Oakley, I., McGee, M. R., Brewster, S., and Gray, P. Putting the feel in 'look and feel'. In *Proceedings of the SIGCHI Conference on Human Factors in Computing Systems*, CHI '00, ACM (New York, NY, USA, 2000), 415–422.

28. Pangaro, G., Maynes-Aminzade, D., and Ishii, H. The actuated workbench: Computer-controlled actuation in tabletop tangible interfaces. In *Proceedings of the 15th Annual ACM Symposium on User Interface Software and Technology*, UIST '02, ACM (New York, NY, USA, 2002), 181–190.

29. Park, W., Park, S., Kim, L., and Shin, S. Haptic mouse interface actuated by an electromagnet. In *Proceedings of the 2011 International Conference on Complex, Intelligent, and Software Intensive Systems*, CISIS '11, IEEE Computer Society (Washington, DC, USA, 2011), 643–646.

30. Parkes, A., Poupyrev, I., and Ishii, H. Designing kinetic interactions for organic user interfaces. *Commun. ACM 51*, 6 (June 2008), 58–65.

31. Patten, J., and Ishii, H. Mechanical constraints as computational constraints in tabletop tangible interfaces. In *Proceedings of the SIGCHI Conference on Human Factors in Computing Systems*, CHI '07, ACM (New York, NY, USA, 2007), 809–818.

32. Pedersen, E. W., and Hornbæk, K. Tangible bots: Interaction with active tangibles in tabletop interfaces. In *Proceedings of the SIGCHI Conference on Human Factors in Computing Systems*, CHI '11, ACM (New York, NY, USA, 2011), 2975–2984.

33. Perelman, G., Serrano, M., Raynal, M., Picard, C., Derras, M., and Dubois, E. The roly-poly mouse: Designing a rolling input device unifying 2d and 3d interaction. In *Proceedings of the 33rd Annual ACM Conference on Human Factors in Computing Systems*, CHI '15, ACM (New York, NY, USA, 2015), 327–336.

34. Poupyrev, I., Nashida, T., and Okabe, M. Actuation and tangible user interfaces: The vaucanson duck, robots, and shape displays. In *Proceedings of the 1st International Conference on Tangible and Embedded Interaction*, TEI '07, ACM (New York, NY, USA, 2007), 205–212.

35. Probst, K., Lindlbauer, D., Greindl, P., Trapp, M., Haller, M., Schwartz, B., and Schrempf, A. Rotating, tilting, bouncing: Using an interactive chair to promote activity in office environments. In *CHI '13 Extended Abstracts on Human Factors in Computing Systems*, CHI EA '13, ACM (New York, NY, USA, 2013), 79–84.

36. Probst, K., Lindlbauer, D., Haller, M., Schwartz, B., and Schrempf, A. A chair as ubiquitous input device: Exploring semaphoric chair gestures for focused and peripheral interaction. In *Proceedings of the SIGCHI Conference on Human Factors in Computing Systems*, CHI '14, ACM (New York, NY, USA, 2014), 4097–4106.

37. Ramstein, C., and Hayward, V. The pantograph: A large workspace haptic device for multimodal human computer interaction. In *Conference Companion on Human Factors in Computing Systems*, CHI '94, ACM (New York, NY, USA, 1994), 57–58.

38. Rasmussen, M. K., Grönvall, E., Kinch, S., and Petersen, M. G. "it's alive, it's magic, it's in love with you": Opportunities, challenges and open questions for actuated interfaces. In *Proceedings of the 25th Australian Computer-Human Interaction Conference: Augmentation, Application, Innovation, Collaboration*, OzCHI '13, ACM (New York, NY, USA, 2013), 63–72.

39. Roudaut, A., Rau, A., Sterz, C., Plauth, M., Lopes, P., and Baudisch, P. Gesture output: Eyes-free output using a force feedback touch surface. In *Proceedings of the SIGCHI Conference on Human Factors in Computing Systems*, CHI '13, ACM (New York, NY, USA, 2013), 2547–2556.

40. Savioz, G., Markovic, M., and Perriard, Y. Towards multi-finger haptic devices: A computer keyboard with adjustable force feedback. In *Electrical Machines and Systems (ICEMS), 2011 International Conference on* (Aug 2011), 1–6.

41. Schmidt, D., Kovacs, R., Mehta, V., Umapathi, U., Köhler, S., Cheng, L.-P., and Baudisch, P. Level-ups: Motorized stilts that simulate stair steps in virtual reality. In *Proceedings of the 33rd Annual ACM Conference on Human Factors in Computing Systems*, CHI '15, ACM (New York, NY, USA, 2015), 2157–2160.

42. Schneegass, S., Alt, F., Scheible, J., and Schmidt, A. Midair displays: Concept and first experiences with free-floating pervasive displays. In *Proceedings of The International Symposium on Pervasive Displays*, PerDis '14, ACM (New York, NY, USA, 2014), 27:27–27:31.

43. Seifert, J., Boring, S., Winkler, C., Schaub, F., Schwab, F., Herrdum, S., Maier, F., Mayer, D., and Rukzio, E. Hover pad: Interacting with autonomous and self-actuated displays in space. In *Proceedings of the 27th Annual ACM Symposium on User Interface Software and Technology*, UIST '14, ACM (New York, NY, USA, 2014), 139–147.

44. Sinclair, M., Pahud, M., and Benko, H. Touchmover: Actuated 3d touchscreen with haptic feedback. In *Proceedings of the 2013 ACM International Conference on Interactive Tabletops and Surfaces*, ITS '13, ACM (New York, NY, USA, 2013), 287–296.

45. Steimle, J., Weibel, N., Olberding, S., Mühlhäuser, M., and Hollan, J. D. Plink: Paper-based links for cross-media information spaces. In *CHI '11 Extended Abstracts on Human Factors in Computing Systems*, CHI EA '11, ACM (New York, NY, USA, 2011), 1969–1974.

46. Taylor, S., Keskin, C., Hilliges, O., Izadi, S., and Helmes, J. Type-hover-swipe in 96 bytes: A motion sensing mechanical keyboard. In *Proceedings of the 32Nd Annual ACM Conference on Human Factors in Computing Systems*, CHI '14, ACM (New York, NY, USA, 2014), 1695–1704.

47. Vonach, E., Gerstweiler, G., and Kaufmann, H. Acto: A modular actuated tangible user interface object. In *Proceedings of the Ninth ACM International Conference on Interactive Tabletops and Surfaces*, ITS '14, ACM (New York, NY, USA, 2014), 259–268.

48. Weiss, M., Schwarz, F., Jakubowski, S., and Borchers, J. Madgets: Actuating widgets on interactive tabletops. In *Proceedings of the 23Nd Annual ACM Symposium on User Interface Software and Technology*, UIST '10, ACM (New York, NY, USA, 2010), 293–302.

49. Wellner, P. Interacting with paper on the digitaldesk. *Commun. ACM 36*, 7 (July 1993), 87–96.

50. Yang, X.-D., Mak, E., McCallum, D., Irani, P., Cao, X., and Izadi, S. Lensmouse: Augmenting the mouse with an interactive touch display. In *Proceedings of the SIGCHI Conference on Human Factors in Computing Systems*, CHI '10, ACM (New York, NY, USA, 2010), 2431–2440.

51. Yankelovich, N., Simpson, N., Kaplan, J., and Provino, J. Porta-person: Telepresence for the connected conference room. In *CHI '07 Extended Abstracts on Human Factors in Computing Systems*, CHI EA '07, ACM (New York, NY, USA, 2007), 2789–2794.

52. Zhang, H., and Li, Y. Gestkeyboard: Enabling gesture-based interaction on ordinary physical keyboard. In *Proceedings of the 32Nd Annual ACM Conference on Human Factors in Computing Systems*, CHI '14, ACM (New York, NY, USA, 2014), 1675–1684.

Technological Caregiving: Supporting Online Activity for Adults with Cognitive Impairments

Anne Marie Piper, Raymundo Cornejo, Lisa Hurwitz, Caitlin Unumb
Northwestern University, Evanston, IL
{ampiper,rcornejo}@northwestern.edu, {lisa.hurwitz,caitlinunumb2015}@u.northwestern.edu

ABSTRACT
With much of the population now online, the field of HCI faces new and pressing issues of how to help people sustain online activity throughout their lives, including through periods of disability. The onset of cognitive impairment later in life affects whether and how individuals are able to stay connected online and manage their digital information. While caregivers play a critical role in the offline lives of adults with cognitive impairments, less is known about how they support and enable online interaction. Using a constructivist grounded theory approach, data from focus groups with caregivers of adults with cognitive impairments reveal four forms of cooperative work caregivers perform in the context of supporting online activity. We find that staying active online is a way of empowering and engaging adults with cognitive impairments, yet this introduces new forms of risk, surrogacy, and cooperative technology use to the already demanding work of caregiving.

Author Keywords
Caregiving; social computing; vulnerable populations

ACM Classification Keywords
H.5.m. Information interfaces and presentation (e.g., HCI): Miscellaneous

INTRODUCTION
Going online is an important aspect of daily life for many people and shapes the way we engage in social interaction, search for information, manage finances, and more. Being active online is important for independence and affects social and emotional wellbeing [13]. With much of the population now online, including many older adults [12,44], it is increasingly important to understand how to help people sustain their online lives through periods of disability. For example, changes in a person's cognitive abilities resulting from Alzheimer's disease, stroke, or a brain injury impact whether and how an individual is able to go about her existing online activities, such as corresponding over email, interacting on social media, and managing bank accounts [29]. Yet, how people sustain such activities in the context of cognitive impairment is an open question with implications for online safety, privacy, social support, and the work of caregivers [3]. Consider the following experience:

Jane is the primary caregiver for her husband, who *"suffers [from] aphasia, mostly communication challenges... But memory is affected when your brain's working on aphasia. I'm very aware of his, you know, when he comes and goes."* She encourages him to go online to keep in touch and look up information about his hobbies. *"Facebook people...would put comments, and it's very nice, because you feel like there's a very caring community that's interested. They can't much do anything except that they can say, 'We're thinking about you.'"* Some days her husband may stare blankly at the computer, and she steps in to help him. Recently, however, her husband *"had his identity stolen... The only reason we knew about it was because somebody tried to get a mortgage... So then, we talked about [the] Internet..."* Despite this unfortunate event, Jane continues to help her husband go online.

Caregiving is a complex and cooperative social practice in which caregivers and other actors support care recipients in a myriad of contexts [35,45]. Prior work details the role of caregivers in supporting activities of daily living (e.g., dressing, bathing, preparing meals, administering medications) [33]. Caregiving can be overwhelmingly stressful work [9], and caregivers often experience high levels of physical, financial, social, and emotional stress – also known as the *burden* of caregiving [11]. Although much work focuses on "offline" or non-technology related caregiver experiences, few studies have examined the impact of technology from the caregiver's perspective [16,34]. Considering how pervasive technology is today, understanding the experience of caregivers is critical given the effects of caregiving on the caregiver's own health and wellbeing [9] and potential to improve overall care by easing the burden on caregivers. While the HCI and CSCW communities are beginning to understand the effects of new technologies on caregiving work, we know much less about how caregivers and care recipients interact in the context of everyday online tools and what staying active online means for the work of caregiving.

This paper reports results from focus groups with 20 caregivers of adults with cognitive impairments, examining the ways in which care recipients interact online, whether

CHI'16, May 07 - 12, 2016, San Jose, CA, USA

ACM 978-1-4503-3362-7/16/05...$15.00
DOI: http://dx.doi.org/10.1145/2858036.2858260

and how caregivers are involved in this online experience, and the benefits and concerns of online activity. Caregivers do much work to support their care recipients' online activities and view staying active online as positive for their care recipients. As the primary contribution of this study, we describe four forms of work caregivers perform in the context of supporting their care recipient's online activity: *guiding*, *stimulating*, *connecting*, and *protecting*. Across these forms of work, caregivers and care recipients cooperatively negotiate the online experience in ways that emphasize empowerment and independence while protecting care recipients through moments of risk and vulnerability. The cooperative use of online tools by caregivers and care recipients introduces tensions related to surrogacy, sharing, and privacy for vulnerable populations. Our analysis contributes insights into how online systems can better support this complex social practice and the dynamics of the caregiver-care recipient relationship.

RELATED WORK

The Work of Caregiving

The health care and nursing literatures often characterize the daily activities of informal caregivers (e.g., family members or friends) as a form of work [17,39,40]. Informal caregivers are unpaid individuals who provide regular care for their care recipient [33]. Providing care consists of assisting and supporting care recipients with various activities of daily living (e.g., dressing, bathing, feeding, etc.) and instrumental activities of daily living (e.g., housekeeping, transportation, medication, etc.).

The literature conceptualizes the emotional and physical strain of providing care for others as the *burden* of caregiving [11]. As part of this framing, prior work has broken this concept into objective and subjective burdens [32]. The objective burden results from concrete events and activities from caregiving (e.g., less personal time), while the subjective burden involves feelings, attitudes, and emotions about caregiving (e.g., resulting loneliness or depression). Objective and subjective burdens may be related to disruptions to a caregiver's life and impact on her wellbeing. Prior studies indicate the ways in which the burden of caregiving impacts the physical health [25], socialization [30], and emotional wellbeing of caregivers [14]. For example, the Alzheimer's Association reported that nearly 40% of caregivers rated their caregiving experience as stressful [1]. Given this intense burden, some caregivers experience high frustration if they do not perceive that their care recipient is making progress [19].

The burden of caregiving often extends beyond simple frustration. Caregivers may struggle to balance the work of caregiving with the emotional burden it entails and ultimately end up neglecting their own needs. For instance, Liu et al. [30] found that caregivers of high-risk infants struggle to reach out for social support and face challenges re-connecting with their social networks. Moreover, caregivers may want to connect with others who are in similar caregiving situations [30]. Chen et al. [9] studied how caregivers balance their personal lives with the work of caregiving for people with a variety of illnesses (e.g. cancer, stroke, diabetes, dementia). Their work describes tensions between providing support and its impact on the caregiver's life. Caregivers' efforts and time invested in providing support for their care recipients goes mostly unnoticed by their relatives and friends. The "invisibility" of caregiving work – or that the burden may only be salient to the person immersed in providing care – limits opportunities for others to step in, collaborate with, and help the primary caregiver. This prior research highlights the importance of understanding and designing to support the work of caregivers, and not simply for care recipients.

Technology to Support Caregiving

The vast majority of technology-related research on caregiving for individuals with cognitive impairments focuses on new tools for supporting remote caregiving and aging in place [16,23,34,42,47]. Prior work [26,41] introduces robotic wheelchairs to support movement among elderly patients, which reduce the caregiver's physical workload. While valuable, this work does not consider caregivers' expectations or needs in other regards, such as coordinating care and social support. To date, few studies have focused on technology to support the needs and practices of caregivers in particular. Some of these efforts aim to alleviate a specific activity performed by the caregiver (e.g. [16,34]). For example, the AwarePad [34] is a mobile application designed to help caregivers manage repetitive questions from care recipients diagnosed with Alzheimer's disease. Chiu and Massimi [10] proposed a digital tool to speed up appointment decisions but also support the caregiver by simplifying communication activities and improving access to community resources. Similarly, the Estrellita system [30] is a collaborative prototype to support caregivers of high-risk infants and their healthcare professionals. Other systems that disseminate health information within a social network (e.g., [43]) stand to help coordinate and catalyze social support for patients and caregivers. New technologies that address caregivers' needs and practices can decrease the burden on caregivers and, in turn, allow caregivers to provide better care for their care recipients.

Supporting Online Activity through Life Transitions

The present study contributes to the literature on how others support online activity for individuals through life transitions. Work by Ammari et al. [2] introduces the notion of parental disclosure management, in which parents decide how and what to share online about their children from birth through adolescence. Hence, children's early online identities are created by their parents and affected by their parents' decisions about what is appropriate to be shared.

In contrast to online identity in childhood, recent studies also investigate cooperative online activity at the end of life (e.g., in hospice [18]) and after an individual passes away [5,6,31].

While family and friends use technology to share information about an individual in hospice, this can lead to privacy violations and conflicts about what should be shared [18]. Our work extends this literature by detailing the cooperative work caregivers perform in the context of their care recipient's online activity, calling attention to issues of vulnerability and surrogacy through life transitions.

METHOD

Participants

We conducted four focus groups with a total of 20 participants (age 27 to 56; *M*=41; *SD*=8; 10 female). All focus group participants were *informal, un-paid caregivers* of an adult with a cognitive impairment, whom we refer to as the *care recipient*. We recruited individuals who indicated that they were a primary caregiver of an individual with cognitive impairment (e.g., memory or speech-language impairment). All caregivers were family related to their care recipient (e.g., provide care for their mother, father, uncle, spouse, or grandparent). Caregivers reported that their care recipients had varying levels of cognitive impairment as a result of conditions such as Alzheimer's disease, stroke, or brain injury from an accident, and all experienced cognitive impairment in middle or older adulthood (i.e., not in early childhood from a developmental disability). Care recipients were between age 51 and 89 (8 female) and were at varying stages of their life (including one who passed away prior to the focus group). All care recipients had been involved in online activity, although with varying levels of independence. All caregivers had some experience going online themselves and supporting care recipients' online activities, and as a result, the average age in our sample of caregivers is somewhat younger than comparable studies that focus broadly on caregiving experiences (e.g. [32]). We aimed to organize groups of caregivers who care for adults with similar conditions (e.g., severe memory loss, speech-language impairment and memory loss), as this cohesion can foster a comfortable environment for participants and help elicit in-depth conversation among participants [27]. Focus groups were conducted in a university conference room.

Procedure

One researcher moderated the focus groups and two other researchers observed and took notes. The moderator guide focused on the ways in which caregivers and care recipients engage online, including using e-mail, social media (e.g., Facebook, Twitter), video chat, banking tools, etc.; benefits and concerns regarding online activity; and any changes in online activity with respect to the care recipient's abilities over time. We allowed the conversation to evolve among participants depending on each group's dynamics, and at times caregivers asked each other questions about their experiences, exchanged strategies, and provided encouragement and empathy to one another. This interaction provides important data about caregivers' shared or conflicting practices, assumptions, concerns, and benefits of online interaction. All focus groups were video recorded and transcribed for analysis. Pseudonyms are used in place of actual names of caregivers and care recipients.

Data Analysis

Data analysis followed a constructivist grounded theory approach [7,8]. Our process of data analysis emerged through interactions with our informants, with our data, and between members of our research team. All researchers read the transcripts, performed initial open coding of data, and discussed the emerging themes. Based on this, we began to view our informants' role in online technology use with respect to their care recipient as a form of "work". This analytic frame is influenced by informant language (e.g., talk of exhaustion from caregiving work, need for support, and constant duties as a caregiver) as well as by prior research in the field that predominantly characterizes caregiving as a form of work [19,20,46]. With this analytic frame in mind, we conducted a second phase of coding to identify the forms of work described by caregivers, how caregivers accomplish this work, and the ways in which various goals in this work support or compete with each other. We iteratively coded data and related these codes to one another through a process of memoing and theorizing. Analysis focused on constant comparison of data, seeking to further refine our understanding of this practice.

Constructivist grounded theory requires reflexivity about how we construct our actions and our position as researchers. Three key factors influence our position as researchers, which both strengthen and limit our analysis. First, our data captures the perspectives of caregivers, which calls attention to their needs in this cooperative social practice. While some care recipients would be able to voice their own opinions, and additional studies should examine this (e.g. [22]), the purpose of the present study is to understand the lived experience of caregivers in the context of their care recipient's online activity. Understanding the perspective of caregivers is important but understudied in HCI [10,30], and our analysis contributes to this literature. Second, our view of this social practice as a form of work risks focusing on functional caregiving activities and the "burden" of caregiving rather than the ways in which caregivers may enable and empower care recipients. We remain cognizant of this in our analysis and return to this point in the discussion. Third, our analysis positions care recipients as a vulnerable population. We note that the positioning as vulnerable is socially constructed and framed by normative ideology, in which the non-disabled person is considered "normal" by society. However, our analysis unpacks the social practices of caregivers of individuals with cognitive impairments as a way of calling attention to how systems could better support transitions in vulnerability and the cooperative nature of online activity for vulnerable populations.

FINDINGS

Caregiving is demanding work, and caring for an adult with cognitive impairments presents unique challenges in the context of helping care recipients engage in and maintain online activity. Before detailing these challenges and the work caregivers perform, we briefly describe our informants' caregiving experiences to contextualize our results. Caregivers in our study provide full-time, unpaid care for an adult with a cognitive impairment. The interaction among focus group participants was both empathetic and supportive. Participants described periods of extreme stress and loneliness from the work of caregiving, to which other participants offered encouragement and advice. Participants had a wide range of experience using the Internet. Caregivers with less experience going online took notes as others shared strategies related to a wide variety of caregiving concerns (e.g., remote activity monitoring, medication reminders, online safety). While the focus group discussion drew out caregiving work related to online activity, this work was in the context of many other responsibilities caregivers assumed – managing medications; scheduling and attending doctor visits; overseeing finances; cooking; cleaning; assisting with bathing and toileting; and providing social and emotional support. Additionally, many caregivers work outside the home and have other family responsibilities.

"Some days, I'm just sitting there, and I just sit and cry, because…this is somebody that used to take care of me, and now the roles are reversed, and [I] need some help, dammit, and I'm not getting it… I work two jobs and take care of my father, along with trying to have a social life, and I have two children of my own. So I'm overwhelmed." (Nancy)

Although care recipients all had a form of cognitive impairment, caregivers detailed care recipients' idiosyncratic memory, speech, language, and/or motor abilities; how this affected their work as a caregiver; and the changes they observed over their care recipients' lives. Caregivers characterized the years between a diagnosis, accident, or other life-changing event, as constant fluctuation – ups and downs – in terms of their care recipient's state.

"Well, for him, it's kind of like a roller coaster. It's up and down… It's a vicious cycle, and it's not just going down and stay down, he'll go down then come back up a little… It's more like a zig-zag than one direction." (Edward)

"Yeah. It's not even day-to-day, it's like hour-to-hour. You can't even say 'This is a good day; this is a bad day.' You've got to just break it down into smaller increments than that." (Constance)

This constant fluctuation requires caregivers to be vigilant of their care recipient's current cognitive, emotional, and physical state, and to constantly assess and monitor their needs. Caregivers learn to recognize when a care recipient is more lucid and cognizant as well as periods of disorientation and declines in memory or communication, and then adjust their own behavior and support accordingly.

"It was really, really hard to gauge just how much I would have to do or not do for him. Because at first you think, 'I have to do all this work for him,' and…he might not have all his faculties, and then the next day he might be…up earlier than I am, doing whatever he wants to do…" (John)

The ongoing changes in a care recipient's cognitive state have significant implications for the ways in which care recipients use technology to go online as well as the work caregivers perform to help care recipients interact online.

"When he's doing really badly, like-- if I walk in on him and he doesn't know what's going on at all… For that moment, I try and…figure out what's going on to see how badly his memory is suffering, or what exactly he's trying to do. And in some cases, he's on the computer when he's doing this. So, he'll be in the middle of writing a Facebook post or something, and he'll just completely blank." (John)

Many caregivers described similar situations, which led them to establish practices around how to facilitate, take part in, and at times prevent online activity for their care recipients. Caregivers described these practices based on their personal experiences, as current educational resources (e.g. caregiver's handbook [37]) do not provide guidance on online activity. The following sections describe these practices as four forms of work, which caregivers perform in the context of their care recipient's online activity. These four forms of work – *guiding*, *stimulating*, *connecting*, and *protecting* – emerged through our qualitative analysis and are the core contribution of this study.

Guiding

A primary way in which caregivers engage in cooperative online activity with their care recipients is through what we call *guiding*. The behavior of guiding includes providing functional assistance, teaching, and mentoring care recipients in online activity.

Caregivers play an important role in supporting functional use of technology due to care recipients' physical impairments that co-occur with their cognitive condition, such as limited motor ability resulting from a stroke or advanced Alzheimer's disease. Functional support often involves working side-by-side with a care recipient to search online for specific information (e.g. typing words in search engines), set up or configure the technology, or operate the computer mouse. Caregivers provide varying levels of guidance depending on their care recipient's needs and abilities – sometimes getting them started with a task and other times completing the entire task for them. Guiding behavior also varies depending on the care recipient's prior technology experience and comfort level. Our sample included older adult care recipients, some of whom had more limited experience going online prior to their impairment. For example, one older care recipient went online minimally before his stroke, but now, being largely confined to his home, works with his caregiver to go online more regularly.

Guiding also involves caregivers' efforts to teach (or re-teach) their care recipient how to use technology. That is, even care recipients who were previously tech-savvy may need to re-learn how to use a specific technology. Teaching care recipients to use technology is a cooperative process in which caregivers use the technology in conjunction with care recipients. Caregivers may work alongside care recipients to demonstrate and teach them how to perform a particular action with a device or application.

"I'm trying to teach my husband to text... Because it--it matters with our kids" (Jane)

Guiding behavior is about teaching a care recipient how to use technology as well as conveying the benefits of this way of interacting, such as Jane's goal of teaching her husband to text message as a way of communicating with their children. In this respect, caregivers encourage and motivate the use of new technology as part of guiding them through initial use, and teaching care recipients in this way can be rewarding.

"I feel good about [helping her online]. I can take care of her. She's been taking care of me forever. That's the least that I can do. Just to make sure you're comfortable and all right. It's like a badge of honor for me to do it." (Derek)

However, teaching care recipients to use technology also may introduce an additional subjective burden for caregivers. That is, caregivers must understand the technology (including its terminology and benefits), keep up with technology updates, and simplify unfamiliar concepts and procedures in ways that their care recipients can understand.

"One example, the first time I said spam to my mom, she goes, 'Spam? What do you mean spam? Like the food, spam?' I go, 'No.' So, she's trying to think. 'Junk mail mom.' Trying to show her over the years, you know, the claims, 'Get a free Walmart card. Gift Card.' Stuff like that. It's like, 'Mom, don't click on those.'" (Joan)

Caregivers guide care recipients through successful technology use by devising strategies to facilitate their care recipient's independent use of technology and avoid routine challenges. Caregivers shared strategies for helping care recipients independently look up login credentials (e.g., usernames/passwords written on whiteboards or notepads), printing information to serve as a reference or for readability, and creating shortcuts on the desktop or tablet for the most used applications.

"I leave my dad logged in because he's not going to remember the password, and even though you got that paper right there [with all of the passwords], he's not going to remember what all them letters and numbers are for. But I leave him logged in so that during the day. I'm at work during the day and so he gets on there himself. And I like the fact that he's into social media because I know he's at least socializing... I know he is using his mind, not watching the same program." (Amy)

As Amy notes, guiding behavior involves configuring the physical and digital environment in ways that afford independence for the care recipient and ease of mind for the caregiver. However, the work of guiding a care recipient through successful technology use is affected by fluctuations in a care recipient's cognitive state and abilities. Caregivers constantly assess and determine the level of support care recipients need when implementing these strategies, and caregivers may need to adjust their strategies on a daily or even hourly basis. The level of support is continually negotiated between caregivers and care recipients. While caregivers work hard to implement strategies that afford independent technology use by care recipients, care recipients may push back and want the caregiver to do more of the work of using technology. At times, providing this guidance can be more difficult for caregivers than having the caregiver "take over" and perform the actions themselves. Furthermore, caregivers monitor their care recipient's aggravation and stress levels when using technology and decide to step in and provide greater assistance in times of high anxiety. Hence, technology use for care recipients is rarely a fully independent activity; caregivers are constantly monitoring, stepping in, and providing guidance when needed. This change in independence has a significant impact on the work of caregivers and the role they now assume.

"Back then, they were really independent, and speaking, probably for everybody here when I say, before anything like this, everybody had their own judgment. They weren't impaired. They could make their own decisions, and they didn't need somebody looking over their shoulder to make sure what they were doing was in their best interest." (John)

As John describes, caregivers now take on a new role and new work associated with ensuring successful online activity for their care recipients, including deciding whether a care recipient's online activity is "in their best interest", which we describe further in the sections below. Prior to experiencing cognitive impairment, care recipients were independent, and actively used e-mail, social media, electronic banking, and other online services. In fact, a few caregivers described that their care recipient was previously the one teaching others how to use new technologies and perform online activities. The onset of cognitive impairment created a role reversal in which caregivers shifted from the ones learning from their care recipients to now filling the role of a guide, teacher, and mentor. In cases in which care recipients were previously quite independent online, it can be frustrating or upsetting for caregivers to shift into this new role.

While supporting online activity for care recipients introduces new work and concerns for caregivers, this interaction has several positive consequences, such as stimulating and connecting care recipients.

Stimulating

The second form of work caregivers perform in the context of care recipients' online activity is what we call *stimulating*. Caregivers and care recipients cooperatively use technology and go online to stimulate care recipients through informational, social, and emotional means. Some caregivers help their care recipients play "brain games" online as a form of cognitive exercise. In this case, caregivers described helping their care recipient access and setup these games and encouraging this type of activity as a form of stimulation. Caregivers also described the cooperative use of Google search, Yahoo News, YouTube, and Facebook as a way of stimulating their care recipient.

"Sometimes I go on Yahoo News, and we'll sit there and go through the new celebrity gossip. That keeps his mind kind of flowing; that's just something he likes to do." (Beth)

Caregivers stressed the importance of finding ways to keep care recipients' minds active and stimulated, and many described viewing online photos of family members, friends, and even famous people as a way of achieving this.

"I also use my e-mail, because my dad is from Memphis. All his family's out there, but my cousins and my aunts, they're able to scan pictures and send them to my e-mail, and I'm able to pull them up there. But they're old pictures... Sometimes...he'll tell a story about that picture, but then sometimes, he'll look at it and be like, 'Who are these? Where did these come from?' So, you know, some days are good, and some days are bad." (Sidney)

As Sidney mentions, jointly viewing family photos is an effective way of stimulating care recipients. Similarly, Beth enthusiastically described the value of social media as a form of social entertainment and stimulation for her care recipient.

"I think Facebook and social media might be a tool to keep dementia patients and people with memory loss motivated... It's more of a social entertainment, but it might actually be helpful to people... When they get likes—any likes, and they're happy... They're like, '100 likes, that's a lot.' They feel appreciated. So it might be a good tool for them, to keep them interactive, to keep the brain going." (Beth)

The stimulation that caregivers aim to provide by using social media with care recipients is related to the work of *connecting*, which we describe below. Jointly viewing online content, such as family photos or familiar movies, also serves as a positive bonding experience between caregivers and care recipients, providing further stimulation.

"I remember we used to watch Blazing Saddles together a couple of times, and [laughing] it's now one of my favorite movies but, kind of on a whim one day...I turned that video on [the computer]... Towards the end...noises come out because it's just a bean scene-- and, then the guy says something like, 'We need more beans,' and the guy's like, 'I think you've had enough,' and all of a sudden, I hear this noise from behind me, and I'm like, 'Dad, I haven't heard you laugh in like two years.'... He's laughing so hard he's crying. [It was] the happiest moment of my year... Such a great moment to be able to experience that with him... " (Constance)

Stimulating a care recipient by helping them engage online introduces new forms of work for caregivers, such as searching for content, identifying meaningful photos or videos, and bringing it into discussion. This interaction, however, also helps alleviate some of the burden on caregivers by providing a mutual source of enjoyment and occupying care recipients. At times, viewing online content can provides a positive outlet for the care recipient without requiring caregivers to be the sole source of entertainment.

"I don't know what I would do without the Internet in this situation. As far as caregiving goes and keeping Adam occupied with social media and current events and things, it's a godsend, seriously. Because he just feels...so abreast about everything that's going on in the world. He can watch newsreels, he can watch friends' videos... If I didn't have that, we-- I think he would go absolutely bonkers." (Jared)

"If we didn't have the Internet in this day and age, our lives as a caregiver would be [taken] up much more... Because of things like the Internet...we have a bit more freedom as a caregiver...because they don't have to be completely occupied by us... They can entertain themselves. They can remind themselves of things. They can be more independent, while having us as more of backline support." (John)

In this way, caregivers depend on the Internet as a way of keeping care recipients busy – as important stimulation, entertainment, and a way of knowing what is going on in the world – and through their online activity caregivers achieve some much needed freedom and separation from their care recipients. Yet, as John mentions, caregivers are still the "backline support" when their care recipient needs help interacting online, echoing the way in which care recipients fade in and out of online independence.

Connecting

Many care recipients interact through e-mail, video chat, and social media websites, and caregivers play a critical role in supporting care recipients' online social activity through the work of *connecting*. This work involves setting up video calls, reading and posting on behalf of care recipients, and mediating their care recipient's online interaction. Video chat, for example, can be a useful way of helping care recipients stay socially connected but presents challenges in remembering who various family members are and understanding the virtual experience (i.e., understanding that video chat enables communication between two parties who are not physically co-located).

"It helps because they actually see the person they're talking to, but just trying to get them to remember is kind of hard." (Trish)

"We would do Skype conversations with people that were on the west coast... We would find her wandering around the house, and we'd say, 'What are you doing?' and she'd say, 'Well, I'm looking for Michael.' And we'd say, 'Well, Michael's not here,' and she says, 'Well he is here, because I was talking with him earlier.'" (Bobby)

Caregivers described that some care recipients do better with text-based communication (e.g., e-mails, comments on social media), which they read with a caregiver and revisit periodically. Caregivers view interacting via social media as a positive experience for their care recipients and help care recipients stay connected through various websites.

"He wanted his own Facebook page. So, we set him up with a Facebook page... and so I have it set up so he doesn't have to keep logging in. He's constantly logged in... He just goes to Facebook...so he can keep in contact... It keeps him occupied... but then again, there's some days that he'll just stare blankly at the screen... 'Who's that?' You know, he doesn't remember people. I think it's good that he is on Facebook, that these images are coming up daily, so maybe it will help him to remember. It will keep his memory hanging by a thread..." (Amy)

Caregivers described Facebook as a particularly important site for care recipients to receive social support and highlighted the importance of social feedback via online mechanisms (e.g., Facebook Likes, comments).

"We use Facebook. He has a thousand people that want to wish him well..." (John)

"I'll post something and I'll get a couple likes. Whenever Adam posts something, it's like, you know, 200 likes, and everybody's commenting... Whenever we're out, I'm like, 'You post this on your page, because I don't get any, as many likes as you get.'" [all laughing] (Jared)

Many caregivers described posting on behalf of their care recipients as a way of helping them stay connected and informing others of their care recipient's condition or needs. Caregivers mentioned posting weekly updates on Facebook, Instagram, Blogger.com, and Caregiver.com.

"Usually it's at the end of the week, how his week's gone, if he was able to put his socks on by himself, with the one hand... That's an accomplishment for him..." (Amy)

"If I happen to bribe him and he goes outside, I put it on Facebook, but if we don't, then I usually use phone calls... I communicate a lot through Facebook without him. But his pictures are included in it... 'Daddy went outside today, or...Daddy was able to dress himself.'" (Nancy)

These online updates provide an important source of encouragement for care recipients, and caregivers relay this social information and support back to care recipients by reading or showing them posts.

"He wants to know the response... He wants to hear what people say. It's entertaining to him..." (Beth)

"People can write comments. That was a really good inspiration for Adam because, you know, I would read to him what I had written and then all the... well wishes that all of his friends were giving back..." (Jared)

This discussion brought up issues of whether and how caregivers involve care recipients in decisions to share information about care recipients online. Some caregivers were mindful about informing care recipients of posting online, although the care recipient may not remember or understand. Others post without their care recipient's consent. For example, Beth's father does not want to be involved with Facebook, but she still posts about him.

"I post[ed] when he was diagnosed with the dementia. When he's having bad days, I post it. I don't tell him... I don't know how he might feel about that that." (Beth)

The ways in which caregivers post online introduces tensions around surrogacy, privacy, and information sharing for vulnerable populations, and we elaborate these concerns in the discussion section. However, posting content about caregiving also provides caregivers with social support for themselves and allows them to voice their own challenges.

"I actually used it for my own cause...to share my story too... Like a tender moment, 'Hey, here we are celebrating his 85th birthday,' but at the same time, 'Hey, here's a man dying from Alzheimer's.... You guys need to know what it's like.' I want to share a part of my story... 'I just spent the last two hours shopping for diapers and Ensure,'... Kind of promoting my cause a little bit too." (Constance).

Caregivers may post about their care recipient to their own profile or even login to their care recipient's account to make posts on their care recipient's behalf. In this way, caregivers and care recipients are establishing a shared online presence that centers on the caregiving experience, which may support both the caregiver and care recipient's online social life. Further, caregivers help mediate and support their care recipients in staying socially connected online. This may include tagging a care recipient in online posts to make them feel included or copying multiple people on emails to make sure a care recipient receives social support.

"[I] tag him in things that he's not tagged in so he feels...part of the group... It's good to feel connected and to be a part of it, and...If he doesn't already have it on his wall, I'll send it his way. It's really important that he feels connected in our little world." (John)

"Our extended family got in the habit of making sure that all of us were included on emails as well... There was this weird place where she had an account, she was maybe accessing it sometimes or forgetting if something had been sent to her and she was kind of reaching out for support..." (Katherine)

Caregivers also help others in their social network understand their care recipient's online behavior, which may go against social norms in information sharing. For example, Amy's father often re-posts photos several times a week, but she explained to her friends online that she "can't stop him" and does not want to stop him "if he's recognizing." Caregivers view online interaction as a way of helping their care recipient stay socially connected, receive valuable social support, and participate more fully in society. Yet, this introduces new work around ensuring safe, meaningful, and inclusive online social experiences.

Protecting

Going online is a useful way of stimulating care recipients and helping them stay connected with others. However, this online activity introduces new challenges for caregivers around *protecting* care recipients by helping them avoid phishing attempts, blocking harmful websites or friend requests, and mediating information disclosure.

Prior work notes that caregivers co-manage and help care recipients take care of finances [32], and we found that caregivers often setup online banking for their care recipients and regularly check the status of care recipients' online bank accounts. Further, caregivers are vigilant of online financial threats to which their care recipients may be vulnerable, such as phishing attempts via email and overspending on unwanted or repeat items online. As Amanda explained, her mother received online offers over email that led to unnecessary purchases.

"... as far as e-mail, I think we all were just too uncertain of what could happen, um, making purchases. I think there may have been a couple times where purchases were made, and we quickly realized that the credit cards needed to be taken away, and this needs to stop, and it all kind of changed at that point." (Amanda)

The challenge is deciding when and under what circumstances a care recipient should not have access to credit card information required for online purchases. Sometimes it is not until an adverse event (e.g., identity theft, extreme over spending) that a caregiver is aware of the need to protect care recipients online. However, caregivers perceived that their care recipients were particularly susceptible to phishing attempts associated with their diagnosis or medical condition, noting care recipients' desperation to find a cure along with not knowing how to protect themselves online.

"When you present someone who has a medical condition, a severe medical condition, with information saying you have a drug like a cancer drug or whatever that's going to cure you, they get excited and want to, you know, purchase it... I've had to control and really train him...not to give out his credit card number online." (Edward)

As part of protecting care recipients online, caregivers learn to use spam filters, set restrictive privacy settings, and block inappropriate content (e.g., adult websites). Although caregivers can block specifics websites, they also work to filter online information that may be particularly distressing to care recipients, such as violent news stories or notices about the passing of loved ones. In fact, many caregivers described instances in which care recipients came across distressing news stories online that greatly affected their emotional and physical state (e.g., shaking from distress). And, some care recipients with memory loss would experience the same distressing content over and over, not remembering that they had already viewed this information.

Filtering online information is a complex task that involves determining which information may harm the care recipient and then blocking or deleting it, and caregivers often lack the controls or options to achieve this.

"Uh, it's rough to do. I have-- there's no filtering device to do that on, because we get the RSS feeds from different websites... There's nothing in place like, to monitor key words... Nothing that sophisticated." (Edward)

Social media provides benefits of stimulating and connecting care recipients but at the same time can be a source of negative information. Caregivers may even avoid sharing or posting such stories on social media to reduce the chance of their care recipients seeing the content.

"We do not post about disasters. Because he gets very agitated... The train accident yesterday. The day before yesterday—the Amtrak. He saw it on the news, and when I came home from work, he was on Facebook reading the Yahoo stories about it." (Amy)

However, caregivers noted a tradeoff inherent in restricting content: protecting care recipients from distressing information may prevent discussion of important topics or reminiscence that can be valuable for stimulation.

"I welcome those things because they open up a conversation. It gets you talking through it... There's a lot of bad news out there, but if it triggers a conversation, then something that can be educational, and it keeps his mind active because he'll want to know how the story turned out. Pique his interest." (Dan)

"Yeah, there is some stuff [in family emails] that's a little too invasive, that I found hard to read and didn't really want to let my mom read. But then we decided as a family that she should..." (Mitch)

Caregivers, sometimes with family member involvement, make decisions about what to share with care recipients and how to best protect them online based on the risks they perceive. Yet, this is also negotiated between caregivers and care recipients over time depending on how a care recipient reacts to certain information and their level of independence in discerning potential online threats. Caregivers also work with care recipients to protect them from negative online experiences by "vetting" their care recipient's friend requests and deciding to block certain online contacts.

"Yeah, either delete or defriend... We figure out ways to cleanse his list of people that are doing inappropriate things... It could be anything. It could be violence, it could be pornographic..." (Edward)

"I don't want to block it from him because it's technically his friends, his friend he had before, and when I put in the security measures...I made it so that anybody new, you know, had to go through the filter, but anybody who was there before, whatever they post is there, so...it's kind of just...I have to deal with it." (John)

As John explains, there is a tension between removing friends his care recipient had before his accident versus allowing him to keep these friendships and dealing with potentially negative situations. Hence, caregivers use both proactive and reactive strategies for protecting their care recipients online, weighing the tradeoffs between potential harm and the benefits of staying socially connected online.

Caregivers also protect care recipients by correcting the spread of misinformation online about their care recipient and guarding against social contacts sharing overly personal information, which can cause family tensions [18].

"When she was getting real bad... She broke her leg at one point, she had some seizures, um, bed wetting issues. It was real personal stuff. He was writing like, you know, hourly details, like how her care was and everything. Just like a little too much." (Mitch)

Similarly, caregivers help their care recipients understand which types of information they should not share online with respect to online privacy risks. This includes posting location-based information (e.g., checking in at the bank or hospital) and other personal details.

"Yeah on Twitter...sometimes he does too many personal details about what we're doing... Like, we're going to the bank, or this or that. He puts some sensitive information that I got to kind of delete. So, you know, we don't want all that exposed... So it's kind of rough." (Edward)

As part of protecting, caregivers must remain vigilant of their care recipient's online activity, monitoring information sharing, and at times moderate, block, filter, or delete certain information. Nevertheless, caregivers perform these actions with the aim of creating a safe and inclusive online environment for their care recipient.

DISCUSSION

While prior research characterizes the "offline" work of caregivers, our analysis identifies caregiving work engendered by everyday online technologies, which has yet to be accounted for by existing nursing, health care, or HCI/CSCW literatures. Although online activity introduces additional work and occasional stress for caregivers, they largely view online activity as a way of empowering their care recipients. Further, transitions in a care recipient's abilities affect online activity and the role caregivers play, through which online activity is cooperatively negotiated from moment-to-moment and over time between the caregiver and care recipient. We describe these themes below and suggest several considerations for design.

Narrative of Empowerment through Online Activity

Caregiving work is often viewed as a burden and characterized by the physical, financial, social, and emotional stress of providing ongoing care. Throughout our analysis we learned that caregivers went to great lengths to enable and support online activity for their care recipients, sometimes at the cost of taking time to learn new technologies, reconfigure settings and accounts for care recipients, instruct care recipients on how to use these tools on a regular basis, and remain vigilant against online threats.

Despite the risks and added work introduced by being online, caregivers view online activity as a positive experience and way of empowering care recipients. Caregivers shared many stories that espoused the benefits of staying up-to-date, stimulated, and connected online, particularly for individuals who are largely confined to their homes. Caregivers configure both physical and digital spaces to promote a sense of independence for their care recipient, even if they are waiting and watching as "backline support". Caregivers act strategically online to ensure their care recipient is included in online interactions and help relay and contextualize these interactions. A care recipient's online profile or blog maintained by a caregiver is a place for family members and friends to provide social support, and caregivers play a role in sharing and interpreting this online support. Receiving hundreds of "Likes" on a Facebook photo of a care recipient accomplishing daily activities such as getting dressed or going outside provides a source of encouragement. These narratives focus on promoting independence and empowering care recipients to live a full life by being active online, which in turn is rewarding for caregivers.

While staying active online is intended to empower care recipients, this also introduces new tensions and challenges for caregivers. Caregivers noted the risks of interacting online and configured accounts to block certain users, filter information, and approve friend requests. Caregivers struggle to balance the conflicting goals of protecting versus empowering: *"I don't like the idea that I'm limiting him... but, unfortunately, I can't let him do that, for his own good," (John).* Many reflected on their own internal conflicts over making decisions aimed at protecting care recipients, as they realize this often leads to disempowerment.

Surrogacy and Transitions in Online Activity

For our population of study, caregivers described significant challenges around assessing, understanding, and supporting the changing abilities of their care recipients – both daily (or even hourly) and over the long term. This constant fluctuation requires caregivers to be vigilant of their care recipient's needs when interacting online and to make decisions about when and how to intervene. Notions of surrogacy in caregiving (e.g., a health care proxy) provide a legal framework for understanding how caregivers make decisions on behalf of care recipients [10,21,38]. This framing, however, focuses on end-of-life decisions and neglects the nuance in how caregivers and care recipients cooperatively negotiate decisions through periods of vulnerability, which may last years or decades.

Our sample includes caregivers who provide care for adults with varying cognitive abilities and at varying stages of life, including one who passed away just before the start of this study. This diversity allows visibility into the transitions that are inherent in caregiving work. For example, caregivers may transition from teaching a care recipient to interact on a social website (e.g., functionally as well as what not to post) to stricter blocking and removal of content when they perceive the care recipient as less able to independently make decisions online. Yet, caregivers constantly assess what constitutes "safe" online behavior in the context of the threats they perceive, which may be financial (e.g., phishing, identity theft) or social/emotional (e.g., hurtful misinformation, distressing news stories).

The cooperative use of accounts between caregivers and care recipients provides additional insights into shifts in online independence and surrogacy. Similar to the account sharing practices within families [15], caregivers and care recipients share accounts explicitly (e.g., financial, medical) and implicitly (e.g., posting photos on behalf of a care recipient). Caregivers and care recipients may assume a shared online presence, which emerges through posting information about the joint experience of caregiving. Tensions may arise around deciding what to share online and how to involve care recipients [18]. Caregivers varied in whether and how they sought approval for performing online actions on behalf of their care recipient, and posting updates and photos of a care recipient without seeking their consent highlights the limited voice some care recipients have in their online presence. Further, privacy research suggests that when an individual is responsible for another person's information disclosure, errors in judgment and even deception may occur [36]. Our analysis highlights many complexities within caregiving work that are introduced by online activity, requiring caregivers and care recipients to continually negotiate online information disclosure [2,28] in the context of vulnerability, risk, and the benefits of interacting online.

Considerations for Design

Our analysis suggests several considerations for designing online systems that better support the dynamics of the caregiver-care recipient relationship as well as the work caregivers perform to empower their care recipients online.

Beyond Individualized Accounts

Our analysis calls attention to yet another context in which the model of an individualized account competes with people's goals and intentions. The notion of "family accounts" was suggested as a way of supporting home computer use among family members [15]. Recent work on how parents manage their children's identities online also suggests shared online accounts to allow cooperative content management and adjustment of privacy settings [2]. Similar features may work well for caregivers and care recipients but should consider how to truly make this a cooperative experience that empowers care recipients, who were at one time autonomous and now need fluctuating levels and types of support. Furthermore, such joint accounts may present ethical and legal challenges [3].

Support Transitions in Vulnerability

Prior work focuses on designing to protect children online before they come of age [2], support the end of life (e.g., hospice care) [18], and manage online information post-mortem [4]. Extending this literature, our data suggest the importance of designing for transitions in vulnerability, in which systems can accommodate the convergence and divergence of online identities (or even accounts) and moments of surrogacy versus independence over the course of one's life. The caregivers we study weave in and out of the online lives of their care recipients, highlighting that vulnerability is not a discrete state or permanent way of being. Rather, vulnerability is socially constructed through perceived risk, abilities, and independence and fluctuates moment-to-moment. Designers should consider periods of life in which vulnerability might be transitory (e.g., gradual recovery after a stroke) or progressive (e.g., from early to late stage dementia) that allows for gradations of support as needed. Opportunities for caregivers to discuss and learn about how to facilitate online activity may also help ease the burden of supporting changes in vulnerability.

Awareness of Online Activity and Perceived Risks

While caregivers strive to empower care recipients by helping them stay active online, they weigh this against their goal of protecting care recipients from various risks inherent in online interaction. The challenge in this balance is staying aware of a care recipient's online activity, particularly when not co-located with the care recipient, and being vigilant of potential risks associated with this activity. This adds to the work of already overburdened caregivers who also monitor medication, food intake, and social and emotional needs. Mechanisms that allow caregivers to cue in on risk-related online situations could help alleviate this burden. For example, a system could detect disclosure of sensitive information (e.g., passwords, credit cards) and hold the transaction for review by or feedback from the primary caregiver. Alternatively, future systems could incorporate responsive interfaces based on how a care recipient is interacting (e.g., linguistic markers [24]).

CONCLUSION

Caregiving is demanding and stressful work. Supporting a care recipient's online activity introduces new responsibilities and concerns but also provides benefits of stimulation and social connectivity. As a first study on this topic, we focus on care recipients with a broad range of cognitive impairments, and future work should examine other groups of care recipients (e.g., young adults with traumatic brain injury) and caregivers (e.g., older non-Internet users caring for a partner). Similarly, our analysis focuses on informal caregivers who are related to their care recipients, and it is likely that the work of supporting online activity and the dynamics of the caregiver-care recipient relationship will be different for paid, non-familial caregivers. Nonetheless, caregivers are grappling with how to support online interaction in ways that empower care recipients while minimizing risk, underscoring the importance of understanding and designing for the experience of caregiving throughout the lifespan.

REFERENCES

1. Alzheimer's Association and National Alliance for Caregiving. 2004. *Families care : Alzheimer's caregiving in the United States*. Retrieved September 1, 2015 from https://www.alz.org/national/documents/report_familiescare.pdf
2. Tawfiq Ammari, Priya Kumar, Cliff Lampe, and Sarita Schoenebeck. 2015. Managing Children's Online Identities: How Parents Decide What to Disclose About Their Children Online. *Proc. of CHI '15*, ACM, 1895–1904. http://doi.org/10.1145/2702123.2702325
3. Rachel Batchelor, Ania Bobrowicz, Robin Mackenzie, and Alisoun Milne. 2012. Challenges of ethical and legal responsibilities when technologies' uses and users change: social networking sites, decision-making capacity and dementia. *Ethics and Information Technology* 14, 2: 99–108. http://doi.org/10.1007/s10676-012-9286-x
4. Jed R. Brubaker, Lynn S. Dombrowski, Anita M. Gilbert, Nafiri Kusumakaulika, and Gillian R. Hayes. 2014. Stewarding a legacy: responsibilities and relationships in the management of post-mortem data. *Proceedings of the SIGCHI Conference on Human Factors in Computing Systems*, ACM Press, 4157–4166. http://doi.org/10.1145/2556288.2557059
5. Jed R. Brubaker, Gillian R. Hayes, and Paul Dourish. 2013. Beyond the Grave: Facebook as a Site for the Expansion of Death and Mourning. *The Information Society* 29, 3: 152–163. http://doi.org/10.1080/01972243.2013.777300
6. Jed R. Brubaker and Gillian R. Hayes. 2011. "We will never forget you [online]": An Empirical Investigation of Post-mortem MySpace Comments. *Proceedings of the ACM 2011 conference on Computer supported cooperative work*, 123–132. http://doi.org/10.1145/1958824.1958843
7. Kathy Charmaz. 2006. *Constructing grounded theory: a practical guide through qualitative analysis*. SAGE Publications. http://doi.org/10.1016/j.lisr.2007.11.003
8. Kathy Charmaz. 2013. Constructionism and the Grounded Theory Method. In *Handbook of Constructionist Research*, James A. Holstein and Jaber F. Gubrium (eds.). Guilford Publications, 832.
9. Yunan Chen, Victor Ngo, and Sun Young Park. 2013. Caring for caregivers: Designing for integrality. *Proceedings of the 2013 conference on Computer supported cooperative work*, 91–102. http://doi.org/10.1145/2441776.2441789
10. Teresa Chiu and Michael Massimi. 2006. A digital support device designed to help family caregivers coordinate, communicate and plan the care of people with brain injury. *AMIA Annu Symp Proc*: 884.
11. Elizabeth C. Clipp, Michael J. Moore, and Linda K. George. 1996. The content and properties of the Caregiver Activities Time Survey (CATS): An outcome measure for use in clinical trial research on Alzheimer's disease. *American Journal of Alzheimer's Disease and Other Dementias* 11, 6: 3–9. http://doi.org/10.1177/153331759601100602
12. Raymundo Cornejo, Daniel Hernández, Jesús Favela, Mónica Tentori, and Sergio Ochoa. 2012. Persuading older adults to socialize and exercise through ambient games. *6th International Conference on Pervasive Computing Technologies for Healthcare (PervasiveHealth), 2012*, 215–218.
13. Shelia R. Cotten, George Ford, Sherry Ford, and Timothy M. Hale. 2012. Internet use and depression among older adults. *Computers in Human Behavior* 28, 2: 496–499. http://doi.org/10.1016/j.chb.2011.10.021
14. Kenneth E. Covinsky, Robert Newcomer, Patrick Fox, et al. 2003. Patient and caregiver characteristics associated with depression in caregivers of patients with dementia. *Journal of General Internal Medicine* 18, 12: 1006–1014. http://doi.org/10.1111/j.1525-1497.2003.30103.x
15. Serge Egelman, A.J. Bernheim Brush, and Kori M. Inkpen. 2008. Family accounts: a new paradigm for user accounts within the home environment. *Proceedings of the 2008 ACM conference on Computer supported cooperative work*, ACM Press, 669–678. http://doi.org/10.1145/1460563.1460666
16. Elizabeth H. Ehleringer and Si Jung Kim. 2013. The wearable lullaby: improving sleep quality of caregivers of dementia patients. *CHI '13 Extended Abstracts on Human Factors in Computing Systems*, ACM Press, 409–414. http://doi.org/10.1145/2468356.2468429
17. Family Caregiver Alliance. 2012. Selected Caregiver Statistics. Retrieved September 10, 2015 from https://caregiver.org/selected-caregiver-statistics
18. Robert Douglas Ferguson, Michael Massimi, Emily Anne Crist, and Karyn Anne Moffatt. 2014. Craving, Creating, and Constructing Comfort: Insights and Opportunities for Technology in Hospice. *Proceedings of the 17th ACM Conference on Computer Supported Cooperative Work & Social Computing*, ACM, 1479–1490. http://doi.org/10.1145/2531602.2531631
19. Georgetown University. 2005. *How Do Family Caregivers Fare? A Closer Look at Their Experiences*. Washington, D.C. Retrieved September 1, 2015 from http://hpi.georgetown.edu/agingsociety/pubhtml/caregiver3/caregiver3.html
20. Mary Jo Gibson and Ari Houser. 2007. Valuing the invaluable: a new look at the economic value of family caregiving. *Issue Brief (Public Policy Institute (American Association of Retired Persons))*, IB82: 1–12.

21. Muriel R Gillick. Medical decision-making for the unbefriended nursing home resident. *Journal of ethics, law, and aging* 1, 2: 87–92.

22. Jacqueline J. Hinckley, Amy Hasselkus, and Ellayne Ganzfried. 2013. What People Living With Aphasia Think About the Availability of Aphasia Resources. *American Journal of Speech-Language Pathology* 22, 2: S310. http://doi.org/10.1044/1058-0360(2013/12-0090)

23. Kristine Holbø, Silje Bøthun, and Yngve Dahl. 2013. Safe Walking Technology for People with Dementia: What Do They Want? *Proceedings of the 15th International ACM SIGACCESS Conference on Computers and Accessibility*, 1–8. http://doi.org/10.1145/2513383.2513434

24. Yoram M Kalman, Kathleen Geraghty, Cynthia K Thompson, and Darren Gergle. 2012. Detecting Linguistic HCI Markers in an Online Aphasia Support Group. *Proceedings of the 14th International ACM SIGACCESS Conference on Computers and Accessibility*, ACM, 65–70. http://doi.org/10.1145/2384916.2384928

25. Janice K Kiecolt-Glaser, Kristopher J Preacher, Robert C MacCallum, Cathie Atkinson, William B Malarkey, and Ronald Glaser. 2003. Chronic stress and age-related increases in the proinflammatory cytokine IL-6. *Proceedings of the National Academy of Sciences of the United States of America* 100, 15: 9090–9095. http://doi.org/10.1073/pnas.1531903100

26. Yoshinori Kobayashi, Yuki Kinpara, Erii Takano, Yoshinori Kuno, Keiichi Yamazaki, and Akiko Yamazaki. 2011. A wheelchair which can automatically move alongside a caregiver. *Proceedings of the 6th international conference on Human-robot interaction - HRI '11*, ACM Press, 407–408. http://doi.org/10.1145/1957656.1957805

27. Richard A. Krueger. 1994. *Focus groups: A practical guide for applied research*. SAGE Publications.

28. Airi Lampinen, Vilma Lehtinen, Asko Lehmuskallio, and Sakari Tamminen. 2011. We're in it together: interpersonal management of disclosure in social network services. *Proceedings of the SIGCHI Conference on Human Factors in Computing Systems*, ACM Press, 3217–3226. http://doi.org/10.1145/1978942.1979420

29. Steve Lauriks, Annika Reinersmann, Henriëtte Gerald Van der Roest, et al. 2007. Review of ICT-based services for identified unmet needs in people with dementia. *Ageing Research Reviews* 6, 3: 223–246. http://doi.org/10.1016/j.arr.2007.07.002

30. Leslie S. Liu, Sen H. Hirano, Monica Tentori, et al. 2011. Improving communication and social support for caregivers of high-risk infants through mobile technologies. *Proceedings of the ACM 2011 conference on Computer supported cooperative work*: 475–484. http://doi.org/10.1145/1958824.1958897

31. Michael Massimi and Ronald M. Baecker. 2010. A Death in the Family: Opportunities for Designing Technologies for the Bereaved. *Proceedings of the SIGCHI Conference on Human Factors in Computing Systems*, 1821–1830. http://doi org/10.1145/1753326.1753600

32. Rhonda J. V. Montgomery, Judith G. Gonyea, and Nancy R. Hooyman. 1985. Caregiving and the experience of subjective and objective burden. *Family Relations* 34, 1: 19–26.

33. National Alliance for Caregiving and American Association of Retired Persons. 2009. Caregiving in the U.S. 2009. *assets.aarp.org*. Retrieved from http://assets.aarp.org/rgcenter/il/caregiving_09_fr.pdf\npapers2://publication/uuid/F95CD001-E1F8-4FDB-87B3-41477D77C8B5

34. René F. Navarro and Jesús Favela. 2011. Usability assessment of a pervasive system to assist caregivers in dealing with repetitive behaviors of patients with dementia. *Proceedings of the 4th International Conference on PErvasive Technologies Related to Assistive Environments*, ACM Press, 1–8. http://doi.org/10.1145/2141622.2141656

35. Jarred Pennington and Tess Knight. 2008. Staying Connected: The Lived Experiences of Volunteers and Older Adults. *Ageing International* 32, 4: 298–311. http://doi.org/10.1007/s12126-008-9020-5

36. Sandra Petronio and Irwin Altman. 2002. *Boundaries of Privacy: Dialectics of Disclosure*. SUNY Press.

37. D K Publishing. 2013. *Caregiver's Handbook*. Penguin.

38. Robin Pugsley. 1988. Guidelines on the Termination of Life Sustaining Treatment and Care of the Dying. *Journal of Medical Ethics* 14, 4: 212. Retrieved from http://www.ncbi.nlm.nih.gov/pmc/articles/PMC1375587/

39. Richard Schulz and Scott R. Beach. 1999. Caregiving as a Risk Factor for Mortality. *JAMA* 282, 23: 2215. http://doi.org/10.1001/jama.282.23.2215

40. Richard Schulz, Alison T. O'Brien, Jamila Bookwala, and Kathy Fleissner. 1995. Psychiatric and Physical Morbidity Effects of Dementia Caregiving: Prevalence, Correlates, and Causes. *The Gerontologist* 35, 6: 771–791. http://doi.org/10.1093/geront/35.6.771

41. Masahiro Shiomi, Takamasa Iio, Koji Kamei, Chandraprakash Sharma, and Norihiro Hagita. 2014. User-friendly autonomous wheelchair for elderly care using ubiquitous network robot platform. *Proceedings of the second international conference on Human-agent interaction*, ACM Press, 17–22. http://doi.org/10.1145/2658861.2658873

42. Katie A. Siek, Danish U. Khan, Stephen E. Ross, Leah M. Haverhals, Jane Meyers, and Steven R. Cali. 2011. Designing a personal health application for older adults to manage medications: A comprehensive case study. *Journal of Medical Systems*, 1099–1121. http://doi.org/10.1007/s10916-011-9719-9

43. Meredith M. Skeels, Kenton T. Unruh, Christopher Powell, and Wanda Pratt. 2010. Catalyzing social support for breast cancer patients. *Proceedings of the 28th international conference on Human factors in computing systems - CHI '10*, ACM Press, 173. http://doi.org/10.1145/1753326.1753353

44. Aaron Smith. 2014. *Older Adults and Technology Use: Adoption is increasing but many seniors remain isolated from digital life*. Pew Research Center.

45. Anselm L. Strauss. 1985. *Social Organization of Medical Work*. University of Chicago Press.

46. Sharon Tennstedt. 1999. Family Caregiving in an Aging Society. *Aging Symposium Longevity in the New American Century*: 14–25.

47. Lin Wan, Claudia Müller, Volker Wulf, and David William Randall. 2014. Addressing the subtleties in dementia care: pre-study & evaluation of a GPS monitoring system. *Proceedings of the SIGCHI Conference on Human Factors in Computing Systems*, ACM Press, 3987–3996. http://doi.org/10.1145/2556288.2557307

Closing the Gap: Supporting Patients' Transition to Self-Management after Hospitalization

Ari H Pollack[1,2], Uba Backonja[4], Andrew D. Miller[4], Sonali R. Mishra[3], Maher Khelifi[4], Logan Kendall[4], and Wanda Pratt[3]

[1]Department of Pediatrics
School of Medicine
University of Washington
Seattle, WA, USA

[2]Division of Nephrology
Seattle Children's Hospital
Seattle, WA, USA

[3]The Information School,
[4]Biomedical and Health Informatics
University of Washington
Seattle, WA, USA

{apollack; backonja; millerad, srmishra; khelifi; kendall5; wpratt}@uw.edu

ABSTRACT

Patients going home after a hospitalization face many challenges. This transition period exposes patients to unnecessary risks related to inadequate preparation prior to leaving the hospital, potentially leading to errors and patient harm. Although patients engaging in self-management have better health outcomes and increased self-efficacy, little is known about the processes in place to support and develop these skills for patients leaving the hospital. Through qualitative interviews and observations of 28 patients during and after their hospitalizations, we explore the challenges they face transitioning from hospital care to self-management. We identify three key elements in this process: knowledge, resources, and self-efficacy. We describe how both system and individual factors contribute to breakdowns leading to ineffective patient management. This work expands our understanding of the unique challenges faced by patients during this difficult transition and uncovers important design opportunities for supporting crucial yet unmet patient needs.

Author Keywords

Health informatics; pediatric; hospital; medical informatics; self-efficacy; self-management; discharge.

ACM Classification Keywords

J.3 Life and Medical Sciences, Health, Medical Information Systems; H.5.m. Information interfaces and presentation.

INTRODUCTION

Hospitals provide acute management for both new and chronic medical conditions with the goal of treating and stabilizing patients so they can return to their life outside the hospital. However, patients face many risks and challenges after leaving the hospital. Re-hospitalization, one such risk has been identified as a major issue within the United States health care system, impacting 1 out of 5 Medicare beneficiaries, leading to $17.4 billion each year in unnecessary spending [35]. Although some hospital readmissions are unavoidable, many are preventable and result from inadequate patient preparation prior to leaving the hospital (i.e. discharge) [11]. Discharge planning, a common component of many health care systems, allows for the development of individualized plans provided to a patient prior to leaving the hospital, with the goal of improving patient outcomes and reducing unnecessary re-hospitalizations. Yet, it has had mixed results [53]. Key remaining challenges include patients having a poor understanding of their medical condition or low health literacy in general [2,34] as well as patients not being able to access the health resources they need after discharge [37,39].

CHI'16, May 07-12, 2016, San Jose, CA, USA
© 2016 ACM. ISBN 978-1-4503-3362-7/16/05…$15.00
DOI: http://dx.doi.org/10.1145/2858036.2858240

June, a 16-year-old competitive soccer player, recently returned home from a three-day hospitalization after being newly diagnosed with Type 1 diabetes. In addition to receiving the medical care necessary to treat and manage her new condition, hospital staff also provided intensive education designed to teach June and her family about what diabetes is and how to manage this chronic condition. Eager to leave the hospital and return to a normal life, June and her family felt empowered with their newly acquired ***knowledge***, ***confident*** *that they had the* ***tools*** *to face whatever challenges lay ahead. However, their feelings of confidence quickly transitioned to feeling overwhelmed and unprepared. Previously simple tasks for June, like grabbing a snack to bring to soccer practice, now required that she read food labels, count carbs, and plan insulin injections. Should she tell her coach or her teammates about her diabetes in case the disease caused her to get ill during an away game, even though she did not want any special treatment? What would she do if she did not have a place at school to take injections in private or to dispose of needles?*

Once discharged, patients and their caregivers need to possess, or know how to obtain, the knowledge (e.g. including both technical/clinical facts as well as patient expertise [58]) and resources (enablers that help individuals manage their illness including social support, access to pharmacies, etc.) required to provide care at home, and respond appropriately to the routine as well as unfamiliar challenges, referred to as self-management [46]. As a result, patients like June (whose scenario is based on a teenaged patient from our study) face a number of challenges immediately after leaving the hospital.

Using human-computer interaction (HCI) methods to redesign technology for use after hospital discharge has the potential to bridge the resource and knowledge gaps faced by patients and caregivers. By designing better tools that consider the holistic needs of patients, clinicians can support patients through their transition to self-management. Although abundant research in HCI and Health Informatics has explored how to best support patients with chronic diseases [12,21,28], we have less understanding of how technology could support patients as they transition to life after an acute hospitalization.

To better understand how information technology could support patients and prepare them as they move from hospital to home, we conducted an interview and observation study with 28 hospitalized patients and their family caregivers, prior to and just after discharge. Through our analysis, we show that many challenges the patients face arise from deficiencies in three key areas: (1) medical **K**nowledge, (2) **R**esources to manage their health (including social support), or (3) **S**elf-efficacy. We describe how these three key areas, referred to as the **KRS** framework, have the potential to help guide design opportunities for HCI and patient-centered information technology to support patients as they transition from hospital-based management to self-management. Based on multiple in-depth interviews, we describe the challenges faced by patients and their families during such a hospital to home transition. We explore how gaps in medical knowledge, in resources needed to care for one's health, and in self-efficacy prevent effective self-management when patients leave the hospital setting. Finally, we outline design recommendations for technologies that could help address these unmet needs and ease the burden of this difficult and fragile transition for patients.

BACKGROUND AND RELATED WORK

With the increasing life expectancy of individuals around the world, the number living with a chronic condition has correspondingly increased [10]. This situation has led individuals to self manage and integrate their health conditions into their daily routine, through self-care [8]. Recently, researchers in the fields of HCI and CSCW have explored broadly how technology supports those living with a chronic illness and have provided suggestions on how to advance both research and design to support individuals living with a chronic illness [24,48].

Although low-tech solutions have shown benefit in reducing undesirable events after discharge (e.g. readmission or no follow-up with their primary physician) [4], they often did not assess the innate skills required for self-management at home.

Given that behavior change is a key component of self-management as individuals need to learn how to adapt their lifestyle as a result living with a chronic illness, Social Cognitive Theory [6] provides a useful lens to help understand and guide the patients' actions post-discharge. SCT has been applied to health promotion interventions [5], and includes the key determinants of the KRS framework. However, SCT alone cannot account for all challenges and constraints faced by individuals self-managing their illness. Therefore, new frameworks are needed in order to understand and design for the needs of this unique population. In the sections that follow, we describe patients' knowledge, resources, and self-efficacy in the context of clinical care and related work.

Knowledge

Traditionally, hospital staff take the primary role in managing patients during the course of a hospitalization. After discharge, patients and their caregivers must take over this management task. Staff try to prepare patients for this transition by providing the appropriate knowledge and resources to ensure a smooth and seamless transition. Interventions that provide patients with medical education at and beyond the time of discharge, facilitate access to needed resources, or support self-efficacy have been successful in improving patient health and quality of life and decreasing readmission rates [13,57,62]. However, not all interventions have been reliably successful, suggesting additional studies are needed to identify useful strategies to reduce readmissions [29].

Despite the education currently provided, patients continue to face many challenges after discharge from the hospital. It has been estimated that up to 20% of patients discharged from US hospitals suffer some type of adverse event leading to re-hospitalization within 90 days, one third of which are preventable [25]. Lack of knowledge is a key factor in these events related to: low health literacy [3,34], and a poor understanding of medication regimens [45]. These knowledge deficits lead to a gap in effective care after discharge.

Some have explored technological solutions to address these gaps in knowledge. For example, researchers have developed relational agents to act as a virtual nurse who helps disseminate information prior to discharge [64] or as a virtual pharmacist who helps detect and resolve issues that arise post-hospitalization [50]. The patients preferred receiving their virtual discharge nurse over their human nurse or doctor and expressed high levels of satisfaction with the virtual agent.

Resources

To successfully manage health and disease outside the hospital setting, patients must also have access to resources that support their transition to home care. Patients face many impediments needed to mange health outside the hospital setting. These impediments include inadequate social and family support [54], challenges with transportation and obtaining medication [40]. These barriers to resources can be particularly exacerbated among vulnerable populations. For example, children and adolescents are often dependent on their families and communities for health-related resources [15], and individuals of low socioeconomic status often lack resources to access health care or engage in healthy behaviors [9,36].

Self-efficacy

Self-efficacy refers to a person's confidence in their ability to accomplish a specific goal [5,6,12]. Lorig and Holman describe that in addition to understanding and managing the medical components of illness, people need to manage their behaviors as well as the emotional sequelea and self-efficacy associated with their illness [43]. Although education programs focusing just on medical aspects of the disease are not sufficient to improve health outcomes in adults [27], those focusing on medical management, self-efficacy, and emotional support, the three tasks required for self-management, have demonstrated benefits in a variety of chronic conditions [44].

Goal setting, a key component of self-efficacy, also plays an important role in helping patients manage their illnesses. Bodenheimer and colleagues describe how these goals help with the creation of action plans, developed by patients through the use of problem solving skills [12]. The creation and successful completion of patient-derived action plans, (which take into account knowledge and resources), support self-efficacy, and provides patients with the confidence to manage their own illness. This results in increased motivation leading to self-management success. In addition, coaching has shown to be effective in enhancing self-management especially during times of transition [49].

Although self-directed goal formation is important for patients, patients often also turn to others with similar conditions for information as well as guidance and support in the goal-forming process. Peers help through informational [18], emotional [51], and instrumental forms of support [32]. With the explosion of online health communities there are many opportunities for individuals to obtain support beyond their immediate social network. Hartzler and colleagues describe how experienced patients do not serve as just "amateur doctors," but rather offer valuable personal information that clinicians often cannot provide [30]. Patient expertise explores "strategies [used] for coping with day-to-day personal health issues gained through trial and error of the lived experience [30]." Integrating patient expertise and promoting social support resources in times of transition should therefore help inexperienced patients with finding and setting realistic goals.

With realistic goals, patients then require decision-making and problem solving skills to support goal attainment. These key skills of self-management require individuals to have access to, gather and interpret data (i.e. sensemaking). Mamykina and colleagues have proposed a sensemaking framework for chronic-disease self-management [46]. With patients in one of two modes based on the familiarity of an experience, they utilize different skills to navigate these experiences.

Recognizing the benefits of self-management, hospitals have an opportunity to integrate knowledge, facilitate access to resources, and support self-efficacy, to aid patients as they transition from hospital care to self care.

METHODS

Our work is part of a larger study, which was approved by the authors' institutional review board and the participating hospitals, exploring how to increase patient engagement in preventing hospital-based errors. We conducted interviews and observations with 28 adult and pediatric (i.e. child and adolescent) patients and their caregivers hospitalized at two different hospitals in Seattle, Washington, United States. One is an adult hospital that serves local patients from various socioeconomic and ethnic backgrounds. The other is a children's hospital that serves pediatric patients from urban and rural areas from various regional states. We chose these two sites because of the different challenges faced by adult and pediatric patients in the discharge process. While adult patients may have a caregiver assisting them post-discharge, pediatric patients almost always rely on the support of adult caregivers because of their minor status and they may not be developmentally capable of caring for themselves. Thus pediatric patients are dependent on caregivers who have their own goals and needs to aid in the patients' self-management. Therefore we sought to understand and include multiple populations to understand the range of complexities and associated with and similarities across self-care strategies.

Study Procedures

Patients were recruited over a four-month period between February 2015 and May 2015. For each patient, we conducted three semi-structured interview or observation sessions that occurred pre- and post-discharge. First, while the patient was in the hospital, the initial sessions with both patients and their caregivers lasted 40-60 minutes. Next we observed the patient while he/she was still in the hospital for 60-90 minutes. Typically, these interviews and observations occurred 1-2 days prior to the patient's discharge. Finally, we carried out a follow-up phone interview within 1-2 weeks after the patient was discharged from the hospital. Follow-up interviews lasted up to 30 minutes and were guided and informed by the initial interviews and allowed us to determine if the patients' needs and expectations were met after discharge.

In the interviews, participants (both patients and caregivers) were asked about their current hospital visit, exploring their experiences in providing and receiving information related to their care. The follow up interviews occurred shortly after discharge and followed up on items discussed and events that occurred after the first interview. All interviews were audio-recorded and transcribed prior to analysis.

We also conducted bedside observations with all the participants, typically after the initial interview. During the observation period, a member of the research team sat in the hospital room and took notes. We focused on discussions regarding the patient's care, communications between patients, caregivers, and providers, and finally the use of technology or other information artifacts in the room.

Study Sites

Our study took place at one adult and one pediatric hospital in a large urban area, Seattle, WA, in the United States. Each hospital serves as a tertiary referral center for a large geographic region. The adult hospital admits over 16,000 patients each year, and the pediatric hospital admits over 15,000 patients each year. Patients at the adult hospital have similar demographics with the local area's population, and two-thirds of the patients are covered by private insurance. The pediatric hospital has a slightly more diverse patient population then the surrounding area, and less than half have private insurance.

Participants

Due to our site selection and sampling methods we had the opportunity to recruit patients with a wide variety of ages and medical conditions. This allowed us to see whether themes were common across age and medical condition. We recruited a total of 48 people to participate: 28 patients and 20 caregivers across both sites. Our methodology utilized a purposeful sampling framework focusing on age, gender, ethnicity, medical service, and disease complexity. Research coordinators employed by each hospital recruited and consented participants on behalf of the research team.

Patient participants had diverse reasons for being in the hospital, which represented varying levels of complexity and medical needs. Fifty percent of the patients, were in the hospital on the surgical service after undergoing different procedures such as a heart or kidney transplant, hip repair, gall stone removal, cleft lip repair, and infection drainage. The other 50% of patients were cared for on medical teams for problems such as a blood infection, diabetes, Chron's disease, chronic obstructive pulmonary disease, kidney failure, pneumonia, and heart disease. Otherwise, patients were equally divided in the following categories: pediatric vs adult, chronic vs. non-chronic conditions, and male vs. female. Though, of the 28 patients, 20 had previously been hospitalized for some reason that could have been related to the current condition for which they were receiving care. Patients' ages ranged between 7 and 76. In the pediatric hospital (14 patients), half of the patients were age 7-13 years and half age 13-17 years. In the adult hospital (14 patients), patients were evenly split between ages 18-39, 40-59, and 60-76 years. Patients were more ethnically diverse than the American population: 18 were White/Caucasian, 6 Black/African American, 3 Hispanic, 2 Asian, and 1 American Indian/Alaska Native. Adult patients had a range of educational levels, with most having had at least some college.

In addition, we enrolled 20 caregivers who were present when patients were recruited. Half were 18-39 and the other half were 40-59. Caregivers were predominantly female, especially at the pediatric hospital. Of the 20 caregivers that participated, 16 were parents of pediatric patients and 4 were caregivers of adult patients.

Analysis

Throughout the interviews and observations, the research team met regularly to discuss preliminary findings and identify themes in the data to identify the gaps associated with discharge preparation. Transcripts were reviewed and coded by three members of the research team using AtlasTi. Initial coding was developed through an iterative process and not guided by a theory or framework identified *a priori*.

FINDINGS

Throughout our analysis, it became clear that the challenges patients experienced during their time of transition to self-management related to three areas: **K**nowledge, **R**esources, and **S**elf-efficacy (KRS). Below we show how the KRS areas frame two key themes: (1) **Gaps in System-based Self-Management support** and (2) **Elements of Individual Self-Management.** Gaps in system-based self-management support relate to the importance of hospital-based practices in supporting individuals as they transition from hospital management to self-management. Elements of individual self-management relate to the various states of individuals in their journey towards effective self-management. Below we describe findings by theme and provide quotations to illustrate each theme. We identify participants with a code: The first letter indicates the site as adult (A) or pediatric (P), the second letter designates patient (P) or caregiver (C), and the number is a unique identification provided by the research team.

Gaps in System-based Self-Management Support

Despite the large amounts of knowledge patients gain during a hospitalization, many patients are still unprepared to successfully self-manage their illness at home. This finding was present in both adult and pediatric populations and across different medical conditions. The gap between hospital management and self-management is related to three key factors: (1) most information transferred to patients occurs verbally, which makes it difficult for patients to process and remember, (2) patients lack the necessary patient expertise to adequately integrate the knowledge back into their lives, and (3) patients and caregivers often have low self-efficacy, preventing them from accomplishing specific tasks. Although the later two items are individual in nature, we identify how all three factors relate back to fundamental system failures.

Challenges with verbal information transfer. Although most hospitals utilize electronic health records (EHR) to document, order, and organize the care provided to patients in the hospital, these systems support the information needs of clinicians rather than patients. Despite the fact that patients are legally entitled to their medical information contained within the EHR, most hospitals do not provide easy or timely access [33,47]. Instead, patients obtain most of their results and the reasoning behind the care they receive verbally from nurses and physicians. However, without a concrete record for patients to refer to, their ability to retain it for future use is called into question. Not to mention the overwhelming volume of information presented over the course of a hospitalization:

I didn't understand and they were talking so fast and I didn't know what was important and what wasn't. Like I wasn't able to tell my family what was going on because there was just so much information. (PC04)

In addition to the lack of tangible information available to patients after a verbal exchange, another important barrier relates to the physical and mental state of patients while in the hospital. Often patients are not capable of interacting with the medical team in a way conducive to effective information transfer.

I really was out of it, I was not the best advocate for myself while I was there, because I was at such diminished capacity that I wasn't advocating for myself like I normally would when I'm in my normal state. (AP06)

Despite the strong efforts of hospitals to educate their patients in preparation for discharge, patients continue to have large gaps in the information or knowledge needed to support them in self-management due to communication challenges stemming from a lack of understanding of complex medical information and being unprepared or unable to process this information.

Lack of patient expertise. Although some discharge information provides a basic framework for re-introduction into life outside of the hospital, many patients are not completely prepared for this transition. Because patient-expertise requires some degree of trial and error through real experiences, it is not surprising that patients are unprepared after discharge. In the controlled setting of the hospital, patients are not exposed to the variety or spontaneity of interactions they are likely to experience once they leave the hospital.

I mean for her, she's like "Am I still going to be able to do my sport?" Even though they keep saying that, she won't believe it until she does. (PC06)

So I felt like I was prepared to take care of him, it was just a matter of taking care of him in our environment that we were going to. That I wasn't sure about - and am still not sure, we're still figuring it out. (PC04)

However, for many, discovering a lack of expertise only occurs after getting back home. Often, the lack of expertise relates to the ability to track important metrics or parameters required for self-management.

If I can't keep track, I forgot and then usually I need my parents to help me keep track of some things, because if I don't keep track of it I lose information. (PP05)

When patients lack expertise they feel overwhelmed or helpless, and not knowing where to turn for help. In this situation patients clearly lack both knowledge and self-efficacy to manager their illness.

Sometimes she'll get sad or she'll feel like she's alone. (PC14)

Fortunately, instead of taking the time to develop their own expertise, patients turn to others for help. Although many have discussed the importance of online patient communities [18,26,52] as well as in-person patient support groups [32] that support the needs of patients with a chronic illness, little is known about how a resource of peer expertise might help people in the hospital prepare for self management. Nonetheless, we found that patients are clearly interested in such a resource.

We haven't [found any other families who need to deal with the same condition]. It's something I would definitely like to do - being that we live in a smaller area, our options are pretty small. (PC14)

Although we know that patient expertise does exist in the hospital, the ability for non-expert patients to obtain this form of support from those more experienced while in the hospital is constrained because of privacy concerns or physical constraints related to an illness.

Due to gaps in knowledge, specifically understanding how to integrate their illness into their daily routines after leaving the hospital, as well as poor self-efficacy, patients clearly lack the expertise or confidence necessary to engage in self-management before leaving the hospital.

Low self-efficacy. Many patients feel completely overwhelmed by their illness, and this feeling leads to the inability to effectively self-manage.

It's been overwhelming, one day at a time. Just trying to - I mean it's just reorganization of your entire life. (PC06)

However, providing patients and their caregivers with simple support tools, allows them to escape the cycle of despair and hopelessness. Support can come in the form of informational, emotional, or instrumental (i.e. providing additional resources) [32].

When I'm really, really worried, I get really stressed out and no one helps me, and I overstress and I get just - but when someone helps me, I stop stressing (PC05)

Although hospital-based systems provide significant and diverse forms of support to patients in the hospital, this support does not adequately prepare all patients for successful self-management after leaving the hospital. We identified specific challenges in ensuring that patients have the necessary knowledge, resources, and self-efficacy to support successful self-management. However, ensuring patients have the emotional and physical support throughout their hospitalization, should help foster self-efficacy earlier, which in turn should help facilitate knowledge acquisition and ultimately the development of patient expertise easing the transition to self-management.

Elements of Individual Self-Management

We found that both adult and pediatric patients and their caregivers discussed knowledge, resources, and self-efficacy as important issues to support self-management. Based on these findings, we developed the Knowledge, Resources, and Self-efficacy (KRS) Framework of Hospital Discharge to describe how these elements intersect to support self-management (Figure 1). We propose this framework because while SCT includes these concepts, it may be limited in the hospital setting where sociocultural influences may be constrained. Also, individuals have less control over their health because they may not (1) be physically or mentally capable of engaging in or have control of their care or (2) have access to key knowledge or resources because of clinician- and system-level issues.

In reality, patients might have two, one, or none of the elements, which can hamper efforts to engage in self-management. We will describe each of the combinations of knowledge, resources, and self-efficacy and illustrate them using quotes from the study.

Knowledge only. Patients could have only knowledge without resources or self-efficacy. This situation is seen often in current hospital discharge practice in which patients are provided information about medications, future appointments, and the plan for managing their health. However, hospital staff do not (1) assess which resources patients have or (2) provide time for patients to learn and practice skills that are needed to carry out the plans.

We saw an example of this in an adult patient (AP02). He had been admitted for Chronic Obstructive Pulmonary Disease (COPD). Although he had been living with the disease before being admitted and knew what medications he needed to take. However, due to financial reasons he had to stop taking the medication, which exacerbated his symptoms and lead to being admitted to the hospital.

I was off for a couple of weeks for financial reasons why I didn't get it refilled and stuff...My condition just became deteriorated. I had trouble breathing and I was real fatigued all the time, and that brought me here.

He also stated that previously he did not have the motivation to adequately care for his health, including proper use of the oxygen tank he had been prescribed.

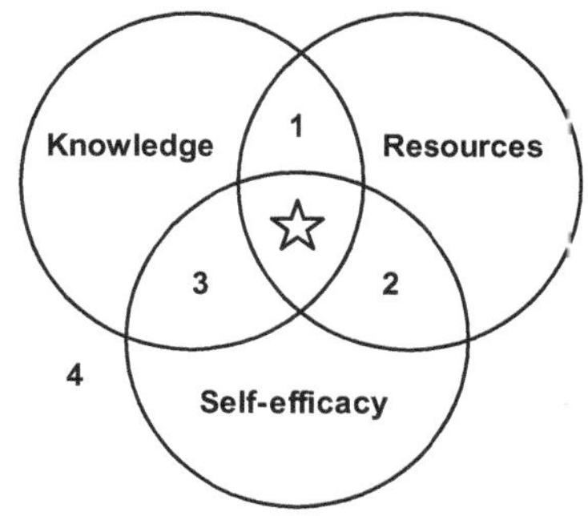

Figure 1. The Knowledge, Resources, and Self-efficacy (KRS) Framework of Hospital Discharge. Self-management (star). When lacking the complete set, patients may posses a combination of elements (1-3), a single element (knowledge, resources, or self-efficacy), or no elements (4).

While he had always cared for himself, he did not have the motivation to listen and learn from the clinicians on how to best manage his health. Ultimately, he appeared to be gaining motivation to support the full development of self-efficacy.

I was just really ready to listen to what they were telling me because I knew there was something that was out of my control, something that I needed to let somebody else take care of and listen to what they were saying ... this was my health, because I didn't like the way I was feeling. So I was ready to listen ... I kind of felt it was time to, like they say, put the cotton in your mouth and open the ears, because I've always taken care of myself, and listen to myself, and make my own decisions based on myself. I never – but I thought it was time to listen to others.

Resources only. Some patients have resources but not knowledge or self-efficacy. These patients have access to social and physical resources (e.g., family caregivers, access to health insurance and a pharmacy to obtain medication). However, the hospital staff did not provide them all the information needed to successfully manage their care because the information was not tailored to their individual needs. Often, the materials that hospital staff utilize are created for a general population, such as exercise and diet pamphlets that do not take into account cultural dimensions. Also, the patients do not have the confidence to perform new tasks because they did not have the opportunity to be taught and practice the skills under the guidance of health professionals at the hospital.

PC04 provides an example of having only resources. The pediatric patient and his caregiver had access to the medications that the pediatric patient needed post-discharge. However, the caregiver did not have the information and skills needed to prepare the medication properly.

... they kept preparing me for the fact that this [medication] would have to be given a certain way until he starts eating

and then we can sprinkle it. It's a tab that has the little sprinkles inside of it. Well, when I went to the pharmacy to get his medications, they didn't give me that version of it. They gave me a like a horse pill that I have to crush, and so they spent so much time preparing me for one thing and then I got a completely different version of the medication ... I kind of wish I would have gotten the medication maybe a couple of days before discharge, so I could have done them in the hospital, like with the nurses, just so I would have had a better idea of that. Because that first night it took me about two hours to do his medications.

Self-efficacy only. Patients with only self-efficacy represent few patients at discharge but could still exist and be impacted by the current discharge practices. These patients have the confidence to manage their health but lack the knowledge and resources to carry out self-management. AP13 provides an illustration of self-efficacy only. She had been living with Crohn's Disease for over 10 years so she had the skills and confidence on how to manage her health. However, she had been admitted to the hospital for a new kidney condition.

It's kind of a habit I've cultivated over the last 13 years with Crohn's, I make sure I have everything – everybody's questions in a row and I get them all answered ... I'm kind of used to all my research being about guts and stuff, and all of a sudden I've got kidneys to deal with...

She did not posses the knowledge about this new condition because the clinicians did not know what was causing the problem and the patient did not know much about kidney disease. Also, she was having problems accessing adequate medical care where she lived.

Trying to get information from here to [Medical clinic] and [Medical clinic] to here, because my insurance company wanted me to have my primary a little closer to home, but I think that's just not going to be a workable thing. We're going to have to figure something out.

Knowledge and Resources (Figure 1, area 1). The patients who would benefit the most from a restructuring of hospital discharge are patients who have knowledge and resources, even though they lack self-efficacy. These patients have an understanding of their disease and its management and have the resources to mange their health; however, they are in need of motivation or confidence in their ability to manage their health.

Pediatric participant PP09 is an example of someone who has knowledge and resources but lacks self-efficacy. The hospital provided the parent with information about post-discharge care. The pediatric patient also had social support – their parent – and access to medical care including on-call help via phone when needed.

I needed to know for the care of my son and they gave me everything what I need, all the numbers, if I had any questions. They gave me my follow up appointment. I mean, basically it was good. They gave me all the information I needed ... I did call them ... because for his blood pressure - I've been doing at home so I did call them on Monday just to make sure that his blood pressure and his pulse was in the right range.

However, the patient did not have the self-efficacy to take their medications. The parent was in the process of providing him the confidence in his ability to take medications through teaching.

Right now, yes, it's just me [the parent giving him the medications], but I'm also training him. I'm telling him you need to know and now I've been training him so he could look at the pills and knows what pill is what.

Resources and self-efficacy (Figure 1, area 2). There may be patients who have the resources and self-efficacy but lack knowledge needed to engage in self-management. It is possible to easily address this by providing tailored information to patients before discharge, which can be facilitated by clinical and/or personal technologies. These patients are likely to have resources, including tangible and informational, available after discharge. In addition, these patients typically have high levels of motivation to get their health back on track.

Caregiver PC05 of a pediatric patient is an example of having resources and self-efficacy but lacking knowledge. This parent was caring for her child and had the resources and self-efficacy to learn about the medications her son was taking and she had resources to purchase these medications. She also had some knowledge about what to expect after discharge.

...we looked up some of the medications like on Google that he's on now ... we talked about what appointments he was going to need after he was out, what appointments we had to come back for ... and following up with the kidney doctor or the urology [doctor].

However, she lacked important knowledge about her son's treatment plan, specifically what medications he needed to take after discharge.

... so like when we left [the hospital] I wasn't sure if I was still supposed to give him the [medication] when we got home, I realized they had been giving him an anti-acid in the hospital but there wasn't anywhere on the form about whether or not we should take them. So I think there was a slight gap in how everything - information passing over.

Knowledge and Self-efficacy (Figure 1, area 3). The situation in which patients have knowledge and self-efficacy but not resources may occur frequently, in particular in areas where there may be system or structural barriers to resources. An illustrative patient could include a patient admitted to a hospital related to their diabetes. They have had the disease for many years so they know about the disease and how to manage it. However, they live in an area with frequent power outages so it is difficult to keep critical medication stored in their refrigerator at the proper temperature.

AP12 exemplifies this scenario. She was admitted for a planned orthopedic surgery and had been given information before being admitted and while in the hospital. She also had the confidence to take her medications and understand much about the medical system and her care specifically because she worked in healthcare.

I had kind of picked her [the surgeon's] brain before on my pre-op appointment, and I did a little research ... she has actually a documentary, like a short four-minute thing on her website, it talks about what they do and what to expect and then six or eight months down the road I should be going back to a more regular routine

However, she lacked the needed resources when the hospital, her health insurance, and her military benefits did not coordinate, resulting in billing concerns.

...when I had called to schedule I had been told from my insurance company that I had approval and I called scheduling, they said they didn't have anything and because I had military stuff pending on my surgery, she said "well, I can send you a bill, but it's going to be $60,000," but they didn't since then. And I called financial aid and all that, they haven't said "well, your patient portion is going to be this, and this is how much," so I have no idea what my bill looks like. And that bothered me a little bit going into this, not knowing if I owe $10,000 or $10.

No knowledge, resources, or self-efficacy (Figure 1, area 4). These patients lack the knowledge, resources, and self-efficacy to engage in self-management. They may be the most challenging at discharge but potentially have the most to gain from any support. Because all of the subjects in our study had access to healthcare, by the very nature of being in the hospital, we have no such examples to describe. However, here we provide a hypothetical example to illustrate this case. Imagine a teenager who is a very recent immigrant, admitted to an emergency department because of injuries from a sexual assault. They come from a culture where sexual assault is not discussed so they do not know about what constitutes sexual assault and consequences of being sexually assaulted. Because of the psychological consequences of being assaulted and being in a new country, they lack confidence in their ability to manage their health or social interactions. Also, because they are not a citizen and in a country with a medical system with which they are unfamiliar, they may lack the resources to medical care after they leave the emergency department.

DESIGN OPPORTUNITIES

Our analysis at the time of transition after a hospitalization has highlighted the presence of a gap between hospital-based care and individual-driven care at home for both adult and pediatric populations and across different medical conditions. This gap leads to challenges for patients recovering from an illness to engage in self-management because often there are not opportunities to (1) support health knowledge, (2) to access resources, and (3) promote self-efficacy, each of which contribute to successful self-management outside the hospital. In addition, hospital-based system challenges and individual personal traits contribute to this problem. With understanding the contributing factors to this gap, designers have an opportunity to focus on specific patient needs that provide support to patients during this risky time of transition from hospital to home. Based on findings regarding expectations and experiences post discharge, we first focus on system support issues ripe for potential design improvements, then discuss the opportunities available to support individual patients who are missing one or more elements required for effective self-management. We focused on the opportunities that take place prior to discharge in preparation for self-management after discharge to address pre-discharge expectations and prevent adverse experiences post-discharge.

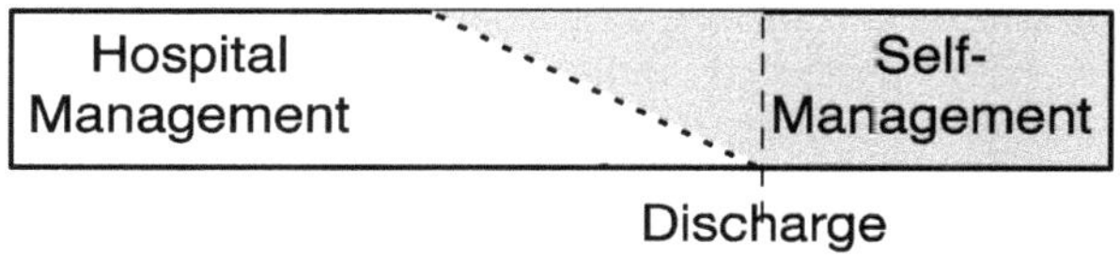

Figure 2. Ideally patients should have the opportunity to develop the necessary self-management elements over time while under the support and guidance of the hospital and its resources prior to discharge.

System Support

Traditionally, hospitals expect patients to begin self-management only at the time of discharge. Although they provide resources to support this transition, we have shown that, in reality, patients still struggle. Given the importance of the knowledge gained from patient expertise and self-efficacy in supporting self-management, it is unrealistic to expect that these elements will be present immediately at the time of discharge. Ideally, a system should support their progressive development over the transition period, culminating with patients completely engaging in their own self-management at the time of discharge (Figure 2). This strategy supports patients as they develop the necessary skills, without having to worry about failure, because they remain supported by the hospital.

Through the KRS framework, we can beging to understand the unique and varying needs of patients throughout their hospitalization and morre importantly how these needs change overtime. The framework will allow tools to be tailored to meet the individual needs of patients in an early yet gradual and supported transition to self-management, taking into consideration the unique constraints (both physical and cognitive placed on patients as a result of their illness. In the following sections, we discuss technology opportunities to allow hospitals to realize this goal.

Capturing and Retaining Verbal Information
We have described multiple issues with information exchange to patients due to communication challenges for hospitalized patients that in turn can impact patients' health knowledge and self-efficacy. These include excessive amounts of information, unfamiliar or confusing medical terms, an inability to process information in real time, and an inability to receive information in the first place, due to altered states of cognition resulting from a patient's illness. Not only is the volume and content of information overwhelming for patients, but so is the speed at which it is delivered, resulting in misunderstandings and errors [60].

In the outpatient setting, others have recommended an automated approach to capturing verbal information [60], and in a cancer consultation setting, simple audio recordings have improved patients recall of the information [61] and been rated highly by patients [1]. However, simple audiotapes provide limited search and retrieval capability. Capturing verbal content during rounds and other hospital based clinician interactions could build on research from the field of ubiquitous computing to go beyond simple audio recordings.

Although embedded capture and access technologies have the potential to encourage the review of recorded conversations [38], further contextualization of this information has the potential to improve its comprehension. For example, medication names, laboratory tests, and even medical problems or diagnoses could be associated with relevant links or InfoButtons (i.e., tailored medical information) [7,17] providing patients the ability to obtain this critical information on demand at a time of their choosing.

Finding Expertise in the Hospital
To gain clinical knowledge and patient expertise, patients, including the patients in this study, are spending more time online searching for health related information, including other patients' experiences, to address various gaps [26,52]. In addition, we know that patient expertise is obtainable from both online communities as well as in-person support groups, but these venues typically support patients outside of the hospital [18,32]. Although preliminary work explores how social interactions support children and adolescents with chronic disease in the hospital setting [59], more work is needed to understand how this technology can support both children and adults during the times of transition at the end of a hospitalization. Work is also needed to explore how hospitals and patients can address the knowledge needs of patients who may not have reliable or any access to online resources (e.g., lack of consistent internet access because they live in a rural area or lack a steady income to pay each internet bill).

Besides directing patients to external resources, hospital-based support has the potential to also fill the patient-expertise gap. Preliminary work [31,41] has shown the potential in cataloging and archiving previous patients' personal histories, experiences, challenges, and solutions in a variety of different formats (e.g. written or video biographies), allowing current patients to obtain this information from a trusted source with minimal effort. At the very least hospitals need to enable patient access to expertise from their peers, and provide ways for them to locate it within the hospital [19].

Supporting Self-Efficacy
Although we have described how gaps in clinical knowledge and patient expertise can lead to low self-efficacy, systems supporting self-efficacy also support self-management, at least in the outpatient setting [12,14]. Preliminary work in hospitals have shown that technology supports patient engagement leading to self-efficacy through contextualized information and communication portals [22,23,63]. Although these systems focus on care planning, goal setting, and medication tracking—all important for improving self-efficacy—our results demonstrate the need for additional support tools.

We have reported patients' challenges in understanding their capabilities and limits related to physical activity and diet. In addition, patients commented on their ability to understand how their actions impact certain clinical parameters—such as blood tests, changes in body weight, or just their overall well-being. Therefore, providing patients with the ability to track a variety of parameters, outcomes or actions may help provide them with a better understanding of (1) how their ability to meet specific goals has changed over the course of their hospitalization and (2) how their behaviors and actions directly impact their clinical course. Work outside the hospital has explored the benefits of self tracking related to general wellness [20] and chronic disease management [55], but little is known about how this technology can influence patients in the hospital. In addition, we need to develop technological solutions that support the integration of self-tracking tools and electronic health records so patients can see this data in context with the rest of their medical information. These tools must minimize the burden of tracking personal information [42], especially in light of the physical and mental constraints faced by hospitalized patients. Finally, we need to expand our understanding how individuals utilize this type of information [16], specifically focusing on how to frame the data to support patient goals and self-efficacy, which are likely different from those needed to support general wellness or chronic disease tracking activities outside the hospital.

Identifying Patients' Needs to Provide Tailored Individual Support
The common thread across the design recommendations we have discussed thus far is that to support patient self-management, hospitals and patients need to work together to identify which of the three elements that patients possess. With this understanding, using the KRS framework, systems can better tailor resources to meet the individual needs of patients. To identify these needs requires both individual- and system-level considerations.

At the individual level, we need to ensure patients have the necessary skills required for self-management (e.g. decision making and problem solving) [43]. By identifying individual deficiencies in one or more of the three elements—knowledge, resources, and self-efficacy—hospital staff can tailor specific strategies to fit the underlying needs. Most often this work will rely on a combination of technologies we just described. However, to ensure resources are allocated efficiently and effectively, understanding individual patient needs will be key. In addition, these tools should support short- and long-term self-management tailored to a specific type or class of medical conditions. Individuals with an acute medical condition, such as a broken bone, and a chronic medical condition, such as diabetes, will need knowledge, resources, and self-efficacy to engage in self-management. The difference lies in how long self-management needs to be sustained. In particular, for individuals with chronic diseases, their knowledge, resources, and self-efficacy needs may change over time and disease progression, and therefore the self-management strategies may need to adjust to those changes requiring the use of flexible tools and strategies.

At the system level, hospitals need to support patients as they transition from hospital management to self-management. This will require multiple changes to existing hospital-based practices. Hospitals and clinicians need to improve how they educate patients about their medical condition, remove the emphasis on verbal lines of transmission, support additional patient-expertise searching, and ensure patients have the confidence necessary to provide their own care without direct medical supervision. Finally, utilization of one or more of these systems will require that hospital staff understand the individual patient and his or her needs.

For both individual- and system-level design recommendations, consideration of the KRS framework and how it supports self-management requires appropriate patient training and education. Knowledge, the most straightforward, requires that patients gain clinical knowledge and patient expertise required to engage in self-management of their illness. Self-efficacy requires that patients gain the confidence and motivation required to change their behaviors and for realistic goal setting. Finally, learning appropriate problem-solving and decision-making skills, both key tasks in self-management [43,46], help individuals find and access social and structural resources needed to mange their health.

Traditional hospital educational programs that only transmit information, which is usually the same across all patients, should be replaced with tailored information that is appropriate for their cognitive development (e.g., toddler vs. older adult) to support active learning. Therefore, designers should explore how the key learning principles of growth, diversity, cognitive development, and motivation [56], support the cultivation of self-management skills. Hospital educational resources should therefore support methods that incorporate these principles to support patients as they prepare for hospital discharge.

Limitations and future work

Although our work provides insight into the challenges facing patients around the time of discharge from a hospitalization, we need to recognize its limitations. Our sample represents the patients from only two different institutions in a single metropolitan area in the United States. Although both institutions provide care to patients from a wide geographic area and diverse sociocultural and medical backgrounds, our findings may not be generalizable and therefore should be validated at additional institutions and locations within and beyond the United States. In future work, we would like to follow patients throughout their hospitalization to understand how best to begin fostering self-management. Finally, our data focused exclusively on patients and caregivers, using their own perspectives and stories. Given the significant role hospital staff play in these issues, they should be included in future studies, not just obtaining their perspective on the challenges related to transitioning to self-management, but more importantly on the development and validation of future technological resources.

CONCLUSION

In this paper, we describe how patients discharged from the hospital often are unprepared as they transition from hospitals managing their illness to their own self-management. We make three primary contributions. First, we show that—despite their best efforts—hospital systems do not utilize their resources in ways that adequately support patients during the transition period. In addition, we describe how patients lack the key elements of knowledge, resources, and self-efficacy required for self-management outside the hospital. Finally, we outline design opportunities for new systems to support patients in their self-management journey. These technological opportunities have the potential to empower patients, affording them the opportunity to focus less on living with an illness, and just living.

ACKNOWLEDGMENTS

We thank our participants, who graciously gave us their time and attention during their hospital stay. We thank the *Patients as Safeguards* team, including Barry Aaronson, Shefali Haldar, Alex Filipkowski, Kelsey Aiello, and Cory Brown. We also thank Virginia Mason and Seattle Children's hospitals. This project was primarily supported by grant #1R01HS022894 from the Agency for Healthcare Research and Quality (AHRQ), with additional funding from the NIH National Library of Medicine Training Grant #T15LM007442.

REFERENCES

1. Gregory D. Abowd and Elizabeth D. Mynatt. 2000. Charting past, present, and future research in ubiquitous computing. *Transactions on Computer-Human Interaction (TOCHI)* 7, 1: 29–58. http://doi.org/10.1145/344949.344988
2. David W. Baker, Julie A. Gazmararian, Mark V. Williams, et al. 2002. Functional health literacy and the

risk of hospital admission among Medicare managed care enrollees. *American journal of public health* 92, 8: 1278–1283.

3. David W. Baker, Ruth M. Parker, Mark V. Williams, and W. Scott Clark. 1998. Health literacy and the risk of hospital admission. *Journal of General Internal Medicine* 13, 12: 791–798. http://doi.org/10.1046/j.1525-1497.1998.00242.x
4. Richard B. Balaban, Joel S. Weissman, Peter A. Samuel, and Stephanie Woolhandler. 2008. Redefining and redesigning hospital discharge to enhance patient care: a randomized controlled study. *Journal of General Internal Medicine* 23, 8: 1228–1233. http://doi.org/10.1007/s11606-008-0618-9
5. Albert Bandura. 1977. Self-efficacy: toward a unifying theory of behavioral change. *Psychological Review* 84, 2: 191–215. http://doi.org/10.1016/0146-6402(78)90002-4
6. Albert Bandura. 2004. Health Promotion by Social Cognitive Means. *Health Education & Behavior* 31, 2: 143–164. http://doi.org/10.1177/1090198104263660
7. David M. Baorto and James J. Cimino. 2000. An "infobutton" for enabling patients to interpret on-line Pap smear reports. *Proceedings / AMIA ... Annual Symposium. AMIA Symposium*: 47–50.
8. Julie Barlow, Chris Wright, Janice Sheasby, Andy Turner, and Jenny Hainsworth. 2002. Self-management approaches for people with chronic conditions: a review. *Patient Education and Counseling* 48, 2: 177–187.
9. Priscilla Barnes, Kelly Caine, Kay Connelly, and Katie Siek. 2013. *Understanding the needs of low SES patients with type 2 diabetes*. ICST (Institute for Computer Sciences, Social-Informatics and Telecommunications Engineering). http://doi.org/10.4108/icst.pervasivehealth.2013.252153
10. Yoav Ben-Shlomo and Diana Kuh. 2002. A life course approach to chronic disease epidemiology: conceptual models, empirical challenges and interdisciplinary perspectives. *International Journal of Epidemiology* 31, 2: 285–293.
11. Jochanan Benbassat and Mark Taragin. 2000. Hospital readmissions as a measure of quality of health care: advantages and limitations. *Archives of Internal Medicine* 160, 8: 1074–1081.
12. Thomas Bodenheimer, Kate Lorig, Halsted Holman, and Kevin Grumbach. 2002. Patient self-management of chronic disease in primary care. *JAMA* 288, 19: 2469–2475.
13. Robert E. Burke, Ruixin Guo, Allan V. Prochazka, and Gregory J. Misky. 2014. Identifying keys to success in reducing readmissions using the ideal transitions in care framework. *BMC Health Services Research* 14, 1: 423. http://doi.org/10.1186/1472-6963-14-423
14. Kristin L. Carman, Pam Dardess, Maureen Maurer, et al. 2013. Patient and family engagement: a framework for understanding the elements and developing interventions and policies. *Health Affairs (Project Hope)* 32, 2: 223–231. http://doi.org/10.1377/hlthaff.2012.1133
15. Richard Charlton, Michael B. Gravenor, Anwen Rees, et al. 2014. Factors associated with low fitness in adolescents - a mixed methods study. *BMC Public Health* 14, 1: 764. http://doi.org/10.1186/1471-2458-14-764
16. Eun Kyoung Choe, Nicole B. Lee, Bonghin Lee, Wanda Pratt, and Julie A. Kientz. 2014. Understanding quantified-selfers' practices in collecting and exploring personal data. http://doi.org/10.1145/2556288.2557372
17. James J. Cimino, G Elhanan, and Q Zeng. 1997. Supporting infobuttons with terminological knowledge. *AMIA Annual Symposium Proceedings*: 528–532.
18. Andrea Civan and Wanda Pratt. 2007. Threading together patient expertise. *AMIA Annual Symposium Proceedings*: 140–144.
19. Andrea Civan-Hartzler, David W. McDonald, Chris Powell, Meredith M. Skeels, Marlee Mukai, and Wanda Pratt. 2010. Bringing the field into focus: user-centered design of a patient expertise locator. ACM Request Permissions, 1675–1684. http://doi.org/10.1145/1753326.1753577
20. Sunny Consolvo, Katherine Everitt, Ian Smith, and James A. Landay. 2006. Design requirements for technologies that encourage physical activity. http://doi.org/10.1145/1124772.1124840
21. Juliet M. Corbin and Anselm Strauss. 1988. *Unending work and care: managing chronic illness at home*. Jossey-Bass.
22. Anuj K. Dalal, Patricia C. Dykes, Sarah Collins, et al. 2015. A web-based, patient-centered toolkit to engage patients and caregivers in the acute care setting: a preliminary evaluation. *Journal of the American Medical Informatics Association : JAMIA*: ocv093. http://doi.org/10.1093/jamia/ocv093
23. Patricia C. Dykes, Diana Stade, Frank Chang, et al. 2014. Participatory Design and Development of a Patient-centered Toolkit to Engage Hospitalized Patients and Care Partners in their Plan of Care. *Proceedings of the AMIA Symposium* 2014: 486–495.
24. Geraldine Fitzpatrick and Gunnar Ellingsen. 2013. A Review of 25 Years of CSCW Research in Healthcare: Contributions, Challenges and Future Agendas. *Computer Supported Cooperative Work (CSCW)* 22, 4-6: 609–665. http://doi.org/10.1007/s10606-012-9168-0
25. Alan J. Forster, Harvey J. Murff, Josh F. Peterson, Tejal K. Gandhi, and David W. Bates. 2003. The incidence and severity of adverse events affecting patients after discharge from the hospital. *Annals of Internal*

Medicine 138, 3: 161–167.

26. Susannah Fox. 2011. *The social life of health information, 2011. Pew internet & American life project*. Retrieved from http://pewinternet.org/Reports/2011/Social-Life-of-Health-Info.aspx
27. Peter G. Gibson, Heather Powell, Amanda J. Wilson, et al. 2002. Limited (information only) patient education programs for adults with asthma. *The Cochrane database of systematic reviews*, 2: CD001005. http://doi.org/10.1002/14651858.CD001005
28. Paul Glasziou, Les Irwig, and David Mant. 2005. Monitoring in chronic disease: a rational approach. *BMJ (Clinical research ed.)* 330, 7492: 644–648. http://doi.org/10.1136/bmj.330.7492.644
29. Luke O. Hansen, Robert S. Young, Keiki Hinami, Alicia Leung, and Mark V. Williams. 2011. Interventions to reduce 30-day rehospitalization: a systematic review. *Annals of Internal Medicine* 155, 8: 520–528. http://doi.org/10.7326/0003-4819-155-8-201110180-00008
30. Andrea Hartzler and Wanda Pratt. 2011. Managing the personal side of health: how patient expertise differs from the expertise of clinicians. *Journal of Medical Internet Research* 13, 3: e62. http://doi.org/10.2196/jmir.1728
31. Andrea L. Hartzler, Shomir Chaudhuri, Brett C. Fey, David R. Flum, and Danielle Lavallee. 2015. Integrating Patient-Reported Outcomes into Spine Surgical Care through Visual Dashboards: Lessons Learned from Human-Centered Design. *eGEMs* 3, 2: 1133. http://doi.org/10.13063/2327-9214.1133
32. Vicki S. Helgeson and Sheldon Cohen. 1996. Social support and adjustment to cancer: reconciling descriptive, correlational, and intervention research. *Health psychology: Official journal of the Division of Health Psychology, American Psychological Association* 15, 2: 135–148.
33. James G. Hodge, Lawrence O. Gostin, and Peter D. Jacobson. 1999. Legal issues concerning electronic health information: privacy, quality, and liability. *JAMA* 282, 15: 1466–1471.
34. Leora I. Horwitz, John P. Moriarty, Christine Chen, et al. 2013. Quality of discharge practices and patient understanding at an academic medical center. *JAMA internal medicine* 173, 18: 1715–1722. http://doi.org/10.1001/jamainternmed.2013.9318
35. Stephen F. Jencks, Mark V. Williams, and Eric A. Coleman. 2009. Rehospitalizations among patients in the Medicare fee-for-service program. *The New England journal of medicine* 360, 14: 1418–1428. http://doi.org/10.1056/NEJMsa0803563
36. Amber E. Johnson, L. Ebony Boulware, Cheryl A.M. Anderson, et al. 2014. Perceived barriers and facilitators of using dietary modification for CKD prevention among African Americans of low socioeconomic status: a qualitative study. *BMC nephrology* 15, 1: 194. http://doi.org/10.1186/1471-2369-15-194
37. Shreya Kangovi, Frances K. Barg, Tamala Carter, et al. 2014. Challenges faced by patients with low socioeconomic status during the post-hospital transition. *Journal of General Internal Medicine* 29, 2: 283–289. http://doi.org/10.1007/s11606-013-2571-5
38. Julie A. Kientz. 2012. Embedded capture and access: encouraging recording and reviewing of data in the caregiving domain. 16, 2.
39. Amy J.H. Kind, Steve Jencks, Jane Brock, et al. 2014. Neighborhood socioeconomic disadvantage and 30-day rehospitalization: a retrospective cohort study. *Annals of Internal Medicine* 161, 11: 765–774. http://doi.org/10.7326/M13-2946
40. Gina Koch, Bonnie J. Wakefield, and Douglas S. Wakefield. 2015. Barriers and facilitators to managing multiple chronic conditions: a systematic literature review. *Western Journal of Nursing Research* 37, 4: 498–516. http://doi.org/10.1177/0193945914549058
41. Danielle C Lavallee, Paul Wicks, Rafael Alfonso Cristancho, and C. Daniel Mullins. 2014. Stakeholder engagement in patient-centered outcomes research: high-touch or high-tech? *Expert Review of Pharmacoeconomics & Outcomes Research* 14, 3: 335–344. http://doi.org/10.1586/14737167.2014.901890
42. Ian Li, Anind Dey, and Jodi Forlizzi. 2010. *A stage-based model of personal informatics systems*. ACM, New York, New York, USA. http://doi.org/10.1145/1753326.1753409
43. Kate R. Lorig and Halsted R. Holman. 2003. Self-management education: History, definition, outcomes, and mechanisms. *Annals of Behavioral Medicine* 26, 1: 1–7. http://doi.org/10.1207/S15324796ABM2601_01
44. Kate R. Lorig, Philip Ritter, Anita L. Stewart, et al. 2001. Chronic disease self-management program: 2-year health status and health care utilization outcomes. *Medical Care* 39, 11: 1217–1223.
45. Amgad N. Makaryus and Eli A. Friedman. 2005. Patients' understanding of their treatment plans and diagnosis at discharge. *Mayo Clinic Proceedings* 80, 8: 991–994. http://doi.org/10.4065/80.8.991
46. Lena Mamykina, Arlene M. Smaldone, and Suzanne R. Bakken. 2015. Adopting the sensemaking perspective for chronic disease self-management. *Journal of Biomedical Informatics* 56, C: 406–417. http://doi.org/10.1016/j.jbi.2015.06.006
47. Kenneth D. Mandl, Peter Szolovits, and Isaac S. Kohane. 2001. Public standards and patients' control: how to keep electronic medical records accessible but private. *BMJ (Clinical research ed.)* 322, 7281: 283–287.

48. Francisco Nunes, Nervo Verdezoto, Geraldine Fitzpatrick, Morten Kyng, Erik Grönvall, and Cristiano Storni. 2015. Self-Care Technologies in HCI: Trends, Tensions, and Opportunities. *ACM Transactions on Computer-Human Interaction (TOCHI)* 22, 6: 33–45. http://doi.org/10.1145/2803173
49. Carla Parry, Heidi M. Kramer, and Eric A. Coleman. 2006. A qualitative exploration of a patient-centered coaching intervention to improve care transitions in chronically ill older adults. *Home Health Care Services Quarterly* 25, 3-4: 39–53. http://doi.org/10.1300/J027v25n03_03
50. Laura M. Pfeifer and Timothy W. Bickmore. 2011. Longitudinal Remote Follow-Up by Intelligent Conversational Agents for Post-Hospitalization Care. *AAAI Spring Symposium - Technical Report, SS-11-01, 33-40.*
51. Jenny Preece. 1998. Empathic communities: reaching out across the Web. *interactions*. http://doi.org/10.1145/274430.274435
52. Jane Sarasohn-Kahn. 2012. *The wisdom of patients: Health care meets online social media. California HealthCare Foundation (2008)*. Retrieved from http://www.chcf.org/publications/2008/04/the-wisdom-of-patients-health-care-meets-online-social-media
53. Sasha Shepperd, Natasha A. Lannin, Lindy M. Clemson, Annie McCluskey, Ian D. Cameron, and Sarah L. Barras. 2013. Discharge planning from hospital to home. *The Cochrane Database of Systematic Reviews* 1: CD000313. http://doi.org/10.1002/14651858.CD000313.pub4
54. Meredith M. Skeels, Kenton T. Unruh, Christopher Powell, and Wanda Pratt. 2010. Catalyzing Social Support for Breast Cancer Patients. *CHI ... conference proceedings / Conference on Human Factors in Computing Systems. CHI Conference*: 173–182. http://doi.org/10.1145/1753326.1753353
55. Brian K. Smith, Jeanna Frost, Meltem Albayrak, and Rajneesh Sudhakar. 2007. Integrating glucometers and digital photography as experience capture tools to enhance patient understanding and communication of diabetes self-management. *Personal and Ubiquitous Computing, 11*(4), 273-286.
56. Elliot Soloway, Shari L. Jackson, Jonathan Klein, et al. 1996. *Learning theory in practice: case studies of learner-centered design*. ACM, New York, New York, USA. http://doi.org/10.1145/238386.238476
57. Kelly D. Stamp, Monique A. Machado, and Nancy A. Allen. 2014. Transitional care programs improve outcomes for heart failure patients: an integrative review. *The Journal of Cardiovascular Nursing* 29, 2: 140–154 http://doi.org/10.1097/JCN.0b013e31827db560
58. Cristiano Storni. 2015. Patients' lay expertise in chronic self-care: a case study in type 1 diabetes. *Health expectations: An international journal of public participation in health care and health policy* 18, 5: 1439–1450. http://doi.org/10.1111/hex.12124
59. Amanda Third and Ingrid Richardson. 2010. *Connecting, supporting and empowering young people living with chronic illness and disability: the livewire online community*. Report prepared for the Starlight Children's Foundation. Retrieved from https://starlight.org.au/sites/all/tmp/files/200-programs/Livewire-Online-Community-Research-Project.pdf
60. Kenton T. Unruh, Meredith Skeels, Andrea Civan-Hartzler, and Wanda Pratt. 2010. Transforming Clinic Environments into Information Workspaces for Patients. *Human Factors in Computing Systems Proceedings of the SIGCHI Conference, 183-192.* http://doi.org/10.1145/1753326.1753354
61. Nienke van der Meulen, Jesse Jansen, Sandra van Dulmen, Jozien Bensing, and Julia van Weert. 2008. Interventions to improve recall of medical information in cancer patients: a systematic review of the literature. *Psycho-oncology* 17, 9: 857–868. http://doi.org/10.1002/pon.1290
62. Simone N. Vigod, Paul A. Kurdyak, Cindy-Lee Dennis, et al. 2013. Transitional interventions to reduce early psychiatric readmissions in adults: systematic review. *The British Journal of Psychiatry : the journal of mental science* 202, 3: 187–194. http://doi.org/10.1192/bjp.bp.112.115030
63. Lauren Wilcox, Janet Woollen, Jennifer Prey, et al. 2015. Interactive Tools for Inpatient Medication Tracking A Multi-Phase Study with Cardiothoracic Surgery Patients. *Journal of the American Medical Informatics Association: JAMIA*. http://doi.org/http://dx.doi.org/10.1093/jamia/ocv160
64. Shuo Zhou, Timothy Bickmore, Michael Paasche-Orlow, and Brian Jack. 2014. Agent-User Concordance and Satisfaction with a Virtual Hospital Discharge Nurse. *Lecture Notes in Computer Science, 8637, 528-541.*

Care Partnerships: Toward Technology to Support Teens' Participation in Their Health Care

Matthew K. Hong[1], Lauren Wilcox[1], Daniel Machado[1], Thomas A. Olson[2], Stephen F. Simoneaux[2]

[1]School of Interactive Computing
College of Computing
Georgia Institute of Technology
{mhong, wilcox, machado}@gatech.edu

[2]Aflac Cancer and Blood Disorders Center
Children's Healthcare of Atlanta
Emory University School of Medicine
{thomas.olson, stephen.simoneaux}@choa.org

ABSTRACT
Adolescents with complex chronic illnesses, such as cancer and blood disorders, must partner with family and clinical caregivers to navigate risky procedures with life-altering implications, burdensome symptoms and lifelong treatments. Yet, there has been little investigation into how technology can support these partnerships. We conducted 38 in-depth interviews (15 with teenage adolescents with chronic forms of cancer and blood disorders, 15 with their parents, and eight with clinical caregivers) along with nine non-participant observations of clinical consultations to better understand common challenges and needs that could be supported through design. Participants faced challenges primarily concerning: 1) teens' limited participation in their care, 2) communicating emotionally-sensitive information, and 3) managing physical and emotional responses. We draw on these findings to propose design goals for sociotechnical systems to support teens in partnering in their care, highlighting the need for design to support gradually evolving partnerships in care.

Author Keywords
Families; Adolescents; Self-Management; Health Information Management; Personal Health; Chronic Illnesses

INTRODUCTION
Among teens, the burden of chronic illness is growing, as rates of cancer, diabetes, heart disease and other conditions are on the rise [49]. Chronic conditions, recognized by the Center for Disease Control and Prevention as a leading health concern for the nation, are still most common among older adults [57]. Yet, estimates of the number of adolescents in the U.S. suffering from *at least one* moderate or severe chronic condition recently reached 31% [64]. Even worse, many health care providers report that the complexity and range of health concerns in teenage adolescents proves more challenging than for other age groups [50, 70]. Recent efforts to design technology to support patient participation in care [32, 39, 74], including efforts to improve personal health record (PHR) systems and patient portals show promise, but largely focus on ill adults [7]. Unanswered questions abound about the applicability of these efforts to younger patients as they represent a particularly vulnerable group with varying social, physical and cognitive abilities. For reasons that we describe in detail below, their involvement in care might be imperative one moment and unwise the next.

Recent computing interventions for chronically ill youth have demonstrated success with symptom recognition [78], promoting healthful physical activity [56, 75], and nutritional competency [29]. However, these efforts assume individualized health goals and view the patient as an independent user. We lack studies examining the role of technology to support *teenage adolescents' ongoing participation as partners in their healthcare.*

Research in this area is particularly important where it concerns complex chronic illnesses [22] (e.g., cancer [38, 71], sickle cell disease [11] and rare blood disorders [41]). People suffering from these forms of illnesses require special attention due to complicated, risky treatments and the unexpected nature of recurrence often leading to hospital readmission. Teenagers grappling with these illnesses face difficult transitions to adulthood [62], and their unique position as both dependent and emerging adult challenges the models of self-management and patient participation typically adopted in HCI research.

To gain a better understanding of common problems faced by teenage adolescents with complex chronic illnesses, we conducted a qualitative field study focused on three stakeholder groups. Informed by nine non-participant observations of clinical consultations, we conducted 38 semi-structured interviews across two pediatric health care settings: 15 interviews with adolescents with chronic forms of cancer and blood disorders, ages 13–17 (referred to henceforth as "teens") along with 15 interviews with parents of these teens and eight interviews with participating clinical caregivers who treated patient participants and also routinely treat teens in the target group. Teens and parents faced

CHI 2016, May 7–12, 2016, San Jose, CA, USA.
Copyright 2016 © ACM 978-1-4503-3145-6/15/04...$15.00.
DOI: http://dx.doi.org/10.1145/2858036.2858508

challenges related to: 1) teens' limited participation in their care, 2) communicating emotionally-sensitive information, and 3) managing physical and emotional responses. Our findings allow us to distill goals for this group that can be addressed through design. In this paper, we:

- Characterize three primary challenges associated with teens' participation in the care of complex chronic illnesses.
- Examine the applicability of HCI research supporting chronic illness self-management to this group and identify opportunities to create teen partnerships with family and clinical caregivers.
- Discuss how technology can support these partnerships by outlining goals for the design of interventions to support teen involvement in their care.

BACKGROUND

We first provide background on the problem space by bringing in perspectives from health and social sciences related to teens' challenges in managing chronic illness. We then summarize the literature describing previous efforts to design technology for ill teens. In doing so, we apply the lens of self-management and related theoretical work to examine the applicability of existing HCI research to this group.

Participation in Care: Necessary but Difficult for Teens

There is now a growing consensus in the medical community that argues for the transformation of the "patient"—from a dependent recipient of care, to an activated participant [23, 28] who is a "whole person" with physical, psychological, social and emotional needs [8].

Teens' activation—and what it means for them to be whole—are complicated prospects. Their physical and psychosocial development vary. Yet, in the pediatric setting, clinical caregivers have limited means to assess the teens' level of psychosocial maturity. There is no clear clinical boundary that sets apart adolescence from adulthood since the patient's age does not reliably mark the progression of their transition to adulthood [60].

Young people often depend on proxy reporting of symptoms and experiences by parents and clinicians [48, 66]. Yet, parents and their children often differ in their assessments of function, behavior, and quality of life [18], place different importance on symptoms and their severity [62], and have different preferences for how they wish to receive medical information [65]. Unfortunately, teens also experience barriers to effective communication during clinical encounters: perceived attitude of the doctor, need for privacy, limited vocabulary or the presence of parents can inhibit discussions that could influence shared decision-making and plans of care [6, 80].

Often, pediatric practice does not even differentiate between childhood and adolescence [59] and the parent-clinician relationship is emphasized. Kientz found that even this relationship is often accompanied by tensions and inequalities [34]. An unintended consequence of these dynamics is that the patient's role as a 'child' during care is perpetuated, while the parents' role as proxy is reinforced, contributing to the difficulties that adolescents face in assuming growing responsibility for their own health.

While there are ongoing efforts in the medical community to ease pediatric-to-adult care transitions, prior research has focused on broad systemic changes needed in healthcare delivery programs and resource management such as staff training and patient education [54] rather than on the role technology can play in supporting patients' participation in their care—an important gap that motivates our work.

Teens and Complex Chronic Illness

Complex chronic conditions, as defined in clinical studies [22], include a range of diseases that "can be reasonably expected to last at least 12 months and to involve either several different organ systems or one system severely enough to require specialty pediatric care and probably some period of hospitalization in a tertiary care center" [22]. Recently, the HCI community has begun to address chronic illnesses that require special needs arising from such complexity [32, 38]. These forms of illnesses, such as cancer and sickle cell disease, have a cyclical nature—often characterized as having repeated cycles of recurrence and remission—even when patients are compliant in their therapies [9]. Their treatment regimens can include frequent blood transfusions, hormonal therapy, and chemotherapy, typically requiring the need to balance effectiveness of the dosage with side effects to the patient. Even when "under control" or in remission, follow-up and continued vigilance are necessary throughout one's lifetime [32].

For teens, these complexities prove especially challenging as their illness affects developmental processes and impacts psychosocial adjustment and quality of life [62]. For example, patients with a cancer diagnosis will typically go through different stages in their illness journey, starting from the initial diagnosis and onto treatment and survivorship, depending upon the recurrence of cancer [26]. As they are required to manage symptoms between visits, their normal daily routines and social roles (e.g., such as going to school and maintaining friendship) are re-established [38], while they are also expected to begin to develop health management skills. Cancer treatments can have a lasting impact on one's physical functioning and appearance, psychosocial wellbeing and other areas of health—with residual effects of chemo or radiation therapy manifesting years later [79].

Self-Management for Chronic Illness

Medical and social science communities alike recognize the importance of *self-management* of chronic illnesses: fostering one's ability to manage symptoms, navigate treatments and cope with the physical, psychosocial, and lifestyle changes they bring about [4]. Corbin and Strauss, guided by extensive ethnographic research with chronically ill patients, specified three sets of self-management tasks involved in living with a chronic illness: medical management, role management, and emotional management [16]. Lorig and Holman [40] and Schulman-Green et al. [63] further expanded on these task sets to identify categories of self-management processes for chronic illness, delineating a comprehensive list of associated skills. For example, chronically-ill people will need to learn to *focus on their illness needs* by monitoring symptoms, taking medications and making day-to-day decisions in response to their experiences, but they will also need to *activate* or effectively *utilize healthcare resources* by reporting accurately about the progression of disease, communicating with clinical caregivers and coordinating care services. In addition, they will need to *develop coping strategies* to deal with various aspects of living with the chronic illness. Our study investigates how we can support teens in partnering with family and clinical caregivers to perform such tasks.

RELATED WORK

Designing for Teens with Chronic Illness

A rich body of HCI research has offered insights into how technology can be designed to support self-management of prevalent forms of chronic conditions [29, 31, 41, 43, 56, 77]. Prior work focused on this goal either draws from theory (e.g., [14, 78]) or emphasizes the involvement of people in the design process (e.g., through user-centered and participatory-based design [45, 55]) with more and more attention being paid to bridging these two approaches [2, 27, 30]. Below, we discuss each approach further and highlight how each has been applied in efforts to design for adolescents.

Theory-based Approaches to Designing for Ill Teens

Behavior change theories feature prominently in self-management interventions aimed at modifying behavioral determinants of health over time. As such, they are well-suited to applications that promote self-management of behaviors to focus on illness needs, such as those related to diet [24], physical activities [13], and medication adherence [17]. While behavioral factors alone were neither the cause nor treatment for the illnesses we studied, it is reasonable to expect that acclimating to new responsibilities, such as recognizing problematic symptoms and administering one's own medications, has dramatic behavioral implications for teens.

Popular models of behavior change include the Transtheoretical Model (TTM), which characterizes an individual's readiness to change behaviors, defining the stages through which she can progress in modifying them and processes governing transitions between those stages [58]. While TTM can be useful in situations in which it is clear how to allocate someone to a stage, adolescents with complex chronic illnesses and their readiness to engage in behavior change is expected to be sporadic as they encounter unexpected illness experiences that are less controllable [9].

On the other hand, the Health Belief Model (HBM) posits that people's *beliefs* (with respect to the severity of their illness, perceived barriers and benefits of self-management) affect the way they behave [5]. Yun and Arriaga [78] advocate for the use of HBM in the design of interventions to increase awareness of symptoms and knowledge of disease process in adolescents, as it allows us to account for their *perceptions* rather than assuming a certain cognitive stage.

Both models have been used extensively in HCI research, but emphasize the individual rather than taking into account social influences such as peers and schooling that are unique to adolescent development. As such, peer-based social cognitive models of behavior such as social validation [12] and social comparison theory [21] have informed the design of persuasive systems for adolescents' health-related activities [46]. These models emphasize the tendency to assess one's abilities in relation to a social group to drive behavior change. For example, Chick Clique [68] made step counts of small groups of adolescent girls visible to each other to motivate physical activity. Other systems such as StepStream [47], AHPC [56] and iFitQuest [42] saw the benefits of school-based deployments as they can leverage existing social structures–rituals, space and time–to promote and sustain physical fitness.

While peer-based social models may work for adolescents who are similar to a target social group, teens with complex chronic illnesses are unlike peers in their existing social structures. They must balance large academic workloads with frequent hospital visits and other care activities. Their social and emotional well-being is challenged due to ongoing stress associated with diagnosis, treatment, social stigma and uncertainty about their future health status [62].

User-Centered Approaches to Designing for Ill Teens

While theories focus on outcome-driven processes mediating behavior, involving ill teens in the design process is critical to understanding their unique needs in various aspects of living with the illness. However, capturing design input from them poses challenges to researchers: the presence of clinicians and researchers can bias teens' reporting of their experiences and preferences [6].

Recognizing these challenges, Peyton and Poole introduced a participatory design research framework, inspired by 'reality TV', that advocates the use of participant-created videos to capture and share illness-related experiences with researchers, as a way to avoid biased responses [45]. Other work has approached this problem through cultural probes and dyadic interviews to mitigate the influence of the researcher [51].

Beyond the Self: Partners in Management

The "self" in self-management suggests a focus on the individual patient; however, the burden of self-management extends to family caregivers rather than the ill person alone [10, 61]. Chen et al. in particular cautioned that the HCI community has placed disproportionate emphasis on sup-

ID	Sex	Age	Disease (Stage of diagnosis/treatment)
T1	F	17	Alveolar Soft-Part Sarcoma (Remission)
T2	F	13	Ewing's Sarcoma (Neoadjuvant Chemotherapy)
T3	M	13	Osteosarcoma (Metastatic disease)
T4	F	17	Osteosarcoma (Neoadjuvant Chemotherapy)
T5	F	16	Alveolar Soft-Part Sarcoma (Remission)
T6	F	17	Clear cell sarcoma (Stage 4 Metastatic)
T7	F	15	Osteosarcoma (Remission)
T8	M	17	Metastatic Testicular Germ Cell (Remission)
T9	M	14	Giant Cell Tumor of Bone (Remission)
T10	M	17	Osteosarcoma (Remission)
T11	F	16	Juvenile Granulosa Cell Tumor (Remission)
T12	M	16	Germ Cell Tumor
T13	F	15	Chronic Idiopathic Thrombocytopenic Purpura
T14	F	13	Sickle Cell Disease
T15	F	14	Osteosarcoma, (Stage 2)

Table 1. Patient demographics and illnesses. Diagnosis and treatment are mainly categorized under therapy, remission, and metastatic stages. Patients in remission are off treatment and may not currently experience symptoms related to the illness. Metastatic cancer is cancer that has spread from the primary site to another part of the body.

porting the execution of caregiving tasks rather than the needs of caregivers themselves [10]. Ethnographic studies helped researchers understand conflicting demands and challenging experiences faced by family caregivers [36, 67, 76]. For example, in their study of bone marrow transplant caregivers, Kaziunas et al. found that, like patients, parents transitioning into the new role of caregivers experience inseparable information and emotion work in their actual caregiving [33]. In parallel, other studies have focused on caregivers' use of social media to better navigate complex information resources to suit their caregiving needs [1, 19].

Parents of ill teens face the typical demands of caregiving, while facing added challenges associated with supporting their teens' participation in care. Our study focuses on understanding both parents' and teens' experiences communicating about and managing health-related needs to better understand and respond to these challenges.

STUDY

Setting

With IRB approval, we conducted observations and semi-structured interviews with parents, teens, and clinicians recruited at Children's Healthcare of Atlanta (CHOA), in two Cancer and Blood Disorders Centers (one urban, one suburban). We recruited patients who were 13–17 years old, through convenience sampling guided by our inclusion and exclusion criteria and IRB-mandated clinician approval. Inclusion criteria included the mental capability to participate in the study (as determined by their oncologist), and the ability to speak English. Non-English-speaking patients, prisoners, and patients with a terminal diagnosis who would not be undergoing treatment or subsequent follow-up were excluded from participation in the study. Prior to the scheduled consultation, we obtained assent from patients, consent from their parents, and HIPAA authorization. Our study

ID	Role	Experience
C1	Physician (Fellow)	2 yrs
C2	Nurse Practitioner	< 5 yrs
C3	Primary Nurse	4 yrs
C4	Physician	4 yrs
C5	Child Life Specialist (Social Worker)	5 yrs
C6	Team Nurse	< 5 yrs
C7	Physician (Fellow)	3 yrs
C8	Physician	16 yrs

Table 2. Clinical caregiver demographics.

included teens with complex chronic illness for which frequent hospitalizations are common, routine diagnostic tests are needed to assess status and management, and treatment decisions involve the consideration of complex symptomatic experiences. Recruitment began in October 2014 and concluded when reaching data saturation in May 2015.

Interviews and Observations

We conducted 38 individual interviews: 15 with patients, 15 with their accompanying parent(s) and eight with clinical caregivers. For nine of the 15 patients, we also observed consultations to note behavioral patterns in the consultation room and contextualize interview responses. Consultations typically involved the reporting of diagnostic tests and an inquiry into patients' symptoms, such as pain levels and experiences with medication. They lasted approximately 15 minutes each, and researchers were present 5-10 minutes before they began (i.e., while patients and parents waited for the physician to arrive).

Interviews with teen patients and parents were conducted in private rooms or separated areas at CHOA: only the parent(s)—not their children or members of the care staff—were present during parent interviews, while only the teen was present during teen interviews. Interviews, conducted by two researchers (one in each room), were audio recorded, and took place after the scheduled consultation. Interviews with clinical caregivers were also audio-recorded and conducted individually. All interviews lasted approximately 30 minutes.

We kept interview topics consistent across the parents and patients while adapting specific question phrasing to each. Topics addressed 1) awareness of illness and diagnostic data, 2) experiences and challenges communicating about aspects of health at the clinic and at home, 3) teens' preferences related to the use of information technologies in their care (such as PHRs), and 4) whether and how commonly-available technologies were appropriated by parents and/or teens to support health management tasks. For clinical caregivers, topics addressed patients' and parents' participation in consultations and other care-related communication (e.g., electronic forms of communication with patients and parents). We also probed their experiences communicating diagnostic information with both patients and parents to learn their perspectives on the impact of computing systems on diagnostic reporting.

Participants

Teens

We conducted 15 interviews with teen patients (10 female). The majority were experiencing varying stages of cancer diagnosis and treatment (therapy, metastatic, or remission). One patient had a chronic form of Idiopathic Thrombocytopenic Purpura (ITP) and one had sickle cell disease. Table 1 provides details on patient demographics.

Parents

In addition to interviews with teens, we conducted in-depth, private interviews with parents of teen patients. Parents' ages ranged from 33–52 (mean=43). In ten cases of 15, the mother alone accompanied the teen and participated. In two cases, the father alone accompanied the teen and participated. In two other cases, both the mother and father participated. Finally, one aunt, who shared parental responsibilities for the teen, participated alone.

Clinical Caregivers

We conducted semi-structured interviews with clinical caregivers individually (details in Table 2). Participants included four physicians with varying levels of experience, two nurses, one nurse practitioner, and a child life specialist.

Analysis

Three researchers created observation notes through regular debriefings following fieldwork. After transcribing all interviews verbatim, we segmented responses by question-answer turn, cross-referencing clusters with observation notes. Together, we conducted affinity clustering with paper copies of the individual turns. We then applied a hybrid approach [20]: after inductive analysis yielding emergent clusters, we reconsidered as a group each cluster in a more deductive fashion. In this way, we together re-evaluated clusters based on our understanding of the domain and prior findings. This resulted in some refinements to cluster composition and resultant codes. Data analysis occurred in an iterative fashion from March 2015 to August 2015.

FINDINGS

We present combined data from both the interviews and observations when discussing themes resulting from our analysis. In reporting on findings, we refer to clinical caregivers with the label "C" and parents with the label "P" while teens are labeled "T" (e.g., C1, P2, and T2).

Teens' Limited Participation in Their Care

While we expected that power relationships between teens, their parents, and their physicians would influence communication about care management, we witnessed several examples of the specific influences of these dynamics on patients' reporting of their health status. Most physicians and nurses asked questions about the patient experience directly to the teen. Still, we observed behaviors indicating frequent deferral to the parent, such as looking to them when the teen was spoken to, speaking with hesitation, and waiting for parents to nod or otherwise give them permission. In some cases, time constraints for parents, or perceived lack of time of clinicians, led to hurried consultations. In these cases, we witnessed more dominance by the parent, manifesting at times in interruption of the teen, and the taking of the teens' turn. Often, once the parent "took over," the remaining portion of the medical consultation was tailored toward the parent.

When asked what they would do if they had a question about a health-related experience, nine out of 11 teens preferred to ask their parents first, before their doctor. Responses revealed two reasons why teens were hesitant to ask questions: previous experiences with explanations that they could not understand, and feeling as though they will not receive a comprehensive answer.

Some teens believed that their doctor perceived them as being unable to understand detailed explanations, and thus do not go into desired details. As T13 put it, *"Sometimes I tell my mom questions to ask them so that I don't have to ask them. [...] they don't want to explain everything to me because they think I won't get it. But if my mom asks a question they'll go into full detail. Because my mom has a strong personality so people usually explain everything to her."* In contrast, T4 told us that she preferred asking her father questions because he spoke to her in ways that were easier to understand. She said, *"Mostly I don't pay attention because I can ask my dad. He explains it better. They [doctors] use too many big words and I don't know all of them, so I just wait 'til my dad tells me."*

While the parents were responding to these preferences, as an unintentional consequence, teens often did not see a need to participate in clinical consultations. In fact, many parents worried that their teens deferred too much to them. P6 described an illustrative example of this, *"Like what you saw in there. Like how she always looks to me, and then I make her say something to whoever she has a question for."* In contrast, T8 provided an illustrative example of the *other side* of this coin, *"I didn't ask too many questions because I knew they knew what they were doing and they definitely knew a lot more than I did."*

Communicating Emotionally-Sensitive Information

The separate interviews revealed insights into how teens and parents handled emotionally-sensitive information. We present how they described preferences related to sensitive topics, as well as instances in which they each found the need to emotionally protect the other, which often resulted in "shielding" information.

Sensitive Topics

In many instances, teen patients and parents expressed the need for a private line of communication with their doctor. Some teens preferred to be seen by clinicians without the presence of their parents. We witnessed this with T3, who cited sexual topics as being the most challenging part of clinical communication. While he hesitated to discuss sex in front of his parents, he needed more clarification about the long-term impact of his treatment on reproduction capability. T8 also preferred to have more private communication with clinicians, particularly concerning certain private parts of his body. As he stated, *"It's a lot easier when they [parents] leave the room. It's something about it's easier for me to talk personally to a stranger than it is to talk to somebody personally that I see everyday. Maybe I can just tell them my story and then never see them again. I guess that's what makes it easier."*

Shielding Information

In other cases, we saw that teens and parents needed a private communication channel for instances typically motivated by the desire to protect one another from emotional distress. Teens shielding information typically manifested as hiding symptoms from parents, not wanting to surprise or worry their parent, and not wanting to delay the parent. T7 expressed this concern, saying that he was hesitant to share details of pain or symptom that he is experiencing. He told us, *"I'll talk to my mom about my health, but only to tell her if I have a new pain or something in my leg. Then I'll be like, 'hey it hurts right here', and she'll say 'how does it feel?' like 'from 1-10', 'do you need medicine?' But like if I want to go into detail. I'll just look it up or see how this pain goes. I don't want to worry her with my problems because I know she'll go insane"*

T13 was protective of both her mother's time and mood, and was cautious not to cause her mom extra work noting that, *"We have to do a lot of extra steps because I'm older I guess [...] She cried a couple times so I feel bad."*

Parents similarly indicated a need for privacy, though the motivations behind it have some variation. Some parents were trying to avoid upsetting their children, hiding the results of a concerning MRI from them, for example, until time had passed and there was a more positive update. A physician, C1, helped to clarify why: *"The first conversation that we usually have with parents, when even we don't know what's going on [...] a lot of parents request we don't let the child know, and I think that's very legitimate because at that point no one knows what's going on, we don't know what it's coming out to be, we don't know what the prognosis is going to be like, we don't know what treatment he's going to get. But once the child is diagnosed, we really stress out that families should talk to their children, and we also talk to them."*

However, at times this approach conflicted with the teen's preferences and information needs. For example, T15 believed that understanding the potential consequences of a treatment could help her better prepare for the next step in her care. She explained, "*After that biopsy, my mom didn't tell me and I guess like, everybody else knew except me [...] I don't want anything held back [...] I really want to know what could be bad because that's how I prepare myself. Like this time, with the surgery, since everything is so close to my nerves, if I come out of surgery without a leg.. I want to be prepared for that. My mom's more like, 'let's just think positive'. But for me, I can't. Through all this, I just can't."*

Managing Physical and Emotional Experiences

Uncertainty in the patient's health status and progression of disease led to increased tensions among teens, parents, and clinical caregivers. Specifically, difficulty in understanding and communicating about the patient's subjective experience (e.g., symptoms, pain level, etc.) seemed to amplify these tensions.

Understanding the Patient Experience

For many parents, talking about teens' experiences was the most challenging part of the communication with physicians. A cancer survivor, P4 lamented on her inability to sympathize with her child's painful experience while receiving chemotherapy, stating, *"It's difficult because all chemo is not the same ... I had like bumble bees stinging me from the top of my head all the way to my toes. She doesn't go through that. So it's kind of hard for me to know. I know she's going through something, but I just don't know what it is."* Seeing that even a previous cancer patient who underwent a similar treatment regimen is struggling to understand her child's experience shows the extent to which parents lack the means to fully ascertain the impact of chronic illness on the patient.

As a common reaction to this struggle, most parents had a persistent desire to probe their child's experiences. Yet patients often complained about inquiries into their physical or emotional state. T8, though he appreciated his parents' concern, tired of questions such as 'how are you feeling?' remarked, *"A lot of times I really don't want to talk to them about how I'm doing. The biggest question I hated being asked is, 'are you okay?' or 'how are you feeling?' I'm feeling fine until you come here asking me all these questions. I mean they want to know and I appreciated it, but if I've got a problem then I'm not afraid to tell anybody."*

C5, a child life specialist[1], shared her thoughts on how and why "prompting" teens every time with questions about their status was not effective. She told us, *"...in terms of sharing how they're feeling about things, that's gonna come in a conversation that's completely unrelated to kids having cancer [..] a lot of times teenagers are so over hearing, 'how are you doing?' or 'how are you coping with everything?' [...] I think the key is not to push it, and it does come out, just in a different way than it does with some of the younger kids who are a little more forthcoming with how they're feeling about things."*

Conflicting Interpretations

Limited means for understanding and empathizing with the patient's symptomatic experience often resulted in conflicting views between patients and their parents when com-

[1] Child life specialists are child development experts who work together with doctors, nurses and other clinical caregivers. They work to assess and meet the emotional, developmental and cultural needs of each child and family.

municating the patient's experience to the doctor. We both witnessed and heard several accounts of teen patients assigning different levels of severity to what might be a symptom. As T5 remarked, *"Sometimes she doesn't really understand, like how I had a fever like a week ago and she was exaggerating about stuff and I was like it wasn't that bad, so sometimes I don't want her to talk because she'll totally make it a bigger deal that it is."*

In these cases, parents require a means of discussing care with the care team without the child present. In fact, P5 took T5's experience to be more serious and addressed this concern to the doctor during the consultation. *"Now I can't say this is front of her because she gets mad, but she's been complaining a lot about her head being dizzy...anytime I say anything she's like "Stop complaining, Mom!" but she really does it at home."* Such differing interpretations about the patient's subjective experience have the potential to influence the doctor's decision-making process toward the patient's treatment. Interestingly, we observed that these differences motivated teens to perceive electronic forms of medical records as a way to *resolve disputes or conflicting interpretations* over the patient's experience and health status. When asked why access to the patient portal might be useful, T8 commented that, *"That way we don't have to question or argue about anything that has happened. All we have to do is look."*

Perspectives on the Role of Computing Technology

Both teens and parents were optimistic about the role of computing technology—such as electronic health records—in their care. When asked if they desired access to electronic medical record data, teens' and parents' views aligned: all parents in our study valued access to the electronic health record, while 12 of the 15 teens indicated that they desired the ability to see *more* of the information in their record and two of the remaining three commenting instead on the importance of electronic care plans and notifications detailing how to prepare for clinical visits.

For both teens and parents, reasons for desiring access to this data included the ability to *share health information in future care scenarios,* and to *make sense of the diagnosis and treatment progress*. In the following sections we explore these desires and bring in clinicians' perspectives on access to patient data.

Making Sense of Diagnosis and Treatment Progress

For patients in our study, the results of diagnostic tests, such as radiology scans of the site of osteosarcoma treatment, or lab results such as the white blood cell count, served to enhance their awareness of the diagnosis. Both teens and parents commented on their desire to access diagnostic data—for both review with clinicians as well as for personal archive and review.

In particular, radiology scans served as a powerful way to relate data back to the teens' physical experience. As T10 explained, *"[The scans] make me feel a little bit like I'm in there. I can see the tumor they point out in my body, so I can see what's wrong with me so they don't have to tell me in some weird way."* These sentiments were echoed by T4, who remarked that he desired ongoing access to his radiology imaging data, *"the MRI—to see what they see—so I could better understand it."*

Teens often commented on the value of visual information as a compelling medium for resolving certain aspects of uncertainty in their care. Several saw the utility of visual information in the context of understanding their illness and preparing for treatment or surgery. T13, when explaining her favorite doctor, commented that, *"she will be like, [this is] what's gonna happen inside my body—but it would be somewhere else. So I can picture it actually happening somewhere else. And sometimes she would draw something out [...] to answer questions about it."*

In addition to the role that radiology scans serve as diagnostic data, they are also taken as salient signs of treatment progress. While it is not uncommon for patients and parents to experience some degree of uncertainty, photographic data was often used in evaluating progress.

Both teens and parents expressed a strong desire for having access to visual signs of progress of the care such as X-rays and MRI scans. P4 saw the need to access the scans to determine whether a treatment has been effective, commenting that, *"When they do an MRI on my daughter, I just like to see what they see. The first time I had to ask them. But I want to see after the chemo, that it [tumor] would disappear... So that's a big relief to see, the progress of what's going on."* While T5 shared that, *"[I] want to see how my platelets have gotten better over time [...] how my MRIs have changed over time: how they were at the very beginning and how they are now—that would be interesting to me."*

Teens were interested in how specific data types changed over time as well as when events unfolded over the course of treatment. As T5 illustrated, *"When I had my first round of chemo; It would have when I started [...] how much weight I lost maybe, and how they had to do blood infusions and all that stuff after that. I want to see that."*

Clinicians' Perspectives

Despite teens' and parents' favorable view toward electronic health data however, a deeper analysis of our findings revealed that clinical caregivers' views related to the availability of this data differed from those of teens and parents. While the patients and parents appreciated having access to these records, care providers on the front line of delivering scanned images cautioned that automatic release of electronic copies is concerning.

Two nurses that we interviewed expressed concerns especially with regards to delivering the 'bad news'. They warned that scans, although seemingly intuitive, could be misleading at times and require careful reviewing of radiologists and oncologists. Both agreed that unless they indicate signs of improvement, scans should not be released automatically and electronically to the patient and family members. Instead, they preferred that the information is communicated verbally via face-to-face or over a phone call prior to the release. Primary nurse, C3, remarked, *"I don't have a problem with them having the information after we've discussed it, but to me the worst thing that can happen is have a parent go in, and read a scan and it's a Friday night, and you're not gonna be able to talk to anyone on your regular team until Monday. [...] So be able to start that discussion so the parents have a time to process that."*

Appropriating Commonly-Available Technologies

We were interested in exploring how families adopted commonly-available technologies to support health-management needs (e.g., internet search, online social networks). The most commonly appropriated technology was Internet search. Teens explained that they searched online during and after their initial diagnosis. Many searched for images online to help them prepare for a procedure or side effects of surgery. T15, an osteosarcoma patient, described that she searched for images to help her prepare for surgery on her leg. "*Pictures—like what the surgery is…I've just mostly been preparing myself – what I've done is preparing myself.*

While we anticipated that teens might look for others like them on the Internet to evaluate their situation, we found that they set strong boundaries around sharing health-related information online. Teens were also specific about whom they would be interested in reading about. The treatment process can vary widely depending on what a patient is diagnosed with, and patients are not as interested in learning about or talking to patients who have gone through different illnesses. As T7 responded, *"I don't wanna hear from a 26 year old that everything's gonna be okay, who had a different cancer than me."*

DISCUSSION

Both teens and parents in our study deal with the burdensome effects of illness while facing challenges unique to their situation. In this section, we discuss both the opportunities and complexities associated with our findings, drawing particular attention to the nuances we found that challenge typical models of self-management and patient participation. Finally, we highlight implications for the design of sociotechnical systems to address the opportunities we see.

Ownership of Health Needs

In Corbin and Strauss' [15] view—and in the view taken in subsequent work to operationalize management of chronic illness [40, 63]—the successful navigation of health management processes is achieved through mastery of a number of skills (e.g., taking medication, reducing stress, keeping appointments). Skills are acquired in service of self-management. Yet, the teens in our study are in need of both parental care and, simultaneously, experiences of autonomy. At times, they were incapable of representing their interests in communication with their physicians and parents played a central role. At other times, the teens' lack of privacy inhibited their communication with physicians.

We can expect that teens will experience varying degrees of psychosocial and physical maturity and varyingly close relationships with their clinical caregivers and parents. Thus, we believe that designing with a view toward mastery of skills for *eventual* self-management can best guide efforts to this group.

Teens with complex chronic illnesses will likely acquire self-management skills more from parents or others who have navigated the experience, rather than from their peer group. Bandura's concept of observational learning [3] aligns with the navigation of health care we witnessed. According to Bandura, observational learning describes a form of role-model-based learning through observing the behavior performed by others and the outcomes that follow. In both the care and home settings of teens with complex chronic illnesses, parents are most likely to assume the role of a model as they directly set an example for communicating with clinical caregivers, navigating the healthcare system, and attending to illness needs. Thus, parents acting as representatives of these teens can be a necessary and important part of teens' acquiring health-management skills.

At the same time, parental involvement *alone* is problematic: while parents can ideally serve as a model for self-management skills, they themselves lack firsthand physical experience of the illness. Teens' participation in their care is essential, yet, as we witnessed in our study, parents often lacked knowledge and means to understand how to support teens' participation. To avoid an abrupt transition to adult care, teens' ability to practice management skills is essential [62]. Supporting eventual self-management for chronically ill teens means strengthening partnerships between parents and teens that allow *a gradual and dynamic process through which teens can learn to take ownership of health-management needs.*

As an overarching goal, we recommend that designers of sociotechnical systems aim to support both teens and parents to *acclimate to the role of partner* in the teens' care. Below, we highlight two particular areas in which we see opportunities for design to better support this goal.

Recognizing and Managing Body Responses

Recognizing when physical responses are present in the body has significant importance for patients especially undergoing long-term treatment cycles such as chemotherapy for which their successful recovery will largely depend on the careful balance between the effectiveness of treatment dosage and its toxicity to the patient. For most teens in our study, parents were predominantly in charge of tracking the patient's symptomatic experience and reporting them to clinical caregivers either remotely or during consultations with the doctor. We saw that parents had difficulty understanding the teen's experience at home while going through chemotherapy treatment (as in the case of T5 and P5) and this led to discrepant interpretations about the patient experience and increased tensions between them.

While previous studies point to the lack of objectivity in proxy-reported health outcomes, proxy reporting by parents is still most common [66]. Teens' assessments and reporting on symptoms can differ qualitatively from their parents', yet our findings show that patients are less prone to raise health concerns directly to their doctors. We also found that, in a conscious effort not to worry the parents, some teens engaged in self-censorship of the symptom severity as they are reporting their experiences to the parents, and would independently decide to raise a health concern only when they felt it became alarming. One concern is that this degree of separation in doctor-patient communication can result in lower care quality as such care is based on approximations of the patient's health.

We recommend that future computing systems accommodate patient- and parent-reported assessments of symptomatic experiences and reconciliation of these assessments during long-term therapies. MacLeod et al. envisioned leveraging similar technology to capture symptoms to provide "evidence" to doctors to aid diagnostic processes [41]—in our case, the role of patient- and parent-reported data, collected in tandem, may contribute to better-informed decision-making after a diagnosis, based on richer data allowing for teens' input. For instance, doctors can consider regularly collected data; patients and parents can point to specific events of concern and provide clinicians with more context when needed.

How to design both the data collection experiences as well as the techniques for reviewing these data—suitable for *teens* in this scenario—is an important area for future work. Hartzler and colleagues have recently demonstrated the feasibility of incorporating patient-reported data into prostate cancer care, through dashboards reviewed collaboratively during consultations [25]. Patel et al. showed that real-time tracking tools for patient-collected data improved psychosocial comfort and symptom communication with clinicians [52]. This work provides starting points on which we can build to explore how a similar interface could be designed for teens and parents to review patient-collected data with physicians. Emerging methods for capturing patient experiences such as symptom severity [52], site of pain or representations of subjective experiences [33] and employing feedback mechanisms [35] to enhance awareness of health status show promise.

The act of collecting assessments periodically can encourage reflective activities, which have the potential to instill agency in health management. Self-reflection has been a proposed mechanism for helping the individual understand more about their behavior and adjust that behavior in response [14]. An important design consideration is that many technologies are designed based on "probe" methods to ask about the patient experience. It is unclear whether teens will respond to these if they don't respond to the spoken equivalent: teens particularly disliked being probed directly about their symptomatic experiences and emotional well-being from their parents.

Our interviews with the Child Life Specialist (CLS) revealed valuable insights about how to encourage teen patients to talk about their health concerns such as, at times, steering the conversation to a topic unrelated to health. More studies are needed to understand these communication strategies, as teens tend to express their feelings in ways that are different from adults. A promising means to better account for these differences includes the **involvement of experts such as CLS's in the user-centered design process, in addition to the typical stakeholders we tend to include (historically, patients, family and clinical caregivers)** as they better understand the delicate communication needs of these teens.

Activating Health-Related Resources

Teens will need to learn how to effectively utilize the health management resources available to them, including non-clinical experts, clinical caregivers in addition to electronic forms of health data.

Connecting with a Community of Experts

Online social communities supporting the connection of patients to others with experience and knowledge (but who are neither clinicians nor caregivers) could potentially satisfy teens' information needs while also potentially reducing the burden on parents to act alone as role models for the teen. However, some teens in our study were not interested in the experiences of older adults—even a decade older. This poses challenges to designers of applications to connect patients with others who have already overcome similar experiences. This suggests that **basing these connections not only on condition but on *skill-attainment* goals** can allow teens to connect with others that they can relate to as peers, based on learned or desired skills, while easing the burden on a family caregiver to serve as role model alone. The "social scaffolding" approach holds promise as a learning environment on which to base a similar application. For example, MAHI [44] supported newly diagnosed diabetics in obtaining self-management skills by connecting them with diabetes educators who could provide personalized guidance.

Augmenting Clinical Consultations

As evidenced by the permission seeking we witnessed in the exam room, teens seemed hesitant to consider themselves an authority on their own experiences and needs. While doctors and other clinical caregivers were inclined to address important concerns to patients, they often did not tailor explanations to the patient's literacy level. Parents were entrusted—and expected—to encode important care information as teens had difficulty understanding medical terminology and plans. Sometimes, parents would unknowingly dominate the conversation as a result. These instances altogether suggest that teens, parents and doctors could be lacking a general awareness of their own actions or beliefs that may interfere with the teen's ability to participate.

We recommend enhancing the situational awareness in clinical environments through the inclusion of cues to action to allow multiple-stakeholder engagement. Multimodal interfaces [73] aimed at detecting nonverbal cues such as gesture and gaze orientation (e.g., teen turning head to parent) in the consultation room show promise because they allow for the capturing of data that could be used in modeling of appropriate moments for providing feedback to effectively inform each stakeholder about their behavior. For example, doctors can be notified during or after the consultation if they are found to talk more to parents than the patient. Of course, technology deployments in clinical consultations could introduce unwanted interruptions as each stakeholder engages in discussions that may have serious implications for the teen's future health outcomes. While more studies are needed to explore the varied effects of feedback mechanisms on the quality of clinical consultations and acceptability of individual stakeholders, recent studies demonstrate this this form of interaction is promising: Patel et al. found that clinicians had favorable attitudes toward reflective visual feedback that provided awareness of their nonverbal communication [53].

Augmenting Personal Health Records

Teens with complex chronic illness will undergo frequent hospitalizations and complicated therapies and electronic health record systems feature prominently in illness management and care. However, personal health records (PHR) systems are currently "one size fits all"—the experience is not different between the parent and adolescent user [7]. As most teenagers have limited prior experience with technologies that report on their personal health data, they must grapple with issues of data privacy, health literacy and emotional preparedness.

We found that medical terminology and teens' limited health literacy presented barriers to their ability to effectively communicate with doctors. These language barriers can similarly transfer to their use of PHRs [37]. Teens favored radiology scans as they allowed for a familiar yet concrete means to make sense of the illness and evaluate the progress of treatment over time. T13 told us that her favorite clinical caregivers used drawings to communicate with her. Realizing teens' strong preference [72] for using abstracted representations of medical information in making sense of their illness experience, we recommend that personal health records made available to teens **embody techniques to vary the level-of-detail of information and apply appropriate timing, linguistic framing and graphical rendering to these data to make their presentation meaningful.**

At times, making medical data more accessible to teens can also mean that there will be unintended consequences that are not in their favor. While electronic forms of health records prioritize the delivery of strictly medical data such as radiology scans and lab results, it is important to realize that teens with chronic conditions are a particularly vulnerable group. As C3 cautions, data that carries any potential for emotional impact needs to be consulted with doctors before its release. However once released, teens will still need to be prepared to understand and process the information that they see. Teens might not only be vulnerable to upsetting medical data, but also while managing symptoms and emotions as they are going through multiple treatment cycles. Capturing and assessing the teen's affective state during this period can help inform system designers to generate more personalized and context-sensitive resources. Work in this direction includes an early prototype of a teen-specific PHR that incorporates new types of information into the teens' health record, including information on mood, peer interactions, aspirations, and goals [51].

LIMITATIONS

Our study has limitations. Like many qualitative studies, we included a relatively small number of participants. Also, we only focus on cancer and blood related disorders in our framing of complex chronic illnesses. Our presence as researchers could have affected certain observed participant behavior or responses during consultations and individual interviews. Finally, while findings of our study may not adequately generalize to a wider population, we expect that knowledge derived from our study can be transferable [69] to similar contexts or situations involving chronically-ill teens and their parents.

CONCLUSIONS

Teenagers grappling with complex chronic illnesses represent a particularly vulnerable population facing difficult transitions from pediatric to adult care. Our study identifies opportunities for teens and parents to develop gradually-evolving partnerships to promote their eventual self-management. First, we discussed the applicability of existing HCI research supporting chronic illness self-management. We then characterized challenges associated with teens' participation in the care concerning specific complex chronic illnesses, including pediatric cancers and blood disorders. Finally, we discussed opportunities for HCI research to address these challenges by outlining a research agenda along with specific recommendations for the design of future sociotechnical systems to better support teens' increased participation in their care.

ACKNOWLEDGMENTS

We thank Aarti Sekhar, Jessica Pater, Beth Mynatt, the study participants and the CHOA staff. This work was supported by an IPaT seed grant and NSF #1464214.

REFERENCES

1. Tawfiq Ammari and Sarita Schoenebeck. 2015. Networked Empowerment on Facebook Groups for Parents of Children with Special Needs. *Proceedings of the 33rd Annual ACM Conference on Human Factors in Computing Systems*, 2805-2814.
2. Rosa I. Arriaga, Andrew D. Miller, Elizabeth D. Mynatt, Claudia Pagliari and Erika Shehan Poole. 2013. Theory vs. design-driven approaches for behavior change research. *CHI*

'13 Extended Abstracts on Human Factors in Computing Systems, 2455-2458.
3. Albert Bandura. 1986. *Social foundations of thought and action: A social cognitive theory*. Prentice-Hall, Inc, 1986.
4. Julie Barlow, Chris Wright, Janice Sheasby, Andy Turner and Jenny Hainsworth. 2002. Self-management approaches for people with chronic conditions: a review. *Patient education and counseling*, 48, 2: 177-187.
5. Marshall H Becker. 1974. *The health belief model and personal health behavior*. Slack, 1974.
6. Bryony A Beresford and Patricia Sloper. 2003. Chronically ill adolescents' experiences of communicating with doctors: a qualitative study. *Journal of Adolescent Health*, 33, 3: 172-179.
7. Patricia Flatley Brennan, Stephen Downs and Gail Casper. 2010. Project HealthDesign: rethinking the power and potential of personal health records. *Journal of biomedical informatics*, 43, 5: S3-S5.
8. JB Brown, W Wayne Weston and Moira Stewart. 1995. The first component: exploring both the disease and the illness experience. *Patient-centered Medicine Transforming the Clinical Method*, 23-52.
9. Yunan Chen. 2011. Health information use in chronic care cycles. *Proceedings of the ACM 2011 conference on Computer supported cooperative work*, 485-488.
10. Yunan Chen, Victor Ngo and Sun Young Park. 2013. Caring for caregivers: designing for integrality. *Proceedings of the 2013 conference on Computer supported cooperative work*, 91-102.
11. Chihwen Cheng, Clark Brown, Tamara New, Todd H Stokes, Carlton Dampier and May D Wang. 2012. SickleREMOTE: A two-way text messaging system for pediatric sickle cell disease patients. *Biomedical and Health Informatics (BHI), 2012 IEEE-EMBS International Conference on*, 408-411.
12. Robert B Cialdini. 2001. The Science of Persuasion. *Scientific American*, 284, 2: 76.
13. Sunny Consolvo, et al. 2008. Flowers or a robot army?: encouraging awareness & activity with personal, mobile displays. *Proceedings of the 10th international conference on Ubiquitous computing*, 54-63.
14. Sunny Consolvo, David W. McDonald and James A. Landay. 2009. Theory-driven design strategies for technologies that support behavior change in everyday life. *Proceedings of the SIGCHI Conference on Human Factors in Computing Systems*, 405-414.
15. Juliet Corbin and Anselm Strauss. 1985. Managing chronic illness at home: three lines of work. *Qualitative sociology*, 8, 3: 224-247.
16. Juliet M Corbin and Anselm Strauss. 1988. *Unending work and care: Managing chronic illness at home*. Jossey-Bass, 1988.
17. Rodrigo De Oliveira, Mauro Cherubini and Nuria Oliver. 2010. MoviPill: improving medication compliance for elders using a mobile persuasive social game. *Proceedings of the 12th ACM international conference on Ubiquitous computing*, 251-260.
18. Christine Eiser and Rachel Morse. 2001. Can parents rate their child's health-related quality of life? Results of a systematic review. *Quality of Life Research*, 10, 4: 347-357.
19. Shelly Farnham, et al. 2002. HutchWorld: clinical study of computer-mediated social support for cancer patients and their caregivers. *Proceedings of the SIGCHI Conference on Human Factors in Computing Systems*, 375-382.
20. Jennifer Fereday and Eimear Muir-Cochrane. 2008. Demonstrating rigor using thematic analysis: A hybrid approach of inductive and deductive coding and theme development. *International journal of qualitative methods*, 5, 1: 80-92.
21. Leon Festinger. 1954. A theory of social comparison processes. *Human relations*, 7, 2: 117-140.
22. Chris Feudtner, Ross M Hays, Gerri Haynes, J Russell Geyer, John M Neff and Thomas D Koepsell. 2001. Deaths attributed to pediatric complex chronic conditions: national trends and implications for supportive care services. *Pediatrics*, 107, 6: e99-e99.
23. Sarah Ford, Lesley Fallowfield and Shôn Lewis. 1996. Doctor-patient interactions in oncology. *Social science & medicine*, 42, 11: 1511-1519.
24. Andrea Grimes, Vasudhara Kantroo and Rebecca E. Grinter. 2010. Let's play!: mobile health games for adults *Proceedings of the 12th ACM international conference on Ubiquitous computing*, 241-250.
25. Andrea L Hartzler, Jason P Izard, Bruce L Dalkin, Sean P Mikles and John L Gore. 2015. Design and feasibility of integrating personalized PRO dashboards into prostate cancer care. *Journal of the American Medical Informatics Associationocv*101.
26. Gillian R Hayes, Gregory D Abowd, John S Davis, Marion L Blount, Maria Ebling and Elizabeth D Mynatt. 2008. Opportunities for pervasive computing in chronic cancer care. Springer, 2008.
27. Eric B. Hekler, Predrag Klasnja, Jon E. Froehlich and Matthew P. Buman. 2013. Mind the theoretical gap: interpreting, using, and developing behavioral theory in HCI research. *Proceedings of the SIGCHI Conference on Human Factors in Computing Systems*, 3307-3316.
28. Judith H Hibbard. 2004. Moving toward a more patient-centered health care delivery system. *HEALTH AFFAIRS-MILLWOOD VA THEN BETHESDA MA-*, 23VAR-133.
29. Deanna M Hoelscher, Alexandra Evans, Guys Parcel and Steven H Kelder. 2002. Designing effective nutrition interventions for adolescents. *Journal of the American Dietetic Association*, 102, 3: S52-S63.
30. Gary Hsieh, Sean A. Munson, Maurits C. Kaptein, Harri Oinas-Kukkonen and Oded Nov. 2014. Personalizing behavior change technologies. *CHI '14 Extended Abstracts on Human Factors in Computing Systems* (107-110. 10.1145/2559206.2560474
31. Jina Huh and Mark S. Ackerman. 2012. Collaborative Help in Chronic Disease Management: Supporting Individualized Problems. *Computer-Supported Cooperative Work (CSCW)*, 853-862.
32. Maia L Jacobs, James Clawson and Elizabeth D Mynatt. 2014. My journey compass: a preliminary investigation of a mobile tool for cancer patients. *Proceedings of the 32nd annual ACM Conference on Human Factors in Computing Systems* (CHI '14), 663-672.
33. Elizabeth Kaziunas, Ayse G Buyuktur, Jasmine Jones, Sung W Choi, David A Hanauer and Mark S Ackerman. 2015. Transition and Reflection in the Use of Health Information: The Case of Pediatric Bone Marrow Transplant Caregivers. *Proceedings of the 18th ACM Conference on Computer Supported Cooperative Work & Social Computing*, 1763-1774.
34. Julie A Kientz. 2010. Understanding parent-pediatrician interactions for the design of health technologies.

Proceedings of the 1st ACM International Health Informatics Symposium, 230-239.
35. Matthew L Lee and Anind K Dey. 2014. Real-time feedback for improving medication taking. *Proceedings of the SIGCHI Conference on Human Factors in Computing Systems*, 2259-2268.
36. Leslie S Liu, et al. 2011. Improving communication and social support for caregivers of high-risk infants through mobile technologies. *Proceedings of the ACM 2011 conference on Computer supported cooperative work*, 475-484.
37. Leslie S Liu, Patrick C Shih and Gillian R Hayes. 2011. Barriers to the adoption and use of personal health record systems. *Proceedings of the 2011 iConference*, 363-370.
38. Leslie S Liu, Kori M Inkpen and Wanda Pratt. 2015. I'm Not Like My Friends: Understanding How Children with a Chronic Illness Use Technology to Maintain Normalcy. *Proceedings of the 18th ACM Conference on Computer Supported Cooperative Work & Social Computing* (CSCW '15), 1527-1539.
39. Yves Longtin, Hugo Sax, Lucian L. Leape, Susan E. Sheridan, Liam Donaldson and Didier Pittet. 2010. Patient Participation: Current Knowledge and Applicability to Patient Safety. *Mayo Clinic Proceedings*, 85, 1: 53-62.
40. Kate R Lorig and Halsted R Holman. 2003. Self-management education: history, definition, outcomes, and mechanisms. *Annals of behavioral medicine*, 26, 1: 1-7.
41. Haley MacLeod, Kim Oakes, Danika Geisler, Kay Connelly and Katie Siek. 2015. Rare World: Towards Technology for Rare Diseases. *Proceedings of the SIGCHI Conference on Human Factors in Computing Systems* (CHI '15).
42. Andrew Macvean and Judy Robertson. 2013. Understanding exergame users' physical activity, motivation and behavior over time. *Proceedings of the SIGCHI Conference on Human Factors in Computing Systems*, 1251-1260.
43. Lena Mamykina, Elizabeth D Mynatt and David R Kaufman. 2006. Investigating health management practices of individuals with diabetes. *Proceedings of the SIGCHI Conference on Human Factors in Computing Systems*, 927-936.
44. Lena Mamykina, Elizabeth Mynatt, Patricia Davidson and Daniel Greenblatt. 2008. MAHI: investigation of social scaffolding for reflective thinking in diabetes management. *Proceedings of the SIGCHI Conference on Human Factors in Computing Systems*, 477-486.
45. Andrew D Miller, Jessica Pater and Elizabeth D Mynatt. 2013. Design strategies for youth-focused pervasive social health games. *Pervasive Computing Technologies for Healthcare (PervasiveHealth), 2013 7th International Conference on,* 9-16.
46. Andrew D Miller. 2014. Social tools for everyday adolescent health.
47. Andrew D Miller and Elizabeth D Mynatt. 2014. StepStream: a school-based pervasive social fitness system for everyday adolescent health. *Proceedings of the SIGCHI Conference on Human Factors in Computing Systems*, 2823-2832.
48. Jake M Najman, et al. 2001. Bias influencing maternal reports of child behaviour and emotional state. *Social psychiatry and psychiatric epidemiology*, 36, 4: 186-194.
49. World Health Organization. 2014. Report: Health for the World's Adolescents. Retrieved May 15, 2015 from http://apps.who.int/adolescent/second-decade/section1/page2/reasons-for-growing-attention.html
50. Donald P Orr, Sarah P Weiser, Donald A Dian and Cheryl A Maurana. 1987. Adolescent health care: perceptions and needs of the practicing physician. *Journal of Adolescent Health Care*, 8, 3: 239-245.
51. Tina Park, Peter Chira, Kimberly Miller and Lisa Nugent. 2015. Living Profiles: an example of user-centered design in developing a teen-oriented personal health record. *Personal and Ubiquitous Computing*, 19, 1: 69-77.
52. Rupa A Patel, Predrag Klasnja, Andrea Hartzler, Kenton T Unruh and Wanda Pratt. 2012. *Probing the benefits of real-time tracking during cancer care*. American Medical Informatics Association, 2012.
53. Rupa A Patel, Andrea Hartzler, Wanda Pratt, Anthony Back, Mary Czerwinski and Asta Roseway. 2013. Visual feedback on nonverbal communication: a design exploration with healthcare professionals. *Proceedings of the 7th International Conference on Pervasive Computing Technologies for Healthcare*, 105-112.
54. American Academy of Pediatrics, American Academy of Family Physicians and American College of Physicians-American Society of Internal Medicine. 2002. A consensus statement on health care transitions for young adults with special health care needs. *Pediatrics*, 110, Supplement 3: 1304-1306.
55. Tamara Peyton and Erika Poole. 2013. "My Mobile Health, My Mobile Life": methods for designing health interventions with adolescents. *CHI '13 Extended Abstracts on Human Factors in Computing Systems*, 481-486.
56. Erika Shehan Poole, Andrew D Miller, Yan Xu, Elsa Eiriksdottir, Richard Catrambone and Elizabeth D Mynatt. 2011. The place for ubiquitous computing in schools: lessons learned from a school-based intervention for youth physical activity. *Proceedings of the 13th Int'l Conference on Ubiquitous Computing* (Ubicomp '11), 395-404.
57. Center for Disease Control and Prevention. 2013. Chronic Disease Indicators. Retrieved May 15, 2015 from https://chronicdata.cdc.gov/health-area/chronic-disease-indicators
58. James O Prochaska, Wayne F Velicer, Carlo C DiClemente and Joseph Fava. 1988. Measuring processes of change: applications to the cessation of smoking. *Journal of consulting and clinical psychology*, 56, 4: 520.
59. John G Reiss, Robert W Gibson and Leslie R Walker. 2005. Health care transition: youth, family, and provider perspectives. *Pediatrics*, 115, 1: 112-120.
60. David S Rosen. 1993. Transition to adult health care for adolescents and young adults with cancer.
61. Polly Ryan and Kathleen J Sawin. 2009. The individual and family self-management theory: Background and perspectives on context, process, and outcomes. *Nursing outlook*, 57, 4: 217-225. e216.
62. Susan M Sawyer, Sarah Drew, Michele S Yeo and Maria T Britto. 2007. Adolescents with a chronic condition: challenges living, challenges treating. *The Lancet*, 369, 9571: 1481-1489.
63. Dena Schulman-Green, et al. 2012. Processes of Self-Management in Chronic Illness. *Journal of Nursing Scholarship*, 44, 2: 136-144.
64. U.S. Department of Health and Human Services. Office of Adolescent Health: Chronic Conditions. Retrieved May 15, 2015 from http://www.hhs.gov/ash/oah/adolescent-health-topics/physical-health-and-nutrition/chronic-conditions.html

65. Kiek Tates and Ludwien Meeuwesen. 2001. Doctor–parent–child communication. A (re) view of the literature. *Social science & medicine*, 52, 6: 839-851.
66. NCM Theunissen, et al. 1998. The proxy problem: child report versus parent report in health-related quality of life research. *Quality of Life Research*, 7, 5: 387-397.
67. Matthieu Tixier and Myriam Lewkowicz. 2015. Looking for Respite and Support: Technological Opportunities for Spousal Caregivers. *Proceedings of the 33rd Annual ACM Conference on Human Factors in Computing Systems*, 1155-1158.
68. Tammy Toscos, Anne Faber, Shunying An and Mona Praful Gandhi. 2006. Chick clique: persuasive technology to motivate teenage girls to exercise. *CHI'06 extended abstracts on Human factors in computing systems*, 1873-1878.
69. Sarah J Tracy. 2010. Qualitative quality: Eight "big-tent" criteria for excellent qualitative research. *Qualitative inquiry*, 16, 10: 837-851.
70. FC Veit, Lena A Sanci, CM Coffey, DY Young and Glenn Bowes. 1996. Barriers to effective primary health care for adolescents. *The Medical Journal of Australia*, 165, 3: 131-133.
71. Pontus Wärnestål, Petra Svedberg and Jens Nygren. 2014. Co-constructing child personas for health-promoting services with vulnerable children. *Proceedings of the 32nd annual ACM Conference on Human factors in Computing Systems* (CHI '14), 3767-3776.
72. Ellen Wartella, Vicky Rideout, Heather Zupancic, Leanne Beaudoin-Ryan and Alexis Lauricella. 2015. Teens, Health, and Technology. A National Survey. *Center on Media and Human Development, School of Communication, Northwestern University*.
73. Nadir Weibel, Colleen Emmenegger, Jennifer Lyons, Ram Dixit, Linda L Hill and James D Hollan. 2013. Interpreter-mediated physician-patient communication: Opportunities for multimodal healthcare interfaces. *Proceedings of the 7th International Conference on Pervasive Computing Technologies for Healthcare*, 113-120.
74. Lauren Wilcox, Dan Morris, Desney Tan and Justin Gatewood. 2010. Designing Patient-Centric Information Displays for Hospitals. *CHI '10: Proceedings of the 28th International Conference on Human factors in Computing Systems*, 2123-2132.
75. Yan Xu, et al. 2012. This is not a one-horse race: understanding player types in multiplayer pervasive health games for youth. *Proceedings of the ACM 2012 Conference on Computer-Supported Cooperative Work* (CSCW '12), 843-852.
76. Naomi Yamashita, Hideaki Kuzuoka, Keiji Hirata and Takashi Kudo. 2013. Understanding the conflicting demands of family caregivers caring for depressed family members. *Proceedings of the SIGCHI Conference on Human Factors in Computing Systems*, 2637-2646.
77. Svetlana Yarosh. 2013. Shifting dynamics or breaking sacred traditions?: the role of technology in twelve-step fellowships. *Proceedings of the SIGCHI Conference on Human Factors in Computing Systems*, 3413-3422.
78. Tae-Jung Yun and Rosa I Arriaga. 2013. A text message a day keeps the pulmonologist away. *Proceedings of the SIGCHI Conference on Human Factors in Computing Systems* (CHI '13), 1769-1778.
79. Brad J Zebrack, et al. 2002. Psychological outcomes in long-term survivors of childhood leukemia, Hodgkin's disease, and non-Hodgkin's lymphoma: a report from the Childhood Cancer Survivor Study. *Pediatrics*, 110, 1: 42-52.
80. Marieke Zwaanswijk, et al. 2011. Communicating with child patients in pediatric oncology consultations: a vignette study on child patients', parents', and survivors' communication preferences. *Psycho-Oncology*, 20, 3: 269-277.

Data-driven Personas: Constructing Archetypal Users with Clickstreams and User Telemetry

Xiang Zhang
Dept. of Statistics
North Carolina State University
Raleigh, NC, USA
xzhang23@ncsu.edu

Hans-Frederick Brown
User Experience
Platfora Inc.
San Mateo, USA
hans@platfora.com

Anil Shankar
User Experience
Platfora Inc.
San Mateo, USA
anilkshankar@gmail.com

ABSTRACT

User Experience (UX) research teams following a user centered design approach harness *personas* to better understand a user's workflow by examining that user's behavior, goals, needs, wants, and frustrations. To create target personas these researchers rely on workflow data from surveys, self-reports, interviews, and user observation. However, this data not directly related to user behavior, weakly reflects a user's actual workflow in the product, is costly to collect, is limited to a few hundred responses, and is outdated as soon as a persona's workflows evolve. To address these limitations we present a quantitative bottom-up data-driven approach to create personas. First, we directly incorporate user behavior via clicks gathered automatically from telemetry data related to the actual product use in the field; since the data collection is automatic it is also cost effective. Next, we aggregate 3.5 million clicks from 2400 users into 39,000 clickstreams and then structure them into 10 workflows via hierarchical clustering; we thus base our personas on a large data sample. Finally, we use *mixed models*, a statistical approach that incorporates these clustered workflows to create five representative personas; updating our mixed model ensures that these personas remain current. We also validated these personas with our product's user behavior experts to ensure that workflows and the persona goals represent actual product use.

Keywords

Personas, User Experience Research, Data-driven design, Machine Learning, Data Science, User Analytics

1. INTRODUCTION

Cooper originated the *Persona* concept for Design and User Experience (UX) practice [3]. He considers a persona as an archetypal user. A persona comprises this user's behaviors, goals, wants, needs, and frustrations when using a product. While designers and user-experience (UX) researchers use personas as a powerful design tool in practice, a cost-effective automatic way to create a persona that can remain current is still an open question [6].

CHI'16, May 07-12, 2016, San Jose, CA, USA
© 2016 ACM. ISBN 978-1-4503-3362-7/16/05...$15.00
DOI: http://dx.doi.org/10.1145/2858036.2858523

In Platfora's case, at the product's inception in 2011 we consulted with *Cooper*, a design strategy consulting agency based in San Francisco, to explore the needs of our product's end-users. Platfora is an enterprise focused big data analytics platform that transforms raw data in Hadoop (or in other data silos) into interactive, in memory business intelligence. Four main Platfora personas emerged from Cooper's research efforts; we discuss the two main user personas here and cover the other while describing the data-driven personas later in the paper. The first, *Jeffrey*, a business analyst, whose primary goal is to understand internal client needs and build out reports for them. Jeffrey would explore both the data import and visualization parts of Platfora to be successful in his work role. The second persona, *Marybeth*, a business analyst, unlike Jeffrey focuses only on explaining the story behind the data to her clients. She would primarily spend time in the visualization component of Platfora. With Platfora's increased adoption in data analytics world, we witnessed new users different from the existing Platfora personas begin to leverage our product. Hence, we started to investigate a data driven approach to refine our existing personas.

Many have suggested creating personas based on data-driven methods. Prutti argued that personas are not believable if they are designed by committee (not based on data) or if the relationship to user data is not clear [15]. To ameliorate Prutti's concern Mulder recommends personas generated by quantitative techniques to avoid human bias [13]. Quantitative or qualitative techniques depend on user data and McGinn opined that persona creation suffers from a common problem of not being based on first-hand customer behavior data, and if so, then the size of data is not statistically significant [10]. So, a quantitative, data-driven approach to create behavior defined personas still remains an open avenue for user research.

In this paper, we propose a fully data-driven approach to construct behavioral personas from raw clicks gathered in telemetry data from our product use. Our approach is different from the existing persona creation approaches in that we approach the problem bottom-up from raw clickstreams without top level features. Instead of relying on survey data, user interviews (transcribed or otherwise), we follow a two stage statistical machine learning approach to create data-driven personas that are solely based on user behaviors.

In the first stage, we aggregate 3.5 million clicks from 2400 users into 39,000 clickstreams to identify ten common workflows. Even though this process is completely data-driven we also validated these ten workflows with user behavior experts in UX research, UX Design, and Product Management within Platfora; these folks were cognizant of existing Cooper personas. The persona experts verified the clustering of workflows and helped to map a few workflows clusters to existing personas, thereby helping us to refine and update Platfora's archetypal users. Since we focus on the quantitative aspect of creating personas we do not provide additional details about these experts reviewing our personas in this paper.

In the second stage, we use a mixed model to group these representative workflows into five personas. To the best of our knowledge, this is the very first attempt to create data-driven personas from raw clickstreams. Our raw clickstream data gathered via product telemetry spans a duration of two years worth of clicks in *Platfora*'s user interface.

The personas that we generated from clickstreams validated two of the existing Platfora personas while showing that the other two personas had evolved into *Full-stack* users. A Full-stack user generates workflows related to Platfora's four main product pages related to *Datasets* (data import and curation), *Lenses*, (creating in-memory data-marts), *Vizboards* (a board populated by multiple visualizations), and *SystemPage* (monitoring the health and status of various Platfora objects).

We next review related work on data-driven personas. The following section describes our approach to leverage clicks from raw telemetry data gathered in the field (from customers) to create common workflows which are then grouped into personas using a mixed model. The subsequent section details our approach to identify ten common workflows with a hierarchical clustering technique on clickstream information to derive five personas. We conclude this paper by identifying the next steps for data-driven persona work that can not only incorporate the clicks in the raw data but also factor the order of the clicks to create richer, more distinguishable personas.

2. RELATED WORK: DATA-DRIVEN PERSONAS

Researchers have relied primarily on survey data to create data-driven personas. Sinha identified three personas for online restaurant finder by using *principal component analysis* on survey data gathered from 63 respondents. In this survey respondents rated 32 dimensions related to restaurant experience [16]. Instead of principal components, Javahery used *clustering* to construct three personas for guiding the new product design for a bioinformatics visualization application [7]. The data gathered from questionnaire and user observations included attributes from 22 users related to domain experience and background.

McGinn used *factor analysis* on the survey data gathered from 1300 respondents to develop eleven personas for customers of a training organization [10]. Each survey included 18 multiple-choice questions on demographic and behavior data. Miaskiewicz used *latent semantic analysis* to create four personas for users of an Institutional Repository (IR) at a large university based on the transcribed text from interviews [12] . The 20 interviews were audio recorded, next transcribed, and then stored in word-by-interview matrices.

Brickey compared several existing qualitative and quantitative persona creation methods for users of an online knowledge management system [1]. He compared the results from manual experts and found that principal component analysis produced the most promising personas for his target user group.

Tobias mined *Tomb Raider: Underworld* game telemetry to predict when a player would stop playing and also the time this player would take to finish the game [9]. Canossas leveraged game telemetry to generate play-personas and focused on improving the player experience for single player action games [2]. Drachen worked in player modeling for the Tomb Raider: Underworld game [5]. They first identified six gameplay features and then clustered these features using a hierarchical clustering technique in the game telemetry data.

Similar to the existing body of data-driven persona construction, we use a clustering algorithm to create Platfora personas. However, unlike the existing approaches that leverage mostly survey data, we harness raw user behavior data from clickstreams captured during Platfora use by thousands of users. Our approach to use this clickstream information about user behavior to create personas is different in two ways from approaches that rely on survey or interview data. First, our approach is more robust due to the large volume of user-behavior data that we harness to generate personas. Second, we use a bottom-up approach that pops out the personas automatically via hierarchical clustering and mixed models. Our approach overlaps with work on player modeling in games in that we leverage product telemetry to generate Platfora personas. We extend this work in player modeling in two ways. First, our approach starts bottom up from raw clickstream instead of identifying any top level features. Second, instead of clustering top level features we use a mixed model to process workflows to generate personas. We describe how we gather clickstreams and product telemetry data in the next section.

3. TELEMETRY AND CLICKSTREAMS

The spacecraft industry was one of the originators of using *telemetry* to gather data remotely from sensors [14]. This telemetry data collection process was designed for efficiency, transparency, and reliability. We designed Platfora's telemetry architecture based on similar goals – to gather user behavior data with efficiency, transparency, and reliability. At the lowest level our telemetry data consists of a click (user interface event) captured whenever a user accesses a user interface element in Platfora. Platfora's customers can opt-in to send their product telemetry back to us.

A *clickstream* is a sequence of clicks generated by a user in one login session. We gathered such clickstream information for two years from July of 2013 to July of 2015. Figure 1 shows the structure of this clickstream data. This data contains four different lev-

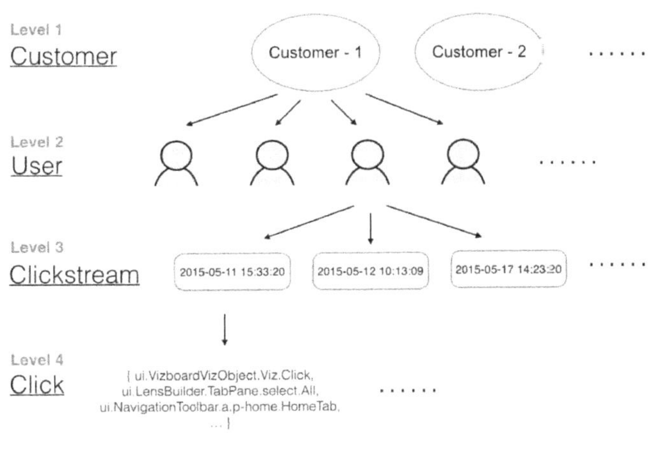

Figure 1: Product Telemetry data with four levels used to create personas.

els. Going up from the bottom, at level 4 is a click; this forms the smallest granularity of telemetry data. These clicks aggregate to form clickstreams at level 3. Higher up, at level 2,we map clickstreams to specific users (whose identification (ID) is anonymized at the customer site). The top most level corresponds to a group of users who represent a Platfora customer site. Since a single user can generate multiple clickstreams at different times, we chunk each clickstream based on the start date and time to create unique clickstream information.

Our initial analysis of clickstream lengths showed that any clickstream with less than 20 clicks was too short to reflect meaningful user behavior during a session. Hence we removed these clickstreams. This resulted in a total of 3.5 million clicks from 39,000 clickstreams generated by 2400 users from 30 customers. The average clickstream length is 92 clicks (3.5 million/39,000). Our persona construction process leverages these clickstreams by first clustering them into common workflows and then characterizing each user by the frequency of common workflows via mixed model.

4. CONSTRUCTING PERSONAS

We construct personas from clickstreams derived from telemetry data using the following algorithm.

Algorithm 1 Data-driven Persona Construction from User Clickstreams

Assume there are P users and N clickstreams in total.
Step 1: Calculate pairwise clickstreams distance
Calculate the $N \times N$ distance matrix, where the (i, j) entry of the distance matrix is the distance between the i-th clickstream and the j-th clickstream.
Step 2: Cluster clickstreams
Implement hierarchical clustering algorithm on the distance matrix to obtain K clusters of clickstreams. The number K is chosen by the user.
Step 3: Map clickstreams to common workflows
Map each clickstream to one of the K common workflow. Record the number of k-th common workflow generated by i-th user as y_{ik}, $i = 1, \ldots, P$, $k = 1, \ldots, K$.
Step 4: Fit mixed model
Fit mixed models with M components on the multinomial data $\{y_{ik}\}_{1 \le i \le P, 1 \le k \le K}$. The number of personas, M, is chosen by the user. The mathematical details of this step can be found below.

Example data and the corresponding R code are available upon request from authors. We next discuss Step 2 and Step 4 in more detail.

4.1 Step 2: Cluster clickstreams

Platfora users follow a few common workflows to accomplish their goal and our telemetry data captures these workflows as clickstreams. Note that each clickstream (as shown in Figure 1) in our telemetry data has timestamp associated with a series of clicks (user interface events). Therefore all the clickstreams generated by users are unique in our dataset. We use *Ward*'s hierarchical clustering algorithm to cluster clickstreams and to identify common workflows [17]. We chose this hierarchical clustering algorithm as it only requires pairwise similarity between clickstreams and it produces a hierarchical treeplot. This treeplot helps to visualize the clustering process and to determine an appropriate number of clusters.

To summarize the common workflows, we first examine the most frequent clicks within a cluster, the average length and duration of clickstreams in each cluster, and the frequency of clicks that comprise key steps in Platfora in all clusters. Next, user behavior experts (UX researchers, UX Designers, Product Managers) review these clusters to verify the representative behaviors of each common workflow.

In the first stage of data-driven persona creation we cluster common clickstreams to identify common workflows. Here is an example. *Jane* can import a dataset into Platfora in two different ways. The telemetry data captures these two workflows as two different clickstreams, say *data1* and *data2*, respectively. The same user, *Jane* can follow different workflows to visualize the imported data and the resulting clickstreams could be *viz1* and *viz2*, respectively. When we cluster *Jane*'s clickstreams, we assume that *data1* is more similar to *data2* when compared to *viz1*. We use the Jaccard index to measure the similarity between two clickstreams [8]. With this index, we define the similarity between two clickstreams as the ratio of the number of common unique clicks over the number of all unique clicks.

For example, say, *Jane* generates two clickstreams S_1 and S_2; these two clickstreams are simply two sequences of clicks; an alphabet represents clicks in these two clickstreams. Assume $S_1 = \{A, B, B, C, D, B, A, C\}$ and $S_2 = \{E, F, F, B, A, C, B, B\}$. For these these two sequences, there are 3 common unique clicks ($\{A, B, C\}$) and the count of union of all unique clicks is 6 ($\{A, B, C, D, E, F\}$). We therefore calculate the similarity between S_1 and S_2 as 0.5 (3/6).

Figures 2 - 4 demonstrate the process of identifying common workflows. We first cluster clickstreams into separate groups based on click similarity and then summarize the common workflow within each cluster. In Figure 2 each dot represents a clickstream. The colors of the dots denote the similarity between clickstreams. A clustering algorithm groups all the clickstreams into separate clusters using the pairwise clickstreams similarity. Figure 3 shows that dots with similar color gradients are grouped together resulting in six clusters.

After the clustering we summarize each cluster by a common workflow which best represents all the clickstreams in that cluster. This process of identifying a workflow is radically different from survey or interview based approaches that only capture a user's self-report of her workflow. Instead of starting top-down, our data-driven approach is bottom-up; we cluster similar clickstreams into a common workflow.

We treat all similar yet distinct clickstreams as a common workflow. Figure 4 shows this clustering process where the bigger dots denote the derived common workflows, with the best representative color in that cluster. For example, in this figure, the clustering process summarized both dark red and light red by the same red color. This process indicates that a cluster of similar clickstreams represent a common workflow even though each clickstream is not exactly the same. Once we identify the common workflows from the raw data clickstreams we can next examine each user based on the different usage of workflows.

4.2 Step 4: Fit mixed model

Users from the same persona have similar goals and behaviors when using the product [3]. We view this frequency of common workflows as a quantitative signature of each user's behavior. That is, we believe users with similar frequency of common workflows are likely to be instances of the same persona. This assumption is the foundation for our *mixed model* to generate personas.

A mixed model is a widely used statistical approach to detect sub-populations [11]. In our telemetry data each persona represents a sub-population of users. A mixed model assigns each user to one of the personas and characterizes the common workflow frequency

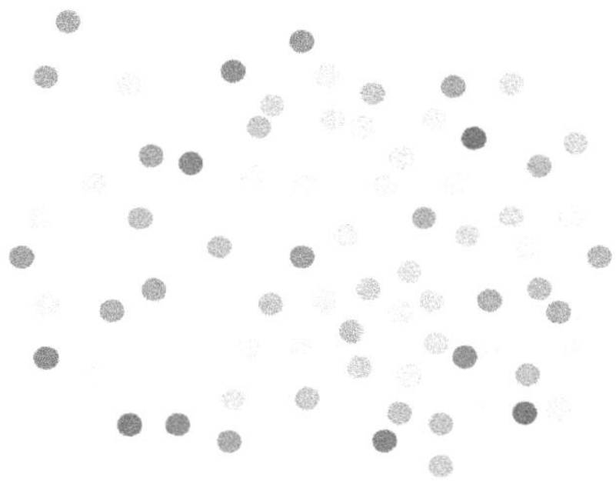

Figure 2: Each dot represents clickstream. Similar colors represent similar clickstreams.

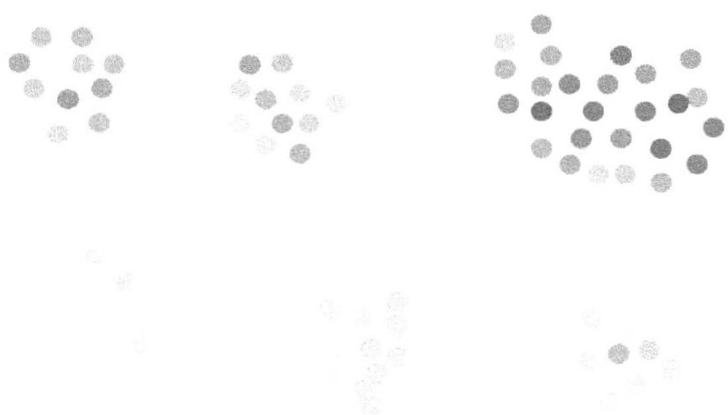

Figure 3: Hierarchical clustering groups clickstreams into six clusters based on their similarity.

Figure 4: A central big dot depicts common workflow. This workflow summarizes clickstreams in each group.

that uniquely defines each persona. Assume there are P users and K common workflows. Denote y_{ik} as the number of k-th common workflow that are generated by the i-th user, for $i = 1, \ldots, P$ and $k = 1, \ldots, K$. Write $\mathbf{y}_i = (y_{i1}, \ldots, y_{iK})$. Assume there are M Personas. Denote Z_i the label of Persona for the i-th user. If $Z_i = m$, the i-th user behaves as the m-th Persona, $m = 1, \ldots, M$. We assume the numbers of common workflows are independently generated from multinomial distribution given the labels of Personas. That is,

$$\mathbf{y}_i | (Z_i = m) \sim \text{Multinomial}(\mathbf{p}_m),$$

where $\mathbf{p}_m = (p_{m1}, \ldots, p_{mK})$, p_{mk} is the chance of m-th Persona to generate k-th common workflow, $m = 1, \ldots, M$, $k = 1, \ldots, K$. Denote $\pi_m = \Pr(Z_i = m)$ and $\boldsymbol{\pi} = (\pi_1, \ldots, \pi_M)$. The full likelihood of the observed data, given the labels of Personas, can be written as

$$L(\boldsymbol{\pi}, \mathbf{p}_1, \ldots, \mathbf{p}_M) = \prod_{i=1}^{P} \sum_{m=1}^{M} (\mathbf{I}(Z_i = m)\pi_m \prod_{k=1}^{K} p_{mk}^{y_{ik}}),$$

where $\mathbf{I}(S) = 1$ if S is true and 0 otherwise. The maximum likelihood estimators (MLE) of $(\boldsymbol{\pi}, \mathbf{p}_1, \ldots, \mathbf{p}_M)$ is simply the maximizer of $L(\boldsymbol{\pi}, \mathbf{p}_1, \ldots, \mathbf{p}_M)$, and we solve this MLE with the Expectation-Maximization (EM) algorithm [4].

Figure 5 shows our mixed model persona creation approach based on the derived common workflows. There are nine users in this ex-

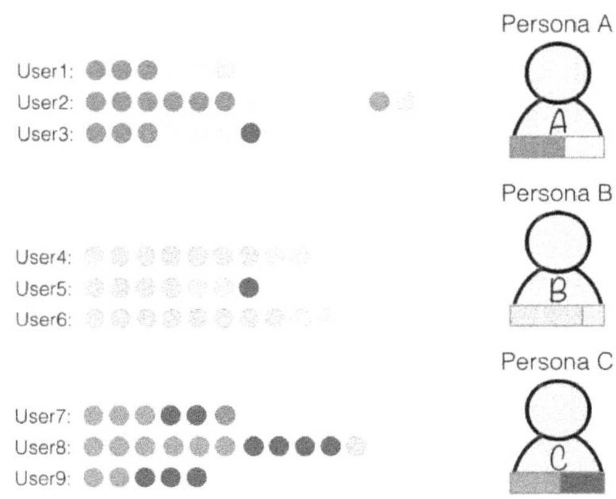

Figure 5: This figure shows the construction of personas based on clickstream types corresponding to each user. The dots following a user id represent clickstreams and colors represent the corresponding workflows. For example, Users 1, 2 and 3 have half of their clickstreams doing *red* workflow and the other half doing *yellow* workflow. Our mixed model summarized this user group as an archetypal user: Persona A.

ample; each user generated multiple clickstreams and these clickstreams are represented by dots. The colors of the dots indicate the common workflows as shown in Figure 4.

For example, User1 generates six clickstreams: three *red* common workflows, two *yellow* common workflows and one *blue* common workflow. This generalization from clickstreams to common workflows makes it possible to easily compare the behavior of two users. Consider User2; even though User2 generates more clickstreams than User1, their behavior patterns are similar: about half of their clickstreams are *red* common workflows and the other half are *yellow* common workflows. Figure 5 shows that this pattern is also shared by User3. Thus we group users with common workflow frequency together to create an archetypal user (persona) to represent this user group. In this example, Users 1, 2, and 3, are represented by the same archetypal user, Persona A.

You can now interpret that Persona A is a type of user who generally spends half of her time in *red* workflow and the other half of the time in *yellow* workflow. Similarly, you can now see that Persona B is predominantly spends time in the *green* workflow whereas Persona C splits time between *pink* and *blue* workflows. As in the first stage, we again consulted with user behavior experts to review both the common workflows discovered by the mixed model and the ensuing personas created by the combination of these workflows. These subject matter experts agreed that these data-driven mixed-model constructed personas derived from raw clickstream data represented archetypal users of our product.

5. FIVE PERSONAS VIA HIERARCHICAL CLUSTERING AND MIXED MODELS

This section first describes our approach to cluster clickstreams to identify common workflows. We next show how to use a mixed model to build data-driven personas. This data-driven approach helps identify ten common workflows and five personas for our product users.

5.1 Ten Common Workflows via Hierarchical Clustering of Clickstreams

Figure 6 shows the result of clustering $39,000$ clickstreams. In this figure the vertical axis shows the dissimilarity between the clusters when they merge together. At the lowest level is each clickstream. This clustering process hierarchically merges similar clickstreams as you traverse up to the root node of the tree. Based on expert views and examining the frequency of the top 25 clicks in each cluster, we chose 10 as an appropriate number of clusters. Increasing the number of clusters did not result in meaningful workflows and reducing the clusters below 10 washed out the differences in workflows. The existing Cooper personas guided the development of these clusters. The red boxes in Figure 6 highlight these ten clusters. We excluded a small group of $1,147$ clickstreams (about 3 percent of the total) from the analysis (between Cluster 6 and 7 in Figure 6). This cluster represented isolated feature testing and not the common workflows.

We examine the clickstream clusters to summarize the behavior of the ten common workflows from Figure 6. This summary provides insight into the key steps triggered by each workflow and we believe that these key steps are specific to different personas. With the help of user behavior experts we identified 14 key steps related to four main Platfora product pages (Datasets, Lenses, Vizboards, and System Page). Figure 7 shows the frequency of clicks on these key steps within the ten common workflows. We order the steps such that steps from the same product page are grouped together. This ordering helps to characterize workflows by the frequency of the key steps.

Figure 8 shows clickstream frequency of steps in Cluster 3 (from Figure 6) for a workflow related to datasets and lenses in Platfora. There is a high frequency of actions for dataset and lens related activities for Cluster 3. Specifically, the frequency is high for *Modify Dataset* and for *Modify Lens*; this is common behavior of users who modify a dataset before building a lens in Platfora. We thus summarize this workflow as *Build lens with optional modification to a dataset.*

Figure 9 shows most frequent dataset related activities in Cluster 1 and Cluster 5. To tease out the difference between these two clusters we examined the top 30 clicks in each cluster with a word cloud. The dataset parsing activity was in Cluster 5's top clicks, whereas this activity was absent in Cluster 1. In Figure 9 you can see that Cluster 5 has higher frequency of clicks for *Create Dataset* step. When compared to Cluster 1, Cluster 5's higher frequency of *Create Dataset* along with the parsing activity reflected a common Platfora workflow in which users parse a dataset (curate it) only when creating a new dataset thus confirming the difference between Clusters 1 and 5. In the same figure, when compared to Cluster 5, Cluster 1 has higher activity for *Modify Dataset*, *View Dataset* and *View Lens*. This is again representative of Platfora user behavior where users are likely to examine a lens or a dataset before modifying an existing dataset. Our key contribution to data-driven persona creation is that we detect the difference between these two workflows *only* from the raw clickstream stream data. Table 1 lists the ten common workflows that we detected by clustering clickstream information. We labeled this workflows after consulting with Platfora's user behavior experts who verified the clustered clickstreams as representative user activities noted in various internal user studies and evaluations.

Table 1: The ten common Platfora workflows identified by clickstream clustering.

Cluster	Workflow
1	Modify dataset
2	Check System Page
3	Build a lens with optional modification to a dataset
4	Create a lens and visualization
5	Create a dataset
6	Create a dataset, a lens, and a visualization all in the same workflow
7	Include data segments in visualization
8	Modify visualization data iteratively
9	Export data from a visualization
10	Explore and view a visualization

5.2 Five Data-driven Personas

We described the identification of common workflows from clickstreams in the previous section. Based on these workflows we next construct data-driven personas. Users with similar workflow frequency share similar behavior even though their individual clickstreams may not exactly be the same. These users are also likely to be instances of the same persona. To generate personas, we focus our analysis on the $1,011$ users who generated at least five clickstreams; these clickstreams comprise 90 percent of the total number of clickstreams in our product telemetry. We dropped users with less than five clickstreams as this number was insufficient to depict meaningful high-level user behavior.

Based on discussion with user behavior experts at Platfora we input five personas to the mixed model. Figure 10 shows the frequency of the ten common workflows for the $1,011$ users where the users are ordered by their personas. Here, we assign each user to a persona that this user is most likely to belong to based on the fitted mixed model. In Figure 10 we were now able to detect groupings of users in the heatmap; we show these groupings by the blue blocks. That is, we detected five groups of users who mapped to

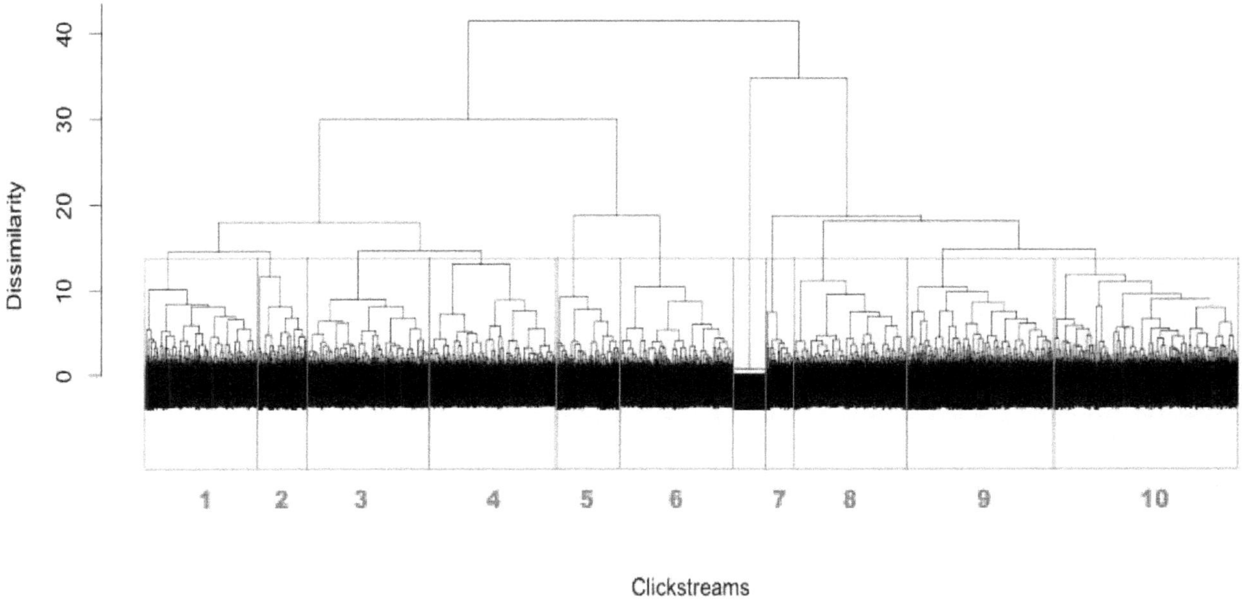

Figure 6: The ten clickstream clusters. At the bottom of the tree is each clickstream. This clustering process hierarchically merges similar clickstreams as you traverse up to the root node of the tree. The red boxes highlight the ten clickstream clusters that we leverage to create personas.

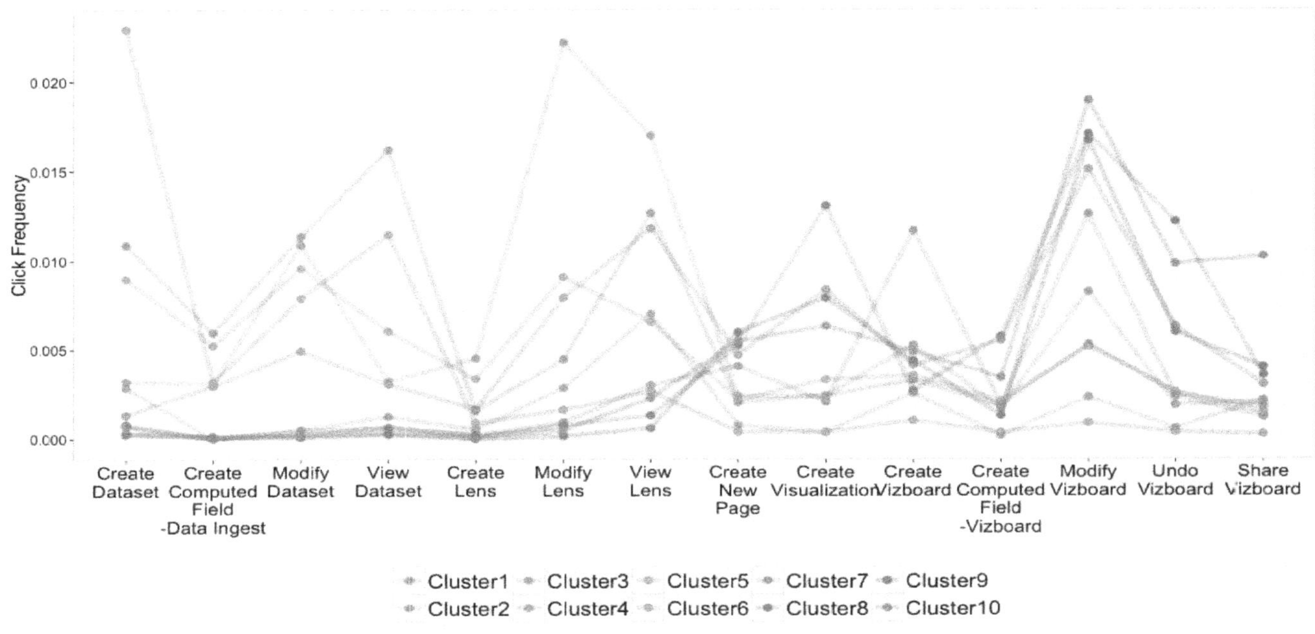

Figure 7: Frequency of 14 key steps in Platfora within each common workflow. You can see the difference in frequency of the key steps across clusters (groups of users) as shown by the different colored lines.

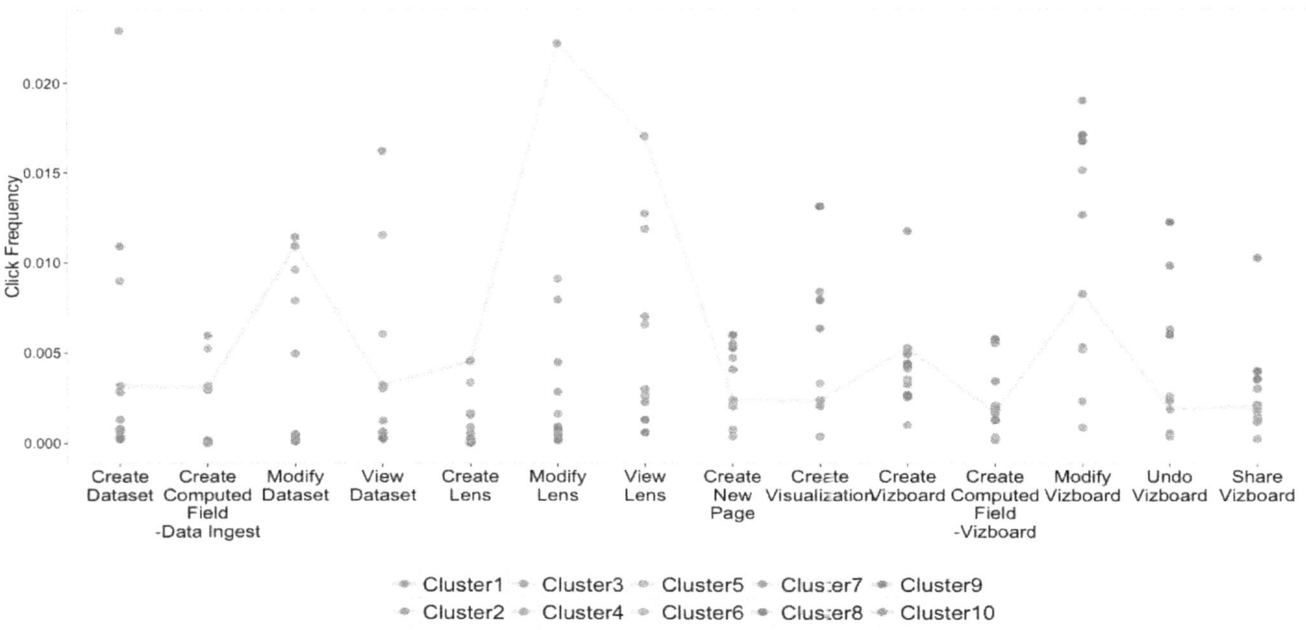

Figure 8: A workflow from Cluster 3: *Build lens with optional modification to a dataset*. Here you can see the high clickstream frequency for *Modify Dataset* and *Modify Lens*.

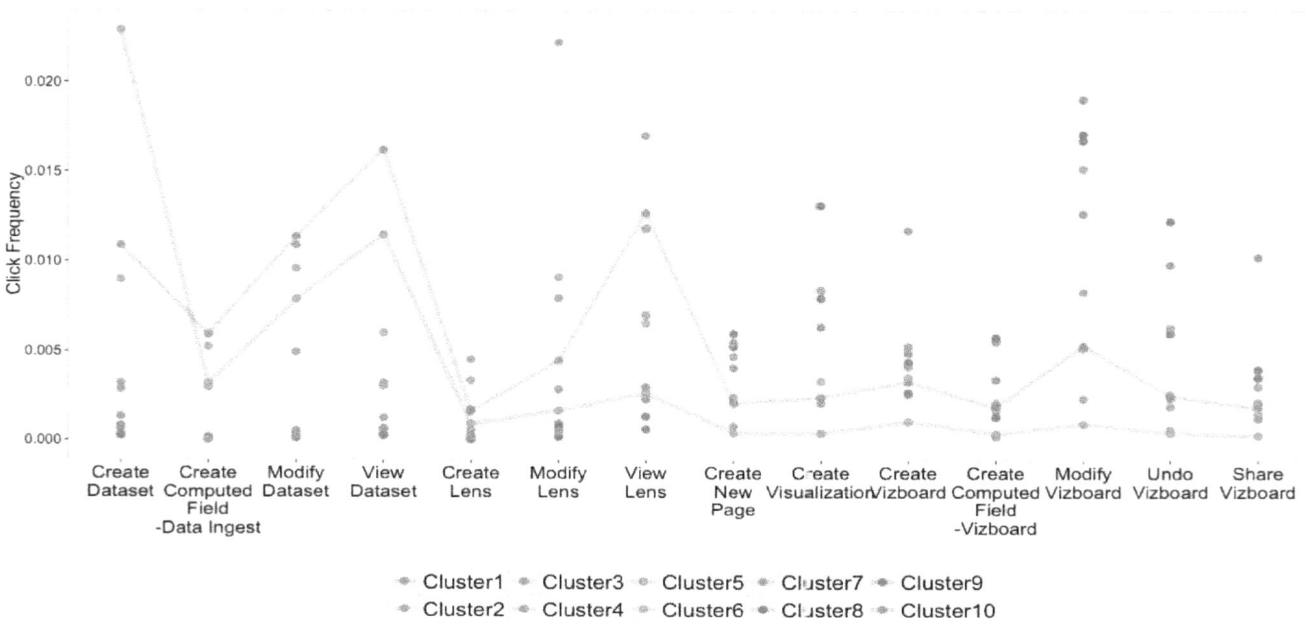

Figure 9: Frequency of dataset related activities in Cluster 1 (red line) and Cluster 5 (green line).

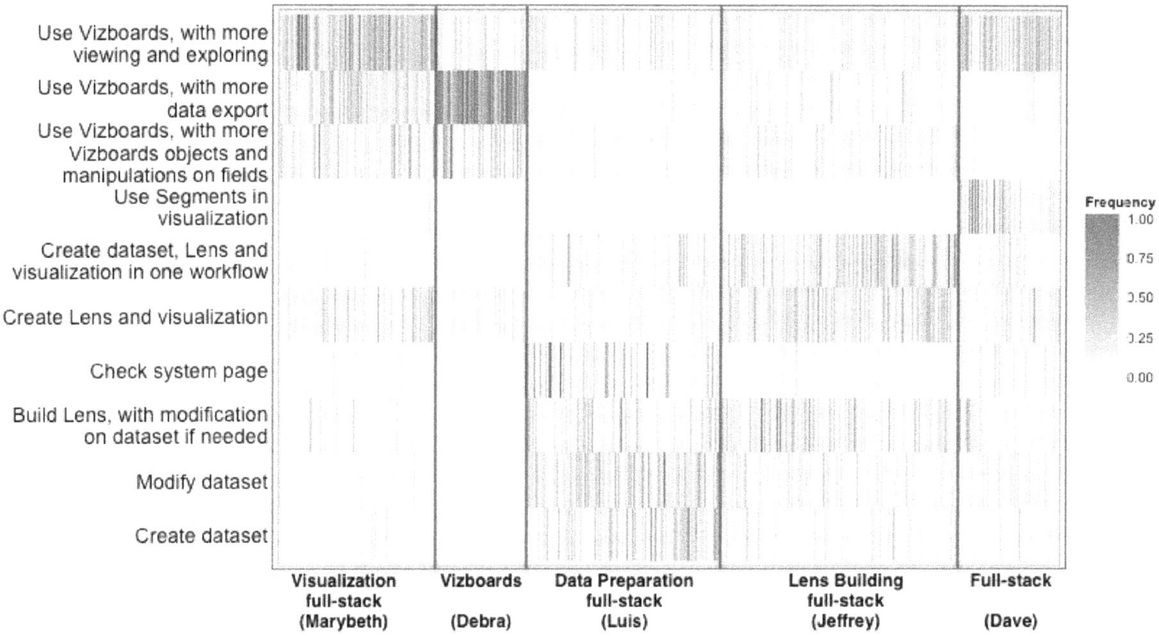

Figure 10: Heatmap of common workflows frequency for each user, ordered by personas. The block of users within the same persona share similar frequency of common workflows.

five personas. We thus harnessed raw clickstream data to identify common workflows that subsequently mapped to personas.

Each persona in our model has a unique probability to generate one of the ten common workflows; this probability is a quantitative signature of each persona. More specifically, these chances are the probability vectors that define the multinomial distribution of each persona. Figure 11 shows these chances of common workflows within each persona; we describe each persona below:

1. *Full-stack user specialized in data preparation (Luis)*: This red line that represents this persona in Figure 11 show that this persona has higher chances for two workflows related to Datasets and Lenses, and for viewing and exploring Vizboards. This persona has the high probability for workflows *Create dataset* and *Modify dataset*; these probabilities add up to 40 percent of this persona's total workflows. Note that these two workflows directly related to datasets appear with the highest chance within the same persona, even though the mixed model does not use the information that these two workflows are related. We believe this co-occurrence does not happen by chance but rather reflects one of the main characteristics of this persona, that is, this archetypal user is similar to a Data Administrator. This user is *Full-stack* with a focus on dataset preparation. By Full-stack, we mean a user who is likely to perform all the workflows related to datasets, lenses, and visualization in Platfora.

2. *Full-stack user specialized in Lens building (Jeffrey)*: This persona has the highest probability related to the following workflows: *Build Lens with optional modification to a dataset*, *Create Lens and visualization* and *Create dataset, Lens and visualization in one workflow*, all of which directly relate to a user's behavior of building a Lens in Platfora. These workflows pertain to actions on multiple objects from Datasets, Lenses and Visualizations within one workflow; these probabilities add up to 50 percent of the workflows within this persona. This persona is interesting as her workflows focus on several main product pages within the same workflow unlike other personas who tend to focus on a single object such a Dataset or a Vizboard.

3. *Full-stack user specialized in Segments (Dave)*: This persona has a 15 percent probability to generate the workflow *Use Segments in visualization*; the other personas have zero chance for the same. We therefore characterize this persona as a full-stack user who focuses on *Segments*; a Segment is an advanced Platfora feature that collects members of a population based on user defined attributes.

4. *Full-stack user specialized in Visualizations (Marybeth)*: This persona has a 70 percent chance that her clickstream is one of the three common workflows related to Vizboards with higher probabilities on leveraging Datasets and Lenses, as well.

5. *Pure Vizboards user (Debra)*: Unlike the previous personas, this persona's clickstreams has a 95 percent probability of representing just one of the three common workflows related to Vizboards. This is the only non Full-stack user among the five personas.

We have thus identified Platfora's personas, bottom-up, based on clustering clickstreams extracted from the product telemetry data.

6. DISCUSSION AND FUTURE WORK

In this paper we proposed a data-driven approach to create personas. Unlike approaches that relied on survey or user interview data to identify workflows, our approach identified workflows by directly incorporating user behavior via clicks and clickstreams. We aggregated these common workflows with a mixed model to

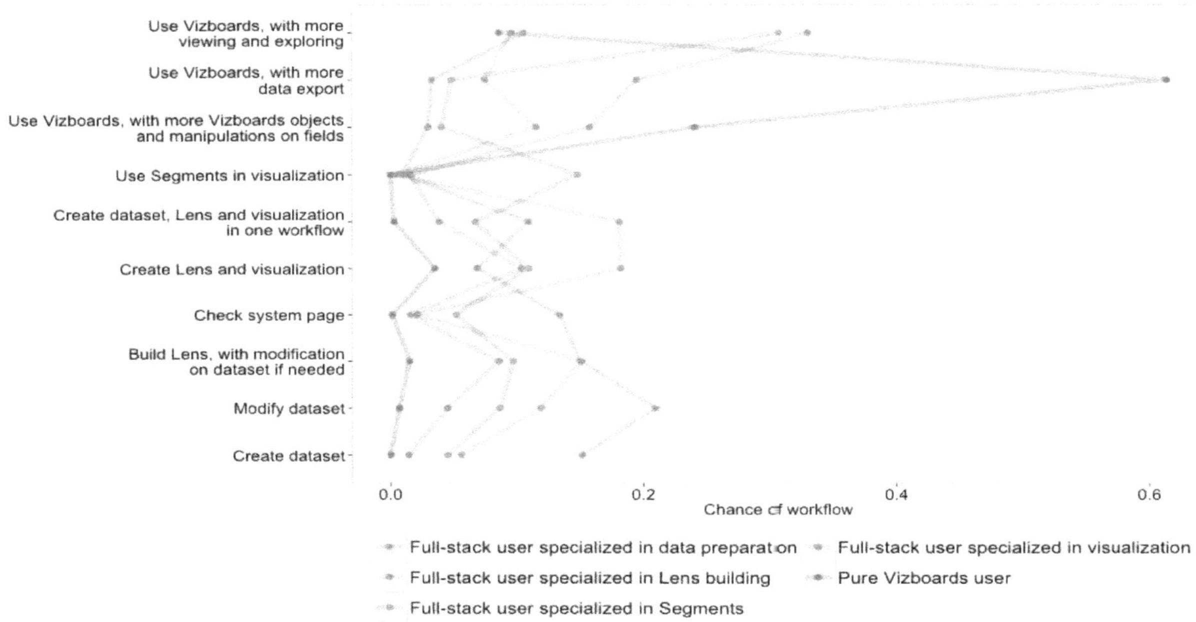

Figure 11: Each data-driven persona has unique behavior as shown by the unique frequency of common workflows as shown on the X Axis.

create data-driven personas. The five personas that we created were also validated by user behavior experts (via interviews) who verified that these personas indeed represented archetypal users of our product. Our approach is not only direct but also low cost as product telemetry is automatically gathered from the field; there is little interference from human interviewers or noisy self-reports.

Clickstream based persona creation based on product telemetry is scalable. Scalability is possible as additional telemetry data can help better understand existing persona characteristics (workflows) either by refining individual personas or by tracking the evolution of personas over time as users increasingly learn and utilize various product features. With 39,000 clickstreams from 2400 users, we also believe that our data is robust enough to generate five personas when compared to existing data-driven approaches that have only relied on a few hundred survey samples or self-reports.

We initiated this data-driven persona work to primarily refine original Platfora personas. The personas that we generated from clickstreams validated two of the existing Platfora personas while showing that the other two personas had evolved into *full-stack* users; we would not have garnered this crucial insight into our product's users without conducting a time-consuming costly persona reconstruction effort via traditional means. For example, we initially assumed that *Jeffrey*, a citizen data-scientist persona, to be *familiar* with datasets, *expert* at data curation and visualization workflows, with not much of an emphasis on sharing of insights via collaborative options (comments or emails). When we mapped existing *Jeffrey*'s to the personas discovered via clickstream clustering, we discovered that this persona was maturing over time in terms of using all four Platfora components eventually morphing into a full-stack user. We believe that it would be tedious and hard to capture such insights into the evolution of a persona over time with surveys or self-reports and that our approach based on clickstreams is a better representation of persona evolution (or maturation) over time.

You can extend our clickstream based approach to incorporate sequence and frequency information of clicks by considering different distance metrics. To use the sequence information, you can consider *n-gram* clicks as the smallest granular element in your current distance metric, where an n-gram click is *n* consecutive clicks in sequence. By considering consecutive clicks, the sequence information is retained as two clickstreams are considered to be similar if they share common clicks and if common clicks appear in the same order. To use the frequency information, you can define the distance between two clickstreams as the Euclidian distance between the two frequency vectors of clicks. With new distance metric, two clickstreams are similar if they share common clicks and the frequency of common clicks are close, so the frequency information is not dropped. The rest of our bottom-up procedure will be exactly the same. The work in this paper was motivated by the need to validate existing Cooper personas with clickstream information. Since calculating the similarity between clickstreams is only one step of our proposed technique, we find it reasonable to use our current simple, yet coarse, distance metric to verify the feasibility of our approach. Incorporating sequence and frequency information is definitely a promising avenue for future research.

We believe that our approach generalizes across applications that capture clickstreams that reflect user behavior. In this work we mined the clickstreams of Platfora users. However, neither the data is limited to clickstream information, nor the underlying system is limited to an analytics platform. Our approach would generalize if applications record a user's behavior in multiple sessions and if each session logs this user behavior as a sequence of actions. For example, our proposed approach would work for an e-commerce website. Here is how: as a user visits the website multiple times, this user is likely to explore a sequence of webpages. Our technique can capture the most common webpage paths that this user explores in the website and build a mixed model for related users based on the frequencies of their most common webpage paths. Thus our approach is domain neutral in all these three critical phases: calculating distance between two sequences of actions, performing hierarchical clustering, and constructing a mixed (user) model.

Our approach to create personas starting with clicks (the atoms of user behavior) can indeed be more rounded by existing approaches that rely on user interviews and surveys. Similar to other research techniques, a triangulation of methods that include data-driven click-stream approaches, surveys, interviews, user observation, and self-reports can ultimately create personas that best represent an archetypal product user.

7. ACKNOWLEDGMENTS

We thank the reviewers for their insightful comments and suggestions that helped us better situate our work and improve the quality of our paper. We also thank the Product Team and the UX experts at Platfora who helped to validate the personas in multiple user interviews.

8. REFERENCES

[1] Jon Brickey, Steven Walczak, and Tony Burgess. 2010. A Comparative Analysis of Persona Clustering Methods.. In *AMCIS*. 217.

[2] Alessandro Canossa and Anders Drachen. 2009. Play-personas: behaviours and belief systems in user-centred game design. In *Human-Computer Interaction–INTERACT 2009*. Springer, 510–523.

[3] Alan Cooper and others. 1999. *The inmates are running the asylum:[Why high-tech products drive us crazy and how to restore the sanity]*. Vol. 261.

[4] Arthur P Dempster, Nan M Laird, and Donald B Rubin. 1977. Maximum likelihood from incomplete data via the EM algorithm. *Journal of the royal statistical society. Series B (methodological)* (1977), 1–38.

[5] Anders Drachen, Alessandro Canossa, and Georgios N Yannakakis. 2009. Player modeling using self-organization in Tomb Raider: Underworld. In *Computational Intelligence and Games, 2009. CIG 2009. IEEE Symposium on*. IEEE, 1–8.

[6] Jonathan Grudin and John Pruitt. 2002. Personas, participatory design and product development: An infrastructure for engagement. In *PDC*. 144–152.

[7] Homa Javahery, Alexander Deichman, Ahmed Seffah, and Thiruvengadam Radhakrishnan. 2007. Incorporating human experiences into the design process of a visualization tool: A case study from bioinformatics. In *Systems, Man and Cybernetics, 2007. ISIC. IEEE International Conference on*. IEEE, 1517–1523.

[8] Lieve Hamers and Yves Hemeryck and Guido Herweyers and Marc Janssen and Hans Keters and Ronald Rousseau and André Vanhoutte. 1989. Similarity measures in scientometric research: The Jaccard index versus Salton's cosine formula. *Information Processing Management* 25, 3 (1989), 315 – 318.

[9] Tobias Mahlmann, Anders Drachen, Julian Togelius, Alessandro Canossa, and Georgios N Yannakakis. 2010. Predicting player behavior in Tomb Raider: Underworld. In *Computational Intelligence and Games (CIG), 2010 IEEE Symposium on*. IEEE, 178–185.

[10] Jennifer Jen McGinn and Nalini Kotamraju. 2008. Data-driven persona development. In *Proceedings of the SIGCHI Conference on Human Factors in Computing Systems*. ACM, 1521–1524.

[11] Geoffrey McLachlan and David Peel. 2004. *Finite mixture models*. John Wiley & Sons.

[12] Tomasz Miaskiewicz, Tamara Sumner, and Kenneth A Kozar. 2008. A latent semantic analysis methodology for the identification and creation of personas. In *Proceedings of the SIGCHI Conference on Human Factors in Computing Systems*. ACM, 1501–1510.

[13] Steve Mulder and Ziv Yaar. 2006. *The user is always right: A practical guide to creating and using personas for the web*. New Riders.

[14] NASA. 1987. Telemetry: Summary of concept and rationale. *NASA STI/Recon Technical Report N* 89 (Dec. 1987), 13455.

[15] John Pruitt and Jonathan Grudin. 2003. Personas: practice and theory. In *Proceedings of the 2003 conference on Designing for user experiences*. ACM, 1–15.

[16] Rashmi Sinha. 2003. Persona development for information-rich domains. In *CHI'03 extended abstracts on Human factors in computing systems*. ACM, 830–831.

[17] Joe H Ward Jr. 1963. Hierarchical grouping to optimize an objective function. *Journal of the American statistical association* 58, 301 (1963), 236–244.

Evaluating the Paper-to-Screen Translation of Participant-Aided Sociograms with High-Risk Participants

Bernie Hogan
Oxford Internet Institute
University of Oxford
bernie.hogan@oii.ox.ac.uk

Joshua R. Melville
Oxford Internet Institute
University of Oxford

Gregory Lee Philips II, Patrick Janulis
Feinberg School of Medicine
Northwestern University

Noshir Contractor
Kellogg School of Management
Northwestern University

Brian S. Mustanski, Michelle Birkett
Feinberg School of Medicine
Northwestern University

ABSTRACT

While much social network data exists online, key network metrics for high-risk populations must still be captured through self-report. This practice has suffered from numerous limitations in workflow and response burden. However, advances in technology, network drawing libraries and databases are making interactive network drawing increasingly feasible. We describe the translation of an analog-based technique for capturing personal networks into a digital framework termed *netCanvas* that addresses many existing shortcomings such as: 1) complex data entry; 2) extensive interviewer intervention and field setup; 3) difficulties in data reuse; and 4) a lack of dynamic visualizations.

We test this implementation within a health behavior study of a high-risk and difficult-to-reach population. We provide a within–subjects comparison between paper and touchscreens. We assert that touchscreen-based social network capture is now a viable alternative for highly sensitive data and social network data entry tasks.

Author Keywords

Participant-aided sociograms; Social networks

ACM Classification Keywords

D.2.1 Requirements/Specifications: Elicitation methods; E.1 Data Structures: Graphs and networks; H.5.3 Group and Organization Interfaces: Web-based interaction

INTRODUCTION

The rise of social media and large scale social data sources has led to significant interest in the collection and analysis of social network data [8]. Much of these data comes from behavioral actions as encoded on platforms, such as Facebook likes, emails sent and messages retweeted. Such 'trace' data can reveal insights about human behavior. However, there are numerous situations when no single passive source of data will be able to capture the specific networks of interest. In particular, the sensitive health behaviors of populations, such as sexual practices and the use of drugs, cannot be reliably captured through trace or non-reactive data. In these cases, self-report data are essential [7].

Since disease transmission often includes a social dimension, health researchers in particular have substantial interest in capturing social network data to develop epidemiological understanding of disease and to inform intervention development. Unfortunately, few data capture tools are designed for such uses. Those that do exist have not kept pace with advances in data management or user interface design. Most social network data capture still requires tedious analog surveying [15]. While some creative solutions have been developed [23, 43], few tools are capable of efficiently capturing complex network data. This is largely due to placing an overly high burden on participants, researchers, or both.

Several technological advancements — in particular the recent emergence of cost-effective capacitive touch screen displays, the increasing power of standardized web technologies, and the development of graph databases — make it plausible to translate the prior analog approach into a digital framework. In theory, this digital translation should significantly improve the usability and decrease the complexity of network data capture for both respondents and researchers.

This paper describes our effort to address the challenges presented by the state of the art in both analog and digital tools for social network capture. We describe the use of a novel open source framework, *netCanvas*[1], built using many of the technological advancements noted above. We apply *netCanvas* to a research study of young men who have sex with men (YMSM), a hard to reach and highly sensitive population, using a specific protocol called *netCanvas-R*. This protocol

[1] http://networkcanvas.io

CHI '16, May 07–12, 2016, San Jose, CA, USA
ACM 978-1-4503-3362-7/16/05...$15.00
DOI: http://dx.doi.org/10.1145/2858036.2858368

was designed to reflect existing analog approaches to data collection and to handle complex multi-layered (i.e., *multiplex*) social, sexual, and drug use networks. We evaluate the efficacy of this protocol compared to a prior analog data capture technique using many of the same participants. When conducting clinical research studies, particularly longitudinal research with vulnerable populations, high respondent satisfaction and ease of use are essential to ensure participant retention and the capture of high quality data. We find that our technique not only captures equivalent data more efficiently than analog techniques, but provides high levels of user satisfaction.

RELATED WORK

Surveying personal networks

Surveying has been an essential cornerstone of social research for over a century. In that time, there have been innumerable studies on methodological advances as well as research on the transition towards computer-based surveying [16]. Social network studies, however, have proven to be especially challenging for existing survey techniques.

For many surveys, there are few dependencies between questions beyond straightforward skip-flow logic. One of the key distinctions between social network surveys and traditional approaches is the need to have alters and relationships persist throughout the survey. In social network visualization it is conventional for people mentioned by a respondent to be represented as nodes, and relationships between them as edges. By treating nodes and edges as discrete classes of objects, these visualization packages not only allow for the drawing of networks, but higher order calculations such as community detection and network layout. The *Prefuse* package, for example, contains methods to automatically arrange nodes using common social network layouts such as Fruchterman Reingold [22].

Most existing survey programs do not have facilities for representing ego (i.e. the respondent) and alters as discrete entities. Instead, alters are reduced simply to names that are piped between questions using a skip-flow logic. Responses to questions concerning network actors are therefore represented as simple fields in the survey data model, and not a special class of object with relational properties (as would be especially useful in managing the collection of social network data).

Here, we discuss the fundamental process of surveying social network data, and link this to advances in social network visualization. While these two practices (data collection and visualization) have often been considered separate, we believe that as research methodologies become more advanced, data collection will necessarily become increasingly intertwined with effective user-centered design.

Name generators as data capture devices

Name generation has been one of the cornerstones of social network analysis (SNA) since its early inception in Moreno's sociometry in the 1930s [19]. In the 1960s, the emphasis shifted from reporting on simply 'who knows who' towards the use of targeted name generators within a sample. In one of the earliest incarnations, the Detroit Area Study [29], name generators were used among a sampled population to assess the breadth and diversity of social support networks. Participants were asked to list N names before completing a 'dyadic census', wherein they systematically indicate any relationships between alters (does A know B, does A know C, does A know D, etc.).[2] This approach has been reproduced with some modifications in numerous sociological studies [45, 17, 10, 33].

The "name generator" approach to social network data collection is comprised of three stages: Name generating, name interpreting, and edge generating.

Name generating is the first stage in network data capture, in which respondents are asked to name members of their network. While the wording of prompts ranges between studies, the boundaries for who is a member of the social network will vary based on the study. There is no universal statement on who should be included or excluded from a social network [31].

Name interpreting is when respondents give additional data about their alters indicated in the prior stage. Name interpretation follows name generation rather than operates in parallel in order to minimize respondent bias. Examples of measures administered during this stage might include alter demographics, ratings of the strength of the relationship between the ego and alter, and the frequency of contact between ego and alter.

Edge generating refers to the respondent providing relational data linking the alters. It is the most complex stage, and the one that has led to substantial differences in research methods. The complexity is due to the fact that for n alters there are $n(n-1)$ possible directed relationships (such as who calls whom) and $\frac{n(n-1)}{2}$ undirected relationships (such as who spends time with whom). In the case of *multiplex* networks, there are even more links. In our study, numerous link types are assessed between alters, such as those who spend time together, use drugs together, have sex with each other, and participate in group sex together. Thus, the complete set of links would rise to $\frac{4n(n-1)}{2}$. As mentioned previously, the earliest method of capturing these data was through a 'dyadic census'. For even 20 alters, a dyadic census requires 190 questions. Responses to this challenge tend to cluster into two camps: visual analog approaches and computer-assisted interviews.

Visual analog approaches

Visual approaches are mentioned by Freeman [20] as a cornerstone of the SNA paradigm. Historically, visualization has provided a means for researchers to view and interact with complex network data, allowing the generation of intuitions and the visual representation of macro-level phenomena. However, when displaying a large number of nodes or relationships, graphs quickly become too complicated to easily interpret, or to be used to develop clear understandings of micro-level structural details. Visualization has been particularly useful, therefore, in studies of close personal networks,

[2] As is convention in social network analysis, we refer to relations (e.g., friendships) between ego and alter are as ties or *ego-alter* ties. The relations between any two alters are referred to as *alter-alter* ties.

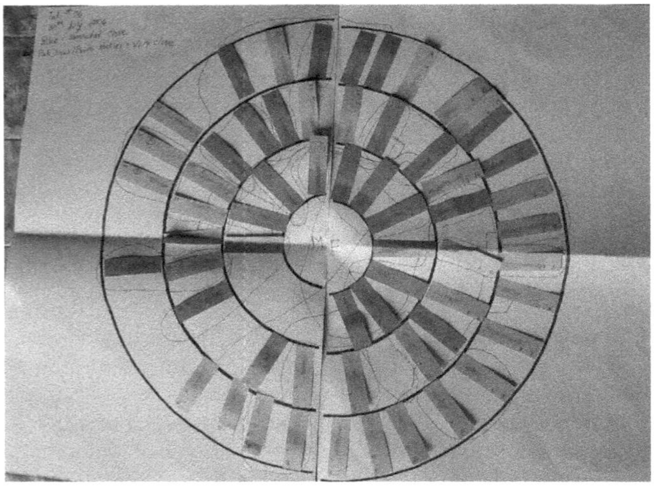

Figure 1. Particpant-aided sociogram from the Connected Lives project. (Previously unpublished image ©Wellman Associates 2005.)

where there are fewer nodes and linkages.[3] In the case of studies that involve the participant in interpreting the visualization, the effectiveness is often further enhanced by their inherent expertise regarding the data [24].

Visual analog approaches in personal network studies begin with visual representations that are built upon the 'scaffolding' of a series of concentric circles around a focal individual. Beginning in the 1980s, the concentric circle approach to network collection was utilized repeatedly by researchers such as Antonucci [3] and Spencer and Pahl [35]. While the arrangement of the nodes was considered important in this work, these studies did not collect alter-alter relational information.

In 2004, Wellman's NetLab extended data collection using a concentric rings approach by adding manipulated physical elements (in this case, post-it notes) that made the interview interactive, tactile, and most importantly, *participant focused* [23]. These physical and interactive elements not only improved the participant experience, but also made the capture of alter-alter relational information more feasible. They titled this approach a 'participant-aided sociogram' (PAS; Figure 1)[23]. Their methods have been subsequently applied in a number of studies, including those examining vulnerable populations [26, 5, 34].

Challenges with current visual analog approaches

Although the recent approaches to PAS networks are highly intuitive for respondents, it remains tedious to code the structural data produced in PAS interviews (e.g. lines drawn in pen between two analog elements). Sometimes lines bend, intersect, or merge in ways that make data imputation slow and prone to errors in dense networks. Further, errors in the imputation of alter names may cause serious issues, particularly in studies interested in matching and consolidating alters across networks [6]. Somewhat counter-intuitively, analog interfaces can quickly become rigid and inflexible once their initial 'openness' is collapsed by the permanence of ink-drawn lines. As an example, consider research examining multiplex networks. On a sheet of paper, one must either erase any existing ties (thus eliminating data) before moving on, or else use different colored pens, thereby multiplying the visual complexity.[4]

As a further illustration, consider a scenario where a question must be asked about an alter with certain qualities. For the interviewer to locate 'the alter with the highest degree' might require tedious manual counting. For a computer this counting is trivial. By extension, there is the matter of sampling within a network. That is, what is the best way to take a subset of alters? The complicated sampling of [12] suggests automation could be an improvement.

Computer-assisted approaches

While analog approaches focus on ease of use and user empowerment, they suffer from complex data collection and a lack of data flexibility *in situ*. Alternative computer-assisted approaches, of which there are now a number, largely bypass these issues through an emphasis on creating structured, manageable data. They range from adaptations of the most direct and generalist survey tools (which simply ask for N alters and then iterate through the dyadic census automatically), to complex real-time network creation as is done in EgoWeb [39].

One of the earliest noted digital capture techniques is McCarty's EgoNet [30]. This tool functions primarily as a survey tool for capturing network data. It is built in Java and requires extensive configuration, but can show real-time features: as one nominates new alters, they appear on a graph. These alters then become connected to the rest of the graph through alter-alter questions that are asked to the respondent. Other tools, such as VennMaker, also utilize a Java-based framework for drawing nodes and edges, and similarly allow the creation of real-time representations [21].

Each of these tools (see Figure 2 for screen-shots of existing digital approaches) were built with small screens and keyboard and mouse interaction in mind. While in-keeping with the technology available at the time, this is at odds with human-computer interaction (HCI) literature indicating that movement and interaction with certain elements is better accomplished with a finger [18, 11].

Compared to analog approaches, computer-assisted approaches front load technical demands. That is, paper-based approaches can be very flexible until before the interview starts. By contrast, computer-assisted approaches require immense specification, both in terms of the interview protocol and the back-end data structure, prior to the start of data collection. Once these are constructed and data captured digitally, it is possible to automate any further processes, such as the act of converting data from its existing format to one amenable to analysis. This is particularly advantageous for longitudinal and ongoing data capture. Removing the time necessary for data entry and validation, while being able to store, analyze,

[3] Nevertheless, work continues to assess how large scale networks can be arranged and visualized in useful ways [42].

[4] See [26] for an example of this process of redrawing multiple networks on a whiteboard.

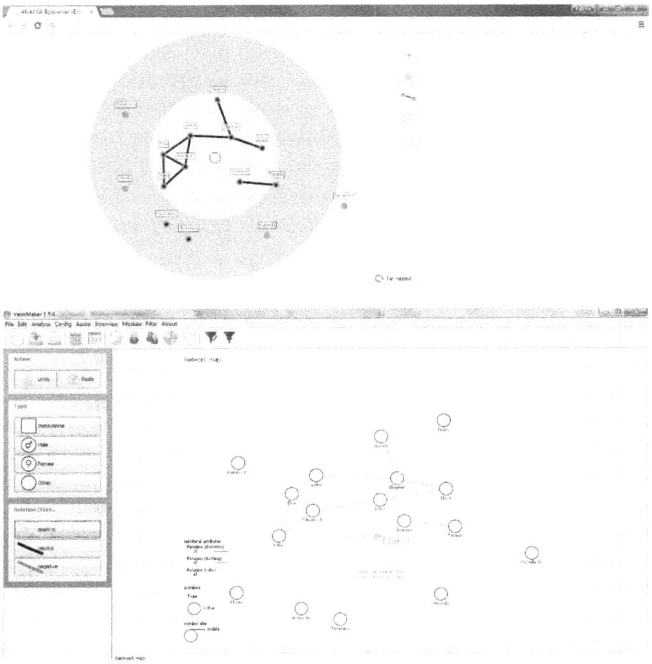

Figure 2. Example digital approaches to the collection of personal networks, Anamia (Top) and VennMaker (Bottom).

retrieve, and query data in near real time is a completely new paradigm in network analysis.

Challenges with current computer-assisted approaches

Despite these advantages, current computational approaches suffer from a series of issues. First they tend to be overly complex in their interface design, predominately as a result of focusing on the requirements of the expert user (often the researcher) rather than the novice (often the research subject). A single screen may be overloaded with controls in order to represent any number of different settings or options. This approach is not without forethought: such interfaces are designed to help an experienced user complete an action they are already familiar with more quickly. An analogy might be made with professional applications in other areas, such as photo-editing or music production, where interfaces often prioritize long-term productivity over short-term intelligibility. VennMaker, for example, functions much akin to a specialized drawing program like OmniGraffle or Visio, with an interface designed around expert requirements rather than co-production.

Though these design goals are reasonable when software is to be used by experienced users, we assert that when interfaces expose novice respondents to complex metaphors, options, and visual representations, they can intimidate and confuse. Tufte's notion of the 'data-ink ratio' [44] seems pertinent: interfaces should in general seek to minimise the redundant 'data ink' used merely to frame the relevant data. Re-enforcing this, past work in human factors has evaluated a number of means for simplifying software, e.g. McGrenere and colleagues demonstrating the benefits of showing fewer elements to novice users [32].

Most existing approaches present interfaces that assume a multi-tasking environment. A review of existing software shows that virtually none offer a full-screen (or single task) experience, or are intended to be used on a large format screen; this severely restricts the space available for interface elements, and makes drawing tasks potentially distraction prone and confusing. Some programs sidestep this issue by not having the sociogram drawn by the participant at all. For example, EgoWeb 2.0 only shows the sociogram after the dyadic census. In this case, the network is drawn algorithmically rather than being co-created. For the designers of EgoWeb 2.0, this was a deliberate decision, since the sociogram is meant primarily as a conversational object rather than one for tie generation. We consider this a design decision rather than a methodological necessity.

The Anamia software by Tubaro and colleagues promotes the sociogram to the status of an interface in its own right, and also operates in a quasi-full screen mode (with only the web-browser and operating system façades still present outside of the software itself) [43]. However, network generation, layout, and edge creation tasks all occur on the same interface, which is restricted by the use of Adobe Flash technology to a predefined screen-size. When combined with the need for the software to be used by an unassisted respondent remotely, all interface elements for all tasks must be visible at the same time, which reproduces many of the issues associated with congested interfaces noted above.

These approaches are also hindered by back-end inflexibility. Much software is intimately tied to a specific data model, often developed for the requirements of a specific study or research exercise. For example, many software requires ties to be uniplex (of only one type), does not allow complex skip-flow logic, or does not allow assignment of complex node attributes such as overlapping group membership. While some software provides a degree of configurability with regards to the data model, this happens primarily via bespoke GUI wizards, or arcane configuration files with proprietary syntax. This limits the type and complexity of data that are able to be captured, as well as the ability to use the software within varied research contexts.

One final challenge with current computer-assisted methods stems from the fact that once data have been captured, existing software is rarely designed for the straightforward aggregation or management of that data. By its nature, network data produces both structural data (ties between nodes) and attribute data (attributes of nodes; attributes of ties).

Storing this data is far from straightforward, yet existing software has been slow to adapt to more recent approaches, and has tended either to defer to notions inherited from relational databases, or to fall back on the even more outmoded system of flat files. If using relational databases, the researcher is often required to create complex queries across many tables to reconstitute the graph from its component parts during analysis. In the case of flat files, equally extensive file manipulation is required.

DESIGN GOALS: A HYBRID APPROACH

The approach taken in our current research has been to draw upon a new framework, *netCanvas*, which seeks to address prior shortcomings of both analog and computer-assisted approaches by using web technologies and a touch-optimized interface. The overall aim of this framework is to replicate as much of the front-end of analog techniques as possible while still preserving the data quality and data flexibility advantages of current digital approaches. Specific requirements which guided the design of this tool were:

1. Similar to PAS techniques, and to improve usability, generated alters should be treated as 'objects' which can be moved and shuffled by the respondent.

2. Similar to PAS techniques and counter to many computer-assisted approaches, data entry must be tactile.

3. Drawing from the HCI literature, interface elements should be designed for optimal respondent ease, engagement, and comprehension. This means simple and colorful displays that are free from excess radio buttons, check boxes, and any elements that are not of use to the interviewee, and that could potentially be distracting[41].

4. The screen should be able to accommodate upwards of 50 nodes clearly without occlusions. We opt for 50 nodes since the literature on personal networks indicates this characterize over 95 percent of personal networks according to past studies[23, 17].

5. Finally, the *netCanvas* framework must be flexible in order to work with multiple diverse protocols that can be specified by various research groups.

While *netCanvas* is the framework, the protocol file defines the specific items, screens, and logic. This paper therefore focuses on the evaluation of one such protocol, *netCanvas-R*.

RESEARCH HYPOTHESES

To evaluate the effectiveness of our implementations of the above requirements, we present four hypotheses:

Hypothesis 1. Users who have completed both an analog-based PAS and *netCanvas-R* will report either equal or more alters on *netCanvas-R*. Further, participants will disclose equal or more information about sexual behaviors with each alter within *netCanvas-R*.

Hypothesis 2. Users who have completed both an analog-based PAS and *netCanvas-R* will be faster on the digital platform.

Hypothesis 3. There will be no evidence that efficiency gains will be due to a learner effect about 'social network thinking'. That is, those who have done a name generator in a different medium will take as long as those who have never done a name generator before.

Hypothesis 4. Users will indicate satisfaction and high usability of *netCanvas-R*. This will include expressions of enjoyment with the data collection process.

These first two hypotheses suggest that *ceterus paribus*, *netCanvas-R* is a preferred approach as it will lead to either no difference or higher levels of disclosure about the social network. Thus, if data quality is either unaffected or improved using *netCanvas-R*, this validates our choice to translate this tool digitally. In addition to these hypotheses, a fourth hypothesis is related to the design and experience of completing the digitized PAS.

METHODS

The design and implementation of the *netCanvas-R* protocol

We use *netCanvas* as a framework that can accommodate the requirements for analog PAS. The framework itself provides a generic set of survey 'screens' (or interfaces) that can be fit to specific tasks, as well as a comprehensive set of APIs for interacting with a network data model and managing an interview session.

To employ *netCanvas*, one must create a 'protocol,' in much the same way as a video game console requires the creation of specific games to run on it. In this case, we implemented a protocol, *netCanvas-R*, that reflects much of the requirements of an analog PAS while also using utilizing novel features like complex skip-flow logic, pan and zoomable maps, and recalling alters between waves that would more complicated within an analog framework.

The interviewer-assisted interview protocol *netCanvas-R* was used to elicit social, drug, and sexual connections by the participant. Below we outline the specifics of how this was implemented, with reference both to the issues with prior approaches set out above, and our stated design goals.

Technological Foundations

The *netCanvas* framework is built entirely using open web technologies, primarily HTML5, CSS, and JavaScript. Historically, these technologies have not been considered sufficiently powerful to create full-fledged applications. As recently as 2011, fundamental interactions, such as scrolling using touch, were unsatisfactory when compared with the 'native' experience provided by applications directly built using operating system APIs [13].

In recent years there have been a number of dramatic improvements in this situation. The ratification of the HTML5 specification introduced APIs for full-screen display, local storage of data, touch events, and hardware-accelerated rasterized rendering using the `<canvas>` element. Of particular importance for an implementation of the analog PAS method are touch interactions and canvas rendering, since, when combined, they allow the arbitrary creation and manipulation of digital 'objects', via touch (or multi-touch) interfaces, wholly within the browser. This functionality gives developers a means to create programmable platform-agnostic applications without choosing between anachronistic UI frameworks (e.g., NetBeans) or proprietary and soon-to-be obsolete technologies such as Flash. Similarly the CSS3 specification has provided a raft of powerful new abilities. Among them is the ability to animate any property of an HTML element with arbitrary or user-defined "easing" functions. These functions allow designers total control over the movement and feel of interface elements, allowing complex and meaningful interaction design. Finally, JavaScript is now robust and performant enough to be used for large-scale applications. The 'Node' server-side JavaScript framework, for example, handles high volume websites such as flickr.com, groupon.com, and yellowpages.com.

This choice of technologies puts *netCanvas*, and by extension *netCanvas-R*, in a unique position compared with contemporaries: it is capable of running across all modern web-browsers on all modern platforms (from Windows, OSX, and Linux, to Apple's iOS platform and Google's Android). While not necessarily advantageous in the context of a single-instance study such as is discussed here, this approach reflects a broader commitment by the authors to create reusable and general purpose academic software, which can be configured to suit specific needs.

Protocol specification

The *netCanvas-R* protocol itself is defined within a protocol file, which is loaded by *netCanvas*. This file consists of a simple and logical JSON schema (See Listing 1) familiar to anyone who has experience with JavaScript syntax. Since the protocol is defined in a clear-text format, it is directly editable by researchers, albeit with the caveat that they must understand the syntax. Still, this represents an improvement over black-box GUI configuration, or proprietary custom configuration files. Our use of open formats also allows the creation of additional tools for developing and managing protocol schemes in the future.

```
var protocol = {
  sessionParameters: {
    name: "RADAR"
  },
  stages: [
    {label:'Introduction', page:'intro.html'},
    {label:'Name Generator', page:'ng.html'},
    {label:'Alter Linking', page:'sociogram.html'},
    {label:'Name Interpreter', page:'ordbin.html'},
    // etc.
  ]
};
```

Listing 1. Example netCanvas protocol file

The protocol is defined as a series of discreet 'stages', with each stage manifest in a single self-contained HTML file. Conceptually, we aim to break the interview process up into logical single-step tasks. This dramatically simplifies the interface requirements for each screen, and establishes a predictable pattern that allows respondents to quickly understand the flow of the interview.

The use of the *netCanvas* framework also enables complex automatic skip logic (also defined in the protocol file) based on data collected from the current session, or even previous visits. This skip logic extends traditional survey programs where skip logic is based solely on responses to specific questions. Since we treat nodes and edges as special classes (creating an underlying network data model during the interview), *netCanvas* operates more like existing social network visualization software than either existing visual network data entry programs like VennMaker or traditional survey programs such as Qualtrics. For example in the case of the GUESS package, one can use

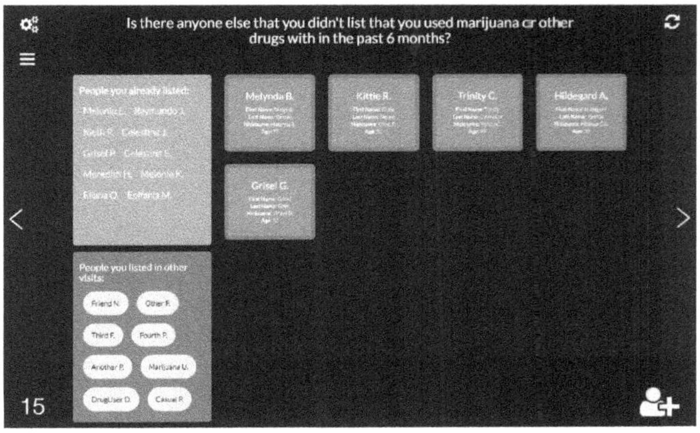

Figure 3. Name generator interface

the modified python (termed gython) to make boolean and set logic queries to nodes and edges[1]. In our case, a specific protocol can make structural queries to the network data model using the netCanvas API. This can be used to, for example, show a screen only if a fully connected clique is present (such as a fully connected set of sex partners).

The *netCanvas-R* protocol embeds automatic skip logic to provide several key benefits. First, by accounting for a participant's prior responses, later items that are deemed irrelevant are able to be skipped, and the length of the survey is greatly reduced. While *prima facie* this is conventional in survey programs, the difference is that we provide a skip logic based on the qualities of nodes. By contrast, fields in conventional surveys do not themselves have queryable attributes. For example, in our case, we can accommodate sensitive issues with gendered pronouns in a straightforward manner that would otherwise require extensive JavaScript hacks in programs such as Qualtrics or LimeSurvey (considering that our participants may be included for having sex with men but identify as either transwomen or genderqueer in addition to the conventional male gender). Although skip logic seems like an obvious inclusion, it is not as easy to permit in studies where all data collection aspects happen on a single screen.

Interfaces and affordances

In keeping with the steps required by the PAS method, *netCanvas* provides predefined interface modules for the three most important steps: name generation, name interpretation, and alter-alter linking on the sociogram. Each stage defined in the *netCanvas-R* protocol file implements one of these interfaces, with simple text fields changed to reflect different prompts, variable names, or other configuration options.

Name Generation (Figure 3) takes place on a simple card-based interface, showing only a prompt, a counter to keep track of alter numbers, and a button for triggering the 'add new alter' panel. Only those interface elements that are necessary for the particular task are shown, with context-specific panels appearing and disappearing as necessary. For example, triggering the new alter form dims all background interface elements, giving the form dramatically increased visual emphasis. Figure 3 demonstrates this minimalist and context-driven ap-

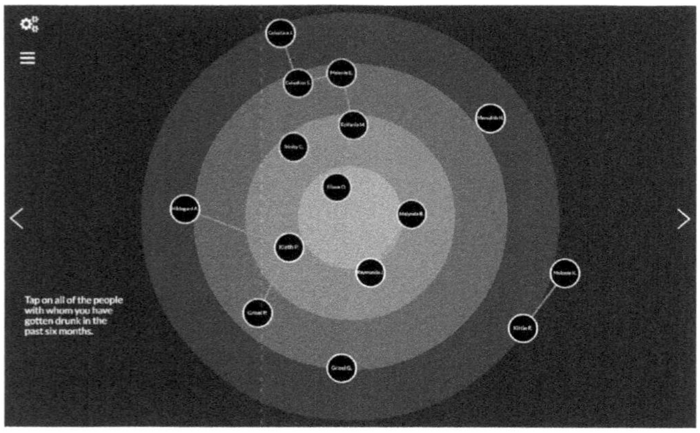

Figure 4. Alter-alter linking (red lines) and alter nomination (yellow highlights)

proach: UI panels are displayed showing previously elicited alters (orange), or alters from a previous interview visit (purple) entirely dynamically, based on the presence of the data they are designed to display. Thus, if a panel has no data to display, it disappears, thereby creating more room for other interface elements to expand into. This process occurs entirely automatically, with no interviewer or respondent involvement.

As with all *netCanvas-R* interfaces, interaction with the name generator interface occurs through touch, gestures, and keyboard for text entry. Since the keyboard is separate from the touchscreen, it can be used by the interviewer or the participant depending on the mobility needs of the participant. Tapping on buttons or cards (representing alters) triggers predictable actions such as opening, editing, or activating. More complex interactions include the ability to drag alters elicited in previous visits into the current interview session. This gesture is both symbolic and practical: it is designed to give participants the sensation of bringing an individual into the present context, while re-enforcing our stated design goal of making alter interactions as tactile as possible. Extending this, we do not use hidden or unconventional user actions, such as long-press for context menus.

The use of longitudinal data in these panels also demonstrates a technique that would have been impractical from a data-management perspective using an analog approach, and formidable from an interface perspective using an existing computational approach.

Within *netCanvas-R*, name generator steps successfully implemented in the earlier LYNC Study were adapted and implemented using the core *netCanvas* interfaces. As in LYNC, the alter's first, last, and nicknames were elicited for each step, along with ego's perception regarding their role(s).

Alter-alter linking (Figure 4) is an example of an interface that benefits particularly from digitization. To indicate a tie, the participant first taps an alter (which is highlighted), and then taps another alter. At this point, an edge is created between the alters, which is anchored to them should either be moved later.

Figure 5. netCanvas-R in situ

In *netCanvas-R* we leverage the flexibility of showing and hiding ties in order to look at three distinct kinds of ties: sexual, social, and drug use.

Finally, **name interpreter** steps take place on one of three interfaces, depending on the type of variable being captured..

For ordinal and nominal variables, we devised a gesture-based binning interface, which allows respondents to quickly categorize alters based on a given prompt. The ordinal and nominal binning interfaces are used within the *netCanvas-R* protocol to collect data on contact frequency, relationship strength, sexuality, gender identity, racial identity, coarse (region level) location, and drug use frequency.

For binary attributes (primarily nomination variables such as 'got drunk with' or 'got advice from') we used the concentric circles interface, drawing again on the analog PAS approach (Figure 4). The participant selects an alter as having a given attribute through a simple tap, which results in it being visually highlighted.

Several other key variables related to the overall aims of the project were also collected, including important attributes of ties (e.g., estimated dates of first and most recent sex), and an interactive map in which alter residence was coded by US Census tract.

Research context

netCanvas-R was designed to understand the social, sexual, and drug use networks of YMSM. YMSM are an important target for HIV research due to their alarming HIV prevalence, as they accounted for 67% of infections in youth in 2008 and increased to 80% in 2013 [2]. They are one of the only risk groups showing an increasing rate of infections [38]. Despite this high prevalence, and despite HIV's high transmission dependence on drug and sexual network dynamics [25, 27], few studies have been able to efficiently capture social, sexual, and drug network data with this population [25].

Data come from two projects focused on understanding the social, sexual, and drug use networks of YMSM. The first is LYNC, an existing study on sexual health, drug use, and networks that collected data from 2011 to 2012. *netCanvas-R* was introduced in the second study, RADAR (hence the use of the '-R' suffix), which began collecting data in 2015. Participants enrolled in LYNC were subsequently invited to join the RADAR study, which allowed a natural experiment where the reliability of the touchscreen interface could be tested.

LYNC
Within the LYNC study, analog SNA interviews were conducted with 175 YMSM who were a part of a larger longitudinal cohort study aimed at characterizing the prevalence, course, and predictors of co-occurring health problems among YMSM in Chicago. To enroll in the parent study, participants must have been assigned male sex at birth, been between the ages of 16 and 20 years at enrollment, resided in the Chicago metropolitan area, and either identified as gay/bisexual/queer or reported sex with another man. SNA interviews described the sexual, support, and drug use networks of YMSM via a method modified from [23]. Network visits occurred between June 2011 and October 2012.

The analog interviews relied on a combination of two interviewer administered procedures to collect these data: 1) completion of a pre-numbered list form (i.e., in paper-and-pencil form) to enumerate alters and to capture alter attributes; and 2) PAS to capture respondent report of interactions between alters (sexual, substance-using, and social networks). Name generators as well as alter characteristic elicitation questions and procedures were based on prior studies of populations at risk of HIV infection [4, 28, 36, 37, 40]. Egos were asked to elicit up to 40 alters on a list that could be moved around on a whiteboard. After the initial list of supportive individuals was generated, participants were then asked which individuals on that list they had "used drugs or alcohol with" or "had sex with." Then they were asked to name anyone else that they had not yet listed that they had "used drugs or alcohol with" or "had sex with." Finally they were asked if there was anyone that they had not listed yet that has "used drugs or alcohol" or "had sex" with at least two the people already mentioned.

RADAR
The second study, RADAR, is an ongoing longitudinal study of a cohort of YMSM in Chicago. Participants came from a combination of recruitment from existing research cohorts of YMSM, venue-based recruitment, and peer referral. To enroll, participants must have been assigned a male sex at birth, been between the ages of 16 and 29 years, and either identified as gay/bisexual/queer or reported sex with another man. Study visits began in 2015 and were comprised of three sections — a network interview (netCanvas-R; Figure 5), a self-report psychosocial interview (H-RASP), and biological testing. The research activities conducted under both RADAR and LYNC were approved by the Northwestern University Institutional Review Board.

The proposed analysis
To evaluate the quality of data captured within *netCanvas-R*, research hypotheses 1-3 will be assessed via two comparisons. First, to allow the most direct comparisons of an analog PAS to the *netCanvas-R* protocol, the subset of the participants recruited into RADAR who had also participated in the LYNC study ($N = 67$) will be analyzed. The number of alters who were indicated to be sex partners and drug partners within LYNC will be compared to data captured later in RADAR. Additionally, to further evaluate research hypothesis 1, the sexual partner information collected by *netCanvas-R* of all current RADAR participants ($N = 280$), will be compared to data captured under self-report via the computerized self-administered HIV-Risk Assessment for Sexual Partnerships (H-RASP) [34]. This instrument evaluates up to 6 sexual partnerships during the 6 months prior to each interview.

To evaluate the efficiency of data capture with *netCanvas-R* versus PAS, interview times will be compared. Comparisons will occur for all participants ($N = 280$) and for all participants minus the subset involved in both LYNC and RADAR ($N = 213$). Research hypothesis 4 will be evaluated by an analysis of two subsets of participants who at the end of the network interview completed surveys assessing *netCanvas-R*. The first subsample ($N = 65$) provided feedback on their experience with using *netCanvas-R* by responding to three Likert scale questions corresponding to three interfaces (network layout, the calendar widget, and the mapping screen) as well as providing qualitative feedback. The second subsample ($N = 60$) completed a modified version of the System Usability Measure [9] indicating their level of support (1 = strongly disagree to 5 = strongly agree) for the measure's usability. To note, our only modification was to change the wording to clarify that the respondent was evaluating the netCanvas application.

RESULTS

Comparing network disclosure across approaches
In order to compare the quality of the data captured in *netCanvas-R*, network size and reported high-risk sexual behaviors were examined across the three approaches: LYNC, which used the analog PAS name generator; *netCanvas-R*, which used the digital name generator; and H-RASP, which asked respondents to provide a single number of sex or drug partners.

Comparing *netCanvas-R* to LYNC PAS
A total of 67 participants completed both the LYNC network survey and the *netCanvas-R* interview as a participant in RADAR. For these participants, the median number of drug partners in the 6 months prior to the interview was 4 (interquartile range [IQR] $= 7.0$) for LYNC and 4 ($IQR = 7.5$) for RADAR (Wilcoxon signed-rank $V = 644, p = 0.86$). Similarly, the median number of sex partners in the six months prior to the interview was 1 ($IQR = 2.0$) for LYNC and 2 ($IQR = 3.0$) for RADAR (Wilcoxon signed-rank $V = 565, p = 0.35$). These results indicated that equivalent numbers of sex and drug

partners were obtained from *netCanvas-R* compared to analog PAS. Additionally, the number of partners respondents indicated under analog PAS was highly correlated with the number indicated under *netCanvas-R*. Results showed significant associations between both the number of drug partners (Spearman $r = 0.56, p < 0.001$) and the number of sex partners (Spearman $r = 0.63, p < 0.001$) named by each participant across interviews, representing strong effect sizes [14].

Comparing netCanvas-R to H-RASP

Of the 280 participants that completed both the *netCanvas-R* interview and the H-RASP as part of the RADAR study, 179 (63.9%) named the same number of sex partners in both data collection tools, while 57(20.4%) named more sex partners in the H-RASP and 41(14.6%) named more sex partners in *netCanvas-R*. The median number of sex alters named during the *netCanvas-R* interview and the H-RASP was 2 ($IQR = 2$ and $IQR = 3$, respectively), indicating there was no significant difference between the two reports (Wilcoxon signed-rank $V = 2269, p = 0.08$).

Accurate estimates of specific sex behaviors are important for understanding HIV transmission. Therefore reports of sexual behavior with up to 6 of the most recent partners were examined. A comparison of the distribution of sexual behavior reported in *netCanvas-R* and H-RASP can be found in Figure 6. Participants reported similar numbers of anal sex acts (ASA) in H-RASP ($Median = 6, IQR = 23$) and in *netCanvas-R* ($Median = 5, IQR = 20$), although this did obtain statistical significance using the Wilcoxon signed-rank test ($V = 6851.5, p = 0.003$). Conversely, there was not a significant difference (Wilcoxon signed-rank $V = 4212.5, p = 0.24$) in the number of condomless ASA (CASA) reported in the H-RASP ($Median = 1, IQR = 11$) as compared to *netCanvas-R* ($Median = 1, IQR = 10$). These results indicated equivalent reports of CASA, but not ASA. However, the number of high risk sexual acts indicated under H-RASP was significantly correlated with the number indicated under *netCanvas-R*. Both the number of ASA (Spearman $r = 0.71, p < 0.001$) and number of CASA (Spearman $r = 0.75, p < 0.001$) were strongly correlated across H-RASP and *netCanvas-R*.

Efficiency during and post-data collection

Despite our results suggesting similarities in data quality, there were stark differences in the time taken for data collection. In a comparison of median times, *netCanvas-R* took participants significantly less time to complete (Wilcoxon signed-rank $V = 35515, p < 0.001$) with the LYNC interview taking approximately 50% longer than *netCanvas-R* (*netCanvas-R*: $Median = 32$ minutes, $IQR = 18.4$; LYNC: $Median = 47$ minutes, $IQR = 36.0$). Furthermore, this difference was unaffected by removing the 67 LYNC participants who also completed *netCanvas-R* (Wilcoxon signed-rank $V = 27105.5, p < 0.001$).

User satisfaction and usability

To assess user satisfaction and usability, we asked a subsample of RADAR participants to provide feedback on their experience with using *netCanvas-R*. The first sample ($N = 65$) were asked to provide a response to three Likert scale questions

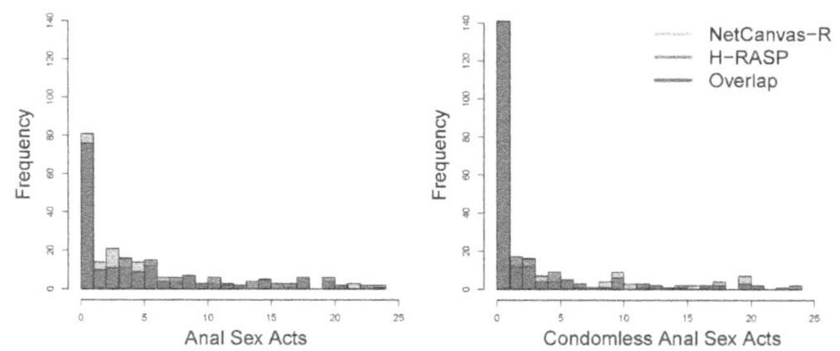

Figure 6. Comparison of distribution of anal sex acts (ASA) and condomless ASA (CASA) in *netCanvas-R* and H-RASP

corresponding to the ease of use (1 = 'very easy' to 5 = 'very hard') of three controls (network arrangement screen, calendar widget, and mapping interface). Across all three controls, scale ratings indicated that respondents found the *netCanvas* system to be very easy to use (network arrangement screen: $Mean = 1.23, SD = 0.52$; calendar widget: $Mean = 1.35, SD = 0.80$; mapping interface: $Mean = 1.72, SD = 1.17$). The respondents were also asked to provide one word descriptions of each of these screens and any suggestions they might have to make the interview more comfortable. Nearly all feedback was strongly positive in nature, with the five most frequently mentioned words being 'Interesting', 'Interactive', 'Fun', 'Simple', and 'Easy.' Further, direct quotes from our query for participant suggestions include: "No, I really enjoyed my time."; "It was pretty fun using the technology!"; "Everything was comfortable"; 'Completely comfortable"; and "It all was pretty cool to see visually".

A second sample ($N = 60$) were asked to complete a modified version of the System Usability Measure [9] indicating their level of support (1 = 'strongly disagree' to 5 = 'strongly agree') for the measure's usability. The scale showed good internal consistency ($\alpha = 0.79$), and participants reported strong support of *netCanvas-R*'s usability, with a mean score of 4.45 ($SD = 0.48$).

DISCUSSION

Hypothesis 1. Users who have completed both an analog-based PAS and *netCanvas* will report either equal or more alters on *netCanvas*. Further, participants will disclose equal or more information about sexual behaviors with each alter within *netCanvas*.

Our results support that the data captured from *netCanvas-R* was of comparable quality to the data captured in both the analog PAS and in the traditional individual self report of specific sexual behaviors (H-RASP). Both the number of partners and the specific behaviors reported with these partners was shown to be equivalent. Given these findings, we can assert that the touchscreen-based approach is comparable to existing research techniques with regards to both data quality and the disclosure of sensitive data.

Hypothesis 2. Users who have completed both an analog-based PAS and *netCanvas* will be faster on the digital platform.

While the data are comparable across platforms, the digital platform demonstrated high efficiency. Interviews were substantially shorter within *netCanvas-R* than in LYNC. Using *netCanvas-R* took a little over half the time taken in LYNC. Also, it is important to note that efficiency extends to the data analytic side as well.The digital platform merges seamlessly with the database and analytic technologies. Therefore, once the data workflow had been constructed, analysis was able to occur immediately after interviews. By contrast, the analog PAS within LYNC required 2-3 hours of additional coding per respondent to enter this data and was unable to accommodate longitudinal observations. These efficiency gains mean lower respondent burden, as well as a better user experience, since alters from time $t-1$ can be pulled into the interview at time t with no additional challenges.

Hypothesis 3. There will be no evidence that efficiency gains will be due to a learner effect about 'social network thinking'. That is, those who have done a name generator in a different medium will take as long as those who have never done a name generator before.

Our analyses controlled for prior experience with the analog PAS, and therefore demonstrated that the efficiency gains observed within *netCanvas-R* were not solely due to a learner effect.

Hypothesis 4. Users will indicate satisfaction and high usability of *netCanvas-R*. This will include expressions of enjoyment with the data collection process.

Results consistently demonstrate that users responded positively to the *netCanvas* platform. Across both open-ended responses and multiple scales of usability, the results show that users were happy with *netCanvas-R*, and especially with the act of laying out and interacting with networks. This suggests that a digital approach does not sacrifice user experience.

CONCLUSIONS

In this paper we describe both a general framework for collecting data on touchscreens termed *netCanvas*, which takes inspiration from paper-based techniques as well as from social network visualization frameworks, and an instantiation of this framework using a protocol tested in the field (*netCanvas-R*). This testing allows us to assess the general claim that touchscreen data collection can now be as reliable and far more efficient than paper based methods.

Because of the need for specific and highly sensitive social data unable to be provided via trace information, tools such as *netCanvas-R* are necessary to facilitate individual data capture. These tools hold a special interest for health and infectious disease researchers, who until now have been limited due to the high participant and researcher burden involved in network capture.

Although in [23] the authors indicated reluctance to use digital tools because of their potential inflexibility, *netCanvas-R* has demonstrated strong success in a large study of the health of a high-risk community. By making use of recent technological advancements and building upon valid participant-aided analog techniques, *netCanvas-R* has been able to strongly improve the capture and management of individual network data. The tool we have designed is able to capture complex multilayered social, sexual, and drug use networks. We find that our technique not only captures equivalent data more efficiently than analog techniques, but provides remarkably high levels of user satisfaction. When conducting clinical research studies, particularly longitudinal research with vulnerable populations, high respondent satisfaction and ease of use are essential to ensure participant retention and the capture of high quality data. Therefore, the prior aphorism of "keep high technology in the lab and low technology in the field"[23] be updated to "keep complexity in the lab and simplicity in the field".

Given the sensitivity of the data collection and the complexity of designing the instrument, it was not possible to directly compare the *netCanvas-R* protocol to other digital approaches. That said, none of the computer-assisted approaches reviewed have incorporated HCI research as thoroughly, nor are they designed to meet the complex requirements we noted such as the importing of longitudinal data, multiplex edges, skip-flow logic with multiple dependencies, and storage of the data within a graph database.

While there are many benefits to the current tool, some limitations still exist. For example, despite the successes demonstrated in this analysis, it must be emphasized that *netCanvas-R* is only a tool and does not substitute for strong interviewer training. For example, netCanvas does not limit the number of nodes one can create. Thus, without interviewer intervention adding more than fifty leads to a very cramped interface. We cannot claim *netCanvas-R* will be as successful in a self-administered setting. Additionally, as of yet there is no easy method for researchers to construct surveys using the *netCanvas* framework without being well versed in HTML5 and JavaScript. However, this team is actively pursuing the development of a survey-building wizard for the development of future protocols. Finally, it must be noted that the *netCanvas-R* protocol exports a notably complex nested JSON file that still must be parsed to be inserted into a Neo4j database or other similar graph structure. Yet, the complexity of data management is hidden from the user. By keeping the design of the interface straightforward and linear, we have been able to capture complex network data with a simplified interface and high fidelity.

The *netCanvas* framework and the *netCanvas-R* interview protocol represent a collaboration between a trans-disciplinary team that spans multiple academic disciplines and institutions. By merging technological advances in network visualization with prior participant-aided sociogram techniques, informed by the needs of a high-risk population, we demonstrate the validity, utility, and feasibility of complex data capture for personal social networks.

ACKNOWLEDGEMENTS

This work was supported by the National Institute on Drug Abuse and the National Institute of Allergy and Infectious Diseases of the National Institute of Health (U01DA036939, PI: Mustanski; R01DA025548-S1, PI: Mustanski; R03DA033906, PI: Birkett; K08DA037825, PI: Birkett; P30AI117943, PI: D'Aquila; P30AI117943-S1, PI: Phillips).

REFERENCES

1. Eytan Adar. 2006. GUESS: A Language and Interface for Graph Exploration. *Proceedings of the ACM Conference on Human Factors in Computing Systems (CHI 06)* (2006), 791800.
2. Centre for Disease Control and Prevention. 2015. Diagnoses of HIV Infection in the United States and Dependent Areas, 2011.HIV Surveillance Report, Volume 23. *HIV Surveillance Report* 25 (2015), 1–82. http://www.cdc.gov/hiv/library/reports/surveillance/2011/surveillance
3. Toni Antonucci. 1986. Measuring Social Support Networks: Hierarchical Mapping Technique. *Generations* 10 (1986), 10–12.
4. Colette L Auerswald, Eiko Sugano, Jonathan M Ellen, and Jeffrey D Klausner. 2006. Street-based STD testing and treatment of homeless youth are feasible, acceptable and effective. *Journal of Adolescent Health* 38, 3 (2006), 208–212.
5. Michelle Birkett, L. Kuhns, C. Latkin, S. Muth, and Brian S Mustanski. 2015a. The sexual networks of racially diverse young men who have sex with men. *Archives of Sexual Behavior* Forthcoming (2015).
6. Michelle Birkett, Lisa M Kuhns, Brian S Mustanski, and Stephen Q Muth. 2015b. The creation and analysis of a macro-network of young men who have sex with men. In *35th International Sunbelt Social Networks Conference [SUNBELT '16]*. Brighton, UK.
7. Stephen P Borgatti, Martin G Everett, and Jeffrey C Johnson. 2013. *Analyzing social networks*. SAGE Publications Limited, Thousand Oaks, CA.
8. Stephen P Borgatti, Ajay Mehra, Daniel J Brass, and Giuseppe Labianca. 2009. Network analysis in the social sciences. *Science (New York, N.Y.)* 323, 5916 (2009), 892–895. DOI: http://dx.doi.org/10.1126/science.1165821
9. John Brooke. 1996. SUS-A quick and dirty usability scale. *Usability evaluation in industry* 189, 194 (1996), 4–7.
10. Ronald Burt. 1984. Network Items and the General Social Survey. *Social Networks* 6, 4 (1984), 293–339.
11. William Buxton, Ralph Hill, and Peter Rowley. 1985. Issues and techniques in touch-sensitive tablet input. *ACM SIGGRAPH Computer Graphics* 19, 3 (1985), 215–224.
12. Juan Carrasco, Bernie Hogan, Barry Wellman, and Eric Miller. 2008. Collecting social network data to study social activity-travel behavior: An egocentered approach. *Environment and Planning B* 35, 6 (2008), 961–980. DOI: http://dx.doi.org/10.1068/b3317t
13. Andre Charland and Brian Leroux. 2011. Mobile application development: web vs. native. *Commun. ACM* 54, 5 (2011), 49–53.
14. Jacob Cohen. 1992. Statistical power analysis. *Current directions in psychological science* 1, 3 (1992), 98–101.
15. Nick Crossley, Elisa Bellotti, Gemma Edwards, Martin G Everett, Johan Koskinen, and Mark Tranmer. 2015. *Social Network Analysis for Ego-Nets: Social Network Analysis for Actor-Centred Networks*. Sage Publications, London, UK.
16. Don A Dillman. 2011. *Mail and Internet surveys: The tailored design method–2007 Update with new Internet, visual, and mixed-mode guide*. John Wiley & Sons.
17. Claude S Fischer. 1982. *To Dwell among Friends: Personal Networks in Town and City* (1 ed.). University Of Chicago Press. 459 pages.
18. Clifton Forlines, Daniel Wigdor, Chia Shen, and Ravin Balakrishnan. 2007. Direct-touch vs. mouse input for tabletop displays. *Proceedings of the SIGCHI conference on Human factors in computing systems - CHI '07* (2007), 647–656. DOI: http://dx.doi.org/10.1145/1240624.1240726
19. Linton C Freeman. 2000. Visualizing Social Networks. *Journal of Social Structure* 1, 1 (2000), 1–20.
20. Linton C Freeman. 2004. *The Development of Social Network Analysis: A Study in the Sociology of Science*. Empirical Press, Vancouver, BC.
21. Markus Gamper, Michael Schönhuth, and Michael Kronenwett. 2012. Social Networking and Community Behavior Modeling : Qualitative and Quantitative Measures. In *Social Networking and Community Behavior Modeling : Qualitative and Quantitative Measures*, Maytham Safar and Khaled A. Madhi (Eds.). IGI Global, Hershey, PA, 193–213.
22. Jeffrey Heer, Stuart K Card, and James A Landay. 2005. Prefuse: a toolkit for interactive information visualization. In *Proceedings of the SIGCHI conference on Human factors in computing systems*. ACM, 421–430.
23. Bernie Hogan, Juan Carrasco, and Barry Wellman. 2007. Visualizing Personal Networks: Working with Participant Aided Sociograms. *Field Methods* 19, 2 (2007), 116–144.
24. Grace YoungJoo Jeon, Nicole B. Ellison, Bernie Hogan, and Christine Greenhow. 2016. First-Generation Students and College: The Role of Facebook Networks as Information Sources. In *Proceedings of the 2016 ACM Conference on Computer-Supported Cooperative Work and Social Computing [CSCW '16]*. San Francisco, CA.
25. Blair T Johnson, Colleen A Redding, Ralph J DiClemente, Brian S Mustanski, Brian Dodge, Paschal Sheeran, Michelle R Warren, Rick S Zimmerman, William A Fisher, Mark T Conner, and Others. 2010. A network-individual-resource model for HIV prevention. *AIDS and Behavior* 14, 2 (2010), 204–221.
26. Lisa M Kuhns, Michelle Birkett, Brian Mustanski, S. Q. Muth, C. Latkin, I. Ortiz-Estes, and R. Garofalo. 2015. Methods for Collection of Participant-aided Sociograms for the Study of Social , Sexual and Substance-using Networks Among Young Men Who Have Sex with Men. *Connections* 35, 1 (2015). DOI: http://dx.doi.org/10.17266/35.1.1

27. Carl A Latkin, Danielle German, David Vlahov, and Sandro Galea. 2013. Neighborhoods and HIV: a social ecological approach to prevention and care. *American Psychologist* 68, 4 (2013), 210.

28. C A Latkin and A R Knowlton. 2005. Micro-social structural approaches to HIV prevention: a social ecological perspective. *AIDS Care* 17, S1 (2005), 102–113.

29. E.O. Laumann, J. Galaskiewicz, and P.V. Marsden. 1978. Community structure as interorganizational linkages. *Annual Review of Sociology* 4 (1978), 455–484. http://www.jstor.org/stable/2945978

30. Christopher McCarty and Sama Govindaramanujam. 2005. A Modified Elicitation of Personal Networks Using Dynamic Visualization. *Connections* 26, 2 (2005), 61–69.

31. Tyler H. McCormick, Matthew J. Salganik, and Tian Zheng. 2010. How Many People Do You Know?: Efficiently Estimating Personal Network Size. *J. Amer. Statist. Assoc.* 105, 489 (mar 2010), 59–70. DOI: http://dx.doi.org/10.1198/jasa.2009.ap08518

32. Joanna Mcgrenere, Ronald M Baecker, and Kellogg S Booth. 2002. An evaluation of a multiple interface design solution for bloated software. *Chi '02* (2002), 164–170. DOI:http://dx.doi.org/{http://doi.acm.org/10.1145/503376.503406{\protect\T1\textbraceright},acmid={\protect\T1\textbraceleft}503406}

33. J Miller McPherson, Lynn Smith-Lovin, and Matthew Brashears. 2006. Changes in Core Discussion Networks over Two Decades. *American Sociological Review* 71, 3 (2006), 353–375.

34. Brian Mustanski, Tyrel Starks, and Michael E Newcomb. 2014. Methods for the design and analysis of relationship and partner effects on sexual health. *Archives of sexual behavior* 43, 1 (2014), 21–33.

35. Ray Pahl and Liz Spencer. 2004. Capturing Personal Communities. In *Social Networks and Social Exclusion*, Chris Phillipson, Graham Allan, and David Morgan (Eds.). Ashgate, Aldershot, UK, 72–96.

36. John J Potterat, Richard B Rothenberg, and Steven Q Muth. 1999. Network structural dynamics and infectious disease propagation. *International journal of STD & AIDS* 10, 3 (1999), 182–185.

37. J J Potterat, D E Woodhouse, S Q Muth, R Rothenberg, W W Darrow, A S Klovdahl, and J B Muth. 2004. Network dynamism: history and lessons of the Colorado Springs study. *Network epidemiology: a handbook for survey design and data collection* (2004), 87–114.

38. Joseph Prejean, Ruiguang Song, Angela Hernandez, Rebecca Ziebell, Timothy Green, Frances Walker, Lillian S Lin, Qian An, Jonathan Mermin, Amy Lansky, H Irene Hall, and for the HIV Incidence Surveillance Group. 2011. Estimated HIV Incidence in the United States, 2006–2009. *PLoS ONE* 6, 8 (2011), e17502. DOI: http://dx.doi.org/10.1371/journal.pone.0017502

39. Harmony Rhoades, Suzanne L. Wenzel, Daniela Golinelli, Joan S. Tucker, David P. Kennedy, Harold D. Green, and Annie Zhou. 2011. The social context of homeless men's substance use. *Drug and Alcohol Dependence* 118, 2-3 (2011), 320–325. DOI: http://dx.doi.org/10.1016/j.drugalcdep.2011.04.011

40. Richard Rothenberg, Julie Baldwin, Robert Trotter, and Stephen Q Muth. 2001. The risk environment for HIV transmission: Results from the Atlanta and Flagstaff network studies. *Journal of Urban Health* 78, 3 (2001), 419–432.

41. Ben Shneiderman and Catherine Plaisant. 2003. *Designing the user interface* (fifth ed.). Pearson Education, Boston.

42. Charles D Stolper, Florian Foerster, Minsuk Kahng, Zhiyuan Lin, Aakash Goel, John Stasko, and Duen Horng Chau. 2014. GLOs: graph-level operations for exploratory network visualization. In *CHI'14 Extended Abstracts on Human Factors in Computing Systems*. ACM, 1375–1380.

43. Paola Tubaro, Antonio. A. Casilli, and Lise Mounier. 2014. Eliciting Personal Network Data in Web Surveys through Participant-generated Sociograms. *Field Methods* 26, 2 (2014), 107–125. DOI: http://dx.doi.org/10.1177/1525822X13491861

44. Edward R Tufte and P R Graves-Morris. 1983. *The visual display of quantitative information*. Vol. 2. Graphics press Cheshire, CT.

45. Barry Wellman. 1979. The Community Question: The Intimate Networks of East Yorkers. *Amer. J. Sociology* 84, 5 (1979), 1201–1233.

Learn Piano with BACh: An Adaptive Learning Interface that Adjusts Task Difficulty based on Brain State

Beste F Yuksel [1], Kurt B Oleson [1], Lane Harrison [1,2], Evan M Peck [3], Daniel Afergan [1,4], Remco Chang [1] and Robert JK Jacob [1]
[1]Department of Computer Science, Tufts University, Medford, MA
[2]Department of Computer Science, Worcester Polytechnic Institute, Worcester, MA
[3]Department of Computer Science, Bucknell University, Lewisburg, PA
[4]Google Inc., Mountain View, CA
{beste.yuksel, kurt.oleson}@tufts.edu, ltharrison@wpi.edu, emp017@bucknell.edu, afergan@google.com, {remco, jacob}@cs.tufts.edu

ABSTRACT
We present Brain Automated Chorales (BACh), an adaptive brain-computer system that dynamically increases the levels of difficulty in a musical learning task based on pianists' cognitive workload measured by functional near-infrared spectroscopy. As users' cognitive workload fell below a certain threshold, suggesting that they had mastered the material and could handle more cognitive information, BACh automatically increased the difficulty of the learning task. We found that learners played with significantly increased accuracy and speed in the brain-based adaptive task compared to our control condition. Participant feedback indicated that they felt they learned better with BACh and they liked the timings of the level changes. The underlying premise of BACh can be applied to learning situations where a task can be broken down into increasing levels of difficulty.

ACM Classification Keywords
H.5.m. Information Interfaces and Presentation : Misc.

Author Keywords
Learning; Brain-Computer Interface (BCI); functional Near Infrared Spectroscopy (fNIRS); Adaptive; Cognitive Workload; Music; Piano

INTRODUCTION
Good teachers, whether they realize it or not, often guide their students into the *zone of proximal development*. That is, they help their students fulfill a learning potential with guidance that the students could not have reached by themselves [51]. However, this is not always an easy task as learning is a complex activity affected by factors such as difficulty of the task to be learned, learner cognitive ability, instructional design, and learner motivation.

Intelligent tutoring systems (ITS) and other computer-based education (CBE) systems have been developed in the last decades to aid this learning process. There have been promising results; meta-analyses revealed that students tend to learn faster and more accurately, and have increased enjoyment of their learning material [27].

Cognitive learning theory (CLT) plays an important role in the designing of instructional learning material and systems. It is based on idea that there is only a finite capacity for working memory available [39, 46] so designers of learning material should avoid overloading students. One approach has been to present learners with tasks of increasing difficulty. Interestingly, meta-analyses have revealed that this is only helpful if the levels of difficulty are increased *adaptively* to learners [52, 53].

Adaptive, interactive learning tasks generally tend to use a mixture of performance and cognitive workload of learners measured by self-reporting on a one-item scale (e.g. [40]). While these studies have made progress one factor is repeatedly highlighted as the weak link in CLT studies and learning studies in general: the measurement of cognitive workload [10, 31, 24, 7]. An adaptive learning system that could adjust task difficulty based on the learner's actual cognitive state, rather than their task performance, would address this issue.

Brain sensing using functional near-infrared spectroscopy (fNIRS) has recently been demonstrated by HCI researchers to measure user cognitive workload in adaptive systems [4, 44, 1] and is resilient to subject movement as might be seen while playing a piano [43]. In this paper, we use brain sensing as the *determining factor* in a learning task by increasing task difficulty adaptively when the learner's cognitive workload falls below a certain threshold, demonstrating that they can handle more information.

We present **Brain Automated Chorales (BACh)**, an adaptive musical learning system that helps users learn to play Bach chorales on the piano by increasing the difficulty of the practice sessions based on cognitive workload using brain sensing. BACh aims to guide learners into the zone of proximal development by measuring when they can cognitively handle

CHI'16, May 7–12, 2016, San Jose, CA, USA.

ACM 978-1-4503-3362-7/16/05$15.00
DOI: http://dx.doi.org/10.1145/2858036.2858388

more information and providing them with the next stage of learning at the right moment.

We use a musical task on the piano keyboard because it lends itself well to task segmentation with increasing levels of difficulty and to high element interactivity due to concurrency. A musical task is also easy to evaluate in terms of accuracy and speed when compared with a control condition. Research has shown that cognitive workload can indeed be measured with fNIRS brain sensing while playing the piano [55].

By analyzing performance data, we found that participants played the pieces faster and with increased accuracy when using our BACh system compared to how they would normally learn a piece of music. Participants also subjectively reported that they played the pieces better, and liked the timings of the level changes.

Thus, the contributions of this paper are as follows:

1. Build an adaptive, interactive musical learning system, BACh, that uses objective measurement of cognitive workload to dynamically increase difficulty levels of Bach chorales.
2. Demonstrate that users could play the musical pieces faster and with more accuracy using BACh than a control condition.
3. Demonstrate through questionnaire and interview data that participants felt they learnt the pieces better with BACh and they liked timings of the level changes.

RELATED WORK

Computer-Based Education

Computer-based education (CBE) is a generic term that is frequently used to encompass a broad spectrum of interactive, adaptive computer applications used in teaching [21]. We will use the term CBE as the broadest umbrella term in this paper, covering all methods of computer aided pedagogy.

A more specific sub-set of computer applications used in teaching is covered by the term intelligent tutoring systems (ITS). These systems are delineated by having knowledge of: (a) *the domain* by having the expert model for the subject, (b)*the student* and following their progress, (c) *tutor model* by making teaching choices based on the student and the material or (d) *user interface model* to tie all models together [33, 32].

CBE has shown that students tend to learn more, take around 30% less time and have increased enjoyment of their subject [27]. This results in students feeling more successful leading to greater motivation to learn and increased self-confidence [6].

In this paper, we develop BACh, based on measuring and adapting to learners' cognitive workload using brain sensing, under the broad category of CBE. We do not profess to our system meeting all the requirements of the definition of an ITS, instead, however, we think that our system can certainly bring benefits to the field of ITS by providing knowledge about the learner that can sway an ITS's teaching choices.

We now discuss the foundations of cognitive load theory and how this fits into our system.

Finite Cognitive Workload and Learning

The fundamental idea behind both Baddeley's working memory model [39] and CLT [46] is that cognitive workload is limited in its capacity to handle information. CLT applies this finite, limited cognitive capacity of working memory to instructional design in order to minimize any unnecessary burdens on working memory and maximize the formation of automated schemas in long-term memory (i.e. learning).

The degree of element interactivity is seen to be the most important characteristic that determines the complexity of learning material. CLT says that an expert differs from a novice because they have previously acquired schemata that have built complex elements into fewer elements. In the example of a pianist, a skilled musician can cognitively group together notes to form chords in their schemata, whereas a beginner has to process each note individually, suggesting that the beginner will have a higher cognitive workload while learning the same piece as the skilled pianist.

Part-task approaches have been investigated to generate instructional design that does not overload the learner. However, artificially reducing cognitive workload by making the learning material easier also reduces understanding therefore it is important to know when to integrate all the parts that have been learned separately. Meta-analyses have found part-task training is only helpful with sequential material, such as playing sequential notes on a piano (e.g. [3]), rather than concurrent tasks, such as playing two hands on a piano at the same time [52, 53]. The missing element in part-task training strategies for this type of learning task is thought to be the opportunity to practice time-sharing skills [9, 53, 52] to allow for the multitask fluency. However, it has been found that increasing-difficulty task *were* helpful if the tasks adapted to the learners individually and not with fixed scheduling [52].

These findings highlight the importance of adaptive learning tasks, especially when using increasing-difficulty strategies. In order for increasing-difficulty training to be adaptive, there has to be some measurement of when the user is ready to move on to the next level of difficulty.

Measurement of Cognitive Workload in Learning Studies

The method of cognitive workload measurement in learning studies have come under criticism and scrutiny in recent years [7, 10, 31, 24]. Moreno [31] has stated that "insufficient attention has been given to the rigorous development of [cognitive load] measures".

Cognitive workload in CLT studies have typically been measured in one of three ways: self-reporting, secondary-task methodology, and physiological measures.

The most frequently used measure is the self-reporting questionnaire created by [35]. De Jong [10] and Moreno [31] raise several issues with the scale's sensitivity, reliability and validity in measuring cognitive workload. Firstly, it is not a direct measurement of cognitive workload, it is measured, instead by interpretation of post-tests [10]. The need for direct measurement of cognitive workload has been highlighted [30]. In fact, more objective measures of cognitive workload using brain sensing have shown discrepancies between self-reported levels and brain activation levels [19].

Another important factor is the timing of the questionnaires, which varies across studies [10]. Many studies only present the questionnaire after learning has taken place, so it is not clear if learners provide an average estimate for the whole task, and it leaves reports open to memory and consciousness effects. However, cognitive workload is a dynamic measure that fluctuates during a learning task [54].

A second method used to measure cognitive workload in CLT studies has been the use of secondary-task or dual-task measures (e.g. [45, 7]). An important disadvantage to this methodology is that the secondary task can interfere considerably with the primary task, especially if the primary task is complex and requires much of the learner's limited cognitive capacity [34, 7]. Furthermore, Brunken et al. [7] points out that the sensory modality of the dual tasks will affect the outcome. According to Baddeley's working memory model [39] different components of working memory use different sensory inputs. However, the different components are not completely independent and still affect each other.

Another set of methods that have been used to measure cognitive workload in learning studies are physiological measures. However, most physiological measures of cognitive workload have only been analyzed offline. This misses the advantage that physiological measures provide which is the continuous availability of data which is especially important for adaptive tasks that can react to learners' needs in real-time.

Heart rate variability (HRV) and electrodermal activity (EDA) (previously called galvanic skin response (GSR)) have been shown to be affected cognitive workload [14, 28, 41]. However, changes physiological measures such as HRV and EDA can also be mapped to other phenomenon [12] such as changes in emotional state. Task-evoked pupillary responses (TEPRs) have also been associated with changes in cognitive workload [49, 20]. However, pupil size is sensitive to a number of factors that are not relative to cognitive workload such as the ambient light in the environment [42].

Brain sensing or neuro-imaging techniques have been discussed in many studies as a promising field for cognitive workload measurements during learning [34, 7, 42, 10]. Brain sensing provides a more direct measurement of the physiological changes occurring in the brain during higher cognitive workload and can be measured continuously which can be used as a real-time determinant in adaptive learning studies.

EEG has been shown to measure cognitive workload via changes in theta and alpha range signals (e.g. [18, 17, 16]). Szafir and Mutlu [48] monitored student attention with EEG and determined which lecture topic students would benefit from reviewing. Szafir and Mutlu (2012) [47] used EEG to detect and recapture dropping attention levels in real-time. They found this improved recall abilities. This is a rare example of how real-time adaptations can help learning using physiological sensing. Instead of measuring attention levels, however, in this paper we will be measuring user cognitive workload.

fNIRS and the Prefrontal Cortex

Functional magnetic resonance imaging (FMRI) and positron emission tomography (PET) studies have established that cognitive workload can be measured in the prefrontal cortex [11, 29]. More recently, brain imaging studies have examined changes in brain function associated with improvements in performance of tasks [15, 38, 5, 25]. Decreases in activation in the prefrontal cortex as users learn have also been found using functional near-infrared spectroscopy (fNIRS). FNIRS is non-invasive imaging technique that measures levels of activation in the brain due to the hemodynamic response. Increased activation in an area of the brain results in increased levels of oxyhemoglobin [13]. These changes can be measured by emitting frequencies of near-infrared light around 3 cm deep into the brain tissue [50] and measuring the light attenuation caused by levels of oxyhemoglobin.

We can therefore use fNIRS to measure levels of cognitive activation in the anterior prefrontal cortex (PFC) by placing sensors on the forehead. The PFC is seat of higher cognitive functioning such as complex problem solving and multitasking [26]. In this paper, we measure activation in the PFC with fNIRS to analyze and respond to differences in cognitive activity while users are engaged in a musical learning task.

The fNIRS signal has been found to be resilient to respiration, heartbeat, eye movement, minor head motion, and mouse and keyboard clicks [43]. It is generally more tolerant of motion than EEG and has a higher spatial resolution. However it does have a slower temporal resolution than EEG with a delay of 5-7 seconds due to the hemodynamic response of blood flow to the brain. Due to its general ease in setting up with users and its relative tolerance of minor motion, fNIRS is an increasingly popular method of brain sensing in the HCI community [43, 4, 44 36, 1, 2, 19].

Studies in HCI have successfully used fNIRS to measure and adapt to cognitive workload in real-time [44, 1, 2, 55]. Such studies have been aimed at increasing task efficiency [1, 2] and automation of systems [44, 55]. However, *real-time* monitoring of cognitive workload to act as determinant in a *learning* task has not yet been explored.

Harrison et al. [19] examined whether cognitive workload could be accurately monitored for incrementally changing task difficulty levels using fNIRS in an *offline analysis*. In an air traffic control simulation, they found oxygenation levels measured by fNIRS increased along with self-reports of increased cognitive workload as the number of aircrafts under operator control increased [19]. Interestingly, they also found a learning effect with lower levels of mean oxygenation values in the last two days compared to the first day [19]. However the authors did not measure task performance such as error rate or task length, so while it is assumed the operators were learning, there are no performance metrics to compare day differences in terms of learning effect. While their

Figure 1. fNIRS equipment and setup. A fNIRS sensor (top-left) that can be placed on the forehead and held in place with a headband (top-right). Experimental setup with participant wearing fNIRS playing at piano keyboard (bottom). The Imagent is visible on the right.

study illustrates the possibility of using fNIRS as a measurement device for cognitive workload during an increasingly difficult air traffic control task, it does not use this signal for the purposes of adaptive learning.

In this paper, we use fNIRS to measure learners' cognitive workload and adapt in real-time to increase levels of difficulty in a musical learning task.

EXPERIMENTAL DESIGN

Sixteen participants (8 female, mean age of 21, SD of 2.4) took part in a within-subject design. All participants first undertook a *training task* where they played 15 easy and 15 hard pieces on the piano. Each piece was 30 seconds long with a 30-second rest between each piece.

After completion of the training task participants received a break and then moved onto the *learning task*. During the learning task, each participant learned two Bach chorales. They had 15 minutes to learn each chorale. One chorale was presented in normal form and participants were instructed to learn the piece the way they normally would. The other chorale was presented with our adaptive interface BACh. The order of the conditions alternated between participants. At the end of the allotted learning time, participants were asked to play the piece once all the way through the best they could. Performance data from both conditions were recorded and evaluated based on the performance where they played the piece all the way through as best they could. Figure 1 shows the fNIRS equipment and experimental setup. Participants wore the fNIRS equipment throughout the entire experiment, including both the control and experimental conditions.

At the conclusion of the learning task, participants were given a questionnaire on how they felt they had learned the two pieces. We also gave participants a short interview on what they thought of the adaptations made by BACh.

All participants were compensated $20. While eleven out of 16 participants rated themselves as beginners, out of the remaining five who rated themselves as intermediate, 3 of them no longer played piano. The median time our participants had played piano was 3 years.

The details of the materials, tasks, and data analysis are given below.

EXPERIMENTAL SETUP

Equipment

We used a multichannel frequency domain Imagent fNIRS device from ISS Inc. (Champaign, IL) for our data acquisition. Two probes were placed on a participant's forehead to measure data from the two hemispheres of the prefrontal cortex. Each probe contains four light sources, each emitting near-infrared light at two wavelengths (690 and 830 nm) and one detector; thus we had sixteen data channels (2 probes x 4 source-detector pairs x 2 wavelengths). The source-detector distances ranged from 1.5 and 3.5 cm, and the sampling rate was 11.79 Hz. The signals were filtered for heart rate, respiration, and movement artifacts using a third-degree polynomial filter and low-pass elliptical filter.

Training Task

All participants carried out a training task so that BACh could classify their high and low cognitive workload. Participants were given 15 easy and 15 hard pieces of music that were chosen by a musicologist to play in random order on the piano. They were given 30 seconds to sight-read each piece (i.e. play a previously unseen piece) followed by a 30 second rest period. A metronome was played at the start of each piece for 4 seconds at a speed of 60 beats per minute. Participants were asked to try to play at this speed but told they could go slower if they needed to.

The criteria for the easy pieces were that a) all notes were in C major (i.e. no sharps or flats), b) there were only whole notes (very slow, long notes), c) there were no accidentals (i.e. no additional sharps, flats, or naturals that are not part of the scale), d) all notes were within the C to G range so that participants did not need to move their hands e) there were no dynamics (i.e. volume of a note or stylistic execution). The hard pieces were chosen by a musicologist and the criteria consisted of pieces that a) had a harder key signature (most pieces had a key signature of at least 3 sharps or flats), b) contained accidentals , c) contained mostly eighth and sixteenth notes (i.e. short, fast notes), d) required some moving of the hands but not too excessively, and e) contained dynamics.

Modeling Brain Data in the Training Task

The easy and hard musical pieces were used to train the system for each individual user's cognitive activity during low and high cognitive workload, respectively. During each piece, the system calculated the change in optical intensity compared to a baseline measurement for each of the sixteen channels. Markers sent at the beginning and end of each trial denoted the segments for each piece. The mean and linear regression slope were calculated for each 30 second trial for each channel resulting in 32 features (16 channels x 2 descriptive features). These features were inputted into LIBSVM, a support vector machine classification tool, with a linear kernel [1].

Learning Task

Music for Learning Task

For the learning task, we chose two Bach chorales. These chorales were chosen because of their similarity in style and difficulty. It is often hard to find two different pieces of music that can objectively said to be similar in level of difficulty. These two chorales, however, were composed using the principles of musical counterpoint. Counterpoint is a set of rules and guidelines that dictate how music can be composed. It is a relationship between the voices of a piece that is interdependent harmonically but independent in contour and rhythm. The two chorales we chose are standardized based on this principle. While they are different pieces of music, they ought to be highly similar in musical difficulty level. They also have an equal number of accidentals (sharps, flats or naturals in the score). Both pieces are the same length, and each has four voices bass, tenor, alto, and soprano. This allowed for an easy way to segment the music in the adaptive condition in order to progressively increase the difficulty. Due to experimental constraints and skill level of participants, the pieces were slightly altered. They were transposed into the same key (G Major) and the eighth notes were removed to maintain rhythmic consistency. We note that by removing some of the notes, some minor counterpoint rules are no longer met. However, the underlying structure and form of both pieces is still intact.

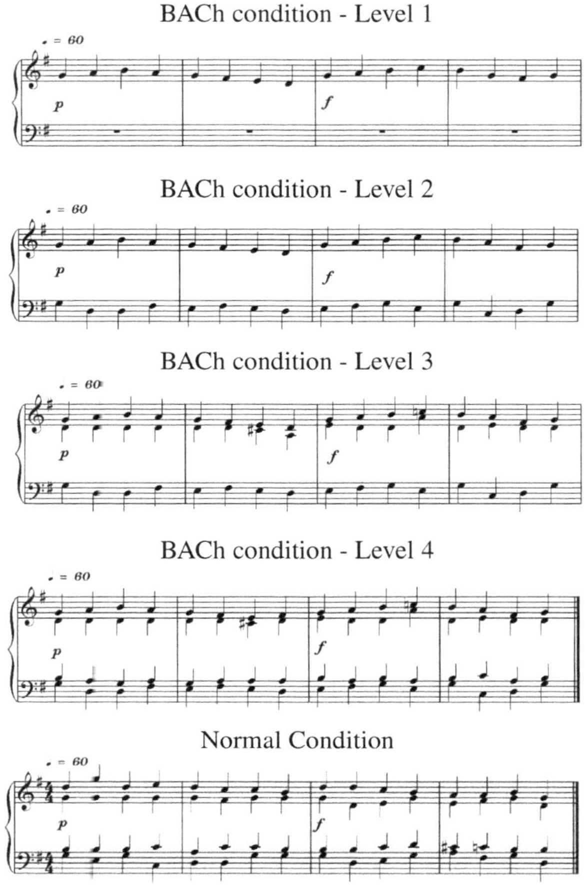

Figure 2. Scores used for BACh and Normal conditions. BACh increased the difficulty level by adding a full line of music when users' cognitive workload fell below a threshold, indicating that they could handle more information. Learners were told that they could learn the normal condition in any way they wished as they normally would. As a consequence, all learners segmented the pieces while they learnt during the normal condition.

Figure 2 shows the musical scores for the BACh and normal conditions. In the BACh condition, each level adds a full line of music until it reaches the full piece at Level 4. In the normal condition, learners were told they could learn the piece the way they normally would. Piano players are typically classically taught to play pieces first with their right hand, then their left hand, and finally both together. During that process, it is not uncommon for learners to play one line of the right or left hand, and add further lines as competency grows. As a result, all participants segmented the pieces while they learnt during the normal condition. Most participants started learning with their right hand only, one participant who was very good with his left hand started with his left hand first. Participants then incorporated the other hand as they progressed while learning. This can be viewed as akin to self-judgment of when to increase task complexity while learning.

MIDI Keyboard and Bitwig

Participants completed tasks on a full-sized Yamaha keyboard with weighted keys. The keyboard was transmitting MIDI data via USB to a computer running Bitwig studio, a digital audio workstation that allows for MIDI recording and playback as well as visual displays of recordings. Participants' musical data was recorded with this equipment for later analysis.

Learning Task Real Time Classification

BACh analyzed the last 30 seconds of real-time fNIRS data in order to calculate a prediction and confidence interval based on the LIBSVM model created by the training task. However, we found during pilot studies that this was not sensitive enough by itself for the varying levels of difficulty presented in BACh. We therefore used an algorithm that took in the LIBSVM model from the training task *and* learners' cognitive workload during each level of difficulty while they were learning the Bach chorales in order to decide when to increase task difficulty.

For each level of difficulty, we measured each learner's cognitive workload for a period of time determined by pilot studies. We started measuring their workload after they started playing *each line of the level that they were on*. For example, if the learner was on Level 3, we started measuring their cognitive workload after they were playing all 3 lines of music. We found that if we started measuring their cognitive workload earlier before the full level of difficulty, BACh would quite correctly think that they were ready to move on earlier as it was reading their cognitive workload for an easier difficulty level.

BACh would then set an individual threshold for each learner for each level based on a combination of brain data from the training task and brain data from the level that the learner was currently on. We ran many pilot studies to create an algorithm that worked for beginners.

EVALUATION OF DEPENDENT VARIABLES

Dependent Variables

We compared the following dependent variables between the BCI and control conditions:

- *Correct notes*: This is the number of correct notes on the musical score given to participants.
- *Incorrect notes*: When an incorrect note is played in the place of a correct note (Figure 3). This is a measure of precision or quality of learning.
- *Extra notes*: A note that is a correct repeat or incorrect extra note. This is different from an incorrect note. Often when learners make a mistake they will play the beat again to correct it, this will result in extra notes (see Figure 3) and is indicative of incomplete learning.
- *Errors*: A temporal group of notes that is a mistake which includes incorrect or extra notes. This is a more lenient measure as it differs from incorrect or extra notes which are counted individually. For example, a user could play several incorrect notes in one temporal group, this would be counted as one error (Figure 3).
- *Missed notes*: This measure is to account for recall (vs. precision which can be measured by the number of correct and incorrect notes). Some people may play very few notes and prioritize precision (i.e. a high number of correct notes out of total notes) but this would not be an accurate representation of learning. The number of missed notes (Figure 3) will account for recall and acts as a measure of completeness.
- *Total time played*: Learners had an unlimited length of time to play the piece once all the way through at the end. The total time it took to play the piece is a good indicator of how well they learned the piece by fast they could play it.
- *Gap between notes*: This is an indicator of well a piece is learned by how long it takes to move from beat to beat. Incomplete learning often involves hesitation and variance between notes as learners try to move from one group of notes to the next.
- *Beats per minute (bpm)*: A faster tempo indicates increased learning as players can move with more ease from beat to beat. This is different from gap between notes which can illustrate greater variance while bpm shows overall speed.

Musical Assessment

The dependent variables total time played, gap between notes and bpm were assessed computationally from the performance data. The others had to be compared to the groundtruth by hand as participants all played at different speeds and score following is an open research problem and beyond the scope of this paper. An expert musician who had taught piano in the past rated participants' learning compared to the groundtruth piano rolls. Figure 3 shows piano rolls from an example of a participant's performance compared to a computer generated groundtruth of how the piece should be played. The figure shows how incorrect notes, missed notes, extra notes and errors were identified and counted.

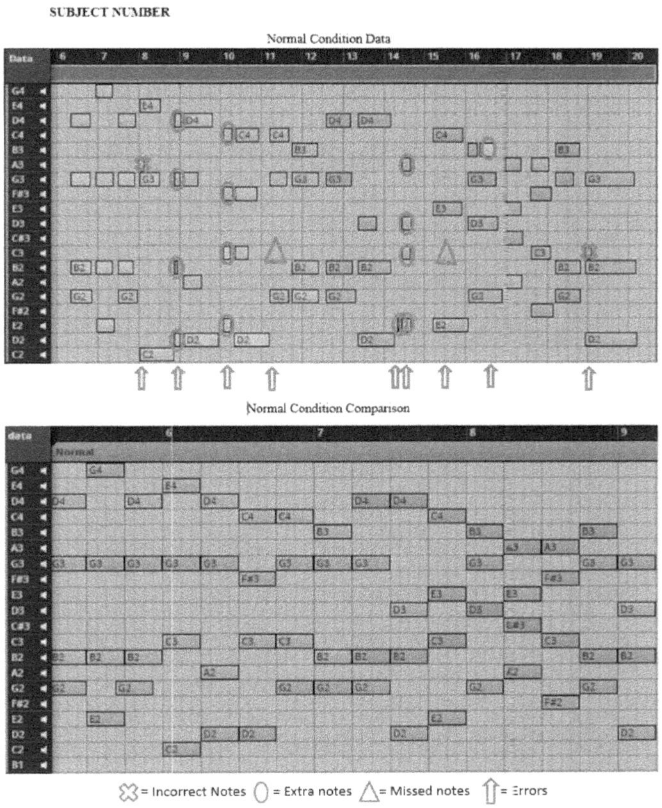

Figure 3. Examples of piano rolls from a participant's performance (top) compared with a computer generated groundtruth of the same piece (bottom). Incorrect notes are denoted by a cross, extra notes by a circle, and missed notes by a triangle. An error is a temporal group of notes and is denoted by an arrow pointing up at the column of notes containing an error.

RESULTS

fNIRS Data

We first verify that the brain data demonstrated effective classification of high and low cognitive workload while users played easy and hard pieces on the piano.

Figure 4 shows the mean and standard error in the oxygenated hemoglobin (oxy-Hb) of participants while they played easy (blue) versus hard (green) pieces on the piano. We present the mean findings across all participants across all 30 trials in Figure 4 to illustrate this general trend.

To investigate differences between hard and easy pieces, we performed a t-test on the mean change in oxygenated hemoglobin. This revealed a significant difference between conditions when participants played an easy piece ($\mu = -0.068, \sigma = 0.077$) versus a hard piece ($\mu = -0.00005, \sigma = 0.124$) on the piano ($t(29) = -2.42, p = .01$). Means and standard errors are shown in Figure 4.

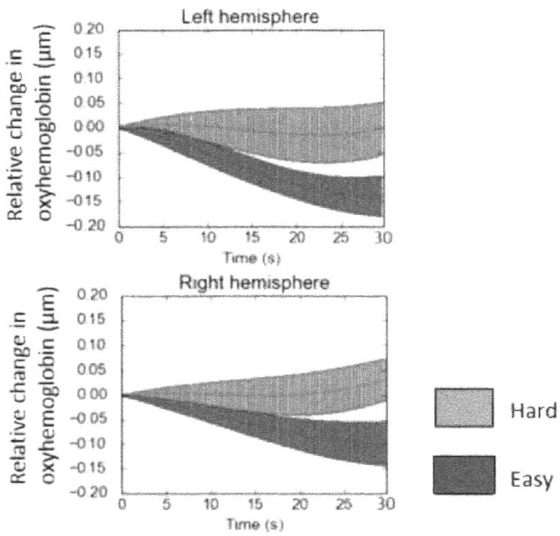

Figure 4. Mean change and standard error in oxy-Hb across all participants. Although each participant was modeled individually, the fNIRS signal exhibited a general trend with higher levels of oxy-Hb corresponding with hard pieces. The mean change in oxy-Hb was significantly higher in participants when they played an hard piece than an easy piece (p = .01).

The significantly higher levels of oxy-Hb when participants were playing harder pieces on the piano correspond with the hemodynamic literature, whereby, when there is increased cognitive activity in an area of the brain, excess oxygen is provided to that area. The increase in oxygen consumption is less than the volume of oxy-Hb provided, resulting in more oxy-Hb [13].

Performance Data

We evaluated the performance data of participants using several dependent variables (Table 1). We carried out Shapiro-Wilk tests that verifed that the data was non-parametric, followed by Wilcoxon Signed-rank tests on all dependent variables (Table 1).

Results indicated a pattern for two traits: 1) *Increased Accuracy*, and 2) *Faster speed* with BACh. We present the results below.

Increased Accuracy

Results showed that participants played significantly more correct notes ($Z = -1.9689, p = .05$), missed significantly fewer notes ($Z = 2.3151, p = .019$), played significantly fewer incorrect notes ($Z = 2.4401, p = .015$) and made fewer errors ($Z = 3.0351, p = .004$) with BACh (Table 1). All of these findings are indicative of higher accuracy with BACh.

The first two graphs in Figure 5 represent the number of incorrect notes and number of errors for each participant. The upward sloping lines (blue) are indicative of better performance with BACh with fewer incorrect notes and errors. Downward sloping lines (green) indicate better performance in the normal condition. Horizontal lines that indicate equality are also indicated in green. Only three participants played fewer incorrect notes in the normal condition, and only one participant played fewer errors in the normal condition.

Dependent Variable	Z	p	effect size
Number of correct notes	-1.9689	**0.05202**	0.304
Number of incorrect notes	2.4401	**0.0153**	0.377
Number of missed notes	2.3151	**0.01911**	0.357
Number of errors	3.0351	**0.003793**	0.468
Number of extra notes	0.8796	0.3633	–
Total time played	2.5337	**0.009186**	0.391
Mean gap between notes	2.482	**0.01099**	0.383
Average BPM	-2.719	**0.00525**	0.419

Table 1. Results from Wilcoxon Signed-rank test. Significant results are highlighted in bold. Findings indicate a pattern for increased accuracy and speed in BACh over the normal condition.

Figure 5 reveals that players who are less skilled (i.e. play more incorrect notes or make more errors) tend to benefit more greatly from BACh with steeper slopes demonstrating that there was a larger difference between the two conditions.

Faster Speed

Results also showed a propensity towards faster playing speed with BACh. With BACh, participants had a faster overall time in the playing the whole piece ($Z = 2.5337, p = .009$), had a lower time in the mean gap between notes ($Z = 2.482, p = .01$), and had a higher beats per minute (bpm) speed ($Z = -2.719, p = .005$) than in the normal condition.

The last two graphs in Figure 5 represent the total time it took to play the whole piece and the mean time in between notes. The upward sloping lines (blue) are indicative of better performance with BACh with faster overall playing time and less time between notes. Downward sloping lines (green) indicate better performance in the normal condition. Horizontal lines that indicate equality are also indicated in green. Only three participants played a faster time in the normal condition and only one participant had less gaps between notes in the normal condition.

Taken together, these results suggest that BACh helps piano players to play with significantly higher accuracy and speed than the normal condition.

Questionnaire Data

Participants' subjective ratings correspond with their performance. Figure 6 shows that participants showed noticeable preferences for BACh in how well they felt they mastered the piece, how correctly they felt they played, and how easy they felt the piece was to learn.

Timings of Level Changes

One of the key contributions of this paper is a learning task where difficulty is increased based on participant cognitive workload falling below a certain threshold. We investigated the timing of these changes while users' were learning the pieces in further detail in two ways: 1) We interviewed participants and asked them what they thought of the changes in the levels of difficulty, and 2) We investigated the variance in timing data to see if there were individual differences in learning times. We present the results below.

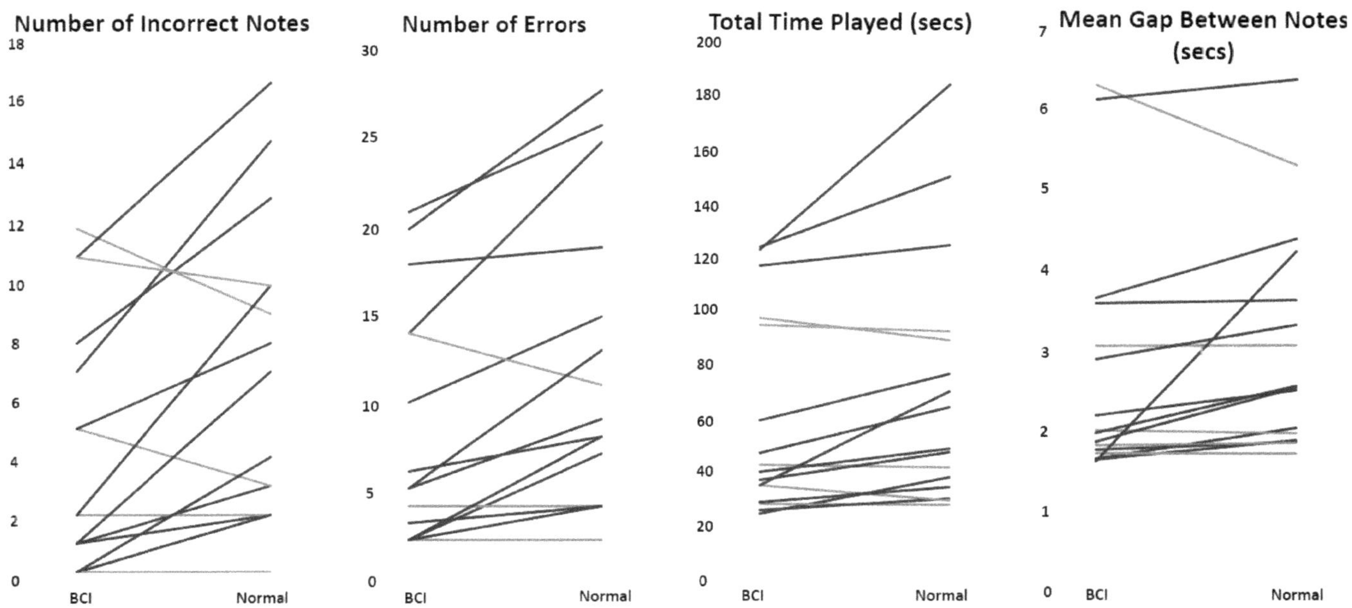

Figure 5. Slopegraphs showing the effects of BACh for each participant. Upward sloping lines (blue) are indicative of better performance with BACh. Downward sloping lines (green) indicate better performance in the normal condition. Horizontal lines that indicate equality are also indicated in green. Participants showed significantly better performance with BACh in all four conditions ($p < .01$). Interestingly, participants who were less skilled seemed to benefit more greatly from BACh.

Interview Data

After the experiment was over we gave participants a recorded interview where we asked them what they thought of the timing of the changes in difficulty levels. The goal of BACh was to change the level of difficulty at a time when the participants' cognitive workload was low enough to handle more information and a higher level of difficulty. When participants were asked about the timings of these changes, which were controlled entirely by the system, their feedback was generally positive:

> *"I thought it was good timings because by the time I learned, it gave me enough time to learn the individual lines, one by one."*

> *"I thought they were good times for changes, all of them."*

> *"Having a timing system can be jarring; you should only add new things when you know that the person has completed the existing part, but these timings were fine."*

One participant even seemed convinced that the experimenters were triggering the changes:

> *"I wasn't sure if you were controlling it or not because when it was added was a pretty appropriate time for me to add on to a part. Especially because in the beginning, one line, for me at least, is very easy to sight read so just getting that melody in my head and figuring out fingering for that one line and then adding on to it very quickly afterwards was helpful. I felt the timing was pretty good. I wasn't sure if it was timed or if you were like, oh she's done with this part, so add on to the second part."*

Such comments suggest that BACh was able to effectively support participants in their learning process by increasing difficulty levels when they were ready and able to handle more information. Some participants were not completely satisfied but in cases like these comments were similar to phrases like this:

> *"Sometimes I wouldn't notice it would change until I would look at the screen; it was a little confusing when I would look up. Yeah, it changed when I had learnt pretty much what I could learn before it changed; it was enough time to learn it."*

or

> *"I thought they [the timings] were pretty good. I think it seemed pretty good overall; the only thing would be the first one was a lot easier to learn because there was only one line, but it wasn't that bad."*

The comment about the levels changing without being noticed can be easily fixed with a small notification sound. The comment about the easiest level taking too long can also remedied by increasing the cognitive workload threshold when levels are very easy. Overall, there were no standalone or overtly negative comments about the timings of BACh. Participants seemed to feel the changes were happening at appropriate times, suggesting that we could help manage their cognitive workload as they were learning by altering the difficulty of a given stimulus.

Individual Differences in Level Changes

While participants spent less time on easier levels and longer lengths of time on levels with increasing difficulty, we did find individual differences in time spent *within* levels. The

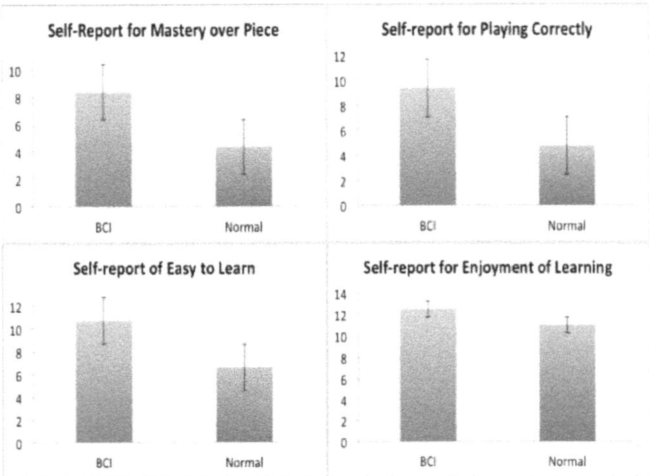

Figure 6. Mean and standard error of participants' ratings of BACh and the normal condition. Participants showed noticeable preferences for BACh in how well they felt they mastered the piece, how correctly they felt they played, and how easy they felt the piece was to learn.

length of time (in seconds) spent on level 1 (μ = 58.58, σ = 33.47), level 2 (μ = 185.60, σ = 64.62), level 3 (μ = 248.49, σ = 151.59), and level 4 (μ = 407.32, σ = 179.80) had high standard deviations, suggesting that BACh was responding to individuals' cognitive workload and learning abilities.

Figure 7 shows the variation in time within levels for each participant and the general pattern of longer time spent on more difficult levels.

DISCUSSION

We presented an adaptive brain-computer interface, BACh, that increases difficulty in a musical learning task when learners' cognitive workload fell below a certain threshold. We showed that BACh significantly increased speed and accuracy compared to a control condition where participants learned pieces the way they normally would. Participant feedback also demonstrated that they felt that they played better and it was easier to learn with BACh. Participants felt that the timings of the difficulty level changes were accurate. Results showed that while there was a general pattern of participants spending longer time on the more difficult levels, there was individual variation on time spent *within* levels, indicating that BACh was responding to individual differences.

We now discuss the challenges of modeling and adapting to learner cognitive workload using brain sensing and designing adaptations accordingly, the importance of responding to learners individually, and designing learning systems based on learner expertise.

Modeling and Adapting to Cognitive Workload

When designing BACh, we were extremely careful to first do no harm to the learning process. We did not want the adaptations made by BACh to impede or interrupt periods of learning in the user. We did this by avoiding disruptive adaptations during periods of cognitive workload that indicated possible learning.

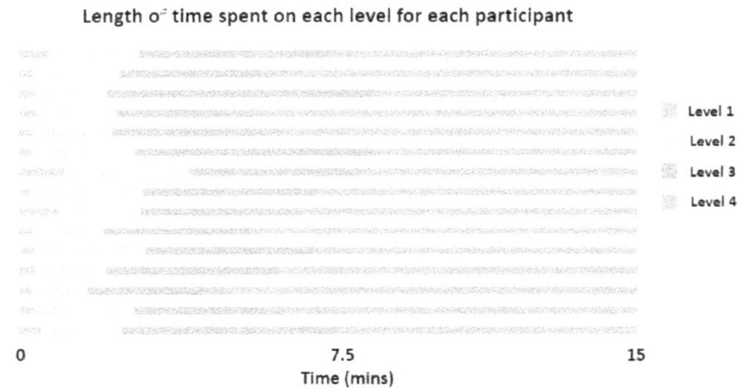

Figure 7. Length of time spent participants spent on each level of difficulty. While participants spent increasing lengths of time as level difficulty increased, there were individual variation within levels, suggesting that they system was responding to user cognitive workload for each participant individually.

One of the limitations of physiological computing is that of mapping from physiological signals to psychological states [12]. For example, if the fNIRS data signals that the learner's cognitive workload is high, this could be indicative of either a phase of learning where the user is being pushed cognitively in a constructive way, or it could indicate that the user is overloaded or overwhelmed and is not able to learn in that state.

We purposefully designed BACh not to interfere when learners' cognitive workload was high in order to avoid disrupting a period of possible learning. This is the reason why the adaptations never *decreased* the difficulty level during periods of high cognitive workload, as this could have proven both disruptive and frustrating to the learners. However, using high cognitive workload as the determining factor in adaptive learning systems would be a very interesting topic to investigate further. The discussion on whether high cognitive workload is 'good' or 'bad' during learning is still an open research problem. It may be that the solution lies in identifying learner emotion, or affect, in conjunction with cognitive workload, to reveal a higher dimensional mapping of the learner's state.

By examining the performance data and participant feedback, it seems that BACh was able to correctly respond to learner cognitive workload to improve playing speed and accuracy. This suggests that we were able to accurately model and adapt to learner cognitive workload in a learning task and guide learners into the zone of proximal development.

Responding to Learners Individually

BACh responds to each learner individually. In the early stages of development, BACh was originally designed to increase difficulty levels during learning when learners' cognitive workload fell below a *fixed percentage threshold*. Early studies showed us very quickly that this was not going to work. Each learner was very individual in their brain measurements, and what worked very well for some, would not even trigger a fixed percentage threshold for others. Furthermore, even if it worked well for one level, it certainly was not guaranteed that it would work for levels of varying difficulty.

Through a series of iterative design techniques, extensive participant feedback, and many pilot studies, we came to an algorithm that would assess learner cognitive workload using both the learner's brain data from the training task and brain data from the *current* level of difficulty that the learner was on to create a threshold for that individual on that level of difficulty.

While there is room for further improvement, our algorithm significantly increased learner speed and accuracy compared to how learners would normally learn a piece of music. Some of this individual responsiveness of BACh can be seen in the variation of the length of time taken by learners on each level. While there was a general pattern of longer periods of time spent on levels with increasing difficulty, there were still individual differences *within* each level. Individual differences in learning is a significant and complex topic and it is important for any CBE system to take it into account.

Expertise of Learners

Learning and CLT literature has explored a phenomenon called *the expertise reversal effect* whereby instructional techniques that are beneficial to beginners can have the reverse effects on more experienced learners [22, 23]. This difference between expert and novice is thought to be due to experts' previously acquired schemata that have built complex elements into fewer elements. In a task, the novice will have to use more of their limited working memory to access and process the individual elements than the expert, reflecting in the difference in skill.

Our results actually suggested that less skilled piano players benefited more from learning with BACh, as demonstrated by the steeper lines in Figure 5 for players who made more mistakes. BACh was designed for beginner piano players. We had originally recruited both beginner and intermediate piano players during our pilot studies, but quickly found that both the musical pieces and the algorithmic parameters of BACh were too easy and frustrating for intermediate players.

We foresee a similar system being of use to intermediate players with harder pieces to learn and different parameter settings for threshold changes. We can also see such a system being frustrating to even more advanced players who might prefer to learn their own way and have access to the whole piece from the beginning. We, therefore, simply suggest that our system is targeted at and useful for *beginner* piano players.

FUTURE WORK

This work takes a first step in using cognitive workload, measured by brain sensing, as a determining factor in a user interface for adaptive learning. While meta-analyses have shown that fixed scheduling when increasing task difficulty is not helpful [52, 53], now that we have sufficient data for the length of time participants spent on each level, we can also investigate and compare other conditions such as using random intervals to increase difficulty level based on means or ranges of the times spent on the different levels in this study.

We can also look at increasing task difficulty based on judgment from an expert such as a piano teacher or self-judgment from the player of when to move onto the next level. The latter is very similar to the normal condition in this paper as learners were encouraged to learn how they normally would. They therefore segmented the piece between the left and right hands and increased the complexity as their competency grew.

We are very enthusiastic about adding the detection of emotion to BACh. There has been much work carried out on the detection of emotion using physiological sensing and facial expression recognition in the field of affective computing for several decades [8]. Such measurements could be used in conjunction with fNIRS or other brain sensing devices that are relatively resilient to motion artifacts. Emotion and learning are very closely tied together [37], with frustration often preceding giving up. If a learning system could detect both cognitive workload *and* affective state, it could be very powerful learning tool indeed.

Lastly, we address the topic of generalizability to other fields of learning. There has been a wealth of learning literature on other subjects such as mathematics or electrical engineering. The underlying premise of BACh is to increase the level of difficulty in a task when cognitive workload falls below a certain threshold measured by brain sensing. This can be applied, or at least investigated, in any field where information can be presented in increasing steps of difficulty.

CONCLUSION

We presented a brain-computer interface, BACh, that measured cognitive workload using brain sensing and increased difficulty levels when learners' cognitive state indicated that they could handle more information. We showed that participants learned musical pieces with increased accuracy and could play with faster speed with BACh compared to a control where they learned the way they normally would. Participants also commented that they felt that they played better and they liked the timings of the changes. We also found individual variations in the time spent within each level of difficulty, suggesting that it is important for tutoring systems to respond to individual differences and needs.

We designed BACh for beginner piano players, however, the underlying premise of BACh can be applied to any learning situation for a complex task that can be broken down into steps of increasing difficulty. By using brain sensing, BACh is able to acquire an objective view into the learner's cognitive state and adjust the learning task to best guide the learner into the zone of proximal development.

ACKNOWLEDGMENTS

We thank Sergio Fantini and Angelo Sassaroli from the Biomedical Engineering Department at Tufts University for their expertise on the fNIRS technology; Erin Solovey from Drexel University for her expertise on processing the fNIRS signal; Kathleen Kuo and Paul Lehrman from the Music Engineering Program and Garth Griffin who is now graduated from the HCI Lab at Tufts University for their musical expertise; and Galen McQuillen from Harvard University for his expertise on pedagogy. We thank the National Science Foundation (grant nos. IIS-1065154, IIS-1218170) and Google Inc. for their support of this research.

REFERENCES

1. Daniel Afergan, Evan M. Peck, Erin T. Solovey, Andrew Jenkins, Samuel W. Hincks, Eli T. Brown, Remco Chang, and Robert J.K. Jacob. 2014a. Dynamic difficulty using brain metrics of workload. *Proceedings of the SIGCHI conference on Human Factors in Computing Systems* (2014), 3797–3806.
2. Daniel Afergan, Tomoki Shibata, Samuel W. Hincks, Evan M. Peck, Beste F. Yuksel, Remco Chang, and Robert J.K. Jacob. 2014b. Brain-Based Target Expansion. *Proc. UIST 2014* (2014).
3. Daniel W. Ash and Dennis H. Holding. 1990. Backward versus forward chaining in the acquisition of a keyboard skill. *Human Factors* 32 (1990), 139–146.
4. Hasan Ayaz, Patricia A Shewokis, Scott Bunce, Kurtulus Izzetoglu, Ben Willems, and Banu Onaral. 2012. Optical brain monitoring for operator training and mental workload assessment. *Neuroimage* 59, 1 (2012), 36–47.
5. Miriam H. Beauchamp, Alain Dagher, John A. D. Aston, and Julien. Doyon. 2003. Dynamic functional changes associated with cognitive skill learning of an adapted version of the Tower of London task. *NeuroImage* 20 (2003), 1649–1660. DOI: http://dx.doi.org/10.1016/j.neuroimage.2003.07.003
6. Ellen R. Bialo and Jay Sivin-Kachala. 1996. The effectiveness of technology in schools: A summary of recent research. (1996).
7. Roland Brünken, Jan L Plass, and Detlev Leutner. 2003. Direct Measurement of Cognitive Load in Multimedia Learning. *Educational Psychologist* 38, 1 (2003), 53–61. DOI: http://dx.doi.org/10.1207/S15326985EP3801_7
8. Rafael A. Calvo, Sidney D'Mello, Jonathan Gratch, and Arvid Kappas (Eds). 2014. *The Oxford Handbook of Affective Computing.* Oxford University Press, 2014.
9. Diane Damos and Christopher D. Wickens. 1980. The identification and transfer of time-sharing skills. *Acta Psychologica* 46 (1980), 15–39.
10. Ton de Jong. 2010. Cognitive load theory, educational research, and instructional design: Some food for thought. *Instructional Science* 38 (2010), 105–134. DOI: http://dx.doi.org/10.1007/s11251-009-9110-0
11. Mark D'Esposito, Bradley R. Postle, and Bart Rypma. 2000. Prefrontal cortical contributions to working memory: evidence from event-related fMRI studies. *Experimental brain research* 133, 1 (2000), 3–11. http://www.ncbi.nlm.nih.gov/pubmed/10933205
12. Stephen H. Fairclough. 2009. Fundamentals of physiological computing. *Interacting with Computers* 21, 1-2 (Jan. 2009), 133–145. DOI: http://dx.doi.org/10.1016/j.intcom.2008.10.011
13. Peter T Fox, Marcus E Raichle, Mark A Mintun, and Carmen Dence. 1988. Glucose During Focal Physiologic Neural Activity Nonoxidaive Consumption. *Science* 241 (1988), 462–464.
14. Tycho K. Fredericks, Sang D. Choi, Jason Hart, Steven E. Butt, and Anil Mital. 2005. An investigation of myocardial aerobic capacity as a measure of both physical and cognitive workloads. *International Journal of Industrial Ergonomics* 35 (2005), 1097–1107. DOI: http://dx.doi.org/10.1016/j.ergon.2005.06.002
15. Hugh Garavan, Dan Kelley, Allyson Rosen, Steve M. Rao, and Elliot A. Stein. 2000. Practice-related functional activation changes in a working memory task. *Microscopy research and technique* 51, 1 (2000), 54–63.
16. Alan Gevins, Michael E. Smith, Harrison Leong, Linda McEvoy Susan Whitfield, Robert Du, and Georgia Rush. 1998. Monitoring working memory load during computer-based tasks with EEG pattern recognition methods. *Human Factors: The Journal of the Human Factors and Ergonomics Society* 40, 1 (1998), 79–91.
17. Alan Gevins, Michael E. Smith, Linda McEvoy, and Daphne Yu. 1997. High-resolution EEG mapping of cortical activation related to working memory: Effects of task difficulty, type of processing, and practice. *Cerebral Cortex* 7 (1997), 374–385. DOI: http://dx.doi.org/10.1093/cercor/7.4.374
18. Alexander Gundel and Glenn F. Wilson. 1992. Topographical changes in the ongoing EEG related to the difficulty of mental tasks. *Brain topography* 5, 1 (1992), 17–25.
19. Joshua Harrison, Kurtulus Izzetoglu, Hasan Ayaz, Ben Willems, Sehchang Hah, Ulf Ahlstrom, Hyun Woo, Patricia Shewokis, Scott C. Bunce, and Banu Onaral. 2014. Cognitive workload and learning assessment during the implementation of a next-generation air traffic control technology using functional near-infrared spectroscopy. *IEEE Transactions on Human-Machine Systems* 44, 4 (2014), 429–440.
20. Shamsi T Iqbal, Xianjun Sam Zheng, and Brian P Bailey. 2004. Task-evoked pupillary response to mental workload in human-computer interaction. *Extended abstracts of the 2004 conference on Human factors and computing systems CHI 04* (2004), 1477. DOI: http://dx.doi.org/10.1145/985921.986094
21. Chen-Lin C. Kulik James A. Kulik and Robert L. Bangert-Drowns. 1985. Effectiveness of Computer-Based Education in Elementary schools. *Computers in Human Behavior* 1 (1985), 59–74.
22. Slava Kalyuga. 2003. The expertise reversal effect. *Educational psychologist* 38, 1 (2003), 23–31.
23. Slava Kalyuga. 2007. Expertise reversal effect and its implications for learner-tailored instruction. *Educational Psychology Review* 19, 4 (2007), 509–539.
24. Slava Kalyuga. 2011. Cognitive Load Theory: How Many Types of Load Does It Really Need? *Educational Psychology Review* 23 (2011), 1–19. DOI: http://dx.doi.org/10.1007/s10648-010-9150-7

25. Clare Kelly and Hugh Garavan. 2005. Human functional neuroimaging of brain changes associated with practice. *Cerebral Cortex* 15, August (2005), 1089–1102. DOI: http://dx.doi.org/10.1093/cercor/bhi005

26. Etienne Koechlin, Gianpaolo Basso, Pietro Pietrini, Seth Panzer, and Jordan Grafman. 1999. The role of the anterior prefrontal cortex in human cognition. *Nature* 399 (May 1999), 148–51. DOI: http://dx.doi.org/10.1038/20178

27. James A. Kulik. 1994. *Technology Assessment in Education and Training*. Eva Baker and Harold F. O'Neil Jr, Chapter Meta-analytic Studies of findings on computer-based instruction., 9–34.

28. Taija M M Lahtinen, Jukka P. Koskelo, Tomi Laitinen, and Tuomo K. Leino. 2007. Heart rate and performance during combat missions in a flight simulator. *Aviation Space and Environmental Medicine* 78, 4 (2007), 387–391.

29. Dara S. Manoach, Gottfried Schlaug, Bettina Siewert, David G. Darby, Benjamin M. Bly, Andrew Benfield, Robert R. Edelman, and Steven Warach. 1997. Prefrontal cortex fMRI signal changes are correlated with working memory load. *Neuroreport* 8, 2 (1997), 545–549. http://www.ncbi.nlm.nih.gov/pubmed/9080445

30. Richard E. Mayer. 2005. Cognitive theory of multimedia learning. (2005).

31. Roxana Moreno. 2010. Cognitive load theory: more food for thought. *Instructional Science* 38, November 2009 (2010), 135–141. DOI: http://dx.doi.org/10.1007/s11251-009-9122-9

32. Roger Nkambou, Riichiro Mizoguchi, and Jacqueline Bourdeau. 2010. Advances in intelligent tutoring systems. (2010).

33. Hyacinth S. Nwana. 1990. Intelligent tutoring systems: an overview. *Artificial Intelligence Review* 4, 4 (1990), 251–277. DOI: http://dx.doi.org/10.1007/BF00168958

34. Fred Paas, Juhani E. Tuovinen, Huib Tabbers, and Pascal W.M. Van Gerven. 2003. Cognitive load measurement as a means to advance cognitive load theory. *Educational psychologist* 38, 1 (2003), 63–71.

35. Fred G Paas. 1992. Training strategies for attaining transfer of problem-solving skill in statistics: A cognitive-load approach. *Journal of educational psychology* 84, 4 (1992), 429.

36. Evan M. Peck, Beste F. Yuksel, Alvitta Ottley, Rob J.K. Jacob, and Remco Chang. 2013. Using fNIRS Brain Sensing to Evaluate Information Visualization Interfaces. *Proceedings of the SIGCHI conference on Human Factors in Computing Systems* (2013), 473–482.

37. Rosalind Picard. 1997. *Affective computing* 252 (1997).

38. Russell A Poldrack. 2000. Imaging brain plasticity: conceptual and methodological issues a theoretical review. *Neuroimage* 12, 1 (2000), 1–13.

39. Grega Repovs and Alan Baddeley. 2006. The multi-component model of working memory: Explorations in experimental cognitive psychology. *Neuroscience* 139, 1 (2006), 5–21.

40. Ron J.C.M. Salden, Fred Paas, Nick J. Broers, and Jeroen J.G. van Merrinboer. 2004. Mental effort and performance as determinants for the dynamic selection of learning tasks in air traffic control training. *Instructional Science* 32, 1-2 (2004), 153–172.

41. Wolfgang Schnotz and Christian Kürschner. 2007. A eeconsideration of cognitive load theory. *Educational Psychology Review* 19 (2007), 469–508. DOI: http://dx.doi.org/10.1007/s10648-007-9053-4

42. Holger Schultheis and Anthony Jameson. 2004. Assessing cognitive load in adaptive hypermedia systems: Physiological and behavioral methods. *Lecture Notes in Computer Science (including subseries Lecture Notes in Artificial Intelligence and Lecture Notes in Bioinformatics)* 3137 (2004), 225–234. DOI: http://dx.doi.org/10.1007/b99480

43. Erin Treacy Solovey, Audrey Girouard, Krysta Chauncey, Leanne M Hirshfield, Angelo Sassaroli, Feng Zheng, Sergio Fantini, and Robert J K Jacob. 2009. Using fNIRS Brain Sensing in Realistic HCI Settings : Experiments and Guidelines. *Proc. UIST 2009* (2009).

44. Erin Treacy Solovey, Paul Schermerhorn, Matthias Scheutz, Angelo Sassaroli, Sergio Fantini, and Robert J K Jacob. 2012. Brainput : Enhancing Interactive Systems with Streaming fNIRS Brain Input. *Proceedings of the SIGCHI conference on Human Factors in Computing Systems* (2012).

45. John Sweller. 1988. Cognitive load during problem solving: Effects on learning. *Cognitive science* 12, 2 (1988), 257–285.

46. John Sweller. 1999. *Instructional Design in Technical Areas*. ACER Press.

47. Daniel Szafir and Bilge Mutlu. 2012. Pay attention!: designing adaptive agents that monitor and improve user engagement. In *Proceedings of the SIGCHI Conference on Human Factors in Computing Systems*. ACM, 11–20.

48. Daniel Szafir and Bilge Mutlu. 2013. ARTFul: adaptive review technology for flipped learning. In *Proceedings of the SIGCHI Conference on Human Factors in Computing Systems*. ACM, 1001–1010.

49. Pascal W M Van Gerven, Fred Paas, Jeroen J G Van Merriënboer, and Henk G. Schmidt. 2004. Memory load and the cognitive pupillary response in aging. *Psychophysiology* 41 (2004), 167–174. DOI: http://dx.doi.org/10.1111/j.1469-8986.2003.00148.x

50. Arno Villringer and Britton Chance. 1997. Non-invasive optical spectroscopy and imaging of human brain function. *Trends in Neurosciences* 20 (1997). http://www.ncbi.nlm.nih.gov/pubmed/9347608

51. Lev Vygotsky. 1978. Interaction between learning and development. *Mind and Society* (1978), 79–91.

52. Christopher D. Wickens, Shaun. Hutchins, Thomas. Carolan, and John. Cumming. 2013. Effectiveness of Part-Task Training and Increasing-Difficulty Training Strategies: A Meta-Analysis Approach. *Human Factors: The Journal of the Human Factors and Ergonomics Society* (2013). DOI: http://dx.doi.org/10.1177/0018720812451994

53. Dennis C. Wightman and Gavan Lintern. 1985. Part-Task Training for Tracking and manual control. *Human Factors* 27, 3 (1985), 267–283.

54. Bin Xie and Gavriel Salvendy. 2000. Prediction of mental workload in single and multiple task environments. *International journal of cognitive ergonomics* 4 (2000), 213–242.

55. Beste F. Yuksel, Daniel Afergan, Evan M. Peck, Garth Griffin, Lane Harrison, Nick Chen, Remco Chang, and Rob J.K. Jacob. 2015. BRAAHMS: A Novel Adaptive Musical Interface Based on Users' Cognitive State. *Proc. NIME 2015* (2015).

#Scanners: Exploring the Control of Adaptive Films using Brain-Computer Interaction

Matthew Pike [1,3], Richard Ramchurn [2], Steve Benford [1] and Max L. Wilson [1]

[1]The Mixed Reality Lab (MRL), University of Nottingham, Nottingham, UK

[2]Horizon Doctoral Training Centre, University of Nottingham, Nottingham, UK

[3]Department of Computer Science, University of Nottingham, Ningbo, China

[pike, richard.ramchurn, steve.benford, max.wilson]@nottingham.ac.uk

ABSTRACT

This paper explores the design space of bio-responsive entertainment, in this case using a film that responds to the brain and blink data of users. A film was created with four parallel channels of footage, where blinking and levels of attention and meditation, as recorded by a commercially available EEG device, affected which footage participants saw. As a performance-led piece of research in the wild, this experience, named #Scanners, was presented at a week long national exhibition in the UK. We examined the experiences of 35 viewers, and found that these forms of partially-involuntary control created engaging and enjoyable, but sometimes distracting, experiences. We translate our findings into a two-dimensional design space between the extent of voluntary control that a physiological measure can provide against the level of conscious awareness that the user has of that control. This highlights that novel design opportunities exist when deviating from these two-dimensions - when giving up conscious control and when abstracting the affect of control. Reflection on of how viewers negotiated this space during an experience reveals novel design tactics.

ACM Classification Keywords

H.5.m [Information Interfaces and Presentation] Miscellaneous

Author Keywords

Control; BCI; TV & Film; Interactive Multimedia.

INTRODUCTION

Building on research into Brain Computer Interfaces (BCI) [39], commercial products have been emerging into the mainstream as a new form of control; moving from research into affordable commercial products for the home[1]. BCI is increasingly being adopted by the entertainment industry [5] both as a tool to understand people's emotional experience [13] and now as a way of controlling emotionally engaging experiences [8, 9].

CHI'16, May 07 - 12, 2016, San Jose, CA, USA

ISBN 978-1-4503-3362-7/16/05. . . $15.00.
http://dx.doi.org/10.1145/2858036.2858276

While entertainment may benefit from BCI, it could also contribute to its development, offering ways of engaging mainstream audiences with the technology and contributing to our understanding of what can and cannot be controlled and how to design for the benefits and limitations of the new technologies. Against this broad backdrop, we report an exploration of using BCI to create an interactive entertainment experience. Following an exploratory 'Performance-led Research in the Wild' methodology [2], we worked with an artist to design and deliver a public experience that was then studied in-situ, qualitatively, in order to reveal wider issues and principles.

In this case the artist created an interactive film which is controlled by levels of Attention and Meditation (provided by a commercial Neurosky EEG[1]), and partially controlled by blinking. The Neurosky device suited this form of artistic installation due to it being minimally intrusive, quick and "dry" to set-up as well as being wireless. In the following sections, we document the artist's rationale behind the work and then report on how 35 people experienced the film when exhibited at a public arts venue. Our study reveals the different ways in which viewers experienced control through BCI, the various tactics they established, and how they experienced tensions between voluntary and involuntary control of the film, versus being aware of their own attempts to control it. We translate these findings into a two-dimensional design space, exploring partial control, that is - not fully understanding control and not thinking about control.

RELATED WORK

Two main areas of related work are pertinent to this project: 1) the interplay of BCI and film-based entertainment, and 2) work on understanding the locus of control within systems.

BCI and Film

Research into Brain Computer Interaction (BCI) typically focuses on one of three main threads: Active, Reactive, and Passive [46]. Active BCI research focuses on systems that try to directly interpret brain data into the active control of an interface. Yuksel et al, for example, interpreted EEG data to allow users to select objects on an interactive tabletop [44]. Reactive BCI focuses on systems that respond indirectly to user control, depending on the situation or external stimuli. Grierson, for example, created a musical instrument, where choice of musical note depended on the selective attention

[1] http://store.neurosky.com/products/mindwave-mobile

of the user [10]. Similarly, Yuksel et al presents a musical instrument that adapts implicitly to users' changing cognitive state during musical improvisation [43]. Zander et al further propose Passive BCI, in which a system autonomously monitors user's brain activity to take independent action, in this case creating a system that identified when users noticed a typing error [46].

As BCI is typically focused on a form of control, most application of BCI in entertainment has focused on interactive experiences like gaming [12]. Yoh et al, for example, created a EEG controller for a storyline-based Hanzel and Grettel game [42]. In a different form of interactive entertainment, Grierson, mentioned above, investigated BCI for control during the creation of music [10]. Very little work has focused on BCI in the context of typically passive entertainment experiences like film [4]. Hasson et al for example, used BCI to evaluate people's reactions to scenes [15], as a passive BCI evaluation of movies. Likewise, Im et al interpreted EEG data to analyse emotional response to film scenes [19]. Marchesi proposed a system that used EEG signals to create an selecting scene while editing a movie - a form of reactive control [25]. In the realm of active control, the BBC recently investigated BCI for control of their digital TV player [40], but their focus is on selecting shows to watch, rather than on experiencing the shows themselves. In this work, we explore a notion of using BCI to create control over a film, where film is typically static in concept and passively watched. The most closely related work to our own, was formative work by Hillard et al, who used neurofeedback to adapt a film experience within focus and attention training for people with ADHD [16].

Traditional control in HCI

It is a central tenet of usability that the locus of control shall remain with the user, to the extent that this is one of Shneiderman's eight golden rules [36]. Direct Manipulation, as a core principle that underpinned the design of graphical user interfaces of HCI, emphasises that, wherever possible, a user should be able to use an interaction that directly maps to what they are trying to achieve [37]. Using a mouse to move an object, for example, provides more direct manipulation over the object than entering desired x and y locations into text boxes. The consideration of Reactive and Active BCI above, however, highlights that HCI is also often concerned with monitoring or modelling the behaviour of users such that they do not have to exert direct control over something. Even in 1992, researchers like Rubine were considering mixing direct manipulation with reactive indirect gesture control [35].

One interesting thread of recent work has focused on forms of partial control that lie somewhere between direct and indirect. Nagashima, for example, investigated the use of biosensing techniques within media arts [30], whilst many others have used bio-feedback to control gaming, such as using heart rate in fitness games [27, 38], relaxation within a shooting game [31], and breathing rate to control the speed of amusement rides [26]. Marshall et al's breathing-controlled bucking bronco [26] directly utilised this limited amount of control; riders had to try to overcome their autonomically-controlled increasing breathing rate associated with the thrilling experience. Their paper further discusses the importance of surrendering control, a topic that also discussed in other areas, such as auto-piloted vehicles [22] and home automation for those observing the Jewish Sabbath [41].

Höök called this interplay between physiological response and physiological control an affect loop [17], in which a user is affected by a system, which is affected by the user, and so on. In this paper, we explore the notion of partial control and affect loops by creating and studying a film that responds to three forms of control: attention, meditation and blinking.

THE #SCANNERS FILM

We worked with an artist to create #Scanners, an interactive film that attempts to deliver a unique immersive viewing experience by having the composition and rhythms of the film match up to the viewers internal rhythms of thought and/or emotion. The artist's inspiration for the experience came from the work of S. Nishimoto et.al and Walter Murch. S. Nishimoto demonstrated the possibility of reconstructing visual experiences from brain activity evoked by natural films using an fMRI machine and advanced machine learning algorithms [32]. Walter Murch postulated that blinking is an automatic response that can reveal rhythms of thought and likens blinking to cuts in film [29]: *"If it is true that our rates and rhythms of blinking refer directly to the rhythm and sequence of our inner emotions and thoughts, then those rates and rhythms are insights to our inner selves and therefore as characteristic of each of us as our signatures."*. In addition to stating the role of blinking in expressing our inner emotions and thoughts, Murch also likens film to dream; thoughts to a shot; and a blink to a cut - a set of relationships we were interested in exploring with #Scanners. More recent research, published since #Scanners began, has directly linked blinking to 'changing scenes' within dreams [1], which is a concept that closely mirrors the experience that the artist envisaged.

Inspired by these ideas, our artist shot and edited an unusual film structure that consciously played with the notions of dreams and reality. The overall film ran for 16 minutes, progressing through 18 scenes. However, each scene was filmed as four distinct layers, two showing different views of the central protagonist's external Reality and the other two showing different views of their internal dream-world. The structure of 18 scenes in 4 layers is shown in Figure 1.

BCI control was then used to move the viewer back and forth between Reality and Dream as the film progressed and also to control the mix of the two layers within each of these. This utilised 3 predefined outputs from the Neurosky EEG device: 1) Blinking[2], 2) Attention and 3) Meditation. Beyond pre-product research [24], the suitability and accuracy of these outputs for HCI have been discussed by others [11, 23], however our research is not focused on these concerns, but on how adaptive multimedia might be controlled by commercially available tools, with the Neurosky being most suitable for the #Scanners experience.

These controls were mapped onto the film's structure as shown in Figure 2. Blinking triggers transitions between the Reality

[2]Whilst not a BCI measure, blinking can be detected by the device.

Figure 1: The #Scanners film shot as four layers synchronized through 18 scenes, with scene cuts aligned between layers

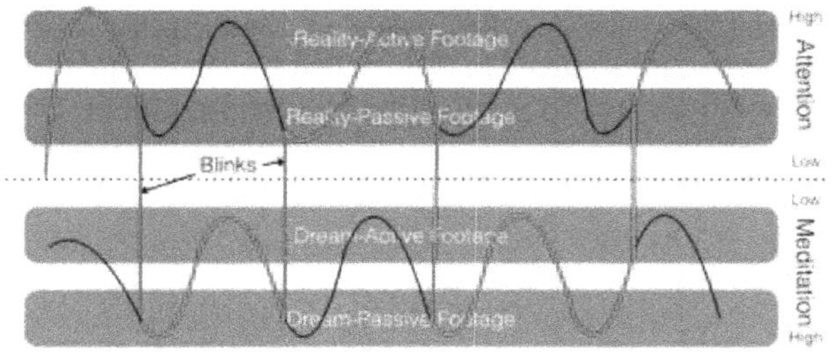

Figure 2: A #Scanners concept diagram, showing how a user moves between and within Dream and Reality layers.

Figure 3: A participant wearing the EEG device, experiencing #Scanners inside the caravan.

and Dream layers. Each time the viewer blinks they move from Reality to Dream or vice versa. When the viewer is watching Reality, their level of measured Attention controls the mix of the two sub-layers. Paying high Attention mixes in more of what is termed the Reality-Active footage layer (Active because the viewer is presumed to be actively attending) whereas low Attention mixes in more of a second layer, the Reality-Passive footage. When the viewer is experiencing the Dream footage, it is the measure of Meditation that controls the mix if the two layers which are corresponding called Dream-Active footage and Dream-Passive footage. Thus, in line with the inspirational sources for the film, Meditation is associated with the control of Dreams, and Concentration with the control of Reality, while Blinking triggers major transitions between them.

Technically, the film is designed such that 2 of the 4 layers are always playing at any one time. The clips are presented such that one clip is always present (opacity = 100%) whereas the second clip varies on e.g. how high their Attention is (0% < opacity < 100%). However, the storyline and number and timings of scenes remain the same regardless of which layers are shown. Thus, each viewer experiences their own unique version of a common story according to their BCI control.

Thematically, the film tackles the topic of bullying, being based on repressed memories of the artist, such that the system could mirror the internal process of recalling childhood memories, repressed memories and dream memories. Memories are not an actual record of what happened, they do not stay the same, and are malleable. Likewise the film is designed to be changed by viewing it, both consciously and unconsciously. Each layer of the film is told from a different point of consciousness, be it from a dream state, impartial matter of fact, day dreaming or high anxiety.

The script was then written over the course of 6 months before being shot at the artist's home town of Stoneyburn, West Lothian, Scotland. The film production consisted of a 10-day shoot with 6 crew members and around 30 actors. The artist and actors explored the themes of bullying and racism in discussions and by work-shopping scenes. In order to create the different layers, several scenes were shot with multiple cameras, whilst others were filmed asynchronously. Each layer had its own set of rules; for example, Dream Passive was shot using a tilt-shift lens in slow motion with a heightened colour palette. In contrast Reality Active was shot with a wide angle at normal speed in realistic colours. Likewise, layers within scenes were thematically separated, antagonism would be set to Reality Active, fantasy to Dream Active.

Preparing and editing the film for the system was very different to the usual editing process. When normally editing a film, an ordered sequence of clips is created that move from the start to the end of the film. Here, however, the artist created four synchronised sequences. Usually the relationship of temporally adjacent clips creates the meaning and flow of the film. However in this case, these attributes of the film are under control of the viewer so the practice of editing was to maximise the possibilities and create parallel potential meanings. This created a major editing challenge where the story had to read linearly both within and across the layers.

STUDYING #SCANNERS

Having made the film, we set about studying it using 'Performance-Led Research in the Wild' as described by Benford et al [2]. As opposed to a scientific experimental methodology, this involves presenting the novel technological experience in an open public space with the aim of gaining rich insights into how people interacted with it. Consequently, we worked with the artist to stage the film at a high-profile public arts venue, and conducted a naturalistic study of public participants who acquired tickets and came along to try it out.

Method and Approach

The film was presented at one of the UK's leading organisations for the development, support and exhibition of video, film and new and emerging media: the Foundation for Art and Creative Technology (FACT) in Liverpool. FACT attracts more than 3000 attendees and showcases more than 350 new media art from across the world, each year. The installation ran from the 14-19th of July 2015 between 10:30 and 17:30 each day. #Scanners was presented in an intimate 6 person capacity cinema, within a caravan (shown in Figure 3) to emulate a rich cinematic experience. The space had no windows, low lighting, plush seating, an eight foot projected image, and stereo speakers.

Participants were recruited in-situ, with advertising placed outside the caravan and through word of mouth, with a number of viewers viewing the experience on the recommendation of a friend. The experience was also advertised on the FACT website. In total, around 75 people had the opportunity to experience #Scanners as the main viewer, sometimes with up to 5 additional spectators. All viewers were told that data, and their unique version of #Scanners, would be recorded for later analysis and were given a chance to opt-out. 35 of these agreed to participate in our study and provided informed consent. Active viewers were fitted with the headset which took on average about 2-3 minutes to set up. Their film experience lasted approximately 16 minutes. Each participant's unique version of the film and brain data was recorded. The session concluded with a semi-structured debriefing interview, focused on people's experiences and feelings whilst using #Scanners, which typically lasted around 10 minutes. Unfortunately, log data for 13 of these participants was incomplete. As such our study focuses on the 24 who had agreed to be interviewed and for whom we have complete logs of BCI data.

Overall Response to #Scanners

We begin by looking at the participants perceived experience on a macro level, identifying that overall, participants were generally positive about #Scanners: *"Yeah it was quite crazy."* - *P35*, *"I felt like I could slow it down, speed it up and I could move on."* - *P33*, whilst *P29* went so far as to say - *"It'd be great to watch on drugs."*

The experience did feature some challenging subject matter, specifically around the subject of bullying - *"[I didn't enjoy] the section where the child is bullied because I got bullied in school when I was a kid and I remember thinking... I didn't actually want to watch that."* - *P33*. *P15* noted that the film *"induced or sort of sense of unease."* Considering the switch between reality and dream footage, *P1* said *"I found it, I don't know if scary is the word, but perhaps a little unnerving in places because usually when you see a film you see outside the character but because you could move to see from inside the characters perspective it was a bit like: oh, I don't want to pick that brick up."*

Figure 4 shows the collective experience of our 24 participants. The bars above zero (X-axis), indicate the number of viewers in the reality state at a given moment, whilst the bars below indicate the number of viewers in the dream state. The graph bars denote the number of viewers in each group at 15 second intervals. The line plots indicate the scaled average intensity of attention (blue) and meditation (green) across all participants. The vertical red lines indicate the timing of synchronised scene changes in the footage. The graph confirms that the control mechanism was reasonably balanced, showing that people did flip between dream and reality and that levels of attention and meditation varied in apparently sensible ways. It gives a first impression that the control mechanism was reasonably well behaved as we might have hoped.

While clearly not a controlled experiment, we have calculated some statistics to help characterise the overall nature of the experience in terms of how much people were deemed to be blinking, attending and meditating and how this shaped the overall viewing patterns of the film. Attention and Meditation values were provided directly from the EEG headset and range from 0 (low) to 100 (high). The average attention level was 53.23 (stdev 5.38), while the average meditation level was 57.75 (stdev 5.09), with a correlation ($r=0.07$) confirming the independence of the two measures. We examined whether Attention and Meditation levels varied between scenes, using a repeated-measures ANOVA. Only Attention varied significantly ($F(17,5)=4.125$, $p<0.0001$), indicating that people's Attention did vary from scene to scene, but their Meditation, or calmness, did not. Pairwise comparisons highlighted that Scenes 3 and 4 drew the highest levels of Attention, during which the primary character in the film experiences an intense and anxious nightmare. Conversely, scenes 17 and 18 drew the lowest levels of attention, which could be explained by decline in interest as time progresses. The focus of scenes 17 and 18, however, is on the main character resolving some of their problems towards a positive ending, involving a calm cycle ride through their neighbourhood. This may have simply commanded less attention than an intense nightmare, or perhaps viewers consciously withdrew attention from a less interesting scene.

There was a large variation in how participants blinked whilst experiencing #Scanners. The normal blinking rate amongst adults is estimated at 10 blinks per minute [7], however, VDU use and watching TV is associated with lower rates of about 5 blinks per minute [33, 20], which Ishimaru et al used to detect when participants were watching TV. In line with such findings, the average number of blinks was 77.6 (stdev 35.5) during the 15:46 minute film, which is about of 5 blinks per minute. The recorded average interval between blinks was 14.6 seconds (stdev 6.5s). Beyond this lower average rate associated with watching TV, however, some participants clearly managed

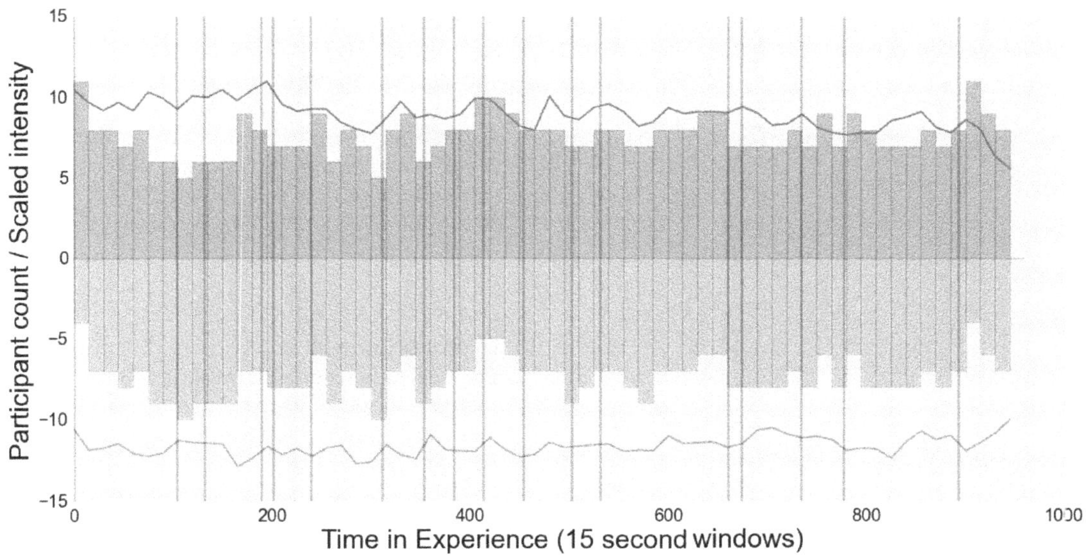

Figure 4: Visualisation of Attention (blue line), Meditation (green line) and state (Reality = purple bars, Dream = red bars).

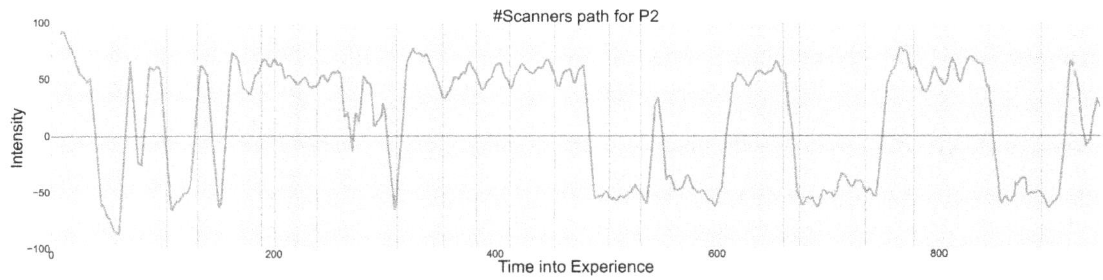

(a) P2 blinked 28 times

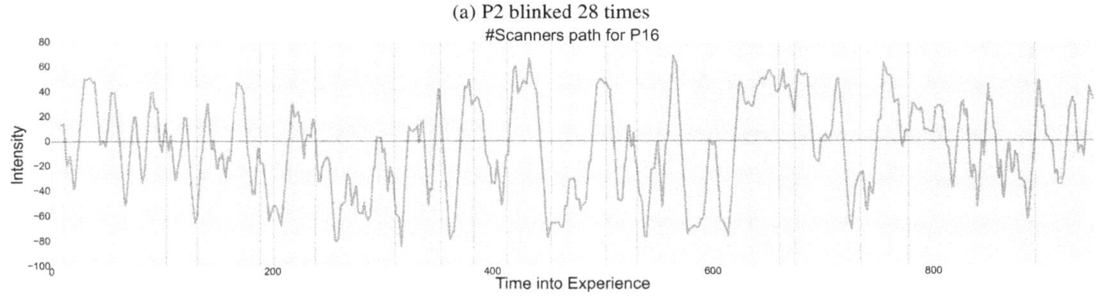

(b) P16 blinked 158 times

Figure 5: Visualisations of viewer's journeys through #Scanners. Above the X-Axis is attention, below it is meditation.

their blinking carefully. *P2*, for example, said *"I definitely had control over the way it was edited as I'd seen that version before I kind of knew I could change the footage that I hadn't seen and see the other version."*. P2 blinked only 28 times, or approximately two times per minute, including a break from blinking for more than two minutes between scenes for 7-11, as shown in Figure 5a (Note - a blink is indicated by the graph line crossing the X-Axis). Others, however, blinked many times throughout the film, as shown by *P16* in Figure 5b who blinked 158 times, or 10 times per minute. *P2*, who had just watched their friend using #Scanners, said *"I think because I watched it before, there was some scenes I didn't want to see or I wanted to see the other side of the scene. So that I found really interesting, so I wasn't passive it was nice to have control over it."* - confirming how they deliberately refrained from blinking as a control tactic

We grouped participants into high and low blinkers. The top third of blinkers were classified as high blinkers, whereas the bottom third were classed as low blinkers. We did this in order to investigate whether there were significant differences between the two. We saw no difference in overall Attention/Meditation levels, but we did see, on a scene-by-scene basis, that the low-blinking group tended to have higher levels of Attention (Shown in Figure 6).

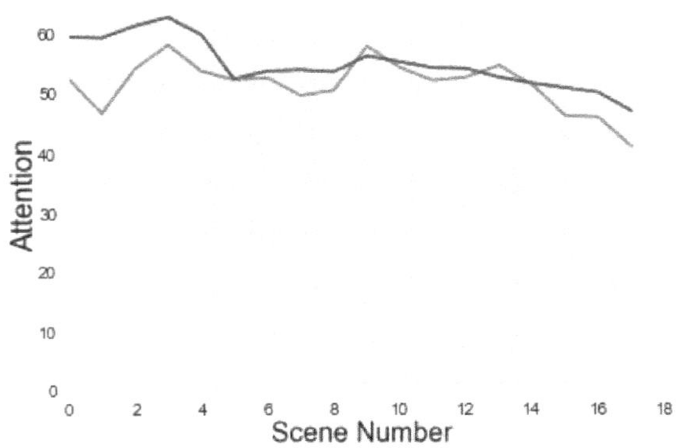

Figure 6: Attention levels of High (red) and Low Blinkers(blue) by scene.

Discovering Control

Having presented some general observations across the whole group of viewers we now turn to looking at the finer details of control as described by the viewers in the subsequent interviews. Many who experienced #Scanners began without knowing how it could be controlled, and the amount that they discovered whilst watching the film varied; some quickly came to understand aspects of the control, even if they did not interpret its effect correctly. Aside from knowing they were wearing a brain scanner, however, a few participants remained unaware that they could have some control over #Scanners: *"I didn't realize there was anything to control" - P19* and *"I thought it was just how it was" - P16*. Some, during the experience, realised that they had some control: *"It did feel like something else was controlling. There was something more kind of [transient] in the edits, you know. It didn't flow in the same way that it would do if you were watching something else..." - P15*. *P28* discovered, during the experience, that blinking was having an effect: *"I noticed that when I blinked, it changed between blue and red, and green and white. And I liked the blue and red so I tried to keep on that as long as I can."*

People didn't necessarily understand how they were controlling it, nor what impact their control was having. *P6* said: *"[I tried to] alter my breathing"* and *"I tried messing about with my hands in front of my eyes"*. *P7* believed they were altering the storyline, saying *"there were little bits where I could control wither people were being aggressive or not."*. Similarly *P10* said *"I did [think I could control characters] near the beginning, especially when I thought: pick that brick up and hit them."*. *P33* thought perhaps they were controlling the temporal flow of the film, saying *"I thought, if I really, really focus on what's going on, it will travel quickly and I will get through this section that I don't really like, if that makes sense and it seemed to do that."*

Some participants knew at the start how the system worked, because they had watched a friend experience, or had spoken to a previous participant. *P5* said *"I enjoyed concentrating because I had the control of the concentrating"*. While some had control over their attention levels, it wasn't always easy for others to so: *"my meditation, I tried to play with that but I wasn't sure if I was having much effect" - P6*. Participants seemed happy, however, with this limited control: *"I was happy with the amount of control, because I didn't know the parameters of how to affect it and trying to manually affect how your brain is reacting is really difficult" - P1*.

Exerting Control

For those that exerted a level of control, some found that this increased their engagement with the film: *"more immersive definitely, I'm used to going along with a storyline and having no control over what's happening and feeling not-connected to the film whereas, that I felt more involved with it, more connected to the film, and to the characters as well"*. Others, like *P2* above, used this control to manage their exposure to difficult material; *P18* said *"The audio became really, really annoying and very abrasive. I was using the opportunity to just switch to a less abrasive... I mean, both were still abrasive but I was switching to the less abrasive at that point and checking in, every so often"*. Using control wasn't always easy due to its semi-autonomic nature: *"yeah I tried to play with [blinking] but sometimes I blinked involuntary, so sometimes where I didn't want it to change it would change" - P6*. Similarly *P22* said *"I think sometimes like I was stopping myself from blinking and then my eyes will get dry."*

Conversely, thinking about control meant that some participants found it hard to fully enjoy the film: *"A lot of the time I found it difficult to remove myself from the thought of the fact that I was changing it and I was controlling it, and I kept thinking like why is my mind doing that pace like what's going on in the film?" - P23*. Similarly, *P31* said *"sometimes you notice that you have the agency, and that flipped you out of flow. But sometimes you've really added to the dramatic effect."* *P28* worried that even more control might reduced the enjoyment of the experience *"I think any more control maybe I think that, maybe more control would have taken away from the immersive elements of the film."*

Based upon interview discussions, we categorised users as to whether they actively tried to Control (N=11) the system or not (N=13). As with High and Low blinkers, we did not see significant differences in Attention and Meditation across the whole film. Looking scene by scene (Figure 7) however, we do see that Controllers had almost consistently higher levels of Meditation. This is different to what we saw for High/Low Blinkers (Figure 6), where we saw the same effect but for Attention. This might imply that, instead of high Attention being associated with low-blinking, low-blinking was more of an autonomic response associated with high Attention. Conversely, those that tried to control their interaction managed to actively control their responses, including Meditation levels. The lack of difference in Attention between those that tried to control the system, and those that didn't, supports the qualitative interview data suggesting that both groups had mixed success at affecting their own attention.

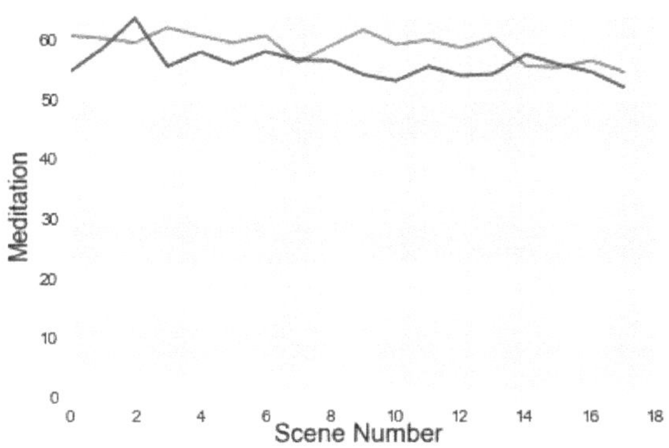

Figure 7: Meditation levels for those that self-identified as trying to Control (Red) and those who did not (Blue).

Releasing Control

Understanding and using control did not mean, however, that users retained control over the film throughout. Some enjoyed giving up the control, with *P31* saying *"So you try not to blink. So that was, I think it did add to it, yeah feels good. I mean I could have let it go as well a little bit, but that was nice. Sometimes I just let go. It's good."*. Some participants even forgot about their control for periods of time, with *P1* saying *"I completely forgot, I was concentrating on the film then a couple of minutes the pressure point there started aching and yeah I'm wearing a headset."*.

In reflection, some said that it would have been better not to know exactly how to control the film. *P13* said *"I wish you hadn't told me before, its not as authentic if you know before"* and *P14* said *"I would have liked to have done it, not knowing anything"*. When asked if *P10* (who did not figure out how to control the system) would have liked to have known in advance, they said *"No [because] then I'd be blinking like anything, and its our observation that changes what happens anyway. I'd have liked to be told that I would be told [how it worked] afterwards. Maybe I would have thrown myself into it more."*

Summary of Findings

Our findings reveals the diverse ways in which viewers experienced #Scanners. No single experience of the film was the same and viewers engaged with the possibilities of BCI control in many different ways. Some actively employed control, adopting deliberate tactics such as not blinking, whilst others did not or were not aware that they could exert control. Some subsequently relinquished control as they became immersed in the film or as their autonomic responses reasserted themselves. Some learned about control for themselves, by experimenting or watching others, while others were told about it. Taken together, these findings present a complex, even bewildering picture. How are we to understand what is happening here? What lessons might filmmakers and other "designers" of interactive entertainment draw from our findings? The following section attempts to answer these questions by setting out a structured design space for BCI control to systematically relate various findings to one another.

DISCUSSION

We now reflect on both the design and viewer experience of #Scanners in order to draw out more general lessons for HCI about the use of BCIs in interactive entertainment. Our discussion takes the form of a gradually building conceptual framework to explain the subtleties of control when using BCI as this - in various guises - emerged as the central issue from our experience. The aim of establishing a conceptual framework is to 1) Define concepts to explain our findings; 2) Ground them in HCI related literature; 3) Reveal unusual strategies and tactics for designing future entertainment.

Our framework involves the definition and comparison of two key dimensions of control - the extent to which control when using BCI can be considered to be voluntary and the extent to which the user is aware or trying to control the system.

Extent of voluntary control

A key motivation for some BCI research, is that people are not fully or directly in control of their interactions, but that systems respond reactively to their behaviour [45], such as with the control of artificial limbs [28]. To be more precise, we would argue that their control of the system is not entirely voluntary. Thus, while we have seen examples that viewers can learn to voluntarily control their blinking in order to try and prolong or break away from scenes in the film, we have also seen how blinking is also an semi-autonomic bodily response to drying eyes, dust and other factors. In short, one cannot refrain from blinking forever. Our findings suggest that our interpretations of attention and meditation were perhaps subject to even more tenuous voluntary control. While viewers often wanted to control them - and some claimed that they could - control was exerted through indirect means such as trying to slow breathing in order to calm down and be more meditative. Whilst users were more able to influence their Attention levels, and we saw a significant difference in Attention levels between different scenes, Meditation levels did not vary significantly throughout the film.

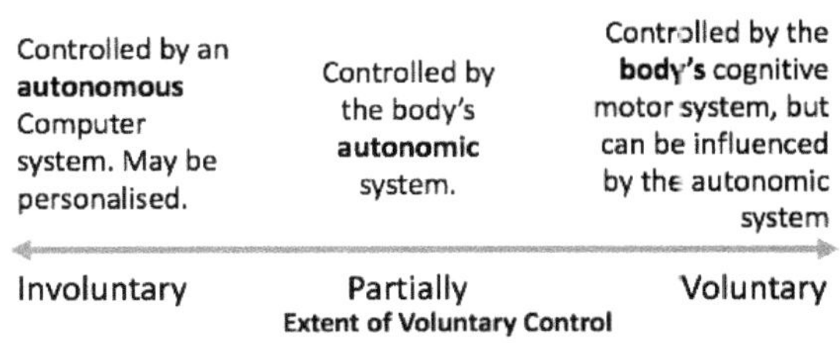

Figure 8: Extent of Voluntary Control as a dimension

Given these observations, it is useful to think of there being a dimension of **Extent of Voluntary Control**. At one end we find forms of control that are largely voluntary, such as choosing to move a mouse or press a key on a keyboard. At the other might be forms of control that are largely involuntary such as sensing the actions of the body's autonomic systems that continue to operate (e.g., the presence of any detectable brain activity at all). Our interpretations of BCI in terms of blinking, attention and meditation are notable for occupying a middle ground along the spectrum where control is partially voluntary. Similar to Marshall et al's breath-controlled bucking bronco [26], the user can choose to blink at certain points, but cannot avoid blinking at others. The user can try to relax, but may be affected by surprise or fear during the film. The user can choose to be more attentive, but may struggle to maintain attention during less action-oriented scenes. The user's position on this spectrum can vary during an experience. Our findings revealed both deliberate and accidental triggers that might cause movement along this spectrum (see Figure 9).

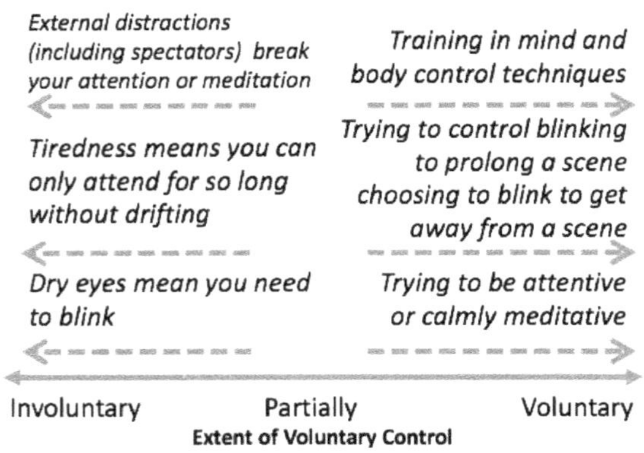

Figure 9: Triggers affecting voluntary control

Extent of Self-Awareness

Our second dimension, shown in Figure 10, concerns the extent to which one is self-aware of one's level of control over one's body, including thinking about controlling the system. This **Extent of Self-Awareness** can vary between being fully conscious of what one is doing, such as when manipulating a mouse or keyboard, to when our attention is focused elsewhere, such when we are deeply immersed in a state of flow when watching a film [6]; like riding a bike without thinking about how to ride it. Our findings reveal that our particular treatments

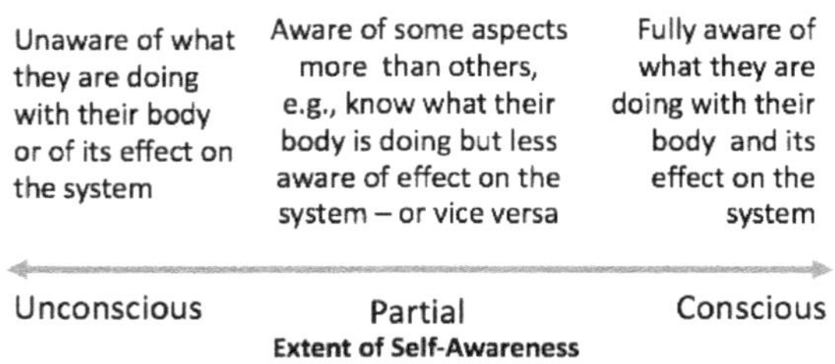

Figure 10: Extent of Self-Awareness of control as a dimension

of BCI in terms of blinking, attention and meditation span various points along this dimension. Users can be consciously aware of trying to control their blinking or unaware of their everyday blinking behaviour. They can be deliberately trying to play close attention, whilst some became immersed in the film and forgot about trying to influence it. Moreover, we have seen how this level of consciousness may vary dynamically throughout an experience as a result of various internal and external triggers that are shown in Figure 11. We noted, for example, how changes in content such as a scene transition in a film might potentially move the user in either direction, re-engaging their attention with the film or causing them to reflect on whether the transition was caused by their blinking.

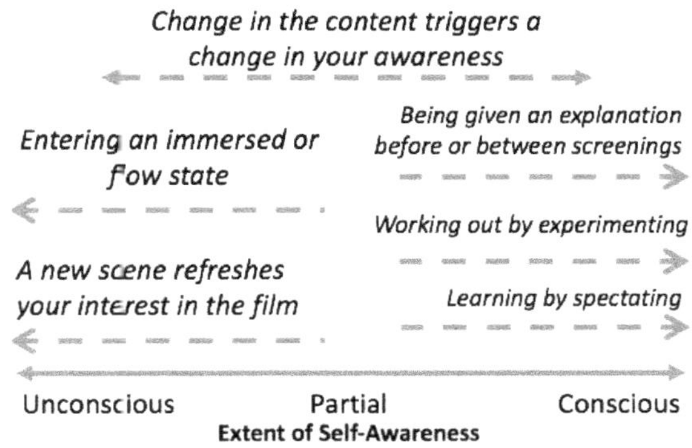

Figure 11: Triggers affecting Self-Awareness of control

A Design Space for Entertaining BCIs

Combining these two dimensions reveals an important design space for the control of BCIs (and possibly other modalities too). Our experience revealed something of a tension in the use of BCIs where users move back and forth between voluntary and involuntary and between conscious and unconscious with different effects. Beyond helping explain our findings, we might also put this taxonomy to use as a design space for BCIs, especially for entertainment. The green diagonal line in Figure 12 represents the traditional locus of control in HCI [36]. This moves between internal locus of control (e.g., direct manipulation) and external locus of control (e.g., autonomous, context-aware and ubicomp sensing systems).

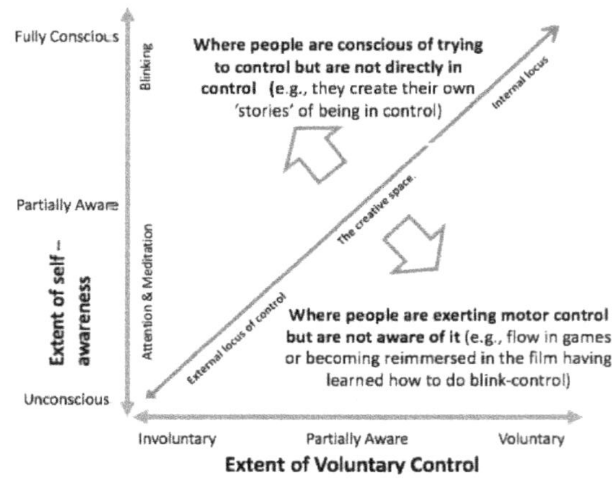

Figure 12: A design space for entertaining BCIs

We suggest that this space away from the central line offers a creative sweet-spot where designers can set up creative tensions and/or trigger users to move between different states: between immersion and self-reflection, and between being in control and surrendering it [26, 3]. This is a liminal space - a space of in-betweenness and ambiguity - that can be particularly productive in creative fields and may encourage people to create their own interpretations or 'stories' of control as we saw in our study.

Our results already suggest some general strategies that involve *thinking off the line*: **Fully-conscious and involuntary** - where we explore physiological measures that people have even less understanding or voluntary control over, such as skin temperature, and **Voluntary but unconscious** - which encourage people into states, perhaps like experiencing flow [6], where people could use voluntary control, but do not need to consciously think about doing it.

Journeys through Control

We return to the idea that this is a dynamic picture - that participants can make various transitions around this space. In an attempt to characterise the many paths taken by those who experienced #Scanners, we developed the state diagram seen in Figure 13. The diagram provides a visualisation of the potential state and transfer of state a viewer may experience during #Scanners. Reflecting on the interview data led us to propose the following states.

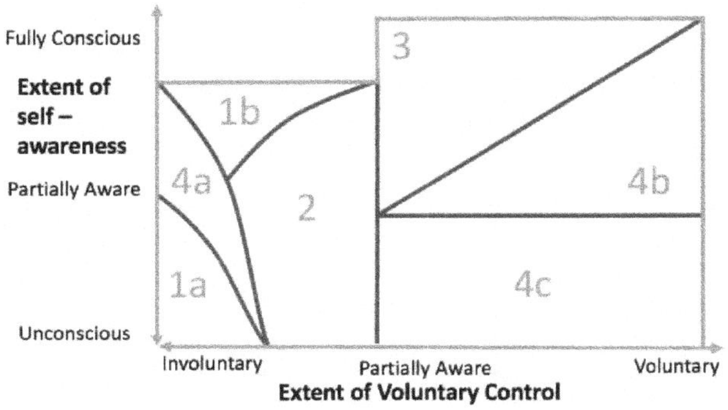

Figure 13: Major states participants travelled through whilst experiencing #Scanners

State (1) indicates one of two entry points into the experience. In (1a), viewers have zero prior knowledge of the system's operation. There may be some awareness of the possibility of some control, since they are wearing the headset, but there is no explicit knowledge. Conversely, (1b) represents the state of knowing. Viewers in (1b) will posses varying degrees of knowledge of the system's operation but have yet to exert any elements of control.

State (2) represents the state of pre-discovery. For viewers transitioning from (1a), this will be the beginning of their discovery, they will begin to notice certain associations between their physiology and manipulation of the experience. Transition from (1b), will begin the process of confirming existing knowledge. Discovery is then witnessed in (3). This is the "*ah-ha*" moment where viewers figure out some/all elements of control associated with the film. Within this state, participants were typically thinking more about how they were controlling, than they understand how it worked; people tried different ways to relax and tried focusing on different things, like controlling the storyline or the actors.

Post discovery occurs in (4). (4a) represents the viewer that never discovers more of the control (partial knowledge). They remain aware that something is effecting the experience but do not discover more. In (4b), some participants enter a stage of

Table 1: Unique identified journeys whilst using #Scanners

ID	Path	Participant	Total
J1	1a	16, 19, 29	3
J2	1b	21	1
J3	1a → 2 → 4a	10, 11, 15, 26	4
J4	1a → 2 → 4b	33, 35	2
J5	1a → 2	12	1
J6	1a → 2 → 3 → 4b	18	1
J7	1a → 2 → 3 → 4b → 4c	1, 28, 30, 31	4
J8	1a → 2 → 3→4c	3, 8	2
J9	1a → 3 →4b	22	1
J10	1b → 3 → 4b	2, 5, 6, 13	4
J11	1b → 2→3 → 4b	23,25	2
J12	1b → 2→3 → 4c	20	1
J13	1b → 2 →3 → 4b → 4c	7	1

understanding with the system control, and begin to use it to control the system. Similarly, those that understand elements of control (e.g. blinking effects the cutting of scenes in some way), may simply slowly relinquish explicit control and fall back into immersion, where their knowledge of control has increased, but they no longer think about doing it (4c).

From detailed analysis of each viewer's interview and video data we were able to identify 13 unique paths through the experience. Table 1 allows us identify some of the interesting characteristics associated with the experience. J1 and J2, for example, shows individuals that never moved beyond the initial state (1). For (1a) this experience would be analogous with watching a standard film (e.g. P16). Perhaps more interesting is P21 who remained in (1b) i.e. they have prior knowledge of some of the systems control, but chose not to explore what exactly they could do with it.

J3 and J4 was the most common journey taken by viewers who did not have prior knowledge of the system's control. The journey indicates that they discovered, based on the system's responses, behaviours that might create a change. Those that never quite work it out, then return to (4a), whilst those that do typically moved to (4b), where they begin to use control. Some, however, went as far as (4c), where in J7 they then forget about control and enter a state of immersion, where they know what is controlling the system but stop thinking it.

For those that knew in advance how the system worked (J10-J13), the path was similar, but typically involved less time in the exploration state, and more time in the 4th states. Realising that some participants knew the operation of the system, however, we can begin to consider two types of transitions: *Intra-experience transitions* that happen during a given experience (i.e. screening of the film) and *Inter-experience transitions* that happen in between experiences, for example as a result of receiving an explanation of how the experience works or perhaps as a result of being a spectator to someone else's experience. In inter-experience contexts, viewers will likely trace a path around our design space as they engage in possibly repeat experiences. In this regards, P33 said *"I want to have another go to see what I can do, because I think I was quite passive. I was very aware of my emotional responses watching it. I was kind of..quite...I guess I was monitoring my emotional responses quite...and allowing them to be quite strong because I kind of had some vague idea that, that might, you know, provide more information for the feedback thing".*

Putting the Framework to Future Work

We now consider the utility of our framework - how might it be useful. The first possibility is a "sensitising concept" to assist in the design or analysis stages of future studies. We might for example, design future studies to explore in greater detail the relationships between voluntary and involuntary control or between conscious and unconscious control, or to explore some of the specific transitions that we have identified in greater depth. Our concepts might also prove useful for analysis data captured from other BCI controlled entertainment experiences. This latter point raises two questions about the generality of our framework:

- To what extent might it apply to other kinds of control that have similar characteristics to BCI?
  With much other work looking at interactions via other physiological data, our framework might equally apply to other forms of broadly physiological control such as breathing and heart rate, but might also be expanded by them.

- To what extent might it apply to applications other than entertainment and non-entertainment?
  Our framework might apply to interactive entertainment like gaming and music creation, but might also apply simply to the control of non-entertainment control concerns such as controlling prosthetics or to help "locked out" users control computers.

The second possibility is as a framework for generating new design ideas. Here we follow Höök and Lowgren's notion of strong concept [18], a form of "intermediate design knowledge" that embodies a core design idea; bridges between specific instances and generalized theory; concerns interactivity; and can help generate new designs. With this in mind, we suggest three ways in which our framework might enable the design of future experiences.

First is the design of interactive content - can the structure of interactive media respond to these transitions. In this paper, we have documented how one film-maker scripted, shot and edited a film. Even this single example reveals various creative strategies, but different types of films might be suitable to different types of physiological control. Suspense thrillers, for example, might monitor users for a difference between being bored and enthralled in order to shorted or extend the scene, where stress is detected from EEG and blink rates [14]. Similarly, designers may ask how to respond to a user that voluntarily closes their eyes for sustained periods of time. During horror films, this could be used as an active controller to skip scenes, or passively to make the film *sound* scarier.

Second is the repeat screening or staging of experiences. Our recognition of inter-experience transitions suggests that more attention needs to be paid to the screening of experiences. Of particular importance here is developing strategies for moving people between different modes of engagement as they re-encounter the experience anew. Should their first experience be a "naive" one before they then find out how it learns? Should they move between spectating and driving as argued by Reeve el al's in their proposals for designing spectator interfaces [34]? What might be the best orders for combining all of these? The notion of varying repeat experiences in this is unusual in film where film-makers are not usually directly concerned whether we enjoy it differently on subsequent viewings. It is perhaps more common to consider the longetivty of enjoying games, but even then the focus is more on progressing through levels than on systematically varying the experience each time.

Third is to explore collective experiences. In its current implementation #Scanners is controlled by an individual user, but films are often watched in groups, whether at the cinema or at home. Within our installation, even, the #Scanners experience can be - and was - witnessed by many viewers concurrently. There is a large opportunity, therefore, to investigate how multimedia might respond to the biological responses of a collective audience. Experiences might monitor the average response across an audience, where Kirke et al, for example, have recently explored the use of audience arousal to vary a film experience with multiple possible endings [21]. Conversely, different people could control different aspects of the experience, where Leslie and Mullen, for example, provided separate control over music streams to each participant [23].

CONCLUSIONS

By creating an interactive film, where the scenes seen by viewers varied depending on their levels of meditation and attention, we have explored a novel design area for including BCI in multimedia experiences. The experience was explored with members of general public as an installation at a week-long national arts exhibition. Most notable, amongst our findings, was that while the BCI based adaptation made the experience more immersive for many viewers, thinking about control often brought them out of the experience. This led us to propose a two-dimensional taxonomy of control, considering both the understanding of the control, and how much users think about control. A traditional belief in HCI is that Direct Manipulation (being able to control exactly what you want to control) sits at the top of both these dimensions. We examined, however, how users deviate from line, and enjoyed the experience more by either not knowing exactly how it worked, or by giving up control and becoming re-immersed in the experience. We conclude that these deviations from the line between knowledge and conscious control over interaction are most interesting design opportunities to explore within future BCI adaptive multimedia experiences.

ACKNOWLEDGEMENTS

This work was supported by the EPSRC ORCHID project (EP/I011587/1), the Horizon Centre for Doctoral Training (EP/G037574/1), the FAST Project (EP/L019981/1), the Arts Council England (27369977) and the International Doctoral Innovation Centre (IDIC), University of Nottingham, Ningbo. **Data access statement:** consent was not gained from participants to release EEG data and interview transcripts online, and so a dataset is not openly available.

REFERENCES

1. Thomas Andrillon, Yuval Nir, Chiara Cirelli, Giulio Tononi, and Itzhak Fried. 2015. Single-neuron activity and eye movements during human REM sleep and awake vision. *Nature communications* 6 (08 2015). http://dx.doi.org/10.1038/ncomms8884
2. Steve Benford, Chris Greenhalgh, Andy Crabtree, Martin Flintham, Brendan Walker, Joe Marshall, Boriana Koleva, Stefan Rennick Egglestone, Gabriella Giannachi, Matt Adams, and others. 2013. Performance-led research in the wild. *ACM Transactions on Computer-Human Interaction (TOCHI)* 20, 3 (2013), 14. http://doi.acm.org/10.1145/2491500.2491502
3. Steve Benford, Chris Greenhalgh, Gabriella Giannachi, Brendan Walker, Joe Marshall, and Tom Rodden. 2012. Uncomfortable Interactions. In *Proceedings of the SIGCHI Conference on Human Factors in Computing Systems (CHI '12)*. ACM, New York, NY, USA, 2005–2014. DOI: http://dx.doi.org/10.1145/2207676.2208347
4. Jon Boorstin. 1995. *Making movies work: Thinking like a filmmaker*. Silman-James Pr.
5. Danny Plass-Oude Bos, Boris Reuderink, Bram van de Laar, Hayrettin Gürkök, Christian Mühl, Mannes Poel, Anton Nijholt, and Dirk Heylen. 2010. In *Brain-Computer Interfaces* (1st ed.). Springer, UK, 149–178.
6. Mihaly Csikszentmihalyi and Mihaly Csikzentmihaly. 1991. *Flow: The psychology of optimal experience*. Vol. 41. HarperPerennial New York.
7. Michael J Doughty. 2002. Further assessment of gender-and blink pattern-related differences in the spontaneous eyeblink activity in primary gaze in young adult humans. *Optometry & Vision Science* 79, 7 (2002), 439–447.
8. Raffaella Folgieri and Roberto Zampolini. 2015. BCI promises in emotional involvement in music and games. *Computers in Entertainment (CIE)* 11, 4 (2015), 4.
9. Gary Garcia-Molina, Tsvetomira Tsoneva, and Anton Nijholt. 2013. Emotional brain–computer interfaces. *International journal of autonomous and adaptive communications systems* 6, 1 (2013), 9–25.
10. Mick Grierson. 2008. Composing with brainwaves: minimal trial P300b recognition as an indication of subjective preference for the control of a musical instrument. In *Proceedings of the ICMC*.
11. Mick Grierson and Chris Kiefer. 2011. Better Brain Interfacing for the Masses: Progress in Event-related Potential Detection Using Commercial Brain Computer Interfaces. In *CHI '11 Extended Abstracts on Human Factors in Computing Systems (CHI EA '11)*. ACM, New York, NY, USA, 1681–1686. http://doi.acm.org/10.1145/1979742.1979828
12. Hayrettin Gürkök, Anton Nijholt, and Mannes Poel. 2012. Brain-computer interface games: Towards a framework. In *Entertainment Computing-ICEC 2012*. Springer, 373–380.
13. Hayrettin Gürkök, D Plass-Oude Bos, van der BLA Laar, Femke Nijboer, and Anton Nijholt. 2011. User experience evaluation in BCI: Filling the gap. *International Journal of Bioelectromagnetism* 13, 1 (2011), 54–55.
14. M Haak, S Bos, S Panic, and LJM Rothkrantz. 2009. Detecting stress using eye blinks and brain activity from EEG signals. *Proceeding of the 1st driver car interaction and interface (DCII 2008)* (2009).
15. Uri Hasson, Ohad Landesman, Barbara Knappmeyer, Ignacio Vallines, Nava Rubin, and David J Heeger. 2008. Neurocinematics: The neuroscience of film. *Projections* 2, 1 (2008), 1–26.
16. Brent Hillard, Ayman S El-Baz, Lonnie Sears, Allan Tasman, and Estate M Sokhadze. 2013. Neurofeedback Training Aimed to Improve Focused Attention and Alertness in Children With ADHD A Study of Relative Power of EEG Rhythms Using Custom-Made Software Application. *Clinical EEG and neuroscience* 44, 3 (2013), 193–202.
17. Kristina Höök. 2008. Affective Loop Experiences–What Are They? In *Persuasive Technology*. Springer, 1–12.
18. Kristina Höök and Jonas Löwgren. 2012. Strong concepts: Intermediate-level knowledge in interaction design research. *ACM Transactions on Computer-Human Interaction (TOCHI)* 19, 3 (2012), 23. http://doi.acm.org/10.1145/2362364.2362371
19. Chang-Hwan Im, Jun-Hak Lee, and Jeong-Hwan Lim. 2015. Neurocinematics based on passive BCI: Decoding temporal change of emotional arousal during video watching from multi-channel EEG. In *Control Conference (ASCC), 2015 10th Asian*. IEEE, 1–3.
20. Shoya Ishimaru, Kai Kunze, Koichi Kise, Jens Weppner, Andreas Dengel, Paul Lukowicz, and Andreas Bulling. 2014. In the blink of an eye: combining head motion and eye blink frequency for activity recognition with google glass. In *Proceedings of the 5th Augmented Human International Conference*. ACM, 15. http://doi.acm.org/10.1145/2582051.2582066
21. Alexis Kirke, Duncan Williams, Eduardo Mir, A Bluglass, Craig Whyte, and Pruthi Andrew Eccleston. 2013. Technical Report on a Short Live-action Film whose Story with Soundtrack is selected in Real-time based on Audience Arousal during Performance. (2013).
22. John D Lee and Katrina A See. 2004. Trust in automation: Designing for appropriate reliance. *Human Factors: The Journal of the Human Factors and Ergonomics Society* 46, 1 (2004), 50–80.
23. Grace Leslie and Tim Mullen. 2011. Moodmixer: Eeg-based collaborative sonification. In *Proceedings of the international conference on new interfaces for musical expression*, Vol. 30. Citeseer, 296–299.
24. An Luo and Thomas J Sullivan. 2010. A user-friendly SSVEP-based brainâĂŞcomputer interface using a time-domain classifier. *Journal of Neural Engineering* 7, 2 (2010), 026010. http://stacks.iop.org/1741-2552/7/i=2/a=026010

25. Marco Marchesi, Elisabetta Farella, Bruno Riccò, and Antonella Guidazzoli. 2011. MOBIE: A Movie Brain Interactive Editor. In *SIGGRAPH Asia 2011 Emerging Technologies (SA '11)*. ACM, New York, NY, USA, Article 16, 1 pages. DOI: http://dx.doi.org/10.1145/2073370.2073385

26. Joe Marshall, Duncan Rowland, Stefan Rennick Egglestone, Steve Benford, Brendan Walker, and Derek McAuley. 2011. Breath Control of Amusement Rides. In *Proceedings of the SIGCHI Conference on Human Factors in Computing Systems (CHI '11)*. ACM, New York, NY, USA, 73–82. DOI: http://dx.doi.org/10.1145/1978942.1978955

27. Soh Masuko and Junichi Hoshino. 2006. A Fitness Game Reflecting Heart Rate. In *Proceedings of the 2006 ACM SIGCHI International Conference on Advances in Computer Entertainment Technology (ACE '06)*. ACM, New York, NY, USA, Article 53. DOI: http://dx.doi.org/10.1145/1178823.1178886

28. Gernot R Müller-Putz and Gert Pfurtscheller. 2008. Control of an electrical prosthesis with an SSVEP-based BCI. *Biomedical Engineering, IEEE Transactions on* 55, 1 (2008), 361–364.

29. Walter Murch. 2001. *In the blink of an eye: A perspective on film editing*. Silman-James Press.

30. Yoichi Nagashima. 2003. Bio-sensing Systems and Bio-feedback Systems for Interactive Media Arts. In *Proceedings of the 2003 Conference on New Interfaces for Musical Expression (NIME '03)*. National University of Singapore, Singapore, Singapore, 48–53. http://dl.acm.org/citation.cfm?id=1085714.1085726

31. Ville Nenonen, Aleksi Lindblad, Ville Häkkinen, Toni Laitinen, Mikko Jouhtio, and Perttu Hämäläinen. 2007. Using Heart Rate to Control an Interactive Game. In *Proceedings of the SIGCHI Conference on Human Factors in Computing Systems (CHI '07)*. ACM, New York, NY, USA, 853–856. DOI:http://dx.doi.org/10.1145/1240624.1240752

32. Shinji Nishimoto, An T Vu, Thomas Naselaris, Yuval Benjamini, Bin Yu, and Jack L Gallant. 2011. Reconstructing visual experiences from brain activity evoked by natural movies. *Current Biology* 21, 19 (2011), 1641–1646. http://dx.doi.org/10.1016/j.cub.2011.08.031

33. S Patel, R Henderson, L Bradley, B Galloway, and L Hunter. 1991. Effect of visual display unit use on blink rate and tear stability. *Optometry & Vision Science* 68, 11 (1991), 888–892.

34. Stuart Reeves. 2005. Designing the Spectator Experience Stuart Reeves, Steve Benford, Claire O'Malley, Mike Fraser. (2005).

35. Dean Rubine. 1992. Combining Gestures and Direct Manipulation. In *Proceedings of the SIGCHI Conference on Human Factors in Computing Systems (CHI '92)*. ACM, New York, NY, USA, 659–660. DOI: http://dx.doi.org/10.1145/142750.143072

36. Ben Shneiderman. 1986. *Designing the user interface: strategies for effective human-computer interaction*. Addison-Wesley Reading, MA.

37. Ben Shneiderman. 1997. Direct Manipulation for Comprehensible, Predictable and Controllable User Interfaces. In *Proceedings of the 2Nd International Conference on Intelligent User Interfaces (IUI '97)*. ACM, New York, NY, USA, 33–39. DOI: http://dx.doi.org/10.1145/238218.238281

38. Tadeusz Stach, T. C. Nicholas Graham, Jeffrey Yim, and Ryan E. Rhodes. 2009. Heart Rate Control of Exercise Video Games. In *Proceedings of Graphics Interface 2009 (GI '09)*. Canadian Information Processing Society, Toronto, Ont., Canada, Canada, 125–132. http://dl.acm.org/citation.cfm?id=1555880.1555912

39. Desney Tan and Anton Nijholt. 2010. *Brain-computer interfaces and human-computer interaction* (1st ed.). Springer, UK.

40. BBC Technology. 2015. BBC develops 'mind-control TV' headset for iPlayer app. (June 2015). http://www.bbc.co.uk/news/technology-33163593

41. Allison Woodruff, Sally Augustin, and Brooke Foucault. 2007. Sabbath Day Home Automation: "It's Like Mixing Technology and Religion". In *Proceedings of the SIGCHI Conference on Human Factors in Computing Systems (CHI '07)*. ACM, New York, NY, USA, 527–536. DOI: http://dx.doi.org/10.1145/1240624.1240710

42. Myeung-Sook Yoh, Joonho Kwon, and Sunghoon Kim. 2010. NeuroWander: A BCI Game in the Form of Interactive Fairy Tale. In *Proceedings of the 12th ACM International Conference Adjunct Papers on Ubiquitous Computing - Adjunct (UbiComp '10 Adjunct)*. ACM, New York, NY, USA, 389–390. DOI: http://dx doi.org/10.1145/1864431.1864450

43. Beste F Yuksel, Daniel Afergan, Evan M Peck, Garth Griffin, Lane Harrison, Nick WB Chen, Remco Chang, and Robert JK Jacob. 2015. *Implicit Brain-Computer Interaction Applied to a Novel Adaptive Musical Interface*. Technical Report. Technical Report TR-2015-01, Department of Computer Science, Tufts University, 2015. www. cs. tufts. edu/Technical-Reports. html.

44. Beste F. Yuksel, Michael Donnerer, James Tompkin, and Anthony Steed. 2010. A Novel Brain-computer Interface Using a Multi-touch Surface. In *Proceedings of the SIGCHI Conference on Human Factors in Computing Systems (CHI '10)*. ACM, New York, NY, USA, 855–858. DOI: http://dx.doi.org/10.1145/1753326.1753452

45. Thorsten O Zander and Christian Kothe. 2011. Towards passive brain–computer interfaces: applying brain–computer interface technology to human–machine systems in general. *Journal of neural engineering* 8, 2 (2011), 025005.

46. Thorsten O Zander, Christian Kothe, Sabine Jatzev, and Matti Gaertner. 2010. Enhancing human-computer interaction with input from active and passive brain-computer interfaces. In *Brain-computer interfaces*. Springer, 181–199.

Inspect, Embody, Invent: A Design Framework for Music Learning and Beyond

Xiao Xiao and Hiroshi Ishii
MIT Media Lab
75 Amherst St.
Cambridge, MA 02142
[x_x, ishii]@media.mit.edu

ABSTRACT
This paper introduces a new framework to guide the design of interactive music learning systems, focusing on the piano. Taking a Reflective approach, we identify the implicit assumption behind most existing systems—that learning music is learning to play correctly according to the score—and offer an alternative approach. We argue that systems should help cultivate higher levels of musicianship beyond correctness alone for students of all levels. Drawing from both pedagogical literature and the personal experience of learning to play the piano, we identify three skills central to musicianship—listening, embodied understanding, and creative imagination—which we generalize to the Inspect, Embody, Invent framework. To demonstrate how this framework translates to design, we discuss two existing interfaces from our own research—MirrorFugue and Andante—both built on a digitally controlled player piano augmented by in-situ projection. Finally, we discuss the framework's relevance toward bigger themes of embodied interactions and learning beyond the domain of music.

ACM Classification Keywords
H.5.m. Information Interfaces and Presentation (e.g. HCI): Miscellaneous

Author Keywords
Reflective Design; Reflexive Design; Music Learning; Musical Expression; Learning Interfaces; Embodied Interaction; Piano; Auto-ethnography; Digital Arts

INTRODUCTION
Playing a musical instrument has many well-documented benefits for both cognitive function and overall health [28]. Of all the instruments, the piano is one of the most popular around the world. Unfortunately, learning to play an instrument, especially the piano, is widely regarded as difficult, tedious, and often unpleasant. Many interactive systems have been designed to support this process, mostly from a novice's perspective, framing the task as one of finding correct notes, learning correct fingering, and repeating enough to solidify muscle memory [7, 11, 17, 22, 25, 26, 33, 41, 46, 52, 57].

This paper aims to support designers to create music learning systems that foster greater expression. Prior research on musical expression within HCI have studied expert performances [12, 30], but relatively little work has been devoted to the process of acquiring expertise from an experiential perspective.

Following a methodlogy articulated by Sengers et al. as Reflective Design [50], we begin with a review of existing music learning systems to tease out their underlying assumptions. Drawing from both music pedagogy literature as well as auto-ethnography, we then present alternative approaches to learning for musicians of all levels where expression plays a key role. From these approaches, we distill the Inspect, Embody, Invent framework, the core of this paper. To concretize this framework, we discuss two of our existing projects on an acoustic player piano augmented with projection, MirrorFugue [68, 69] and Andante [70]. Finally, we discuss how our framework may generalize to domains beyond music.

This paper offers two potential contributions by connecting a well-established perspective from the art of music performance to the HCI discourse. Firstly, our framework and examples may guide the design of new music learning interfaces. Though our examples center on the piano, ideas presented are applicable across instruments. Additionally, ideas from this paper may also contribute to a deeper understanding of both embodied interaction and the learning process for creative expression. This may inform the design of systems for diverse domains beyond music.

RELATED WORK
Interactive technologies for music learning encompass a broad range of existing work from toys that convey simple musical concepts to integrated tutorial systems. To narrow our scope, our review focuses on piano learning. Learning systems are generally classified by their intended use-case, such as support for lessons (traditional and remote), tools

CHI'16, May 07 - 12, 2016, San Jose, CA, USA

ACM 978-1-4503-3362-7/16/05···$15.00
DOI: http://dx.doi.org/10.1145/2858036.2858577

for practice, and self-learning. In contrast, our review categorizes prior work across usage scenarios based on what specific roles systems have adopted to support learning. In the vast majority of existing work, systems depart little from the traditional role of the instructor, which may be divided into two main tasks: presentation of new material and feedback on student progress.

Presentation of Material

The presentation of new material by a traditional instructor typically involves some physical demonstration on the instrument. Video tutorials, as found on a number of online courses [2], seek to virtually emulate the teacher's demonstrations for distance learning. Computer generated 3D graphics have also been employed for more technical demonstrations, such as fingering of phrases [25, 33].

The teacher may also use the written score as reference, explaining its structure and pointing out important details. In a similar vein, many systems begin with information from the score, which is then translated to visuals or haptics that facilitate the mapping of score to instrument [7, 11, 13, 17, 22, 25, 46, 57]. For visuals, light-up keyboards have long been used for learning [5], and many systems have adopted the piano-roll notation to depict the score, where blocks representing notes fall onto a keyboard to indicate note strikes. This may be shown in a separate display or projected onto a physical piano [13, 26, 46]. Research on haptics have developed wearable devices that stimulate the fingers to passively learn note sequences [17].

Feedback on Progress

Based on listening and observing student playing, a traditional teacher gives feedback, which includes pointing out mistakes as well as description and demonstration of new sounds, new methods of playing, and exercises for practice. Tutorial systems have thus modeled their interactions after this process. The computer would capture some facets of the student's playing, which is then analyzed and presented back to the student [13, 15, 22, 33, 35, 36, 45, 46, 51]. Capture and analysis may focus on sound or physical movements. Systems based on sound typically capture either audio or MIDI from the student, which is then analyzed for accuracy of pitch and rhythm, sometimes articulation and dynamics to a limited degree [13, 22, 45, 46, 48, 51]. Systems based on movement have employed sensors as well as motion capture to give feedback on the lower-level mechnical aspects of playing, such as posture and muscle usage [15, 32, 33, 36].

Feedback from interactive systems may be classified into three types. On the most basic level, technology may act as a neural mirror through which students may gain awareness of their own playing. To this end, audio recording is frequently used by amateurs and professionals alike, and video has been increasingly adopted by teachers and students to inspect performances [60]. Researchers have explored the presentation of various data streams for feedback either during or after playing. For example, data from physical sensors has been sonified as real-time indicators of a student's arm movements while visual renderings of MIDI have been used to study accuracy of timing [13, 15].

As some data streams may be difficult to understand in isolation, a second type of feedback presents data from student playing in comparison with either the written score or with an expert performance. This approach allows students to inspect their own playing for deviations from the score or example. Some systems involve analysis and modeling of audio and gesture to enable score following [48]. Others present data visually, as graphs, charts, or annotated 3D models [33, 36].

Finally, feedback from a system may intervene to point out mistakes and weaknesses in a student's playing [13, 22, 46, 51, 57]. In order to identify mistakes, systems must include some notion of what is correct. To avoid the subjectivity of interpretation, existing systems tend to define correctness based on what is specified by the score, focusing on accuracy of pitch, timing, dynamics, and articulation based on a literal reading of notation.

Motivation

As practicing regularly is commonly acknowledged as challenging [41], another approach centers on motivating the student to play [11, 38, 39]. Systems have been designed to encourage practice with game-like mechanics, where students are rewarded with points for successful performances [26, 41]. To avoid the discouragement from frequent errors, projects have relaxed the criteria for what is deemed correct, increasing strictness as students progress [11, 38]. Using simular technology, interfaces have introduced an element of social playing by allowing non-musician family members to accompany their children learning the piano [39].

THE NOVICE MINDSET

Within the HCI Community, piano learning systems have predominantly focused on supporting novice classical students. From their designs we may trace a set of underlying assumptions about piano playing rooted in the priorities of the novice. We describe three key assumptions that have motivated a large number of existing projects described in the previous section.

Correctness is Paramount

Many see the primary goal of playing music as reproducing a sequence of correct notes with correct timing based on what a composer has specified in the score. For the beginner, there are two major difficulties: deciphering the score into notes on the instrument and the long repetitive process to cement muscle memory. Systems rooted in this idea attempt to present the relationship between notes and instrument in a more legible way as well as offer practice support by pointing out mistakes in the student's playing [7, 13, 22, 46, 51, 57].

Physicality is Mechanics

Playing any musical instrument requires knowing how to act through the body. The prevailing view dictates that a beginner must first acquire basic technical facility to emit sounds with the instrument before considering musicality. Finger usage, considered the most important physical component of piano playing, is the focus of several systems [17, 22, 25]. Interfaces have also been designed to train posture as well as control of various muscle groups used in playing [32, 33].

Expression is Limited

How to play the correct notes and how to use the body is usually treated as independent from expression. Based on an assumption that expression will naturally emerge from a solid technical foundation, some designers of novice learning systems forgo teaching expression altogether [17, 57]. When considered, expression is often seen as an extension of decoding the score. Thus, systems have been made to present dynamics and articulation markings as well as analyze playing for "accuracy of expression" [46, 52].

BEYOND THE NOVICE MINDSET

HCI pioneer Alan Kay once remarked that "the problem with being a beginner is that you get a lot of practice staying a beginner" [21]. The biggest preoccupation for beginners is finding and playing correct notes. Advanced players, however, focus not on the notes but on now to *speak* through them. While the beginner phase is almost universally seen as a frustrating and tedious process [7, 22, 25, 46, 57], advanced musicians derive pleasure from playing. Most interactive systems treat the beginner phase as unavoidable and focus efforts on helping students through it. We argue that designers of interactive systems should focus on fostering core musicianship skills for players of all levels. By looking beyond the novice mindset, we may bypass the usual frustrations of of the novice to find more fun and fulfillment in learning.

As background, we first discuss the aspects of playing most imporant for acquiring musicality. We then describe the concrete process to learn a classical piano piece. Finally, we demonstrate the relevance of these ideas for learners of all levels, with a note on learning outside of the Western Classical tradition.

SKILLS FOR MUSICIANSHIP

To illustrate the contrast between music learning for novices and experts, we paraphrase an analogy used by a number of respected musicians [23, 29, 66]. The novice approach of music learning is compared to classrooms that teach foreign languages through the memorization of rules, rewarding correctness over communication on exams. As a result, students may recite rules and repeat phrases but struggle to express thoughts and feelings through the language.

How people learn to speak their native language gives insights on a better way to learn music. Native language learning begins in an immersive entironment, where people first learn to listen. They gradually attune their ears to the tones and rhythms of the language and gain the ability to distinguish sounds and phrases. At the same time, people learn to create sounds with their body. Through imitation, often unconscious, they practice not only the muscles of the mouth but also the idiomatic facial expressions and gestures of the new language. Most importantly, the speaker always practices expression using the new language through constant attempts to communicate with others in the environment.

Though people learn their mother tongue as children, several courses have adapted a similar process for adults to learn foreign languages, which emphasize listening, speaking, and conversation from the outset even with a limited vocabulary [3, 60]. Though grammar rules are introduced to help the adult's analytical mind, correctness is not enforced at the expense of communication.

Ear, Body, Imagination

The above analogy highlights three aspects of language learning—listening, bodily engagement, and frequent expression—which correspond to the three aspects of music most central to an expert's musician's craft: the ear, the body, and the creative imagination. As with language learning, almost anyone can gain proficiency with playing music if they focus on developing these key skills.

Ear

Expert musicians always stress the importance of developing the ear [4, 29]. Though all students are told to "listen", most untrained ears attend to content by default, focusing on notes rather than the quality of sounds [63]. Learning to listen in the musical sense means cultivating a sensitivity for qualities such as tone, rhythm, and phrasing. True listening transforms a piece from a sequence of correct notes with correct timing into a statement in a tonal language with its own motivic vocabulary, logic, and flow.

Body

Though training the body requires much practice time for any musician, novices and experts differ drastically in their approach. Novices by default target the extremities directly responsible for producing sound [64]. On the piano this translates to a preoccupation with correct fingering. Other concerns of the body, such as the arms, wrists, and posture are later introduced and trained in isolation. The expert musician, however, feels music in the whole body. Abby Whiteside describes this phenomenon as feeling the *basic rhythm* of a piece which then coordinates the various muscle groups responsible for manipulation of the instrument [64]. Though the keyboard is the interaction locus, pianists must not think of playing as simply pressing keys but as music from the body flowing through the arms, wrists, fingers into the keys to emanate sound. As Whiteside notes, rhythm coordinates the body, but it must be internalized as feeling rather than intellectualized counting. The student must learn to *speak* through the body, inflecting and coloring the shape and timing of phrases.

Attendance of live performance is highly encouraged among serious music students, for learning to use the body relies heavily on imitation. Studies in mirror neurons have shown that the human brain possesses specialized hardware for imitation [31], which enables people to observe and copy complex, coordinated movements difficult to explain analytically. Through imitation, students may absorb not only technique but also how music is felt in the body of another player.

Imagination

For expressive playing, a student must not only develop the ear and the body but also the imagination. In musical parlance, this is also referred to as "developing the ear" [4, 63], showing the close link between perception and imagination. To avoid the confusion of terms, we will distinguish the imagination as the *inner ear*.

Training the inner ear means growing the ability to hear music without the instantiation of physical sounds. Composers hone this skill for their craft, exemplified by Beethoven's ability to compose even while deaf. Expert performers must also develop their inner ear for expressive playing. In *The Art of Piano Playing,* Heinrich Neuhaus instructs classical pianists to develop a crystal-clear *artistic image* of how a piece ought to sound with full expression, which then guides the body's movement to physically render the piece [34].

Even though classical performers no longer improvise original material[1], practicing written pieces still requires an active imagination. To discover the artistic image of a new piece, the expert practices by replaying passages in different ways (varying speed, dynamics, phrasing, etc.) while carefully listening to craft an original interpretation. Studies have shown that creative variation during practice boosts both their effectiveness and enjoyment [23].

PROCESS TO LEARN A PIECE

To understand how these skills translate to the practical task of learning pieces, we draw from both pedagotigal literature and personal experience. In the classical tradition, any musician—from the novice to the virtuoso—always learns from the score written by a composer. While the amateur translates instructions from the score directly into motions on the instrument, the expert first converts the score into an *artistic image* (or *aural image*) in the mind, which then guides the body's movement. When training the body, practice methods should reinforce performance habits [23]. Students must always aim to play with ease and expression, never slipping into auto-pilot mode where the mind wanders elsewhere. In practice as in performance, students should listen carefully and make physical adjustments based on what they hear.

First Person Perspective

For a glimpse into the process of learning a classical piece, we turn to the first-person perspective of the first author. Employed by David Sudnow in the now classic *Ways of the Hand* [55], first-person methodologies are gaining increasing traction within the field of HCI. In particular, first-person approaches have been applied to themes of embodied cognition and aesthetic experience to derive insights often overlooked by traditional third-person research practices [16, 43, 46].

The first-author studied piano for 18 years in the typical classical approach before taking an interest in alternative methods of learning music. For the past six years, she has studied intensively with a world class pianist and composer. She has documented her progress in journal entries, which include take-aways from weekly lessons and notes from daily practice. To reflect her personal perspective, the following section is presented in the first person voice.

Reference, Reduction, Reconstruction

When I begin to learn a new piece, the first step is always to familiarize myself through *reference* material. Generally, I try to listen to recordings from different artists. It also helps to watch videos of performances. Through these materials, I begin to form a high-level impression of how the piece might sound and feel. To get into the sound, I sometimes sing along with recordings, move my hands as if conducting, or even dance to the music.

Training myself to play the piece involves two main processes, which I will call *reduction* and *reconstruction. Reduction* means creating a sketch. I would first map out its structure, delineating sections and seeing their logical flow. In each section, I would find and play the melody by itself, which also helps with finding its internal structure and shape. In this phase, it is useful to understand some theory, which helps with identifying structure. However, it's important not to get caught up in intellectualizing for its own sake at the expense of playing musically. For the performer, theory is just a tool to help us with greater expression.

The *reduction* phase also involves pinpointing the difficulties of the piece. These could be due to complexity in content (e.g. unusual harmonies, dense counterpoint), in physical techniques that need more training (e.g. fast passages, octaves), or even in expressive interpretation (e.g. rapid changes in dyanmics). A good goal for the *reduction* stage is to be able to play every section of the piece only as melody, with full dynamics (and perhaps a simple harmony if you are able). In a way, it's like creating your own jazz lead sheet.

[1] It is worth noting that the current predominant culture of classical performance has not always been the norm throughout history. Until well into the 19th century, improvisation played an integral role in what we now know as "classical" music, especially for the piano [49].

After an initial sketch has been made, then comes the *reconstruction* phase, where I gradually begin to fill it in. There are a few strategies I typically use. For musically complex spots, I start with an outline, then gradually add more details as each version becomes fluent. Starting with the melody, I first add a bassline, then more of the harmony. If the material is too complex to play well, I simplify it. Sometimes, I ignore rhythm in the accompaniment and play it only as block chords. Singing along with the melody also helps to maintain musicality.

For technical difficulties, the trick is to invent exercises for yourself in order to keep your mind engaged. An easy way to do this is through octave displacement, playing a passage at different parts of the piano. I can also change the rhythm of the passage, or break it apart into smaller units and play the units in a different order. In the end, it doesn't matter too much what type of exercises you invent, as long as you maintain a flow state, where you are neither frustrated nor bored [6].

Finally, I can save a lot of practice time by grouping similar passages. Many pieces are built up from motifs, which are then repeated and varied. Recognizing them means what I have already practiced may be applied to speed up learning new material. This strategy also works from piece to piece. Let's say one piece uses a lot of octaves. If we encounter another piece that also has octaves, we should use our existing knowledge of the technique to help us learn the new piece faster. It's really just a switch in mindset and may seem simple, but even in practice, I often have trouble thinking in this way because of my own long training in the typical brute-force approach.

Though I segment practice into three distinct stages, the reality is never such a strict forward progression. It's very helpful to keep *referencing* recordings and videos (and to attend performances) even in more advanced stages of learning a piece. It's also helpful to go back to *reduction* every so often to not lose track of the underlying structure.

LEARNING FOR ALL LEVELS

Focus on listening, embodied understanding, and creative imagination is not only reserved for the already advanced. Several established methods for beginners focus on developing exactly this set of skills. For example, the Suzuki method advocates learning by ear [56], and Dalcroze Eurhythmics presents music as full-body exercises that connect physical movements with sound [20]. Dalcroze practitioner Claire-Lise Dutoit summarizes the principles of eurhythmics as cultivating "the ability to hear", to "understand and express music in movement", and "the call made on the pupil to improvise and develop freely his own ideas" [9]. These guiding principles also underlie several other teaching systems such as the Kodály, Willems, and Orff methods [53, 37, 1]. In all these approaches, symbolic notation is introduced only after the feeling of music is firmly grasped by the ear and the body. While these methods were originally conceived for children, they have also been effectively adapted for adult beginners.

Role of the Teacher

Teaching music for all levels should share the same priorities; instruction for the less advanced only differs in the level of guidance from the teacher. A good teacher may use demonstrations to tune the student's ear to different qualities of sound and to show how sounds manifest in bodily movements. The teacher may also break down a complex piece into more manageable parts, distill a knotty passage into its essence, and introduce intermediary exercises to guide a student through difficulties. Ultimately a good teacher also instills self-sufficiency—teaching students how to teach themselves.

Music Across Cultures

With few exceptions, discussion of music within HCI has primarily centered on the Western Classical tradition. While our ideas of piano learning readily apply across instruments in Western Classical music, it is important also to look beyond our own cultural defaults [50]. The perspective espoused by this paper may go against the "typical" view of music learning within HCI, but the same ideas are the accepted norm in many cultures around the world.

Historian Craig Wright observes that notation made the West an "odd culture out", for its adoption of a symbolic and quantitative representation. Other cultures described music differently in writing if they did so at all [67]. The Japanese, for example, record gestures instead of specific notes in *shakuhachi* scores. In cultures without a precise quantitative notation, primacy of the ear, the body, and the imagination take on greater importance during learning. Often, as in the case of Brazilian Samba Schools, learning to play is a social activity where imitation and interpersonal communication play a crucial role [40]. Samba derives in part from African drumming traditions, where a robust rhythm felt in the body animates performances coordinates ensemble playing. African traditions played a key role in the birth of American Jazz, which has in turn influenced much of popular music. In these traditions, development of the ear, an embodied understanding, and the creative imagination pervade all stages of the learning process [14, 19].

FROM DOMAIN KNOWLEDGE TO DESIGN

The previous sections offered a condensed overview of the knowledge and experiences that have shaped our thinking. From this background, we now turn to consider the design of interactive systems, introducing a design framework and discussing two example projects. The framework distills our desired learning process into three key components—Inspect, Embody, and Invent. We summarize each and put forth general guidelines for design. Two projects from our own prior research show how actual systems may support the desired learning process.

The same background has shaped both the framework and the two projects, though the framework had not yet been formalized when the projects were designed and deployed. To correlate the framework with concrete designs, we reinterpret interactions on the two projects in light of Inspect, Embody, Invent. Though it may not qualify as a formal evaluation of the framework, this exercise enriches the connection between domain knowedge, design theory, and working prototypes.

THE FRAMEWORK: INSPECT, EMBODY, INVENT

To open opportunities for the design of novel music learning systems, we summarize the main takeaways of the previous sections, which we term Inspect, Embody, and Invent.

Inspect

refers to the necessity to convey an understanding of repertoir beyond surface correctness:

- Learning should tune the ear to the quality of sounds, such as tone, phrasing, and rhythm.
- Students should learn to recognize underlying structure beyond individual notes (e.g. broad harmonic shifts, cadences, and motifs).
- It's important to present musical structures and qualities not just as intellectualized symbols. The eye should support the ear, not take its place.

Embody

refers to the crucial role played by the body when learning to play music:

- Music should be felt through the whole body, with a basic rhythm corrdinating the body's movements.
- Imitation is an effective way to learn to use the body for both technique and expression.
- During practice, students should always feel the music so that it flows with ease and expression, even if they have to simplify a piece to its essence.

Invent

refers to the development of the creative imagination.

- Students should not only train the ear for physical sounds but should also learn to "hear" music with the *inner ear*.
- It is helpful to invent exercises for difficult passages to decrease frustration and to engage the mind for more effective practice.
- Like learning to speak a language, the ultimate goal of playing music is to *speak* through the music.

EXAMPLE SYSTEMS

To bridge theory with actual designs of interactive systems, we describe two existing projects from our own research. Both projects augment a Yamaha Disklavier player piano with projection [71]. The first, MirrorFugue, is inspired by reflections on the lacquered surface of a grand piano and simulates the presence of a virtual pianist playing the physically moving keys [68, 69]. The second, Andante, visually echoes the bodily sensation of musical phrases through the silhouettes of miniature figures walking and dancing on the keys [70]. Both are already documented in their respective publications. We describe here only their technical implementation and musical content in order to ground the discussion of interactions in light of Inspect, Embody, Invent.

Figure 1. Learning through imitating a virtual performer on MirrorFugue

MirrorFugue

Setup

To create the illusion of a virtual reflection playing the piano, 720p video of a pianist's hands and upper body is projected onto the piano's keyboard and music stand. Video of the hands is calibrated to align with the physical keyboard and is naturally reflected on the fallboard (the vertical surface in front of the keys). For the upper body display, a 39"x11" piece of ¼" plywood treated with projection paint is placed on the music stand. Both videos are beamed from a a short throw projector mounted above the piano bench 7' from the ground. This setup ensures that a person seated normally at the piano does not occlude the projected images.

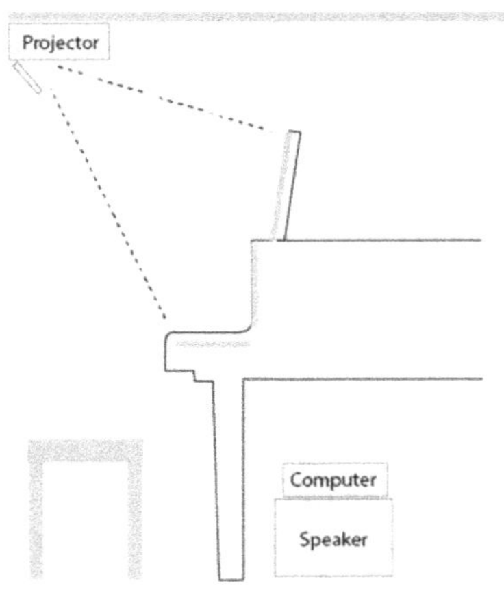

Figure 2. System diagram showing projection setup for both MirrorFugue and Andante

Data for a MirrorFugue performance comprises one MIDI sequence and two videos, one to capture the piano keyboard and the other to capture the pianist's head and shoulders. MIDI output from the Disklavier is fed to a computer through a MIDI-to-USB cable and is recorded along with an audio stream from the computer's own microphone. Video and MIDI data are then manually edited using their accompanying audio for synchronization. The causal link between the life-sized projected video, the physical movement of the keys, and the acoustic sound from the piano creates a striking illusion of the pianist's physical presence. The effect is especially vivid for someone seated at the piano bench.

A custom Java program controls MirrorFugue for demonstrations and exhibits. For demonstrations, selected performances may be triggered from the keys of a wireless numpad. For exhibits, the program supports looping playlists that are either predefined or randomized. We are currently developing a new version of the program in JavaScript that allows playback at various speeds, fast-forward, and rewind. The new program runs from the Chrome web browser, thanks to an extension of the Web MIDI specification published in June 2015 [65].

Content

Performances from 15 pianists were recorded for MirrorFugue. This roster includes 8 professionals, among them three Steinway Artists and several well-known names (e.g. Allen Toussaint, Vijay Iyer, and Ryuichi Sakamoto) [54]. Other recorded players include two children, one piano teacher, and two professors from the MIT Media Lab (Marvin Minsky and Joe Paradiso), as well as the first-author herself. These recordings showcase a range of musical styles and levels of expertise.

Many aspects of playing the piano may be absorbed by listening and watching a MirrorFugue performance more effectively than watching a video on a screen [68, 69]. From the hands on the keyboard, a student may observe fingering as well as shifts in hand position and weight balance. From the upper body, a student may understand the relationship between breath and phrase, how rhythm is felt, and how a performer may personify characters and moods. Additionally, a student may pick up elements of personal style, delving into multiple interpretations of the same piece or emulating the technique of artists whose hand and body type is most similar to theirs.

Andante

Setup

Andante retains the same projector setup as MirrorFugue. To display on the fallboard, the reflective keyboard cover is replaced with a projection surface made form the same material as the MirrorFugue upper body display.

For the original implementation of Andante, all animations were drawn by hand using a lightboard for precise control of character's movements. Frame sequences were organzed based on type of step (e.g. whole step between white keys). A Java program controls playback by reading MIDI recorded from a human player and selecting the appropriate frame sequences to display for each note played by the Disklavier. We are currently working on a new version of Andante in JavaScript that procedurally generates character animations with lifelike movement from human input of musical phrases.

Figure 3. (left) Rendering polyphonic music on Andante. (right) A screenshot from the new JavaScript program that shows symbolic notation with Andante.

Content

To show a range of content for Andante, the original implementation featured three example applications: scales played by a variety of characters, a blues baseline to accompany improvisers, and a Bach canon that maps polyphony into a different figure for each voice. Unlike MirrorFugue, which seeks to reflect reality, Andante abstracts and miniaturizes the figure, which personifies the shape and structure of musical lines. Since people easily emphathize with characters in animated films from their expressive form and movement [42], Andante's figures invite the user to project themselves into a virtual microcosm.

The cartoon nature of the figures makes Andante especially well-suited for teaching children. The characters' appearance and gait echoes and amplifies the shape of musical phrases and may help attune the ear to qualities of sound. We may also use Andante to introduce symbolic notation, taking advantage of the resemblance between a figure's head and how notes are written. The head may be shown with variations in stem and filling to indicate the type of note, and it may be raised or lowered on a staff to reflect what keys are played by the figure. This maintains a connection to a body-based intuition of music when introducing symbolic notation.

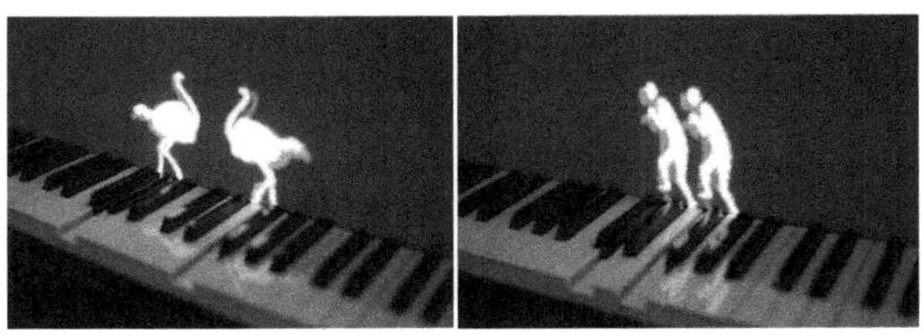

Figure 4. Different characters on Andante

INTERACTIONS

MirrorFugue has been shown to 12 concert-level pianists and 2 professional teachers. In-depth interviews were conducted with 5 of these expert musicians while quotes and general impressions were recorded from the rest. We also observed interactions of MirrorFugue "in the wild" at a public exhibition in New Orleans over two week in December 2015. The exhibit featured recordings from 4 local pianists and allowed visitors to sit at the piano and interact with the instrument.

Andante has been shown to 5 professional performers, with 3 of whom we conducted in-depth interviews. Andante was also integrated into lesson of 30-50 minutes with 8 children between the ages of 7 and 12, following 15-20 hours of design discussions with a Dalcroze certified piano teacher over the course of 9 months.

Based on comments from the expert interviews as well as observations from the MirrorFugue exhibit and Andante lessons, we derived three main ways to engage with both projects: listening, imitating, and playing a duet. These are not rigid modes of interaction, but instead allow a user to fluidly go from one mode to another. These interactions may be linked to the Inspect, Embody, and Invent stages of learning, which we describe in more detail along with illustrative scenarios.

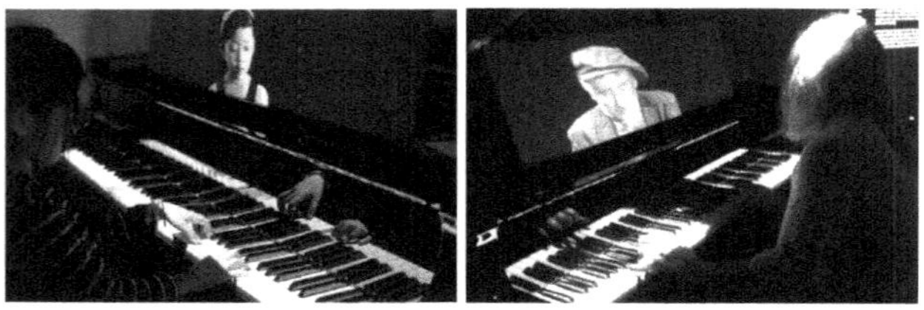

Figure 5. (left) A child improvises with her own reflection. (right) A visitor imitates blues pianist Jon Cleary.

Inspect

Most basically, a user may sit at the piano to review recordings on both MirrorFugue and Andante. All the pianists who saw MirrorFugue expressed that it was an excellent tool to understand fingering as well as musical expression. At the exhibit, we observed that children would rest their hands on the moving keys as they listened to the performance. After the Andante lessons, the teacher observed that his students listened more carefully to pieces play with Andante and retained a better memory of what they had heard.

We hypothesize that both MirrorFugue and Andante may help students develop their ear as visual elements may draw attention to nuances in quality of sound. Both systems also relate the perception of sound to other dimensions of musical understanding. MirrorFugue presents sound in relation to actions of the performer while Andante brings forth the symbolic, structural aspects of a piece. Additionally, students may also capture their own playing on the piano and review it on either system. On MirrorFugue, students may become more aware of their own body during playing, observing technique, posture, as well as expressive gesture. A recording mapped to Andante figures may help focus attention to the shape of phrases and the feeling of rhythms. Both systems may teach students to assess the quality of their own playing.

Embody

MirrorFugue and Andante both advocate learning through imitation. Both support playback at slower speeds as sound is generated on the piano from MIDI instructions. Through copying the physical movement of playing, expression is absorbed as an integral part of the overall musical statement.

A striking example of this interaction took place at the MirrorFugue exhibit, where a fan of one of the recorded pianists sat down in front of the piano and began to imitate her virtual idol. Though she has no training in piano, she was able to mirror almost exactly the overall movements of the virtual body and hands. This demonstrates how MirrorFugue may allow students to grasp the larger gestures of a piece before preoccupation with specific notes.

During the Andante lessons, the difference between quarter notes and eighth notes were introduced as "walk" vs "run", which allowed children to grasp patterns more quickly than from the score alone. Andante may help students internalize rhythms before learning specific notes on the piano. This may speed up learning by breaking down the process, decreasing cognitive load at each step.

Figure 6. (left) A lesson using Andante. (right) Playing the blues with a virtual figure walking a bass line.

Invent

More advanced pianists who sat at the bench of MirrorFugue and Andante almost always began to play with the recordings without prompt. They were often highly motivated by the experience of playing a duet with famous virtual pianists. We also observed younger users, in this case children below the age of 10, who couldn't help "accompanying" the pianist in MirrorFugue by playing along.

These interactions demonstrate how students may play virtual duets with Andante and MirrorFugue as a part of their training. This may be useful when the student needs to repeat a phrase several times to secure it in the ear and the body. In such cases, MirrorFugue may provide a background that varies as the student repeats, to help focus the student's ear. As the student becomes more fluent with the material, MirrorFugue and Andante may provide a base against which the student may improvise with the material. For example, the system might provide a harmonic progression, allowing room for the student to invent melodies.

BEYOND MUSIC

To close, we reflect on how insights from the music learning process may inform the understanding of learning and embodiment in general. We first connect ideas presented in this paper to existing theories from the congnitive sciences. We then consider the broader relevance of Inspect, Embody, Invent by applying it to diverse domains beyond music.

Connection to Cognition

The prevailing view of music learning for novices and alternative approaches advocated by this paper echo contrasting views of human cognition. Descended from the likes of Plato and Descartes, the dominant view in Western philosophy has long held that humans live in an objective, external world. Thus, cognition is the process of forming and manipulating mental representations of that world [62]. Following this tradition, Cognitivists (as termed by Varela et al.), particularly in the field of Artificial Intelligence, liken the human mind to a computer, where representations are abstract symbols, which the brain manipulates independent of the body, the physical world, and any deeper meaning.

Underlying assumptions of typical classical piano learning align closely with a Cognitivist worldview. Playing music is seen as the process of programming the body to perform instructions encoded in abstract symbols to produce sound. Practice requires repetition only because human muscles (unlike machines) must repeat to remember. After instructions are programmed into muscle memory, the player then adds expression, like applying formatting to a text document.

In contrast, the approach to learning music summarized by our framework correspond to ideas of embodied cognition, a topic of growing interest among HCI researchers in recent years [8, 16, 18, 27, 43, 48, 58]. Embodied cognition argues that the body's ability to perceive and act within an environment plays a crucial role in how humans understand the world [19, 62]. Learning to play music can thus be seen as the process to acquire the perception (listening) and motor skills (technique) to act within the environment of the instrument.

Compelling arguments across disciplines place embodiment at the root of human cognition. In his work with children, Piaget described a progression from pure sensory-motor experience to symbolic logical thinking in human cognitive development [21]. Within linguistics, Lakoff and Johnson argue that abstract concepts are understood in terms of the more concrete, ultimately scaffolding upon basic sensory-motor experience [24]. The effectiveness of music learning methods like Dalcroze Eurythmics [44], which begin by cultivating a body-based musical intuition, also support theories of embodied cognition.

Generalizing the Framework

The Inspect, Embody, Invent framework is relevant for diverse skills that include a physical and creative component. Examples include dance, sports, martial arts, cooking, crafts, as well as plastic arts such as drawing and sculpture.

In the generalized framework, **Inspect** calls for systems to support the development of the senses. For example, learning to draw requires learning to see [10], dance requires enhanced kinesthesia, and cooking requires a heightened sensitivity to taste. To support the development of perception, reference materials as well as feedback methods provided by a system should emphasize the qualitative and the sensorial more than quantitative, intellectualized representations.

Embody calls for systems to support and enhance the role of the body during learning. Video is already a popular medium for people around to world to learn new skills, demonstrating the efficacy of imitation. Novel interfaces might consider how to go beyond the simple video in supporting imitation. Systems might also explore strategies to coordinate movements of the entire body.

Finally, **Invent** calls for systems to encourage and support users to creatively engage with what they have learned. This includes not only making personal statements through the medium (e.g. inventing new dishes or dance moves) but also creative experimentation during practice to acquire basic skills. Systems may provide examples to inspire the user as well as create environments to motivate creative output.

Though Inspect, Embody, Invent is most immediately applicable for domains involving physical skill, it may also have broader relevance for more abstract subjects. A compelling example is Seymour Papert's work with the LOGO programming language to teach children mathematics [40]. Papert introduced math concepts through a programmable *turtle* with both a virtual and a physical manifestation. Programming LOGO enabled children to solve problems not by blind symbol manipulation but by projecting themselves into the perspective of the *turtle* (Embody). Papert also observed that effective learning environments invite participants in with sensorially rich discoveries (Inspect) and foster learning through varied enactments that allow room for expression (Invent).

CONCLUSION

Our ultimate goal in writing this paper is to help designers create more effective and enjoyable music learning systems that promote a deeper understanding of musicality. To this end, we first uncovered the assumptions within the prevailing view of music learning in the Western classical tradition, tracing how these assumptions have shaped the design of existing music learning systems. Next, we presented an alternative view of music learning drawing from domain literature and first person experience. Finally, we distilled key points of the alternative view into a new framework—Inspect, Embody, Invent—and used it to reinterpret two existing projects on the piano. This paper also tried to connect the dots between the process of music learning to broader domains for design, relating ideas from music learning to existing theories of embodiment and cognition and applying our framework to the learning of other skills beyond music.

We recognize that our general approach may be seen as unorthodox against the de facto rules of HCI research. Thus, we included references to methodologies and precedents (e.g. Reflexive design and auto-ethnography) as necessary to justify our course of research. Conversely, we observe that traditional HCI methodologies with their focus on optimizing quantifiable metrics risk blinding researchers to the richness and nuance of artistic practices. We hope that this work may contribute to a broader discussion on appropriate research methods to design for the arts on their own terms.

CODA

The field of HCI is always seeking new metaphors and frameworks to guide the design of new interactions with the computer. For us, music has been a rich source of inspiration, with the piano an especially interesting example. Unlike other musical instruments, which feature a direct connection between the human body and the sound-producing object, the piano keyboard is an artificial interface used to operate a back-end machine. It thus has striking parallels with the early form-factors of the computer—a machine accessed through commands on the keyboard. (Interestingly, another name for the first typewriters was "literary piano" [61]).

The piano keyboard interface allows a single person to play more complex music than on any other instrument. Consequently, learning to play all too often prioritizes a symbolic understanding over embodiment and emotional expression, drawing an interesting parallel with the many problems of using the traditional computer. However, experts on the piano do learn to play the machine with the command of the entire body, authentic emotional expression, and a fluent grasp of sophisticated musical structures. We believe that deeper understanding of all these facets of of musical performance may yield valuable insights for designing more engaging, more *human* interactions with the computer.

This paper has attempted to shed some light on these topics, providing a primer for deeper music learning. There is still much unexplored territory, and we have offered pointers to some promising areas of future research for musical applications and beyond. As Alan Kay called for all aspiring technologists to delve into the liberal arts for an "endless well of inspiration" [21], we encourage researchers to delve more deeply into the endlessly fascinating world of music.

ACKNOWLEDGEMENTS

This paper was motivated by learnings from several years of piano lessons with Donal Fox. Conversations with Pablo Puente, Hanoi Hantrakul, Edith Ackerman, and Ken Perlin also contributed much to our thinking. We are grateful to Yamaha for their generous loan of a Disklavier piano over the past 4 years and to the Tangible Media Group for continual support. Thanks to the anonymous reviewers for their constructive feedback.

REFERENCES

1. American Off-Schulwerk Association. What is Orff Schulwerk? http://aosa.org/about/what- is- orff-schulwerk/. Accessed: 2015–09–25.
2. Berklee. Berklee Online. https: //online.berklee.edu/school/courses/music_education. Accessed: 2015–08–25.
3. Berlitz. The Berlitz Method. http://www.berlitz.us/berlitz- method/. Accessed: 2015–09–25.
4. Ran Blake. 2010. Primacy of the Ear. Lulu.com.
5. Casio. Lighted Keys. http://www.casio-usa.com/ products/Digital_Pianos_%26_Keyboards/Lighted_Keys/. Accessed: 2015–09–20.
6. Mihaly Csikszentmihalyi. 1990. Flow: the Psychology of Optimal Experience. Harper Perennial.
7. Roger B. Dannenberg, M. Sanchez, A. Joseph, P. Capell, R Joseph, and R Saul. 1990. A Computer-Based Multi-Media Tutor for Beginning Piano Students. Interface - Journal of New Music Research 19 (1990), 155–173. Issue 2-3.
8. Paul Dourish. 2004. Where the Action: The Foundations of Embodied Interaction. The MIT Press.
9. Claire-Lise Dutoit. 1965. Music Movement Therapy. The Riverside Press.
10. Betty Edwards. 1989. Drawing on the Right Side of the Brain. Tarcher.
11. Y. Fukuya, Takegawa Y., and H. Yanagi. 2013. A Piano Learning Support System Considering Motivation. (2013).
12. Rolf Inge Godoy and Marc Leman (Eds.). 2010. Musical Gestures: Sound, Movement, and Meaning. Routeledge.
13. W. Goebl and G. Widmer. 2006. Unobtrusive Practice Tools for Pianists. In Proceedings of the 9th International Conference on Music Perception and Cognition.

14. Lucy Green. 2002. How Popular Musicians Learn: A Way Ahead for Music Education. Ashgate Publishing, Ltd.
15. A. Hadjakos, E. Aitenbichler, and M. Mühlhäuser. 2008. The Elbow Piano: Signification of Piano Playing Movements. In Proceedings of NIME '08.
16. Kristina Höök. 2010. Transferring Qualities from Horseback Riding to Design. In Proc. NordiCHI '10.
17. Kevin Huang, Ellen Yi-Luen Do, and Thad Starner. 2008. PianoTouch: A Wearable Haptic Piano Instruction System for Passive Learning of Piano Skills. In Proc. ISWC '08. IEEE Computer Society, Washington, DC, USA, 41–44.
18. Caroline Hummels, Kees C. Overbeeke, and Sietske Klooster. 2007. Move to Get Moved: A Search for Methods, Tools and Knowledge to Design for Expressive and Rich Movement-based Interaction. Personal Ubiquitous Comput. 11, 8 (Dec. 2007).
19. Vijay S. Iyer. 1998. Microstructures of Feel, Macrostructures of Sound: Embodied Cognition in West African and Africa-American Musics. Ph.D. Dissertation. UC Berkeley.
20. Emile Jacques-Dalcroze. 1967. Rhythm, Music, and Education. The Riverside Press.
21. Alan Kay. Doing with Images Makes Symbols. https://archive.org/details/AlanKeyD1987. Accessed: 2015–09–25.
22. T. Kitamura and M. Miura. 2006. Constructing a Support System for Self-Learning Playing the Piano at the Beginning Stage. In Proceedings of the 9th International Conference on Music Perception and Cognition.
23. Gerald Klickstein. 2009. The Musician's Way: A Guide to Practice, Performance, and Wellness. Oxford University Press.
24. George Lakoff and Mark Johnson. 2003. Metaphors We Live By. University of Chicago Press.
25. Chih-Chun Lin and Damon Shing-Min Liu. 2006. An Intelligent Virtual Piano Tutor. In Proc. VRCIA '06.
26. Synthesia LLC. Synthesia. http://www.synthesiagame.com/. Accessed: 2015–09–20.
27. Lian Loke and Toni Robertson. 2013. Moving and Making Strange: An Embodied Approach to Movement-based Interaction Design. ACM Trans. Comput.-Hum. Interact. 20, 1 (April 2013).
28. Michael Matthews. 18 Benefits of Playing a Musical Instrument. http: //www.effectivemusicteaching.com/articles/directors/ 18- benefits- of- playing- a- musical- instrument/. Accessed: 2015–09–25.
29. David McGill. 2007. Sound in Motion: A Performer's Guide to Greater Musical Expression. Indiana University Press.
30. Andrew P. McPherson, Adrian Gierakowski, and Adam M. Stark. 2013. The Space Between the Notes: Adding Expressive Pitch Control to the Piano Keyboard. In Proc. CHI '13 (CHI '13).
31. P. Molenberghs, R. Cunnington, and J. Mattingley. Is the Mirror Neuron System Involved in Imitation? A short review and meta-analysis. Neuroscience and Biobehavioral Reviews 33, 975–980. Issue 7.
32. R. Montes, M. Bedmar, and M. Sol Martin. 1993. EMG Biofeedback of the Abductor Pollicis Brevis in Piano Performance. Biofeedback and Self-Regulation 18, 67–77. Issue 2.
33. J. Mora, W.-S. Lee, G. Comeau, S. Shiromohammadi, and A. El Saddik. 2006. Assisted Piano Pedagogy Through 3D Visualization of Piano Playing. (2006).
34. Heinrich Neuhaus. 1995. The Art of Piano Playing. Hollowbrook Pub.
35. K. Ng and P. Nesi. 2008. i-Maestro: Technology-Enhanced Learning and Teaching for Music. In Proceedings of NIME '08.
36. Kia C. Ng, Tillman Weyde, Oliver Larkin, Kerstin Neubarth, Thijs Koerselman, and Bee Ong. 2007. 3D Augmented Mirror: A Multimodal Interface for String Instrument Learning and Teaching with Gesture Support. In Proceedings of the 9th International Conference on Multimodal Interfaces (ICMI '07). ACM, New York, NY, USA, 339–345.
37. The Swiss Website of Willems Music Education Teachers. Willems Music Teaching System. http://www.willems.ch/en/education.htm. Accessed: 2015–09–25.
38. C. Oshima, Y. Miyazawa, and K. Nishimoto. 2002. Color-in Piano: A Piano that Allows a Performer to Concentrate on Musical Expression. In Proceedings of the 7th International Conference on Music Perception and Cognition.
39. Chika Oshima, Kazushi Nishimoto, and Norihiro Hagita. 2007. A Piano Duo Support System for Parents to Lead Children to Practice Musical Performances. ACM Trans. Multimedia Comput. Commun. Appl. 3, 2, Article 9 (May 2007).
40. Seymour Papert. 1993. Windstorms: Children, Computers, and Powerful Ideas. Basic Books.
41. Graham Percival, Ye Wang, and George Tzanetakis. 2007. Effective Use of Multimedia for Computer-assisted Musical Instrument Tutoring. In Proc. EMME '07.

42. Ken Perlin and Athomas Goldberg. 1996. Improv: A System for Scripting Interactive Actors in Virtual Worlds. Computer Graphics 29, 3 (1996).
43. Sebastiaan Pijnappel and Florian Mueller. 2013. 4 Design Themes for Skateboarding. In Proc. CHI '13.
44. P. Puentes and P. Godall. 2012. Evaluation of the Dalcroze Rhythmic Approach in First Steos of Music Education. Master project research. Barcelona: UAB.
45. Kathleen Riley. 2007. New Views of Piano Playing Through Motion Analysis and MIDI Technology. Journal of Technology in Music Learning 4 (2007), 17–30. Issue 1.
46. Katja Rogers, Amrei Röhlig, Matthias Weing, Jan Gugenheimer, Bastian Könings, Melina Klepsch, Florian Schaub, Enrico Rukzio, Tina Seufert, and Michael Weber. 2014. P.I.A.N.O.: Faster Piano Learning with Interactive Projection. In Proc. ITS '14 (ITS '14). ACM, New York, NY, USA, 149–158.
47. Thecla Schiphorst. 2011. Self-evidence: Applying Somatic Connoisseurship to Experience Design. In CHI '11 Extended Abstracts.
48. N. Schnell, F. Bevilacqua, D. Schwarz, N. Rasamimanana, and F. Guédy. 2006. Technology and Paradigms to Support the Learning of Music Performance. (2006).
49. Harold C. Schonberg. 1987. The Great Pianists: From Mozart to the Present. Simon and Schuster.
50. Phoebe Sengers, Kirsten Boehner, Shay David, and Joseph 'Jofish' Kaye. 2005. Reflective Design. In Proc. Critical Computing '05 (CC '05). ACM, New York, NY, USA, 49–58.
51. S. Shiromohammadi, A. Khanafar, and G. Comeau. 2006. Midiator A Tool for Analyzing Students' Piano Performance. Revue de recherche en Education Musicale 24 (2006).
52. Stephen W. Smoliar, John A. Waterworth, and Peter R. Kellock. 1995. pianoFORTE: A System for Piano Education Beyond Notation Literacy. In Proc. ACM Multimedia '95.
53. International Kodály Society. The Kodály Concept. http://www.iks.hu/index.php/home1/the- kodaly- concept. Accessed: 2015–09–25.
54. Steinway & Sons. Steinway Artists. http://eu.steinway.com/en/concert-artist/artists-alphabet/. Accessed: 2016–01–07.
55. David Sudnow. 1993. Ways of the Hand. The MIT Press.
56. Shinichi Suzuki. 1974. The Suzuki Concept: An Introduction to a Successful Method for Early Music Education. Diablo Press.
57. Yoshinari Takegawa, Tsutomu Terada, and Masahiko Tsukamoto. 2012. A Piano Learning Support System Considering Rhythm. In Proc. ICMC '12.
58. Jakob Tholander and Carolina Johansson. 2010. Design Qualities for Whole Body Interaction: Learning from Golf, Skateboarding and BodyBugging. In Proc. NordiCHI '10.
59. Michel Thomas. The Michel Thomas Method. http://www.michelthomas.com/. Accessed: 2015–09–25.
60. Mary Tov. 2003. The Video Camera: A Teacher's Best Friend. The Piano Adventures Teacher (2003).
61. *Type Writing Machine*. Scientific American. Vol. 1017. Issue 1.
62. F.J. Varela, E. T. Thompson, and E. Rosch. 1992. The Embodied Mind: Cognitive Science and Human Experience. The MIT Press.
63. Kenny Werner. 1996. Effortless Mastery: Liberating the Master Musician Within. James Aeberold.
64. Abby Whiteside. 1955. Indispensables of Piano Playing. Charles Scribner's Sons.
65. Chris Wilson, Google, and Jussi Kalliokoski. Web MIDI API. https://webaudio.github.io/web- midi- api/. Accessed: 2015–06–15.
66. Victor Wooten. Music As a Language. http://http://ed. ted.com/lessons/victor- wooten- music- as- a- language. Accessed: 2014–02–04.
67. Craig Wright. 2013. City, Chant and the Topography of Early Music. Harvard University Press, Chapter Quantification in Medieval Paris and How it Changed Western Music.
68. Xiao Xiao and Hiroshi Ishii. 2011. MirrorFugue: Communicating Hand Gesture in Remote Piano Collaboration. In Proc. TEI '11.
69. Xiao Xiao, Anna Pereira, and Hiroshi Ishii. 2013a. MirrorFugue III: Conjuring the Recorded Pianist. In Proc. NIME '13.
70. Xiao Xiao, Basheer Tome, and Hiroshi Ishii. 2014. Andante:. In Proc. NIME '14.
71. Yamaha. Disklavier Pianos. http://usa.yamaha.com/ products/musical- instruments/keyboards/disklaviers/. Accessed 2016–01–07.

TimeFork: Interactive Prediction of Time Series

Sriram Karthik Badam,[1] Jieqiong Zhao,[2] Shivalik Sen,[3] Niklas Elmqvist,[1] and David Ebert[2]

[1]University of Maryland
College Park, MD, USA
{sbadam|elm}@umd.edu

[2]Purdue University
West Lafayette, IN, USA
{zhao413|ebertd}@purdue.edu

[3]Birla Institute of Technology and Science
Goa, India
shvlksen@gmail.com

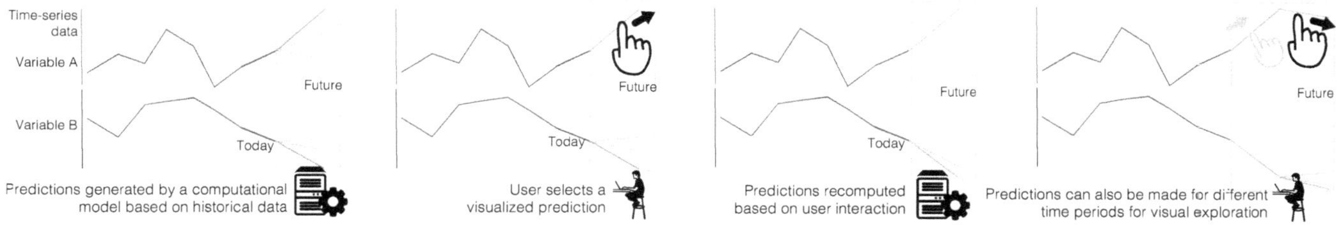

Figure 1. TimeFork is a technique for interactive prediction of time-series data. It uses computational models to create and show predictions on time-series visual representations. They are explored through a dialogue, driven by interaction, to see how predictions for time-series variables change based on others. This approach harnesses user knowledge of external factors and the ability of computational models to predict based on past trends.

ABSTRACT

We present TimeFork, an interactive prediction technique to support users predicting the future of time-series data, such as in financial, scientific, or medical domains. TimeFork combines visual representations of multiple time series with prediction information generated by computational models. Using this method, analysts engage in a back-and-forth dialogue with the computational model by alternating between manually predicting future changes through interaction and letting the model automatically determine the most likely outcomes, to eventually come to a common prediction using the model. This computer-supported prediction approach allows for harnessing the user's knowledge of factors influencing future behavior, as well as sophisticated computational models drawing on past performance. To validate the TimeFork technique, we conducted a user study in a stock market prediction game. We present evidence of improved performance for participants using TimeFork compared to fully manual or fully automatic predictions, and characterize qualitative usage patterns observed during the user study.

Author Keywords

Visual Analytics; Human-in-the-loop; Time Series; Visual Prediction; User Study

ACM Classification Keywords

H.5.2 Information Interfaces and Presentation: User Interfaces—*Interaction styles*; I.3.6 Computer Graphics: Methodology and Techniques—*Interaction techniques*

CHI'16, May 07-12, 2016, San Jose, CA, USA
© 2016 ACM. ISBN 978-1-4503-3362-7/16/05...$15.00
DOI: http://dx.doi.org/10.1145/2858036.2858150

INTRODUCTION

Time-series data is prevalent across many domains, including financial markets, healthcare, meteorology, seismology, and astronomy. Information visualization (InfoVis) and visual analytics (VA) techniques are commonly used to analyze such time-series datasets. Recent techniques [52, 53] in these fields visualize time series and related statistical metrics to enable analysts to interactively reason about the temporal data. Their goal is to better leverage the human ability to gain understanding from visualizations, including identifying the underlying trends, anomalies, and correlations, through an interactive and undirected search [28]. However, going beyond understanding time-series data to predicting its future behavior remains a very challenging task, and few interactive exploration models exist that support this activity.

Prediction information has been integrated into time-series representations in the past [18]. Hao et al. [16] called this approach *visual prediction*: the act of visually predicting a time-series variable by observing the predictions from a computational model, shown alongside the time-series representations. However, traditional approaches cannot fully support visual exploration of future trends in complex multivariate datasets such as stock markets, weather, and healthcare data, mainly due to their lack of consideration of inter-variable relationships (e.g., if A increases, B decreases). Exploring these relationships through "what-if" questions (e.g., what if A increases?) can help us better judge the future than blindly trusting computational models that lack contextual information (e.g., legislation on fracking affecting oil stock prices).

In this paper, we present **TimeFork**, an interactive prediction technique for visual prediction of multivariate time series through visual exploration of predictions from computational models and the time-series data itself. To understand the motivation behind this technique, let us consider a potential use-case scenario involving prediction of the stock market. Stock traders have access to stock price and trade volume information, and they might also be following news, Twitter, and the earning reports of the companies they are interested in. Visualizations can aid them in understanding this data, e.g., how the stocks have changed over time, the current state of each stock, and how people are reacting on Twitter. However, knowing this information, they now have to make an estimate of the future for investment in each stock, even though they may not fully understand how to optimally account for their observations from the visualizations, the events happening during that time (such as product releases, mergers, and acquisitions), and the dynamic relationships among their stocks. By using a computer-supported technique such as TimeFork, traders can engage in an interactive dialogue with the computer to show them multiple predictions (with different confidences based on the historical data), account for different "what-if" scenarios (e.g., what if stock A increases due to their increased earnings), and come to a shared set of predictions with the computer through visual exploration.

The predictions generated by the computational models in TimeFork reflect the temporal (based on the past data of a variable) and conditional trends (based on the past relationships between variables), and are explored through an iterative process of judging what will happen to each variable based on specific future trends selected by the user for others (Figure 1). This interactive dialogue between the computer and the data analyst continues until the analyst finds sufficient information to make a decision. To showcase TimeFork, we developed STOCKFORK, a stock market VA application that instantiates the TimeFork technique using machine learning models trained on stock market data. Furthermore, we evaluated the effectiveness of TimeFork for visual prediction through a simulated stock trading experiment. In this study, participants were given an opportunity to invest virtual money on three stocks and make decisions based on their predictions. We found that the presence of a dialogue in TimeFork led to higher monetary gains compared to traditional automatic and manual prediction approaches in specific scenarios. The results of these analyses and our observations along with their implications are explained in later sections after descriptions of the related work, the technique, and the StockFork tool.

BACKGROUND

The motivation for TimeFork comes from the philosophy of visual analytics [46] itself: using computational models (for prediction) closely coupled with visual exploration (of time series). Below we discuss the literature related to time-series visualizations, time-series analytics, and visual prediction.

Time-Series Visualization

Heer et al. [19] provide examples of simple charts used for visualizing time-series data including index charts, horizon graphs, stacked graphs, and small multiples. More contextual representations for time-series include cluster and calendar-based visualizations [47], spiral visualizations [49] that map periodic sections of time-series into ring layouts, trend and trajectory visualizations [40] in financial markets, and multi-resolution layouts for handling overplotting in large time-series by switching between aggregated and detailed representations [17, 31]. Beyond static and interactive representations, there have also been animated representations to show trajectories of time-series variables. Moere et al. [35] built a 3D visualization based on information flocking [39] to show static and dynamic patterns arising in stock markets.

For large datasets, techniques [14] for visualizing the essence of the time series through perceptually important points—points that are most informative to visual identification—have been proposed. From an interaction standpoint, Hochheiser and Shneiderman's TimeSearcher [22] enabled dynamic quering of time-series visualizations through timeboxes—rectangular regions drawn on the 2D representations—to show details-on-demand. This tool was further developed to search time-series trends through similarity measures [6]. More recently, Zhao et al. [52] supported visual exploration of derived values and correlations within time-series data using lenses to transform time-series representations.

Time-Series Analytics and Prediction

Fu et al. [13] reviewed data mining models for time-series data including methods for representation, classification, segmentation, and pattern discovery. They identify two important pattern matching tasks: discovering frequent vs. surprising patterns. Approaches for motif discovery [9, 45], anomaly detection [8, 50], and novelty detection [33] answer these challenges. Of special interest to TimeFork are clustering and classification techniques that help to identify similar patterns across time series using distance measures [26] to quantify the relationships between time-series variables. Examples of such approaches [30] include using self-organizing maps [29], agglomerative clustering, and distance-based metrics. Rule mining [13, 21] to find rules defining the inter-variable relationships, is also of interest to computer-supported prediction techniques such as TimeFork.

Time-series prediction has often been attempted using statistical approaches such as regression analysis [18], as well as soft computing approaches such as neural networks, fuzzy logic, and evolutionary computation [37]. Among the latter, both supervised (e.g., multilayer perceptron) and unsupervised learning architectures (e.g., self-organizing maps [2]) have been applied. In financial markets, neural networks have been successful not only in predicting stocks based on their past price trends [48], but also based on the mood observed on Twitter [3]. However, stock prediction through automated techniques has mostly been restricted to individual stocks without generalizations. Beyond this, weather and healthcare data prediction has also relied on soft computing [32, 44].

Mixed-Initiative Techniques and Visual Prediction

Our TimeFork technique resembles mixed-initiative interaction [23], which targets a natural interleaving of contributions by people and computers to solve a task together [24]. These interaction techniques engage the user in an efficient dialogue with the system through interaction to resolve uncertainties. Mixed-initiative techniques have recently been used to analyze data on visual interfaces, where the user can interact with the parameter space of a computational model for classification to eventually come up with better results [27]. In visual analytics, semantic interaction [12] follows a similar ideology by coupling analyst's interaction with statistical models that incrementally learn and update visualizations (in their case, document layouts). Similar to these techniques, TimeFork aims at achieving an interactive dialogue between analysts and computers to make better predictions.

TimeSearcher3 [7] visualized predictions in a time-series visualization following a data-driven forecasting method. This system extrapolated time-series data by finding similar past sequences, while allowing the user to control the similarity metrics. Hao et al.'s [16] approach to supporting visual prediction went beyond TimeSearcher3 to support integration of multiple prediction models including autoregressive integrated moving average (ARIMA), Holt Winters (a seasonal method), and similarity-based models. They extended this approach to visualize peak-preserving predictions [18] for seasonal trends, interact with the model to adjust smoothing parameters, and connect predictions to similar past trends through brushing-and-linking. Malik et al. [34] presented a VA approach to explore correlations in multivariate spatiotemporal data. Still, visual prediction of multivariate time series—very common in financial, scientific, and medical domains—remains a challenge, due to the lack of support for visual exploration of possible futures across variables.

TIMEFORK: INTERACTIVE VISUAL PREDICTION

The TimeFork technique is designed to support interactive prediction of multivariate time-series data by integrating computational models with interactive visual analysis. Due to this inherent coupling with computational models, the design of TimeFork is based on the guidelines established by Horvitz [24] for mixed-initiative techniques including maintaining an efficient human-computer dialogue, transparently conveying the computer's capabilities [43], and preserving the working memory of the user during interaction. The basic TimeFork workflow is an iterative dialogue between the analyst and the visual analytics system as follows (Figure 1, 2):

1. **System – Show and predict:** The system shows the current state of the data as well as predictions for the future at the selected position in time using visual representations.
2. **Analyst – View and select:** The analyst views the visualized current state and predictions (and their likelihoods), and can make one of three choices about future change:
   (a) *Manual:* The analyst has knowledge or intuition that conflicts with the predictions proposed by the system, so chooses an entirely different projection for the future than suggested by the system.
   (b) *Hybrid:* The analyst selects one of the proposed future predictions suggested by the system.
   (c) *Automatic:* The analyst accepts the system's choice as the most likely prediction.
3. **System – Accept and update:** The system uses the analyst's prediction as a "what-if" question (what if the chosen prediction is true) to create new predictions (conditional predictions) for the time series, essentially *forking time*. Return to Step 2 (or Step 1 if no predictions exist).

Step 2 is the analyst's input point in this dialogue. Beyond making a choice about the next prediction action, this is also where the analysts can change the time step (allowing for a different prediction duration), move to a different point in time (essentially abandoning the current line of prediction), and go back to previous actions (equivalent to forking the prediction). This is also where an analyst can decide to stop entirely, presumably because the new prediction state provides sufficient information to make a decision.

An actual implementation of TimeFork in a visual analytics system needs to be instantiated with specific computational models, visual representations, and a prediction interface that are all specific to the domain and dataset.

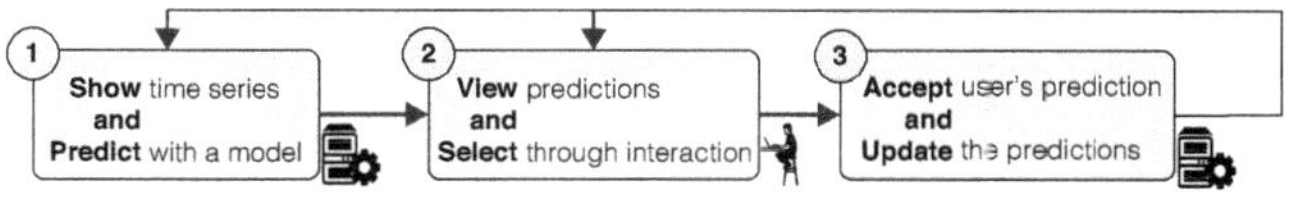

Figure 2. The three-step TimeFork workflow maintains a dialogue between the analyst and the computer for visual prediction.

TIMEFORK FOR STOCK DATA

To showcase the TimeFork technique, we developed a stock market analytics tool, STOCKFORK, that uses the TimeFork technique to support visual prediction of the stock prices. Our dataset consisted of end-of-day stock price (*adjusted closing*) and trade volume for stocks from the technology and consumer goods sectors (data from 2012 to 2015). TimeFork's interactive prediction workflow strongly relies on user understanding of the time-series data and also the factors influencing it. Therefore the StockFork interface is designed to visualize the stock prices and trade volume, which is the primary quantitative information stock traders and analysts follow, as well as aid analysis across stocks through derived attributes (e.g., cross-correlation) [52]. Besides this, external information from the domain is also shown to aid prediction. Our visualization design makes it easy to plug in the TimeFork technique, thus, exemplifying how it can be supported in other time-series visual analytics tools [6, 22, 52, 53].

StockFork: Visual and Interaction Design

StockFork (Figure 3) contains an overview+detail layout following Shneiderman's guideline [42] for visual exploration—overview first, zoom & filter, details on demand. The overview captures overall patterns in the stock market data, and the detail views visualize selected time periods.

Overview representation. The overview in StockFork captures the overall patterns for multiple stocks of interest, selected from a stock list available in the interface. While there are many design choices for showing multiple time series in a single view (as outlined by Javed et al. [25]), our overview design contains horizon graphs [20] stacked vertically visualizing stock prices in a space-efficient layout (seen in Figure 3). Horizon graphs are effective for discrimination (is point A higher than point B?) [25] and thus enable the users quickly understand the past trends. Other design choices for horizon graphs include offset and mirror representations with different band count and height, which have their own effects on graphical perception [20].

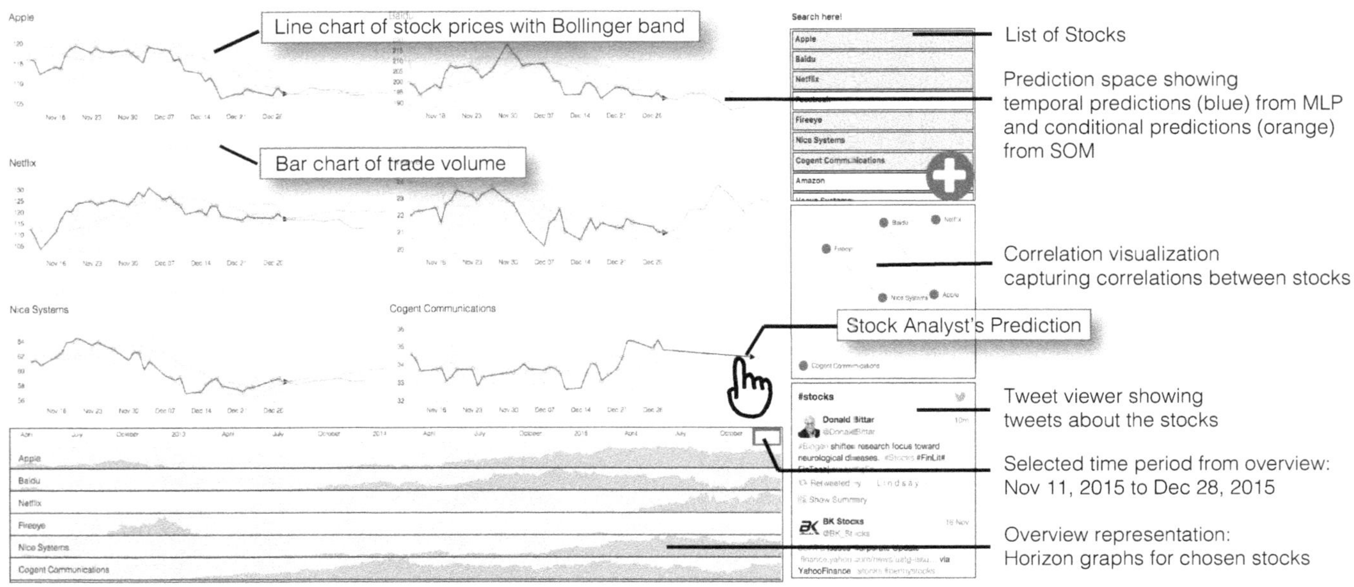

Figure 3. StockFork presents line charts of stock prices along with other visualizations and prediction space to support TimeFork for visual prediction.

The overview also supports selection of a time period on the time axis to show specific data in the detail views. This helps the analyst view different time scales (e.g., past week vs. month), which is common in stock trading, and also test TimeFork on a past time period against ground truth data.

Detail representations. The detail views capture visual information that can aid in visual prediction using the TimeFork technique. StockFork has three detail views:

- *Small multiple charts:* These charts visualize the stock price and trade information. Our design includes line charts for stock prices and bar charts for trade volume (one per stock), as they are common representations for time-series data. The line charts also show Bollinger bands [4] capturing moving averages and moving standard deviations, which indicate bullish/bearish trends in stock prices. Furthermore, the bar charts use color (green, red) to distinguish trades leading to rise/fall of stock price. These features are commonly seen in stock trading tools [41]. More design choices do exist including circular layouts [53] and complex representations such as Candlestick plots [36].

- *Correlation visualization:* Exploratory analysis of time series also requires supporting elaborate tasks such as visualizing derived values and identifying correlations [52]. In StockFork, we chose to visualize correlations between stocks to understand which stocks show similar trends (a task pursued by analysts working with multiple stocks). We use a visual design inspired by Moere et al. [35] for this purpose—a node-link diagram using position of nodes (stocks) to encode Pearson correlation (r) between stock prices in the selected time period. The links in the diagram are colored (green, red) based on the sign of r $(+, -)$, with opacity capturing $|r|$. Stocks that are positively correlated are placed closer to each other (using a force-directed layout), thus, implying they might follow similar price trends.

- *Tweet viewer:* Beyond the stock market dataset, external information from public opinions and company reports are often used as qualitative information sources for prediction. StockFork streams tweets related to the stocks using a Twitter widget to represent such information.

Enabling TimeFork's Interactive Prediction Workflow

To support the TimeFork workflow, the line charts are attached with a prediction space showing predictions from the computational models and supporting user interaction.

Step 1: Show and Predict (System)

In this step, temporal predictions are generated by a computational model for the stocks based on the past values in the selected time period. The model driving this step is a multilayer perceptron (one MLP model per stock), a feed-forward neural network model, trained on the stock price data from our dataset for each stock. Each neural network model has five layers: input layer of 6 neurons, hidden layers of sizes (50, 60, 70), and an output layer of one neuron, with Sigmoid activation function. The input to each model is the past six relative price changes (ratio of price change to previous stock price), and the output is the relative future change (decoded using the current stock price). The models are trained on these (*input*, *output*) pairs from the historical data using the standard backpropagation algorithm. Trained models showed more than 90% accuracy with the training dataset.

Apart from these predictions directly obtained from the past values, alternative predictions of lower confidence values are also created at the same time by changing one or more input elements (by a 10% fixed margin) and recording the model's output. The confidence value ($c \in [0, 1]$) of an alternative prediction was scaled inversely by the number of changes made to the input. Also, the choice of the margin was based on a manual verification of different margins (5%, 10%, and 20%) to find the one that reinforces top (best) predictions from the

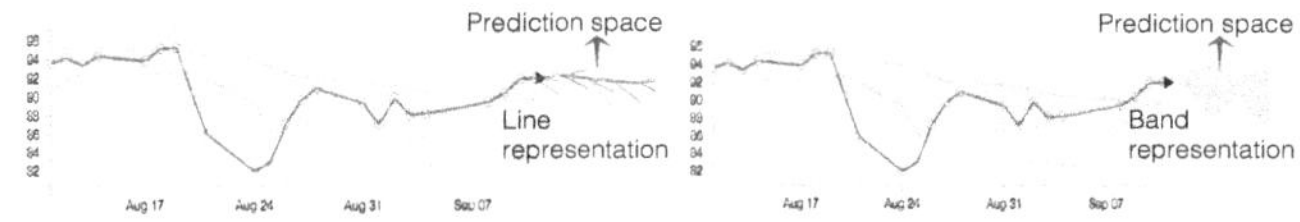

Figure 4. Two different forms of visualized prediction information: lines showing individual predictions of different confidences mapped to opacity and bands showing the range of possibilities.

training data with less-variant alternatives. These alternative predictions can therefore give a sense of variation of the predictions based on the change in the input pattern, and provide an awareness of the model's confidence in the predictions. Although predictions are for a single day each, longer time periods (e.g., a week) can be predicted using individual predictions for each day as ground truth to predict the next. We refer to this approach as *prediction chaining*. Note that prediction chaining can lead to a tree structure of predictions, however, we have chosen to work with the main trunk (high confidence predictions) and its alternatives rather than all branches to minimize visual clutter when rendered (leading to the structure in Figure 4).

Step 2: View and Select (Stock Analyst)

The predictions from Step 1 can be visualized individually or through aggregations showing a range [7]. Figure 4 shows both prediction representations from the StockFork interface. The line representation is a direct presentation of the predictions, with each line showing the change, and the opacity capturing the prediction's confidence. For the band representation, the individual predictions are processed to compute a weighted mean (μ) and standard deviation (σ) for each day in future to visualize a band ($\mu \pm 2\sigma$). The choice of the prediction representation is based on the time-series visualization itself: while line and band representations fit well with a line chart, other visualizations may require a different prediction representation that aligns better with the overall design.

User interactions with the prediction space are then enabled. Analysts can proceed with the gained visual knowledge from the detail views and the visualized model predictions in three ways: (1) neglect the visualized predictions altogether and make their own prediction (manual prediction); (2) select one of the proposed predictions that best suites their understanding (hybrid prediction); and (3) accept the most likely prediction provided by the computational model (automatic prediction). Analysts make one of these interactions directly on the prediction space by choosing a direction and a time period of predicted movement (by dragging an arrow on the prediction space signifying movement using mouse or touch input). This interaction is then fed into the system in the next step.

Step 3: Accept and Update (System)

The Accept and Update step is the most crucial part of the TimeFork technique to create and maintain an interactive dialogue with the system. Analyst predictions from the previous step reflects their understanding of what might happen to a stock. Given that stocks patterns may co-occur—e.g., Apple releasing an iPhone can effect Samsung's stock—computational models in this stage consider the predictions for some stocks and generate new (conditional) predictions for others to reflect the analyst's understanding. Therefore, models for this step must cluster or classify similar co-occurrence patterns from the historical data (e.g., Apple and Tesla increased together by 5% each over 100 times in the past), and enable quick lookup of similar patterns (if Apple increases, what will happen to Tesla?). For this purpose, we used a self-organizing map (SOM) [29] of 625 neurons and trained it on the co-occurrences from the dataset (e.g., Apple and Tesla have relative price changes of 0.05 and 0.03 on a day). Each neuron after training captures a co-occurrence pattern across all stocks, and neurons are clustered by the Euclidean distance between these patterns. Upon receiving the user interaction, which is divided into day-level predictions through the *closest fit* in the prediction space, the SOM is searched for the cluster of neurons with similar trends for the stocks predicted by the user and conditional predictions are obtained from it. Prediction confidences are mapped to the Euclidean distance of the cluster neurons from the pattern.

Similar to the predictions from Step 1, conditional predictions are generated for each time step and are chained to cover longer time periods. The conditional predictions can be integrated with the visualized temporal predictions from the previous step, or presented as a new band/line. This step thus enables the computer to communicate its own assessment for other stocks based on the analyst's prediction, enabling visual exploration of predictions and maintaining a continuous dialogue (Figure 5), which ends with the analyst gaining enough information to make an investment decision.

Other interactions. StockFork also supports storing the user predictions from Step 2 (*save*) and reverting to a previous state of the prediction space (*undo*) in the interface.

StockFork: Implementation

Our StockFork implementation uses a server-client architecture and is available as open source[1], along with sample stock market data and prediction models. The client interface was developed with web technologies—HTML5, JavaScript (JS), and CSS3—with D3 visualization framework [5] for the overview and detail views. StockFork's server uses Node.js to (1) collect stock market data using Yahoo Finance API (through Historic library [11]), and (2) train the models to enable TimeFork's interactive prediction workflow on the client. To refresh, two types of models were used: multilayer perceptrons (MLP) in Step 1 for temporal predictions and a self-organizing map (SOM) in Step 3 for conditional predictions.

Temporal Predictions

The multilayer perceptrons (one per stock) were implemented with the Brain library [1]. This model is trained on relative price changes, as described earlier, and predicts the future changes thus providing temporal predictions. The training procedure happens ahead of time and each trained MLP is converted into a serialized format (a JSON file) capturing all neuron weights. The pre-trained model can be recreated on the client using this file and the Brain JS API. This is carried out by a StockFork wrapper, which also accesses the pre-trained model to generate the temporal predictions.

[1] `https://github.com/karthikbadam/TimeFork`

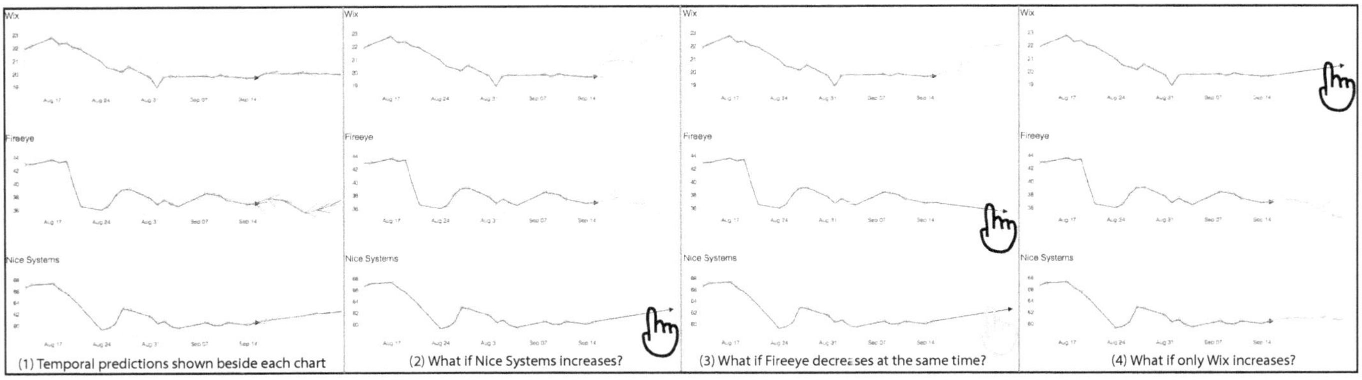

Figure 5. A typical dialogue in StockFork: the analyst interacts and the computer updates the predictions in the visualizations for further exploration.

Conditional Predictions

The self-organizing map was implemented with the ML-SOM library [51]. The SOM is trained on co-occurrence patterns of relative changes ahead of time. It is converted into a JSON file consisting of the weights and passed to the client where the model is recreated. A StockFork wrapper takes input (i.e., user's prediction for one or more stocks), accesses this pre-trained model on the client to generate conditional predictions, thus, answering the "what-if" questions.

New models for temporal and conditional predictions can be easily added by developing client-side JS wrappers that take the corresponding input (e.g., past relative price changes for temporal prediction) and return the model predictions.

USER STUDY

The TimeFork technique creates a human-computer dialogue by visualizing predictions, allowing the user to predict through manual, hybrid, and automatic predictions, and updating the predictions for further exploration. While manual and automatic prediction reflect traditional approaches in stock market (and time series in general), the presence of all three choices in TimeFork helps the analysts account for their own knowledge and understanding to come to a shared set of predictions with the computer. Therefore, the focus of our user study was not only to understand if TimeFork leads to better predictions, but also when/why it does so and how it changes the analyst's approach towards prediction and the entailing decisions. For this reason, we used simulated stock trading tasks where the participants can read multiple visualizations of stocks and information about the companies, gain an understanding, and engage in the dialogue.

Participants

We recruited 13 participants (5 female, 8 male) from the general population (including students, faculty, and staff) within our university campus. The participants were between 18 and 50 years of age. They were paid $10 for participation. All participants self-reported as proficient computer users with 6+ years of experience. Furthermore, 11 participants had previously used visualizations for data analysis and 7 of them had experience following stock markets; however, it was limited to either investing through a trader or novice-level experience in technical analysis of stock markets.

Dataset and Task

We picked stock market analysis due to the natural interest that many people have in stock trading and the potential opportunity to gamify the task by providing the participants with virtual money to invest. This gamification can help incentivize our participants to engage in TimeFork's workflow and make informed decisions to succeed at the tasks, while still maintaining the ecological validity of our experiment. The participants were given $100,000 in virtual money and asked to invest in three stocks: Apple, Facebook, and Tesla, on a simplified StockFork interface that shows line charts for stock prices, summarized earnings reports (1-2 paragraphs per company), and the prediction information from the models (when TimeFork is enabled). Quarterly earnings reports were used instead of Twitter, as they are publicly available and more commonly used by traders. These reports detailed the earnings and profits made by each company (and its products) compared to previous quarters, as well as investments in new ventures. The stocks were picked after a discussion with a stock trader as a representative set of a popular long-term player (Apple), a growing stock (Facebook), and a volatile stock (Tesla). The selection criteria for these stocks is not related to TimeFork but rather a representative of a stock portfolio with stocks of different risk values.

The task consisted of asking participants to predict the behavior of each stock and make a decision on how much to invest on them. Following this, they had to click an *evaluate* button on the interface that invests the said amount over the chosen time period and calculates their final earnings from this trade.

Experiment Factors

The prediction technique is a factor (T) influencing participant performance. Since fully automated prediction does not require a user, our experiment consisted of two conditions:

(A) TIMEFORK PREDICTION: In this condition, the participants are shown the simplified StockFork interface with TimeFork enabled (Figure 6). The prediction information is shown and the system reacts to user interaction.

(B) MANUAL PREDICTION: Here, the interface is similar to the previous condition except it lacks the prediction information due to the absence of TimeFork.

Experimental Design and Procedure

During the study, each participant predicted the stocks in both Technique (T) conditions. To counter learning effects, we picked two sets of data for using the techniques (one per technique) and introduced a factor D that represents the stock data shown: (***D*1**) data after the second quarter reports in July 2014 (Jul-Aug 2014), and (***D*2**) data after the fourth quarter reports of 2014 released in Jan 2015 (Jan-Mar 2015).[2] The participants were asked to invest their earnings on an assigned interface (technique + data combination) through four time steps (repetitions) within the assigned data. They were shown stock price data over 3-4 weeks and were asked to make predictions spanning between 1 and 20 days into the future based on their assessment in each time step. The participants were also shown the performance of their prediction in the previous time step (in the assigned D), to revise their strategies if needed. Overall, the participant's goal in an interface is to maximize their overall profit by investing their current earnings in the three stocks at each time step. The order of the technique (T) and data (D) factors was counterbalanced.

An experiment session began with the participant arriving, and reading and signing a consent form. The participants then completed a demographic survey. Following this, they were shown how to use the interface for the assigned first condition, including how to read the line charts, how to explore the prediction space, and how to invest on the stocks. The participants trained using the interface (with a training dataset), during which they were encouraged to ask questions, until they were comfortable. They then finished the tasks, followed by completing a Likert scale survey rating the efficiency, ease of use, and enjoyability of the technique. After the first condition, the participants continued to do the same with the second condition. Each session lasted between 45 and 60 min.

We recorded the profit/loss made during the tasks, along with the investment information. The participant interactions were recorded for further analysis. The participants were also encouraged to "think aloud" and announce their understanding of the stock behavior. The sessions were followed up with a post-session interview to examine their strategies to understand the time-series data, deal with the reactions of the computer to their interaction, and decide on the investment.

Study Design Rationale

Here we discuss our study design decisions and rationale.

- *Real stock market data.* TimeFork strongly relies not only on the analyst's understanding of the visualized data but also on user's domain knowledge that is not captured by the models. We therefore used stock market data along with earnings reports. Furthermore, we used real stock names to maintain the practicality (also, the reports contain other identifiable information). Counterbalancing the conditions helps reduce any participant bias linked to this decision.
- *Novice participants.* We recruited from the general university population rather than expert traders to ensure that the prior knowledge of the stock trends is minimal. Furthermore, we envision TimeFork to be accessible not just to experts but also novice analysts who are computer literate. Our participants were requested to make decisions based on the understanding gained during the experiment.
- *Simplified study interface.* We chose to limit the study to a simplified interface of StockFork to focus on the mechanism being studied here—prediction of time series. None of the removed views were necessary for the study.
- *Multiple datasets.* Two separate sets of stock market data are chosen to work with the two techniques (since exposure to a data once would influence the performance if used again). Within each set, the prediction task is repeated four times using four time steps. This procedure reduces the effects of randomly guessing the future.

[2]The prediction models were trained only with the stock market data from July 2012 to February 2014 for the study.

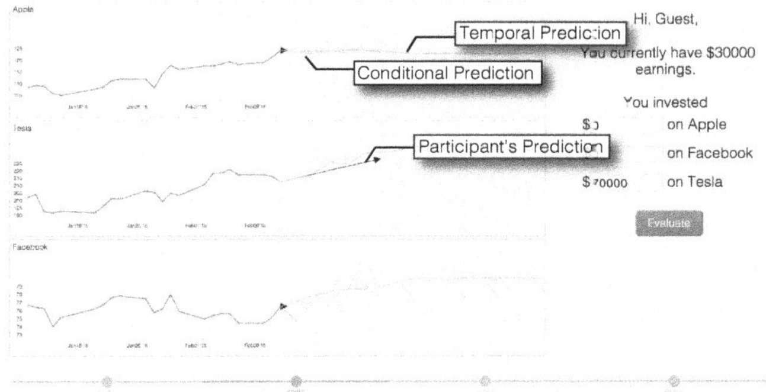

Figure 6. StockFork interface used in the user study (with TimeFork).

RESULTS AND OBSERVATIONS

Below we report the results from the statistical analysis and the qualitative analysis, as well as the participant feedback.

Quantitative Performance

Similar to Green et al. [15], we used a (linear) *mixed effects model* for our analysis of profit to avoid the fixed-effect fallacy [10]. We modeled participant and data D as random effects with a random intercept term for participant and random slope+intercept for data. Technique T was our fixed effect. Overall, we found no significant main effect ($\chi^2(1, N = 26) = .809$, $p = .37$) of technique—TimeFork (mean = \$14,907.18, s.d. = \$11,978.27) was similar to Manual prediction (mean = \$7,474.32, s.d. = \$4,944.23). However, we found differences in the coefficients (intercept, slope) for the effect of TimeFork in data $D1$ and $D2$ (discussed in the supplementary material).

Performance Differences in Data Conditions

We then analyzed the participant performance individually for both data conditions (Figure 7)—stock data from Jul-Aug 2014 ($D1$) and Jan-Mar 2015 ($D2$)—using the independent-samples T-test (with Bonferroni correction). In 2014 data ($D1$), there was a significant performance difference between TimeFork and Manual ($t(11) = -3.34$, $p = .013$). Participants using TimeFork (mean = \$23,467.20, s.d. = \$9,061.30) outperformed Manual prediction (mean = \$9,831.10, s.d. = \$4,454.80) for tasks with data $D1$. In 2015 data ($D2$), there was no significant difference between the two techniques.

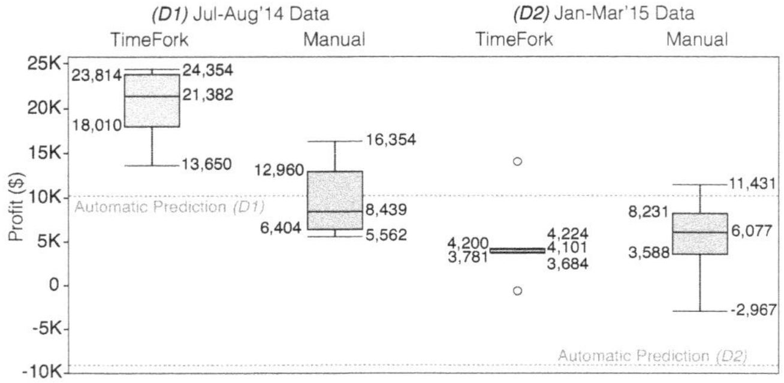

Figure 7. Box plot capturing the distributions—median (center line in each box), interquartile range (box), extrema (whiskers), and outliers (circles)—of performance using TimeFork and Manual prediction with Data *D*1 and *D*2. Performance of automatic prediction is highlighted.

Performance of Automatic Prediction

We analyzed the capabilities of the computational models by calculating the performance if the model's best predictions were followed (automatic prediction). The investment strategy here consists of following the high confidence predictions till the day when their direction changes from a rise to fall in stock price. The slopes of these rising prediction trends are used to split the earnings proportionally across stocks. No investment is made on stocks whose best predictions show an immediate fall in stock price. For example, if Apple increases for the next 3 days by 5% and Tesla increases for the next 10 days by 5% (while Facebook decreases), more money is invested in Apple, than Tesla, due to the promise of a quick turnover. Based on this, we found that our models generate $10,225.60 profit for the initial $100,000 virtual money provided for 2014 data (*D*1). For 2015 (*D*2), the model lost $9,094.80 showing that the model failed to predict the stocks.

Investment Differences

Since the participants were free to invest any fraction of the total earnings, we were interested in observing the differences in investment across stocks for each data condition. Similar analyses as before with T-tests revealed significant differences in investment between TimeFork and Manual in data *D*1 for Apple ($t(38) = 3.46$, $p = .008$) and Tesla ($t(45) = -3.65$, $p = .004$). For Tesla, TimeFork (mean = $47,389, s.d. = $28,776.20) had higher investments than Manual (mean = $20,420.40, s.d. = $19,699.70). In contrast for Apple, Manual prediction (mean = $53,008.60, s.d. = $24,640.80) had higher investments than TimeFork (mean = $29,929.50, s.d. = $16,226.40). In *D*2, there were no significant differences in investment between the two techniques.

Qualitative Analysis

To understand the results from statistical analysis and the extent to which participants explored StockFork, we present our observations from the study in the following five categories:

Visual Understanding of Time Series through StockFork

All tasks began with the participants observing the stock price trend in the line charts, reading the earnings reports, the performance of their previous prediction, and sometimes, directly exploring the predictions shown by the system (when TimeFork is enabled). In TimeFork condition, eight participants (P1, P2, P5-P8, P10, P13) started their tasks by looking at the reports, line charts, and their past predictions. The rest started by first reading the predictions shown in the TimeFork condition. In Manual prediction, all participants started by reading the reports and the line charts along with their previous predictions. While reading the charts, the participants looked for (1) a dominant trend in the past 7-10 days to see if it's going up or down (P1-P13), (2) the range of the stock price and the variance seen in the line chart (is stock price fluctuating and by how much—P4, P8, P12), and (3) the number of times the stock price changed direction (P3 in Manual).

Dialogue through TimeFork

In StockFork, the information sources described earlier often give a conflicting impression of what might happen. For example, Apple might be doing well on the earnings report in terms of its product sales and profits, but the current trend in its line chart might be decreasing. TimeFork's predictions added within the interface can complicate this further as it might not be fully agreeing with other visualized information. The user interactions in the TimeFork workflow—manual, hybrid, and automatic predictions—are therefore useful to come to a common understanding through an interactive dialogue. Overall, there were three levels of dialogue observed:

- **Minimal Dialogue:** Participant (P9), in two of the four task repetitions, started his prediction process by selecting the best temporal prediction path given by the system for a stock (automatic prediction), to see that the predictions for others are fluctuating (i.e., the variations in the lower confidence conditional predictions are high). He resolved this conflict by accepting the best temporal prediction path for each stock, and neglecting other visualized information.
- **Moderate Dialogue:** Eleven participants (except P3 and P11) preferred to start exploring the computer's predictions by either making a manual prediction (based on earnings report and chart trend) or choosing the system's best temporal prediction. This led to conditional predictions for other stocks, which are explored through 3-4 interactions to either make a manual prediction for these stocks, or find a prediction pattern that they most agree with based on the earnings reports and the chart trends. In the latter case, participants mostly chose a lower confidence computer prediction (hybrid). Participant P1 said that he wanted the computer to "*weigh in*" on what might happen, but he did not necessarily follow the best suggestion that was provided. The performance of the participants engaging in moderate dialogue was varied depending how they approached the time period of prediction and the investment.
- **Extended Dialogue:** Five participants (P3, P4, P6, P8, P11) indulged in an extended dialogue, with P3 and P11 using it for all task repetitions. In this case, the participants would interact through all three types of predictions—manual, hybrid, and automatic—to find the conditional prediction trend that best aligns with the reports and the charts, and shows least variance in the prediction space. These participants also adjusted the time period for their predictions during this process. They would typically go

through more than six interactions (with P3 making up to 20 interactions), to arrive at their answer. It is worth noting that participants P3, P4, P6, P11 used TimeFork with data *D*1 and performed better than both automatic and manual prediction conditions, with P3 making the highest profit.

Strategies: Direction of Prediction
In TimeFork condition, the direction of the user's prediction was directly influenced by their dialogue with the system. P9, who preferred minimal dialogue, used the direction of the system's best temporal prediction. Participants in moderate dialogue, had multiple strategies for direction: (1) when they encounter conflicting predictions (predictions that do not reflect the reports, chart trends, or too different to each other), made a manual or hybrid prediction based on the earnings reports (P1, P4, P7, P12, P13) and the chart trends (P2, P4, P5, P9, P12, P13); and (2) the more popular strategy, was to come up with a manual prediction that is between the temporal predictions and the conditional predictions for the stocks, in case of conflicts. The second strategy was observed at least in one repetition for ten participants (all except P3, P9, P11). Between P3 and P11, who had an extended dialogue, the direction was based on the best conditional predictions from visual exploration. Finally, in Manual prediction, participants either extrapolated the trend in the past 10 days (all participants) or selected an increase/decrease direction based on the earnings reports (all participants except P3). P8 also incorporated his previous prediction performance in his strategy.

Strategies: Time Period of Prediction
In TimeFork, P9 followed the system's best predictions to decide the time period. Participants in a moderate dialogue used different strategies based on their exploration: (1) for hybrid predictions, the time period was based on the computer's (lower-confidence) predictions (11 participants); and (2) for manual predictions it was a selection of a short time period (2-5 days—P1, P2, P5, P7, P10, P13). Participants in the extended dialogue made this decision based on the dialogue. In Manual, the participants chose a short (2-5 days—P2, P8, P10) or long time period (6-15 days—P3, P4, P11, P12, P13) without a significant reason. Some participants (P5, P6, P7, P9) chose a time period based on the trend in the chart.

Strategies: Investment
The investment in both techniques was mainly based on the participant's predictions—for twelve participants (P2-P13) in TimeFork and eleven (P1, P4, P6-P13) in Manual prediction. In TimeFork, participants (P1, P5, P7, P10) also used the variance of the computer's predictions and the chart trends for their investments. In Manual condition, participants P2, P5, P10 used the reports as a measure of "confidence" for investment, and participant P4 invested more in charts with less variance. After reviewing his previous predictions, P3 invested all his earnings on a single stock that he concluded was increasing the most based on his visual exploration.

Subjective Ratings and Feedback
After each session, the participants rated the techniques on three metrics: efficiency, ease of use, and enjoyability, on a Likert scale ranging from 1 (e.g., strongly disagree) to 5 (e.g., strongly agree). We analyzed these ratings with Wilcoxon Signed Rank tests and found no significant differences between the two techniques. However, most participants (P2-P4, P8, P10-P13) mentioned that Manual prediction required more guess work. They also felt that it took them more time to get used to the TimeFork's workflow. P2 stated that TimeFork gave her "*someone else's point of view*," while P3 and P4 expressed that the conditional and lower-confidence predictions showed how sensitive other stocks to a particular stock.

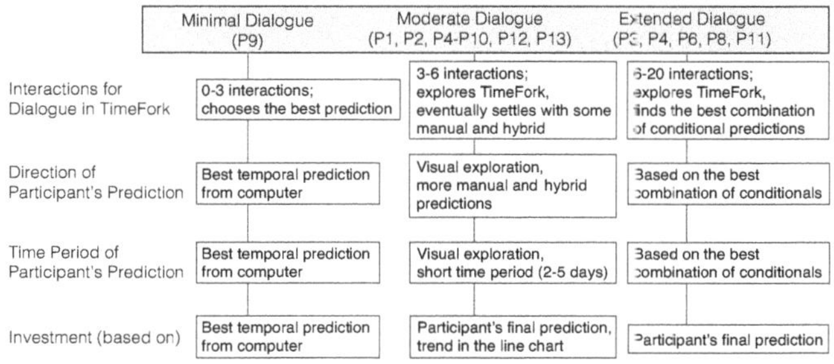

Figure 8. Three forms of dialogue and corresponding usage patterns of the TimeFork technique observed through a qualitative analysis.

DESIGN IMPLICATIONS
Our StockFork application instantiates TimeFork using neural network models to provide temporal and conditional predictions that contribute to the dialogue with the analyst. However, this also severely influences the visual prediction. In our experiment setup, the computational models performed better for 2014 data (*D*1) compared to 2015 (*D*2), and this led to participants performing better with TimeFork for *D*1, compared to no difference between TimeFork and Manual prediction in *D*2. This suggests that having a dialogue with an intelligent partner (accurate model) affects the analyst's ability for the better—it led to significantly higher profits in TimeFork outperforming both automated and manual prediction. On the other hand, TimeFork's current design did not manage to overcome the model weaknesses (inaccuracies in prediction). Participant performance was not affected by the presence of a weak model in *D*2, but it changed the level of dialogue with the computer. More work is required not only to measure the effects of weak models, but also to create methods for visualizing the weakness of computational models.

As expected, most participants (twelve) always engaged in the dialogue (moderate or extended) with the computer; however, the amount of dialogue affected the visual predictions and the decisions following it. This explains the investment differences—the presence of a good dialogue in *D*1 guided the distribution among stocks. Participants in extended dialogue explored a range of "what-if" scenarios that led them to shared predictions with the system. They were observed to be consistent in their decisions: direction and time period of prediction (directly obtained from this exploration) and investment (mapped to their predictions), and also performed better than the automatic, manual prediction, and average performance in their condition. However, TimeFork currently only succeeded in motivating five out of the thirteen participants to explore an extended dialogue. Also, participants (4 of 5) using the strong (accurate) model in $D1$ mostly engaged in this dialogue. Participants preferred to override the computer to some extent and make manual predictions rather than engage in a fully extended dialogue. For this reason, we recognize a potential weakness of TimeFork in lacking an overview representation of "what-if" scenarios to engage the user.

The decisions entailing predictions are often more important than the predictions themselves. For example, an energy provider analyzing the consumption of gas and electricity may visually predict that the gas consumption might increase while electricity decreases. However, they would be more interested in understanding how to deal with this and distribute their energy resources. In our study, participants mostly mapped their investments directly to their predictions, but, four of them also considered the confidence of the computer itself into account ("if the computer's predictions are too varied, maybe I should not invest too much"). This effect may lead to positive or negative results as it connects to why the computer's predictions are varied and also the user's interaction itself. More work is required to understand ways to mitigate this effect either by decoupling prediction and decision making, or by embedding solutions that propose possible answers to these decisions based on the user interactions.

Limitations. Our study design decisions have unique influences on the outcome. Firstly, the two datasets (D) follow the release of the quarterly earnings reports to ensure that there is an external factor (the earnings reports) influencing the stocks, and they are separated by six months so that the trends are not influencing each other a lot. However, this choice has led to a performance difference in automatic prediction mainly since data $D2$ had more instances of stock prices falling. Also, earnings reports may reflect only a subset of all external factors affecting the stock prices. Secondly, investing in three stocks at once in each task meant that the profits made on one stock influenced others (therefore, overall performance was analyzed). A more controlled study is needed to understand the effects of TimeFork on individual stocks and specific trends. Finally, real stock names may have impacted the performance of our novice participants; however, this is important as knowledge of external factors facilitates the users better express their opinions in the dialogue with the computer system to find the best predictions.

APPLICATION SCENARIOS

While we demonstrated our TimeFork technique with stock market data, we believe that the technique is applicable to other scenarios as well. In this section, we provide two short application scenarios inspired by real-world challenges.

Household Resource Consumption

Consider an energy provider company interested in understanding resource consumption (electricity, water, and gas) in a household neighborhood. The company wants to manage their resource reserves using years of usage data, along with data from temperature, humidity, and moisture sensors in the households and the neighborhood. In the presence of such fine-grained, high-volume, and high-velocity streaming data, the company is trying to understand which household will have an increased consumption of electricity.

Since there are often relationships between the variables in that data, interactive visual prediction through TimeFork works well. The company's analysts would look at the visualized time series from the neighborhood and the households, and start by predicting what might happen in the neighborhood (based on TimeFork or their own knowledge). They would then see updated predictions for the electricity, water, and gas consumptions for each individual household. They could further filter these predictions by choosing a trend for the temperature within these households. They could choose not to agree with the system at this stage, and make a different prediction based on temperature and humidity, to find the predictions to be more conclusive. Upon finding the households with predicted increase in electricity consumption, they could use a similar visual exploration to estimate the gas and water consumptions for proper resource allocation or maintenance.

Movie Earnings

Let us consider a more casual example in the entertainment industry. Hundreds of movies are released per year just in the United States. Often the earnings of the movies over time depend on the cast, genre, and also other movies releasing in the same time period. To figure out the ideal release date for a new movie [38], an analyst can access the historical patterns of movie earnings and releases on a TimeFork-enabled VA interface. She would then try to find the seasonal effects on the new movie of a particular genre (say comedy) and cast, by expressing that there will be a comedy movie in April-June season, to see the predictions for earnings. Following this, she can also postulate that there might be three other movies releasing in the same week with different genres, to see their effect on the earnings of the original movie. She could further change the season, and also query based on the cast, to find the ideal time period for the movie release.

CONCLUSION AND FUTURE WORK

We have presented the TimeFork method for interactive visual prediction based on combining predictions from computational forecasting models with analyst input in an interactive interface. To showcase the idea, we have further applied it to stock market data. Our user study showed significantly better performance in the presence of an efficient dialogue when using TimeFork compared to manual (in data $D1$) and automatic prediction (in data $D1$ and $D2$). In other words, our work shows that involving both humans as well as computational models in the sensemaking loop is a useful approach.

The TimeFork method represents a canonical example of visual analytics [46] and we are eager to continue exploring such explicit human-computer collaborations. However, one of the biggest challenges in visual analytics design is to identify the inflection points where the analyst can provide the most useful feedback to the system. The TimeFork method provides one such design, and we see much potential for applying the method to other datasets and domains.

ACKNOWLEDGMENTS

We thank the anonymous reviewers, Catherine Plaisant, Cody Buntain, Matthias Nielsen, and Senthil Chandrasegaran for their feedback that substantially improved our manuscript.

REFERENCES

1. Heather Arthur. 2013. Brain Node.js Library. (2013). https://www.npmjs.com/package/brain, accessed December 2015.
2. Guilherme A. Barreto. 2007. Time series prediction with the self-organizing map: A review. In *Perspectives of Neural-Symbolic Integration*. Springer, 135–158.
3. Johan Bollen, Huina Mao, and Xiaojun Zeng. 2011. Twitter mood predicts the stock market. *Journal of Computational Science* 2, 1 (2011), 1–8.
4. John Bollinger. 2001. Bollinger On Bollinger Band. (2001).
5. Michael Bostock, Vadim Ogievetsky, and Jeffrey Heer. 2011. D^3: Data-Driven Documents. *IEEE Transactions on Visualization and Computer Graphics* 17, 12 (2011), 2301–2309.
6. Paolo Buono, Aleks Aris, Catherine Plaisant, Amir Khella, and Ben Shneiderman. 2005. Interactive pattern search in time series. In *Proceedings of SPIE Electronic Imaging*. 175–186.
7. Paolo Buono, Catherine Plaisant, Adalberto Simeone, Aleks Aris, Ben Shneiderman, Galit Shmueli, and Wolfgang Jank. 2007. Similarity-based forecasting with simultaneous previews: A river plot interface for time series forecasting. In *Proceedings of the International Conference on Information Visualization*. 191–196.
8. Philip K. Chan and Matthew V. Mahoney. 2005. Modeling multiple time series for anomaly detection. In *Proceedings of the IEEE International Conference on Data Mining*. 90–97.
9. Bill Chiu, Eamonn Keogh, and Stefano Lonardi. 2003. Probabilistic discovery of time series motifs. In *Proceedings of the ACM International Conference on Knowledge Discovery and Data Mining*. 493–498.
10. Herbert H Clark. 1973. The language-as-fixed-effect fallacy: A critique of language statistics in psychological research. *Journal of verbal learning and verbal behavior* 12, 4 (1973), 335–359.
11. Nick Desaulniers. 2013. Historic Node.js Library. (2013). https://www.npmjs.com/package/historic, accessed December 2015.
12. Alex Endert, Patrick Fiaux, and Chris North. 2012. Semantic interaction for visual text analytics. In *Proceedings of the ACM Conference on Human Factors in Computing Systems*. 473–482.
13. Tak-chung Fu. 2011. A review on time series data mining. *Engineering Applications of Artificial Intelligence* 24, 1 (2011), 164–181.
14. Tak-chung Fu, Fu-lai Chung, Ka-yan Kwok, and Chak-man Ng. 2008. Stock time series visualization based on data point importance. *Engineering Applications of Artificial Intelligence* 21, 8 (2008), 1217–1232.
15. Spence Green, Jeffrey Heer, and Christopher D Manning. 2013. The efficacy of human post-editing for language translation. In *Proceedings of the ACM Conference on Human Factors in Computing Systems*. 439–448.
16. Ming Hao, Halldór Janetzko, Ratnesh Sharma, Umeshwar Dayal, Daniel Keim, and Malu Castellanos. 2009. Poster: visual prediction of time series. In *Poster Compendium of the IEEE Symposium on Visual Analytics Science and Technology*.
17. Ming C. Hao, Umeshwar Dayal, Daniel A. Keim, and Tobias Schreck. 2007. Multi-resolution techniques for visual exploration of large time-series data. In *Proceedings of the Joint Eurographics / IEEE VGTC Conference on Visualization*. 27–34.
18. Ming C. Hao, Halldor Janetzko, Sebastian Mittelstädt, Water Hill, Umeshwar Dayal, Daniel A. Keim, Manish Marwah, and Ratnesh K. Sharma. 2011. A Visual Analytics Approach for Peak-Preserving Prediction of Large Seasonal Time Series. In *Computer Graphics Forum*, Vol. 30. 691–700.
19. Jeffrey Heer, Michael Bostock, and Vadim Ogievetsky. 2010. A tour through the visualization zoo. *Communications of the ACM* 53, 6 (2010), 59–67.
20. Jeffrey Heer, Nicholas Kong, and Maneesh Agrawala. 2009. Sizing the horizon: the effects of chart size and layering on the graphical perception of time series visualizations. In *Proceedings of the ACM Conference on Human Factors in Computing Systems*. 1303–1312.
21. Magnus Lie Hetland and Pål Sætrom. 2005. Evolutionary rule mining in time series databases. *Machine Learning* 58, 2-3 (2005), 107–125.
22. Harry Hochheiser and Ben Shneiderman. 2004. Dynamic query tools for time series data sets: timebox widgets for interactive exploration. *Information Visualization* 3, 1 (2004), 1–18.
23. Eric Horvitz. 1999. Principles of mixed-initiative user interfaces. In *Proceedings of the ACM Conference on Human Factors in Computing Systems*. 159–166.
24. Eric J. Horvitz. 2007. Reflections on challenges and promises of mixed-initiative interaction. *AI Magazine* 28, 2 (2007), 3.
25. Waqas Javed, Bryan McDonnel, and Niklas Elmqvist. 2010. Graphical perception of multiple time series. *IEEE Transactions on Visualization and Computer Graphics* 16, 6 (2010), 927–934.
26. Young-Seon Jeong, Myong K. Jeong, and Olufemi A. Omitaomu. 2011. Weighted dynamic time warping for time series classification. *Pattern Recognition* 44, 9 (2011), 2231–2240.
27. Ashish Kapoor, Bongshin Lee, Desney S. Tan, and Eric Horvitz. 2012. Performance and Preferences: Interactive Refinement of Machine Learning Procedures. In *Proceedings of the AAAI Conference on Artificial Intelligence*.

28. Daniel Keim, Florian Mansmann, Jörn Schneidewind, and Hartmut Ziegler. 2006. Challenges in visual data analysis. In *Proceedings of the International Conference on Information Visualization*. 9–16.

29. Teuvo Kohonen. 2001. *Self-Organizing Maps*. Springer.

30. T. Warren Liao. 2005. Clustering of time series data—a survey. *Pattern Recognition* 38, 11 (2005), 1857–1874.

31. Jessica Lin, Eamonn Keogh, and Stefano Lonardi. 2005. Visualizing and discovering non-trivial patterns in large time series databases. *Information Visualization* 4, 2 (2005), 61–82.

32. Andrew C. Lorenc. 1986. Analysis methods for numerical weather prediction. *Royal Meteorological Society, Quarterly Journal* 112 (1986), 1177–1194.

33. Junshui Ma and Simon Perkins. 2003. Online novelty detection on temporal sequences. In *Proceedings of the ACM International Conference on Knowledge Discovery and Data Mining*. 613–618.

34. Abish Malik, Ross Maciejewski, Yun Jang, Whitney Huang, Niklas Elmqvist, and David Ebert. 2012. A Correlative Analysis Process in a Visual Analytics Environment. In *Proceedings of the IEEE Conference on Visual Analytics Science and Technology*. 33–42.

35. Andrew Vande Moere. 2004. Time-varying data visualization using information flocking boids. In *Proceedings of the IEEE Symposium on Information Visualization*. 97–104.

36. Steve Nison. 2001. *Japanese candlestick charting techniques: a contemporary guide to the ancient investment techniques of the Far East*. Penguin.

37. Ajoy K. Palit and Dobrivoje Popovic. 2006. *Computational intelligence in time series forecasting: theory and engineering applications*. Springer Science & Business Media.

38. Predictive Analytics for Movie Openings 2013. VAST Mini Challenge 1: Visualize the box office. (2013). `http://vacommunity.org/VAST+Challenge+2013`, accessed December 2015.

39. Glenn Proctor and Chris Winter. 1998. Information flocking: Data visualisation in virtual worlds using emergent behaviours. In *Virtual Worlds*. Springer, 168–176.

40. Tobias Schreck, Tatiana Tekušová, Jörn Kohlhammer, and Dieter Fellner. 2007. Trajectory-based visual analysis of large financial time series data. *ACM SIGKDD Explorations Newsletter* 9, 2 (2007), 30–37.

41. Shobhit Seth. 2014. The Best Technical Analysis Trading Software. (2014). `http://www.investopedia.com/articles/active-trading/121014/best-technical-analysis-trading-software.asp?header_alt=c`, accessed December 2015.

42. Ben Shneiderman. 1996. The eyes have it: A task by data type taxonomy for information visualizations. In *Proceedings of the IEEE Symposium on Visual Languages*. 336–343.

43. Ben Shneiderman and Pattie Maes. 1997. Direct manipulation vs. interface agents: A debate. *Interactions* 4, 6 (1997), 42–61.

44. K. Srinivas, B. Kavihta Rani, and A. Govrdhan. 2010. Applications of data mining techniques in healthcare and prediction of heart attacks. *International Journal on Computer Science and Engineering* 2, 02 (2010), 250–255.

45. Yoshiki Tanaka, Kazuhisa Iwamoto, and Kuniaki Uehara. 2005. Discovery of time-series motif from multi-dimensional data based on MDL principle. *Machine Learning* 58, 2 (2005), 269–300.

46. James J. Thomas and Kristin A. Cook. 2005. *Illuminating the Path: The Research and Development Agenda for Visual Analytics*. IEEE Computer Society.

47. Jarke J. Van Wijk and Edward R. Van Selow. 1999. Cluster and calendar based visualization of time series data. In *Proceedings of IEEE Symposium on Information Visualization*. 4–9.

48. K. R. Venugopal, K. G. Srinivasa, and L. M. Patnaik. 2009. Fuzzy Based Neuro - Genetic Algorithm for Stock Market Prediction. In *Soft Computing for Data Mining Applications*. 139–166.

49. Marc Weber, Marc Alexa, and Wolfgang Müller. 2001. Visualizing Time-Series on Spirals. In *Proceedings of IEEE Symposium on Information Visualization*. 7–14.

50. Li Wei, Nitin Kumar, Venkata Lolla, Eamonn J. Keogh, Stefano Lonardi, and Chotirat Ratanamahatana. 2005. Assumption-Free Anomaly Detection in Time Series. In *Proceedings of the International Conference on Scientific and Statistical Database Management*. 237–242.

51. Michaël Zasso. 2014. ML-SOM Node.js Library. (2014). `https://www.npmjs.com/package/ml-som`, accessed December 2015.

52. Jian Zhao, Fanny Chevalier, and Ravin Balakrishnan. 2011a. KronoMiner: using multi-foci navigation for the visual exploration of time-series data. In *Proceedings of the ACM Conference on Human Factors in Computing Systems*. 1737–1746.

53. Jian Zhao, Fanny Chevalier, Emmanuel Pietriga, and Ravin Balakrishnan. 2011b. Exploratory analysis of time-series with ChronoLenses. *IEEE Transactions on Visualization and Computer Graphics* 17, 12 (2011), 2422–2431.

The Effect of Visual Appearance on the Performance of Continuous Sliders and Visual Analogue Scales

Justin Matejka, Michael Glueck, Tovi Grossman, and George Fitzmaurice
Autodesk Research, Toronto Ontario Canada
first.last@autodesk.com

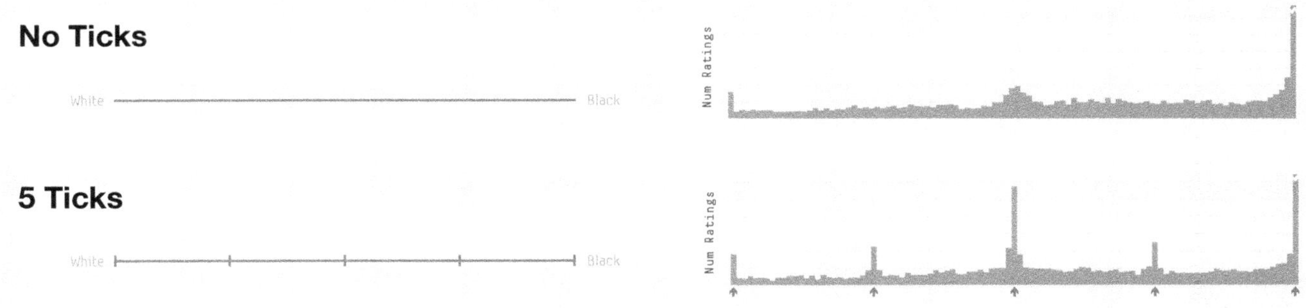

Figure 1. Distribution of survey responses when asked to "rate the blackness" of 50 shades of grey, spread at perceptually equal distances between white and black. The only difference between the surveys is the visual presentation of the slider (on the left), shown with no tick marks, or 5 tick marks. Arrows on the x-axis of the graphs indicate the locations of the tick marks.

ABSTRACT
Sliders and Visual Analogue Scales (VASs) are input mechanisms which allow users to specify a value within a predefined range. At a minimum, sliders and VASs typically consist of a line with the extreme values labeled. Additional decorations such as labels and tick marks can be added to give information about the gradations along the scale and allow for more precise and repeatable selections. There is a rich history of research about the effect of labelling in discrete scales (i.e., Likert scales), however the effect of decorations on continuous scales has not been rigorously explored. In this paper we perform a 2,000 user, 250,000 trial online experiment to study the effects of slider appearance, and find that decorations along the slider considerably bias the distribution of responses received. Using two separate experimental tasks, the trade-offs between bias, accuracy, and speed-of-use are explored and design recommendations for optimal slider implementations are proposed.

INTRODUCTION
Rating scales are a commonly used tool for collecting responses from subjects and participants in many fields of research, including psychology, human-computer interaction, medicine, and sociology. One of the most widely used approaches for survey research is the Likert scale [22], where a participant chooses a response from a discrete number of choices along a single-dimension linear scale.

CHI'16, May 07 - 12, 2016, San Jose, CA, USA

ACM 978-1-4503-3362-7/16/05...$15.00
DOI: http://dx.doi.org/10.1145/2858036.2858063

An alternative to the Likert scale is the visual analogue scale (VAS), in which respondents specify their response by indicating a position along a continuous line between two end points [16]. Continuous sliders have the implicit assumption that users are equally likely to make their selection at any point along the line. Prior work has shown that VASs provide some advantages over categorical scales [11,12,31]. In particular, the continuous data collected with VASs can be used for a greater number of statistical tests and goodness of fit tests may be more powerful [11].

Recently, major attention has been given to web-based research methods and data collection [17,21]. Online survey systems [39,40], as well as crowd-sourcing systems [41], allow researchers to rapidly recruit and collect responses to survey questions and allow for the use of multimedia stimuli. VASs are commonly used for such research methods, and it has thus become important to understand the design and characteristics of VASs. Given the volume of responses which web-based surveys can produce, it is important that such responses are collected efficiently and without any artificial bias from the design of the response mechanism. In particular, it has been shown that subtle changes in the layout and appearance of rating scales can affect responses [20,30].

However, little research has been conducted on how the visual design and mechanics of VASs may impact the collection of responses. More specifically, the presence of decorations such as labels and tick marks can be added to give information about the gradations along the scale and allow for more precise and repeatable selections [35]. While such visual attributes have been studied in detail for the labelling of discrete scales [38], their impact on VASs, and their effect on the distribution of collected responses has not been rigorously examined.

Our work explores if and how visual design variations of VASs impacts the results obtained from web-based collection systems. We perform a 2,000 user, 250,000 trial Mechanical Turk experiment, to study the impact of slider decorations on VAS responses. We test a number of design variations that involve the mark-up of the slider scale with tick marks, labels, and other decorations. We provide a thorough analysis of the collected results, which help identify designs which should be avoided due to the induced bias in responses. Furthermore, through the use of two separate experimental tasks, we are able to analyze the trade-offs between bias, accuracy, and speed-of-use.

Our results show that the presence of decorations along the slider (and in particular tick marks) can considerably bias the distribution of responses received. However, the use of decorations can favourably increase precision and reduce response time. Our analysis of the trade-offs of these factors lead us to a grounded discussion on design recommendations for optimal slider implementations. In particular, a banded slider design was shown to outperform the traditional undecorated slider in terms of speed and accuracy, while maintaining a similar level of response bias.

RELATED WORK

Visual analogue scales (VASs) have a history of use in psychology, psychiatry, and healthcare, to measure a range of subjective experiences, such as mood, depression, pain, and physical exertion [23]. The VAS was introduced by Hayes & Paterson in 1921 as a method for factory foremen to rate the performance of workers [16]. In 1923 Freyd discussed the broader application of the technique in the field of psychology, providing heuristic guidelines for visual appearance [10]. VASs have traditionally been displayed on paper, with their key advantages over other techniques being that they can be self-administered with little training, and provide extremely sensitive (granular) measurement. Their disadvantages have traditionally been that they are visual, cannot be administered aurally, and take longer to encode (measure/transcribe). However, when administered on a computer, the measuring step can be automated, making VASs a viable alternative to discrete Likert scales. Software tools allow for the automatic creation and encoding of VASs [23,31] generating a renewed interest in VASs. Our paper aims to better understand the nature of responses generated by VASs to ensuring they are collected without artificial bias.

There is a large body of research comparing the effectiveness of VASs compared to other rating systems [15,18,24,26,36], looking at the effect of labelling on discrete rating systems [2,4,37], and looking at how question phrasing influences participant response [13,25,27,29]. However, there has been relatively little research investigating the how changes in visual appearance or labelling affect VASs. In the 1970s Scott & Huskisson looked at how the graphical representation of paper-based VASs influenced the results of a pain severity questionnaire and found that a vertical orientation of the slider lead to more "clumping" than horizontal orientations [34] and that the presence of labels could attract responses [19]. Later, Dauphin *et al.* [28] performed a similar study and found the orientation of the scale affected the number of ratings at the end points. Performed at a small scale (~100 trials per condition), the visible effects were limited. In this paper we systematically explore the potential causes of bias in VASs on a large scale for digitally administered surveys.

STUDY #1: PERCEPTUAL JUDGEMENT TASK

In this first study, we investigate the effect that the appearance of visual analogue scales has on the rating behaviour of survey respondents. Through a series of conditions, we explore visual decorations used to markup scales such as tick marks, labels, and banded sliders. We also explore the shape of the thumb which marks the selected value, and test a "dynamic" slider which continuously displays the currently selected value. Each condition was tested using a perceptual judgement task, requiring participants to rate the "blackness" of a shade of grey.

Task – Shades of Grey

Developing a set of stimuli to use as a test of rating behaviour is a difficult and well-studied problem [33]. We chose a task which presents the participant with a shade of grey and requires them to rate the shade on a scale between "White" and "Black". Borg and Borg [1] extensively studied using a "scale of blackness" as a stimulus and concluded that it serves as a good test of general rating behaviour. Our task is modelled on the task used by Neely and Borg to test the performance of a VAS compared to a graduated Likert scale [15]. A collection of 50 shades of grey (Figure 2) were selected in perceptually equal steps between white and black according to the CIE L*a*b* colour space [3].

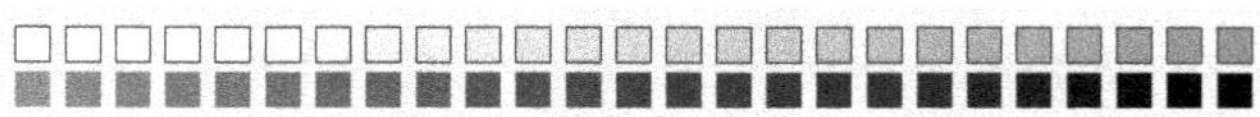

Figure 2. 50 shades of grey used for the perceptual judgment task of Study #1, selected at perceptually equal distances using the CIE L*a*b* colour system.

While each shade of grey does have a theoretically "correct" position on the scale, pilot tests suggested a relatively wide range of responses could be entered for any given shade. For example, Figure 3 shows the distribution of responses from a pilot study for two selected shades.

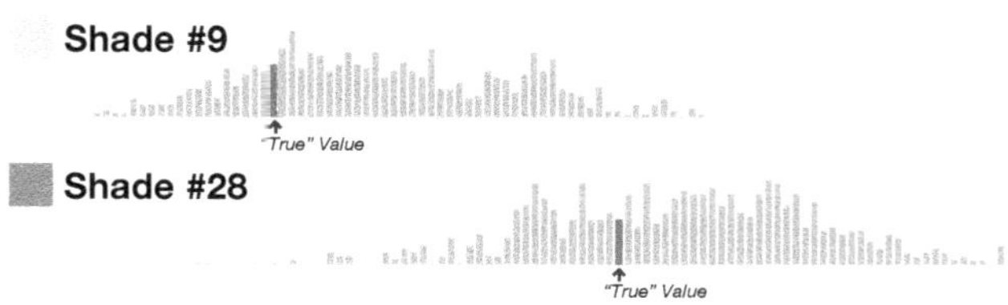

Figure 3. Response distributions for two representative shades of grey from a pilot study.

Crowdsourcing

Participants for the study were recruited using Amazon's Mechanical Turk. Previous work [14,17] has shown "turkers" to be suitable participants for visualization research and to represent a comparatively diverse participant pool [32]. The short time between posting a study and getting results allowed exploration of more variations than practical for an in-person study. The study took ~ 6 minutes to complete and participants were compensated $1 USD.

Experimental Design

To investigate the issue of whether the visual appearance of a slider influences the data collected, we divided the problem into a number of questions we wanted to answer:

- *Does the* ***presence*** *of tick marks have an effect?*
- *Does the* ***number*** *of tick marks matter?*
- *Does the* ***visual weight*** *of the ticks matter?*
- *Do alternating* ***major/minor*** *tick weights have an effect?*
- *Does the* ***shape of the slider thumb*** *matter?*
- *What is the effect of* ***labels*** *vs.* ***ticks*** *vs.* ***labels and ticks****?*
- *What is the effect of* ***banded representations****?*
- *What is the effect of a* ***dynamically labelled*** *thumb?*

We describe the specific conditions to answer each of these questions within the results section.

Apparatus

The experiment was developed as a JavaScript application and embedded on a standard HTML webpage compatible with all modern browsers and operating systems.

Before each trial, the slider (measuring 600 pixels wide) is positioned on screen without the thumb graphic. To prevent leaving the cursor in the same place for multiple trials, a blue "start position" circle is placed below the slider (Figure 4, Step 1). After the cursor is moved over the start position, the trial begins and the stimulus is displayed (Figure 4, Step 2). Once the cursor is within 100 pixels of the slider, the thumb appears at the current x-coordinate of the cursor, and the user clicks the left mouse button to register their rating. After clicking, the stimulus disappears and the blue "start position" is displayed again (counterbalanced to appear on both the left and right side equally). For all slider conditions the input space and slider response was exactly the same; a one-to-one mapping between cursor's x-coordinate and slider thumb position, and in all cases the slider thumb moved freely and continuously along the scale and never "snapped" to any of the tick or label locations. The only difference between any two conditions is the visual appearance of the scale.

Participants were given the instructions to *"Please move the cursor and click to indicate your perceived level of 'blackness' for the below square"*. To disable comparing the colour of the stimulus to the white background of the page, the stimulus was presented over a greyscale noise pattern.

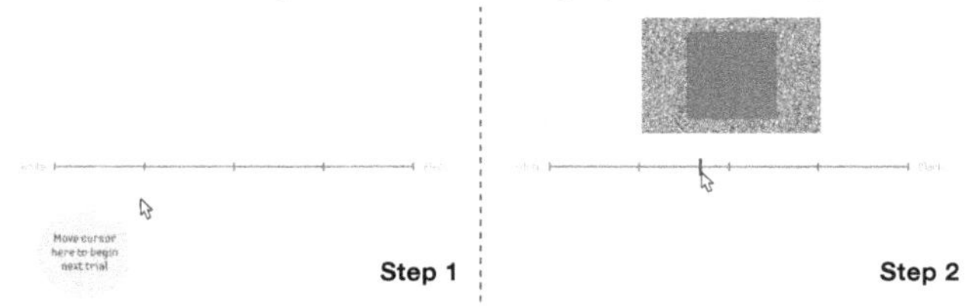

Figure 4. The two steps of a single trial.

Organization

The study was structured as a between-subjects design with each participant completing 200 trials, all with the same slider condition. Once a participant completed one condition, they were excluded from participating in any other conditions of the experiment. The 200 trials were organized into 4 blocks of 50 trials, where each block consisted of one trial for each of the 50 shades of grey presented in a randomized order. Thus, the participant rated each shade of grey 4 times. The location of the "start position" was counter-balanced between these 4 trials. Results from the first and last blocks were compared to verify fatigue was not a substantial factor over the duration of the study. Differences in monitor calibration, lighting conditions, individual colour perception, etc. prevents us from reliably calculating an "absolute error" for any particular trial. However, by repeated measurements over multiple blocks with the same set of stimuli we are able to measure the "consistency" of individual participants.

For each condition, 75 participants were recruited. Individual trials further than half the slider width away from their "true" location on the scale were identified as probable accidental clicks and removed. Anomalous participants were identified using Tukey's outlier filter based on inter-block consistency. Between those participants who left before completing all trials, and those removed as outliers, each condition ended with between 53 and 67 participants, resulting in between 10,399 and 13,170 trials for each condition.

Metrics

Given that the greyscale stimuli are selected at perceptually linear increments across the range of the scale, a "perfect" set of responses would be evenly distributed between the minimum and maximum points of the scale (Figure 5, A). If monitor calibration, lighting conditions, or individual perceptual variation caused a participant's responses to skew either high or low, we would still expect to get a smooth distribution of responses, perhaps skewed to one side (Figure 5, B). We consider either of these as "low bias" distributions.

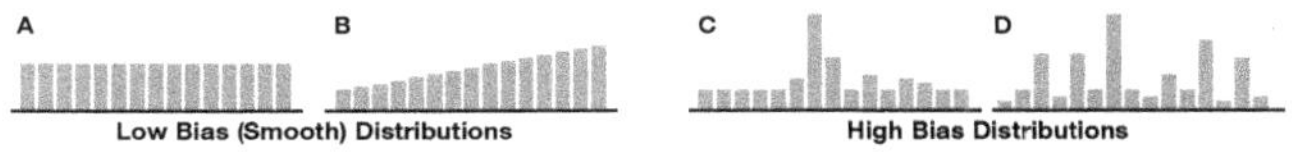

Figure 5. Example low and high-bias rating distributions.

A noisy, or irregular distribution of responses with one or multiple "spikes" along the range of values (Figure 5, C/D) is not consistent with the evenly distributed stimuli used in the study and would be considered a "high bias" distributions. To mathematically represent the bias in a distribution of responses we calculate the "smoothness" by grouping the data into 100 bins and calculating the standard deviation of the difference between all adjacent bins:

$$bias = \sqrt{\frac{1}{N_b}\sum\left((x_i - x_{i-1}) - \frac{\sum(x_i - x_{i-1})}{N_b}\right)} \quad (1)$$

where N_b is the number of bins and x_i is the number of ratings falling in each bin. With this calculation, a smooth, or low-bias distribution will have a *low* bias score, and distributions with large differences between successive bins will have a *high* bias score. Since the slider implementation clamps values to the end points (0 and 600) creating artificially larger input regions than the other points on the range, the extreme values are removed before performing the bias calculation. The overall bias of a condition is calculated as the mean of the individual participant biases.

Results

Due to growing concerns in various research fields over the limitations of null hypothesis significance testing for interpreting and reporting experimental results [5,8,9,42] we base our analyses and discussions on effect sizes and confidence intervals [6]. The 95% confidence intervals (CIs) are computed using bootstrapping [7].

Q1: Do Ticks Marks Matter?

The first, and most basic, question we wanted to investigate was to see if the presence of tick marks along a slider would have an effect on data collected. For this we compared the results for two designs: *No Ticks*, a slider without any tick marks, and *5 Ticks*, a slider with 5 equally spaced tick marks along the width of the slider (Figure 6).

Figure 6. Slider conditions used to answer the question "Do Ticks Matter?"

Since the two slider conditions have the exact same input space, and the tick marks are "non-functional" in the sense that the slider does not automatically "snap" to these locations, we expected the effect of the tick marks to be minimal. However, looking at the distribution of responses for each of the conditions, the effect of tick marks is apparent (Figure 7).

The y-axis intervals in the above charts are normalized to the expected number of responses. If the responses for each shade were evenly distributed around their "true" locations on the slider, we would expect each bin of the histogram to reach the '1x' level. Locations above the 1x line have received more responses than should be expected, and those below have received less. For example, the spike at location 300 (the middle of the slider) in the *5 Ticks* condition indicates that location received >5.5 times more responses than would be expected with a uniform distribution.

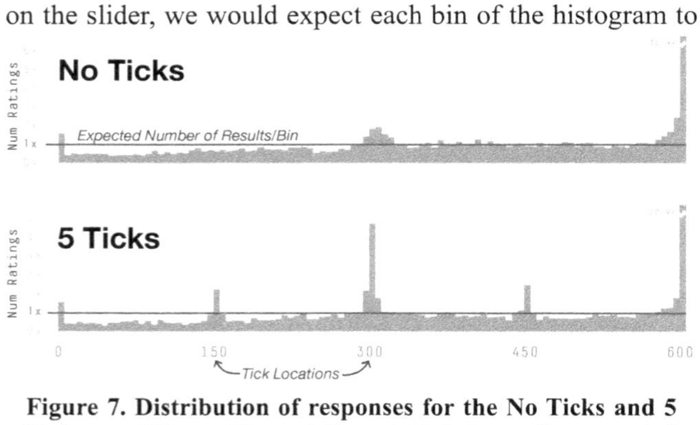

Figure 7. Distribution of responses for the No Ticks and 5 Ticks conditions. The red line at '1x' shows the expected number of results in each bucket of the histogram. The x-axis labels (and dashed lines) show the location of the tick marks displayed on the slider.

In these (and all other) conditions there is considerable bias towards the end points, particularly at the "black" end of the spectrum. As mentioned above, due to enlarged hit zones and increased susceptibility to monitor calibration differences, the end points are removed before performing the bias calculations. However, perhaps notable is that these two conditions have very similar results at both the low (1.69x vs. 1.68x) and high (10.9x vs. 10.9x) ends of the scale. To improve the visualization of the data in the middle of the scale, the vertical axis has been capped at 6x and the value of the right-most bin displayed alongside the broken bar.

Visual inspection of Figure 7 suggests that tick marks do indeed have a bearing on the distribution of results, and agrees with analysis of the mean bias metric (Figure 8).

Figure 8. Mean bias scores for the *No Ticks* and *5 Ticks* conditions. Error bars show 95% CIs.

For each condition, the bias metric is calculated for each user and the mean and 95% confidence intervals is computed using bootstrapping. On the chart, values towards the left indicate a smoother, less biased distribution, and values to the right indicate a less smooth, more biased set of results.

It is interesting to note that even without any ticks or labels, the *No Ticks* conditions still exhibits a "bump" around the middle of the scale, suggesting that even without any decorations (and disregarding the end points) the distribution of responses on a VAS is not fully uniform.

The mean *completion time* for the *No Ticks* and *5 Ticks* conditions were very close, at 1.63s and 1.69s respectively. In fact, the *completion times* for all slider conditions for this task bunched very tightly between 1.6 and 1.8 seconds and were not analyzed further.

Q2: Does the Number of Tick Marks Matter?

Having established that the presence of tick marks affects the results, we next wanted to see what effect varying the number of tick marks would have. Besides the *5 Tick* condition tested above, five other variations were tested: *2 Ticks*, with tick

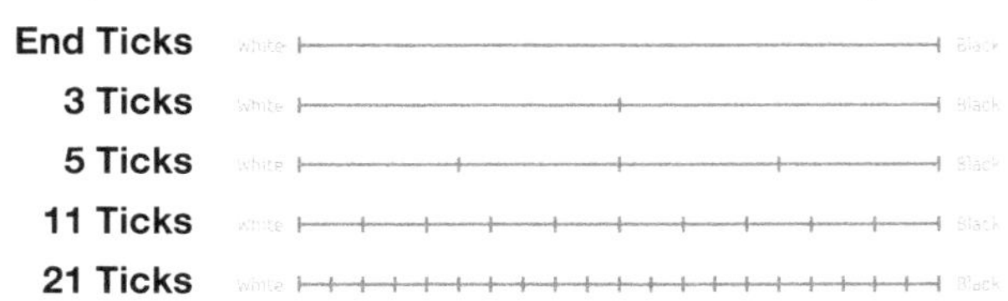

Figure 9. Slider conditions used to investigate the effect on varying the number of ticks.

marks only at the extremes; *3 Ticks*, tick marks at the ends and in the middle; and *11 Ticks* and *21 Ticks*, with 11 and 21 evenly spaced tick marks respectively (Figure 9).

For the higher number of tick conditions, we believed the effect of the ticks would be diminished – that if there are too many tick marks, spaced too tightly, that they will no longer influence the user and the results will trend back towards those from the *No Ticks* condition. The resulting distributions from this set of conditions are shown in Figure 10.

We can see that the *End Ticks* distribution closely resembles that from the *No Ticks* condition (Figure 7) and the two conditions also have very similar bias distributions (Figure 11). For the 3, 5, 11, and 21 *Tick* conditions, the effect of the individual tick marks is clearly visible. The individual spikes at the tick locations are smaller in the *21 Ticks* condition, and the large spike seen at the middle location (300) in the 3, 5, and 11 tick conditions is also reduced (2.2x in the *21 Ticks* condition compared to 4.8x in the *11 Ticks* condition).

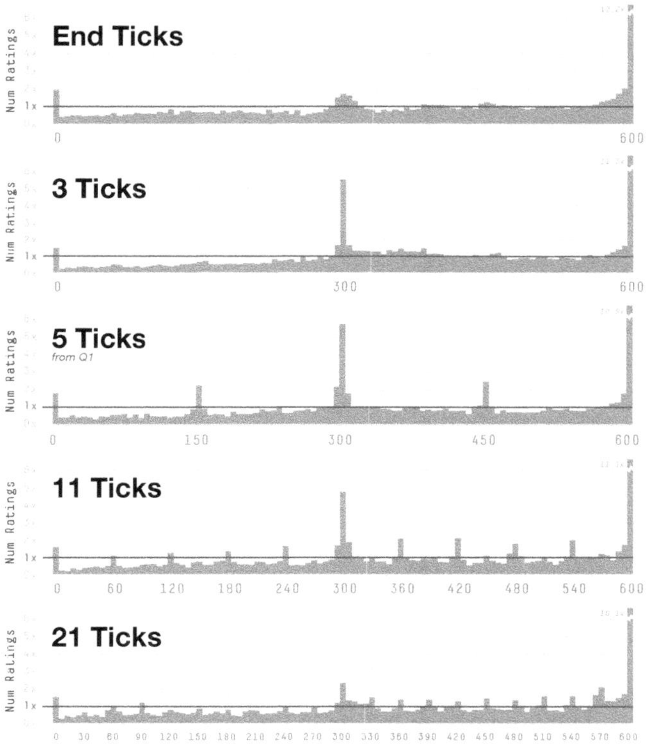

Figure 10. Distributions of responses for the various *number-of-tick* conditions.

Figure 11. Mean bias scores for varying number of tick marks. Error bars show 95% CIs.

The overall amount of tick bias in the *21 Ticks* condition also appears to be somewhat reduced compared to the 3, 5, and 11 Tick conditions (Figure 11), however all of the 3, 5, 11, and 21 Tick conditions produced markedly more biased results than the *No Tick* and *End Tick* conditions.

Q3: Does the Visual Weight of the Tick Marks Matter?

Besides the number of tick marks, we suspect that varying the appearance of the tick marks could have an effect on how likely it is for responses to gravitate towards them. Namely, we suspect that visually less imposing, or "lighter" tick marks will introduce less bias towards the ticks, and visually "heavier" ticks marks will increase bias.

To test this theory, we created two additional variations of the *5 Tick* slider: *Light Ticks* has very short, thin tick marks, and *Heavy Ticks* has wider and taller tick marks (Figure 12).

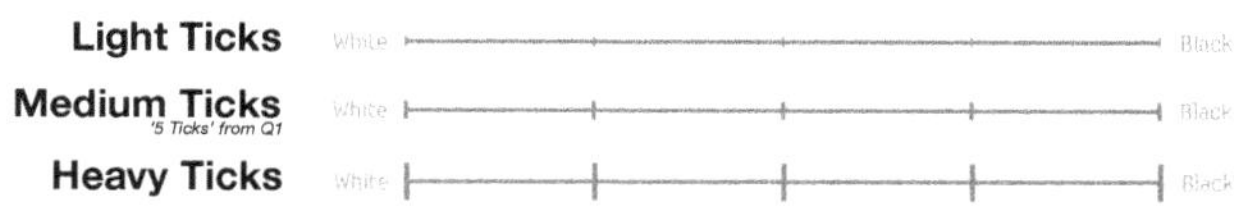

Figure 12. Variations on the visual weight of tick marks.

Rather unexpectedly, the visual weight of the tick marks did not appear to have much of an effect on the amount of tick bias. Visual inspection of the resulting distributions (Figure 13) does not reveal any particular difference among the conditions, and analysis of the mean bias metric also suggests that the tick weight did not substantially change the amount of bias (Figure 14).

Prior to running the study we were concerned that the tick marks in the *Light Ticks* condition were *too* minimal – that

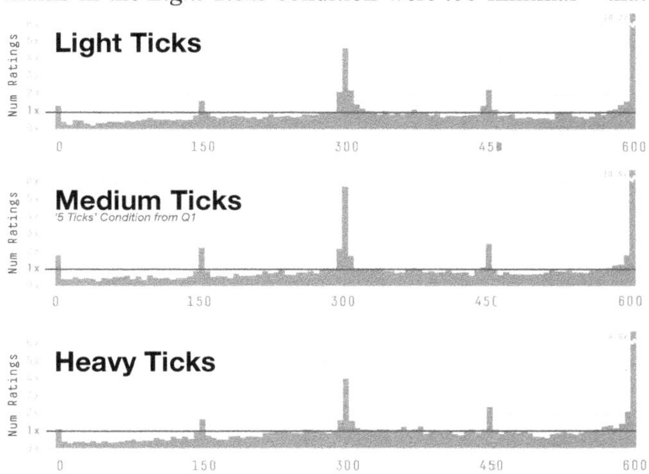

Figure 13. Distributions of responses for the tested *weight-of-tick* conditions.

Figure 14. Mean bias scores for varying the weight of the tick marks. Error bars show 95% CIs.

participants would have trouble even noticing that they existed, much less have them bias their responses. It is hard to imagine using tick marks any less visible in practice, but it would be an interesting exercise to see just how slight the ticks need to be to have no effect on the collected responses.

Q4: What is the Effect of Major/Minor Ticks?

All of the slider designs tested to this point have had a consistent tick appearance over the length of the slider. A commonly used design variation is to use "major" and "minor" tick marks along the length of a scale. We tested two variations of in this category: *Major/Minor* has the same tick locations as the *5 Tick* condition, but the 1st, 3rd, and 5th ticks are rendered more heavily than the 2nd and 4th ticks, and *Ruler*, which employs 4 levels of tick weights (Figure 15). We suspect that in these conditions the smaller/lighter "minor" tick marks may influence the results less than the larger/heavier "major" ticks.

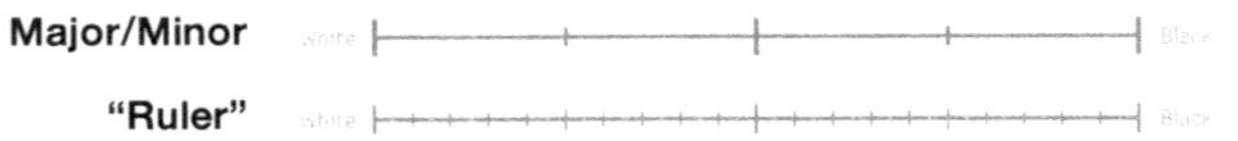

Figure 15. Sliders used to test the effect of "major" and "minor" ticks on the same scale

The distribution of responses in the *Major/Minor* condition (Figure 16) is very similar to that of the *5 Ticks* condition, and the means and confidence intervals are also similar (Figure 17), suggesting that in this case, the presence of major/minor ticks did not greatly affect the level of bias.

The three largest tick sizes in the *Ruler* condition have the same positions as the ticks in the *21 Ticks* design. When there were 21 equally-weighted ticks in the (*21 Ticks* condition), the spikes around each of the ticks were relatively constant, with a small increase at the middle location (300). However, the *Ruler* condition has larger spikes at the larger tick marks, namely 150, 300, and 450, resulting in considerably more overall tick-bias than present in the *21 Ticks* condition. Of note, the 4th level of very faint tick marks did not seem to noticeably influence the results.

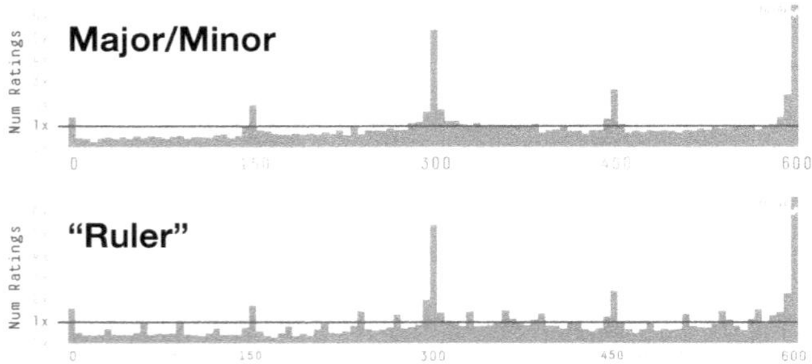

Figure 16. Results for Major/Minor Tick Mark examples.

Figure 17. Mean bias results for the Major/Minor tick mark conditions.

Q5: Does the Shape of the Thumb Matter?

For visual analogue scales, it is common to represent the mark on the line as an 'X'. The X mark is what respondents are asked to mark the line with when answering a VAS question on paper, and the convention has made its way to digital representations as well [31]. In desktop environments, the slider thumb is most commonly rectangular in shape, while in mobile scenarios, the slider is often a circle. We do not anticipate the shape of the slider will materially affect the distribution of responses, but to confirm, we ran the *5 Tick* slider with three different thumb shape conditions: *Rectangle Thumb*, *Circle Thumb*, and *'X' Thumb* (Figure 18).

Figure 18. Thumb slider styles used.

Comparison of the result distributions among the three *slider type* conditions did not suggest any differences between the conditions, and looking at the bias scores for the conditions similarly suggests that the shape of the thumb does not greatly affect the distribution of responses (Figure 19).

Figure 19. Mean bias scores for varying the shape of the thumb slider. Error bars show 95% CIs.

Q6: Labels vs. Ticks vs. Labels and Ticks

In the previous conditions, the demarcations along the slider have been solely indicated by tick marks. It is also common to use labels, either on their own or in combination with tick marks, to represent positions on the continuum (Figure 20).

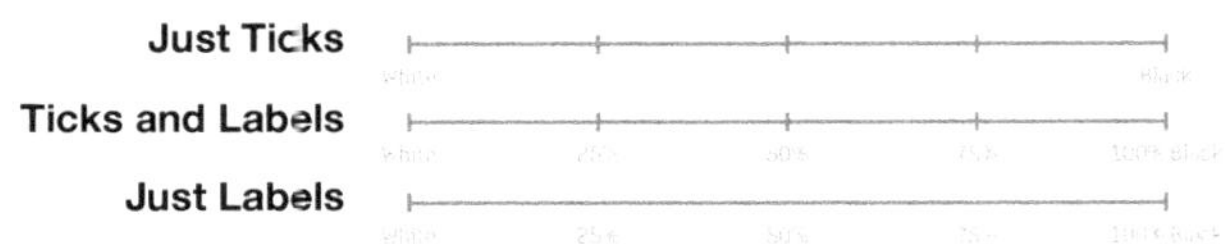

Figure 20. Sliders to test the effect of the combination of labels and ticks.

We suspected that perhaps the addition of labels to the tick marks (*Ticks and Labels*) would cause more clustering at the tick points than just the ticks alone (*Just Ticks*). When displaying only the labels, but not the ticks (*Just Labels*) we hypothesized that there would still exist bias towards the label positions but it would be less pronounced than in the conditions with ticks.

The result distributions between the *Just Ticks* and *Ticks and Labels* conditions turned out to be quite similar (Figure 21), and while the *Ticks and Labels* condition had a marginally higher average measure of bias than *Just Ticks* (2.58 vs 2.41) the confidence intervals overlap substantially. The *Just Labels* condition exhibits more rounded spikes around the label positions, as expected, and overall exhibited less bias than the other two conditions (Figure 22).

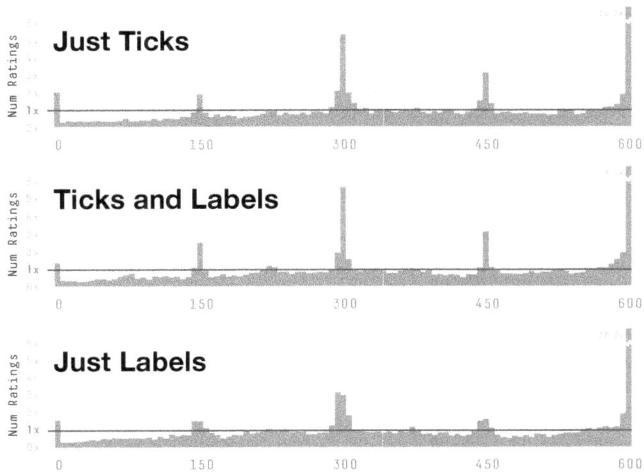

Figure 21. Results for ticks and/or labels.

Figure 22. Mean bias scores for ticks and/or labels.

Q7: What is the Effect of 'Banded' Representations?

Besides simply adding ticks and labels to the basic line of the slider track we were interested in exploring how more substantial changes to the design of the slider track might work. As one possible alternative, we tested the idea of a "banded" slider (Figure 23).

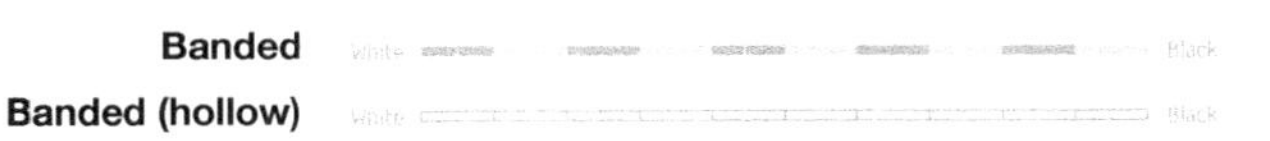

Figure 23. Two variations of a "banded" slider.

We tested two variations of the "banded" slider: *Banded* consists of alternating filled rectangles of dark and light shades of grey, and *Banded (hollow)* has the same rectangles, but filled with white and outlined. These variations contain the same amount of information, and in fact, display the same information as the *11 Ticks* condition (the boundaries between segments of the banded designs correspond to the tick mark locations in the *11 Ticks* design). The results from these conditions were rather unexpected (Figure 24).

The *Banded (hollow)* design produced a similar distribution pattern (and had substantially overlapping CIs) with the *11 Ticks* condition. However, quite surprisingly, the distribution of results in the *Banded* condition shows almost no bias in results towards the boundaries between bands except for a small spike in the middle (300). In fact, the mean bias-effect for the *Banded* condition is very similar to that of the *No Ticks* condition (Figure 25), suggesting that a banded representation of a slider might be a good way to provide the additional information afforded by tick marks, without introducing the associated bias.

We were quite surprised by the results of the *Banded* slider. To ensure that the results were not due to the particular set of participants who were assigned this condition, we collected

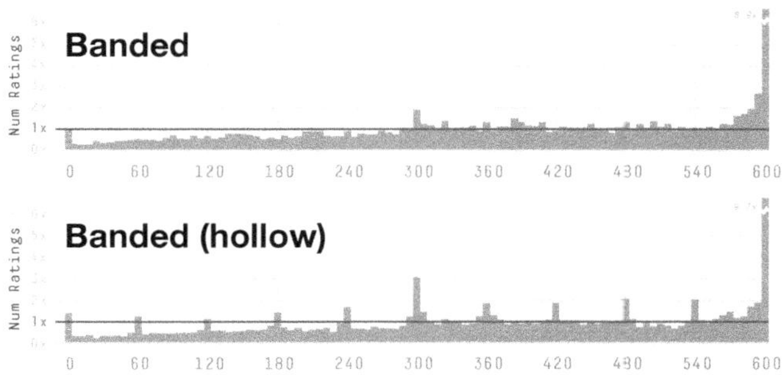

Figure 24. Results for banded slider variations.

Figure 25. Mean bias scores for the banded and banded (hollow) conditions. No Ticks and 11 Ticks are included for comparison. Error bars show 95% CIs.

data from an additional 80 participants and found that they produced similar results. We hypothesize that the solid regions in the *Banded* condition "smooth out" the bias found in the *Banded (hollow)* condition by emphasizing the wide "band" areas, rather than the boundaries between the bands.

Q8: Effect of Dynamically Labelled Thumb Slider

The final design variation we explored is a dynamically updating label showing the current value of the slider. We designed this condition to appear the same as the *No Ticks* condition, with the addition of a text label over the thumb indicating the current value (Figure 26).

Figure 26. Dynamically labelled slider design.

The label above the slider ranged from 0% at the "white" to 100% at the "black" end. We were not sure if this slider would encourage the relatively un-biased distribution generated by the *No Ticks* slider, or if perhaps the presence of the dynamic label above the thumb might bias the results towards "round" numbers. Looking at the distribution of responses (Figure 27) suggests that indeed the presence of the dynamic label did bias responses towards specific round values as observed by the spikes at 10%, 50%, 75%, etc.

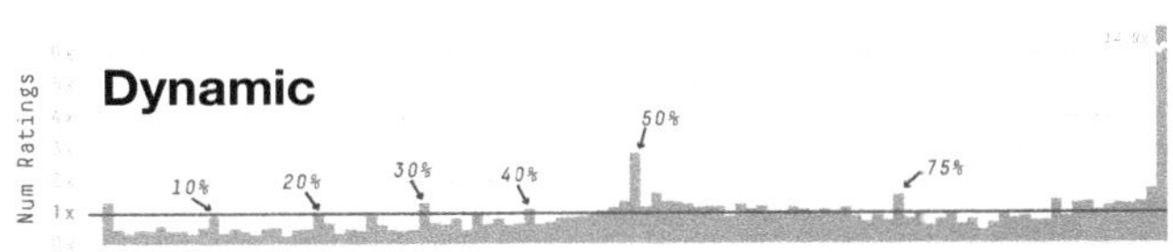

Figure 27. Distribution of results for the *dynamic* slider.

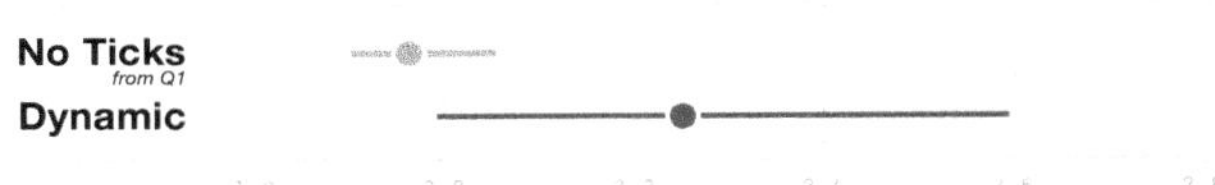

Figure 28. Bias comparison between *Dynamic* and *No Ticks*.

Looking at the bias ranges shows that the mean level of bias is higher with the *Dynamic* slider than the *No Ticks* design. However, compared to other conditions the *Dynamic* slider has a wide 95% CI, suggesting that the bias induced with this technique is not uniformly applied to all users (Figure 28).

Summary

Overall, we found that the visual design of VASs can heavily influence the responses which are obtained from online experiments. In particular, tick marks were found to bias the results towards the locations of the ticks. Bias was not affected by the visual weight of the ticks or the shape of the thumb. Labels on their own resulted in somewhat less bias than labels+ticks. The most promising result may be that the visual appearance of shaded bands reduces bias substantially when compared to the equivalent "ticked" design, and produces bias levels similar to that of the scale with no ticks.

STUDY #2: OBJECTIVE PRECISION TASK

With the first set of experiments we were interested in exploring how the visual presentation of a slider altered the responses in a *judgement* task – one where a wide range of values could be reasonably selected for a particular stimulus (Figure 3). In this second set of experiments, we want to see how the visual appearance of the slider influences results to an *objective* question – one where a participant is instructed to select a specific value along the scale with as much accuracy as possible. This simulates a scenario when a respondent has a desired value they wish to specify. This study will allow us to test the accuracy and efficiency of the previously tested conditions.

Task – Percentage Finding

We created a "percentage finding" task to test the precision of the sliders when attempting to select a known target. The task was set up in much the same way as the task from the first study, however instead of a slider ranging from "white" to "black" and presenting the participant with a shade of grey to rate, in this task the slider ranged from "0%" to "100%" and the participant was presented with a particular percentage (e.g., 32%) to locate and select on the scale.

Experimental Design

Participants were again recruited from Mechanical Turk using the same criteria as in the first set of experiments. The study was divided into two blocks, each randomly presenting each of the 101 whole number percentages between 0% and 100%. The slider mechanics were the same as in the first study, with the side of the "start position" counterbalanced for each of the individual percentages over the two blocks. The 202 total trials took an average of 7 minutes to complete and participants were compensated $1 USD. Pilot tests suggested this task would have less individual variation between participants so 25 users were recruited for each condition. Individual trials more than 35 percentage points from the target were removed as outliers and anomalous participants were removed using Tukey's outlier filter on *magnitude of response error*, leaving between 18 and 24 participants for analysis in each condition.

Conditions

We selected a range of slider designs from the first study and expanded the set to include more conditions and variations on the number of labels being shown (Figure 29).

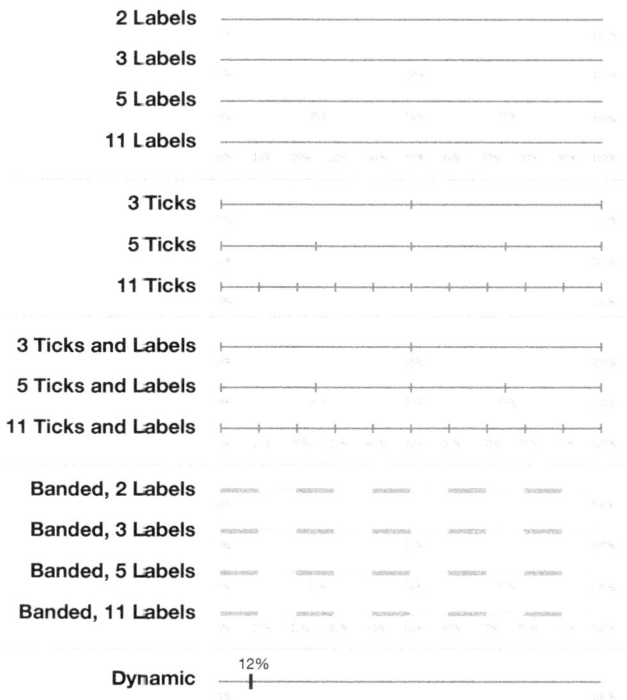

Figure 29. Slider designs tested in the second set of objective precision experiments.

Results

For each trial the *completion time* and *error* were recorded, with *completion time* being the elapsed time from when the cursor left the "start position" to when the mouse button was clicked to register the response, and *error* being the difference between the registered and target value. We calculate the *precision* of a participant as the median absolute error, and the *precision* of a technique as the mean of the participant precisions. As before, the stimulus was hidden until the cursor entered the start position.

Error/Precision

For each slider condition we created an "error map" which includes one dot for each completed trial, with the x-position representing the target value for the trial, and the y-position showing the error between the target and registered response. Two representative error maps are shown in Figure 30.

Looking at the error map for the *5 Labels* condition we notice several interesting properties. Because the labels serve as references for specific values along the scale, we can see the distribution of errors "pinch in" at the label points showing that users are unsurprisingly, more precise at selecting a value which is close to a value marked on the slider. The second, less expected property is the asymmetric shape of the error curve between adjacent labels. Values just to the right of a label (e.g., 54) tend to have positive errors and values just to the left of a label (e.g., 69) tend to have negative errors. Put another way, the trend is to make the selection further away from the nearest label than it should be. Further, this asymmetric error distribution between demarcations appears to be consistent across the various conditions tested.

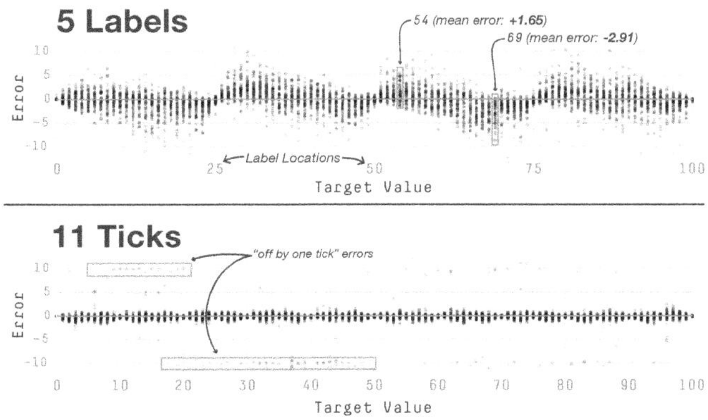

Figure 30. "Error maps" for the *5 Labels* and *11 Ticks* conditions from the second set of experiments.

Looking at the *11 Ticks* error map we see that errors are generally closer to '0', which we would expect since there are more landmarks on the slider to aid with positioning. However, it is interesting to note the clusters of errors at +10 and -10. In this condition the ticks are not labelled with their value, and are 10 units apart from one another, so these errors appear to be the result of "mis-counting" the tick marks and placing the selection nearly exactly one-tick away from the proper location. These "off-by-one" errors do not appear in the *11 Ticks and Labels* condition, since the labels eliminate the need for the user to "count" the tick marks themselves.

Speed

Besides precision of responses, we are also interested in the *speed* of responses. For pollsters, speed is an important factor to allow respondents to answer more questions in a shorter time. Unlike in the first study, the completion times for this study do appear to vary meaningfully among the conditions. In Figure 31 we plot the *speed* vs. *precision* for each of the conditions (with *Average Completion Time* calculated as the average of the median completion times per participant).

For this task an optimal slider has a combination of fast speed (low on the chart) and high precision (left on the chart). Unsurprisingly, the *Dynamic* slider with a label showing the exact value has the greatest precision. However, this comes at the cost of speed, as it is also one of the slowest techniques.

For pairs of designs which vary only in their inclusion of labels (for example, *11 Ticks* and *11 Ticks and Labels*) we would expect that since they demark the same positions on the line, they would enable similar levels of precision. Additionally, we would expect the variant without labels to be slower since the user needs to "count" the ticks to find the correct location. We see this trend very clearly with the *11 Ticks* and *11 Ticks and Labels* conditions; they have similar levels of precision, but *11 Ticks and Labels* is considerably

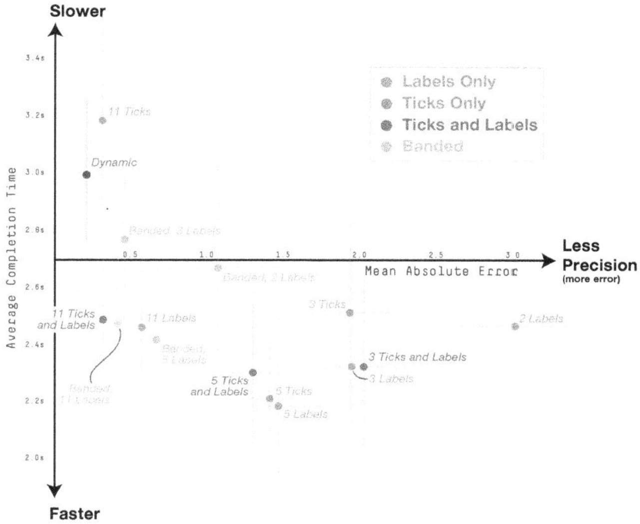

Figure 31. Speed vs. Precision results from the second set of experiments. Error bars show the 95% CIs for *completion time* vertically, and for *mean absolute error* horizontally. *(Note: horizontal error bars on the most precise conditions are too short to extend beyond the bounds of their mark.)*

faster (3.2s vs 2.5s). Further, we might expect conditions which vary only in their inclusion of ticks (for example, *11 Labels* and *11 Ticks and Labels*) to have similar completion times, but the 'ticks' variant enabling more precision. We see this occurring with *11 Labels* and *11 Ticks and Labels*, and to a lesser extent in the 3 and 5 tick/label conditions as well.

Another general, and logical, trend is for conditions which vary only in the number of marks (for example, *2/3/5/11 Labels*), precision decreases as the number of marks decreases. This can be seen most clearly in the "*2/3/5/11 Labels*" and *"3/5/11 Labels and Ticks*" conditions.

Finally, there is an interesting difference between the *11 Ticks* condition and the *Banded, 2 Labels* condition. They each present the exact same information to the user: values at the end points and 9 unlabeled demarcation points in between. However, the *11 Ticks* design produced results with more precision (and a longer time) than did *Banded, 2 Labels.* In the first set of experiments using the perceptual judgement task, users seemed to be less drawn to the division between bands than to the tick marks, and a similar effect is seen here.

COMBINED RESULTS

The previous two studies have looked at three main properties of Visual Analogue Scale performance:

- ***Judgement Bias**:* How much the design of the scale pulls the responses away from the baseline response curve when answering a judgement question. (Study One)
- ***Objective Precision**:* How accurately responses can be entered in relation to the desired value when answering an objective question. (Study Two)
- ***Speed**:* How long it takes to enter a response. (Study One did not see meaningful differences in completion times between the conditions, but Study Two, did).

For most cases it will be desirable to choose a slider design which *minimizes* the amount of bias and *maximizes* the amount of precision. It may also be desirable to choose a design which *minimizes* the time required to enter each response. In order to explore the trade-offs between these three properties, we ran the "greyscale test" from Study One on the 6 conditions from Study Two which were not originally tested in Study One (*3 Labels*; *11 Labels*; *3 Ticks and Labels*; *Banded, 3 Labels*; *Banded, 5 Labels*; *Banded, and 11 Labels*). After running those remaining 7 slider designs through perceptual judgment greyscale task, we have a set of 15 slider designs for which we can compare their *bias* and *precision.* Figure 32 plots the relationship between bias and precision for these conditions, with the point size correlating to *completion time* in the "percentage" test. The desirable "high precision, low bias" designs are found in the lower-left quadrant of the plot.

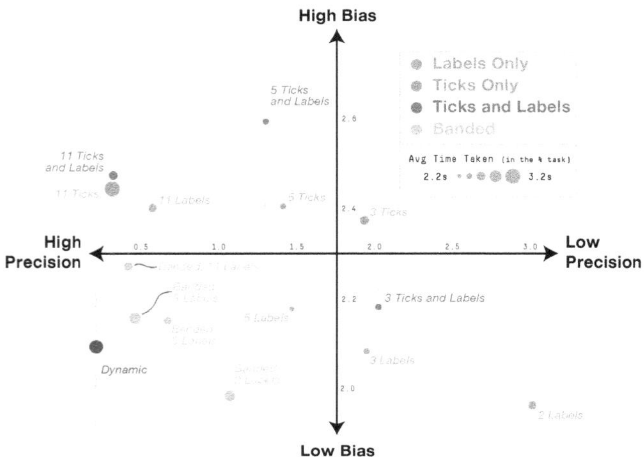

Figure 32. Bias vs. Precision results. Bias is measured using the perceptual judgement greyscale task, while precision (and speed) are measured using the objective percentage finding task. The best combination of properties is "High Precision" and "Low Bias", in the lower left hand corner.

DESIGN GUIDELINES

While the "optimal" scale design will be dependent on the type of question being asked, through these studies we have developed some general design guidelines for VASs:

Avoid Tick Marks: Tick marks can have a positive impact on the precision of responses, but they introduce an undue amount of bias in the results towards their location. The *Banded* designs enable the precision of tick marks, without the bias.

Use *Dynamic Feedback* for Precision: If high precision is a primary concern, use a slider which reports the slider's current value. While it increases response time, it affords more precision than including many ticks or labels, while introducing less bias into the results.

Use *Banded, 2 Labels* for Low Bias: The most commonly used VAS design is similar to *2 Labels*, with the only decoration being labels at the end points. *Banded, 2 Labels*, produces similarly low levels of bias, but enables higher precision should the situation call for it.

FUTURE WORK & DISCUSSION

We reported on the results for 18 designs for the perceptual judgement task, and for 15 designs for the objective precision task. Given the promise of the *banded* design, exploring further variations such as altering the number of bands, using gradients, or varying the thickness of the bands would be worthwhile. Additionally, it would be valuable to look at combining the traits of some conditions with favourable properties; in particular looking at a *banded* design with *dynamic* feedback could be a promising direction to enable the low bias that both techniques independently promote, combined with the high precision of the *dynamic* feedback with the higher speed of the *banded* design.

For our studies we choose two tasks; the *subjective judgment* task of rating the blackness of a greyscale shade for Study One, and the *objective precision* task of finding a particular percentage value for Study Two. For another project we ran a fairly large study (160 participants, 32,000 trials) on a *completely* subjective task (where participants were presented a social media profile picture and asked to "*rate the suitability of this image for use as a headshot in a corporate environment*") and found that the level of bias closely matched what was found in the *subjective judgement* greyscale task used in the first study. In the future it would be interesting to explore and test the biases for differing VAS designs over an even wider range of question types.

All of the scales we used in our studies were fixed at 600 pixels wide, which results in different real-world lengths depending on the DPI of the monitor used. While fixed-pixel width sliders are the norm in digital VASs systems, it would be worth studying if the actual display length materially affects the results, and considering if the displayed length of the scale should be normalized between respondents. Additionally, our conditions used the standard VAS input paradigm (point, click) rather than the workflow for traditional UI sliders (point, click, drag, release). Initial testing suggests that the observed results from VASs apply to traditional UI sliders as well, but follow up studies could explore this. Finally, as mentioned in the related work, prior studies have shown that the orientation of paper-based VAS scales may influence a user's responses. While such scales are predominately horizontal, it would be interesting to study what influence a vertical scale would have on our results.

CONCLUSION

We presented the results from two high-volume online experiments to explore and quantify the effects of visual analogue slider design on response bias, accuracy, and speed of use. Our results show the presence of certain decorations along the slider can considerably bias the distribution of responses received, however, a banded slider design was shown to outperform the traditional slider in terms of speed and accuracy, while maintaining a similar level of response bias. Given the current tends towards online surveys and web-based research methodologies, we believe our work serves as an important reference for online survey design.

REFERENCES

1. Gunnar Borg and Elisabet Borg. 1991. *A General Psychophysical Scale of Blackness and Its Possibilities as a Test of Rating Behaviour*. Department of Psychology, Stockholm University.
2. Lei Chang. 1994. A psychometric evaluation of 4-point and 6-point Likert-type scales in relation to reliability and validity. *Applied psychological measurement* 18, 3: 205–215.
3. C. Connolly and T. Fleiss. 1997. A study of efficiency and accuracy in the transformation from RGB to CIELAB color space. *IEEE Transactions on Image Processing* 6, 7: 1046–1048. http://doi.org/10.1109/83.597279
4. Mick P. Couper, Michael W. Traugott, and Mark J. Lamias. 2001. Web survey design and administration. *Public opinion quarterly* 65, 2: 230–253.
5. Geoff Cumming. 2013. The New Statistics Why and How. *Psychological Science*: 0956797613504966. http://doi.org/10.1177/0956797613504966
6. Geoff Cumming and Sue Finch. 2005. Inference by eye: confidence intervals and how to read pictures of data. *The American Psychologist* 60, 2: 170–180. http://doi.org/10.1037/0003-066X.60.2.170
7. Thomas J. DiCiccio and Bradley Efron. 1996. Bootstrap confidence intervals. *Statistical Science* 11, 3: 189–228. http://doi.org/10.1214/ss/1032280214
8. Pierre Dragicevic, Fanny Chevalier, and Stephane Huot. 2014. Running an HCI Experiment in Multiple Parallel Universes. *CHI '14 Extended Abstracts on Human Factors in Computing Systems*, ACM, 607–618. http://doi.org/10.1145/2559206.2578881
9. John E. Hunter Frank L. Schmidt. 1997. Eight common but false objections to the discontinuation of significance testing in the analysis of research data.
10. M. Freyd. 1923. The Graphic Rating Scale. *Journal of Educational Psychology* 14, 2: 83–102. http://doi.org/10.1037/h0074329
11. Frederik Funke and Ulf-Dietrich Reips. 2012. Why Semantic Differentials in Web-Based Research Should Be Made from Visual Analogue Scales and Not from 5-Point Scales. *Field Methods* 24, 3: 310–327. http://doi.org/10.1177/1525822X12444061
12. Joachim Gerich. 2007. Visual analogue scales for mode-independent measurement in self-administered questionnaires. *Behavior Research Methods* 39, 4: 985–992. http://doi.org/10.3758/BF03192994
13. Eric Gilbert. 2014. What if We Ask a Different Question?: Social Inferences Create Product Ratings Faster. *Proceedings of the 32Nd Annual ACM Conference on Human Factors in Computing Systems*, ACM, 2759–2762. http://doi.org/10.1145/2556288.2557081
14. Michael Gleicher, Michael Correll, Christine Nothelfer, and Steven Franconeri. 2013. Perception of Average Value in Multiclass Scatterplots. *IEEE Transactions on Visualization and Computer Graphics* 19, 12: 2316–2325. http://doi.org/10.1109/TVCG.2013.183
15. G. Ljunggren G Neely. 1992. Comparison between the Visual Analogue Scale (VAS) and the Category Ratio Scale (CR-10) for the evaluation of leg exertion. *International journal of sports medicine* 13, 2: 133–6. http://doi.org/10.1055/s-2007-1021244
16. Mary HS Hayes and Donald G. Patterson. 1921. Experimental development of the graphic rating method. *Psychol Bull* 18, 1: 98–9.
17. Jeffrey Heer and Michael Bostock. 2010. Crowdsourcing Graphical Perception: Using Mechanical Turk to Assess Visualization Design. *Proceedings of the SIGCHI Conference on Human Factors in Computing Systems*, ACM, 203–212. http://doi.org/10.1145/1753326.1753357
18. Marianne Jensen Hjermstad, Peter M. Fayers, Dagny F. Haugen, et al. 2011. Studies Comparing Numerical Rating Scales, Verbal Rating Scales, and Visual Analogue Scales for Assessment of Pain Intensity in Adults: A Systematic Literature Review. *Journal of Pain and Symptom Management* 41, 6: 1073–1093. http://doi.org/10.1016/j.jpainsymman.2010.08.016
19. E. C. Huskisson. 1974. Measurement of pain. *The Lancet* 304, 7889: 1127–1131.
20. Don A. Dillman Jolene D. Smyth. 2006. Effects of Using Visual Design Principles to Group Response Options in Web Surveys. *International Journal of Internet Science*.
21. Aniket Kittur, Ed H. Chi, and Bongwon Suh. 2008. Crowdsourcing User Studies with Mechanical Turk. *Proceedings of the SIGCHI Conference on Human Factors in Computing Systems*, ACM, 453–456. http://doi.org/10.1145/1357054.1357127
22. R. Likert. 1932. A technique for the measurement of attitudes. *Archives of Psychology* 22 140: 55.
23. Dawn M. Marsh-Richard, Erin S. Hatzis, Charles W. Mathias, Nicholas Venditti, and Donald M. Dougherty. 2009. Adaptive Visual Analog Scales (AVAS): A Modifiable Software Program for the Creation, Administration, and Scoring of Visual Analog Scales. *Behavior research methods* 41, 1: 99–106. http://doi.org/10.3758/BRM.41.1.99
24. Heather M. McCormack, David J. de L Horne, and Simon Sheather. 1988. Clinical applications of visual analogue scales: a critical review. *Psychological medicine* 18, 04: 1007–1019.
25. Hendrik Müller, Aaron Sedley, and Elizabeth Ferrall-Nunge. 2014. Designing Unbiased Surveys for HCI Research. *CHI '14 Extended Abstracts on Human Factors in Computing Systems*, ACM, 1027–1028. http://doi.org/10.1145/2559206.2567822

26. Gregory Neely. 1995. *Properties of a category ratio scale (CR-10) and the visual analogue scale (VAS): a comparison with magnitude estimation, line production, and category scaling*. Dept. of Psychology, Stockholm University.
27. Bing Pan, Arch G. Woodside, and Fang Meng. 2014. How Contextual Cues Impact Response and Conversion Rates of Online Surveys. *Journal of Travel Research* 53, 1: 58–68. http://doi.org/10.1177/0047287513484195
28. Agnès Paul-Dauphin, Francis Guillemin, Jean-Marc Virion, and Serge Briançon. 1999. Bias and Precision in Visual Analogue Scales: A Randomized Controlled Trial. *American Journal of Epidemiology* 150, 10: 1117–1127. http://doi.org/10.1093/oxfordjournals.aje.a009937
29. Philip M. Podsakoff, Scott B. MacKenzie, and Nathan P. Podsakoff. 2012. Sources of method bias in social science research and recommendations on how to control it. *Annual Review of Psychology* 63: 539–569. http://doi.org/10.1146/annurev-psych-120710-100452
30. Ulf-Dietrich Reips. 2010. Design and formatting in Internet-based research. In *Advanced methods for conducting online behavioral research*, S. D. Gosling and J. A. Johnson (eds.). American Psychological Association, Washington, DC, US, 29–43.
31. Ulf-Dietrich Reips and Frederik Funke. 2008. Interval-level measurement with visual analogue scales in Internet-based research: VAS Generator. *Behavior Research Methods* 40, 3: 699–704. http://doi.org/10.3758/BRM.40.3.699
32. Joel Ross, Lilly Irani, M. Six Silberman, Andrew Zaldivar, and Bill Tomlinson. 2010. Who Are the Crowdworkers?: Shifting Demographics in Mechanical Turk. *CHI '10 Extended Abstracts on Human Factors in Computing Systems*, ACM, 2863–2872. http://doi.org/10.1145/1753846.1753873
33. Paul van Schaik and Jonathan Ling. 2003. Using on-line surveys to measure three key constructs of the quality of human–computer interaction in web sites: psychometric properties and implications. *International Journal of Human-Computer Studies* 59, 5: 545–567. http://doi.org/10.1016/S1071-5819(03)00078-8
34. J. Scott and E. C. Huskisson. 1976. Graphic representation of pain. *Pain* 2, 2: 175–184.
35. Daniel R. Smith and Bruce N. Walker. 2002. Tick-marks, axes, and labels: The effects of adding context to auditory graphs. *International Conference on Auditory Display (ICAD)*. Retrieved March 31, 2015 from https://smartech.gatech.edu/handle/1853/51392
36. George W. Torrance, David Feeny, and William Furlong. 2001. Visual Analog Scales Do They Have a Role in the Measurement of Preferences for Health States? *Medical Decision Making* 21, 4: 329–334.
37. Roger Tourangeau, Mick P. Couper, and Frederick Conrad. 2004. Spacing, Position, and Order Interpretive Heuristics for Visual Features of Survey Questions. *Public Opinion Quarterly* 68, 3: 368–393. http://doi.org/10.1093/poq/nfh035
38. Li-Jen Weng. 2004. Impact of the Number of Response Categories and Anchor Labels on Coefficient Alpha and Test-Retest Reliability. *Educational and Psychological Measurement* 64, 6: 956–972. http://doi.org/10.1177/0013164404268674
39. SurveyMonkey: Free online survey software & questionnaire tool. Retrieved March 30, 2015 from https://www.surveymonkey.com/
40. Google Forms - create and analyze surveys, for free. Retrieved March 30, 2015 from http://www.google.ca/forms/about/
41. Amazon Mechanical Turk - Welcome. Retrieved March 30, 2015 from https://www.mturk.com/mturk/welcome
42. Beyond Significance Testing: Statistics Reform in the Behavioral Sciences, Second Edition. *http://www.apa.org*. Retrieved March 25, 2015 from http://www.apa.org/pubs/books/4316151.aspx

Making Sense of Temporal Queries with Interactive Visualization

Leilani Battle[1], Danyel Fisher[2], Robert DeLine[2], Mike Barnett[2], Badrish Chandramouli[2], Jonathan Goldstein[2]

MIT
Cambridge, Massachusetts 02139
leilani@csail.mit.edu

Microsoft Research
Redmond, Washington 98052
{danyelf, rdeline, mbarnett, badrishc, jongold}@microsoft.com

ABSTRACT

As real-time monitoring and analysis become increasingly important, researchers and developers turn to data stream management systems (DSMS's) for fast, efficient ways to pose temporal queries over their datasets. However, these systems are inherently complex, and even database experts find it difficult to understand the behavior of DSMS queries. To help analysts better understand these temporal queries, we developed StreamTrace, an interactive visualization tool that breaks down how a temporal query processes a given dataset, step-by-step. The design of StreamTrace is based on input from expert DSMS users; we evaluated the system with a lab study of programmers who were new to streaming queries. Results from the study demonstrate that StreamTrace can help users to verify that queries behave as expected and to isolate the regions of a query that may be causing unexpected results.

Author Keywords

Streaming Data; Data Visualization; Data Analysts

ACM Classification Keywords

H.5.m. Information interfaces and presentation (e.g., HCI): Miscellaneous.

INTRODUCTION

Academia, industry, and individuals are increasingly monitoring temporal data. Companies track changes in sales and inventory; app designers on the Internet of Things coordinate and monitor continuous signals from home, office and wearable devices. Medical and health-monitoring devices contain logic to process multiple temporal signals, combining GPS, heart rate, and accelerometers to determine and log when the user is running, walking and even sleeping. In e-businesses, cloud-hosted services capture both user behavior and service performance into live telemetry data. Analysts create dashboards from this data to monitor software quality and to produce game leaderboards, search results, and other client-facing products. Given the integral role of streaming data in these endeavors, programmers and data scientists need tools to analyze temporal data quickly and efficiently.

CHI'16, May 07-12, 2016, San Jose, CA, USA
© 2016 ACM. ISBN 978-1-4503-3362-7/16/05...$15.00
DOI: http://dx.doi.org/10.1145/2858036.2858408

To make temporal analyses scale to massive datasets, the database community has developed *data stream management systems* (DSMS's) [1],[4],[5],[8],[24]. DSMS's support fast, continuous computation over temporal data streams. A DSMS supplements a classic relational database management system (DBMS) by maintaining a first class notion of time. Time is not simply an extra column in a relational table. Rather, *streams* of temporal data represent facts and relationships that vary over time. Each "row" in a stream, called a *stream event*, has a start and end time. Entities and relationships are valid only within their temporal range.

To write a DSMS query, a data analyst reasons about both the data's content and temporal range. For instance, consider an online store with a data stream of customer shopping transactions. Both the number of customers and the contents of their carts vary over time. A simple query in a relational data model—for example, the average number of items per cart—instead becomes a windowed moving average in a streaming system. This requires the data analyst to consider temporal issues, like the duration of the window for the moving average and how to combine the time range of a customer's shopping session with the time ranges of items in the cart. In short, queries within DSMS's can be confusing for data analysts to understand and construct (Figure 1).

In this paper, we look at data analysts as a user group with specialized skills and distinctive needs (as in Fisher et al. [12] and Kandel et al. [19]). Supporting data analysts who work with streaming data raises unique and difficult challenges; we address them by applying user-centric design principles and methodologies.

We make the following contributions in this paper:

1) We discuss the complexity of understanding and debugging DSMS queries, and explore a case study;

2) We present a visualization design for illustrating the behavior of DSMS queries;
3) We present results from a user study showing that this visualization can help analysts better understand and construct queries.

CHALLENGES FOR USERS WITH DSMS QUERIES

The fundamental difference between streaming and relational databases is reflected in the way that these systems respond to queries. While relational queries in DBMS's produce static results (e.g., the count is 3), stream queries in DSMS's produce *result streams* (e.g., the count is 3 at time stamp 1, then 4 at time stamp 2, etc.). This distinction makes interpreting query output challenging for users who are unfamiliar with DSMS's: users need to learn to track how answers in the output stream change over time, and verify that these shifts match the input.

If interpreting stream query results can be difficult and error-prone, writing stream queries is even more challenging. DSMS's utilize specialized stream query languages, which are designed to support both relational and temporal operations. Some operations in a stream query language, like filtering ("where") and projection ("select"), are the same as in relational query languages. However, other query operators, like join, are "false friends" in that they have different interpretations from their relational counterparts. For example, a relational join over two tables compares every row in the first table with every row in the second, and outputs any matching pairs that are found. In contrast, a join in a DSMS will only output a matching pair of stream events if the events also overlap in time. Some DSMS operations have no equivalent operation in relational languages, such as trimming the duration of stream events, or shifting the start and end times of events.

Nor is understanding each operator individually enough: streaming queries often entail multiple phases of projection, joining, and filtering; events flow through a series of operators before they reach their final state. Analysts can find it challenging to see how those components combine, and to connect output events to the input they came from.

Expert Interviews on the Challenges of DSMS Queries

To better understand how these complexities affect users, we interviewed two expert DSMS users. Both work on data science teams at a large software company[1]. John processes the history of software modifications across a very large codebase; his temporal queries look at how the codebase and its contributors are changing over time.

Mark supports advertising features for a large-scale website. He produces live dashboards for advertisers on the effectiveness of their campaigns, and runs spot analyses of tools and features to understand adoption and usage.

In building their analytics, whether for offline use (as John does) or live streaming (as Mark does), both analysts create streaming queries in the DSMS – and, as such, can run into questions of whether their query is doing the right thing. We are generally interested in the process of constructing, testing, and iterating on a query; activities we collectively call "debugging".

Small-Scale Versus Large-Scale Debugging

John and Mark both reported that they typically debug their queries in two phases: first a small-scale *prototyping phase;* then a large-scale *performance-testing phase*. In the prototyping phase, they use small test datasets (less than 20 stream events) to manually track each input in the data stream and each output from the query. Here, each input event represents a specific test case—a strategy reminiscent of unit tests in software engineering. During this phase, they carefully check their queries for correctness, and improve their understanding of how query operators behave and interact. Once they are confident that their queries exhibit correct behavior, they try a larger dataset for full-scale performance testing. This performance testing can sometimes drive them to change the underlying query, and they return to the prototyping phase.

John and Mark also told us that they lack tools for effectively debugging their queries during the prototyping phase. Instead, they manually create query diagrams on the whiteboard in order to manually trace them. There is a design opportunity to support the prototype phase. A design can trade scalability for specificity, and show how queries act on small-scale data examples, rather than its aggregated effect on the dataset as a whole.

Challenges in Writing & Debugging Streaming Queries

Consider a motivating example based on a scenario from Mark, who wants to analyze user session data for a new online store. The raw data is stored as a single stream of aggregated shopping cart events, where each stream event represents the current number of items in a particular user's cart. An example of the stream is provided in the left-hand table in Figure 2a. Mark wants to write a single DSMS query to answer the following questions every 60 minutes:

- How many users are signed into the store over time?
- On average, how many products are in their shopping carts?

The DSMS query needed to answer Mark's questions is shown in Figure 1a (written in Trill-LINQ[2] [8]). This query demonstrates a common pattern for computing multiple statistics over streams. There is no guarantee that two queries will process the same stream events at the exact

[1] Names were changed to protect the privacy of these users.

[2] Trill-LINQ is a DSMS written in functional query language supported by the .NET Framework; the techniques in this paper apply equally for other DSMS dialects.

```
var oneHourVar = 60;
var offsetVar = 0;
var stats =
cartEvents.TumblingWindowLifetime(oneHourVar,offsetVar)
.Multicast(s => s.Aggregate(w=> w.Count())
      .join(s.Aggregate(w => w.Average(e => e.cartSize)),
            lhs=> true, rhs=> true,
            (lhs, rhs) => new {count = lhs, averageCart = rhs}));
```

(a) Correct Query

```
    var oneHourVar = 60;
    var offsetVar = 0;
    var stats = cartEvents.Multicast(s =>
(E)->s.TumblingWindowLifetime(oneHourVar,offsetVar)
          .Aggregate( w=> w.Count())
          .join(s.Aggregate(w => w.Average(e => e.cartSize)),
                lhs=> true, rhs=> true,
                (lhs, rhs) => new {count = lhs, averageCart = rhs}));
```

(b) Mark's (Incorrect) Query

Figure 1. A correctly written example query (left), and Mark's query (right). Mark's error – placing the TumblingWindowLifetime inside the Multicast, rather than outside -- is labeled as E.

Event	Start	End	UserID	countVal
0	0	30	1	1
1	0	60	2	1
2	30	120	1	2
3	60	120	2	2
4	120	195	1	3
5	120	140	2	1
6	180	225	2	1
7	225	290	2	2
8	290	305	2	1

(a) Shopping cart input

Start	End	count	average-Cart
0	30	2	1
30	60	2	1.5
60	120	2	2
120	140	1	1.5
140	180	1	3
180	195	2	2
195	225	2	1
225	240	2	2
240	290	1	2
290	300	1	1
300	305	1	1

(b) Query output

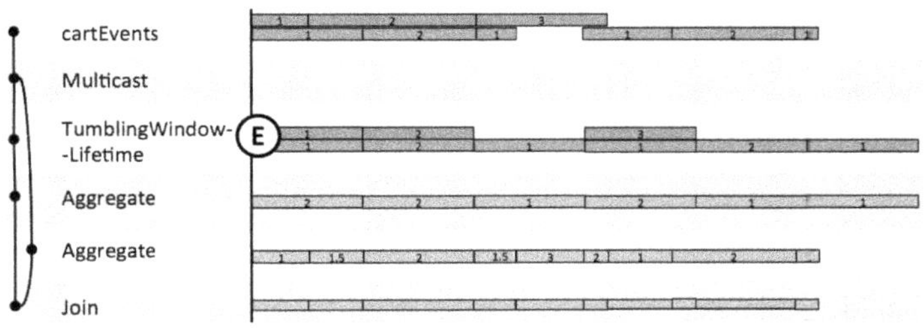

(c) StreamTrace diagram.

Figure 2. Table and Timeline representations for Mark's query (right-hand side of Figure 1). The results of the left-side TumblingWindowLifetime (at E) are out of step with the results of the right-side Aggregate

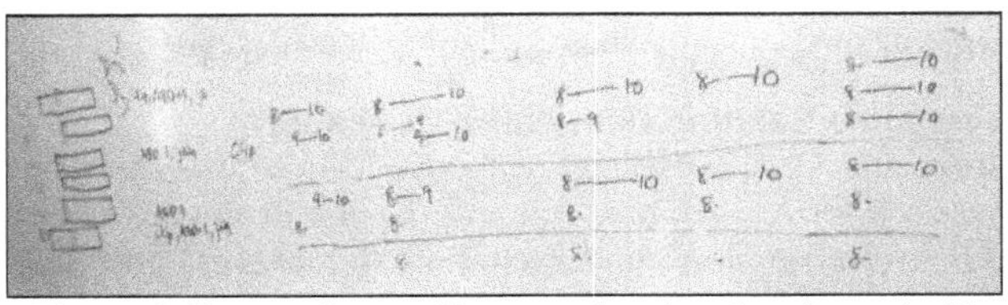

Figure 3. Expert-drawn diagram showing timed events. It shows (at left) a query plan, and (at right) horizontal bars showing time segments.

same time, and thus no guarantee they will provide matching results. This mismatch can be problematic for dashboards and other use cases that require a suite of statistics over fixed time windows. Hence relevant statistics must be computed within a single query.

In this example, a correct approach to thinking about how to construct the stream query is to consider how to augment or redirect the flow of timeline events. For example, if we want to compute multiple statistical operations in parallel over the stream, we can think of this process as creating multiple branches (or copies) of the stream (known as *Multicasting* the stream), and applying a different statistical operation to each branch. Similarly, to produce a single stream of statistics, we can view this process as *joining* the two Multicast branches back together, which will consolidate the duplicated events. In the query shown in Figure 1(a), these operations are represented as: 1) mapping the aggregated result to non-overlapping, 60-minute windows (TumblingWindowLifetime); 2) copying the stream into *two identical branches* (Multicast); 3) computing a separate aggregate statistic on each branch (Aggregate + Count, Aggregate + Average); and 4) joining the two branches together to consolidate the aggregate statistics (Join).

Mark originally wrote the erroneous query shown in Figure 1b. Though very similar to the correct query at left, Mark's query contains one error, at the letter E. When Mark's query is executed, it produces the incorrect result shown in Figure 2b, which is not broken into the desired 60-minute intervals. We see in Figure 2b that the time windows produced by Mark's query seem random and hard to fix, but Mark's query was actually very close to being correct. He chose the correct windowing operator (TumblingWindowLifetime), and even placed it in a reasonable location (on the first of the two Multicast branches). However, Mark failed to notice that the second branch of the Multicast operation was not mapped to 60-minute windows. This error is exacerbated when the two branches are then joined together: the events from each branch end up overlapping at weird times, resulting in output events with strange durations.

The correct query moves the TumblingWindowLifetime operator to be before the Multicast operator, eliminating the issue of applying windowing to each branch separately. However, when looking only at Mark's query in Figure 1b, or the output stream in Figure 2b, it is very challenging to detect and fix the error.

The Need for Visualizations

When Mark recounted this story during our interview, we noticed that although he was not able to produce the correct DSMS query to his problem, he was able to easily describe the correct *behavior* of the query. Mark provided us with hand-drawn diagrams showing the behavior he wished to see; John similarly provided us with Figure 3 to show how he thinks about temporal data and DSMS operators. As this language is an intuitive way of thinking about queries, we (manually) produced a visualization of the logic behind Mark's erroneous query shown in Figure 2(c).

This visualization highlights Mark's logical error: while the Multicast operation creates two separate branches, only the left branch is extended to 60-minute windows using the TumblingWindowLifetime operator. As a result, in Figure 2c, the events in the left-hand branch look noticeably different from the events in the right-hand branch.

John and other DSMS users shared these difficulties with writing stream queries: while they can reason about the high-level logic behind a query, they can have difficulties externalizing that into a correct query. With the help of a visualization, they can quickly identify the effects of each operation, and how these operations interact with each other across multiple data streams.

Common Mistakes in Writing Streaming Queries

We followed up our conversations with John and Mark with broader interviews, speaking to their teams and two other teams who create and use DSMS queries. In the interviews, we learned that even accomplished developers on their teams often had trouble formulating queries that behaved in the ways they expected; DSMS experts found it extremely difficult to explain temporal queries to novices.

We asked our interviewees to provide us with examples of their challenging DSMS queries, and access to the datasets they used to test the queries. The most challenging queries consistently included operators that both cause two streams to interact (such as join operations), and that change the temporal scope of an event (such as windowing functions). Data streams only interact with each other when their events overlap in time; as such, subtle bugs can arise from mismatched temporal extents in queries (like in Mark's query in Figure 1(b)). When these challenges are considered together, we found that they can be grouped into three categories of unmet needs:

1) Users have trouble inferring the combined behavior of multiple operators pipelined together in a single query.
2) Users struggle to mentally track temporal extents when validating the output of DSMS queries, and often have to write out timelines by hand.
3) Users lack intuition for the DSMS-specific temporal manipulation operations.

These three categories of challenges, combined with our focus on supporting query prototyping, represent our high-level design goals. In the remainder of this paper, we describe our visualization design, and show how it can be used to address these challenges and help DSMS users to better write and interpret temporal queries.

A Visual Approach to Reducing Complexity

We propose a new approach for capturing and visualizing the behavior of stream queries, making them easier to understand and debug. Our tool, StreamTrace, incorporates this visualization into an interactive DSMS. Our visualization is designed to help improve users' understanding of both how individual DSMS operators manipulate the data being queried, and the relationships between these operators. It visualizes the intermediate state of the query output after executing each operator, in order to show how each step of the query impacts the final result.

Our visualization scheme is based on in-person interviews and iterative design sessions with domain data analysts who work with a DSMS on a daily basis. We evaluated StreamTrace by conducting a lab study of 15 developers who were new to DSMS's, and conclude from our qualitative surveys from the study that StreamTrace can improve their ability to understand temporal query results and produce accurate DSMS queries in less time.

BACKGROUND

The StreamTrace system integrates aspects of several well-known visualization types, and builds upon existing software and concepts from several research domains.

Leveraging Existing Debugging Concepts

Parnin and Orso's debugging model [28] consists of three phases: *fault localization* (identifying the erroneous code); *fault understanding* (understanding the cause); and *fault correction* (fixing the bug). Translating this model for DSMS queries requires incorporating debugging features to figure out what a query is doing, trace the causes of query errors, and confirm that bugs are fixed. Unfortunately, most querying systems function as a black box, so users cannot see the results of intermediate steps. Our goal is to open that box to expose the interactions to users.

Several dataflow-focused debugging tools inspired our system design for analyzing DSMS queries. The Java Whyline [20] allows users to backtrack and identify the steps carried out by a program; users can ask why specific objects were assigned given values. JIVE [23] visualizes the steps of a procedural execution of a program to help a user understand what paths were chosen. Both of these visually lay out the progress that data makes through complex code, and to work forward and backward between outputs, antecedents, and inputs.

Temporal Visualizations

Temporal data analysis and exploration is a well-studied area of data visualization [2]. Coordinating multiple timelines can help users understand how data relates

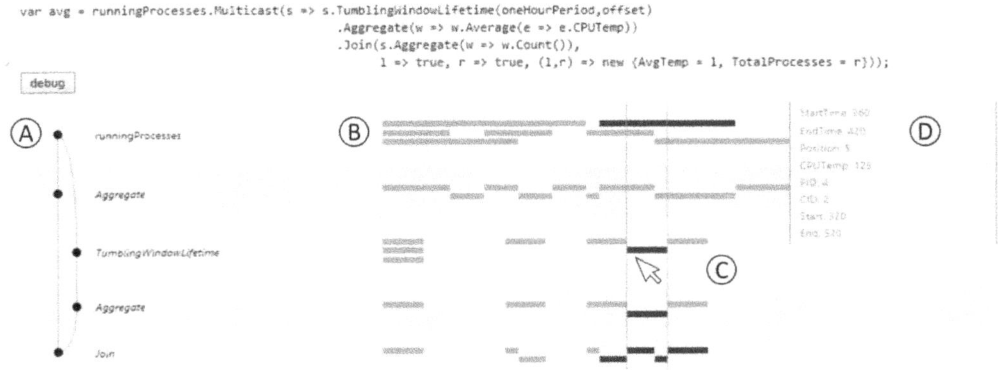

Figure 4. A debugging visualization produced by StreamTrace, with the following components: (A) a workflow diagram; (B) a timeline; (C) provenance highlighting, where one time entry is highlighted; and (D) a tooltip. This query `Multicasts` the `runningProcesses` stream to two branches (or copies), applies an `Aggregate` operation to each branch, and consolidates the final statistics by `join`ing the two branches together.

between different groups. Kosara and Miksch [21] use a hierarchical arrangement of coordinated timelines to visualize clinical guidelines as time-based plans. Gschwandtner et al. [15] use a hierarchical arrangement of timelines to support exploration of patient outcomes given time-stamped clinical treatment information. We similarly use a timeline approach, coordinated with other views, to help unpack temporal data.

Another area of work highlights alternative techniques for specifying event patterns as temporal searches [11],[18],[22],[26], where the focus is on creating new languages or specification schemes, rather than debugging queries for existing systems.

Related Visual Debugging Systems

To the best of our knowledge, StreamTrace is the first GUI-based tool for open-ended temporal query writing and debugging. The visualization systems that are most closely related to StreamTrace are focused primarily on monitoring complex scientific workflows. VisTrails [29] is an interactive workflow analysis system that supports data analysis and exploration. It is oriented toward allowing users to re-execute a precise workflow, and to modify that workflow in a predicable way. The Perfopticon visualization system supports interactive analysis of workflows that perform batch execution of queries on a distributed DBMS [27].

We know of only one other system intended for direct interaction with data streams. System S [10] is a visual debugger based on showing the query plan, or the low-level sequence of compiled operations that describes how the query will be executed. In contrast, StreamTrace operates at the *user* level, showing the stages of the query that map directly to the clauses in the user's input. However both visualizations share a timeline view, and track the histories of individual events. We believe that the results from our user test would also speak to the System S visualizations.

THE DESIGN OF STREAMTRACE

Our visualization scheme is designed both to help new DSMS users quickly learn how DSMS queries work, and to support the techniques that experts like John and Mark already use when interpreting temporal queries. As such, we chose three goals for the design of our visualizations, one for each class of debugging problems we found through our interviews. DSMS visualizations should:

1) Clarify the input-output relationships between all stream operators in the query, to show how these operators are connected.
2) Illustrate the timeline relationships between events at each stage of operations, as in John and Mark's hand-drawn diagrams.
3) Convey how individual events flow through each stream operator in a query, to show how these individual operators behave.

Given that the open-endedness of scripting has been shown to be a good fit for data exploration tasks [12],[19], we chose to support a scripting-based design for users to write and edit their queries, alongside our DSMS visualizations.

In the remainder of this section, we explain how we distilled our design goals into concrete visualization components, implemented these components, and validated our design choices through feedback from Mark and a third DSMS expert Hank[3].

Three Visualization Components

In choosing how to visualize query execution, we looked to ways that the experts thought about DSMS queries. During our expert interviews, we noticed John and Mark already

[3] John had moved to a new job role by the time our StreamTrace prototype was completed, and could not provide feedback.

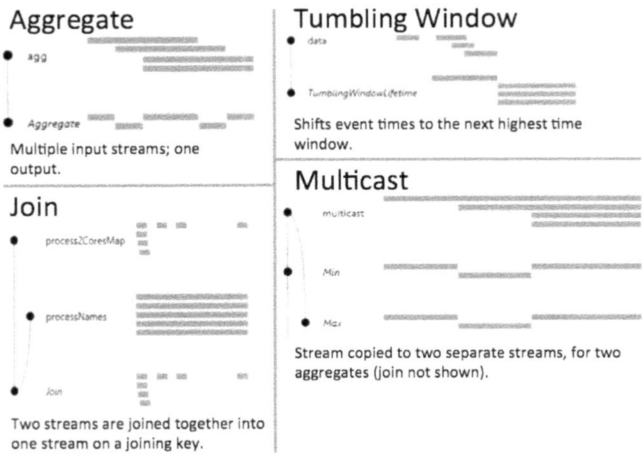

Figure 5. Four major operators in Trill, with their visual representation in StreamTrace. "Tumbling Window" manipulates the timeline, while the others keep events in their fixed timeslots.

had diagrams visible in their offices of query sequences: a real example from John's office can be seen in Figure 3; Hank sent us sample queries that included an ASCII representation of a query timeline (Figure 6).

Mark explained that he also manually generates workflow diagrams of query operations. In these diagrams, he works with his team to decide what data they want the query to represent, and work out the sequence of operations that will generate it. These hand-drawn diagrams support the first design goal, of illustrating events on a timeline.

We developed three major components for StreamTrace's visualizations. Figure 4 is a screenshot of a StreamTrace visualization. First, StreamTrace draws a *workflow diagram* representing the input streams and the sequence of query operations executed on the inputs (labeled A). Second, StreamTrace draws a *timeline view* for each operator (and input) in the workflow diagram (labeled B), where the timeline view captures the result of executing this particular query operator. Last, StreamTrace provides *linked highlighting* across timeline views (labeled C), allowing the user to explore the complete history of an individual stream event—both what that event would become later in the query, and where this event came from. We refer to this history as the *provenance* of the event.

The first design goal is addressed through StreamTrace's workflow diagram. This diagram acts as a flow chart, showing the order in which the operators are executed, and which operators are responsible for producing the inputs to future operators later in the diagram.

StreamTrace's timeline views support the second design goal. Each streaming operator updates the output stream as the query is executed. The series of timeline visualizations allows a user to pinpoint which operator introduced errors.

StreamTrace's linked highlighting across timeline views addresses the third design goal. The linked highlighting feature allows users to figure out how a single event changes in duration or temporal position, no matter how complex, by tracing its provenance forward and backward. This fine-grained view enables users to get a very detailed view of their data

Implementation of Visualization Components

Here, we provide a more detailed description of the design of the three visualization components.

Workflow Diagram

StreamTrace represents the workflow diagram as a directed acyclic graph. Root nodes in the graph are inputs to the query; other nodes are query operators. The edges represent the ordering and relationship between query operators: operators that take a single input are drawn as straight lines, while operators that take multiple inputs or that produce multiple outputs are drawn as branches. The diagram is read from top to bottom; we narrow the layout to ensure that it could be seen as an annotation for the timelines. StreamTrace italicizes labels for query operator nodes; this allows users to distinguish easily between query operators and inputs.

For example, the workflow diagram in Figure 4 has one starting node, labeled `runningProcesses`, which is the only input stream to the query. This input is passed to a single *`Multicast`* operation, which we see in the graph by the edge between the starting node and the node labeled *`Multicast`*. The *`Multicast`* operation creates two branches (i.e., copies) of the stream, shown by the two outgoing edges from the `Multicast` node. The right-hand branch contains a *`TumblingWindowLifetime`* operation and an *`Aggregation`* operation. The left contains only a single *`Aggregation`* node. Last, the branches are brought back together with a *`Join`* operation.

While the workflow diagram resembles familiar DBMS query execution plans, there is an important difference: an execution plan shows the path *after* the database system has optimized it which might include a number of transformations that users do not expect, such as the reordering of operations. As StreamTrace is meant to support the logical stages of query construction, we chose a workflow diagram that is a direct translation of the operations in the original query.

Timeline View

The timeline view is designed to help users understand how each stream event is manipulated by a given query. Inspired by diagrams drawn by our experts—as in Figures 3 and 7—the timeline view is represented as a series of bars, each representing an event in the stream. The position and length of each bar is mapped to the start time and duration of the event. All of the events that emerge from a single operator are arranged in a lane together; within that lane, vertical position is arbitrary, but chosen to prevent overlap between events. When a user hovers over an event, a tooltip at the right side (labeled D in Figure 4) shows the detailed begin and end times for the event, as well as any contents associated with the event.

Figure 5 shows a selection of Trill operators that manipulate either query graphs (e.g., Multicast) or temporal operators (e.g., TumblingWindowLifetime). The combination illustrates how StreamTrace uses bars to present temporal changes and extents.

Linking Timeline Views

The goal of this feature is to allow the user to ask *why* a specific event is part of the output—or to figure out what happened to an event as it propagated through the query. When a user hovers over a specific event in the timeline, StreamTrace displays this link using *provenance highlighting*, which shows the history of the event. In Figure 4, the user has hovered their mouse over an output event from executing a `TumblingWindowLifetime` operation; all relevant stream events are highlighted (i.e., colored black) by StreamTrace. Events highlighted above the current event represent inputs that contributed to the creation of the current event earlier in the query's execution; we call this *backward provenance*. For example, StreamTrace highlights the events in the input stream(s) that were used to compute the current event. Similarly, events highlighted *below* the current event represent intermediate and final outputs that the current event contributed to later in the query's execution; we call this *forward provenance*.

Validation through Expert Feedback

After we created our initial prototype of StreamTrace, we showed it to Mark and Hank to collect feedback. Hank is the lead of a performance analysis team. Like John and Mark, Hank is the DSMS expert for his team of six people. We met with Hank and the rest of his team, all of whom were in the process of learning Trill, after our first designs for StreamTrace were implemented.

They expressed interest in having a canonical set of basic queries for training their team. This inspired us to add tutorial materials as part of the StreamTrace design: a view in the analytics environment that shows core operations and allows the user to see their implementations; and a tutorial booklet with StreamTrace views of common Trill operators. After seeing the final design, Hank and his team expressed immediate interest in using StreamTrace to analyze their existing DSMS queries, and explained how they saw clear value in using a tool like StreamTrace in the future.

After learning more about StreamTrace's final design, Mark said that StreamTrace would allow his team to *verify* that they are doing the right thing, and that their plan is being carried out correctly.

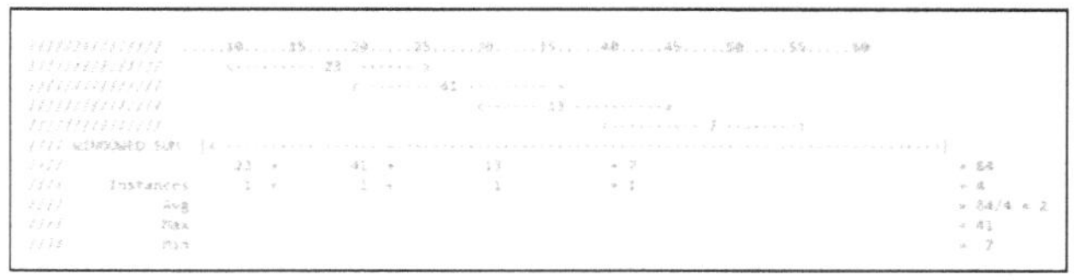

Figure 6. This comment, embedded in a sample query from Hank, shows a timeline view drawn with ASCII art.

THE IMPLEMENTATION OF STREAMTRACE

StreamTrace's back-end design is based on a notion of tracing fine-grained provenance through queries. To capture the intermediate steps of a query, we developed a new approach for provenance recording. The key aspect is to have each event store its own list of the previous input events that contributed to it. To do this, each stream event is assigned a *provenance identifier*. As a query is executed, these identifiers are propagated through each query operator to the related output events. We implement these provenance lists in two parts: (1) each event is annotated with a list of past inputs; and (2) the core Trill operators are wrapped in specialized code to propagate provenance identifiers from input events to the corresponding output events. The wrapper code executes *outside* of the DSMS, making it applicable to other systems beyond Trill.

Without provenance tracking, StreamTrace would lack the necessary metadata for visualizing query behavior. This technique was inspired by past work in the database community on recording provenance for workflows [17] and data streams [16],[31],[13],[14]. The focus of these projects is to ensure that provenance data can be efficiently tracked and stored. This past work does not address how to make the resulting histories easy to interpret for non-DSMS experts, which is precisely what we address in StreamTrace.

StreamTrace breaks each operation out of the query expression separately through a process of query rewriting. Query rewriting happens automatically behind the scenes; users still see the original query when provenance is enabled. Users enable StreamTrace with a single click, which triggers provenance annotations, rewrites the current query, executes this new query, and shows the output. Provenance tracking is enabled for all core Trill operators; as such, StreamTrace supports all of standard relational algebra, with enhancements for time manipulations. Collectively, these operations are common to other DSMS streaming engines, too; there is nothing specific to Trill about the broader design.

LABORATORY STUDY

After iteratively refining StreamTrace with expert users, we validated our design with a laboratory study.

Hypotheses and Tasks

The goal of our quantitative evaluation was to learn whether users better understand and debug temporal queries with the assistance of our visualization. The feedback we received from expert DSMS users encouraged us to believe that StreamTrace would be good for helping novice users understand queries. We carried out a laboratory user study to test two hypotheses: using StreamTrace, subjects will

H1: identify errors in Trill queries more easily.
H2: find queries easier to write.

To test these hypotheses, we wanted to observe analysts in the process of working through specific queries. We created four synthetic datasets, each containing roughly a dozen events. We chose these datasets to help participants debug the intent of the temporal query, as opposed to its runtime performance where larger datasets would be necessary. For guidance, we directly referenced the test datasets given to us by our experts John and Mark when creating our own synthetic datasets. This ensured that our datasets had the same structure and relative size as test datasets used in the real world. We then created one query per dataset that we expected users to be able to solve in the study.

In choosing our tasks, we strove for a balance to accommodate the lab setting: we chose tasks that were complex enough to manifest query comprehension and authoring problems, but not so complex to overwhelm and intimidate participants. To achieve this, we collected real queries from our DSMS experts to use as starting points for our tasks, grouped the queries by difficulty (e.g., easy, medium and hard), and modified the queries as necessary to match our test datasets and reflect appropriate difficulty levels for the study. The final tasks challenged users either to expand a simpler query into a more complex one or to debug an erroneous complex query. Each query required the user to tweak two or three operations. For example, one task asked users to change a query from filtering and showing a single value, to showing a value across multiple filters in parallel. In doing so, users would need to change from a filtering operator to a grouping one, and find the appropriate syntax. Figure 4 illustrates the initial conditions for Task B in the visualization condition. Users were told they needed to debug the query so that that *all* of the output was mapped to a set of fixed time windows (as in our motivating example with Mark).

We carried out a series of pilots to ensure that the queries were of roughly similar difficulty. To reduce learning effects, we ensured the tasks had minimal overlap—none of the four require the same Trill operators in their solutions.

The study was carried out within-subjects. Participants carried out four rounds of tasks, alternating between with- and without the StreamTrace enhancements. We alternated which condition was first. We used a Latin-square design to counterbalance tasks and conditions in order to balance out difficulty and learning effects.

We measured the amount of time to get a correct query for each task. All sessions were audio- and video-recorded. Users filled out a brief survey after completing each of the

Table 1: The four tasks for the user study

Task	Description	Operations
A	Find the max temperature across multiple CPUs in one stream	GroupApply; Aggregate
B	Ensure that a multicast stream has consistent time windows. (e.g., Figure 2(c))	Multicast; TumblingWindow-Lifetime
C	Join a stream with a second stream on a key	Join; Where
D	Match "start" and "end" pairs within a log	AlterEventDuration; ClipEventDuration

four tasks, then a concluding survey that compared tasks to each other. After each session, we interviewed users to get additional thoughts on their experience with the system.

Testing Environment

StreamTrace is implemented within the experimental data science environment Tempe [9], which executes its data analysis operations in Trill. Tempe works in an interactive C# interpreter designed for live coding, which allows a user to modify any line of a program, and see a recomputed result immediately. Tempe also provides intelligent code-completion; when a user types part of a command, the system shows available methods on an object, the parameters of a method call, and what objects match the appropriate types. This allows us to focus on query semantics, rather than syntax.

Study Procedure

We first introduce users to Trill with a paper guide specifically created for the study, a modification of the guide we created for Hank. The guide illustrates the syntax and grammar for the eight Trill operators used in the study. While Trill has dozens of other operators, this subset allows us to capture all of the query types provided by our experts. The guide illustrates its functions in a number of different ways, including timelines similar to the visualization. After spending approximately ten minutes reading the Trill guide, subjects are then introduced first to the analytics environment, then to the StreamTrace visualizations. They are given a list of queries; the experimenter works with them for another five minutes to ensure that they can correctly write a query, accurately interpret the results of queries; the experimenter also answers subjects' questions.

Each of the four timed tasks began with two simple "warm-up" tasks to teach subjects about the current dataset and to familiarize them with the Trill operators they might need for the task. When the subject announces that they are ready to proceed, the experimenter starts a timer and the subject starts on the test query. When the participant announces they are done, the experimenter records the time and checks their answer. Participants were asked to continue attempting the task until they found the correct answer. Participants who did not complete the task correctly were stopped after twenty minutes per task and marked as "did not finish".

Participants

We recruited professional developers, data scientists, and data-oriented testers from within a large software company. We chose a random sample from three internal distributions lists. We sent personalized email invitations to screen for experience in C# and LINQ, and interest in data analysis.

From this pool, 18 participants took part in the study. We dismissed three for lacking the required skills. The remaining 15 (1 female) reported an average of

- 8.3 years of professional experience;
- 5.7 years of C# experience; and
- 3.4 years of LINQ experience;

In terms of job roles, 8 described themselves as developers, 4 as testers, and 3 as data scientists. We noted that seven participants had just 1 or 2 years of experience with LINQ. This was the first time any of our study participants encountered any DSMS, including Trill.

RESULTS

Observations

We watched each user work through the problems and recorded both screen captures and sessions. This allowed us to track how users were interacting with the visualizations.

We found the visualizations **were useful for different types of queries.** P1, a LINQ beginner, started with the visualization for his first task. When he moved on to the second task (task B) he said "The visualization would really help here!" Task B requires the user to align time windows together; the visualization makes it immediately apparent which items are out of alignment (as shown in Figure 4). Without the visualization, he was more frustrated. P11, also working on Task B without the visualization, similarly complained, "I couldn't tell why the data didn't correspond to the correct [temporal] window."

During times when users felt they had strong intuitions, this verification was less important: P13 did not use the visualization on Task C: "This one," he said, "uses standard [non-temporal] LINQ queries; I don't need it."

The visualizations were helpful to **verify and confirm** that a query was working as expected. P1, for example, did not use the visualization during the course of working on Task C—but used afterward to show that he had succeeded. Similarly, P13 used the visualization after he had completed Task A to check whether he had the segments he expected. P8 said, "visually seeing the result, it's easier to verify correctness instead of reading individual items."

Last, the visualization helped **shape people's mental models.** P5 did not use the visualization during his study at all. However, during his tutorial period, he spent a long time studying the visualizations and their interactions. Afterward, he reported that the visualization was "helpful" but not quite worth turning on. We interpret P5 as building a more-detailed mental model of the queries based on the visualizations.

Three Phases of Debugging

We used these observations to assess StreamTrace's effectiveness across the three phases of the debugging process as described by Parnin and Orso [28]: fault understanding, fault localization, and fault correction. We found that StreamTrace was generally helpful across a majority of these phases.

For tasks like Task B, where participants greatly benefitted from seeing the temporal scope/alignment of events, we found that our visualizations **helped with the fault understanding phase** of debugging for some participants.

Some users also found the visualizations to be **helpful during the fault localization phase** of debugging queries. P12, for example, reported that he found Task B to be ambiguous—but when he saw the initial view, he figured out what needed to be done. P15 was struggling with Task D—after he turned to the visualization to walk step-by-step through the behavior he expected to see, he was able to quickly solve the problem.

Our visualizations also had their limitations. Several users struggled with the Trill syntax; while fighting compiler errors, the visualization had no extra information to show them. Thus our visualizations were less effective during fault correction. As we note above, some users found StreamTrace effective for *verifying* that their fixes had worked; this phase is not accounted for in this model.

Quantitative and Survey Results

We measured time to accurate completion for each question. All participants were able to make it through all four questions within twenty minutes each; most took far less. However, with programming tasks, there is often high variability within users on task performance, and our study was no exception. For example, there was high variance both within- and between-users across tasks in our study. Even when compared within the same condition and for the same user, completion times could vary by 6 minutes or more for over a third of our participants. Correcting syntax errors, or understanding the question, often took some time. Disappointingly, as Figure 7 shows, the visualizations did not obviously make users quicker for any of the tasks. But we were not surprised when there was no "home run" performance measure that clearly shows a large difference between conditions. We believe that this variability is inherent in the complexity of the streaming concepts and the tasks, rather than a flaw of our study.

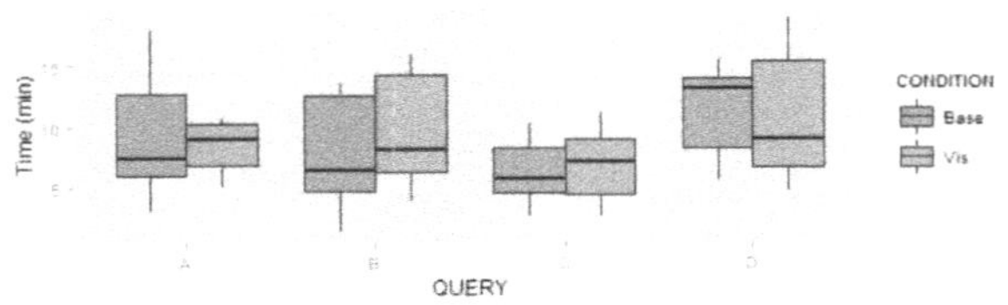

Figure 7. Time distribution for each query, by condition. The visualization did not obviously speed users.

We turn, then, to our survey results. Amidst other questions, we asked users to estimate the value of the visualization to them. Figure 8 shows that users felt that the visualization was more helpful for B and D, the temporal queries, than for the others. We saw similar results for the statement "the visualization helped me solve the task faster;" and (reversed) for "the visualization was useless."

DISCUSSION

The laboratory experiment tested very specific scenarios. High variance, both within- and between-subjects, meant that we did not come to a quantitative result showing that users were faster to debug or create queries using StreamTrace. However, we did see that the visualizations assisted in query debugging in a variety of ways. Users used the visualizations, guide, and the tutorial to better understand how Trill queries were structured and to how to think about the sequence of events. During the tasks, they used StreamTrace to identify what was wrong with the data, and to check that they got the right answer at the end.

Some types of queries seem more amenable to this visualization than others: in tasks that entail manipulation of the timeline, the visualization could help users keep track of the time. As a result, users talked much more often about the visualization challenges of the temporal tasks B and D over the non-temporal tasks, A and C.

The real queries carried out by the experts tended to combine temporal and non-temporal aspects. As a result, it is likely that StreamTrace might be more generally useful for them then for the more specialized queries.

We conclude that seeing how events flow through streaming queries helps users with two specific debugging subtasks: identifying faulty code regions, and identifying the causes of erroneous or unexpected behavior within these code regions. We attribute these benefits to the use of timelines to make temporal semantics explicit, and the ability to "drill in" to see the effect of individual operators on specific stream events. Alternative query debugging designs, such as for non-temporal queries, can still utilize a "drill in" feature to show users how individual records are modified as they are processed by a query. Our timeline-based visualization design could potentially be applied to high-level pipelines outside of DSMS's (e.g., command-line scripts, execution workflows), given appropriate input-output provenance data.

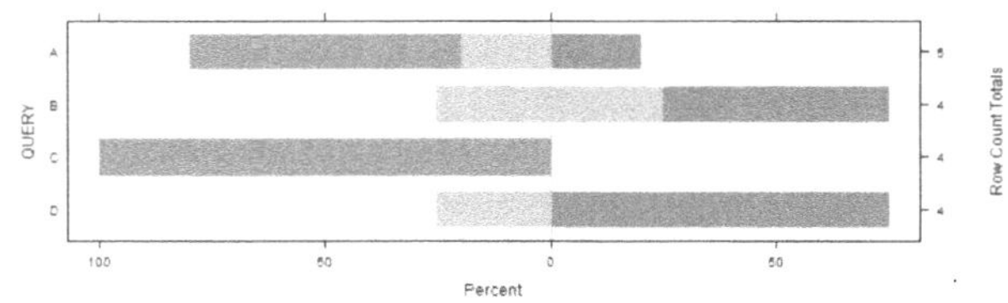

Figure 8. Likert survey question: agreement by task: "The visualization was helpful for this task." Scale from dark red ("Strongly Disagree") to dark blue ("Strongly agree")

Future Opportunities

Our study focused primarily on evaluating small-scale debugging techniques. As such, it is unclear how StreamTrace scales up in both visualization design and dataset size. For example, in the current implementation, the timeline remains fixed; this is a limitation on visual scalability. We plan to extend our visualizations and provenance tracking to larger event streams, which will allow users to do both small-scale prototyping and large-scale performance testing within a single debugging tool.

Both the expert users and our participants provided many suggestions to improve the system. Our participants suggested several new features and colorings to improve StreamTrace's visualizations. With aggregate operations, users wanted to directly render *aggregation values* on the timeline bars, perhaps even transforming the result into a line chart. This would make the visualization more powerful as a signal processing view. Several users also wanted to be able to link the query text itself to the visualization by cross-highlighting between the workflow diagram on the left and the text above. These features would enhance the StreamTrace experience.

CONCLUSION

In this paper, we have presented a visualization design to help DSMS users better understand their temporal queries. Our prototype, StreamTrace, helps improve users' understanding of how individual DSMS operators manipulate data streams, and the relationships between these operators within temporal queries. We evaluated StreamTrace by carrying out a lab study with 18 analysts new to DSMS's. We concluded from our user study that StreamTrace can help users at two critical points in debugging tasks: when locating faulty code regions in their queries, and when understanding and identifying the causes for unexpected query behavior.

ACKNOWLEDGEMENTS

We thank Remco Chang for his insightful feedback and suggestions, which helped improve the paper. We also thank the DSMS experts who helped design our visualizations for StreamTrace.

REFERENCES

[1] Abadi, D., et al. The Design of the Borealis Stream Processing Engine. In *Proc. CIDR* 2005, 277-289.

[2] Aigner, W., Miksch, S., Schumann, H., & Tominski, C. *Visualization of time-oriented data*. Springer Science & Business Media (2011).

[3] Amsterdamer, Y., Davidson, S.B., Deutch, D., Milo, T., Stoyanovich, J., Tannen, V. Putting Lipstick on Pig: Enabling Database-style Workflow Provenance. In *Proc. VLDB Endow. 5, 4* (2011), 346–357.

[4] Babcock, B., Babu, S., Datar, M., Motwani, R., and Widom, J. Models and issues in data stream systems. In *Proc. PODS 2002*, ACM Press (2002), 1-16.

[5] Babu, S., and Widom, J. Continuous Queries over Data Streams. *SIGMOD Record 30*, 3 (2001), 109-120.

[6] Cao, J., Rector, K., Park, T.H., Fleming, S. D., Burnett, M., and Wiedenbeck, S. A Debugging Perspective on End-User Mashup Programming. In *Proc. IEEE Symp. on VL/HCC 2010*, ACM (2010), .

[7] Carney, D., et. al. Monitoring streams: a new class of data management applications. In *Proc. VLDB 2002*, VLDB Endowment (2002), 215-226.

[8] Chandramouli, B., et al. Trill: A High-performance Incremental Query Processor for Diverse Analytics. In *Proc VLDB Endow* 8 (2014), 401–412.

[9] DeLine, R., Fisher, D., Chandramouli, B., Goldstein, J., Barnett, M., Terwilliger, J. F. and Wernsing, J. Tempe: Live Scripting for Live Data, In *Proc. of IEEE Symp. on VL/HCC* 2015, ACM (2015).

[10] De Pauw, W., Leţia, M., Gedik, B., Andrade, H., Frenkiel, A., Pfeifer, M., and Sow, D. Visual Debugging for Stream Processing Applications. In *Proc. RV*, Springer-Verlag (2010), 18-35.

[11] Fails, J. A., Karlson, A., Shahamat, L. & Shneiderman, B. A Visual Interface for Multivariate Temporal Data: Finding Patterns of Events across Multiple Histories. in *Visual Analytics Science And Technology, 2006 IEEE Symposium On* 167–174 (2006).

[12] Fisher, D., DeLine, R., Czerwinski, M., and Drucker, S. 2012. Interactions with big data analytics. interactions 19, 3 (May 2012), 50-59.

[13] Glavic, B., Esmaili, K.S., Fischer, P.M., Tatbul, N. The Case for Fine-Grained Stream Provenance. *In Proc. BTW Workshops 2011*.

[14] Glavic, B., Esmaili, K.S., Fischer, P.M., Tatbul, N. Ariadne: managing fine-grained provenance on data streams. *In Proc. DEBS 2013*, ACM (2013), 39-50.

[15] Gschwandtner, T., Aigner, W., Kaiser, K., Miksch, S., Seyfang, A. CareCruiser: exploring and visualizing plans, events, and effects interactively." *Pacific Visualization Symposium (PacificVis)*, IEEE Computer Society (2011), 43-50.

[16] Huq, M.R., Wombacher, A., and Apers, P.M. Inferring fine-grained data provenance in stream data processing: reduced storage cost, high accuracy. In *Proc. DEXA 2011*, Springer Berlin Heidelberg (2011), 118-127.

[17] Ikeda, R., Park, H., and Widom, J. Provenance for Generalized Map and Reduce Workflows. In *Proc. CIDR 2011*.

[18] Jin, J. & Szekely, P. Interactive querying of temporal data using a comic strip metaphor. in *2010 IEEE Symposium on Visual Analytics Science and Technology (VAST)* 163–170 (2010).

[19] Kandel, S., Paepcke, A., Hellerstein, J. M., and Heer, J. (2012). Enterprise data analysis and visualization: An interview study. *Visualization and Computer Graphics, IEEE Transactions on*, *18*, 12 (2012), 2917-2926.

[20] Ko, A.J. and Myers, B.A. Finding Causes of Program Output with the Java Whyline. In *Proc. CHI 2009*, ACM (2009), 1569-1578.

[21] Kosara, R., and Miksch, S. Metaphors of movement: a visualization and user interface for time-oriented, skeletal plans. *Artificial Intelligence in Medicine* 22 (2001), 111-131.

[22] Krause, J., Perer, A. & Stavropoulos, H. Supporting Iterative Cohort Construction with Visual Temporal Queries. *IEEE Transactions on Visualization and Computer Graphics* **22,** 91–100 (2016).

[23] Lessa, D., Jayaraman, B., and Chomicki, J. A Temporal Data Model for Program Debugging. In *Proc. DBFL 2011*.

[24] Madden, S. and Franklin, M.J. Fjording the Stream: An Architecture for Queries over Streaming Sensor Data. In *Proc. ICDE 2002*, IEEE Computer Society (2002), 555.

[25] Meijer, E. The world according to LINQ. *Comm. ACM* 54, 10 (October 2011), 45-51.

[26] Monroe, M. *et al.* The Challenges of Specifying Intervals and Absences in Temporal Queries: A Graphical Language Approach. in *Proceedings of the SIGCHI Conference on Human Factors in Computing Systems* 2349–2358 (ACM, 2013).

[27] Moritz, D., Halperin, D., Howe, B. & Heer, J. Perfopticon: Visual Query Analysis for Distributed Databases. *Comput. Graph. Forum* 34 (2015), 71–80.

[28] Parnin, C. and Orso, A. Are Automated Debugging Techniques Actually Helping Programmers? In *Proc. ISSTA 2011*, ACM (2011), 199-209.

[29] Scheidegger, C., Koop, D., Santos, E., Vo, H., Callahan, S., Freire, J., and Silva, C. Tackling the provenance challenge one layer at a time. *Concurrency and Computation: Practice and Experience 20*, 5 (2008), 473-483.

[30] Subrahmaniyan, N., Beckwith, L., Grigoreanu, V., Burnett, M., Wiedenbeck, S., Narayanan, V, Bucht, K., Drummond, R., and Fern, X. Testing vs. Code Inspection vs. What Else?: Male and Female End Users' Debugging Strategies. In *Proc. CHI 2008*, ACM (2008), 617-626.

[31] Vijayakumar, N., and Plale, B. Tracking Stream Provenance in Complex Event Processing Systems for Workflow-Driven Computing. In *VLDB EDA-PS Workshop 2007*.

Investigating Time Series Visualisations to Improve the User Experience

Muhammad Adnan
University of Leeds
Leeds, UK
m.adnan1@hotmail.com

Mike Just
Heriot-Watt University
Edinburgh, UK
m.just@hw.ac.uk

Lynne Baillie
Heriot-Watt University
Edinburgh, UK
l.baillie@hw.ac.uk

ABSTRACT

Research on graphical perception of time series visualisations has focused on visual representation, and not on interaction. Even for visual representation, there has been limited study of the impact on users of visual encodings and the strengths and weaknesses of Cartesian and Polar coordinate systems. In order to address this research gap, we performed a comprehensive graphical perception study that measured the effectiveness of time series visualisations with different interactions, visual encodings and coordinate systems for several tasks. Our results show that, while positional and colour visual encodings were better for most tasks, area visual encoding performed better for data comparison. Most importantly, we identified that introducing interactivity within time series visualisations considerably enhances the user experience, without any loss of efficiency or accuracy. We believe that our findings can greatly improve the development of visual analytics tools using time series visualisations in a variety of domains.

Author Keywords

Visualisation; graphical perception; evaluation; interaction technique; visual encoding; coordinate system; time series.

ACM Classification Keywords

H.5.2. [Information interfaces and presentation (e.g., HCI)]: User Interfaces---Evaluation/methodology, Interaction styles (e.g., commands, menus, forms, direct manipulation).

INTRODUCTION

The staggering volume of continuously generated data today creates extraordinary opportunities for businesses to improve decision making with deeper insights into their data. However, most organisations collect more data than they can analyse and present in a meaningful way [19,28]. This has led to an increasing interest and effort from both industry [40] and academia [15] in developing usable and scalable visual analytics (VA) solutions. VA is commonly defined as: "the science of analytical reasoning facilitated by interactive visual interfaces" [37, p.4]. Whether simple or complex, a VA system is essentially composed of two main components: *visual representation* and *interaction* [39]. The former deals with the mapping of underlying data to alternative visual representations, while the latter facilitates the dialog between the user and the VA system. Despite consistently stating the value and importance of interaction for visual data analysis [12,37], the focus of the research by much of the VA community has been on the visual representation of data rather than on the interaction, as has been noted by others [2,24,30].

Graphical perception is defined as the ability of users to interpret the visual encoding and thereby understand the information presented in a graph [8]. The aforementioned trend of focusing more on visual representation than on interaction is also predominant in graphical perception of time series visualisations, which is a well-studied area in visual analytics. A common practice in quantitative graphical perception studies of time series visualisations [4,10,14,16,21] is to conduct them in a static setting, i.e., not allowing the users to interact with the time series visualisations, thereby limiting our knowledge of the user experience. In addition, the overall coverage of different visual representations of time series data is lacking. Several previous studies [4,10,14,16,21] have compared the effectiveness of time series visualisations within and across the categories of positional (e.g., Figure 1(a&b)) and colour visual encodings (e.g., Figure 1(c&d)). However, to the best of our knowledge, there has been no study that compares the effectiveness of time series visualisations that use area visual encoding (e.g., Figure 1(e&f)) with their positional and colour counterparts. We use the term 'area' throughout even though we encode area-based visualisations using only segment (or arc) length, i.e., the width is fixed. Area does consist of length and width, however due to a relatively large segment/arc width, we believe it is more accurate to describe our testing as the stimulus of area. Similar to visual encodings, limited empirical evidence is available for the strengths and weaknesses of Cartesian (e.g., Figure 1(a,c&e)) and Polar (e.g., Figure 1(b,d&f)) coordinate systems for time series visualisations, using different visual encodings.

To address this research gap, we performed a comprehensive graphical perception study that measured

CHI'16, May 07-12, 2016, San Jose, CA, USA
© 2016 ACM. ISBN 978-1-4503-3362-7/16/05...$15.00
DOI: http://dx.doi.org/10.1145/2858036.2858300

the effectiveness (i.e., completion time, accuracy, confidence and ease of use) of time series visualisations with different interactions, visual encodings and coordinate systems for several tasks. Our work makes three primary contributions:

C1: We systematically examine the effects of two commonly used interaction techniques (i.e., highlighting and tooltips) on the effectiveness of different time series visualisations.

C2: We compare the effectiveness of time series visualisations that use three different visual encoding techniques: position, colour and area.

C3: We investigate the impact of two coordinate systems (Cartesian and Polar) on the effectiveness of time series visualisations within each of the aforementioned visual encoding techniques.

Through these contributions, we hope to contribute to some very practical problems that rely on effective data visualisation of large time series data sets, such as analysing network security data to counter cyber-threats. We also believe that our work will motivate the visual analytics research community to focus equally on interaction and visual representation of data. In the next section we review related work. Then, we present our quantitative graphical perception study and explain the choice of time series visualisations, interaction techniques, study tasks and our time series data generation method. Finally, we present the results, discuss their implications and highlight further research opportunities.

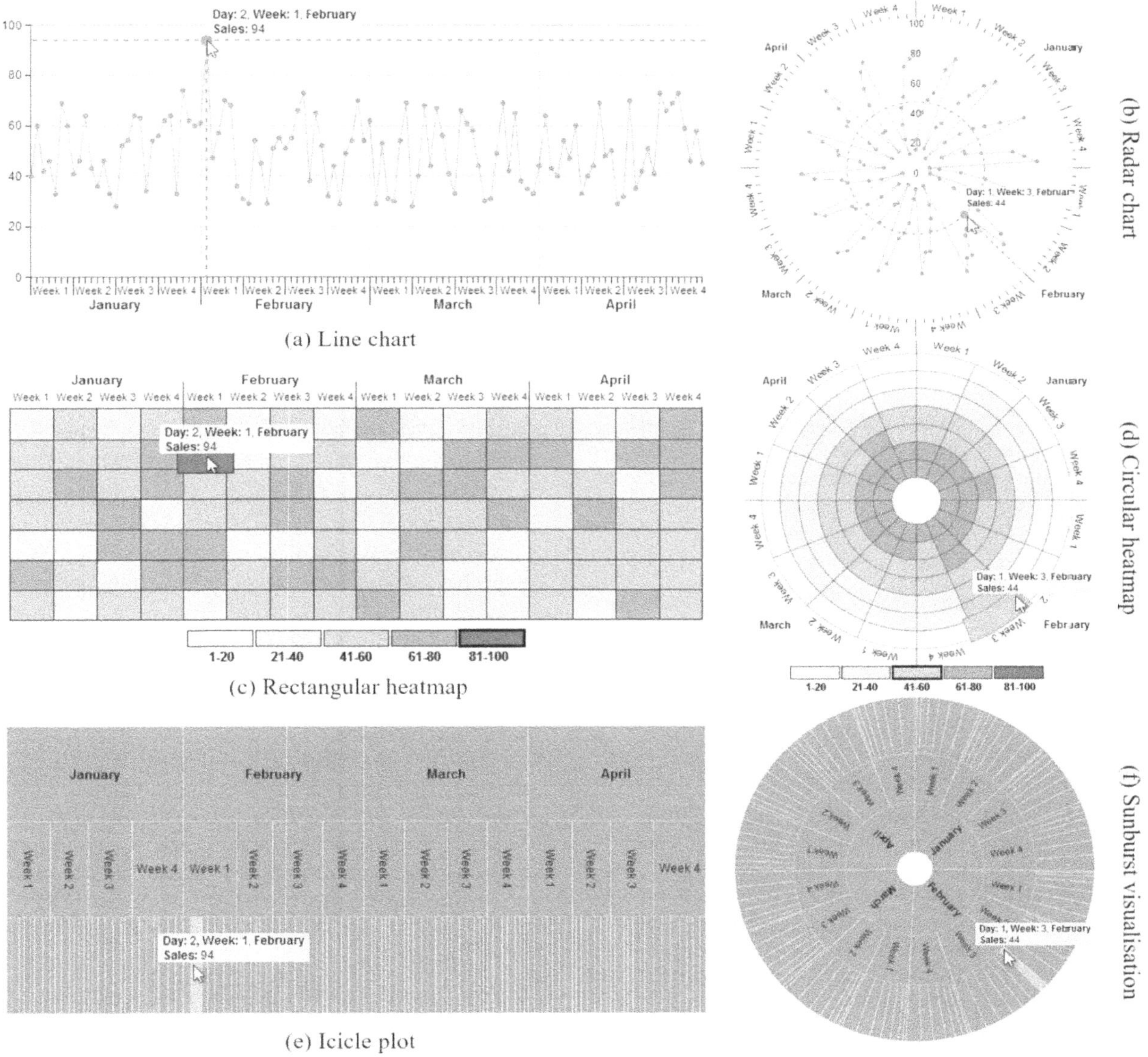

Figure 1. Selected time series visualisations with highlighting and tooltip interaction techniques. Visual encodings: positional (a) & (b); colour (c) & (d); area (e) & (f). Coordinate systems: Cartesian (a), (c) & (e); Polar (b), (d) & (f). Tasks: maxima (a), (c) & (e); trend detection (b), (d) & (f).

RELATED WORK

We review the related work for three areas that are key to our research, and the impact of each on the graphical perception of time series visualisations, namely the effects of interaction techniques, and then the impact of different visual representations, first with visual encodings and then with coordinate systems.

Interaction Techniques

The visual analytics (VA) research community has focused more on the visual representation of data rather than on different aspects of interaction, unlike the closely related research field of Human-Computer Interaction (HCI) that places equal emphasis on both the design and user experience. The small set of VA papers that discuss interaction largely concentrate on the classification and characterisation of interaction techniques [12,18,34,35,39], capturing interaction processes [31], designing and operationalising interactions [20,25,38] and identifying challenges and opportunities for further research [13,30]. However, limited attention has been paid to measuring the exact effects of commonly used interaction techniques on visual representations, both in general and specific to quantitative graphical perception studies of time series visualisations. There are two exceptions in this regard. Lam et al. [23] examined the effects of interactive low- and high-resolution visual representations of time series data on search and comparison tasks. Also, Perin et al. [29] compared interactive horizon graphs with static horizon graphs and small multiples of line charts for multiple time series datasets. The focus of these two quantitative studies was on comparing the effectiveness of alternative visual representations of time series data, rather than on assessing the effects of individual interaction techniques. A more quantitative approach to assess the impact of alternative interaction techniques for different time series visualisations remains an under-researched area.

Therefore, one of the main contributions (C1) of this work is to systematically examine the effects of commonly used interaction techniques (i.e., highlighting and tooltips) on the effectiveness of different time series visualisations.

Visual Encodings

Prior work on graphical perception found that the choice of visual encoding matters a great deal to users. In their seminal work in 1984, Cleveland and McGill [8] presented various charts to participants and asked them to compare the values of two marked objects by estimating the percentage of a smaller value versus a larger. This accuracy measure was then used to rank the following visual encodings (ordered from most to least accurate) for quantitative data: (1) position along a common scale, (2) position along non-aligned scales, (3) length, direction and angle, (4) area, (5) volume and curvature, and (6) shading and colour saturation. More recently, Heer and Bostock [17] in 2010, successfully replicated these results by conducting a crowdsourced experiment using Amazon's Mechanical Turk. Based on existing psychophysical results and analysis of different perceptual tasks, Mackinlay [27] extended the ranking of the effectiveness of visual encodings to ordinal and nominal data.

Time series data is among the most common type of data explored in quantitative graphical perception studies. The focus of such studies has been on evaluating the effectiveness of time series visualisations within and across the categories of positional (e.g., Figure 1(a&b)) and colour visual encodings (e.g., Figure 1(c&d)). Within the category of positional visual encoding, Heer et al. [16] compared the effectiveness of line charts with horizon graphs. They investigated the effects of chart size and layering on user performance for a single task of value comparison. Similarly, Javed et al. [21] evaluated the effectiveness of four different line chart techniques, involving multiple time series datasets. This study involved three tasks of comparison, slope and discrimination. On the other hand, Correl et al. [10] investigated how time series visualisations, using both positional and colour visual encodings, can be specifically designed to support aggregate comparisons. Albers et al. [4] also compared the effectiveness of eight different time series visualisations, using both positional and colour visual encodings, for a number of point and summary comparison tasks. The results from these studies [4,10,16,21] highlight the strengths and weaknesses of both positional and colour visual encodings for representing time series data and suggest that no individual visual encoding dominates in every task and data density. In particular, these findings indicate limited generalisability of the results of generic, non-time series studies conducted by Cleveland and McGill [8] and Heer and Bostock [17] to time series visualisations.

This encouraged us to compare the effectiveness of time series visualisations using area visual encoding with visualisations using positional and colour visual encodings. To the best of our knowledge, ours is the first study that compares the effectiveness of time series visualisations using three different visual encodings of position, colour and area. This relates to the second contribution (C2) of our work.

Coordinate Systems

The strengths and weaknesses of visualisations based on Cartesian and Polar coordinate systems have been discussed by developers but empirical evidence is limited. Some studies exist that compared the Polar visualisations with competing Cartesian counterparts [7,36]. However, the non-time series nature and limited control of confounding factors within these studies constrains the generalisability of their findings.

Cleveland and McGill [9] compared the effectiveness of bar charts with their polar counterparts, pie charts. They found bar charts to be more effective than pie charts, because comparing lengths is more accurate than comparing angles. However, Schonlau and Peters [33] found the effectiveness of pie charts closely comparable to that of bar charts. More recently, Diehl et al. [11] compared the effectiveness of a matrix-based Cartesian visualisation with its Polar counterpart. They employed the generic study task of memorising positions of visual elements. The findings from their user study suggested using a Cartesian coordinate system unless there are clear reasons in favour of a Polar coordinate system. While conducted with better control over confounding factors than [7] and [36], the findings of these generic, non-time series studies are not easily generalisable to Cartesian and Polar time series visualisations, mainly due to the large number of tasks with varying complexity, different data densities and the variety of available visual representations of time series data.

With regards to the impact of coordinate systems on time series visualisations, the study conducted by Fuchs et al. [14] is closest to our work. They compared the effectiveness of two Cartesian and two Polar time series visualisations in a small multiple setting (called "glyphs"). One set of glyphs (one Cartesian and one Polar) used positional visual encoding, while the other set used the colour visual encoding. They found that line glyphs generally performed better for peak and trend detection tasks, while the Polar glyphs were better suited for reading values at specific temporal locations. In contrast to Fuchs et al. [14], we investigated the impact of coordinate systems on normal-sized, temporally labelled time series visualisations, not only based on positional and colour visual encodings but also using an area visual encoding (i.e., Figure 1(e & f)). This relates to the third contribution of our work (C3).

USER STUDY

To better understand the impact on the user experience, we conducted a lab-based user study to evaluate the effectiveness of different time series visualisations that use varied interaction techniques, visual encodings and coordinate systems for four tasks.

Time Series Visualisations

Time series data is a set of quantitative values changing over time, and it is predominant in a variety of domains ranging from banking and finance to computing to climate measurements. It is also extremely conducive to visualisation. Aigner et al. [3] provides an extensive review of time series visualisations.

We selected two time series visualisations (one Cartesian and one Polar) from each of three visual encoding categories of position, colour and area. Firstly, a Cartesian line chart (Figure 1(a)) was used as a well-known baseline for the positional visual encoding; the radar chart (Figure 1(b)) is the Polar counterpart. Secondly, following similar studies [4,10,14], rectangular (Figure 1(c)) and circular heatmaps (Figure 1(d)) were chosen to serve as the Cartesian and Polar counterparts from the category of colour visual encoding. We used ColorBrewer 2.0 [6] to choose a colour-blind safe sequential colour scheme for heatmaps. Lastly, considering the hierarchal nature of time series data, the Cartesian icicle plot (Figure 1(e)) and Polar sunburst visualisation (Figure 1(f)) were selected to represent the area visual encoding. While we could have used Cartesian and Polar treemaps [22] for our area encoding, icicle plots and sunbursts offer a more logical and space-efficient way of representing time series data. Further, sunburst provides an accurate Polar representation of the Cartesian icicle plot, unlike treemaps, thereby providing some consistency with the pairings for positional and colour encodings.

Interaction Techniques

In this study, we investigated the effects of two commonly used interaction techniques: highlighting and tooltips. In its simplest form, highlighting acts as the viewing control to attract a user's attention to a subset of data within a visualisation [26]. On the other hand, a tooltip is a text message that appears when a cursor is positioned over an element in a graphical user interface. In our case, the purpose of both of these techniques was to facilitate the identification of the temporal location and quantitative value of a particular data point as accurately as possible. The primary difference was that highlighting tried to achieve this visually, whereas the tooltip explicitly provided the required information in textual form.

The implementation of both of these interaction techniques was achieved through mouseover. The implementation of highlighting varied for each visualisation pair, mainly due to the inherent structure of the visual encodings. However, the design principle remained the same in each case, i.e., to have maximum visual impact, while avoiding visual occlusion. In the case of line chart, the highlighting of a particular data point increased its radius and introduced two dashed lines, each stretching from the selected data point to the X and Y axis respectively (Figure 1(a)). The same highlighting technique was used for radar chart, except following the Polar coordinate system (Figure 1(b)). In the case of the colour-encoded heatmaps, highlighting a data point increased its size and added an outline around the corresponding legend (Figure 1(c&d)). Lastly, in the case of the area-encoded icicle plot and sunburst visualisations, the highlighting of a data point changed its colour (Figure 1(e&f)). Note that the visualisations that were using the colour visual encoding limited our choice of highlighting to alteration in the size of data points, as opposed to changing their colours. The opposite was true for time series visualisations that use the area visual encoding.

The implementation of tooltips was the same for all visualisations, regardless of the type of visual encoding and coordinate system being used. We derived the following four interaction scenarios from these two commonly used interaction techniques: no interaction (where neither highlighting nor tooltips were used), only highlighting, only tooltips, and both highlighting and tooltips (highlighting-tooltips).

Tasks

Following Fuchs et al. [14] our selection of tasks was based on two criteria: (1) their ecological validity and (2) their heterogeneity in terms of the elementary perceptual tasks. To meet the first criterion, our tasks were informed by investigations into the work practices of network security professionals, particularly the activity of data correlation to find new and unexplained patterns for further analysis [1]. However, we believe that the study tasks are also widely applicable to other domains, e.g., climate measurement and banking and finance. Heterogeneity was ensured by selecting tasks that were composed of distinct elementary perceptual tasks. The time series data was presented to participants in the form of sales data of a fictitious company, spanning over 16 weeks (with 7x16=112 data points) to provide an easy-to-understand context. Based on these criteria, we selected the following four tasks for this study:

1. Maxima: To identify the highest absolute value in a dataset (e.g., the highlighted day in Figure 1(a,c&e)). Specifically, we asked participants to "discover the day when the sales were at their highest".
2. Minima: To identify the lowest absolute value in a dataset. Specifically, we asked participants to "discover the day when the sales were at their lowest". This was functionally identical to the maxima task, except that "highest" was changed to "lowest". Despite their similarities, prior work [4,32] suggests that there are differences in the performance of these two tasks and that different visualisations may be more suitable.
3. Comparison: To compare two sets of data points to find out which set has the highest aggregated value. Specifically, we asked participants to "discover which of the following weeks has the highest aggregated sales: <week X> or <week Y>".
4. Trend detection: To identify a subset of data (i.e., a week) with the lowest value increase (or upward trend) within the dataset (e.g., 3rd week of February in Figure 1(b,d&f)). Specifically, we asked participants to "discover the week with the smallest difference in sales between the first and last day".

In terms of ecological validity, maxima and minima tasks aim to identify the highest and lowest network traffic respectively, when detecting bandwidth depletion denial of service (DoS) attacks using data correlation. On the other hand, the comparison task aims to compare two subsets of data to identify unexplained patterns requiring further analysis. Lastly, the task of trend detection aims to identify increasing or decreasing trends in network traffic when performing the activity of data correlation.

Experiment Design

We followed a within-subject design with independent variables of 4 interaction scenarios (no interaction, highlighting, tooltips and highlighting-tooltips), 3 visual encodings (position, colour and area), 2 coordinate systems (Cartesian and Polar) and 4 tasks. This within-subject factorial design yielded a total of 96 (4x3x2x4) experimental conditions for each participant. The dependent variables used to measure the impact on users were the completion time of each experimental condition, answer correctness, confidence regarding the given answer, and the ease of use of the visualisation. The experiment was approved by our University's ethics board.

Following Javed et al. [21], the order of the tasks was not counterbalanced, but rather presented in the order of simple to complex, to better prepare the participants for the more difficult tasks at the end. We believed this would not have a significant effect on the validity of the study results since our purpose was not to compare the effectiveness of one task against another, but rather to compare the effectiveness of alternative time series visualisations within the selected tasks. We counterbalanced the order of time series visualisations and interaction scenarios between subjects using a balanced Latin square to minimise the systematic effects of practice.

Time Series Data

Following previous graphical perception studies [4,10,14,16,21], we used synthetic time series data in order to have greater control on the data values and their corresponding visual representation. We generated 96 distinct time series datasets, one for each experiment condition. These were assigned randomly to minimise the learning effect of a correct answer repeatedly appearing at a particular temporal location or having a particular value. Each dataset had 112 data points (1 per day) and spanned over a period of 16 weeks. Based on our pilot testing and the data density of datasets used by similar studies [4,10,14], we estimated that this scale of data would be substantial enough to achieve the appropriate level of difficulty for the different tasks of our study.

We adopted the methods of Fuchs et al. [14] and Correl et al. [10] to generate synthetic data for this experiment. All data values were drawn from a normalised range 0 to 100 to make the data generalisable across different display conditions. Below we explain the data generation method for each of the four study tasks:

Maxima: We selected a data point (p) at random in terms of its temporal placement and value. The value of p was drawn from the range 65 to 100. Following Albers et al. [4] and Fuchs et al. [14], we set the offset d=20, which is the difference between the maxima (p) and randomly generated noise. The remaining data points within the time series dataset were randomly drawn from the range 1 to (p - d).

Minima: Similar to maxima except that p was drawn from the range 1 to 35 and the remaining data points within the time series dataset were randomly drawn from the range (p + d) to 100, with offset d=20.

Comparison: We selected two weeks (w1 and w2) at random in terms of their temporal placement. Data points within w1 were drawn at random from the range 20 to 80. The sum (s1) of values within week 1 was then calculated. The values of data points within w2 were randomly drawn with the constraint that the sum of values (s2) was either 20% (offset d) lower than s1 to simulate the aggregated value of w1 > w2, or s2 was 20% higher than s1 to simulate the aggregated value of w2 > w1. The remaining data points within the time series dataset were randomly drawn from the range 1 to 100.

Trend Detection: First, we created 15 distractor weeks. In each week, the value of the 1st data point was drawn from the range 1 to 20 and the value of the 7th data point was drawn from the range 70 to 100. From these distractor weeks, we identified the week with the smallest difference between the first and last day (sDif). Then, we created the winner week and added it to the dataset at a random temporal place. In this week, the value of the 1st data point (p1) was drawn from the range 1 to 50 and the value of the 7th data point was calculated by using the formula 'p1 + sDif - offset (d)', where d=20. The middle 5 data points within each week were drawn along the trend line with a random variation of 1 to 5.

Participants

We recruited 24 participants (14 male, 10 female). All participants had normal or corrected-to-normal vision and did not report colour blindness. The age of participants ranged from 18-44 years. 11 participants (46%) were students, 1 participant (4%) was part-time employed and 12 participants (50%) were in full-time employment. The education level of participants was diverse with 5 participants (21%) enrolled as undergraduate or graduate students, 8 (33%) had a Bachelor's degree, 8 (33%) received a Master's degree and 3 participants (13%) had a Ph.D. degree. Following Javed et al. [21], we also screened participants to have reasonable computer experience, which was defined as using a computer more than 20 hours per week. All the participants were given a £10 voucher upon completion of the study.

Apparatus

The experiment was conducted on a 15.6 inch Samsung laptop with a 2.5GHz Intel i5 processor, 6 GB of RAM and screen resolution set to 1366x768. A standard, wired mouse was also connected with the laptop to facilitate the interaction with the study software.

The study was implemented as a web application using HTML5, CSS and JavaScript. Time series visualisations were developed using D3.js [5]. Based on our pilot studies, for the Cartesian time series visualisations, a width of 700 pixels and a height of 300 pixels was found to be of appropriate size on the 15.6 inch laptop with the screen resolution set to 1366x768. The size of Polar visualisations was set to 458x458 pixels to assign an approximately equal number of pixels for both the Cartesian and Polar visualisations.

Study Procedure

The experiment took place in a quiet room. The participants sat in front of a table at a distance of approximately 50cm from the laptop and interacted with the study software using only a mouse.

The experiment began by briefly explaining the purpose and procedure of the study. The participant was asked to sign a consent form and to complete a short demographic survey. The experimenter then explained (using a script) the time series visualisations, interaction techniques, data, and the first task. After completing the training for the first task, the participant completed 24 (4 interaction scenarios x 3 visual encodings x 2 coordinate systems) experimental conditions for the task in which he/she selected the correct answer using drop-down menus of week and month. After each condition, the participant answered two 5-point Likert scale questions, ranging from strongly agree (5) to strongly disagree (1): (i) I feel confident about the given answer and (ii) I think this visualisation is easy to use for this task. The participant completed the training and all experimental conditions for the task of maxima, then minima, comparison and trend detection respectively. Thus, training was completed at the start of each of the four tasks. Participants were advised that they should only move on to the actual study task once they were comfortable with the study software and fully understood the task.

Participants were advised to perform each experimental condition as quickly as possible to keep it in line with our 1st criterion of task selection (i.e., ecological validity); however, no strict time limits were imposed. The study duration ranged from 50 to 75 minutes.

RESULTS

In this study, completion time was the only continuous dependent variable and it was not normally distributed. Data normality was tested using the Shapiro-Wilk test, which identified 73.95% (71 out of 96) experimental conditions that were not normally distributed ($p<0.05$). The remaining 3 dependent variables in this study were either binary (accuracy) or ordinal (confidence and ease of use), which by definition could not be normally distributed. Therefore, we analysed the results using a non-parametric Friedman test. Pairwise comparisons were conducted with Wilcoxon signed-rank test. Significance levels were adjusted with the Holm-Bonferroni correction for multiple testing. We categorise the results into three sub-sections, corresponding to the three contributions of this paper. We only report on the statistically significant results at $p<0.05$.

Effects of Interaction Techniques

We compared the effectiveness (i.e., completion time (seconds), accuracy (percentage), confidence (Likert) and ease of use (Likert)) of four selected interaction scenarios (i.e., no interaction, highlighting, tooltips, and highlighting-tooltips) for three visual encodings (i.e., position, colour and area) and four tasks. Figure 2 provides an overview of statistically significant results.

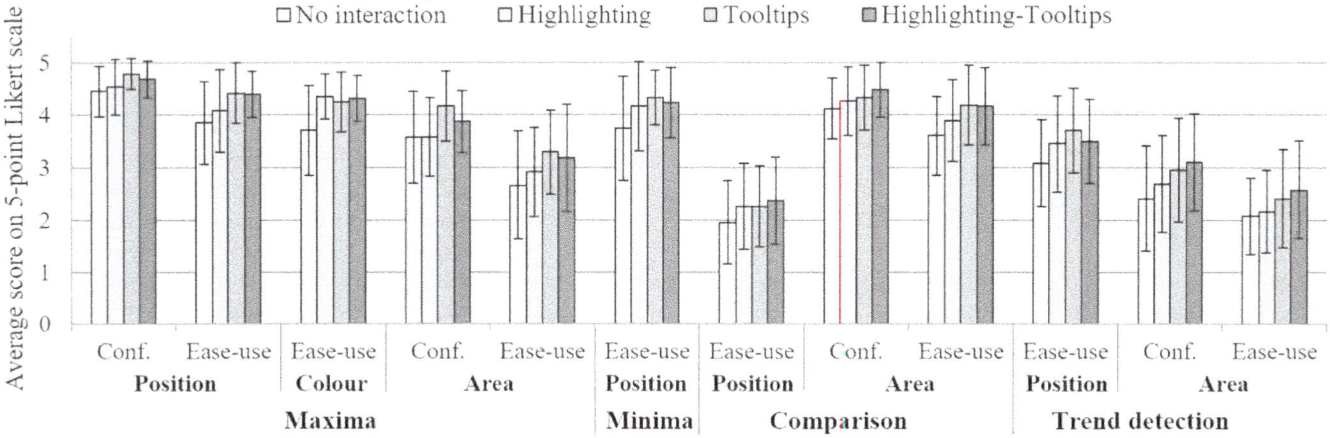

Figure 2. Overview of results for interaction scenarios. Conf. = confidence and ease-use = ease of use.

Maxima Results

For visualisations using positional visual encoding, there was an overall effect of interaction scenarios on confidence ($\chi^2(3)=11.53$, $p=0.009$) and ease of use ($\chi^2(3)=15.26$, $p=0.002$). Pairwise comparisons showed that participants had more confidence regarding their answers when using visualisations with tooltips than no interaction ($Z=-2.84$, $p=0.005$) and highlighting visualisations ($Z=-2.81$, $p=0.005$). Similarly, visualisations with tooltips were easier to use than no interaction ($Z=-3.03$, $p=0.002$) and highlighting visualisations ($Z=-2.91$, $p=0.004$). Visualisations with highlighting-tooltips were also found to be easier to use than no interaction visualisations ($Z=-2.89$, $p=0.004$).

For visualisations using colour visual encoding, there was an overall effect of interaction scenarios on ease of use ($\chi^2(3)=15.70$, $p=0.001$). Pairwise comparisons showed that visualisations with highlighting ($Z=-3.12$, $p=0.002$), tooltips ($Z=-2.80$, $p=0.005$) and highlighting-tooltips ($Z=-3.22$, $p=0.001$) were easier to use than no interaction visualisations.

For visualisations using area visual encoding, there was an overall effect of interaction scenarios on confidence ($\chi^2(3)=14.30$, $p=0.003$) and ease of use ($\chi^2(3)=17.31$, $p<0.001$). Pairwise comparisons showed that participants had more confidence regarding their answers when using visualisations with tooltips than no interaction visualisations ($Z=-2.74$, $p=0.006$). Moreover, visualisations with tooltips ($Z=-3.14$, $p=0.002$) and highlighting-tooltips ($Z=-3.06$, $p=0.002$) were easier to use than no interaction visualisations.

Minima Results

For visualisations using positional visual encoding, there was an overall effect of interaction scenarios on ease of use ($\chi^2(3)=10.35$, $p=0.016$). Pairwise comparisons showed that visualisations with highlighting ($Z=-2.99$, $p=0.003$) and tooltips ($Z=-2.76$, $p=0.006$) were easier to use than no interaction visualisations.

Comparison Results

For visualisations using positional visual encoding, there was an overall effect of interaction scenarios on ease of use ($\chi^2(3)=10.36$, $p=0.016$). Pairwise comparisons showed visualisations with highlighting ($Z=-2.68$, $p=0.007$) and highlighting-tooltips ($Z=-2.55$, $p=0.010$) were easier to use than no interaction visualisations.

For visualisations using area visual encoding, there was an overall effect of interaction scenarios on confidence ($\chi^2(3)=10.32$, $p=0.016$) and ease of use ($\chi^2(3)=17.01$, $p<0.001$). Pairwise comparisons showed that participants had more confidence regarding their answers when using visualisations with highlighting-tooltips than no interaction visualisations ($Z=-2.80$, $p=0.005$). Moreover, visualisations with tooltips were easier to use than no interaction ($Z=-3.12$, $p=0.002$) and highlighting visualisations ($Z=-2.66$, $p=0.008$). Visualisations with highlighting-tooltips were also found to be easier to use than no interaction visualisations ($Z=-3.12$, $p=0.002$).

Trend Detection Results

For visualisations using positional visual encoding, there was an overall effect of interaction scenarios on ease of use ($\chi^2(3)=24.05$, $p<0.001$). Pairwise comparisons showed that visualisations with tooltips ($Z=-3.40$, $p=0.001$) and highlighting-tooltips ($Z=-2.69$, $p=0.007$) were easier to use than no interaction visualisations.

For visualisations using area visual encoding, there was an overall effect of interaction scenarios on confidence ($\chi^2(3)=18.02$, $p<0.001$) and ease of use ($\chi^2(3)=13.04$, $p<0.005$). Pairwise comparisons showed that participants had more confidence regarding their answers when using visualisations with tooltips ($Z=-3.10$, $p=0.002$) and highlighting-tooltips ($Z=-3.17$, $p=0.002$) than no interaction visualisations. In addition, visualisations with highlighting-tooltips were easier to use than no interaction ($Z=-2.89$, $p=0.004$) and highlighting visualisations ($Z=-2.73$, $p=0.006$).

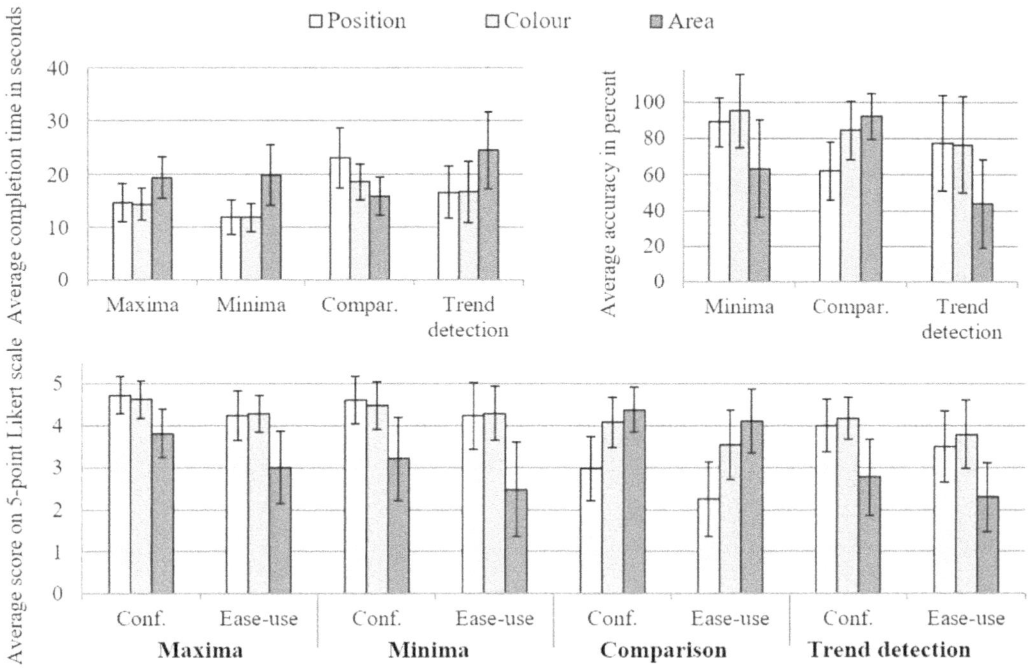

Figure 3. Overview of results for visual encodings. Conf. = confidence, ease-use = ease of use, compar. = comparison.

Impact of Visual Encodings

We compared the effectiveness (i.e., completion time, accuracy, confidence and ease of use) of visualisations using three different visual encoding techniques (i.e., position, colour and area) for the tasks of maxima, minima, comparison and trend detection. Figure 3 provides an overview of statistically significant results.

Minima Results

There was an overall effect of visual encodings on accuracy ($\chi^2(2)=33.74$, $p<0.001$). Pairwise comparisons showed that the participants gave more correct answers when using visualisations with colour visual encoding, compared to position ($Z=-2.36$, $p=0.018$) and area ($Z=-4.18$, $p<0.001$). Participants also gave more correct answers when using visualisations with positional visual encoding than area ($Z=-3.89$, $p<0.001$).

Comparison Results

There was an overall effect of visual encodings on completion time ($\chi^2(2)=37.00$, $p<0.001$), accuracy ($\chi^2(2)=33.09$, $p<0.001$), confidence ($\chi^2(2)=31.08$, $p<0.001$) and ease of use ($\chi^2(2)=31.63$, $p<0.001$). Pairwise comparisons showed that the completion time was lower for visualisations with colour ($Z=-4.11$, $p<0.001$) and area visual encodings ($Z=-4.29$, $p<0.001$) than position. The completion time was also lower for visualisations with area visual encoding than colour ($Z=-3.46$, $p=0.001$). In addition, participants gave more correct answers when using visualisations with colour ($Z=-3.67$, $p<0.001$) and area visual encodings ($Z=-3.96$, $p<0.001$) than position. Pairwise comparisons also showed that participants had more confidence in their answers when using visualisations with colour ($Z=-3.79$, $p<0.001$) and area visual encodings ($Z=-3.95$, $p<0.001$) than position. Participants also had more confidence in their answers when using visualisations with area visual encoding than colour ($Z=-2.12$, $p=0.034$). Lastly, visualisations with colour ($Z=-3.64$, $p<0.001$) and area visual encodings ($Z=-3.94$, $p<0.001$) were easier to use than position. Visualisations using area visual encoding were also easier to use than colour visual encoding ($Z=-2.72$, $p=0.007$).

For all other cases, there were no statistically significant differences between positional and colour visual encodings, however both were more effective than area visual encoding. Also, no statistically significant differences were found for the dependent variable of accuracy within the task of maxima.

Impact of Coordinate Systems

We compared the effectiveness (i.e., completion time, accuracy, confidence and ease of use) of Cartesian and Polar coordinate systems for three visual encodings (i.e., position, colour and area) and four tasks (i.e., maxima, minima, comparison and trend detection). Figure 4 provides an overview of statistically significant results.

Maxima Results

For visualisations using positional visual encoding, the participants had more confidence regarding their answers for the Cartesian coordinate system than Polar ($Z=-2.08$, $p=0.038$). Similarly, the Cartesian visualisation was easier to use than Polar ($Z=-2.75$, $p=0.006$). For visualisations using area visual encoding, the completion time was lower for the Cartesian coordinate system than Polar ($Z=-2.46$, $p=0.014$). In addition, the Cartesian visualisation was easier to use than Polar ($Z=-2.49$, $p=0.013$).

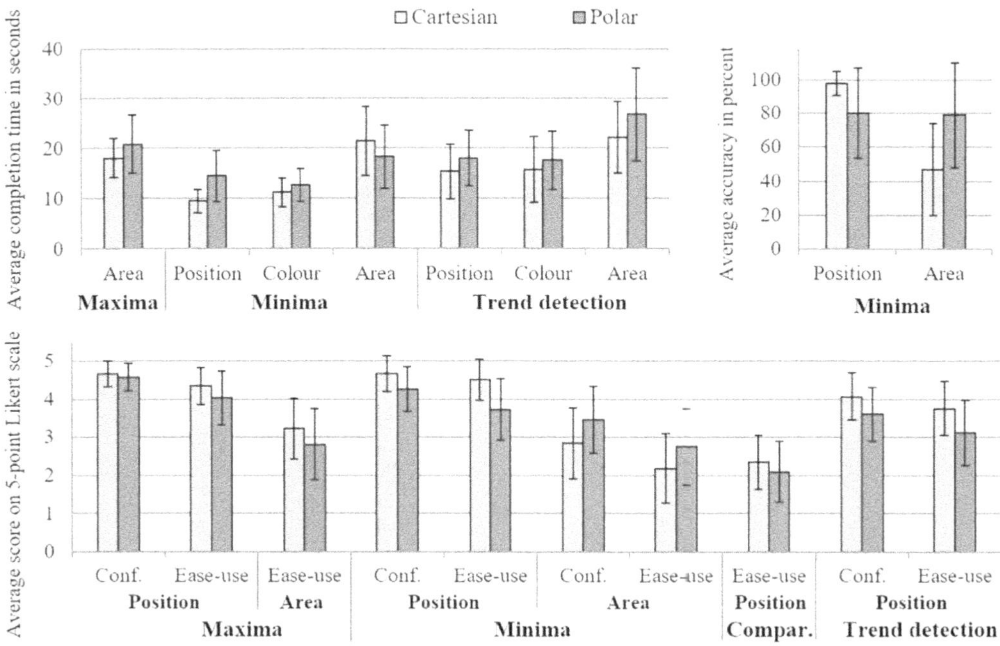

Figure 4. Overview of results for coordinate systems. Conf. = confidence, ease-use = ease of use and compar. = comparison.

Minima Results

For visualisations using positional visual encoding, the completion time was lower for the Cartesian coordinate system than Polar ($Z=-4.00$, $p<0.001$). The participants gave more correct answers when using the Cartesian coordinate system compared to Polar ($Z=-2.80$, $p=0.005$) In addition, the participants had more confidence in their answers for the Cartesian coordinate system than Polar ($Z=-3.33$, $p=0.001$) and found it easier to use, compared to Polar ($Z=-3.92$, $p<0.001$).

On the other hand, for visualisations using colour visual encoding, only completion time was lower for the Cartesian coordinate system than Polar ($Z=-2.11$, $p=0.034$).

In contrast to positional and colour visual encodings, the Polar visualisation performed better than its Cartesian counterpart for area visual encoding. The completion time was lower for the Polar coordinate system than Cartesian ($Z=-2.14$, $p=0.032$). The participants gave more correct answers when using the Polar coordinate system than Cartesian ($Z=-4.00$, $p<0.001$). Also, participants had more confidence regarding their answers for the Polar coordinate system than Cartesian ($Z=-3.60$, $p<0.001$) and found it easier to use, compared to Cartesian ($Z=-3.11$, $p=0.002$).

Comparison Results

For the task of comparison, the only statistically significant result was for the visualisations using positional visual encoding. The participants found the Cartesian visualisation to be easier to use than its Polar counterpart ($Z=-2.59$, $p=0.010$).

Trend Detection Results

For visualisations using positional visual encoding, the completion time was lower for the Cartesian coordinate system than Polar ($Z=-2.46$, $p=0.014$). In addition, the participants had more confidence regarding their answers for the Cartesian coordinate system than Polar ($Z=-2.98$, $p=0.003$). They also found it easier to use compared to Polar ($Z=-3.47$, $p=0.001$).

On the other hand, for visualisations using colour visual encoding, only completion time was lower for the Cartesian coordinate system than Polar ($Z=-2.07$, $p=0.038$). Similarly, for visualisations using area visual encoding, only completion time was lower for the Cartesian coordinate system than Polar ($Z=-2.49$, $p=0.013$).

DISCUSSION

We divide the findings into three sub-sections, corresponding to the three contributions (C1-C3) of this paper.

Effects of Interaction Techniques

We found that introducing interactivity for time series visualisations could considerably enhance the user experience (i.e., confidence and ease of use), without the loss of any efficiency or accuracy. Further, there are clear differences in the effectiveness of selected interaction scenarios (i.e., highlighting, tooltips, and highlighting-tooltips). Our findings indicate that visualisations with tooltips were not only considerably more effective than the visualisations with highlighting, but they were also slightly better than visualisations with both the highlighting and the tooltips (highlighting-tooltips). In terms of design implications for time series visualisations, this finding suggests that users prefer clear textual instructions (i.e., tooltips) than highlighting, when it comes to facilitating the identification of temporal location and quantitative value of a particular data point.

The trend of interactive time series visualisations resulting in better user experience was observed considerably less for the task of minima and visualisations that use colour visual encoding. This confirms the findings of prior work [4,32] that indicate that despite the similarity between minima and maxima, there are differences in the performance of these two tasks and that different visualisations may be suitable. This finding has two design implications for time series visualisations. Firstly, introducing interactivity may add little value for time series visualisations using colour visual encoding. Secondly, the effect of interactivity on the performance of minima task is very negligible.

Impact of Visual Encodings

Our findings suggest that for maxima, minima and trend detection tasks, time series visualisations that use positional and colour visual encodings were more effective than area visual encodings. However, for the task of comparison, visualisations that use area visual encodings were more effective than their positional and colour counterparts.

This confirms that the findings of generic, non-time series graphical perception studies [8,17] are not fully generalisable to time series visualisations. In other words, while visualisations using positional visual encodings are quite a strong option to visualise time series data, there are many scenarios where visualisations that use colour visual encoding are comparable or more effective. In addition, we have a new finding that there are certain scenarios (e.g., comparison task) where visualisations that use area visual encoding are better suited, compared to visualisations from both the visual encodings of position and colour.

In terms of design implications, our findings suggest that the choice of a time series visualisation should be based on the type of tasks and the metric used to measure the effectiveness, since there is no *"one-size-fits-all"* solution.

Impact of Coordinate Systems

We found that visualisations that are based on a Cartesian coordinate system are generally comparable or more effective than Polar, except for visualisations that use area visual encoding for the task of minima.

This confirms the findings of two generic studies conducted by Diehl et al. [11], which suggest using a Cartesian coordinate system unless there are clear reasons in favour of Polar. In our case, the only scenario where a visualisation based on the Polar coordinate system (i.e., sunburst visualisation) were more effective than its Cartesian counterpart (i.e., icicle plot) was from the category of area visual encoding, for the task of minima. There could be several possible reasons for this finding. We believe that this was due to the increased space to encode data values of days, provided by the outermost ring of the sunburst visualisation compared to the lowermost segment of the icicle plot.

Also note that, the effect of coordinate systems is negligible for time series visualisations that use colour visual encoding. In terms of design implications, this finding suggests that time series visualisations using colour visual encoding may be an appropriate choice when the coordinate system is not known beforehand.

LIMITATIONS AND FUTURE WORK

While comprehensive enough to explore three different aspects (C1-C3) of time series visualisations, this approach was not without limitations. To begin with, we investigated the effect of two commonly used interaction techniques (i.e., highlighting and tooltips) on the effectiveness of different time series visualisations. In the future, we would like to extend this study to other commonly used interaction techniques, e.g., selection, filtering and zoom in/out.

In addition, our experiment considers a small but diverse set of time series visualisations and tasks. We believe that our findings would be generalisable to a wider range of situations, but we have not confirmed this empirically. In our future endeavours, we plan to extend these findings by including additional time series visualisations (e.g., scatter plots and horizon graphs) and tasks (e.g., range and outliers). The same is true for the selected size and aspect ratio of time series visualisations, density of time series datasets and the offset between the correct answers and randomly generated noise.

CONCLUSION

In this paper, we presented the results of a comprehensive graphical perception study. The purpose of this study was to examine the effects of two commonly used interaction techniques on time series visualisations (C1), to compare the effectiveness of time series visualisations using the positional, colour and area visual encodings (C2) and to investigate the impact of Cartesian and Polar coordinate systems on the effectiveness of time series visualisations (C3).

Our results show that the time series visualisations that use positional and colour visual encodings were more effective than area visual encodings for maxima, minima and trend detection tasks. However, for the task of comparison, visualisations that use area visual encodings were more effective than their positional and colour counterparts. We also found that the time series visualisations that are based on the Cartesian coordinate system are generally comparable or more effective than Polar. Most importantly, we identified that introducing interactivity within time series visualisations considerably enhances the user experience, without any loss of efficiency or accuracy. We believe that our findings could vastly assist visual analytics tool developers when choosing time series visualisations for different tasks in a variety of domains. We also believe that our work will motivate the visual analytics research community to focus equally on interaction and visual representation of data.

REFERENCES

1. Muhammad Adnan, Mike Just, Lynne Baillie, and Hilmi G. Kayacik. 2015. Investigating the work practices of network security professionals. *Information & Computer Security* 23, 3: 347-367.
2. Wolfgang Aigner. 2011. Understanding the role and value of interaction: First steps. In *Proceedings of the International Workshop on Visual Analytics* (EuroVA '11), 17-20. http://dx.doi.org/10.2312/PE/EuroVAST/EuroVA11/017-020
3. Wolfgang Aigner, Silvia Miksch, Heidrun Schumann, and Christian Tominski. 2011. *Visualization of time-oriented data*. Springer Science & Business Media.
4. Danielle Albers, Michael Correll, and Michael Gleicher. 2014. Task-driven evaluation of aggregation in time series visualization. In *Proceedings of the SIGCHI Conference on Human Factors in Computing Systems* (CHI '14), 551-560. http://dx.doi.org/10.1145/2556288.2557200
5. Michael Bostock, Vadim Ogievetsky, and Jeffrey Heer. 2011. D^3 data-driven documents. *IEEE Trans Vis Comput Graph* 17, 12: 2301-2309.
6. Cynthia A. Brewer, Mark Harrower, and Pennsylvania State University. 2015. ColorBrewer 2.0 – color advice for cartography. Retrieved July 10, 2015 from http://colorbrewer2.org/
7. Michael Burch, Felix Bott, Fabian Beck, and Stephan Diehl. 2008. Cartesian vs. radial – a comparative evaluation of two visualization tools. In *Proceedings of 4th International Symposium on Visual Computing* (ISVC '08), 151-160. http://dx.doi.org/10.1007/978-3-540-89639-5_15
8. William S. Cleveland and Robert McGill. 1984. Graphical perception: Theory, experimentation, and application to the development of graphical methods. *Journal of the American statistical association* 79, 387: 531-554.
9. William S. Cleveland and Robert McGill. 1986. An experiment in graphical perception. *International Journal of Man-Machine Studies* 25, 5: 491-500.
10. Michael Correll, Danielle Albers, Steven Franconeri, and Michael Gleicher. 2012. Comparing averages in time series data. In *Proceedings of the SIGCHI Conference on Human Factors in Computing Systems* (CHI '12), 1095-1104. http://dx.doi.org/10.1145/2207676.2208556
11. Stephan Diehl, Fabian Beck, and Michael Burch. 2010. Uncovering strengths and weaknesses of radial visualizations---an empirical approach. *IEEE Trans Vis Comput Graph* 16, 6: 935-942.
12. Alan Dix and Geoffrey Ellis. 1998. Starting simple: adding value to static visualisation through simple interaction. In *Proceedings of the working conference on Advanced visual interfaces* (AVI '98), 124-134. http://dx.doi.org/10.1145/948496.948514
13. Niklas Elmqvist, Andrew V. Moere, Hans-Christian Jetter, Daniel Cernea, Harald Reiterer, and T. J. Jankun-Kelly. 2011. Fluid interaction for information visualization. *Information Visualization* 10, 4: 327-340.
14. Johannes Fuchs, Fabian Fischer, Florian Mansmann, Enrico Bertini, and Petra Isenberg. 2013. Evaluation of alternative glyph designs for time series data in a small multiple setting. In *Proceedings of the SIGCHI Conference on Human Factors in Computing Systems* (CHI '13), 3237-3246. http://dx.doi.org/10.1145/2470654.2466443
15. John R. Harger, and Patricia J. Crossno. 2012. Comparison of open-source visual analytics toolkits. In *Proceedings of the SPIE 8294, Visualization and Data Analysis*, 82940E. http://dx.doi.org/10.1117/12.911901
16. Jeffrey Heer, Nicholas Kong, and Maneesh Agrawala. 2009. Sizing the horizon: the effects of chart size and layering on the graphical perception of time series visualizations. In *Proceedings of the SIGCHI Conference on Human Factors in Computing Systems* (CHI '09), 1303-1312. http://dx.doi.org/10.1145/1518701.1518897
17. Jeffrey Heer and Michael Bostock. 2010. Crowdsourcing graphical perception: using mechanical turk to assess visualization design. In *Proceedings of the SIGCHI Conference on Human Factors in Computing Systems* (CHI '10), 203-212. http://dx.doi.org/10.1145/1753326.1753357
18. Jeffrey Heer and Ben Shneiderman. 2012. Interactive dynamics for visual analysis. *Communications of the ACM* 55, 4: 45-54.
19. Intel IT Center. 2013. Big Data Visualization: Turning Big Data into Big Insights. Retrieved July 5, 2015 from http://www.intel.co.uk/content/dam/www/public/us/en/documents/white-papers/big-data-visualization-turning-big-data-into-big-insights.pdf
20. Yvonne Jansen and Pierre Dragicevic. 2013. An interaction model for visualizations beyond the desktop. *IEEE Trans Vis Comput Graph* 19, 12: 2396-2405.
21. Waqas Javed, Bryan McDonnel, and Niklas Elmqvist. 2010. Graphical perception of multiple time series. *IEEE Trans Vis Comput Graph* 16, 6: 927-934.
22. Brian Johnson and Ben Shneiderman. 1991. Tree-maps: A space-filling approach to the visualization of hierarchical information structures. In *Proceedings of the IEEE Conference on Visualization* (Visualization '91), 284-291. http://dx.doi.org/10.1109/VISUAL.1991.175815

23. Heidi Lam, Tamara Munzner, and Robert Kincaid. 2007. Overview use in multiple visual information resolution interfaces. *IEEE Trans Vis Comput Graph* 13, 6: 1278-1285.
24. Heidi Lam. 2008. A framework of interaction costs in information visualization. *IEEE Trans Vis Comput Graph* 14, 6: 1149-1156.
25. Hai-Ning Liang, Paul Parsons, Hsien-Chi Wu, and Kamran Sedig. 2010. An exploratory study of interactivity in visualization tools: 'Flow' of interaction. *Journal of Interactive Learning Research* 21, 1: 5-45.
26. Jie Liang and Mao L. Huang. 2010. Highlighting in information visualization: A survey. In *Proceedings of the 14th International Conference on Information Visualisation* (IV '10), 79-85. http://dx.doi.org/10.1109/IV.2010.21
27. Jock D. Mackinlay. 1986. Automating the design of graphical presentations of relational information. *Acm Transactions On Graphics* 5, 2: 110-141.
28. Andrew McAfee and Erik Brynjolfsson. 2012. Big data: The management revolution. *Harvard Bus Rev* 90, 10: 61-67.
29. Charles Perin, Frédéric Vernier, and Jean-Daniel Fekete. 2013. Interactive horizon graphs: improving the compact visualization of multiple time series. *In Proceedings of the SIGCHI Conference on Human Factors in Computing Systems* (CHI '13), 3217-3226. http://dx.doi.org/10.1145/2470654.2466441
30. William A. Pike, John Stasko, Remco Chang, and Theresa A. O'connell. 2009. The science of interaction. *Information Visualization* 8, 4: 263-274.
31. Margit Pohl, Sylvia Wiltner, Silvia Miksch, Wolfgang Aigner, and Alexander Rind. 2012. Analysing interactivity in information visualisation. *KI-Künstliche Intelligenz* 26, 2: 151-159.
32. Jibonananda Sanyal, Song Zhang, Gargi Bhattacharya, Phil Amburn, and Robert J. Moorhead. 2009. A user study to compare four uncertainty visualization methods for 1d and 2d datasets. *IEEE Trans Vis Comput Graph* 15, 6: 1209-1218.
33. Matthias Schonlau and Ellen Peters. 2008. Graph comprehension: An experiment in displaying data as bar charts, pie charts and tables with and without the gratuitous 3rd dimension. *Social Science Research Network Working Paper Series.*
34. Kamran Sedig, Paul Parsons, and Alex Babanski. 2012. Towards a Characterization of Interactivity in Visual Analytics. *Journal of Multimedia Processing and Technologies* 3, 1: 12-28.
35. Kamran Sedig, Paul Parsons, Mark Dittmer, and Robert Haworth. 2014. Human-centered interactivity of visualization tools: Micro-and macro-level considerations. In *Handbook of Human Centric Visualization*, Weidong Huang (eds). Springer, New York, 717-743.
36. John Stasko, Richard Catrambone, Mark Guzdial, and Kevin McDonald. 2000. An evaluation of space-filling information visualizations for depicting hierarchical structures. *International Journal of Human-Computer Studies* 53, 5: 663-694.
37. James J. Thomas and Kristin A. Cook (eds.). 2005. *Illuminating the path: The research and development agenda for visual analytics*. IEEE Computer Society Press.
38. Christian Tominski, Camilla Forsell, and Jimmy Johansson. 2012. Interaction support for visual comparison inspired by natural behavior. *IEEE Trans Vis Comput Graph* 18, 12: 2719-2728.
39. Soo J. Yi, Youn ah Kang, John T. Stasko, and Julie A. Jacko. 2007. Toward a deeper understanding of the role of interaction in information visualization. *IEEE Trans Vis Comput Graph* 13, 6: 1224-1231.
40. Leishi Zhang, Andreas Stoffel, Michael Behrisch, Sebastian Mittelstadt, Tobias Schreck, René Pompl, Simon Weber, Holger Last, and Daniel Keim. 2012. Visual analytics for the big data era - A comparative review of state-of-the-art commercial systems. In *Proceedings of IEEE Conference on Visual Analytics Science and Technology* (VAST '12), 173-182. http://dx.doi.org/10.1109/VAST.2012.6400554

Smartwatch *in vivo*

Stefania Pizza[1], Barry Brown[2], Donald McMillan[2], Airi Lampinen[2]

[1]CoRiS
Sapienza University of Rome, Italy
stefania.pizza@uniroma1.it

[2]Mobile Life Centre
University of Stockholm, Sweden
[barry, don, airi]@mobilelifecentre.org

ABSTRACT
In recent years, the smartwatch has returned as a form factor for mobile computing with some success. Yet it is not clear how smartwatches are used and integrated into everyday life differently from mobile phones. For this paper, we used wearable cameras to record twelve participants' daily use of smartwatches, collecting and analysing incidents where watches were used from over 34 days of user recording. This allows us to analyse in detail 1009 watch uses. Using the watch as a timepiece was the most common use, making up 50% of interactions, but only 14% of total watch usage time. The videos also let us examine why and how smartwatches are used for activity tracking, notifications, and in combination with smartphones. In discussion, we return to a key question in the study of mobile devices: how are smartwatches integrated into everyday life, in both the actions that we take and the social interactions we are part of?

Author Keywords
Smartwatches, wrist watches, wearable computing

ACM Classification Keywords
H.5.m. Information interfaces and presentation (e.g., HCI): Miscellaneous

INTRODUCTION
The wristwatch is one of the oldest wearable technologies, allowing a user to quickly glance at the time and related information. This paper addresses the most recent evolution of the wristwatch in the form of connected 'smartwatches'. Google's range of licensed "Android Wear" watches and Apple's self named "Apple Watch" adopt functionality from the mobile phone, although in a new form factor and with a number of new design innovations. While technologically these devices are not radical advances on concepts that have been tested in the wearable technology community, they do collect together a range of functionality in well-designed and consumer-accessible technological form. The adoption of these devices, albeit at this point only at an early stage, presents some interesting user research questions.

For example, what does a wrist worn technology support in contrast to the screen of a mobile phone? The mobile is now the world's computational form factor of choice, supporting a range of different activities and types of media consumption. What then does the smartwatch add? Second, much of the functionality of commercial smartwatches is build around notifications, or gaining information quickly 'at a glance'. This has the potential to cause considerable distraction if it takes users' attention away from focal concerns such as interacting with others. How does the stream of notifications received on a smartwatch and mobile phone compare in this regard? Third, the health tracking functions of watches are central to their design and marketing, with watches tracking users' heart rates and exercise – echoing the function of popular devices such as the FitBit and the increasing mainstreaming of Quantified Self concepts as a path to wellness [14]. How are these functions actually used and in what way do they integrate themselves with daily practice? Lastly, what limitations and possibilities can we identify from closely studying smartwatches *in vivo* [44] for future design and innovation?

To answer these questions we provided twelve participants with a smartwatch for one month, with the final three days of use recorded with pairs of wearable cameras. These recordings were combined with interviews with each participant. This data gives us a uniquely detailed view on how smartwatches are used, what for, and in what contexts. From 34 days of recording we have over 168 hours of dual-aspect recording covering 1009 incidents of watch use – around 6 uses per hour, with each use being on average 6.7 second long. Moreover, our videos let us look in more detail at what and why watches are used in particular situations. We discuss the importance of *time* as a straightforward application for a watch, activity tracking, and the role of notifications. We go on to unpack why a wrist worn technology fits into situations and activities a phone might not, before examining how mobile computing could develop further with the watch. We offer these results not only to inform the future design of such devices, but also as a reflection on wider lessons for wearable technology. In discussion, we reflect upon what smart watches can teach us about the ways in which computational assistance – and interruption – come to be fused into everyday life and practice.

CHI'16, May 07-12, 2016, San Jose, CA, USA.
© 2016 ACM. ISBN 978-1-4503-3362-7/16/05...$15.00.
DOI: http://dx.doi.org/10.1145/2858036.2858522

BACKGROUND

The wristwatch became common for women in the late 1800s, followed post-war by men in the early 1900s [43]. The original design of the watch came from the adoption of pocket watches by the military. With military manoeuvres co-ordinated so as to happen simultaneously, watches were an important tool of war – yet, with hands full a pocket watch could not be consulted as easily as one tied to a solder's wrist [ibid].

More technological advances followed with the advent of the digital watch [54], and then HP's calculator watch in 1978, followed quickly by watches with a range of different features – from radio to television [4]. In moving towards the smartwatch platform we see today, there have been a number of computer-watches such as the Swatch/HP's Webwatch [63], the Microsoft SPOT [37], and the Fossil PalmOS powered Wrist-PDA. Recently the Android Wear platform as well as Apple's Watch devices have achieved some popularity [57]. Running in parallel, there has been an increase in the amount of wrist worn non-watch wearables – primarily aimed at health, fitness, and the quantification of personal action [66].

There has been a wealth of work on input modalities for this form factor. The mechanics of touch on small devices have been examined in detail [3, 27, 28, 34, 51, 59] as has text entry for small devices [11, 13, 16, 29, 35, 46, 50, 55, 70] as well as other input modalities such as tilting and twisting the screen [71], tracing letters on other surfaces with your finger [68], interacting around the device [36, 49], interacting with just gaze and attention [2], and even blowing on the watch [12]. However, there has been relatively little study of the use of smartwatches. Lyons [41] looked at traditional watch wearers' practices to learn lessons for the smartwatch. Giang *et al* compared notification distraction between smartwatches and smartphones [18], Cecchinato *et al* [9] and Schirra & Bentley [62] interviewed smartwatch wearers to better understand how and why they used the device. This last paper emphasised the importance of notifications as a watch function, as well as the importance of appearance in choosing a watch device. Giang *et al* moved the study of notifications, disruption, and distraction from the smartphone to the smartwatch, contrasting these with studies of notifications on the desktop e.g. [15, 31, 67]. On mobile phones, Pielot *et al* [53] found that over 60 notifications a day was usual, and Leiva *et al* [38] looked at the effect of task interruption by incoming phone calls.

WHAT IS A SMARTWATCH?

The two leading types of smartwatch, Android Wear and the Apple Watch, share much of their functionality. The most basic functionality is displaying the time, and users can choose from a library of watch faces that also display other data along with the time, such as the weather or a step counter. When not being used, the Apple Watch turns its display off to preserve battery power, illuminating the screen only when it detects motion of the user's hand, or when the user touches the screen. Each watch is coupled to a user's phone, relaying information from the phone to the watch. Notifications that arrive on the phone (resulting from text messages, phone calls, or applications) are 'forwarded' to the watch, where they create a sound or small haptic vibration on the user's wrist. If the user raises their hand within a few seconds, the details of the notification are then shown. After being read, notifications on the watch are kept on the watch for reference (in the 'notification centre'), until deleted by the user. Both Google and Apple's smartwatches allow users to send messages, launch apps, or perform other tasks using voice commands, and a range of other applications are offered for download on the app store. Lastly, users' steps and exertion are measured through a variety of sensors, monitoring physical activity.

METHODS

To understand smartwatches *in vivo*, we wanted to record what watches were used for and the situation and context of use. Research using tracking of mobile device use has grown in popularity as devices have become important parts of a broader range of activities [6-8, 24, 44]. In particular, naturalistic video recording of mobile device use has advantages for capture and analysis in that it allows for the study of the moment-by-moment details of how the environment and device are connected in use [6]. Accordingly, for this study, we had participants wear multiple portable wearable cameras that recorded their actions relatively unobtrusively, while allowing us to see and understand smartwatch use *in vivo* [44]. We made a small 'sensor bag' (Figure 1) which contained two cameras with long-life batteries that allowed them to record for eight hours each. One of the cameras was directed to record the scene around the participant (pointing forward). The second camera was connected to a small 'stalk' camera that was

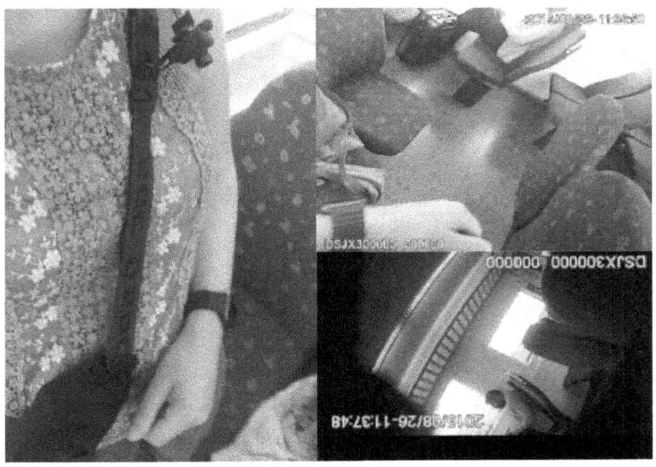

Figure 1: Participant wearing watch and camera. The 'stalk camera' gives a rough analogue of the participant's view of their wrist (and the watch). The camera bag visible on the strap at the bottom left contains a front-facing camera that records the user's context. Camera views are on the right.

mounted at the shoulder of the participant (looking downwards), so as to capture the participant's body and wrist. This angle captured interactions with the watch.

We recruited twelve participants using social media and advertising on local activity websites (Couchsurfing and a student group on Facebook). Our sample was somewhat skewed in terms of age (between 23 and 36, median age 30), and five out of the twelve participants were students. The other participants' occupations included management consultant, entrepreneur, accounts clerk, medical researcher and fraud analyst. Seven of the twelve participants were female. All participants regularly used an iPhone, and had not previously owned a smartwatch or fitness tracker. Three of them regularly wore conventional watches. Participants were given an Apple Watch, with a choice of a small (38mm) or large (42mm) version, and were asked to use it for a month with the last three days of usage recorded using our camera setup. On the day the recording started, participants were given the cameras and asked to record the rest of their day, with a researcher meeting with them the next day to collect the recordings from the cameras and to address any problems or concerns. On the third day, the cameras and the smartwatch were collected by a researcher and if possible an interview was carried out there and then. In this way, we aimed to collect at least two full days of video of each participant, although participants were allowed to stop the cameras when they wanted, to preserve their privacy or that of others around them.

As with any wearable camera study, there were some issues concerning when cameras could be worn, and permission from those caught on camera but not part of the research.

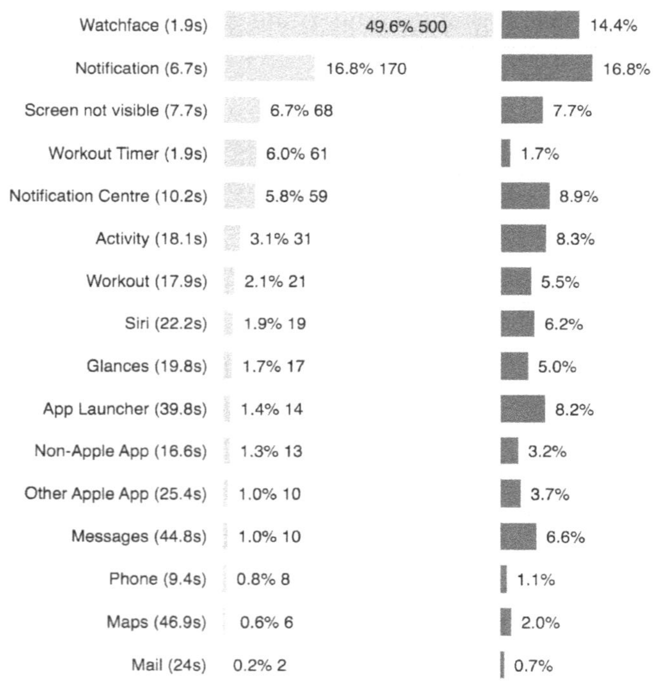

Figure 2: Watch usage by frequency of use (from 1009 incidents) and as % of time using watch (from 6777 seconds). Average use time per app is listed in brackets.

Therefore, we asked our participants to turn the cameras off when appropriate, as well as allowed them to choose on which days they were recorded. For practical reasons, two participants only recorded on 2 days making a total of 34 days of recording – 23 workdays, 11 weekend days. After the study all participants were interviewed for between 45 minutes and 1 hour, with questions covering their experiences of the watch and the recording procedure.

Our analysis started by watching the video and extracting clips where there was any interaction around or with the watch. For nearly all the video, the watch was visible, or if the watch itself was obscured (such as when it was under a coat sleeve) then the arm was at least captured such that the time of interactions with the watch would be visible (if not the actual interaction). For timing we counted from illumination to either the hand moving back to its original position or the screen going off. For each interaction with the watch, we extracted a video clip including ten seconds before and after to retain a sense of the surrounding activity. Each clip was logged with details including who was present, the type of watch interaction, and the length of interaction. This allowed us to gain an overview of watch use, in terms of the number of clips and the watch functions being used. For our analysis sessions, all authors collectively watched all 'watch use event' clips, around 8 hours of video in total. We selected for closer analysis clips that were particularly revealing of smartwatch use – either due to interaction with another person around the watch, or action involving the use of the watch. This smaller corpus of 110 clips was used for a more lengthy analysis of the interaction around the watch to examine patterns of talk, device, and bodily interaction. We drew on interactional analysis and the broader body of work in HCI that looks closely at the moment-by-moment interaction with technology [7, 17, 20-22]. Accordingly, our analysis took the form not of the repetition of a formal method, but a much more crafted set of analysis sessions and informed inspection of clips. Each extract was thus looked at as an individual, unique incident of use – but also inspected for exemplifying patterns that we can extrapolate to be present in other situations.

OVERVIEW OF RESULTS AND DATA

Our 12 participants recorded 168 hours and 21 minutes worth of video, from 34 days of recording. Each participant recorded on average just over 14 hours of video (with min 5hrs 29 min and max of 22hrs 15 minutes). These videos contained 1009 incidents of watch use. The range of watch use went from 1.5 per hour to 8.6 per hour, with a mean of 5.4 per hour. Watch use was on average 6.7 seconds long (max=205s, min=0.2s, median=2s). Clearly this is very different from the 38 seconds median usage for smartphones [7].

We can examine individual incidents of watch use by the app used, as outlined in Figure 2. The use of the watch is dominated by checking the time – making up 50% of watch

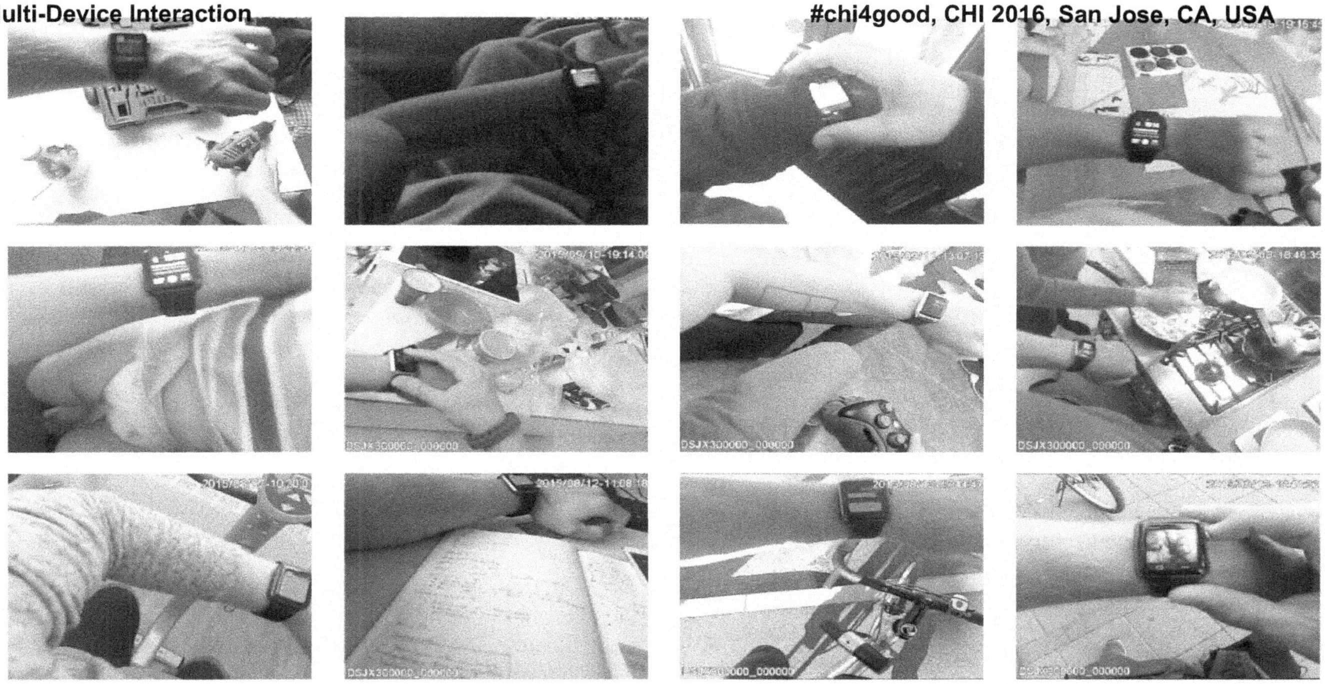

Figure 3: Diversity of smartwatch use, from left to right: Stepping down from a chair to read a notification while drilling, reading a message in bed, notification on getting off a bus, checking time during a child's art project, breastfeeding, cooking, playing an Xbox game, cooking, exercise bike, working, reading a message on bike, viewing Instagram while waiting outside supermarket.

uses. The time spent glancing at the watch was relatively short, though, averaging only 1.9 seconds, and this means that of the total time using the watch, checking the time drops to 14.4%. So while basic time functionality is important it is not as dominant as might first appear.

Notifications came second at 17% of usage, with a longer duration of 6.7 seconds. After clips where the watch is not visible (7%) the Workout Timer and Notification Centre come next ("Notification centre" refers to the Apple Watch's interface for managing notifications). Non-Apple third party applications make up a low amount of usage – only 1%. In terms of notifications, Messages was the most popular at 34%. Activity was the second most common notification at 20%. Other notifications came from non-Apple apps (20%), non-visible applications (16%), Mail (4%), phone calls (1%) and Timer (5%). However, these percentages come from a fairly small sample of only 170 notifications.

WHAT IS THE WATCH USED FOR?

Our detailed video data affords, however, not only an overview on smartwatch use but also the ability to understand in detail how the smartwatch is used in particular situations. Figure 3 illustrates this with frames taken from different situations of use: cooking, childcare, travelling, sleeping. Perhaps not surprisingly, a wearable supports multi-activity [19] both sequentially and simultaneously. Having access to the audio/visual recording of each of these moments of interaction allows us to begin to understand not just what the watch was used for, but why. In this section, we look at the most prominent uses for the watch in turn: Timekeeping, Notifications, Activity Tracking, and Applications.

Time

Just as phone calls are an essential role of the smartphone, so the smartwatch is used to tell the time. Glancing at a watch face can also be a potential site for information beyond the time. So, an initial question we asked was: why look at the time?

Prospection, retrospection, and 'scalloping'

From activity around watch looking, we can differentiate between *prospective* and *retrospective* checking of the time. Prospective is looking forward to an event or time that has some relevance to what you are doing now. So, for example, participants would look at their watch when they got onto a train or bus as part of their daily commute, calculating when they would arrive. In Figure 4 (left), one participant has put on a load of washing, and will need to go and move the washing to the dryer at a set time. Looking at their watch then lets them look prospectively into the future, calibrating their sense of time of current action with what is planned. In this example our participant must return to the task of washing at a set time in the future. Ceci [10] described this as strategic time-monitoring with three distinct phases: calibration where a cluster of clock-checking calibrates an individual's psychological clock, an

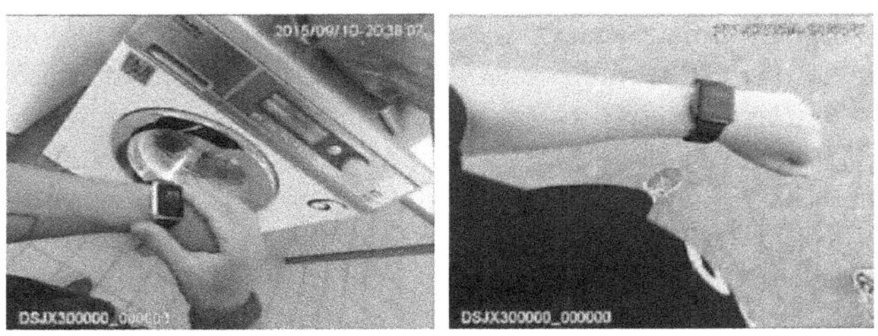

Figure 4: Prospective and retrospective time

intermediate phase of reduced clock-checking where other tasks can be performed, and what they called a "scalloping phase" wherein the frequency of clock-checking increases as the deadline approaches. We noticed that this would often happen in bursts during incidents of focal attention (such as working at a laptop, or reading). While looking at the watch is hardly a strenuous activity, it does involve a defocusing from the task at hand, and a slight physical movement. Clock watching can perhaps be seen as an indication that attention is waning from the primary task.

In contrast, looking at the watch *retrospectively* involves reflecting on how much time has elapsed. This can be done specifically, by looking at the watch face as in Figure 4 (right), or referentially, by reflecting on time as it makes itself known in the currently visible outcomes of its passing. In Figure 4 we see a participant who is going on a run and has started a workout timer on their watch. In this case, they checked the watch on four occasions during the run, each time looking at the time to see how long had passed.

Smartwatches can display more information than just the time: six of our participants chose the 'modular' watch face which displayed activity circles, weather, date, calendar entries, alarms, timers, and world clocks customisable by the user. So, in many cases there is a range of possible pieces of information that are being consulted. However, checking the time was a particularly short event, and while the user may have gathered other information – such as if there were waiting notifications (indicated by a red dot on the top of the screen) – time spent looking at the time was only 3.8 seconds on average.

Notifications

We now look at the second most dominant function of the smartwatch by the frequency of interactions in our data. *Notifications* are interesting in that unlike clock-checking the action is initiated by the watch (in the form of a haptic and/or audio notification). This can either be ignored or responded to by a user. With the Apple Watch we gave our participants, lifting their wrist within 5 seconds of the incoming message will show the notification instead of the watch face. It is not entirely clear from the data how many notifications are ignored (since this is not a visible action), although our participants in the interviews mentioned that notifications were usually read immediately on their receipt.

One important question concerning notifications is how much they interrupt activity. This has been an issue which has motivated much discussion. For example, prior work on smartphones in classrooms has found damaging effects on educational outcomes, and there has been considerable discussion of the costs of interruption on task resumption [61]. One immediate focus of our analysis, then, was to find examples of notifications interrupting or disrupting an on-going activity. As can be seen in Figure 3, clearly the watch is used in a range of different settings, while participants are engaged in a variety of different activities. Some activities took place in so called "dead time" [52] such as commuting on public transport, waiting for service, or in queues of different sorts. Other activities such as cooking, cleaning, and personal hygiene, while not 'dead time' were at least interruptible without much damage to the activity itself. Indeed, despite the HCI focus on the damage that disruptions cause, in our videos it appeared that little damage was done to the activities being carried out by the short watch interactions that we recorded. One possibility is that, in actuality, much of our daily activity is interruptible at little cost. If we look at some of the tasks being undertaken during watch notifications – doing the washing, reading a newspaper, drilling a hole in the ceiling – these were tasks that have natural breaks within the task (such as getting back down off the chair to fetch another part, or getting to the end of a story). Moreover, since they may not be particularly cognitively challenging undertakings, interruption may come at a relatively low cost, weighed against the possible (projected) benefits of reading the notification. Activities already feature micro-breaks and self-interruptions [1], and a watch notification might provide an opportunity to take a break from a task. Work done on micro-breaks in data entry [23] and crowdsourcing [60] has identified the potency of breaks of three seconds and longer in intensive tasks.

Text messages

Text messaging has been a longstanding use of mobile phones from SMS to IM, and it has gained recent renewed attention with the popularity of services such as WhatsApp and iMessage [47]. Receiving text messages on the watch is not an entirely different experience from a phone, although our participants talked about how when wearing the watch text messages would be read much quicker than when they were received on the phone, since any message coming in would trigger a notification and then, potentially, a quick glance at the watch to read the message. What impact does reading messages slightly earlier have on text messaging? Drawing on our data, we could see three potential advantages. The first was the ability to quickly triage incoming notifications, and possibly reply to those that were urgent, or could be quickly replied to using canned messages or emoticons. This allowed the wearer to attend *less* to the messages and notifications they deemed a lower priority than their current task – foregoing the action of taking out the phone to check the sender or content – while still giving sufficient attention to what they considered higher priority messages. This means less engagement with the phone, and therefore less physical disengagement from the current task and chance of the check of a notification to be sidetracked by the plethora of other apps. As one participant put it:

> *I think I reduced my phone time by I would estimate around 60%. I would see the messages and I wouldn't maybe reply directly to them.*

So something that would take a discrete amount of time on the phone could be done in small bursts throughout the day, potentially during activities where a small rest from the main task would be beneficial, or alternatively where the current engagement could easily be interrupted. Indeed, while we saw relatively little *replying* to messages on the watch (only 13 cases), messages were frequently read, and (as one participant put it in the interview), relevant answers composed before being later entered and sent on the phone:

> *I would wait a while so I could think about them. [...] I think in general I was better in answering my text messages [..] It was easier to answer them quicker than before. I could wait an hour or two to answer.*

This increase in the speed with which incoming messages are noticed by the recipient also has the result of raising expectations on the part of the sender. Our participants talked about how senders expected that messages would now get a quicker response, adding to the already prevalent social pressure to be reachable and connected at all times.

Activity tracking

Perhaps the most mentioned application from our interviews was the activity tracking software. The watch passively tracks activity as well as allowing users to explicitly log exercise. This was used to produce a running log of steps taken, calories burnt, and hours where the user stood, visualised as circles that showed completion towards a set goal. Our participants used the built in Workout application as well as more specialised ones for particular activities, such as running.

These applications provided information during and after exercise. They present the time elapsed during a particular session of exercise, and time until a particular goal. The watch also supplied exercise information during other daily activities (through step counts) and prompted users to stand up to break up sedentary periods. The Activity application provided an overview of the day in terms of time and activity, too, and this feature supplied a new retrospective outlook on a day – echoing that seen by people using other quantified self technologies. When asking about this in the interview, we obtained explanations that were not unlike those discussed above for the use of the time – prospective and retrospective purposes. The prospective purpose of looking at the 'rings' of completed activity was to see what activity might need to be put into the day to be able to meet the goals of completing the rings and hitting the exercise goal. On a daily basis, then, activity could be added to a day when necessary. Alternatively, there was a retrospective purpose of looking at the activity in that it offered a short overview of the participant's day. While this was only in terms of physical activity, it was still enough to support reflection on the day. While our data is suggestive then that the smartwatch did have a positive influence on physical activity it must be noted that we only have data from a short period of use.

Talking to the Watch

With recent improvements in the quality of speech recognition [26, 30], one feature of the watch that we were interested to see in practice was the use of speech recognition to interact with the devices' intelligent agent. This allows a user to speak commands to the watch, as well as have messages transcribed to be sent. Speech recognition is a challenging function for any device, although clearly it has considerable potential for a device such as a watch where free-text entry is not available.

We have only a very small number of incidents from our participants involving the use of Siri (17 or 2% of usage). Siri seemed to divide our participants, with most saying that they would never use it, but others claiming to be occasional users. While such a small set of examples is not heavily indicative, eight of our extracts involved setting a timer, and five sending a message. For the timer examples, Siri seemed to set the timer correctly in the cases we saw. It had less success with messages: in one case it incorrectly cropped the message that was being sent before its second sentence, and the participant had to use their voice to send a second message. In another case, the participant attempted twice to transcribe a message saying that she was going to a friend's house. The second attempt resulted in laughter at the proposed transcription and the user abandoning the watch to reply on the phone. Previous work on speech has discussed how participants format their voice and interaction to be "machine listenable" – attempting to talk in a format that they think will be more appropriate for the recognition algorithm [64]. This might extend to the tasks which the speech system was used for, in that setting a timer is a fairly straightforward recognition task. When we asked participants why they did not make greater use of Siri, explanations were given in terms of its low accuracy rate. This might be something of a hangover from earlier speech systems, or alternatively the lower accuracy obtained while the system trains itself to the speaker. Despite recommendations in the literature [65], there are no speech correction features supported in Siri, and this means that if a speech command has a fatal mistake, it must be repeated in total.

Other Applications

As we conducted the study, the Apple Watch was a relatively new device – and although it had managed to collect a surprisingly large library of applications, the actual software development kit restricted considerably the functions that an application could carry out on the watch. This said, most of our participants had tried to make use of a third party application. Notable third party apps used by our participant included Instagram, Twitter, Nike Plus, and various news applications. They still accounted for only a very small 2% of the interactions we recorded with the device. Notifications were an exception to this proportion. Notifications from non-watch apps are still displayed on the watch, and this means that any application that displays notifications on the phone can have a lightweight partial interface on the watch. 20% of notifications (34) received on the watch were from non-Apple applications.

THE WATCH IN EVERYDAY LIFE

Our analysis so far has given us an overview of some of the basic functions of the watch and how it was used. Our videos, however, let us examine in more depth the role of the watch in everyday activities. As with any new device, the smartwatch finds its home not simply by meeting particular user goals, but rather in how it is a "thread in the complex tapestry of everyday interaction" [6].

The Materiality of the Smartwatch

One of the most interesting aspects of the watch was the physical role that the watch played in action. Here, we will look at the role the watch plays on the body, and as another physical device to be managed and maintained by users.

On the Wrist, not in the Hand

The body-mounted nature of the device obviously makes it different from a phone. In a straightforward way the watch is more *convenient*, even if it has more limited functionality than other, larger devices. If we were to attempt an expanded description, we might describe the materiality of the watch, in how the way it is physically designed to sit on your wrist enables a set of interactions with the body and the world. Indeed, in Ferreira and Hook's [25] ethnography of phone use amongst Pacific Islanders, they describe how, in that setting, the prevalence of water mandates a different orientation to mobile devices and the physical environment. Islanders make use of their phones for messaging and the like, but since much of their life is spent in or above water, the use of their phones was different from those of us who live on dry land. This reminds us that our own orientations of our bodies and hands to mobile technology are not natural or universal but are a product of conventions of use, and the environment we find ourselves in. With the watch then we can see in our videos a similar emergent set of material engagements of body, the watch, and the environment. The watch is 'always there' and can be consulted by simply moving your wrist to bring the watch into your visual frame – the same gesture which triggers the screen. This attachment of the device to the wrist provides a context independent 'look' gesture that will obtain the watch screen in visual range. Interestingly, even though considerable amounts of our participants' time was spent using phones or laptops, both of which have always present clocks in the corner of the screen, the context insensitive familiarity of the gesture would mean that participants would often turn to their watch to get the time.

The always-available nature of the device means that a user did not have to go and find the watch, or take the watch out of a bag or pocket. Interestingly, this seemed to be a particular advantage when participants were at home. In these cases, the phone would likely not be carried around in a pocket, and this meant that using the phone involved going to get the phone. This was made visible in cases where participants received phone call notifications on their watches and would then quickly go to, or search for, the phone in order to answer the call. Few calls were made by participants through the watch. They reported not trusting the quality of the audio they would send to others. When a participant was out of their home or office, the phone would usually be available in a pocket or bag – and we saw cases where a participant gets a message on the watch and then quickly moves to their phone (which was available nearby) to continue the conversation.

If we unpack 'convenience' further, then, it is not only about location but also about the nature of the watch as a wearable device. Having a device mounted on the body means that it can be consulted without having to use one's hands to hold or control a device. In Figure 3, on the first image we can see a participant reading a notification with a power drill in one hand. While interaction with the device does demand a free hand, reading can be done while both hands are occupied. The lack of required hands, combined with the lack of needing to go anywhere to fetch the phone, means that one does not need to physically disengage from an ongoing activity that requires one's body. One example of this is physical exercise – when running or on an exercise bike, consulting the watch can be done while retaining physical involvement in the activity.

While phones can be used in these situations, taking out a phone can potentially create more physical disruption. A watch can interrupt a task with a short notification, and then the task can be continued quickly. This can also be seen in childcare or cooking (Figure 3). In these cases, the task quickly continues after the watch is consulted. Similarly in Figure 5 we can see a cooking activity involving a couple, where one grates cheese. The cheese grating only takes a few seconds during which the alarm goes off on the other person's watch. The watch user consults their watch, dismisses the alarm, then moves the pot of pasta (which the alarm indicated was cooked) off the heat. The watch alarm is elegantly incorporated into the cooking with little or no disruption.

This said, the watch does make some demands for physical interaction. Elements of the screen need to be touched, as well as the watch's controls. Indeed, the watch allowed for two modes of physical interaction. Scrolling or swiping was a function where the accuracy of the gesture was not particularly important and so the device could be held in the air and a finger placed on the screen to control the scrolling.

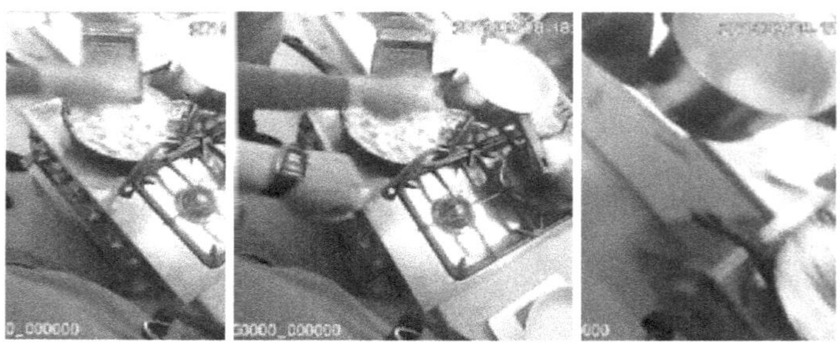

Figure 5: Cooking Pasta

Yet, certain functions of the watch required more fine grained pointing and manipulation – such as picking an application to launch or touching screen controls (choosing a reply to, or dismissing a text message). As Lyons and Profita [40] point out, usage of wearables moves between different physical configurations (which they call 'dispositions') over time. In our data, for closer interaction, the watch would be touched on the side with one or two fingers to stabilise and orient the rest of the hand, and another finger used to make the desired selection. While this was not universally the case, it seemed that placing a 'stabilising' finger on the watch allowed greater accuracy (as can be seen in three of the images in Figure 3). An ongoing panel survey of Apple Watch users has even suggested that the *nose* is a common way of interacting with the watch [69].

Lastly, the nature of our study gave us little data on reactions to the appearance of the watch (although obviously this is an important longstanding role for watches). The novelty of the watch did trigger conversations, as did our participants wearing cameras, but in our interviews participants were ambivalent towards the watch design. Clearly different methods and design work would fit better with examining questions around fashion and the physical design of the watch [33].

The Smartwatch as Screen

One interesting feature resulting from the physical location on the watch on the wrist is its arrangement in the visual field. O'Hara and colleagues present one of the most detailed discussions of the importance of materiality with technology in their discussion of writing from multiple sources [48], and the combination of paper documents with writing documents on screen. Their work clearly points out the importance of the visual field in arranging materials used in writing – such as being able to maintain a writing book alongside paper documents when writing. Back in Figure 3, again, we can see examples where arrays of documents are arranged. In one case a user arranged their credit card, a paper notebook, an iPhone, the keyboard of a desktop computer next to the watch. In that case a banking transaction was being made that required the card number and a text message code. The participant holds up the watch next to the keyboard and looks between the two to type in the code. In other cases we could see how the watch would be held in the visual field so it could be consulted in combination without requiring movement.

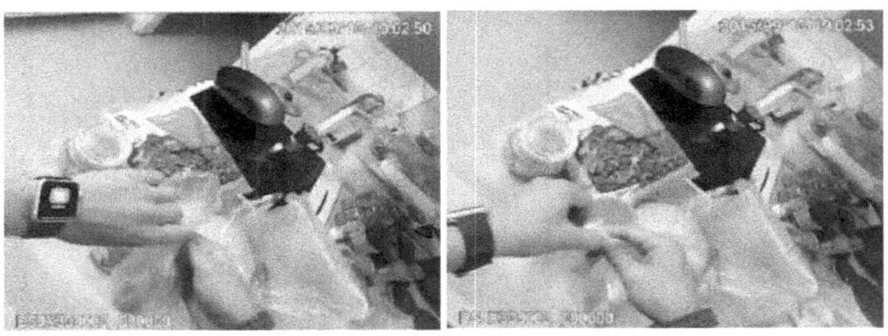

```
W:  It was supposed to be next week
A:  Yeah
W:  But because she has hosted the club
    before so
    many times|                  <<left image>>
A:            |Okah
W:   Emm (1.0) She (0.7) made a big party
     for our school          <<right image>>
                   <<opens bag while speaking>>
```

Figure 6: Checking notification during conversation Numbers in brackets indicate a (timed pause) **in talk**

Earlier research has described the watch as an 'extra screen' for the phone [62]. Indeed, much of the functionality of the Apple Watch relies upon the phone being close by. We did see some cases where use of the watch led directly to use of the phone – particularly in the form of text messages received on the watch that led to a reply being composed on the phone. Around 3% of watch uses were followed by iPhone use. Another combination of devices can be seen in 'second screening' where the smartwatch is another screen added to the already complicated tapestry of multi-device use many people manage on a day-to-day basis [32]. In traditional second screening behaviour, the primary focal device, such as the television, had the waxing and waning attention of the user who shifts to a complimentary – or in some cases unrelated – task on the second device. The cases we saw with the watch were different. When the phone was active for a particular task the participant would move attention to the watch to quickly consult some details without having to change their application on the mobile device. The limited multi-tasking capabilities of mobile devices go some way to explain this, yet we saw participants consulting the watch while using a laptop or a desktop computer simultaneously.

The watch in social interaction

Let us now turn to the place the smartwatch holds in social interaction. As we discussed above, there is potential for the watch to cause disruption, as a source of interruption for conversation and interaction with others. Indeed, some have argued that the smartphone is a disruptive and negative influence on social interaction [56, 58]. In contrast, our past video analytic work has argued for the ways in which smartphones can, rather than interrupting social interaction, actually benefit and initiate conversation by providing topic and being an ongoing agent in conversation [8].

We looked through our videos for situations where social interaction and use of the smartwatch influenced each other. In particular, we sought examples of where social interaction was disturbed by the watch and its notifications; in terms of a delayed response, a hesitation or halt in talk, or a turn that was later repaired where evidence could be found of the notification having a role. To our surprise, we could not find any incidents where talk was disturbed. This could have been a side effect of the data we collected – participants were on their own in 68% of our watch use cases. We found 117 clips, or 18% of watch use, involved conversation while the watch was being used. Figure 6 is one example of a notification coming in and being managed, in that the notification is read while the participant tells a story about the previous night, with the user pausing slightly after they read the notification. Yet, the conversation still continues afterwards. Indeed, while they speak the next turn they simultaneously open a bag of sugar, which may have led to the pauses in talk as much as the notification. This clip also emphasises the complexity of users' everyday activity – here, the participant is talking about last night, arranging some ingredients for cooking, and quickly reading a notification on the watch.

This is not to say that notifications did not influence or potentially disrupt interaction in other subtle ways. In our interviews some participants reflected upon this:

"It's like, something vibrated, I know something happened. I'm curious now, but I don't want to be rude so I'm not going to look. There are two processes, trying to listen to somebody and trying to not listen to your watch."

This temptation and potential distraction was balanced with the possible even greater distortion of using a phone:

"With the watch I also pick it up but it's much faster, so I think a process of check and go is actually better."

"I noticed that myself when my classmate who has an Apple Watch, I don't look at his watch very often but if he'll take up his phone, I would probably"

Visibly interacting with the watch

There is also potential for the device to *positively* contribute to conversation. For example, we saw a case where a news notification was read aloud by the participant – the notification in this case provided a topic of conversation of interest to the couple. Having a watch also means that a participant can use looking at the watch, in conversation, as part of gesturing to or emphasizing a planning or time related task. So, for example, in one clip (Figure 7) a participant is sitting outside having lunch. Before lunch they had mentioned the one pm meeting they had after lunch, and at 12:45 they turn to the watch to look at it, say "I need to get back" and then quickly pack their belongings to leave. To their lunch participants this gesture and exclamation is legible as 'lateness' – and indeed, the others

```
A: What is the time have you kept track of it?
W: [*] Oh quarter to [.] fuck, I need to get back
   (stands up)
B: Can we wait five minutes?
W: I have a meeting with ((my boss))
```

Figure 7: Lunch and meeting (translated from Swedish)

quickly pack up alongside their watch-wearing friend. Yet, in other settings, this gesture could be problematic. We frequently noticed participants checking their watch 'under the table' – in one extract a participant is in a day-long meeting and they frequently discreetly turn their hand under the desk. The watch does not detect this move, however, and the watch does not turn on until the participant touches the watch. The action here is seeable to others as 'looking at my watch', which might impart impatience or boredom.

Usability problems

While we did not conduct an extensive evaluation of the watch's interface it is perhaps worth mentioning that in our clips we do not see much in the way of confusion about the interface with some notable exceptions. Launching apps caused some problems in that users would get quickly lost in the overview of applications, sometimes abandoning the task. The touch screen itself also sometimes caused problems and would not register touches (it is not clear if this was a hardware problem, or a problem with the device becoming unresponsive). Interestingly, swipe gestures were quickly carried out unproblematically, and much of the interactional problems seemed to come from touching buttons. As the work on interaction with small displays has shown, it might be better to support swipe gestures more universally, than relying on having users touching small targets on a moving watch face [50].

For some participants they regularly attempted to turn the watch 'off' after they had finished interacting with it, a little like hitting the power button on a phone. They would do this by hitting the crown button. Yet while in some cases this returns the watch to the time screen (which seemed to fit with the notion of being 'off'), in other cases it would return the watch to the application launch screen and they would hesitate before touching the button again (which would return them to the time).

DISCUSSION

Clearly, the smartwatch in use is not a simple device. As a relatively new form factor it introduces new possibilities and problems. In discussion, we turn to three of these briefly. First, we will consider the broader issue of distraction and activity. Second, we mention the role of the watch, and the pressures of time and sociality. Finally we discuss the design of this generation of smartwatches.

Distractions

One topic we have engaged with in different ways is that of distraction. The link between notification, interruption, and distraction is not as strong as it may appear at first. In HCI, distraction has been a topic that, in its contribution to cognitive models of task activity [5, 67], has shown the challenge of managing interruptions alongside primary tasks. Our study has collected together an interesting corpus of watch notifications during activity. As we have discussed above, it is not clear that these are best understood in terms of interruptions. One alternative approach, growing out of conversation analysis is to use video to look at behaviour in terms of multi-activity. As Haddington *et al* put it "the organisation of multiple tasks and activities is a collective, collaborative and intersubjective process; it relies on participants' finely-tuned coordination practices and on the real-time and *in situ* organisation of joint activities." [19, p6].

Our data, ranging from cooking to multi-party conversation, demonstrates that a short refrain from a conversation or task can be unproblematic. Indeed, many tasks are arranged so that breaks and subtasks are a natural part of their execution. We might remark upon the watches ability to be consulted without changing bodily comportment, or engagement with an activity. So, for example, in cooking or preparing food the physical arrangement of the task need not be changed while a watch is quickly consulted. The watch may simply reduce the need, or temptation, to take the phone out. A notification, which may have caused the phone to sound an alert or vibrate, carries with it the mystery of what is being notified until the phone is retrieved. With the watch the compulsion to find out the source of the notification can be readily sated, and glancing at the watch may be less of a distraction than the cognitive load of wondering about the incoming message and negotiating access to the phone around the current task.

Time and sociality

"I have less patience with someone who doesn't wear a watch than with anyone else, for this type is not time-conscious. In all our deeds, the proper value and respect for time determines success or failure." ([42], p. 392)

A related issue concerns the potential for the watch as a part of the 'cultural norm of busyness' as Leshed and Sengers put it [39]. Certainly there is potential for use of a smartwatch to contribute to stress or unhappiness through the immediacy of notifications, or its use as a technology for intensification of work and life activity. Even the basic wristwatch sits in a long tradition of the clock and the intensification of industrial processes [45]. For the smartwatch we studied it appeared that it was not time as such, but the flood of messages that had the potential of intensification, and while messages were felt to be important they potentially drew participants away from where they were. For these reasons many of our participants were equivocal about the benefits of the device. Yet, this can be balanced by the potential to manage or hold back some temporal and social demand. Indeed, the value of the device may be in its role as an intermediary. The watch can serve as a way of reducing time spent on the phone, and to also balance availability to others with one's own concerns and demands. With a device that is only perhaps at the beginning of its development it is difficult to foresee how it will evolve, but clearly there is the possibility of the watch not as a device which simply renders busyness, but as something that can balance the forces and demands of sociality, leisure and work.

Design and the watch

As an empirical study, we have focused on documenting the uses of the smartwatch. Yet, some design possibilities are worth mentioning in passing. Three of our participants remarked upon the current need for the watch to be close to a phone for its functionality – remarking that the watch would potentially be more useful as a device that could be used when the phone had been left at home.

Considering our discussion of prospective and retrospective time, a watch face might prospectively display time – showing graphically, for example, how long it is until the end of the working day, or even bedtime, or helping concentration by dividing up activities into shorter parts that can be completed. In terms of retrospection, we were interested in how the activity tracker comes to be used not only as a way of looking back at calories and exercise, but also as a record of the day. Similarly, we might think about applications that allow for retrospection. A simple application might, for example, record times spent in different places, or time spent in different activities (such as conversation). Secondly, clearly notifications are a large part of the value of a smartwatch. Yet, notifications as they are currently implemented support only limited interaction. Notifications have the potential to at least support some broader forms of interaction – for example using voice to give a command after a notification has been read or using a hand gesture to answer a notification.

More broadly, we have discussed and demonstrated at length the ways in which the watch supports a form of 'task embeddedness' in that watches can be used without disturbing tasks that are in motion. Advice given to designers of smartwatch apps broadly has been focused on designing quick and simple interaction — and our results here do nothing to question this aim. Yet, a broader set of possibilities might exist in thinking about not only how as smartwatch might be used to enhance a task. For example, furniture assembly instructions could be given while construction was in progress.

CONCLUSION

In this paper, we have opened up the use of the smartwatch, drawing on naturalistic video recordings from 34 days of use across twelve participants. We have used these recordings to document the ways in which the smartwatch is integrated into participants' lives, and the possibilities for assistance but also disruption. From our data we have seen that the materiality of the watch lends itself well to its perceived role as a companion device for the mobile phone – providing quick, unobtrusive, and less disrupting access to incoming information. While it is early in its development, in a similar way that talk of the 'smartphone' has given way to simply talking about 'the phone' perhaps the term 'smartwatch' will disappear as wrist-mounted technology creates a place for itself on the wrist.

REFERENCES

1. Rachel F Adler and Raquel Benbunan-Fich. 2013. Self-interruptions in discretionary multitasking. *Computers in Human Behavior*, 29 (4). 1441-1449. DOI: 10.1016/j.chb.2013.01.040
2. Deepak Akkil, Jari Kangas, Jussi Rantala, Poika Isokoski, Oleg Spakov and Roope Raisamo. 2015. Glance Awareness and Gaze Interaction in Smartwatches. in Proceedings of the 33rd Annual ACM Conference Extended Abstracts on Human Factors in Computing Systems, ACM, 1271-1276. DOI: 10.1145/2702613.2732816
3. Patrick Baudisch and Gerry Chu. 2009. Back-of-device interaction allows creating very small touch devices. in Proceedings of the SIGCHI Conference on Human Factors in Computing Systems, ACM, 1923-1932. DOI: 10.1145/1518701.1518995
4. Dennis B. Beringer. 1984. Caculator Watches as Data Entry Devices: The Fundamental Things Apply as Time Goes by. *Proceedings of the Human Factors and Ergonomics Society Annual Meeting*, 28 (3). 253-257. DOI: 10.1177/154193128402800313
5. Jelmer P. Borst, Niels A. Taatgen and Hedderik van Rijn. 2015. What Makes Interruptions Disruptive?: A Process-Model Account of the Effects of the Problem State Bottleneck on Task Interruption and Resumption. in Proceedings of the 33rd Annual ACM Conference on Human Factors in Computing Systems, ACM, Seoul, Republic of Korea, 2971-2980. DOI: 10.1145/2702123.2702156
6. Barry Brown, Moira McGregor and Eric Laurier. 2013. iPhone in vivo: video analysis of mobile device use. in Proceedings of the SIGCHI Conference on Human Factors in Computing Systems, ACM, DOI: 10.1145/2470654.2466132
7. Barry Brown, Moira McGregor and Donald McMillan. 2014. 100 days of iPhone use: understanding the details of mobile device use. in Proceedings of the 16th international conference on Human-computer interaction with mobile devices & services, ACM, Toronto, ON, Canada, 223-232. DOI: 10.1145/2628363.2628377
8. Barry Brown, Moira McGregor and Donald McMillan. 2015. Searchable Objects: Search in Everyday Conversation. in Proceedings of the 18th ACM Conference on Computer Supported Cooperative Work & Social Computi, ACM, Vancouver, Canada., 508-517. DOI: 10.1145/2675133.2675206
9. Marta E Cecchinato, Anna L Cox and Jon Bird. 2015. Smartwatches: the Good, the Bad and the Ugly? in Proceedings of the 33rd Annual ACM Conference Extended Abstracts on Human Factors in Computing Systems, ACM, 2133-2138. DOI: 10.1145/2702613.2732837
10. Stephen J Ceci and Urie Bronfenbrenner. 1985. "Don't Forget to Take the Cupcakes out of the Oven": Prospective Memory, Strategic Time-Monitoring, and Context. *Child development*. 152-164. DOI: 10.2307/1130182
11. Jae-Min Cha, Eunjung Choi and Jihyoun Lim. 2015. Virtual Sliding QWERTY: A new text entry method for smartwatches using Tap-N-Drag. *Applied ergonomics*, 51. 263-272. DOI: 10.1016/j.apergo.2015.05.008
12. Wei-Hung Chen. 2015. Blowatch: Blowable and Hands-free Interaction for Smartwatches. in Proceedings of the 33rd Annual ACM Conference Extended Abstracts on Human Factors in Computing Systems, ACM, 103-108. DOI: 10.1145/2702613.2726961
13. Hyeonjoong Cho, Miso Kim and Kyeongeun Seo. 2014. A text entry technique for wrist-worn watches with tiny touchscreens. in Proceedings of the adjunct publication of the 27th annual ACM symposium on User interface software and technology, ACM, 79-80. DOI: 10.1145/2658779.2658785
14. Kate Crawford, Jessa Lingel and Tero Karppi. 2015. Our metrics, ourselves: A hundred years of self-tracking from the weight scale to the wrist wearable device. *European Journal of Cultural Studies*, 18 (4-5). 479-496. DOI: 10.1177/1367549415584857
15. Mary Czerwinski, Edward Cutrell and Eric Horvitz. 2000. Instant messaging and interruption: Influence of task type on performance. in OZCHI 2000 conference proceedings, 361-367.
16. Mark D Dunlop, Andreas Komninos and Naveen Durga. 2014. Towards high quality text entry on smartwatches. in CHI'14 Extended Abstracts on Human Factors in Computing Systems, ACM, 2365-2370. DOI: 10.1145/2559206.2581319
17. Grace de la Flor, Paul Luff, Marina Jirotka, John Pybus, Ruth Kirkham and Annamaria Carusi. 2010. The Case of the Disappearing Ox: Seeing Through Digital Images to an Analysis of Ancient Texts. in Proceedings of the 28th international conference on Human factors in computing systems, ACM, Atlanta, Georgia, USA, 473-482. DOI: 10.1145/1753326.1753397
18. Wayne C. W. Giang, Inas Shanti, Huei-Yen Winnie Chen, Alex Zhou and Birsen Donmez. 2015. Smartwatches vs. smartphones: a preliminary report of driver behavior and perceived risk while responding to notifications. in Proceedings of the 7th International Conference on Automotive User Interfaces and Interactive Vehicular Applications, ACM, Nottingham, United Kingdom, 154-161. DOI: 10.1145/2799250.2799282
19. Pentti Haddington, Tiina Keisanen, Lorenza Mondada and Maurice Nevile. 2014. *Multiactivity in social interaction. Beyond multitasking*. John Benjamins Publishing Company.

20. Christian Heath, Jon Hindmarsh and Paul Luff. 2010. *Video in Qualitative Research*. SAGE.
21. Christian Heath and Paul Luff. 2000. *Technology in action*. Cambridge university press.
22. Christian Heath, M S Svensson, J Hindmarsh and P Luff. 2002. Configuring awareness. *Computer Supported Cooperative Work (CSCW)*, 11 (3). 317-347. DOI: 10.1023/A:1021247413718
23. Robert A Hennfng, Steven L Sauter, Gavriel Salvendy and Edward F Krieg JR. 1989. Microbreak length, performance, and stress in a data entry task. *Ergonomics*, 32 (7). 855-864. DOI: 10.1080/00140138908966848
24. Niels Henze, Enrico Rukzio and Susanne Boll. 2011. 100,000,000 taps: analysis and improvement of touch performance in the large. in Proceedings of the 13th International Conference on Human Computer Interaction with Mobile Devices and Services, ACM, 133-142. DOI: 10.1145/2037373.2037395
25. Tony Hey and Anne Trefethen. 2003. The Data Deluge: An e-Science Perspective. in *Grid Computing: Making the Global Infrastructure a reality*, John Wiley & Sons, Ltd 809--824.
26. Geoffrey Hinton, Li Deng, Dong Yu, George E Dahl, Abdel-rahman Mohamed, Navdeep Jaitly, Andrew Senior, Vincent Vanhoucke, Patrick Nguyen and Tara N Sainath. 2012. Deep neural networks for acoustic modeling in speech recognition: The shared views of four research groups. *Signal Processing Magazine, IEEE*, 29 (6). 82-97.
27. Christian Holz and Patrick Baudisch. 2010. The generalized perceived input point model and how to double touch accuracy by extracting fingerprints. in Proceedings of the SIGCHI Conference on Human Factors in Computing Systems, ACM, 581-590. DOI: 10.1145/1753326.1753413
28. Christian Holz and Patrick Baudisch. 2011. Understanding touch. in Proceedings of the SIGCHI Conference on Human Factors in Computing Systems, ACM, 2501-2510. DOI: 10.1145/1978942.1979308
29. Jonggi Hong, Seongkook Heo, Poika Isokoski and Geehyuk Lee. 2015. SplitBoard: A Simple Split Soft Keyboard for Wristwatch-sized Touch Screens. in Proceedings of the 33rd Annual ACM Conference on Human Factors in Computing Systems, ACM, 1233-1236. DOI: 10.1145/2702123.2702273
30. Xuedong Huang, James Baker and Raj Reddy. 2014. A historical perspective of speech recognition. *Communications of the ACM*, 57 (1). 94-103.
31. Shamsi T Iqbal and Eric Horvitz. 2007. Disruption and recovery of computing tasks: field study, analysis, and directions. in Proceedings of the SIGCHI conference on Human factors in computing systems, ACM, 677-686. DOI: 10.1145/1240624.1240730
32. Tero Jokela, Jarno Ojala and Thomas Olsson. 2015. A Diary Study on Combining Multiple Information Devices in Everyday Activities and Tasks. in Proceedings of the 33rd Annual ACM Conference on Human Factors in Computing Systems, ACM, 3903-3912. DOI: 10.1145/2702123.2702211
33. Oskar Juhlin. 2015. Digitizing fashion: software for wearable devices. *interactions*, 22 (3). 44-47.
34. Amy K Karlson, Benjamin B Bederson and John SanGiovanni. 2005. AppLens and launchTile: two designs for one-handed thumb use on small devices. in Proceedings of the SIGCHI conference on Human factors in computing systems, ACM, 201-210. DOI: 10.1145/1054972.1055001
35. Andreas Komninos and Mark Dunlop. 2014. Text input on a smart watch. *Pervasive Computing, IEEE*, 13 (4). 50-58.
36. Sven Kratz and Michael Rohs. 2009. HoverFlow: expanding the design space of around-device interaction. in Proceedings of the 11th International Conference on Human-Computer Interaction with Mobile Devices and Services, ACM, 4. DOI: 10.1145/1613858.1613864
37. John Krumm, Gerry Cermak and Eric Horvitz. 2003. Rightspot: A novel sense of location for a smart personal object. in (Dey, A., Schmidt, A. and McCarthy, J. eds). *UbiComp 2003: Ubiquitous Computing*, Springer Berlin Heidelberg, 36-43.
38. Luis Leiva, Matthias Bhömer, Sven Gehring and Antonio Krüger. 2012. Back to the app: the costs of mobile application interruptions. in Proceedings of the 14th international conference on Human-computer interaction with mobile devices and services, ACM, San Francisco, California, USA, 291-294. DOI: 10.1145/2371574.2371617
39. Gilly Leshed and Phoebe Sengers. 2011. I lie to myself that i have freedom in my own schedule: productivity tools and experiences of busyness. in Proceedings of the SIGCHI Conference on Human Factors in Computing Systems, ACM, 905-914. DOI: 10.1145/1978942.1979077
40. K. Lyons and H. Profita. 2014. The Multiple Dispositions of On-Body and Wearable Devices. *Pervasive Computing, IEEE*, 13 (4). 24-31. DOI: 10.1109/MPRV.2014.79
41. Kent Lyons. 2015. What can a dumb watch teach a smartwatch?: informing the design of smartwatches. in Proceedings of the 2015 ACM International Symposium on Wearable Computers, ACM, 3-10. DOI: 10.1145/2802083.2802084
42. X Malcolm, Alex Haley and MS Handler. 1992. *The autobiography of Malcolm X*. Ballantine Books New York.

43. Thomas L Martin. 2002. Time and time again: Parallels in the development of the watch and the wearable computer. in Wearable Computers, 2002.(ISWC 2002). Proceedings. Sixth International Symposium on, IEEE, 5-11. DOI: 10.1109/ISWC.2002.1167212

44. Donald McMillan, Moira McGregor and Barry Brown. 2015. From in the wild to in vivo: Video Analysis of Mobile Device Use. in Proceedings of the 17th International Conference on Human-Computer Interaction with Mobile Devices and Services, ACM, 494-503. DOI: 0.1145/2785830.2785883

45. Lewis Mumford and Langdon Winner. 2010. *Technics and civilization*. University of Chicago Press.

46. Michael Nebeling, Anhong Guo, Alexandra To, Steven Dow, Jaime Teevan and Jeffrey P Bigham. 2015. WearWrite: Orchestrating the Crowd to Complete Complex Tasks from Wearables. in UIST '15 Adjunct Proceedings of the 28th Annual ACM Symposium on User Interface Software & Technology, ACM, 39-40. DOI: 10.1145/2815585.2817782

47. Kenton P. O'Hara, Michael Massimi, Richard Harper, Simon Rubens and Jessica Morris. 2014. Everyday dwelling with WhatsApp. in Proceedings of the 17th ACM conference on Computer supported cooperative work & social computing, ACM, Baltimore, Maryland, USA, 1131-1143. DOI: 10.1145/2531602.2531679

48. Kenton P. O'Hara, Alex Taylor, William Newman and Abigail J. Sellen. 2002. Understanding the materiality of writing from multiple sources. *International journal of human-computer studies*, 56 (3). 269-305.

49. Ian Oakley and Doyoung Lee. 2014. Interaction on the edge: offset sensing for small devices. in Proceedings of the SIGCHI Conference on Human Factors in Computing Systems, ACM, 169-178. DOI: 10.1145/2556288.2557138

50. Stephen Oney, Chris Harrison, Amy Ogan and Jason Wiese. 2013. ZoomBoard: a diminutive qwerty soft keyboard using iterative zooming for ultra-small devices. in Proceedings of the SIGCHI Conference on Human Factors in Computing Systems, ACM, 2799-2802. DOI: 10.1145/2470654.2481387

51. Pekka Parhi, Amy K Karlson and Benjamin B Bederson. 2006. Target size study for one-handed thumb use on small touchscreen devices. in Proceedings of the 8th conference on Human-computer interaction with mobile devices and services, ACM, 203-210. DOI: 10.1145/1152215.1152260

52. M. Perry, K. O'Hara, A. Sellen, B. Brown and R. Harper. 2001. Dealing with Mobility: Understanding access anytime, anywhere. *ACM Transactions on computer human interaction*, 8 (4). 323-347.

53. Martin Pielot, Karen Church and Rodrigo de Oliveira. 2014. An in-situ study of mobile phone notifications. in Proceedings of the 16th international conference on Human-computer interaction with mobile devices & services, ACM, 233-242. DOI: 10.1145/2628363.2628364

54. Christian Piguet. 2002. The First Quartz Electronic Watch. in (Hochet, B., Acosta, A. and Bellido, M. eds). *Integrated Circuit Design. Power and Timing Modeling, Optimization and Simulation*, Springer Berlin Heidelberg, 1-15.

55. Frederic Pollmann, Dirk Wenig and Rainer Malaka. 2014. HoverZoom: making on-screen keyboards more accessible. in CHI'14 Extended Abstracts on Human Factors in Computing Systems, ACM, 1261-1266. DOI: 10.1145/2559206.2581173

56. Andrew K Przybylski and Netta Weinstein. 2013. Can you connect with me now? How the presence of mobile communication technology influences face-to-face conversation quality. *Journal of Social and Personal Relationships*, 30 (3). 237-246.

57. Reza Rawassizadeh, Blaine A Price and Marian Petre. 2014. Wearables: has the age of smartwatches finally arrived? *Communications of the ACM*, 58 (1). 45-47.

58. James A Roberts and Meredith E David. 2016. My life has become a major distraction from my cell phone: Partner phubbing and relationship satisfaction among romantic partners. *Computers in Human Behavior*, 54. 134-141.

59. Anne Roudaut, Stéphane Huot and Eric Lecolinet. 2008. TapTap and MagStick: improving one-handed target acquisition on small touch-screens. in Proceedings of the working conference on Advanced visual interfaces, ACM, 146-153. DOI: 10.1145/1385569.1385594

60. Jeffrey M Rzeszotarski, Ed Chi, Praveen Paritosh and Peng Dai. 2013. Inserting micro-breaks into crowdsourcing workflows. in First AAAI Conference on Human Computation and Crowdsourcing,

61. F. Sana, T. Weston and N.J. Cepeda. 2012. Laptop Multitasking Hinders Classroom Learning for Both Users and Nearby Peers. *Computers & Education*

62. Steven Schirra and Frank R Bentley. 2015. It's kind of like an extra screen for my phone: Understanding Everyday Uses of Consumer Smart Watches. in Proceedings of the 33rd Annual ACM Conference Extended Abstracts on Human Factors in Computing Systems, ACM, 2151-2156. DOI: 10.1145/2702613.2732931

63. Mark T Smith. 2007. Reconciling ICT and Wearable Design: Ten Lessons from Working with Swatch. *The Role of Design in Wearable Computing*, 16

64. Hagen Soltau and Alex Waibel. 1998. On the influence of hyperarticulated speech on recognition performance. in ICSLP-98. International Conference on Spoken Language Processing,

65. Bernhard Suhm, Brad Myers and Alex Waibel. 1996. Interactive recovery from speech recognition errors in speech user interfaces. in Spoken Language, 1996. ICSLP 96. Proceedings., Fourth International Conference on, IEEE, 865-868. DOI: 10.1109/ICSLP.1996.607738

66. Melanie Swan. 2012. Sensor Mania! The Internet of Things, Wearable Computing, Objective Metrics, and the Quantified Self 2.0. *Journal of Sensor and Actuator Networks*, 1 (3). 217.

67. J Gregory Trafton and Christopher A Monk. 2007. Task interruptions. *Reviews of human factors and ergonomics*, 3 (1). 111-126.

68. Wouter Van Vlaenderen, Jens Brulmans, Jo Vermeulen and Johannes Schöning. 2015. WatchMe: A Novel Input Method Combining a Smartwatch and Bimanual Interaction. in Proceedings of the 33rd Annual ACM Conference Extended Abstracts on Human Factors in Computing Systems, ACM, 2091-2095. DOI: 10.1145/2702613.2732789

69. Daisuke Wakabayashi. 2015. Apple Watch Users Discover Another Way to Go 'Hands Free'. Retrieved December, 27, 2015 from http://www.wsj.com/articles/nosy-apple-watch-users-discover-another-way-to-go-hands-free-1451077454

70. Junjue Wang, Kaichen Zhao, Xinyu Zhang and Chunyi Peng. 2014. Ubiquitous keyboard for small mobile devices: harnessing multipath fading for fine-grained keystroke localization. in Proceedings of the 12th annual international conference on Mobile systems, applications, and services, ACM, 14-27. DOI: 10.1145/2594368.2594384

71. Robert Xiao, Gierad Laput and Chris Harrison. 2014. Expanding the input expressivity of smartwatches with mechanical pan, twist, tilt and click. in Proceedings of the SIGCHI Conference on Human Factors in Computing Systems, ACM, 193-196. DOI: 10.1145/2556288.2557017

When Tablets meet Tabletops: The Effect of Tabletop Size on Around-the-Table Collaboration with Personal Tablets

Johannes Zagermann[1], **Ulrike Pfeil**[1], **Roman Rädle**[1], **Hans-Christian Jetter**[2], **Clemens Klokmose**[3], **and Harald Reiterer**[1]

[1]HCI Group, University of Konstanz,
{johannes.zagermann,ulrike.pfeil,roman.raedle,harald.reiterer}@uni.kn
[2]University of Applied Sciences Upper Austria, hans-christian.jetter@fh-hagenberg.at
[3]Department of Computer Science, Aarhus University, clemens@cs.au.dk

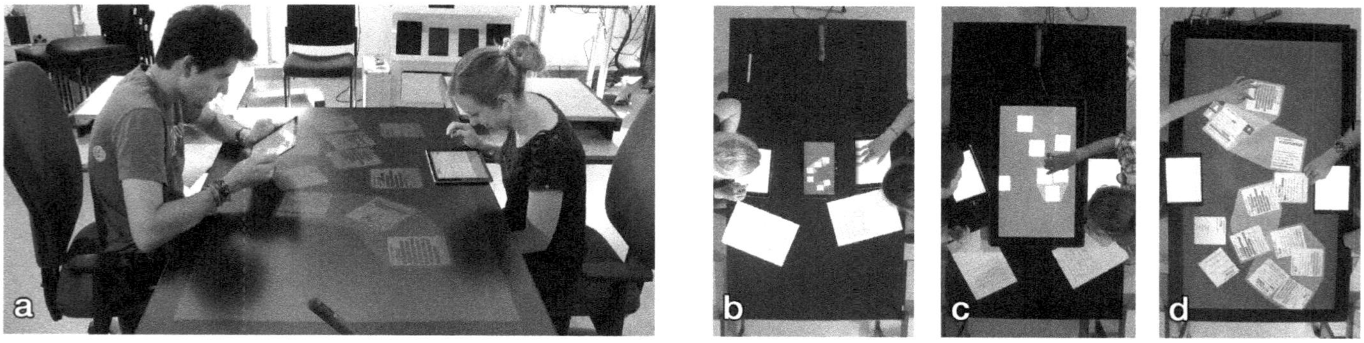

Figure 1. Setting of the study (a) and bird's-eye views on the three tabletop sizes 10.6″(b), 27″(c), and 55″(d).

ABSTRACT

Cross-device collaboration with tablets is an increasingly popular topic in HCI. Previous work has shown that tablet-only collaboration can be improved by an additional shared workspace on an interactive tabletop. However, large tabletops are costly and need space, raising the question to what extent the physical size of shared horizontal surfaces really pays off. In order to analyse the suitability of smaller-than-tabletop devices (e.g. tablets) as a low-cost alternative, we studied the effect of the size of a shared horizontal interactive workspace on users' attention, awareness, and efficiency during cross-device collaboration. In our study, 15 groups of two users executed a sensemaking task with two personal tablets (9.7″) and a horizontal shared display of varying sizes (10.6″, 27″, and 55″). Our findings show that different sizes lead to differences in participants' interaction with the tabletop and in the groups' communication styles. To our own surprise we found that larger tabletops do not necessarily improve collaboration or sensemaking results, because they can divert users' attention away from their collaborators and towards the shared display.

Author Keywords

cross-device interaction; group work; tabletops; tablets; display size

CHI '16, May 07–12, 2016, San Jose, CA, USA
© 2016 ACM. ISBN 978-1-4503-3362-7/16/05...$15.00
DOI: http://dx.doi.org/10.1145/2858036.2858224

ACM Classification Keywords

H.5.3 Information Interfaces and Presentation (e.g. HCI): Collaborative Computing

INTRODUCTION

Tabletops can greatly benefit collaborative activities such as visual analytics, search, and sensemaking [6, 9, 13], mainly because of enabling natural face-to-face communication around a shared workspace [7], providing a high level of awareness and fluid interaction [5, 19], and supporting natural territoriality during collaboration [21]. However, a large tabletop is also costly and difficult to maintain compared to other common off-the-shelf devices such as tablets. This is particularly true for environments like libraries or classrooms in which tabletops are often unavailable due to budget and space restrictions whereas tablets are quite common. Some researchers therefore aim at natural cross-device interaction and sensemaking with mobile devices *instead of* tabletops [10, 4, 17], while Tang et al. [22] recommend combining mobile devices *with* tabletops. Such combined cross-device systems (e.g. [11, 14, 18, 23]) are thought to be helpful for *mixed-focus collaboration* [3, 22] where users frequently transition from tightly-coupled collaboration to loosely-coupled parallel work, e.g., for reading or annotating a document or reviewing a long list of items on their own. Indeed, Wallace et al. [23] observed that in such scenarios the presence of a tabletop (39″) leads to better sensemaking performance than with tablets alone. To better understand why, we closely studied the effect that three tabletops with different sizes had on users' attention, awareness, and efficiency during cross-device mixed-focus collaboration. Investigating these effects enabled us to understand size-related advantages and disadvantages and to compare large tabletops with lower-cost, smaller-than-tabletop devices that could potentially serve as alternatives. We conducted an experimental study of a collaborative sensemaking task that was executed by 15 groups of two users with two personal tablets (9.7″) and a shared workspace. We varied the size of the shared workspace over three conditions corresponding to off-the-shelf devices (10.6″ tablet, 27″ portable tabletop, and 55″ large tabletop). To observe authentic collaboration during the study, we built a collaborative multi-device application for solving a complex analytical task based on the "Stegosaurus" data set from the VAST 2006 Challenge [16].

Our goal for the study was to better understand the implications of the size of the shared space and to contribute a nuanced description of its role in collaborative sensemaking activities. We address this overall research question by investigating the following subquestions both qualitatively and quantitatively:

- RQ1: How does the size of the tabletop affect users' interaction with the devices?
- RQ2: How does the size of the tabletop affect the communication between the participants?
- RQ3: Does the size of the tabletop affect group awareness, the quality of the results of the group work, and participants' satisfaction with the support by the system?

RELATED WORK

There are multiple studies in HCI and CSCW of how different physical affordances of interactive technology affect co-located collaboration, e.g. studies examining different tabletop sizes [20], different orientations (vertical vs. horizontal) [19], or different input modalities (touch vs. mouse) [5]. These studies pursued the goal of understanding how the physical affordances of a technology affect the kinds of cognitive and social interactions that will result, e.g. accessibility, visibility, 'sharability', etc. [19]. Our study follows this tradition of research and shares the goal of studying the effect of different affordances on co-located collaboration.

Understanding Affordances & Tabletop Collaboration

Rogers and Lindley [19] compared collaborative problem-solving around horizontal tabletops with collaboration at large vertical screens. They found that tabletops made it easier for all members to contribute to the problem-solving, encouraged group members to swap roles more often, and to explore more alternative solutions. Ryall et al. [20] compared collaborative word-puzzle solving with different tabletop sizes (80 cm vs. 107 cm diagonal) and group sizes (2-4 members). Their study revealed that users preferred a large tabletop for this particular task, but that size had no effect on completion time and the distribution of work. Interestingly, Ryall et al. mention that examining size-related issues for multi-device and mixed-surface interaction should be part of future work.

Morris et al. [12] provide a survey of collaborative search on tabletops and identify benefits of tabletops such as face-to-face collaboration that encourages more equal working styles than shoulder-to-shoulder situations. However, they mention that orientation of content on tabletops is an issue that could be solved with additional devices like tablets that enable e.g. text input or reading of documents.

Tang et al. [22] analyzed collaboration in tabletop settings with groups of two. In two studies they identified different coupling styles during *mixed-focus collaboration* [3] that range from closely coupled collaborative situations to loosely coupled parallel work activities. To support the latter, Tang et al. recommend providing mobile high resolution personal territories (e.g. tablet PCs or PDAs) as an addition to the horizontal shared surface of the tabletop.

This related work on physical affordances and size-related issues for multi-device/cross-device interaction serves as a motivation for our study and for better understanding the role of tabletops of different sizes in mixed-focus collaboration.

Tablets and Tabletops

With the growing popularity of cross-device and multi-device interaction, researchers have proposed working with multiple mobile devices instead of a tabletop. Lucero et al. [10] have introduced several cross-device mobile applications for seamless collaboration across smartphones, e.g., for photo sharing. Hamilton and Wigdor [4] propose Conductor, a system facilitating multiple tablets for single-user analytical sensemaking. Like we did in our study, they used the VAST 2006 data set to study the use of their system. They found that users used between 5-10 tablets for their task and that the parallel and combined use of the tablets was found to be highly useful.

Other systems have explored a close integration of mobile interaction with tabletops, e.g., for visual exploration [11], for sensemaking [23], for discussing and annotating work results in a science lab [14], or for collaborative Web search in schools [18]. McGrath et al.'s Branch-Explore-Merge system uses a private view on a tablet and a public view on a tabletop for collaborative visual exploration [11]. Private and public views are coupled using a branch-explore-merge protocol similar to revision control systems for source code, so that the results of individual explorations on the tablets can be merged back into the group results at any time. Wallace et al.'s prototype system was used to study collaborative sensemaking with only tablets, only a tabletop, or a combination of both [23]. They found that the presence of a tabletop led to improved sensemaking performance and supported a group's ability to prioritize information, to make comparisons between task data, and to form and critique the group's working hypothesis. They also found a positive correlation with equity of member participation using the shared digital table and a negative correlation of equity of member participation using personal tablets. Albeit similarities in system functionality like document transfer from tablet to tabletop and vice versa, the key difference between their work and our investigation is the variation of tabletop size as an independent variable as compared to tabletop being present or not.

This related work, in particular Wallace et al. [23], inspired varying table size as an independent variable during a study. We hereby contribute a better understanding of the nuances of the role of the tabletop during collaborative sensemaking.

Studies Using VAST 2006 Challenge Data

HCI, CSCW, and InfoVis researchers have long been interested in understanding the benefit of tabletops or tablets for sensemaking. For this reason, many used the data and tasks from the VAST 2006 Challenge to observe authentic sensemaking activities during a controlled and sufficiently demanding task. The VAST 2006 Challenge was developed by the National Visual Analytics Center at Pacific National Labs and can be considered a standardized visual analytics task [16]. Andrews et al. [1] have used it to analyze how a large high-resolution display affects the use of space and working styles. Hamilton et al.'s tablet-based sensemaking system Conductor was also studied using VAST 2006 data [4]. Isenberg et al.'s Cambiera used the same data to study collaboration activities in tabletop settings for dyads and identified different coupling styles describing the groups' activities [6]. Jakobsen and Hornbæk used VAST data on high-resolution wall displays to study co-located collaboration [8]. Their system resembled Cambiera and they found that a wall display also supports various coupling styles and can be used to observe them and their relation to the proximity of participants.

In the light of this extensive use of the data and tasks of the VAST 2006 Challenge for studying (collaborative) sensemaking, we also chose to use them for our study.

STUDY

In order to investigate the effect of tabletop size on collaborative cross-device sensemaking, we designed and implemented a multi-device system that enabled groups to search, read, and make sense of documents from a database. The system served as experimental platform for observing (close to) authentic collaborative behavior. Obviously, the use of a specific system with a particular interaction design influences user behavior and thus restricts the extent to which we can generalize from our findings to all collaborative tasks and systems. We discuss such limitations in greater detail later.

Pre-Study

Our research questions, our study design, and the system design were informed by a pre-study. It was conducted with an earlier version of our system, where 15 pairs were asked to work on a general search-related group task. Already the very initial analysis of the collected video data indicated that the efficiency gain from a larger display was far smaller than expected – or even negative. In order to look into this phenomena more systematically, we refined our system for the main study and focused the UI and study design on our identified sub-topics: the interaction with the devices (RQ1), the communication activities (RQ2), and the quality of group work results and users' satisfaction with system support (RQ3).

Task

To provide a documented, authentic, and sufficiently demanding collaborative sensemaking task, we used the "Stegosaurus" data from the VAST 2006 Challenge [16] that was already used by [1, 4, 6, 8]. VAST 2006 describes a fictional story with 238 news articles, images, and data sheets. Groups have to search and find relevant information from this data, filter non-important articles, and connect important facts that lead to new insights and suppositions in order to come up with a solution to a hidden plot. The task involves solitary activities like searching for and reading relevant information as well as group activities like sharing and sorting relevant documents in order to solve the case. The task is difficult enough to require participants to work together for an extended period of time (we limited it to 90 minutes).

We did not expect groups to completely solve the task within the time frame. However, participants were handed questions about the plot at the beginning of each session to focus their behavior and stimulate an authentic collaboration.

System Description

Our system supported groups during phases of solitary and collaborative work. On their tablets, participants could execute full text searches in the VAST 2006 data by typing one or more keywords into a search box. Search results were presented in a ranked list (right tablet in Figure 2). Each item in this list represented a document and contained a document ID for clear verbal reference, a preview of sentences that contained the keyword(s), and icons indicating whether a document was already read, favored, or edited before. To access the document users tapped on the respective search list item to open a document view (left tablet in Figure 2). This view enabled them to read and highlight text in a document, add comments to it, share it on the tabletop, or send it directly to the tablet of their group partner on which the document then was also displayed in a document view. Each participant was assigned with an individual color (green or yellow). This color-coding was used for the background-color of their tablet, as the highlight-color of selected parts of documents, and as an indicator for the origin of each shared document.

Figure 2. Overview of the system with two tablets and one tabletop.

Shared documents appeared on the tabletop in boxes containing the document ID, an excerpt of its content, and buttons for document-related actions (tabletop in center of Figure 2). The possible actions enabled participants to reread documents on their personal tablet or to remove documents from the tabletop. Each box was additionally marked with a bookmark icon with a participant's color to indicate who shared the document. Boxes could be moved and rotated freely on the tabletop to allow for spatial arrangements or to form tableaux to embody the groups working hypotheses [23]. Multiple boxes could be grouped into visual clusters using touch input to encircle them with a lasso. This created a colored convex hull around the selected boxes as a visual grouping. This hull remained around the boxes and its shape was updated whenever the boxes were rearranged by participants. For a rapid exchange of information users could send documents to the tablet of the other group member. Adding documents to the tabletop enabled users to externalize ideas, store documents for later use and to create a common ground for group communication. Clustering of snippets helped to find connections between relevant events, persons, and places. The color-coding provided a visual connection between the participants, their tablets, and their contributions to the tabletop.

Apparatus

Figure 1a shows the study setup, which consisted of a conventional office table (1.4 × 0.8 m) on which the tabletop that served as the shared space was placed. For the study, we chose three multi-touch devices of different sizes as tabletops (Figure 1b, c, and d): 10.6″ (Microsoft Surface 2 Pro), 27″ (Lenovo Horizon), and 55″ (Microsoft Perceptive Pixel). Each of them represented a typical size for a personal mobile device, a personal workspace, and a multi-user workspace. All three devices had the same display resolution of 1920 x 1080 pixels to guarantee for a higher internal validity of the study.

The two participants sat on office chairs and were facing each other. Each one was provided with an Apple iPad 2 (9.7″) as their tablet. Next to each participant was a small mobile desk for filling out the questionnaire and as a space for notes or to place the tablet.

We used two cameras to record the study. One camera was installed with a bird's-eye view above the table (Figure 1 right) and a second camera recorded the scene from the side to be able to see gestures, postures, and interactions of both participants (Figure 1 left).

Participants

30 participants (15 female, 15 male) were recruited for the experiment. The mean age was 22.4 years (SD = 2.9, aged 15-28). 29 participants were right-handed and one left-handed. None of the participants had color vision deficiency, consequently they had no problems with the employed color-coding. 25 participants were undergraduate students and 4 participants PhD students from non-technical subjects such as psychology, biology, or politics. One participant did not answer this question. To recruit the participants we used postings and flyers looking for "detectives". By this we hoped to find participants who were interested in puzzles, crime stories, or mysteries and thus were motivated by the VAST 2006 data and task. We assigned five groups of two participants to each tabletop size. Two groups were both female, two were both male, and one group was mixed. Group members did not know each other and had not worked together before.

Procedure

We chose a between-subjects design with the tabletop size as independent variable with three conditions (10.6″, 27″, 55″). In total, we investigated five pairs in each condition resulting in 15 pairs and 30 participants respectively. Like Isenberg et al., we chose a group size of two, because in their study two group members working on VAST 2006 were already sufficient to identify differences in coupling styles and collaboration strategies [6].

At the beginning of each study participants were seated at the two mobile desks. They were asked to fill out a questionnaire about demographics and tech-savviness. Then they were seated facing each other on the long sides of the table. Participants received an introduction into all features of the system and were given time to explore its functionality with a sample data set until they felt comfortable enough using it. The experimenter then introduced them to the VAST 2006 task. During the 90 min. session, they could look up task instructions at any time on their tablet or on a printed sheet of paper. The experimenter answered general questions about the procedure or prototype but did not answer questions about participants' performance or how to solve the given task. Participants were free to move the mobile desks and office chairs as desired. The session stopped after 90 min or when participants felt that they had solved the case and found the plot. Then, both group members were asked to individually fill out a second questionnaire about their findings about the plot. Finally, we conducted a short semi-structured interview in order to ask participants about the strategy that they employed during the task and how much they felt that the system supported their activities. Each session lasted about 2 hours in total, and afterwards participants were compensated for their time.

DATA ANALYSIS

We employed several data collection methods in order to investigate our research question: We gathered video data in order to analyze participants' group work behavior, data logs in order to analyze and quantify participants' interactions with the included digital devices, and a questionnaire and interviews in order to investigate participants' results of group work and to what extent participants felt supported by the system.

Video Data

To address the subtopics of our research questions, we developed a coding scheme to analyze our video data. Doing so, we placed the focus on participants' interaction with devices, their communication behavior, as well as the object they focused on during the task. After initial viewings of our videos, we started to describe and distinguish between different codes that apply to our research questions as well as offering a sound description of the video data. This coding scheme was refined until we felt that it was saturated. After this, an inter-coder reliability test was conducted for three 10 minute samples of video data to ensure objective coding by our two independent coders. Cohen's Kappa was calculated individually for the categories Focus ($\varkappa$ = 0.96), Communication ($\varkappa$ = 0.85), and Interaction ($\varkappa$ = 1.0), revealing a high intercoder reliability in each category for the final coding scheme that is presented below.

0.0 Focus: In order to investigate where participants placed their visual focus during the task, we distinguish between the codes *0.1 Tablet*, *0.2 Tabletop*, *0.3 Person* and *0.4 Other*

1.0 Communication: To analyze the extent to which participants were talking, we code *1.1 Talk* and *1.2 Silence*. Utterances and mumblings were coded as *1.2 Silence*.

2.0 Interaction: To investigate participants' interaction with the tabletop, we code *2.1 add document* for sending documents from the tablet to the tabletop, *2.2 delete document* for deleting documents from the tabletop, *2.3 move document* for moving documents to another place on the tabletop as well as *2.4 cluster documents* for participants' activities to collect documents in a cluster in order to sort them.

We used the coding scheme for both qualitative and quantitative investigation. In our qualitative analysis, the creation of the coding scheme helped us to elicit the main aspects of the group work. Also, it allowed us to focus on specific subparts of the video for a more detailed observation. We could, for example, only view sequences when participants where focusing on the table in order to further investigate this event by describing its context and related events in more detail. In addition, we also calculated the frequencies and durations for the coded events in order to investigate how the qualitative findings are reflected in the quantitative data.

Data Logs

In addition to the video data, we also collected logs of users' interaction with the system. We logged the number of document manipulations (e.g. move) on the tabletop and how often documents were transferred from the tabletop to a tablet or vice versa. We also logged the number of times a document was transferred from one tablet to another. We did this in order to analyze whether the tabletop size had an effect on how and how often users interacted with documents.

Questionnaire and Interview

We used a questionnaire with questions about the solution (i.e. plot) of the VAST 2006 challenge to understand (1) the quality of the group results based on individual answers to the questions and (2) the extent to which group members had the same knowledge of their results and solutions to the task. Also, we concluded each session with a semi-structured interview focusing on group strategies when working on the task and to what extent participants felt supported by the system.

FINDINGS & DISCUSSION

In this section we report on our findings and discuss them in relation to our research questions. In particular, we focus on the differences across the three different sizes of the tabletop (SMALL: 10.6″, MEDIUM: 27″, LARGE: 55″) with respect to users' interaction with the devices (RQ1), the group's communication activities (RQ2), and the differences regarding user perceptions and the quality of group work results (RQ3). For each research question, we elaborate on specific subtopics based on our qualitative observations and interview data. Quotes from participants in the following section were slightly modified to prevent publishing the solutions of the VAST 2006 Challenge tasks.

In addition, we report our quantitative results in relation to our observations. In our analysis, we employed a mixed-effects models approach to analyze individual scores taking participants' group membership as an additional source of variance into account. We used the nmle package by Pinheiro and Bates [15] for R.

RQ1: Findings on Device Interaction

To answer RQ1, we distinguish between three different aspects of the participants' interactions with devices that could be influenced by the size of the tabletop: (1) participants' visual focus and attention, (2) participants' frequency of searching and transferring documents, and (3) participants' manipulation of documents on the tabletop.

Focus and Attention

In our qualitative analysis of video data, we observed that participants used the system mostly as we expected and intended in all three conditions. They used the tablets for searching or reading activities and the tabletop for collecting and grouping documents. But we also observed the following differences between the conditions: Participants in the SMALL condition used the tabletop in a more goal-oriented fashion and only focused on it when actively using it. In comparison, participants in the LARGE condition stayed visually focused on the tabletop even during phases of reflection or for visually scanning over shared documents. Interestingly, this was notable even during phases that did not require visual focus on the tabletop (e.g. when reflecting about next steps) but during which the tabletop apparently attracted most participants' visual attention. For example, participants sometimes looked at and "played" with documents on the tabletop (i.e. playfully moving them back and forth with their fingers without the intention of actually reordering them) while thinking about how to proceed with the task and even while verbally coordinating next steps with their partner ("What could we search for that we don't already have on the table?") or reflecting on the progress so far ("What do have we already? How is all this related?").

In contrast, participants in the SMALL condition were visually focusing on and directly referring to their group partner when they were reflecting or coordinating their activities (e.g. one participant who was finished reading a document on his tablet looked up and directly addressed his group partner: "Did you find anything yet?"). These observations are also reflected in our quantitative results. Table 1 shows the average percentage of the session time that participants focused on the tablet, tabletop, group member, and other objects across the three conditions.

Our analysis revealed no overall statistically significant effect of "focus on other person" ($F(2,12) = 2.74$, $p = .10$). But as Table 1 shows, participants using the small tabletop focused three times longer on the other person (14% of the time) than participants using the large tabletop (4% of the time). With a statistically significant difference between LARGE and SMALL ($b = 9.77$, $t(12) = 2.22$, $p < .05$). There were, however, no statistically significant differences for this

	Focus on Tablet	**Focus on Tabletop**	**Focus on Person**	Focus on other
SMALL	71.47 (SD=9.57)	6.40 (SD=2.32)	14.21 (SD=10.06)	7.92 (SD=2.83)
MEDIUM	77.27 (SD=7.62)	5.69 (SD=2.36)	8.77 (SD=6.11)	8.27 (SD=3.91)
LARGE	78.37 (SD=4.97)	9.57 (SD=2.64)	4.43 (SD=2.25)	7.63 (SD=3.38)

Table 1. Mean percentage of time that participants focused on tablets, tabletop, other persons, or other objects. Statistically significant differences ($p<.05$) are shown in bold.

between the SMALL and MEDIUM conditions and no statistically significant differences between the MEDIUM and LARGE conditions.

The analysis also shows statistically significant differences for "focus on tabletop" ($F(2,12) = 6.50$, $p < .05$) between LARGE and SMALL ($b = -3.17$, $t(12) = -2.63$, $p < .05$) and LARGE and MEDIUM ($b = -3.88$, $t(12) = -3.21$, $p < .05$). Participants using the LARGE tabletop focused almost twice as long on the tabletop (10% of the time) than in the MEDIUM condition (6% of the time). There were, however, no statistically significant differences for this between the SMALL and MEDIUM conditions. Focusing on other things (e.g. on the information sheet or just looking around) happened to the same extent in all conditions.

Finding 1.1. Our results show that participants' visual attention in cross-device settings can be drawn towards a large tabletop, even in situations where there is no pragmatic reason to focus on the tabletop. This can result in non-"face-to-face" verbal communication without eye contact between collaborators. On the contrary, a small tabletop received less visual attention and was used in a more goal-oriented fashion. Users did not "play" with objects on the small tabletop and focused significantly longer on their collaborator.

The choice of the size of a tabletop should therefore not been taken too lightly. Larger does not necessarily mean better. Depending on the context of use, it can be desirable to increase eye contact within a group, (e.g., to build trust in collaborators or creating a sense of intimacy) or to increase the focus on the shared tabletop (e.g. to support collaborative activities).

Search and Transfer

Our qualitative data revealed differences in the strategies that participants employed to access documents across the conditions. We observed that participants worked more *filing-oriented* in the LARGE condition and more *search-oriented* in the SMALL condition.

By *filing-oriented* we mean that the tabletop served as a space to collect, file, and pile found documents in space and to use visual and spatial cues to quickly access and then transfer documents to the tablets. We observed that the large tabletop display was used as external memory and "space to think" as described in [1].

By *search-oriented* we mean that even after a found document was filed or piled on the tabletop, participants frequently accessed these previously found documents by repeated searches with the tablet using memorized keywords rather than looking up documents on the tabletop and sending them to the tablets.

We found evidence for these two different strategies in our video data (e.g. one user commented "I will just search for 'basement' - this will get me the document about the groundskeeper." Another user asked "Where did we put the documents with the wine export?" while trying to find a document on the tabletop). However, we could not directly confirm these findings with a quantitative analysis. For this analysis we attempted to use the number of document transfers across devices as indicators for the two strategies. We distinguished between (1) the transfer of documents from a tablet to the tabletop, (2) the transfer of documents from the tabletop to a tablet, and (3) the transfer of documents between tablets. We expected that a filing-oriented strategy should lead to more frequent tabletop-to-tablet transfers than a search-oriented strategy.

	Tablet to Tablet	Tablet to Tabletop	Tabletop to Tablet
SMALL	3.3 (SD=4.76)	6.2 (SD=2.94)	12.6 (SD=8.06)
MEDIUM	5.1 (SD=5.09)	6 (SD=3.74)	14.3 (SD=10.41)
LARGE	1.3 (SD=1.25)	6.5 (SD=3.21)	23.7 (SD=12.6)

Table 2. Document transfers across devices per participant.

Table 2 shows the mean number of document transfers per participant across the three conditions. The results show differences, but none are statistically significant. There is only a non-significant tendency that the larger the tabletop, the more documents were generally transferred from tabletop to tablet (e.g. almost twice as many in condition LARGE than in condition SMALL).

Finding 1.2. There was qualitative evidence in our data that a larger tabletop affords more spatial and visual organization schemes for digital content, which is also considered one of the key qualities of large high-resolution displays [1] or tabletops [9] for sensemaking.

Nonetheless, we observed how users skillfully used the search function and memorized keywords to successfully compensate for the lack of space on a medium-size or small tabletop. This is noteworthy, since (as we discuss later) there was no significant difference in the objective quality of group results for the different tabletop sizes.

Document Manipulation

During video analysis, we found that document manipulation differed across the three conditions. As mentioned above, participants in the SMALL condition used the tabletop in a very goal-oriented fashion, primarily for quick collection and organization of documents. In contrast, participants in the LARGE condition did not always interact purposefully with documents but tended to "play" with documents by moving them on the tabletop. Participants also spent a lot of time browsing and arranging the content of the tabletop while seemingly getting sidetracked from the task at hand. This could imply that the larger tabletop affords a more spatial, but also more playful and serendipitous interaction with the documents, while the smaller tabletop affords a limited but more goal-oriented interaction.

In Table 3, we summarize our quantitative analysis of participants document manipulation on the tabletop. It shows the mean number of different manipulations (*add*, *delete*, *move*, *cluster*) per session.

	Add	Delete	**Move**	Cluster
SMALL	5.1 (SD=2.43)	0.6 (SD=0.80)	9.7 (SD=6.12)	4.1 (SD=2.84)
MEDIUM	5.8 (SD=3.74)	1.5 (SD=1.20)	9.7 (SD=6.72)	2.5 (SD=3.26)
LARGE	5.8 (SD= 2.75)	0.9 (SD=0.94)	21.7 (SD=14.51)	2.8 (SD=1.72)

Table 3. Mean number of different manipulations of documents on the tabletop per session. Statistically significant differences (p<.05) are shown in bold.

The analysis shows how tabletop size did indeed affect the number of document movements on the tabletop. It revealed a significant effect of the number of *move*-manipulations ($F(2,12)$ = 3.98, p <.05) between LARGE and SMALL (b = -12.0, $t(12)$ = -2.32, p <.05) and LARGE and MEDIUM (b = -12.0, $t(12)$ = -2.32, p <.05).

Participants in the LARGE condition moved documents almost twice as often as participants working with MEDIUM or SMALL while there were no significant differences in *add*, *delete*, or *cluster*. This hints at a more exploratory working style with frequent rearrangements of documents and a more playful style of interaction.

Finding 1.3. Based on our qualitative and quantitative analysis, we found that a larger tabletop can invite a more explorative or playful interaction with objects on the tabletop that is also reflected in a significantly higher number of movements. Other kinds of manipulations (e.g. clustering) showed no statistically significant differences.

This more frequent movement of objects is not necessarily connected to purposeful rearrangement of objects in space for sensemaking. Instead, larger tabletops seem also to invite more playful and serendipitous interactions that happen between and during the actual goal-oriented manipulations or conversations.

RQ2: Findings on Communication Activities

Our analysis differentiates between the *amount* of communication and *characteristics* of communication. Both are discussed in the following.

Amount of Communication

Our qualitative observations indicate that the amount of communication differs across the three conditions. The larger devices seemed to attract and hold attention and reduce verbal communication.

For example, we observed that participants in the SMALL condition often explicitly dedicated time to engage in communication with their group partner. Doing so, they would lean back in their chairs and shift their attention to the other participant and away from the devices. This "leaning back" was intended for signaling readiness to communicate to the other group member. Typically this was followed by direct verbal communication about the current results and the next steps. It occurred during group work, when participants stepped out of their current activity in order to reflect on the work done so far and think about next steps. Thus it can be regarded as an active measure to create group awareness.

In the LARGE condition, participants only rarely took the time to directly address their group partner without focusing on the tabletop. They reflected on their work not by directly addressing their group partner but through activities mediated by the tabletop such as browsing and rearranging the content on the tabletop. This was not necessarily accompanied by verbal communication.

	Talk
SMALL	16.51 (SD=9.03)
MEDIUM	13.68 (SD=4.95)
LARGE	8.39 (SD=4.68)

Table 4. Percentage of time that participants were talking to each other.

The differences in the amount of verbal communication were also part of our quantitative analysis. Table 4 shows the percentage of time that participants were talking as opposed to being silent during the session. Participants talked most in the SMALL condition (16% of the time) and least in the LARGE condition (8% of the time). However, the analysis revealed that the differences were not statistically significant ($F(2,12)$ = 2.55, p = .12) with p = 0.057 for LARGE vs. SMALL being only marginally greater than .05 (b = 8.12, $t(12)$ = 2.11).

Finding 2.1. Based on our qualitative analysis, we found that participants talked more and more directly to each other when using a small tabletop than when using a large tabletop. We observed that this face-to-face talk seemed to be more important when using a smaller tabletop and that participants introduced phases exclusively dedicated to verbal communication for coordinating actions and creating awareness. This suggests that verbal communication was used to compensate for a smaller shared space that provided less overview and only allowed for less effective deictic references. However, a quantitative analysis did not reveal a statistically significant difference in the total amount of communication.

Characteristics of Communication

In order to investigate what mediates communication across the three conditions, we analyzed where participants were looking while they were talking to each other.

Based on our video observations, we also found differences in communication with respect to how participants used deictic references by pointing to documents on the tabletop for elaborating their arguments. For example, participants working with the large tabletop were often already engaged in sensemaking discussions while they were interacting with the documents on the tabletop. This was also reflected in the prevalence of deictic references that accompanied their communication. For instance, "What do we have here? We have the groundskeeper cleaning the basement (participant *pointing* at the tabletop), we have the event at the town hall (*pointing*), and the sick grandparents (*pointing*). How could these three be related?" In the MEDIUM and LARGE condition the two group work activities *structuring documents on the tabletop* and *talking about and making sense of the gathered information* blended into each other and participants frequently switched between them. When group partners talked during such activities, this happened often without eye-contact between the collaborators and was mediated by the tabletop.

In contrast, the two activities *structuring documents on the tabletop* and *talking about and making sense of the gathered information* rarely overlapped in the SMALL condition. After participants clustered the documents on the tabletop according to document topic, they would disengage from the tabletop and address their group partner in order to reflect on the information. For example, one participant was silently clustering documents on the tabletop while the other participant was reading a document on his tablet. Once the participant was finished with his sorting activity, he withdrew from the tabletop, rubbing his face, and addressing his partner by saying: "Let's think about what we have so far," upon which his partner looked up and they started a discussion about the information that they have read and found so far without using deictic references.

Our quantitative results confirm these differences for the visual focus. Table 5 shows the average percentage of the session time that participants focused on the tablet, tabletop, group member, and other objects while talking. Results indicate that participants mostly focused on their tablet while talking. This is not surprising and lies in the nature of the task, in which the tablets were the source of the information that participants wanted to convey to their partner. For instance, they looked at it to read important information aloud or to verify that their contribution was correct.

	Talk & Focus Tablet	**Talk & Focus Tabletop**	Talk & Focus Person	Talk & Focus Other
SMALL	49.27 (SD=10.13)	11.53 (SD=6.65)	29.76 (SD=15.41)	9.44 (SD=4.66)
MEDIUM	53.73 (SD=11.53)	12.33 (SD=8.08)	24.96 (SD=11.92)	8.98 (SD=5.07)
LARGE	49.36 (SD=14.84)	24.61 (SD=8.88)	18.11 (SD=7.60)	7.92 (SD=5.00)

Table 5. Individuals' focus while talking. Statistically significant differences ($p<.05$) are shown in bold.

Our analysis revealed a significant effect on the time participants focused on the tabletop while talking ($F(2,12) = 8.03$, $p < .05$) for LARGE and SMALL ($b = -13.08$, $t(12) = -3.39$, $p < .05$) and LARGE and MEDIUM ($b = -12.27$, $t(12) = 3.18$, $p < .05$). In the LARGE condition, participants focused almost twice as long on the tabletop (24.6%) than in the MEDIUM (12.33%) or SMALL condition (11.53%). In addition, Table 5 also shows that participants in the SMALL condition focused more on the other person while talking, whereas participants in the LARGE condition focused more on the tabletop than on the other person.

> **Finding 2.2.** Our data shows that the large tabletop attracted the visual attention of group members during verbal communication. It also enabled a close integration of actively structuring and manipulating items on the tabletop with talking about and making sense of the items including the use of deictic references.
>
> This close integration did not happen for the small tabletop where active structuring and talking rarely overlapped. Instead these activities happened sequentially with frequent phases that were exclusively dedicated to verbal face-to-face communication (including eye contact) without interacting with the tabletop.

RQ3: Findings on User Perceptions and Group Results

We analyzed data from our interviews and questionnaires to understand (1) participants' collaboration strategies during group work, (2) participants' satisfaction with the system support, and (3) the objective quality of the results of group work.

Group Strategy and Awareness

Concerning collaboration strategies, participants in the SMALL condition reported that they had not explicitly distributed tasks among themselves. Rather they worked mostly solitarily while keeping their group partner informed about their current progress. They also stated that most of the time they were aware of their group partners' activities and that "there was no need to communicate the strategy – only findings needed to be communicated." They stated that their main focus was on reading and that clustering and sorting on the small tabletop was considered as taking "too much time."

Participants in the MEDIUM condition reported that they occasionally distributed tasks among each other, but that a more explicit assignment of subtasks would have improved group work. Despite the division of labor, they were mostly aware of their partner's activities, but they sometimes needed to ask their partner for a progress update ("What are you currently working on?") to actively create group awareness.

In the LARGE condition, participants stated that they frequently distributed tasks among themselves. They also reported that they were only partially aware about their group partner's activities, but some awareness was mediated by the tabletop. Clustering and sorting activities were perceived to help them in sensemaking and reflection. One participant said: "If I didn't know how to proceed, I just looked at the table."

User Satisfaction with System Support

Participants in the SMALL condition valued the support for direct document transfer between tablets and the highlighting function to emphasize important parts of a document. They were also satisfied with the ability to cluster documents. Other advantages of the tabletop were not mentioned. They reported that they did not divide the tabletop into personal and group territories [21], but, in contrast, explicitly valued the clear distinction between personal activities on the tablet and shared activity on the tabletop (as suggested by Tang et al. [22]).

Participants in the MEDIUM condition mainly valued the tabletop as an information and memory pool that allowed them to quickly access relevant documents. Furthermore, they reported using the space in order to sort documents thematically. Most of them stated that they were satisfied with the size of the table, however some mentioned that a larger tabletop might have allowed for additional personal spaces on the interactive table.

Finally, participants in the LARGE condition explicitly stated their appreciation of the tabletop as an efficient but also playful way of accessing documents, while providing a good overview. They additionally stated that they divided the tabletop into different areas that they used to distinguish between kinds of documents. For example, one group reported that they "stuck all the unimportant stuff in the corner and focused on the main documents of the plot in the center of the table" which resonates with the observations of Andrews et al. about sensemaking on large screens [1]. Participants used the tabletop to structure documents and to compare them with documents displayed on the tablets. Furthermore, they valued being able to work on the tabletop simultaneously and reported the interaction with the system to be fun. Regarding the size of the display, participants were satisfied and positively reported that it even allowed them to have a personal territory on the shared table as well. Some of the participants expressed a wish to also have a reading function on the tabletop in addition to that on the tablet.

Results of Group Work

To assess the results of the participants' group work we asked them to fill out a questionnaire about facts on the plot they were investigating. This questionnaire consisted of nine multiple-choice questions. In total, participants were able to get 44 points, depending on their answers.

Table 6 summarizes participants' general performance across the three conditions as well as the level to which they agreed on an answer irrespective of whether it was right or wrong. For the Performance Score significance was tested based on individual scores using the mixed-effects model approach. For the Conformity Score we applied a one-way ANOVA based on group scores that show how consistent the group partners performed.

The results show no statistically significant differences for the Performance Score or for the Conformity Score. This lets us conclude that in all three conditions the participants were provided with sufficient support and flexibility to establish successful collaboration styles and strategies. Neither the system nor the task unfairly privileged one condition compared to another.

	Performance Score	Conformity Score (p=.187)
SMALL	83% (36.5 / 44 - SD 4.86)	81.8% (36.0 / 44 - SD 3.08)
MEDIUM	76% (33.3 / 44 - SD 3.67)	73.6% (32.4 / 44 - SD 2.3)
LARGE	76% (33.3 / 44 - SD 5.16)	76.8% (33.8 / 44 - SD 3.27)

Table 6. Mean Performance Scores (mixed-effects model, based on individual scores) and Levels of Conformity per group (one-way ANOVA, based on group scores).

The qualitative analysis of how participants made use of the different tabletop sizes confirms the benefit that is usually attributed to large displays or tabletops for increased awareness [13, 19] or for spatial sensemaking [1, 6]. The appreciation of the large tabletop by participants and the desire for a larger tabletop by the participants in the MEDIUM condition fit into this picture and resonate with earlier findings about the desire for more space during around-the-table collaboration [20]. The positive attitude towards a clear separation between private territories on mobile devices vs. group territories on tabletops is in accordance with earlier work on territories and coupling styles around tabletops [21, 22].

However, we found it surprising how the subjective preference for larger tabletops was not reflected in the objective quality of the results of the group work. While there were clear differences in group awareness and task distribution, there were no statistically significant differences in Performance and Conformity scores. This indicates that the participants were perfectly able to perform sensemaking and maintaining awareness using face-to-face communication, rather than it being primarily mediated by the tabletop.

Strategies included the introduction of different styles of communication with eye-to-eye contact, using search-oriented strategies instead of filing-oriented strategies, and relying more on direct exchange of information between tablets than sharing documents via the tabletop.

> **Finding 3.** From our observations we can conclude that the users working with small tabletops during cross-device collaboration were perfectly capable of maintaining awareness and performing sensemaking primarily mediated by face-to-face communication. They were able to adapt and improvise and succeeded in achieving an objective quality of work results that was not significantly different from those working with medium-sized or large tabletops.

LIMITATIONS

As mentioned in the study description, the system design and the given task naturally influenced the collaboration behavior that we observed. There are specific aspects of our study that limit the generalizability of our findings to all cross-device systems for sensemaking: First, the VAST 2006 Challenge made it necessary to frequently search for documents and to closely read them. This shifted the overall nature of the collaboration towards many phases of solitary parallel work and fewer phases of tightly-coupled collaboration. Users focused on their tablets at least for 71% of the time (Table 1). A different task (e.g. collaborative design or gaming) might afford more tightly-coupled collaboration and thus emphasize the role and the importance of the tabletop. This could also lead to a generally greater importance and benefit of larger tabletops than we observed. Second, our groups consisted of two users. We chose pairs like Isenberg et al. [6] who demonstrated that pairs are sufficient to identify differences in coupling styles and collaboration strategies. Choosing larger groups in followup studies might reveal a greater need for display space than in our study. In larger groups there will also be an increased importance of group awareness – whether it is actively created through verbal conversation or is mediated by the size and physical affordances of the tabletop. Third, our participants were students whose analysis skills differ from that of professional analysts. But as our study focused on observed differences between the three conditions and their UI and demands for technical proficiency were almost identical, our findings should be independent from education and technical skills of participants. Observed differences should not be substantially different for non-students. However, age-related differences in memory, eye-sight or motor skills could have an impact (better eye-sight and memory could benefit SMALL, motor impairments could hamper LARGE).

Nonetheless, we believe that our study employed a balanced task set and also realistic setting for collaboration. That none of the conditions can be considered unfair or unsolvable becomes evident through the absence of statistically significant differences in the groups' performance scores.

IMPLICATIONS FOR FUTURE RESEARCH

Our findings point towards the need for a more nuanced understanding of the role of a shared tabletop and its size in co-located multi-device collaboration. We have observed that for the particular kind of collaborative sensemaking task that we studied, a larger tabletop did not lead to a better task performance or user experience. In particular, we found evidence that the large tabletop attracted significantly more attention than the smaller ones – for good and for ill.

However, a major part of our sensemaking task consisted of individual work with personal tablets, e.g., searching for documents and reading text. It would be interesting to contrast our results with a study of a task where the major part of the work requires tightly-coupled collaboration. It would also be interesting to see to what extent the found strengths of SMALL tabletop sizes (i.e. increased group awareness, focused work strategy) hold true for group sizes larger than two. Some effects that we considered to be positive in our study setting (e.g. focus on other person) might be detrimental to the quality of collaboration in larger groups.

Although we did not analyze territoriality in our study, findings suggest that the size of the tabletop influences how people manage personal and shared work spaces in cross-device settings. Research investigating the effect of shared display size on territoriality in group collaborations would further help to understand the role of the tabletop in relation to personal devices.

In addition, we are interested on how our findings relate to a study investigating the effect of a shared display size in a vertical setting. Changing the orientation of the shared display also implies changes to the physical user position and interaction with the system which might strongly influence the effects that we found. We would especially expect different results in how participants would refer to the shared display if it were vertically oriented.

Research on shared interactive surfaces has primarily focused on large tabletops or large interactive wall displays with up to 200″ [2]. Our findings imply that under certain conditions small shared interactive surfaces could outperform large ones. While tablets are typically designed for personal tasks, our results encourage research on re-purposing tablet-sized devices as shared interactive surfaces for mixed-focus and cross-device collaboration, or even to ad hoc expand the shared surface using additional devices (as proposed by [17]).

CONCLUSION

While interactive tabletops are increasingly combined with mobile personal devices such as tablets, the effect of size of such shared space is still unexplored. In this paper, we studied the effect of the size of a shared horizontal tabletop on users' attention, awareness, and efficiency during cross-device mixed-focus collaboration. We conducted an experimental study of a collaborative sensemaking task using the "Stegosaurus" data set from the VAST 2006 Challenge [16]. We studied 15 groups of two users working with our collaborative multi-device application existing of two personal tablets (9.7″) and a tabletop with a variable size over three conditions (10.6″, 27″, and 55″). In detail, we focused on participants' interaction with devices (RQ1), communication activities (RQ2) and user preferences and quality of work (RQ3). We found that larger tabletops do not necessarily improve collaboration or sensemaking results, because they can divert users' attention away from their collaborators and towards the shared display. This has implications on participants' interaction with the tabletop as well as on their communication style.

We conclude that the choice of size for a shared tabletop for cross-device collaboration is not obvious, but should depend on the task at hand, and that a larger tabletop is not necessarily the better choice.

ACKNOWLEDGEMENTS

We thank the German Research Foundation (DFG) for financial support within project C01 of SFB/Transregio 161.

REFERENCES

1. Christopher Andrews, Alex Endert, and Chris North. 2010. Space to Think: Large High-resolution Displays for Sensemaking. In *Proceedings of the SIGCHI Conference on Human Factors in Computing Systems (CHI '10)*. ACM, New York, NY, USA, 55–64.
2. M. Beaudouin-Lafon, S. Huot, M. Nancel, W. Mackay, E. Pietriga, R. Primet, J. Wagner, O. Chapuis, C. Pillias,

J.R. Eagan, T. Gjerlufsen, and C. Klokmose. 2012. Multisurface Interaction in the WILD Room. *Computer* 45, 4 (April 2012), 48–56.

3. Carl Gutwin and Saul Greenberg. 1998. Design for Individuals, Design for Groups: Tradeoffs Between Power and Workspace Awareness. In *Proceedings of the 1998 ACM Conference on Computer Supported Cooperative Work (CSCW '98)*. ACM, New York, NY, USA, 207–216.
4. Peter Hamilton and Daniel J. Wigdor. 2014. Conductor: Enabling and Understanding Cross-device Interaction. In *Proceedings of the SIGCHI Conference on Human Factors in Computing Systems (CHI '14)*. ACM, New York, NY, USA, 2773–2782.
5. Eva Hornecker, Paul Marshall, Nick Sheep Dalton, and Yvonne Rogers. 2008. Collaboration and Interference: Awareness with Mice or Touch Input. In *Proceedings of the 2008 ACM Conference on Computer Supported Cooperative Work (CSCW '08)*. ACM, New York, NY, USA, 167–176.
6. Petra Isenberg, Danyel Fisher, Sharoda A. Paul, Meredith Ringel Morris, Kori Inkpen, and Mary Czerwinski. 2012. Co-Located Collaborative Visual Analytics around a Tabletop Display. *IEEE Trans. Vis. Comput. Graph.* 18, 5 (2012), 689–702.
7. Robert J.K. Jacob, Audrey Girouard, Leanne M. Hirshfield, Michael S. Horn, Orit Shaer, Erin Treacy Solovey, and Jamie Zigelbaum. 2008. Reality-based Interaction: A Framework for post-WIMP Interfaces. In *Proceedings of the SIGCHI Conference on Human Factors in Computing Systems (CHI '08)*. ACM, New York, NY, USA, 201–210.
8. Mikkel R. Jakobsen and Kasper Hornbæk. 2014. Up Close and Personal: Collaborative Work on a High-resolution Multitouch Wall Display. *ACM Trans. Comput.-Hum. Interact.* 21, 2, Article 11 (Feb. 2014), 34 pages.
9. Hans-Christian Jetter, Jens Gerken, Michael Zöllner, Harald Reiterer, and Natasa Milic-Frayling. 2011. Materializing the Query with Facet-streams: A Hybrid Surface for Collaborative Search on Tabletops. In *Proceedings of the SIGCHI Conference on Human Factors in Computing Systems (CHI '11)*. ACM, New York, NY, USA, 3013–3022.
10. Andrés Lucero, Jussi Holopainen, and Tero Jokela. 2011. Pass-them-around: Collaborative Use of Mobile Phones for Photo Sharing. In *Proceedings of the SIGCHI Conference on Human Factors in Computing Systems (CHI '11)*. ACM, New York, NY, USA, 1787–1796.
11. Will McGrath, Brian Bowman, David McCallum, Juan David Hincapié-Ramos, Niklas Elmqvist, and Pourang Irani. 2012. Branch-explore-merge: Facilitating Real-time Revision Control in Collaborative Visual Exploration. In *Proc. of the 2012 ACM International Conference on Interactive Tabletops and Surfaces (ITS '12)*. ACM, New York, NY, USA, 235–244.
12. Meredith Ringel Morris, Danyel Fisher, and Daniel Wigdor. 2010a. Search on Surfaces: Exploring the Potential of Interactive Tabletops for Collaborative Search Tasks. *Inf. Process. Manage.* 46, 6 (Nov. 2010), 703–717.
13. Meredith Ringel Morris, Jarrod Lombardo, and Daniel Wigdor. 2010b. WeSearch: Supporting Collaborative Search and Sensemaking on a Tabletop Display. In *Proceedings of the 2010 ACM Conference on Computer Supported Cooperative Work (CSCW '10)*. ACM, New York, NY, USA, 401–410.
14. Gerard Oleksik, Hans-Christian Jetter, Jens Gerken, Natasa Milic-Frayling, and Rachel Jones. 2013. Towards an Information Architecture for Flexible Reuse of Digital Media. In *Proceedings of the 12th International Conference on Mobile and Ubiquitous Multimedia (MUM '13)*. ACM, New York, NY, USA, Article 12, 10 pages.
15. Jose Pinheiro, Douglas Bates, Saikat DebRoy, Deepayan Sarkar, and R Core Team. 2015. *nlme: Linear and Nonlinear Mixed Effects Models.* `http://CRAN.R-project.org/package=nlme` R package version 3.1-122.
16. Catherine Plaisant, Georges Grinstein, Jean Scholtz, Mark Whiting, and et al. 2008. Evaluating Visual Analytics at the 2007 VAST Symposium Contest. *IEEE Comput. Graph. Appl.* 28, 2 (March 2008), 12–21.
17. Roman Rädle, Hans-Christian Jetter, Nicolai Marquardt, Harald Reiterer, and Yvonne Rogers. 2014. HuddleLamp: Spatially-Aware Mobile Displays for Ad-hoc Around-the-Table Collaboration. In *Proceedings of the Ninth ACM International Conference on Interactive Tabletops and Surfaces (ITS '14)*. ACM, New York, NY, USA, 45–54.
18. Roman Rädle, Hans-Christian Jetter, and Harald Reiterer. 2013. TwisterSearch: A Distributed User Interface for Collaborative Web Search. In *Distributed User Interfaces: Usability and Collaboration*, Mara D. Lozano, Jose A. Gallud, Ricardo Tesoriero, and Victor M.R. Penichet (Eds.). Springer London, 53–67.
19. Yvonne Rogers and Sian Lindley. 2004. Collaborating around vertical and horizontal large interactive displays: which way is best? *Interacting with Computers* 16, 6 (Dec. 2004), 1133–1152.
20. Kathy Ryall, Clifton Forlines, Chia Shen, and Meredith Ringel Morris. 2004. Exploring the Effects of Group Size and Table Size on Interactions with Tabletop Shared-display Groupware. In *Proceedings of the 2004 ACM Conference on Computer Supported Cooperative Work (CSCW '04)*. ACM, New York, NY, USA, 284–293.

21. Stacey D. Scott, M. Sheelagh T. Carpendale, and Kori M. Inkpen. 2004. Territoriality in Collaborative Tabletop Workspaces. In *Proceedings of the 2004 ACM Conference on Computer Supported Cooperative Work (CSCW '04)*. ACM, New York, NY, USA, 294–303.

22. Anthony Tang, Melanie Tory, Barry Po, Petra Neumann, and Sheelagh Carpendale. 2006. Collaborative Coupling over Tabletop Displays. In *Proceedings of the SIGCHI Conference on Human Factors in Computing Systems (CHI '06)*. ACM, New York, NY, USA, 1181–1190.

23. James R. Wallace, Stacey D. Scott, and Carolyn G. MacGregor. 2013. Collaborative Sensemaking on a Digital Tabletop and Personal Tablets: Prioritization, Comparisons, and Tableaux. In *Proceedings of the SIGCHI Conference on Human Factors in Computing Systems (CHI '13)*. ACM, New York, NY, USA, 3345–3354.

Enhancing Cross-Device Interaction Scripting with Interactive Illustrations

Pei-Yu (Peggy) Chi[1,2 *], **Yang Li**[1], **Björn Hartmann**[1,2 *]
Google Inc.[1]
Computer Science Division, UC Berkeley[2]
peggychi@cs.berkeley.edu, yangli@acm.org, bjoern@cs.berkeley.edu

ABSTRACT
Cross-device interactions involve input and output on multiple computing devices. Implementing and reasoning about interactions that cover multiple devices with a diversity of form factors and capabilities can be complex. To assist developers in programming cross-device interactions, we created DemoScript, a technique that automatically analyzes a cross-device interaction program while it is being written. DemoScript visually illustrates the step-by-step execution of a selected portion or the entire program with a novel, automatically generated *cross-device storyboard* visualization. In addition to helping developers understand the behavior of the program, DemoScript also allows developers to revise their program by interactively manipulating the cross-device storyboard. We evaluated DemoScript with 8 professional programmers and found that DemoScript significantly improved development efficiency by helping developers interpret and manage cross-device interaction; it also encourages testing to think through the script in a development process.

Author Keywords
Cross-device interaction; scripting; interactive illustration; storyboards.

ACM Classification Keywords
H.5.2. User Interfaces — prototyping, input devices and strategies, graphical user interfaces.

INTRODUCTION
Wearable and mobile devices have introduced new ways for interaction with their unique capabilities and form factors. As consumers embrace a multi-device ecosystem, interactions spanning multiple devices can bring significant benefits beyond operating single devices. Examples that have been shown include: cross-display content manipulation [29, 32, 37], watch-phone interactions [6, 11, 16], multiple cube-size device gaming [34], and interactive augmented space via smart eyewear [10, 27].

Implementing cross-device interactions poses several challenges to developers. First, *it is difficult to account for the wide variety of form factors and capabilities* of devices *and their combinations* that a program may be run on. For example, a cross-device camera app may have to provide several versions to offer similar interactions on a phone and a watch or an eyewear for consistency. Second, *it is challenging to express and reason interaction flows that span multiple devices*. The higher-level relationships between cross-device inputs and outputs are often defined in a variety of callback functions spread across a codebase. Third, *testing cross-device interactions remains difficult*, especially when various physical inputs across devices are involved. Developers often have to resort to stepping through applications and manually provide input to test these interactions.

Prior work has aimed to lower the complexity in cross-device development through programming frameworks or toolkits by abstractions. Panelrama introduced a constraint-based approach for specifying cross-device UIs [37]. Weave's scripting framework allows developers to create cross-device behaviors using a high-level API inspired by Web programming models [7]. WatchConnect provides a platform for prototyping watch-centric apps considering watch-specific capabilities [16]. In this paper, we take a complementary but independent approach: We hypothesize that a key difficulty lies in bridging the gap between envisioning concrete examples of interactions and abstracting specification in code. When designing cross-device interactions, developers have to translate device-specific scenarios into abstract specifications to a range of devices at runtime. *The gulf of execution* [30, 25]—writing device selection and event handler statements—and *the gulf of evaluation*—reasoning whether existing statements specify the correct set of devices and interactions—can be significant when number of devices and form factors increase. Our goal is to minimize these gulfs by 1) illustrating the behavior of code with concrete examples,

CHI'16, May 07-12, 2016, San Jose, CA, USA
ACM 978-1-4503-3362-7/16/05.
http://dx.doi.org/10.1145/2858036.2858382

* This work was done while the first and the third authors were respectively an intern and an academic consultant at Google.

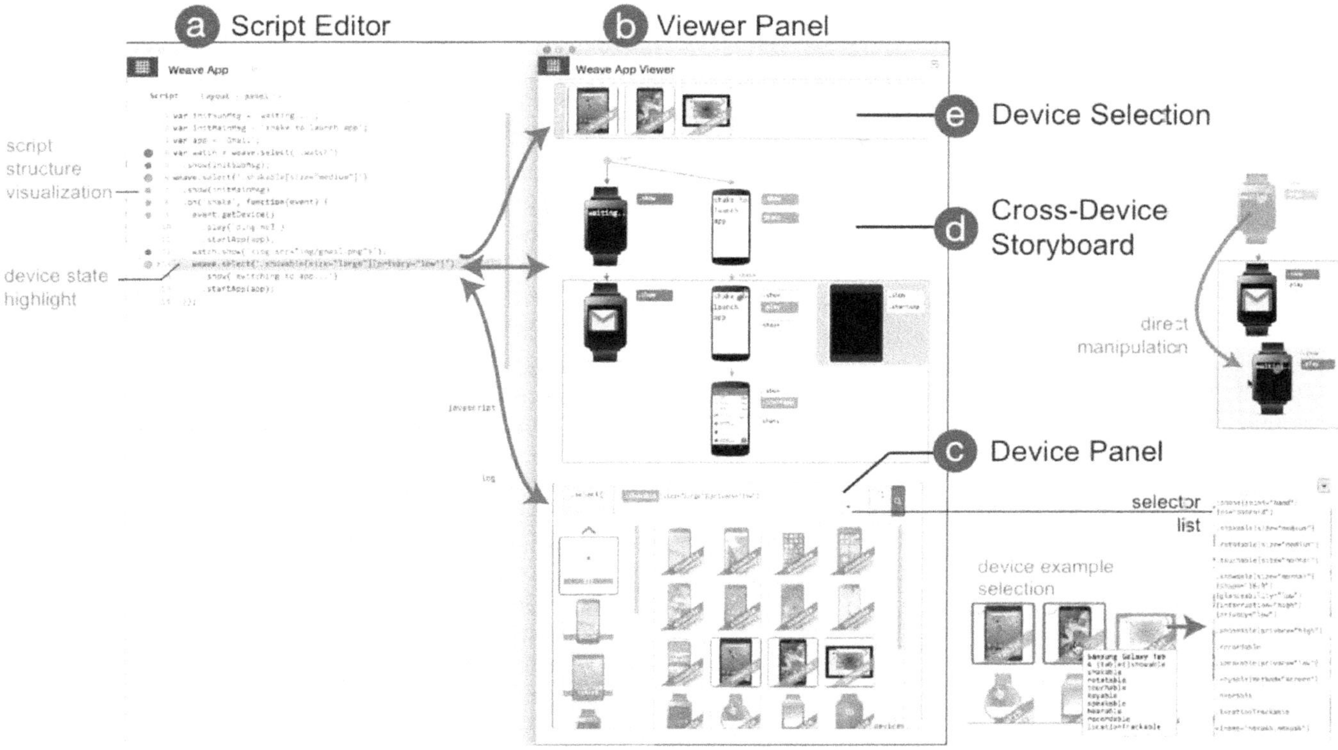

Figure 1. DemoScript allows developers to script the abstract logic in the Script Editor (a) and in real-time observe and manipulate the simulation in the Viewer (b). Developers can specify device examples in the Device Panel (c), observe the device selection (e), and verify the application logic in the cross-device storyboard (d). The storyboard employs a grid layout where each column represents a device selection, and each row shows the device state progress in time connected by arrows to show the interaction flow.

and 2) the opposite direction—generating code from direct manipulation of the visual illustration.

We present DemoScript, a novel technique that assists developers in programming cross-device interaction by interactively illustrating the behavior of the program. Based on an understanding of the syntax and semantics of a cross-device UI framework, DemoScript analyzes the program as the developer enters it, and in real-time automatically generates and presents a visual illustration of the scripted behavior as a cross-device storyboard (see Figure 1).

In our approach, developers move between authoring code (*i.e.*, abstract application logic) and manipulating visualizations (*i.e.*, examples of concrete run-time executions) of aspects of their code. The visualizations focus on key aspects of cross-device interactions—device selection and interaction flow—and show examples of how the written behaviors give rise to different behaviors across multiple devices. Developers can navigate in code line-by-line to see the partial, step-by-step execution, which helps them connect the abstract code to run-time behaviors. Through the cross-device storyboard, developers can revise their program for a range of aspects by directly manipulating the elements in the storyboard. Our approach effectively encourages testing and visually verifying cross-device interactions that involve various device form factors and interaction capabilities.

An evaluation of DemoScript with 8 professional programmers indicated that our technique significantly improves the efficiency for programming complex interaction behaviors such as cross-device interaction, in comparison with a baseline approach. In particular, our work makes the following contributions:

- A novel approach for programming cross-device interactions, based on a seamless coupling of scripting and interactive visual illustration of scripted behaviors;
- Interactive cross-device storyboards—a novel visualization of interaction logic, and a set of initial findings on the usefulness and usability of cross-device storyboards. Storyboards allow developers to revise a script by direct manipulation and visualizing code fragments as well as entire programs;
- A set of methods for analyzing a cross-device interaction script in a given UI framework.

RELATED WORK

Our work touches on three research topics: enhanced code editors, cross-device IDEs, storyboards in interaction design, and iterating with examples. We here discuss how our work is related to each of these areas.

Enhanced Code Editors

Tools that visualize different aspects of source code and allow direct manipulation of abstractions can successfully lower the complexity of programming [28]. Prior work has attempted to integrate many software visualization techniques into code editors [8]. For example, Codelets shows interactive examples and documentation inside an IDE [31]. Stacksplorer visualizes the structure of call graphs [18]. Beyond enhancing IDEs for general programming tasks, research has also focused specifically on techniques for supporting the development of interactive applications. Most IDEs nowadays ship with a GUI builder to enable developers to graphically layout user interfaces. Xcode further allows developers to create UI sequences for Apple Watch and interactively monitor variables in a program [2, 3]. Juxtapose allows programmers to explore interface alternatives [14] using a linked editing technique [35], and DejaVu helps programmers understand computer vision-based applications that extract interaction logic from camera input [19].

Similar to prior work, we intend to enhance program editors for interactive systems. However, we specifically focus on the unique challenges emerged from cross-device interaction development. We designed DemoScript based on a fundamental understanding of programming frameworks for cross-device interactions.

Cross-Device Interaction

In multi-device research, authoring support tends to focus either on graphical, direct manipulation authoring, or on programming frameworks without visual editors. In the first category, Damask provides a GUI for designers to specify UI patterns across devices [26], while XDStudio supports authoring distributed UIs visually on emulators or actual devices [29]. In the second category, the WatchConnect toolkit comprises both hardware and software components for rapid prototyping of watch-centric cross-device applications [16]. Panelrama uses a constraint-based approach for specifying cross-device UIs [37]. Our work seeks to find a middle ground between these two approaches. On one hand, we focus on preserving the flexibility and high complexity ceiling of authoring interactions in a general purpose programming language. On the other hand, we contribute interactive storyboards that help developers understand the interactions in code.

Storyboards

Screenflow diagrams or UI storyboards are widely used in practice to help developers visualize the flow and think through the logic of an application [36]. They show a sequence of UI screens, each representing application output triggered by user inputs. Researchers have proposed systems that use storyboards to author various kinds of interactive prototypes without code, including sketch-based GUIs [21], sensor-driven mobile prototypes [13], and activity-based applications [23]. Storyboards can also be generated from user demonstration. For examples, FrameWire extracts interaction logic from a paper prototype walkthrough [24] and the Designers' Outpost captures site maps on a smart whiteboard [20].

In contrast to these approaches, we extend the expressiveness of storyboards by introducing a new format based on the unique aspects of cross-device interaction. In addition, our storyboards are closely coupled with scripting—the changes in a script are reflected in the storyboard instantaneously and vice versa.

Iterating with Examples

Examples help concretize and illustrate abstract concepts and can serve as a guide for exploring design spaces. Research has contributed example-centric systems for using examples to search, filter and explore information spaces. For example, users can look for visual website designs by navigating a corpus of specific examples and indicate preferences such as "show more like these selections" [33, 22]. Other efforts include refining and manipulating database queries interacting directly with example results [1], and improving image search results by learning similar features from user-specified examples [9]. In our work, we employ examples to help developers specify selection queries for devices from a wide range of options.

SCRIPTING WITH DEMOSCRIPT

DemoScript helps developers author and test a cross-device interaction script using interactive illustrations. It automatically analyzes a script as it is entered or modified by a developer, based on a cross-device UI framework—in our current implementation, we use the Weave framework proposed previously [7]. DemoScript identifies code relevant to device specification, user input events, and device actions (UI output), and visualizes the interaction flow for an entire program or a subset of code as a cross-device storyboard and presents it side-by-side along the script editor (see Figure 1).

Our cross-device storyboard illustration is based on a grid layout (see Figure 2f). Each column of the grid represents a selected device, and each row presents a state of the cross-device application that is characterized as the combination of device states (across columns). Each cell in this storyboard thus shows the state of a specific device at a particular point of the script execution. If there is no change on a device at an execution step, its representation is omitted on the row such that the developer can easily spot devices that have state changes. The directional arrows that connect cells are transitions, which visualize the interaction flow from one device state to another. A transition can be triggered by a device action (e.g., showing an image on the display) or a user event (e.g., shaking the device).

To discuss how a developer would benefit from DemoScript in scripting a cross-device behavior, assume a developer, Megan, wants to create a photo sharing application such as Instagram. In her design, a watch shows notifications of incoming photos as thumbnails, and tapping on a thumbnail on the watch will open a larger view of this photo on a device with a larger-form factor device, such as a smartphone or a tablet. As the photo is opened on another device, the watch then switches to the Maps application showing the geographical location of this photo. We demonstrate how Megan uses a scripting tool enhanced by DemoScript. We highlight how our tool helps developers on a set of key tasks in cross-device development.

Specifying Target Devices and Transitions

Megan starts by specifying her target devices for this application. To do so, she creates a device selection in the Script Editor (see Figure 1a) by entering `weave.select(':watch')`. As she enters the script, she immediately sees an LG G Watch emulator rendered on the storyboard (see Figure 2a). The top ribbon of the Viewer shows a Device Selection list of four smart watches (see Figure 1e) that match this selector. Megan can choose a target emulator by selecting a device from the list. At the bottom, a Device Panel shows the device repository in which she can browse through possible devices (see Figure 1c). To specify the device for photo viewing, she creates another selection for a phone by entering `weave.select(':phone')` in the Script Editor. Megan sees a phone emulator displayed on the storyboard column next to the watch emulator (see Figure 2b).

Megan then realizes that the phone is needed only when the user shakes the watch. Without manually modifying her script, she adds a transition from the watch to the phone by double-clicking the two device states in sequence in the storyboard and associates the "shake" event to it in the popup. This direct manipulation automatically refactors the script by attaching an event callback to the watch selection and nesting the photo selection within the callback:

```
.on('shake', function(event) {
    weave.select(':phone');
})
```

Correspondingly, the phone emulator is pushed down a row in the storyboard and connected with a transition from the watch, which indicates the use of watch is triggered by the shake event from the watch (see Figure 2c). To help Megan understand the scope of the callback function (see Line 2-4), DemoScript visualizes the scope as an *event block* that encapsulates any device states that take place *only* in this callback function scope. A transition arrow tagged with an input event is added from the *source* device that triggers the event—the watch that fires the shake event (Line 2)—to the event block.

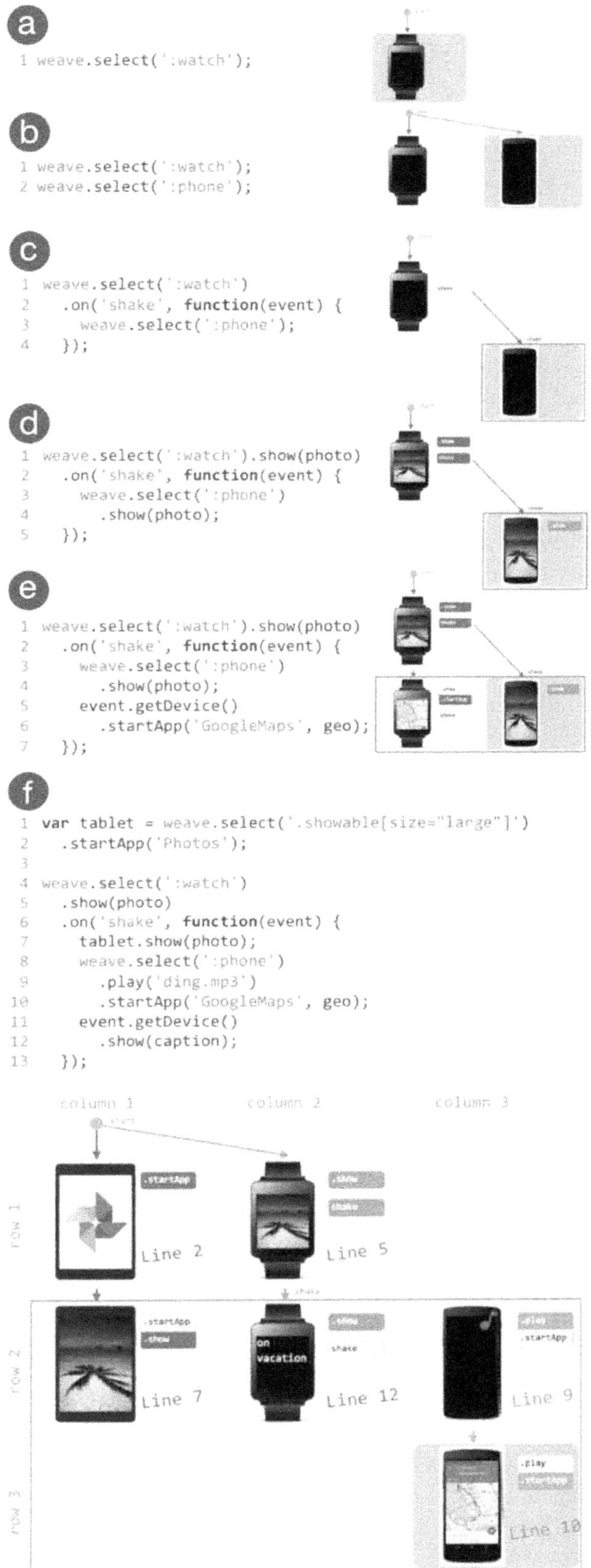

Figure 2. An example of scripting cross-device interaction enhanced by DemoScript.

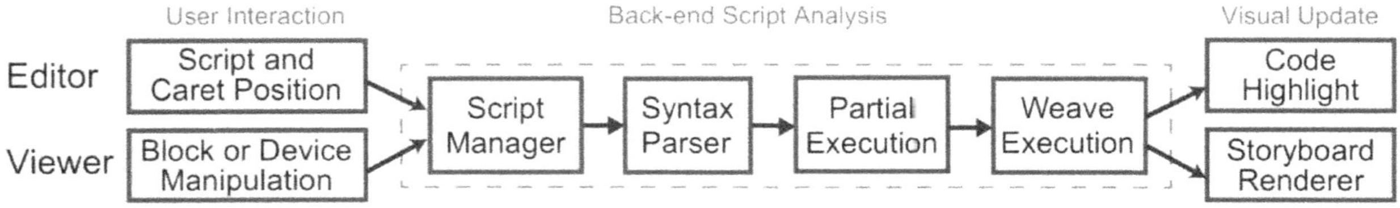

Figure 3. The processing pipeline of DemoScript. The system analyzes developer manipulations and scripting edits in the background to provide real-time, visual feedback in the IDE.

Specifying Device Actions

Next, Megan starts designing the device outputs that users would want to see. To simplify our discussion, assume the program has predefined the resource handle to the photo and its metadata as variables `photo`, `geo`, and `caption` respectively. In the Script Editor, Megan adds `.show(photo)` to the watch selection before the event callback, which lets the watch show a thumbnail of the `photo`. Similarly, she adds `.show(photo)` to the phone selection to show a large view of the `photo` on the phone in response to the shake event. In the process, she immediately sees a sample photo being rendered on both device emulators (see Figure 2d).

While the phone offers a large view of the image, Megan wants the watch to display the photo's geographical location in a Maps application. To do so, in the callback (see Figure 2e) she adds:

```
event.getDevice().startApp('GoogleMaps', geo)
```

With that, the watch switches to a map view the moment when the photo is opened on the phone. All these changes in the script are automatically captured and presented in the storyboard. Both devices are shown on the same row because their states all have changed in response to the shake event (see Figure 2e). Note that the event block has also been expanded to include the device state updates of both the watch and the phone.

Revising Device Selection Criteria with Examples

Megan acquires a good understanding of the look and feel of her choice of devices for the application. From the phone visualization in the storyboard, Megan realizes that users might prefer an even larger view of the photo such that users can easily annotate the photo. To this end, she decides to modify the device selection for the phone, she points to the line where the selector, `weave.select(':phone')`—is declared (see Line 3 in Figure 2e). In response to this action, DemoScript automatically selects the column of the phone selection, updates the Device Selection ribbon at the top of the Viewer Panel, and opens the device repository panel at the bottom (see Figure 1e and 1c).

Megan then selects a few tablets from the device repository, including a Nexus 9 and a Surface Pro. Given these device examples, DemoScript infers a list of selector options based on the attributes of these devices, including device types and capabilities. We will discuss the underlying mechanism in the following section. In particular, DemoScript suggests `':tablet[os="android,windows"]'` as a top choice. After reviewing device examples resulted from this selector in the Device Selection list, she discovers that this selector does not cover laptops that can be converted to a tablet. As such, she explores other suggestions in the selector list offered by DemoScript (see Figure 1c) by testing them out—clicking on each option to view matched device examples. She finally chooses the selector `'.showable[size="large"]'` that better matches her expectation. She then clicks the "Send" button to commit the selector to the script.

Reusing Interaction Behaviors by Drag-and-Drop

After testing her application in the storyboard, Megan decides that showing the map on a phone would be preferable to the watch that has limited display real estate. To do so, instead of modifying the script, she directly drags the map view on the watch to the third, unoccupied column. This direct manipulation creates another instance of the watch selection with the map shown on the third column. Meanwhile, DemoScript creates another selection in the callback function. Because the developer will most likely change the device selection, instead of having two watches in the application, DemoScript automatically prompts the developer to specify a selector. She updates the selector with `':phone'`. Once again, the change is immediately reflected in the storyboard.

Finally, Megan adds more user feedback to enrich this application and sees her complete storyboard as shown in Figure 2f. As the script grows to be more complicated, she could select a block of code to *partially render* the storyboard. For example, selecting Line 7-10 in Figure 2f will re-render the storyboard to show only a tablet showing a photo (Line 7) and a phone playing sound and then launching an app (Line 9-10).

From these examples, we show that DemoScript is closely integrated with script editing. DemoScript enables the developers immediately see the dynamic update on the storyboard based on the position of the script in the Editor. This helps understand the mapping between a portion of code to its runtime execution. Our cross-device storyboard enables a set of visual representations and direct manipulation operations that correspond critical tasks in scripting a cross-device interaction. It also provides an effective visualization of the interaction flow. For example, by looking at how often transitions run across columns, a developer can easily understand the amount of attention shift during an interaction behavior, which is a critical factor of the usability of a cross-device application.

THE DEMOSCRIPT SYSTEM

In this section, we discuss the underlying mechanisms of our system. DemoScript is integrated with a scripting editor and continuously analyzes the script to dynamically generate a cross-device storyboard visualization. Particularly, our implementation analyzes Weave scripts written in JavaScript [15], by obtaining the syntax tree of the code and partially executing it to provide visual assistance in real-time (see Figure 3).

Script Analyses

DemoScript first parses the script into an abstract syntax tree (AST). An AST represents the essential syntactic structure of source code in a tree structure. ASTs have been widely used for program analysis [4] and can be used for program slicing to enable automatic partial testing [38] and potentially usability evaluation [17].

We traverse an AST and recursively build a simplified tree that expresses hierarchical relationships between key constructs of the Weave API, which includes 1) device selectors, 2) actions that change UI state, and 3) events and their handlers that define which input events trigger the actions. *Device selectors* use a declarative query language to define desired properties, similar to CSS selectors for choosing elements on Web pages. For example, `.select('.showable')` selects devices that have a display to show visual outputs. *Actions* are declarations to change the device states, such as updating UI, launching existing application, or playing sounds. An action can be triggered in a callback function that listens to any specific *event* emitted by a device, e.g., touching the screen or shaking the device. DemoScript also identifies and tracks location information for each Weave construct, including its line and column indices to the source code.

Cross-Device Storyboard Generation

DemoScript renders the cross-device storyboard by traversing the AST. It focuses on visualizing device selections and their interaction relations. DemoScript first generates an initial view by rendering emulators for each selection shown in different columns. It then partially executes the code based on the caret position in the Script Editor and dynamically adjusts the layout.

Device Selection Rendering

For each selection statement in the script, DemoScript creates a new column in the storyboard view. To visualize the lifecycles of device selections (*i.e.*, if a device is operated *only* when a certain event is fired), it differentiates the top-level selections $\{selection_{\text{top}}\}$ and those exist in event callbacks $\{selection_{\text{event}}\}$ by presenting them on different rows—pushing $\{selection_{\text{event}}\}$ down one row. For example, in the script in Figure 2f, two new selections via `weave.select` (from Line 1 and 4) are shown in the first and second columns. Inside the *shake* callback function, another new selection (from Line 8) is added to the third column but pushed to the second row.

Next, it is important to visualize the specific "scope" in an interaction flow for developers to visually track the device states before and after an event. Therefore, DemoScript renders an *event-associated arrow* and an *event block* to highlight the relation between devices. To help viewers follow the interaction flow, DemoScript adds a transition arrow from the $selection_i \in \{selection_{top}\}$ that triggers the event *i* to another $selection_j \in \{selection_{event\_i}\}$ that exists in the callback. The transition arrow is tagged with an event type, such as "shake" or "rotate". It then applies an event block to wrap $\{selection_{event\_i}\}$, *i.e.*, all the selections created in the callback. If there is no new selection, it adds an empty block. The initial view is shown in Figure 4 top-left. The default opacity to these visual elements is set to be low and will be highlighted when the script is executed.

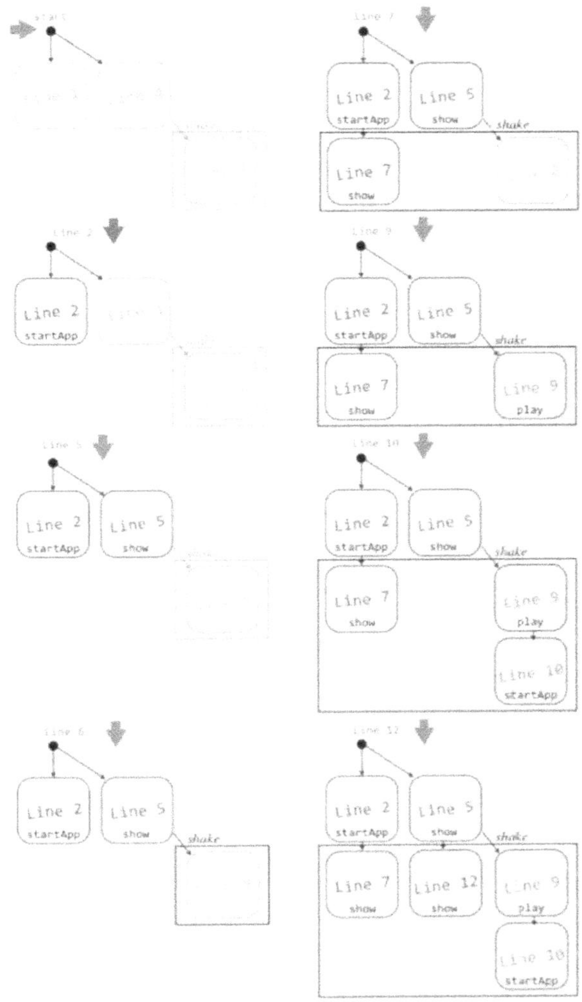

Figure 4. Storyboard adjustments by partial execution of a script based on the developer's navigation in the code.

Code Fragment Execution

When a developer navigates in the script, DemoScript receives the caret position $p = (line_m, column_n)$ from the Script Editor. It finds the specific element in code at p and identifies all the other Weave elements from the entry point of the script to p. For example, if $m = 10$ and n is between [7, 36] as `startApp('GoogleMaps', geo)` shown in Figure 2f, the relevant elements include several actions (`'startApp'` in Line 2 and 10, `'show'` in Line 5 and 7, and `'play'` in line 9) and an event (`'shake'` in Line 6) for three different device sets, sorted by closures and positions in code. For each partial execution sequentially from the entry point to p, DemoScript dynamically executes these partial elements and simulates the events in the sequence in the Weave framework. It then adjusts the storyboard (see Figure 4) and inserts the updated UI view for any execution that triggers a user feedback (e.g., showing a message, playing a sound, or starting an app).

Next, DemoScript adjusts the event block to wrap all the UI states triggered by the corresponding callback. For example, when developer navigates to Line 7 that is inside the "shake" callback, a new UI for the watch is appended below the initial view of the device, and the "shake" event block is dynamically expanded to include this view (see Figure 4 top-right). In other words, the developer would only see the partial view of the entire storyboard with all screens created prior to the first execution of Line 7. This interactive method that generates a partial view of the entire script allows developers to easily find the mapping between code and execution. In addition, because DemoScript maps the storyboard and code elements, it enables interactions for developers to directly manipulate device state or selection and update the script automatically.

If the caret is at a selection, it then shows the Device Panel that allows developers to manually specify device examples (see Figure 1e). Any update of the selector will replace the original selector string based on its start and end position retrieved from the AST.

Deriving Device Selection from Examples

DemoScript enables developers to specify a selector by giving examples from a device catalog. Given q device examples $[d_1, \ldots, d_q]$ in a repository of N devices where $q \in [1, N]$, DemoScript adopts a rule-based principle to generate a selector list. Each device d_i with k capabilities is represented as a vector $(cap_i prop_j,\ cap_i prop_{j+1},\ \ldots,\ cap_{i+1} prop_j,\ cap_{i+1} prop_{j+1},\ \ldots,\ cap_k prop_{j+r})$, where cap is a device capability for d_i (e.g., `'.showable'` and `'.shakable'`) and $prop$ is a property of this capability, such as `'privacy'`, `'glanceability'`, and `'size'`. This device-specific information is presumably defined by manufacturers; we modeled it manually from published device specifications.

DemoScript generates a list of selectors for each common $cap_i prop_j$ of these capability vectors between the selected devices as: {$selector_1$=`'cap₁[prop₁₋₁="valueₐ", prop₁₋₂="value_b"]'`, $selector_2$=`'cap₂[prop₂₋₁="value_c"]'`, …}. Each

Figure 5. Examples of DemoScript storyboard results.

selector$_i$ will match a list of devices in the repository so that the examples $[d_1,...,d_q]$ are contained in the device selection. In addition to capabilities, DemoScript also considers selectors by more relaxed—such as using device types, e.g., `':phone[os="android"]'`—or constrained attributes—such as device names, e.g., `'*[name="Nexus5, GalaxyNote4"]'`.

Finally, the list of selector options are ranked based on the number of device matches resulted from each selector in an ascending order, i.e., the more constrained the selector is, the higher it is ranked. In this way, developers can choose a selector based on their coverage and how well the coverage matches their desired devices.

RESULTS

Figure 5 shows two additional examples of the DemoScript storyboard results. The script in Figure 5a assigns one of the devices a different role from an annotation palette (Line 7) to a chat panel (Line 16) when an event happens (*i.e.*, phone calling triggered by the user, Line 12-17). This role change is visually depicted by the second column and the event block. In Figure 5b, the columns show the individual functions of each device (a volume controller, a music player, and a video player respectively) and their progress in time considering device capabilities.

IMPLEMENTATION

The DemoScript system consists of both a backend server and a frontend user interface. Our Node.js-based[1] web server has several functions: 1) it hosts the developers' scripts, 2) runs the Weave framework, 3) stores the device repository in the JSON format, and 4) maintains the DemoScript logic. A user interacts with the frontend application, which includes the web IDE and the Viewer, implemented as a Chrome app [12]. When the developer edits in the Script Editor of the IDE, the front-end app updates the edited script and the current caret position in the code to the back-end server. To analyze the JavaScript code, we integrated an ECMAScript AST parser Esprima [15] into our server to obtain the full syntax tree, which maintains the code hierarchy. If the edited script is executable, the server partially executes Weave code by traversing the AST in order to store information, including device selections and properties. This data is sent in JSON back to the front-end UI, which highlights the code in the Editor, visualizes the storyboard using D3 [5], and handles developer interaction via jQuery[2] and Bootstrap[3]. To avoid unnecessary visual update and flickering while the developer focuses on code editing, we included a 500ms idle time for invoking updating. This architectural design makes it flexible to integrate the DemoScript Viewer with standalone IDEs such as Sublime Text[4] or Android Studio[5].

[1] https://nodejs.org/
[2] https://jquery.com/
[3] http://getbootstrap.com/
[4] http://www.sublimetext.com/
[5] https://developer.android.com/sdk/

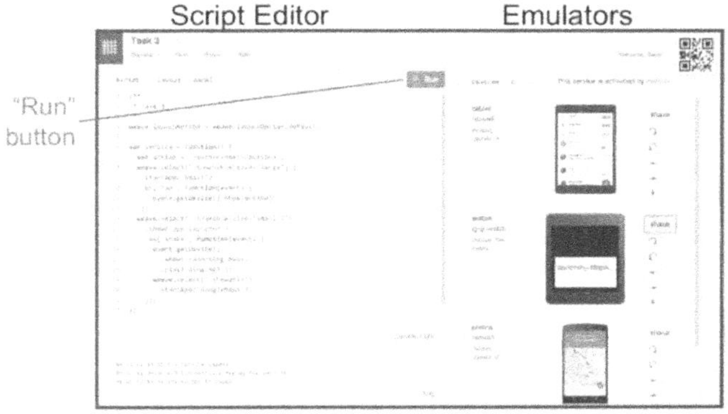

Figure 6. The baseline condition in our evaluation. Similar to conventional IDEs, it provides a script editor and a set of emulators for testing.

EVALUATION

We hypothesized that DemoScript could help developers easily manage various aspects of the tasks for programming cross-device behaviors that would otherwise be challenging. To validate this hypothesis, we conducted a study to compare DemoScript with a baseline condition that provides a script editor and emulators—a typical setup for UI programming. Specifically, we used the Weave IDE that was previously introduced (see Figure 6) [7]. In the study, we asked participants to interpret the cross-device behaviors that are fulfilled a set of scripts, and then identify and fix issues in these scripts for achieving different behaviors. We garnered both quantitative measurement such as task completion time and qualitative feedback on their reactions to DemoScript.

Participants and Setups

We recruited 8 professional programmers (2 females), aged between 21 and 45 years (Mean=26) from an IT company. Participants were required to have moderate JavaScript programming knowledge and were selected randomly from volunteers via an internal study invitation. 5 out of 8 participants had limited mobile programming experience; only 1 had programmed wearable devices. None of them had used the Weave framework.

The study was conducted in a laboratory environment. A MacBook Pro running OS X and Google Chrome browser was connected to a 24-inch LCD display with 1920x1200 pixel resolution. We provided an external mouse and a keyboard. Each participant was compensated with a $40 gift card for their participation in a 90-minute session.

Procedures and Tasks

At the beginning of the session, we introduced the Weave framework to the participants and asked them to walk through a web tutorial by following a cross-device launch pad app design, which approximately took 10 minutes. The Weave API documentation was available to participants during the experiment.

We then asked the participants to perform two sets of tasks in sequence, denoted Set I and Set II, where Set I is assigned to the first condition and Set II for the second condition. We counterbalanced the order of the two conditions to guard against learning effects in our analysis. Each set consists of two tasks with varying complexity: the first task is relatively *easy* (denoted as Task 1) and the second one is *hard* (denoted as Task 2). Task 1 in each set has three subtasks, while Task 2 has two. We designed the tasks in the way that both sets have comparable complexity, shown as follows:

Task 1. Given a script with three device selections, two of them each had a callback for different event types, and the third selection was only initiated once inside a callback function. Not all the selections and actions matched the instructions. At most 15 minutes was given to finish the task.

Subtask 1. [*Script understanding*] Explain how a user would achieve the following goal: {set I – to see an image, set II – to launch the Maps app}. Describe what the user would see on each device.

Subtask 2. [*Script refinement*] Suppose the script's developer intended to show the {I – photo launch button, II – application} on a {I –wrist-worn, II – large-display} device, answer if the script works properly as described. If not, fix the script to match the app description.

Subtask 3. [*Interaction enhancement*] To improve the user experience, modify the script so that {I – a prompt is shown on the target device before the photo appears, and II – whenever there is any UI update, play a "ding" sound on the same device as an indication}.

Task 2. The provided script had the same number of selections as Task 1.

Subtask 1. [*Script understanding*] Given the app description, does the script work as described? What works and what is different? The app enables user to {I – shake her phone to launch Gmail with both auditory and visual feedback before switching the app; meanwhile, she would see the Gmail icon on a wearable device; II – shake a wearable device that has a thumbnail displayed in order to see a large view of the photo on another device with the Photos app; a "ding" sound is played before launching the Photos app}.

Subtask 2. [*Debugging*] Correct the script so that it matches the description.

Finally, participants were asked to complete an online questionnaire with 5-point Likert-scale questions and debrief their thoughts.

RESULTS AND DISCUSSION

We discuss participants' performances and experience in terms of both quantitative results and qualitative feedback on comparing the baseline system and DemoScript.

Task Performance

All the participants completed the given tasks in both conditions. The average completion time for each subtask is

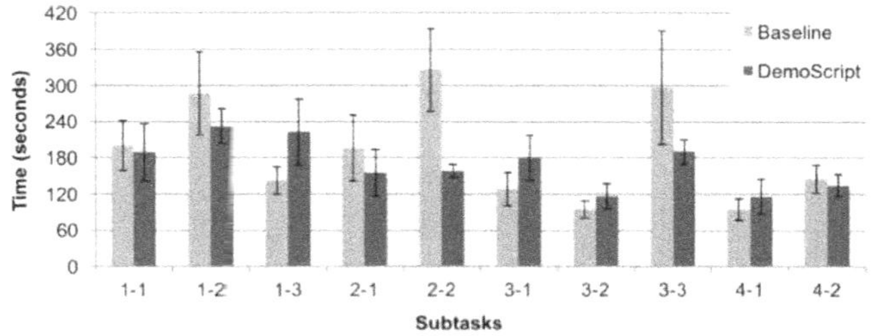

Figure 7. Average completion time for each subtask of the baseline system and DemoScript.

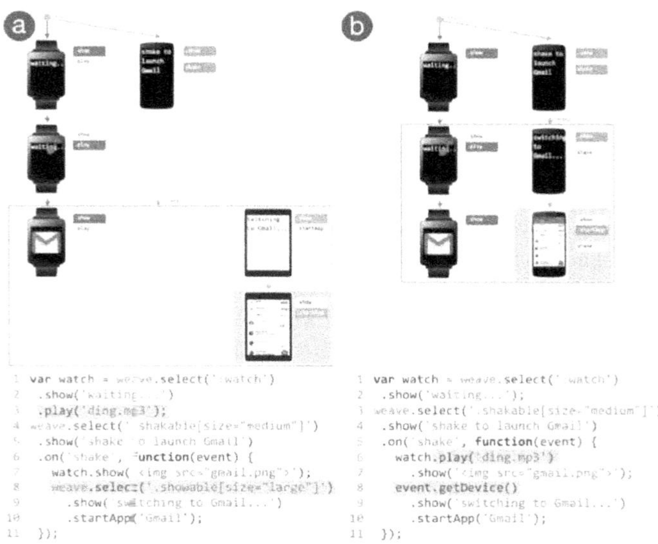

Figure 8. An example showing how developers can identify and correct errors with the support of storyboard.

shown in Figure 7. Overall, using the baseline system, participants needed more time to fix and test a script (Mean=3.2 minutes compared to 2.8 minutes using DemoScript on average). Furthermore, participants had a higher error rate using the baseline method (17.5% compared to 2.25% with DemoScript). We recorded an error when the oral interpretation was incorrect or incomplete (for script understanding subtasks) or the script failed to fully achieve the instruction (for scripting tasks). We discuss these errors and participants' coding behaviors that we observed in the following section.

Coding Behavior

Identifying Design Patterns and Redundancy

DemoScript's storyboard visualization helped participants identify errors where the provided script did not match the provided application description. For example, in the original script of task 3 (see Figure 8a), auditory feedback was played before the event is triggered, and the script incorrectly specified a wrong device selection to initiate the application. These errors were visually distinguishable in the storyboard, and all the 4 participants were able to fix the script with DemoScript (see Figure 8b), whereas 2 of the other 4 participants failed to correct all the errors using the baseline system.

The storyboard also helped participants to quickly identify the redundant code. Only 2 of 4 participants using the baseline correctly removed the redundant code in Task 3. Participants explained, the advantages of DemoScript include "*Being able to see the various device actions in sequence*" (P3) and to see "visualization of subsequent events" (P6) or a "*full overview over the execution flow; event listeners are clearly visible*" (P7).

Encouraging Testing When Scripting

Using DemoScript, participants actively navigated in the Editor to test the logic in the given scripts line-by-line and to verify their code changes (25.35 line navigations on average). They found the concept of the multi-device storyboard straightforward (4.5, SD=0.76) and it was easy to test (4.625, SD=0.52). On the contrary, participants only tested the code 2.23 times on average using the baseline system, which provided a "Run" button to deploy the code to emulators. P5 explained, with DemoScript, "*You can clearly see your code running on the screen, which makes it easier to debug and understand what you are doing instead of trying to play the scenes inside your head. It was very clean and well designed interface and it was easy to interact with it.*" Compared to standard IDEs for mobile devices, P2 shared, "*It was a big advantage to have an emulator for each device class running simultaneously and it was nice that the emulators ran the program instantly.*"

In the baseline condition after using the DemoScript system, two participants answered and scripted without testing the scripts. One of them asked if he could pull up the device list as what DemoScript showed. The participant later explained that he preferred to focus on coding, so DemoScript made it easy to see the runtime results while he scripted, whereas using the baseline system, he thought through the code and was confident in his interpretation or fixes (note that 2 of 5 subtasks failed).

We suspect that the ability of line-by-line testing improved the task success rate as it helped developers identify errors early. Participants constantly verified the script visually when coding, which was especially effective when learning a new framework. When participants found an error, they could quickly identify, reason, and correct the code. This might also lead to the fact that for some subtasks (1-3, 3-1, 3-2, 4-1), participants spent more time using DemoScript.

Visualizing Device Examples

Participants preferred how DemoScript presented a list of emulators and showed the mapping between selectors and emulators (4.625, SD=0.52): "*With the initial IDE, it was more difficult to find out which devices were being selected*" (P1). For the subtasks of fixing the selector, 4 of 8 participants chose to create a selector from device examples. P2 noted that "*The other nice thing was the device selector string generator.*"

Participants found it easy to learn (4.5, SD=0.53), script cross-device interactions (4.75, SD=0.46), and felt capable of scripting the provided tasks (4.875, SD=0.35) with DemoScript. Participants also expressed the interests in using DemoScript if it becomes available (4.75, SD=0.46): "*It is awesome and I want to use it :D cant wait for it.*" (P5)

Opportunities and Limitations

We also collected user feedback on the additional supports that they expected DemoScript could provide. First, handling more complicated logic, such as conditioning when a callback function breaks into two different behaviors based on certain condition using `if-else` and `switch`. Our revised design providing basic support of language-based condition is to arbitrarily select one condition and render the storyboard but provide other paths for developers to test. Second, two participants suggested combing the baseline and DemoScript IDEs—to provide a new tool that can interactively shows the step-by-step execution but also allow them to do formal testing with emulators. Debuggers of popular IDEs enable developers to test application logic by inspecting execution states (e.g., checking variable values at breakpoints). In contrast, DemoScript provides high-level visualization of application logic and execution, which allows developers to easily grasp important aspects of interaction flows. These two approaches complement rather than compete with each other. A developer might find it beneficial to switch between the unique advantages of both. Third, the storyboard can be possibly generated as a visual instruction for consumers who would interact with the final application at runtime.

Beyond supporting cross-device programming based on the Weave framework, we argue that many components of DemoScript could apply to other types of app development. Techniques for selecting interactive elements (devices in our case) and providing UI feedback and listening to user events (such as touch or sensor input) are common in interaction or mobile frameworks such as Android. To apply our techniques, one would need to analyze UI constructs in the framework, which is conceptually straightforward. However, it would require additional engineering effort to analyze a program at various levels.

CONCLUSION

We presented DemoScript, a technique that automatically analyzes and visualizes a cross-device interaction program while it is being written. Particularly, we introduced cross-device storyboards, a novel visualization for cross-device development. It is closely coupled with scripting by offering step-by-step execution of a selected portion or the entire program. Via the storyboard, a developer can revise various aspects of a program by direct manipulation. We evaluated DemoScript with 8 professional programmers and found that it outperformed the baseline condition in many ways to simplify programming tasks for complex interaction behaviors.

REFERENCES

1. Azza Abouzied, Joseph Hellerstein, and Avi Silberschatz. 2012. DataPlay: interactive tweaking and example-driven correction of graphical database queries. In *Proc. UIST '12*, 207-218.
2. Apple Inc. Swift. 2015. https://developer.apple.com/swift/
3. Apple Inc. WatchKit. 2015. https://developer.apple.com/watchkit/
4. Ira D. Baxter, Andrew Yahin, Leonardo Moura, Marcelo Sant'Anna, and Lorraine Bier. 1998. Clone Detection Using Abstract Syntax Trees. In *Proc. ICSM '98*, 368-377.
5. Michael Bostock, Vadim Ogievetsky, and Jeffrey Heer. 2011. D3 Data-Driven Documents. *IEEE Transactions on Visualization and Computer Graphics* 17, 12, 2301-2309.
6. Xiang 'Anthony' Chen, Tovi Grossman, Daniel J. Wigdor, and George Fitzmaurice. 2014. Duet: exploring joint interactions on a smart phone and a smart watch. In *Proc. CHI '14*, 159-168.
7. Pei-Yu (Peggy) Chi and Yang Li. 2015. Weave: Scripting Cross-Device Wearable Interaction. In *Proc. CHI '15*, 3923-3932.
8. Stephan Diehl. 2007. *Software Visualization: Visualizing the Structure, Behaviour, and Evolution of Software*. Springer-Verlag New York, Inc., Secaucus, NJ, USA.
9. James Fogarty, Desney Tan, Ashish Kapoor, and Simon Winder. 2008. CueFlik: interactive concept learning in image search. In *Proc. CHI '08*, 29-38.
10. Jens Grubert, Matthias Heinisch, Aaron Quigley, and Dieter Schmalstieg. 2015. MultiFi: Multi Fidelity Interaction with Displays On and Around the Body. In *Proc. CHI '15*, 3933-3942.
11. Google Inc. Android Wear. 2015. https://www.android.com/wear/
12. Google Inc. Chrome Apps. 2015. https://developer.chrome.com/apps/
13. Björn Hartmann, Scott R. Klemmer, Michael Bernstein, Leith Abdulla, Brandon Burr, Avi Robinson-Mosher, and Jennifer Gee. 2006. Reflective physical prototyping through integrated design, test, and analysis. In *Proc. UIST '06*, 299-308.
14. Björn Hartmann, Loren Yu, Abel Allison, Yeonsoo Yang, and Scott R. Klemmer. 2008. Design as exploration: creating interface alternatives through parallel authoring and runtime tuning. In *Proc. UIST '08*, 91-100.
15. Ariya Hidayat. Esprima: ECMAScript parsing infrastructure for multipurpose analysis. 2015. http://esprima.org/
16. Steven Houben and Nicolai Marquardt. 2015. WatchConnect: A Toolkit for Prototyping Smartwatch-Centric Cross-Device Applications. In *Proc. CHI '15*, 1247-1256.
17. Melody Y. Ivory and Marti A Hearst. 2001. The state of the art in automating usability evaluation of user interfaces. *ACM Comput. Surv.* 33, 4, 470-516.
18. Thorsten Karrer, Jan-Peter Krämer, Jonathan Diehl, Björn Hartmann, and Jan Borchers. 2011. Stacksplorer: call graph navigation helps increasing code maintenance efficiency. In *Proc. UIST '11*, 217-224.
19. Jun Kato, Sean McDirmid, and Xiang Cao. 2012. DejaVu: integrated support for developing interactive camera-based programs. In *Proc. UIST '12*, 189-196.
20. Scott R. Klemmer, Mark W. Newman, Ryan Farrell, Mark Bilezikjian, and James A. Landay. 2001. The designers' outpost: a tangible interface for collaborative web site. In *Proc. UIST '01*, 1-10.
21. James A. Landay and Brad A. Myers. 1996. Sketching storyboards to illustrate interface behaviors. In *Proc. CHI '09*, 193-194.
22. Brian Lee, Savil Srivastava, Ranjitha Kumar, Ronen Brafman, and Scott R. Klemmer. 2010. Designing with interactive example galleries. In *Proc. CHI '10*, 2257-2266.
23. Yang Li and James A. Landay. 2008. Activity-based prototyping of ubicomp applications for long-lived, everyday human activities. In *Proc. CHI '08*, 1303-1312.
24. Yang Li, Xiang Cao, Katherine Everitt, Morgan Dixon, and James A. Landay. 2010. FrameWire: a tool for automatically extracting interaction logic from paper prototyping tests. In *Proc. CHI '10*, 503-512.
25. Henry Lieberman and Christopher Fry. 1995. Bridging the gulf between code and behavior in programming. In *Proc. CHI '95*, 480-486.
26. James Lin and James A. Landay. 2008. Employing patterns and layers for early-stage design and prototyping of cross-device user interfaces. In *Proc. CHI '08*, 1313-1322.
27. Microsoft Inc. HoloLens. 2015. https://www.microsoft.com/microsoft-hololens/
28. Brad Myers, Scott E. Hudson, and Randy Pausch. 2000. Past, present, and future of user interface software tools. *ACM Trans. Comput.-Hum. Interact.* 7, 1, 3-28.
29. Michael Nebeling, Theano Mintsi, Maria Husmann, and Moira Norrie. 2014. Interactive development of cross-device user interfaces. In *Proc. CHI '14*, 2793-2802.
30. Donald A. Norman and Stephen W. Draper. 1986. *User Centered System Design; New Perspectives on Human-*

Computer Interaction. L. Erlbaum Assoc. Inc., Hillsdale, NJ, USA.

31. Stephen Oney and Joel Brandt. 2012. Codelets: linking interactive documentation and example code in the editor. In *Proc. CHI '12*, 2697-2706.
32. Roman Rädle, Hans-Christian Jetter, Mario Schreiner, Zhihao Lu, Harald Reiterer, and Yvonne Rogers. 2015. Spatially-aware or Spatially-agnostic?: Elicitation and Evaluation of User-Defined Cross-Device Interactions. In *Proc. CHI '15*, 3913-3922.
33. Daniel Ritchie, Ankita Arvind Kejriwal, and Scott R. Klemmer. 2011. d.tour: style-based exploration of design example galleries. In *Proc. UIST '11*, 165-174.
34. Sifteo Inc. Sifteo Cubes. 2015. https://www.sifteo.com/
35. Michael Toomim, Andrew Begel, and Susan L. Graham. 2004. Managing Duplicated Code with Linked Editing. In *Proc. VLHCC '04*: the 2004 IEEE Symposium on Visual Languages - Human Centric Computing, 173-180.
36. Khai N. Truong, Gillian R. Hayes, and Gregory D. Abowd. 2006. Storyboarding: an empirical determination of best practices and effective guidelines. In *Proc. DIS '06*, 12-21.
37. Jishuo Yang and Daniel Wigdor. 2014. Panelrama: enabling easy specification of cross-device web applications. In *Proc. CHI '14*, 2783-2792.
38. Mark Weiser. 1981. Program slicing. In *Proc. ICSE '81*: the 5th International Conference on Software engineering, 439-449.

XDBrowser: User-Defined Cross-Device Web Page Designs

Michael Nebeling and Anind K. Dey
Human-Computer Interaction Institute, Carnegie Mellon University, Pittsburgh, PA, USA
{ mnebelin, anind }@cs.cmu.edu

ABSTRACT

There is a significant gap in the body of research on cross-device interfaces. Research has largely focused on enabling them technically, but when and how users want to use cross-device interfaces is not well understood. This paper presents an exploratory user study with *XDBrowser*, a cross-device web browser we are developing to enable non-technical users to adapt existing single-device web interfaces for cross-device use while viewing them in the browser. We demonstrate that an end-user customization tool like XDBrowser is a powerful means to conduct user-driven elicitation studies useful for understanding user preferences and design requirements for cross-device interfaces. Our study with 15 participants elicited 144 desirable multi-device designs for five popular web interfaces when using two mobile devices in parallel. We describe the design space in this context, the usage scenarios targeted by users, the strategies used for designing cross-device interfaces, and seven concrete mobile multi-device design patterns that emerged. We discuss the method, compare the cross-device interfaces from our users and those defined by developers in prior work, and establish new requirements from observed user behavior. In particular, we identify the need to easily switch between different interface distributions depending on the task and to have more fine-grained control over synchronization.

Author Keywords

Cross-Device Web Design; End-User Customization Study.

INTRODUCTION

The current proliferation of new devices ranging from smartwatches and phones, to tablets, to interactive tabletops and walls has prompted researchers to investigate combined use of multiple devices. We identify three main research streams.

First, a number of studies have been conducted on multi-device workflows [6, 17, 28, 30] and specifically cross-device web use [18, 20, 19, 34]. These studies clearly identified a need to support sequential and parallel use of multiple devices to more easily share tasks and interfaces between them. However, they were insufficient for producing concrete guidelines on how to adapt existing interfaces for cross-device use.

CHI'16, May 07–12, 2016, San Jose, CA, USA

ACM 978-1-4503-3362-7/16/05$15.00
DOI: http://dx.doi.org/10.1145/2858036.2858048

Second, many different cross-device interaction techniques [3, 4, 29, 31, 32] have been explored. While they are promising for improving cross-device interactions, most techniques are limited to a particular set of applications or combination of devices, and are generally not available in current interfaces.

A third stream of research has investigated new cross-device design tools [5, 7, 8, 9, 11, 12, 13, 14, 25, 36]. The vast majority of these tools, however, are targeted at developers, allowing them to distribute interfaces between devices programmatically or using special authoring tools. While a number of possible cross-device interfaces were showcased to illustrate technical support, whether or not these address actual user needs and are desirable by end-users was not explored.

As part of the *XDBrowser* project, we are investigating how existing web browsers can be extended to support parallel usage of multiple devices as motivated by previous studies. This paper presents a prototype of XDBrowser that enables non-technical users to adapt existing single-device interfaces for cross-device use. We use XDBrowser primarily as a tool for conducting a user-driven elicitation study on cross-device interfaces. Asking users to customize and try out alternative cross-device designs during active use, enabled us to observe user behavior both when designing and when using cross-device interfaces. The main contribution of this paper is therefore our study, which aims to build a better understanding of when and how users want to use cross-device interfaces.

Our work is inspired by the early cross-device paper prototyping study by Hutchings and Pierce [15]. In their study, users were asked to demonstrate how they would want interfaces to be distributed between devices when used in different multi-device environments. Our own research also started out using paper prototyping to experiment with different cross-device interfaces and considered designing for many different cross-device settings. However, we quickly realized that a crucial element for users is to experience the interaction as closely as possible to the final interface. We wanted to avoid the three main limitations we found with their study design.

First, paper prototyping has strong limitations when testing response times and when comparing small variations of an interface. The latter became particularly evident when designing for a combination of handheld mobile devices, where interfaces are small and preferences depend on the details of the interaction, making the paper prototyping method unsuitable.

Second, they studied three multi-device settings that resulted in a rather high-level analysis of user-defined distributions, mostly showing that users wanted to distribute interfaces in all conditions, but providing little detail on how. We focus on one likely cross-device setting using two mobile devices in parallel to study this in detail.

Third, their study asked users to customize each interface for one particular task. Our study instead is exploratory in nature, asking users to customize for all the tasks that they would like to perform with the cross-device version of the interface and use the think-aloud protocol to describe how their interactions and tasks would benefit from cross-device use.

In our study, 15 participants created 144 desirable multi-device designs for five popular types of interfaces when using two mobile devices in parallel. We report on usage scenarios suggested by users, the design strategies employed by users when designing for this cross-device setting, and seven mobile multi-device design patterns underlying the user-defined interfaces. Based on user feedback, we analyze both ease of design and ease of use of different cross-device interfaces and identify the reasons why some cross-device interfaces were more difficult to create than others, and how to better support those in future cross-device design tools. We close with a discussion of our method and how the user-defined designs from our study compared to developer-defined designs from prior work, as well as suggesting ways of using our results in future research.

RELATED WORK

We build on prior work on *multi-device workflows*, *cross-device systems and toolkits*, and *end-user customization*.

Multi-Device Workflows

Early studies by Oulasvirta and Sumari [28] and Dearman and Pierce [6] in the context of mobile information work identified a strong need for seamless multi-device interaction because many activities spanned multiple devices. However, multi-device workflows had to be carefully planned as they were commonly hindered by two facts. First, information and actions are tied to the device rather than the user. Second, devices are not aware of their role in the user's larger task.

In addition to the more serial workflows identified by these works, a recent study by Santosa and Wigdor [30] found new patterns of parallel device use. Despite widespread adoption of cloud services for multi-device synchronization, the authors still report a lack of support for parallelism in cross-device interactions. Jokela *et al.* [17] distinguish between resource lending, related parallel use, and unrelated parallel use. They identify three challenges users commonly face when using multiple devices in parallel: deciding which devices to use, accessing content between devices, and keeping devices updated and charged. Display size, input capabilities, and level of multi-tasking support are the main factors in choosing which device to use in a specific situation.

With a particular focus on cross-device web use, Kane *et al.* [18] analyzed web-based usage data across devices and found that often the same sites were visited in desktop and mobile settings. Follow-up studies by Karlson *et al.* [20] using log analysis identified temporal usage patterns with information workers as well as strong device preferences for certain tasks, such as preferring the smartphone for keeping track of emails and device switching rarely occurring within a given task. A second screenshot-based diary study [19] found that smartphone tasks were often suspended until they could be completed on the PC. They identified and discussed major task completion barriers such as missing functionality, input/output challenges, complex tasks and cost/benefit choices.

Together, these studies identify a lack of support for synchronizing relevant task state across devices to make it easy to transition a task between devices. They also highlight that, in order for users to benefit from using multiple devices to complete a task, they need to be able to decompose the task into meaningful subtasks that they can then distribute and perform using multiple devices. Our work adds to these studies by detailing when and how users want common web browsing tasks to be distributed between multiple devices and the cross-device interactions demanded by users.

To enable our study, we first studied the technical support available in existing cross-device systems and tools. Using this knowledge, we developed our prototype of XDBrowser and used it as a tool to study user-defined cross-device interfaces.

Cross-Device Systems and Toolkits

Johanson *et al.* [16] introduced the idea of *multibrowsing* and developed special software enabling users to send web pages to, or open them from, other devices. A lot of the research since then has focused on improving the technical aspects of multibrowsing. For example, Ghiani *et al.* [9] developed push-and-pull techniques that are not limited to transferring URLs between devices, but provide advanced support for HTML DOM capture and JavaScript state persistence. This enables full migration between devices and even multiple users, but comes at the cost of additional infrastructure and requires its own web proxy-based migration environment [10].

Recently, a number of cross-device systems and toolkits were proposed. We focus our review on those that informed the design of XDBrowser's distribution tools the most.

Panelrama [36] is a web-based toolkit with support for interface division and automated distribution between devices based on developer-specified groups of web page elements, so-called panels, and their suitability for distribution. Panels need to be specified in HTML and panel state captured and synchronized in JavaScript using shared variables.

With the Tandem Browsing Toolkit [12], developers can create multi-display web sites consisting of multiple parts which can be viewed on several devices in parallel. Geared towards web applications that have stages, *e.g.,* a shopping web site that consists of a login, item selection and checkout stage, the toolkit synchronizes transitions from one stage to another across multiple devices through a finite state machine.

Frosini and Paterno [8] propose a flexible framework based on the idea of dynamically migrating engines that provides developers with an API for interface distribution and/or migration between dynamic sets of devices. Distribution can be dynamically controlled based on the types of a specific device or group of devices and the roles associated to a specific user or groups of users, which can be switched at any time.

XDStudio [25] is the first distributed interface builder following a long line of previous multi-device authoring tools such as Damask [22], Gummy [24] and D-Macs [23]. The specific focus of XDStudio is on enabling interactive development of cross-device interfaces by adding cross-device capabilities to the authoring environment itself. Distributed interfaces can be designed by simulating target devices, by directly involving them *via* on-device authoring, or both. At its core is the notion of distribution profiles that enable reuse of existing interface distributions and their adaptation to new cross-device settings not originally designed for at run-time.

While this past work is very motivating to the goal of enabling more seamless cross-device interaction, the techniques have so far been limited to developers. Our goal with XDBrowser is to adapt and integrate the cross-device support that has already been implemented and demonstrated as separate systems targeted at developers. We want this support to be available directly in a web browser without requiring developers to modify interfaces to enable cross-device use and without requiring users to install and use special migration infrastructure and browsing clients. To avoid these constraints, our prototype necessarily does not offer a full range of support for cross-device interfaces. With our prototype, however, non-technical users are able to browse existing single-device interfaces and customize them for serial or parallel usage of multiple devices *via* built-in visual tools. Most importantly, browser view state and input can be flexibly controlled and synchronized between multiple devices. This was crucial for letting users experiment with different kinds of cross-device interfaces and eliciting both technical and design requirements from the usage of XDBrowser and observed user behavior.

End-User Customization

End-user customization techniques commonly aim to empower non-technical users with simple and easy-to-use tools for adapting existing interfaces to their requirements. Our prototype of XDBrowser adds to the research in this area and shares commonalities with the following systems.

PageTailor [2] provides end-users on PDAs with a direct manipulation interface and simple controls for hiding, resizing and repositioning elements in a web page. Using PageTailor, web pages can be customized over multiple browsing sessions and are automatically reconfigured when a page is loaded.

The Highlight [27] system takes the inverse approach in that, while browsing a web page on the desktop PC, end-users can demonstrate interactions central to the application for browsing on mobiles. The interaction sequences and corresponding web page elements are learned and used to generate a smaller, mobile-friendly version of the original page. Highlight uses a separate authoring tool that provides a storyboard view and a preview to browse and refine the mobile versions.

The PlayByPlay system [35] shares browsing sessions in the form of instant messages that can be executed in another browser using the CoScripter technology [21]. This is particularly powerful for collaborative web browsing with multiple users and can also be used for synchronizing web browsing actions across multiple desktop and mobile devices.

CrowdAdapt [26] builds on crowdsourcing and introduces new adaptation operations to support, not only desktop-to-mobile adaptation, but a much wider range of devices including large screens. With CrowdAdapt, users can interactively adapt the web page layout similar to PageTailor and share their customizations so that others browsing with similar devices can immediately benefit from user-contributed layouts.

Our XDBrowser prototype extends these techniques so that existing interfaces can be partitioned, copied and moved between devices as they are viewed in the browser. Compared to previous developer-oriented techniques [10, 14, 26, 25, 36] which are all based on HTML DOM element selection, XDBrowser does not require the user to understand the page's internal structure and composition of the layout. In fact, it works independent of the HTML DOM and easily caters to cases where page elements are specified at different levels of the DOM hierarchy. Inspired by WinCuts [33], we implemented a rectangular selection tool allowing users to frame any part of the web page that they want to share between devices. In addition, multi-select is supported so that different parts of the same page can be shared. As a result, web interfaces can be cut, copied and moved between devices, making it as easy as constructing paper prototypes for multi-device environments [1, 15], but allowing this directly in the browser *via* visual tools that are suitable for non-technical users.

CROSS-DEVICE INTERFACES WITH XDBROWSER

Our larger goal with XDBrowser is to support more seamless cross-device use when browsing on multiple devices in parallel. We developed a prototype to better understand user needs and study when and how users want to use cross-device interfaces. The main idea of our study was to ask users to adapt popular single-device interfaces for cross-device use as they view and interact with them using the browser.

XDBrowser supports three common functions for multi-device interface distribution adapted from existing cross-device systems and tools: *(1)* pushing an entire page to a device, *(2)* pushing user selected parts of a page, and *(3)* pulling a page from another device. When pushing or pulling pages using these functions, XDBrowser opens the URL in a new tab on the target device and checks whether the user selected regions within the page. If that is the case, the page will be split into the corresponding regions.

To illustrate the three functions and the resulting actions in XDBrowser, let us use an example. Figure 1 shows a scenario in which XDBrowser was used to combine a smartphone and a tablet to work around individual device limitations and maximize screen usage by distributing parts of a mail interface. The phone is used for viewing the inbox and selecting mails (Step *1*), while the tablet is used as the primary device for reading mails (Step *2*)). Clicking a message on the phone loads the respective mail on the tablet. This is an example of the *overview+detail* design pattern commonly employed by users to view details on the larger device and keep an overview on the smaller device.

Users can choose which tabs or shared page they want to keep in sync. When synchronization is activated for a page,

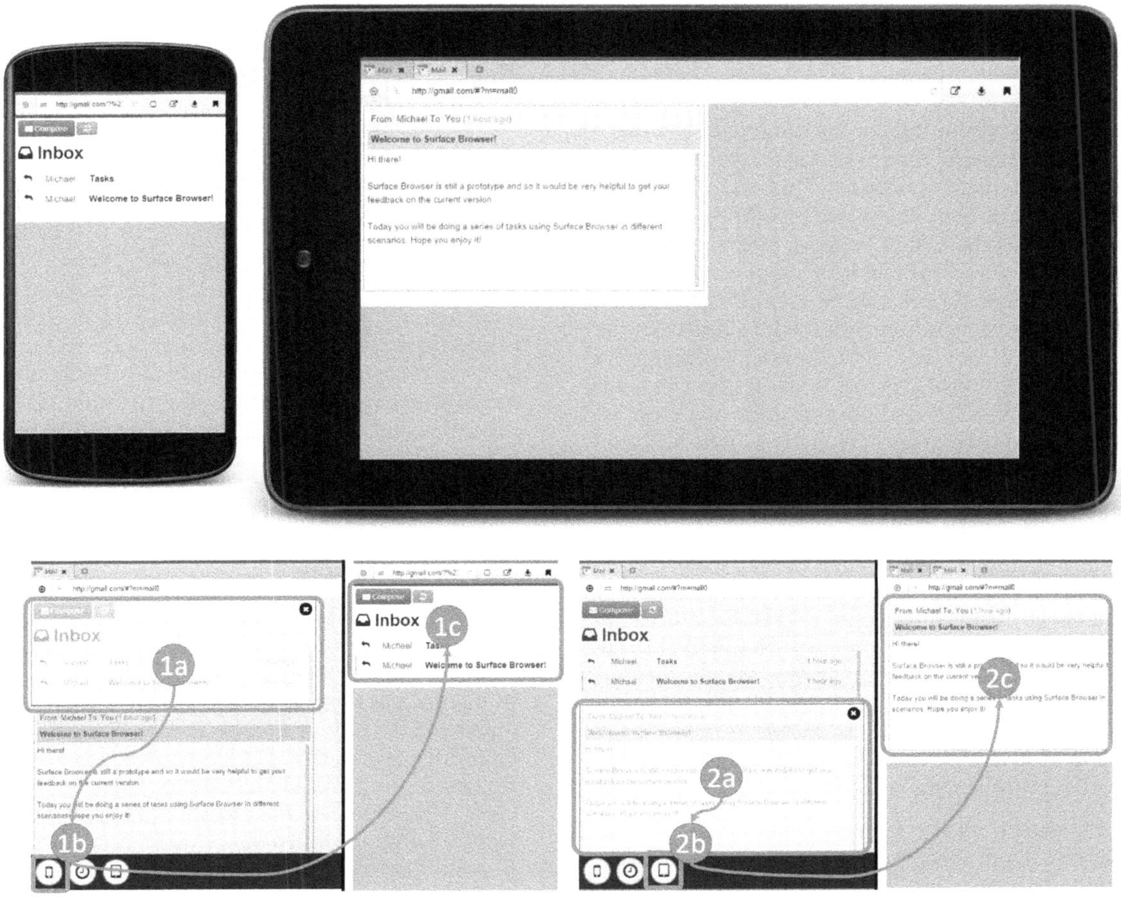

Figure 1. Mail interface customized using XDBrowser to view the inbox on a smartphone (Steps *1a)* select inbox on tablet; *1b)* push inbox from tablet to phone; *1c)* inbox on phone) and read selected mails on a tablet (Steps *2a)* select message on tablet; *2b)* push message to tablet; *2c)* message on tablet)

XDBrowser will broadcast changes of the viewport and input provided by the user to connected devices. All tabs that have the same page loaded will be updated with the new view state and input. XDBrowser automatically activates synchronization for pages pushed to, or pulled from, another device. Users can toggle synchronization at a per-tab level, or can disable synchronization for all tabs at once to operate the device completely independently from other connected devices.

XDBrowser supports four synchronization options that can be toggled to achieve different cross-device interactions:

1. *Click sync* captures click events at the document level, therefore covering the entire page, and replays them in all synced tabs by locating the target element and triggering the associated click handler. To prevent multiple form data submissions, clicks on submit buttons are not replayed.

2. *Scroll sync* monitors scrolling along both axes and maintains the scroll state by transferring and setting the scroll position in proportion to the viewport size on synchronized devices.

3. *Input sync* captures keyboard, mouse and touch input on any form input field (text fields, checkboxes and radio buttons, comboboxes and multi-selects) part of the page. For each field, the current value is serialized and restored in synced browser tabs opened on the same and connected devices.

4. *URL sync* tracks changes to the URL loaded into a tab including changes to the fragment or hash part. The hash is not only used by web browsers to jump to anchor links, but also by many modern web applications, such as GMail, Google Maps, or YouTube, to store page-internal state, such as the selected mail folder or message, the location and zoom level of the map, or the video and timeline index. When a change of the URL is detected, XDBrowser updates all synchronized tabs with that URL so that page-internal state is transferred and updated on all connected devices.

In combination, these four synchronization options enable XDBrowser to fully restore the browser's view state and input when a page is shared between devices. Synchronization keeps the interactions in one tab or shared page synchronized with all other tabs on the same device or on connected devices that have the same page opened. Therefore, with all synchronization options enabled, clicking buttons, scrolling the page, entering form data, and jumping to anchors or modifying the URL on one device will perform the same action on all connected devices. Disabling synchronization means that the interactions on the current device will have no effect on the other devices. Synchronization can be toggled at any time so that it is possible to decouple devices to operate them independently and reintegrate and resynchronize them on demand. Note that this all still works when pages are cut into regions and even if multiple cuts of the same page are shared with other devices since XDBrowser only restricts the viewport according to the user's selection. This essentially hides, but does not extract or remove, HTML DOM elements and therefore does not run the risk of breaking web pages. While these features may not be sufficient to support all the cross-device interfaces that could possibly be created with previous systems and toolkits, our study reported later shows that they do make XDBrowser a powerful tool for users to explore and experiment with the kinds of cross-device interfaces they find useful and usable. We developed the synchronization options prior to the study and believe they are generic and could apply to a wider range of applications than the ones we studied.

XDBROWSER IMPLEMENTATION

XDBrowser is implemented as a fullscreen browser interface running within the OS's default web browser. The fact that only native browser features based on HTML5 and CSS3 are used enables XDBrowser to run on any web-enabled device providing modern browser support, with *no need for modification or special software*, making it a lightweight solution that can readily be adopted. The browser interface is responsive to the device in use, enabling its interface to adapt to a wide range of mobile devices including phones, tablets, and laptops.

XDBrowser uses a client-server architecture. The two main client-side components are: (1) *browser windows* containing the browser's navigation controls and wrapping the actual web pages in iframes and (2) *selection boxes* for cutting browser windows and transferring parts of a page. When distributing pages, first the iframe wrapping the entire page is cloned. For each selection box, the cloned iframe is then wrapped again in a new container sized to fit the selection box and translated to match the scroll position. The main components are implemented using the jQuery Widget Factory. Modernizr and CSS3 media queries are used for XDBrowser's responsive design. Depending on the device's screen dimensions and available touch support, either jQuery UI or Hammer.js are used for draggable and resizable behaviors. The server is based on Node.js. Socket.IO is used for realtime bidirectional event-based communication between all connected devices.

While sufficient for our study, this implementation has some limitations. Our approach works best with pages served locally or stored offline. Many top sites forbid iframe embedding and browsers prevent cross-site scripting, but a proxy server fixes this [9]. For sites that maintain a session, the user needs to login on each device, but a remote-control architecture [27] or shared virtual browser such as PhantomJS resolves this [14].

STUDY DESIGN

Our end-user customization study with XDBrowser comprised three parts. First, a questionnaire collected data on participants' use of devices and interfaces, their experience using touch as input and designing interfaces, and demographic information. They were then introduced to the core features of XDBrowser, explaining the push-and-pull functions and means for synchronization by showing examples of multi-device distributions. This part of the study was used both for training and priming of participants regarding possible cross-device interfaces.

Second, participants were asked to perform five customization tasks for the interfaces shown in Figure 2. Task order was randomized and counterbalanced between participants. For each task, participants used XDBrowser on two mobile devices of different size, a Nexus 4 phone and a Nexus 7 tablet. Using the features of XDBrowser and the think-aloud protocol, they were asked to perform each customization task in three steps: *(1)* demonstrate a task they commonly perform with the interface, *(2)* create desirable interface distributions to perform the task using the two devices in parallel, and *(3)* perform the task using the custom cross-device interface. Immediately after each customization task, participants were given a short questionnaire where they rated three statements related to the task: *"I would enjoy operating the browser in this manner"*, *"It was easy to do the task"*, and *"The available features were effective for this task"*.

At the end of the study, users filled in a detailed questionnaire rating various features of XDBrowser. We recruited 15 participants (10 male, 5 female, median age 28) with high experience using touch as input (median 6 using 7-point Likert scale) and intermediate UI design skills (median 5). All participants indicated high familiarity with the five web sites that our versions resembled, and owned and used multiple devices on a regular basis. There was no time limit in the study and participants were encouraged to try out as many different designs as they wanted. The study took roughly one hour per participant.

Below we describe the five interfaces used for customization: mail client, media player, maps viewer, article reader and slideshow presenter (Figure 2). These interfaces were commonly reported in the cross-device literature [4, 8, 11, 25, 36]. We believed that this selection would give us a variety of interfaces with different requirements and best allow us to compare the cross-device interfaces designed by our users to those designed by developers in previous work. All interfaces were based on real web sites; however, these are highly dynamic and personalized. Our versions ensured that the same content is shown to all participants. Rather than five specific existing sites, we wanted to test representative but simplified versions of them to focus users on core page elements.

Mail Interface

Similar to many email clients, the *mail* interface is composed of two pages: an inbox and a compose page. The inbox lists mails and shows the content of a mail selected from the list. The compose page for writing mails is opened when the compose button or the reply icon next to each mail is pressed. With this interface, we were interested in understanding how users would deal with synchronized pages, showing details of selected mails, and text input in a multi-device scenario.

Media Interface

Inspired from and implemented using YouTube, the *media* interface contains a video player and a playlist with controls for pausing/resuming playback, muting and unmuting, seeking

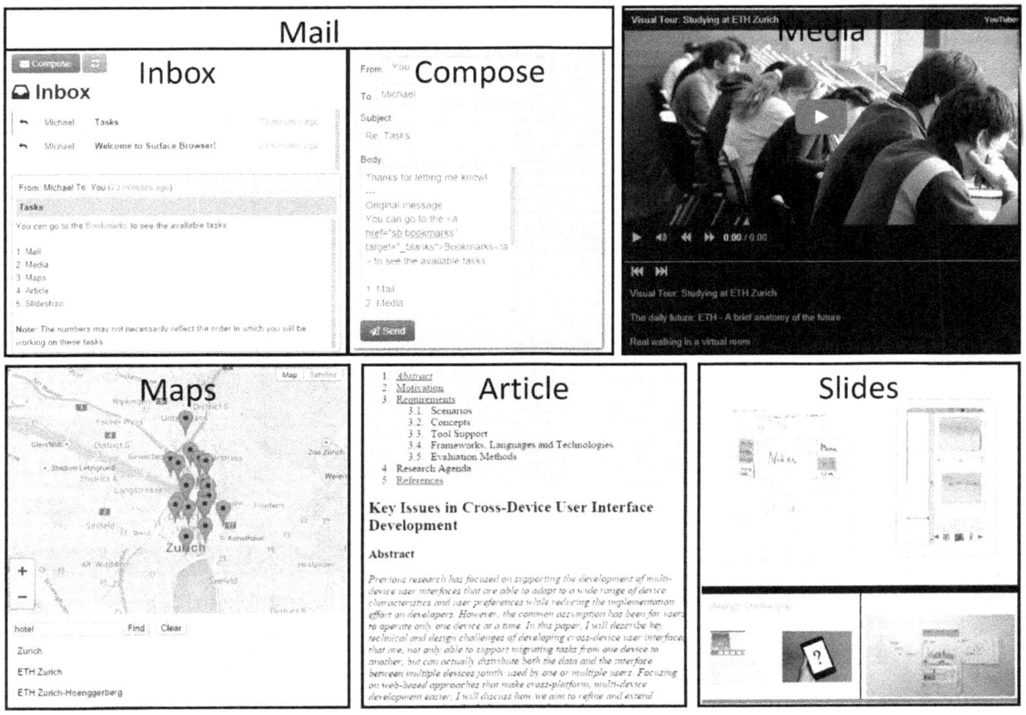

Figure 2. The five customization tasks used for the study involved a mail client, a media player, a maps browser, an article reader and a slides viewer.

through the video, as well as rotating through the playlist. The playlist was restricted to three selected videos. This is an interesting interface for our study as it raises the question of which device(s) should play video and/or audio as well as issues of synchronizing media and controlling playback.

Maps Interface

Based on Google Maps, the *maps* interface embeds a map that can be panned and zoomed using gestures. It also has controls for switching between the map, terrain and satellite views as well as increasing/decreasing the zoom level. Located below the map is an input field for text search based on the Google Places service. For each place found in response to a query (*e.g.*, "hotel"), a marker will be added to the map. Markers can be clicked to show additional information. The *maps* interface also lists three places that center and zoom the map on the target location when selected. This interface is interesting due to the many possible configurations of the map across devices and in terms of what should and should not be synchronized.

Article Interface

Similar to many online newspapers, blogs and wikis, the *article* interface shows a table of contents with links to the respective sections in the text, an excerpt of the actual text, and a list of the references for citations in the text. This interface is interesting for exploring scrolling and navigation within larger pages and how the need for these may be reduced with cross-device use.

Slides Interface

Finally, to cover tasks common to gallery browsing and slideshow presentations, we included the *slides* interface. It consists of the current slide that can be clicked to go to the next slide, as well as thumbnail previews of the previous and next slides. Each preview can be clicked to set it as the current slide. In addition, the interface contained a textarea for notes. This interface is interesting as all page elements control and provide a different view on the state of the slideshow.

RESULTS

The main results of our study comprise the usage scenarios suggested by participants for parallel device use, the design strategies employed by participants when customizing each interface, and the design patterns emerging from the different designs created by participants. They also include participant feedback in terms of whether they would enjoy using XD-Browser, its ease of use when customizing each interface, and the effectiveness of its distribution and synchronization tools.

Cross-Device Interfaces and Usage Scenarios

In total, participants created 144 desirable designs with XD-Browser for the five interfaces using the two mobile devices. With an average of 9.6 different designs per participant and 1.92 per participant and task, participants could almost always think of at least two different ways of customizing and using each interface in the cross-device setting. We discuss the highlights of each customization task below, showing the variety of cross-device interfaces created using XDBrowser.

Mail Interface

For the *mail* interface, participants commonly customized for two primary tasks: reading mails and writing mails. A popular design for the first task was to use the phone for checking the inbox and selecting messages that participants then read on the tablet (Figure 3(a)). However, when they considered customizing for the second main task, writing mails, they

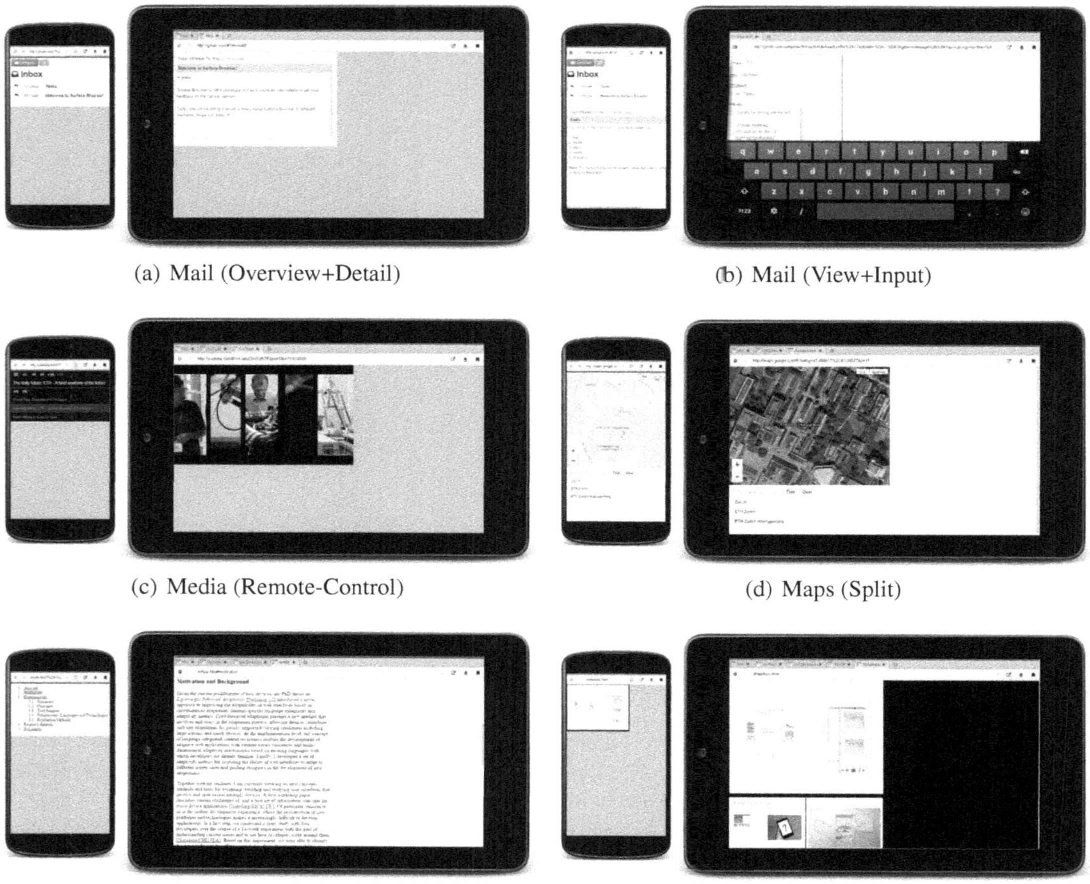

(a) Mail (Overview+Detail) (b) Mail (View+Input)

(c) Media (Remote-Control) (d) Maps (Split)

(e) Article (Overview+Detail) (f) Slides (Extend)

Figure 3. Examples of user-defined cross-device interfaces and the five cross-device design patterns that were most popular for these interfaces.

opted for a different cross-device design. In order to dedicate one device to input only, in this case, many participants used the tablet for composing mails and the phone for checking the inbox *and* reading mails (Figure 3(b)). They explained that the on-screen touch keyboard on the tablet is larger and more comfortable for typing. Since both tasks typically go hand in hand, participants wanted to quickly switch between the two different versions optimized for each task. To achieve this with our current prototype, participants opened two tabs with the *mail* interface, one for the customizations for reading and the other for writing mails. They then synchronized them and switched tabs according to the task.

Media Interface

The *media* interface was commonly customized for one task: playing media. The most frequent cross-device design showed the video in fullscreen on the tablet and the playback controls and the playlist on the smartphone (Figure 3(c)). However, participants distinguished between watching videos by themselves and showing videos to others, and made minor modifications in each case. In the first case, one participant copied one half of the video player on one device and the other half on the other device to make full use of the combined screen real estate. In the second case, another participant kept a smaller preview of the video on the smartphone for their own reference. In both cases, participants debated which devices should play sound. Participants often muted sound on the smartphone to limit audio to the tablet where speakers are usually better compared to those on smartphones. Some however played sound on both devices to have a better stereo effect when watching videos alone. One participant only played sound on the smartphone *via* headphones and watch the video on the tablet without having to worry about headphone cables. Participants also commonly suggested at some stage during the task that they might want to look up related information on the smartphone, *e.g.,* movie actors or lyrics for music videos. They could do this by disabling synchronization on the smartphone to use it independently from the tablet.

Maps Interface

The *maps* interface was customized for two primary tasks, namely for looking up a location on the map and for comparing maps. For looking up a location, the most popular cross-device design showed the map using a higher zoom factor on the tablet for a detailed view and a lower zoom level on the smartphone for an overview (Figure 3(d)) However, keeping the map views synchronized was a challenge since participants only wanted to synchronize the center of the map and not the zoom factor. This was tricky for XDBrowser's URL sync since the maps URL contains both parameters and hence synchronized both the center and the zoom level of the map view. For comparing maps, participants created different designs for comparing either the same location using two different map views or two different locations. In the first case, designs commonly showed the default map view on the phone and the terrain or satellite view on the tablet. These were considered useful for planning a bike trip and exploring the surroundings for walks and hikes. In the second case, the phone was used to zoom on one location and the tablet to zoom on another location. This was considered helpful for planning a road trip and deciding where to make a stop. For either task, participants found that the way XDBrowser currently synchronizes URLs was not ideal. They therefore only used synchronization up to the point of loading the *maps* interface on both devices and then disabled it to browse the maps independently on each device.

Article Interface

The *article* interface was customized for the primary task of reading the text and occasionally checking references. The most common cross-device design showed the article text on the tablet for reading and the table of contents and list of references on the smartphone (Figure 3(e)). When clicking on links in the table of contents or the references on the smartphone, participants commonly wanted XDBrowser to jump to the respective passage in the article on the tablet, rather than scrolling the page on the smartphone. To keep a lock on these parts of the page, participants cut the interface into two regions, one containing the table of contents and the other the references, to remove the article text from the smartphone. They explained that this design allowed them to use the smartphone for overview and reference purposes in support of the primary task of reading on the tablet.

Slides Interface

Participants customized the *slides* interface for a primary task, showing slides, and a secondary task, taking notes. For the primary task, the most common cross-device design showed the current slide on the tablet and the slide's previous and next previews on the smartphone (Figure 3(f)). For the secondary task, many wanted to exclusively use the smartphone for taking notes and show the rest of the interface on the tablet. Compared to the *mail* interface, however, they anticipated that switching between the two designs would not frequently occur while using the interface. They would either show slides or review slides and take notes. These two separate activities therefore did not create the same challenges as for the *mail* interface, where quickly switching between different customizations was commonly requested.

Design Strategies

In general, while customizing interfaces, participants considered and weighed the cost associated with using both devices, and necessarily having to switch between them, as opposed to just using one device for the task at hand. Although the vast majority of designs created by participants involved parallel use of both devices, not all of them did. If participants did not see the benefit in using both devices, they simply just used one of the devices for the task.

In observing participants customizing most interfaces for parallel multi-device use, we identified three common design strategies: *(1)* optimize for screen space, *(2)* optimize for input, and *(3)* minimize device switching.

The first strategy is motivated by participants' understanding that combining two devices provides more space for viewing content than using the devices in isolation. An obvious example of this strategy was the *media* interface with the player stretching across both devices. Other examples include the mail design for reading tasks where moving the inbox to the phone afforded more space on the tablet for reading messages, and the *maps* interface with overview and detail views on the tablet and phone. While we did not measure user performance during tasks, participants expected that optimizing along the screen size dimension reduces the time and effort required for between-page navigation (*e.g.,* inbox *vs.* compose mail), within-page navigation (*e.g.,* scrolling the article page), and panning/zooming (*e.g.,* viewing maps).

The second strategy was based on participants' preference for typing on the device with the larger keyboard where they felt they could type faster and with fewer errors. Clear instances of this strategy were observed for the *mail* and *slides* interfaces, where synchronization between the smartphone and the tablet allowed participants to view content on the smartphone while writing messages or taking notes on the tablet.

The third strategy was to keep the number of device switches during tasks low. This was exhibited through participants keeping the interface parts that they commonly required during a task together on the same device. On the other hand, the interface parts that helped them transition between tasks were commonly copied or moved to the other device. Again a good example is the *mail* interface where the tablet was used for the main task, reading messages, and the smartphone for opening messages on the tablet. This cross-device design only requires switching between devices when the user wants to select a different message for reading, which corresponds to starting a new task. However, when the larger task was writing messages, participants changed the design to keep the inbox and reading pane together on one device and used the tablet for writing.

Design Patterns

We reviewed each of the 144 designs created by participants, extracted common features and grouped the results into the largest classes. Seven multi-device patterns from three groups—*async patterns*, *copy and sync patterns*, and *move and sync patterns*—were identified in two separate passes and discussed with an independent cross-device researcher. Figure 4 gives an overview of the design patterns and how frequently they were employed in each customization task, while Figure 3 illustrates popular designs for the top five patterns. Below we present the groups and each pattern in turn.

1. Async Patterns

The first group consists of asynchronous multi-device use patterns, *i.e.,* using devices independently or not in full sync.

Single

While the vast majority were cross-device designs, three designs (2%) used only a single device. Three participants did not find it beneficial for the *media*, *maps* and *article* tasks

Pattern/Interface	Mail	Media	Maps	Article	Slides	Total
Async						
Single	0	1	1	1	0	3
Split	1	1	8	6	0	16
Overview+Detail	9	2	6	12	3	32
Copy and Sync						
Mirror	1	2	1	1	1	6
Extend	4	6	4	2	6	22
Move and Sync						
Remote-Control	4	13	10	4	14	45
View+Input	13	0	2	0	5	20
Total	32	25	32	26	29	144

Figure 4. Seven multi-device patterns, including five for cross-device use in parallel, and how often each was suggested in the five customization tasks. Highest-scoring patterns per task are indicated in gray shading.

to be able to use the two devices in combination and instead suggested using the original interface on just one of them.

Split
16 designs (11%) used the same interface on both devices in parallel, but in a not fully synchronized split view. This was popular for *maps*, *e.g.,* for route planning and exploring the surroundings using different map views (Figure 3(d)).

Overview+Detail
With 32 designs (23%), the second most popular pattern was to have only the parts of the interface that were useful for overview purposes on one device, and only the parts with details on the other. This was the most common proposal in the *article* task with 12 designs (8%) (Figure 3(e)).

2. Copy and Sync Patterns
The second group consists of patterns in which the page is copied and fully synchronized between devices.

Mirror
Six designs (4%) assigned equal roles to devices and duplicated the interface. Participants expected that the state of the interface would be fully synchronized between devices, *e.g.,* two suggested it in the *media* task for playback in stereo.

Extend
22 designs (15%) replicated parts of the interface on the second device so that the interface extended across both devices. For example, a common design for *slides* was to replicate the current slide on the second device (Figure 3(f)).

3. Move and Sync Patterns
The third group consists of patterns that move parts of the page from one device to the other and keep them in sync.

Remote-Control
The most popular pattern with 45 designs (31%) moved parts of the interface to another device for remote control. This was most common in the *media* and *slides* tasks where it was popular to have all controls only on the phone (Figure 3(c)).

View+Input
20 designs (14%) used one device for viewing content and the other for text input. This was most popular for *mail* with the phone used for viewing the inbox and the tablet for writing messages as input was perceived to be easier on the tablet given the larger virtual keyboard (Figure 3(b)).

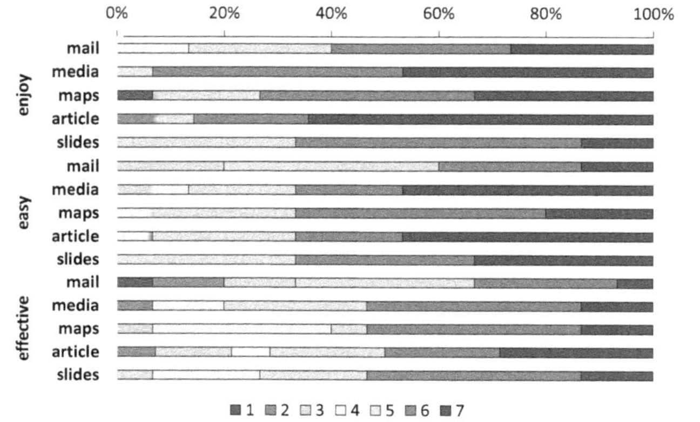

Figure 5. Post-task feedback on whether participants enjoyed operating XDBrowser, found the task easy to perform and provided tools effective.

User Feedback
When asked about the main benefits of XDBrowser, one participant said: *"It lets you take advantage of the strengths of each device, so that you have the smoothest overall experience"* (P1). It was considered useful for *"combining display and input devices for an improved user experience"* (P4) and for *"the fact that you can easily switch from one device to the other by means of sync"* (P9). Participants appreciated XDBrowser's *"distribution of the view area and the input area to maximize the view area"* (P13) and the ability to *"move typing tasks to the tablet"* (P12). Other aspects they highlighted included that *"less scrolling is necessary because I can navigate using a second device"* (P15) and that they could use XDBrowser *"to show to another person what I see on my screen"* (P14).

We also asked participants what they think are the main shortcomings of our prototype. In line with the challenges of creating cross-device interfaces for some tasks, it was considered necessary to *"make it easier to switch between tabs when combined"* (P1). Currently, *"too many steps are required for selecting content to be shared, should be automated for me"* (P3). For some interfaces, some participants were *"not sure all the time what gets synced and what doesn't"* (P15) and found that *"sync control could be more sophisticated"* (P5).

From the post-task feedback shown in Figure 5, we can see that participants enjoyed using XDBrowser for the tasks, found it easy to perform the tasks and the customization tools creating cross-device designs effective. Across all tasks, the median ratings were at or above 5 on a 7-point Likert-scale (7 = best).

Enjoyment
Overall, participants enjoyed using XDBrowser. Two participants answered that, while the tasks were easy and the features seemed effective, they would not enjoy using the two devices in combination for the *maps* and *article* interfaces and gave it a low rating for that reason.

Ease of Use
The *mail* task was not so easy for three participants who wanted to open the compose page directly on the other device without having to first open it on, and then push it to, the target device, which is currently required. The *media* task was not so easy for some participants due to the fact that autoplay is not available on mobile devices as enforced by the HTML5

standard, which required the video player to be started once on each device before it could be synchronized.

Effectiveness

The browser's features were generally deemed effective with some differences between tasks. Again, participants gave lower ratings in the *mail* and *media* task for the same issues noted above. The *maps* task received several slightly negative to neutral ratings mainly due to the fact that synchronizing the map's bounds between devices meant that also the zoom level remained in sync. This was contrary to some proposals of participants who wanted to maintain the same location, but have different views and zoom levels on the two devices. The lower ratings in the *article* task were given by participants who, as also requested for the mail application, wanted to open links in the text directly on the other device, rather than jumping to the anchor on the current device. Finally, the *slides* task received lower effectiveness ratings by participants who wanted to scale the current slide to fill the viewport. This was also often requested in the *media* task; however, there it was not an issue since YouTube supports fullscreen playback.

DISCUSSION

At the highest level, we differentiate distribution and synchronization, and distinguish two distribution methods, *copy/move*, and four synchronization options, *click/scroll/input/URL sync*. Many different designs were possible and a pattern analysis grouped the results into the seven largest classes. Our patterns can be seen as distinct but not disjoint, *i.e.*, a particular design can have elements in common with more than one pattern. Two pieces of information were used for disambiguation: *(i)* main function of distributed elements based on separation of content, navigation and presentation, *(ii)* participants' stated intent behind each distribution and role of each device. Figure 3(c) is a *remote-control* example because all navigation elements were moved to the phone with the intent to control video playback on the tablet. Figure 3(e) is *overview+detail* rather than *remote-control* although the table of contents with some navigation elements was moved to the phone because the intent was still to navigate the article primarily on the tablet.

Several recent works have presented cross-device designs for mail clients, media players, map browsers, document readers and gallery viewers similar to the five tasks we studied [4, 8, 11, 25, 36]. However, these were commonly designed by developers. Many of the designs proposed by developers can be classified as *mirror*, *extend*, *remote-control* and *overview+detail* patterns. While there is agreement in terms of classification, overall we found much less usage than expected for some of these patterns in our study. For example, *mirror* and *extend* designs from the *copy and sync* category were not very popular among participants. We suspect that this may have to do with our study only using two devices and that duplication or replication of interfaces may be more desired with additional devices. However, this is something that remains to be established.

Much more popular in our study were the *move and sync* patterns instead. Here, the examples shown in the literature missed some designs frequently created by our participants. For example, Duet [4], Conductor [11] and Panelrama [36] all present similar cross-device designs for the *mail* and *maps* interfaces. However, we find two major differences in the results of our study. First, our study showed a lot of variety with many different designs from the *move and sync* pattern category especially for these two interfaces. Second, none of them considered different tasks for each interface whereas our participants distinguished between primary and secondary tasks for which they wanted different cross-device designs.

The design strategies and patterns we extracted from user-defined designs establish the variety of desired designs and the data we collected on user preferences can guide designers in making informed decisions about choosing the right pattern for different tasks. Our study helps to provide a better picture of the mobile cross-device design space and can inform future design in this context. Our motivation to focus on two mobile devices was to generate a rich set of patterns for a setting that is increasingly common [17, 29, 30]. If existing web sites were to implement our patterns, users would immediately benefit.

Our study also raises new technical and design issues. First, while users often associated specific roles with devices, the same users frequently switched them depending on the task. Our attempt to tackle the issues at the browser rather than interface level is therefore a step in the right direction since the users themselves can use the tools to easily switch device roles making their own customizations without having to rely on developers to make the necessary changes for them. Second, an important question raised by participants is *what is* and *what is not* synchronized. XDBrowser currently supports four synchronization options that proved sufficient for customizing the interfaces for most tasks. However, in some cases, participants asked for more control while others wanted XDBrowser to make the decision for them. Our study therefore motivates further research into the means of providing fine-grained support and automation of different interface distributions with synchronization control at the content, navigation and presentation levels. It will also be interesting to study cross-apps tasks involving multiple web sites. Building on the results of this paper, these are important avenues for future research.

CONCLUSION

This paper has presented a user study around XDBrowser, a new kind of web browser we are developing to enable a better cross-device web browsing experience. XDBrowser extends previous end-user customization techniques to cross-device use. Our user study demonstrates its potential to support a wide range of common web browsing tasks and elicit desirable cross-device interfaces leading to seven design patterns.

The results generated so far are useful in at least three ways. First, they provide an overview of possible cross-device designs able to guide developers of distributed interfaces. Second, they aid classification of cross-device designs. Third, they provide a basis for comparison in future cross-device studies.

Acknowledgments

Michael Nebeling started this research with support from ETH Zurich. It was continued at CMU under mobility grant, P300P2_154571, by the Swiss National Science Foundation.

REFERENCES

1. Brian P. Bailey, Jacob T. Biehl, Damon J. Cook, and Heather Metcalf. 2008. Adapting paper prototyping for designing user interfaces for multiple display environments. *PUC* 12, 3 (2008), 269–277. DOI: http://dx.doi.org/10.1007/s00779-007-0147-2
2. Nilton Bila, Troy Ronda, Iqbal Mohomed, Khai N. Truong, and Eyal de Lara. 2007. PageTailor: Reusable End-User Customization for the Mobile Web. In *Proc. MobiSys*. 16–29. DOI: http://dx.doi.org/10.1145/1247660.1247666
3. Nicholas Chen, François Guimbretière, and Abigail Sellen. 2013. Graduate Student Use of a Multi-Slate Reading System. In *Proc. CHI*. 1799–1808. DOI: http://dx.doi.org/10.1145/2470654.2466237
4. Xiang 'Anthony' Chen, Tovi Grossman, Daniel J. Wigdor, and George W. Fitzmaurice. 2014. Duet: Exploring Joint Interactions on a Smart Phone and a Smart Watch. In *Proc. CHI*. 159–168. DOI: http://dx.doi.org/10.1145/2556288.2556955
5. Pei-Yu (Peggy) Chi and Yang Li. 2015. Weave: Scripting Cross-Device Wearable Interaction. In *Proc. CHI*. 3923–3932. DOI: http://dx.doi.org/10.1145/2702123.2702451
6. David Dearman and Jeffrey S. Pierce. 2008. It's on my other computer!: computing with multiple devices. In *Proc. CHI*. 767–776. DOI: http://dx.doi.org/10.1145/1357054.1357177
7. Eli Raymond Fisher, Sriram Karthik Badam, and Niklas Elmqvist. 2014. Designing peer-to-peer distributed user interfaces: Case studies on building distributed applications. *IJHCS* 72, 1 (2014), 100–110. DOI: http://dx.doi.org/10.1016/j.ijhcs.2013.08.011
8. Luca Frosini and Fabio Paternò. 2014. User Interface Distribution in Multi-Device and Multi-User Environments with Dynamically Migrating Engines. In *Proc. EICS*. 55–64. DOI: http://dx.doi.org/10.1145/2607023.2607032
9. Giuseppe Ghiani, Fabio Paternò, and Carmen Santoro. 2012. Push and Pull of Web User Interfaces in Multi-Device Environments. In *Proc. AVI*. 10–17. DOI: http://dx.doi.org/10.1145/2254556.2254563
10. Giuseppe Ghiani, Fabio Paternò, and Carmen Santoro. 2013. Interactive Customization of Ubiquitous Web Applications. *VLC* 24, 1 (2013), 37–52. DOI: http://dx.doi.org/10.1016/j.jvlc.2012.10.005
11. Peter Hamilton and Daniel J. Wigdor. 2014. Conductor: Enabling and Understanding Cross-Device Interaction. In *Proc. CHI*. 2773–2782. DOI: http://dx.doi.org/10.1145/2556288.2557170
12. Tommi Heikkinen, Jorge Goncalves, Vassilis Kostakos, Ivan Elhart, and Timo Ojala. 2014. Tandem Browsing Toolkit: Distributed Multi-Display Interfaces with Web Technologies. In *Proc. PerDis*. 142–147. DOI: http://dx.doi.org/10.1145/2611009.2611026
13. Steven Houben and Nicolai Marquardt. 2015. WatchConnect: A Toolkit for Prototyping Smartwatch-Centric Cross-Device Applications. In *Proc. CHI*. 1247–1256. DOI: http://dx.doi.org/10.1145/2702123.2702215
14. Maria Husmann, Michael Nebeling, Stefano Pongelli, and Moira C. Norrie. 2014. MultiMasher: Providing Architectural Support and Visual Tools for Multi-Device Mashups. In *Proc. WISE*. 199–214. DOI: http://dx.doi.org/10.1007/978-3-319-11746-1_15
15. Heather M. Hutchings and Jeffrey S. Pierce. 2006. Understanding the Whethers, Hows, and Whys of Divisible Interfaces. In *Proc. AVI*. 274–277. DOI: http://dx.doi.org/10.1145/1133265.1133320
16. Brad Johanson, Shankar Ponnekanti, Caesar Sengupta, and Armando Fox. 2001. Multibrowsing: Moving Web Content across Multiple Displays. In *Proc. Ubicomp*. 346–353. DOI: http://dx.doi.org/10.1007/3-540-45427-6_29
17. Tero Jokela, Jarno Ojala, and Thomas Olsson. 2015. A Diary Study on Combining Multiple Information Devices in Everyday Activities and Tasks. In *Proc. CHI*. 3903–3912. DOI: http://dx.doi.org/10.1145/2702123.2702211
18. Shaun K. Kane, Amy K. Karlson, Brian Meyers, Paul Johns, Andy Jacobs, and Greg Smith. 2009. Exploring Cross-Device Web Use on PCs and Mobile Devices. In *Proc. INTERACT*. 722–735. DOI: http://dx.doi.org/10.1007/978-3-642-03655-2_79
19. Amy K. Karlson, Shamsi T. Iqbal, Brian Meyers, Gonzalo Ramos, Kathy Lee, and John C. Tang. 2010. Mobile Taskflow in Context: A Screenshot Study of Smartphone Usage. In *Proc. CHI*. 2009–2018. DOI: http://dx.doi.org/10.1145/1753326.1753631
20. Amy K. Karlson, Brian Meyers, Andy Jacobs, Paul Johns, and Shaun K. Kane. 2009. Working Overtime: Patterns of Smartphone and PC Usage in the Day of an Information Worker. In *Proc. Pervasive*. 398–405. DOI: http://dx.doi.org/10.1007/978-3-642-01516-8_27
21. Gilly Leshed, Eben M. Haber, Tara Matthews, and Tessa A. Lau. 2008. CoScripter: Automating & Sharing How-To Knowledge in the Enterprise. In *Proc. CHI*. 1719–1728. DOI: http://dx.doi.org/10.1145/1357054.1357323
22. James Lin and James A. Landay. 2008. Employing Patterns and Layers for Early-Stage Design and Prototyping of Cross-Device User Interfaces. In *Proc. CHI*. 1313–1322. DOI: http://dx.doi.org/10.1145/1357054.1357260
23. Jan Meskens, Kris Luyten, and Karin Coninx. 2010. DMacs: Building Multi-Device User Interfaces by Demonstrating, Sharing and Replaying Design Actions. In *Proc. UIST*. 129–138. DOI: http://dx.doi.org/10.1145/1866029.1866051

24. Jan Meskens, Jo Vermeulen, Kris Luyten, and Karin Coninx. 2008. Gummy for Multi-Platform User Interface Designs: Shape me, Multiply me, Fix me, Use me. In *Proc. AVI*. 233–240. DOI: http://dx.doi.org/10.1145/1385569.1385607

25. Michael Nebeling, Theano Mintsi, Maria Husmann, and Moira C. Norrie. 2014. Interactive Development of Cross-Device User Interfaces. In *Proc. CHI*. 2793–2802. DOI:http://dx.doi.org/10.1145/2556288.2556980

26. Michael Nebeling, Maximilian Speicher, and Moira C. Norrie. 2013. CrowdAdapt: Crowdsourced Web Page Adaptation for Individual Viewing Conditions and Preferences. In *Proc. EICS*. 23–32. DOI: http://dx.doi.org/10.1145/2480296.2480304

27. Jeffrey Nichols, Zhigang Hua, and John Barton. 2008. Highlight: A System for Creating and Deploying Mobile Web Applications. In *Proc. UIST*. 249–258. DOI: http://dx.doi.org/10.1145/1449715.1449757

28. Antti Oulasvirta and Lauri Sumari. 2007. Mobile Kits and Laptop Trays: Managing Multiple Devices in Mobile Information Work. In *Proc. CHI*. 1127–1136. DOI: http://dx.doi.org/10.1145/1240624.1240795

29. Roman Rädle, Hans-Christian Jetter, Mario Schreiner, Zhihao Lu, Harald Reiterer, and Yvonne Rogers. 2015. Spatially-aware or Spatially-agnostic?: Elicitation and Evaluation of User-Defined Cross-Device Interactions. In *Proc. CHI*. 3913–3922. DOI: http://dx.doi.org/10.1145/2702123.2702287

30. Stephanie Santosa and Daniel Wigdor. 2013. A Field Study of Multi-Device Workflows in Distributed Workspaces. In *Proc. UbiComp*. 63–72. DOI: http://dx.doi.org/10.1145/2493432.2493476

31. Dominik Schmidt, Julian Seifert, Enrico Rukzio, and Hans Gellersen. 2012. A Cross-Device Interaction Style for Mobiles and Surfaces. In *Proc. DIS*. 318–327. DOI: http://dx.doi.org/10.1145/2317956.2318005

32. Teddy Seyed, Chris Burns, Mario Costa Sousa, Frank Maurer, and Anthony Tang. 2012. Eliciting Usable Gestures for Multi-Display Environments. In *Proc. ITS*. 41–50. DOI:http://dx.doi.org/10.1145/2396636.2396643

33. Desney S. Tan, Brian Meyers, and Mary Czerwinski. 2004. WinCuts: Manipulating Arbitrary Window Regions for More Effective Use of Screen Space. In *Proc. CHI EA*. 1525–1528. DOI: http://dx.doi.org/10.1145/985921.986106

34. Minna Wäljas, Katarina Segersthl, Kaisa Väänänen-Vainio-Mattila, and Harri Oinas-Kukkonen. 2010. Cross-Platform Service User Experience: A Field Study and an Initial Framework. In *Proc. Mobile HCI*. 219–228. DOI: http://dx.doi.org/10.1145/1851600.1851637

35. Heather Wiltse and Jeffrey Nichols. 2009. PlayByPlay: Collaborative Web Browsing for Desktop and Mobile Devices. In *Proc. CHI*. 1781–1790. http://doi.acm.org/10.1145/1518701.1518975

36. Jishuo Yang and Daniel Wigdor. 2014. Panelrama: Enabling Easy Specification of Cross-Device Web Applications. In *Proc. CHI*. 2783–2792. DOI: http://dx.doi.org/10.1145/2556288.2557199

"With most of it being pictures now, I rarely use it": Understanding Twitter's Evolving Accessibility to Blind Users

Meredith Ringel Morris[1], Annuska Zolyomi[2], Catherine Yao[1,3], Sina Bahram[4], Jeffrey P. Bigham[5], Shaun K. Kane[6]
[1]Microsoft Research; [2]The University of Washington; [3]Massachusetts Institute of Technology; [4]North Carolina State University; [5]Carnegie Mellon University; [6]University of Colorado Boulder
merrie@microsoft.com, annuska@uw.edu, catyao@mit.edu, sbahram@ncsu.edu, jbigham@cmu.edu, shaun.kane@colorado.edu

ABSTRACT
Social media is an increasingly important part of modern life. We investigate the use of and usability of Twitter by blind users, via a combination of surveys of blind Twitter users, large-scale analysis of tweets from and Twitter profiles of blind and sighted users, and analysis of tweets containing embedded imagery. While Twitter has traditionally been thought of as the most accessible social media platform for blind users, Twitter's increasing integration of image content and users' diverse uses for images have presented emergent accessibility challenges. Our findings illuminate the importance of the ability to use social media for people who are blind, while also highlighting the many challenges such media currently present this user base, including difficulty in creating profiles, in awareness of available features and settings, in controlling revelations of one's disability status, and in dealing with the increasing pervasiveness of image-based content. We propose changes that Twitter and other social platforms should make to promote fuller access to users with visual impairments.

Author Keywords
Social media; Twitter; blindness; accessibility.

ACM Classification Keywords
H.5.m. Information interfaces and presentation (e.g., HCI).

INTRODUCTION
Worldwide, 39 million people are blind [32]. Blind computer users typically use screen reader software that converts on-screen information to aural speech or refreshable Braille; screen readers require accessible content in order to work. In particular, images require an alternative text description (called "alt text," since web page authors can specify such text in the "alt" field of an image's HTML tag). On web pages, alt text is often absent or insufficiently detailed [3, 15, 24]. Automated image description generation (e.g., [2, 4, 5, 14, 19, 30]) is not robust enough to be useful in practice.

Social media have become an increasingly important part of modern life. For example, more than 302 million people use Twitter every month, sending more than 500 million tweets per day [28]. Many people who are blind use social media to stay connected with friends, family, colleagues, and people with shared interests [5, 34]. However, with the ease of taking and sharing photos afforded by smartphones, social media are becoming increasingly image-based. For instance, Facebook users uploaded over 350 million photos per day in 2013 [25]. Twitter was created in 2006, and initially had a very simple text-based interface (consequently making it popular among people who are blind [5]), but began hosting embedded images in tweets on June 1, 2011 [11].

Although some blind people take and share images [18], the increasing pervasiveness of imagery lacking alt text is problematic for this constituency (to our knowledge, no major social media platforms support alt text). The rising image-heaviness of social media impedes blind users' ability to engage fully with this increasingly important medium, as explained by one blind participant in our study:

> *"In an increasingly visual culture, it's vital that people with visual impairments have equal access to information on social media... one of the most frustrating experiences I encounter is sitting down after a long day of work to scroll through my tweets and have a few laughs with my friends, only to realize that an article I want to read or a picture or video a friend has tweeted is inaccessible."*

Our research aims to pave the way toward making social media more accessible to people who are blind. In this paper, we focus on Twitter since prior studies have indicated that Twitter is disproportionately popular among blind people due to its history as a simple, text-based medium [5] and since the majority of tweets are publically accessible for analysis due to the medium's default privacy conventions. We address the following research questions:

RQ1: What are blind users' goals in engaging with Twitter? What barriers exist to achieving these goals, and how might technology be designed to facilitate them?

CHI'16, May 07 - 12, 2016, San Jose, CA, USA

ACM 978-1-4503-3362-7/16/05...$15.00
DOI: http://dx.doi.org/10.1145/2858036.2858116.

RQ2: How are people who are blind currently using Twitter? How does their use differ from sighted users? Do these differences reflect different goals, or do they reflect accessibility problems? Do usage differences between blind and sighted users represent possible privacy leakages about disability status?

RQ3: Is Twitter becoming less accessible to people who are blind over time? What types of inaccessible content are prevalent, and what types of technologies might be appropriate to mitigate accessibility challenges associated with different Twitter behaviors and content types?

RELATED WORK

Social media use is on the rise; more than 70% of online American adults were using social media as of September 2014 [12]. Researchers have begun to examine the extent to which social technologies are used and usable by people impacted by disabilities, such as parents of children with special needs [1, 23] and other serious health concerns including postpartum depression [10] and eating disorders [7]. Our focus is on social media use and usability for people who are blind. Three prior studies have looked specifically at how people who are blind use social media [5, 31, 34]. Brady et al.'s research [5] provided the first insights into this area; their survey results established that people who are blind do indeed use social media, and identified that Twitter adoption is higher than typical for this user group due to Twitter's (historically) relatively simple, text-based interface. Wu and Adamic [34] conducted a log-based study of the activity patterns of Facebook users who were accessing the service via a screen reader; unlike [34], we supplement logs with survey data that provides subjective and qualitative feedback from blind social media users, and we model traits differentiating blind and sighted users. Voykinska et al. [31] also studied blind users of Facebook via interviews and surveys that offered insights into the strategies blind Facebook users adopt to work around the accessibility challenges of interpreting the image-heavy site. Buzzi et al. [6] report a case study of a blind user's difficult interactions with Twitter. Our research builds upon these findings – like [31] and [34], we are providing deep insight into how people who are blind interact with a specific social technology (in this case, Twitter, a choice of technology inspired by Brady et al.'s findings regarding its importance to this constituency; Wu and Adamic [34] noted that their findings may not extend to other media such as Twitter, so our work complements prior work to provide a richer picture of how findings generalize or differ across media).

Twitter is a microblogging social media service on which users post messages ("tweets") limited to 140 characters. Since June 1, 2011, visual content (images and video) can be embedded directly into a tweet to supplement the 140 characters of text [11]. Twitter was identified by Pew as among the most popular social media platforms, being used by 23% of online American adults in September 2014 [12]. Twitter's dual role as a social network and a news source makes it particularly important for many users [22]. There are several Twitter client applications designed specifically for screen reader users, such as EasyChirp [13], Chicken Nugget [8], and TheQube [26]. These apps often provide special functionality, such as compatibility with refreshable Braille displays; keeping abreast of evolving functionality and use trends is a challenge for third-party clients.

The increased pervasiveness of smartphones with high-quality cameras has made it simple for people to capture and share imagery. This trend is reflected in the quantity of images being shared in social media – several hundred million photos are uploaded to Facebook every day, for instance [25]. This paper is the first to present data demonstrating the growing proportion of and importance of images embedded in Twitter posts.

In addition to posting photos of daily life or news events, people also use imagery in tweets in informal ways that further confound accessibility for blind users by taking formerly accessible content (text) and rendering it as imagery that cannot be interpreted by a screen reader. For example, "screenshorting" [17, 33] is a trend in which users post photos or screen captures of blocks of text as images embedded in a tweet, thereby circumventing Twitter's 140 character text limit. Many users also circumvent the official "retweet" functionality by instead posting a photo or screen capture of an original tweet as an embedded image; these unofficial retweets may have a variety of motives, such as avoiding implicitly "liking" a tweet by not adding to its official retweet count, circumventing the 140 character limit by giving the retweeter more room to add commentary, and/or making it more difficult for government regimes to track who is supporting various ideologies [27].

Web protocols have long supported and encouraged site designers to add "alt" tags to their HTML code in order to provide verbal descriptions for images – this text is read aloud by a screen reader when a blind user visits a compliant web page; however, there is no affordance in Twitter (or any other major social media that we are aware of) for adding alt text to images embedded in posts. One grassroots effort to retrofit alt text into tweets is the Alt Text Bot [9]; if a Twitter user forwards a tweet with an embedded image to the Alt Text Bot's account, then the service uses the Cloudsight API (an undisclosed mix of human-powered and computer-vision-powered captioning), and tweets back a short caption. Some Twitter users may choose to use the 140 characters of their tweet to describe an embedded image; our findings reveal that this is quite rare, with only 11% of multimedia tweets having text that might serve as a useful description.

Many researchers are working to develop automated captioning technologies. Semi-automated captioning systems (i.e., human-in-the-loop labeling provided via crowd-powered systems [2, 4, 5, 30]) or fully-automated systems (i.e., approaches combining computer vision, machine learning, and natural language generation technologies [14, 19]) currently exist, but are not practical for automatically captioning social media imagery for blind users due to issues such as cost, privacy, and response time for human-in-the-loop systems, and issues such as accuracy and generalizability beyond limited training image types for ML-based approaches. Our findings contribute information about the variety and types of imagery being shared on Twitter that can inform the design of enhanced automated approaches for captioning such imagery for blind users.

METHODS

We created an online survey to gather the perspectives of current Twitter users who are blind on their needs and concerns regarding this form of social media. The survey also collected the Twitter handles of the respondents, which we used to gather account features from the Twitter "firehose," a data source containing all tweets from public accounts. We also gathered the same firehose data for a control set of users to compare the characteristics of blind user's accounts with those of sighted users.

Survey Method

We used SurveyGizmo to design an online survey, and pilot-tested the survey with screen reader users to help ensure accessibility. The survey was available from March 4th to March 15th, 2015. It had 26 questions, and took a median of 12 minutes to complete.

Because the survey was about Twitter use, we recruited participants via Twitter by sending tweets advertising the survey from our personal and organizational accounts; these tweets used hashtags that people in our target demographic are likely to attend to such as *#a11y* (a general hashtag related to accessibility) and *#csun* (a hashtag related to a conference on accessible technologies that occurred during the survey period). We also purchased advertising on Twitter to promote our tweets. Twitter does not offer blindness as a demographic for ad targeting; instead, we targeted our ads to users who had ever tweeted with the hashtag *#a11y* or who followed accounts related to blindness, such as accounts associated with prominent advocacy organizations (e.g., AFB, NFB) or with services used by people who are blind (e.g., screen reader companies, guide dog organizations). To incentivize participation, we contributed $1 to participants' choice of the AFB, NFB, Benetech, or Lighthouse International for each completed survey.

The survey's consent form indicated that participants must be at least 18 years old, have a Twitter account, and be blind (as defined by needing to use a screen reader to interact with computers or mobile devices). We also informed participants that their Twitter profile page and public tweets would be analyzed as part of the study. To facilitate accessibility and privacy, all questions not relating to qualifying criteria were not required, so some participants left some items blank if they did not feel comfortable disclosing them.

Survey Participants

We received 117 completed surveys and 20 that were partially complete. We manually checked the validity of all 137 Twitter handles provided by these respondents by viewing the associated profile page in a web browser. Five handles did not resolve to valid profile pages; those respondents' data were removed from analysis, leaving 132 users (112 with completed surveys, 20 partially complete).

Table 1. Motivations for using Twitter among 112 blind users.

Motivation to use Twitter	%
Become informed of news/current events	88.4%
Enjoy entertainment and/or humor	72.3%
Learn about research/issues related to blindness	70.5%
Socialize with friends or family	63.4%
Participate in advocacy related to blindness	58.0%
Facilitate career/professional networking	52.7%
Meet new people	50.9%
Meet new people who are also blind	43.8%

All 132 respondents used screen readers (most commonly VoiceOver, JAWS, and NVDA). Respondents' ages ranged from 18 – 67 years old, with a median age of 35 and a mean of 37.8 years. 70.5% identified as male and 19.7% as female (9.8% didn't specify). Respondents were from a diverse set of 19 countries; the most common were the U.S. (47.7%), U.K. (13.6%), Canada (11.4%), and Australia (4.5%).

All 132 respondents' Twitter handles were used for our analysis of account properties, but we only analyzed the answers from the 112 fully-completed surveys.

Firehose Analysis

We used the Twitter firehose to analyze public account and tweet properties of the 132 Twitter handles provided by our survey participants. We analyzed data from the six months preceding our survey (Sept. 1, 2014 through Feb. 28, 2015).

In order to compare the properties and activities of blind users of Twitter to sighted users, we assembled a control set of an additional 132 accounts. To create the control set, we used the Twitter firehose to randomly sample all distinct Twitter handles that sent at least one public, English tweet on February 28, 2015. We manually verified that each account belonged to a non-celebrity, non-spammer person (and not to an organization or business) by viewing the associated profile page. We also made sure the profile page contained no indications the user was blind, since our intent was for the control sample to represent sighted Twitter users.

Of the 132 valid Twitter handles provided by our blind survey participants, 16 had to be eliminated from firehose analysis – 13 of these were protected accounts whose tweets were not available to us, and 3 of these were accounts that sent no tweets during the six-month data collection period (presumably those account owners use their accounts primarily to read others' tweets). This left us with 116 accounts known to belong to people who are blind. We reduced the size of the control set to 116, to match. Thus, our firehose data consisted of six months of tweets and profile properties from 232 public Twitter accounts, 116 belonging to our blind survey takers and 116 from our control sample.

Figure 1. This sample Twitter profile page uses the default *profile image* (an egg) and the default *header image* (a solid blue rectangle). The user's *Twitter handle* appears below the profile image, followed by the *bio*.

FINDINGS

In this section, we present the findings from the survey, firehose analysis, and manual inspection of profile pages.

Motivations for Using Twitter

We asked respondents why they use Twitter, allowing them to select options from a list (Table 1), as well as a write-in option. 8.0% provided write-in responses, such as "to state opinions," "to discover new music," and "to document my daily life." 84.8% of respondents identified with at least one motivation for using Twitter that was related to blindness (rows 3, 5, and 8 in Table 1).

Visual Imagery in Tweets

We asked how often respondents asked others on Twitter to describe the contents of images in tweets. Choices were *frequently (nearly every day)*; *occasionally (a couple times a week)*, *rarely (a couple times a month)*, or *never*. The majority (55.4%) reported never asking other Twitter users to describe imagery. 28.6% reported doing this rarely, 12.5% occasionally, and 3.6% frequently. We also asked whether respondents intentionally follow users who retweet images and add descriptions to them; 20.5% reported doing so. One respondent noted not only following such users, but actively engaging with them, "In the past, I've reached out to people who use good image descriptions and thank them..." Another noted that finding users who can give good descriptions is challenging, "I'm hesitant to ask for photo descriptions because people don't know how to give them..."

We asked respondents what information they want about the visual content of tweets. A few people indicated this would not interest them (e.g., "None. I would not be interested in looking at visual content on Twitter at all"; "None – if people tweet inaccessibly, I stop following them."). However, the vast majority expressed interest in having alt text for images (e.g., "tags or descriptions"; "short alternative description"; "what it is, color, and what's in the background"). Many noted nuance that would be appreciated in captions ("if there is a visual joke, then to understand why it is humorous"; "clear description of: colours, shapes, patterns, lighting, focus, facial expression, action, body language, clothing, location, whether image contains text and what it says"; "Anything the author of said visual media wishes to highlight… I might as well know what the author intends to display when tweeting visual media."). Some noted that videos often posed less of a challenge than still images, due to the audio track providing some additional context (e.g., "Videos, as long as they have audio, don't bother me").

Profile Page Characteristics

Figure 1 shows an example Twitter profile page, illustrating the placement and defaults for visual components. A user's *Twitter handle* (username) and *profile image* appear adjacent to every tweet they send; clicking on a particular Twitter handle or searching for a particular user takes one to that user's profile page, where the *header image* and optional 160 character *bio* and location fields are also visible. If the account is public, all of that user's tweets are also shown on the profile page in reverse chronological order.

We manually inspected the profile pages associated with all 132 Twitter handles of blind users collected through our survey. We performed the same coding process on the 132 control accounts (before each the sets were reduced to 116 to accommodate protected tweets – all 132 accounts in each set had public profile pages that could be examined).

Each profile page was coded on the following dimensions:

- Did the bio field explicitly state that the user was blind, allude to blindness (e.g., by mentioning interests in accessible technology, guide dogs, screen readers, Braille, etc.), or provide no clues as to the user's vision abilities?
- Was the profile image the default (egg)?
- Was the header image the default (solid rectangle)?

We examined the blind users' accounts' bio fields to see whether they disclosed information about vision status. 20.5% had blank bios. 19.7% explicitly mentioned visual impairment (e.g., "Went blind in Nov. 2012"; "chocoholic who happens to be blind"; "Blind sportswriter"). 25.0% alluded to blindness by mentioning related concepts (e.g., "Seeing Eye grad not currently working a dog"; "Braille transcriber by trade"). The remaining 34.9% had bios that did not provide any clues regarding the user's vision status.

We asked participants if their primary Twitter profile image was the default (Figure 1), or whether they had customized it. 22.3% reported that their image was the default, 50.0% reported having customized it, and 27.7% reported being unsure what their profile image was. We then compared this self-report to our manual coding of these users' profile images. For those who reported being unsure of whether they had a non-default profile image, most (23 of 31) did indeed have the default (including in this number two people who had non-egg but completely blank profile images). Of the 55 who reported having customized their image, only 85.5% were correct (8 actually did have the default egg). Of the 25 people who reported having the default profile image, 76.0% were correct, but 6 actually did have a customized image. Some survey respondents didn't even realize there was a default; one participant noted, "Just learned of the 'egg' terminology [from the description provided in the survey]."

For the respondents who said that they had customized their profile image, we asked how they selected the image. We analyzed the responses only from the 47 people who truly had a non-default image. The methods of choosing a profile image fell into three categories – help from a sighted friend, using a known (pre-existing, labeled) image, and taking or creating a new image oneself. Four responses were ambiguous and couldn't be placed with certainty into any of these three categories (e.g., "uploaded a photo"). 51.1% asked a sighted friend for assistance in creating a profile image (e.g., "My wife took the photo of me on my iPhone and said it looks good"; "I am a Star Trek fan, so I had a friend who can see choose a good [Star Trek] image for me"). 29.8% were cases where the person used a known photo (e.g., "I used a portrait taken for work purposes"). 12.7% were images created specifically for their Twitter profile by the blind user (e.g., "I took the picture with my phone").

We asked those who indicated that they had left the image as the default to explain why. Some said that imagery is not important to them (e.g., "I don't care about pictures"). Others mentioned privacy concerns (e.g., "Because I do not want my picture displayed on social media or on the internet"). A few indicated not taking time (e.g., "I just never bothered…"). However, the most common response theme related to accessibility issues, either not being aware the profile existed or being unable to make the changes easily (e.g., "I've not been able to change it on the Twitter page with my screen reader"; "didn't know you could change it, or how to do it").

We also asked whether respondents had customized their profile's "header image" (Figure 1). 17.0% reported being unsure, 8.0% reported that they had customized it, and 75.0% reported they had not. As with profile images, our participants were sometimes incorrect about the content of their header images – five who reported that they did not customize their header image actually had, and five who reported that they had changed it actually had the default.

Of the 132 control accounts, only 1.5% had not customized their profile image, and only 16.7% had not customized their header image. A Pearson chi-square test shows that the proportion of blind vs. control users with a custom profile image is significantly different (57.6% of blind users vs. 98.5% of control users): $\chi^2(1, N=264) = 64.4$, $p < .001$. A Pearson chi-square test also shows that the proportion of blind vs. control users who have customized their header image is significantly different (11.4% of blind users vs. 83.3% of control users): $\chi^2(1, N=264) = 137.1$, $p < .001$.

Based on the firehose analysis of the 116 blind and 116 control accounts' properties, 23.3% of control users had empty bios in their profile and 19.8% of blind users did. This is not a statistically significant difference. We also analyzed the length in characters of the bio field. Blind users had significantly longer bios (92.9 characters vs. 51.6 for control users), $t(230) = -5.685$, $p < .001$.

Account Characteristics

We measured users' account age in days as of March 1, 2015. For the control users, this was 1103.97 days, and for blind users it was 1749.88 days. This is a significant difference, $t(230) = -7.816$, $p < .001$, suggesting that blind users were more likely to be relatively early adopters of Twitter, a finding consistent with prior self-report studies on the social media habits of people who are blind [5] (an alternative possibility may be that more experienced blind Twitter users than typical self-selected to participate in our survey).

We also examined the number of followers the accounts in each set had, normalizing by the account age in days (since accounts accumulate followers over time). The normalized follower count for control users is .732, while blind users have a much lower normalized follower count of .261, which is a significant difference, $t(230) = 2.601$, $p = .01$.

Examining the number of friends, also normalizing by account age, control users had .896 normalized friends, whereas blind users had .763; this was not a statistically significant difference. There was also no significant difference in friend-to-follower ratio.

The final account property we examined was whether or not the account had geolocation enabled; if geolocation is enabled, a precise latitude/longitude is attached to each tweet when the tweet is made from a device (such as a smartphone) that is able to provide this data. 44.8% of control users had geo-location enabled on their account, and 56.0% of blind users had geolocation enabled. This difference is marginally significant according to a Pearson Chi-Square test, $\chi^2(1, N=232) = 2.914$, $p = .088$.

Tweet Characteristics

Normalizing tweet volume by account age provides a rate of tweeting (mean tweets per day). For control users this was 7.77, for blind users it was 9.12. This was not a statistically significant difference ($t(230) = -.754$, $p = .452$).

Our data indicated whether a tweet contained embedded multimedia, such as a photo or video (note that this refers only to multimedia embedded directly within a tweet, not to URLs within tweets that may point to media hosted elsewhere). Blind users are much less likely to share embedded visual content on Twitter than the control users – 23.43% of control users' tweets contained embedded multimedia, compared to 4.78% of blind users' tweets, which is a significant difference: $t(230) = 10.990$, $p < .001$.

We also examined what percent of tweets were "original" tweets as opposed to retweets. Blind users are much less likely to retweet messages than control users, with 27.33% of blind users' tweets being retweets, compared to 34.66% of control users' tweets, $t(230) = 2.257$, $p = .025$.

We analyzed the most frequently used hashtags among the blind and control user accounts. All words in which a "#" character preceded a sequence of letters and/or numerals were parsed out as hashtags. Any punctuation appearing at

Table 2. The most popular hashtags used by the 116 blind and 116 control group Twitter users over a six-month period.

Hashtag	# users	# tweets	category
Blind Users			
a11y	73	3014	disability
blind	60	320	disability
fb	57	3808	tech
accessibility	56	1575	disability
audio	42	1307	tech
Control Users			
wcw	22	62	meme
tbt	17	31	meme
ferguson	15	98	news
neverforget	15	39	news
relationshipgoals	13	43	meme

the end of terms was removed, and case was normalized to lowercase. We then counted the number of tweets from our data set containing each hashtag, as well as how many unique users from our set ever used that hashtag.

Table 2 shows the most popular hashtags for each group. The blind users have much more convergence (higher numbers of unique users) on common hashtags, which may reflect shared interests of this group and common purpose in their use of Twitter (i.e., to find and/or share information related to blindness). The most popular hashtags for the blind users related to disability/accessibility and/or to technologies (such as "audio"), whereas the most popular hashtags for the control group appear to be memes ("wcw" = "women crush Wednesday"; "tbt" = "throwback Thursday") and terms related to trending news events, suggesting differential uses of Twitter by these two groups (advocacy and seeking and sharing information related to accessibility and technology for the blind users, contrasted with entertainment, socializing, and news consumption for the sighted users). Note that there may be some biases toward the use of certain hashtags among our blind user set as an artifact of our recruitment method (some of our recruitment was accomplished through tweets and twitter ads targeted toward disability-related hashtags such as #a11y).

Predictive Power

Our findings indicate that there are statistically reliable differences in the properties and behavior associated with the Twitter accounts of people who are blind versus people who are sighted. This suggests that there may be privacy leakage regarding peoples' vision status – while a subset of the participants in our study chose to explicitly indicate in their Twitter profile that they were blind, most did not. However, our findings indicate that implicit cues that users may not be aware of could nonetheless reveal their disability status; this privacy leakage carries with it a risk of discrimination, such as online harassment or differential advertisement targeting.

To explore the extent to which automatic detection of visual impairment status may be possible, we performed a binomial logistic regression analysis on the 116 blind users' accounts and 116 control users' accounts for which we had complete data. This model correctly classified 94.0% of control users as being sighted and 92.2% of the blind users as being blind. The Nagelkerke R Square value for this model is .805 (i.e., the model accounts for 80.5% of the variance between the blind and control accounts).

Table 3. Binomial logistic regression model to differentiate blind and sighted Twitter users. $R^2 = .805$.

Variable	B	Exp(B)	S.E.	Sig.
Bio length in chars	.013	1.013	.006	.033
Bio is blank	1.138	.871	976	.888
Account age in days	.001	1.001	001	.072
Normalized # friends	.449	1.567	.589	.446
Normalized # followers	-.655	.519	.729	.369
Friend/follower ratio	-.026	.974	.067	.693
Mean tweets per day	.007	1.007	.019	.727
Percent photo tweets	-10.336	.000	2.892	.000
Percent RTs	.023	1.023	.013	.077
Geolocation enabled	1.168	3.216	.559	.037
Default profile photo	3.000	20.085	1.300	.021
Default bkgd image	2.596	13.405	.630	.000

The most significant predictor variables in this model were the percent of tweets originating from the account that contained multimedia ($p < .001$), whether the account had the default background image on the profile page ($p < .001$), whether the account had the default "egg" as the profile photo ($p = .021$), the length of the account's bio ($p = .033$), and whether the account had geolocation enabled ($p = .037$). Table 3 shows the details of the model. Note that we did not include linguistic characteristics of tweets (such as hashtags) as features in our model, but the commonalities in hashtags used by many people who are blind suggests that content-related features may also represent a similar privacy leakage.

A conservative rule of thumb to avoid overfitting is to have at least ten examples per factor [29], which we do. However, to further address possible concerns about overfitting, we re-ran the data with ten-fold cross validation using Weka; overall accuracy was 90.5%, with true positive rates of 92.2% for control and 88.8% for blind classes.

Prevalence of multimedia tweets

To analyze whether the amount of multimedia content in tweets is increasing over time, we sampled all public English language tweets sent between noon and 2 p.m. UTC on the first day of each month for the eighteen-month period from January 2014 through June 2015, a total of 159,163,658 tweets. We examined the tweets' metadata to determine if they contained multimedia. Both embedded photos and embedded videos count as multimedia and are not differentiated in the metadata available to us since videos are embedded as a "photo thumbnail" of the first video frame. For the subset of tweets made from February 2015 onwards, we have additional metadata that allows us to distinguish whether embedded multimedia is a video thumbnail versus a static image; from this data, we find that video is still relatively rare –93.6% of embedded multimedia in tweets consists of static imagery, while 6.4% are videos. The proportion of tweets containing embedded multimedia has been rising. In January 2014, 15.4% of tweets contained multimedia, rising to 28.4% by June 2015 (Figure 2).

Separating out tweets as "original" tweets (the first time a tweet is sent) versus retweets, we find that multimedia was embedded in 13.2% of original tweets in January 2014, rising to 23.2% by June 2015. However, retweets exhibit a far higher percentage of embedded multimedia, rising from 22.8% of retweets in January 2014 to 42.2% in June 2015. A paired samples t-test comparing the percent of multimedia original tweets versus retweets each month shows a significant difference, $t(17) = 31.81$, $p < .001$. This suggests that tweets containing imagery are among the most "important" according to popularity and interest levels.

To better understand the nature of imagery being shared on Twitter, we randomly sampled 900 English tweets issued on June 1, 2015 that contained embedded imagery. We coded these tweets and images with regards to three questions:

- What is the type of image embedded in the tweet?
- How important is the embedded image to interpreting the meaning of the tweet?
- Would the text of the accompanying tweet serve as a useful description for the image?

Using an open-coding methodology, two researchers iteratively developed coding schemes for these questions by

Table 4. Frequency of image types embedded in 900 English-language image-containing tweets from June 1, 2015.

Image Type	Frequency
Photographs	64.4%
Images with Embedded Text (e.g., ads)	11.5%
Pictures of Text	9.0%
Screenshots	7.0%
Drawings	5.4%
Graphs	1.1%
Inspirational Quotes	0.9%
Unofficial Retweets	0.7%
Memes	0.0%

viewing and labeling a separate random sample of embedded-imagery tweets. To illustrate the robustness of the coding scheme, these two researchers then redundantly coded 200 tweets from the set of 900 (inter-rater reliability measures for each question are reported as we discuss the findings for each, below); a single researcher then labeled the remaining 700 tweets. Because of the size of images, the firehose feed does not store the actual embedded image, but rather a URL pointing to the image; about 16% of these URLs were broken links, likely because either Twitter or the user deleted the tweet after posting. Tweets containing broken image links were discarded from analysis, leaving 756 of the original 900 tweets (and leaving 172 of the 200 in the set used for computing IRR measures).

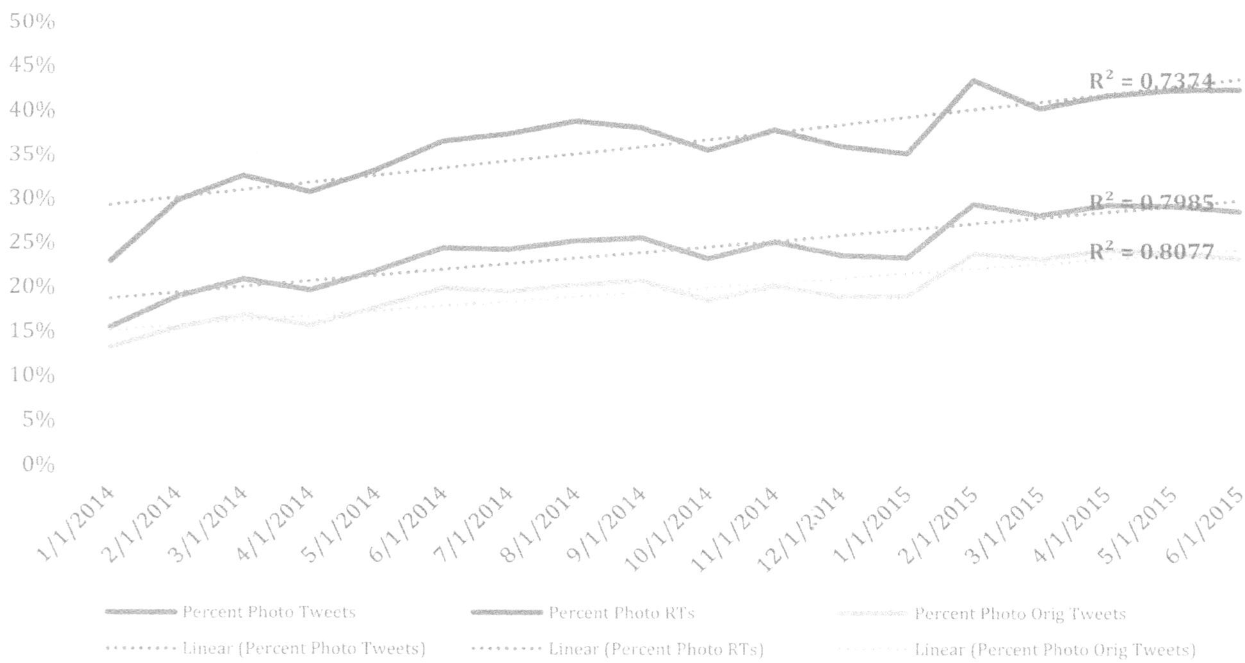

Figure 2. The percent of English-language tweets that contain embedded multimedia is increasing over time. The dashed lines show best-fit line and associated R^2 values for linear regression. Blue represents the percentage of all tweets that contain multimedia, green represents only original tweets, and red represents retweets.

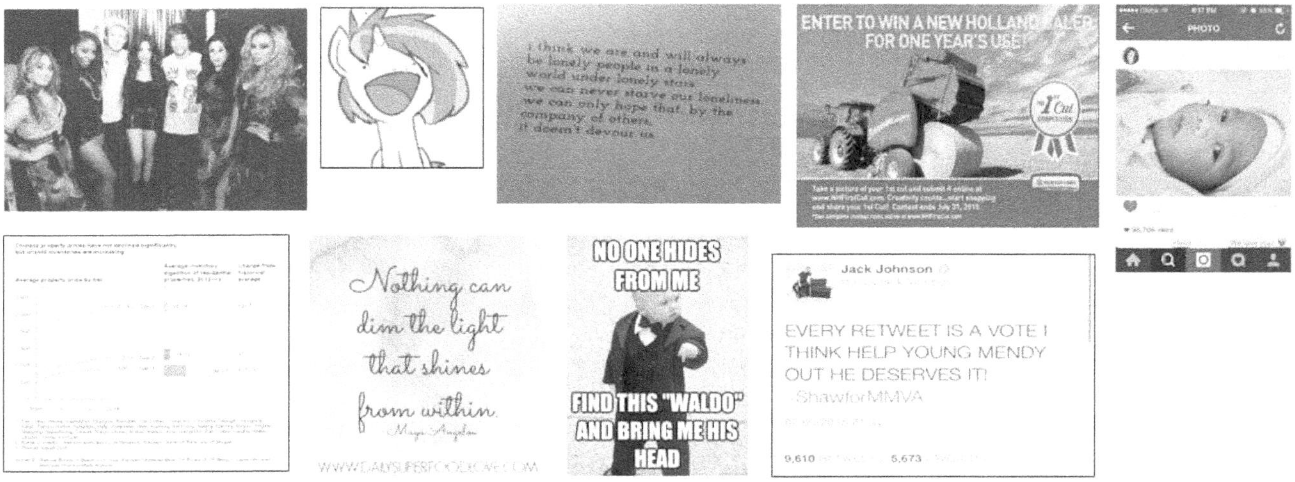

Figure 3. Nine types of imagery commonly embedded in tweets. Top row: photograph; drawing; picture of text ("screenshort"); image with embedded text; screenshot. Bottom row: graph; inspirational quote; meme, unofficial retweet.

What is the type of image embedded in the tweet?

Determining the types of images embedded in tweets facilitates identifying what captioning solutions might be most appropriate. Our coding scheme identified nine categories of imagery appearing in tweets (Figure 3). To illustrate the robustness of the scheme, we calculated the Cohen's Kappa for the 172 images coded by two raters; the Kappa score was 0.8595, indicating substantial agreement (particularly given the large number of categories). Table 4 shows the distribution of image types in our sample of tweets. When people think of "images" in tweets, the default assumption is typically of photos; while photos comprised the largest category of imagery (64%), the diversity of image types on Twitter suggests that a variety of different captioning approaches may need to be merged to adequately cover the types of imagery shared in social media.

How important is the embedded image to interpreting the meaning of the tweet?

Answering the question of how important the embedded image is to the point of the tweet provides insight into whether the abundance of embedded imagery significantly degrades blind users' Twitter experience; if the majority of images add no significant value to their tweets, then captioning solutions may not be necessary. Our coding scheme used an ordinal scale with the codes being *very important* (a user hearing the text of the tweet without viewing the image would not be able to understand the tweet's meaning), *somewhat important* (a user hearing the text of the tweet without viewing the image would be able to partially interpret the tweet's meaning), and *nonessential* (a user hearing the text of the tweet without viewing the image would be able to fully appreciate the point of the tweet). To measure inter-rater reliability, we calculated the Spearman's correlation coefficient between the two researchers' answers to this question, finding $r = 0.53$, an indication of moderate to strong agreement. Overall, 55.6% of the 756 embedded images were rated as very important to interpreting the meaning of the tweet, 19.4% as somewhat important, and 25.0% as nonessential. This indicates that embedded imagery are generally integral to interpreting their respective tweets, and thus that accessible descriptions of this imagery is important for blind users' Twitter experience.

Would the text of the accompanying tweet serve as a useful description for the image?

We wanted to know if tweets themselves provide text that could serve as a caption for blind users, so we coded how well tweet text described embedded images' contents. Using a three-point scale, we coded the tweet's utility as a caption as either *good* (a blind user hearing the tweet would have a detailed understanding of the accompanying image's contents), *minimally acceptable* (a blind user hearing the tweet would have a rough idea of the accompanying image's contents), or *poor* (a blind user hearing the tweet would have no insight into the accompanying image's contents). We again used Spearman's correlation coefficient as a measure of inter-rater reliability, with $r = 0.60$, reflecting moderate to strong agreement. Of the 756 tweet-image pairs labeled, 61.8% of the tweets would be poor captions. 27.0% of the tweets would have made a minimally acceptable caption, and the remaining 11.2% would have been good captions. These findings indicate that, for the great majority of tweets, tweet text would not adequately serve as a description of the embedded imagery for people who are blind.

DISCUSSION

Our survey of blind Twitter users combined with our analysis of blind and sighted users' public Twitter profiles and tweets and our analysis of the volume and nature of embedded imagery in public tweets allow us to reflect on our research questions, and to suggest design guidelines for improving the accessibility of social media for people who are blind.

RQ1: *What are blind users' goals in engaging with Twitter? What barriers exist to achieving these goals, and how might technology be designed to facilitate them?*

Our survey of 132 blind Twitter users revealed that this user group uses social media for many of the same reasons as sighted users – for keeping up with news, for entertainment, for socializing with existing ties, and for professional networking. Additionally, the majority (85%) of our survey respondents also reported using Twitter for reasons specifically related to their visual impairment, including participating in advocacy on behalf of people who are blind, meeting new contacts who are also blind, and learning about issues and news related to blindness. Our analysis of the hashtags most prevalent among blind Twitter users provides further evidence of this specialized use of social media, reflecting the popularity of terms relating to disability and accessible technologies among this user group.

Some user goals (such as meeting new contacts who are also blind) could be facilitated more automatically if Twitter were to automatically identify users who are blind, either by searching for explicit self-identification within the user's profile bio (45% of the blind participants in our survey had bio fields revealing or strongly hinting at their vision status) or by identifying people with a high probability of being blind through more implicit means, which our regression analysis suggests is possible. Automatic or opt-in identification might also facilitate other goals of Twitter use, such as by attempting to use automated captioning technology to label tweets with embedded images in blind users' feeds, and/or to remind the people with blind followers that they should use images judiciously or label them clearly. However, anything involving self-identification or automatic identification of blind users raise serious privacy concerns.

Other approaches to mitigating the barriers blind users currently face in achieving their goals on Twitter are to provide data about all accounts, rather than only those associated with people who are blind. For example, in addition to listing stats such as the number of friends and followers any user has, a user's profile page might also list stats such as what percent of their tweets contain embedded images; this information could help a blind user decide whether or not to follow a particular account. Community-generated ratings (such as ratings about whether users' tweets provide good descriptions of embedded imagery) might also be appropriate to include in profiles, particularly for certain types of user accounts (i.e., accounts that might be expected to uphold a higher standard for accessibility than an average user, such as corporate accounts, news organizations, and/or verified celebrity accounts).

Providing the ability to add alt text for screen readers to images embedded in tweets (which would not count against a post's character limit) would be a valuable platform-level enhancement for Twitter and other popular social media platforms. Alt tag compliance rates by typical users is likely to be low, so another important platform-level enhancement might be to facilitate letting motivated users supplement the accessibility of others' posts (as happens with other forms of user-generated content, such as Wikipedia [21]). For instance, platforms could pay employees or crowd workers to add in any missing alt text to embedded imagery in highly retweeted tweets, or could provide facilities to allow motivated volunteers who use the medium to add alt text to a tweet originating with another user. Providing a way that blind users can request a description of a particular image, such as by forwarding the image to a special account or marking a flag indicating the need for an automated or community-generated caption would also be a valuable addition to Twitter and other social media platforms.

RQ2: *How are people who are blind currently using Twitter? How does their use differ from sighted users? Do these differences reflect different goals, or do they reflect accessibility problems? Do usage differences between blind and sighted users represent possible privacy leakages about disability status?*

Our analysis of profiles and tweets associated with 116 blind and 116 control users indicated several differences in Twitter use. Many of these differences seem to reflect usability and accessibility challenges. For example, blind users were significantly less likely to complete their profile page (profile picture and header image) than sighted users, and many reported confusion over whether or not they had updated these fields and/or surprise that these fields existed, indicating accessibility issues with completing profiles. More blind users than control users had geolocation features enabled in their account; most users prefer to obscure their precise location for privacy reasons [16], leading us to infer the blind users may have this option enabled because the status of privacy settings and/or the ability to modify them are both not easily accessible to screen readers.

Our analysis of the most common hashtags among each user group also revealed differences. The prevalence of hashtags related to accessibility issues and technology is likely due to some of the unique social media usage motivations that our blind survey respondents described. However, the absence of certain types of hashtags, such as popular memes, from the list of top tags may reflect the usability challenges of an increasingly image-centric medium. For example, among the most common hashtags used by the control group were tags such as *#tbt* and *#wcw* that are typically associated with posting embedded imagery (for "tbt" aka "throwback Thursday" people typically post a nostalgic image, and for "wcw" aka "women crush Wednesday" people typically post images of women they admire or find attractive). This differential hashtag use, along with our finding that tweets with images are more likely to be retweeted than those not containing imagery, suggests that many popular aspects of Twitter are not currently accessible to blind users.

Our regression analysis indicates that many blind users may be able to be automatically identified as blind, even if they are like the 55% of our sample that didn't explicitly mention topics related to visual impairment in their user bio; implicit indicators such as profile page characteristics, retweeting rates, and tweet content provide a reliable basis for inferring vision status. This may represent a privacy leakage [20] that could have negative implications for these users – for example, the platform could identify their vision status to advertisers, resulting in discrimination.

RQ3: *Is Twitter becoming less accessible to people who are blind over time? What types of inaccessible content are prevalent, and what types of technologies might be appropriate to mitigate accessibility challenges associated with different Twitter behaviors and content types?*

Our analysis of a large sample of tweets over an eighteen month period indicates that Twitter is quickly morphing from a primarily text-based medium to a primarily multimedia one. As of June 2015, 28.4% of tweets contained embedded multimedia (not including tweets containing URLs that link to external sources of imagery or video). We found that image-containing tweets are among the most popular, being retweeted at a far higher rate than text-only tweets. The prevalence of images, and the lack of a mechanism for providing alt text for embedded images, means that Twitter, once a preferred medium for people who are blind [5], is becoming increasingly inaccessible.

Our analysis of the types of embedded imagery found on Twitter reveals that images do not simply refer to photographs, but to a wide variety of visual content types. This finding suggests that automated solutions for captioning these images may not be straightforward, and may require systems that combine different technologies (computer vision for recognizing items in photos, OCR for recognizing text in "screenshorts," etc.). Some types of embedded media might be best dealt with by platform changes or social engineering approaches rather than attempts at automated or manual captioning. For example, the rise of the "screenshorting" trend [17, 33] suggests that increasing the character limit may be desirable to end users and would reduce the inaccessible images used to circumvent current limits. The use of embedded screenshots of tweets as an unofficial retweet mechanism is another example of users taking something that could be screen reader accessible text and instead sharing it as inaccessible images – Twitter may wish to consider addressing the situations that cause people to circumvent the official retweet mechanisms (which may include things like a desire to circumvent the 140 character limit in order to add long commentary to a retweet, the desire to avoid "liking" or boosting the stats of a retweet, and/or the desire to avoid being officially linked to the sender of a tweet in regimes that monitor political tweets [27]).

Limitations

Readers should bear in mind that the blind people who chose to participate in our study may have been somehow non-representative of other blind Twitter users who chose not to participate. Although we used an accessible survey template and pilot-tested with screen reader users, feedback from some participants indicated that some screen reader versions may have had compatibility issues, which may have biased our survey sample in ways that are difficult to quantify.

While rich, our Twitter firehose data does not contain information about who a given user follows; this prevented us from doing some analyses that may have provided interesting perspectives, such as identifying what percent of each blind user's feed actually contained imagery (i.e., providing insight into whether blind Twitter users tend to follow people who tweet less imagery than is typical).

Also, note that this research implicitly assumes that our sample of control users is sighted (we manually screened their bios for any implications that they were blind and did not find any); however, it is possible (though statistically unlikely) that some members of the control set were blind.

Our study does not investigate the accessibility of Twitter to people with other disabilities; however, improved text equivalents for imagery may benefit other populations, such as other users of screen readers (people with low vision) and users with cognitive challenges (who may gain deeper understanding of content with a clear text description).

While our research focused on Twitter, we believe many of our findings have implications for other social media. Our work joins prior work [5, 31, 34] in providing evidence that people who are blind are interested in using social media; the lack of alt text capabilities on major social platforms should be a top design concern for such services. Our findings on the variety of imagery types shared socially provide new challenges that social platforms and computer vision researchers must consider when thinking of the breadth of imagery to service with emerging captioning tools. This work also illustrates how a platform that was previously quite accessible to the blind can evolve over time to become increasingly inaccessible due to a combination of new features introduced and changing end-user behaviors; this finding should be a reminder to all platforms that accessibility may not be a one-time solution, but must evolve along with a platform and its users.

CONCLUSION

In this paper, we used a multi-method approach to explore how and why people who are blind use Twitter, and the challenges they face in doing so. Our findings revealed that blind users have many goals in common with sighted social media users, but also use social media for reasons related specifically to advocacy for, education about, and socializing amongst others who are blind. We also demonstrated that profile page characteristics and tweet patterns provide reliable, albeit unintentional, means of distinguishing blind from sighted users. Our findings also showed that Twitter is becoming more image-heavy over time, and that image-based tweets are diverse, largely inaccessible, and not clearly amenable to any existing automated captioning methods. We provided several suggestions for solutions that might allow Twitter to continue to be accessible to people with visual impairments; ensuring the accessibility of social media is increasingly important given the prominent role of such new media in social and political life.

REFERENCES

1. Ammari, T., Morris, M.R., and Schoenebeck, S.Y. Accessing Social Support and Overcoming Judgment on Social Media among Parents of Children with Special Needs. *Proceedings of ICWSM 2014*.
2. Be My Eyes. http://bemyeyes.org.
3. Bigham, J.P., Kaminsky, R.S., Ladner, R.E., Danielsson, O.M., and Hempton, G.L. WebInSight: Making Web Images Accessible. *Proceedings of ASSETS 2006*.
4. Bigham, J.P., Jayant, C., Ji, H., Little, G., Miller, A., Miller, R.C., Miller, R., Tatarowicz, A., White, B., White, S., and Yeh, T. VizWiz: Nearly Real-Time Answers to Visual Questions. *Proceedings of UIST 2010*.
5. Brady, E., Zhong, Y., Morris, M.R., and Bigham, J. Investigating the Appropriateness of Social Network Question Asking as a Resource for Blind Users. *Proceedings of CSCW 2013*.
6. Buzzi, M.C., Buzzi, M., and Leporini, B. Web 2.0: Twitter and the blind. *Proceedings of CHItaly 2011*.
7. Chancellor, S., Pater, J., Clear, T., Gilbert, E., and De Choudhury, M. #thyghgapp: Instagram Content Moderation and Lexical Variation in Pro-Eating Disorder Communities. *Proceedings of CSCW 2016 (to appear)*.
8. Chicken Nugget. https://q-continuum.net/chicken_nugget/.
9. Cundiff, C. "Alt Text Bot." *AT&T NYU Connect Ability Challenge*, June 23, 2015. http://connectability.challengepost.com/submissions/37785-alt-text-bot
10. De Choudhury, M., Counts, S., and Horvitz, E. Predicting Postpartum Changes in Emotion and Behavior via Social Media. *Proceedings of CHI 2013*.
11. Dorsey, J. "search + photos." *The Official Twitter Blog*, June 1, 2011.
12. Duggan, M., Ellison, N., Lampe, C., Lenhart, A., and Madden, M. Social Media Update 2014. *Pew Internet and American Life Project*, January 9, 2015.
13. EasyChirp. http://easychirp.com.
14. Fang, H., Gupta, S., Iandola, F., Srivastava, R.K., Deng, L., Dollár, P., Gao, J., He, X., Mitchell, M., Platt, J.C., Zitnick, C.L., and Zweig, G. From Captions to Visual Concepts and Back. *Proceedings of CVPR 2015*.
15. Goodwin, M., Susar, D., Nietzio, A., Snaprud, M., and Jensen, C.S. 2011. Global web accessibility analysis of national government portals and ministry web sites. *Journal of Information Technology & Politics*, 8(1), 41-67.
16. Hecht, B., Hong, L., Suh, B., and Chi, E.H. Tweets from Justin Bieber's Heart: The Dynamics of the "Location" Field in User Profiles. *Proceedings of CHI 2011*.
17. Honan, M. The Rise of the Screenshort. *BuzzFeed News*. December 19, 2014.
18. Jayant, C., Ji, H., White, S., and Bigham, J.P. Supporting Blind Photography. *Proceedings of ASSETS 2011*.
19. Karpathy, A. and Fei-Fei, L. Deep Visual-Semantic Alignments for Generating Image Descriptions. *Proceedings of CVPR 2015*.
20. Kosinski, M., Stillwell, D., and Graepel, T. Private traits and attributes are predictable from digital records of human behavior. *Proceedings of the National Academy of Sciences*, Vol. 110 No. 15, Feb. 12, 2013, pp. 5802-5805.
21. Kuksenok, K., Brooks, M., and Mankoff, J. Accessible Online Content Creation by End Users. *Proceedings of CHI 2013*.
22. Kwak, H., Lee, C., Park, H., and Moon, S. What is Twitter, a social network or a news media? *Proceedings of WWW 2010*.
23. Morris, M.R. Social Networking Site User by Mothers of Young Children. *Proceedings of CSCW 2014*.
24. Shi, Y. E-Government Web Site Accessibility in Australia and China: A Longitudinal Study. *Social Science Computer Review*, Fall 2006. 24: 378-385.
25. Smith, C. "Facebook Users are Uploading 350 Million New Photos Each Day." *Business Insider*, Sept. 18, 2013.
26. TheQube. http://thequbc.oire.org
27. Tufecki, Z. Big Questions for Social Media Big Data: Representativeness, Validity and Other Methodological Pitfalls. *Proceedings of ICWSM 2014*.
28. Twitter. "Twitter Usage/Company Facts." https://about.twitter.com/company, retrieved July 27, 2015.
29. Vittinghoff, E. and McCulloch, C.E. Relaxing the Rule of Ten Events per Variable in Logistic and Cox Regression. *American Journal of Epidemiology*, March 2007, 165(6): 710-8.
30. Von Ahn, L. and Dabbish, L. Labeling Images with a Computer Game. *Proceedings of CHI 2004*.
31. Voykinska, V., Azenkot, S., Wu, S., and Leshed, G. How Blind People Interact with Visual Content on Social Networking Services. *Proceedings of CSCW 2016 (to appear)*.
32. World Health Organization. "Visual Impairment and Blindness" factsheet, August 2014. http://www.who.int/mediacentre/factsheets/fs282/en
33. Williams, O. R.I.P. Blogging, Killed by Screenshorts. *The Next Web News*. April 14, 2015.
34. Wu, S. and Adamic, L. Visually Impaired Users on an Online Social Network. *Proceedings of CHI 2014*.

Sleep Debt in Student Life: Online Attention Focus, Facebook, and Mood

Gloria Mark[1], Yiran Wang[1], Melissa Niiya[2], Stephanie Reich[2]

[1]Department of Informatics
University of California, Irvine
{gmark,yiranw2@uci.edu}

[2]School of Education
University of California, Irvine
{mniiya,smreich@uci.edu}

ABSTRACT

The amount of sleep college students receive has become a pressing societal concern. While studies show that information technology (IT) use affects sleep, here we examine the *converse*: how sleep duration might affect IT use. We conducted an *in situ* study, and logged computer and phone use and collected sleep diaries and daily surveys of 76 college students for seven days, all waking hours. We examined effects of sleep duration and sleep debt. Our results show that with less sleep, people report higher perceived work pressure and productivity. Also, computer focus duration is significantly shorter suggesting higher multitasking. The more sleep debt, the more Facebook use and the higher the negative mood. With less sleep, people may seek out activities requiring less attentional resources such as social media use. Our results have theoretical implications for multitasking: physiological and cognitive reasons could explain more computer activity switches: related to less sleep.

Author Keywords

Multitasking; sleep; productivity; computer logging; *in situ* study; sensors; social media; Facebook; mobile phone; mood

ACM Classification Keywords

H.5.3 [Information Interfaces and Presentation]: Group and Organization Interfaces; K.4.m [Computers and Society]: Miscellaneous.

INTRODUCTION

"O magic sleep! O comfortable bird,
That broodest o'er the troubled sea of the mind...."

John Keats, in Endymion, 1818

CHI'16, May 07 - 12, 2016, San Jose, CA, USA

ACM 978-1-4503-3362-7/16/05 $15.00
DOI: http://dx.doi.org/10.1145/2858036.2858437

This reflection on sleep by the poet Keats was written almost 200 years ago. Yet in our current digital age, the topic of sleep (or lack thereof) is as important as ever, widely discussed in the academic community as well as in the popular press. One dominant theme has been how people rarely get enough sleep--the term "sleep debt" is actively discussed in the public sphere. Sleep deprivation can have serious consequences, leading to errors in the workplace [23], accidents [2], and even to falling asleep involuntarily at critical times, such as while driving [2]. However, how sleep deprivation might affect how people use information technology (IT) has yet to be explored.

Considering the current tendency of information workers and students to be online and accessible for interruptions much of the day (and night), the relationship of IT use and sleep is an important issue. Over the last decade, there has been discussion of how constant connectivity is associated with multitasking [32], interruptions [12], and checking email [32], during what might normally be sleeping hours, disrupting or shortening sleep.

In human-computer interaction (HCI), attention has been given to prototypes and apps that provide novel ways to measure sleep [3, 11, 24], including sensing social data [38]. In other fields, although studies suggest that IT use might interfere with sleep, cf [1], there have not yet been studies showing the *converse*: how sleep duration might affect IT use. Why is it important to consider how sleep might affect IT use? First, if a connection between sleep duration and IT use is indeed found, then this would point to the notion of sleep as a variable that should be considered in HCI research, particularly as it relates to user performance with digital media. Second, this research could identify specific computer behaviors that are present when people are lacking sleep, which could prevent human error. Third, such research could inform the design of technological interventions that might lead people to improve their sleep habits, e.g. by recognizing and informing about digital media behaviors that might be impacted by sleep deprivation.

The purpose of this study is to examine how sleep might affect IT use. Rather than rely on laboratory settings, we conducted an *in situ* study to capture real world contingencies that could play a role in the relationship between sleep and IT use. Sleep deprivation in young people, especially college students, has been given much attention, particularly on how sleep is affected by technology use (cf 1, for a review). As a first step to studying this converse relationship, we examine how technology use is affected by sleep duration with college students. Our results show that with less sleep, students perceive higher work pressure and productivity, spend shorter durations of time focusing their attention online, increase their time on Facebook, and experience more negative mood. These results contribute to the growing body of research examining the relationship of sleep and IT use.

SLEEP AND INFORMATION TECHNOLOGY USE

Sleep Duration and Performance

Lack of sleep is linked to numerous negative cognitive and health outcomes [23]. Lack of sleep can lead to reduced memory and cognitive functioning [23, 30], poor academic and work performance [23, 43], and safety risks such as falling asleep while operating vehicles [2]. Sleep deprivation and its effects remain prevalent among the US adult population, with 37% of adults aged 20-39 years reporting less sleep than the recommended 7-9 hours per night [11]. Those people who stay up late or who are categorized as "evening types" report attentional and emotional problems [35].

Sleep debt

Sleep debt is the cumulative loss of, and consequent pressure for sleep, that results from an inadequate amount of physiologically normal sleep [51]. Sleep debt can accrue in a variety of ways including going to bed later but keeping wake time the same, having untreated sleep disorders, or experiencing external sleep disturbances. Since people vary in the amount of sleep they need, sleep debt is based on the "*cumulative hours of sleep loss with respect to the subject-specific daily need for sleep*" [51]. Numerous studies have found sleep debt to impact a host of outcomes such as mood [18], weight gain [4], performance [42], and health [29].

College Students and Sleep Duration

Young adults may be particularly at risk for sleep disturbances and deprivation [6]. Lack of sleep is prevalent among college students, especially women [8]. Poor sleeping habits have negative impacts on undergraduate physical and mental health as well as academic performance such as lower test scores and grade point averages [43, 49]. Poor sleep quantity and quality, which include late nights, earlier wakeup times [49], and irregular sleep-wake patterns [28] are associated with lower academic performance, suggesting that routines around sleep, in addition to sleep amount, affect college students.

Constant availability via mobile phones and the Internet may lead to sleep disturbances. For example, among a sample of young people, smartphones were often used before bed and caused frequent sleep interferences [25]. Among adolescents, IT use tends to stretch late into the evening with negative effects on sleep as well as on academic performance [9]. Thus, while there is mounting evidence that IT use consequently affects sleep, no one has looked at the opposite relationship, which we explore in this study.

Sleep and Social Media Use

Increasingly, research has documented how social media might contribute to sleep deficiencies, largely from people staying awake to stream videos, peruse profiles, and chat online [39, 50]. However, studies are lacking on how sleep duration might affect social media and computer usage. Such relationships are quite plausible. Social media is often viewed as a lightweight activity [52] with socializing, escape, and distractions being common reasons people report for using social media [1, 47]. There is evidence of an association between more time on social networking sites and less effortful thinking [55]. Thus, sleep deprived individuals who are online may likely engage in less cognitively demanding and more distracting activities such as social media use.

Sleep and Multitasking

A number of studies have examined multitasking, or activity switching, while working with digital media, [e.g. 12, 19]. Multitasking can occur by switching attention not only among computer screens but also between devices [22]. These studies have often pointed to the role of interruptions (from external sources or oneself) [19], email [32], or habitual behavior [19] in influencing multitasking. Although not as thoroughly explored, sleep may also affect technology use and multitasking. For instance, one study found that those who ended their daily activity and went to sleep earlier tended to multitask less the next day [33]. This suggests that perhaps sleep patterns might be associated with attention shifting.

Studies of sleep deprivation and attention have found insufficient sleep to result in decreased visual and auditory attention [20] Less sleep could thus contribute to less cognitively taxing behaviors while on the computer such as having less persistent attention with more switching of focus between windows and applications. This alteration in attention also applies to task switching [17]. It is quite plausible that similar low-attention behaviors, due to less sleep, could occur while on the computer as well. Thus, less sleep could contribute to higher online multitasking in the following ways. It could lead to more frequent switching of attention to different computer screens. This switching could be due to more self-interruptions, which comprise almost half of all interruptions in the workplace and can lead to task switches [12, 19]. Self-interruptions could be due to higher distractibility, and lack of sleep could make people more prone to distraction and thus more likely to switch focus from their current task at-hand.

RESEARCH QUESTIONS

In contrast to prior studies, which focused on how IT use affects sleep, we look at the converse: how sleep duration might affect how people use IT. While numerous studies point to the detrimental effects of having less sleep [23, 30, 43, 49], amount of sleep could also affect IT use. Further, while we expect sleep debt to be related to sleep duration, there are differences. One night of short sleep may affect some performance measures the next day and not others. However, sleep debt represents an accumulation of the effects of loss of sleep. In other words, consistently sleeping shorter than one's ideal amount could accumulate and produce effects on different variables than sleep duration. We thus examine sleep duration the night before and sleep debt with different variables. The following are our research questions and hypotheses.

RQ1: What are the impacts of sleep on college students' perceptions of productivity and work pressure? Before examining sleep effects on IT use, we begin by looking at related experiences to sleep duration. Decades of research have shown that sleep and health are related and that deficits in sleep can lead to personal and fiscal costs [23]. Studies of worker productivity and sleep patterns have found that decreased sleep leads to reduced memory, cognitive functioning, and work performance [30]; and for college students, sleep deficits result in lower academic performance [43, 49]. Conversely, when students are well rested, they tend to perform better academically and exercise more [5]. Thus, we explore whether less sleep duration the night before is associated with higher subjective work pressure and lower perceived productivity. We hypothesize that:

H1: Students with shorter sleep duration the night before will have higher perceived work pressure the next day.

H2: Students with shorter sleep duration the night before will rate their productivity to be lower the next day.

RQ2: Is sleep related to college students' multitasking on the computer? Surveys of college students have found high association between online computer use and sleep deficits for that evening [37]. Other research shows that longer duration of focus on the computer is related to less stress [32]. Coupling these patterns with evidence that decreased sleep reduces attention and focus [26], computer behavior when people had less sleep might involve more switching and less focused attention. A higher frequency of switching on the computer has been considered as a measure of higher multitasking [32]. In other words, from a fine-grained perspective it is an indicator of switching attention between different activities as screens and content change. Thus, we expect that less sleep should be associated with higher multitasking, as reflected by shorter attention duration on any computer screen. Thus, we expect that:

H3: Students with shorter sleep duration the night before will have shorter focus duration on computer windows the next day.

RQ3: Is sleep debt associated with Facebook use? Social media consumption (as opposed to production) is often lightweight, requiring little effort and often serving as a quick break (see [52]). As such, it is not surprising that youth report using social media for such things as distraction, a way to fill time, and as a mechanism for socializing [47]. Further, college students who use social media, especially social networking sites like Facebook, report feeling a need to check these sites regularly to stay connected to others [48]. This is consistent with other research that suggests that Facebook use is habitual [13]. We would not expect social media habits like Facebook use to change so easily after one night of sleep loss but rather would expect to see changes over longer term sleep loss accumulation (i.e. sleep debt). For this research question we examine sleep debt, as we are interested in whether we find a relationship of accumulated sleep loss with the tendency to increase lightweight activities.

When students are more sleep deprived and using technology, they might seek out activities involving fewer cognitive resources [15]. When working online, they may also be more likely to be distracted from work, and social media is reported as a common form of distraction [47]. A study of Facebook use and student engagement, using the National Survey of Student Engagement (NSSE) showed a negative relationship of Facebook use and engagement in educational activities [21]. It has also been observed in the workplace that when people are engaged in computer work Facebook affords a light break from work [31]. The most common social media site among adults ages 18-29 is Facebook, with 87% reporting using it in 2014 [14]. Others have also reported Facebook as the most popular social media site among college students [21]. We therefore focus on Facebook use and thus expect that when students have higher sleep debt, when online they would be more likely to spend more time doing Facebook as a lightweight activity and also as a distraction.

H4: Students with more sleep debt will engage in more Facebook use.

RQ4. How is sleep debt related to mood? A meta-analysis of laboratory sleep studies found that sleep deprivation significantly negatively impacts mood [42]. However, in contrast, a study of college students who were sleep deprived for 24 hours showed no significant changes in mood, such as negative mood states of anger and anxiety [43]. The authors explain this to the notion that 24 hours of sleep deprivation is long enough to affect fatigue but not long enough to impact mood. A large cross-sectional survey study of college students though did find a relationship between self-reported sleep disturbances and negative mood [28]. Because sleep loss over 24 hours did not affect mood, we expect that longer accumulated sleep could affect mood. Therefore in this research question we examine sleep debt. Based on these studies we expect that the more sleep debt one has, the more it would negatively impact mood. Most studies of the effects of sleep deprivation and mood have been done in the laboratory or with surveys. We are not aware of studies that have examined the relationship of sleep deprivation and mood where people have been tracked in an *in situ* environment. Therefore, we hypothesize:

H5: Students with more sleep debt will experience more negative mood.

METHODOLOGY

We conducted an *in situ* observational study at a large public university on the U.S. west coast in Jan.-May of 2014. We used a mixed-methods approach with automatic computer and phone logging as the primary method of data collection. In order to capture the context of students' life at school, their sleep schedule, and mood, we also used daily surveys and a one-time general survey about attitudes and demographic information. Computer and phone logging and other data collection occurred over seven days.

Participants and Procedure

Participants were recruited from undergraduate courses, student residences, and snowball sampling. In total, we collected data from 76 undergraduates: 34 males and 42 females. Due to the availability of monitoring software and its limitations, the study was restricted to students who used both Windows computers and Android phones. Students' ages ranged from 18 to 23 years (mean=19.3) and the median college year was sophomore.

On Day 1 of the study, participants visited a campus laboratory where the computer and phone logging software were installed on their devices. Students who also had desktop computers were given software installation instructions. Participants were sent a link to an online general survey on Day 1 and instructed to complete it before the end of the study (by Day 7). Two daily surveys were sent each day: one at 7 a.m. (a sleep diary for the night before), asking participants to complete it once awake and another at 9 p.m. (an end-of-day survey), asking them to complete it before going to bed. On Day 7, semi-structured exit interviews (for about 30 minutes) were conducted. Participants were asked about their experiences during the study, their technology habits, and their beliefs about how technology could affect stress, productivity, and mood. Descriptive coding was used to identify key themes that emerged from these interviews [46]. Participants were paid $100 for their participation.

Measures

A total of 71 people were used in the analysis. Five people were excluded due to missing computer data (logging software problems, software getting uninstalled by antivirus software, and one participant uninstalling the software). For these 71 participants, we collected computer and phone logs, sleep duration, social media use and daily surveys, and single general surveys.

Computer and phone logging. Computer activity over seven days was captured with Kidlogger (kidlogger.net). This Windows freeware generated one log record each time a user opened a new window or switched between already open windows. A window was an application or a web browser tab. Each log record included the start time and duration of the active window, the name of the application, a URL if the window was a web browser tab, and idle time. Timestamps were recorded to the second. Only time spent in the current window was measured. For example, if a webpage was open in the background when the user used Word in the foreground, Kidlogger only counted the time spent in Word. Computer idle time was not included. Phone logging over seven days was collected using the AWARE Framework application (www.awareframework.com). A log record was generated each time a user opened an application, web browser tab or switched between apps. The log captured activity to the millisecond. Data from computer and phone logging was partitioned into daily logs and numbered, generating at least seven days of computer/phone use per person. Due to scheduling issues, for some participants more than 7 days of data was collected. The distribution of full days of data collection was as follows: 58 students have 5 full days (7 days in total); 9 students have 6 full days (8 days in total); 1 student has 8 full days (10 days in total); 3 students have 7 full days (9 days in total); and 1 student has 8 full days (10 days in total).

Facebook (FB). Measures of FB usage from both the computer and phone logs were used to calculate frequency and duration of visits. The duration of time on FB from computer and phone logs were added together to produce a total daily time on Facebook.

Focus duration. Multitasking can be considered from different perspectives: at a broad level examining task switching, or at finer-granularity, examining attention shifts among different activities which could be within the same task. We adopt this fine-granularity perspective to investigate the relationship of sleep and its effects on how people shift their attention when working on the computer. We feel that measuring duration of focus on computer screens is a reasonable proxy for attention duration with computer work, and this has been used as a measure of attention in multitasking, cf [32]. By computing its inverse, average duration of focus can alternatively be converted into a measure of average switching among different computer windows per time unit. Focus duration is measured as the average duration spent on any active window, based on the logging software.

Sleep duration. Daily sleep duration was measured via a self-report sleep diary, modified from [36]. Starting from Day 2 of their study, participants were asked to enter the time they went to bed the previous day (hour and minute) and the time they woke up (hour and minute). Thus, data were collected for at least six nights (sleep on Days 1-6). Five days is considered sufficient to produce reliable measures of sleep [45]. Sleep diaries have been found to be very accurate [7], are commonly used in sleep studies [5, 8,

9, 41] and have been used as a gold standard when testing sleep-monitoring devices, e.g. [34]. Self-reported sleep has also been validated with actigraphs [54]. Sleep diary reports were included in the end-of-day surveys described below.

Sleep debt. People can accumulate sleep debt on days when they work and they generally compensate for loss of sleep on free days. Sleep debt is operationalized as follows. The larger the difference between mid-sleep time on free days compared to mid-sleep time on work days, the larger is considered the sleep debt [44]. The mid-sleep time is calculated as the mid-point between sleep onset and awakening. The analysis by Roenneberg and colleagues [44] shows that most people compensate for sleep loss during the week (work days) by sleeping longer on weekends (free days). Therefore, the ideal mid-sleep time on free days is calculated from observed mid-sleep time on free days, corrected by the weekend and weekday sleep durations, by the following formula recommended by [44]:

$$MS_{FSC} = MS_F - .05*(SD_F-(5*SD_W + 2*SD_F)/7)$$

where MS_F=mid-sleep time on free days, SD_F=sleep duration on free days, and SD_W is sleep duration on work days. $(5*SD_W + 2*SD_F)/7$ is the average weekly sleep need.

Based on students' schedules, we used weekday as a "workday" and weekends were "free days". We took the difference between the mid-sleep time of each workday and the ideal mid-sleep time, as the daily sleep debt. We took the absolute value, since the theory of sleep debt is that it is the absolute departure from the ideal mid-sleep time that is representative of sleep debt. It is the disruption from ideal sleep that matters. As sleep debt has a long tail, we used a log transformation to make the distribution normal.

Mood. Mood was measured using the PANAS scale at the end of every day. The PANAS [53] is a well-validated scale that measures two dimensions of mood: positive and negative affect. Following [27], we created a measure of Affect Balance, which refers to a balance between positive and negative affect, where the negative score is subtracted from the positive score.

Survey measures. Participants filled out daily end-of-day surveys where they answered questions on work pressure and perceived productivity. Other daily measures were also asked but are not covered in this paper. A general survey asked students for demographic information, technology use habits, course load, and class standing.

Measures used

The following are definitions of our measures used.

- *Work Pressure: (End-of-day survey): I feel that I was under work/study pressure today* (using a Likert scale, 1=Strongly disagree; 5=Strongly agree).
- *Perceived Productivity: (End-of-day survey): How productive do you feel you were today?* (using a Likert scale, 1= Not at all; 5=Extremely).
- *Sleep Duration: (Sleep diary)* the amount of sleep self-reported daily based on time to sleep the previous night and time one woke up the next morning. Greater values for sleep duration reflect a greater amount of sleep.
- *Sleep Debt:* calculated by the formula above, based on self-reported daily sleep. Greater values represent a greater amount of sleep debt.
- *Total Computer Duration:* the total daily active time on the computer, based on the logging software.
- *Focus Duration:* the average duration spent on any active computer window, based on the logging software. One outlier was removed.
- *FB Duration on Computer/Phone*: the total daily FB use on the computer and phone combined, based on the logging software. One outlier was removed. A square root transformation was done to improve normality.
- *Affect balance:* the positive daily PANAS score minus the negative daily PANAS score (End-of-day survey)
- *Interviews*: participant responses to semi-structured interviews of their technology experiences.

Control variables:

- *Age, gender* (General survey)
- *Workload*: number of course credit units taken at the time of the study (General survey)
- *Deadlines: (From the end-of-day survey): How much did deadlines influence you today?* (using a Likert scale, 1= Not at all; 5=Extremely) (End of day survey).

RESULTS

We collected more than 1,720 hours of computer logs from 71 participants, excluding computer idle time. Most participants reported in exit interviews that the week of the study was representative of a typical school week.

Overview of results

We begin by reporting an overview of the results. Table 1 shows descriptive statistics of the measures of interest. The average sleep duration in our sample was 7.9 hours, with a wide range of 2.6 to 14.0 hours. Students showed a positive sleep debt, meaning that on average they accumulated sleep loss. Focus duration on any computer window averaged 1 minute, 38 seconds. Sleep duration and sleep debt are weakly negatively correlated: r= -.11, p<.05.

Research questions and analyses

For our analyses we used linear mixed-effects models (LMM) using SPSS, with Subjects as random effects, to handle the nested nature of the data (each participant has multiple days of data). We used a random intercept for participants; all other factors in the model were entered as fixed effects. Parameters were estimated using the maximum likelihood method. For LMM, SPSS calculates

Type III F tests and uses the Satterthwaite approximation for calculating denominator degrees of freedom. For our analyses, we used the measure of sleep duration the night before (Sleep Duration) (H1-H3) and the measure of sleep debt (Sleep Debt) (H4-H5) to examine the association with the variables of interest on the current day. We controlled for age, gender, workload (i.e. Credit Units), and deadlines. We only analyzed full days of data collection and days when the computer usage was greater than zero. We removed four cases (i.e. four days of different individuals) when computers were not used, as these did not represent typical computer usage for these four students. Thus, for each person we averaged six days of measures used for sleep duration, for calculating sleep debt, and for the other measures. We used thematic coding of the exit interviews to identify themes on sleep and computer use.

RQ1: Impacts of sleep on perceptions of work pressure and productivity

Our first research question addressed the effects of sleep duration on students' perceived work pressure and reported productivity. At the end of each day, participants reported how much work pressure they felt they were under, and how productive they felt they had been. For Hypothesis 1, using a LMM, controlling for deadlines, workload, age, and gender, we found a strong trend that sleep duration the night before was negatively associated with reported work pressure the next day (Table 2). An R^2 statistic for LMM must account for the variance explained by both the fixed and random effects. As there is no standard method for specifying an R^2 in LMM [16], we can provide an estimate of the R^2 using fixed effects alone. This value will *underestimate* the amount of variance explained, as random effects are not included, but it will provide a reasonable estimate. For this model, the adj. R^2 = .56. (Table 2). Not surprisingly, the control variable of deadlines was positively correlated with work pressure. Control variables of age, gender, and workload were not significant. The results thus weakly support H1: the less sleep people had the night before, the higher their reported work pressure.

Daily measures	Mean (SD)	Median	Min	Max
Sleep Duration (hr)	7.95 (2.03)	8.00	2.58	14.00
Sleep Debt	.89 (.76)	.70	.01	3.90
Total Computer Duration (hr)	3.93 (2.88)	3.51	.001	13.02
Total Phone Duration (hr)	1.54 (2.89)	1.28	0	10.75
Focus: Avg. duration/window (min)	1 min 39 sec (1.15)	1 min, 13 sec	0	6 min 17 sec
Duration of FB on computer [1] (min)	33 min 31 sec (38.8)	19 min 36 sec	0	3 hr 19 min
Duration of FB on phone[1] (min)	16 min 16 sec (23.25)	8 min 54 sec	13 sec	2 hr 6 min
Work pressure (1, low-5, high)	2.94 (1.46)	3.00	1	5
How productive (1, low-5, high)	2.75 (1.03)	3.00	1	5

Table 1. Average daily measures for participants. Measures are based on full days of computer logging, and only on days when the computer was used. [1]Descriptive measures of FB in this table are based on days when FB was used.

H1: Work Pressure	Coeff (SE)	t	p
Intercept	-.59 (1.16)	-.51	.61
Sleep Duration	**-.05 (.03)**	**-1.90**	**.06**
Controls:			
Age	.09 (.05)	1.66	.10
Female (ref. to males)	-.20 (.13)	-1.56	.13
Workload	.01 (.02)	.52	.61
Deadlines	.73 (.04)	19.43	.001

Table 2. RQ1. H1: results of the effect of sleep duration the night before on daily work pressure.

Hypothesis 2 stated that longer sleep duration the night before would be associated with higher ratings of productivity for the current day. Results are in Table 3. Surprisingly, the results showed the opposite effect: the longer the sleep duration, the lower the reported productivity, adj. R^2 = .17. The control variable of deadlines was positively correlated with productivity. None of the other control variables were significant. Thus, we reject H2, as the result was in the opposite direction that we expected.

H2: Productivity	Coeff (SE)	t	p
Intercept	2.64 (1.24)	2.14	.04
Sleep Duration	**-.06 (.03)**	**-2.22**	**.03**
Controls:			
Age	-.03 (.06)	-.44	.66
Female (ref. to males)	.18 (.14)	1.31	.19
Workload	.01 (.02)	.42	.68
Deadlines	.28 (.04)	7.73	.001

Table 3. RQ1. H2: results of the effect of sleep duration the night before on daily productivity.

In interviews, several common ideas emerged around sleep, work, and technology. First, staying up late was associated with increased pressures the next day. The reasons for this pattern of sleep deprivation and work pressure varied. Some students reported staying up late in order to study for tests or complete high stakes assignments, such as P9, who explained: "*I want to sleep but I need to get this done. There's just so much work to do, you know*?" Participants also cited "wasting time" on technology as a reason for staying up late and having to work harder the next day. For example, P57 described the reciprocal relationship between his sleeping and SM use. He noted that his SM use is "*bad because I notice after a while, 'Why am I still on this? I need to do my lab homework or something.' And then I was like, 'Okay, I guess I'm not sleeping until late tonight.'*" A theme among participants was that longer sleep was associated with a more relaxed schedule, thus providing context for rejecting H2 and the finding that longer sleep duration was associated with lower productivity. Lower productivity may also be associated with shorter sleep duration because participants chose to catch up on sleep during times with fewer obligations. Several participants described sleeping in on weekends, such as P56, who reserved "*stress-free days so I don't check my phone as much because I'd rather sleep.*" Similarly P32 had "*an actual routine Monday through Friday…versus weekends where I'll sleep in.*"

RQ2. Sleep and computer usage

Our next set of hypotheses examined the relationship of sleep duration on people's computer focus duration the next day, shown in Table 4. Hypothesis 3 stated that sleep duration should be positively related to Focus Duration. As a proxy for focus, we measured the amount of time that a computer window was in active use. We then computed the average duration of focus on all computer windows in active use for that day. The results show a significant effect of sleep duration on Focus Duration: with less sleep the night before, the average focus duration on any computer window the following day correspondingly became significantly shorter, adj. $R^2 = .04$. The control variable of deadlines was significantly negatively correlated with focus duration: $F(1, 302)=8.23$, $p < .004$). The more deadlines participants had, the shorter was their focus duration on any computer screen. The other control variables were not significant. Therefore, the results support Hypothesis 3.

H3: Focus Duration	**Coeff (SE)**	**t**	**p**
Intercept	192.28 (117.54	1.64	.11
Sleep Duration	**3.79 (1.59)**	**2.38**	**.02**
Controls:			
Age	-3.82 (5.53)	-.69	.49
Female (ref. to males)	-12.37 (13.51)	-.92	.36
Workload	-1.63 (2.34)	-.70	.49
Deadlines	-6.24 (2.13)	-2.93	.004

Table 4. RQ2. H3: results of the effect of sleep duration the night before on online focus duration. All measures taken on a daily basis.

In the interviews, one theme regarding focus duration recurred throughout: sleep deprivation resulted in distraction the following day, particularly in class. P68, for example, described how switching focus helped her stay awake after staying up late: "*In class I get really sleepy and then I'll go do something on the Internet…then I'll be like okay, I'm awake now.*" For one participant, lack of sleep also led him to feeling out of control and distractible: "*When I'm tired I have no control, I get distracted left and right.*" This example highlights a potential feedback loop, with poor sleep causing distractibility, leading to further sleep deprivation.

RQ3. Sleep and Facebook and Other Social Media use

We next examined sleep debt (as opposed to duration) and FB use. H4 stated that the higher the sleep debt, the longer the duration spent on FB. The results show that sleep debt does show a significant positive relationship with FB use on the computer and phone, adj. $R^2 = .06$ (Table 5). The control variables of Workload and Deadlines showed a significant positive correlation with Facebook use. We thus find support for H4.

The interviews provided some insight on the findings. Participants described a relationship of sleep and social media use. Increased social media use after short sleep duration may in part be a strategy, as mentioned in RQ1, to stay awake. For example, P65 stated that she used it during lectures: "*When I fall asleep I use it to wake myself up and get back to class.*" P7 described a similar behavior as part of his waking routine: "*So that I don't go back to sleep, I forcibly open Instagram and I forcibly open Facebook so I don't go back to sleep. I made it a habit to look at something and process stuff so I can wake up.*"

Students also discussed use of other social media sites as a lightweight activity that was integral to sleep and wake

H4: FB Duration	**Coeff (SE)**	**t**	**p**
Intercept	-75.12 (45.67)	-1.65	.11
Sleep Debt	**4.17 (1.99)**	**2.10**	**.04**
Controls:			
Age	3.53 (2.15)	1.64	.11
Female (ref. to males)	.19 (5.29)	.04	.97
Workload	2.01 (.91)	2.20	.03
Deadlines	1.45 (.72)	2.02	.04

Table 5. RQ3. H4: results of the effect of sleep debt on Facebook duration on computer and phone.

routines. Social media use was viewed as undemanding: "*it's easy to just scroll through Reddit. Just mindless behavior. Like procrastination time. And it's just easy. Scroll down, open a funny picture, move on to the next thing*" (P76). Twenty students described how social media use was a common practice as part of their before-bed routines. This use was for a variety of purposes, including relaxing and keeping up with information. For example, P9 reported: "*I go on Tumblr every night before I go to sleep to relax or debrief for the day.*" Similarly, P25 described her sleep routine: "*I watch videos until I fall asleep, and that's every single night. I noticed that starting this year in college, I always do that. It helps me fall asleep.*"

The interview results that social media was used as a lightweight activity to relax before sleep makes sense given that out of 71 informants, 51 reported using social media to take breaks during schoolwork. Some illustrative comments included those by P43 who said that she switched to Facebook as a way to escape the stress of schoolwork: "*I feel refreshed because I have a break time to not think about school work.*" P59 said that his social media routine included "*scrolling down through posts over and over again. It's a good way to get my mind off of school work and stress.*" Participants also noted that social media use was part of their waking routines: "*I check Reddit a lot…before I go to sleep and also when I wake up….Just to see if there is anything new*" (P66). However, some reported that social media as part of their sleep routine interfered with their ability to get adequate sleep: "*I would be like 'What am I doing? I'm supposed to be sleeping.' But then I use [YouTube] like 10 minutes….I use it a lot before I go to sleep*" (P3).

RQ4. Sleep and Mood

Our last hypothesis examined the relationship of sleep debt and mood. We expected that more sleep debt would be related to more negative affect. Our dependent variable was Affect Balance [27], which is an indicator of positive well-being based on the PANAS scores [53]. Results in Table 6 show that there is a significant negative relationship of sleep debt with Affect Balance: the more sleep debt one has accumulated, the more negative is one's mood, adj. R^2 = .10. Gender was significant: $F(1, 67)=13.13$, $p<.001$: females have significantly more positive mood than males. The other controls were not significant. Therefore, we found support for H5.

H5: Affect Balance	**Coeff (SE)**	**t**	**p**
Intercept	-11.43 (12.62)	-91	.37
Sleep Debt	**-1.83 (94)**	**-1.94**	**.05**
Controls:			
Age	.97 (.60)	1.61	.11
Female (ref. to males)	5.36 (1.45)	3.69	.001
Workload	-.02 (.25)	-.06	.95
Deadlines	-.30 (.33)	-.91	.37

Table 6. RQ4. H5: results of the effect of sleep debt on mood.

DISCUSSION

Although studies have documented the effects IT use can have on sleep patterns, our results point to the converse: sleep duration can impact IT usage. Shorter sleep duration the previous night was related to higher work pressure and perceived productivity the next day. We also found that the shorter the sleep duration the night before, focus duration was shorter on the computer the next day. With more sleep debt, people spend more time on Facebook the next day. Sleep debt negatively impacts mood.

Our findings contribute to the growing body of research that has been examining the interplay of sleep and IT use. To date, studies have examined how IT use impacts sleep, generally finding that more time online leads college students to receive less sleep [1, 39, 50]. Other work has examined measurement of quality and quantity of sleep, e.g. through the use of smart phones, wearable devices, or sensing social behavior [3, 11, 24, 38]. Our work instead sheds light on the converse phenomenon: how sleep patterns can affect people's IT use and mood.

There has been much research interest in HCI on the topic of multitasking. Further, there has also been a body of research documenting that college students experience poor sleep habits, which in turn can lead to reduced cognitive functioning [30] and poor academic performance [44]. Our result that less sleep is associated with shorter duration of focus is related to multitasking behavior; the shorter the duration of focus on a computer screen, the more frequently one switches between screens, i.e. switching attention to different content [32]. Multitasking is also associated with lack of cognitive control and focus [40]. Our finding of shorter attention duration is consistent with other findings that show that when people are more tired, they are more distractible [25]. Thus, our results build on prior work showing that poor sleep affects cognitive functioning: we found that effects of poor sleep can be manifest in computer activity as well, specifically in terms of shorter focus duration while using the computer.

This result has theoretical implications for multitasking in HCI. It suggests that it is not just external interruptions, applications such as email, habitual behavior, or amount of projects that influence duration of focus [19, 32], but that there could be physiological and cognitive reasons for switching computer activities, due to lack of sleep. As we controlled for deadlines and workload, the shorter focus duration result implies that there is a factor beyond a student's work situation that could be affecting their attention duration. The association of amount of sleep with multitasking suggests that people's tendency to multitask can vary not only with task and the environment, but also can potentially change with sleep patterns. Thus, poor sleep patterns may contribute to explaining why online multitasking occurs, which is of theoretical interest for HCI.

Our results of sleep patterns on work pressure and productivity also contribute to the research literature. There is an established pathway of less sleep and lower productivity for adults, e.g. [23]. For college students, sleep patterns have been examined with lab-based performance tests (e.g. math or attention tasks after sleep-deprivation) and GPA [54] but never with *in situ* observation. Thus, our results show that poor sleep patterns can impact perceptions of work pressure and productivity for students. Future research can examine how these perceptions might be mediators of student performance.

The result showing that less sleep is associated with higher reported work pressure and higher productivity suggests that with less sleep, students may be spending more time on work activities. Less sleep can also mean that people are getting more work done, which would explain the result of higher perceived productivity. Fewer hours of sleep enables more time available to spend on work. Combining this idea with the result of higher work pressure suggests that with less sleep people could be experiencing a higher cognitive workload, e.g. due to deadlines, which we found to positively correlate with work pressure. Thus, less sleep can provide benefits, but may have repercussions in terms of higher work pressure and the ability to maintain focus.

Higher work pressure can place more cognitive demands on an individual. Some research has suggested that social media use is associated with less effortful thinking [55]. Combining our results, it is possible then that with less sleep, and with feeling more work pressure, people may turn to lightweight activities such as Facebook.

Shorter focus suggests being more distractible. The combination of shorter attention focus (and possibly more distractibility), and higher Facebook use leads us to posit that less sleep may lead to more self-interruptions. It is plausible that people self-interrupt to view Facebook, as its habitual use has been documented, cf [13, 52]. The qualitative results combined with the quantitative results help us better understand a potential role of Facebook with respect to work. Facebook might provide a mental break or distraction while conducting work on the computer. Consistent with this idea are data from the interviews where most students reported that social media was used as a work break. However, it is important to note that more Facebook use and increased multitasking may reflect, rather than result from, less sleep. This relationship can be tested in a laboratory setting. We also need to be cautious that not all Facebook use is for leisure activity or breaks. Although not a strong theme of Facebook use, four participants did mention that they used Facebook groups for school-related activities such as sharing information for group projects, organizing club activities, or participating in Q&A for class materials. We urge future studies to investigate sleep variables and types of Facebook activities.

College students are the cohort of highest users of social media. We explored social media use other than Facebook use in our sample post facto with sleep debt and found no relationship. One reason could be that social media is very heterogeneous. Social media can be used for a variety of purposes: e.g. information seeking, communication, or keeping up with friend networks. Different social media are also associated with different social norms; thus, we expect that behavior with social media can be quite diverse. It is possible that even with less sleep, people's needs that are satisfied by many types of social media may not change, but with Facebook, perhaps with sleep debt there is increased pressure to keep up with one's social network. Another reason could be that patterns of general social media use for this college student cohort might be highly variable, unlike with Facebook use which most college students use. Some support for this idea is found in the 2014 Pew study which shows that Facebook use is much higher than the next most popular social media site, Instragram, which 53% of young adults use [14]. Thus, it could be that aside from Facebook, the use of social media is fairly diverse in our sample and differences in its use may not be manifest with changing sleep patterns. This suggests further exploration with specific social media sites. As new social media sites gain in popularity, there may arise new relationships with patterns of sleep debt.

Our results that show that sleep debt is associated with negative mood corroborate laboratory studies, which show the same findings [28, 42, 43]. However, our contribution is that we show that these results occur in *in situ* environments in the course of natural day-to-day activities. In addition, the relationship of sleep debt and a more negative mood could be mediated by higher work pressure, as we discovered. We feel that these results lead to an opportunity for further research to test the interaction of sleep patterns, specific social media sites, and mood.

We looked at a one-way directional relationship of sleep duration on behaviors. However, more broadly, our study suggests that the relationship of sleep and IT use can be bidirectional. Identifying a relationship in the opposite direction is important, especially if these variables are reciprocal in nature (in other words, less sleep leads to more Facebook use and in turn more Facebook use could lead to less sleep). While our study of examining the role of sleep duration on IT use is a first step, future research should look at iterative processes. There may in fact be a cyclic relationship of sleep duration and certain behaviors.

Designing for sleep patterns

Our results inform some ideas of how technology could be designed to help remedy the effects of lack of sleep. We present the following suggestions. Our results suggest that sleep patterns should be considered when designing interfaces. People experience "social jet lag" [38], when people's circadian rhythms are mismatched to their work schedules or social lives. Interfaces could be customized to adapt to individuals' practices, as they are affected by their sleep patterns. For example, if an individual's attention focus is markedly decreased (as evidenced by shorter attention duration on computer screens or switching screens), then this could be a signal to trigger an intervention to take a relaxation break. Our results also suggest that people may gear their IT usage depending on their level of mental alertness. For example, lightweight computer activity could be beneficial in the morning to ease into computer work. There is utility to understanding computer usage as students wake or go to sleep that could help in their performance. Lastly, our results suggest that amount of sleep may be a variable of interest when doing user experience studies or *in situ* observations of IT use.

Limitations

Though our primary independent variables were sleep duration the night before, and sleep debt, which occur before the other measures temporally, we cannot state a causal relation. There may be any number of other underlying variables that mediate the relationship between sleep and IT usage. A limitation is that phone Facebook use may be overestimated; the highest durations of phone Facebook use were captured late at night, perhaps after participants had fallen asleep. Some participants stated that they used social media—especially on their phones—to fall asleep. Another limitation is that we did not measure quality of sleep but only focused on sleep duration. However, because we took multiple measures over different days for each individual, we can take into account variations of sleep duration within individuals. Still, it would be important in a future study to consider quality as well as quantity of sleep, including daytime naps. Lastly, sleep was based on self-report, which has been validated in previous studies. Nevertheless, future studies could use unobtrusive observational measures such as actigraphs for more precise estimates.

Our results apply to college students, based on our sample. It is unclear whether our results would generalize to other groups and domains, such as in the workplace. We do however strongly suspect that some relationships we found would generalize more broadly, such as with sleep and duration of computer window focus. Considering the importance of sleep in job performance, this could be an important area for further research.

CONCLUSIONS

As new sensors, biosensors and other innovative tools for measuring behavior continue to be developed, we envision that the results they yield will prove useful to the HCI community in improving the user experience. Our results point to sleep duration as one factor that is associated with IT usage. Although there is growing evidence of social media and computer usage disrupting sleep, this study shows that sleep affects IT usage as well. We hope that our research can spark future research into other techniques to explore more deeply the relationship of sleep and IT use.

ACKNOWLEDGEMENTS

This material is based upon work supported by the National Science Foundation under grant #1218705. We thank Fernando Rodriguez for his valuable comments.

REFERENCES

1. Sue K. Adams, Jennifer F. Daly, and Desireé N. Williford. 2013. Adolescent sleep and cellular phone use: Recent trends and implications for research. *Health Services Insights* 6: 99-103.
2. Torbjörn Åkerstedt. 1988. Sleepiness as a consequence of shift work. *Sleep* 11, 1: 17-34.
3. Jared S. Bauer, Sunny Consolvo, Benjamin Greenstein, Jonathan Schooler, Eric Wu, Nathaniel F. Watson, and Julie Kientz. 2010. ShutEye: encouraging awareness of healthy sleep recommendations with a mobile, peripheral display. In *Proc. of CHI'10*, 1401-1410.
4. Virginie Bayon, Damien Leger, Danielle Gomez-Merino, Marie-Françoise Vecchierini, and Mounir Chennaoui. 2014. Sleep debt and obesity, *Annals of Medicine* 46, 5: 264-272.
5. Craig M. Becker, Troy Adams, Caroline Orr, and Lyndsay Quilter. 2008. Correlates of quality sleep and academic performance. *Health Educator 40*, 2: 82-89.
6. Michael H. Bonnet and Donna L. Arand. 1995. We are chronically sleep deprived. *Sleep* 18, 10: 908–911.
7. Richard R. Bootzin and Mindy Engle-Friedman. 1981. The assessment of insomnia. *Behavioral Assessment* 3: 107-126.
8. Walter C. Buboltz Jr, Franklin Brown, and Barlow Soper. 200_. Sleep habits and patterns of college students: a preliminary study. *J of American College Health* 50, 3: 131-135.
9. Christina J Calamaro, Thornton BA Mason, and Sarah J. Ratcliffe. 2009. Adolescents living the 24/7 lifestyle: effects of caffeine and technology on sleep duration and daytime functioning. *Pediatrics* 123, 6: e1005-e1010.
10. Center for Disease Control. Unhealthy sleep-related behaviors—12 States, 2009. 2011. *Morbidity and mortality weekly report* 60, 8: 233-238.
11. Eun Kyoung Choe, Sunny Consolvo, Nathaniel F. Watson, and Julie A. Kientz. 2011. Opportunities for computing technologies to support healthy sleep behaviors. In *Proc of CHI'11*. 3053-3062.
12. Mary Czerwinski, Eric Horvitz, and Susan Wilhite. 2004. A diary study of task switching and interruptions. In *Proc of CHI '04*, 175-182.

13. Bernhard Debatin, Jennette P. Lovejoy, Ann-Kathrin Horn, and Brittany N. Hughes. 2009. Facebook and online privacy: Attitudes, behaviors, and unintended consequences. *Journal of Computer-Mediated Communication* 15, 1: 83-108.

14. Maeve Duggan, Nicole B. Ellison, Cliff Lampe, Amanda Lenhart, and Mary Madden. 2014. 2014. Social Media Update 2014. Pew Research Center. http://www.pewinternet.org/2015/01/09/social-media-update-2014/. Accessed Sept. 2015.

15. Jeffrey S. Durmer and David F. Dinges. 2005. Neurocognitive consequences of sleep deprivation. *Seminars in neurology* 25, 1: 117-129.

16. Lloyd J. Edwards, Keith E. Muller, Russell D. Wolfinger, Bahjat F. Qaqish, and Oliver Schabenberger. 2008. An R2 statistic for fixed effects in the linear mixed model. *Statistics in medicine* 27, 29: 6137-6157.

17. Shirley Fisher. 1980. The microstructure of dual-task interaction: IV. Sleep deprivation and the control of attention. *Perception* 9, 3: 327-337.

18. J. Friedmann, G. Globus, A. Huntley, D. Mullaney, P. Naitoh, and L. Johnson. 1977. Performance and mood during and after gradual sleep reduction. *Psychophysiology* 14: 245–50.

19. Victor M. Gonzalez and Gloria Mark. 2004. "Constant, Constant, Multi-tasking Craziness": Managing Multiple Working Spheres. In *Proc of CHI '04*, 113-120.

20. Christopher M. Jung, Joseph M. Ronda, and Charles A. Czeisler. 2011. Comparison of sustained attention assessed by auditory and visual psychomotor vigilance tasks prior to and during sleep deprivation. *Journal of sleep research* 20, 2: 348-355.

21. Reynol Junco. 2012. The relationship between frequency of Facebook use, participation in Facebook activities, and student engagement. *Computers & Education*, *58*(1), pp.162-171.

22. Amy K. Karlson, Shamsi T. Iqbal, Brian Meyers, Gonzalo Ramos, Kathy Lee, and John C. Tang. 2010. Mobile task flow in context: A screenshot study of smartphone usage. In *Proc of CHI'10*, 2009-2018.

23. Gerald Krueger. 1989. Sustained work, fatigue, sleep loss and performance: A review of the issues. *Work & Stress*, *3*, 2: 129-141.

24. Shaun Lawson, Sue Jamison-Powell, Andrew Garbett, Conor Linehan, Erica Kucharczyk, Sanne Verbaan, Duncan A. Rowland, and Kevin Morgan. 2013. Validating a mobile phone application for the everyday, unobtrusive, objective measurement of sleep. In *Proc. of CHI'13,* 2497-2506.

25. Uichin Lee, Joonwon Lee, Minsam Ko, Changhun Lee, Yuhwan Kim, Subin Yang, Koji Yatani, Gahgene Gweon, Kyong-Mee Chung, and Junehwa Song. 2014. Hooked on smartphones: an exploratory study on smartphone overuse among college students. In *Proc of CHI'14*, 2327-2336.

26. Julian Lim and David Dinges. 2008. Sleep deprivation and vigilant attention. *Annals of the New York Academy of Sciences* 1129, 1: 305-322.

27. Ya Liu, Zhenhong Wang, and Wei Lü. 2013. Resilience and affect balance as mediators between trait emotional intelligence and life satisfaction. *Personality and Individual Differences* 54.7: 850-855.

28. Hannah G. Lund, Brian D. Reider, Annie B. Whiting, and J. Roxanne Prichard. 2010. Sleep patterns and predictors of disturbed sleep in a large population of college students. *Journal of Adolescent Health 46*, 2: 124-132.

29. Faith S. Luyster, Patrick J. Strollo, Jr., Phyllis C. Zee, and James K. Walsh. 2012. Sleep: A Health Imperative. *Sleep* 35, 6: 727 -34.

30. Pierre Maquet. 2001. The role of sleep in learning and memory. *Science 294*, 5544: 1048–1051.

31. Gloria Mark, Shamsi T. Iqbal, Mary Czerwinski, and Paul Johns. 2014. Capturing the mood: Facebook and face-to-face encounters in the workplace. In *Proc. of ACM Conference on Computer Supported Cooperative Work (CSCW'14),* 1082-1094.

32. Gloria Mark, Steven Voida, and Armand Cardello. 2012. A pace not dictated by electrons: An empirical study of work without email. In *Proc of CHI'12*, 555-564.

33. Gloria Mark, Yiran Wang, and Melissa Niiya. 2014. Stress and multitasking in everyday college life: An empirical study of online activity. In *Proc of CHI'14*, 41-50.

34. Jun-Ki Min, Afsaneh Doryab, Jason Wiese, Shahriyar Amini, John Zimmerman, and Jason I. Hong. 2014. Toss'n'turn: smartphone as sleep and sleep quality detector. In *Proc. of CHI'14*, 477-486.

35. Timothy H. Monk, Daniel J. Buysse, Jaime M. Potts, Jean M. DeGrazia, and David J. Kupfer. 2004. Morningness-eveningness and lifestyle regularity. *Chronobiol Int'l* 21, 3: 435–443.

36. Timothy H. Monk, Charles Reynolds, David J. Kupfer, Daniel J. Buysse, Patricia A. Coble, Amy J. Hayes, Mary Ann Machen, Susan R. Petrie, and Angela M. Ritenour. 1994. The Pittsburgh sleep diary. *Journal of Sleep Research,* 3: 111–120.

37. Janet Morahan-Martin and Phyllis Schumacher. 2000. Incidence and correlates of pathological Internet use among college students. *Comp in Human Beh 16*, 1: 13-29.

38. Elizabeth L.,Murnane, Saeed Abdullah, Mark Matthews, Tanzeem Choudhury, and Geri Gay. 2015. Social (media) jet lag: How usage of social technology can modulate and reflect circadian rhythms. In *Proceedings of the 2015 ACM International Joint Conference on Pervasive and Ubiquitous Computing*, 843-854.

39. Gwenn Schurgin O'Keeffe and Kathleen Clarke-Pearson. 2011. The impact of social media on children, adolescents, and families. *Pediatrics127*,4: 800-804.

40. Eyal Ophir, Clifford Nass, and Anthony D. Wagner. 2009. Cognitive control in media multitaskers. *Proceedings of the National Academy of Sciences* 106.37: 15583-15587.

41. June J. Pilcher, Douglas R. Ginter, and Brigitte Sadowsky. 1997. Sleep quality versus sleep quantity: relationships between sleep and measures of health, well-being and sleepiness in college students. *Journal of psychosomatic research 42*, 6: 583-596.

42. June J. Pilcher and Allen J. Huffcutt. 1996. Effects of sleep deprivation on performance: a meta-analysis. *Sleep* 19: 318–26.

43. June J. Pilcher and Amy Walters. 1997. How sleep deprivation affects psychological variables related to college students' cognitive performance. *Journal of American College Health* 46, 3: 121-126.

44. Till Roenneberg, Tim Kuehnle, Peter P. Pramstaller, Jan Ricken, Miriam Havel, Angelika Guth, and Martha Merrow. 2004. A marker for the end of adolescence. *Current Biology* 14, 24: R1038-R1039.

45. Avi Sadeh. 2011. The role and validity of actigraphy in sleep medicine: an update. *Sleep medicine reviews* 15, 4: 259-267.

46. Johnny Saldaña. 2012. *The Coding Manual for Qualitative Researchers*. Sage.

47. Kaveri Subrahmanyam, Stephanie M. Reich, Natalia Waechter, and Guadalupe Espinoza. 2008. Online and offline social networks: Use of social networking sites by emerging adults. *J of Applied Developmental Psychology*, *29*, 6: 420-433.

48. S. H. Thompson and Eric Lougheed. 2002. Frazzled by Facebook? An exploratory study of gender differences in social network communication among undergraduate men and women. *College Student J* 46, 1: 88-99.

49. Mickey T. Trockel, Michael D. Barnes, and Dennis L. Egget. 2000. Health-related variables and academic performance among first-year college students: implications for sleep and other behaviors. *J of American college health 49*, 3: 125-131.

50. Jan Van den Bulck. 2004. Television viewing, computer game playing, and Internet use and self-reported time to bed and time out of bed in secondary-school children. *Sleep 27*, 1: 101-104.

51. Hans Van Dongen, Naomi Rogers, and David Dinges. 2003. Sleep debt: theoretical and empirical issues. *Sleep and Biological Rhythms,* 1, 5-13.

52. Yiran Wang, Melissa Niiya, Gloria Mark, Stephanie Reich, and Mark Warschauer. 2015. Coming of age (digitally): An ecological view of social media use among college students. In *Proc of CSCW'15,* 571-582.

53. David Watson, Lee A. Clark, and Auke Tellegen. 1988. Development and validation of brief measures of positive and negative affect: The PANAS scales. *Journal of Personality and Social Psychology* 56, 6: 1063-1070.

54. Amy R. Wolfson, Mary A. Carskadon, Christine Acebo, Ronald Seifer, Gahan Fallone, Susan E. Labyak, and Jennifer L. Martin. 2003. Evidence for the validity of a sleep habits survey for adolescents. *Sleep,* 2: 213-216.

55. Bu Zhong, Marie Hardin, and Tao Sun. 2011. Less effortful thinking leads to more social networking? The associations between the use of social network sites and personality traits. *Computers in Human Behavior 27*, 3: 1265-1271.

"Tell It Like It Really Is": A Case of Online Content Creation and Sharing Among Older Adult Bloggers

Robin Brewer and Anne Marie Piper
Northwestern University, Evanston, IL, USA
rnbrewer@u.northwestern.edu, ampiper@northwestern.edu

ABSTRACT
While the majority of older adults are now active online, they are often perceived as passive consumers of online information rather than active creators of content. As a counter to this view, we examine the practices of older adult bloggers (N=20) through in-depth interviews. We study this group of older adults as a unique case of content creation and sharing. We find that the practice of creating and sharing through blogging meets several important psychological and social needs for older adults. Specifically, blogging supports the development of identity in older adulthood; fosters self-expression that supports older adults' values; provides meaningful engagement during retirement; and enables a sense of community and social interaction that is important for wellbeing in late-life. We argue for a focus on *designing for late-life development* and detail opportunities for online systems to better support the dynamic experience of growing older through online content creation and sharing.

Author Keywords
Blogging; older adults; creative expression; identity

ACM Classification Keywords
H.5.3. Group and Organization Interfaces: Computer-supported cooperative work

INTRODUCTION
More than half of American older adults (people age 65+) go online on a regular basis [17], and increasing numbers of seniors are using social network sites (SNSs) such as Facebook, Twitter, and LinkedIn [16]. Interacting online is an important way in which younger people express themselves and develop their identities [23], but relatively few older adults actively publish content online or use online platforms in the same way [24]. Currently, older adults in the U.S. are often characterized as consumers of online content rather than creators [65]. Older adults may lurk in online communities, which may be a result of the complexity of interfaces for sharing content, concerns about privacy, and differences in attitudes towards sharing information online [21,26,29,33,48,67].

Yet, online engagement in older adulthood has implications for late-life health and wellbeing [56]. Being active online is associated with positive health outcomes among older adults (e.g., less depression [13]). As people age, they can experience significant change from moving to a new community [36] and retiring from the workforce [61]. These changes can have an impact on older adults' emotional health [60] and evolving identity [51] as well as relationships with family members and friends [12,27]. Prior work has shown that creative expression can be beneficial to seniors and promote healthy aging [8,41]. The perceived control people derive from participating in creative activities and social engagement that creative expression affords can lead to reduced depression and loneliness and increased morale among older adults [8]. Given this, recent work in HCI focuses on how to engage seniors in creative activities and online sharing with family and friends [2,44,54,65]. Existing HCI literature tends to focus on novel prototype sharing systems. While studying such systems is valuable, the literature contains sparse examples of how older adults contribute and share content on mainstream platforms (see [25] as a noteworthy exception), leaving open many questions about how older adults appropriate existing technology to address their need for sharing, disclosure, and community during this phase of life.

This paper analyzes a specific case of online content creation and sharing: older adults who blog. We conducted interviews with 20 older adult bloggers to understand why and how these individuals blog as well as what this practice affords for people in older adulthood. We find that blogging is an important way in which older adults satisfy a variety of needs and embrace the experience of growing older. Specifically, we find that blogging: (1) supports the development of identity in older adulthood; (2) fosters self-expression in ways that support older adults' values; (3) provides meaningful engagement during retirement; and (4) enables a sense of community and social interaction that is important for wellbeing in late-life.

Our case analysis makes two primary contributions to HCI. First, studying blogging provides a lens through which we examine how older adults engage in online content creation and sharing as a way of achieving a variety of goals in late-

ACM 978-1-4503-3362-7/16/05...$15.00
DOI: http://dx.doi.org/10.1145/2858036.2858379

life. From this, we argue for a focus on *designing for late-life development*, which characterizes older adulthood as a period of growth and reflection. This is in contrast to how much research in HCI frames designing for older adults, which treats aging as a form of decline and problematizes age-related changes as something that technology can solve (see [63] for a review). Second, we contrast our findings with existing literature on technologies to support content creation and sharing for older adults, highlighting converging evidence in this space and areas in which systems could better support the dynamic experience of growing older.

BACKGROUND AND MOTIVATION

As a way of understanding online participation and sharing among older adults, scholars in HCI and CSCW largely focus on studying older adults' behaviors on and attitudes towards SNSs, such as Facebook and Twitter. This work often contrasts older adults' behaviors to those of young adults and teenagers, who frequently use SNSs for staying in touch with family members and friends [24,32,64], connecting with people from their past [57], and self-expression [32]. Older adults also use SNSs to connect with family and friends [26] and with people who have shared interests [29]. Older adults, however, are less likely than younger users to actively contribute on these sites by leaving comments or posting status updates [26,30,38]. Prior work suggests that older adults find sharing brief updates on SNSs to be superficial and "meaningless" [26]. Further, older adults have privacy concerns about sharing information on SNSs and view these websites as a place to show off and seek attention [21,29,67], suggesting that the social practices associated with these sites and affordances of the medium (e.g., unclear privacy policies) may turn off older adults.

While recent press articles suggest that the popularity of blogging in a traditional sense is diminishing [28,43], perhaps due to the introduction of "micro-blogging" platforms (e.g., Twitter), blogging may still be an important online activity for many older adults [31]. Further, the medium of a blog and social practices of blogging provide an interesting contrast with studies of older adults using SNSs. Studying older adult bloggers, although anachronistic, is a valuable way of understanding how older adults engage in the social practice of online content creation and sharing using mainstream technology.

The field of HCI has a long history of blogging studies. Beginning in the late 1990s, blogging emerged as an important social practice for younger people [47]. The initial concept of a blog – which has a dedicated URL and organizes posts in reverse chronological order – is one of the oldest online content publishing platforms and still persists today. For example, twenty years later, Tumblr is one of the most widely-used blogging platforms with nearly 253 million blogs[1] hosted on the site [18]. Early work by Nardi et al. indicates that people blog to document their lives, communicate with their social contacts, express their views and opinions, update people, seek feedback, release emotional tension, and share their thoughts and feelings [46,47]. These studies, however, only include younger people.

Blogging can also be a source of empowerment [50] and address needs of affiliation and self-disclosure [6] for communities with shared interests or needs. From studying weight loss bloggers, researchers found that these individuals were empowered through blogging because of their ability to voluntarily disclose information to a community of like-minded people and that blogging helped to improve their self-worth [50]. Additionally, Chen [6] found that affiliation and the need for self-disclosure motivates women to blog. Other studies note benefits of blogging for people with chronic diseases such as chronic pain [15] and cancer [7]. Similarly, people with chronic diseases, including some older adults, were more likely to reach out for support through blogs or online forums compared to SNSs [7,15]. This prior work indicates that sharing online can be beneficial for these populations when systems allow for asynchronous communication [15], reminiscence [1,52], and sharing of personal histories or identities [62]. Blogs give voice to vulnerable populations, thus strengthening "the blogger's attachment to the blogging community" [50]. As a result, people who feel highly stigmatized report that blogging helps to improve their self-esteem.

Despite this extensive prior work, little is known about what the social practice of blogging affords for people in older adulthood, who may deal with identity changes introduced by retirement [51], negative stereotypes of aging [63], and the desire to stay socially connected [34]. Although the field has yet to examine existing older adult bloggers, one prior study investigated older adults' attitudes towards social media and blogging as well as how to introduce blogging to older adults [67]. This prior work details older adults' perceptions of blogs as a safe alternative to Facebook, and we further elaborate the differences between SNSs like Facebook and blogs in the present paper. Additionally, our analysis extends these findings by studying the views of older adults who are already deeply engaged in the practice of blogging, revealing how these individuals blog as a way of grappling with the experience of growing older.

Research has also studied and introduced research prototypes aimed at engaging older adults in creation and sharing. In focus groups about reminiscing, older adults describe their openness about using technology to express themselves and see the value of intergenerational sharing [45]. Another study describes seniors who used the Enmesh iPad application to share pictures and messages with each other [65], and found that older adults liked being able to express themselves creatively and wanted to share with a responsive audience. One outlet for creative expression with older adults is

[1] https://www.tumblr.com/about

through art therapy, in which technologies may provide greater independence and choice in sharing for older adults [44]. The SPARCS, Tlatoque, and Wayve systems, prototypes for sharing photos, messages, and calendars with family members, are other examples that aim to engage older adults in family sharing [2,11,35]. Finally, Rogers et al. [54] argues that older adults can be motivated to create and share in the technological design space if provided with ways that "tap into the huge diversity of skillsets of retired people." This work provides a foundation for understanding how to design for content creation and sharing among older adults, and we return to this literature in the discussion.

METHOD

We conducted semi-structured interviews with 20 older adult bloggers (age 65-82; M=73 years old; 18 female). We recruited people who were over the age of 65, had a public blog in English with at least one post created since January 2015, and had publically available contact information (e.g., an e-mail address on their blog home page, about page, or blog profile description). Participants were recruited via snowball sampling either through blogrolls, a feature commonly used by bloggers to list other blogs they follow, or word-of-mouth as recommended by participants at the end of their interviews. The initial list of bloggers was created by searching for older adult bloggers on a public search engine.

On average, our participants have blogged for 7.4 years and eight participants authored more than one blog. The older adults we interviewed use Blogger's BlogSpot platform, WordPress, and Typepad. On average, participants have made 128 posts in 2015 alone (January through August; min = 4 posts, max = 369 posts,). Participants were also active on popular SNSs like Facebook (n=11) and Twitter (n=15) and described using these sites to promote their blogs. Only one participant who used her blog as a professional outlet used Twitter as a form of micro-blogging (vs. using it to promote her blog). Other than SNSs and traditional blogs, one participant had created podcasts in addition to blogging. Participants were from a variety of occupational backgrounds (e.g. retail, personal trainer, and producer) and discussed many different topics (see Table 1). All but one participant blogged from the United States.

We conducted semi-structured interviews by phone or Skype, with one participant requesting to complete the interview via e-mail. Our interview protocol focused on older adults' motivations to start and continue blogging, topics that they blog about, challenges encountered, and their blogging process (e.g. creating and editing posts). We used this to open up a discussion with participants about how they share online more broadly, including on other platforms. Each interview lasted approximately one hour and older adults received a $15 Amazon gift card for participating.

We transcribed all interviews, and multiple researchers reviewed, discussed, and coded the data following a grounded theory approach [5]. Initial open coding revealed themes such as "blogging about aging" and "increasing readership through commenting". We further refined these themes through axial coding and constant comparison of data in which we related new data back to emerging themes. Through an iterative process of memoing and theorizing, four high-level themes emerged around how and why older adults blog, which we present below.

P#	M/F	Age	Years Blogging	# of Blogs	# of Posts	Blog Topic
1	F	69	1	1	28	Retirement
2	F	75	10	1	134	Personal
3	F	80	9	1	7	Politics
4	F	77	9	3	62	Personal, quilting
5	F	71	3	2	12	Personal, dreams
6	F	82	9	2	4	Politics and feminism, knitting
7	F	74	15	3	357	Technology, writing, pop culture
8	M	65	9	2	249	Personal satire, technology
9	F	74	10	1	78	Politics
10	F	74	11	2	369	Aging
11	F	75	6	1	15	Travel
12	F	68	2	1	16	Fitness
13	F	68	7	1	31	Personal
14	F	72	8	1	238	Writing
15	F	72	6	2	140	Hiking, personal
16	F	80	7	1	120	Personal
17	F	72	5	1	224	Education
18	F	68	10	2	375	Personal, travel
19	F	72	6	1	10	Family
20	M	73	5	1	106	Travel

Table 1. Participant demographics and blogging profile. Number of posts represents total over last nine months.

RESULTS

Our analysis examines older adults who are active bloggers as a case of successful online content creation and sharing, and through this, we identify four key ways in which blogging helps older adults satisfy important psychological and social needs associated with this period of life.

Development of Identity through Blogging

Our analysis suggests that creating and sharing through blogging provides an important outlet for older adults to continue to refine their identity and reflect on new identities (e.g., as a retiree, grandparent, older person) throughout older adulthood.

Many of our participants have a blog that focuses on a particular theme in which they write about specific topics, such as HTML and website design, hiking, politics, knitting, feminism, or personal events that occurred in their daily lives. The theme of the blog represents part of that author's identity (e.g., being an avid hiker or political commentator). Participants said they created multiple blogs if they wanted to talk about more than one topic, and rarely did older adults mix personal and thematic blogs. For example, P4 has a blog for her crafting hobby and started a blog to discuss aging. People in older adulthood often desire to maintain and separate multiple identities, each addressing a social need [61]. Here, we learned that older adults purposefully separate themes (e.g., gardening enthusiast) across different blogs, which helps them to express and keep distinct different dimensions of their identity.

Beyond hobbies and interests, an older adult's identity is also influenced by their previous profession [51]. For some participants, blogging was a natural extension of their work-related identity as a writer or journalist. Writing was already part of their identity, both personally and professionally, and blogging helped them carry this identity into older adulthood. One participant who identifies as a writer said that blogging was a natural progression when she entered retirement: "*... I was telling my daughter, 'What am I going to do? I am sitting here all by myself.' You know, poor me, and she said, 'Well, you like to write. Writing is what you do...'*" (P1). Another participant was also a writer before she retired and said that she started blogging because "*I wanted to have an outlet for writing, creative writing and expressing myself in a way that I didn't have to look for a publisher,*" (P15). In this way, blogging allows free expression without having constraints imposed upon her writing style, topic, and timeline. Similarly, P19 who was previously a writer said, "*In retirement it just feels very natural to come to my desk and sit down and be at my computer and be writing. The fact that I'm writing for myself in my own voice is something that I like.*" Writing as a blogger allows for more freedom than writing professionally, providing older adults with greater control over what and how they share online.

Blogging is also a way in which these older adults negotiate and reflect on new identities as they enter new stages of life, such as retiring or becoming a grandparent. P19 said:

"*...all of my working life I identified myself by my job. ...When you retire, you start thinking, and 'Well what am I going to say that I am?' My new identity became, 'I'm a grandmother who is doing full time daycare.... [Blogging] helped me describe what I was doing, it helped me get a lot of positive feedback from people who saw the value in that.*"

Indeed, an important part of an older adult's identity is shaped by their former occupation, and the transition to retirement can be traumatic if their prior employment is the main source of their identity [51]. Blogging helps older adults deal with their changing identities associated with retirement as well as new family roles that they may now assume. This life change is significant, and some older adults blog to share and reflect on their transitioning identity:

"*My intended audience are people over 55 who are either getting ready to retire or who are already retired... I figured other people were in the same boat as I was, and I am going to write about how to cope with this. What am I going to do now that I have lost the meaningful work that I had?... I began to study what retirement is for different people, how it is handled by different people, what problems do retirees face, and those topics form the basis for most of my blogging.*" (P1)

Beyond coping with new life roles in retirement, many participants explained that their blog is linked to their identity as an older adult, through which they share the experience of aging. For example, P12 said, "*[My blog] shows that I'm in my 60s...I would assume people would be interested if they're older.*" This participant and others describe how their blog topics center on aging, and how the blogs they read are also about people's experiences with aging. Participants described presenting themselves on their blog as being "*an advocate for old people*" (P10) or that people they follow "*tell it like it really is*" (P3) for aging. For example, P5 said, "*My theme is getting old. Aging and exposing to the community at large what it's really like.*" This includes sharing both positive and negative aspects of growing older. For example, P5 said:

"*I talk to a lot of seniors and I try to give voice to some of their concerns. . 'What am I even for? Why am I still here?' and I find a lot of older people say that and I try to search for that answer. I try to give voice to that concern and pull that answer if I can find it.*"

Participants highlighted the importance of being a voice for older adults more broadly and conveying the true experience of aging, which motivates them to blog and allows them reflect on and develop their identities throughout older adulthood.

Participants also described developing their voice through the practice of blogging, which is another way in which they manage their online identity. All but one participant said their online identity closely reflected their offline identity. This participant (P8) said that he writes using a persona who:

"*swears a LOT more than I do and tends to take a direct approach to subjects. On the rare occasions I do meet with a reader they tend to be surprised that I'm such a mild mannered quiet person! [Persona name] is my darker alter ego!... [My persona] is a heavy drinker and womaniser while I am happily married [for nearly 40 years] and rarely touch a drop. While I don't hide my true identity I don't advertise it either as it might spoil the fun for some.*"

Having this online identity, which is starkly different from his offline identity, allows him to retain a level of anonymity to be able to write about events that occurred and people he knows in real life. Other studies have shown that older adults have strong concerns about being able to control their privacy online [21,26], and here we see that assuming an alternate persona or online identity is one way older adult bloggers can conceal their offline identity.

Although only one participant blogs using a different persona, some participants described differences in their online and offline voices. As P19 describes, "*There are times when I get depressed, in the middle of winter for example. I try not to represent that online, but I might say I'm depressed, and then talk about what I know I have to do.*" Here P19 describes presenting herself more positively online, but other participants describe being more open or using more humor online through their blog posts. Older adult bloggers are aware that an online audience, even if imagined [40], is reading their posts, and they may change their voice depending on their audience. For example, P15 said, "*I'm aware that anybody, anywhere can read it, so I'm aware even if I only imagine the audience, there is an audience…There's an awareness that it is a public form.*" She further explained that this awareness of her audience affects the formality of her voice while writing and topics she posts about, which we elaborate upon below.

Older adults in our study took pride in their ability to learn to blog. Generally they started by reading other people's blogs and commenting on posts. Over time, they realized that they had a unique voice, and wanted to start their own blogs. Several participants proudly described how they taught themselves to blog, rather than relying on help from family members. That is, the way older adults described their independence in learning to blog was an attempt to contrast their abilities with views of older adults being "digital immigrants" and less adept at using technology [29]. Blogging was a way in which older adults reflected on and developed their identities, and at the same time, their identity was further shaped by identifying as a blogger.

Fosters Self-Expression that Supports Seniors' Values

Younger people regularly express themselves online, including through blogging [30,31], and we find that blogging provides a means of self-expression for older adults in ways that support their values. Older adults in our study appreciate the ability to construct longer and well thought out messages as they blog. For example, P19 said she does not use Twitter because "*I can't keep myself to so few words.*" Our participants view SNSs as a place for shorter updates and staying connected with close social contacts (e.g., family members and friends). Blogs, on the other hand, were a place for expressing oneself in depth. For example, P5 said, "*That's another good thing about writing and blogging. It does reveal more inner you than people might see at first in their blog personally.*" Similarly, P6 said "*I go into much more depth when I post a blog. It's something more in-depth than anything I would put on Facebook.*"

Self-expression through blogging is not simply about the length of a post, as P6 explains. Older adults view depth of thought, clarity in writing, and continuity across posts as core elements of blogging. This view of blogging resonates with prior work that describes the importance of "heavyweight" interactions for older adults (e.g., written letters, phone calls), which demonstrate a commitment of time and dedication and provide a sense that a real connection was made [34,35]. The desire for so called heavyweight interactions is in contrast to the nature of exchanges over SNSs, which older adults may view as "trivial" and "meaningless" [26]. Aligned with this prior work, we learned that older adults contrasted the depth of self-expression they achieve through blogging to what they consider to be more superficial sharing. P14 explained, "*I don't want to post just everything like 'I got up and had breakfast' type of thing. I prefer to post about something that might interest people.*" Similarly, P5 said, "*I don't want to hear about their trip upstate to the Empire State Building unless they're making some broader statement.*" Participants described what they have personally experienced in terms of "meaningless" sharing as well as their view of the culture of sharing on SNSs.

Further, older adults in our study view blogs as a space for serious and meaningful self-expression whereas they use SNSs for short family updates or sharing family photos. While participants have social network site accounts, few said they frequently posted updates to Twitter, Facebook, Instagram, Pinterest, or other similar sites. Instead, they occasionally viewed posts from their social contacts on these platforms and used these tools to advertise their blogs. Twitter was used to "*promote the blog by using the titles' of the different blog posts*" (P1) to a broader audience, and Facebook was used to share posts with friends and family members. These older adults use automatic posting features built into SNSs, through which they "*use [Facebook and Twitter] to generate readership*" (P13) or '*as secondary distribution channels*" (P10). Importantly, participants are making key distinctions in how they approach different online platforms; they viewed their blogs – not SNSs – as their central online space for self-expression.

For these older adults, self-expression on blogs is also distinct from a diary or journal, similar to views of younger bloggers [47]. Participants viewed blogs as more professional than a diary. P10 said, "*It's nowhere near any— it's not a diary at all. It's a professional publication.*" Several participants described how the intended audience further distinguishes a blog from a diary:

"*If I wrote a diary it would be completely different. The blog is for public consumption – a fact of which I am constantly aware – so there are topics, particularly about my family I would never discuss or even mention. The diary would be for me, whereas the blog is for [persona name].*" (P8)

These participants describe how the "imagined audience" dictates the different topics that would be discussed on blogs as compared to diaries. Older adults also described the intentionality of blogs as they are more focused with themes and have a more specific purpose than diaries and journals. However, one participant (P17) was in the process of transcribing her offline diary into a blog as a public reference for her former classmates. She said, "*Once in a while there would be a sentence that I would either delete completely and not read, not transcribe into my blog…*" She noted deleting details that were too personal and anonymizing posts to conceal the identities of certain individuals, again emphasizing older adults concerns about online privacy [21,26].

In contrast to both diaries and SNSs, participants identified blogs a safe space for expressing highly personal concerns to which they thought others could relate (e.g., being laid off, transitioning into life as a grandparent) and their thoughts on "taboo" topics (e.g. politics, religion). P9, who writes a political blog, said that she is "*maybe not quite so political offline [laughs]. You know, when I grew up, there were three things you didn't discuss: money, politics, and religion*". Yet P9, P18, and P19 specifically discuss politics on their blog and P5 discusses religion. For these older adults, their blog provides them with an online space in which they are comfortable voicing their opinions and invite feedback from others, similar to what other research suggests about why younger people blog [46,47].

While older adults used their SNS accounts to advertise their blogs, they viewed their blogs as having a fairly separate audience with only a few overlapping family members or friends. Part of what may contribute to older adults' willingness to express themselves and disclose their personal views on their blog is the perceived separation of these audiences. This may help older adults prevent context collapse, in which multiple aspects of one's identity are flattened into a singular online space [40]. Indeed the "work" of maintaining separate identities may be easier to understand and perform on blogs than other social platforms in which self-presentation is influenced by many other factors (e.g., others posting photos/text about you). Maintaining separate identities may also be easier to do on blogs, which provide opportunities to have multiple profiles, than on SNSs, which support a single user profile.

As we highlight here and elaborate below, blogging opens up older adults to new social circles, which are distinct from their social networks on other platforms, and as such provides a new space for online self-expression and disclosure. This underscores the importance of understanding older adults' values in self-expression online vis-à-vis the affordances and practices associated with various platforms. While our participants view Facebook, for example, as a central and important space for connecting with family (echoing [9,21,26]), blogs provide these older adults with a forum for self-expression that enables depth of thought and continuity as well as a safe space for discussing sensitive topics.

Provides Meaningful Engagement during Retirement

We also find that blogging fills a void for many of our participants' by providing a focal activity and purpose in retirement. That is, blogging serves as a form of "work" for older adults, through which participants established routines and created regular posting schedules. P10 said, "*I have a regular schedule. Up until three or four months ago, I posted seven days a week… I just then switched to three days a week: Monday, Wednesday, Friday.*" Similarly, P1 explained, "*It has become more or less my job. Even though I do not make money on it, I spend three or four hours a day on it. So it has given me a focus for my time…*"

Older adults described the extensive time and effort they put into maintaining and publishing on their blog. They talked about taking time to conduct research for posts, write posts, and often edit and iterate on multiple drafts before publishing posts. The research phase involves looking for statistics and facts so that their blog posts are accurate in the context of writing about one's own opinions. Bloggers perceive this research to be valuable to their audience but it is also information for themselves and helps them reflect on the topic of their post. After conducting the necessary research for a post, many participants stated that they would write multiple drafts of their posts and continuously edit them until they were satisfied. This involved revising to present facts related to their post, refining the language (often with the aim of not offending readers), and anonymizing names and places to protect their privacy or the privacy of those they are writing about.

Older adults in our study carefully craft, edit, and refine their blog posts as part of the work of maintaining a blog. While most of our participants have been blogging for at least five years, some described the time required to create and edit posts as being a downside. For example, P10 said, "*It takes all my life to do this blog,*" and noted that she recently cut back on blogging. Others described that their blogging ebbs and flows depending on other activities throughout the year. Nonetheless, starting a blog requires a commitment of time, which older adults take seriously, and they emphasized the long-term nature of blogging.

"*I don't think people understand what a commitment it is. When you start a blog, you're committing yourself to writing once a week or however often. …It's not something you just do for a week and then stop… I keep doing it because I keep enjoying it.*" (P7)

Part of what contributes to older adults' sense of meaningful engagement through blogging is the act of creating an artifact that they perceive is of value to others. In fact, many of our participants began blogging because they felt they had something worthwhile to share and thought of blogging as a way of helping others. P1 explained, "*I am happy that I can express myself. I am happy that I can look for information and present it to people in ways that I hope can help them."* Specifically, several participants perceived that their blogs describing the aging process or experience of growing older would benefit others, both immediately and in the future. When asked what types of posts would be worth preserving, participants often described that posts that give clues about aging would be most important.

"I think that what they would look for out of my things is mostly how to lend your way through the harder things that are going to come hitting you in the head after you're 50." (P13)

Participants saw benefit in saving or printing the posts for their children or grandchildren to reference in the future.

"My great grandkids ...60 years from now maybe they would be interested in what I was like, and what my thoughts were. Because of ancestry.com most of it is born, died, and maybe if you are lucky what kind of work they did. Something like this would give more of my views and stuff." (P2)

These older adults perceive of imagined audiences relative to both the present and the future. Existing literature on the "imagined audience" tends to describe benefits and consequences of having such an audience as something that occurs within a short time frame (e.g., the intended or unintended audience that may see your update on Twitter moments after you tweet it) [40]. However, in our study older adults described their "imagined audiences" as groups that may use their blogs as an artifact in the future for the purposes of legacy preservation. In this way, older adults conceived of their blogs as something of value to hand down to future generations, similar to a digital heirloom [49].

Blogging plays an important role in how these older adults achieve meaningful engagement in retirement, and while older adults report that the time and effort required to maintain a blog is extensive, this activity is a worthwhile way to share their histories, views, and knowledge with other people.

Blogging as Community and Social Interaction

Staying socially connected is important for late-life health and wellness [55,60], and blogging enables older adults to achieve this in critical ways. Some participants began blogging as a way of disseminating information to a larger group of social contacts. For example, P20 said he "*had a big staff...and trying to keep in touch with them and help them find jobs, so I created a newsletter for the group...*" Soon the newsletter's subscribers grew to over one hundred people and maintaining it became difficult so he decided to start a blog. Another participant commented, "*I think it's positive. I think it's a whole lot easier to do emails and blogging than it is to use more traditional formats.* (P13)" She talked about how blogging has "*reduced the amount of personal emails I send, and letters,*" but saw this as a positive change.

While older adults in our study use their blog as a way of interacting with existing offline contacts, some began blogging with the aim of expanding their group of social contacts by connecting with new older adults online.

"My goal when I started in 2006 was-- I wanted to interact with other women who were retiring and lived in different parts of the country and find out...what were they thinking about." (P6)

After starting to blog, the interactive nature of blogs and the feedback they got from other people motivated these older adults to continue blogging. P20 said, "*...I'd probably stop doing [it] if people didn't ever look.*" Another participant, whose blog was picked up by USA Today and CNN said:

"People read it would write to me and say 'Gee, I think this is really cool' or some such thing and I'd always answer them and we'd start a communication back and forth, many of which I've kept...and we're still friends to this day". (P9)

When asked about their favorite part of blogging, participants responded: "*when I connect to somebody that was totally unexpected and it turns into a relationship*" (P9), and "*I started liking them as people I do not know at all*" (P4). Another said that she posts because of "*those people who tell me that they look forward to reading it every morning*" (P14). While prior work examines how older adults keep in touch with existing ties online [10,15,26,34], participants in our study described many new online friendships found through blogging that led to meaningful offline relationships. A few participants even attend in-person blogging conferences where they interact with each other.

"[Another blogger] wrote to several women a few years ago to see if we wanted to get together and have a meeting, our group, to meet. Six of us went down to [location] and had a meeting three years ago. We got together again last year and we're going to get together again this year." (P15)

This older adult explained that she thinks of many of her blogging friends from around the world as family. Blogging allows older adults to have a social support network outside of known, offline family and friends, which helps them to stay socially connected in important ways. P6 said, "*This technology which can really isolate people has the potential to connect them.*" That is, while technology has the potential to further isolate some older adults, blogging can foster important new social interactions and help older adults stay connected.

"This has kept me from being isolated... when I'm lonely or I'm upset about my husband's Alzheimer's, I can go on the blog ... and I feel like I am with friends even though they are not right here. It's better than having someone from here." (P11)

Interestingly, P11 notes that her online friendships provide her with support and a sense of community that may be better than her local in-person support network. Indeed, some participants described living far away from family members and having friends who have moved or passed away, leading them to seek new friendships online. Similarly, some older adults have followers who check on them if they have not posted recently. P15 has a friend who "*sends [her] an email and it says, 'Are you okay? Is everything all right?'*" when she does not post according to her regular schedule.

"*If I don't post, she [friend] wants to know if I am okay. I feel like almost an obligation almost where I let her know I am going to be away from the computer this week or something like that.*" (P2)

The perceived "obligation" to post regularly further highlights the strength of the social bonds older adults establish through blogging. This also echoes the presence of routines and patterns (e.g., calling every evening) as a way of coordinating communication about whether an older adult is all right [26,34].

While the concept of having online and offline friends in a virtual "blogger world" is not a new phenomenon [47], the ability to share in-depth with a broader community of people with similar interests (outside of family members and friends) seems to be what makes blogs uniquely appealing to these older adults. Yet, these older adults act strategically to build online community and social relationships. Many participants said they kept track of their readership through widgets and audience statistic software that are embedded in their blog. A couple of participants used external services such as Google Analytics for more advanced statistics (e.g. predicted readership interests and city). Similar to prior research, some participants use reader statistics to change how they blog [47]. For example, if a post about a certain topic decreases readership, they may not continue to post about those topics. P15 describes how she creates posts based on what she thinks her readers will like:

"*I have an app that shows me who's looking at my blog, how many a day, all the rest of this kind of stuff and you can see where they came from… I wrote in a couple of posts about stinging nettle, people will want to know about that for instance and my blog posts will come up.*"

This participant also explained that she views how people arrive at her blog (e.g., specific search terms) and then posts more about those topics to attract more readers. Similarly, P9 said she avoids changing topics too drastically and is "*careful with that because that isn't where my following is at the moment.*" Older adults display a high level of awareness of and sensitivity towards their audience, and reflect on their writing in ways that cultivate their following. As part of this, participants learned that maintaining readership means that they are writing about topics that are valued by other people, which contributes to their self-worth. Older adults also explained that they learn about and follow norms in the blogging community, such as social exchange rules.

"*I discovered that the way that you gain readers is ... when somebody makes a comment on my blog, I will go look at theirs…then I'd start following them. They follow me…as the years go by, you begin to sort of know these people and they sort of know me. It's just sort of like commenting on somebody else's blog and paying attention to who is interested in what you're interested in.*" (P15)

Older adults have expectations for high levels of reciprocity in online interaction [26], in which they feel obligated to respond to comments on their blog. Participants described the time intensive nature of responding to comments, which adds to the work of blogging. P5 said, "*…at some point in time, I disabled the comment thing on my blog because I didn't want to deal with comments and back and forth.*" For her, enabling comments on her blog meant that she had a responsibility to respond to and interact with people who commented on her posts. This responsibility became "very time-consuming" and felt similar to a having a full time job. Older adults also edit comments posted to their blog. Participants described deleting particularly negative comments to portray their blog as a safe space for people to present their views on issues without backlash.

Overall, blogging provides an important source of community and social interaction for these older adults. Learning and following community norms, such as reciprocity in commenting, resulted in increased readership and community support, which motivated seniors to continue creating and sharing online.

DISCUSSION

Analyzing the practices, experiences, and values of older adults who blog provides a case through which the field of HCI can better understand online content creation and sharing for older people more broadly. This case provides an instructive lens for examining late-life development in the context of older adults' online behaviors as well as informs the design of systems to better engage this demographic and support the experience of aging.

Towards Late-Life Development

Much work in HCI focuses on designing for disability associated with aging, such as addressing challenges of mobility limitations [20], motor impairments [39], memory loss [37], and communication [53]. While addressing these issues is important, considerably less work has examined the design of technology to support the personal and social development that takes place in the later part of life (e.g., [54]). Further, Vines et al. assert that:

> "the HCI research community has tended to render ageing as a 'problem' that can be managed by technologies. In doing so, it focuses on the deterioration of cognitive and physical abilities, health-related problems and associated risks, and the shrinking of social opportunities and networks resulting in loneliness and social isolation." [63]

Rather than "deficit-driven design" [3] and focusing on "the downside of aging" [54], a more holistic view of the aging experience is needed. Towards this end, we argue that one way to avoid problematizing aging as something technology can solve is to shift the focus to *designing for late-life development* in ways that help people embrace and manage the dynamic experience of growing older. Our analysis reveals how a particular group of older adults engages in creating and sharing through blogging as a way to embrace, deal with, and voice their concerns about growing older. The need to express oneself extends into older adulthood [4,8,45], and blogging fills this need in an important way.

While it is easy to assume that identity is static and solidified early in life, we actually continue to develop our identities throughout the lifespan, including into older adulthood [51,61]. Indeed, older adulthood is a time of self-development and change, often brought about by transitioning from the workforce to retirement and consequently needing to establish a new routine or activities that provide a sense of purpose [51,58,61]. The activity of blogging provides a focus for older adults in retirement as well as a space for reflecting upon this change.

Blogging is also a purposeful and meaningful activity for these older adults, and participation in meaningful activities is associated with better psychological well-being and health-related quality of life in older adulthood [19]. Through blogging, these older adults perceive that the artifacts they are producing are (or will be) valuable to others. This perception contributes to their self-worth in a time when they may be questioning their role in society [51]. Similarly, blogging affords self-expression in ways that promote articulation of and reflection upon one's changing identity in older adulthood, which is influenced by shifts in work-life routines, family roles and responsibilities, and the broader experience of aging.

Further, older adults often experience changes in social interaction and the composition of their social groups, resulting from retirement, relocation, and/or the passing of a partner, family members, or friends [42]. Blogging provides important community and social interaction for older adults, who may seek like-minded peers to jointly navigate the experience of growing older or come together around shared interests. Additionally, older adulthood involves a more complex or multifaceted emotional experience due to the positive and negative emotions associated with aging [4]. While participants were an active voice for aging, many described how they did not want to write negative posts. When a participant did describe a seemingly negative event about aging on their blog, they reframed it positively by saying that blogging allowed them to receive support from their community of readers. We show how older adults can develop their voice through blogging about major life transitions, and some may share the complexity of their emotions to call attention to the aging process. Other older adults may mask such feelings (e.g., using humor) to promote readership and foster their online following.

Blogging can be a way older adults fight against negative stereotypes of aging, both by assuming the identity of a "tech-savvy senior" through blogging and by telling "it like it really is" for aging. A growing debate in the disability studies literature involves the social construction of disability [66], in which society creates the notion of disability by operating under the assumption that the non-disabled person is "normal". Similarly, older adults' voices and online identities resonate against a backdrop of normative views of aging, in which aging is a form of decline plagued by impairment and social isolation [63]. Rather, creation and sharing through blogging or with other digital artifacts [54] is a source of empowerment for oneself while also building community in ways that empower others. Therefore, rather than designing for disability and decline in older adulthood, shifting the focus towards *designing for late-life development* may help prevent reinforcement of these stereotypes and begin to empower the individuals we aim to engage with the new systems we introduce.

Opportunities for Design

While our analysis focuses on the specific practices of a select group of older adults, we study their values and needs in the context of technology use as a way of informing the design of systems for content creation and sharing more broadly. We revisit the four themes from our results section in the context of related work and describe the design opportunities within each.

Support Multiple, Changing Identities in Older Adulthood

As we described earlier, people continue to develop their identities and even take on new identities throughout older adulthood. Older adults in our study blog as a way of reflecting on their changing identities and performing online self-presentation work in the context of their evolving identity [22]. Prior work suggests that older adults may want to maintain multiple identities [61], each with a different social need. Having multiple distinct blogs that embody these identities may be one way older adults achieve this (e.g., blogging as a quilting/sewing enthusiast versus the experience of aging). Designers should consider ways to support complex and multi-faceted identities of older adults in online systems, realizing that older adults may prefer separate online spaces to express different identities, rather than forcing them to adopt a unitary online profile.

Promote Depth of Thought and Reflection in Self-Expression

Prior work has shown that bloggers frequently contribute content across multiple online platforms [31], but older adults in our study reported that they rarely contributed (i.e., by posting, commenting) on other platforms such as Facebook or Twitter. Indeed, this passive behavior on other social platforms is characteristic of older adults more broadly [24]. Among our sample of older adults, their preference for self-expression on a blog is due to both the design of the medium as well as the social practice of blogging. A blog allows for long-form self-expression, which our informants contrasted with the challenges of constraining oneself to so few characters on Twitter, and a continuous and centralized space for viewing posts. In contrast to micro-blogging, in which small excerpts are posted sporadically throughout the day, older adults valued the depth of thought, time, and effort they spent crafting each blog entry – wanting it to read like a "college essay" and a "professional publication".

The ways in which older adults described deep, careful, and meaningful sharing through blogging is akin to older adults' sharing through letter writing as a valued form of communication (e.g., [26,34]). With both letters and blog posts, older adults spend time carefully crafting an artifact for a particular audience in ways that convey a level of thoughtfulness and care. Both blogging and letter writing afford the ability to create and save drafts, edit this content over time, and then share content (i.e., post the blog or mail the letter when ready). The reflexivity and iteration inherent in these practices is in contrast to the seemingly spontaneous nature of self-expression on more traditional SNSs. Recent prototypes (e.g., [2,11,35]) push the boundaries between so called "lightweight" and "heavyweight" sharing, illustrating gradations of sharing that are valuable and rich in their own way [35]. Nevertheless, future systems that aim to facilitate self-expression for older adults should consider ways to support iteration, reflection, and revising activities.

Support Meaningful Work, Meaningful Artifacts

Among younger bloggers, 84% describe their blog as a hobby and something they do not spend much time on [31]. In contrast, our informants view blogging as something that is worthy of time and investment. Some equate blogging to a job and treat it as their "work" in older adulthood. Blogging provides a source of meaningful engagement for older adults by providing a focal activity, around which older adults create routines and regular posting schedules. Prior work involving the SPARCS system suggests that it is important to prompt older adults to share routinely and that these routines help develop a captive and interactive audience [2]. Older adult bloggers are doing precisely this, and their intearction with their audience depends on this routine to the point that followers check on older adults if they deviate from their posting patterns. Designing to encourage similar structure and routines in sharing may help foster meaningful engagement and successful interaction with one's audience.

Deriving a sense of meaningful engagement through blogging also stems from creating an artifact that is valuable to others. Older adults view their blog as something that will help or be of interest to others. They described printing out blog posts or saving them in some way so that others may benefit from this information in the future. Older adults' perceptions of the archival and artifactual nature of blogs suggests that they may serve as a digital heirloom [49]. Similarly, other prototypes that have successfully engaged older adults center around sharing family histories [49,52] and artifacts [59]. The motivation to document life experiences heightens in older adulthood as people view the end of life drawing near [14], and future online sharing systems with archival and tangible qualities are likely to resonate well with the goals of older adults.

Foster Community and Interaction with New Social Groups

Blogs are a space in which older adults created friendships and extended their social circles to include many people who they had not met in-person. Indeed, prior work suggests that creating and sharing content may be a way of fostering new social connections [25,54,65], and our analysis provides a detailed example of this occurring in practice. Interaction through their blog was a way of reaching out to "virtual friends" or initially, weak ties. Prior work on the Enmesh system also notes that sharing with strangers is challenging without having an interactive audience [65], and here we observe that the culture of blogging and artifacts produced help enable a level of interaction that older adults desire. Providing appropriate spaces for sharing and interacting with weak ties can benefit older adults by expanding their social support networks. Yet, older adults have expectations around online reciprocity [26,34], and features that allow them to customize the level of expected reciprocity (e.g., ability to enable/disable comments) are important.

Interacting with new social groups (and being motivated to continue doing so) was largely influenced by older adults' visibility of their online audience. Older adults appreciated that they could see which posts were popular with readers and learn more about their readers with advanced analytics. This transparency of their audience, even if by size alone, let participants know that their posts were being viewed and that others found this information to be worthy of reading. In this sense, audience awareness influences older adults' self-perception that what they are expressing is relevant, impacting their self-worth. Designers should consider ways to make audience information transparent, easy to understand, and useful for self-reflection.

CONCLUSION

This paper provides a case analysis of older adults who actively engage in online content creation and sharing, which stands in contrast to current views of older adults as lurkers and passive members of online social communities. Through the practice of blogging, older adults find ways to meet a variety of psychological and social needs that arise in older adulthood. Our case analysis, however, has limitations due to the small, homogenous sample. Our sample includes two men, who may have slightly different perspectives and values around online self-expression, disclosure, and social interaction [6]. Additionally, our sample consists of current bloggers, who are likely more active online than the broader older adult population. Lastly, we recruited participants with public blogs, and older adults with private blogs may exhibit different online behaviors. Nonetheless, our analysis provides insight into how older adults create and share content online, through which we highlight *designing for late-life development* as a productive framing for creating new technologies to empower people in older adulthood.

ACKNOWLEDGEMENTS

We thank our study participants and Karina Sirota for her help transcribing interviews. This work was supported by NSF grant IIS-1533340.

REFERENCES

1. Robin N. Brewer and Jasmine Jones. 2015. Pinteresce: Exploring Reminiscence as an Incentive to Digital Reciprocity for Older Adults. *Proceedings of the 18th ACM Conference Companion on Computer Supported Cooperative Work & Social Computing - CSCW'15 Companion*, ACM Press, 243–246. http://doi.org/10.1145/2685553.2699017

2. A.J. Bernheim Brush, Kori M Inkpen, and Kimberly Tee. 2008. SPARCS: exploring sharing suggestions to enhance family connectedness. *Proceedings of the ACM 2008 conference on Computer supported cooperative work - CSCW '08*, ACM Press, 629. http://doi.org/10.1145/1460563.1460661

3. John M. Carroll, Gregorio Convertino, Umer Farooq, and Mary Beth Rosson. 2012. The firekeepers: Aging considered as a resource. *Universal Access in the Information Society* 11, 1, 7–15. http://doi.org/10.1007/s10209-011-0229-9

4. Laura L. Carstensen and Susan Turk Charles. 1998. Emotion in the Second Half of Life. *Current Directions in Psychological Science 7*, 144–149. http://doi.org/10.1111/1467-8721.ep10836825

5. K Charmaz. 2006. *Constructing grounded theory: a practical guide through qualitative analysis*. http://doi.org/10.1016/j.lisr.2007.11.003

6. Gina Masullo Chen. 2012. Why do women write personal blogs? Satisfying needs for self-disclosure and affiliation tell part of the story. *Computers in Human Behavior* 28, 1, 171–180. http://doi.org/10.1016/j.chb.2011.08.024

7. Deborah S. Chung and Sujin Kim. Blogging activity among cancer patients and their companions: Uses, gratifications, and predictors of outcomes. *Journal of the American Society for Information Science and Technology* 59, 2. http://doi.org/10.1002/asi.v59:2

8. Gene D Cohen. 2006. Research on Creativity and Aging : The Positive Impact of the Arts on Health and Illness. *Generations* 30, 1, 7–15.

9. Graeme W Coleman, Lorna Gibson, Vicki L Hanson, Ania Bobrowicz, and Alison McKay. 2010. Engaging the disengaged. *Proceedings of the 8th ACM Conference on Designing Interactive Systems 2010*, ACM Press, 175–178. http://doi.org/10.1145/1858171.1858202

10. Raymundo Cornejo, Jesús Favela, and Mónica Tentori. 2010. Ambient displays for integrating older adults into social networking sites. *Collaboration and Technology*, 321–336. Retrieved from http://link.springer.com/chapter/10.1007/978-3-642-15714-1_24

11. Raymundo Cornejo, Mónica Tentori, and Jesús Favela. 2013. Enriching in-person encounters through social media: A study on family connectedness for the elderly. *International Journal of Human-Computer Studies* 71, 9. http://doi.org/10.1016/j.ijhcs.2013.04.001

12. Erin York Cornwell and Linda J Waite. 2009. Social Disconnectedness, Perceived Isolation, and Health among Older Adults. *Journal of Health and Social Behavior* 50, 1, 31–48. http://doi.org/10.1177/002214650905000103

13. Shelia R Cotten, George Ford, Sherry Ford, and Timothy M Hale. 2012. Internet use and depression among older adults. *Computers in Human Behavior* 28, 2, 496–499. http://doi.org/10.1016/j.chb.2011.10.021

14. Masashi Crete-Nishihata, Ronald M Baecker, Michael Massimi, et al. 2012. Reconstructing the past: Personal memory technologies are not just personal and not just for memory. *Human-Computer Interaction* 27, May, 92–123. http://doi.org/10.1080/07370024.2012.656062

15. Jessica M. David, Alison Benjamin, Ronald M. Baecker, Diane Gromala, and Jeremy Birnholtz. 2011. Living with pain, staying in touch: exploring the communication needs of older adults with chronic pain. *in Proc. CHI EA '11*, 1219–1224. http://doi.org/10.1145/1979742.1979751

16. Maeve Duggan, Nicole B. Ellison, Cliff Lampe, Amanda Lenhart, and Mary Madden. 2014. *Social Media Update 2014*. Retrieved from http://www.pewinternet.org/2015/01/09/social-media-update-2014/

17. Maeve Duggan and Andrew Perrin. 2015. *Americans' Internet Access: 2000-2015*. Retrieved from http://www.pewinternet.org/2015/06/26/americans-internet-access-2000-2015/

18. Maeve Duggan. 2015. *Mobile Messaging and Social Media 2015*. Retrieved from http://www.pewinternet.org/2015/08/19/mobile-messaging-and-social-media-2015/

19. Aaron M. Eakman, Mike E. Carlson, and Florence A. Clark. 2010. The Meaningful Activity Participation Assessment: A Measure of Engagement in Personally Valued Activities. *The International Journal of Aging and Human Development* 70, 4, 299–317. http://doi.org/10.2190/AG.70.4.b

20. Kathrin M. Gerling, Regan L. Mandryk, Matthew Miller, Michael R. Kalyn, Max Birk, and Jan D. Smeddinck. 2015. Designing Wheelchair-Based Movement Games. *ACM Transactions on Accessible Computing* 6, 2, 1–23. http://doi.org/10.1145/2724729

21. Lorna Gibson, Wendy Moncur, Paula Forbes, John Arnott, Christopher Martin, and Amritpal S Bhachu.

2010. Designing Social Networking Sites for Older Adults. *BCS '10 Proceedings of the 24th BCS Interaction Specialist Group Conference*, BCS, 186–194. Retrieved from http://dl.acm.org/citation.cfm?id=2146303.2146331

22. Erving Goffman. 1982. The presentation of self in everyday life. In *The Presentation of Self in Everyday Life*. 1–10.
23. Rebecca Gulotta, William Odom, Haakon Faste, and Jodi Forlizzi. 2014. Legacy in the age of the internet: reflections on how interactive systems shape how we are remembered. *Proceedings of the 2014 conference on Designing interactive systems - DIS '14*, ACM Press, 975–984. http://doi.org/10.1145/2598510.2598579
24. Keith N Hampton, Lauren Sessions Goulet, Lee Rainie, and Kristen Purcell. 2011. Social networking sites and our lives. *Pew Internet American Life Project* 47, 9, 85. Retrieved from http://pewinternet.org/Reports/2011/Technology-and-social-networks.aspx
25. Dave Harley and Geraldine Fitzpatrick. 2008. YouTube and intergenerational communication: the case of Geriatric1927. *Universal Access in the Information Society* 8, 1, 5–20. http://doi.org/10.1007/s10209-008-0127-y
26. Alexis Hope, Ted Schwaba, and Anne Marie Piper. 2014. Understanding digital and material social communications for older adults. *Proceedings of the 32nd annual ACM conference on Human factors in computing systems*, ACM Press, 3903–3912. http://doi.org/10.1145/2556288.2557133
27. Azmina Karimi and Carman Neustaedter. 2012. From high connectivity to social isolation: communication practices of older adults in the digital age. *Proceedings of the ACM 2012 conference on Computer Supported Cooperative Work Companion*. Retrieved from http://dl.acm.org/citation.cfm?id=2141559
28. Verne C. Kopytoff. 2011. Blogs Wane as the Young Drift to Sites Like Twitter. *The New York Times*. Retrieved from http://www.nytimes.com/2011/02/21/technology/internet/21blog.html
29. Vilma Lehtinen, J Nasanen, and Risto Sarvas. 2009. "A little silly and empty-headed": older adults' understandings of social networking sites. *BCS-HCI*, British Computer Society, 45–54. Retrieved from http://portal.acm.org/citation.cfm?id=1671011.1671017
30. Amanda Lenhart, Deborah Fallows, and John Horrigan. 2004. *Content Creation Online*. Retrieved from http://www.pewinternet.org/2004/02/29/content-creation-online-2/
31. Amanda Lenhart and Susannah Fox. 2006. *Bloggers: A portrait of the internet's new storytellers*. Retrieved from http://www.pewinternet.org/2006/07/19/bloggers/
32. Amanda Lenhart. 2015. *Teens, Social Media & Technology Overview 2015*. Retrieved from http://www.pewinternet.org/2015/04/09/teens-social-media-technology-2015/
33. Siân E Lindley, Richard Harper, and Abigail Sellen. 2008. Designing for Elders : Exploring the Complexity of Relationships in Later Life. *BCS-HCi*, 77–86.
34. Siân E Lindley, Richard Harper, and Abigail Sellen. 2009. Desiring to be in touch in a changing communications landscape. *Proceedings of the 27th international conference on Human factors in computing systems - CHI 09*, ACM Press, 1693. http://doi.org/10.1145/1518701.1518962
35. Siân E. Lindley. 2011. Shades of lightweight: supporting cross-generational communication through home messaging. *Universal Access in the Information Society* 11, 1, 31–43. http://doi.org/10.1007/s10209-011-0231-2
36. Siân Lindley and Jayne Wallace. 2015. Placing in Age. *ACM Transactions on Computer-Human Interaction* 22, 4, 1–39. http://doi.org/10.1145/2755562
37. Stephen Lindsay, Katie Brittain, Daniel Jackson, Cassim Ladha, Karim Ladha, and Patrick Olivier. 2012. Empathy, participatory design and people with dementia. *Proceedings of the 2012 ACM annual conference on Human Factors in Computing Systems - CHI '12*, ACM Press, 521. http://doi.org/10.1145/2207676.2207749
38. Mary Madden. 2010. *Older Adults and Social Media*. Retrieved from http://www.pewinternet.org/2010/08/27/older-adults-and-social-media/
39. Aqueasha Martin-Hammond, Abdullah Ali, Catherine Hornback, and Amy K. Hurst. 2015. Understanding design considerations for adaptive user interfaces for accessible pointing with older and younger adults. *Proceedings of the 12th Web for All Conference on - W4A '15*, ACM Press, 1–10. http://doi.org/10.1145/2745555.2746645
40. Alice E. Marwick and Danah Boyd. 2011. I tweet honestly, I tweet passionately: Twitter users, context collapse, and the imagined audience. *New Media & Society* 13, 1, 114–133. http://doi.org/10.1177/1461444810365313
41. Susan H. McFadden and Anne D. Basting. 2010. Healthy Aging Persons and Their Brains: Promoting

Resilience Through Creative Engagement. *Clinics in Geriatric Medicine 26*, 149–161. http://doi.org/10.1016/j.cger.2009.11.004

42. Miller McPherson, Lynn Smith-Lovin, and Matthew E. Brashears. 2006. Social Isolation in America: Changes in Core Discussion Networks over Two Decades. *American Sociological Review* 71, 3, 353–375. http://doi.org/10.1177/000312240807300610

43. Robinson Meyer. 2015. What Blogging Has Become. *The Atlantic*. Retrieved from http://www.theatlantic.com/technology/archive/2015/02/what-blogging-has-become/386201/

44. Alex Mihailidis, Scott Blunsden, Jennifer Boger, et al. 2010. Towards the development of a technology for art therapy and dementia: Definition of needs and design constraints. *The Arts in Psychotherapy* 37, 4, 293–300. http://doi.org/10.1016/j.aip.2010.05.004

45. Luca Morganti, Giuseppe Riva, Silvio Bonfiglio, and Andrea Gaggioli. 2013. Building collective memories on the web: the Nostalgia Bits project. *International Journal of Web Based Communities* 9, 1, 83–104. http://doi.org/10.1504/IJWBC.2013.051373

46. Bonnie A Nardi, Diane J Schiano, Michelle Gumbrecht, and Luke Swartz. 2004. Why we blog. *Communications of the ACM* 47, 12, 41. http://doi.org/10.1145/1035134.1035163

47. Bonnie A. Nardi, Diane J. Schiano, and Michelle Gumbrecht. 2004. Blogging as social activity, or, would you let 900 million people read your diary? *Proceedings of the 2004 ACM conference on Computer supported cooperative work - CSCW '04*, ACM Press, 222. http://doi.org/10.1145/1031607.1031643

48. Chris Norval, John L. Arnott, and Vicki L Hanson. 2014. What's on your mind?: investigating recommendations for inclusive social networking and older adults. *Proceedings of the 32nd annual ACM conference on Human factors in computing systems - CHI '14*, ACM Press, 3923–3932. http://doi.org/10.1145/2556288.2556992

49. William Odom, Richard Banks, David Kirk, Richard Harper, Siân Lindley, and Abigail Sellen. 2012. Technology Heirlooms?: Considerations for Passing Down and Inheriting Digital Materials. *Proceedings of the SIGCHI Conference on Human Factors in Computing Systems*, ACM, 337–346. http://doi.org/10.1145/2207676.2207723

50. Anne-Marie Oostveen. 2011. The internet as an empowering technology for stigmatized groups: a case study of weight loss bloggers. *Proceeding BCS-HCI '11 Proceedings of the 25th BCS Conference on Human-Computer Interaction*, 114–119. Retrieved from http://dl.acm.org/citation.cfm?id=2305316.2305337

51. John W Osborne. 2012. Psychological effects of the transition to retirement. *Canadian Journal of Counselling and Psychotherapy* 46, 45–58. http://doi.org/10.1080/13642537.2012.734472

52. S Tejaswi Peesapati, Victoria Schwanda, Johnathon Schultz, Matt Lepage, So-yae Jeong, and Dan Cosley. 2010. Pensieve: Supporting Everyday Reminiscence. *Proceedings of the 28th international conference on Human factors in computing systems - CHI '10*, ACM Press, 2027. http://doi.org/10.1145/1753326.1753635

53. Anne Marie Piper, Nadir Weibel, and James D. Hollan. 2010. Introducing multimodal paper-digital interfaces for speech-language therapy. *Proceedings of the 12th international ACM SIGACCESS conference on Computers and accessibility - ASSETS '10*, 203. http://doi.org/10.1145/1878803.1878840

54. Yvonne Rogers, Jeni Paay, and Margot Brereton. 2014. Never Too Old: Engaging Retired People Inventing the Future with MaKey MaKey. *Proceedings of the SIGCHI Conference on Human Factors in Computing Systems - CHI '14*, 3913–3922. http://doi.org/10.1145/2556288.2557184

55. Carol D. Ryff. 1995. Psychological Well-Being in Adult Life. *Current Directions in Psychological Science 4*, 99–104. http://doi.org/10.1111/1467-8721.ep10772395

56. Na'ama Shapira, Azy Barak, and Iddo Gal. 2007. Promoting older adults' well-being through Internet training and use. *Aging & mental health* 11, 5, 477–484. http://doi.org/10.1080/13607860601086546

57. Aaron Smith. 2011. *Why Americans use social media*. Retrieved from http://www.pewinternet.org/2011/11/15/why-americans-use-social-media/

58. Hanna van Solinge and Kène Henkens. 2008. Adjustment to and satisfaction with retirement: Two of a kind? *Psychology and Aging* 23, 2, 422–434. http://doi.org/10.1037/0882-7974.23.2.422

59. Molly M. Stevens, Gregory D. Abowd, Khai N. Truong, and Florian Vollmer. 2003. Getting into the Living Memory Box: Family archives & holistic design. *Personal and Ubiquitous Computing* 7, 3-4, 210–216. http://doi.org/10.1007/s00779-003-0220-4

60. S Shyam Sundar and Anne Oeldorf-Hirsch. 2011. Retirees on Facebook: can online social networking enhance their health and wellness? *CHI'11 Extended* ..., 2287–2292. http://doi.org/10.1145/1979742.1979931

61. Ursina Teuscher. 2010. Change and persistence of personal identities after the transition to retirement. *International journal of aging & human development* 70, 1, 89–106. http://doi.org/10.2190/AG.70.1.d

62. Elizabeth Thiry, Siân Lindley, Richard Banks, and Tim Regan. 2013. Authoring personal histories: Exploring the timeline as a framework for meaning making. *Proceedings of the 2013 SIGCHI conference on Human Factors in computing systems (CHI 2013)*, 1619–1628. http://doi.org/10.1145/2470654.2466215

63. John Vines, Gary Pritchard, Peter Wright, Patrick Olivier, and Katie Brittain. 2015. An Age-Old Problem: Examining the Discourses of Ageing in HCI and Strategies for Future Research. *ACM Transactions on Computer-Human Interaction* 22, 1, 1–27. http://doi.org/10.1145/2696867

64. Kerryellen G. Vroman, Sajay Arthanat, and Catherine Lysack. 2015. "Who over 65 is online?" Older adults' dispositions toward information communication technology *Computers in Human Behavior* 43, 156–166. http://doi.org/10.1016/j.chb.2014.10.018

65. Jenny Waycott, Frank Vetere, Sonja Pedell, et al. 2013. Older adults as digital content producers. *Proceedings of the SIGCHI Conference on Human Factors in Computing Systems - CHI '13*, ACM Press, 39. http://doi.org/10.1145/2470654.2470662

66. Susan Wendell. 1996. The rejected body : feminist philosophical reflections on disability. In *Routledge*. 57–68.

67. Bo Xie, Ivan Watkins, Jen Golbeck, and Man Huang. 2012. Understanding and Changing Older Adults' Perceptions and Learning of Social Media. *Educational Gerontology* 38, September 2014, 282–296. http://doi.org/10.1080/03601277.2010.544580

Social Media Image Analysis for Public Health

Venkata Rama Kiran Garimella
Aalto University
Helsinki, Finland
kiran.garimella@aalto.fi

Abdulrahman Alfayad
Carnegie Mellon University
Doha, Qatar
afayad@qatar.cmu.edu

Ingmar Weber
Qatar Computing Research Institute
Doha, Qatar
iweber@qf.org.qa

ABSTRACT
Several projects have shown the feasibility to use *textual* social media data to track public health concerns, such as temporal influenza patterns or geographical obesity patterns. In this paper, we look at whether geo-tagged *images* from Instagram also provide a viable data source. Especially for "lifestyle" diseases, such as obesity, drinking or smoking, images of social gatherings could provide information that is not necessarily shared in, say, tweets. In this study, we explore whether (i) tags provided by the users and (ii) annotations obtained via automatic image tagging are indeed valuable for studying public health. We find that both user-provided and machine-generated tags provide information that can be used to infer a county's health statistics. Whereas for most statistics user-provided tags are better features, for predicting excessive drinking machine-generated tags such as "liquid" and "glass" yield better models. This hints at the potential of using machine-generated tags to study substance abuse.

INTRODUCTION
The annual cost of "lifestyle diseases" in the U.S. is estimated at up to a *trillion* U.S. dollars. In order to target these diseases and induce required lifestyle changes it is useful to first gain a better understanding of the phenomenon through (i) identifying the population groups most affected, (ii) understanding the interaction between environment, population and other variables, and (iii) tracking changes over time to monitor the effect of any campaign or interventions.

Over the last couple of years, social media has emerged as a viable data source to use for large-scale public health studies. Using social media seems particularly appropriate for studying lifestyle diseases, such as obesity, as more and more of people's life and social interaction is publicly shared online.

CHI'16, May 07 - 12, 2016, San Jose, CA, USA

ACM 978-1-4503-3362-7/16/05 ... $15.00
DOI: http://dx.doi.org/10.1145/2858036.2858234

One type of social media data that, to the best of our knowledge, has not been tapped into for large-scale public health studies is *images*. More than 1.8 billion images are shared online every day [1], (compared to 500M tweets per day), making rich media content a prolific data source.

In addition to its sheer size, social media image data might contain complementary data that is not shared in textual status updates. For example, after or even during a social gathering it is often customary to share images taken with a smart phone, rather than post a textual summary of the event. Images shared might or might not be annotated by the user. Until recently, automatically processing the *content* of images was beyond the realm of technical feasibility. Due to advances in deep learning [9], it has become possible to automatically understand objects in images and generate textual descriptions. In this paper, we look at whether the *content* of images shared on Instagram provides health-related information, and, in particular, whether machine-generated tags add value over user-provided ones.

The use of automatic image annotation tools holds a range of potential advantages one of which is language agnosticism. Here, "language" refers both to English vs. say, Spanish but it also refers to different and inconsistent conventions of what users might label as, say, "#healthy". Another advantage is the inference of "hidden" labels that an image owner would not assign. Studies have shown that a large fraction of young social media users have posted a picture depicting substance use [15]. Such images about alcohol or drug intake may not be explicitly labeled as, say, "#alcohol" and hence difficult to track using text-based methods. The insights obtained from this study could be of use in designing systems for understanding and monitoring substance abuse and other stigmatized behaviors.

We find that both user-provided and machine-generated labels for geo-tagged Instagram images hold valuable information in predicting county-level health statistics. Though for most variables user-provided labels outperform machine-generated ones, the opposite holds for "Excessive Drinking".

[1] `http://read.bi/1ouGzgQ`, last accessed on July 13, 2015.

RELATED WORK

Social media data for public health analysis Traditional methods to track public health metrics are based on pooling data from doctors, pharmacies and other sources which comes with certain drawbacks related to latency and cost. For tracking lifestyle diseases, where latency is not an issue, survey-based approaches have difficulties in collecting a "holistic" view of a patient that includes many facets of their lifestyle.

Recent studies have shown that a large scale, real time, non-intrusive monitoring can be done using social media to get aggregate statistics about the health and well being of a population [7, 23, 11]. Twitter in particular has been widely used in studies on public health [17, 21, 16, 12], due to its vast amount of data and the ease of availability of data.

Culotta [5] and Abbar et al. [1] used Twitter in conjunction with psychometric lexicons such as LIWC and PERMA to predict county-level health statistics such as obesity, teen pregnancy and diabetes. Paul et al. [18] make use of Twitter data to identify health related topics and use these to characterize the discussion of health online. Mejova et al. [14] use Foursquare and Instagram images to study food consumption patterns in the US, and find a correlation between obesity and fast food restaurants.

Social media has also enabled large-scale studies linking lifestyle and health data at an *individual* level. For example, Sadilek et al. [22], build a classifier to identify the health of a user based on their Twitter usage. Many more "hidden", yet important conditions such as depression [6, 4, 3], sleep problems [13], eating disorders [26], and substance use [20] have been studied using social media data. Our study is different from the ones discussed above in that we propose the use of image data to study public health.

Abdullah, et al. [2] use smile recognition from images posted on social media to study and quantify the overall societal happiness. Andalibi et al. [3] study depression related images on Instagram and "establish[ed] the importance of visual imagery as a vehicle for expressing aspects of depression". In our work, we study if the use of image recognition techniques helps in understanding a broader range of health related issues.

Image recognition, Deep learning Almost all the methods above rely on textual content though images and other rich multimedia form a major chunk of content being generated and shared in social media. Automatic image annotation has greatly improved over the last couple of years, owing to the development in deep learning [8]. Object recognition [27] and image tagging [9] have become possible because of these new developments, e.g. Karpathy et al. [9] use deep learning to produce descriptions of images, which compete with (and sometimes beat) human generated labels. A few studies already make use of these advances to identify [10] and study [25] food consumption from pictures.

DATA COLLECTION

The social media data used in our analysis consists of geo-referenced Instagram images (mostly taken at restaurants, related to food) obtained by Mejova et al. [14]. From this data, we are using the November subset consisting of 18M images. The choice of a smaller subset was randomly made to cater to the hard rate-limit restrictions imposed by Imagga and the choice for food related images was to maintain topical focus.

Each image is associated with various types of meta data, such as geographic location (latitude, longitude), user-provided hashtags, time stamp and comments. Using the (latitude, longitude), we mapped an image to a U.S. county (represented by a unique FIPS code) using an API provided by Federal Communication Commission.We then considered the top 100 counties in terms of image count and sampled 2,000 images uniformly at random from each of these 100 counties, due to computational restrictions imposed by the image annotation API.

We make use of two types of meta data obtained from images in this study: (i) machine-generated tags from a commercial service, and (ii) user-provided textual tags (hashtags).

Machine-Generated Tags

Each image was tagged using a state-of-the-art commercial image recognition tool from Imagga.com.[2] Figure 1 shows an example image along with the tags and their confidence. For 189,293 of our 200,000 images we managed to obtain at least one tag via Imagga. For the remaining 10,707 images the Instagram image was no longer publicly available, either due to deletion, changes in privacy settings, or account suspension by Instagram.[3]

Imagga API returns, for each image a set of tags along with a 'confidence' score. We only considered those tags with a confidence score above 20%. We experimented with different threshold values in the range of [5,60]. Based on the macro-averaged correlation for the nine different indices, we selected a global value of 20%. Though different threshold values might lead to slightly better results for a given index, we preferred not to explore this route to avoid the risk of overfitting. Tags appearing in less than 10 distinct counties were also ignored, leaving us with 1,750 distinct tags. Using this tag set, we created a representation of the tags used in each of the 100 counties by counting how many images were assigned a particular tag by Imagga. Imagga is not a restaurant- or food-specific annotation tool and its model is trained on general images. The ten most commonly returned machine annotations for the images in our data set were 'food', 'delicious','cocktail','people','gold'

[2]`http://docs.imagga.com/#auto-tagging`

[3]The Imagga tags dataset is available for download at `https://users.ics.aalto.fi/kiran/imagga_tags_data`

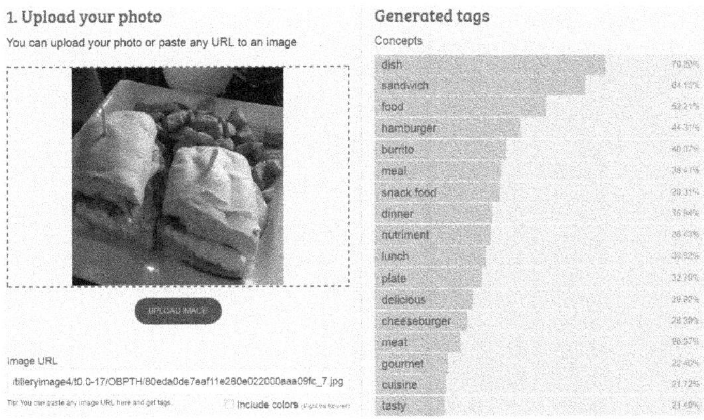

Figure 1. Example output for the Imagga Auto-Tagging Demo for one of the Instagram images in our data set. Each tag is associated with a confidence score (shown on the right).

, 'healthy', 'adult', 'caucasian', 'person', 'kitchen'. We observe that the tags contain references to food, restaurants and people. In general, the Imagga generated tags include a wide range of information from identifying types of food ('spaghetti'), drinks ('cappuccino'), objects ('stringed instrument'), people ('male'), and actions ('drunkard').

User-Provided Tags

Many images are provided with textual tags by the user uploading the image. For example, the image shown in Figure 1 comes with the tags #breakfastsandwich, #brunch, and #amazingpotatoes. Note that images might or might not have textual tags assigned by the user (in our dataset, 49% of the images have at least one tag). To have an equal size comparison to the machine-annotated data set, we sampled 200k images with at least one user-provided tag, 2,000 images for each of the 100 counties. Only user-provided tags appearing in at least 10 distinct counties were kept, leaving us with 5,865 distinct tags.

Demographic variables

As a baseline, we also obtained a list of demographic variables from the County Health Rankings website.[4] For each of the 100 counties we used same the demographic features that were used in Culotta [5], representing information related to (i) age distribution, (ii) racial distribution, and (iii) income. The ground-truth offline data on public health was obtained from the same County Health Rankings site. This data contains a wealth of health-related variables ranging from "Teen births" to "Diabetic monitoring". Given that our image data was obtained from *food* locations, we decided to focus our analysis on the following nine variables: (i) % *Smokers*, (ii) % *Obese*, (iii) *Food environment Index*, (iv) % *Physically inactive*, (v) % *Excessive drinking*, (vi) %*Alcohol – impaired driving deaths*, (vii) % *Diabetics*, (viii) %*Food insecure*, and (ix) % *Limited access to healthy food*.

[4]http://www.countyhealthrankings.org/rankings/data

METHODS

To test whether social media image data helps in studying public health, we perform regression to predict each of the nine health-related variables (dependent variables) using the image meta data features described above (independent variables). Given the high-dimensionality of our feature vectors relative to the number of validation points (N=100 counties), we use ridge regression to avoid over fitting (with a smoothing parameter of α=0.1 as in [5]). We perform 10 fold cross-validation, training a model on 90 counties and testing it on the remaining 10 to evaluate the accuracy of the regression.

For each county, the number of images containing a tag was used to create a county x tags matrix (size 100 x 1,750 for Imagga, 100 x 5,865 for user tags). We normalized each row (county) in this matrix using Euclidean norm in order to remove differences in image counts across counties. We also tried out various extensions of the text tags using external dictionaries such as LIWC [19] and PERMA [24]. We do not report results for these here as they did not lead to improvements, neither applied to human-generated nor to machine-generated tags.

To measure the accuracy, we used (i) Pearson's r - Correlation between the actual and predicted values (larger values are better), and (ii) Symmetric Mean Absolute Percentage Error (SMAPE, smaller values are better).

RESULTS

Table 1 summarizes the prediction performance for different combinations of (i) user-provided tags as features ("U"), (ii) machine-generated tags as features ("I"), and (iii) county-level demographics ("D"). We observe that using user-provided tags in conjunction with demographic features helps significantly improve the performance over just using demographic features, both in terms of Pearson's r and SMAPE.

To understand the performance of the models in more detail, we decided to zoom in on the four variables with the largest absolute improvement in Pearson's r over the demographics-only baseline: physically active (U+D), excessive drinking (I), alcohol impaired driving deaths (U), and limited access to healthy food (U).

Figure 2 shows scatter plots for these four health statistics. Each dot corresponds to a county with its actual health value on the x-axis and the predicted value, using the best-performing model, on the y-axis. As it might be of interest to domain experts, we labeled some of the outliers on the scatter plot with the name of the area.

According to our data, Arlington, VA "looks" healthier than it actually is, whereas the opposite holds for Hamilton, TN. In future work, it would be interesting to see what differences exist between such counties.

To understand *why* a particular model works, we performed a feature analysis for the same set of four statistics. In each case we computed the top 10 features with

Table 1. Prediction performance for nine health statistics across 100 counties in a 10-fold cross validation setting. Feature sets used were (U)ser tags, (I)magga tags, (D)emographics and combinations of these. Statistical significant improvement over the demographics-only baseline was tested using a Fisher r-z transform paired test between the two correlations * = .05, ** = .01, * = .001.**

	Pearson's r						SMAPE					
	U	I	D	U+D	I+D	U+I+D	U	I	D	U+D	I+D	U+I+D
Smokers	0.55	0.53	0.72	0.73	**0.75**	0.73	8.1	8.7	7.1	6.8	**6.7**	6.9
Obese	0.42	0.48	0.81	**0.84****	0.82	0.84	6.5	6.2	4	**3.7**	3.9	3.7
Food Env. Index	0.54	0.45	0.87	**0.91*****	0.87	0.90	4.2	4.3	2.4	**2**	2.4	2
Physically active	0.46	0.58	0.70	**0.79***	0.74	0.79	7.7	7.4	5.9	**4.8**	5.6	4.9
Excessive Drinking	0.22	**0.49****	0.38	0.33	0.48	0.38	6.2	**5.2**	6.1	6.3	5.7	6
Alcohol Impaired	**0.51****	0.26	0.25	0.43	0.28	0.44	**7.9**	8.9	9.1	8.5	8.9	8.2
Diabetic	0.34	0.40	0.77	**0.83****	0.78	0.82	7.7	7.2	5.1	**4.5**	4.9	4.6
Food insecure	0.37	0.38	0.84	0.86	0.84	**0.87**	7.8	7.2	4.4	**4.2**	4.5	4.3
Limited access	**0.61***	0.40	0.46	0.58	0.48	0.58	**19.7**	22.6	21.5	20.5	20.9	20.8

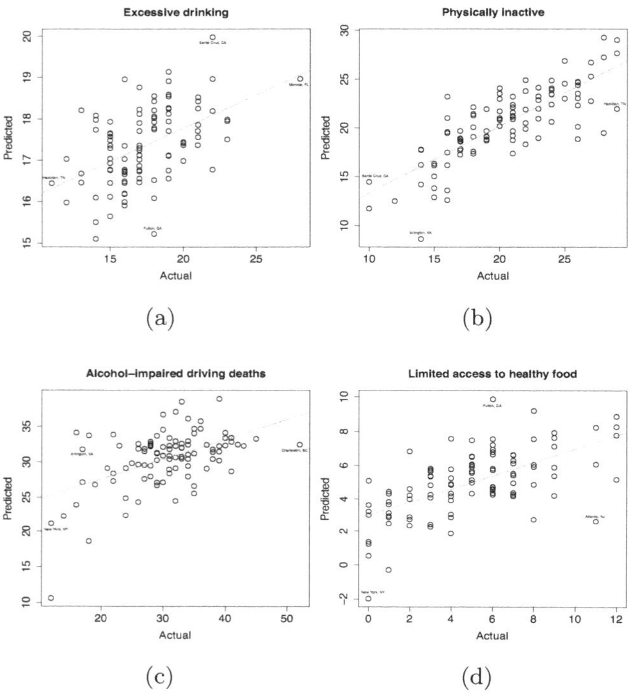

Figure 2. Predicted vs. actual health statistics value using (a) Imagga tags for predicting excessive drinking, (b) User-provided tags + demographics for predicting physically inactive, (c) User-provided tags for predicting alcohol-impaired driving deaths, and (d) User-provided tags for predicting limited access to healthy food.

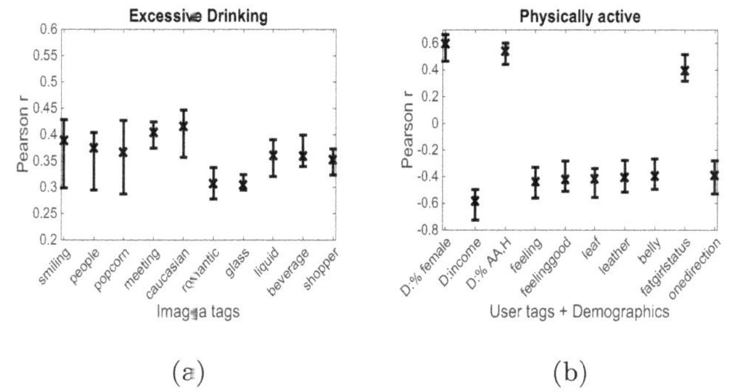

Figure 3. Feature analysis, showing the top ten features with the highest absolute value of correlation, for Imagga tags for predicting excessive drinking, (b) User-provided tags + demographics for predicting physically inactive. In (b), features with "D:" indicate demographic features, "D: AA,H" indicates demographic features pertaining to African Americans and Hispanics. Error bars indicate 95% confidence interval.

the highest (absolute) value of correlation. Figure 3 shows the results.

Among the machine-derived tags most predictive of excessive drinking (Fig. 3 (a)), "liquid","beverage" and "meeting" (c.f. "party") and others make intuitive sense. These tags are especially interesting since such tags might not be part of human annotations. For the user-provided tags predictive of physical inactivity (Fig. 3 (b)), the hashtag #fatgirlstatus makes sense. It is used in a self-ironic manner to refer to food obsession and related topics.In addition to these intuitive features, there are also many that require further investigation. As the goal of this study was to test the general feasibility of using *images* for public health studies, rather than to fully explain the social dynamics behind one particular health issue, we leave this for future work.

CONCLUSIONS

In this paper, we studied if social media image data can be used to understand public health. We used both user-provided as well as machine-generated tags to see if they can predict county-level health statistics. Our study relies on recent advances in deep learning for image analysis, a very active field that is undergoing constant advances. We show that both user-provided and machine-generated tags provide information that improves over models using only demographic information. Whereas in most cases, models based on user-provided tags outperform machine-generated ones, for statistics on excessive drinking the opposite holds. Machine-generated tags such as "glass", "liquid" and "beverage" (Figure 3) are all found to be good predictors, and such tags might not be part of human annotations. Machine-generated tags might prove of particular value in the case of stigmatized behaviors such as substance abuse, where explicit hints are unlikely to be added by the image owner. This could also be used in designing interfaces that could identify and help users in need of support.

REFERENCES

1. Sofiane Abbar, Yelena Mejova, and Ingmar Weber. 2015. You Tweet What You Eat: Studying Food Consumption Through Twitter. In *CHI*. 3197–3206.
2. Saeed Abdullah, Elizabeth L Murnane, Jean MR Costa, and Tanzeem Choudhury. 2015. Collective Smile: Measuring Societal Happiness from Geolocated Images. In *Proceedings of the 18th ACM Conference on Computer Supported Cooperative Work & Social Computing*. ACM, 361–374.
3. Nazanin Andalibi, Pinar Ozturk, and Andrea Forte. 2015. Depression-related Imagery on Instagram. In *Proceedings of the 18th ACM Conference Companion on Computer Supported Cooperative Work & Social Computing*. ACM, 231–234.
4. Sairam Balani and Munmun De Choudhury. 2015. Detecting and Characterizing Mental Health Related Self-Disclosure in Social Media. In *Proceedings of the 33rd Annual ACM Conference Extended Abstracts on Human Factors in Computing Systems*. ACM, 1373–1378.
5. Aron Culotta. 2014. Estimating County Health Statistics with Twitter. In *CHI*. 1335–1344.
6. Munmun De Choudhury, Michael Gamon, Scott Counts, and Eric Horvitz. 2013. Predicting Depression via Social Media.. In *ICWSM*.
7. Mark Dredze. 2012. How Social Media Will Change Public Health. *IEEE Intelligent Systems* 27, 4 (2012), 81–84.
8. Geoffrey E Hinton, Simon Osindero, and Yee-Whye Teh. 2006. A fast learning algorithm for deep belief nets. *Neural computation* 18, 7 (2006), 1527–1554.
9. Andrej Karpathy and Li Fei-Fei. 2014. Deep visual-semantic alignments for generating image descriptions. *arXiv preprint arXiv:1412.2306* (2014).
10. Yoshiyuki Kawano and Keiji Yanai. 2015. FoodCam: A real-time food recognition system on a smartphone. *Multimedia Tools and Applications* 74, 14 (2015), 5263–5287.
11. Patty Kostkova. 2013. A Roadmap to Integrated Digital Public Health Surveillance: The Vision and the Challenges. In *WWW*. 687–694.
12. Patty Kostkova. 2015. Public Health. In *Twitter: A Digital Socioscope*, Yelena Mejova, Ingmar Weber, and Michael Macy (Eds.). Cambridge University Press, 111–130.
13. D.J. McIver, J.B. Hawkins, R. Chunara, A.K. Chatterjee, A. Bhandari, T.P. Fitzgerald, S.H. Jain, and J.S. Brownstein. 2015. Characterizing Sleep Issues Using Twitter. 17 (2015), e140.
14. Yelena Mejova, Hamed Haddadi, Anastasios Noulas, and Ingmar Weber. 2015. #FoodPorn: Obesity Patterns in Culinary Interactions. In *DigitalHealth*.
15. Elizabeth M Morgan, Chareen Snelson, and Patt Elison-Bowers. 2010. Image and video disclosure of substance use on social media websites. *Computers in Human Behavior* 26, 6 (2010), 1405–1411.
16. Jon Parker, Yifang Wei, Andrew Yates, Ophir Frieder, and Nazli Goharian. 2013. A Framework for Detecting Public Health Trends with Twitter. In *ASONAM*. 556–563.
17. Michael J. Paul and Mark Dredze. 2011. You Are What You Tweet: Analyzing Twitter for Public Health. In *ICWSM*. 265–272.
18. Michael J. Paul and Mark Dredze. 2014. Discovering Health Topics in Social Media Using Topic Models. *PLOS ONE* 9 (2014), e103408. Issue 8.
19. J. Pennebaker, J. Francis, and R. Booth. 2007. Linguistic inquiry and word count: LIWC 2001. (2007). `http://homepage.psy.utexas.edu/homepage/faculty/pennebaker/reprints/liwc2007_operatormanual.pdf`.
20. Salimian P.K., Chunara R., and Weitzman E.R. 2014. Averting the perfect storm: addressing youth substance use risk from social media use. *Pediatric Annals* 43 (2014), e242. Issue 10.
21. Kyle W Prier, Matthew S Smith, Christophe Giraud-Carrier, and Carl L Hanson. 2011. Identifying health-related topics on twitter. In *Social computing, behavioral-cultural modeling and prediction*. Springer, 18–25.
22. Adam Sadilek and Henry Kautz. 2013. Modeling the Impact of Lifestyle on Health at Scale. In *WSDM*. 637–646.
23. Abeed Sarker, Rachel E. Ginn, Azadeh Nikfarjam, Karen O'Connor, Karen Smith, Swetha Jayaraman, Tejaswi Upadhaya, and Graciela Gonzalez. 2015. Utilizing social media data for pharmacovigilance: A review. *Journal of Biomedical Informatics* 54 (2015), 202–212.
24. Martin Seligman. 2012. *Flourish: A Visionary New Understanding of Happiness and Well-being*. Atria Books.
25. Kyoko Sudo, Kazuhiko Murasaki, Jun Shimamura, and Yukinobu Taniguchi. 2014. Estimating Nutritional Value from Food Images Based on Semantic Segmentation. In *UbiComp*. 571–576.
26. Morgan Walker, Laura Thornton, Munmun De Choudhury, Jaime Teevan, Cynthia M. Bulik, Cheri A. Levinson, and Stephanie Zerwas. 2015. Facebook Use and Disordered Eating in College-Aged Women. *Journal of Adolescent Health* 57 (2015), 157–163.
27. Ren Wu, Shengen Yan, Yi Shan, Qingqing Dang, and Gang Sun. 2015. Deep image: Scaling up image recognition. *arXiv preprint arXiv:1501.02876* (2015).

It Matters If My Friends Stop Smoking: Social Support for Behavior Change in Social Media

Corbin Reno and Erika S. Poole
College of Information Sciences and Technology
The Pennsylvania State University
University Park, PA 16802 USA
{cfr5045, esp13}@psu.edu

ABSTRACT
A growing body of research has examined whether and how an individual can leverage online social networks to receive social support for health behavior change. This prior research largely focuses on attributes of the post content and the experiences and concerns of people posting. Less is known about moderators and mediators that influence whether and how one's social network will respond to a request for support. Using a factorial survey experiment, we find evidence that attitudes toward specific types of health behaviors greatly increase likelihood of response to a post, and that targeting close-tie relationships may increase effectiveness of social media based behavior change interventions, particularly related to smoking cessation.

Author Keywords
Social media; health behavior change

ACM Classification Keywords
H.5.m. Information interfaces and presentation (e.g., HCI): Miscellaneous.

INTRODUCTION
Making changes to health habits can be difficult, but research shows *social support* can positively influence motivation and adherence to health behavior change (HBC) [9]. Given benefits of social support, many consumer-oriented diet/fitness tracking mobile apps and wearable devices include functionality allowing users to automatically share health behavior successes (e.g., walking a certain distance or losing weight) over social media. Social media posts may offer several benefits: they reach a broad audience of one's peers, are cheap to implement, and by requiring little to no explicit effort on behalf of the user, they can fit into a person's daily routines. If implemented well, people making positive changes for their health may receive more support from people in their lives—and may be more likely to maintain these changes long-term. However, it is unclear whether these posts are effective at eliciting social support for behavior change, or if they just clutter social media information streams [12]. Thus, in this study we examine the question: *Which factors influence whether a person will respond to a social media post discussing behavior change?*

To answer this question, we conducted a full-factorial survey experiment investigating moderators and mediators of response to social media behavior change posts, and provide guidance on the design of health information sharing mechanisms for social media. In contrast to prior work, which focuses either on attributes of engaging posts (e.g., including pictures) or the needs and concerns of those who are asking for support, we instead focus on the needs and concerns of those who would be *giving support;* that is, we focus on needs of the people who would have their social media streams cluttered by requests for support.

CHI'16, May 07-12, 2016, San Jose, CA, USA
© 2016 ACM. ISBN 978-1-4503-3362-7/16/05…$15.00
DOI: http://dx.doi.org/10.1145/2858036.2858203

RELATED WORK
One of the most accessible and popular ways to share user-generated content online is through social media sites—especially when it comes to sharing information about oneself. Seventy-one percent of all Internet users in the U.S. are users of Facebook, and 2.5 million pieces of content are shared per minute on the social media site [4,8]. Given the reach of social media, a variety of HBC devices and applications have capitalized on social media to foster social support for HBC. Early reports on the effectiveness of these supports have been mixed [12], highlighting the potential advantages and hardships in eliciting social support from one's social network. Concerns about cluttering others' information streams with meaningless content may reduce when, how, and why a person asks for support from their social networks [5,13]. In Newman *et al.*'s study of health information sharing on Facebook as well as Lee and Lim's study of online and app-based social support for runners, the researchers found tensions between social conventions and needed social support. For example, concerns about impression management might lead to conservative posting strategies, while at the same time accountability for behavior change may indicate more information sharing. Yet we know little about how to account for these tensions in the design of mechanisms for social support via social media. That being said, there is some guidance on factors that make social media appealing to its intended audience (e.g. [11,16]). With

respect to social media for health and wellness, Epstein et al. provide guidance on how to structure Twitter posts that are more likely to garner audience response. In their study of recreational runners, post sentiment, images, and human generated content (as opposed to system-generated by an activity tracking device) predicted responses [5]. We build upon this growing body of literature on audience response to social media. Using Facebook as the primary platform of investigation, we examine moderators and mediators that influence whether or not a person responds to a HBC post viewed on social media. In contrast to prior research on social media for health and wellness, which provides guidance on post features that are attractive (e.g., inclusion of images), we provide complementary insight by identifying whether and how characteristics of the audience and type of health behavior influence engagement.

METHODS

We designed a between-subjects factorial survey experiment to identify whether attitudes, norms, relationship, and behavior type predict intention to respond to a social media post about HBC. While factorial survey experiments are not traditionally an HCI research method, they have been used in a variety of social science disciplines to study preferences and decision in ways that simultaneously approximate real-world complexity while also controlling for bias [1].

The theoretical lens guiding the research is the theory of reasoned action (TRA), a cognitive theory used to understand human behavior and predict behavior change in a variety of settings [7]. TRA focuses on how an individual's *attitudes* and *subjective norms* about a behavior (e.g., beliefs about what others think or what is appropriate) influence behavioral intentions and actions. Although behavior and intention are not always perfectly aligned, research repeatedly finds a strong positive link between the two, particularly for behaviors that are familiar and well-practiced [14].

To operationalize the construct *attitude*, we decompose it into three facets: (1) perceived importance of the HBC, (2) firsthand, personal experience with the behavior change, and (3) secondhand exposure to the HBC. With respect to *subjective norms*, we focus on audience perception of whether it is appropriate to post content about specific health behaviors on social media. Finally, we explored stable factors that may influence intention to respond, including demographics, social media usage habits, and relationship between content creators and consumers.

Survey Experiment Design

The survey experiment was created using Qualtrics (Qualtrics, Provo, UT). Participants were first asked demographics and qualification questions including gender, age, education, ethnicity, social media usage in past 12 months, and an attention check question.

Participants were then presented with a randomly assigned situational vignette and faux Facebook post containing factors systematically varied between the participants. The factors varied included (1) *relationship to poster* and (2) *type of behavior in post*. Table 1 lists all conditions and the number of participants. Figure 1 shows an example vignette.

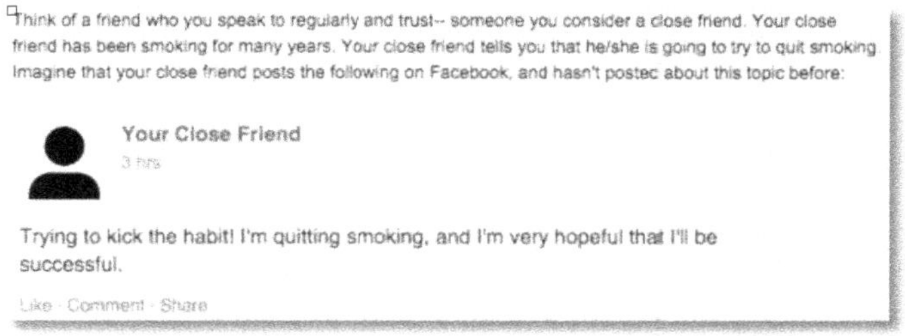

Figure 1: Example Vignette

Following the vignette, participants were asked were three questions focused on ***attitude towards the health behavior*** described in the vignette:

- **Opinion:** "Do you personally feel that the behavior found in the Facebook post is an important issue in the world?"
- **Personal Experience:** "Have you personally attempted to achieve this behavior?"
- **Secondhand Exposure:** "Do you know someone who has attempted to achieve this behavior?"

If respondents indicated "yes" for the personal experience or secondhand exposure questions, they were asked whether the HBC was a current attempt, a past success, or a past failure.

Subjective norms about social media were measured via a question asking for a rating of how appropriate it would be to post about this behavior change on social media (1 = absolutely inappropriate, 7 = absolutely appropriate).

Intentions to respond were measured via multiple-select question in which participants could indicate no intention to respond, social media-based interaction (*like, comment, share, private message*), or other forms of communication (*text message, phone call, or in-person contact*). Participants were also asked a question about the impact of post frequency on response intention, but it was omitted from analysis due to an error in the statistical plan.

Participant Recruitment and Characteristics

Participants (n=1299) from the United States were recruited from Amazon Mechanical Turk, and received $0.15. Participants under 18, non-users of Facebook, and those who incorrectly answered the attention check were screened out of further participation, leaving 877 participants in the dataset used for analysis. Summary demographics indicate majority white (74%), female (59%), age 25-44 (57%), with at least some college education (79.2%).

HBC	Relationship	Participants
Quitting Smoking	Close Friend	98
	Family	90
	Acquaintance	94
Eating Healthy	Close Friend	102
	Family	111
	Acquaintance	92
Exercising More	Close Friend	94
	Family	85
	Acquaintance	111
Total:		877

Table 1. Number of Evaluable Participants by Treatment

RESULTS

Survey data was analyzed using binary logistic regression. Checks for multi-collinearity indicate no strong correlations ($r \geq 0.4$), so no predictors were initially removed. Outliers were identified by computing Cook's distance; 49 instances fit outlier criteria, and were excluded from analysis (N = 828). Finally, we conducted a preliminary examination of the number of cases in each level of our predictors. A general rule of thumb when conducting a regression is that each predictor level has at least 10 observations. Education, age, and race all had levels with 10 or less observations, and were omitted from further analysis. An initial binary logistic regression model was built with the remaining predictors. This initial model was statistically significant (X^2 (15) = 293.053, $p < .001$) and correctly classified 89.3% of all cases. However, some predictor levels were not statistically significant. In order to find a reduced model with the best predictive power, we created several models with and without each predictor that had at least one level where $p > 0.05$. A likelihood ratio test was used to determine model fit. If the likelihood ratio test (LRT) is statistically significant, then the predictor in question should remain in the model. From the LRT, the predictors Gender, LinkedInUser, Google+User, InstagramUser, Exposure, and Behavior were excluded due to statistical insignificance. External factors that were left in the model after checking observation counts and coefficient significance included Twitter user, Pinterest user, and Tumblr user. The final regression model was statistically significant (X^2 (10) = 289.407, $p < .001$), correctly classifying 89% of all cases. Additionally, a Hosmer and Lemeshow test was conducted to ensure model goodness-of-fit, and the results of that test confirm our model (X^2 (8) = 10.673, p = .221; an HL test confirms goodness-of-fit when $p > 0.05$). The full results of the final binary logistic regression model are located in Table 2. Note that to interpret

Predictors[=Level]	B	df	p	Exp(B)
(Constant)	-63.380	1	.000***	.000
TwitterUser=False	.619	1	.028**	2.090
PinterestUser=False	-1.028	1	.000***	0.429
TumblrUser=False	.639	2	.034**	1.895
Relationship=Acqtce.	Base	2	.000***	Base
Relationship=Friend	2.347	1	.000***	10.452
Relationship=Family	2.276	1	.000***	9.736
Behavior=Exercise	Base		.000***	Base
Behavior=Smoking	2.191	1	.000***	8.948
Behavior=Eating	-0.207	1	.483	0.813
Opinion=True	1.844	1	.000***	6.325
Personal Exp.=True	1.145	1	.000***	2.811
PostAppropriateness	0.873	1	.000***	2.395

*** p < .001 ** p < .05 * p < .10

Table 2. Results from the Binary Logistic Regression

the logistic regression, it is more intuitive to look at the odds ratio shown as *Exp(B)* in Table 2.

Predictors of Post Response

Relationships Matter: If the poster is a close friend, the post is over 10.452 times more likely to receive a response than if the poster is an acquaintance. If the poster is a family member, the odds ratio also remains elevated (OR=9.736).

Experience Can Help, But Attitude Matters More: Individuals who have personally attempted the HBC referenced in the post are over 2.811 times more likely to respond compared to those who have not attempted the HBC. However, a subtler and stronger indicator of response likelihood is whether the respondent holds a belief in the perceived importance of the specific health behavior referenced in the post. If a specific behavior is considered important to the person, he or she is 6.325 times more likely to respond to a post about that health behavior.

Behavior Type is an Important Factor: We also found evidence that response likelihood differs based on type of behavior. The baseline in the regression analysis for type of behavior was posts involving *exercising more*. Of particular interest is that *quitting smoking* posts have 8.948 times the likelihood of response compared to the baseline of *exercising more* posts. The predictor level for the difference in response likelihood between *exercise* and *eating healthy* posts was found to be statistically insignificant.

DISCUSSION

If the goal of integrating social media into an intervention is to receive supportive responses, ensuring the post gets to the right audience matters. Here we provide guidance on how to accomplish that goal.

When will the audience respond?

When will the audience respond to a HBC post? This answer depends in part on the HBC genre in question. Our study revealed that posts involving quitting smoking are far more likely to receive engagement from the audience than posts about diet or exercise. This finding is an important but underexplored factor in existing design frameworks focused on when and how to share health and wellness information online [5].

Who should be in the audience?

If our goal is to maximize supportive responses, our findings indicate two genres of responders: (1) people who care about the poster or (2) people who take an interest in or relates to the post's content. For the HBCs we considered, one of the most effective ways to ensure response is to target posts to close friends and family. Incorporating or targeting close family and close friends on social media could provide further improve the effectiveness of smoking cessation interventions with social media components. While an intuitive finding, it does provide some empirical support for the question of whether it is better to target HBC content to a subset of audiences or whether to broadcast content widely. This provides complementary support for the work of of Paay et al, who argue for the importance of tailored content in digital smoking cessation programs [15].

Identifying and targeting audience members interested in *content,* however, is a slightly more nuanced undertaking. While one might initially think that someone who has gone through the same experience in the past may be the most likely to provide support, we find that merely having the *belief* that a specific HBC is an "important world issue" is a better predictor. Put another way, in order to get supportive responses, there is no need to artificially limit audience of HBC posts to people who have who have prior or current experience with a specific HBC (e.g. a private group of peers changing a behavior together). In fact, it could be argued that targeting a selective yet slightly wider audience would be beneficial, as it would circumvent the attrition that is common in HBC programs and potentially stymies effective long-term peer support [6].

System Design Recommendations

We provide the following system design recommendations for incorporating social media into HBC applications. The first is to automatically route content to close friends and family. From a technical standpoint, routing content to people who have close tie relationships could be operationalized via computational approaches to estimating tie strength [3]. The second recommendation is to identify content-interested audience. This can be done in at least two ways. One method could be to provide an in-interface single-question survey. Prompt potential audience members with a single-question that asks whether they perceive of specific health behavior in question as an "important world issue." This could either be done independent of any specific HBC post (e.g. as an account setting or a pop-up survey), or it could be asked when a post suggestive of HBC is shown on a newsfeed. Alternatively, topic modeling, which has been used in non-health related social media research, could be used to tailor audience. For example, Hong and Davison utilized the popular Latent Dirichlet Allocation (LDA) topic modeling method to identify Twitter users based on the category of their posts [10]. A similar approach could be used for health-specific content, but taken one step further: users that typically create or share posts relating to health could be shown HBC posts to encourage responses from a like-minded audience.

CONCLUSION AND FUTURE WORK

The study contributes and understanding of how relational and contextual factors influence intentions to respond to HBC posts on social media. Internal factors including relationship to the poster and attitude toward the HBC influenced likelihood to respond. Furthermore, we identified that not all types of HBC elicit the same volume of response, which has previously been underexplored in the literature.

That being said, we recognize that this work does not account for every and all health condition, health behavior, or patient population. Our strategy was to focus on a limited number of health behaviors that each are strongly linked to the most common and often preventable chronic health conditions (e.g. heart disease, stroke, cancer, diabetes, obesity, arthritis) [2]. Ultimately, more research is needed to better understand how social media fits into the context of rarer or stigmatized health conditions. Moreover, there is also a need for comparative research rigorously assessing the benefits and drawbacks of general purpose social media versus patient-centered, tailored online communities.

In closing, we aim for this work to open avenues for future human-computer interaction research focused on better understanding when, where, and how social media and other technological tools are—and are not—effective in supporting HBC. We strongly urge more discussion and investigation into the circumstances in which general purpose social media leads to effective social support—and the circumstances in which it may fail to do so. Understanding of social media for health-related social support remains a critical gap in human-computer interaction and medical informatics literature. By addressing the gap, we can build systems that are more effective for HBC support, and provide much needed advisement to healthcare providers incorporating social media into patient engagement initiatives.

ACKNOWLEDGEMENTS

A research grant from the Penn State Schreyer Honors College funded this work. In addition, we thank our anonymous reviewers and Jofish Kaye for their invaluable feedback on earlier drafts of this paper.

REFERENCES

1. Katrin Auspurg and Thomas Hinz. 2014. *Factorial Survey Experiments*. SAGE Publications.

2. Ursula E Bauer, Peter A Briss, Richard A Goodman, and Barbara A Bowman. 2014. Prevention of chronic disease in the 21st century: elimination of the leading preventable causes of premature death and disability in the USA. *The Lancet* 384, 9937: 45–52.
3. Moira Burke and Robert E. Kraut. 2014. Growing Closer on Facebook: Changes in Tie Strength Through Social Network Site Use. *Proceedings of the 32nd Annual ACM Conference on Human Factors in Computing Systems*, ACM, 4187–4196.
4. Maeve Duggan, Nicole B. Ellison, Cliff Lampe, Am, a Lenhart, and Mary Madden. 2014. Social Media Update 2014. *Pew Research Center: Internet, Science & Tech.* Retrieved July 29, 2015 from http://www.pewinternet.org/2015/01/09/social-media-update-2014/
5. Daniel A Epstein, Bradley H Jacobson, Elizabeth Bales, David W McDonald, and Sean A Munson. 2015. From nobody cares to way to go!: A Design Framework for Social Sharing in Personal Informatics. *Proceedings of the 18th ACM Conference on Computer Supported Cooperative Work & Social Computing*, ACM, 1622–1636.
6. Gunther Eysenbach. 2005. The law of attrition. *Journal of Medical Internet Research* 7, 1.
7. Martin Fishbein and Icek Ajzen. 2011. *Predicting and changing behavior: The reasoned action approach.* Taylor & Francis.
8. Gunelius, Susan. 2014. The Data Explosion in 2014 Minute by Minute - Infographic. *ACI*. Retrieved July 29, 2015 from http://aci.info/2014/07/12/the-data-explosion-in-2014-minute-by-minute-infographic/
9. Catherine A Heaney and Barbara A Israel. 2008. Social networks and social support. *Health behavior and health education: Theory, research, and practice* 4: 189–210.
10. Liangjie Hong and Brian D Davison. 2010. Empirical study of topic modeling in twitter. *Proceedings of the First Workshop on Social Media Analytics*, ACM, 80–88.
11. C.J. Hutto, Sarita Yardi, and Eric Gilbert. 2013. A Longitudinal Study of Follow Predictors on Twitter. *Proceedings of the SIGCHI Conference on Human Factors in Computing Systems*, ACM, 821–830.
12. Carol A. Maher, Lucy K. Lewis, Katia Ferrar, Simon Marshall, Ilse De Bourdeaudhuij, and Corneel Vandelanotte. 2014. Are health behavior change interventions that use online social networks effective? A systematic review. *Journal of Medical Internet Research* 16, 2.
13. Mark W. Newman, Debra Lauterbach, Sean A. Munson, Paul Resnick, and Margaret E. Morris. 2011. It's not that i don't have problems, i'm just not putting them on facebook: challenges and opportunities in using online social networks for health. *Proceedings of the ACM 2011 Conference on Computer Supported Cooperative Work*, ACM, 341–350.
14. Judith A Ouellette and Wendy Wood. 1998. Habit and intention in everyday life: the multiple processes by which past behavior predicts future behavior. *Psychological Bulletin* 124, 1: 54.
15. Jeni Paay, Jesper Kjeldskov, Mikael B Skov, Lars Lichon, and Stephan Rasmussen. 2015. Understanding Individual Differences for Tailored Smoking Cessation Apps. *Proceedings of the 33rd Annual ACM Conference on Human Factors in Computing Systems* ACM, 1699–1708.
16. Emilee Rader, Alcides Velasquez, Kayla D. Hales, and Helen Kwok. 2012. The Gap Between Producer Intentions and Consumer Behavior in Social Media. *Proceedings of the 17th ACM International Conference on Supporting Group Work*, ACM, 249–252.

Author Index

Aagesen, Peter Tolstrup 3126
Abbas, Malath 3812
Abdolrahmani, Ali 2034
Abdulin, Evgeniy 1503, 2969
Abdul-Rahman, Alfie 1
Abe, Kaho 277
Abe, Tetsuya 2395
Abney, Andrea 3597
Abowd, Gregory 3453
Abram, Gregory 700
Aced López, Sebastián 1654
Achituv, Tal 2467
Ackad, Christopher 2343
Acquisti, Alessandro 587
Adachi, Takuya 2705
Adamic, Lada A. 564
Adams, Ross K. 365
Adar, Eytan 587
Aditya, Vikram 56
Adnan, Muhammad 5444
Afergan, Daniel 3770, 5372
Agapie, Elena 1072
Aggarwal, Deepti 188
Agrawala, Maneesh 38
Ahmad, Muhammad Aurangzeb 397
Ahmad, Muneeb Imtiaz 2234
Ahmed, Muzamil 1869
Ahmed, Nova 459
Ahmed, Syed Ishtiaque 1073, 1403, 5063
Ahn, June 3317, 3607
Ahrens, James 700
Aida, Daiya 1322
Aitamurto, Tanja 3604
Aizpurua, Amaia 2766
Ajuruchi, Obinna 3339
Akazue, Moses 4401
Akik, Chaza 331
Akkil, Deepak 1151, 1573
Akleman, Ergun 2249
Al Moubayed, Samer 7, 4933
Alabdulhafith, Maali 2976
al'Absi, Mustafa 4489
Alan, Alper T. 2012, 5262
Alavi, Hamed S. 3408
Albaghli, Reem 4884
Albaugh, Lea 285
Alborno, Paolo 1629
Alcaidinho, Joelle 193
Alcock, Celena 384
Alexa, Marc 791
Alexander, Jason 2778, 2845, 3492
Alfayad, Abdulrahman 5543
Alghamdi, Elham 1362
Ali, Haider 375
Ali, Syed 2299
Alkly, Lana H.A. 3975
Almeida, Teresa 1810, 2599, 3635
Aloimonos, Chloe 2072
Alqarni, Abdulhadi 2758, 2976
Alshammari, Mohammad 2984
Alt, Florian 309, 1344, 1349, 1415, 2156, 3736, 3766, 5076
AlTarawneh, Ragaad 1222
Altimira, David 1681
Altmeyer, Maximilian 1813, 2026
Alves, Thamara 1362
Amaral, Telmo 4464
Amarvaj, Likhith 56
Amershi, Saleema 3553
Amma, Christoph 3639
Ammari, Tawfiq 610
Amores, Judith 1, 2
Amr, May 3723
Anagnostopoulos, Theodoros 4711
Anane, Rachid 2984
Andalibi, Nazanin 3906
Andersen, Erik 957
Andersen, Jeff 4298
Andersen, Kristina 1352, 3423, 4968
Anderson, Fraser 409
Anderson, Jennings 2783
Anderson, Kenneth M. 2783
Ando, Mitsuhito 1561
Ankolekar, Anupriya 3324
Annetta, Michael 1945
Antaki, James F. 4477
Anthony, Lisa 1752, 1921
Antonijoan, Marc 2387
Antunes Ferreira, Marilia 3643
Aoyama, Shuhei 2403
Apaolaza, Aitor 2766
Appert, Caroline 4189
Araujo, Bruno 2857, 4610
Archambault, Daniel 2396
Arefin Shimon, Shaikh Shawon 3822
Arents, Rogier 1794
Arif, Ahmed Sabbir 2992, 3469, 5151
Asad, Mariam 827, 3293
Asadzadeh, Parvin 284
Asenov, Dimitar 5040
Ashbrook, Daniel 1510
Ashktorab, Zahra 3895
Asthana, Siddhartha 343
Atkins, Cheralyn 2982
Au, Irene 1043
Auriemma, Joshua R. 5252
Avle, Seyram 2233
Avrahami, Daniel 673, 1072
Aylett, Matthew P. 501, 1821, 3379, 3612, 3643
Ayobi, Amid 2774
Azaria, Amos 1555
Azenkot, Shiri 4896
Azhar, Saad 680
Azmandian, Mahdi 3, 1968, 3647
Baarslag, Tim 2012
Babic, Teo 3754
Baccino, Thierry 4850
Bach, Benjamin 3670
Bächer, Moritz 3806
Back, Jon 1359
Backonja, Uba 5324
Badam, Sriram Karthik 5409
Bader, Patrick 509
Bae, Byung-Chull 2563
Bae, Seok-Hyung 2548
Bahram, Sina 5506
Bai, Xue 1533
Bailey, Brian P. 4086
Baillie, Lynne 4401, 5444
Bailly, Gilles 445, 1438, 1548, 4189, 5298
Bakhshi, Saeideh 575
Bakker, Saskia 1608, 2334
Balaam, Madeline .. 331, 343, 1810, 2599, 3635
Balakrishnan, Aruna 1063
Balakrishnan, Ravin 59, 3683, 4587
Balcı, Fuat 1538
Bales, Elizabeth 635
Balestra, Martina 661
Ball, Madeleine 661
Ballay, Laura 1111
Ballweber, Christy 2348
Balta, Andra 2410
Baltodano, Sonia 3542
Bandara, Arosha K. 2417
Banerjee, Amartya 1828
Banka Johnson, Eva-Carin 305
Banks, Richard 2549, 2869
Banovic, Nikola 248
Baquerizo, Priscilla 3620
Barbosa, Simone D. J. 933
Bardzell, Jeffrey 1051, 1390, 3550, 4325
Bardzell, Shaowen 1051, 1390, 3293, 3550, 4325
Barkhuus, Louise 864, 2430
Barmaki, Roghayeh 86
Barnes, Cathy 2999
Barnett, Mike 5433
Barrio, Pablo J. 2729
Barsilowski, Dietrich 5595
Barthet, Mathieu 313
Bartindale, Tom 2705
Bartkowski, Wiesław 3707
Bartneck, Christoph 1681
Bartram, Lyn 1959
Barz, Michael 1813
Basharat, Amna 92
Bastarache-Roberge, Marie-Christine 1980
Bateman, Scott 1548
Battle, Leilani 5433
Baudisch, Patrick ... 936, 944, 2175, 3431, 3970
Bauer, Christine 609
Bauer, Lujo 101, 527, 3748
Bauman, Adrian 3211
Baumann, Nicola 3007
Baumgartner, Nina 3069
BD, AC 609
Beale, Russell 2923

Beaudouin-Lafon, Michel 2075
Beck, Austin 3607
Beckmann, Nils 1637
Bedi, Rishi 261
Bedwell, Ben 3049, 4061
Bee, Penny 2124
Bees, Jonathan 3748
Beitra, Robin 1597
Bekker, Tilde 1123
Bektas, Kenan 5812
Bellotti, Victoria 1644, 3508
Benadda, Tarik 14
Benavides, Xavier 1, 2
Benenson, Zinaida 3870
Benford, Steve 293, 1163, 3651, 5385
Benko, Hrvoje .3, 1221, 1233, 1968, 2869, 3647
Bennett, Cynthia L. 1745
Bennett, Peter 2020, 2609, 3461
Bentley, Frank R. 823, 1893, 3761, 5710
Bentley, Logan J. 164
Benton, Laura 969
Berghmans, Brent 168, 2744
Berkovich, Marianne 5921
Bernhard, Orlando 2940
Bernhaupt, Regina 940
Bernstein, Michael S. ... 237, 2645, 2893, 3167, 3500, 4111, 4647
Berry, Daniel M. 5228
Berseth, Glen 2119
Berst, Andreas 3796
Bertenshaw, Emma 3049
Bertini, Enrico 3659
Bethancourt, Matthew 2504, 3683
Betke, Margrit 1952
Bevan, Nigel 2999
Bevilacqua, Frédéric 2829, 3558, 3667
Beyls, Peter 3816
Bhangaonkar, Sourabh 2782
Bi, Xiaojun 49, 3532, 4699
Bian, Yuanzhe 1991
Bian, Yulong 433
Bianchi-Berthouze, Nadia 1092, 5698
Bichard, Jo-Anne 2474
Bickel, Bernd 3806
Bidwell, Nicola J. 3574, 5063
Biehl, Jacob T. 673
Bigham, Jeffrey P. .. 621, 1555, 3500, 3834, 5506
Billinghurst, Mark 1257, 1681
Billman, Dorrit 2969
Bilogrevic, Igor 5215
Bimamisa, David 1193
Bird, Jon 3453, 3485
Birk, Max V. 2982, 3007, 4562, 5595
Birk, Morten 791
Birkett, Michelle 5360
Bishop, Ann P. 859
Bixler, Robert 1661
Bjorn, Pernille 3550
Blackwell, Alan F. 2533, 2886
Blackwell, Lindsay 610
Blandford, Ann 1028, 2906
Bleumers, Lizzy 3484
Blevis, Eli 1324, 3581
Blythe, Mark 387, 3484, 4968
Bodak, Rebeka 1781
Bødker, Susanne 984, 2538
Boehner, Kirsten 2970
Bogdan, Cristian 1300
Bohne, René 3788
Boisvert, Jacques 261
Bok, Jinwook 4658
Bolchini, Davide 2027
Boll, Susanne 2049, 2285, 2601, 3738
Bonny, Justin W. 3473
Bonsignore, Elizabeth 3317, 3607
Booker, Jennifer 473
Booten, Kyle 2401
Booth, Kellogg S. 188
Booth, Tracey 3485
Bopp, Julia Ayumi 2996
Borchers, Jan 1067, 2497, 3062, 3232, 3522, 3788
Borgman, Christine L. 1585
Boring, Sebastian 5862
Borriello, Gaetano 5675
Bosch, Lilian Bernadina Josefina 2790
Bosch, Nigel 1661
Bose, Raja 2697
Bossavit, Benoît 1294
Bostan, İdil 3944
Boucharenc, Christian Gilles 1937
Boucher, Andy 1597
Boucher, Christina 3822
Bouchigny, Sylvain 2632
Boussayoud, Anfal 1180
Bousseau, Adrien 397
Bower, Peter 2124
Bowers, John 1597
Bowey, Jason T. 2982, 3007
Bowler, Leanne 1187
Boy, Jeremy 3659
Boyd, LouAnne E. 4872
Boyle, Frederick 786
Brade, Marius 3006
Bradford, DanaKai 910, 2014
Brady, Erin L. 621, 1100
Braley, Sean 770
Brander, Fran 1781
Brandt, Eva 3331
Brandt, Joel 3232
Branham, Stacy M. 2034, 3387
Braude, David A. 3643
Brawner, Stephen 3227
Bresin, Roberto 1092
Bresson, Jean 3671
Brewer, Robin 2246, 5529
Brewster, Stephen A. 1670, 1744, 1779, 2319, 4401, 4838
Briggs, Pam 2920, 3379, 3566
Britton, Lauren M. 2882
Brock, Anke 445
Brockmeyer, Eric 5885
Brönmark, Jonas 680
Brooks, Christopher 2693
Brooks, Conner 1729
Broth, Mathias 4921
Brown, Andy 2766
Brown, Barry 852, 1632, 2933, 5456
Brown, Deana 321
Brown, Hans-Frederick 5350
Brown, Quincy 1921
Brown, Richard 3820
Brownbridge, Carly 1398
Broy, Nora 509, 961
Brubaker, Jed R. 2895, 2908
Brucker-Cohen, Jonah 3824
Bruckman, Amy S. 2574
Brule, Emeline 445
Brumby, Duncan P. 1028, 3311
Brunskill, Emma 2623, 4142
Bruun, Anders 3975
Bryan-Kinns, Nick 313, 1055, 3477
Bryant, Kimberly 3909
Bubel, Mark 68
Buehler, Erin 1100
Bueno, Andre de Oliveira 198
Buie, Elizabeth 1367
Bulling, Andreas 1379, 1519, 2156, 3299
Burg, Christine 3181
Burggraaff, Jessica 261
Burkhardt, Hugh 1159
Burleson, Winslow 919
Burmester, Michael 3013
Burnett, Margaret M. 1104, 1449, 2586, 3509
Burnside, James 2655
Burrows, Alison 1526, 3584
Burstyn, Jesse 3649, 3675
Burtner, Russ 955
Buruk, Oğuz Turan 3944, 3655
Busch, Marc 1835
Buschek, Daniel 1344, 1349, 2041, 3736
Büschel, Lukas 2570
Büschel, Wolfgang 2592
Butler, Crystal 2798
Butscher, Simon 4634
Butt, Asad Imtiaz 3263
Buttlar, Benjamin 3007
Butz, Andreas 309, 3234
Buxton, William 2869
Buzali, Tofi 248
C, Varun Perumal 5765
Cai, Carrie J. 3143, 3500
Caine, Kelly 981
Cairns, Paul 1088
Callison-Burch, Vanessa 2908
Calvi, Licia 3347
Calvo, Rafael A. 988, 3438
Camci, Anil 3827
Cameron, David 1597
Camurri, Antonio 1629
Canat, Mert 3655, 3944
Canfield, Kramer 3084
Cao, Sabina 648
Cao, Yang 2640
Cao, Yiqun 598
Cao, Yu 3255

Čapkun, Srdjan 540
Capra, Licia 1608
Capra, Robert 3508
Caramiaux, Baptiste 3428, 3558
Caraway, Monica 1109
Carcedo, Marta G. 3572
Cardona-Rivera, Rogelio E. 3438
Cardonha, Carlos Henrique 2171
Carey, Lisa 4477
Carlson, Jennifer Lee 755
Carlsson, Isabella 3877
Carpendale, Sheelagh 3670
Carrascal, Juan Pablo..... 2726, 3649, 3762, 3781
Carroll, Alexander K. 710
Carroll, John (Jack) 1047
Carroll, John M. 1644, 3919
Carter, Elizabeth J. 140, 5885
Carter, Marcus 3355, 3415
Carvalho, Lucila 2062
Casiez, Géry 4250
Castaneda, Lisa M. 3473
Castellucci, Steven J. 996
Castet, Julien 2283
Catala, Alejandro 2474
Cater, Kirsten 2020
Caton, Simon 3400, 3536
Cauchard, Jessica R. 3261
Causegic, Haris 3114
Cazes, Marjolaine 14
Cecchinato, Marta E. 1200, 1389
Cen, Keting 1745
Centivany, Alissa 1126
Cesar, Pablo 959
Chacholiades, Christos 2661
Chalmers, Matthew 284, 1904
Chamberlain, Alan 1163, 3651
Chan, Christine 1757
Chan, Edwin 3403
Chan, Joel 2717
Chan, Liwei 1526
Chan, Rosanna Yuen-Yan 1533
Chan, Stephen C. F. 5169
Chancellor, Stevie 1157, 2111
Chandra, Priyank 372
Chandramouli, Badrish 5433
Chandwani, Rajesh 3091
Chang, Daphne 587
Chang, Joseph 2258
Chang, Joseph Chee 3180
Chang, Kerry Shih-Ping 2497
Chang, Remco 5372
Chang, Shanton 1798
Chapuis, Olivier 2075, 2829
Charness, Neil 1131
Chatterjee, Shre Kumar 1476
Chatting, David 685, 2474
Chattopadhyay, Debaleena 2027, 2487
Chaudhry, Beenish M. 5645
Chavaillaz, Alain 4828
Cheema, Salman 1159
Chen, Binbin 4647
Chen, Bing-Yu 8, 1526, 4228, 4233
Chen, Chia-Yu 152, 3272
Chen, Dennis 4309
Chen, Fang 2808, 3035
Chen, Guanling 2821, 3247, 3255
Chen, I-Chun 3867
Chen, Jenn 3335
Chen, Jiawei 1644
Chen, Kevin 4098
Chen, Ke-Yu 1504
Chen, Mei-Ling 1615
Chen, Min 1
Chen, Mu-Tsz 20
Chen, Stephanie 3167
Chen, Te-Yuan 156
Chen, Wei 3792
Chen, Weixuan 'Vincent' 2134
Chen, Xi 1533
Chen, Xiang 'Anthony' 5909
Chen, Xu 781
Chen, Yan 3192
Chen, Yen-Yu 3272
Chen, Yineng 1760
Chen, Yue 20
Cheng, Bernard 3781
Cheng, Chin-Yi 13, 5743, 5753
Cheng, Janette L. 3261
Cheng, Jinghui 2038, 3021, 3659
Cheng, Tony 2072
Cheng, Waikuen 3883
Cheok, Adrian D. 3285
Cherek, Christian 3522
Cherng, Fu-Yin 2185, 4378
Cherston, Juliana 1647
Cheshire, Coye 1669, 3204
Chevalier, Fanny 248, 4587, 5003
Cheverst, Keith 2490, 3574
Cheyer, Adam 1032
Chi, Ed H. 3335
Chi, Pei-Yu (Peggy) 5482
Chia, Shue Ching 1295
Chiang, Yih-Harn 20
Chiauzzi, Emil 2178
Chien, Wei-Chi 1375
Chilana, Parmit K. 384, 1462
Chisik, Yoram 1127
Chiu, Justin 1563
Cho, Juhee 2563
Cho, Jun-Dong 2563
Choe, Eun Kyoung 272
Choi, Jeanie 3877
Choi, Koeun 4658
Choi, Seungwoo 998, 1165
Choi, Woohyeok 1692
Choi, Younggeun 3774
Chong Loo, Elena 420
Chorianopoulos, Konstantinos 1872
Chorley, Martin 3400
Chou, Kuan-Ting 156
Chou, Po-Lin 44
Chouchane, Amir 3227
Chourasia, Priyesh 745
Christensen, Kurtis C. 164
Christin, Nicolas 527, 3748
Chu, Hao-Hua 5704
Chu, Sharon Lynn 2782
Chua, Soon Hau 3572
Chun, Matthew 3248
Chung, Yi-Ju 3272
Church, Karen 1893
Churchill, Elizabeth 3408, 3566
Churchill, Robyn 2612
Cila, Nazli 889, 3091
Ciolfi, Luigina 3363
Claes, Sandy 5824
Clark, Gradeigh D. 1656, 3722
Clark, Joshua 4337
Clark, Sean M. 3477, 3663, 3885
Clarke, Jenny 1681
Clarke, Rachel 4968
Clawson, James 3309, 3469
Clear, Adrian K. 3581
Clegg, Eileen 952
Clegg, Tamara 3607
Clinch, Sarah 2872, 2947, 4793
Cockburn, Andy 4005, 4663, 4687, 5608
Cockton, Gilbert 1020
Cohen, Phil 1032
Coldham, George 738
Cole, Sara 786
Coles, Tim 2014
Colley, Ashley 2490, 3574
Colley, James A. 4061, 5933
Colter, Aubrey 2425
Colucci, Lucas 2141, 3020
Coman, Alina 2947
Comber, Rob 26, 1810, 2599, 2958, 3516, 3625, 3635, 5015
Conejo-Toledo, Andrea 4872
Coninx, Karin 2192
Connelly, Kay 804, 5645
Conner, Caleb 3028
Connolly, Philip 1415
Consolvo, Sunny 5921
Contractor, Noshir 5360
Conway, Dan 3035
Cook, Kristin 955
Cooper, Emily A. 1211
Cooper, Seth 2348
Čopič Pucihar, Klen 1842, 1849
Coppers, Sven 487
Coppersmith, Glen 2098
Cordeiro, Felicia 5632
Corenthy, Loic 3446
Corley, Courtney D. 1215
Cornejo, Raymundo 5311
Corno, Fulvio 1654
Coros, Stelian 3431
Correia, Nuno N. 899, 1055
Corsten, Christian 3062
Cosley, Dan 2271
Costanza, Enrico 4061, 4908, 5262, 5933
Coulton, Paul .. 375, 583, 1383, 1842, 1849, 4032
Counts, Jared 2764
Counts, Scott 3378

Courtemanche, François 1980, 4850
Coutrix, Céline 3793
Cowan, Benjamin R. 2805
Cox, Anna L. 1028, 1088, 1385, 1389, 2774, 2932, 3311
Cox, Jasmine 5874
Coyle, David 3584
Crabtree, Andy 5933
Craddock, Ian 1526
Craig, Brittany 1921
Crandall, David 4309
Cranor, Lorrie Faith 101, 527, 1047, 3748
Cranshaw, Justin 4722
Cremonesi, Paolo 1540, 2257
Crivellaro, Clara 1073, 1096, 2958
Culbertson, Gabriel 957
Czerwinski, Mary 1717, 1739, 3699
Dachselt, Raimund 1713, 2592
Dahl, Yngve 3079
Dahlinger, André 2813
Dai, Guozhong 1760
Daiber, Florian 1097, 1998
Dalal, Nishtha H. 98
d'Alessandro, Nicolas 3558
Dalsgaard, Peter 2562, 4435, 4991
Dalton, Nicholas S. 365
Dang, Steven 2717
D'Angelo, Sarah 2492
Daniel, Maxime 2283
Daniele, Antonio 3831
Daniels, Jena 2348
Darbar, Rajkumar 2431
Darch, Peter T. 1585
Darzentas, Dimitrios 1163, 3651
Das, Juthika 1921
Das, Sauvik 598
Dasgupta, Sayamindu 1486
Daughtry, John 849
Davies, Edward 2609
Davies, Nigel 2872, 2947, 4793
Davis, Hilary 3387
Davis, Jasmine 661
Davis, Pryce 1828
Davivongsa, Patlapa 2425
Day, Margot 3211
Dcosta, Malcolm 1483, 5665
De Angeli, Antonella 4622
De Araujo, Bruno 4587
De Choudhury, Munmun 1157, 2098, 2111, 3906
de Freitas, Adrian A. 3834, 5909
de Juan, Paloma 575
De la Cruz Pineda, J. Andrés 762
De Luca, Alexander 1349, 3736, 4320, 4806, 4823
De Russis, Luigi 1654
de Souza, Cleidson R. B. 3204
de Souza, Paulo 2057
de Vries, Roelof A. J. 297
De Weyer, Tom 2192
de Wit, Jan 1250
Dearden, Andy 3620
Deber, Jonathan 2857
Degraen, Donald 487, 2744
Deka, Biplab 2383
Delalonde, Charles 1308
DeLappe, Joseph 3812
Deldjoo, Yashar 1540
DeLine, Robert 5433
Dell, Nicola 2220, 3620
Demajo, Tom 3812
Demeyer, Serge 1272
den Broeder, Lea 889
Denis, Grégoire 445
Denman, Pete 1445
Densmore, Melissa 3620
Depping, Ansgar E. 3462
Derthick, Katie 4423
Desjardins, Audrey 2549
Desjardins, Audrey 5274
Deterding, Sebastian 3931
Devendorf, Laura 3431, 6028
Devries, Richard 5228
Dey, Anind K. 248, 1591, 1644, 1915, 3847, 4413, 5494, 5909
Dezfuli, Niloofar 2617, 2688
Dhareshwar, Anupama 5063
Dhenki, Suprabho 56
Di Cuia, Danilo 26
Di Rienzo, Antonella 2257
Diakopoulos, Nicholas 1114
Diamond, Sara 3695
Diaz-Tula, Antonio 3533
Dickerson, Robert F. 5126
Dickson, Gary 4056
Diefenbach, Sarah 3234
Dierk, Christine 1338
D'Ignazio, Catherine 2612
Dill, Katie 1043
DiMicco, Joan Morris 872
Dimitrov, Hristo 2667
Dimond, Jill P. 2635, 3293
Dinakar, Karthik 2134, 3438
Dindler, Christian 984
Ding, Xiang 2821, 3247
Ding, Xianghua (Sharon) 3532
Dingler, Tilman 1459, 4793
Dinneen, Jesse David 3508
DiSalvo, Betsy 623, 4459
DiSalvo, Carl 827, 2970, 3516, 4979
Divinsky, Anna 1315
D'Mello, Sidney 1661
Do, Ellen Yi-Luen 3395
Dobbelstein, David 203, 2439, 3679
Dobrev, Dobromir 4838
Doeweling, Sebastian 1598
Dogangün, Aysegül 1637
Dolejšová, Markéta 436
Dombrowski, Lynn 1256, 2895, 3293
Domin, Christian 1173
Domínguez, Ignacio X. 3438
Domova, Veronika 680
Dong, Lan-Xi 3695
Dorin, Camila 3042
Döring, Tanja 2446
Dorn, Jonas F. 261
Doroudi, Shayan 2623
Dorr, Michael 2681
Doryab, Afsaneh 609, 1644
Doshi, Prachi 2141
Dosono, Bryan 2882
Dove, Andrew 3498
Dove, Laura 880
Dow, Andy 3625
Dow, P. Alex 564
Dow, Steven P. 1243, 2717, 3834
Downs, John 3415
Doyle, Judith 3835
Drachen, Anders 3597
Dragicevic, Pierre 596, 1081
Dray, Susan M. 1047, 3620
Dredze, Mark 2098
Drossaert, Constance H. C. 297
Druin, Allison 3595
D'Souza, Marcus 261
Du, Fan 2217
Du, Ruofei 2454
Duan, Jun 1497
Duarte, Carlos 899
Dublon, Gershon 5753
Ducasse, Julie 2186
Duente, Tim 3758
Dugan, Casey 3061
Duggal, Mona 343
Duh, Henry 3395
Duke, Jon 2027
Dulake, Nick 1033
Dumas, Cedric 2014
Dunlop, Mark 1131, 3469
Dunn, Elizabeth W. 1011
Dunne, Robert 1827
Dunnigan, Anthony 1577
Dunphy, Paul 4464
Dupont, Rémi 14
Dupree, Janna Lynn 5228
Durham, Lenitra 1445
Durie, Steve 3839
Durrani, Haris 2299
Durrant, Abigail C. 2819
Dutoit, Thierry 1548
Duyan, Yalçın 1538
Duysburgh, Pieter 3331, 3484
Dworman, Garett 840
Dzodom, Gabriel 1857
Eady, Alexander Keith 2482
Easley, William 2034
Ebbinghaus, Sigrid 4320
Ebert, Achim 1222, 2292
Ebert, David 5409
Echtler, Florian 1374, 3796
Ede, Meghan 840
Edge, Darren 1692
Edmonds, Ernest 3477, 3663
Edwards, Isabelle 360
Effner, Troy 1063
Efrat, Tamara Anna 5984

Egelman, Serge 4806, 4823, 5257
Eiband, Malin 2041
Eichmann, Philipp 2362, 3049
Eickhoff, David 3970
Ekbia, Hamid 1822, 4997
El Ali, Abdallah 2049
El Kaliouby, Rana 1032
El Mimouni, Houda 473
Elahi, Mehdi 1540
Elarief, Noha 2586
Elblaus, Ludvig 265
Elgar, Ben 2655
Ellison, Nicole B. 89
Elmqvist, Niklas 1114, 5409
Elsden, Chris 685, 2819, 5015
Elwin, Albert 3812
Encinas, Enrique 387
Engelen, Lina 3211
Engelke, Ulrich 2057
Engeln, Lars 1713
Engels, Rutger C.M.E. 1945
England, David 3477
Engström, Arvid 2933
Epp, Felix 1288
Epstein, Daniel A. 673, 1109, 5632
Epstein, David H. 4489
Erete, Sheena 1180
Erich, Floris 3851
Erkut, Cumhur 560
Ernst, Matthew 2088, 2097
Escalona, Francisco 2264
Escobar, Dariela 1720
Eslami, Motahhare 2371
Evans, Adam 4447
Evans, Michael 475, 2766, 5874
Evans, Susan 165
Everitt, Aluna 2778
Evers, Vanessa 297
Exe, Nicole L. 2314
Exposito, Marc 2462
Ezaiza, Hafez 1222
Faes, Axel 168, 2744
Fagerlin, Angela 2314
Fagerlund, Janina 1007
Faiola, Anthony 4502
Fakourfar, Omid 1548
Faloutsos, Petros 2119
Fan, Mingyue 1187
Fanello, Sean 5138
Fardeen, Sarah 2992
Farnsworth, Carol 1077, 1115
Farve, Niaja 2134, 2467
Farzan, Rosta 3061
Fast, Ethan 237, 4647
Faucett, Heather 1256
Favory, Xavier 3671
Feary, Michael 1069
Fei-Fei, Li 3167
Feijs, Loe M.G. 1794
Feiner, Steven 3731, 5114
Feinstein, Carl 2348
Feit, Anna Maria 4262
Fekety, Drea K. 5776
Feld, Yannick 2049
Felix, Cristian 3659
Fellion, Nicholas 2482
Fels, Sidney 965
Feltwell, Tom 3339
Feng, Catherine 4896
Feng, Wenxin 1952
Fernaeus, Ylva 5970
Fernando, Piyum 2064
Ferrario, Maria Angela 1270
Ferreira, Denzil 1869, 4711
Ferreira, Pedro 840
Ferreira, Renato Pina 3204
Ferreira, Vinicius 1362
Fetter, Mirko 1193
Fiebrink, Rebecca 3558
Fiesler, Casey 2574
Figueira Filho, Fernando 3204
Findlater, Leah 4884
Finn, Kate 1011
Finnegan, Daniel J. 200
Fischer, Joel E. 5933
Fisher, Danyel 5433
Fisher, Karen E. 859
Fitzmaurice, George ... 6, 409, 908, 4599, 5421, 5996
Fitzpatrick, Geraldine 2474
Fitz-Randolph, Marcy 2178
Fjeld, Morten 2447, 3572
Flack, Robert 3335
Flanagan, Mary 2773, 4122
Flatla, David R. 2693, 5191
Fleck, Mathias 3056
Fleck, Rowanne 2923
Flores, Huber 1869
Flores Cano, Cesar 2661
Florez, Omar 1445
Foehrenbach, Stephanie 973
Fogarty, James 1109, 5632, 5658
Follmer, Sean 1607, 2764, 3706
Folmer, Eelke 1250
Foong, Pin Sym 1016
Forlines, Clifton 2857
Forlizzi, Jodi 3301, 4142
Forshaw, Stephen 1270
Forte, Andrea 3906
Fox, Sarah 1426, 3293
Françoise, Jules 2829, 3667
Fraser, C. Ailie 458
Fraser, Mike 2332, 4734
Frauenberger, Christopher 130, 341, 3373
Fredette, Marc 1980, 4850
Freeman, Euan 1670, 2319
Freeman, Guo 4325
French, Fiona 3355, 3355
Frey, Jérémy 1865, 2283
Frick, Lennart 2601
Friedberg, Earl 1312
Friedman, Batya 4423
Friedrich, Kai 1706
Friedrichs, Thomas 2285
Frigo, Alberto 541
Frishberg, Leo 1024
Frisson, Christian 1548
Froehlich, Jon E. 1757, 2072
Fröhlich, Peter 1835
Fromm, Josh 5675, 5885
Fu, Wai-Tat 3352, 4538
Fuchsberger, Verena 3550
Fujiwara, Kazuki 104
Fukuhara, Shiho 4216, 6028
Fukushima, Shogo 1322
Funk, Mathias 1794
Furr-Holden, C. Debra 4489
Furuyama, Yoshikazu 1980
Fussell, Susan R. 1038, 3363
Gajos, Krzysztof Z. 944, 2635, 4098
Galbraith, Caroline 2034
Gallacher, Sarah 1608
Gamberini, Luciano 4203
Gambino, Andrew 2837
Gannon, Derek 2805
Gannon, Madeline 3431, 5996
Gao, Fengqiang 433
Gao, Wei 897
Gao, Xianyi 1656
Gao, Yang 3255
Gao, Yanjun 2081
Garbett, Andrew 26, 685
Garcia, Jérémie 3339, 3558, 3671
Garcia, Sarah E. 777, 1013
Garcia-Sanjuan, Fernando 2474
Gardner, Bruce 3839
Gardner, Henry 2295
Garimella, Venkata Rama Kiran 5543
Garrett, Tanner 571
Garzotto, Franca 1540, 1684, 2257
Gatti, Elia 1677
Gaver, William 1597, 3423
Gavrilo, Katerina 1250
Ge, Jun 2837
Gebhardt, Christoph 2508
Geerts, David 959
Gellersen, Hans 2845
Gelsomini, Mirko 1684
Gelsthorpe, David 1827
Genç, Çağlar 1538
Georges, Vanessa 4850
Georgi, Marcus 3639
Gerber, Elizabeth M. 3500
Gerber, Lukas C. 1000
Gerding, Enrico H. 2012
Gergle, Darren 2492
Gerling, Kathrin M. 4447, 5595
Gerritsen, David B. 1187
Geyer, Werner 3061
Ghassemian, Shaghayegh 4423
Ghattas, Hala 331
Ghazali, Masitah 3395
Ghazinejad, Ali 1822
Ghosh, Ishita 355
Ghosh, Sanjay 768
Ghosh, Sarthak 2640

Giaccardi, Elisa ... 3347
Gibbs, Martin ... 3956
Gibson, Madeleine C. ... 5104
Gilardi, Marco ... 1398, 1677
Gilbert, Stephen ... 2864
Gill, Brian ... 4423
Gillies, Marco ... 3558
Gilutz, Shuli ... 927
Ginige, Athula ... 2234
Giordano, Richard ... 3066
Girotto, Victor ... 919
Girouard, Audrey ... 2088, 2097, 2482, 3461
Glass, Brian ... 3870
Gleason, Cole ... 621
Glicksman, David ... 3871
Glöss, Mareike ... 1632
Glover, Kevin ... 1163, 3651
Glueck, Michael ... 5003, 5421
Glushko, Bobby ... 1126
Go, Kentaro ... 3190
Gobbo, Daniela ... 647
Goel, Mayank ... 5675
Goggins, Sean ... 3559
Goguey, Alix ... 4250
Goh, Joslin ... 4098
Göksun, Tilbe ... 3944
Gold, Nicolas E. ... 5698
Goldfarb, Steven ... 1647
Goldstein, Daniel G. ... 2729
Goldstein, Jonathan ... 5433
Gollakota, Shyamnath ... 1515
Golsteijn, Connie ... 1608
Gombač, Leo ... 1849
Gomer, Richard C. ... 2012
Gomes, Antonio ... 770, 3492
Gomez, Randy ... 3612
Goncalves, Jorge ... 1869, 4711
Gong, Nan-Wei ... 4216, 6028
Gontarek, Sarah ... 4000
Gonzalez, Dario C. ... 164
Gooberman-Hill, Rachael ... 3584
Gooch, Daniel ... 969, 2105
Good, David A. ... 2886
Good, Judith ... 3373
Good, Nathaniel ... 3415
Goodyear, Peter ... 2062
Gopalakrishnakone, Ponnampalam ... 3285
Gordon, Eric ... 1096
Gordon, Mitchell ... 3817
Gorinova, Maria I. ... 2533
Gorm, Nanna ... 4315
Gotsch, Daniel ... 3675
Gotsis, Marientina ... 1945
Gould, Sandy J. J. ... 1028, 1385, 1389, 3311
Goyal, Nitesh ... 2447
Gradinar, Adrian ... 1270, 1383
Gradmann, Michael ... 2844
Graham, T.C. Nicholas ... 2681
Grandhi, Sukeshini A. ... 1337
Granic, Isabela ... 1945, 1989
Gray, Colin M. ... 328, 4044
Grbac, Jan ... 1849
Green, David P. ... 11, 3379
Green, George ... 5874
Green, Jeremy ... 2751
Green, Keith E. ... 1407
Greenhalgh, Chris ... 1163, 3651
Greuter, Stefan ... 3122
Grierson, Mick ... 1781
Grinberg, Nir ... 564
Grinter, Rebecca E. ... 321, 3620
Groeger, Daniel ... 420
Groen, Maarten ... 889
Groh, Rainer ... 3006
Grønbæk, Jens Emil ... 791
Grønbæk, Kaj ... 152
Gross, Harriet ... 2920
Gross, Mark ... 2504, 3683
Gross, Tom ... 1193, 2844, 3069
Grossauer, Eva-Maria Beatrix ... 5849
Grossman, Tovi ... 6, 90, 409, 4599, 4610, 4663, 5421, 5996
Grow, April ... 285
Gruning, Jane ... 208, 1176
Gu, Heng ... 1459
Gu, Xiaochi ... 1991
Gu, Yu ... 5126
Guan, Dongdong ... 433
Guczka, Sascha R. ... 3115
Guerra-Gomez, John Alexis ... 113, 5710
Gugenheimer, Jan ... 1996, 3679
Guha, Mona Leigh ... 3595
Guha, Shion ... 1081
Guimbretière, François ... 887
Guinness, Darren ... 2519
Güldenpfennig, Florian ... 728
Gullstrom, Charlie ... 269
Gulotta, Rebecca ... 1187
Günther, Sebastian ... 2617
Guo, Anhong ... 621, 3834
Guo, Jiayi ... 20
Guo, Jingru ... 1563
Guo, Jinlong ... 3219
Guo, Philip J. ... 1462
Guo, Shitao Stan ... 1510
Gupta, Aakar ... 59, 3683
Gupta, Neha ... 3604
Gupta, Shreya ... 50
Gupta, Siddharth ... 796
Gupta, Surabhi ... 2014
Gurevich, Michael D. ... 3339
Guthals, Sarah ... 3909
Gutierrez, Francisco J. ... 2112
Gutwin, Carl ... 3462, 4663, 4687, 5608, 5836
Guy, Amy ... 552
Guy, Ido ... 3025
Guydish, Andrew ... 1729
Ha, Byeongwon ... 3843
Haag, Maren ... 4017
Haas, Gabriel ... 1996, 3679
Haber, Nick ... 2348
Habib, Hana ... 101
Hachet, Martin ... 2283
Hachisu, Taku ... 1282
Haddad, Donald Derek ... 2425
Haescher, Marian ... 2209
Haeuser, Hendrik ... 11, 2832, 3800
Haeuslschmid, Renate ... 5076
Hagen, Kristoffer ... 1872
Haghighi, Mo ... 1526
Hagiya, Toshiyuki ... 733
Hahn, Nathan ... 2258, 3180
Hahnloser, Richard H. R. ... 5812
Hailpern, Joshua ... 3324
Haimson, Oliver L. ... 2895, 3906
Haines, Robert ... 2766
Håkansson, Maria ... 3581
Hakizimana, Jean ... 4423
Häkkilä, Jonna ... 2490, 3574
Haldar, Shefali ... 3103
Hale, Scott A. ... 1208
Halfaker, Aaron ... 13
Hall, Andrew ... 13
Hall, Brian D. ... 110
Hall, Kyle Wm. ... 3670
Hall, Margeret ... 3400, 3536
Hall Jr., Phillip ... 1921
Haller, Michael ... 3754, 5138, 5849
Halskov, Kim ... 791, 984, 2562, 4435
Halvey, Martin ... 4401
Hämäläinen, Perttu ... 758
Hamdan, Nur Al-huda ... 2497, 3062
Hamilton, Keith ... 2751
Hamilton, Kevin ... 2371
Hamilton, William ... 213
Hamilton-Fletcher, Giles ... 2162
Hammerla, Nils Y. ... 11, 2832, 3800
Hammond, Laura M. ... 777, 1013
Han, Gyeol ... 6058
Han, Kyungsik ... 1215
Hancock, Jeff ... 3857
Hancock, Mark ... 3, 1968, 3647
Handberg, Leif ... 269
Hanenberg, Stefan ... 1104
Hankerson, David ... 473
Hanneton, Sylvain ... 2829
Hanrahan, Benjamin V. ... 1644
Hänsch, Norman ... 3870
Hansen, Derek L. ... 3317
Hanson, Erica ... 3395
Hanssen, Geir Kjetil ... 3079
Hansson, Karin ... 3604
Hantrakul, Lamtharn Hanoi ... 12
Hara, Kotaro ... 1757
Harbach, Marian ... 4806, 4823, 5257
Hardy, Jean ... 610
Harman, Alex ... 2667
Haroz, Steve ... 1081
Harper, Richard ... 4781
Harper, Simon ... 317, 2766
Harrell, D. Fox ... 1896, 1906
Harriman, Jiffer ... 2504, 3683
Harris, Helen ... 3335
Harris, Jeffrey ... 1769
Harris, Owen ... 1989
Harrison, Chris ... 1491

Harrison, Daniel 2932
Harrison, Lane 5372
Hartmann, Björn 1607, 5482
Hartmann, Fabian 3736
Hartmann, Johannes 3796
Hasegawa, Satoshi 3238
Hasholzner, Regina 2156
Hasselqvist, Hanna 1300
Hassenzahl, Marc 1375, 2999
Hassib, Mariam 1415, 1570, 2156
Hata, Kenji 3167
Hauenstein, Mark 1597
Hawkey, Kirstie 1362
Hawkins, Dan 931
Haworth, Brandon 2119
Hayasaki, Yoshio 3238
Hayes, Gillian R. 1256, 2895, 4872
Hayes, Kate 313
Hayward, Vincent 3808
Hazzard, Adrian 1163, 2669, 3651
He, Liang 2072, 2454
He, Yan 4533
Healer, Sam 2655
Hearst, Marti A. 5028
Hecht, Brent 13, 515, 2442
Heeffer, Caspar 1359
Heffernan, Kayla J. 1798
Heibeck, Felix 5753
Heidbrink, Scott 4298
Heintz, Matthias 3975
Hekler, Eric B. 2178, 3988, 4521
Heldstab, Christian 973
Heller, Florian 1067, 2497
Heloir, Alexis 3558
Hendley, Robert J. 1021, 2923, 2984
Hendriks, Niels 3331
Hengeveld, Bart 2549
Henneman, Richard L. 1111
Hennig, Shannon 3643
Henrich, Dominik 2844
Henrikson, Rorik 4587
Henry Riche, Nathalie 3670
Henze, Niels 509, 1706, 2576, 4793
Henzler, Philipp 2439
Heo, Seongkook 2869
Hepp, Benjamin 2508, 3806
Hernandez, Javier 4000
Herr, Sascha 2844, 3069
Herring, Susan C. 1038
Herrmanny, Katja 1637
Hesselgren, Mia 1300
Hettiarachchi, Anuruddha 1957
Heun, Valentin 4
Heuten, Wilko 2049, 2285, 3738
Hewapathirana, Roshan 2234
Hewett, Rattikorn 2306
Heyden, Klaus 4828
Heyer, Clint 3126
Hicks, Catherine M. 458
Hicks, Kieran 4447
Hicks, William S. 1691
Hieda, Naoto 3835
Higuch, Keita 5180
Hill, Alexander 2655
Hill, Benjamin Mako 1152, 1486
Hill, Charles 2586, 3509
Hill, Ewan 1647
Hill, Jennifer 3076
Hille, Diana 2879
Hilliges, Otmar 2508, 3806, 5040
Hillman, Serena 1879
Hiltz, Starr Roxanne 2430
Hinckley, Ken 2869
Hinder, Heidi 2020
Hiniker, Alexis 648, 4743
Hinrichs, Uta 1833, 4634
Hinsberger, Hayley 125
Hoare, Michaela 1163, 3651
Hodges, Steve 11, 2832, 3800
Hodgins, Jessica K. 140
Hödl, Oliver 728
Hofman, Jake M. 2729
Hofmann, Megan 1769
Hogan, Bernie 5360
Hoggan, Eve 3446
Hohenstein, Jess 3034
Holden, Amey 343
Holla, Akshay 1921
Holland, Simon 3339
Hollis, Victoria 1729
Holroyd, Patrick 1398
Holsti, Leo 758
Holtzblatt, Karen 1063, 1077
Holz, Christian 2869, 3761
Homewood, Sarah 273
Hong, Hwajung 4538
Hong, Matt H. Y. 1691
Hong, Matthew K. 5337
Hong, Sungsoo (Ray) 4746
Hong, Yidi 5
Hook, Jonathan 11, 2832, 3800
Höök, Kristina 305, 840, 3131, 3301
Hope, Alexis 2512
Horiuchi, Toshiharu 733
Horn, Michael S. 1691, 1328
Hornbæk, Kasper 596, 2050, 2726, 2740, 2752, 3767, 4509, 4956, 5862
Horvitz, Eric 1032, 2523
Horwege, Sebastian 2601
Hoshi, Takayuki 3238
Hosio, Simo 1869, 4711
Hou, Hsincheng 156
Houben, Steven 1608, 3366
Hourcade, Juan Pablo 1123, 1127
Houston, Lara 1403
Hovsepian, Karen 4489
Howell, Noura 6028
Hsiao, Dun-Yu 2348
Hsiao, Hsu-Fu 3241
Hsieh, Gary 1084, 3020, 5632
Hsieh, Yi-Ta 4203
Hsu, Anne 470
Hsu, Jane Yung-jen 3715
Hsu, Ting-Ying 38
Hu, Jun 1794
Hu, Yunqi 5
Huang, Da-Yuan 1526
Huang, Elaine May 5958
Huang, Jin 1760
Huang, Ke 3247
Huang, Michael Xuelin 5169
Huang, Ming-Chyi 5704
Huang, Ting-Hao Kenneth 1555
Huang, Xun-Yi 2185
Huang, Yitong 3049
Huber, Bernd 470
Huber, Jochen 2697
Huck, Jonny 1383
Hudin, Charles 2719, 3687
Hudson, Matthew 1886
Hudson, Nathaniel 384
Hudson, Scott E. 1769, 5885, 5897
Hudson-Smith, Andy 375
Huh, Jina 6040
Hui, Julie 218
Hullman, Jessica R. 38, 5092
Humă, Bogdana 487
Humayoun, Shah Rukh 1222
Hummels, Caroline 3301, 3691
Hung, Yi-Ping 1526, 3867
Hunsucker, Andrew J. 647
Hurley, Ursula 1415
Hurst, Amy 2034, 3453
Hurwitz, Barak 3042
Hurwitz, Lisa 5311
Hussain, Mustafa 2126
Hußmann, Heinrich 1947, 2041, 4320, 5034
Husu, Tuomas 1007
Hutson, Holly 2057
Hwang, Inseok 5126
Hyde, Jennifer 140
Iacovides, Ioanna 1389
Igarashi, Takeo 2520
Ihrke, Stephan 2592
Iida, Kazuki 1282
Ijiri, Takashi 3325
Ikeda, Kazushi 4111
Im, Hyejin 2851
Inkpen, Kori M. 4770
Inoue, Seki 1980
Introne, Joshua 3559
Ioannidis, Zac 2655
Iqbal, Shamsi T. . 1717, 1739, 2657, 3143, 3500
Irani, Lilly C. 1051, 1057, 3604, 4573
Irani, Pourang 498, 3612
Irannejad Bisafar, Farnaz 3620
Irwin, Germaine 1921
Isbister, Katherine 277, 1430, 2225, 3301
Ishak, Clarissa 931
Ishak, Edward W. 796
Ishii, Akira 2511
Ishii, Hiroshi ... 12, 13, 2425, 2764, , 5397, 5743, 5753
Iskander, Nancy 2087
Islam, MD Rasel 4238
Isley, Vicky 3847

Isokoski, Poika 1151, 1573
Israr, Ali 3285
Istance, Howell 2648
Ivanov, Vyacheslav D. 3144
Iversen, Ole Sejer 984, 1123, 4435
Iyer, Vikram 1515
Izadi, Shahram 5138
Jaccheri, Letizia 1872
Jack, Margaret 2209
Jackson, Daniel 2136
Jackson, Steven J. 1403, 2209
Jacob, Robert J. K. 3770, 5372
Jacovi, Michal 3025
Jacucci, Giulio 4203, 5789
Jaeger, Paul 4884
Jaen, Javier 1737, 2474
Jain, Dhruv 1563
Jakobsen, Mikkel R. 2050, 5862
Jalaliniya, Shahram 5801
James, Jobin Mathew 1151
Jamir, Limalemla 343
Jamison-Powell, Sue 2920
Jang, Gunmin 3774
Jang, Sungjune 3706
Janneck, Monique 3115
Janovica, Jelizaveta 26
Jansen, Bernard J. 1315, 2081
Jansen, Guido 889, 3091
Jansen, Yvonne 596
Janßen, Lukas 921
Janssens, Daan 1272
Janulis, Patrick 5360
Janzen, Izabelle 188
Jaques, Natasha 2134
Jarusriboonchai, Pradthana 4366
Jarvis, Nadine 1597
Jay, Caroline 1827, 2766
Jayaram Masti, Ramya 540
Jayaratne, Keisha 116
Jazbec, Maša 3851
Jeffries, Robin 1047
Jelen, Ben 804, 5645
Jenkins, Edward 26, 2945
Jenkins, Tom 827, 3423, 4979
Jeon, Jae Ho 272
Jeong, Hayeon 1165
Jeong, Yunwoo 9
Jernigan, Will 1449
Jetter, Hans-Christian 5470
Jewell, Michael O. 4061, 5933
Jezler, Olivia 1677
Jheng, Jyun-Fong 152
Ji, Sookyoung 5620
Jia, Haiyan 4286
Jia, Shuang 1533
Jia, Yuan 2001
Jiang, Lijun 4818
Jiang, Pei-Yu 3241
Jiang, Ruiwen 68
Jiang, Zhenhui 5715
Jin, Weina 172
Jitkoff, Nicholas 3335
Jofre, Ana 3695
Johanson, Colby 3450
Johns, Paul 1717, 1739, 3699
Johnson, Daniel 1930, 5583
Johnson, Ian G. 2945
Johnson, Isaac L. 13, 515
Johnson, Jeff 931, 1011, 3897
Johnson, Paula 2136
Johnson, Rose 1608
Johnston, Andrew 3339
Johnston, Chuck 1109
Jokinen, Jussi P. P. 4390
Jolly, Stephen 2766, 5874
Jones, Keith S. 2306
Jones, Matt 475, 969, 3793
Jones, Michael D. 876
Jones, Quentin 1337, 2430
Jones, Sara 3485
Jones, Simon L. 3099
Jones, William 571, 3508
Jonsson, Martin P. 305, 3131, 3301
Joshi, Ajjen 1952
Joshi, Raj 3572
Joshi, Varun 5
Jota, Ricardo 2857
Jouffrais, Christophe 445, 2186
Ju, Wendy 980, 3542
Jude, Alvin 2141, 2519
Jung, Eun Hwa 3107
Jung, Hyunggu 1644
Jung, Jiwon 2857
Jung, Malte 957
Just, Mike 5444
Jylhä, Antti 4203
Kaasinen, Eija 833
Kadar, Cristina 2148
Kafai, Yasmin B. 1473
Kaijanaho, Antti-Juhani 1104
Kaipio, Johanna 4129
Kairam, Sanjay 113
Kajastila, Raine 758
Kajimoto, Hiroyuki 281, 3717
Kaliouby, Rana el 3723
Kalnikaite, Vaiva 1729
Kalvani, Pranshu 527
Kalyn, Michael 4447
Kamal, Kapil Kant 745
Kamar, Ece 2623
Kaminski, Matthijs 168, 2744
Kamm, Christian P. 261
Kane, Shaun K. ..1100, 1934, 2034, 4884, 5506
Kang, Bumsoo 6040
Kang, Laewoo (Leo) 1403, 3855
Kang, Yunho 32
Kangas, Jari 1151
Kanis, Marije 2790, 3091
Kannuri, Nanda Kishore 343
Kao, Dominic 1896, 1906
Kao, Hsin-Liu (Cindy) 3699, 3703
Kapadia, Apu 4309
Kapadia, Mubbasir 2119
Kaptelinin, Victor 352
Karachiwala, Baneen 5063
Karagozler, M. Emre 6028
Karagozler, Mustafa Emre 4216
Karahalios, Karrie 2371, 4538
Karale, Ajinkya 56
Karanam, Saraschandra 5720
Karanam, Yamini 2001
Karat, Clare-Marie 1047
Karlsson, Anna 305
Karthikeyan Ranithangam, Akshaye Shreenithi Kirupa 5909
Kasahara, Shunichi 1561
Kashani, Salma 3248
Kato, Jun 3325
Kaufman, Geoff 2773, 4122
Kaul, Oliver Beren 2526, 2533
Kay, Alan 3910
Kay, Judy 2062, 2343, 3211
Kay, Matthew 1081, 4521, 5092
Kaye, Joseph 'Jofish' 113, 575, 4533, 5710
Kazakos, Konstantinos 343
Kazemitabaar, Majeed 2072
Kazi, Rubaiat Habib 6, 908, 4599
Keating, Shelby 1698
Keegan, Brian C. 4337, 4351
Keller, Sean 1504
Kelly, Kate 1781
Kelly, Norene 2864
Kelly, Ryan 2105, 3099
Kendall, Logan 3103, 5324
Kennedy, Jessie 3670
Kennedy, Lyndon 575
Kerber, Frederic 1813, 2332, 2540
Kerlin, Lianne 5874
Kerracher, Natalie 3670
Kerrigan, Finola 3379
Ketcheson, Mallory 2681
Kettunen, Marju 1007
Khairuddin, Irni Eliana 2872
Khajah, Mohammad M. 5571
Khaled, Rilla 969
Khalilbeigi, Mohammadreza 1598, 2617
Khamis, Mohamed 1415, 2156
Khan, Azam 5003
Khan, Hani 3084
Khan, Salman "Sal" 3906
Khan, Vassilis-Javed 1250
Khanipour Roshan, Parisa 623
Kharrufa, Ahmed 11, 2832, 3800
Khatri, Ashik 2249
Khayatkhoei, Mahyar 2119
Khelifi, Maher 3103
Khelifi, Maher 5324
Khot, Rohit Ashok 1119
Khurana, Rushil 4533
Khurelbaatar, Sugarragchaa 281, 3717
Khut, George 3301, 3859
Kiciman, Emre 2098
Kiefer, Tobias 2540
Kiene, Charles 1152
Kientz, Julie A. 165, 648, 3988, 4746
Kim, Byungmoon 2585

Kim, Chang Min 2555, 2673
Kim, Chul-Joo 2548
Kim, Da-jung 699
Kim, David 5138, 5958
Kim, Hanbit 2548
Kim, Han-Jong 213, 2307
Kim, Honesty 1000
Kim, Hwan 3694
Kim, Hyeong Cheol 2640
Kim, Hyunsoo 3774
Kim, Jaejeung 2165
Kim, Jennifer G. 4538
Kim, Jeong-Whun 5620
Kim, Ji Eun 2258
Kim, Jinhan 6040
Kim, Jinyoung 2837
Kim, Joohee 2563
Kim, Joohyun 1692, 4758
Kim, Jooyeon 4351
Kim, Juho 470
Kim, Ju-Whan 213, 2307
Kim, Juyoun 1229
Kim, KwonHyun 272
Kim, Kyung-Joong 1915
Kim, Lawrence H. 3706
Kim, Man-Je 1915
Kim, Min Kyung 62
Kim, Minhwan 3694
Kim, Nam Wook 2851
Kim, SeungHyun 2857
Kim, SeungJun 1591, 1915
Kim, Shin 1922
Kim, Soohee 2900
Kim, Sunjun 5151, 5163
Kim, Yea-Seul 38
Kim, Yongkwan 2548
Kim, Yoochan 1229
Kim, Yoojung 1280, 5620
Kim, Young-Ho 272
Kinder-Kurlanda, Katharina 1288
King, Jen 3415
King, Jung-Tai 4378
Kinneen, Justin 2805
Kinoshita, Yuichiro 3190
Kipling, Mathew 2136
Kirk, David S. 685, 1620, 2474, 2819, 3408, 5015
Kirk, Pedro 1781
Kirlik, Alex 2371
Kirst, Dominik 1519
Kitamura, Yoshifumi 3325
Kitsos, Christos 1904
Kittur, Aniket 598, 2258, 3180
Kizilcec, René F. 2390
Klaassen, Sebastian 700
Klarkowski, Madison 1930, 5583
Klemmer, Scott 458
Kljun, Matjaž 1842, 1849
Klokmose, Clemens Nylandsted 2538
Klokmose, Clemens 3366, 5470
Klooster, Sietske 3301
Knees, Peter 1352
Knibbe, Jarrod 4734
Knowles, Bran 3581
Knowles, Sarah 2124
Ko, Andrew J. 1449
Ko, Minsam 998, 1165
Ko, Yooyoung 62
Koch, Janin 1423
Kocksch, Laura 1288
Koedinger, Ken 4142
Koelemeijer, Dorien Neema 309
Kogan, Marina 2783
Koh, Eunyee 1583, 2585
Koh, Kyle 4658
Koh, Raymond K.C. 1937
Kohn, Josh 1973
Kohno, Tadayoshi 4746
Koike, Hideki 553
Kola, Tara 5092
Kolathumani, Radhika 5
Komogortsev, Oleg 1503
Kong, Danielle 3770
Kong, Ha Kyung 4538
Kong, Haixun 2241
Konrad, Robert 1211
Kontschieder, Peter 261
Kopp, Kristopher 1661
Korayem, Mohammed 4309
Korge, Andreas 3114
Korger, Christina 2570
Korn, Oliver 3114
Korsgaard, Henrik 3366
Kort, Joke 269
Korzetz, Mandy 2570
Kosch, Thomas 1570
Kosmalla, Felix 1097, 1998
Kostakos, Vassilis 1869, 2751, 4711
Kostiainen, Kari 540
Kothaneth, Shreya 635
Kothari, Neel 3263
Kou, Yubo 3883
Kouper, Inna 1822
Kovacs, Robert 2175
Kow, Yong Ming 3532, 3883
Koyama, Yuki 2520
Koźmiańska, Kamila 3707
Krämer, Jan-Peter 3232
Kratz, Sven 1577
Kraus, Kari 3317
Krause, Josua 3659, 5686
Krause, Markus 1173, 3536
Kraut, Robert E. 125, 598, 1243, 3899
Kravitz, Joshua 3167
Krebs, Bethany 3355
Krebs, Sebastian 1996
Kreutz, Kerstin 1067
Krischkowsky, Alina 3434
Krishna, Ranjay A. 3157
Kristensson, Per Ola 1991, 3459
Kristoffersson, Annica 1038
Krome, Sven 3122, 3542
Kröse, Ben 839
Krüger, Antonio ..1097, 1813, 1998, 2026, 2332
Krupka, Erin L. 587
Kry, Paul G. 3806
Kubo, Yuki 3852
Kucharski, Przemysław 2447
Kuenen, Stoffel 10
Kühn, Romina 2570
Kulesza, Todd 3558
Kulic, Dana 1092
Kulik, Lars 745
Kulkarni, Vaibhavi 3091
Kulshreshth, Arun 177
Kumagai, Kota 3238
Kumar, Janaki 1043, 1115
Kumar, Manish 745
Kumar, Mrinal 2098
Kumar, Neha 2220, 3620
Kumar, Ranjitha 2383, 3263
Kumar, Santosh 4489
Kumar, Saurabh 343
Kun, Andrew L. 961, 5776
Kunze, Kai 1257, 1459, 2321
Kuo, Han-Chih 8, 4228, 4233
Kurauchi, Andrew 1952
Kurbak, Ebru 3881
Kurilova, Darya 527
Kurowska, Magdalena 3707
Kuscher, Alexander 3335
Kushlev, Kostadin 1011
Kuttal, Sandeep Kaur 3509
Kuznetsov, Stacey 1786, 2064, 3516
Kwan, Irwin 880
Kwint, Sigrid 297
Kwok, Tiffany C. K. 5169
Kwon, Bum Chul 993
Kwon, Kyeong-An 1483
Laakso, Karri-Pekka 1007
Laaksolahti, Jarmo 840
Lääveri, Tinja 4129
Labonté-LeMoyne, Élise 1980
Ladha, Cassim 2136
Ladha, Karim 2136
Ladner, Richard 1100
Lafreniere, Benjamin 4663, 5608, 5836
Lahaye, Marcel 3062
Lai, Chien-Tung 1236
Laib, Magdalena 3013
Laiola Guimarães, Rodrigo 2171
Lalanne, Denis 3408
Lam, Michelle S. 2645
Lamas, David 2712
Lambdin, Charles 1024
Lambie, Alan 1510
Lampe, Cliff 89, 610, 5240
Lampinen, Airi 852, 1669, 2933, 3415, 5456
Landay, James A. 3261
Landwirth, Robert 3870
Lang, Johannes 3114
Lank, Edward 1312, 2087, 5228
Lankes, Michael 1835
Lantz, Vuokko 2319
Laput, Gierad 1491
Larson, Eric C. 5675

Lasecki, Walter S. 3192
Laskowski, Paul 5028
Latulipe, Celine 3477
LaViola Jr., Joseph J. 177, 1729
Law, Edith 4098
Law, Effie Lai-Chong 3975
Lawler Kennedy, Sally 1115
Lawo, Dennis 921
Lawson, Shaun 501, 2920, 3339
Lazar, Jonathan 933, 3901
Le, Huy Viet 2576, 4793
Le, Khanh 4238
Le Dantec, Christopher A. 827, 1096
Leavitt, Alex 4337
Lechelt, Zuzanna 26, 3711
Lecolinet, Eric 2075
Lee, Alexandra 2396
Lee, Bongshin 272, 993, 3558
Lee, Byungjoo 1857, 3863, 5203
Lee, Chao-Hui 5704
Lee, Christine H. 68
Lee, DoYoung 4238
Lee, Geehyuk 5151, 5163
Lee, Genehee 2563
Lee, Gun 1681
Lee, Hung-Chi 3715
Lee, Hyunjeong 5620
Lee, Ja Young 5104
Lee, Jihyun 2585
Lee, Jisoo 2178
Lee, Jiyun 3227
Lee, John D. 5104
Lee, Joongseek 5620
Lee, Jung Lin 6028
Lee, Kun-Lin 2141
Lee, Kun-Pyo 1922, 2857
Lee, Kwang-Jae 2563
Lee, Mankyung 2563
Lee, Min Kyung 1057
Lee, Nahyeon 2563
Lee, SangJeong 2548, 3173
Lee, Sangwook 32
Lee, Seunghyun "Tina" 4861
Lee, Soobin 3774
Lee, Sooyeon 1644
Lee, Taeyoung 1280
Lee, Tzu-I 20
Lee, Uichin .... 998, 1165, 1229, , 2165, 2857, 3173, 4758
Lee, Woohun 3694, 3746
Lee, Yeoreum 699
Lee, Yi-Chen 4378
Lee, YuKyoung 32
Lefelt, Todd 1043
Léger, Pierre-Majorique 1980, 4850
Leidinger, Cornelius 1813
Leigh, Darren 2857
Leigh, Sang-won 3719, 6053
Leister, Andreas 2688
Leitersdorf, Dean 1644
Leithinger, Daniel 2764
Lemmens, Ryanne 2192
Lennon, Marilyn 3461
Lenz, Tomt 3639
Leong, Hong Va 5169
Leong, Joanne 5849
Leshed, Gilly 2271
Lessel, Pascal 1813, 2026
Levine, Mark 3566
Lewkowicz, Myriam 3545
Li, Cheng-Yuan 5704
Li, Chengzhao 3462
Li, Hanchuan 7, 4933, 5885
Li, Jie 3129
Li, Jinhui 2961
Li, Junhui 80
Li, Liyuan 1295
Li, Sheng 26
Li, Simon Y. W. 1788
Li, Toby Jia-Jun 13
Li, Wenjuan 4818
Li, Xincheng 71
Li, Yang 5482
Li, Yiu 2667
Li, Zong-Yu 38
Liang, Jiajie 2141
Liang, Rong-Hao 8, 1526, 4228, 4233
Liao, Kerwell 5921
Liao, Q. Vera 3352
Liccardi, Ilaria 1, 2012
Liikkanen, Lassi A. 816
Lilija, Klemen 1705
Lim, Calvin 2279
Lim, Daniel 1607
Lim, Joo Hwee 1295
Lim, Youn-kyung 699, 2549
Lin, Feng 2038
Lin, Hung-Yeh 38
Lin, Jiaxin 3129
Lin, Kuan-Yu 1236
Lin, Long-Fei 4228
Lin, Veronica 655
Lin, Wen-Chieh 2185, 4378
Lin, Ya-Fang 5704
Lin, Yilun 13
Lin, Yin 2141
Lin, Yi-Tien 44
Lin, Yun-Ting 74
Lin, Zhiyuan (Jerry) 1157
Lindahl, Carina 4238
Lindlbauer, David 791, 1705
Lindley, Joseph G. 375, 583, 4032
Lindley, Siân 261, 1176, 2136
Lindqvist, Janne 1656, 3722
Lindsey, Robert V. 5571
Lindtner, Silvia 1051, 1390, 2233, 3550
Linehan, Conor 2669, 2920, 4447
Lingel, Jessica 815
Liou, Yu-Han 38
Lischke, Lars 1706, 2447
Littman, Michael L. 3227
Liu, Can 2075
Liu, Chenxi 285
Liu, Cynthia 156
Liu, Feng 2093
Liu, Leslie 3628
Liu, Shuai 1497
Liu, Yilin Elaine 4861
Liu, Yun-En 5571
Liu, Zhengjie 1047, 2999, 3620
Livingston, Ivy J. 944
Lo, I-Wen 44
Lo, Joanne 6028
Lo, Katherine 3293
Lobel, Adam 1945, 1989
Locascio, Joanne 4533
Löchtefeld, Markus 1097, 2332, 2540
Lodato, Thomas 827, 4979
Loitsch, Claudia 2879
Loke, Lian 3301
Loksa, Dastyni 1449
Lomas, J. Derek 4142
Lombrozo, Tania 470
Long, Elenore 1786, 3516
Lopes, Pedro 223, 944
Lotte, Fabien 2283
Lovell, Karina 2124
Lovell, Sarah T. 423
Löw, Christian 728
Lozano, Cecil 919
Lu, Di 3061
Lu, Nannan 2328
Lu, Yujia 1497
Luc, Annie 1921
Lucero, Andrés 3136, 3309
Lüdtke, Andreas 2285
Ludwig, Thomas 3604
Luger, Ewa 5286
Lugmayr, Artur 3395
Lukanov, Kristiyan 4011
Lukate, Johanna M. 2886
Lund, Arnold (Arnie) 1047
Lundberg, Jonas 1490
Lundgren Lyckvi, Sus 2808
Lundström, Anders 301
Luo, Chu 1869, 4711
Luo, He-Lin 3867
Luo, Qiong 409
Luo, Xu 1526
Lushaj, Valon 728
Lustig, Caitlin 1057
Lutchyn, Yuliya 1717
Lutton, Courtney 3822
Luyten, Kris 487, 2192, 2744
Lykourentzou, Ioanna 1243
Lyons, Michael J. 965
Ma, Haiwei 3784
Ma, Ruisha 2667
Ma, Wenjuan 4568
Ma, Xiao 3857
Ma, Xiaojuan 409, 5715
Macé, Marc J-M 2186
Machado, Daniel 5337
Macías Ruvalcaba, Fernando 762
Mackay, Wendy E. 397, 3339, 3558
MacKenzie, I. Scott 996

MacKenzie, Scott 3770
MacLean, Karon E. 3248
MacLeod, Haley 229, 804
Macvean, Andrew 849
Maddock, Jim 360
Madeira, Cheryl 2272
Madgwick, Seb 2609
Madjaroff, Galina 2200
Maes, Pattie .... 2, 4, 2134, , 3438, 3719, 6053
Mahmoud, Abdelrahman 3723
Mahoney, Jamie 3339
Mai, Jens-Erik 3400
Maior, Horia A. 4011
Makhaeva, Julia 130
Makino, Yasutoshi 1980
Malacria, Sylvain 1548, 5298
Malaka, Rainer 541, 5595
Malapaschas, Aris 4366
Maldonado Branco, Rita 3331
Malik, Sana 1583, 2217
Malkin, Nathan 4823
Malloch, Joseph W. 3339
Maly, Martin 849
Mamykina, Lena 2635, 3628
Manakhov, Pavel 3144
Mancini, Clara 3355
Mancini, Maurizio 1629
Mandryk, Regan L. 1088, 2982, 3007, 3450, 3462, 4562, 5595, 5608
Manikam, Subhashini Arcot 343
Manindla, Amarendar Reddy 343
Manja, Philip 2570
Mankoff, Jennifer 248, 285, 1100, 1769, 5897
Mann, Anne-Marie 1833
Mann, Nancy 872
Mann, Samuel 3581
Manojlovic, Stefan 1250
Mao, Mao 2886
Marcos, Mari-Carmen 3637
Marcu, Gabriela 3628
Mardanbegi, Diako 5801
Marforio, Claudio 540
Marinie, Celia 976
Mark, Gloria 1717, 1739, 3508, 4502, 5517
Markopoulos, Panos 1250, 3792
Markussen, Anders 5862
Marlow, Jennifer 1072
Marquardt, Nicolai 1092, 1608, 3309, 3366, 3453, 3711
Marques, Rodrigo 1563
Márquez Segura, Elena 6014
Marreiros, Helia 2012
Marroquin, Juan C. 2645
Marschner, Steve 887
Marsden, Nicola 4017
Marshall, Andrea R. 473
Marshall, Catherine 3508
Marshall, Joe 1119, 2669
Marshall, Justin 2945
Marshall, Mark T. 1033
Marshall, Matthew 1620
Marshall, Paul 152, 1028, 2774, 2906, 2932
Martelaro, Nikolas 980
Marti, Patrizia 3301
Martin, Charles 2295
Martin, Fiore 1055
Martin, Michael 2295
Martinez Plasencia, Diego 4734
Martínez Sandoval, Carlos A. 762
Martinez-Maldonado, Roberto 2062
Martinie, Célia 1069
Marzo, Asier 1952
Marzo, Asier 3277
Masai, Katsutoshi 1257
Massimi, Michael 931
Matejka, Justin 5421
Matias, J. Nathan 1138, 1486
Matic, Nada 2625, 2697
Matsumura, Kohei 3325
Mattheiss, Elke 1835
Matthews, Tara 5921
Matthies, Denys J.C. 2209
Mattos, Andrea Britto 2171
Matulic, Fabrice 1713, 2592
Matviienko, Andrii 2049, 2601
Mauderer, Michael 5131
Maurer, Bernhard 3434
Maurer, Frank 3403
Mauriello, Matthew Louis 2217, 3595
Mavadati, Mohammad 3723
Mayer, Julia M. 2430
Mayer, Marissa 3907
Mayer, Sven 2447, 2576
Mazalek, Ali 5151
Mazarakis, Athanasios 3400
Mazarakis, Athanasios 3604
Mazurek, Michelle L. 101, 527
McAvinia, Claire 2315
McBride, Simon J. 2014
McCann, James 285, 5397
McCarthy, John 2136
McCracken, Megan 1662
McDuff, Daniel J. 3723, 4000
McEwan, Mitchell 5583
McGarry, Brynne 1264
McGookin, David 1720, 3461
McGrath, William 1237
McGregor, Moira 1632
McGrenere, Joanna 4154
McInnis, Brian 2271
McIntosh, Jess 2332
McKay, Christian 1328
McLachlan, Ross 1301
McLaughlin, Janice 2417
McMillan, Donald 852, 2933, 5456
McNally, Brenna 3595
McNaney, Roisin 3387, 4464
McNeill, Charlie 2332
McPherson, Andrew P. 3339
McRoberts, Sarah A. 3784
Meban, Margaret 3781
Medhi-Thies, Indrani 3620
Mehrotra, Abhinav 1021
Mehta, Vikram 2417
Mekky, Sherif 3136
Mekler, Elisa D. 2996, 3166, 4509
Melcer, Edward F. 1430, 2225
Meldah, Eman 2661
Melicher, William 101, 527
Mellor, Sebastian 5015
Melville, Joshua R. 5360
Mendelowitz, Eitan 3871
Mendez, Christopher J. 1449
Méndez, Gonzalo Gabriel 3727, 4073
Meng, Liying 4818
Meng, Weizhi 4818
Meng, Xiangxu 433
Meng, Xiaojun 1016
Mengucci, Michele 2162
Mennicken, Sarah 3227, 5958
Mentis, Helena 2200
Mercado, David Jan 1438
Mercer, Eduardo 2712
Mercurio, Johanna 305, 3131
Merget, Daniel 3227
Merritt, Timothy 3492
Merz, Benedikt 3152
Meschtscherjakov, Alexander 3542
Mesmar, Sandra 331
Metatla, Oussama 1055
Metaxa-Kakavouli, Danaë 2893
Meurer, Johanna 921
Meyer, Thomas D. 2136
Meys, Wouter 889
Miau, Daniel 3731, 5114
Michalowicz, Stephanie 2798
Michelson, Becky 2612
Milam, Adam 4489
Miller, Andrew D. 3103, 5324
Miller, David 234, 3542
Miller, Laurie 721
Miller, Matthew K. 4562
Miller, Nick 4464
Mills, Kelly 3607
Miniukovich, Aliaksei 4622
Miralles, David 2387, 2462
Miranda, Müller 3204
Mirza-Babaei, Pejman 3159, 3597
Mishra, Sonali R. 3103, 5324
Mitchell, Luke 2655
Mitchell, Tom 2609
Mitra, Tanushree 2111
Mitros, Piotr 1045
Miyashita, Homei 1846
Mizouni, Rabeb 4758
Mizrahi, Moran 5984
Moffatt, Karyn 3508
Mogk, Cory 908
Mohan, Manisha 3703
Mohd Noor, Mohammad Faizuddin 1909
Möller, Sebastian 2355
Momeni, Ali 3735
Moncur, Wendy 3387, 3408
Monroy-Hernández, Andrés 1152, 4722
Moore, Dana 3620

Moore, Florencia 3181
Moore, Halla 2425
Moore, Joanne 1385
Moosajee, Naeem 3159
Morales González, Rafael 4189
Moreau, Rebecca 365
Moreno Rocha, Mario A. 762, 3620
Morgan, Alexander 1904
Morgans, Amee 745
Morimoto, Carlos H. 1952, 3533
Morishige, Hironao 3804
Morris, Meredith Ringel 2246, 5506
Morris, Richard 3035
Morrison, Alistair 284
Morrison, Briana 623
Morrison, Cecily 261
Morrison, Shannon 2574
Morrison-Smith, Sarah 3822
Mortensen, Cody V. 164
Moser, Carol 1881
Moser, Christiane 3597
Moser, Kilian 309
Mosher, Matthew 289
Mott, Martez E. 1934
Mottelson, Aske 3492
Motupali, Anil 1698
Mozer, Michael C. 5571
Mtenzi, Fred 2915
Mubin, Omar 2234
Mudd, Tom W. 3339
Mueller, Florian "Floyd" 940, 1119, 1681
Mueller, Stefanie 936, 2175, 3431, 3970
Muender, Thomas 4562
Mühlhäuser, Max 1598, 2617, 2688
Muldner, Kasia 919
Mulholland, James 3021
Muller, Michael 3604
Müller, Florian 1598, 2617, 2688
Müller, Heiko 3738
Müller, Jens 1245, 4634
Müller, Jörg 152, 791, 1705
Müller, Livia J. 3166
Müller, Marc 2026
Müller, Peter 5040
Mumm, Jesse 1180
Munson, Sean A. 1109, 3020, 5092, 5632
Munteanu, Cosmin 992, 1131, 3387, 3612
Munzner, Tamara 2264
Muralidhar, Srihari H. 5063
Murer, Martin 3550
Murgia, Alessandro 1272
Murray-Rust, Dave 552
Murthy, GVS 343
Musolesi, Mirco 1021
Mustanski, Brian S. 5360
Mutlu, Bilge 1038
Myers, Brad A. 1104, 2497
Myers, Christopher 1338
Naaman, Mor 564, 1301, 3857
Nabi, Tahmid 3498
Nacenta, Miguel A. 3727, 4073, 5191
Nachbar, Katrin 1637
Nachman, Lama 1445
Nacke, Lennart E. 1088, 3597
Naeem, Muhammad 2299
Naemura, Takeshi 1322
Nafus, Dawn 1057, 1445
Nägeli, Tobias 2508
Nahar, Papreen 343
Nahum-Shani, Inbal 4489
Nakadai, Kazuhiro 3612
Nakagaki, Ken 2764
Nakai, Yuriko 281, 3717
Nakamura, Hiromi 3325
Nakamura, Keisuke 3612
Nam, Chaebong 2271
Nam, Tek-Jin 213, 1922, 2307, 2555, 2673
Nancel, Mathieu 4250
Nandakumar, Rajalakshmi 1515
Nappey, Thomas 2136, 3800
Narasimhan, Sindhuja 360
Nardi, Bonnie 423, 1057
Nardi, Bonnie 4997
Narula, Abhishek 2504, 3683
Nathan, Lisa 1127
Naumann, Philipp 2442
Neate, Timothy 475
Nebeling, Michael 3834, 5494, 5909
Needham, Chris 1385
Needham, S. A. 4722
Nelson, Gregory L. 4521
Nembrini, Julien 3408
Neustaedter, Carman ... 931, 1038, 1959, 3197, 3317
Newbold, Joseph W. 5698
Newell, Edward 3155
Newhouse, Nikki 239
Newman, Nicholas 1781
Ng, Alexander 1744
Ng, Jamie 1295, 2279
Ng, Joy 2241
Ng, Kenney 5686
Ngai, Grace 5169
Nguyen, Anna 1966
Nguyen, Cuong 2093
Nguyen, Huyen 2057
Nguyen, Michelle 1607
Nicholson, James 3566
Nicol, Emma 1131
Nicole, Love 1180
Niels, Adelka 3115
Nieminen, Marko H.T. 4129
Niewiadomski, Radoslaw 1629
Niezen, Gerrit 3453
Nigay, Laurence 3793
Niiya, Melissa 5517
Nishida, Jun 3742
Nishida, Takeshi 3325
Nisi, Valentina 718
Nissen, Bettina 685, 2958
Noh, Boram 9
Noh, Seung-Tak 6058
Norton, Juliet 423
Not, Elena 1033
Nov, Oded 661
Nowacka, Diana 2136
Nozaki, Hiroki 3804
Nuernberger, Benjamin 1233
Nunes, Nuno Jardim 718
Nunnari, Fabrizio 3558
Nuseibeh, Bashar 2417
Nuutinen, Maaria 833
Nylander, Stina 1119
Nyström, Jimmy 269
Oakley, Ian 4238
Obaid, Mohammad 3572
Obel, Carsten 152
Obrist, Marianna .. 959, 1398, 1677, 2162, 3285
Ochiai, Yoichi 3238, 3431
Ochoa, Sergio F. 2112
Odom, William 1187, 2549, 3423, 5945
Oehlberg, Lora 397, 804
Ofek, Eyal 3, 1233, 1968, 3647
Ogata, Masa 3325
Ogawa, Masaki 3804
Ogbonnaya-Ogburu, Ihudiya F nda 1180
Oh, Alice 4351
Oh, Changhoon 1280
Oh, Jeongmin 1692, 3173
Oh, Soo Youn 2900
O'Hara, Kenton 2487, 2869, 3309, 3355, 3415, 4781
O'Hara, Kieron 552
Ohta, Naohisa 2321
O'Kane, Aisling Ann 2906, 3453
Okazaki, Ryuta 281, 3717
O'Keefe, Eanna 2805
Okerlund, Johanna 661
Ölçer, Selim 1538
O'Leary, Ciarán 2915
Oleson, Alannah 1449
Oleson, Kurt B. 5372
Oliveto, Luigi 2257
Olivier, Patrick 11, 26, 331, 343, 1073, 1096, 2136, 2832, 3566, 3800, 4464, 5015
Olopade, Dayo 3904
Olsen, Dan R. 876
Olsen, Jennifer K. 1187
Olson, Thomas A. 5337
Olsson, Thomas 4366
Olwal, Alex 3754
Omirou, Themis 2661, 2667
O'Modhrain, Sile 3339
O'Neill, Eamonn 200
O'Neill, Jacki 5063
O'Neill, Mark 4298
Oney, Steve 3192
Onishi, Kazusa 2705
Opila, Claire 1301
Opwis, Klaus 2996, 3152, 3166
Orji, Rita 1835
Orso, Valeria 4203
Ortlieb, Martin 5215
Ostberg, Anna 2625
Othman, Mohammad 4464
Ou, Jifei 13, 5743, 5753

Oualil, Youssef 1379
Oulasvirta, Antti 1131, 1423, 1857, 3722, 3780, 4262, 4956, 5203
Ouyang, Tom 3817
Ovalle, Liliana 1597
Oviatt, Sharon 3612
Ozanne, Elizabeth 745
Özcan, Oğuzhan 1538, 3655, 3944
Page, Xinru 3415
Paget, Susan 1359
Pahud, Michel 2869
Paine, Garth 3875
Pak Yong Ho, Melwyn 3227
Palanque, Philippe 976, 1069
Palen, Leysia 2783, 2796
Palleis, Henri 1947
Pan, Rui 1959, 3197
Pan, Shimei 3612
Pandelakis, Matthew 2064
Pandey, Anshul Vikram 3659
Pandey, Vineet 458
Panëels, Sabrina 2632, 2719, 3687
Pappalardo, Alessandro 1684
Parab, Chinmay 50
Paradiso, Joseph A. 1647, 3703
Paredes, Luis 897
Pares, Narcis 1123, 3373
Paritosh, Praveen 3536
Park, Deokgun 1114
Park, Hyung Kun 3746
Park, Joonyoung 2165
Park, Jung Wook 1591
Park, Sangkeun 1229, 2857, 4758
Park, SoHyun 1280
Park, Sungjoon 4351
Park, Taiwoo 6040
Park, Young-Woo 9
Parker, Andrea G. 3620
Parkinson, Adam 2150, 3750
Parsons, Sarah 1294
Parzer, Patrick 3754, 5138
Pasquetto, Irene V. 1585
Patel, Kanika 4872
Patel, Kishan 4142
Patel, Nirmal 4142
Patel, Shwetak N. 7, 1504, 4933, 5675, 5885
Patra, Abhisekh 3197
Patterson, Donald J. 423
Paul, Sharoda A. 710, 3038
Paulos, Eric 1338, 6028
Pauw, Daniel 3607
Pavlidis, Ioannis 1483, 2249, 5665
Pead, Daniel 1159
Pearce, Celia 3877
Pearson, Jennifer 3793
Pease, Zachary 1453
Pece, Fabrizio 3806
Peck, Evan M. 5372
Pedell, Sonja 745
Peer, Eyal 5257
Peesapati, S. Tejaswi 1893
Peeters, Jeroen 10
Pejovic, Veljko 1021
Pelachaud, Catherine 1438
Pelikan, Hannah R. M. 4921
Pellicone, Anthony 244
Peng, Huaishu 887
Penn, Gerald 992, 3612
Pennington, Sarah 1597
Perer, Adam 5686
Perez Cano, Rocio 3084
Pérez-Quinones, Manuel 2406
Perkins, Daniel F. 3919
Perrault, Simon T. 1016, 2640, 3572
Perrotta, Andre 3816
Perteneder, Florian 5849
Peters, Anicia 2586, 3620
Peters, Dorian 988
Peters, Isabella 3400
Petersen, Marianne G. 2740, 3301
Petersen, Mark 700
Petit, Grégory 690
Petrelli, Daniela 1033
Petrie, Helen 1085
Pfeiffer, Max 944, 2526, 3758
Pfeil, Ulrike 5470
Pfeuffer, Ken 2845
Pfleging, Bastian 961, 3542, 5076, 5776
Phat, Pham Tan 2961
Phelan, Chanda 5240
Phillimore, Peter 343
Phillips, Cody 1930, 5583
Phillips, Stephanie 2136
Phillips II, Gregory Lee 5360
Piana, Stefano 1629
Piazzolla, Pietro 1540, 2257
Picard, Noah 3227
Picard, Rosalind W. 2134, 3438, 4000
Pielot, Martin 3637
Pieper, Christian 3738
Pierce, James 3423
Pietriga, Emmanuel 4189
Pietrzak, Thomas 3261, 3683, 5298
Pike, James 1597
Pike, Matthew 293
Pike, Matthew 5385
Pina, Laura R. 5658
Pinder, Charlie 2923
Pine, Katie 1057
Ping, An 1109
Piorkowski, David 3509
Piper, Anne Marie 2246, 5311, 5529
Pisetti, Anna 1033
Pittman, Corey 1729
Pizza, Stefania 5456
Plaisant, Catherine 2217
Plank, Meghan M. 98
Pletikosa Cvijikj, Irena 2148
Podlubny, Martin 1904
Poeller, Susanne 3007
Pogrund, Rona 2306
Pohl, Henning 1173
Politis, Ioannis 3542
Pollack, Ari H. 3103, 5324
Pollalis, Christina 661
Poller, Andreas 1288
Ponnada, Aditya 768
Pons, Patricia 1737
Ponsard, Antoine 2264, 4154
Poole, Erika S. 5548
Poonwala, Nikhil 4142
Poor, G. Michael 2519, 3028
Popović, Zoran 2348
Porcheron, Martin 3309
Poronnik, Philip 3211
Porter, Victoria 3762
Posch, Irene 3881
Potard, Blaise 3643
Poupyrev, Ivan 4216, 6028
Prabhakar, Annu 804
Prasad, Eswar 5665
Pratt, Wanda 3103, 5324
Preece, Jenny 1201
Preist, Chris 1308, 1324
Preston, Kenzie L. 4489
Price, Blaine A. 2417
Pritchard, Gary W. 3566
Priyadarshana, Lahiru Lakmal 3762
Probst, Kathrin 3754
Procyk, Jason 931, 1879
Profita, Halley 4884
Proulx, Jason 1011
Proulx, Michael J. 200
Prpić, John 3536
Pullin, Graham 3643
Punjasthitkul, Sukdith 4122
Purewal, Harpreet 26
Pursel, Bart 1315
Pursglove, Bradley 11, 2832, 3800
Putnam, Cynthia 2038, 3659
Qaurooni, Danial 1822
Qu, Huamin 409
Quek, Francis 2782
Quigley, Aaron 1833, 3309
Quinn, Philip 83, 4005
Quintana, Chris 2272
Quintana, Rebecca 2272
Rädle, Roman 1245, 2487, 5470
Rafiev, Ashur 2136
Raghavan, Barath 423
Rahman, Md Mahbubur 4489
Räihä, Kari-Jouko 2648
Rajendran, Chandni 50
Rajendran, Vasanth K. 188
Rajpurkar, Pranav 237
Ralph, Maria 680
Ramakers, Raf 409
Ramani, Karthik 897
Ramchurn, Richard 293, 5385
Ramchurn, Sarvapali D. 4908, 5262, 5933
Ramos, Laura 721
Ramos Rojas, Julian 3847
Ramraika, Anmol 2592
Ranasinghe, Nimesha 3285
Randall, David 3364
Randall, Emily 122

Rangel, Alejandro ... 4872
Rank, Stefan ... 1966
Rank, Stefan ... 1973
Rankin, Yolanda A. ... 670
Rantakari, Juho ... 2490
Rashidi, Yasmeen ... 3215
Rasmussen, Majken K. ... 2740
Ratan, Rabindra ... 3542
Rau, Andreas ... 1359
Read, Janet C. ... 927, 1123, 1833, 2410
Rector, Kyle ... 165
Reddy, Madhu ... 2081, 3628
Reeder, Robert ... 5921
Regan, David ... 5874
Reich, Stephanie ... 5517
Reichl, Peter ... 728
Reilly, Derek ... 1362
Reinach, Stephen ... 880
Reinecke, Katharina ... 1881, 2693
Reiners, Torsten ... 738
Reiter, Andreas ... 3550
Reiterer, Harald ... 1245, 3366, 4634, 5470
Rekimoto, Jun ... 1561
Rello, Luz ... 3637
Ren, Fei ... 80
Ren, Shuang ... 2947
Ren, Xiangshi ... 1131
Rendl, Christian ... 3754, 5138
Renfree, Ian ... 1389, 2932
Rennert, Kara ... 718
Rennick-Egglestone, Stefan ... 2124
Reno, Corbin ... 5548
Resnick, Paul ... 5240
Resseguier, Beverly ... 1980
Ressel, Christoph ... 2601
Revelle, Glenda ... 1123
Reynolds, Erin ... 1945
Rho, Saeyoung ... 699
Rhodes, Emily ... 1063
Riaz, Waleed ... 2299
Rice, Mark ... 1295
Rice, Mark ... 2279
Rich, Travis ... 2134
Richard, Gabriela T. ... 1473
Richardson, Dan ... 4464
Rickman, Aimee ... 2371
Ricks, Rebecca ... 184
Riedel-Kruse, Ingmar H. ... 1000
Riemann, Jan ... 1598, 2688
Rieser, Denise Christine ... 2940
Rigas, Ioannis ... 1503
Rigoll, Gerhard ... 2681, 3227
Ringland, Kathryn E. ... 1100, 1256
Rintel, Sean ... 2487, 4781
Rispoli, Zachary ... 3735
Rivera-Loaiza, Cuauhtémoc ... 1127
Roads, Brett D. ... 5571
Robert, Lionel P. ... 2461
Roberts, David L. ... 3438
Robertson, Toni ... 3301
Robinson, Karen E. ... 4216
Robinson, Simon ... 969, 3574, 3793
Rodden, Tom ... 3049, 4061, 5933
Rode, Jennifer A. ... 473, 1100
Rodger, Sunil ... 2417
Rodolfo, Inês ... 899
Rodríguez López, Abril I. ... 762
Rogers, David H. ... 700
Rogers, Simon ... 1909
Rogers, Yvonne ... 1608, 3711
Rogerson, Melissa J. ... 3956
Rohde, Markus ... 3364
Rohn, Janice ... 1108
Rohrer, Christian P. ... 786
Rohs, Michael ... 944, 2526, 2533, 3758
Rolinson, Esther ... 3885
Romeo, Pietro ... 1779, 1904
Romppainen, Mikko ... 1007
Ronch, Judah ... 2200
Ronen, Inbal ... 3025
Rooke, Christianne ... 5608
Rooksby, John ... 284
Rosen, Allyson ... 948
Rosenbaum, Stephanie ... 755
Rosés Brüngger, Raquel ... 2148
Roseway, Asta ... 3699
Rosner, Daniela K. ... 1403,1426, 1745, 6008
Rossitto, Chiara ... 864
Rosso, Juan ... 3793
Rosson, Mary Beth ... 2837, 3919
Rost, Mattias ... 284, 1904
Rostami, Asreen ... 6014
Rota Bulò, Samuel ... 261
Rother, Carsten ... 2592
Roto, Virpi ... 833
Roudaut, Anne ... 498, 2655, 2661, 2667
Rouleau, Stéphanie ... 14
Roumen, Thijs ... 2175
Roussel, Nicolas ... 3683
Rovelo Ruiz, Gustavo Alberto ... 487
Row, Yea-Kyung ... 2673
Rozner, Eric ... 5126
Rubens, Calvin ... 770
Rubya, Sabirat ... 3784
Rudzicz, Frank ... 3612
Rughiniş, Cosima ... 487
Rughiniş, Razvan ... 487
Ruiz, Jaime ... 3822
Rukzio, Enrico ... 1996, 2439, 3679
Runge, Nina ... 541
Ruoti, Scott ... 4298
Rusak, Gili ... 2893
Russo, Edoardo ... 1904
Ruths, Derek ... 3155
Ruzic, Ljilja ... 4861
Ryan, James Owen ... 160
Ryokai, Kimiko ... 6028
Sá, Paulo ... 899
Saakes, Daniel ... 6058
Saba, Elliot ... 5675
Sabiescu, Amalia ... 3347
Sachar, Simranjit ... 1114
Sadeghian Borojeni, Shadan ... 2285
Saegusa, Hidekazu ... 6008
Sahay, Saurav ... 1445
Sahdev, Sidharth ... 5298
Sahoo, Deepak Ranjan ... 3767
Sajadieh, Sahar ... 297
Sakaguchi, Saki ... 3325
Sakamoto, Daisuke ... 2520, 3325
Saksono, Herman ... 3620
Salehi, Niloufar ... 2645
Salinas, Lara ... 1383
Sallnäs Pysander, Eva-Lotta ... 1359
Samanta, Debasis ... 2431
Sampalli, Srinivas ... 2758, 2976
Sample, Alanson P. ... 7, 4933, , 5897
Samsel, Francesca ... 700
Samsonov, Pavel ... 2442
Samuel, Ben ... 160
Sanchez, Susana ... 1459
Sánchez, David A. ... 3788
Sanders, Steven ... 2857
Sands, Ashley E. ... 1585
Sandvig, Christian ... 1057, 2371
Sanford, Jon ... 4861
Sänger, Johannes ... 3870
Sanna, Claudio ... 1684
Sano, Akane ... 1717, 1739
Santana, Christina J. ... 1786, 3516
Saraf, Dean ... 1810
Sarasua, Alvaro ... 3428
Sarcar, Sayan ... 1131
Sari, Eunice ... 3395, 3620
Sarkar, Advait ... 261, 1467, 2533
Sarkar, Dan ... 1264
Sarker, Hillol ... 4489
Sarma, Anita ... 3509
Sas, Corina ... 2872, 2947, 4793
Sasse, M. Angela ... 3870
Sathyanath, Shreyaswi ... 343
Sato, Toshiki ... 553
Sato, Yoichi ... 5180
Sato, Yuka ... 1766
Sauer, Hanno ... 1637
Sauer, Juergen ... 4828
Sauro, Jeff ... 786
Savage, Evan ... 1445
Savage, Valkyrie ... 1607
Savisaari, Olli ... 5203
Scaffidi, Christopher ... 3498
Schaefbauer, Christopher ... 5645
Schatzl, Bernhard ... 728
Scheipl, Gregor ... 5138
Schenk, Simon ... 2681, 3227
Scherer, Aaron M. ... 2314
Schiano, Diane J. ... 3181
Schiefsky, Mark ... 944
Schien, Daniel ... 1324
Schiphorst, Thecla ... 3197, 3301, 3667
Schippert, Katharina ... 3013
Schlager, Mark ... 2406
Schlegel, Thomas ... 2570
Schmandt, Chris ... 1563, 3703
Schmidt, Albrecht ... 1570, 1706, 3114, 5776
Schmidt, Ryan ... 908

Schmidt, Thomas ... 728
Schmitt, Rachel ... 3808
Schmitz, Martin ... 1598, 2688
Schneegass, Stefan ... 1379, 1415
Schneider, Hanna ... 309
Schneider, Oliver S. ... 3248
Schoenebeck, Sarita Y. ... 610, 635, 1881
Schoenfeld, Alan ... 1159
Schöffel, Sebastian ... 2292
Schofield, Guy ... 2705
Scholtz, Jean ... 955
Schöning, Johannes ... 13, 515, 541, 2442, 3366, 3574
Schoop, Eldon ... 1607
schraefel, m.c. ... 1476, 2012
Schramm, Katherine ... 4687
Schreiner, Mario ... 3366
Schröder, Svenja ... 728
Schulze, Diane ... 3227
Schwank, Johannes ... 2292
Schwesig, Carsten ... 4216
Schwind, Valentin ... 1706
Seah, Sue Ann ... 3446
Seamons, Kent ... 4298
Seeley, Damon ... 3871
Seevinck, Jennifer ... 3889
Sefercik, Buğra Can ... 3944
Segreti, Sean M. ... 527, 3748
Segundo Díaz, Rosa Lilia ... 2923
Sehl, Anja ... 3006
Seifi, Hasti ... 3248
Seipp, Karsten ... 525
Sellen, Abigail ... 261, 1200, 2869, 3415, 5286
Selvaraj, Senthil Kumar ... 2279
Semaan, Bryan C. ... 2882, 3559, 3883
Sen, Prasanta Kr ... 2431
Sen, Shivalik ... 5409
Senecal, Sylvain ... 4850, 1980
Sengupta, Subhasree ... 515
Seo, Jinwook ... 272, 4658
Seppänen, Marko ... 833
Seppi, Kevin ... 876
Serafin, Stefania ... 560
Serim, Baris ... 5789
Serrano, Marcos ... 498, 2186
Seshagiri, Sarita ... 768
Seuken, Sven ... 5262
Seyed, Teddy ... 3403, 4675
Shadbolt, Nigel R. ... 552, 3066
Shaer, Orit ... 655, 661, 3461
Shah, Neha ... 1301
Shahid, Suleman ... 2299
Shahriaree, Nina ... 3988
Shakeri, Gözel ... 1744
Shamma, David A. ... 113, 575, 621, 3167, 3379, 5710
Shankar, Anil ... 3021, 5350
Shann, Mike ... 5262
Shapira, Lior ... 1
Sharma, Nikhil ... 3612
Sharma, Nirwan ... 128
Sharma, Sangita ... 1445
Sharmin, Moushumi ... 4489
Shastri, Dvijesh ... 2249, 5665
Shaw, Alex ... 1752, 1921
Shay, Richard ... 527
Shebanek, Mike ... 823
Sheik-Nainar, Mohamed ... 2625, 2697
Shen, Chia ... 433
Shen, Michael ... 156
Shen, Yicong ... 2185
Sherwen, Sally ... 3355
Shi, Jiamin ... 1344, 3766
Shi, Lei ... 4896
Shi, Wen ... 68
Shi, Yuanchun ... 71, 4699
Shibata, Tomoki ... 3770
Shieber, Stuart M. ... 944
Shim, Young Mog ... 2563
Shima, Keigo ... 2705
Shimizu, Junichi ... 2321
Shin, Jaemyung ... 6040
Shinoda, Hiroyuki ... 1980, 3446
Shipman, Frank ... 1857
Shipp, Victoria ... 3049
Shiraga, Shota ... 3190
Shirazi, Ali Sahami ... 1415
Shizuki, Buntarou ... 2395, 2403, 2511, 2705, 2736, 3852
Shklovski, Irina ... 4315
Shmorgun, Ilya ... 2712
Shneiderman, Ben ... 1047, 2217
Shodhan, Sharan ... 4142
Shokouhi, Milad ... 1200
Shrivastava, Soumya ... 745
Shum, Venus ... 3711
Siami Namin, Akbar ... 2306
Siegel, Martin A. ... 647
Siek, Katie A. ... 804, 3461, 3628, 5645
Siewiorek, Daniel ... 4413
Siirtola, Harri ... 2648
Sikich, Danielle ... 1921
Sikka, Vishal ... 3910
Silberman, M. Six ... 4573
Silic, Mario ... 2954
Silpasuwanchai, Chaklam ... 1131
Silva, Luis ... 5028
Silvennoinen, Johanna M. ... 4390
Šimbelis, Vygandas 'Vegas' ... 301, 840
Simha, Rahul ... 3076
Simm, Will ... 1270
Simoneaux, Stephen F. ... 5337
Simonsen, Jakob G. ... 2740
Sing, Keng Hua ... 130
Singer, Leif ... 3204
Singh, Aneesha ... 1092
Singh, Harmeet ... 56
Singh, Karan ... 4537
Singh, Meenu ... 343
Singh, Pushpendra ... 343
Singh, Rishabh ... 1462
Singhal, Samarth ... 3197
Sirkin, David ... 980
Sivaraman, Venkatesh ... 1045
Skatova, Anya ... 3049
Skriloff, Sarah Justine Guy ... 164
Slaats, Yanti ... 3091
Slavin, Kevin ... 2134
Sleeper, Manya ... 101
Slegers, Karin ... 512, 3331, 3484, 5824
Slotta, James D. ... 2272
Slyper, Leeyat ... 62
Smailagic, Asim ... 4413
Smeddinck, Jan D. ... 5595
Smit, Niki ... 1989
Smith, Anthony Nalan ... 3181
Smith, Gillian ... 285, 3877
Smith, Ian ... 1270
Smith, Paul ... 3847
Smith, Simon ... 1930, 5583
Smith, Wally ... 3956
Smyth, Gavin ... 1200, 2869
Smyth, Thomas N. ... 2635
Snow, Stephen ... 1476
Sobek, Ismael ... 62
Sobel, Kiley ... 165, 249
Soden, Robert ... 2783, 2796
Soles, Justin ... 690
Solheim, Martin ... 3778
Soll, Marcus ... 2442
Solomon, Jacob ... 2314, 4166, 4568
Solovey, Erin ... 1698
Sonderegger, Andreas ... 4828
Song, Hoyeong ... 3774
Song, Hyunchang ... 3049
Song, Hyunjoo ... 4658
Song, Junehwa ... 6040
Song, Yale ... 575
Sonne, Tobias ... 152
Soomro, Shoaib ... 1538
Soriente, Claudio ... 540
Soska, Anna ... 1476
Soto Mino, Gustavo ... 1385
Sousa, Marta ... 899
Špakov, Oleg ... 2648
Spelmezan, Daniel ... 3788
Spence, Charles ... 3285
Spiel, Katharina ... 130
Spielberg, Andrew ... 5897
Spiro, Emma ... 360
Sra, Misha ... 1563
Srinivas, Preethi ... 4502
Srinivasa Ragavan, Sruti ... 3509
Srinivasan, Vasant ... 4945
Stach, Tad ... 1879
Ståhl, Anna ... 305, 3131, 3301
Stallings, Michael ... 647
Standell, Toni ... 1007
Stangl, David ... 2175
Starbird, Kate ... 360
Stark, Luke ... 3415
Starling, Summer ... 3204
Stärz, Jan ... 2292
Stawarz, Katarzyna ... 2932
Stead, Mike ... 375
Steele, Katherine M. ... 1745

Stefik, Andreas ... 1104
Steimle, Jürgen ... 420
Steiner, Helene ... 13
Steinfeld, Aaron ... 4477
Steinhardt, Stephanie B. ... 2198
Steinheimer, Saskia ... 261
Stella, Erica ... 1684
Stern-Rodriguez, Eva ... 4
Stevšić, Stefan ... 2508
Stewart, Lauren ... 1781
Stewart, Margaret ... 1043
Stiber, Maia ... 5675
Stockman, Tony ... 1055
Stolterman, Erik ... 4056
Stone, Maria ... 823
Stowell, Elizabeth ... 661
Strachan, Steven ... 2632, 2719, 3687
Strawn, Devon ... 1445
Striner, Alina ... 1201
Stringer, Helen ... 4464
Strohmaier, Markus ... 3352, 3400
Strohmeier, Paul ... 2726, 3492, 3781
Stuedahl, Dagny ... 3347
Stuerzlinger, Wolfgang ... 3403, 5151, 5849
Stumpf, Simone ... 3485
Sturdee, Miriam ... 375
Su, Hsiao-Ching ... 44
Su, Xiaojun ... 1760
Subramanian, Lakshmi ... 2798
Subramanian, Sriram ... 3446, 3767
Sugano, Yusuke ... 3299
Suganuma, Kiyoshi ... 1561
Sugimoto, Maki ... 1257
Sugiura, Kazunori ... 2321
Suh, Bongwon ... 1280, 2585
Suh, Hyewon ... 648, 3988
Suh, Jihoon ... 134
Suh, Minhyang (Mia) ... 1084
Summerville, Adam J. ... 160
Sun, Emily ... 1301
Sun, Ke ... 71
Sun, Min ... 2348
Sun, Wangshu ... 184
Sun, Weize ... 1991
Sun, Xu ... 1329
Sun, Yingze ... 1821
Sundar, S. Shyam ... 2837, 3107, 5252
Sung, Ching-Ying ... 2185
Suzuki, Kenji ... 1282, 3742
Suzuki, Ryo ... 2645
Svanæs, Dag ... 3301, 3778
Swaminathan, Saiganesh ... 2175
Swanson, Tom ... 3473
Swift, Ben ... 2295
Syme, Don ... 2533
Szigeti, Steve ... 3695
Szostak, Dalila ... 3542
Ta, Kevin ... 1548
Ta, Stephanie ... 5034
Taamneh, Salah ... 1483
Tachtler, Franziska Maria ... 309
Tadic, Borislav ... 3364
Tag, Benjamin ... 2321
Taher, Faisal ... 2778
Tajadura-Jiménez, Ana ... 1092, 5698
Takada, Ryosuke ... 2705, 2736
Takayama, Leila ... 4945
Takeuchi, Yuichiro ... 449
Talhouk, Reem ... 331, 1073
Talton, Jerry O. ... 2383
Tan, Desney ... 1515
Tanaka, Atau ... 2150, 3428, 3558, 3750
Tanaka, Jiro ... 2395, 2403, 2511, 2705, 2736, 3852
Tanaka, Katie G. ... 4550
Tanaka, Serena ... 2348
Tandong, Cedrick N. ... 5063
Tang, Anthony ... 1548, 3197
Tang, John C. ... 4770
Tang, Lie Ming ... 3211
Tang, Ning ... 781
Tang, Richard ... 1548
Tang, Shiliang ... 225
Tanner, Kesler ... 3706
Tao, Ye ... 2328
Tasse, Dan ... 1187, 3324
Tausch, Sarah ... 5034
Tavares Smith, Marcia ... 1270
Tay, Hong Huei ... 1295, 2279
Taylor, Alex ... 2958
Taylor, Brandon ... 4413
Taylor, Nick ... 1415, 2945
Te, Yiea-Funk ... 2148
Tearo, Khalid ... 1362
Tedjasaputra, Adi ... 3395
Teevan, Jaime ... 2657, 2893, 3143, 3500, 3508, 3834
Temir, Elizaveta ... 2906
Templeman, Robert ... 4309
Templier, Thomas ... 5812
Tentori, Monica ... 1092, 4872
Teras, Marko ... 738
Terry, Michael A. ... 4098
Tew, Philip ... 2609
Teyssier, Marc ... 4
Tezcan, Mustafa Ozan ... 3655, 3944
Thar, Jan ... 2497, 3788
Theng, Yin-Leng ... 2961
Theodore, Michael ... 2504, 3683
Thepvongsa, Brandon ... 571
Thieme, Anja ... 331, 2136, 3387
Thies, William ... 3620
Tholander, Jakob ... 1119
Tholander, Jakob ... 3301
Thomas, Lisa ... 3379
Thomaszewski, Bernhard ... 3806
Thomer, Andrea K. ... 3219
Thompson, Carola ... 1108
Thompson, Kate ... 2062
Thomson, Shelby C. ... 3007
Thorsteinson, Caleb ... 571
Tiab, John ... 2752
Tian, Feng ... 1760, 3532
Tian, Rundong ... 1338
Tice, Brian ... 2425
Tiefenbacher, Philipp ... 2681, 3227
Tiefenbach-Keller, Stephen ... 3695
Tilmanne, Joëlle ... 3558
Timmermans, Annick ... 3792
Tixier, Matthieu ... 3545
Tiza, Eran ... 3944
To, Alexandra ... 3834
Tobias, Crystal ... 140
Tochihara, Naoya ... 553
Todi, Kashyap ... 168, 2744, 3780
Toeters, Marina ... 3792
Tokuda, Hideyuki ... 3804
Tomimbang, Helen ... 4872
Tomitsch, Martin ... 2343
Tomlinson, Bill ... 423
Toms, Gill ... 2124
Tong, Xin ... 172
Toombs, Austin L. ... 328
Torquato, Matheus Fernandes ... 3793
Towner, Auriell ... 2178
Träger, Christoph ... 1713
Tran, Thomas ... 6008
Tran Luciani, Danwei ... 1490
Treacy, Stephen M. ... 710
Tregillus, Sam ... 176, 1250
Treude, Christoph ... 3204
Trimpop, John ... 2209
Trocchianesi, Raffaella ... 3347
Troiano, Giovanni M. ... 2740, 3492
Trotto, Ambra ... 10
Truong, Khiet P. ... 297
Tsai, Chia-Ling ... 38
Tsai, Yu-Lun ... 5704
Tsaknaki, Vasiliki ... 5970
Tsandilas, Theophanis ... 397
Tscheligi, Manfred ... 1069, 1835, 3542, 3550
Tse, Audrey ... 68
Tsiamyrtzis, Panagiotis ... 2249, 5665
Tsui, Katherine ... 1038
Tu, Pei-Yun ... 1615
Tuan, Tina ... 1063
Tuch, Alexandre N. ... 3152
Tucker, William D. ... 3620
Tung, Samuel ... 3084
Turbak, Franklyn ... 1104
Turcot, Jay ... 3723
Turmo Vidal, Laia ... 6014
Turner, Anna ... 5921
Turner, Dan ... 1644
Turton, Terece L. ... 700
Twidale, Michael B. ... 3219
Tyburski, Matthew ... 4489
Tyllinen, Mari ... 4129
Uchidiuno, Judith Odili ... 3607
Uddin, Md. Sami ... 5836
Ueoka, Ryoko ... 1766
Ulas, Servet ... 172
Ullrich, Daniel ... 3234
Umetani, Nobuyuki ... 6, 4599
Unander-Scharin, Åsa ... 265
Unander-Scharin, Carl ... 265

Unumb, Caitlin 5311
Unver, Baris 3784
Ur, Blase 527, 3227, 3748
Urban, Bodo 2209
Ürey, Hakan 1538
Uriu, Daisuke 5945
Usman, Muhammad 2119
Uyanik, Ilyas 2249
Väänänen, Kaisa 2430
Vaara, Elsa 840
Vacca, Ralph 1772
Vaccaro, Kristen 2371
Valderrama Bahamondez, Elba 3620
Valentin, Frederic 445
Valfre Piazza, Serenela V. 14
Vallgårda, Anna 3423
van Alphen, Erik 2334
van Berkel, Niels 1869, 4711
van den Hoven, Elise 721
Van Der Veer, Gerrit 1047
Van Kleek, Maximus 552, 3066, 3508
van Oostendorp, Herre 5720
van Rooij, Marieke 1989
Vanacken, Davy 487
Vance, James K. 3438
Vande Moere, Andrew 5824
Vandenberghe, Bert 512, 3331
Vandenheste, Sebastien 4073
Vaniea, Kami 3215
VanLehn, Kurt 1159
Vasalou, Asimina 969
Vashishtha, Ishan 2141
Vasilescu, Bogdan 1272
Vasilevitsky, Tatyana 5731
Vassileva, Julita 2112
Vatavu, Radu-Daniel 1003, 1934, 3390
Vaziripour, Elham 4298
Vazquez-Alvarez, Yolanda 1821
Vega, Katia 3703
Veinot, Tiffany 610
Velasco, Carlos 3285
Velloso, Eduardo 3415
Venolia, Gina 4770
Verame, Jhim Kiel M. 4908
Verbert, Katrien 525
Verma, Nitya 2341
Vermeeren, Arnold P.O.S. 3347
Vermeulen, Jo 1021, 3366
Vertanen, Keith 3469
Vertegaal, Roel 770, 3649, 3675, 3762, 3781
Vetere, Frank 745, 1798, 3415
Vi, Chi Thanh 3285
Vicencio-Moreira, Rodrigo 3462
Vigo, Markel 1827
Vines, John 685, 1620, 2417, 2945, 3387, 3625, 4464
Vink, Luke 2764
Virtanen, Lasse 2490
Visser, Aaron 3762
Vitak, Jessica 3415, 3895
Vlachokyriakos, Vasilis 1073, 1096, 2958
Vlahovic, Tatiana A. 1187
Vogel, Daniel 4250, 4274, 4675
Vogl, Anita 3754
Voida, Amy 2341, 4550
Voida, Stephen 2001
Volkova, Svitlana 1215
Volpe, Gualtiero 1629
von Veh, Curtis 2657
von Zezschwitz, Emanuel 2041, 2156, 3736, 4320
Voss, Catalin 2348
Wacharamanotham, Chat 2497, 3788
Wacker, Philipp 1067, 3788
Waddell, T. Franklin 3107, 5252
Wadler, Philip 1104
Waern, Annika 803, 1359, 6014
Wagner, Linda 1111
Wahid, Shahtab 796
Waje, Aniruddha 1362
Wakkary, Ron 2549
Wakkary, Ron 5274
Walker, Erin 919, 1698
Walker, Ian D. 1407
Walker, Imani 473
Walker, Luke 2681
Wall, Dennis 2348
Wallace, James R. 2087
Wallace, Jayne 2136
Walsh, Greg 1453
Walsh, Jenny 2805
Walsh, Lorcan 261
Walter, Robert 1705
Walz, Steffen P. 3122
Wan, Marcus 1295
Wanderley, Marcelo M. 3339
Wang, Alf Inge 1872
Wang, Dakuo 255
Wang, Dennis 152
Wang, Fan 1526
Wang, Gang 225
Wang, Guanyun 13, 2328, 5743
Wang, Hao-Chuan 1236, 1615, 2185, 5704
Wang, Hongan 1760
Wang, Honghao 3255
Wang, I-Fang 152
Wang, Katie 2072
Wang, MinJuan 2808
Wang, Nai-Ching 146
Wang, Ninglu 80
Wang, Pan 1937
Wang, Pengfei 74
Wang, Qi 3792
Wang, Shannon 1243
Wang, Shiyu 957
Wang, Shuo-Ping 1236
Wang, Wen 13, 5743
Wang, Yanan 1497
Wang, Yao 2406
Wang, Yi-Chia 125
Wang, Yiran 5517
Wang, Yixiao 1407
Wang, Yun 409
Wang, Yuying 2661
Ward, Jamie 2162
Ward, Nick 1781
Warr, Andrew 3335
Wash, Rick 4568
Washington, Peter 2348
Watten, Phil L. 1398, 2162
Watters, Jason 3355
Waycott, Jenny 745, 3387
Webber, Sarah 3355
Weber, Gerhard 1085, 2879
Weber, Ingmar 5543
Wechsung, Ina 2355
Weeks, Christopher 1308
Wehbe, Rina R. 796
Wei, Jyh-Da 3241
Wei, Weijie 2999
Wei, Zhiyong 781
Weibel, Nadir 2126
Weie, Stian 1872
Weilenmann, Alexandra 852
Weir, Daryl 3780, 4262
Weisling, Anna 3893
Weißker, Tim 3796
Weitzner, Nathan 297
Welge, Julika 1375
Wen, Hongyi 3847, 4699
Wendt, James 786
Wessels, Arne 2640
West, Peter 3066
Westendorf, Lauren 661
Westermann, Tilo 2355
Westort, Liliana 661
Wetzstein, Gordon 1211
Whalen, Tara 3415
Wheldon, Pete 5015
White, Brooke 823
Whitehouse, Sam 2667
Whitmire, Eric 5675
Whittaker, Steve 1032, 1729
Whittle, Jon 1270
Wickersham, Alice 3311
Widauer, Christopher 728
Wiehr, Frederik 1097, 1998
Wiese, Jason 1187
Wiethoff, Alexander 2562
Wigdor, Daniel 1957, 2857, 4610, 5765
Wijayarathne, Jayathri 2234
Wilcox, Lauren 5337
Wilkie, Katie L. 3339
Wilkinson, Gerard 11, 2832, 3800
Williams, Amanda CdC 5698
Williams, Diane L. 140
Williams, Joseph Jay 470, 3536
Williams, Kaiton 1051
Williams, Michele A. 2034
Williamson, John 1744, 1909, 2751, 3433
Williamson, Julie R. 2751
Willis, Karl 5753
Wilson, Andrew D. 3, 1233, 1968, 3647
Wilson, Graham 1779, 4838
Wilson, Max L. 293, 4011, 5385
Wilson, Rob 3625

Windham, Daniel ... 2764
Windle, Karen ... 2920
Winkler, Christian ... 3679
Winnen, Fabian ... 3639
Winograd, Terry ... 2348, 3907
Wiseman, Sarah ... 1385
Wisniewski, Pamela ... 1729, 3415, 3919
Witteman, Holly O. ... 2314
Wittenhagen, Moritz ... 3522
Wobbrock, Jacob O. ... 1934, 3390
Wolf, Christine T. ... 1256
Wolf, Dennis ... 1996
Wolf, Katrin ... 509, 2576
Wolff, Christian ... 2026
Wong, Jian-Syuan ... 1315
Woo, Woontack ... 6058
Wood, Gavin ... 11, 1810, 2832, 3635, 3800
Wood, Lincoln C. ... 738
Woodward, Julia ... 1921
Worgan, Paul ... 2655, 2667, 4734
Wortmann, Felix ... 2813
Wouhaybi, Rita H. ... 1445
Woźniak, Paweł ... 2447, 3572
Woznowski, Przemyslaw ... 1526
Wright, Peter ... 343, 1096, 2136, 2705, 2958, 4968
Wu, Bing-Hsun ... 74
Wu, Chieh-Lin ... 74
Wu, Ellick ... 2279
Wu, Hongkai ... 1622
Wu, Justin ... 4298
Wu, Pei-Jung ... 156
Wu, Raymond ... 1563
Wu, Rundong ... 887
Wu, Stephanie ... 2038
Wu, Y. Wayne ... 4086
Wu, Yanhong ... 5003
Wu, Yongmeng ... 313
Wulf, Volker ... 921, 1073, 3364
Wyche, Susan ... 3620
Wyeth, Peta ... 1930, 5583
Xia, Haijun ... 4610
Xiao, Lu ... 3532
Xiao, Robert ... 1221
Xiao, Sa ... 433
Xiao, Shuangjiu ... 781
Xiao, Xiao ... 12, 5397
Xie, Linxin ... 2805
Xie, Wei ... 180
Xiong, Wei ... 4699
Xu, Bin ... 2001
Xu, Chenren ... 2821
Xu, Heng ... 3919, 4286
Xu, Jing ... 2821, 3247
Xu, Liming ... 1163, 3651
Xu, Pingmei ... 3299
Xu, Xiao-hong ... 1533
Xu, Xuexin ... 2961
Xu, Zichun ... 3822
Yadav, Deepika ... 343
Yalla, Sai ... 2038
Yamada, Suguru ... 3804
Yamaguchi, Mami ... 1766
Yamanaka, Shota ... 1846
Yang, Chenglei ... 433
Yang, Chi-Lan ... 1615
Yang, De-Nian ... 1526
Yang, Dongseok ... 3774
Yang, Hui ... 1622
Yang, Junrui ... 5909
Yang, Michael Ying ... 2592
Yang, Qian ... 4477
Yang, Shuo ... 1526
Yang, Xing-Dong ... 3403, 4675
Yang, Yi ... 5
Yang, Yulong ... 3722
Yao, Catherine ... 5506
Yao, Cheng ... 1497, 2328
Yao, Hsin-Yun ... 3808
Yao, Lining ... 13, 5743
Yarosh, Svetlana ... 635, 3784
Yatani, Koji ... 998
Yazaki, Tomonori ... 733
Ye, Xu ... 3255
Yefimova, Katya ... 859
Yem, Vibol ... 281, 3717
Yen, Ching-Chiuan ... 1937
Yeo, Hui-Shyong ... 6058
Yeung, W. L. ... 1788
Yildirim, Irem Gökçe ... 2005
Yin, Ming ... 4098
Ying, Fangtian ... 1497, 2328
Yip, Jason C. ... 1127, 3607
Yoder, Matthew J. ... 3219
Yonetani, Ryo ... 5180
Yonezawa, Takuro ... 3804
Yong, Seraphina ... 1236
Yoo, Chungkuk ... 5126
Yoo, Daisy ... 4423
Yoo, Sooyoung ... 5620
Yoon, Dongwook ... 1045
Yoon, Susik ... 2857
Yoshida, Natsuko ... 1322
You, Chuang-Wen ... 5704
Young, Alexandra ... 3049
Young, Meg ... 1403
Yousef, Hanna ... 2632
Yu, Bin ... 260, 1794
Yu, Chun ... 71, 4699
Yu, Haizi ... 2383
Yu, Kai ... 80
Yu, Kun ... 3035
Yu, Liyue ... 1187
Yu, Neng-Hao ... 3272
Yu, Shuang ... 598
Yue, Yanzhen ... 5715
Yuksel, Beste F. ... 3770, 5372
Yurdakul, Celalettin ... 3655, 3944
Yurman, Paulina ... 2474
Zade, Himanshu ... 5063
Zagermann, Johannes ... 5470
Zammitto, Veronica ... 1879
Zanella, Michele ... 1684
Zaphiris, Panayiotis ... 1127
Zappala, Daniel ... 4298
Zaykov, Yordan ... 261
Zeiner, Katharina M. ... 3013
Zeising, Anja ... 1123
Zeleznik, Robert ... 2362
Zelzer, Idan ... 4896
Zgraggen, Emanuel ... 2362, 3049
Zhai, Shumin ... 49, 83, 3817
Zhang, Amy X. ... 3378
Zhang, Caowei ... 2328
Zhang, Carrie ... 184
Zhang, Chi ... 2321
Zhang, Jia ... 2141
Zhang, Jingxian ... 3263
Zhang, Lanyun ... 1329
Zhang, Leshao ... 313
Zhang, Peijin ... 7
Zhang, Peijin ... 4933
Zhang, Qing ... 910
Zhang, Ruofan ... 80
Zhang, Xiang ... 5350
Zhang, Xiaolong (Luke) ... 1760
Zhang, Xiaoyi ... 5658
Zhang, Xinyi ... 225
Zhang, Xujing ... 3675
Zhang, Yang ... 1491
Zhang, Yifei ... 1991
Zhang, Yunbo ... 897
Zhang, Zuoyi ... 3784
Zhao, Ben Y. ... 225
Zhao, Jian ... 5003
Zhao, Jieqiong ... 5409
Zhao, Peijun ... 71
Zhao, Shengdong ... 1016, 2640, 3572
Zhao, Xuan ... 89
Zheng, Haitao ... 225
Zheng, Jingjie ... 4274
Zhenyu, Zhu (Cole) ... 3597
Zhong, Mingyuan ... 71
Zhou, Andrew Jie ... 1622
Zhou, Dao ... 1991
Zhou, Huiyuan ... 1362
Zhou, Jianlong ... 3035
Zhou, Junhan ... 1491
Zhou, Kaitlyn ... 360
Zhou, Sharon ... 944
Zhou, Yi ... 781
Zhou, Yining ... 74
Zhu, Fengyuan ... 184
Zhu, Haiyi ... 598
Ziat, Mounia ... 3808
Ziegler, Jürgen ... 1637
Zikmund-Fisher, Brian J. ... 2314
Zimmerman, John ... 1051, 1187, 4477
Zirkl, Martin ... 5138
Zolyomi, Annuska ... 5506
Zoran, Amit ... 5731, 5984
Zuckerman, Ethan ... 2612
Zuyev-Grabovitch, Irena ... 3025
Zwerdling, Naama ... 3025
Zytko, Doug ... 1337

www.ingramcontent.com/pod-product-compliance
Ingram Content Group UK Ltd.
Pitfield, Milton Keynes, MK11 3LW, UK
UKHW051416290926
15471UKWH00009B/1623

9 781450 346320